DATE DUE			
Sep 27 '72			
Oct 2 '72			
Oct 5 '73			
Sep 25 '81			

MUSIC IN ANCIENT ISRAEL

The captured vessels of the Jerusalem Temple, with the sacred silver trumpets, which Titus carried in his triumphal procession. Stone-relief from the Arch of Titus, Rome. (After Alfred Jeremias, *The Old Testament in the Light of the Ancient East*, London, 1911).

MUSIC IN ANCIENT ISRAEL

by

ALFRED SENDREY

PHILOSOPHICAL LIBRARY
New York

15 East 40th Street, New York, N. Y. 10016

Library of Congress Catalog Card No. 66-20218
Manufactured in the United States of America

To the Memory of

CURT SACHS

CONTENTS

ACKNOWLEDGMENTS

It is the author's pleasant duty to express his appreciation to all the persons who, through the long development and the many transmutations of the present work, gave him encouragement and valuable advice.

In the first place, he is deeply indebted to Prof. CURT SACHS and Dr. JOSEPH YASSER, who read the entire manuscript and whose suggestions and constructive criticism were invaluable for the final formulation of the text.

Sincere thanks are also due Mr. ROBERT STRASSBURG, who helped with the reading of the proofs and who, furthermore, gave the author unstintingly of his time and effort.

To the Jewish Community Library at Los Angeles and its librarians, Rabbi RUDOLPH LUPO and SHIMEON BRISMAN, the author hereby conveys his gratitude for extended library facilities and much helpful advice accorded him.

The production of a voluminous work such as this would not have been possible without the material aid of two generous sponsors. They wish to remain anonymous; the author's heartfelt gratitude should be expressed for their unselfish and high-minded support.

Finally, the author expresses thanks to the editorial staff of the Philosophical Library. The co-operation between editors and author could not have been more harmonious.

Los Angeles, California, May 1968.

INTRODUCTION

The scrutiny of music of all the ancient peoples raises special problems in many cases because of the subtle imponderabilia which the scholar is bound to come across, and to take into account in his investigations. Working with such delicate material frequently necessitates deviations from the traditional methods of musicology.

This is particularly true of the music of the ancient Hebrews, and for a special reason: the main sources for our knowledge of their tonal art bear the imprint either of canonicity (Bible), or that of hallowed Jewish or Christian traditions (rabbinic and patristic literature).

This situation has for centuries caused a serious handicap for musicology in the matter of critically evaluating the available sources. The present study endeavors to evade these handicaps and to approach the problems under investigation without any preconceived ideas.

o
o o

Historic truth is not always immediately apparent from the text of our sources. This applies in general to the historical records concerning the music of Ancient Israel. In our protracted investigations we were frequently faced with the necessity of extracting meanings from scanty data. And without deviating from the principle of scholarly objectivity, we came to grips with problems which had to be approached subjectively in order to arrive at some logical solutions. Nevertheless, we refrained in all instances from any forced conclusions, even if they were otherwise in conformity with the spirit of the music under investigation. In all such cases we left the adoption or rejection of our personal interpretation to the discretion of the reader.

o
o o

By resorting partly to a somewhat unusual—because essentially musical—approach to the problems of this study, we have endeavored to clarify a number of hitherto unexplained or misinterpreted matters. In several respects, however, we probably will never be able to eliminate the last doubt. Even in an epoch relatively close to the national life of the ancient Hebrews, in which the knowledge of their musical practice could reasonably be expected, many facts pertaining to their activity were misunderstood and distorted, because some of their musical customs had fallen into complete oblivion.

The numerous and contradictory attempts of talmudic and patristic writers, as well as of authors through the Middle Ages and even up to our own days, at interpreting the musical terms of the ancient Hebrews created a confusion which arduous scholarly work failed to eliminate. It will be one of our main tasks to clarify this situation. We could not escape, therefore, dealing not only with the logical and largely accepted conclusions of ancient and modern writers, but also discussing critically the numerous obsolete and seemingly illogical reasonings, as well as outright errors and misconstructions, which abound in the vast literature concerning our subject. All this explains why our study includes the history of literary *misinterpretation* of the music of Ancient Israel in addition to its normal interpretation. Without overstressing the value of that negative secondary material, we hold that the exposition of trials and errors in conjunction with our interpretation rightfully belongs to the scope of our investigation.

This being so, the reader is emphatically warned *not* to take the quotations pertaining to this "secondary material" as the author's inability to reach the primary sources or, worse still, as his agreement with some obsolete views found among these quotations. At the same time, the author does not entirely exclude the possibility that certain views considered today as "patently obsolete" may contain a grain of truth and that, with partial revision in the future, they may yet turn out to be useful for a more adequate interpretation of some controversial points. Experience in many scholarly fields abounds with modified "resurrections" of opinions that for a long time have been branded as antiquated. Under these conditions, the sheer impracticality of presenting impartially all the existing views and opinions, quite apart from their purely historical interest, becomes self-evident.

o
o o

By their very nature, certain topics are within the scope of more than one section of this study. In numerous instances it was neither possible, nor advisable, to exhaust all the characteristics of a particular item in a single chapter. Therefore, returning to already familiar items in connection with some other phases of the musical life in Ancient Israel, was sometimes indispensable. Dealing each time anew with the same facts, persons, or institutions in various chapters of this study should be considered as a different treatment of the same topic from another angle or within a changed situation. Ample cross-references will indicate whenever a subject had to be discussed on more than one occasion.

o
o o

For the chronology of biblical and historical events and of biographical data we follow the *History of the Jews* by HEINRICH H. GRAETZ (English edition, Philadelphia, 1898). To be sure, modern historiography may have arrived in some instances at other conclusions; but in a musicological treatise such slight chronological differences have only a minor significance.

o
o o

Our system of transliteration is given in a separate table. For the transliteration of Hebrew proper names we have availed ourselves of the rendering in the *Jewish Translation of the Scriptures* (Philadelphia, 1917). In transliterating textual passages from the Hebrew and Aramaic into English, we follow the system of transliteration adopted by the *Jewish Encyclopedia* (New York, 1901-06).

In some cases our transliterations may seem to be incongruous. Such differences, however, are always made obvious in our text itself by typographical devices: words or names taken over from the English text of the *Jewish*

Version appear in ordinary type, whereas transliterated Hebrew passages and those of other ancient languages are printed in *italics.*

The transliteration of Yiddish texts follows a system introduced by the Yiddish Scientific Institute ("YIVO") in New York, which uses a phonetic transcription instead of transliterating a text letter by letter. This system does justice to the Yiddish language and complies at the same time with English phonetics. It was also adhered to in the present author's *Bibliography of Jewish Music* (New York, 1951).

o
o o

The principle of distributing our material into the various sections of this book requires some brief comments.

The Music of the Earlier and of the Neighboring Civilizations (Section I) is touched in our study merely in its bare outlines, stressing the elements which have some bearing upon the music of the Hebrews, or reveal some common or similar traits. A more exhaustive representation of this vast subject would have exceeded by far the space allotted to it in our work. Besides, the music of Antiquity has been discussed in numerous special essays which may be readily consulted if further information is desired. The most important ones are enumerated in the general bibliography appended to this book.

The Sources of Jewish Music (Section II) would have required a more extensive treatment than was possible within the framework of our study. In any but a musicological treatise, the biblical as well as talmudic and patristic sources should have been dealt with much more emphasis upon their historical, philosophical and religious aspects. The restrictions imposed upon ourselves in this regard will be compensated by the abundant use and exegesis of all these sources in the chapters dealing with the actual musical practice of the Jews.

The Survey of Biblical References to Music (Section III) has been compiled innumerable times in the existing literature but, as far as we know, never before in a comprehensive and systematic order. The purpose of this survey is twofold: first to show the wealth of musical information contained in the Bible, thus refuting the wide-spread belief that the Bible tells us relatively little about the music of the Israelites; then, to demonstrate the overall influence of music upon Jewish life, thinking and feeling.

For purely musical research, *The Book of Psalms* (Section IV) assumes a place of specific significance. No other portion of the Scriptures contains so many musical terms. That is not surprising if we realize that the Psalter, as will be shown, constituted in its primitive as in its final form the liturgical hymnal and song book of the Israelites. It matters little that, for posterity at least, the meaning of a goodly number of these musical terms became hidden, camouflaged as it were. It was not always so. To their originators these terms must have served as quite useful practical indications and instructions for the musical rendition of the psalms. Their meaning became lost only in later centuries, especially after the destruction of the Jerusalem sanctuary and, as a consequence, the annihilation of the Temple's musical service. In the form they survived in the Bible, these terms have perpetually challenged the historians, biblical exegetes and musicologists to rediscover their true meaning.

In accordance with its towering place in the music of Ancient Israel, *Singing* (Section V) has been given the most extensive treatment in our book. All the facets of vocal art had to be thoroughly examined, historically (chapters 1-9), artistically (chapters 11, 13-15), aesthetically (chapter 12), and ethically (chapter 17). Among these, the chapters "Hebrew Melody," "Hebrew Rhythm," and "The Dynamics of Hebrew Singing" represent investigations scarcely attempted before on such an extensive scale.

The portion of our study devoted to the *Instruments* (Section VI) distinguishes between instruments mentioned in the Bible and those which can be found only in post-biblical writings. In both categories, in contradistinction to modern classification, the division into stringed, wind and percussion instruments is self-explanatory. While biblical instruments have been dealt with in innumerable treatises, the instruments of the talmudic epoch were hitherto rather neglected. Only a few of these are mentioned, or superficially described, by some of the ancient or modern writers. Having been rescued here from an undeserved oblivion, some of the post-biblical instruments are dealt with musicologically for the first time in this work.

While various single instruments mentioned in the Bible have been described (though not always exhaustively) again and again in the existing literature, their combinations in smaller or larger ensembles, i.e. bands or *Orchestras* (Section VII), were grossly neglected. We have tried our best to remedy this deficiency.

As a rule, *The Dance* (Section VIII) of the Israelites has been treated more or less cursorily in quite a number of writings dealing either with the music of the ancient Hebrews, in general, or with their religious and popular customs, in particular. Our treatment of the subject tends to complement the general history of ancient civilizations and to shed light upon an important aspect of the musical practice of the Israelites.

The Music Instruction in Ancient Israel (Section IX) represents an initial attempt at uncovering the intrinsic reasons for the high musical culture of the Hebrews. These chapters unravel historically and pedagogically the music teaching in Israel at its different stages of development. Furthermore, they afford some insight into the sociological and economic connotations of this side of music in biblical times.

The Supernatural Power of Music (Section X) dealing with "Music and Superstition" and "Prophecy and Music," is a composite picture in which a great many bits of evidence have taken part and which was put together here for the first time in order to give a comprehensive exposition of these two important and musically imbued factors of Jewish spiritual and religious life.

Women in the Music of Ancient Israel (Section XI) and *The Musical Organization* (Section XII) are, basically, concentrated accumulations of many previously discussed facts, viewed here, however, from a different angle and on a higher plane. Thus, their treatment in separate sections needs no further justification.

LIST OF ILLUSTRATIONS

Illustration 31
The sacred instruments on Jewish coins.

Illustration 32
Vase from Megiddo, showing a lyre (c. 1025 B.C.E.) (After The Biblical Archaeologist)

Illustration 33
A Semitic lyre player enternig Egypt, as depicted on the Beni-Hassan monument (c. 1900 B.C.E.) (After Sachs)

Illustration 34
Ivory from Megiddo (c. 1200 B.C.E.), showing a lyre player (After Heston)

Illustration 35
Enlargement of the lyre player on Illustration 34.

Illustration 36
Bronze-figure from Megiddo, representing a Jewish flute-girl (1300-1200 B.C.E.). (After Schumacher)

Illustration 37
Levitical singing groups in the First Temple, as depicted in the Codex of Kosmas Indikopleustes, Cod. Vat. Graec. 699. (After Zenner)

Illustration 38
Assyrian dulcimer player (After Stainer)

Illustration 39
Instrument in the shape of an ox-head (After Engel)

Illustration 40
Hittite lutanist, from Eyuk (After Sachs)

Illustration 41
Trumpets found in Tut-Ankh-Amen's tomb. Left to right: Silver trumpet; its wooden core; bronze trumpet; its wooden core (After Kirby)

Illustration 42
Different shapes of the *shofar* (After Jewish Encyclopedia, vol. XI)

Illustration 43
Probably the oldest known signs for *shofar*-calls, in a Hebrew manuscript of the 13th century, the *Codex Adler* (in the Jewish Theological Seminary, New York, No. 932)

Illustration 44
Yemenite *shofar,* richly carved, about 54 inches long (At the Mount Sinai Memorial Park, Los Angeles)

Illustration 45
Moses. Sculpture by Claus Slutter (At the Museum in Dijon)

LIST OF ABBREVIATIONS

A

AmbrosMus	Ambros, August Wilhelm, Musikgeschichte (Breslau, 1862-82), 5 vols.
ArnoldRhythms	Arnold, William R., The Rhythms of the Ancient Hebrews, in *"Old Testament and Semitic Studies in Memory of William Rainey Harper"* (Chicago, 1908).
Athen	Athenaeus, Deipnosophistēs (The Sophists at Dinner) ed. Loeb Classical Library (London, New York, 1927), 7 vols.
AuthVer	Authorized Version

B

BaethPsalm	Baethgen, Friedrich, Die Psalmen übersetzt und erklärt (Göttingen, 1892).
BuddeGesch	Budde, Karl, Geschichte der althebräischen Literatur (Leipzig, 1906).

C

CalmetDict	Calmet, Augustin, Dictionary of the Holy Bible (Engl. ed. Boston, 1832).
ChantRelig	Chantepie de la Saussaye, Pierre Daniel, Lehrbuch der Religionsgeschichte (Tübingen, 1925), 2 vols.
CornCult	Cornill, Karl Heinrich, The Culture of Ancient Israel (Chicago, 1914).
CornMus	Cornill, Karl Heinrich, Music in the Old Testament (Chicago, 1909).

D

DelPsalms	Delitzsch, Franz, Biblical Commentary on the Psalms, transl. by Francis Bolton (Edinburgh, 1892), 3 vols.

E

EngMus	Engel, Carl, The Music of the Most Ancient Nations (London, 1864).
ERE	Hastings James, Encyclopedia of Religion and Ethics (New York, 1908-21), 12 vols.
ErmanRel	Erman, Adolf, Die Ägyptische Religion (Berlin, 1905).
EwaldAnt	Ewald, Heinrich August, The Antiquities of Israel (Engl. ed. Boston, 1876).
EwDicht	Ewald, Heinrich August, Die Dichter des Alten Bundes (Göttingen, 1866).

F

FarOrg — Farmer, Henry George, The Organ of the Ancients from Eastern Sources (London, 1931).

FétisHist — Fétis, François Joseph, Histoire générale de la Musique (Paris, 1869-76), 5 vols.

FineInstr — Finesinger, Sol Baruch, Musical Instruments in OT, in *Hebrew Union College Annual* (Cincinnati, 1926), III, pp. 21-76.

FineShof — Finesinger, Sol Baruch, The Shofar, in *Hebrew Union College Annual* (Cincinnati, 1931-32), VIII-IX, pp. 193-228.

ForkelGesch — Forkel, Johann Nicholaus, Allgemeine Geschichte der Musik (Leipzig, 1788-1801). 2 vols.

G

GalpSum — Galpin, Francis William, The Music of the Sumerians and Their Immediate Successors the Babylonians and Assyrians (Cambridge, 1937)).

GesHandw — Gesenius, Wilhelm, Hebräisches und Chaldäisches Handwörterbuch über das A.T. (Leipzig, 1915).

GesLex — Gesenius, Wilhelm, A Hebrew and English Lexicon of the Old Testament, including the Biblical Chaldee (Boston, 1906).

GesThes — Gesenius, Wilhelm, Thesaurus philologicus et criticus linguae Hebraeae et Chaldaeae Veteris Testamenti (Leipzig, 1829-58).

GlaserPsalm — Glaser, Otto, Die ältesten Psalmmelodien, in *Zeitschrift für Semistik* (1935), X, pp. 324-25.

GraetzPsalms — Graetz, Heinrich H., Kritischer Commentar zu den Psalmen (Breslau, 1882-83).

GressMus — Gressmann, Hugo, Musik und Musikinstrumente im Alten Testament (Giessen, 1903).

H

Hark — Harkavy, Alexander, Translation of the Old Testament (New York, 1916), 2 vols.

HarrisHer — Harris, C. W., The Hebrew Heritage, a Study of Israel's Cultural and Spiritual Origins (New York, 1935).

HastDict — Hastings, James, A Dictionary of the Bible (New York, 1898-1904).

HerdSpirit — Herder, Johann Gottfried, The Spirit of Hebrew Poetry, transl. by James March (Burlington, 1833), 2 vols.

I

IdelJewMus — Idelsohn, Abraham Zevi, Jewish Music in its Historical Development (New York, 1929).

IdelThes — Idelsohn, Abraham Zevi, Hebräisch-Orientalischer Melodienschatz (Jerusalem, Berlin, Vienna, 1914-1932), 10 vols. The same in an English and in a Hebrew edition.

J

JahnArch — Jahn, Johann, Biblical Archaeology (New York, 1853).

JastDict — Jastrow, Marcus, A Dictionary of the Targumim, the Talmud Babli and Yerushalmi and the Midrashic Literature (New York, 1943).

JBL — Journal of Biblical Literature (Syracuse, N.Y.).

JerATAO — Jeremias, Alfred, Das Alte Testament im Lichte des Alten Orients (Leipzig, 1903).

JerHand — Jeremias, Alfred, Handbuch der altorientalischen Geisteskultur (Leipzig, 1913).

JewTransl — The Holy Scriptures according to the Masoretic Text (Philadelphia, 1917)

JosAnt — Josephus, Ioudaikē archailogia (Antiquities of the Jews).

JosApio — Josephus, Contra Apionem (Against Apion).

JosWar — Josephus, Peri tou Ioudaikou polemiou (The Jewish War).

JQR — Jewish Quarterly Review (New York).

JRAS — Journal of the Royal Asiatic Society (London).

K

KraussSynAlt — Krauss, Samuel, Synagogale Altertümer (Berlin-Vienna, 1922).

KraussTA — Krauss, Samuel, Talmudische Archäologie (Leipzig, 1910-12), 3 vols.

L

LangdLit — Langdon, Stephen Herbert, Babylonian Liturgies (Paris, 1913).

LangdTerms — Langdon, Stephen Herbert, Babylonian and Hebrew Musical Terms, in *JRAS,* Part II, April, 1921, pp. 169-91.

LeitGes — Leitner, Franz, Der gottesdienstliche Volksgesang im jüdischen und christlichen Altertum (Freiburg, i.B., 1906).

M

M	Mishnah
MGWJ	Monatsschrift der Gesellschaft für die Wissenschaft des Judentums (Krotoschin).
Midr	Midrash
MowPsalm	Mowinckel, Sigmund, Psalmenstudien (Christiania-Oslo, 1921-23), 6 vols.

N

NowackArch	Nowack, Wilhelm, Lehrbuch der hebräischen Archäologie (Freiburg, i.B., 1894).

O

OesterPsalms	Oesterley, Emil Oscar William, The Psalms in the Jewish Church (London, 1910).

P

PfeifferIntro	Pfeiffer, Robert H., Introduction to the Old Testament (New York, 1941).
PfeifferMus	Pfeiffer, Augustus Friedrich, Über die Musik der alten Hebräer (Erlangen, 1779).
PG	Migne, Jacques Paul, Patrologia Graeca (Paris, 1857-66), 81 vols.
PGL	———, Patrologia Graeco-Latina (*ibid.*), 161 vols.
PhiloLaws	Philo Judaeus, Peri tōn en merei diatagmatōn (On the Special Laws).
PhiloMos	Philo Judaeus, Peri biou Mouseōs (About the Life of Moses).
PhiloTher	Philo Judaeus, Peri biou theorētikou hē iketōn (About the Contemplative Life).
PL	Migne, Jacques Paul, Patrologia Latina (Paris, 1844-55), 221 vols.
PortShilṭe	Portaleone, Abraham, Shilṭe ha-Gibborim (Mantua, 1612).

R

RiehmHandw	Riehm, Eduard Carl August, Handwörterbuch des biblischen Altertums (Bielefeld and Leipzig, 1893-94).

S

SaalArch	Saalschütz, Joseph Lewin, Archäologie der Hebräer (Königsberg, 1855).
SaalForm	Saalschütz, Joseph Lewin, Von der Form der hebräischen Poesie (Königsberg, 1825).

SaalGesch — Saalschütz, Joseph Lewin, Geschichte und Würdigung der Musik bei den Hebräern (Berlin, 1829).

SachsAlt — Sachs, Curt, Die Musik des Altertums (Breslau, 1924).

SachsDance — Sachs, Curt, World History of the Dance (New York, 1937).

SachsGeist — Sachs, Curt, Geist und Werden der Musikinstrumente (Berlin, 1929).

SachsHist — Sachs, Curt, The History of Musical Instruments (New York, 1940).

SachsRhythm — Sachs, Curt, Rhythm and Tempo, (New York, 1953).

SachsRise — Sachs, Curt, The Rise of Music in the Ancient World East and West (New York, 1943).

SchneidKult — Schneider, Hermann, Die Kulturleistungen der Menschheit (Leipzig, 1927), 3 vols.

SieversMetr — Sievers, Eduard, Metrische Studien, Part I, Studien zur hebräischen Metrik, in *Abhandlungen der Philologisch-historischen Klasse der Königlich Sächsischen Gesellschaft der Wissenschaften* (1901), XXI, No. 1.

StainMus — Stainer, Sir John, The Music of the Bible, New ed. by F. W. Galpin (London, 1914).

T

T.B. — Babylonian Talmud.

ThirProblems — Thirtle, James William, Old Testament Problems (London, 1916).

ThirTitles — Thirtle, James William, The Titles of the Psalms (London, 1904).

T.Y. — Palestinian Talmud.

U

UgThes — Ugolino, Blasius (Biagio), Thesaurus antiquitatum sacrarum . . . (Venice, 1744-67), 34 vols.

W

WeissInstr — Weiss, Johann, Die musikalischen Instrumente in den heiligen Schriften des Alten Testaments (Graz, 1895).

WellPsalms — Wellhausen, Julius, The Book of Psalms (New York, 1898).

WilkEgypt — Wilkinson, Sir Gardner, The Manners and Customs of the Ancient Egyptians (London, 1878).

WincklerKeil — Winckler, Hugo, Keilinschriftliches Textbuch zum Alten Testament (Leipzig, 1909).

ZMW — Zeitschrift für Musikwissenschaft (Leipzig).

ZNTW — Zeitschrift für Neutestamentliche Wissenschaft (Giessen).

TABLE OF TRANSLITERATIONS

Hebrew and Aramaic

Consonants.

א not noted at the beginning; replaced by ʾ

בּ ב : b	ט : ṭ	פּ (with dagesh) : p
ג : g	י : y	פ (without dagesh) : f
ד : d	כּ כ : k	צ : ẓ
ה : h	ל : l	ק : ḳ
ו : v	מ : m	ר : r
ז : z	נ : n	שׁ : sh
ח : ḥ	ס : s	שׂ : s
	ע : replaced by ʿ	תּ ת : t

Vowels.

◌ָ : a	◌ִ : i	◌ֶ : e	◌ֲ : a	וּ : u
◌ֳ : o	◌ֻ : u	◌ַ : a	◌ֱ : e	וֹ : o
◌ְ : e	◌ֵ : e	◌ֹ : o	◌ִי : i	

Kamez ḥatuf is represented by *o*. The so-called "continental" pronunciation of the English vowels is implied.

The Hebrew article is transcribed as *ha*, followed by a hyphen, without doubling the following letter.

The presence of *dagesh lene* is not noted, except in the case of *pe*. *Dagesh forte* is indicated by doubling the letter.

Greek

Α α : a	Ι ι : i	Ρ ρ : rh
Β β : b	Κ κ : k	Σ σ : s
Γ γ : g	Λ λ : l	Τ τ : t
Δ δ : d	Μ μ : m	Υ υ : y
Ε ε : e	Ν ν : n	Φ φ : ph
Ζ ζ : z	Ξ ξ : x	Χ χ : ch
Η η : ē	Ο ο : o	Ψ ψ : ps
Θ θ : th	Π π : p	Ω ω : ō
	ʽ : h	

MUSIC IN ANCIENT ISRAEL

acknowledged by the world. Not so in music. Here we are witnessing a general attitude oscillating between sheer scepticism and complete denial of the aptitude of the Jews for music.

It is surprising to find a similar attitude even among scholars of great repute. As great a student of the spirit of Jewish culture and religious philosophy as MUCKLE failed to recognize the spark that, under proper conditions, would kindle the innate Jewish musical faculties. He readily acknowledges that

> "where the Jewish soul is replete with the power of a great heart, the messianic ideal spreads the luster of transfiguration upon all the peoples," [1]

but vitiates his panegyric by simply denying to the Jews any artistic aptitude:

> "Architecture, painting, sculpture, and music have to be eliminated. In all these fields the Jewish people failed to produce original works, and were we to try to explain this phenomenon, we would have to refer to the mystery of the Jewish soul. The Jews tried to be active in all these fields; we know how the prophets raged frantically against the worship of images; we know the role of the music in the people's life and especially at religious festivals; we know that the Temple, though built by foreign hands, was firmly established in the heart of every Jew. In these instances, however, the intrinsic spiritual power of the Jewish people failed, just as in all these fields their accomplishments have fallen behind those of other nations in later centuries." [2]

By reason of some strange aberration, it simply did not occur to MUCKLE that the lack of accomplishments of the Jews in the visual arts was due not to their inborn incapacity for the latter, but to the strict religious laws prohibiting the making of "any graven image, or any manner of likeness of any thing that is in heaven above, or that is in the earth beneath, or that is in the water under the earth" (Exod. 20:4).

And as to the alleged inaptitude of the Jews for the tonal art, we shall see as a result of the present study, whether this opinion can be maintained in view of the accomplishments in this field, by the ancient Israelites.

o
o o

And now, as we are about to launch our investigation, three preliminary questions emerge quite conspicuously from the very start:

(1) What are the origins of Jewish music and of the musical culture of the Jews?

(2) What kind of music did the Jews find upon entering Cana'an, their future homeland, and what use did they make of it?

(3) How did music develop among the Jews after the establishment of their national existence? Did the Israelites succeed in transforming and assimilating the elements borrowed from other civilizations, so that a new, autonomous Jewish musical art came into being?

To answer these questions, let us have a glance at the musical culture of the great civilizations that made up the ancient Near-East.

I. THE MUSIC OF THE EARLIER AND OF THE NEIGHBORING CIVILIZATIONS*

In examining the ancient civilizations of the Near-East, the first thing we realize is the close interrelation that existed among them for millennia. Wars, diplomatic intercourse, exchange of ideas, intermarriage, and an extensive trade resulted in a cultural assimilation that left its definite mark in all domains; political, economic, religious, and social, on these otherwise different peoples.

The music of these regions, too, was strongly and mutually influenced in its development by the common cultural undercurrents. The widespread trade between the peoples brought about a continuous exchange of commercial goods and articles of luxury; thus, among other things, instruments of music were interchanged and knowledge of their use was disseminated. Through the mushrooming of religious groups and sects, all types of hymns, litanies and other sacred songs were created, which eventually were transplanted from one people to another. In urban life, there developed a class of skillful craftsmen, among them builders of instruments, whose inventiveness brought about better and finer instruments of music. Such instruments were considered *objets de luxe* in Oriental life, and as such, they were among the most desirable articles of trade.

History teaches us that it was not always the smaller or politically weaker people which succumbed to the spiritual influence of a mighty conqueror. Cultural interrelations were not determined by mere political force; one may cite many instances to show that often the weaker people was the giver in the intellectual field, while the conqueror turned out to be on the receiving end. This is particularly obvious in the music of Antiquity, which—in those times—was regarded less as an art in itself, than as a general aspect of intellectual life. In this respect, the music of the ancient Orient represents a unity, in which mutual influence and fructification were governed by the laws of natural evolution.

1. SUMERIA

Our oldest records concerning the musical organization and the music system of the nations of Antiquity are from Sumeria and Egypt. Not so long ago scarcely anything was known about the music of the Sumerians. Fortunate discoveries during recent decades have enabled us to obtain a rather accurate insight into the musical culture of this nation. Through the pioneering research work of SACHS, EBELING and LANGDON, light has been shed on the prehistoric obscurity of the religion, the customs, and also the music of the Sumerians. As a matter of fact, so many resemblances have been found between their music and that of Ancient Israel that, for some time, the question was seriously discussed as to whether or not the Israelites had taken over their musical art directly from the Sumerians. This assumption, however, overlooks the considerable time difference between the decline of the Sumerian

* See Introductory Notes on p. 15.

empire and the beginning of the Jewish national existence; despite all the similarities, there is scarcely any room for such an hypothesis.

How did this idea originate?

We know that Abraham's home-town was the Sumerian-Chaldaean city of ʾUr. From there, his father Terah planned to emigrate to Canaʿan with his sons and his grandson Lot, whose father died at an early age. Terah, however, settled at Haran in northwestern Mesopotamia, so that henceforth this town was regarded as the domicile of his tribe (Gen. 11:31). Abraham, his wife Sarah, and his nephew Lot continued the journey to Canaʿan. Soon after they settled in the already heavily populated country, Abraham and Lot separated by mutual agreement, because there were not sufficient pastures for their numerous flocks. Abraham took up residence at Hebron, where he led a nomadic life. According to the biblical chronicler, he had all in all 318 servants, "born in his house, all trained men" (Gen. 14:14).

Even if we were to assume that some of these "trained men" sang or played instruments, it is unthinkable that a single, relatively small, group of men could have transplanted from one country to another all the ramifications of its musical practice. This would scarcely have been possible for a clan, or even an entire tribe. It is rather safe to assume that the music of the Sumerians entered Israel in a roundabout way, namely by the continuous cultural intercourse which took place between the Hebrews and the Egyptians on the one hand, and the Hebrews and the Babylonians and Assyrians on the other. It is commonly known that the Israelites borrowed from other civilizations all elements in conformance with their individuality, their religion, and their artistic conceptions. The similarities in musical practice of the Sumerians and the Israelites, so widely separated in point of time, can be explained for the most part by the fact that the ethos of their music, its "emotional connotation," was very much alike. The following brief outline shows not only the affinities, but also the differences between the music of Sumeria and that of Israel.[3]

Sumerian texts of the 3rd millennium B.C.E. often make mention of religious music. In historical reports of Sumeria there are frequent references to it; the various records about the musical performances of the Sumerians are mostly connected with their religious rites and temple ceremonies.

Secular music and musical customs drew their vital energy from popular sources; preserved documents show that, apart from a highly developed sacred music, the Sumerians possessed a vigorous folk music.

The pastoral life of the Sumerian herdsmen and peasants gave to the bulk of the population ample opportunity for music making. Singers and musicians were employed at the court and by the nobility. On the famous standard of ʾUr (ca. 2700 B.C.E.) we see the reproduction of a royal banquet with court dignitaries; a female singer accompanied by a harpist (or lyre-player) entertains the revelers.[4]

A catalogue of Sumerian and Assyrian hymns and secular songs[5] contains the initial lines of numerous poems and songs of diverse categories, such as liturgies, royal psalms, festival songs and lamentations; poems of victory and of heroic acts alternate with popular songs for workmen and shepherds, and with musical recitations; the list contains, furthermore, numerous love songs for both sexes. Originally, this catalogue was much more abundant, since only the upper part of the stone slab on which the list was engraved is preserved. Nevertheless, this collection of titles affords an excellent insight into the pattern of secular music of the Sumerians, such an insight having been impossible without this archaeological discovery.

Our sources reveal even more information about the liturgical music of Sumeria. This is obvious, if we consider the predominance of the cult and of religious ceremonies in the life of the Sumerians. Attached to all their largest temples were schools of music, in which the young clergy was trained systematically in musical liturgy.[6]

The musical service of the temples was performed by "liturgists" (*kalū*) and "psalmists" (*narū*), whose functions consisted of administering the daily sacred ceremonies and providing a vocal background for them. In the temple of Ningirsu at Lagash, a special officer was in charge of the singers; another had the function of supervising the thorough preparation of the choir, consisting of male and female singers. The choral group was divided into several classes or sections. Sacred singers had their own guilds;

> "they became at last a learned community, a kind of college, which studied and edited the official liturgical literature . . . We have . . . a considerable liturgical literature of the learned college attached to the temple of Bel in Babylon." [7]

The Sumerian word *gala* (*narū* or *kalū*) indicated the "psalmist," the leader of the liturgical chant. He also officiated at funerals, in which an instrument called *balag (balaggu)* was used.

The musical service of Sumerian temples used instruments of all categories.

In the temples, the psalmists and singers were accompanied mainly by stringed instruments. Among these, the harp *(al* or *zag-sal)* and the seven-stringed lyre *(shebitu)* were preferred.

> "The lyre was the favorite accompaniment for the voice owing to its sweet tone." [8]

Another accompanying instrument was the two-stringed lute *(ẓinnitu)*, probably a long-necked, guitar-like instrument, on which the differences of pitch were produced by stopping the strings with the fingers.

Besides the *balaggu,* the flute and the drum were used most in sacred music. There is a reference to these two instruments in a litany to the sun-god.[9]

The most frequently mentioned wind instrument of the Sumerian temple music were

> "the 'covered' pipe *(kanzabu)*, the single-pipe, an oboe-type *(malilu)*, the double-pipe *(shem,* in Akkadian *ḫalḫalattu)*, sometimes combined with the timbrel *(me-ze)*."

There must have been other instruments in the Sumerian orchestra which are not mentioned by their names, as proven by the indication "and other instruments," found frequently in the original sources.[10]

The priests pronounced their oracles

> "to the strains of the (cross-strung) harp (*zag-sal*) or of the lyre *(al-gar)*, a custom continued by the Hebrew prophets and psalmists,

who 'opened their dark sayings upon the harp.' "[11]

Is it a mere accident that the Sumerian graphic word-symbol for *ḥul,* "to rejoice," has a striking similarity to the form of a harp?[12] In the Hebrew language, the same word, *ḥul,* indicates "dance."

Galpin ventures a hypothetical claim that he discovered an actual example of instrumental accompaniment for a Sumerian song.[13] According to his theory, the lyrics in Sumerian songs were put to music in a free recitative style; the rhythm of the melodic line was determined by the word accent, and these accents were punctuated by the accompanying of harps and occasional drum-beats.[14]

Recent research in the field of musical notation as probably employed in high Antiquity arrives at entirely different conclusions. In several pertinent essays, Sachs proves that Galpin's theories are untenable, being based upon arbitrary suppositions. Contrary to Galpin, he states that in this Babylonian discovery

> "there are no signs for single notes. They indicate intervals, ascending or descending."

Furthermore, he points out the fact that

> "the vocal notations used in connection with religious texts indicate stereotyped groups of notes. They provide evidence of that particular ornamental style that we roughly call 'oriental.'"[15]

Foreign conquerors, like the Chaldeans, invaded Sumeria, burned the houses and temples of Lagash, and carried the inhabitants into captivity. The laments in metrical form, composed on this occasion, and addressed to the deities of the city, are very similar to those the Hebrew psalmist would write in times of national disaster.[16]

ILLUSTRATION NO. 1

Sumerian musicians. Vase fragment from Bismaya, ca. 3200 B.C.E. (After Curt Sachs, *Musik der Antike,* Potsdam, 1928).

As may be seen, there are obvious similarities between the musical practice of the Sumerians and the Israelites. This will become even more evident when we scrutinize the musical aspects of Ancient Israel.

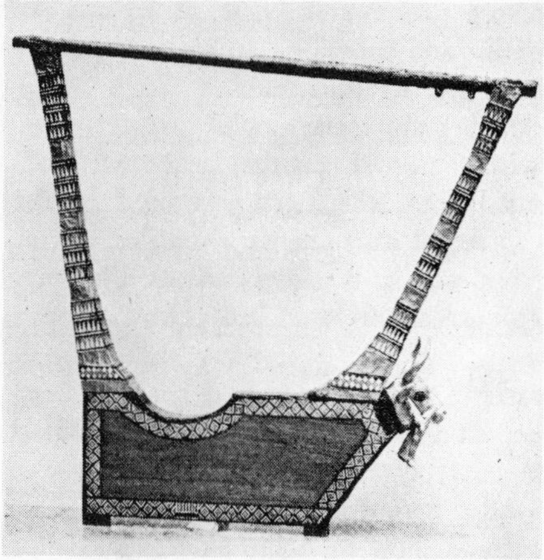

ILLUSTRATION NO. 2

Gold and mosaic kithara found in the Great Death-pit at ʾUr (ca. 2700 B.C.E.). Baghdad Museum (After Sir Leonard Woolley, *ʾUr of the Chaldees*, London 1950).

2. EGYPT

The general Egyptian civilization, thousands of years old, and rich in sciences and arts, is well known in almost all its aspects through its own historical records and through the preservation of foreign documents. About the music of the Egyptians, however, we know relatively little. This highly civilized nation, whose literature contains specimens of supreme quality, among them the oldest known art-poem of mankind, left scarcely more than pictorial representations of its musical culture.

The murals in temples and tombs, paintings and bas-reliefs, preserved to this day in great number, show a rich inventory of musical instruments in the Old as well as the New Empire. In Babylonian and Assyrian monuments, too, there are numerous reproductions of the musical instruments that were used by these nations. In general, however, it may be said that the forms of the Egyptian instruments were richer and more varied than those of the Babylonians and Assyrians. This leads to the conclusion that the instruments of the Egyptians were more advanced in their construction and more developed technically; consequently, the quality of their sound must have been superior to that of other peoples.

Among the Egyptian instruments the family of harps (*ben* or *bīn*) had a prominent place.[17] The Egyptians developed several varieties of harps, such as the shoulder-harp, the horizontal and vertical angular-harp, etc. The family of lyres (*k·nn·r*) was also much in use, with numerous species in form and design.

The predominance of stringed instruments in Egyptian bas-reliefs affords clues as to the character of Egyptian music, especially of their sacred music. In all probability, this must have been soft, solemn and sedate, in keeping with the dim *claire-obscure* of the temple halls and providing an appropriate tonal background for the mystic ceremonies of the Egyptian rites.

Among the wind instruments we find mainly the double-clarinets (with parallel pipes), the double-oboes (with pipes in angular position), and a kind of short-oboe.[18] Apart from woodwinds, the Egyptians used in their secular music metal trumpets, mainly as signal instruments in battles, but also in popular festivities. Several scholars suppose that the Egyptians used bagpipes. This, however, is an error, since bagpipes cannot be traced prior to the 1st century C.E.[19]

The Egyptians possessed a great variety of percussion and shaking instruments. Entire families of drums are depicted in ancient monuments, from the small hand-drum to the big, barrel-shaped type; also large and small cymbals, concussion sticks, castanet-like rattles, and different kinds of sistra.

As to singing in Egypt, historical records show that solo singers and choral groups, accompanied by instruments, participated in musical performances at the court and in the houses of the nobility. But we possess only scant information as to whether music, particularly vocal music, had taken root in the daily life of the people and had become a popular pastime, as was the case later with the Israelites.

The Egyptians knew no musical notation. The facts related by the Greeks about the music theory of the Egyptians are mostly Pythagorean, *i.e.* later Hellenistic attributions.

An outstanding feature of Egyptian festivals was antiphonal singing, performed by choral groups of dancing men and women. In honor of the bull-shaped god Apis, young men would march in processions and would perform songs until, possessed by the spirit, they would begin to prophesy.[20]

The Egyptians performed dramatic plays in which episodes of mythology were presented in dramatic form, with songs accompanied by instruments.[21]

Sacred music, highly praised owing to its effect upon the human soul,[22] was performed by a special guild of temple singers and musicians. Their functions were hereditary; the songs were transmitted orally from father to son.

Along with priestly musicians of the Middle Empire, a secular class of musicians came gradually into being which, at least in a general way, made successful inroads into the heretofore exclusive art of the privileged temple musicians. The main feature of the musical practice of secular musicians was external display, showing off by means of virtuosity. PYTHAGORAS, who lived in Egypt in the 6th century B.C.E., reports that the temple musicians were violently opposed to this abuse of musical art. Their objections had no effect,—indeed could not have any,—since the people enjoyed this *ars nova* of the new era. In a general way, this period brought profound changes in the life and customs of the Egyptian people, with the result, in the sphere of music, that artificiality won a higher recognition than the intrinsic quality of musical art. Virtuosity in musical performance was not only favored, but frankly requested. Slowly, the sublime art of a great epoch degenerated and became the servant of a society addicted exclusively to luxury and the pleasures of an easy and carefree life.[23]

ILLUSTRATION NO. 3
Egyptian harpists, with large bow-shaped harps. Wall painting in the tomb of Ramses III (XIX. Dynasty, 1320-1200 B.C.E.) (After Julius Wellhausen, *The Book of Psalms,* New York, 1898).

ILLUSTRATION NO. 4
Egyptian harp, lute, double pipe, lyre and square drum. (After Sir Gardner Wilkinson, *The Manners and Customs of the Ancient Egyptians,* London, 1878).

ILLUSTRATION NO. 5
Egyptian lyres from a tomb of the XIX. Dynasty (1320-1200 B.C.E.) (After Carl Engel, *The Music of the Most Ancient Nations,* London, 1864).

ILLUSTRATION NO. 6
Lute player from Tell el Amarna (After Friedrich Behn, *Musikleben im Altertum und frühen Mittelalter*, Stuttgart, 1954).

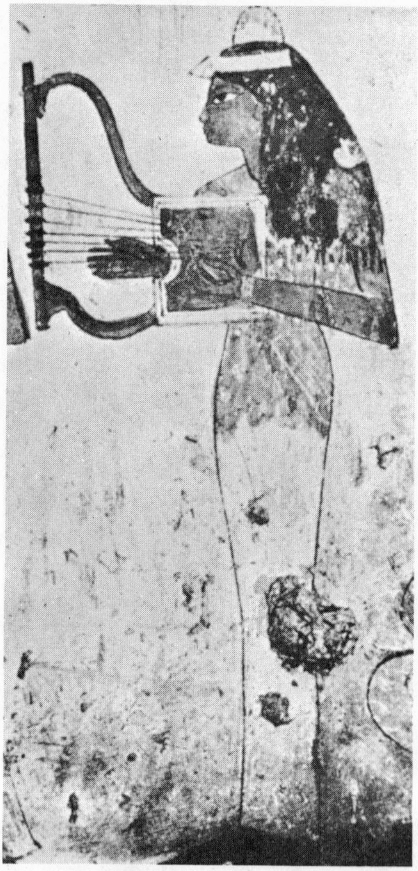

ILLUSTRATION NO. 7
Egyptian lyre. Wall painting from tomb 38, Thebes. (XVIII. Dynasty, 1580-1320 B.C.E.) (After Curt Sachs, *The History of Musical Instruments*, New York, 1940).

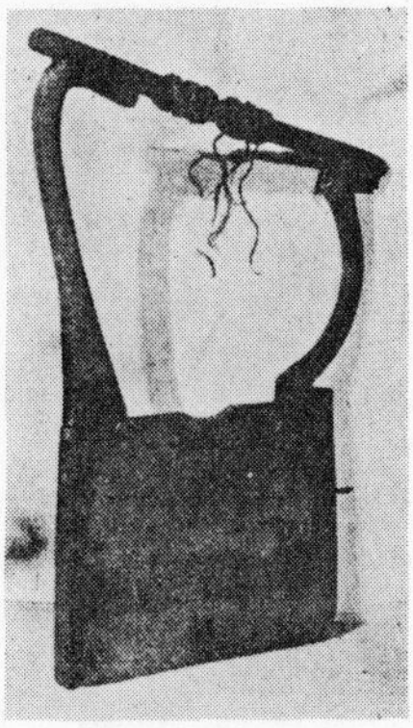

ILLUSTRATION NO. 8
Egyptian lyre. Probably from Der el-Medinah (New Empire, 1580-1090 B.C.E.). (After Hans Hickmann, *Musikgeschichte in Bildern*, Leipzig, 1961).

ILLUSTRATION NO. 9
The long-necked lute (New Empire, 1580-1090 B.C.E.). (After Curt Sachs, *The History of Musical Instruments*. New York, 1940).

ILLUSTRATION NO. 10
Small bow-shaped Egyptian harp with twenty strings. Found at Thebes (After Julius Wellhausen, *The Book of Psalms*, New York, 1898).

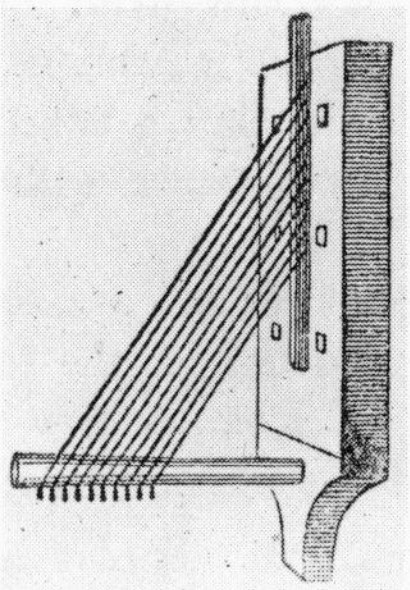

ILLUSTRATION NO. 11
Small Egyptian angular harp (ca. 1300 B.C.E.) In the Museum, Cairo. (After Julius Wellhausen, *The Book of Psalms*, New York, 1898).

ILLUSTRATION NO. 12.
Statuette of an Egyptian girl playing a triangular harp (XXV. Dynasty, ca. 1300 B.C.E.) British Museum (After Sir John Stainer, *The Music of the Bible,* London, 1914).

3. BABYLONIA AND ASSYRIA*

It is reasonable to assume that the Babylonians inherited their civilization from an earlier people. Until recently, however, the nation that might have been the predecessor of the Babylonian empire was unknown. Modern science has established the fact that this historical role was played by the Sumerians.

Together with the other elements of their culture, the music of the Sumerians was taken over by the Babylonians, and with it the terms of their musical practice as well as most of the instruments, including their names.

When the Babylonians appropriated the old Sumerian prayers, they considered them sacred, just as they did the old language of the Sumerians.

> "Their priests inserted the Sumerian songs, hymns, litanies and prayers in their own religious service, and recited or sang them in the original language, just as Hebrew songs are chanted and sung . . . even to-day in our synagogues."[24]

The music in the Babylonian cult was performed by the *kalû* (priest), the *zammarû* (singer) and, for the lamentations, by the *lallarû* (singer of wailing). A representation in the sacrificial picture of Teloh shows an instrument with eleven strings, as used at a Sumerian sacrificial festival.[25] Other instruments depicted in antiquities found at Bismaya have five and seven strings,[26] and represent furthermore a procession of musicians, with boys, female singers and instrumentalists from the Assyrian period.[27] Among the Hittite excavations at Sandchirli was found a bas-relief, showing a minstrel playing a long-necked lute; a man listens fascinated by his performance. (Illustr. 26).

The most important Babylonian and Assyrian pictures, however, are those in which the triumphant return of victorious kings is reproduced. In the royal palace of SENNAḤERIB, excavated in the neighborhood of what is now the village of Kuyundchik, there are well-preserved bas-reliefs in which musicians

* Babylonia and Assyria, owing to the close affinity of their music, are treated here in the same chapter.

and singers are shown exalting the glory of the king. In one of these pictures, SENNAḤERIB is depicted in his chariot, after a victorious battle, reviewing his prisoners; the conquered people are characterized by the wearing of an inverted Phrygian cap. In front of the king are musicians playing harps and praising the victor. Another bas-relief represents a victorious campaign against another people. In the conquered capital city, palm-trees are felled; musicians with drums and, possibly, with cymbals seem to perform some kind of ritual dance. Singing women, marking the rhythm by clapping their hands, are seen marching to welcome the king.

Even more pompous is the reception by the inhabitants of the conquered city of Susa of SENNAḤERIB's grandson, ASHUR-IDANNI-PAL (or ASHUR-AK-BAL, 668-626 B.C.E.). This picture gives important disclosures about the composition of an Elamite orchestra. There are nine singing boys, clapping their hands to mark the rhythm. Three men play upon harps with sixteen or more strings; two of the men are represented with one foot lifted, as though they were dancing. One man blows a double-oboe; another, marching also with dance steps, plays a sort of psaltery, an instrument built of a hollow sounding board with strings stretched upon it. His right hand holds a plectrum, the fingers of the left hand either strike the strings or seem to produce different pitches by stopping the strings. Four women play upon large harps, another blows a double-oboe; still another beats a small drum attached to her body. In addition, we see six singing women, one of them applying a pressure to her throat and cheeks, a procedure used in the Orient to produce a shrill tone. (Illustr. 27).

The composition of this group of musicians affords an illuminating insight into the character of the music of the Assyrians. It shows that, in their orchestras, the percussion instruments were of minor significance, compared with the main feature of their musical practice, vocal music. The use of nine singing boys and six female singers indicates that the singing must have been of a dominant volume, in general. Besides, there are seven stringed instruments, but only two double-oboes; single flutes (or oboes) are entirely absent. Yet, it must be considered that this procession represents the jubilant reception of a king after a victorious battle. Two small hand-drums and a pair of cymbals for the triumphant entrance of a conqueror is indeed a modest percussion inventory, to say the least. This peculiarity leads to the conclusion that the basic trend of Assyrian music, at least in the period of the great kings, was that of refinement, the same trend we witnessed in the golden age of Egyptian music.

In general, the music of Babylonia and Assyria was not basically different from that of Egypt. In all these countries, the types of principal instruments were similar: the horizontal and vertical angular harps, the different kinds of lyres, the double-oboe, as well as the drums, cymbals, and other percussion instruments. For love-songs a "ten-stringed" instrument was used; sometimes flutes also accompanied these songs.

Occasions on which music was abundantly used in Babylonia were the processions and plays performed at the new year's festival, in which actors and choral groups took part. Such pantomimic displays were probably presented in a dramatic form. This is no more than a reasonable conjecture, however, since we have no detailed reports about such plays.

Just as in Sumeria, the young priests in Babylonia were trained in special schools. Such a school was attached to every big temple. The temples were provided with well stocked libraries, serving as fountain-heads of knowledge for future priests and priestly musicians.

The priestly office just as that of the singers was hereditary, as in Israel. The difference, however, was that, according to Mosaic law, priesthood in Israel was the exclusive privilege of Aaron's descendants, while no such genealogical restrictions are reported from Babylonia and Assyria.

There exists no direct knowledge of a musical notation in these two countries. Yet, it is not impossible that the Babylonians attempted to apply some sort of notation for the direction of chanting or singing, or the instrumental accompaniment.[28]

It must be mentioned that the hymns and supplications of the Assyrians were performed in antiphonal form, as in Israel. Such chants sung responsively by the priest (precentor) and the congregation, or by two choral groups antiphonally, were employed by the Babylonians and Assyrians long before their use was historically recorded by the Israelites. Furthermore, if we consider the fact that the character of the Assyrian music must have been somewhat akin to that of the Hebrews, we may reasonably assume that the Israelites borrowed not only from the Egyptians but also from the Assyrians the elements that gave rise to the future flourishing of their music.

ILLUSTRATION NO. 13
Babylonian harp (ca. 7th cent. B.C.E.) (After Julius Wellhausen, *The Book of Psalms,* New York, 1898).

ILLUSTRATION NO. 14
Semitic musicians from Gudea's epoch. Sacrificial act with musical accompaniment, showing an eleven-stringed harp. Bas-relief from Lagash (Telloh), ca. 2400 B.C.E. In the Louvre, Paris (After Fritz Hommel, *Geschichte Babyloniens und Assyriens,* Berlin, 1885-88).

ILLUSTRATION NO. 15
Semitic captives (probably Israelites) playing lyres under the eye of an Assyrian guard. Stone-relief from Lagash (Telloh), ca. 7. cent. B.C.E. British Museum. (After Julius Wellhausen, *The Book of Psalms,* New York, 1898).

ILLUSTRATION NO. 16
Assyrian (Aramaean) musicians. Stone-relief found in the palace of King Barrekub at Sandchirli (ca. 7th cent. B.C.E.) (After Friedrich Behn, *Musikleben im Altertum . . . , Stuttgart,* 1954).

ILLUSTRATION NO. 17
Assyrian double oboe in conical form (After Carl Engel, *The Music of the Most Ancient Nations,* London, 1864).

ILLUSTRATION NO. 18
Assyrian quartet. Bas-relief found at Kuyundchik (ca. 680 B.C.E.) Louvre, Paris. (After Carl Engel, *The Music of the Most Ancient Nations,* London, 1864).

ILLUSTRATION No. 19
Assyrian musicians playing dulcimers with small sticks. Bas-relief found at Kuyundchik (ca. 9th cent. B.C.E.) British Museum (After Carl Bezold, *Ninive und Babylon* (Bielefeld and Leipzig, 1903).

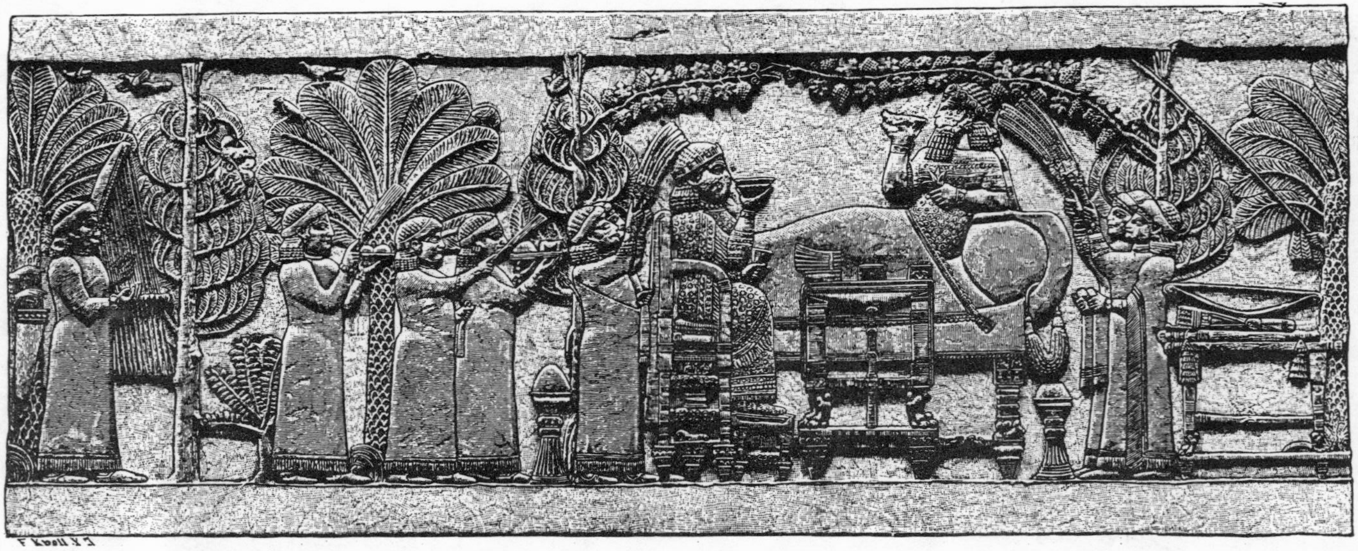

ILLUSTRATION No. 20
"Garden Party." Ashur-Idanni-Pal with his Queen at a banquet in the garden, entertained by musicians. Stone-relief found at Kuyundchik (ca. 7. cent. B.C.E.) British Museum (After Fritz Hommel, *Die Geschichte Babyloniens und Assyriens,* Berlin, 1885).

ILLUSTRATION NO. 21
Sacrifices with musical accompaniment in Assyria. Stone-relief found at Kuyundchik (ca. 7. cent. B.C.E.). British Museum (After Carl Bezold, *Ninive und Babylon,* Bielefeld and Leipzig, 1903).

ILLUSTRATION NO. 22
Assyrian quartet. Two harps, a double-oboe and a dulcimer. The players are apparently dancing. Stone-relief found at Kuyundchik (ca. 680 B.C.E.). British Museum (After Francis W. Galpin, *The Music of the Sumerians . . . ,* Cambridge, 1937).

ILLUSTRATION No. 23
Assyrian harpist with an instrument of 22 strings. The performer appears to be marching. Stone-relief found at Kuyundchik (628-626 B.C.E.), British Museum (After Carl Engel, *The Music of the Most Ancient Nations,* London, 1864).

ILLUSTRATION No. 27
Solemn reception of Ashur-Idanni-Pal after the conquest of Susa, the capital city of Elam. Stone-relief found at Kuyundchik (ca. 628-626 B.C.E.). British Museum. (After Carl Engel, *The Music of the Most Ancient Nations,* London, 1864).

ILLUSTRATION No. 24
Assyrian lyre with five strings. The player seems to use a plectrum (7. cent., B.C.E.) (After Carl Engel, *The Music of the Most Ancient Nations,* London, 1864).

ILLUSTRATION No. 25
Assyrian long-necked lute (7. cent. B.C.E.) (After Carl Engel, *The Music of the Most Ancient Nations,* London, 1864).

ILLUSTRATION No. 26
Babylonian minstrel playing a long-necked lute, with a raptured listener. Stone-relief, found at Sandchirli (time of the Mitanni, 15. cent. B.C.E.). Berlin Museum (After Alfred Jeremias, *Handbuch der altorientalischen Geisteskultur,* Leipzig, 1913).

ILLUSTRATION NO. 28
Musicians on a phoenician bowl from Cyprus. Double-oboe, lyre and hand-drum. British Museum. (After Fritz Behn, *Musikleben im Altertum* . . . , Stuttgart, 1954).

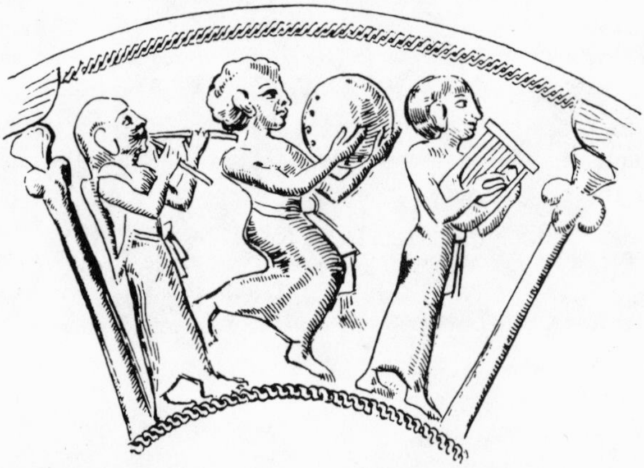

ILLUSTRATION NO. 29
Musicians on a phoenician bowl from Olympia. Double-oboe, hand-drum and lyre. British Museum. (After Fritz Behn, *Musikleben im Altertum* . . . , Stuttgart, 1954).

4. CHALDAEA

The country of Chaldaea *(ereẓ kasdim),* mentioned repeatedly in the Bible (Gen. 11:28,31; Jer. 24:5, 25:12, 50:8,10; 51:24; Ezek. 23:23, etc.), is considered by many to be identical with Babylonia. This, however, is a misconception historically, geographically, and ethnographically. The Chaldaeans were of Indo-European origin, whereas the Babylonians were Semites.[29] The Chaldaeans were bellicose and eager for conquest; they first captured certain parts of Sumeria and subsequently adopted the civilization of the conquered nation. They spread out over the entire southern part of Mesopotamia bordering the Persian Gulf; their ancient capital city was Bit Yakin. From there, they first subdued Babylonia (ca. 1300 B.C.E.), and later, after the collapse of Assyria, established the Greater Babylonian Empire, *mat kaldu,* which included Babylonia, Assyria, and several other smaller countries, such as Peḳod, Shoʿa and Koʿa (Ezek. 23:23).

Other historians think that the *kaldi* were Aramaeans, *i.e.* Semites.[30] Against this the fact can be cited that the Babylonian king SENNAḤERIB (705-681 B.C.E.) always made a clear distinction between the *kaldi* on the one hand, and the Arabians and Aramaeans, on the other.[31] This seems to indicate that the *kaldi* must have belonged to another race. The Bible, too, for the most part, uses different terms for the Babylonians *(benē Babel)* and the Chaldaeans *(kasdim),* an indication that they were considered different peoples (*cp.* Ezek. 23:23; Jer. 25:12; 50:8; 50:24,25; 50:35; 51:24; 51:35, and other places).

Such a controversy would be of no significance for the history of music of the ancient Hebrews, were there not a special circumstance to be considered. As already mentioned, the home-town of the patriarch Abraham was the "Chaldaean" city of ʾUr *(ʾur kasdim),* from where he emigrated to Canaʿan (Gen. 11:28, 31). This fact brought about the theory that it was Abraham who transplanted the music of the Chaldaeans *(i.e.* virtually of the Sumerians) to Canaʿan. It has already been shown that this would scarcely have been possible for a detached tribe, or even a larger section of a people, let alone for a single clan. The music of Sumeria-Chaldaea came to Israel by way of the general cultural intercourse between the ancient nations of the Near-East.

Following the conquest of Sumeria by the *kaldi,* the ancient bellicose customs of the new rulers were gradually softened by the infinitely higher civilization of the vanquished. With the general culture of the Sumerians, the *kaldi* adopted also the musical tradition of the subjugated people. The *kaldi,* subsequently, were instrumental in transplanting this tradition to Babylonia, and in this indirect way, Sumerian music might have been introduced into Israel.

5. PHOENICIA

The geographical location of Phoenicia and the cultural intercourse carried on for centuries with its neighboring nations, determined the civilization of this people, famous in Antiquity for its trading and colonizing activities.

The evaluation of the civilizatory role the Phoenicians played in Antiquity recently underwent some changes. While formerly historiography attributed to them a paramount importance in the civilization of the Mediterranean basin, modern science is challenging this opinion. Now the pendulum swings to the other extreme, denying them creative capacities in almost all domains of their intellectual life, asserting that their cultural achievements had been taken over exclusively from other peoples. To a certain extent this would be understandable, considering the centuries old close commercial ties the Phoenicians entertained with the entire civilized world of Antiquity. Still, the truth seems to lie between these two extremes, since in certain fields (e.g. architecture, sculpture, handicrafts, etc.) the Phoenicians proved to be such accomplished masters that their creative talents cannot be questioned. This is the case mainly in the domain of architecture.

o
o o

We know from the Bible that, toward the end of David's reign, HIRAM I, king of Tyre (980-947 B.C.E.), built for the Jewish monarch a splendid palace of precious cedar-wood (2 Sam. 5:11). Furthermore, David planned to erect, with the assistance of HIRAM, a magnificent temple that would replace the modest tabernacle built by Jewish hands (2 Sam. 7:1-2).

David's project did not materialize before Solomon's accession to the throne (1 Kings 5:15 ff). HIRAM sent to his friend (to the "tyrant of Jerusalem," as the historian DIOS calls him)[32] his most skilled carpenters and craftsmen, together with all the necessary material.

The Second Temple, too, was built, after the return from the Babylonian exile, by stone-masons, carpenters and craftsmen from Sidon and Tyre (Ezra 3:7).

Thus, biblical, and other, sources attest to the proficiency in architecture and to the skill in arts and crafts of the Phoenicians. As to their music, however, we have no more than conjectures, since historical records in this field are few and highly contradictory.

In view of the close cultural intercourse with the Egyptians and especially owing to the fact that for several centuries Phoenicia was occupied by Egyptian rulers, we might assume that the Phoenicians derived their musical culture mainly from Egypt. The Egyptian civilization was older than that of the Phoenicians; this alone would presuppose the influence of Egyptian music upon that of the Phoenicians. Even the statement of the priests of Baal-Melkart, patron of Tyre, that their temple had existed for 2300 years,[33] would not contradict this assumption. Yet, the music of the Phoenicians might have been influenced also by their immediate neighbors, the Assyrians.

As for their instruments, the lyre *(kinnor)*, considered by many to have been a Phoenician "invention," was likely to have had as its model a similar Egyptian instrument (*k·nn·r*). Much more credit is due to the statement of SOPATROS that the *nabla*, another much used stringed instrument of the Phoenicians, had been invented by the Sidonians and was called, therefore, *sidonian nabla*.[34] Among the other popular instruments in Phoenicia, IOUBA mentions the *lyrophoinikos* and the small triangular harp, the *trigōnon* (called also *epigoneion*).[35] JULIUS POLLUX, in enumerating the instruments of his time, mentions two stringed instruments the names of which are indications of their Phoenician origin: the *phoinix* and the *lyrophoinikos* (see above); he gives, however, no further description of them.[36] (Illus. 28 and 29.).

The ethnographic, economic and cultural intercourse between Phoenicia and Israel might lead to the assumption that the music of both peoples have many similarities. Such a conclusion would be logical, were it not for one serious obstacle: the gap between the religious ethics of the two neighboring peoples.

The Phoenician religion was based upon the cult of Ishtar (or Astarte) and indulged in the cruel service of Moloch, in which human sacrifices had to be offered to the gods.

PLUTARCH reports that such sacrifices took place to the accompaniment of flutes and drums, "so that the cries of the wailing should not reach the ears of the people." [37]

One of the sacred institutions of the Ashera cult were the innumerable hierodules maintained in the temples. These were the ill-famed *kedeshot* (lit. "dedicated ones"), practicing religious prostitution in the temples. The money so earned was delivered as offerings to the goddess. The *kedeshah* also had to take care of the music and singing in the regular morning and evening sacrificial rites.[38] At the big temples, their number was 3000 to 6000 and even more. Their favorite instruments were the *ʾabub* and the *trigōnon,* already mentioned. Phoenician Syria provided the Near-East and the Mediterranean basin with large groups of those *ʾabub*-playing girls, the *ambubaiae,* who populated the streets and places of the great cities, and whose playing and singing was but the cloak for a less honorable trade.[39]

The comparison of these savage customs with the enlightened conceptions of the Jewish religion speaks for itself. The Israelites declared human sacrifices an "abomination" (Deut. 12:31; 18:10, 2 Kings 16:3; 17:17; 21:6; 23:10; 2 Chron. 28.3; 33:6; Jer. 7:31; 19:5; 32:35; Ezek. 16:21; Lev. 18:21; 20:2-5; Kings 15:12); severely condemned religious prostitution (Deuter. 23:18, 19; *cp.* also 1 Sam. 2:22). The Mosaic law also established the strong prohibition of harlotry as a means of increasing the Temple's treasury (Deut· 23:19).

Strangely enough, the music of the Phoenicians was characterized by the writers of Antiquity in a peculiar way; they based their reports solely upon the orgiastic rites of the Phoenician religion, without the slightest hint that the Phoenicians might have had another kind of musical art as well. Among the ancient reports one in particular should be mentioned, because it gave rise to an entirely biased conception of the music of this nation, a conception which lasted up to our own time.

ARISTIDES QUINTILIANUS (fl. 1-2 century C.E.), in his book *De Musica,* investigated the musical practice of the peoples in the Near-East of his time, and arrived at the following conclusion:

> "In the realm of [musical] education there are two degenerate trends: one is the entire lack *(amousia),* and the other the wrong practice, of art *(kakomousia).*"

He gave examples of both phenomena among the peoples of this region; according to his statement, the second category included, among others,

> "those who cultivate the sensuous instincts, who are too enervated psychically and not hardened enough physically, such as the Phoenicians and their descendants [the colonists living] along the northern coast of Lybia." [40]

LUCIAN (ca. 125-ca. 190 C.E.) also gives a detailed account of the spring festival at Hieropolis and says:

> "But the greatest of all feasts is kept in the first summer season, some call it Fire-Feast, and some Torch-Feast. . . . They cut their own arms and beat each other upon their backs. And many that stand there play flutes and many beat timbrels and others sing sacred songs." [41]

This report is generally considered a confirmation of ARISTIDES' opinion about the music of the Phoenicians. Actually, LUCIAN states merely the facts, but gives no evaluation of the music itself. Thus, the only contemporary judgment about the music of the Phoenicians is that of ARISTIDES.

His report might be authentic, perhaps, for the epoch in which he lived. At that period, the mores and the art of the Phoenicians must already have shown a marked decline. Furthermore, it must be remembered that the report of ARISTIDES concerns only a special aspect of Phoenician music. He did not elaborate upon other possible musical manifestations of this people, who gave so many irrefutable proofs of their outstanding artistic qualities in other fields, such as painting, sculpture, architecture, and handicrafts.

There are several indirect indications that the Phoenicians at least at the height of their civilization, must have had a nobler and more refined tonal art, than the *kakomousia* intimated by ARISTIDES. The Phoenicians had probably taken over part of their music from the Egyptians. As we already know, Egyptian music in its classical period was solemn, sedate, and full of dignity. The music of the Assyrians, too, apart from its orgiastic features at religious festivals, also showed a nobler aspect on other occasions. We know, moreover, that the Lydians, whose religion contained orgiastic rituals similar to those of the Phoenicians, had a more dignified music in addition to the sensuous type (see *infra)*. If we recall the cultural relationships which existed among the nations of the ancient Near-East, we may assume that the artistic quality of the music of the neighboring civilizations might have exercised a definite influence upon the musical practice of the Phoenicians, a nation so obviously gifted in the arts.

There is strong, though indirect proof for this assumption. The principal stringed instruments, *kinnor* and *nebel,* were identical among the Phoenicians and the Israelites. We know of the highly artistic use the Hebrews made of these two "sacred" instruments. It would not be unreasonable, therefore, to conclude that the Phoenicians also used these instruments in an artistic manner.

In addition, we may point out another fact, considered by SACHS as a definite sign of aesthetic trends in the complex character of the Phoenicians. SACHS proved that the Spanish dance, the basic aspect of which is dignity and beauty of form, originated in Phoenicia.[42] A people that possessed such dances, could not have been barbarous without some discernment in its art, but must have had nobler, aesthetically and ethically loftier spheres of artistic activity.

For want of direct and authentic source material about the music of the Phoenicians, the conclusions as ventured above are conjectures, to be sure, but they possess a high degree of probability. The analogies with the musical civilization of their immediate neighbors, especially of Israel, are the strongest supports for this assumption.

6. PHRYGIA AND LYDIA

One cannot avoid mentioning, in this survey, two other peoples of Antiquity whose music was sufficiently wide-spread to have had an influence upon the musical practice of the Israelites. These peoples were the Phrygians and the Lydians.

Statements of Greek philosophers and historians carry repeated indications that the Phrygians and Lydians were the instructors of the Hellenes in musical art. The reports suggest even the approximate time (7th century B.C.E.) in which this musical fertilization took place. According to the sources, the Greeks took over from these nations some specific modes and were taught by them the art of playing instruments.[43]

The reliability of these historical records is proven by the fact that the forms of musical practice among the ancient peoples of the Near-East were basically the same. The only, though important, difference was the particular ethos attributed by these peoples to their music. The instruments used by the various nations were basically identical, with only minor regional differences.

A people which took over an instrument from another people, would experiment with it and attempt more or less essential changes. Even if the basic form was left intact, something would be added here, or taken away there, so that ultimately a different handling of the instrument became necessary; this changed technique possibly transformed the character of its sound. This should be borne in mind if, in the ancient records, we sometimes come across instruments having the same name, but serving entirely opposite purposes and being used at completely different occasions.

For instance, the pipe (oboe) was blown strongly by the Syrians; its tone, therefore, had a savage character. This is how the instrument was used at the feasts of the slain and resurrected Adonis. The Phrygians, on the other hand, accompanied a specific dirge, the *lytierses,* with similar pipes which, however, were blown softly. The pipes used for such funeral dirges were called *monauloi thrēnētikoi,* "lamenting pipes." [44] Yet, among the Israelites, the pipe *(ḥalil)* was the instrument of joyous popular festivals, as well as the typical mourning instrument which was used at every funeral.[45]

The character of the Lydians showed qualities which might appear contradictory: a propensity toward licentiousness and debauchery on the one hand, and fierce warrior virtues on the other. HERODOTUS states that he knows no people more valiant and virile. Like other nations of Antiquity, the Lydians, too, worshipped Cybele whose rites contained orgiastic ceremonies and a noisy music that created a state of sensuous ecstasy among the worshippers. It seems, however, that they also cultivated another type of music, which was serious and dignified, for ARISTOTLE considered it particularly appropriate for the education of young men. The Phrygian and Lydian modes were early introduced into Greek music and constituted, together with the native Dorian mode, the basic feature of the future music theory of the Hellenes.

7. GREECE

Strictly speaking, in the survey of the musical civilization of Israel's neighbors the music of the Greeks should not be lacking. If, however, we do bypass that music, it is for a special reason.

The main source of our knowledge about the music of the Israelites, the Bible, came to a temporary close in the 5th century B.C.E. At this time, the influence of the Greek civilization upon Jewish life in general was by no means so decisive as to leave any recognizable marks in the field of Jewish cultural endeavors. Jewish music, in particular, was still mainly under the spell of Egypt, Babylonia and Assyria. Greek influence gained foothold in Jewish life only several centuries later, when it had succeeded in creating a new spiritual movement, a new way of life. At this time, Hellenism had spread quite conspicuously among certain strata of society of the Hebrews, especially in the large cities. Almost no branch of social life remained untouched by the new trend. In the field of music, however, Greek influence was quite negligible.

It is not difficult to discover the reason for this situation.

In the Hellenistic period of Jewish cultural life, Hebrew music already possessed a strength of its own; the sacred as well as secular music of the Jews had developed characteristics so idiomatic that Greek interference—if any—could not penetrate below the surface. At any rate, the essence of Jewish music remained unscathed by the Hellenistic philosophy of art and its resultant practice.

In biblical as well as in post-biblical sources, there is not the slightest indication that Greek music would have left any trace in Jewish tonal art. The music of the Israelites, conscious of its individual nature, successfully avoided the temptations of Greek music. The inimical attitude of the talmudic sages regarding Greek song,[46] and the general hostility of Judaism, faithful to its traditional past, to the inroads of the Hellenistic spirit into Jewish cultural life are indirect, but nevertheless strong indications that music in Israel remained virtually untouched by Greek music.

For this reason, passing over the music of the Greeks, as being immaterial for the development of Jewish music, seems to be fully justified for the present limited survey.

8. CANAʿAN

Historical research has established that the land of Canaʿan, the future homeland of the Israelites, possessed no civilization of its own prior to its occupation by the Hebrews. This is explained by its geographical location between the two greatest centers of culture in early Antiquity, Egypt and Babylonia. For thousands of years, not only the courts, but also the peoples themselves, sustained continuous communication, and the route between them always passed through Canaʿan. Soldiers, ambassadors, trading caravans maintained a steady flow from one country to the other. Letters, reports and gifts were sent from one ruler to the other. All cultural and political exchange centered in Canaʿan as a focal point.

The entire coast of the Mediterranean north of Canaʿan was a string of minuscule principalities, mostly reduced to the environs of a city. The most important ones were the Phoenician cities Arvad, Byblos (Gebal), Beirut, Sidon, the island-city of Tyre and the cities on the coast Usu and Akko.

The territory of Cana'an, too, was splintered into small city-states, which constantly rivaled each other, and had their own *ba'alim* as well as their own ritual customs. The language of the land was similar to the Hebrew. Traces of Aramaic can not be found yet at this period.[47]

Whether the music of the Cana'anite religious rites was similar to that of the Phoenicians, or whether it had its own features, can only be surmised. Yet, it is highly probable that the music of the ancient inhabitants of the country exerted its influence upon the newcomers. At the beginning, there might have been a certain blending of the religion of Yahveh with the cult of the Cana'anites; in this stage, the rites of both must have been similar.[48] Yahveh was worshipped with pagan ceremonies, consequently with pagan songs. The "high places," mentioned in numerous passages of the Scriptures, were the sites of such ceremonies.[49]

After the death of the judge Yaïr, we find, among the Israelites, Syrian, Phoenician, Moabite, Ammonite, and Philistine rites, furthermore the worship of *ba'alim* and *'asherim,* as practiced by the Cana'anites (Judg. 10:6,10). With these rites the Hebrews adopted the usual forms of worship, called the names of the deities (1 Kings 18:24), and gave them praises (Josh. 23:7); the songs of these rites were the same as those used in the heathen religions. About their character we are informed by the description of the divine judgment at Mount Carmel (1 Kings 18:26-28). The delirious ecstasy, the invocations *(i.e.* "singing") accompanied by savage dances and noisy music, were the outstanding features of the ceremonies of the priests of Ba'al. They give us a vivid picture of the orgiastic character of this kind of ritual music.

Soon, however, the spiritually and ethically higher religion of Israel prevailed over the temptations of the sensuous worship of pagan deities. These Jewish qualities carried the victory in the struggle of the Yahveh religion against the established crude forms of the heathen cults. Thus, the basis was given for the transformation of the music of the pagan Cana'anite rites into the spiritually loftier music of the Jewish cult.

Yet, the Jewish people could never have withstood the surrounding pagan influences, it could never have created its own musical art, had it not been gifted by nature in matters musical. From Egypt and the desert, Israel brought to Cana'an the joy of singing, a vivid phantasy in music, as well as a wealth of old songs.[50] Its natural gifts must have been stronger than the music found in Cana'an. This explains why Jewish music prevailed, despite its still undeveloped form. The musical culture of the Israelites, coming into bloom relatively soon after the conquest of Cana'an, approximately in Samuel's time, shows that the Hebrews succeeded rapidly in overcoming pagan preponderance and in finding their own form of musical expression,—a development leading within a remarkably short period to the highly organized musical institutions of David and Solomon.

And just as the Israelites succeeded almost from the beginning in extricating themselves from foreign ideological influences, so did they also learn during their later national existence how to preserve their musical culture from dangerous and disintegrating inroads.

II. THE BIBLE AND OTHER HISTORICAL SOURCES OF JEWISH MUSIC

If we compare our relatively limited knowledge of the music of the great nations of Antiquity with whatever the Bible reveals about the music of Israel, it will be evident that the biblical information is at bottom far more eloquent and meaningful than all the other records of Antiquity concerning music, except those of the Greeks. As a matter of fact, the musical references of the Bible are almost the first records in the history of mankind that afford a comprehensive insight into the musical culture of a people of high Antiquity.

At the time when the Old Testament came to a temporary closing, music in Jewish life has already reached the stage of its inner consolidation. In Israel's early history, music has been mostly an implement for superstition and magic. In the intermediate stage it was the necessary background for religious rites. Only in its further development it became possession of the entire people. At this stage, it was deeply rooted in the people's consciousness; it was no more a mere accessory of religion, or the privilege of a single class, but the common property of a whole nation. Music became a people's art, in the broadest sense of the word.

This universal significance of music in the life of the Jewish people, this indivisible unity between people and art, is the explanation for the fact that the references of the Bible concerning music are mostly of a general nature. The biblical authors took it for granted that the people were thoroughly familiar with musical matters, so that they considered it unnecessary to indulge in long descriptions and minute details.

A further proof of the importance of music in the life of the Jewish people is a legend related almost at the beginning of the Old Testament. There, music is mentioned as being one of the three fundamental professions: that of the herdsman, of the metal forger, and of the musician (Gen. 4:20-22). Even in those archaic times, music was looked upon as a necessity in every day's life, enjoying equal rights with the other two primitive professions, as a beautifying and enriching complement of human existence.

We find a similar legend in the mythology of other ancient peoples. In the Sumerian epos *Tagtug and Dilmun,* there is an obvious parallel to Gen. 4:21,22:

> "The Sumero-Accadian god Enki, 'Lord of the Earth,' has numerous titles as patron of the arts, of the singers and psalmists."

The Sumerian Lumḫa, like the Hebrew Lamech, is said to have been the father of three sons. This myth seems to have been taken over and transformed by the Hebrews.[1]

Jubal of the Jewish legend was the first musician in history, the "inventor" of musical instruments and, through this, the creator of the musical profession and musical art, and the "father," *i.e.* the patron, of musicians. This, of course, cannot be measured or evaluated by way of historical standards.

The biblical tale about the three primeval professions, though only a myth, has nevertheless a symbolic meaning. Some biblical commentators believe that once there might have existed a specific saga about the origin of human civilization. This might have been used by the biblical author.

In the genealogy of Lamech's three sons, the name of Kain needs no further explanation, since the word, in Arabic, signifies "smith." This is the personification of a profession, a procedure often to be found in the mythology of Antiquity.

It is assumed that Jabal is identical with Kain's brother Habel or Hebel, mentioned in Gen. 5:2 ff. The initial letters of Habel and Jabal are different, but variants of the first letters of such names are rather frequent. The meaning of the word is the same as the Arabic *ʾabil,* "the shepherd (of camels)." Thus, the analogy is established to Kain, the "smith." Abel, the shepherd, called in one passage of the Bible Habel, in the other Jabal, are variants of the same name, with an identical profession.[2]

Jubal, the patron of music, is Kain's half-brother. The word Jubal is very similar to *yobel,* the "horn." Probably the punctuation of the noun *yobel* underwent some changes and was thus transformed into Jubal. It can hardly be doubted that Jubal is the personification of the "horn," just as ʾAharon, the brother of Moses, is the symbolization of ʾAron, the "ark of Covenant." Or, to quote an even more appropriate, though non-Hebrew, example of Antiquity, the mythical hero KINNYRAS of Phoenicia, who is the personification of the *kinnyra* (the *kinnor,* "lyre"). In mythology, hypostasis is a frequent procedure to determine the originator of an art or craft. In the case of Lamech's three sons, the ancestors of the three professions so essential to nomadic life,—herdsmen, forging and music,—the hypostasis was the given procedure for the personification.

o
o o

In primeval times music is completely subjected to daily functions; it represents the pure and exclusive form of *music for practical use* or *utilitarian music* ("Gebrauchsmusik"). A higher importance was attributed to it as soon as it became a part of the religious ceremony. This was a decisive step in the development of music since only when it ceased to be exclusively the servant of daily life and a helper for physical work, could it rise into a higher and more independent sphere. The music of the cult, too, was not yet a full-manifestation of free art, supposed to provide mankind with feelings of happiness, *i.e.* to provide the element of sheer pleasure in aesthetic experience, but it was a significant step in this direction.

In the archaic stage of civilization, the music for practical use represents mainly the rhythmical support and accentuation of daily manual work. There is a long way from this stage to music as an embellishment of religious ceremonies. The transition was not a sudden one, of course; it entailed a gradual development that cannot be examined here. One phase, however, should be mentioned at this point, namely: music as implement in magic and sorcery. Music in magic was certainly older than its use in the cult. For a long time it served both purposes. Cultural history furnishes innumerable examples for the use of music to chase away demons, heal madness, and for its participation in all kinds of magic practices. There are in the Scriptures more vestiges of all these uses than one would ordinarily suppose. They are, however, mostly veiled as to their real meaning, often even purposely blurred, so that it is sometimes difficult to detect their original meaning.

o
o o

Apart from the Bible, there are a few historical writings of Antiquity which contain some rather substantial even if occasional information about the music of Ancient Israel. Among them, the two books of FLAVIUS JOSEPHUS (37-ca. 100 C.E.), "Wars of the Jews," and "Antiquities of the Jews" occupy an outstanding place. The advantage of these works is that their author possessed a close and intimate knowledge of many things he actually described. Their weakness lies in the fact that their author indulges almost continuously in glorifying his people. This led him to some exaggerations and often impaired his credibility.

The other famous Jewish writer who still lived during the period of the independent Jewish state, was PHILO OF ALEXANDRIA, called PHILO JUDAEUS (ca. 20 B.C.E.-ca. 40 C.E.). His numerous historical and philosophical essays, both large and small, reveal, on the whole, a good understanding of the general musical culture of his time. But his treatment of the subject is completely under the spell of the musical theory and philosophy of the Hellenes. Facts concerning the music of his own people are almost entirely missing in his writings; the few historical references to that effect do not constitute any substantial enrichment of our knowledge of the music of Ancient Israel. On the other hand, his description of certain musical usages of the Jewish sect of the Therapeutae has been made with care and allows us to draw, retrospectively, a few conclusions with regard to the musical practice of the ancient Hebrews.

The writings of the Greek and Roman historians and philosophers contain, as far as they deal with the history and customs of the Jews, quite a number of valuable references to Jewish music, but also many erroneous statements and many details they did not observe as eyewitnesses. The principal authors in this field are TACITUS (ca. 55-ca. 117 C.E.), DIODORUS SICULUS (1st century B.C.E.) and, in some respects also ATHENAEUS (ca. 200 C.E.), whose writings contain a multitude of references to the music practice of coeval Greece and thus, shed indirectly some light upon that of the Israelites. A few works which are known to have contained valuable information about the music of the Hebrews, are lost, one of them by NICOLAS DAMASCENUS (ca. 100 B.C.E.), which was partly used by JOSEPHUS.

Further important sources of information about the ancient Jewish music are contained in the early rabbinical literature, such as the Mishnah, Gemara, Tosefta, the Babylonian and Palestinian Talmud, and—as far as these are preserved,—the Targumim, the Aramaic versions of the biblical text. The collection of Jewish legends and tales, the Midrashim, contains also quite a number of references to music, but its credibility with regard to Ancient Israel is naturally limited, especially in the parts added at later times.

The value of the early rabbinic literature for musicological research is rather uneven. The rabbinic writers obviously tried to clarify some obscure passages of the biblical text and to explain obsolete musical terms.

Some of their explanations are useful, others merely add to the existing confusion. Sometimes, the rabbinic opinions contain inner contradictions, or else they are patently erroneous. Amidst good observations, they contain exaggerations easily recognizable to anyone familiar with music.

All this is not surprising if we realize that these interpretations of musical terms were made by men who had only a superficial relation to music and no special musical knowledge to speak of. Their opinions, therefore, mostly fail to clear up doubtful notions about the music of the Jews.

Thus, if the value of the rabbinical writings for musicology is rather limited, their significance for the history of civilization cannot be overlooked. The aim of the talmudic sages was to preserve and to expound tradition. In this field, their work is highly meritorious. Quite a few musical notions and terms, and a goodly number of musical traditions would be irremediably lost without their retrospective care.

There is another reason why the rabbinical literature of the early Diaspora is important for our subject. It shows that, in spite of all the severe religious prohibitions, the Israelites have never given up their music entirely after the destruction of the Temple. As sign of mourning for the ravaged sanctuary, all musical activity was supposed to be abandoned. This interdiction was carried out in one field only, where the spiritual leaders of the dispersed people retained their full sway: in the religious service. Instrumental music, as part of the ceremony, ceased to exist with the downfall of Jerusalem.[3] Singing, however, as practiced in the Synagogue, never was seriously threatened by rabbinic prohibitions.

In still another field, the Jews of the Diaspora succeeded in saving their musical tradition. The secular music, especially its intimate forms, the music at home, the singing of *zemirot* in the family, etc., survived all the vicissitudes. Music was kept in a subdued tone, to be sure, it was cultivated mainly in closed circles, and appeared only at very rare occasions in public life. Yet, this intimate type of musical activity was the indispensable spiritual bridge connecting the Jew with his musical past; it gave consolation to the individual, poured balm upon the wounds of a tormented people, kindled the hope for a better future. Besides his religion, music was the only stimulus for his inner life, and history proves that he never gave up, even for a short while, this comfort to his soul. The early rabbinical literature is the indirect but irrefutable confirmation of this, though it gives us only a rather abstract and hazy picture of the musical practice in the Galut.

A further source of knowledge concerning the music of the Jews in the centuries following the destruction of their national existence are the writings of the early Fathers of the Church. Everything that the patristic literature relates about music, refers directly or indirectly to the musical practice of the Israelites. We know that the early Christian Church was the immediate successor to the Jewish cult. The sacred ceremonies of the Temple, or of the Synagogue, were taken over almost without any change by the Judaeo-Christians. The music of the Temple, at least its vocal aspect, constituted an important element in their sacred service, as it also did, later on, in that of the apostolic Christians. Singing of psalms, hymns, spiritual songs and responses, with or without instrumental accompaniment, was considered by early Christian congregations an indispensable form of worship, just as it used to be in the service of the Temple. The statements of the Church Fathers about the music of the early Christians give us, therefore, a valuable insight into the practice of the direct predecessors of the new Church, the Temple, as well as the Synagogue.

The significance of the patristic literature for Jewish musical research is not minimized by the fact that the writings containing references to music, Jewish and Christian, extend over a relatively long period, until about the sixth century. The development of matters spiritual in those times was slow and hesitant. Christian religion, particularly in its beginnings, aimed not to obliterate, but to preserve basic Jewish tradition. Jesus himself said: "I am not come to destroy, but to fulfill" (Matth. 5:17). Only after a longer period Christian sacred ceremonies show a departure from Jewish rites. Until then, the Church continued the Jewish tradition, especially so in its musical part.

Furthermore, the patristic literature affords a valuable insight into the secular music of the Jews in the Roman Diaspora. From many indications one may see that music had an important part in Jewish secular life, then as before. Besides containing interesting features for the history of civilization, numerous statements of the early Church Fathers are indirect proof that Jewish music survived in those centuries, in spite of every ordeal of fate.

o o o

Written sources provide an impressive amount of material for our subject. However, authentic visual reproductions concerning ancient Jewish music, are very scarce. Pictures published in later times, especially in humanistic literature, are altogether products of the imagination, stemming obviously from Western musical usage.

The few preserved authentic pictures showing Jewish instruments can be quickly enumerated.

On the Arch of Triumph in Rome, erected to the glory of the emperor TITUS after the destruction of the Temple of Jerusalem, are shown the sacred silver trumpets *(ḥaẓoẓerot)*, together with the sacred vessels of the sanctuary, which TITUS carried as booty in his triumphal procession. (Frontispiece)

A coin of Bar Kokba issued during the war of liberation against the emperor HADRIAN (132-135 C.E.), shows a pair of trumpets; they are designed in such a shortened and clumsy fashion that it is somewhat difficult to reconstruct their original shape. According to SACHS, they do not represent trumpets, but oboes.[4] (Illustr. 30).

Nevertheless, we maintain that they are reproductions of the sacred trumpets of the Temple. In these numismatic designs the exact shape of the depicted instruments was only of a secondary importance; the main objective must have been a patriotic demonstration, on coins issued by the victorious national hero, of a sacred symbol of the Jewish religion. The oboe *(ḥalil)* was far from having the same symbolic meaning for the Jews as the *ḥaẓoẓerot,* the use of which was instituted by the commandment of the Lord Himself (Num. 10:2). Bar Kokba's revolt was the first successful resistance of Judaism against a powerful oppressor after the destruction of its national existence. The stamping of their own coins served as a visible and tangible sign of the urge for national survival. The fact that on the coins *two* instruments are represented, is an unmistakable sign that they are the sacred trumpets.

ILLUSTRATION No. 30
The sacred temple instruments (*ḳinnor* and *ḥaẓoẓerot*) shown on Bar-Kokba's coins (132-135 C.E.). British Museum.

ILLUSTRATION No. 31
The sacred Jewish instruments shown on Bar-Kokba's coins (132-135 C.E.) British Museum.

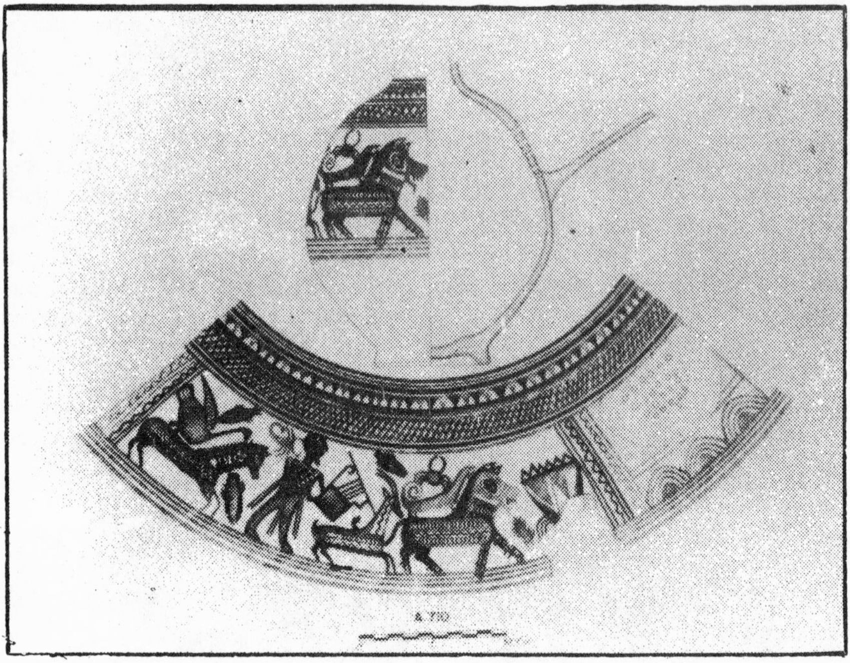

ILLUSTRATION No. 32
Fragment of a Philistine vase found at Megiddo, showing a procession of animals, with a lyre-player (ca. 1150-1000 B.C.E.) (After *The Biblical Archaeologist,* New York, 1941)

ILLUSTRATION NO. 33
Fragment of an ivory-carving found at Megiddo. A lyre-player entertains a Cana'anite king. (ca. 1180 B.C.E.). Rockefeller Museum in Jerusalem. (After R. W. Heaton, *Everyday life in Old Testament Times,* New York, 1956).

ILLUSTRATION No. 34
Enlargement of the *kinnor*-player in Illustr. 33. The instrument has nine strings, a rather bulky four-square resounding body. In all probability this is the prototype of the Jewish *kinnor*.

ILLUSTRATION No. 35
A Semitic lyre-player entering Egypt with his clan. Stone-carving on the Beni-Hassan monument (ca. 1900 B.C.E.) (After Curt Sachs, *History of the Musical Instruments*, New York, 1940).

ILLUSTRATION NO. 36.
Bronze-figurine on a tripod, showing a Jewish flute-girl. The figure had originally on its upper part a head-piece, and served probably as a lamp. The instrument is a double-oboe with two identical pipes. Details cannot be distinguished (ca. 1300-1200 B.C.E.) (After Gottfried Schumacher, *Tell el-Muteselim,* Leipzig, 1929)

Several other coins of Bar-Kokba, issued during the same period, show a further symbol of the once glorious Temple music, the biblical *kinnor* in several varieties. (Illustr. 31) The design of these coins is likewise crude, the strings are represented by thick lines, showing mostly three, on some coins five or six strings. The technique of coinage in those times probably did not allow the application of finer lines. As a matter of fact, Jewish instruments of the lyre-type possessed more strings. It is interesting to observe that the string instruments reproduced on these coins show a great similarity either to the Greek *lyra,* or the Greek *kithara.* They might represent later forms of the ancient Jewish instrument, designed after actual Greek patterns.

The earlier form of the Jewish *kinnor,* probably that of David's time, is depicted on a vase (about 1025 B.C.E.) found at Megiddo. It shows curved side-arms, a straight, horizontal cross bar, protruding on both ends, to which four strings are attached; but the number of strings in this picture is inconclusive, just as in Bar Kokba's coins,—the *kinnor,* especially its *ʿasor* variety, in fact had ten strings. The instrument has on its base a square, fair-sized sounding board, which might have given to it a relatively ample sonority. (Illustr. 33, 34).

This instrument reveals a striking similarity to a lyre on a wall-painting found in Tomb 38 at Thebes (ca. 1420 B.C.E.). Here, as there, the same square sounding board, the same curved side-arms, the same cross bar protruding on both ends; the only difference is that the Egyptian instrument shows seven strings. (Illustr. 7).

It seems that the instrument represented on the vase from Megiddo is the reproduction of such an Egyptian lyre, brought along by the Israelites, or imported earlier by the Canaʿanites and found by the Hebrews in their new homeland. This Egyptian lyre might have served as a model for the Jewish *kinnor* as used by David himself and introduced by him into the music of the Temple. (Illustr. 32).

Furthermore, a portrayal of a Semitic lyre-player should be mentioned, found in a fresco of a sepulchral grotto at Beni-Hassan, in the tomb of a prince named NEHERA-SI-NUM-HOTEP, who lived in the epoch of the Pharaoh AMENEMHET II of the 12th Dynasty (1938-1904 B.C.E.). In this mural the prince is approached by a procession of Semitic, or, as some think, Hebrew, nomads, asking the royal permission for settling in Egypt. Among the immigrants a musician is portrayed, holding under his right arm an instrument, seemingly an eight stringed lyra, which he manipulates partly with his bare left hand, perhaps "stopping" the strings,[5] while his right hand plucks the strings with the aid of a plectrum. The body of the instrument is a square board, having an opening at the upper part, which apparently serves as a hole in the resonance body. This instrument was considered to be the prototype of the Hebrew *kinnor.* (Illustr. 35).

We are of the opinion that it is rather the lyre depicted in the tomb of Thebes, which may be considered the prototype of the *kinnor.* (See Illustr. 7).

Another possible model, or forerunner, of the Jewish *kinnor* might be a lyre depicted on an ivory from Megiddo (dated about 1200 B.C.E.). It shows a Canaʿanite king sitting on a throne flanked by winged lions with human heads. He drinks from a bowl, as one of his musicians entertains him on the lyre. The instrument has nine strings, which are strung horizontally and plucked with the fingers of the left hand. A rather large resonance body is held under the left arm of the player; his right hand, however, is hidden by the corpus of the instrument, so there is no way of finding out what its role might have been in playing the instrument. This picture evidently represents a pre-Israelitic instrument, therefore it is reasonable to assume that it might have been either copied by the Israelites, or at least have influenced the form and structure of the later Jewish lyre. (Illustr. 33. Illustr. 34 is an enlargement of the lyreplayer of Illustr. 33).

If we mention, in addition, a discovery at Megiddo, a bronze-figure (35 cm high), apparently representing a Jewish flute-girl, we have enumerated all the extant and authentic pictorial reproductions of ancient Jewish instruments recovered to date. (Illustr. 36).

Present day notions about these instruments would be rudimentary, indeed, had we not the possibility to complete our knowledge and to reconstruct the missing details through analogy and comparison with the instruments of the musical culture of Egypt and Babylonia. Fortunately, there exists a wealth of pictorial material of Egyptian and Babylonian-Assyrian instruments, so that the lack of pictures of Jewish origin does not exclude useful conclusions with regard to the instruments of Ancient Israel.

Musicological research is greatly handicapped by the fact that soon after the destruction of the Temple in Jerusalem the knowledge of the instruments of the sanctuary and of their technique was lost through disuse. Even the simplest data of the musical practice fell into oblivion. The learned scribes of rabbinical literature were often in doubt whether a term indicated a stringed or a wind-instrument. Certain expressions in the headings of the psalms, being without any doubt pertinent musical indications, could not be understood even in early talmudic times, and thus gave rise to the most contradictory interpretations.

The numerous doubts, contradictions and misinterpretations still existing to-day cannot be solved by historians and linguists alone. Anthropology and sociology must often lend a helping hand. In the long run, however, the assistance of the musician will be needed. Seemingly insoluble problems sometimes allow for new and unexpected interpretations when treated in the light of to-day's musical practice. In our investigations we will adopt this approach—but without any claim to finality—in all instances where the attempts at solutions by means of traditional methods have yielded intangible or unsatisfactory results.

o
o o

In 1963, a remarkable little booklet was published, which is destined to revolutionize our knowledge of the musico-archaeological discoveries in Israel. The booklet was published by the "Israel Music Institute," Tel-Aviv, sponsored by the Israeli Ministry for Education and Culture. The author is the musicologist Dr. BATHJA BAYER.

The title of the work is *"The Material Relics of Music in Ancient Israel and its Environs."* It is an inventory of archaeological items, which the author, for the most part, has discovered herself, or newly interpreted from reports of archaeological excavations. This "preliminary" inventory is highly remarkable for its wealth and diversity, since up to now most of the described items were completely unknown to musicology.

Still in 1957, the *New Oxford History of Music* (I, p. 295) had this to say:

> "Of the instruments themselves not a single example has as yet come to light, and from the pre-Hellenistic period no native representation of a Palestinian instrument survives."

According to her publication, Dr. BAYER identified the following examples or representations of:

131 idiophones, 72 membranophones, 57 chordophones, adding to these the representations of 19 items relating to the dance, altogether the impressive figure of 280 archaeological discoveries.

Of these, about 100 refer to pre-biblical and biblical times, i.e. up to the 3rd cent. B.C.E. The time-limit of the inventory is the middle of the 6th cent. C.E., which allows us to harmonize the material with the post-biblical literature, especially the Mishnah.

Since the publication of *"The Material Relics,"* the inventory of the registered discoveries has been considerably augmented, especially by recent reports of excavations.

It would be premature, after this preliminary report, to pass judgment on the value of these discoveries for the musical culture of Ancient Israel. The author plans, however, to publish the results of her research in a book with numerous photographic illustrations.

III. SYSTEMATIC SURVEY OF BIBLICAL REFERENCES TO MUSIC*

Following the initial reference to music in association with the Scriptural Ur-musician Jubal (discussed above), Lamech's address to his wives Adah and Zillah (Gen. 4:23) is generally considered to be the first "song" of the Bible,[1] though not yet in the same sense as for instance Miriam's "Song at the Red Sea," or Deborah's and Barak's triumphal song. Poetry in olden times was always "sung," by which term history of primitive civilizations always understands a rhythmic accentuation of pertinent words or syllables, coupled with an elevated speech that now and then approaches real singing. It is virtually this rhythmically accentuated, though intervallically loose, speech-melody that, at an early cultural stage constitutes poetry as different from prose.

The Bible mentions music again after the flood at the chase of Jacob by his father-in-law Laban (Gen. 31:27). The joyous escort mentioned here, "with mirth and with songs, with tabret and with harp"[2] is an indication that already in the times of the patriarchs music accompanied the cheerful events of life. It is true that Laban was no Israelite but an Aramaean (Syrian); he was the brother of Rebekah, mother of Jacob. But in olden times the forms of living of neighboring peoples were practically identical.

After the crossing of the Red Sea "sang Moses and the children of Israel" a song of thanksgiving to exalt the Lord and to give thanks for their miraculous rescue (Exod. 15). As the climax of this thanksgiving "Miriam, the prophetess, the sister of Aaron, took a timbrel in her hand; and all the women went out after her with timbrels and with dances. And Miriam sang unto them" (Exod. 15:20,21).

Both these songs of thanksgiving, as well as—with some reservations—the song and dance around the golden calf (Exod. 32:18,19) are indications that the Jewish people must have had some musical knowledge at the Exodus from Egypt and that, on appropriate occasions, the urge for music found its spontaneous outlet.

The dramatic description of God's apparation at Mount Sinai (Exod. 19:13,16,19; 20:15), at which, besides thunder and lightning, "the voice of a horn exceeding loud" was heard, has a mystical as well as a symbolic meaning.

The next biblical passages in which music is mentioned, show music for the first time in the service of the cult. In the enumeration of the high holidays, the first day of the seventh month is hallowed as a "memorial proclaimed with the blast of the horn" (Lev. 23:24). The fiftieth year, the sacred year of the Jubilee, shall be announced

> "with the blast of the horn on the tenth day of the seventh month; in the day of atonement shall ye make proclamation with the horn throughout all your land" (Lev. 25:9).

In the description of the high priest's garment, the Bible twice mentions little golden bells *(paʿamonim),* (Exod. 28:33; 39:25,26). This description

*The following survey does not intend to give an historic or artistic evaluation of the references to music in the Old Testament. This will be the aim of the subsequent sections.

contains the indication that the lower fringe of the garment should be garnished with bells,

> "and the sound thereof shall be heard when he goeth in unto the holy place before the Lord, and when he cometh out, that he die not."

This is an unmistakable sign that in olden times the Jewish religion was permeated with superstition and magic. We have here a remnant of magic, although biblical authors tried to becloud its meaning, as they have also tried to eliminate, as far as possible, traces referring to other ancient superstitious practices.

The increasing importance of music in religious rites and in actions of the state become evident through God's commandment to Moses: "Make thee two trumpets of silver" (Num. 10:2-10). The biblical text contains precise instructions when and how the trumpets should be blown, when the army should go to the battle, when the people, or the princes might gather, etc. The trumpets have to be blown when the people celebrate feasts, "for a memorial before your God." To blow the sacred trumpets was for all times to come the privilege of Aaron's sons (descendants), the priests (Num. 10:8).

A special day in the Jewish cycle of holidays in the "seventh month, on the first day of the month" was called "the day of blowing the horn" (Num. 29:1).

The last quoted passages show us the trumpets as implements of the cult. Besides, assuming important secular functions already in olden times, they were the attributes of royal might and dignity. At all solemn state ceremonies trumpeters accompanied the kings.

Among the holy vessels sent by Moses into the army camp, there were also "trumpets for the alarm" (Num. 31:6).

The destruction of the walls of Jericho by the sound of "rams' horns" is less a musical occurrence than an act of sympathetic magic (Josh. 6). Other peoples of Antiquity possessed numerous legends, and entertained strong beliefs concerning the destructive or constructive power of music.[3]

From here on, the blast of the horn is very often mentioned in the Bible. The horn *(shofar)* is used by the Israelites in the most diversified manner. Generally, it prepares the people for impending disaster, or to spread horror and fright. The horn blasts in the Book of Judges (3:27, 6:34, 7:8,16,18-20,22) are war signals. In Gideon's army there were three hundred horn-blowers who, divided into three groups of a hundred each, spread anguish and fear among the enemy and put him to flight (Judg. 7:16 ff). The victorious conclusion of the campaign was announced by a horn blast (2 Sam. 2:28).

On the other hand, the horns were never lacking at joyous or solemn occasions, such as the bringing in of the ark of covenant to Jerusalem by David, the ointments of kings, etc.

Absalom announced his succession to the throne "with the sound of the horn" (2 Sam. 15:10). After a battle "blowing the horn" was the signal for rallying the scattered troops (2 Sam. 18:16). Revolt and its crushing were announced with "blowing the horn" (2 Sam. 20:1,22). Solomon's succession to the throne (1 Kings 1:34) and his ointment (1 Kings 1:39,41) were introduced by sounding "rams' horns," just as was later the coronation of Jehu as king of Israel (2 Kings 9:13).

The trumpeters were the heralds of the king's majesty and might; "as the manner was," their place was "on the platform by the king" (2 Kings 11:14). When Athalia was killed, "the captains and the trumpets [stood] by the king" (2 Kings 11:14; 2 Chron. 23:13). These and numerous other biblical passages attest to the multifarious use of trumpets and horns as signal and heraldic instruments.

Outside of the cult, the exclusive signal instrument was the *shofar*. In many English versions of the Bible it is translated as "trumpet," which is misleading; the correct translation of *shofar* is "horn."

From times immemorial the heroic tales of the people were transmitted orally from generation to generation. This is attested by several biblical passages: "And thou shalt tell thy son in that day . . ." (Exod. 13:8). "Now therefore write ye this song for you, and teach thou it the children of Israel. . . . So Moses wrote this song the same day, and taught it the children of Israel" (Deuter. 31:19,22). "And [David] said to teach the sons of Judah the bow" [Luther's translation: "the song of the bow"] (2 Sam. 1:18).

In the heroic times of Israel, scribes used to write down the songs of the bards as well as other popular songs, and they compiled several collections containing songs of war and triumph, ballads, and songs of the ancient glory. These collections either were lost, or deliberately destroyed by the later editors of the biblical books in order to establish and perpetuate the idea of unique genuineness of the Holy Writ as an "inspired" document. Several of the collections which existed prior to the Old Testament are even mentioned with their titles by some of the biblical chroniclers. Thus, we know that a "Book of the Wars of the Lord" (*Sefer milḥamot Adonay*) has existed (Num. 21:14). Furthermore, the chroniclers mention a "Book of the Righteous" (*Sefer ha-Yashar,* Josh. 10:13; 2 Sam. 1:18-27), and a "Book of Lamentations" ([*Sefer*] *ʿal ha-ḳinot,* 2 Chron. 35:25).

Once in a while we find references to "Chronicles of the Kings of Israel" and "Chronicles of the Kings of Judah" (1 Kings 22:39,46, a.o.). These books are not identical with the First and Second Chronicles of the Old Testament. The authors of these two biblical books plainly admit that they took over certain portions from the above mentioned historical records into their own writings.[4]

The digging of a life-giving well was an important and solemn event among the Israelites, as among Oriental nomads in general. It was accompanied by certain ceremonies and also by songs. The lyrics of one of these songs are preserved in the Bible (Num. 21:17,18).

We are confronted here with a typical example of a work-song, used in all civilizations, low and high, ancient and contemporary. Another such work-song is that of the wine-pressers, referred to indirectly but not quoted, in Jer. 25:30.[5]

Deborah's and Barak's triumphal song is a worthy counterpart to Miriam's song of thanksgiving (Judg. 5:2). According to the chronicler, Miriam's song was accompanied by the dance of women and by playing of instruments. There is no specific mention of instrumental background to Deborah's song. In those archaic times, however, songs at solemn occasions were mostly accompanied by instruments. We might very well assume the same treatment of Deborah's triumphal paean.

The dance in Ancient Israel was mainly performed by women. Jephtha's daughter came to meet her returning father "with timbrels and with dances" (Judg. 11:34). At the Feast of the Lord "the daughters of Shiloh came out to dance in the dances" (Judg. 21:21). The victorious David was received by the women of all the cities in Israel with "singing and dancing," "with timbrels, with joy, and with three-stringed instruments" (1 Sam. 18:6,7; 21:12).

> "And the women sang one to another in their play [in dancing], and said: Saul hath slain his thousands, and David his ten thousands" (1 Sam. 18:7; 29:5).

Here, for the first time, the Bible mentions antiphonal singing, a specific form of choral performance, characteristic in the Jewish musical practice, especially in the singing of psalms.

Sometimes even men danced in Israel, as the Scriptures state:

> "And the men . . . went out into the field, and gathered their vineyards, and trod the grapes, and held festival" (Judg. 9:27).[6]

To deride the captured Samson, the Philistines sent for him "that he make sport" [*i.e.* "dance"] (Judg. 16:25).

Hannah's song of praise (1 Sam. 2) belongs to the category of "sung" poetry. The performance of this song of praise might have been similar to the accentuated speech-melody of poetry in ancient times.

> "The band of prophets coming down from the high place with a psaltery, and a timbrel, and a pipe, and a harp, before them" (1 Sam. 10:5)

was a fair-sized group of musicians that may be considered, within the customary musical practice of Ancient Israel, a "band," or an "orchestra."

The prophets uttered their deliverances with musical accompaniment. The close affinity between prophecy and music[7] is evident from the events described in 1 Sam. 19:20-24. We see there that the propretic ecstasy affected one group after the other. The prophet Elisha, needing the stimulus of music for his prophecy, asked for a minstrel, and announced his prediction to the sounds of the *kinnor* (2 Kings, 3:15).

In Ancient Israel the belief was wide-spread that music has the faculty of affecting strongly, or even radically, man's innermost feelings. It creates states of ecstasy (1 Sam. 19:20-24), sometimes, on the contrary, has a soothing effect upon the soul and the emotions. In order to overcome his melancholy, king Saul sent to "seek out a man who is a skillful player on the harp" (1 Sam. 16:16). Thus came David, the simple shepherd-boy, to the court of the king who, from the very start, became fond of him and made him his armour-bearer. Every time when Saul was plagued by fits of melancholia, David had to play for him (1 Sam. 19:9).

David's skill in playing the *kinnor* must have been exceptional, since the fame of it reached even the officers of the court. David attended to his art with diligence and "played with his hand, as he did day by day" (1 Sam. 18:10).

At the transfer of the ark of the covenant to Jerusalem, which was one of the most outstanding and solemn events in the religious and national life of Israel, music played a prominent role. (2 Sam. 6:5, 14,15; 1 Chron. 13:8).

In Ancient Israel music had a triple significance: singing, playing of instruments, and dance. All these forms of musical art were considered worthy to serve God and glorify His name. David's dance was a sacred action; the king was possessed by a sort of religious transport, about which the chronicler says:

> "And David danced before the Lord with all his might."

The joy the ancient Hebrews derived from music is evident from the answer given to king David by old Barzillai, when he was invited to accompany the king to Jerusalem:

> "I am this day fourscore years old; can I discern between good and bad? can thy servant taste what I eat or what I drink? can I hear any more the voice of singing men and singing women?" (2 Sam. 19:36).

In this answer music is shown as an essential part of the elementary enjoyment of life.

Yet, another fact becomes evident from Barzillai's answer: the existence of female singers in the early history of Israel.

We might assume that they belonged to a group of male and female palace-singers, as it was a general institution in Antiquity at princely courts. Several other biblical passages corroborate this assumption (*cp.* Eccles. 2:8; Amos 8:3).[8]

David's song of thanksgiving for his deliverance from his enemies (2 Sam. 22:2) can be assumed to represent a real "song" that employed an existing or a specially composed melody. This item of praise also appears in the Book of Psalms (Ps. 18), a proof that we are confronted here with a poem that in the ritual was performed as a real song. David's last words (2 Sam. 23:2-7) are not termed a "song;" nevertheless, there are good reasons to put it into the same category, since its form, meter and contents show the same characteristics as the above mentioned song of thanksgiving.

The carrying of the ark of the covenant from the tabernacle built by David into the new sanctuary erected by Solomon in Jerusalem, took place in a solemn procession and with a colorful display (1 Kings 8:1 ff). Although there is no mention of music at all on this occasion, we may well assume a rich musical accompaniment, all the more so since in the description of the first transfer (2 Sam. 6:5 ff) the chronicler refers to music and singing as essential elements of the ceremony. Here, just as in other passages, the biblical author dispenses with elaborating on facts which must have been familiar to anyone in Ancient Israel.

There is no end of making music on joyous occasions. At Solomon's coronation "the people piped with pipes, and rejoiced with great joy" (1 Kings 1:40). When king Joash was crowned

> "all the people of the land rejoiced, and blew with trumpets; the singers also [played] on instruments of music, and led the singing of praise" (2 Chron. 23:13).

The pipe must have been a popular and wide-spread instrument, since the description of the chronicler intimates a multitude of pipers.

The authors of the two Books of the Chronicles were evidently levitical singers or musicians, since the most abundant references to music are to be found in these parts of the Scriptures. They contain detailed reports on music of the Temple in the times of David and Solomon. These indications are of great value for our knowledge of the musical organization of the First Temple.

To be a Temple singer was the privilege of the tribe of Levi (1 Chron. 6:16 ff). There were other functions reserved for the Levites in the sacred service, but the singers were exempted from all other duties "for they were employed in their work day and night" (1 Chron. 9:33).

The chronicler gives a detailed account about the distribution of the singers in various groups, tells the names, mostly also the parentage of the singers (1 Chron. 15:16-22).

This description affords a clear idea as to the organization of the Temple music in its initial stage. Heman, Asaph and Ethan were the precentors and, at the same time, the leaders of the choir, to whom belonged the honorable function of giving the signal with cymbals to start singing. The following eight singers were the prefects of the groups, leading the song and accompanying themselves with psalteries *ʿal ʿAlamoth.* Six other prefects either doubled the melody with the harps *ʿal Sheminith,* a larger type of instrument, or played a kind of "accompaniment" to the melody. Chenaniah assumed the function of the supreme choir-master, and was the instructor of the entire levitical singing group.

All the above mentioned singers played some instruments (1 Chron. 16: 41,42). They were the group-leaders of a goodly number of levitical musicians. Besides, there must have been numerous other non-levitical singers and musicians, as the chronicler states (1 Chron. 13:8; 15:28).

Both passages report two phases of the same event and in almost identical ways, with the only difference that the first passage emphasizes the singing brought out at the beginning of the procession, whereas the second passage points more to the instrumental part of the ceremony.

After the transfer of the ark to David's city, a solemn service was held with singing and music (1 Chron. 16:4-6).

In this enumeration, Asaph has the office of the first, Zechariah that of the second precentor; the other singers named are group-leaders. "Continually," as applied to the priestly trumpeters, specifies that the blowing of the sacred trumpets was the exclusive privilege of the Aaronites.

From this time on, music had its permanent place in the ceremonial of the

Temple (1 Chron. 16:7,37).

The principal offices of the permanent music service were held, besides Asaph, by

> "Heman and Jeduthun,[9] to sound aloud with trumpets and cymbals, and with instruments for the songs of God" (1 Chron. 16:42).

The "instruments for the songs of God" *(kle shir ha-ʾElohim)* were the stringed instruments assigned mainly to accompany the singing in the ritual, to wit the soft lyre *(kinnor)* and the tuneful harp (*nebel*). It is not difficult to imagine from these indications the general character of the Temple music of David (and also that of Solomon, that carried on the Davidic tradition). It was solemn and dignified; singing was the predominant element, instrumental music, largely as an accompaniment to singing, assumed, in general, a secondary importance.

When David started with his preparations for a future sanctuary, he made a survey of the Levites to be picked for the sacred offices and counted among the singer-musicians

> "four thousand [who] praised the Lord 'with instruments which I made to praise therewith'" (1 Chron. 23:5).

These were only singers of thirty years old or more, since they were not admitted to the service before this age (1 Chron. 23:5).[10] And similarly to the other office-holders among the priests and Levites, the Temple singers had

> "to stand every morning to thank and praise the Lord, and likewise at even" (1 Chron. 23:30).

From these four thousand levitical singers David made a selection according to the clans they belonged to, but mainly according to their talents; for we see that a short time later the number of the sacred singers was two hundred and eighty-eight,

> "all that were instructed in singing unto the Lord, even all that were skillful" (1 Chron. 25:7).

These two hundred and eighty-eight singers were divided into twenty-four "wards," *i.e.* groups, consisting of twelve singers each. Every one of these groups was headed by a group leader, their names being mentioned by the chronicler. In order to avoid jealousy and any dispute for precedence, the distribution into the groups was carried out by casting a lot. From the very beginning, the Temple musicians were organized as a guild, or corporation, in which all were equal, having the same privileges and the same duties, for all were

> "skillful, as well the small as the great, the teacher as the scholar" (1 Chron. 25:8).

The strict discipline to which the musicians of the sacred service were subject, the continuous practicing required by their office, must have given to their performances an extraordinarily high level of perfection. Even the dispassionate chronicler, reporting mainly facts and events, was at one specific occasion induced to abandon his sober approach and to express his unrestrained admiration for the accomplishments of the Temple musicians. This "musical criticism," the very first in human history, was applied on the occasion of the dedication of Solomon's Temple. The all-important role of the music in the solemn service and its magnificent performance find their expression in the following appreciation of the chronicler: "it came even to pass, when the trumpeters and singers were *as one, to make one sound to be heard* in praising and thanking the Lord" (2 Chron. 5:12,13).

This supreme perfection concerning the "ensemble" aspect of the performance which apparently was unusual even with the thoroughly trained Temple musicians, accomplished by more than four hundred singers and musicians, seems to have created among the worshippers a kind of religious ecstasy. In this rapture *en masse* the people imagined

> "that the house was filled with a cloud, even the house of the Lord, so that the priests could not stand to minister by reason of the cloud; for the glory of the Lord filled the house of God" (2 Chron. 5:13,14).

With this, the chronicler wanted to intimate that such perfection of a musical performance, never attained before, was rewarded by a heavenly sign, maybe even by the grace of the divine presence.

At the conclusion of this memorable feast of dedication which lasted seven days, the chronicler again recalls the important part played by the musicians (2 Chron. 7:6). As the climax of the dedication, Solomon confirmed anew the Temple music as an everlasting sacred institution (2 Chron. 8:14).

Soon, the simple instruments of David were replaced by luxurious specimens which

> "Solomon made of the sandal-wood . . . harps and psalteries for the singers; and there were none such seen before in the land of Judah" (1 Kings 10:12; 2 Chron. 9:11).

Solomon the wise prince of peace, the builder of the sanctuary, the firm consolidator of Temple music, eclipses in the consciousness of posterity Solomon the poet and musician. Nevertheless, the Old Testament gives testimony to the creative power of the king and to his artistic accomplishments:

> "He spoke three thousand proverbs; and his songs were a thousand and five" (1 Kings 5:12 [4:32]).

Only fragments of this output are preserved in the Book of Psalms, Proverbs, and Ecclesiastes, maybe also in the "Song of Songs," being equally attributed to Solomon.[11] All this proves the universality and artistic creativeness of Solomon, one which, in its variety and fecundity, has no equal among crowned rulers.

After Solomon's death, (931 B.C.E.), the disruption of the nation into two kingdoms, northern Israel and southern Judah, had fateful consequences. The people, weakened externally and shattered internally by frequent disturbances, were dangerously wedged in between the two rival powers Egypt and Assyria. Just as the people could not raise a political resistance, it could not ward off the cultural and spiritual influences of paganism, including those in the field of music.

Under Jeroboam, king of Israel, (931-910 B.C.E.), the true faith deteriorated, the people took to idolatry, the priests and Levites were driven out of the Temple of God, and music fell into the hands of pagan leaders. The prophet Elijah fought vigorously against ungodliness. At the divine judgment on the Mount Carmel he encountered, alone and without assistance, four hundred and fifty priests of Ba'al who—among other heathen ceremonies—"danced in halting wise about the altar" (1 Kings 18:26).

The country was in distress, the people abandoned the God of Israel, "the priests with the trumpets of alarm" called for repentance and summoned the faithful to fight against unbelief (2 Chron. 13:12, 14). Not before Asa, king of Judah (911-871 B.C.E.), succeeded to the throne, was idolatry abolished. The people renewed its covenant with the true God,

> "and they swore unto the Lord with a loud voice, and with shouting, and with trumpets, and with horns" (2 Chron. 15:14).

Under his successor, Jehoshaphat (871-847 B.C.E.), the religion of the fathers was even more strengthened. The king restored the sacred service in all its splendor, including the musical part of it. (2 Chron. 20:19).

In the war against the Ammonites and Moabites singing Levites marched ahead of the army to implore God's assistance (2 Chron. 20:21,22). After the victory upon his enemies, Jehoshaphat rallied his people in the "Valley of Berakah" (Valley of Blessing),

> "for there they blessed the Lord; therefore the name of that place was called the Valley of Berakah, unto this day" (2 Chron. 20:26).

Then they marched to Jerusalem

> "with psalteries and harps and trumpets unto the house of the Lord" (2 Chron. 20:28).

Again, a period of apostasy and ungodliness followed. Not before the time of Joash, king of Judah (835-796 B.C.E.) was the cult of Ba'al again abolished and traditional sacred music reinstituted. The high priest

> "Jehoiada appointed the offices of the house of the Lord under the hand of the priests and Levites, . . . with rejoicing and with singing, according to the direction of David" (2 Chron. 23:18).

After Joash, the people again abandoned the true faith and, with it, the noble musical tradition. Good and bad rulers followed each other, and it was only after several generations that a king acceded to the throne who restored Yahveh's cult, the sacred service, and with it the music of the Temple. This was Hezekiah, king of Judah (714-686 B.C.E.) (2 Chron. 29:25-30).

At this re-dedication of the sanctuary the priests and the Levites vied with each other in the service of the Lord (2 Chron. 29:34). At the subsequent celebration of the Passah-feast, the levitical singers must have particularly distinguished themselves, since even the king was induced to praise them publicly (2 Chron. 30:22).

This Passah-feast, at which "the Levites and the priests praised the Lord day by day, singing with loud instruments unto the Lord" (2 Chron. 30:21), was celebrated in such an inspiring way that

> "the whole congregation took counsel to keep other seven days with gladness. . . . For since the time of Solomon . . . there was not the like in Jerusalem" (2 Chron. 30:23,26).

The whole-hearted praise given by Hezekiah to the musicians of the Temple seems to indicate that this unusual prolongation of the Passah-feast was in no small measure due to the accomplishments of the sacred singers and musicians. The immediate result of it was that Hezekiah not only restored the ancient organization of the singers, acknowledging the privileges of their corporation, but that he also took a particular care to provide for the welfare of his singers (2 Chron. 31:2 ff).

The fame of king Hezekiah's singers spread gradually far beyond the boundaries of Israel; so much so, in fact, that when the Assyrian conqueror SENNAḤERIB besieged Jerusalem (711 B.C.E.), he demanded as price for sparing the city, and apart from a heavy tribute, the delivery of the king's male and female singers. To save David's city from destruction, Hezekiah had to comply with the victor's demand.

King Josiah of Judah (639-609 B.C.E.) ordered the repair of the Temple, badly dilapidated during centuries of numerous vicissitudes. On this occasion, the neglected levitical instruments also underwent a thorough restoration under the supervision and assistance of the levitical musicians themselves. (2 Chron. 34:12).

After the renewal of the covenant between Yahveh and the people of Israel, king Josiah made preparations to celebrate the Passah-feast with great pomp. The report about this gorgeous festival fills an entire chapter of the Chronicles. The priests were so overloaded by their sacrificial duties that the Levites had to assist them in preparing the sacrifices (2 Chron. 35:15).

Josiah died on the field of honor in the war against the Pharaoh Neko, deeply mourned by his people, but especially by his singers (2 Chron. 35:25).

Soon, however, the Jewish people was struck by the greatest national catastrophe in its history. NEBUCHADREZZAR conquered Israel, destroyed Solomon's Temple, and led the flower of the nation to Babylonia into captivity (586 B.C.E.). The music of the Temple ceased; singing was abolished; in its mourning for the lost sanctuary, the captives renounced the joys of music. At least, this is what the psalmist says (Ps. 137:2).

However, music and singing never ceased actually even in the oppression of the Babylonian exile. The practice of music in public might have been abandoned, or restricted to a bare minimum. In close company, however, in the family, perhaps in special reunions, the tradition was kept alive, the ancient precious possession of sacred songs was cultivated with increased zeal. For, when after nearly five decades the first group of repatriates returned to the old country, there were among them—besides priests, Levites, doorkeepers, and other office-holders of the former Temple—hundred and twenty-eight sacred singers, "children of Asaph," *i.e.* the descendants of the families of the original Temple singers (Ezra 2:41). The parallel passages in the Book of Nehemiah gives even a larger number of the returning Temple singers, namely hundred and forty-eight (Neh. 7:44). Furthermore,—and this is of paramount importance—there were among the repatriates two hundred non-levitical male and female singers (Ezra 2:65). At a census held later by Neḥemiah in order to establish the total number of the repatriates, two hundred and forty-five non-levitical male and female singers were counted (Neh. 7:67).

Would it have been possible to have that many sacred and secular singers among the repatriates, if music and singing had been abandoned in the exile, as hinted by the psalmist?

After the return, the singers settled in villages and hamlets which, prior to the exile, served as domicile to their ancestors (Ezra 2:70). The earlier settlements for the Levites were established soon after the conquest of Cana'an. The Bible mentions forty-eight such levitical cities (Num. 35:7; Josh. 21:41), but it is doubtful whether all of them actually existed. Under the new living conditions after the return from Babylonia, only a fraction of the Levites could stay in Jerusalem; the others had to settle in villages and hamlets not too far from the Temple. In a register drafted by Nehemiah (Neh. 11:10-19), the number of the Levites living in Jerusalem was two hundred and eighty-four (Neh. 11:18). Some of the settlements outside of Jerusalem are named by the chronicler (Neh. 12:28,29).

The singers occupied a special status in the hierarchy of the Temple. This is evidenced by the fact that, in enumerating the office-holders of the sanctuary, the musicians always were mentioned separately (Ezra, 2:41,70; 7:7,24; Neh. 7:44,73; 10:29,40; 12:29; 13:5,10).

Among the priests and Levites who, in the exile, married foreign women and now, under the pressure of the zealots, were compelled to divorce their non-Jewish wives, the levitical singer Eliashib is mentioned by his name (Ezra 10:24).

Once the bare necessities of life were secured, the Jews proceeded with the erection of a new Temple, starting already in the second year after the return from the exile. In the meantime the music of the sacred service must have been re-established, for at the laying of the foundation for the new sanctuary a solemn service was held, "at which the Levites sang one to another in praising and giving thanks to the Lord" (Ezra 3:10,11). As this report indicates, not only the ancient Davidic songs survived the Babylonian captivity, but also the forms of musical practice, among them antiphonal singing.

To protect the city of David and the new sanctuary, the Israelites started to build new strong walls around Jerusalem, despite the advice of certain antagonists to the contrary. In building the wall the utmost precautions were taken to be safe from sudden hostile attacks.

> "And the builders, every one had his sword girded by his side, and so builded."

Nehemiah who supervised the construction, always had a horn-blower at his side to give a warning in case of danger. (Neh. 4:12-14 [18:20]).

Once the new walls made the city and the sanctuary safe from attacks, the next step was the resumption and reorganization of the pre-exilic national and religious institutions, among them the regular sacred service and the Temple music. The Persian King DARIUS who granted the permission for the erection of a new sanctuary, issued a decree to the effect that the priests and the other office-holders of the Temple, among them the singers, should receive "expenses, and that which they have need of" (Ezra 6:9).

Ezra the Scribe obviously enjoyed special favors of the king ARTAXERXES, successor to DARIUS, for he procured from the sovereign a decree that can be considered a veritable *magna charta* of the new liberties and privileges granted to the servants of Yahveh's cult.

To begin with, this decree explicitly confirmed the late DARIUS' edict with regard to the re-establishment of the sacred service. Ezra obtained from his royal benefactor the assurance of every moral and material assistance. Apart from other statutes, the decree contained specific stipulations as to the fees due to the priests and Levites. As the height of the royal favors, the monarch granted to all office-holders, and also to the singers, complete exemption from taxes (Ezra 7:24).

These royal privileges were not all that Ezra procured from ARTAXERXES. As tangible proof of his benevolence, the monarch released the sacred vessels and other implements, among them the musical instruments, that were taken as booty after the destruction of Solomon's Temple, and he gave Ezra permission to bring them back to Jerusalem. Thus, after the Temple was restored (516 B.C.E.), the sacred service was resumed in its ancient glory (Neh. 7:1).

The re-establishment of the sacred music was the beginning of a new bloom of the musical culture in Ancient Israel that, in some respect, even eclipsed the time of Solomon. The levitical singers had the lion's share in this new flourishing of musical art.

Once the sacred service was firmly re-established, the artistic as well as the social standing of the Temple musicians improved more and more. The singers formed a professional corporation, that watched jealously over the interests of its members. Several of their special privileges are mentioned by the chroniclers; in enumerating the office-holders of the cult, the singers were always mentioned by themselves (Neh. 10:29, a.o.); their service and their dues were precisely circumscribed (Neh. 10:40); like the priests, they had *Nethinim* (literally "given ones") at their disposal. These were originally foreign slaves, who later were set free and had to perform the low services of the Temple. The descendants of these slaves, the *Nethinim,* constituted a separate class of servants and always were specially mentioned by the chroniclers.

In the newly built Temple, Uzzi, of Asaph's progeny, was the master of the levitical singers (Neh. 11:22; 12:42). His activity must have been highly beneficial for the sacred music, which is proven by the fact that the chronicler preserved his name for posterity. Since David's and Solomon's times such an honor has not been bestowed upon any leader of sacred music.

The singers received for their services a sort of payment that mainly consisted in natural products (Neh. 12:47). These were tributes offered by the people according to a special assessment (Neh. 13:5). Furthermore, the Levites received a daily "salary" from the king's treasury (Neh. 11:23). The tributes for the Levites were stored in special chambers which were situated around the Temple court.

The prefect of these chambers was the priest Eliashib. He was an unfaithful steward of his office, because he accorded unfair favors to one of his relatives of the name of Tobiah, the same who scoffed at the builders of the new walls

(Neh. 3:35 [4:3]) and conspired against them (Neh. 4:2 [4:8]). Eliashib gave Tobiah one of the chambers and put

> "into it the offerings which were given by commandment to the Levites, and the singers, and the porters" (Neh. 13:4,5),

thus creating a strong resentment among the unjustly treated Levites.

Since all protests remained ineffectual, the Levites and the singers took a radical step: they discontinued their service. The singers suspended their work, resulting in the first "strike" recorded in human history. The chronicler reports in detail about this extraordinary events[12] (Neh. 13:10).

The public reading of the law by Ezra took place in a solemn manner. In a festive procession "Ezra the priest brought the Law before the congregation" (Neh. 8:2). Though the chronicler does not mention any music at this procession, it may be assumed, nevertheless, that the carrying of the scroll of the Law was accompanied by sacred songs, as in the earlier religious ceremonies of this kind.

The dedication of the newly erected walls of the city is described in detail by the chronicler. He reports the great number of singers and musicians who performed at this occasion (Neh. 12:27-46).

As this report shows, the musical part of the festivity was performed according to the ancient tradition, *i.e.* using the songs that were sung in the sacred service in David's time. (Neh. 12:24,25). The two large singing companies that met at the house of God, performed their songs antiphonally, in the ancient Jewish tradition, under the direction of Jezrahiah, the new leader (Neh. 12:42).

Gradually, the status of the musicians of the Temple became more and more similar to that of the priests. It was, therefore, a logical development that the singers, overstraining their ambition, tried to achieve complete equality with the priests also in their outward appearance. They eventually reached this goal under king AGRIPPA II (reign. 49-70 C.E.) who, with the consent of the Sanhedrin, granted them the privilege to wear, when on duty, the white priestly robe.[13] How this ambition, stretched too far, contributed to the eventual downfall of the singers' organization, will be recounted later.

o
o o

It is common knowledge that in the popular life of all nations musical feeling manifests itself mainly in singing. In the secular music of Israel, singing of popular songs had practically the same importance as singing of psalms in sacred music· It is, therefore, natural that the Bible quite frequently mentions some of these songs, either in the form of references to their various kinds, or else by actually quoting their texts, or portions thereof. The following species of secular songs are mentioned in the Old Testament:

War songs (Num. 21:14,15; 21:27-30).

Songs of triumph (Exod. 15:20; Judg. 5:1 ff; 1 Sam. 21:12; Isa. 14:4).

Marching songs (Num. 10:35,36; 2 Chron. 20:21).

Work songs (Num. 21:17,18; Judg. 9:27; Isa. 5:1; 16:10; 27:2; 65:8; Jer. 25:30; 48:33; Hos. 2:17).

Song of the builders, at laying the corner-stone (Job 38:7), at laying the top stone (Zech. 4:7).

Song of the watchman (Isa. 21:12).

Love songs (Psalm 45; Song of Songs 2:14; 5:16; Ezek. 33:32).

Wedding songs (Gen. 31:27; Jer. 25:10; 33:11).

Drinking songs (Job. 21:12; Ps. 69:13; Isa. 24:9; Am. 6:5).

Dance songs (Exod. 15:20; 32:18,19; 1 Sam. 18:6,7; 21:12; 29:5; Ps. 26:6; 68:26; 87:7).

Songs of the palace (2 Sam. 19:36; Amos. 8:3).

Songs of the courtesan (Isa. 23:15,16).

Songs of derision (Job 30:9; Lament. 3:14,63).

Songs of mourning and lamentation (2 Sam. 1:18-27; 1 Kings 13:30; 2 Chron. 35:25; Eccles. 12:5; Jer. 9:16,17; 22:18; Ezek. 27:30,32; Amos 5:16; Zech. 12:12-14).

A mixed category (partly religious and partly secular) are those sung by the Israelites at pilgrimages (Psalms 120-134; *cp.* Ps. 119:54). These fifteen "Songs of Ascents," as they are called in their headings, were sung, according to the tradition, by pilgrims coming every year from all parts of Israel to the Feast of the Lord (Isa. 27:13, 30:29, 31:4; Jer. 31:12).[14] The Temple was situated on a high ground to which steps led up; these psalms, therefore, also were called "Songs of Degrees."

There are strong indications that these songs, prior to their incorporation in the Book of Psalms, were sung at secular occasions and served only later as musical background for religious ceremonies.

The most important feature of Jewish musical culture, the singing in connection with religious ceremonies, was paralleled by the complete permeation of secular life, public as well as private, with popular song. Joy as well as sorrow expressed themselves in singing. The revelers "sing to the timbrel and harp, and rejoice at the sound of the pipe" (Job 21:12). In remembering his lost happiness, Job says:

> "The blessing of him that was ready to perish came upon me; and I caused the widow's heart to sing for joy" (Job 29:13).

There are in the Scriptures a few examples of musical metaphors derived from the animal world. The noble horse "swalloweth the ground with storm and rage" when it hears the sound of the horn (Job 39:24). The song of the turtle-dove (Song of Songs 2:12) and of the birds at dawn (Eccles. 12:4; Ps. 104:12) are common expressions in the vocabulary of all peoples, therefore it is not unusual to find them in the biblical text. An impressive description, however, is given of the horror in a city punished by God; in the destroyed Nineveh

> "all beasts of every kind shall lie down in the midst of her in herds" and "voices shall sing in the windows" (Zeph. 2:14). *(Cf.* Isa. 38:14; 59:11; Micah 1:8).

Nature is quite frequently pictured in musical symbols, as for instance:

> "Then shall the trees of the wood sing for you before the Lord" (1 Chron. 16:33).

In other realistic musical metaphors the voices of Nature, the raging of the sea, the rustling of the woods are blended with the idea of worshipping the Creator. The most significant ones are:

> "Sing, O ye heavens . . . break forth into singing, ye mountains, O forest, and every tree therein" (Isa. 44:23);—
>
> "The wilderness and the parched land . . . and the desert . . . shall blossom abundantly, and rejoice, even with joy and singing" (Isa. 35:1,2);—
>
> "Sing, O heavens, and be joyful, O earth, and break forth into singing, O mountains" (Isa. 49:13);—
>
> "The mountains and the hills shall break forth before you into singing, and all the trees of the field shall clap their hands (*i.e.* dance)" (Isa. 55:12).—

And when the chronicler looks for an especially imaginative symbol, he recurs to the singing of the stars:

> "When the morning stars sang together, and all the sons of God shouted for joy" (Job 38:7).

The fields, the meadows praise the Lord by their fertility. Man, enjoying these blessings of God, joins in an exulting song of praise (Ps. 65:14).

o
o o

From the standpoint of musical research, the Book of Psalms deserves a special place. No other part of the Old Testament contains so many references to the practice of music. These are of paramount importance for the understanding of the sacred music of Israel; their interpretation occupied countless exegetes of the Old Testament. There exists a huge literature on the headings and the other musical terms of the psalms, containing most contradictory opinions. The musical terms will be examined in the following section; here we want merely to summarize the references to music in the Book of Psalms:

"I will sing unto the Lord," "Sing praises unto the Lord," and "Sing unto the Lord a new song" are usual and stereotyped formulae in the psalms. There are no less than 35 such passages: 13:6; 27:6; 28:7; 30:5; 30:13; 40:4; 47:7; 57:10; 59:17; 61:9; 66:2; 66:4; 68:5; 68:33; 69:31; 81:2; 89:2; 92:2; 95:2; 96:1,2; 98:1; 98:4; 101:1; 104:33; 105:2; 108:2,4; 135:3; 144:9; 147:1,7; 149:1,3.

Praising God with the sound of instruments is also a formula frequently used. So for instance:

> "Give thanks unto the Lord with harp, sing praises unto him with the psaltery of ten strings (*'Asor*)" (Ps. 33:2). The latter term is mentioned in two other passages of the Psalter: "to sing praises . . . with an instrument of ten strings and with the psaltery" (Ps. 92:4), and "upon a psaltery of ten strings will I sing praises unto Thee" (Ps. 144:9).

Exalting the Lord with stringed instruments, and with music in general, is a preferred expression of the religious fervor that filled the authors of the psalms. (Pss. 57:9; 71:22; 81:3,4; 98:5,6; 108:3,4; 147:7). And, as the climax of the expressive power of religious music, in the two last psalms (149, 150), song, play and dance are joined to the glory of the Eternal.

To encircle the altar is an ancient religious ceremony with dancing evolutions. It is mentioned in Ps. 26:6. Further references to this ancient rite are: "Walk about Zion, and go round about her" (Ps. 48:13), and (Ps. 118:27).[15]

God's approach is announced "amidst the sound of the horn" (Ps. 47:6). The instrument is used here to proclaim the revelation, and its sound is the symbol of the splendor and glory emanating from the Lord's apparition.

Esoteric riddles (*ḥidot*), parables, like some prophetic sayings, were often uttered with musical accompaniment. (Ps. 49:5), and (1 Sam. 10:5).

The triplicity of music in Ancient Israel was the basic principle of the thinking and feeling of the people, as evidenced in the Psalter (Ps. 68:25; 81:3; 87:7). The most meaningful expression of this triplicity occurs in the last two psalms, 149 and 150.

Music affords consolation to man in his affliction (Ps. 77:7; cp. Job. 35:10).

Singing and the divine laws were spiritually linked in the consciousness of the Hebrews: "Thy statutes have been my songs in the house of my pilgrimage" (Ps. 119:54).

In Babylonia, in captivity, disgrace and humiliation, the joy of singing has ceased (Ps. 137:2-4), at least temporarily.

After this pessimistic note, however, the subsequent psalms radiate reliance and trust in God, and from there on the glorification of God through music takes increasingly eulogistic forms. The last six psalms are a single continuously intensified song of praise to the glory of the Eternal. All phenomena of human life, all impulses of nature, the forceful play of the elements, all utterances of human emotions are used to exalt the greatness and mercy of the Creator. After the psalmist exhausted all notions of the language, he turns to the expressive power of musical metaphors in order to give vent to the exuberance of his feelings. Music becomes for him the epitome of worshipping God. More than literal language, more than all other phenomena of life, music is destined to glorify God (Pss. 149:3; 150:3-5).

After this climax in displaying music's symbolic power, there is nothing left for the psalmist but to exclaim: "Let every thing that hath breath praise he Lord. Hallelujah!" (Ps. 150:6).

o o o

In contrast to the Book of Psalms, the "Song of Songs" has only a minor importance for our subject. This jewel of lyric poetry is completely devoid of any indication as to how it was sung in Ancient Israel. The Canticle is ascribed to king Solomon, the poet and musician; therefore it has been surmised that like the psalms, it was sung with instrumental accompaniment. There is, however, not the slightest foundation for such an assumption, either in the text itself, or in contemporary or later sources.[16]

The only reference to music in the "Song of Songs"—if we disregard its very title and two amorous allusions to the "sweet voice" of the girl friend (2:14) and the voice of the beloved (5:2,16)—is the passage where spring is called "the time of singing," (2:12). Furthermore, the author alludes to the "dance of Maḥanaim" (7:1) which, similar to antiphonal singing, was performed by two groups of dancers. The poet used here as a comparison an episode from Jacob's story to whom, at Maḥanaim, two groups of angels appeared (Gen. 32:2 [1]).[17]

Some passages of the "Ecclesiastes" reveal a close relationship of the author to music. He counts among the princely entertainments the bliss of music:

> "I got me men-singers and women-singers, and the delights of the sons of men, as musical instruments (*shiddah*), and that of all sorts" (Eccl. 2:8).[18]

Rational philosophy is expressed by a metaphor in which "dance" is a synonym for "music":

> "To everything there is a season . . . a time to weep, and a time to dance" (Eccl. 3:4).

The contempt for frivolous singing is expressed by the contrast:

> "It is better to hear the rebuke of the wise, than for a man to hear the song of fools" (Eccl. 7:5).

Under "songs of fools" we have to understand either drinking songs of licentious revelers, or perhaps insincerely flattering songs. The incantations of snake-charmers (Eccl. 10:11) must have had definite musical elements, as intimated also by Ps. 58:5, Jer. 8:17, and Ecclus. 12:13.

At God's judgment

> "one shall start up at the voice of a bird, and all the daughters of music shall be brought low" (Eccl. 12:4).

The ancient Jewish custom of professional mourners, singing dirges at funerals, is reflected in the passage:

> when "man goeth to his long home, the mourners go about the streets" (Eccl. 12:5)

The "Proverbs" declare daily musical activity a wise undertaking and a joy pleasing God (Prov. 8:30,31). For a God-fearing man singing is an intrinsic joy (Prov. 29:6). One cannot utter a merry song with an afflicted heart (Prov. 25:20). In the conception of the "Proverbs,"

> "wisdom crieth" (1:20); . . . "she crieth aloud" (8:3).

[THE SEPTUAGINT translates: "she *chants* her *song*"]. When

> "the city rejoiceth, . . . there is shouting (*rinnah*)" (11:10). The

silliness of fools is drastically commented on by a simile with the dance:

> "The legs hang limp from the lame; so is a parable in the mouth of fools" (26:7)

The real meaning of the passage becomes evident by LUTHER's translation:

> "Wie einem Krüppel das Tanzen, also stehet dem Narren an, von Weisheit reden" ("Like the dancing of a crippled man, so is wisdom in the mouth of fools").

Perhaps also King Lemuel's "Song of a virtuous woman," as verses 31:10-31 are sometimes called,[19] may be included among the musical references of the "Proverbs."

o
o o

When certain classes of the people became wealthy, luxury and debauchery began to spread. Formerly, music served as an embellishment of life; the merriness of a company and the joys of a banquet were enhanced by song and music. With the increased luxurious living the essence of music underwent a radical change. It became more and more the noisy accompaniment of carousals; it served to excite the senses and became the helper of sybaritic epicurianism. Puritanic prophets stormed against revelry and licentiousness, and since music became a part of it, also against music; they admonished the people to repent and summoned them to return to a life pleasing to God. Job poured out his wrath against the ungodly ones who

> "sing to the timbrel and harp, and rejoice at the sound of the pipe," and "send forth their little ones like a flock, and their children dance" (Job 21:11,12).

Isaiah scourged even stronger the abuses of luxury, gluttony and debauchery:

> "Woe unto them that rise up early in the morning, that they may follow strong drink; that tarry late into night, till wine inflame them! And the harp and the psaltery, the tabret and the pipe, and wine, are in their feasts" (Isa. 5:11,12).

Amos, too, was inflamed by the increasing pleasure-hunting of the nobles; and because their revelry was always accompanied by music, he thundered also against it:

> "Woe to them that are at ease in Zion . . . that lie upon beds of ivory, and stretch themselves upon their couches . . . that thrum on the psaltery, that devise for themselves instruments of music, like David, that drink wine in bowls" (Am. 6:4-6).

The divine judgment will be announced by sounding the horn:

> "All ye inhabitants of the world, and ye dwellers on the earth, when an ensign is lifted up on the mountains, see ye; and when the horn is blown, hear ye" (Isa. 18:3).

Also:

> "And it shall come to pass in that day, that a great horn shall be blown" (Isa. 27:13).

In describing the divine judgment, the prophet foretells:

> "The mirth of tabrets ceaseth, the noise of them that rejoice endeth, the joy of the harp ceaseth; they drink not wine with a song" (Isa. 24:8,9).

The redeemed humanity will sing again:

> "God the Lord is my strength and song, and He is become my salvation" (Isa. 12:2). "In that day shall this song be sung in the land of Judah,"

and then follows a song of praise in honor of the righteous God (Isa. 26:1 ff).

The pilgrimage to the yearly Feast of the Lord took place in a solemn procession, with songs and music:

> "Ye shall have a song as in the night when a feast is hallowed; and gladness of heart, as when one goeth with the pipe to come into the mountain of the Lord, to the Rock of Israel" (Isa. 30:29).

The victory over the enemy always was celebrated with music:

> "It shall be with tabrets and harps; and in battles of wielding will He fight with them" (Isa. 30:32).

In the song of triumph at the downfall of the king of Babylonia (Isa. 14:4) the prophet scourges the luxuries of the beaten ruler, to which belonged music:

> "Thy pomp is brought down to the nether-world, and the noise of thy psalteries" (Isa. 14:11).

At the defeat of the Babylonian king

> "the whole earth is at rest, and is quiet; they break forth into singing" (Isa. 14:7).

According to the concept of the prophets, the divine character of song originates from a commandment of God Himself:

> "For thus saith the Lord: Sing with gladness for Jacob" (Jer. 31:7).

Chroniclers and prophets use by preference musical similes and metaphors to characterize sudden changes of moods. Especially, they like to express the transition from merriment to mourning, from happiness to despair by using musical images. Job describes his misery by a comparison borrowed from music:

> "My harp is turned to mourning, and my pipe into the voice of them that weep" (Job 30:31).

When the prophet mourns for Moab, he laments:

> "Wherefore my heart moaneth like a harp for Moab" (Isa. 16:11).

The most dreadful punishment that will befall the sinful people is an existence without song:

> "Then will I cause to cease from the cities of Judah, and from the streets of Jerusalem, the voice of mirth and the voice of gladness, the voice of the bridegroom and the voice of the bride" (Jer. 7:34; 25:10).

At the downfall of Moab "there shall be no singing in the vineyards" (Isa. 16:10). In his prophecy about the destruction of the city of Tyre, the prophet threatens:

> "And I will cause the noise of thy songs to cease, and the sound of thy harps shall be no more heard" (Ezek. 26:13).

God's punishment implies the end of singing and dancing:

> "And the songs of the palace shall be wailings in that day" (Amos 8:3), and "the elders have ceased from the gate, the young men from their music. The joy of our heart is ceased; our dance is turned into mourning" (Lament. 5:14,15).

But even in misery, in sufferings, and with a burning heart it is a duty to sing the song of the Lord, praise Him in songs (Jer. 20:13). The formula "Sing unto the Lord a new song" is seldom found outside the Psalter, and only on solemn occasions (Isa. 42:10).

When Israel will be forgiven by the Lord, the entire universe will break forth into singing:

> "Then shall the lame man leap as a hart, and the tongue of the dumb shall sing" (Isa. 35:6).
>
> "And the ransomed of the Lord shall return, and come with singing unto Zion" (Isa. 35:10).
>
> "With a voice of singing declare ye, tell this, utter it even to the end of the earth" (Isa. 48:20).
>
> "Joy and gladness shall be found therein [in the garden of the Lord], thanksgiving, and the voice of melody" (Isa. 51:3).

The watchmen of Zion

> "lift up the voice, together they sing" (Isa. 52:8).

"Break forth into joy, sing together, ye vast places of Jerusalem . . . for the Lord hath redeemed His people" (Isa. 52:9).

"Sing . . . break forth into singing" (Isa. 54:1).

"Behold, My servants shall sing for you of heart" (Isa. 65:14).

Also Isa. 35:2, 44:23, 49:13, 55:12, quoted already above.

In songs of thanksgiving, musical metaphors are frequently used. In the Psalm for the dedication (or re-dedication) of the sanctuary it is said:

"Thou didst turn for me my mourning into dancing" (Ps. 30:12).

And when Hezekiah recovered from grave illness, he made a vow:

"Therefore we will sing songs to the stringed instruments all the days of our life in the house of the Lord" (Isa. 38:20).

When the repentant people again were accepted in God's grace, the chroniclers never failed to make allusions to the joys of music, as a contrast to the past affliction and distress. After repentance and atonement

"shall proceed thanksgiving and the voice of them that make merry" (Jer. 30:19). "And they shall come and sing in the height of Zion" (Jer. 31:12). Israel "shall go forth in the dances of them that make merry" (Jer. 31:4). "Then shall the virgin rejoice in the dance, and the young men and the old together" (Jer. 31:13). "The daughter of Zion shall sing again" (Zeph. 3:14), for the Lord anew will show mercy to His repentant people, "He will rejoice over thee with joy, . . . He will joy over thee with singing" (Zeph. 3:17).

All these prophecies reflect the spiritual attitude of the Jewish people to music. It is the universal dispenser of joy, the epitome of life's bliss, an indispensable element of human existence. These pronouncements of the prophets are all the more significant as they mostly represent God's own words, revealed by the mouth of the prophets. These sayings of God, using musical metaphors, are the outstanding proof of the ethical loftiness of music in the concept of Ancient Israel.

Trumpets and horns as announcers of solemn, menacing, or tragic events are used in many passages of the Bible in a metaphoric sense. The powerful sound of a voice is like the blowing of the horn (Isa. 58:1; Hos. 8:1). The horn warns and threatens (Isa. 18:3). It rallies the people to war (Jer. 4:5). "The sound of the horn" mingles with the uproar of the battle (Jer. 4:19,21). Horns and trumpets call Israel to the fight (Hos. 5:8). War is announced by sounding the horn (Jer. 42:14; 51:27; Ezek. 7:14). The blowing of the horn proclaims approaching disaster (Jer. 6:1,17). It warns the people of danger (Ezek. 33:3-5). It is the harbinger of impending catastrophe (Joel 2:1). It calls the people to repentance (Joel 2:15).

The sound of the horn causes terror and alarm when "Moab shall die with tumult, with shouting, and with the sound of the horn" (Amos 2:2), and spreads horror at the divine judgment (Amos 3:6).

"A day of the horn and alarm" is "a day of wrath . . . of darkness and gloominess" (Zeph. 1:15,16). "A great horn shall be blown" when the lost and outcast have found the way back to God (Isa. 27:13).

And when the redemption comes, the Lord will reveal Himself to the daughter Zion and, as a sign of His mercy, "the Lord will blow the horn" (Zech. 9:14).

In this succinct survey the manifold significance comes to the fore which, in the mind of the Israelites, was attributed to the sound of the trumpets and horns.

Mourning for the deceased with music was at all times a significant Jewish custom. The funeral ceremony took place with lamentations of professional wailing women (1 Kings 13:30).[20] Their dirges were accompanied by pipes (*cp.* Matth. 9:23). Even the poorest man had to hire for the funeral of his wife at least two *ḥalil*-players and a wailing woman.[21] The sound of the pipe, in certain metaphors, was synonymous with deep mourning:

> "Therefore my heart moaneth for Moab like pipes, and my heart moaneth like pipes for the men of Kir-ḥeres" (Jer. 48:36).

Funeral lamentations are frequently mentioned in the Bible (1 Kings 13:30; 2 Chron. 35:25; Eccl. 12:5; Jer. 9:16; 22:18; Amos 5:16,17). A reference to funeral lamentation in responsive form is intimated by the biblical passage:

> "And the land shall mourn, every family apart, and their wives apart" (Zech. 12:12-14).

The close affinity between musical terms and general thinking in Israel is a leading motif throughout the Scriptures. Thus, the pleasant manners of a man and the degree of his popularity are characterized by a musical simile:

> "And, lo, thou art unto them as a love song of one that has a pleasant voice, and can play well on an instrument" (Ezek. 33:32).

Musical instruments, dispensers of joy, belong to the most cherished goods of life. Among the treasures of the prince of Tyre "tabrets and pipes" are mentioned (Ezek. 28:13).[22]

The bells (*meẓillot*) hung on the neck of horses and other useful domestic animals, served to protect them against evil spirits (Zech. 14:20).[23]

The instruments of NEBUCHADREZZAR's orchestra, mentioned in the Book of Daniel, belong to a special category:

> "At what time ye hear the sound of the horn (*ḳarna*), pipe (*mashroḳita*), harp (*ḳathros*), trigon (*sabbeka*), psaltery (*pesanterin*), bagpipe (*sumponiah*), and all kinds of music (*v'kol benē zimra*), ye fall down and worship the golden image that Nebuchadrezzar the king hath set up" (Dan. 3:5,7,10,15).

The music at NEBUCHADREZZAR's court does not belong to the realm of Jewish musical culture. The names of most of the instruments in the Book of Daniel indicate that they are of alien origin. The author of that book obviously wanted to stress the pagan character of the ceremonies and of the music at NEBUCHADREZZAR's court by choosing exotic musical terms. He also wanted to emphasize the difference between the character of Jewish and Babylonian music.[24]

This systematic survey shows the material referring to music in the Old Testament. It contains a multitude of tessarae of mosaic which, seen isolated, do not reveal much. Pieced together in an appropriate way, however, they afford a vivid picture of the conception and practice of music in Ancient Israel. Their real meaning is not always what they say ostensibly, but what they intimate or even silently pass by as self-evident.

Our task will be to elucidate the seemingly obscure passages of the biblical text, so that their real significance presents itself with clarity and logic.

IV. THE BOOK OF PSALMS

The Book of Psalms (Hebrew: *Sefer Tehillim,* Greek: *Psaltērion,* Latin: *Psalterium*) is a collection of 150 lyric poems,[1] in five sections or books. The Hebrew title refers to the internal contents of the book, as praises in honor of God, whereas the Greek and Latin titles define the external form of the book, as hymns sung to the sounds of the psaltery, one of the principal instruments for the accompaniment of singing in Ancient Israel.

The psalms contain, mainly in their headings, musical instructions and other indications which are supposed to refer to the music of the psalms or to their musical performance. This attaches to the Psalter a particular importance for our inquiry.

It is outside of our task to examine the psalms historically and philologically. This has been performed abundantly by reputed scholars in a great number of books and essays. But we will refer occasionally to their findings inasmuch as it will be necessary to elucidate our subject from the viewpoint of history and philosophy.

Originally, the Psalter contained probably more than the present number of poems. Some might have been lost; others deleted from the main body by later editors. Whatever remained after the final editing, is a unique anthology of lyrico-religious poetry. It surely is not accidental that the Psalter became, and remained until today, the fundamental liturgical song book of the Israelites.

o o o

The oldest Hebrew words for song are *shir* and *shirah.* Primitively, the word was not used in the sense of a religious song, it simply meant any poem sung. The Psalter contains not merely religious, but also secular (even if religiously colored) songs of various categories, a sign that the compilers of the Psalms drew from all sources of popular poetry.

In the olden times, songs of praise for the use in the cult might have constituted a sort of primitive hymnal. The strong religious alliance of the people of Israel with his God was likely to inspire the folk-bards to compose individual poems in which Yahveh's might, kindness and loving care for His people were exalted. Songs of praise and thanksgiving, songs of prayer and repentance might well have been the principal categories of the initial compilation. They constitute, in fact, the foundation of the later Book of Psalms.

Another species of song incorporated into the Psalter was the historic ode, intended to preserve the memory of some great national event.

Examples of this species are Psalm 30, "a Song at the Dedication of the House," and Psalm 137, which portrays the sufferings of the oppressed Jews in the Babylonian captivity, and a few others.

Further sources of the Psalter are the various popular songs, such as work-songs, songs of the harvest and vintage, love songs and nuptial songs, a great number of which may have existed in the early period of folk poetry. The names or the initial words of such popular songs are sometimes preserved in the headings of the psalms. Needless to say, a liturgical hymnal, such as the

Psalter, could not simply incorporate popular songs that had a manifest secular character without imparting them with a certain religious color. Nevertheless, some of the psalms contain, though in a modified form, elements clearly pointing to their popular origin, as for instance the song of thanksgiving of the people in Psalm 65:10-14. Some vestiges of former popular songs may also be traced in Pss. 104:13-16 and 147:7-9.

Finally, there are certain prayer-like meditations that, because of their archaic traits, may be considered as the precursors of later psalm-writing. Such poems may have been inspired in relatively early times by the strong religious sentiment of the Israelites, particularly by their occasional immersion into the spirituality of their faith.

A sublime example of this type is David's hymn of praise, which he offered to the Lord when He saved him from his enemies (2 Sam. 22), and which is incorporated almost without any change in the Psalter (Ps. 18).

Biblical exegesis assumes that the "penitential" hymns of the Babylonians might have prepared, or even influenced, the compositions of the psalms, perhaps giving them material as well as form.

o
o o

The voluminous and basically diverging opinions of biblical exegesis about the origins and the final order of the Psalter can only be slightly touched in our survey. Biblical commentators disagree even upon such elementary questions as to whether the Psalter, or certain portions of it, have originated before or after the Babylonian exile. On the other hand, there is almost complete unanimity among most of the commentators that the Psalter received its final form around 200 B.C.E.

The majority of the psalm-commentators place the origin of the Psalter in the period of the early kingdom (11th-10th cent. B.C.E.). Some of its parts may have been added conceivably in Hezekiah's time (8th cent. B.C.E.). The fourth book was presumably written at the time of the Babylonian exile or shortly thereafter (6th cent. B.C.E.), and the remaining portion during the two or three following centuries.

These chronological data, widely accepted as the most probable ones, will serve us as general guide-posts of our own investigations. Apart from being fundamentally logical, they are in perfect agreement with the historical development of the musical culture in Ancient Israel, as we shall presently see. Indeed, when examined closely, the parallelism between the gradual growth of the Psalter and the evolution of the sacred music of the Hebrews can hardly be overlooked.

o
o o

Considering the many analogies between the civilizations of Babylonia and Israel, already alluded to in our foregoing chapters, it is not surprising to discover certain similarities between the poetical outputs of both nations. Scholars have established some striking parallels in form, language and ideas between the Hebrew psalms and certain Babylonian poems.[2] On the other hand, there are substantial differences between them, mainly because of the higher religious ethics of the Israelites.

Aside from the Babylonian influence, not a few Egyptian traits have likewise penetrated the Hebrew psalms. The best known of these is the resemblance between IKHNATON'S (AMENOPHIS IV, 1370-1358 B.C.E.) "Hymn to the Sun," and Psalm 104.[3] Another similarity may be observed between the "Precepts of Amenophis" (AMENEMHET I, c. 2000-c. 1970 B.C.E.) and the "Proverbs of Solomon" of the Old Testament (Prov. 22:17-23). Psalm 29 is believed to be of Cana'anite origin.[4]

Despite these occasional foreign infiltrations, however, modern exegesis of the psalms has convincingly proved that, on the whole, the Psalter is a genuine creation of the Jews.

1. THE HEADINGS (OR SUPERSCRIPTIONS) OF THE PSALMS

The majority of the psalms include in their headings the supposed author's name. Out of the one hundred and fifty psalms, seventy-three are ascribed to David, twelve to Asaph, eleven to the children (the progeny) of Korah, two to Solomon, one each to Moses, Heman and Ethan. According to the tradition, David was the most prolific author of psalms, for which reason his name has been attached to the entire collection. As commonly known, the Psalter is often called "The Book of Psalms of David."[5] In view of the fame of king Solomon and of his recognized talent as a poet, it is rather surprising that no more than two psalms are ascribed to him, the more so since the Bible reports elsewhere that "he spoke three thousand proverbs; and his songs were a thousand and five" (1 Kings 5:12 [4:32]). It might well be that a number of these was actually incorporated into the Psalter, although it would be difficult to understand, in such a case, why the name of the famous author has not been mentioned. The most probable assumption is that in the turbulent centuries following Solomon's reign the majority of his proverbs and also of his songs (=psalms) were lost.

The children (descendants) of Korah belonged to a levitical clan. The tradition says that they originated in the desert. They were members of a group of scribes who, from the time of Hezekiah until the return from the Babylonian exile (ca. 724-ca. 444 B.C.E.), carried on an extended and prolific literary activity. The psalms attributed to them contain a goodly number of historical records and references, a fact that seems to hint at their possible participation in authoring the historical books of the Bible.

The psalms ascribed to Asaph have likewise originated in a levitical school. This name, like that of the children of Korah, refers to a family of Levites whose literary activity extended over several centuries. The psalms mentioning Heman and Jedithun as their authors, are certainly of levitical origin, since these men and their descendants belonged to the tribe of Levi.

Fifty-one psalms carry no author's name. In the talmudic literature these are called, characteristically, "orphaned psalms."[6]

o
o o

At all times, the headings, as well as the various descriptions, directions and names contained in the psalms have intrigued biblical exegetes. It is generally agreed that they are important allusions to the origin, the character, the purpose and, most of all, the musical rendition of the psalms.

The indications of the headings fall into two categories:

(1) Either they are general terms referring to the species or to the character of the psalm, that have but a loose relationship to music, if any.

(2) Or they are terms of the musical practice itself, pointing to some particular feature, such as the melody to be used as a pattern for the music of the psalms, the choice of the accompanying instruments, the way of actual performance, etc.

Both categories contain terms the meaning of which is clear from their etymology or other unmistakable characteristics; and they also include terms that are obscure and even patently incomprehensible. Commentators of all times have exerted their utmost efforts to unravel the secrets of these mysterious terms. Thus, countless opinions, interpretations and hypotheses have arisen, often diametrically opposed to each other, creating a confusion that largely continues to this day, although recent exegesis has removed many a doubt and straightened out a number of errors in this respect.

Up to now, the commentators of the psalms have availed themselves of general history, philology, and history of religions as their main tools for tackling the still existing difficulties. The specific musical approach has only been used whenever the meaning of the headings themselves happened to be quite obvious and thus would hardly justify any other treatment. The Psalter was born out of the spirit of music itself, as it were; this is why the musical background of the psalms is prevalent in all their parts. As a matter of fact, one is inclined to suspect that the purely musical implications of the headings are even much more extensive than it is generally assumed. A greater clarity might be obtained, in this respect, if we try to examine the headings from the angle of sheer musical practice. Such an approach would perhaps be contrary to traditional biblical exegesis. It may indeed be looked upon by some as a perfectly arbitrary choice, especially by those who deny the Psalter having any character of a "music book" altogether.[7]

2. GENERAL TERMS

The canonical text of the Bible has no general designation for the Book of Psalms, as a whole, only special terms for individual psalms in their headings, such as *shir, mizmor,* etc. In the Jewish liturgical use, however, the Psalter has long been called *Sefer Tehillim,* "Book of Songs of Praise." This colloquial title of unknown historical date is an indication of the purpose of the collection.

Tehillah, "song of praise," is derived from *hallel,* "to praise." *Hallel* is the commonly used word for laudatory singing in the Hebrew cult. The song of the Levites is so-called in several biblical passages (1 Chron. 16:4,23; 23:5,30; 25:3; 2 Chron. 5:13; 7:6; 8:14; 31:2).

However different the songs of the Psalter may appear with regard to their form and content, they have one thing in common: they are lyrico-religious songs destined for liturgical use. The Psalter went through different stages of evolution before attaining its final form. Several smaller collections were unified, single songs were added or omitted, slightly edited or markedly changed. Yet, the ultimate purpose of the primitive collection was the same as of the final book: it served as a hymnal for the public worship at the Temple.

Curiously enough, the specific term *tehillah* (SEPTUAGINT: *ainēsis,* VULGATE: *laudatio,* AQUILA: *hymnēsis,* JEROME: *hymnus*)[8] is used only once in the subtitles of the psalms, namely in the heading of Ps. 145. It appears, however, frequently in the psalmodic text itself, and also in other portions of the Scriptures. The general term "Song of Praise" seems to have been omitted from other headings. Probably all psalms were primitively called *tehillim,* as they are conveniently called in our days.

The principal English versions render the word either as "[Psalm of] Praise," "Song of praise," or simply "Praise" (*Douay*). *Wycliffe* has "preising" in the early, and "ympne" [the Old-English spelling for "hymn"] in the later version.

Moulton's translation of the psalms has the peculiarity of leaving out, in general, the superscriptions. The few exceptions from this rule will be indicated at the proper places.

o
o o

Tefillah is the common term for "prayer," especially for "supplication"; it is to be found at the head of four psalms (17, 90, 102, and 142), and furthermore in Habakkuk 3. In the postscript to Ps. 72:20 all psalms up to and including this number are called *tefillot.*

In the headings, the word seems to refer to a specific poetic form of prayer, the "threnodic psalm." The term was not restricted, however, to plaintive prayers, but—as evidenced by Ps. 72:20—it comprised also prayers of thanksgiving, and may have been the generic name for ritual psalms.

Most of the English Bibles translate *tefillah* as "prayer." *Moffat* avails himself of this word for Pss. 90 and 102, but uses "ode or prayer" for Ps. 142.

The earlier version of *Wycliffe* has "orisoun" [Old-English for "oration," *cp.* with the French "oraison"] for all three psalm-headings, whereas his later version has "preier" for Pss. 90 and 102, and "salm" for Ps. 142.

o
o o

The headings of fifty-seven psalms carry the subtitle *mizmor,* a term not to be found elsewhere in the Bible. In the early Greek and Latin translations of the Old Testament the respective equivalents of this subtitle are used more frequently than in the original Hebrew. The SEPTUAGINT sets *psalmos,* the VULGATE and the other Latin translations *psalmus,* AQUILA *melōdēma,* SYMMACHOS *ōdē,* and JEROME *canticum.*

The etymology of *mizmor* (from the root *zmr*) indicates a song accompanied by instruments, a song to be performed independently, in contrast to the dance-song (the "roundelay" of the Old Testament) which was mostly accompanied by rhythmical instruments or by clapping of hands. A frequently used instrument to accompany singing was the *nebel* (Gr. *psaltērion,* Lat. *psalterium*), rendered in the English translations as "psaltery." Eventually, the Greek (or Latin) name of this stringed instrument was affixed to the collection of songs themselves which were anciently accompanied by it, hence the name "Psalter."

Mizmor is uniformly rendered, in the principal English Bibles, as "Psalm," its Old-English spelling being "salm" in *Wycliffe,* both early and later versions. Only a few modern versions, among them *Moffat,* use "song."

o
o o

Another of the several subtitles is *shir* (Gr. *asma ōdē,* Lat. *canticum,* or *hymnus*). The word signifies "song" (*cp.* Pss. 7, 45, 46). This must have been the earliest term of the psalms and was probably used in the headings at the early stage of the Psalter.[9] Originally, the word designates a lyric poem, intended for singing, especially at joyous occasions. Eventually, the name was given primarily to songs of praise used in the cult, particularly to songs performed by the levitical choir.

Shir is mostly coupled together with *mizmor,* five times immediately before,[10] and eight times after this latter term.[11] By itself, it appears in Ps. 46 and, in a slightly changed form as *shirah,* in Ps. 18. The double term is rendered by the Latin versions of the Bible as *canticum psalmi* or *psalmus cantici,* meaning in both cases "song to be sung."

The Midrash interprets *mizmor* as a psalm accompanied by instruments, and *shir mizmor* as a psalm sung by a choral group alone.[12]

Elsewhere, *shir* is also used to designate a secular song (Isa. 23:16; Amos 6:5; 8:10). In the Psalter, the double term *shir mizmor* seems to refer only to religious songs. Yet, there is no internal or external evidence showing any tangible difference between psalms called *shir, mizmor,* or *shir mizmor.* One of the explanations for these variants could be that the various manuscripts arbitrarily used one term alone or the two terms together. It is also possible that the double term *shir mizmor* came about as a reconciliation of the various single-term readings found in the earlier collections at the time of the ultimate integration of the Psalter.

The root *zmr* is of Assyrian origin and means "to play" or "to sing"; it may have been commonly used for singing as well as for playing musical instruments. Another meaning of the root is "to pinch" or "to pluck," and in this sense it implies the action of plucking stringed instruments. *Zamar she-e-ri* is the Assyrian equivalent for *mizmor shir* and indicates, in this language, a song in the mood of an "elegy."[13] *Zmr* and its derivatives remained foreign terms in the Hebrew language, while *shir* was the vernacular word for the song. *Shir* is applied in the Bible to songs of the ritual as well as to songs of general religious character outside of the ritual, whereas *mizmor* is the specific term for religious songs. In the meaning of a drinking song, *shir* is used in Amos 6:5 and in the Book of Ecclesiasticus: "music at a hanquet of wine" (Ecclus. 49:1).

Shir as a single term is rendered, in the English Bibles, as "Song," in *Wycliffe* as "salm" (early and later versions). *Shir mizmor* is translated as "A Song; a Psalm," *mizmor shir* as "A Psalm; a song." *Douay* sets "A Psalm of a canticle," and "A canticle of a Psalm," respectively.

Moffat is rather inconsistent in his renderings; for the double term he puts indiscriminately either "song" alone (Pss. 30, 65), or "A song for music" (Pss. 48, 66, 68, 75, 76, 83, 87, 88, 108). For Ps. 67 he uses "A song for a string accompaniment," and for Ps. 92 "A song to be accompanied."

The double term is rendered by *Wycliffe* as "the salm of the song" (early) and "the salm of song" (later) for Ps. 30, "the song of the loode" (early) and "song of lernyng" (later) for Ps. 45 "salm" (early), and "song" (later) for Ps. 46, and "the preising of the song" (early), and "the song of psalm" (later) for Ps. 48.

o o o

Still another subtitle appears in fifteen psalms following consecutively, 120 to 134, namely *shire ha-maʿalot,* with the variant in Ps. 121, *shir la-maʿalot.*

The SEPTUAGINT translates them *ōdē tōn anabathmōn,* the VULGATE and JEROME *canticum graduum,* both meaning "Songs of Degrees." In his description of the sanctuary, JOSEPHUS mentions the fifteen steps leading from the Court of the Women up to the court of the Israelites, which he calls *bathmoi.*[14] The oldest rabbinical tradition connects these fifteen steps with the fifteen psalms referred to, saying that the Levites used to stand at the former, while singing the latter at the Feast of Tabernacles during the ceremony of the Water-libation.[15] Since the number of the psalms and of the steps was identical, the rabbinic writers concluded that each psalm was sung on one of the steps.[16]

The Church Fathers, while maintaining the ancient Jewish tradition concerning the fifteen steps, attribute to them, in addition, a mystico-religious meaning:

> *Siquidem quindecim sunt carmina in Psalterio, et quindecim gradus per quod ad canendum ascendunt Deo* ("Just as there are fifteen songs in the Psalter, there are fifteen steps on which [the faithful] could rise to God [by means of] singing").[17]

The later Greek translators, AQUILA, THEODOTION and SYMMACHOS abandoned the idea of the "degrees" and translated *asma tōn anabaseōn* (*eis tas anabaseis* for Ps. 121), meaning "Song of the Ascents." The explanation of the change was that these were the psalms sung by the repatriates from the Babylonian captivity when they "ascended" to Jerusalem. Indeed, Ezra called the return from Babylonia *ha-maʿalah mi-Babel* (Ezra 7:9). As for the plural, *ha-ma'alot,* the expounders try to elucidate this particularity by referring to the historical fact that the return from Babylonia took place in successive groups, as if "by degrees," first under Zerubbabel in 537 (Ezra 2:2 ff), then in the seventh year of the reign of ARTAXERXES, under Ezra, in 458 (Ezra 7:6-8). Against this interpretation, however, stands the fact that Psalms 122 and 134 intimate the existence of a newly built Temple, a well organized cult, and the completion of the walls of Jerusalem. All this could have been accomplished only after the return from the exile.

The third, and most probable, traditional interpretation maintains that these fifteen psalms have been sung by the pilgrims going annually to Jerusalem for the three great agricultural festivals, when they offered to the Temple the first fruits and the products of their harvest. Thus, *shir ha-ma'alah* would imply "Song of the Ascending Pilgrims," or "Song of Pilgrimage." The contents of these short, popular songs are indeed very appropriate for the occasion, some of them even containing direct allusions to pilgrimage, like Pss. 121, 122, 132, 133. Jerusalem had an elevated geographical location, the Temple itself being situated on a high ground; it was therefore logical to term the pilgrimage to the sanctuary an "ascent," as it is done, in fact, in other parts of the Bible, as, for instance, in the verse

> "Ye shall have a song as in the night when a feast is hallowed; and gladness of heart, as when one goeth with the pipe to come into the mountain of the LORD, to the Rock of Israel" (Isa. 30:29; see also Exod. 34:24, 1 Kings 12:27, 28; Ezra 7:9; Jer. 31:6; Ps. 24:3, etc.).

According to WILSON,

> "there is no doubt that 'go up' was the ordinary term in use for the yearly, or other, ascents to the house of the Lord at Jerusalem."[18]

The yearly pilgrimage to Jerusalem was a ritual action, prescribed by the Law (Exod. 34:24), and it was carried out in the form of a solemn procession. Several authentic and detailed descriptions of this religious ceremony are preserved. According to PHILO[19] and to the rabbinic scribes,[20] the offering of the first fruits was always a joyous popular feast. The husbandmen gathered in the larger places and marched to Zion with singing and piping. By the time the procession arrived at the outer court of the Temple, the Levites would intone the 30th Psalm.

As the numerous praying assemblies (synagogues) came gradually into being, the congregations in the provinces established the semi-annual custom of sending *ma'amads* to Jerusalem, where these were instructed in the rites and ceremonies of the Temple and also in the sacred songs.[21] The Mishnah states:

> "When the time was come for a Course [of *ma'amads*] to go up, the priest and the Levites thereof went up to Jerusalem."[22]

This phraseology, too, conveys the idea of one's "ascending" to Jerusalem.

As THIRTLE thinks, all these views of the numerous commentators are mutually exclusive, because their advocates discredit one another in their conclusions. True enough, he admits that

> "perhaps the most plausible of these theories, and the one which finds most favour among modern scholars, is that which would discern in the title a description of the Songs as designed for the use at the three

pilgrim feasts, i.e. 'to be sung on the way up to Jerusalem'."[23]

Nevertheless, and despite all the historical and liturgical evidence to the contrary, THIRTLE gives to these psalms an entirely different interpretation. In basing his theory on a passage in Isaiah 38:20, in which Hezekiah offers the Lord his thanksgiving for his miraculous recovery from mortal sickness ("therefore we will sing songs to the stringed instruments all the days of our life in the house of the Lord"), THIRTLE ventures a new and rather problematical hypothesis. He maintains that

> "the Songs of the Degrees were specifically compiled and in a definite manner associated with King Hezekiah and his experiences on the throne of Judah."[24]

The historical events during Hezekiah's reign, mostly the Assyrian invasion, but also the king's sickness and recovery, his service in the Lord's House and his Passover celebration, are considered by THIRTLE as underlying "motives" for the psalms. The Songs of the Degrees, some originally written in Hezekiah's time, some selected from ancient poems, constitute supposedly a commentary upon these events. Thus, THIRTLE views these fifteen psalms as being simply commemorative of Hezekiah, that is, written or adapted for the purpose of underscoring the most important occurrences of his reign.[25] Especially the coincidence between the years that were miraculously added to the king's life and the number of the Songs (fifteen) are taken by THIRTLE as validating his theory.[26]

THIRTLE's assumptions are in sharp contradiction with the findings of a host of biblical exegetes, traditional and modern, proving with great probability that the Psalter as a whole (but not necessarily the fifteen "Songs of Ascents" as an independent unit) in its final shape is the result of an organic development during at least eight centuries.

Most of the biblical scholars agree that the fifteen psalms constituted formerly a small, independent collection. And the title of this minuscule song book may well have been *Shire ha-ma'alot.* When this collection was incorporated eventually into the complete Book of Psalms, the former plural title might have been superimposed in singular to each one of these fifteen psalms.

Later translators of the Bible either follow one of the traditional interpretations, or have their own, different approach to the meaning of *Shire ha-ma'alot.* LUTHER translates the term as "Ein Lied im höhern Chor," intimating that the psalms were sung either on an elevated and "graded" place, or by a greater number of singers. English Bibles either use "Song of Degrees" (*Authorized Version, Harkavy*), or "Song of Ascents" (*Jewish, American* and *Revised Standards Versions*). *Moffat* has "A pilgrim song," and even *Moulton,* contrary to his general practice, gives a generic title to these fifteen psalms: "The pilgrims' Songs of Ascent."

Wycliffe too has "Song of Degrees," though in the Old-English spelling: "the song of the grees" (early), and "the song of greces" (later version). *Douay* sets "A gradual canticle."

However, the classical as well as the modern biblical exegesis accepts the traditional explanation only in part. HERDER, EWALD,[27] and others agree that *shir ha-ma'alah* means the song of the pilgrims marching to Jerusalem, either on their return from Babylonia, or on their yearly pilgrimages to the

Feast of Yahveh. With certain reservations, BUDDE, too, follows this idea.[28] He maintains that all the texts of the *ma'alah*-psalms are written in a popular vein, so pure and unaffected as seldom found in later periods. In some of them (Pss. 121, 122, 125, 132, 133, 134) the longing for Zion finds an especially adequate expression. Consequently, to use his own words,

> "we may legitimately assume that they orginated among the caravans of pilgrims marching from far away to Jerusalem; they were compiled and, eventually, formed a small collection of their own."

Another hypothesis is advanced by GESENIUS and, after him, by DE WETTE, DELITZSCH, and WINER.[29] They supposed that the term in question refers to a specific rhythm in poetry, the so-called "rhythm of degrees" (Gr. *anadiplosis*). This belief is based on a particularity found in several of these psalms, namely the poetical formula according to which a certain phrase or expression at the end of a verse is transferred to the beginning of the following verse, where it serves as the starting point of a new, similar or contrasting, idea. If this procedure is applied repeatedly within a poem, the verses are linked like "degrees."

This principle prevails indeed in some of the Psalms of the Degrees, most distinctly perhaps in Ps. 121. In other psalms, however, (*e.g.* 120, 127, 129, 131) it is only sporadic and in Pss. 128 and 132 it is entirely lacking. On the other hand, this "rhythm of degrees" can be found in other psalms not belonging to the Psalms of the Degrees, *e.g.* in Ps. 29, and also in other portions of the Bible (Judg. 5:3-6; Isa. 26:5,6, etc.). It is, therefore, highly questionable whether *ma'alah* in reality refers to this particular technique of poetry.

In a comprehensive study of the psalms, SIGMUND MOWINCKEL established an entirely new theory concerning the origin and purpose of the Psalter.[30] His unusual approach was highly commended by some, and rejected, at least in part, by others. We will discuss his findings only insofar as they have any bearing upon the music of the psalms.

The main tendency of his study, the "leit-motif" of his entire approach to the Psalter, is to show that after David's reign the Judeans adopted the Cana'anitic annual festival of the enthronement of Ba'al, which was based upon a similar festival held in the Temple of Marduk at Babylon. According to MOWINCKEL, this pagan festival was subsequently celebrated in honor of Yahveh at the Feast of Tabernacles, an assumption which, in the light of history, is quite improbable.

MOWINCKEL interprets the terms appearing in the headings either as indications for certain ritual actions, or as directives on how to perform specific religious ceremonies.

According to him, *ma'alah* means neither degrees, nor ascent, nor even pilgrimage, but the solemn procession that took place on New Year's day at the festival of Yahveh's ascension to the throne.

As he maintains, there is a weighty argument against the traditional interpretation, namely the circumstance that several *ma'alah*-psalms were not meant to be sung in the procession, but in the Temple itself. He points out, for instance, that Ps. 134 was sung at the nocturnal feast in the court of the sanctuary; Pss. 124 and 129 are liturgical chants in antiphonal form, consequently songs of the cult in the proper sense of the word. Ps. 128 is a priestly benediction and Ps. 121 a liturgical antiphonal chant with a priestly blessing. All this seems to indicate that these psalms have been performed in the Temple proper.[31]

From all these allegedly "clear" explanations MOWINCKEL draws the amazing conclusion that *ma'alah* cannot be interpreted in any musical sense whatsoever.

o
o o

The headings of thirteen psalms contain the term *maskil* (Pss. 32, 42, 44, 45, 52-55, 74, 78, 88, 89, 142), which, furthermore, is to be found in the text itself of Ps. 47:8. The SEPTUAGINT translates it as *syneseōs* or *eis synesin,* "on understanding" or "to an instruction," SYMMACHOS as *synesis* (Ps. 44). The VULGATE has *intellectus* or *intelligentia,* AQUILA *epistimōn,* JEROME *eruditio.* The Targum uses the paraphrase *Sekla ṭoba,* "good discernment," based quite obviously on *sekel-ṭob* of 2 Chron. 30:22.

The word is probably derived from the verb *sakal,* "to have insight" or "comprehension"; about its meaning, however, as a designation for a poem or song, the opinions of the commentators are divided.

GESENIUS thinks *maskil* was primarily a "didactic poem" with changing meters; he bases his opinion on Ps. 32:8. Now, a didactic content can at most be admitted for Pss. 32 and 78; in the other psalms, such or similar implication is doubtful or missing altogether. Ps. 45 is headed, besides *maskil,* by the indication "A Song of Loves," and Ps. 142 by "A Prayer." These two subtitles cannot easily be reconciled with the idea of a "didactic poem." Nevertheless, this belief is shared by quite a number of other commentators, among them CALMET and DE WETTE.[32] HENGSTENBERG, THOLUCK,[33] and others, likewise interpret the term in the sense of a "didactic poem" or "poem for instruction," but they derive it from *haskil* (Hiph. form of *sakal*), "to teach," "to make one prudent."

ROSENMÜLLER considers the word as a designation for a specific form of poetry;[34] he takes Ps. 47:8 as a basis for his assumption. LUTHER's translation, "Unterweisung" ("instruction") also clings to the idea of a didactic poem. DELITZSCH, on the other hand, explains *maskil* as "meditation," which has little probability. Impetuous complaints, such as contained in Pss. 44 and 74, can hardly be considered as belonging to the category of meditative poems.

All these interpretations have one thing in common, namely that the thirteen psalms under consideration have a didactic posture and are written in a metrical form that displays artful structure of their stanzas and refrains, a structure which they share, however, with some other non-*maskil* psalms.

MOWINCKEL's interpretation differs substantially from all those discussed above.[35] He does not deny that the term *maskil* refers to a poem of a specific kind or to a specific use. But he maintains that the heterogeneous contents of these psalms preclude their definition as "didactic poems." Besides, such poems have in the Hebrew language a special term: *mashal.* The psalms called *maskil* must be considered,—invariably, according to MOWINCKEL,—as songs intended for the cult alone. In an illuminating passage of the Old Testament it is stated that

> "Hezekiah spake encouragingly unto all the Levites that were skilled (*hamaskilim*) [or: "taught the good knowledge"] in the service of the Lord" (2 Chron. 30:22).

Zammeru maskil in Ps. 47:8 means:

> "sing ye praises in a skillful song," or "sing ye praises with understanding" (*Authorized Version*).

Furthermore, MOWINCKEL refers to the fact that, according to the conception of Ancient Israel,

> "there existed a close relationship between the composition of psalms and acts of prophecy; both were considered as manifestations of a specific endowment, which in later times was identified with rapture or inspiration."[36]

Ps. 49:2-5 and 1 Chron. 25:1-3 plainly reveal that the authors of psalms as well as the sacred singers had a firm belief in their respective poetic and musical talents as stemming from prophetic inspiration.

From all this, MOWINCKEL concludes that *maskil* must have been a song for the cult, performed with musical instruments, and induced by a particular "insight" or "intelligence," or by a specific power of inspiration, a very general statement, which could be applied with equal reason to many psalms outside the *maskilim.*

The question arises, however, as to why only thirteen psalms out of one hundred and fifty carry the term *maskil.* If poetry was a matter of divine inspiration, all the psalms, not only a handful of them, should be called *maskilim.* The fact that only a limited number of psalms were thus termed leaves some doubt open as to whether *maskil* may not have had, after all, a somewhat different meaning.

In our opinion, of all the different interpretations of *maskil,* the most probable is that of a penitential song. All the *maskil*-psalms, with the exception of the wedding ode (45), and perhaps of the lengthy Ps. 78, in which God's loving care for His erring people is praised, could—at least according to their contents—considered as belonging to the category of penitential songs.

The principal English versions have taken over the term phonetically. *Wycliffe* has "understonding," or "undirstondying" (early), and "lernyng" (later), the *Douay Version* "understanding," and *Moffat* "(an) ode."

o
o o

The headings of six psalms contain the term *miktam* (Pss. 16, 56, 57, 58, 59, 60), the meaning of which created considerable controversy. Etymologically, the term is connected with the Hebrew *katab* or *katam;* its meaning would respectively be either "scripture," "poem," or "riddle," "maxim," depending on the root it is derived from. GESENIUS thinks the word originated from *katam,* meaning "to conceal."[37] Other commentators trace it back to *ketem,* "gold," and accordingly, invest the term with the meaning "golden (psalm)." By way of analogy they point to the existence in the Arabic literature of some poems called *mudhahhabāt,* "guilded poems." These constitute a small compilation of seven items called *Qasida,* which also are surnamed *muʿallaqāt,* or "the suspended ones."[38] The two terms served apparently as somewhat loose titles for this small Arabic anthology at its first publication, as there seems to be no relationship between them and the contents of the *Qasida.*

LUTHER's translation of *miktam* as "ein gülden Kleinod" ("a guilded gem"), comes rather close to the same idea. Probably following up this meaning, HORNE and d'HERBELOT[39] have advanced a hypothesis that on some special occasions at the Jerusalem Temple, the psalms termed *miktam* were written in guilded letters and suspended in the sanctuary.

The ancient translators of the psalms follow entirely different paths in their efforts to find the true meaning of this word. The SEPTUAGINT and THEODOTION have *stēlographia,* the VULGATE *tituli inscriptio.* In his *Psalterium juxta Hebraeos,* JEROME renders the term as *humilis et simplex* (Pss. 16, 56-59) and as *humilis et perfectus* (Ps. 60). He obviously follows the Targum which ordinarily divides *miktam* into two words, *mik* and *tam,* rendering it as *makik ushelim,* "tender and perfect" (Pss. 56-59); as *parshegen,* "copy" or "explanation" (Ps. 60); and as *gelipa teriẓa,* meaning an "upright sculpture."[40] AQUILA and SYMMACHOS agree with the Targum in dividing the word into two. All these interpretations seem to refer to certain ancient religious customs of Oriental peoples, which may have been preserved in some form in the rites of the Israelites. In Egyptian and Babylonian excavations supplications were found written on steles, which were erected "before the gods," with the purpose of lending a special emphasis to the request of the donor, or of perpetuating the memory of the author or the donor. In the Phoenician cult, too, the donation of votive steles was considered an action pleasing the gods. Such steles sometimes contained a mere inscription with the name of the deity, or a short, stereotyped votive formula, occasionally symbolic images or pictures. They were erected in gratitude for a received favor and with the pre-calculated intention of putting the deity under obligation.[41]

All six psalms under consideration have the character of lamentations or supplications which, in the light of the above analogy, would suggest that *miktam* indicates a species of supplications that was presented to the deity in a written form.

HITZIG associates *miktam* with the Arabic *mâktum* (secret, hidden) and interprets it as *"anekdoton,"*[42] *i.e.* a song heretofore unknown and first published by the compiler of the Psalter. In the later Hebrew usage, the word assumed the meaning of "epigram."[43]

HENGSTENBERG thinks that *miktam* signified a "secret," and concludes from this that the psalms so termed have had an occult meaning. In the opinion of ALEXANDER,[44] the term indicates "the depth of doctrinal and spiritual import" of the respective psalms. GESENIUS, ROSENMÜLLER, THOLUCK, DE WETTE, and other commentators assume that the word may have originally ended with the letter *b,* instead of *m,* and was eventually transformed into *miktam* through an inversion, or an error of a scribe. As a proof, they refer to Hezekiah's song of thanksgiving (Isa. 38:9), in which the word appears in the form of *miktab,* with the meaning of "scripture," "poem," "song," or "song of praise."

Some authors, on the contrary, consider *miktab* to be a corruption of the allegedly original *miktam.* So OESTERLEY[45] and BRIGGS.[46]

LANGDON submits an entirely different reasoning and interprets *miktam* as a musical instrument.[47] According to this theory, the word is philologically connected with the Babylonian noun *naktamu,* "metal cover (for a vessel)," and is—as LANGDON thinks—the name of a percussion instrument, possibly the tambourine or cymbal. Peculiarly, in an earlier passage of the same essay he says that, following the analogy of *shushan* "that probably means a flute," *miktam* too signifies a similar wind instrument.[48]

LOUIS SEGOND, the author of the best modern French translation of the Bible, renders the term as "hymn."

English versions of the Scriptures evade the pitfalls of doubtful interpretations and take over *miktam* mostly in its original Hebrew form. Following closely the VULGATE, *Wycliffe* and *Douay* translate "inscripcioun of the title" (early), or "salm or song" (later), and "inscription of a title," respectively. *Moffat* has adopted the idea of *ketem,* "gold," and translates accordingly "a golden ode," which, in a modern Bible, seems to be out of place.

MOWINCKEL tries to find his own solution on the basis of the concordant contents of the respective psalms.[49] He derives the word from the Assyrian *katamu,* "to cover." The root of this word is the same in Hebrew and Syrian, and in both instances has assumed the meaning "to defile," "to besmirch." Accordingly, *miktam* would designate a song

> "the purpose of which would be 'to cover,' *i.e.* 'to expiate' sin, impurity, sickness, guilt,—all these notions being synonymous."

Consequently, MOWINCKEL suggests "a psalm for atonement" as an appropriate translation, especially since it seems to correspond, as he thinks, to the content of the psalms. The same holds true for Isa. 38:9-20.

VULGATE's translation, *tituli inscriptio,* points to still another conception. Some commentators suppose that *miktam* was a musical indication the meaning of which fell into oblivion with the passing of time. Should one try to find a proof for this assertion from the musical point of view, one would immediately discover, in the first place, that the word *miktam* is practically always connected with certain titles which seemingly have no relationship whatever with the contents of the psalms. Such titles are: *ʿal yonat ʾelem reḥoḳim* (Ps. 56) (LUTHER: "of the mute dove among the strangers"); *ʿal tashḥet* (Pss. 57, 58, 59) (LUTHER: "that he may not perish"); *ʿal shushan ʿedut* (Ps. 60) (LUTHER: "the rose of the testimony"). Many exegetes of the Bible consider these indications to be the titles of well-known songs or melodies, serving as melodic patterns for the respective psalms. From this, they conclude that *miktam* might have signified an instruction to employ a borrowed melody, the title of which appears in the heading of the psalm.

This assumption is corroborated by the fact that ancient Syrian hymn-writers used to place at the head of their poems certain musical titles, such as

> "to the melody (*ʿal kālāh db'* . . .) 'I will open my mouth with knowledge.' "[50]

Assyrian excavations have yielded a slab of stone containing a veritable catalogue of Sumerian and Assyrian songs, such as psalms, liturgies, popular and love songs.[51] This catalogue comprises numerous titles of songs, whose melodies were supposed to be applied to a number of different psalmodic and liturgical texts.[52] It is evident, therefore, that the indication of widely familiar melodies by means of textual titles belonging to various psalms or hymns, so that they could easily be sung with changed lyrics, must have been a persistent practice in the music of Antiquity.

Vestiges of the very same songs referred to in the headings of the psalms are even found occasionally in other parts of the Scriptures. Such as, for instance, the line *ʿal tashḥet,* "destroy not," already mentioned in connection with Pss. 57, 58, 59. We find it again in Isa. 65:8, though in a slightly modified form:

> "as, when wine is found in the cluster, one saith: 'Destroy it not (*ʿal tashḥitehu*), for a blessing is in it.' "

This might have been the first stanza of an ancient vintage song, a species frequently mentioned in the Bible. There is also a trace of *yonat ʾelem reḥokim,*

> "the silent dove of the far-off pine grove" (Ps. 56:1),

transferred in a somewhat modified form to Ps. 55:6-7:

> "Oh that I had wings like a dove! (*kayonah*) Then would I fly away, and be at rest. Lo, then would I wander far off (*ʾareḥik*) I would lodge in the wilderness."

It is possible that these may have been some very popular songs in those times, so that their sheer mention in the headings of the psalms was sufficient for the immediate implementation of their respective melodies not merely by the Levites, well versed in musical matters, but also by the congregation itself.

The objection could be raised that *miktam* is used once in the superscriptions (Ps. 16) without being connected with a song-title; furthermore, that a certain number of headings contain song-titles without the word *miktam.* These titles are: *ʿal mut-labben* (LUTHER: "of the beautiful youth," Ps. 9:1); —*ʿal ʿayyelet hashaḥar* (LUTHER: "of the hind hunted, at dawn," Ps. 22:1); —*ʿal shoshannim* (LUTHER: "of the roses," Pss. 45:1; 69:1; 80:1);—*ʿal maḥalat* (LUTHER: "in chorus, responsively," Ps. 53:1);—*ʿal maḥalat leʿannot* (LUTHER: "of the weakness of the distressed ones," Ps. 88:1). Besides, we find in Ps. 75:1 *ʿal tashḥet* ("destroy not") without *miktam,* in contrast to Pss. 57, 58 and 59, which have the very same song-title, accompanied by the word *miktam.*

Yet, all this is no conclusive proof against the assumption that *miktam* implied the use of some current popular melody for the psalm. It is an established fact, first noticed by THEODORE of MOPSUESTIA, a theologian of the school of Antioch (d.ca.428 C.E.), that the headings and superscriptions were a later addition to the psalm texts; in the Christian versions of the Old Testament they do not even belong to the canonical text. The original SEPTUAGINT lacked the historical titles of Pss. 51, 52, 54, 57, 63, and 142. On the other hand, the SEPTUAGINT contains liturgical and historical data in the psalm headings which are not included in the Masoretic Hebrew text. Moreover the Syriac version of the Bible has entirely different titles.[53]

These headings might well have been originally some marginal notes for the choir-leaders or precentors. They represent certain instructions for the musical performance of the psalms; or they may have indicated the melody as well as the instruments to be chosen and may have reminded the singers of certain particularities pertaining to their interpretation. The biblical scribes of earlier times may have been aware of the fact that the headings had no relationship with the psalm text proper. Therefore, they probably did not transfer these headings into later copies as scrupulously as they handled the text itself. This explains the various readings in the preserved ancient manuscripts, the frequent inversions of letters, and other incongruities, as for instance, the fact that some manuscripts contain words that are left out in others.

This alone would explain why a term may occasionally be lacking in certain headings. Yet, another circumstance has to be taken into account with regard to these musical instructions. As long as the primary tradition of the Temple music was alive and the meaning of the musical terms was familiar to anyone connected with sacred music, a great many indications, however important, could be omitted from the superscriptions, without endangering their correct understanding. This could serve as a further explanation why *miktam* has been left out in some of the headings, where—by analogy—we would expect to find it. On the other hand, *miktam* stands alone at least on one occasion (Ps. 16). This must have been an instance when, because of the practical necessity to change sometimes the musical material of the sacred service, the choice of a song was left to the discretion of the levitical choirmaster. A situation like this would naturally preclude the specific mention of the song in the heading of the psalm. This, of course, is but a surmise, having nevertheless some probability.

Later scribes copied the headings with all these simplifications and abbreviations; in the end, they were taken rather naively as representing the "authentic" version and, since the establishment of the Jewish canon, accepted as a sacred and unimpeachable text. Thus, the musical terminology in the headings of the psalms has been preserved with all its "mysteries" and apparent inconsistencies.

o
o o

In the superscription of Ps. 60 there is, in addition to *miktam le-David,* the term *le-lammed.* The SEPTUAGINT and SYMMACHOS translate it as *eis didachēn,* the VULGATE as *in doctrinam,* JEROME as *ad docendum,* all in the sense of "to teach." The Targum adopted the same meaning, and all the modern Bible versions follow this interpretation. According to the conventional biblical exegesis, this psalm was intended for teaching the young people. There is an analogy to this in 2 Sam. 1:18:

> "And [David] said—To teach the sons of Judah the [song of the] bow,"[54] but mainly in Deuter. 31:19,22: "Now therefore write ye this song for you, and teach thou it the children of Israel."

The question arises, however, whether this should have been the only psalm to be taught to the young. The practice of singing psalms was preserved from generation to generation by oral tradition. Therefore, it may well be taken for granted that numerous other psalms, texts as well as melodies, were taught, *i.e.* rehearsed and continually repeated until they were indelibly engraved in the memory of the young generation. It is difficult to explain why this psalm alone contains the instruction *le-lammed,* or why the author of this psalm should have considered it necessary to specially indicate an accepted procedure for this particular psalm, which certainly has been customarily applied to other psalms as well.

It is rather safe to assume that all or most of the psalms headed by *miktam* were poems to be taught to the youth. The term *le-lammed,* may very well have withered away gradually and, intentionally or by oversight, it was preserved in this one heading. It might also be that all the psalms superscribed with *miktam* originally constituted a small independent collection. This is corroborated by the fact that in the final order of the Psalter they are grouped together, immediately following each other, with the sole exception of Ps. 16. Perhaps Ps. 60 was originally the initial poem of this small collection and contained in its heading the underlying purpose of the entire set, *le-lammed,* that is "to be taught to the youth." When the Psalter took its final shape, the first piece might have been transferred for some reason to the end, and so *le-lammed* lost its meaning as a generic term and was retained merely in a single psalm.

All these are no more than conjectures, to be sure, but they furnish at least a plausible explanation for the fact that the indication *le-lammed* appears only once in the Psalter.

The principal English Bibles render the word in its original meaning "to teach," or "for instruction" (*Revised Standard Version*). *Wycliffe* sets "in to lernyng" (early), and "to teche" (later), *Douay* "for doctrine." Whereas *Moffat* puts surprisingly "for recitation," thereby divesting the psalm of its musical character.

o

o o

The superscriptions of two psalms contain the indication *le-hazkir* (Pss. 38 and 70). The SEPTUAGINT renders the term as *eis anamnēsin,* "in remembrance," AQUILA as *tou anamimnēskein,* "in commemoration," the VULGATE as *in rememorationem,* JEROME as *in commemoratione* (Ps. 38) and *ad recordandum* (Ps. 70); all three Latin forms express nearly the same idea, "in remembrance." Most of the scholars explain the insertion of this term as the expressed desire of the psalmist to be remembered by God.[55]

The translation of the Targum, however, implies another idea; it points to a certain sacrificial ceremony at which, with a handful of flour and oil, incense was thrown into sacrificial fire. If the interpretation of the Targum is correct, both psalms were parts of this sacrificial rite, called *ʾaskara* ("memorial," *cf.* Lev. 2:2,9,16).

The translation of the SEPTUAGINT to Ps. 38, *eis anamnēsin,* with the additional remark *peri sabbatou,* seems to be an indication that both psalms were not sung at the regular daily *ʾaskara,* but only at that of the Sabbath.[56]

English versions, though following the same general idea, paraphrase the term quite differently. *Wycliffe* has for Ps. 38 "in remembering of the saboth" (early), and "to bythenke on the sabat" (later), furthermore for Ps. 70 "in remembering" (early), and "to haue mynde" (later). *Douay* sets "for a remembrance" (Ps. 38), and "to bring to remembrance" (Ps. 70). The *Authorized Version, Harkavy,* and the *American Version* likewise render the term as "to bring to remembrance," whereas the *Jewish Version* has "to make memorial," the *Revised Standard Version* "for the memorial offering," and *Moffat,* in specifying this particular offering, sets "to be used when incense is offered." As in several other instances, *Moulton* leaves out the word in both psalm-headings.

o
o o

Finally, there is in the headings of the psalms the subtitle *shiggayon* (Ps. 7). The same word, in a somewhat altered form, *ʿal shiggionot,* appears in Habakkuk 3:1.

The SEPTUAGINT translates *shiggayon* as *psalmos,* the VULGATE as *psalmus,* AQUILA as *agnoēma,* SYMMACHOS and THEODOTION as *hyper agnoias,* JEROME as *ignoratio* or *pro ignoratione.* For Habakkuk 3:1 the SEPTUAGINT puts *meta ōdēs,* AQUILA and SYMMACHOS *epi agnoēmatōn.*

All these early Greek and Latin translators interpreted *shiggayon* as a synonym for *shegiʾot,* "error," "fault" (*cp.* Ps. 19:13).[57] The Midrash and RASHI follow the same idea, while speaking of "David's transgression." The etymology of the word is evidently connected with the verb *shagah,* "to wander." In a wider sense, this verb has the meaning "to reel," "to err," "to go astray." According to this, *shiggayon* would mean a psalm with a changing meter or a changing melody.

Modern exegesis assumes that psalms usually show strophic patterns with as a rule fairly regular meter. Psalm 7 and Habakkuk's song of praise have both a heptasyllabic meter with three distinct parallels in each verse. Therefore some biblical commentators consider *shiggayon* to be either an indication of a poetical structure metricized in this fashion, or else of the melodic form set to it. The same meter, however, is used in other psalms and songs of praise, to which the term *shiggayon* is not appended. Again, the point must be stressed that the headings have not always been treated by the scribes with the same solicitude as the canonical text proper.

Another meaning of the verb *shagah* is "to be large." In the Piʿel form, it would signify "to enlarge," "to perform a song with great excitement." Both from this and the original meaning of the word, modern commentators derive the most diverse interpretations. DE WETTE, ROSENMÜLLER, CALMET, and others believe the term to indicate a "plaintive song" or an "elegy." HENGSTENBERG, and others, maintain that the word refers to the errors and delusions of the miserable and, as such, is connected with the contents of the psalm. They call it "a wandering song" or a "song of wanderings" (PARKHURST). HOUBIGANT interprets *shiggayon* as *cantio erratica,* "chant mixte." As an explanation of "mixte" he says:

> "chant qu'on peut mettre sur plusieurs airs, ou à plusieurs parties,"

that is a song set for several parts.[58] This, however, is an obvious anachronism, for the music of Antiquity did not know part-setting in the Occidental sense. (See, however, p. 439 ff).[59]

PARKHURST and others explain *shiggayon* as "a song of wanderings."[60] According to this view, David wrote the psalm during his years of wandering when, as a fugitive, he tried to escape from Saul's pursuits. EWALD, DELITZSCH, and others, interpret it as a "dithyramb," or a "reeling poem." This, however, is quite incompatible with the contents of Ps. 7. DELITZSCH maintains that

> "*shiggayyon* (related to *shigaon,* "madness") may mean, in the prosodic parlance, a reeling poem, *i.e.* one endowed with a most excited movement and a rapid change of the strongest emotions, therefore a dithyrambic poem."[61]

And he adds by way of general musical observation:

> "The musical accompaniment also had its part in the general effect produced. Moreover, the contents of the psalm corresponds to this poetic musical style."[62]

Quite obviously, however, this represents a perfectly arbitrary interpretation. From the beginning to the end, the psalm expresses reliance on a righteous God who saved the innocent David from an unjust enemy and to whom, in the concluding verse, David expresses his gratitude. All this cannot possibly be associated with the idea of a "reeling poem."

A more appropriate explanation of the term can be obtained by way of examining its equivalents and parallel uses in other ancient religions. The word seems to be connected with the Assyrian liturgical term *shigū,* meaning a plaintive song of several stanzas. In Babylonia, such poems were performed with musical accompaniment and with special rites.[63] In the Assyrian language, the verbal form of *shigū* means "to rave," "to lament vehemently." From this, GESENIUS derives the meaning of an "ode" or a "dithyramb," *i.e.* "a wild, passionate song, with rapid changes of rhythm."[64] EWALD, RÖDIGER and DELITZSCH, on the other hand, adhere to earlier interpretations and explain the term as an indication for a special rhythm, or a specific kind of lyric poetry.

MOWINCKEL likewise views the word as related to the Assyrian *shegū* (or *shigū*), "plaintive psalm." Its verbal form ("to wail," "to lament") is used to indicate a threnody in religious ceremonies. MOWINCKEL surmises furthermore that this term came anciently to Cana'an being first introduced into the rites of the local tribes and then, in a roundabout way, into the Hebrew cult. Accordingly, he interprets *shiggayon* as a "psalm of lamentation (of a sick man.)"

Shiggionot (Hab. 3:1) is supposed to be the plural form of *shiggayon.* This would give to this heading a logical meaning, in the sense of "in the manner of lamenting songs," which would correspond to the contents of the poem, despite its hopeful ending (verses 18 and 19). Nevertheless, MOWINCKEL claims that *shiggayon* could not be directly derived from the Hebrew *shagah* and that there must have been another root at the origin of it. He advances a theory based upon SEPTUAGINT's translation, *meta ōdēs* ("with a song"), to the effect that *shiggionot* might be a corrupted spelling, and therefore suggests *'al neginot* as a probably correct reading. Yet, should we accept *shiggayon* as authentic, it would signify, according to MOWINCKEL, not so much a lamenting song but rather the ritual ceremony at which such psalms were sung.[65]

Most of the English Bibles have taken over the term phonetically for the psalm-headings as well as for Habakkuk. The exceptions are: *Wycliffe,* using "for the ignoraunce" (early), and "for vnkuunynge men" [*i.e.* "for ignorant men"] (later), both settings for the psalm only, since the word is omitted in Habakkuk altogether. *Douay,* on the contrary, leaves out the term in the psalm-headings, but puts "for ignorances" in Habakkuk. *Moffat* translates the psalm-heading as "dithyramb," and Habakkuk as "in dithyrambic measure."

3. TERMS OF MUSICAL PRACTICE

Accustomed to a strict orderliness, characteristic of the ancient tradition, Jewish liturgical functionaries must have surely tended toward putting down in writing the important guiding marks pertaining to the musical aspect of their rites. This would especially apply to psalms, in so far as any such markings were possible at the time when musical notation in Occidental sense was still unknown. This indeed may have been the aim of certain indications inserted occasionally in the headings of the psalms which, no doubt, represent instructions for musical performances. These instructions were useful to the contemporaries of the psalmists as well as to their immediate successors, because their meaning was understood by everyone connected with sacred music.

Eventually, however, their true meaning fell gradually into oblivion, which is not surprising if we consider how vague these terms are *per se.* In the fourth and fifth books of the Psalter (Pss. 90-150), which are later additions to the collection, scarcely any one of these indications can be found, a proof that their meaning must have become rather obscure even in a relatively short time after the first three books were compiled. Even the translators of the SEPTUAGINT (completed in the 3rd cent. B.C.E.) no longer understood these terms, and thus were compelled to take them over phonetically from the original Hebrew, the same method having been also applied by the later Old Latin translators. Owing to the unintelligibility of these terms, whose meaning was entirely lost by subsequent desuetude, the early Fathers of the Church completely refrained from giving them any rational interpretation and, in accordance with the general tendency of early Christianity, attributed to them all sorts of moral, allegorical, and mystical implications.

o
o o

Since no musical notation was known at that period, the Levites were confronted with the problem of perpetuating in some other way the music of the psalms, both the melody and the accompaniment The continuity of the well established tradition depended mainly on finding a method for the best possible transmission of the current musical practice to further generations. Levitical singers, the chosen guardians of the tradition, were bound to invent and further develop such a method. They solved this problem as effectively as was feasible in those days. To begin with, they had to establish a musical terminology which, in a nutshell, would contain all that the levitical singers and musicians with an average professional education had to know. The proper application of these terminological indications was supposed to furnish future generations with the key to correct musical rendering of the psalms. Where and how have these indications been put into effect?

From the very beginning of Temple music, there may have existed a scroll of the Psalter reserved for the exclusive use of the master of the levitical musicians. Such a copy would represent, in a way, a "score," serving the choir-leader for rehearsals. Choir conductors of all times had to have some kind of score, or lead-sheet; and it is unlikely that this useful device was created exclusively by our Western musical practice. In his *Shilṭe ha-Gibborim* (Mantua, 1612), PORTALEONE postulates the use of a score by the levitical choir-masters. Describing the details of the Temple institutions, he enumerates the order of precedence of the Levites and says in paragraph 16:

> *ha-memunah ʿal hazilẓal v'ʿal kol kle ha-niggunim v'ʿal kol seferi ha-parṭiṭurah v'seferi ha-inṭavolaṭurah,* "the prefect of the cymbals and of the instruments for the accompaniment of the song, as well as of all the books known as *partitura* or *intavolatura.*"[66]

In this *partitura, i.e.* "score," all the indications considered essential for the proper rendering of music would have been inscribed, such as the melody to be chosen for the psalm, sometimes also the accompanying instrument to be used, and other instructions pertaining to the musical performance.

The only place where such indications could be inserted was the heading (or the subscriptions) of the psalms. It goes without saying, therefore, that such indications pointing merely to the performance of music did not belong to the text proper and also that their corresponding words were *not* sung in ancient times.

°°°

Here we have to refer to an important and entirely new interpretation of the musical instructions of the Psalter, which heretofore were unanimously considered as headings, *i.e.* superscriptions of the individual psalms.

Greek, Latin, Hebrew and other ancient manuscripts used to be written in a way that the text ran without any break or division between words and without the indication of chapters or paragraphs. The biblical verses themselves were divided not by their authors or the scribes who wrote them down initially, but by subsequent editors, priestly and levitical functionaries, and mainly by the Masoretes, who were chiefly responsible for the actual form of the Holy Writ.

This situation is of special significance for the Book of Psalms. Similarly to other ancient manuscripts, the psalms followed one another without divisions, leaving the door open to all kinds of personal interpretations as to where a psalm had to begin or to end. It is well known how this incertitude resulted in different arrangement of psalms in the various Bible Versions (Hebrew, Greek, Latin, Syriac, Arabic, etc.).

THIRTLE, after closely investigating the textual relationship between the psalms and the terms contained in the headings, has made the important discovery that some of these terms apply not to the following, but to the preceding psalm.[67]

THIRTLE found two Scriptural instances outside the Psalter which undeniably corroborate his contention and which must be considered as typical examples of what the psalms of Israel were in point of form. One is the "Song of Thanksgiving of Habakkuk" (Hab. 3), which opens with "A Prayer of Habakkuk upon Shiggionoth," and ends with "To the Chief Singer on my Stringed instruments." The other is Hezekiah's Thanksgiving, "when he had been sick, and was recovered of his sickness" (Isa. 38:10-20), ending with:

> "Therefore we will sing songs to the stringed instruments all the days of our life in the house of the Lord."

These two poems are looked upon by THIRTLE as the normal or standard procedure for all psalms. He concludes that words of instruction, which to-day stand in the SEPTUAGINT and all subsequent versions of the Bible as *super*scriptions, belong in reality not to the psalm that follows them but as *sub*scriptions to the psalm that precedes them.

It is surprising that none of the innumerable biblical scholars ever sensed even the remotest possibility of the headings belonging as subscriptions to the preceding psalm. If nothing else, a striking analogy from Antiquity should have pointed to it. Sumerian and Babylonian psalms have always in subscription that which Hebrew psalms have in their headings: the name of an author, the musical instrument to be used as accompaniment, the tune to which it was to be sung, the kind of musical composition, the purpose of the psalm, and sometimes even the collection to which it belonged.

THIRTLE's discovery establishes indeed a closer relation between the contents of certain psalms and their musical rendition. Though in some isolated cases (*e.g.* Pss. 49, 150, etc.) the musical instructions would be more appropriate as *headings* than as *subscriptions* to the preceding psalm, there is, in general, all reason to accept THIRTLE's arrangement as representing the true meaning of most of the musical instructions.

For the sake of uniformity, we will refrain from re-numbering in our treatise all the indications of THIRTLE as attached to the various psalms. Only in special instances will we assign them to the psalms to which, according to his system, they rightly belong.*

o
o o

To the musicologist of to-day, most of the terminological "enigmas" in the psalm-headings yield an instant solution by way of viewing them mainly in the light of our days' rudimentary musical necessities.

Some of these indeed include terms the meaning of which is often so obvious that, contrary to what has actually taken place in many instances, their interpretation should not have ever raised any doubt. Such is especially the case with the indication *la-menazzeah,* used so frequently in the Psalter.

(*) The reader may find a complete rearrangement of the psalm-headings in conformity with this system in "*The Companion Bible*" published by the Lamp Press, Lmtd., (London, n.d.).

The word is derived from the verb *naẓẓaḥ*, "to shine," "to triumph," and signifies, in the Pi'el conjugation, "to lead." *Menaẓẓeaḥ* in 2 Chron. 2:1,17 means the "overseer." The verbal form of the word appears in three passages of the Scriptures, in 1 Chron. 23:4 and Ezra 3:8,9, in the sense of "presiding," or "administering," and in 1 Chron. 15:21, where it indicates a definite function in the music of the Temple namely "to lead" or "to direct" the song.

It is surprising that, having at hand such an unmistakable meaning of the word, the early translators of the Bible failed to do justice to its real implication. The translations of the SEPTUAGINT, *eis to telos,* and the VULGATE, *in finem,* both meaning "unto the end," give quite an erroneous sense. The same holds true for the rendering of AQUILA, *tō nikopoiō,* "for the victor," of SYMMACHOS, *epinikios,* "song of victory," and of THEODOTION, *eis tos nikos,* "for the victory." JEROME translates either *victori,* "for the victor," or *pro victoria,* "for the victory," following obviously the footsteps of his early Greek predecessors.

The Targum renders the word as *leshabbaḥa,* "in praise of . . ." The same expression is used by the Targum, however, for *la-shir* in 1 Sam. 18:6, a fact difficult to explain.

Outside of psalms, *la-menaẓẓeaḥ* is to be found only in one other passage of the Bible, namely Habakkuk 3:19. This "song of thanksgiving" of Habakkuk, according to the author's own indications, was designed for performance with musical accompaniment, just as were the psalms. While *la-menaẓẓeah* stands in the Psalter always in the headings, it appears in Habakkuk at the end. It has been surmised that Habakkuk's poem represents a displaced psalm, which, for some reason, was not incorporated into the Psalter, or was removed from it in later times. This assumption is supported by the unusual fact that this song of thanksgiving contains three times the term *selah.* Outside of the Psalter, this is the only place in the Scriptures where this term is used.

Out of one hundred and fifty psalms fifty-five contain the indication *la-menaẓẓeaḥ* and, of these, fifty-two in the first three books, indeed in more than half of the eighty-nine psalms they contain. In the fourth book the term is entirely lacking, in the fifth book it appears three times (Pss. 109, 139, 140).

Menaẓẓeaḥ is the singer chosen to lead the music or to officiate as precentor, who probably also instructed the choir, or at least supervised the rehearsals, and was a specially qualified artist with a superior musical knowledge. Furthermore, he must have been entrusted with the occasional solo passages in psalm-singing. Thus, he may be considered the precursor of later days' *ḥazzan,* the precentor of the synagogal sacred service.

The first singing master of the Davidic music organization was Chenaniah, of whom the chronicler says:

> "He was master in the song, because he was skillful" (1 Chron. 15:22).[68]

In the later books of the Scriptures only two names of leaders of singing are preserved: Matthaniah, of Asaph's progeny (Neh. 11:17), and Jezrahiah (Neh. 12:42). Besides Matthaniah, as the second and third soloist of the Second Temple, Bakbukiah and Abda (or Obadiah, *cp.* Neh. 12:25) are mentioned.

Why do only fifty-five psalms carry the indication *la-menaẓẓeaḥ?* And why is the indication lacking in the remaining ninety-five psalms, a great number of which, were, no doubt, publicly sung?

There are relevant indications that *la-menaẓẓeaḥ* was only put at the head (or at the end) of such psalms which either were designed to be sung by a soloist, or which contained passages for a solo singer. The other psalms were performed by the choir alone.

There seems to be a remarkable affinity between psalm-singing in Ancient Israel and one of the vocal forms of our Occidental music, the cantata. A comparative scrutiny will reveal a striking similarity between the formal principle of the two, as will be shown in the following review.

Some of the psalm texts strongly suggest that these psalms used to be performed either by a solo singer throughout, or the chorus singing antiphonally, —or else alternating only in the ritornellos—with the soloist. Those psalms, therefore, superscribed with *la-menaẓẓeaḥ,* would correspond either to the Occidental "solo cantata," or "mixed cantata," in which soloists and choir alternate. On the other hand, psalms without any specific indication in their headings would be considered as having been sung throughout by the chorus alone and would represent the parallel to our "choral cantata."[69]

A simple philological examination of the texts of certain psalms will corroborate this theory. The alternation of the subjects "I" and "We" within the same psalms justifies the assumption that these psalms were originally congregational songs which must have been performed antiphonally by the precentor as soloist, and the worshippers in the capacity of a responding choral body.[70] At a later, artistically more elaborate stage of sacred music, the function of the precentor was retained, but the singing of the congregation was taken over by the levitical choir.

Psalm 5, for example, provides the pattern for a meaningful division of the text into passages for solo and choral singing. In verses 2-4, the psalmist speaks in the first person (solo), in verses 5-7 in the third person (choir), in verses 8-9 again in the first person (solo), in verses 10-11 in the third person (choir). The contents of verses 12-13 is very well suited for ending the psalm by the soloist together with the choir.

Psalm 9 has, in general, the same structure. Verses 2-6 solo; verses 7-13 choir; verses 14-15 solo; verses 16-17 choir. Here the psalmodic text is interrupted by the indication *Higgayon Selah,* believed to be a sort of musical interlude.* Verses 18-19 again would be sung by the soloist, 20-21 by the chorus, while the concluding *Selah* would here signify a sort of postlude, (if we assume that this term has had its legitimate place at the end of the psalm).

In accordance with their introspective contents, Psalms 13 and 54 are well suited for the performance by the soloist alone.

Psalm 59 displays a remarkable symmetry for a cantata-like musical forma-

* For these terms see pp. 146 and 156.

tion. Verses 2-5 would be the part for the soloist, verse 6 for the chorus, followed by *Selah.* Verses 7-11 would be sung by the soloist, verses 12-14 by the chorus. After another *Selah,* the choir would continue with verses 15-16, the precentor would end with verses 17-18.

These few examples could be increased at will (f.e. Ps. 12, 18, 39, 41, 46, 47, 62, 70, 75, a.o.); they suffice however to demonstrate that the contents of the psalms favor their arrangement according to solo and choral units. One could hardly raise a serious objection to this surmise, either philologically, or musically. Furthermore, there were likely to allude to certain aspects of human nature which, in the absence of any direct historical accounts, must now be given a bit of hypothetical consideration.

At all times and in all places, the performing artist was subject to human vanity. Whether he was a sacred or a secular musician, a singer or an instrumentalist, his aim was to put his artistry into the brightest possible light (*cp.* the original meaning of the verb *naẓẓaḥ,* "to shine") and to entice his audience by the merit of his performance. The levitical singers "that were instructed in singing unto the Lord," "were all skillful" in their craft—so the Scriptures tell us most explicitly (1 Chron. 25:7). The precentor, however, was the *primus inter pares,* the singing virtuoso *par excellence* of those days, and as such, without any doubt, the artistic "attraction" of the sacred service. With all the solemnity of the Jewish religious ceremonies, and with all the fervor of the participants, the effect which the singing virtuoso of yore used to exercise upon his audience must have been considerable. This fact was bound to procure for him great popularity among the congregants and increased authority in his relations with the priests. Both factors were certainly used to the full by the precentors.

In actual practice, this may have resulted in the request of the precentor for an opportunity of displaying his virtuosity during the sacred services. This, of course, could be effected only during the performance of the psalms. It is reasonable to assume that the psalms, in relation to which the precentor was granted his much desired opportunity, have been specifically designated in advance.

The singer-virtuoso might not have been satisfied with the given verbal assurance that certain psalms would be permanently reserved as his "showpieces." He might have asked, in addition, that his privilege should be stipulated in writing. The priests had to consent to this demand. And so, their pledge found its expression in the heading (or at the end) of the psalms. This is, in our opinion, the real significance of the term *la-menaẓẓeaḥ.* The fact that fifty-five out of one hundred and fifty psalms carry this indication shows the extent of the prestige the precentors must have enjoyed in Ancient Israel. Because of their indispensability in the sacred service and their popularity with the worshippers, the precentors could well afford to make demands, being sure in advance that these would not be denied.

If our assumption is correct, then sacred musical practice of biblical times divulges the same phenomena of artists' vanity, the urge to show off, and other traits of spoiled virtuosos, which the *ḥazzanim* of the Synagogue were so frequently accused of displaying at later periods.

THIRTLE furnishes another explanation of *la-menazzeaḥ,* which would divest the word of any musical connotation. It is therefore unnecessary to deal with it in extenso.[71]

MOWINCKEL, who tries to explain most of the terms in the headings as marks for ritual procedures, offers a corresponding interpretation also for *la-menazzeaḥ*.[72]

He rejects the very idea of "leading," especially "to conduct a band," or "a choral group," as "impossible to prove." According to him, both passages, 1 Chron. 15:21 and 2 Chron. 34:12, 13, generally quoted as supporting the notion of "leading," are untenable.

MOWINCKEL concludes that *lebashmi'a* and *la-menazzeaḥ* indicate the main purpose of sacred music: first, to draw, by clashing cymbals, the attention of Yahveh to the worshippers, then, to please Him and to obtain His mercy through singing and playing.

Basically, this is the unadulterated meaning of the verb *nazzaḥ,* as exposed above, referring to the portions of the Psalter, in which opportunity was given to the precentor, the virtuoso singer of those days, "to shine" and "to triumph," for the higher glory of God, in whose honor the sacred music was performed.

English Bibles show wide discrepancies in the interpretation of this term. The *Authorized Version* and *Harkavy* have "to the chief Musician," for the psalms, but "to the chief Singer," for Habakkuk. The *American Version* has invariably "for the chief Musician," the *Jewish Version* "for the Leader," the *Revised Standard Version* "to the Choirmaster." *Moulton,* as usual, leaves out the term in the psalm-headings, but puts "for the chief Musician" in Habakkuk. *Moffat* follows the basically correct idea that the Psalter was composed of several smaller hymnals and, interpreting the compilation of *la-menazzeaḥ*-psalms as an earlier unit, renders the term as "from the Choirmaster's collection."

The Old-English versions follow the early Greek and Latin translations and render accordingly: *Wycliffe* for Ps. 4, "in to the end" (early), and "to the victorie in orguns" (later); for Ps. 5, "in to the end" (early), and "to the ouercomere (on the eritagis)," (later); for Ps. 6, "in to the end" (early), and "to the ouercomere in salmes" (later); for the other psalms, "in to the ende", and "to the victorie" (both in the later version). *Douay* gives for the psalms a literal rendition of the VULGATE as "unto the end," but a very circumstantial paraphrase for Habakkuk, "and the conqueror will lead me upon my high places singing psalms."

o o o

Another musical term in the headings is *neginah.* Its various derivatives in singular, as well as in plural form *neginot,* appear in the superscriptions of Pss. 4, 6, 54, 55, 61, 67, 76, furthermore, in Ps. 77:7, in Lamentations 5:14, in Hezekiah's song of thanksgiving (Isa. 38:20), and also in Habakkuk's song of praise (Hab. 3:19).[73]

The meaning of the word is unmistakably expressed by its etymology. It stems from the Hebrew root *naggen,* "to touch the strings" (Greek: *psallein*).[74] The SEPTUAGINT, AQUILA and THEODOTION translate *neginah* as *en psalmois* or *en hymnois,* the VULGATE *in carminibus,* JEROME *in psalmis.* SYMMACHOS has best rendered the meaning of the original; he translates *dia psaltērion,* "on stringed instruments," more correctly "[to accompany] on the psaltery."

The vocal parallel term to *naggen* "to play on stringed instruments," is the verb *zammer,* "to sing with musical accompaniment" (Pss. 71:22, 149:3), or, more precisely, "to sing with the accompaniment of the *kinnor*" (1 Chron. 16:42; 2 Chron. 5:13; 7:6; 35:12; Am. 6:5).

The procedure of accompanying singing with instruments is indicated in the Hebrew by the prepositions *be* or *bi,* "with" (*cp.* Ps. 150:3-5) and *'al,* "upon" (*cp.* Ps. 92:4), both having the same musical implication. Connected with *neginah,* the headings use always *bineginot,* except in Ps. 61, which has *'al-neginot.* The term always appear jointly with *la-menaẓẓeaḥ,* their combined meaning being, therefore,

> "to the master of song (or precentor), (to be accompanied) on stringed instruments."

Whether there exists a strict correlation between *bineginot* and the preceding *la-menaẓẓeaḥ,* cannot be positively proven. If both terms belong together, their meaning is the one given above. If, however, they represent instructions independent from each other, their meaning would be broken up into two sentences:

> "To the master of song" (or "to the precentor");—"to sing to the accompaniment of stringed instruments."

The difference is but a slight one; it lies in the grammatical structure.

MOWINCKEL translates both terms as belonging together: "to induce [God's] mercy by playing on stringed instruments" ("zur Gnädigstimmung durch Saitenspiel").[75]

Neginah and *neginot* have greatly diversified renderings in the English Bibles.

Wycliffe has "in ditties" (early), and "in orguns" (later), for Ps. 4. Both versions leave out the word in Ps. 6, but put "in ditees or ympnes [hymns]" (early), "in orguns, ether in salmes" (later) for Pss. 54, 55, and 76, "in ympnes" (early), and "on orgun" (later) for Pss. 61 and 67. For Ps. 77:7 both versions use a circumstantial paraphrase: "and I sweteli thogte in the nigt with myn herte" (early), and "and Y thougte in the night with myn herte" (later). Isa. 38:20, too, is paraphrased as: "and oure salmes wee shal singe alle the dages" (early), and "and we schulen synge oure salmes in all the daies" (later). Habakkuk 3:19 is rendered as "singynge in psalmes" (early), and "syngynge in salmes" (later). Lamentations 5:14 is translated as "quer [choir] of syngeres" (early), and "queer of syngeris" (later).

Douay has "in verses" for the seven psalm-headings, "I meditated" for Ps. 77:7, "psalms" for Isa. 38:20, "choir of singers" for Lam. 5:14, whereas Habakkuk 3:19 is paraphrased as "and the conqueror will lead me upon my high places singing psalms."

The *Authorized Version* and *Harkavy* take over phonetically the psalm titles "On Neginoth," but use "song" for Ps. 77 and Isaiah, "music" for Lamentations, and "on my stringed instruments" for Habakkuk.

The *American Version* renders "On stringed instruments" for the psalm-headings, "song" for Ps. 77 and Isaiah, "music" for Lamentations, and "on my stringed instruments" for Habakkuk.

Moulton leaves out the word in the psalm titles, but has "song" for Ps. 77:7, "song to the stringed instruments" for Isaiah, "music" for Lamentations, and "on my stringed instruments" for Habakkuk.

The *Jewish Version* has "with string music" for the superscriptions of the psalms, "song" for Ps. 77 and Isaiah, "music" for Lamentations, and "with my string music" for Habakkuk.

Moffat translates the psalm titles and Habakkuk as "to a string accompaniment," Ps. 77:7 as "thinking to myself," Isaiah as "we shall make music in thy house," Lamentation simply as "music."

The *Revised Standard Version* has "with stringed instruments" for the psalm-headings and Habakkuk, "I commune with my heart" for Ps. 77, "and we will sing to stringed instruments" for Isaiah, "music" for Lamentations.

o
o o

It is worthy of note that none of the many instruments mentioned frequently in other portions of the Old Testament appears in the headings, whereas they are repeatedly quoted in the text proper of the psalms. This is by no means a lack of reportorial precision, but rather corroborative evidence to the effect that common knowledge needs no minute description. *Neginot* was a collective term for the family of stringed instruments, so those responsible for the headings considered it superfluous to mention a particular species.

The harp-player was called *menaggen* (1 Sam. 16:18; 2 Kings 3:15; Ps. 68:26). By the familiar transferring the manner of playing the instrument to the species of song accompanied by it, *neginah* obtained the meaning of "song with the accompaniment of stringed instruments," or, in a general way, "accompanied song." This is expressed by the various nuances of the early Greek and Latin versions of the Old Testament, such as *en psalmois, en hymnois, in canticis, in psalmis,* etc.

In later times *neginah* obtained still another meaning. The signs of the accents for biblical cantillation were called *neginot, ta'ame haneginah,* or, briefly *ta'amim.* These signs were added to the text of the Scriptures and their primary function was syntactic-punctuating. As time passed, they became a sort of rudimentary musical notation, indicating groups of tones and, in some respect, differences of pitch of the cantillation. Gradually, the *ta'amim* developed into a complex pattern of notation, designating ascending and descending figures, scale patterns, slurs, trills, tremolos, and other devices, thus constituting an elaborate method for traditional cantillation. In this stage of evolution, *neginah* implied the entire system of accentual signs, as well as the rules of their application.

o
o o

The term *'al 'alamot,* which appears in the heading of Ps. 46 and in a single other passage of the Scriptures, in 1 Chron. 15:20, has given rise to the most diversified interpretations.

The Hebrew noun *ʿalmah* means "maiden"; the majority of the translators implement this meaning in various ways. There is, however, a second meaning of the word, implying "secret." The early translators of the Bible used sometimes one, sometimes the other sense. Thus, the SEPTUAGINT translated *hyper tōn kryphiōn,* "upon 'the secrets'," AQUILA *epi neaniotētōn,* "upon 'youth'," SYMMACHOS *hyper tōn aiōnōn,* "upon 'the eternities'," a rendering used also in the Midrash. The VULGATE used partly *pro arcanis* (Ps. 46), "for the secrets," partly *super puellarum* (sc. *modulum*), which means "after the melody 'young maidens'." JEROME translated *pro juventutibus,* "for the young." LUTHER's translation "about youth" ("Von der Jugend") follows up this idea.

Most of the modern English Bibles again avoided these difficulties by taking over the term phonetically from the Hebrew, the sole exception being the version of *Moffat,* who gives the term a definite musical meaning (see p. 124).

The earliest English versions follow closely the SEPTUAGINT and VULGATE. Thus, *Wycliffe* translates "for the priue thingis" (early), and "for gongthis" later) for Ps. 46, "in orgnys sungyn priue thingis" (early), and "sungun pryuetees in g官ternes" (later) for 1 Chron. 15:20. The *Douay Version* has "for the hidden" in the psalm, and "(sung) mysteries upon psalteries" in 1 Chron. 15:20.

Despite the glaring discrepancies in the interpretation of the word, there is a logical solution, which presents itself naturally if we apply to it, like in other instances, the considerations of normal musical practice.

We know that since the earliest times women have been employed in the rites of Yahveh. The passages referring to this custom were intentionally obscured in, or apparently eliminated from, the Scriptures for the purpose of textual "purification." This may be inferred from the fact that in certain cases the latter procedure was not carried out radically enough, and thus some vestiges remained, hinting at the existence of female participants in religious rites. Female singers are mentioned, for instance, in 2 Sam. 19:36, 2 Chron. 35:25, Ezra 2:65, Neh. 7:67, and Eccles. 2:8. True enough, all these passages are ambiguous since they do not state explicitly whether these women belonged officially to the sacred service, or were secular professional or non-professional singers. The same applies to the information on this subject found in a non-biblical source.[76]

Apart from these historical records, there are several indirect references in the Scriptures, as well as in the early rabbinic literature, to the participation of women in the cult, especially as singers in the sacred service. The traces of it, even though cryptically veiled most of the time, are nevertheless sufficiently revealing to support our assumption.

It is obvious that purely ritual functions of a higher or even lower degree were denied to women. In the Yahveh-cult, such functions were reserved exclusively to men. Besides singing in the levitical choir, the principal task of women in the cult was performing the sacred dance (Exod. 38:8).

Judging from the religious customs of the Israelites, the participation of women in Temple ceremonies was well-nigh indispensable. Numerous pilgrims, among them women, came from all the provinces to the great agricultural festivals in Jerusalem. Following the sacred services in the Temple, the people indulged in song and dance. Women who knew how to lead these groups of singers and dancers were, therefore, a necessary institution in the sanctuary. It would not be far-fetched to assume that these were the same women who participated in the daily musical services and performed the Temple dances. Psalm 68:26 points clearly to this fact.

The most weighty evidence, however, for the participation of women in the music of the Temple is contained in the term *ʿal ʿalamot.* Some commentators interpret this word as the title of a well known song; others attach to it the meaning of a musical instrument (see later). Yet, it refers more likely to the *range of the female singing voice.* This is corroborated by the musical hints contained in certain indirect and veiled allusions of the biblical text, of which more presently. One may, therefore, safely assume that *ʿal ʿalamot* in reality signifies "women's voices," or, more precisely, "the range of female voices," *i.e. "soprano."* The heading of Psalm 46, consequently, contains the instruction that this psalm be sung by a woman's chorus. If we assume, with THIRTLE, that this heading represents in reality a subscription to Ps. 45, things become even more evident. This psalm, surnamed "A Song of Loves,"—a nuptial ode,—is more than any other suited for female voices.

> "It would be incongruous," comments THIRTLE, "to assign the second half (verses 10-18) to any other than a Maiden's Choir."[77]

Moffat translates Ps. 46:1 as "for soprano voices," which applies even more so to Ps. 45.

A hidden reference to female singers is to be found in Am. 8:3. The original says:

> "And the songs (*shirot*) of the palace shall be wailings in that day."

Some expounders, however, believe that instead of *shirot,* "songs," the text should be read *sharot,* "female singers," and, accordingly, the passage should mean:

> "Then will the women-singers in the Temple howl."[78]

In later times, the participation of female singers in the cult was abolished. The Second Temple replaced them by boy singers.[79] The meaning of *ʿal ʿalamot,* "in the range of women's voices," has not changed because of this innovation.

Even more obvious is the meaning of this term in 1 Chron. 15:20. "Psalteries set to *ʿalamot"* indicates here a psaltery (*nebel*) in the range of women's voices, *i.e.* in the "higher tessitura" ("high" according to Western conception; see *infra*), namely a smaller, therefore high-pitch type of *nebalim,* which must have played an essential role in the music of the Temple. (For the interpretation of *ʿalamot* as a musical instrument see pp. 320ff.)

The traditional, and most logical, explanation of the two terms *ʿal ʿalamot* and *ʿal ha-sheminit* (see *infra*) refers to two contrasting vocal ranges, high and low. In our general musical parlance, the high range is termed as the treble, and the low range as that of the male voice, the bass, this being usually an "octave" lower. But the Oriental (and also the Greek) conception of vocal ranges is quite different from our theory of "high" and "low" sounds. In our acoustic system we determine and measure the differences of pitch by the number of vibrations per second produced by sounding bodies. The higher the number of vibrations, the higher the sound.

This is different in the Orient, and especially in Semitic usage. There, "high" and "low" of the tone and, accordingly, the "raising" or "falling" of the voice (or of a melodic line) is not determined by the number of vibrations, but by the manner in which the sound was produced. A "large" pipe or a "long" string has a "high" tone, while a "small" pipe or a "short" string produces a "low" sound.[80] On the Greek *kithara* the longest string was called *hypatē*, "the highest," and with the diminishing length of the strings the tones gradually became "lower" (this being in diametrical opposition to our Occidental terminology).

The same principle prevails in Hebrew phonetics. Hebrew grammarians consider the vowels *u* and *o* "high" sounds; accordingly the punctuation in written texts is *above* the consonants. The vowels *a, e,* and *i* are "low" sounds, consequently the punctuation is *below* the consonants.

All this would seemingly undo the theory that *ʿalamot* represented the range of the high voice, whereas *sheminit* would be the opposite, low range. In reality, however, both conceptions are not incompatible, as will be seen presently.

The interpretation of *ʿalamot* in the sense of the "range of women's voices" should not necessarily be excluded, if we abandon the idea that the Israelites were thinking of this range in terms of either "highness" or "lowness." In the conception of the Hebrews, *ʿalamot* might have simply represented the sound whose pitch corresponded generally to that of women's voices, regardless of whether it was actually designated as "high" or "low." The opposite was *sheminit,* indicating, as it were, the sound whose pitch was characteristic of male voices. This interpretation is based quite logically upon the differentiation of the pitch quality of human voices, without interfering with the Oriental conception of "high" and "low," and does not exclude the assumption that the Israelites considered women's voices as "low," and men's voices as "high."

A different interpretation of *ʿal ʿalamot,* but still maintaining the idea of women's voices, is given by CORNILL.[81] He thinks

> "if Psalm 46 were sung according to its inscription 'after the manner of maidens,' we must assume that the men sang in falsetto, just as not so very long ago when women's voices were in the same manner excluded from the service of the Evangelical church, falsetto was regularly practiced and belonged to the art of church music."

CORNILL's hypothesis of falsetto-singing is not as far-fetched as it may seem at first sight. In the Oriental musical practice, this manner of singing is quite popular and, in fact, is a common feature even in our own days.

All these arguments lead to the logical conclusion that in the musical practice of Ancient Israel *ʿalamot* indicated the range of women's voices, and *sheminit* that of male voices, doubling the same melody, that is—according to our Western conception—singing it in the interval of an octave.

MOWINCKEL tries to explain all doubtful or seemingly inexplicable words of the headings as indications of some ritual action.[82] Thus, he interprets *ʿalamot* as a term pointing to some rites at the festival of Yahveh's enthronement, and concludes that Psalms 46 and 48 belonged to a ritual ceremony used at this festival. They were sung "upon" (or "at") the mysteries, an assumption which, in the light of history, is quite improbable.

o
o o

Similar to *ʿal ʿalamot,* the term *ʿal ha-sheminit* has also brought forth a number of most diverse opinions. The latter term appears in Pss. 6 and 12, also in 1 Chron. 15:21. Its literal meaning in Hebrew is "on the eighth," or, if the linguistic vocalisation is correct, "over the eighth." The SEPTUAGINT expresses this sense by translating the term as *hyper tēs ogdoēs,* the VULGATE as *pro octava.* AQUILA's rendering is *epi tēs ogdoēs,* SYMMACHOS translates *peri tēs ogdoēs,* JEROME *super octava* (Ps. 6) and *pro octavam* (Ps. 12). The Targum paraphrases "on the zither with eight strings." Again, the modern English versions have taken over phonetically the original Hebrew term, with the exception of *Moffat,* who interprets it in a musical sense as "harps set for bass voices." *Wycliffe* draws, of course, on the Latin and Greek translations, and renders the term "in harps for the eygetethe sungyn cynychion" (early), and "sungen in harpis for the eightithe, and epynychion" (later). Following the same models, the *Douay Version* has "a song of victory for the octave upon harps."

The majority of modern commentators are inclined to believe that the term designates an eight-string instrument (*neginah*). We know that the *kinnor* (lyre) had ten strings;[83] another similar accompanying instrument, the *ʿasor* (Pss. 33:2; 92:4; 144:9), had likewise ten strings, while the *nebel* (harp) had twelve strings. Nevertheless, the possibility should not be discarded that there also might have existed a larger, and consequently lower sounding type of a string instrument with only eight strings. Proceeding from analogies with Babylonian instrumental nomenclature, LANGDON supposes that *sheminit,* in fact, has been a harp-like instrument with eight strings.[84]

Other commentators, however, offer different interpretations. EWALD and OLSHAUSEN[85] maintains that *sheminit* was the indication of a key (or mode). GESENIUS and DELITZSCH say that it pointed to the low range of the human voice, namely the bass.[86] Other exegetes assume that *ʿal ha-sheminit* refers to a change of pitch, meaning "in the eighth tone," *i.e.* "in the octave." Practically, this would indicate that the melody was to be sung, or doubled, in a lower range. The question now arises whether one would be justified to assume that the ancient Hebrews knew the notion of the "octave" in its intervallic sense, being the higher or lower repetition of the same tone.

About the music system of Ancient Israel no direct information has been preserved. It is not impossible, however, that inasmuch as the music of the Hebrews belonged to the Oriental musical culture, it possessed more subtle fractional intervals than the later Occidental music. To be sure, we have no more positive knowledge about these intervals, than about the Israelites' notion of an "octave" as the eighth tone in the established scale. Yet, it may well be surmised that a people which cultivated so assiduously the playing on stringed instruments, would fairly soon discover the simple acoustic law of the division of a string in two equal halves, resulting in the sound of the octave.[87] Thus, the interpretation of *sheminit* as the "octave," jointly with its numerical application (the "eightness"), presupposes the existence, in the musical practice, of a seven-tone scale, in which the eighth tone, the octave, would represent the repetition of the initial tone in another range.

Among the string instruments of the Greeks there existed a large species, the *magadis,* with twenty strings, but only ten different tones, which were duplicated in the interval of an octave (*dia pasōn*). The procedure of playing two strings simultaneously was called *magadizein,* which in fact doubled the melody in the higher (or lower) octave.

In view of this historical evidence, the question now arises whether it may not have been possible that the notion of the "octave" (or of the Greek *dia pasōn*) found its application in the music of the Hebrews. The answer is given by the religious history of the Jews.

Hellenism, a pagan conception of the world, a material philosophy of life, was met with deep hatred by the Jews faithful to their ancestral creed. Between the Hellenizers and the Jews clinging to the ancient religious laws, there was a deep cleavage for centuries. Like in all their religious institutions, the Jews were intent on preserving the pristine character of their past in their sacred music as well. Consequently, in all likelihood they most emphatically opposed any inroads of Greek musical ideas, theoretical as well as practical.

Yet, some of the levitical musicians of the Second Temple may have been familiar with the music theory of the Hellenes. Possibly, the system of Greek music was also known to others than to Levites.[88]

However, between the mere possibility of the knowledge of the Greek music system and its actual application in the practice of the Temple, there is an abysmal gap. The guardians of the sacred tradition, the priests and Levites, would scarcely have tolerated the incursion of Hellenistic notions into the sacred precincts of their liturgical hymnal. The sound effect of *sheminit* might, in fact, have been recognized by some levitical singers as that of doubling the voice in the octave; the terminology in the intervallic sense of "eightness" was certainly not applied in this meaning.

The simplest interpretation of this controversial term is to be found not in the headings of these three psalms, but in 1 Chron. 15:21. The narration about the installation of the levitical music service according to the commandment of David enumerates the precentors Heman, Asaph and Ethan

> "with cymbals of brass to sound aloud; and Zechariah, and Aziel, and Schemiramoth, and Jehiel, and Unni, and Eliab, and Maaseiah, and Benaiah, with psalteries set to Alamoth (*binebalim* ʿ*al* ʿ*alamot*); and Mattithiah, and Eliphalehu, and Mikniahu, and Obed-Edom, and Jeiel, and Azaziah, with harps on the Sheminith, to lead (*bekinnorot* ʿ*al hasheminit, lenaẓẓeaḥ*)."

The solution is hinted by the uncommon use, in this passage, of the terms ʿ*alamot* and *sheminit. Nebalim* and *kinnorot,* as names of musical instruments, are generally used by the chroniclers without any specific epithets or other qualifications. Why is this different here, as well as in the three psalm headings? Everything points to the possibility that different species of instruments are meant for both categories: a smaller, therefore higher pitched type of *nebalim* which—in this case—could very well lead (*i.e.* double) the melody in the upper register, and a larger, consequently lower sounding species of *kinnorot,* for doubling the same melody (perhaps with discreet ornamentations) in the subjacent register.

THIRTLE, too, stresses the contradiction of *sheminit* and *ʿalamot,* and arrives at the conclusion that "whatever 'the eighth' may mean, it would seem to describe the Male Choir."[89] However, he offers still another, extra-musical, interpretation of *sheminit,* alluding to the liturgical fact that "some of the most solemn seasons of worship were on the *eighth* day."[90] (*Cp.* Lev. 23:26; Num. 29:35; Neh. 8:18). The "holy convocation," the "solemn assembly" on the eighth day of Tabernacle might have been connected with certain rites to which the *sheminit*-psalms may have furnished the appropriate musical surrounding. "In that case, *the eighth* would imply association with special solemnities."[91]

THOMAS K. CHEYNE thinks that *ʿalamot* and *sheminit* are corruptions of the names of clans or guilds. Thus, *ʿalamot* would signify "of Salmath," or the Salmaeans, a division of Temple singers, and *sheminit* would stand for "of the Ethanim," or "Nethinim," the body of Temple servants.[92] It is quite inconceivable that the performance of a psalm would have been entrusted to the lowest class of the Temple functionaries, who did merely menial work in the Sanctuary.

MOWINCKEL's interpretation differs here, as usual, from all solutions that would be considered practical from the musical point of view. He thinks that *sheminit* refers neither to an instrument, nor to a term of musical practice in the sense of the octave-interval, but draws from the text of Pss. 6 and 12 a new and peculiar conclusion.[93]

He endeavors to prove that these psalms were used during the rites of purification. Then, he quotes analogies from the history of religions in order to demonstrate that, at such rites, the number eight has played an important part. For several such rites, the eighth day was decisive. In certain instances, seven attempts at purification must be made; the eighth of these attempts determines whether the purification may be taken as accomplished.

Since, according to MOWINCKEL, Psalms 6 and 12 were "doubtless" designed to serve as the climax of purifying rites, he concludes that they probably belonged to the final, the "eighth act of purification." Consequently, the logical interpretation of *ʿal ha-sheminit* would be "the eighth time," or "the eighth (act of purification)," intimating that the psalm was performed at this particular rite.

o
o o

The headings of Psalms 53 and 88 contain the indication *ʿal maḥalat.* The meaning of this term was not clear even to the early translators of the Bible, for which reason they did not attempt to render it in their respective languages, but took over the word phonetically from the original Hebrew: *hyper maeleth* in the SEPTUAGINT, *pro maëleth* (Ps. 53) and pro *maheleth* (Ps. 88) in the VULGATE.

According to THIRTLE, it is part of the subscription to Pss. 52 and 87 which, together with the immediately preceding musical indication, would read: "To the Chief Musician, relating to *maḥalat.*"

The extant interpretations of the word are again most contradictory. Some commentators derive it from the Hebrew *maḥaleh* or *maḥalah,* "sickness," and consider these psalms as poems having been written on the occasion of their author's illness. Looking into the contents of the psalms, this conception could possibly be adopted for Ps. 88, but scarcely for Ps. 53.

The translators of early Christian times rather followed the meaning of the Hebrew *maḥol,* "dance." AQUILA translates *epi choreia,* SYMMACHOS *dia chorou,* THEODOTION *hyper tēs choreias,* JEROME *pro chore* (Ps. 53) and *per chorum* (Ps. 88). All these translations express the idea "for the dance," or "for the roundelay."

Songs as a musical background for dancing are frequently mentioned in the Scriptures (Exod. 15:20; 32:18,19; 1 Sam. 18:6,7; Pss. 26:6; 68:26; 87:7). Consequently, it would by no means be unexpected to find dance songs mentioned in the superscriptions of the psalms, possibly connected with sacred dances, or with the ceremony of a processional encompassing the altar. On the other hand, however, the textual examination of both psalms—53 and 88—in no sense justifies the assumption that these psalms were used to accompany dances.

The translation of the Targum to Ps. 53 makes use of a circumlocution:

> "Upon the punishment of those who profane the Lord's name."

Here, *maḥalat* is interpreted in the sense of *ḥalal,* "to profane." The verb *ḥalal,* however, has also another meaning, "to pierce." This has been adopted by RASHI, who explains *maḥalat* as "a pierced," that is, a flute-like instrument.

In Psalm 88, *maḥalat* is supplemented by *le'annot.* This word is derived from *'anah,* having various meanings; first, "to shout," "to cry," "to sing" (all three in Exod. 32:18, "to sing" also in Isa. 27:2); then, "to answer in singing, in response," (1 Sam. 18:7; 21:12; 29:5; Hos. 2:17); furthermore, in the Pi'el form "to oppress," "to afflict," in the Po'al form, "to be afflicted," and in Hithpa'el, "to humble oneself." The SEPTUAGINT renders it by *tou apokrithēnai,* the VULGATE by *ad respondendum,* both expressing the idea of "to justify oneself." JEROME translates (*per chorum*) *ad praecinendum,* . . . "to lead the singing," the Targum *leshabbaḥa,* "to praise." According to its meaning as "oppression," "weakness," *le'annot* may be interpreted as "to bring down," that is "(to perform) with a reduced voice," which would correspond to singing *piano.*

In THIRTLE's opinion, Ps. 52 was apparently designed for celebrating the great victory over the Philistines,

> "the event recalled in simple fashion by the 'Great Dancing' which followed it."[94]

This could have occurred in the incident recorded in 1 Sam. 18:6,7, and referred again in 21:12 and 29:5.

Maḥalat (for *meḥolot*) *le'annot,* as subscription to Ps. 87, is interpreted by

THIRTLE as "dancing with shoutings."[95] This was intended to remind one of the greatest events in the national and religious history of Israel, the bringing over of the ark to Zion (2 Sam. 6:12-15; 1 Chron. 15:15-20).

LUTHER renders the two passages differently. For Ps. 88 he adopts the meaning of "sickness" and translates the passage as "upon the weakness of the miserable" ("von der Schwachheit des Elenden"); while for Psalm 53 he renders "singing in choir, alternately" ("im Chor umeinander vorzusingen"). However, the structure of the latter psalm does not favor the idea of antiphonal singing. The text expresses a homogeneous thought, without showing any phraseological symmetry in its construction, which is a pre-requisite for the antiphonal style.[96]

MOWINCKEL tries to establish a relation between *maḥalat* and some kind of a ritual action.[97] In his opinion, the performance of the two psalms was a feature at the rites of the New Year's festival, intended as magic means against diseases. Therefore, he suggests as translation of the term: "against the sickness," or—considering the external circumstances in performing these psalms—"above the sickness," or "above the sick spot (of the body)."

Thus, we are left with one, and musically satisfactory interpretation, that suggested by RASHI: "(accompanied) by pipes." Unquestionably, the contents of both psalms (53 and 88), one in a pensive, the other in a joyous mood, favor the idea of accompanying the singing with now softly, now vigorously, blown *ḥalilim.* Should the term *maḥalat* have any relation to music (and all the evidence seems to support this assumption), then RASHI's explanation is to be given the preference.

English versions of the Scriptures follow the procedures of the SEPTUAGINT and the VULGATE by taking over the term phonetically from the Hebrew, with the exception of *Moffat,* who sets "to the tune of 'Suffering' " (Ps. 53), and "to the tune of 'Suffering sore' " (Ps. 88).

Wycliffe has for Exod. 15:20 "daunces," (early), and "cumpanyes" (later), for Exod. 32:19 "companyes (of men)" (early), and "dauncis" (later), for Judg. 21:21 "dauncis (daunsis)," whereas in other passages it follows AQUILA, SYMMACHOS, THEODOTION and JEROME, who avail themselves of the connotation of the Greek *choros* and the Hebrew *maḥol,* "dance." Accordingly, *Wycliffe* translates Ps. 149: 3 as "(preise thei the name of hym) in quer [Old-English spelling of "choir"] (early), and "(herie thei his name) in a queer" (later), and Ps. 150:4 as "in timbre and quer" (early), and "in tympane and queer" (later).

o
o o

There was until now no clear-cut explanation for the term *ʾel ha-neḥilot*[98] in the superscription of Ps. 5. The SEPTUAGINT and THEODOTION translate the expression as *hyper tēs klēromousēs,* "for the heritage," the VULGATE as *pro ea, quae hereditatem consequitur,* "for that which follows the heritage," AQUILA as *hyper klērodosiōn,* SYMMACHOS as *hyper klērouchōn,* both meaning "for the distribution (by lot)" or "for the allotment," and JEROME as *pro hereditatibus,* "for the inheritances," or as LUTHER rendered it, "for the hereditament" ("für das Erbe").

The origin of the word has been explained in various ways. HENGSTENBERG derives it from the verb *naḥal,* "to possess." This meaning comes close to "inheritance"; he thinks, therefore, that the SEPTUAGINT's translation is correct.

The majority of the biblical expounders, however, trace the word back to *ḥalal,* "to pierce," attaching to it the meaning of a "pierced" instrument, the flute or the pipe.[99]

Among the English Bibles, *Moffat* and the *Revised Standard Version* translate "for flutes," and "for the flutes," respectively, while other modern versions have taken over the term phonetically from the Hebrew as "upon the Nehiloth," or "with the Nehiloth" (*American Version*). As in other instances, *Moulton* leaves the term out. The earliest English versions follow, as usual, the Latin and Greek models, in setting "for hir that getith the eritage" (early), and "to the ouercomer on the eritagis" (later) in the *Wycliffe Bible,* and "for her that obtaineth the inheritance" in the *Douay Version.*

Only for the sake of completeness we want to mention that, as in other instance, MOWINCKEL tries to establish a relation between the term and some kind of ritual action. He maintains that the psalm has been used specifically to heal diseases (cp. verse 4) and, consequently, attributes to *ʾel ha-neḥilot* the same meaning, "against sickness," as to *maḥalat* of Pss. 53 and 88.[100]

The superscriptions of Pss. 8, 81 and 84 contain the indication *ʿal ha-gittit,* which, too, gave rise to the most diversified explanations. Since the majority of the expounders hold that the term signifies a musical instrument, it will be examined in the section dealing with the instruments of the Hebrews.

o

o o

Among other musical indications in the headings *shir ḥanukkat ha-bayit,* "Song at the Dedication of the House" (Ps. 30), should be mentioned. This title intimates that the psalm was sung either at the dedication of Solomon's Temple or of the Second Temple, possibly also at the re-dedication of the desecrated sanctuary under Hezekiah's newly established reign. All English Bibles follow this idea, with slight nuances as to the interpretation of *bayit.*

Thus, *Wycliffe* sets "in the dedicacioun of the hous of Dauyd" (early), and "for the halewyng of the hows of Dauid" (later). *Douay* has "at the dedication of David's house," and the heading of the vicinal Psalm 28 of this biblical version has a related notion, which is lacking in the Hebrew original or elsewhere, "at the finishing of the tabernacle." The *Authorized Version, Harkavy,* the *American* and *Jewish Versions* render the title of Ps. 30 as "Song at the Dedication of the House," the *Revised Standard Version* as "at the dedication of the Temple," *Moffat* as "for the Dedication Festival," and *Moulton* even extends the idea of dedication by translating "for the Inauguration of Jerusalem."

OESTERLEY maintains that this psalm originated in the time of the Maccabees, or at least the superscription was added to it following some historical events that took place at this period.[101] The Books of the Maccabees relate that, after the desecration of the Temple by ANTIOCHUS EPIPHANES, the sanctuary was "dedicated afresh, with songs and harps and lutes, and with cymbals" by JUDAS MACCABAEUS in 165 B.C.E. (1 Macc. 4:54). The Talmud also refers to this event, adding that at this ceremony the "Hallel" was sung.[102] From these precise indications referring to the musical part of this consecration, OESTERLEY concludes that the psalm "at the Dedication" was sung on this occasion. This assumption does not exclude, of course, the possibility that the psalm is much older and has been used at former dedications or re-dedications.

o
o o

The superscription of Ps. 45 contains the expression *shir yedidot,* translated as "a Song of Loves," (LUTHER: "A Bridal Song"). Apparently, this psalm was sung in Ancient Israel at wedding ceremonies.

o
o o

Some psalm headings include terms, the meaning of which has no bearing upon the contents of the psalms; their implication, therefore, is obscure, at least at first sight. These terms are:

ʿal mut labben (Ps. 9),
ʿal ʾayyelet ha-shaḥar (Ps. 22),
ʿal shoshannim (Pss. 45, 69, 80).
ʿal shushan ʿedut (Ps. 60),
ʿal yonat ʾelem reḥoḳim (Ps. 56), and
ʿal tashḥet (Pss. 57, 58, 59, 75).

The simplest, and musically the most logical, explanation of these terms would be that they represent either the names or the first words of the lyrics of certain secular songs, which were popular in the epoch when the Psalter was compiled, and the melodies of which (but not the text) served as the pattern for singing the psalms. Thus, the musical practice of the Temple would foreshadow a similar procedure in the synagogue-singing during medieval times, when some *ḥazzanim* adopted popular melodies to liturgical texts for use in Synagogue worship.

A direct analogy to this procedure can be found in the catalogue of Sumerian and Assyrian liturgies and hymns, referred to earlier in this study. Line 44 of this catalogue is Semitic and represents the title of a religious hymn. Other items contained in this catalogue are titles of secular songs.[103]

Despite the fact that the interpretation of the above biblical terms as song-titles or lyrics of songs appears logical and is corroborated by historical records, it did not seem to satisfy the classical biblical exegetes. More than once, these titles were suspected of having a hidden meaning, and expounders tried hard to solve these alleged mysteries.

We shall confine ourselves to the exposition of a few selected theories in all three categories.

ʿAl mut labben (Ps. 9), literally "on 'death for the son,'" or, according to another interpretation, "on 'the pale death,'" is paraphrased variously in the early versions of the Bible. The SEPTUAGINT translates *hyper tōn kryphiōn tou hyiou,* the VULGATE *pro occultis filii,* both meaning "on 'the son's secret,'" AQUILA *neaniotētos tou hyiou,* "the son's youth," THEODOTION *hyper akmēs tou hyiou,* "on 'the son's flourishing time,'" JEROME *pro morte filii,* "on 'the son's death.'" The Targum's interpretation incorporates the idea of "youth," and LUTHER is obviously influenced by this in his translation "of the beautiful (age of) youth" ("von der schönen Jugend").

The expounders are divided with regard to the real meaning of the expression. Some of them suspect that *ʿal mut* is a corrupted spelling of *ʿal ʿalamot* or *ʿal ʿalamut.* In fact, in some Hebrew manuscripts *ʿalmut* is written as one word.

Apart from the heading of Psalm 9, *ʿal-mut* also appears as the concluding word of Ps. 48; here, too, it was interpreted in most different ways. The SEPTUAGINT translates it as *eis tous aiōnas,* the VULGATE *in saecula,* both "in eternity," AQUILA as *athanasia,* literally "no death," *i.e.* "deathlessness," "immortality."

The English Versions show marked differences in rendering this passage. The *Authorized Version, Moulton* and *Harkavy* have: (God will be our guide) "unto death." The *Jewish Translation* interprets: (He will guide us) "eternally," *Douay* and *Moffat*: "for evermore," and the *American* and *Revised Standard Versions*: "for ever and ever." LUTHER has adopted an entirely different idea: (He guideth us) "like youth" (Er führet uns "wie die Jugend"). The French translations use: "jusqu' à la mort," "unto death."

According to GESENIUS, *ʿal mut* in the title of Ps. 9 is an indication that the psalm should be sung "in the manner of maidens," or "in the range of maidens' voices," consequently by a women's choir.[104] He also suggests another solution: "with high sounding instruments," using as analogy the Greek terms for the high-pitched species of pipes: *parthenikoi,* or *gynaikēioi auloi.*

ALEXANDER asserts that *mut labben* represents the title, or the initial words, or the main thought of some well-known poem or song, and that the psalm was either written in this style or was actually adapted to this melody.[105]

GRAETZ advocates the strange but untenable theory that *ʿal mut* (like *ʿalamot,* discussed earlier) signifies the accompaniment "with Elamite instruments."[106]

ʿAl mut labben is, after MOWINCKEL, a kind of historical note referring to the initial occasion on which this psalm was used for purification. Accordingly, he suggests as translation: "against the death which threatens the son (of some king)."[107]

Even more strange is THIRTLE's interpretation of the controversial term. He refers to the Targum, in which this inscription reads:

> *leshabbaḥa ʿal mituta degabra di nafaḳ mebeyini mashrita,* that is: "to praise, regarding the death of the man who went out between the camps."

In this Aramaic title *ben* is spelled as *beyn* "champion." In 1 Sam. 17:4, 23, Goliath is called *ʾish ha-benayim,* translated in the English Bibles as "champion." Now, THIRTLE assumes that the Masoretic spelling as *ben* is incorrect and that it should be substituted by the variant *beyn* found in the Targum. From this he concludes that the psalm-heading (in this case the subscription of Ps. 8) means in reality: "On the death of the champion" (*i.e.* Goliath), and that the psalm was composed by David in commemoration of his victory.[108]

THIRTLE attributes still another psalm (the *maḥalat*-psalm, No. 52) as having been written by David on the occasion of his victory over the Philistines, and goes even so far as to assert in all seriousness that

> "one may well conceive David holding in his hand the sword of the fallen giant, and writing this psalm."[109]

In so far as the contents of the two psalms (8 and 9) are concerned, a simple comparison will show that Ps. 9 would be far more appropriate for the celebration of such an outstanding event as Goliath's death, which would contradict THIRTLE's hypothesis in this particular instance. His merits in having discovered that a number of musical superscriptions of the psalms belong in fact as subscriptions to the preceding psalm, should not blind us to his obvious errors in interpreting some of the other psalm-headings.

Most of the principal English Bibles have taken over the term phonetically from the original. Following literally the ancient Latin and Greek translations, *Wycliffe* sets "for the hid thingus of the sone" (early), and "for the pryuytees of the sone" (later), while *Douay* has "for the hidden things of the son." *Moffat* interprets *ʿal mut* in the sense of *ʿalamot,* namely "voices in the maidens' range," and translates accordingly "for a soprano boys' choir."

o
o o

ʿAl ʾayyelet ha-shaḥar (Ps. 22), literally "on 'the doe at dawn,'" is rendered by the SEPTUAGINT as *hyper tēs antilēpseōs tēs heōthinēs,* "on 'the apparition in the morning,'" by SYMMACHOS as *hyper tēs boētheias tēs orthrinēs,* by AQUILA as *hyper tēs elaphou tēs orthrinēs,* "on 'the aid at daybreak.'" VULGATE's version is *pro susceptione matutina,* "for the matutinal action (sacrifices?)," that of JEROME *pro cervo matutino,* "for the deer in the morning." LUTHER amplified this idea by adding the notion of hunting, and translated: "Of the hart hunted at daybreak" ("Von der Hindin, die früh gejagt wird").

The Targum refrains from giving a literal translation; instead, it interprets the superscription as "the power of the matutinal Tamid-sacrifice," which would seem to indicate that the psalm was sung at this religious ceremony. The Midrash is still aware of this paraphrase.[110] The traditional interpretation explains *ʾayyelet ha-shaḥar* as the first light prior to the rise of the sun, the shape of which resembles the antlers of a stag.

According to MOWINCKEL, *ʾayyelet ha-shaḥar* is supposed to indicate a ritual action, in this instance a ceremony of atonement. *ʾAyyelet* is, allegedly, not the feminine of *ʾayyal,* "stag," but the feminine of *ʾayil,* "sheep." From this MOWINCKEL concludes that at a certain phase of the religious ceremony a female sheep was sacrificed, just as the dawn arose in the East; Ps. 22 was sung "above" this sheep, *i.e.* when it was slaughtered and offered.[111]

Again, THIRTLE's explanation takes to more speculation. "The Hind of the Dawn" is, according to him, an Oriental word picture of the sun as it sheds its rising rays.

> "In Oriental figure, the hind is an emblem of grace and beauty; the morning, or dawn, is that for which the watchman waits. Hence the

title suggests, in metaphor, an object toward which the heart goes out in warm desire."

How this can be harmonized with THIRTLE's assumption that

"this psalm . . . seems to have been chosen to recall the coronation of David,"

is difficult to figure out. THIRTLE calls Ps. 21 the "National Anthem" of the Jewish people,[112] a designation which would be objectionable even without representing an obvious anachronism.

As in many other instances, the principal English versions have adopted the phonetic spelling of the original, with some notable exceptions. *Wycliffe* sets "for that taking to, or, for the morutid undertaking" (early), and "for the morewtid hynd" (later). *Douay* translates "for the morning protection," *Moffat* and the *Revised Standard Version* interpret the term as the title of a coeval song, or melody, rendering the heading as "to the tune 'Deer of the Dawn,'" and "according to 'The Hind of the Dawn,'" respectively.

o o o

ʿAl shoshannim (Pss. 45, 69), literally "on 'the lilies,'" and *ʿal shushan ʿedut* (Ps. 60), literally "on 'the testimony of the lily,'" as well as *ʾel shoshannim ʿedut* (Ps. 80), belong together inasmuch as in all three expressions the substantive is identical. It is amazing how differently the early Greek and Latin translators rendered the term. The SEPTUAGINT has *tois alloiōthēsomenois eti* (Ps. 60), "those who will be changed," and *hyper tōn alloiōthysomenōn martyrion* (*tō Asaph*) (Ps. 80) "on 'the changing testimony' (for Asaph)," AQUILA sets *hyper tōn krinon martyrias,* "on 'the testimony of the flowers,'" SYMMACHOS *hyper tōn anthōn martyria,* "on 'the testimony of the flowers,'" the VULGATE *pro iis qui commutabuntur,* "for those who will be changed," and JEROME *pro liliis testimonii,* "on 'the lilies of the testimony.'"

The Targum follows an entirely different idea in relating the word obviously to *shonim,* "teachers." It renders Ps. 45 and 80 as "the members of the Sanhedrin," and Ps. 69 as "the captivity of the Sanhedrin." This may be explained by the historical fact that during the national life of Israel the Great Sanhedrin was entrusted with the duty of sitting and passing judgment.[113]

LUTHER's rendering departs from the meaning of *shushan,* "lily"; he uses instead "Von den Rosen," ("of the roses") (Pss. 45, 69, 80), and "Von der Rose des Zeugnisses" ("of the rose of the testimony") for Ps. 60.

For RASHI's interpretation of *shushan* see p. 302.

It is certainly an interesting coincidence that the Greek word *krinon,* "white lily," has still another meaning: it signifies a kind of "dance of the chorus," or "round-dance." Would it be possible, theoretically at least, to establish a relation between *shushan* and the notion of a dancing choral group? In the light of many analogies between the religious customs of the Hebrews and other ancient peoples, it would not be far-fetched to assume that the Israelites accompanied certain psalms with ritual dances. Thus, one could perhaps give some thought to the hypothesis that—in conformity with the second meaning of the

Greek word—the psalms superscribed with *shushan* represents poems for the dance" ("Reigenlyrik" in Germanic terminology).

As MOWINCKEL asserts, the three terms in question are not suited for an interpretation as ritual actions, but rather as ritual objects, lilies, or flowers. ʿ*Edut* means literally "testimony" (Exod. 25:16, etc.), and, in a figurative sense "revelation." In the Jewish, and in other Oriental religions, the oracle of flowers was a well-known rite. Such oracle, or the "revelation," was delivered with special ceremonies, at which psalms were sung. These are the psalms which, according to MOWINCKEL, were performed "above" the lily or revelation.[114]

THIRTLE's interpretation deviates completely from all traditional and modern explanations. Since his definition of this term is closely connected with that of *gittit,* we will take them up jointly at this place.

Shoshannim's simple meaning is "lilies," but the word was used for spring flowers in general.

> "It is not surprising that the Passover, falling in the month ʾ*abib* ("growing green"), should be associated with the flower season and expressed by such a word."

Gittit, on the other hand, meaning "winepress," suggests the vintage season. *Shoshannim* and *gittit* belong to nature and agriculture; they represent "flowers" and "fruit," one telling us of spring, the other of autumn. Passover was the spring feast, Tabernacles the autumn feast. From this, THIRTLE draws the conclusion that the *shoshannim*-psalms belong to the Festival of Passover, the *gittit*-psalms to the Festival of Tabernacles.[115]

The psalms headed by *shushan* ʿ*edut* (Pss. 59 [60] and 79 [80]) are explained by THIRTLE as having been destined for a "Second Passover." The original institution was to be held in the first month (Num. 9:5). But for those who, by reason of ceremonial uncleanness, or "being in a journey afar off," could not keep the Passover, there was an ordinance to celebrate it "in the second month on the fourteenth day at dusk" (Num. 9:11). The psalms bearing the subscript term *Lilies*: *Testimonies,* were selected according to THIRTLE, for use at the Second Passover,

> "a Passover qualified by the word *Testimonies* to show that it was the one contemplated by the special command of the Lord."

However logical this interpretation of *gittit* may appear, the contents of the three *gittit*-psalms (in THIRTLE's numbering) fail to bear out this explanation. At least two of the psalms to which *gittit* is *super*-scribed, correspond, in their contents, infinitely better to the idea of the "joyous shout" in treading the new wine (*cp.* Pss. 81:2-4; 47:2).

Most of the English versions reproduce the expression phonetically. *Wycliffe* sets for Ps. 45: "for hem that shul ben with chaungid" (early), "for the liles" (later);—for Ps. 69: "for hem that shuln ben al chaungid," (early), and "on the roosis" (later);—for Ps. 60: "for hem that shul ben holli chaungid" (early), and "on the witnessyng of roose" (later);—for Ps. 80: "for hem that shul ben al holli chaungid" (early), and "(this salm is) witnessing (of Asaph) for lilies" (later).

The *Douay Version,* disregarding ʿ*edut* in Pss. 60 and 80, sets for all four headings "for them that shall be changed." *Moffat* has "to the tune of 'The

Lilies'" for Pss. 45 and 69, and "to the tune of 'Lily of the Law'" for Pss. 60 and 80. The *Revised Standard Version* uses three times (Pss. 45, 69, 80) "according to Lilies," and, surprisingly, takes over the term phonetically for Ps. 60.

o o o

ʿAl yonat ʾelem reḥokim (Ps. 56), literally "on 'the silent dove of the far-off pine grove,'" is paraphrased circumstantially by the SEPTUAGINT as *hyper tou laou apo tōn hagiōn memakrymenou,* "on 'the people which is removed from the holy life' (or: 'from the sanctuary')." The VULGATE expresses a similar thought, *pro populo qui a Sanctis longe factus est,* "for the people that is far away from sacred places (or: from the Saints)." The Targum, however, follows another idea: "For the assembly of Israel which is like a silent dove at the time when it is far from its cities." AQUILA has *hyper peristeras alalou makrysmōn,* "on 'the silent dove of the far removed.'" LUTHER's rendering seems to have been inspired by AQUILA: "of the silent dove among strangers" ("Von der stummen Taube unter den Fremden"). According to the expounders, the silent dove, in all these translations, symbolizes the exiled and defenseless people of Israel.

Among the other numerous interpretations we may mention one by ALEXANDER, who maintains that the term refers to David, characterized as an innocent and silent sufferer in foreign lands. The majority of commentators agree on one point, namely that these superscriptions have no bearing on the musical performance, unless they are taken as titles or the initial words of a song. This appears to be the most logical conclusion.

MOWINCKEL opines that the heading signifies a rite, having as its purpose purification and healing.[116] The singing of the psalm was done "above" the dove, which was supposed to carry away the impurity caused by *ʿaven, i.e.* "magic." (*cf.* verse 8).[117]

THIRTLE, in assigning the superscription of Ps. 56 as subscription to Ps. 55, associates it with the contents of the last named psalm, in which verses 6-8 indeed constitute a logical connection with the "Silent Dove in the far-off pine grove" of the title.[118] THIRTLE's other assumption, namely that the psalm was "probably sung in commemoration of the conflicts in David's career,"[119] belongs to the sort of exegesis which presupposes that the historical superscriptions of the psalms represent authentic events in David's life.

Again, the English versions solve the problem by retaining phonetically the original Hebrew expression in its entirety. *Moffat* and the *Revised Standard Version* interpret it in a musical sense, as the title of a coeval popular song, "to the tune of 'Dove in isles afar,'" and "according to The Dove of Far-off Terebinths," respectively.

Wycliffe has even three alternative translations: "for the puple that fro seintis is maad aferr" (early), and is reproducing in the later version the idea of the Hebrew original, as well as that of the VULGATE: "(In Ebreu thus,) to the overcomyng on the doumb culuer of fer drawing awei," and "(In Jeroms translacioun thus,) to the ouercomer for the doumb culuer, for it gede awei far." *Douay* follows closer the ancient Latin and Greek translations, by setting "for a people that is removed at a distance from the sanctuary."

o
o o

ʾ*Al tashḥet* (Pss. 57, 58, 59, 75) is uniformly given a literal translation, *mē diaphteirēs,* "destroy not," by the SEPTUAGINT, AQUILA and SYMMACHOS. For Ps. 75 alone, SYMMACHOS puts *peri aphtharsias,* "for immortality." The VULGATE has two variants, *ne dispersas* (Pss. 57, 58, 59), "disperse not," and *ne corrumpas* (Ps. 75), "destroy not." JEROME's translation, *ut non disperdas,* is close to VULGATE's first version. LUTHER hints at another thought: "lest he perish" ("Dass er nicht umkäme"); however, this nuance, too, does not provide us with a satisfactory solution.

ALEXANDER offers a rather tortuous explanation of the term, the justification of which, as he asserts, may be found in the Chaldaean version of the Bible. His reasoning is that the four psalms in question originated in that period of David's life, when he had constantly been compelled to repeat: "Destroy not!" This saying was subsequently adopted as a sort of motto for these psalms. On the other hand, GESENIUS, DELITZSCH and BAETHGEN believe that the word signifies the title or the beginning of a song supposed to serve as a melodic pattern for the psalm. The majority of the expounders support this view. EWALD even thinks that ʾ*al tashḥet* might have been borrowed from the beginning of an ancient penitential song, the initial words of which may have been: "Destroy not, O God, Thy people!"[120]

The term is considered even by MOWINCKEL the opening words of the lyrics of a song or melody which was supposed to be used for the music of the psalms. Strangely enough, he almost immediately drops this idea, since—as he thinks—"there are no analogies for it in the ancient Orient."[121]

In THIRTLE's numbering, the four ʾ*al-tashḥet*-psalms (56, 57, 58, 74) have unquestionably a penitential character. In these psalms the entire nation implores Divine clemency. They all could have been inspired by incidents in the life of Moses and David, as related in Deuter. 4:30,31 and 2 Sam. 24:16, in which the Lord is implored not to destroy his repentant people. In the hour of the people's rebellion against the Lord's commands, Moses prayed forty days and forty nights to the Lord: ʾ*al tashḥet* ʿ*ammeḥo v'naḥalateḥo,* "destroy not thy people and thine inheritance" (Deuter. 9:26). Moses' prayer seems to have constituted the leitmotif of these psalms, designed to be sung in circumstances of national disaster.[122]

In view of this logical explanation, the suggestion that ʾ*al tashḥet* represents a catchword of an ancient vintage song, as appearing in Isa. 65:8, can easily be discarded.

The English versions adopted the original expression phonetically, with some exceptions. *Douay* has "Destroy not" for Pss. 57, 58, 59, and "Corrupt not" for Ps. 75. *Moffat* and the *Revised Standard Version* invest the term with a musical meaning, by translating it as "to the tune of 'Destroy not' " ("Destroy it not," *Moffat,* Ps. 75), and "according to 'Do not Destroy' " (*Revised Standard Version*).

Again, *Wycliffe* has three different translations, one for the early version as "ne desroge thou," and two for the later version: "(In Ebreu thus), to the victorie, lese thou not semeli song," and "(In Jeroms translacioun thus,) for victorie, that thou lese not Dauid."

o
o o

SUMMARY AND CONCLUSIONS

All the foregoing interpretations of the terms in the headings of psalms represent a cross-section of a research pursued during almost two millennia. In making an appropriate selection of these highly contradictory opinions, it was our aim to demonstrate the strange and sinuous ways followed sometimes by the psalm exegetes seeking to discover the meaning of the seemingly obscure terms.

However, the expounders did not always stand on shaky ground. Whenever they were guided mainly by musical considerations, they were able, in most cases, to offer natural as well as logical interpretations. In other instances, they were bound to lose themselves in fruitless speculations, which necessarily ended in a blind alley.

Our investigations would be incomplete without attempting to extract from the maze of the exposed opinions and delusions the basic set of what are true, or at least probable, facts. We will endeavor, therefore, to restore (as far as is humanly possible) the original sense of the controversial terms at the time of their initial introduction into musical practice and to figure out how these terms were understood by those for whom they were intended. One should never lose sight of the fact that these terms had been conceived by musicians, intended for musicians, and applied by musicians. There is, consequently, no more effective way of recovering their original meaning than to guide oneself constantly by the musical needs which the artists of those times have been admittedly confronted with.

The two paramount needs in the field of sacred music of Ancient Israel have been:

(1) A "score" for the choir-leader, which he used during rehearsals and which also served as a depository for all the minutiae of the performance;

(2) recording for posterity, in a written form, the essentials of the correct musical practice.

It has been shown earlier that the most convenient place where instructions with regard to the musical rendering could be inserted were the headings (or the postscripts) of the psalms. It is obvious, therefore, that the bulk of the terms in the headings are direct references to the musical apparatus of the psalms and instructions for their performance.

A. GENERAL TERMS OF THE HEADINGS (LITURGICAL AND GENERIC)

(1) *Tehillah,* the liturgical name for psalm. Appears only once in the Psalter.

(2) *Tefillah,* signifies the prayer in liturgy. It is used in four superscriptions.

(3) *Mizmor,* indicates an accompanied psalm to be sung by the precentor, or in which the precentor and chorus sang in a responsorial form. Fifty-seven headings contain this term.

(4) *Shir* is the specific name for a song of praise, mostly performed by the choir alone. Fifteen psalms are thus termed.

(5) *Shir ha-maʿalot* is a popular type of song used by pilgrims on their way to Jerusalem to attend the yearly festival of Yahveh's ascension to the throne. These songs constitute a series of fifteen psalms.

(6) *Shir yedidot,* "a love song," which probably was sung at wedding ceremonies. One psalm has this distinction.

(7) *Shir ḥanukkat ha-bayit* was used for the dedication or re-dedication of the house of God. Appears in one psalm.

(8) *Maskil* stands for a song of praise of a special kind, possibly sung by a soloist with occasional participation of the chorus. Appears in thirteen psalms.

(9) *Miktam* means, in all probability, that a certain type of popular song is to be selected as a melodic pattern for the psalm. If divested of a musical meaning, it may be explained as a personal or private prayer or meditation. Six headings carry this term.

(10) *Le-lammed* indicates that the psalm had to be taught to young people. It is prescribed only for a single psalm, though there can be no doubt that numerous other psalms had thus be taught.

(11) *Le-haskir* implies that the psalm was sung at the sacrificial rites of the *ʾaskara.* Heads two psalms.

(12) *Shiggayon* is a penitential or lamenting song. A single psalm is thus termed.

B. TERMS REFERRING TO THE MUSICAL PERFORMANCE

(1) *La-menaẓẓeah,* "for the precentor," an indication that in such a psalm substantial solo-passages, with or without participation of the chorus, have been assigned to the leader in song. Fifty-five titles carry this label.

(2) *ʿAl-neginot* and *bineginot* are instructions to accompany the singing with stringed instruments. Is to be found in eight psalms.

(3) *ʿAl ha-gittit,* another collective term for stringed instruments, indicating that these are prescribed for the accompaniment of the psalm. More probably, however, the psalms were designed to be sung at the Festival of Tabernacles. Three psalms contain it.

(4) *ʿAl ʿalamot* is a specific instruction for the accompaniment of the song with high-pitched instruments; the psalm might have conceivably been sung by a women's or boys' choir. Applied to one psalm.

(5) *ʿAl ha-sheminit* is, in a sense, the opposite indication for the accompaniment with larger, low-pitched instruments, as probably used for a male choir. Two psalms are thus termed.

(6) *ʿAl maḥalat* signifies accompaniment with pipes. If read as *meḥolot,* it would refer to a victory celebration with dancing. To be found in two headings.

(7) ʾ*El ha-neḥilot* has the same implication as ʿ*al maḥalat,* indicating wood-winds for accompaniment. If read as *neḥalot* ("inheritance"), it would signify the commemoration of taking possession of the Land of Promise. One heading carries this instruction.

(8) ʿ*Al mut labben,* ʿ*al* ʾ*ayyelet ha-shaḥar,* ʿ*al shoshannim,* ʿ*al shushan* ʿ*edut,* ʿ*al yonat* ʾ*elem reḥokim,* and ʿ*al-tashḥet* are the titles or the catchwords of popular songs serving as melodic patterns for psalms. Six such titles appear in eleven superscriptions.

If we divest these titles of their musical connotation, they could be interpreted as historical or seasonal psalms and would probably mean:

mut labbeyn, "the Death of the Champion,"
ʾ*ayyelet ha-shaḥar,* "the Hind of the Dawn,"
yonat ʾ*elem reḥokim,* "the Dove of the Distant Terebinths,"
shoshannim, psalms destined for the Passover Feast,
shushan ʿ*edut,* psalms destined for the Second Passover,
ʿ*al-tashḥet,* "Destroy not," as a motto for penitential psalms.

4. THE PROPER NAMES IN THE HEADINGS

Let us now cast a glance upon the names of persons and families included in the headings, which are supposed traditionally to have been the authors of the respective psalms.

That these names refer to the authors is inferred mainly from the preposition *le,* appearing immediately before the names. Many commentators, however, do not consider this preposition to be the *lamed auctoris,* but interpret it in the sense of "for." Accordingly, the heading would not mean "A Psalm of David," but "A Psalm for David." This, of course, would invalidate the assumption of David's authorship.

The preposition "of" would even be less appropriate in connection with the names of Asaph, Heman, Ethan (Jeduthun), and the Sons of Korah. In the last-appearing case, particularly, it is quite unlikely that entire families would figure as collective authors of certain psalms. It is more probable that the names refer to certain groups of Temple singers and that the *lamed* is either an indication that the respective psalm belonged to the choice repertoire of a given choral group, or that it has been taken from a hymnal originally compiled (not created) by this family or choral group. Presumably, every choral group, or most of them, had their favorite hymns; possibly also various groups might have shown preference for certain songs or melodicles (*maḳamat*), which they used as patterns for the music of the psalms. It seems logical therefore that such selected psalms should have been characterized by specific inscriptions using the names of these families or groups of singers.

Other hymns and psalms selected in this fashion have been, as some commentators believe, those superscribed with *shir, miktam, maskil,* etc. To all appearances, psalms taken from an earlier compilation were given the generic name of such a collection, and these names, attached to the individual psalms, were retained in the headings in the final order of the Psalter.

There is another valid argument against considering the *lamed* as an indication for authorship, namely the fact that in some headings more than one individual is mentioned. Thus, the names of David and Jeduthun in Pss. 39 and 62, and those of Asaph and Jeduthun appear in Ps. 77. The SEPTUAGINT attributes Ps. 137 to David and Jeduthun, Ps. 138 even to three authors, David, Haggai and Zechariah. Psalm 88 names, besides the "Sons of Korah," "Heman the Ezrahite." Here, two different traditions seem to clash, since both cannot possibly be correct at the same time. Heman, a sage of early times, compared in wisdom to Solomon (1 Kings, 5:11), was the son of Zerah, consequently belonged to the tribe of Judah (1 Chron. 2:6). The Korahites, on the contrary, were Levites. The content of the psalm, too, shows that it could not have been a product of Solomon's time, but probably was composed in the Babylonian exile.

Biblical criticism has gradually abandoned the assumption that the proper names in the headings represent the author of the psalms.[123] The opinion prevails that they rather refer to previous collections from which they were taken over.

As to the period, or periods, in which the psalms were created, the modern dating of the majority of the psalms after 400 B.C.E. is seriously questioned by many scholars of note. GUNKEL, for instance, maintains that the majority of the psalms was written before 200 B.C.E. He also defends the view that the origin of various types of psalms goes as far back as the period of the early monarchy, and even the Judges.[124] WILSON goes even further in claiming that

> "comparative literature and history are in favor of the probability of psalms having been composed in Hebrew as early as the time of David, of Moses, and even of Jacob."[125]

CHEYNE[126] and DUHM,[127] on the other hand, doubt the existence of any Davidic psalms and maintain that all the psalms were written in the post-exilic period. BRIGGS declares that

> "David in the titles of seventy-four psalms indicates not the authorship, but, with few exceptions, the first of the several minor Psalters, gathered under the name of David in the late Persian period, from which these psalms were taken by later editors of the major Psalter."[128]

As to the time in which they may have originated, BRIGGS says that

> "eight belong to the Greek period . . . All the others . . . not later than the middle Persian period."[129]

OESTERLEY, on the contrary, opines that a considerable portion of the Psalter, at least in its primitive shape, must have originated in pre-exilic times.[130] Historical evidences are in favor of this assertion. The Sumerians, Babylonians and Egyptians used hymns and psalms in their liturgy already in primeval times.[131] Considering the close interrelation of these cultures with that of the Israelites, it may be assumed that this liturgical custom was in early times adopted by the Hebrews.

Yet, it is well-nigh impossible, to determine the time of origin of a collection such as the Psalter, into which items from a period extending over almost nine centuries have been incorporated. An additional handicap is that, in all probability, some of these hymns and psalms have not been written down immediately upon composition, but were no doubt preserved orally for a certain length of time. This must have resulted in all kinds of unintentional or arbitrary changes, additions or deletions, rendering even more difficult the determination of their original dates. Furthermore, the introduction into public worship of certain psalms which primarily were not intended for this purpose, might have caused certain re-adjustments in the original text. Before the Psalter became, through the canon, a sacred book of the Jews, "the post-exilic Jewish leaders did not refrain from replacing some archaic forms or obsolete expressions with those in common use at the time."[132] Since it is an established fact that "compiling the Psalter was not motivated by a literary urge, but by a practical religious need, it may be assumed that this need justified even more radical changes of the text, in order to adapt the songs to the actual requirements of the worship."[133]

THIRTLE asserts in all seriousness that

> "the text of the Psalter comes into history, not as so many fugitive poems, but rather as a *single document continuously written.* [The italics are ours]. Though arising in different ages, and originally written in various styles, the constituent psalms as a whole were reduced to a common character, and had impressed upon them a literary complexion, generally speaking, peculiar to one age,"[134]

a statement, which is in glaring contradiction with the generally accepted findings of biblical exegesis.

It has already been mentioned that the major Psalter was gradually assembled from several small collections, which existed from the early kingdom until the times of the Maccabees. Even a century later, at the time of POMPEIUS' reign (67-48 B.C.E.), the urge to compose psalms has not subsided, as proven by the apocryphal "Psalterium Salomonis," which originated at this time. This compilation, which, of course, has nothing to do with Solomon except the name, was not included into the Book of Psalms, an indication that the canonical Psalter was closed at the time of POMPEIUS.

After the destruction of the Temple by the Romans, devout and poetically gifted writers continued to compose psalms, imitating the style and form of the canonical psalms. Sometimes these "new songs" were nothing but a mosaic of biblical quotations. In some instances, however, they give testimony of real inspiration which, had they been composed in biblical times, would probably have warranted their inclusion into the canonical Psalter. Their number must have been considerable. TIMOTHEUS I, Nestorian Patriarch of Seleucia (726-819 C.E.), reports in a letter to SERGIUS, Metropolitan of Elam, that in a cave near the Dead Sea, about 800 C.E., ancient Hebrew manuscripts have been discovered, adding: "We have found more than 200 psalms of David among our books."[135] Of course, these were all non-canonical psalms, the name of David being attached to them but pseudo-epigraphically. But if this number was found in a single cave, the chances are that other places, such as libraries of sects, monasteries, early churches, etc. held also a great number of post-biblical psalms. This assumption is borne out by the recently discovered Dead Sea Scrolls, which contain a considerable collection of post-biblical

Psalms (or *Hymns*) *of Thanksgiving,* which will be discussed in another chapter of our study.[136]

Many commentators, ancient as well as modern, maintain that a number of canonical psalms originated in the Maccabean period. Others, however, among them GESENIUS, EWALD, HUPFELD, EHRT, BAETHGEN, WILSON and THIRTLE, are opposed to this belief. They cite all sorts of historical and philological arguments in support of their theory, but the conclusive proof against the Maccabean origin of psalms is furnished by EHRT.[137]

The Greek translator of the apocryphal book of "Ecclesiasticus," Jesus the son of Sirach, states in the prologue to this book, that his grandfather, the author of the book, after having diligently studied the Law, the Prophets and the other portions of the Scriptures,

> "was drawn on also himself to write something pertaining to learning and wisdom; to the intent that those which are desirous to learn, and are addicted to these things, might profit much more in living according to the law." (Ecclus., Prologue).

The translator asks the indulgence of his readers if his rendering does not always conform to the original, which was written in Hebrew,

> "for the same things uttered in Hebrew, and translated into another tongue, have not the same force in them."

As an excuse, he refers to the fact that the Greek translation of the Holy Writ (meaning the SEPTUAGINT) also shows substantial deviations from the Hebrew original.

This prologue may serve as the evidence that the author of the book of "Ecclesiasticus" has been a student of the Hebrew Scripture, and that his grandson, the translator, knew the SEPTUAGINT. The time of both, author and translator, can rather accurately be established by precise historical data given by the translator in his prologue (. . . "in the eight and thirtieth year coming to Egypt, when Euergetes was king . . ."). This gives us the time when the Greek translation of "Ecclesiasticus" was completed, *viz.* ca. 180 B.C.E. The fact that Jesus, the son of Sirach, knew the Greek translation of the Bible, including the Psalter, proves conclusively that the canon of the Psalter must have been concluded at this time. Which, in turn, precludes the possibility that psalms from the Maccabean times (167-165 B.C.E.) have been incorporated into the Psalter.

As to the authorship of David and the other persons and families named in headings, there are historical and philological arguments against this assumption.

It is common knowledge that literary production of Antiquity was mostly anonymous. No stress was laid, in those times, upon the preservation of an author's name for posterity.

The great Egyptian, Persian, Indian, Babylonian and Assyrian poems were created by the concerted work of numerous and anonymous authors during long periods of time. The same holds true for the Bible. With the exception of the Prophets and the books of Ezra and Nehemiah, the authors of the biblical books are not known by their names.

Even the prophetical books, though they carry the name of an "author," were apparently not written by the prophets themselves. They do not represent "literature" in the proper sense of the word, but are rather pamphlets for fight and propaganda. Their aim was to preserve the true religion and its institutions, and they also comprised exhortations and commandments for a life pleasing God. The names of the prophets have been put at the head of these writings not for the mere attestation to their authorship, but because it was indispensable for the prompt success of these books to proclaim whose teaching they contained.[137a]

The books of Ezra and Nehemiah are the documentary evidence of one of the most important national events in the history of the Jewish people: the return from the Babylonian exile. Again, the authority of the two famous scribes had to attest to the authenticity of the reports, whether they wrote it or not. This is the reason why their chronicles carry their names.

All the other portions of the Scriptures are anonymous, despite the fact that some of them are attributed to an "author." Moses, for instance, is supposed to be the author of the Pentateuch, as the synagogal tradition maintains.

> "In reality, the work was handed down to posterity without any name of an author, like all other historical literature of the Hebrews; wherever Moses appears, the Pentateuch not only speaks of him in the third person, but it makes a clear and impartial distinction between the narrator on the one hand, and Moses on the other."[138]

True enough, the "Song of Songs," "Proverbs," and "Ecclesiastes" are ascribed to Solomon, yet biblical exegesis is extremely doubtful about his authorship. The Psalter is certainly no exception to the general rule.

The Jewish inner direction for establishing national symbols erected, in later times, a "Davidic tradition," by creating, as it were, an idealized figure of the king, which deviates considerably from the historical person. It was in keeping with this tradition to represent David, apart from his other virtues, as the famous author of psalms. This is the reason why seventy-three psalms have been ascribed to him. The Greek version of the Psalter contains even additional Davidic psalms, and the Syriac version attributes almost all the psalms to him.[139]

There are no historical, philological, or other methods for determining David's authorship. The most outstanding expounders of the Psalter are at variance in pointing out the particular psalms that could be ascribed to him. Delitzsch thinks that thirty-four are David's, Ewald admits only thirteen[140] while Baethgen, in the final analysis, reduces the number to three (1, 3, and 4), and considers as certain only Psalm 1. Thirtle, on the contrary, asserts that the "Davidic Psalter" originally started with Ps. 3, and that Pss. 1 and 2 were prefixed as a kind of preamble to the oldest Davidic collection in Hezekiah's time.[141] Pfeiffer also maintains that

> "none of the psalms could have been written by David, even if we disregard anachronisms such as the numerous allusions to the Temple of Zion or even to the Exile (Ps. 69:35 [69:36]); the language, style, and religious conceptions of the psalms of David are radically different from those of his time."[142]

One should remember, however, that posterity often identifies the name of a compiler with the material of his collection. We speak of Gregorian and Ambrosians chants, although Pope GREGORY and Bishop AMBROSE have been merely compilers and editors, but not the authors of these chants. We may, therefore, use the term of "David's Psalter," without necessarily considering David as the author of the poems ascribed to him.

The authorship of Moses for Ps. 90 is highly doubtful, if for no other reason than that this psalm appears in the fourth book of the Psalter, which—as mentioned above—originated much later than the first three books. Should a psalm composed by Moses have ever existed, it would most certainly be incorporated into an earlier, even the earliest psalmodic collection.

Solomon's authorship, too, meets with some doubts, although, in so far as the time factor is concerned, the first of the two psalms ascribed to him (Ps. 72) and incorporated in the second book, could have been written by him.

The "Sons of Korah" were Levites who acquired fame as scribes of religious literature. Their outstanding merit, however, was that a branch of their clan, similar to the Asaphites and Hemanites, distinguished itself in the sacred musical service.

The headings of the psalms indicate ten or twelve poems as having been composed by the Korahites, *viz.* Pss. 42-49, of which Ps. 43 has no specific inscription, but originally may have belonged to Ps. 42, and Pss. 84, 85, 87 and 88, the last one having also the name of "Heman the Ezrahite," apart from the "sons of Korah." These poems have different stylistic features, but all seem to have belonged to a special hymnal of the Korahite singer-guild, from which they were transplanted into the major Psalter.[143]

The Asaphites, too, were a levitical family of singers (2 Chron. 20.14; 29:30; Ezra 2:41; Neh. 7:44; 11:22, etc.).

Jeduthun (or Jedithun) is the name of one of the three early protagonists of the sacred music; he is called by this name in 1 Chron. 16:41 ff, 25:1 ff, 2 Chron. 5:12, 29:14 and 35:15. In other passages, however, the names of the three precentors are Asaph, Heman and Ethan. According to a modern view, Jeduthun and Ethan are supposed to have been the same person, the difference being merely in the spelling of the name.[144]

The difference of the preposition *le* (Ps. 39) and *ʿal* (Pss. 62, 77), which precede the name of Jeduthun, gave rise to all sorts of speculations. For Pss. 39 and 62 THEODORET assumes the preposition to have indicated that the psalm was composed by David, and sung, or perhaps reshaped, by Jeduthun. Something similar was intimated by the Targum in paraphrasing the heading "by the mouth of Jeduthun," or simply "by Jeduthun." Some modern expositors see a connection between *le-yeditun* (or *ʿal-yeditun*) and the preceding *lamenazzeaḥ,* and arrive at the conclusion that the heading should signify:

> "to the leader (or to the chief musician) of the family of Temple singers named after Jeduthun."

EWALD disqualifies completely the assumption that Jeduthun is a proper name and interprets it as a term referring to a key (or mode, "Tonart").[145] LAGARDE thinks that it is a corrupt spelling of (*ʿal*) *yede ʿethan,* "(upon) the hands of Ethan," *i.e.* in charge of the guild led by Ethan.[146]

MOWINCKEL endeavors to propound his own theory.[147] Jeduthun, he says, might be a verbal abstract derived from *yada,* "to praise," "to give thanks." In the Hithpaʿel-form, the verb assumes the meaning "to admit," "to confess," "to submit his case (to Yahveh)." Jeduthun, therefore, would signify "confession," or something similar. In MOWINCKEL's opinion, nothing seems to stand in the way of this interpretation, since all three psalms are complaints which include confessions.

Furthermore, MOWINCKEL sees an error in the general assumption that the psalmists have taken over the name Jeduthun from the Chronicles. Just the contrary is true, namely that the chroniclers and their later copyists and interpolators misunderstood the word in the headings and transformed it into the name of a non-existing levitical singer.[148]

o
o o

Inasmuch as most of the psalms were either composed or adapted for ritual use, it is not too difficult to determine the circle from which they have emanated. Everything intimates that the authors of the psalms are to be traced back to the ranks of functionaries of the Temple, especially to levitical singers.

"The singers were the performers, the guardians and the preservers of the sacred song. They were the 'experts,' the 'sages,' who knew the songs and their characteristics, and knew how to make them. Consequently, we can assume that they were the poets who wrote them; it was their circle, which maintained the tradition of poetry. As preservers of the inherited wealth of songs, they were the *soferim,* the writers, who recorded them; between the scribe and the author, there was virtually no difference in Ancient Israel. Therefore, the creation of new songs constituted one of the functions of the singers; it was their responsibility to provide for songs required for the cult."[149]

It is obvious that, individually or collectively, the singers also took care of the musical adaptation of the psalms by selecting and arranging the melodies (or melodicles) which served as patterns for the psalms. We may mention, finally, that through their unflagging work, and despite all the vicissitudes of history, the levitical singers must be credited with the preservation, for many centuries, of the tradition of singing the psalms. All this is the living testimony of the paramount role of the levitical singers as authors, composers and performers of psalms.

o
o o

In conclusion, we should mention briefly Psalm 151, incorporated into the SEPTUAGINT, which has been rejected by the Jewish canon.[150] All councils of the Apostolic Christian Church have likewise opposed its admission into the Psalter. On the other hand, it was incorporated into the Syriac, Arabic and Coptic versions of the Scriptures. Its heading reads: "A Psalm, in the hand-writing of David, composed by David, when he fought in single combat with Goliath."[151]

It is evident that the psalm is much older than the Codex Alexandrinus of the Bible (6th century C.E.), in which it is preserved. Since the linguistic features of this psalm are quite different from those of the canonical psalms, biblical criticism unanimously brands it as spurious.

The psalm has certain bearing on our subject, inasmuch as verses 2 and 3 contain a couple of musical terms:

Verse 2. My hands made the organ,
And my fingers jointed the psaltery.
Verse 3. And who is who taught me?
The Lord himself, he is my Master.

The original words are *organon* and *psaltērion,* the Greek equivalents for *ʿugab* (*cp.* Ps. 150:4) and *nebel,* unless we assume that these are collective terms, *organon* for wind, and *psaltērion* for stringed instruments. We may mention in passing that this is the only psalm in which David is portrayed as a builder (or perhaps a designer) of musical instruments (but *cf.* 1 Chron. 23:5, translated by the SEPTUAGINT as "he made," instead of the Hebrew "I made").

5. SELAH

More than any other technical term of the Psalter, the mysterious word *selah* excited the imagination of scholars of all times.

Ṣelah appears in the Psalter 71 times, 67 times of it within the psalmodic text and 4 times at the end of a psalm. In the first book nine psalms have *selah* (Pss. 3, 4, 7, 9, 20, 21, 24, 32, 39), in the second book seventeen psalms (Pss. 44, 46, 47, 48, 49, 50, 52, 54, 57, 59, 60, 61, 62, 66, 67, 68), in the third book eleven psalms (Pss. 75, 76, 77, 81, 82, 83, 84, 85, 87, 88, 89), in the fourth book the term is entirely lacking, and in the fifth book it appears only in two psalms (Pss. 140, 143).[152]

Out of 39 psalms which contain *selah,* 31 also have the indication *la-menaẓẓeaḥ* in their heading. Since psalm-exegesis agrees upon the musical connotation of the last-mentioned term, it was concluded that *selah,* too, refers, in one way or another, to music. This conclusion is corroborated by another biblical passage, the only one outside the Psalter, in which *selah* is used (Hab. 3), and where the word has unmistakably a musical implication.

Habakkuk's "prayer," more precisely "song of praise," seems to have originally belonged to the canonical Psalter, from which it has been subsequently removed for reasons unknown to us.[153] That this song of praise is in reality an abrogated psalm is proven by the fact that *selah* appears in it three times, and furthermore by the musical instruction *la-menaẓẓeaḥ bi-neginotai,* "For the leader. With my string-music." The only difference between this song of praise and the regular psalms is that the latter carry the musical instruction exclusively in their headings, while in Habakkuk it stands as a postscript.

Outside of the Bible *selah* is used only in the *Shemoneh ʿEsreh* ("the eighteen prayers"), where it appears once after the third and the eighteenth blessing. This series of prayers has many affinities with the psalms, so that *selah* in them does not represent a special characteristic. It demonstrates, at any rate, that in the times when the *Shemoneh ʿEsreh* originated, the term *selah* was well known in the liturgy.

Not all the early translators of the Bible have attributed to *selah* a musical meaning. The SEPTUAGINT translates *diapsalma,* "a pause in singing," *i.e.*

"an instrumental interlude." The VULGATE, however, had no equivalent for this word and simply left it out altogether. AQUILA renders it as *aei,* "always," in five places, however, he translates, similarly to the Syriac version, *asma,* "song," "melody." SYMMACHOS and THEODOTION translate in some passages *diapsalma,* in others *eis tous aiōnas,* "in all eternity," *eis telos,* "until the end," and *diapantos,* "always." JEROME uses *semper,* "always," the Targum has in most instances *le-ʿalemin,* "in eternity," sometimes *tedira,* "for ever." HIPPOLYTUS (died ca. 230 C.E.) gives a circumstantial definition of the word.[154] He says that it indicates some change of rhythm or of melody in the psalm, or else a change of contents, or a modification of thought or of verbal expression. AUGUSTINE, in his commentary on the 4th Psalm, tries to define the term:

> "the inserted [word] *diapsalma* forbids the connection [of a verse] with the preceding one. It is (as some think) either a Hebrew word meaning "So be it!" [Amen!], or a Greek word indicating a break in the psalmody (whenever the psalm is performed with singing). In fact, *diapsalma* signifies a pause in singing. Just as *synpsalma* stands for the connection of the lyrics while singing, so *diapsalma* means the separation of phrases where a pause in the sentences becomes evident. Whatever meaning prevails, this is probable: when *diapsalma* is inserted, the phrase has to be interrupted and disconnected [from the preceding one]."[155]

JOHN CHRYSOSTOM gives a different, and musically even more relevant definition of *diapsalma.* In referring to David as to the composer of the Psalter, he says that David used to assign each psalm to one of the choral groups of the divine service. Sometimes, however, when the text contained different moods within the same psalm, he felt that it should be divided into different parts, and so he let these contrasting parts sung by alternating groups. Such a change from one group to another was indicated by the interpolated word *diapsalma,* and a psalm in which hymnic and pastoral (bucolic) parts alternated, was called *Canticum diapsalmatis.*[156]

The Mishnah reports a similar custom in later times: the psalms, in this period, were sung in several sections, the breaks between these being filled with blasts of trumpets.[157] Hence commentators concluded that *selah* stood at places where interruptions occurred.

The majority of classical and modern commentators is inclined to accept the SEPTUAGINT's translation, *diapsalma,* "a pause in singing." Yet, the specific meaning and implementation of this pause are by no means clarified either by the SEPTUAGINT, or by the expounders.

Writers of Antiquity derive *diapsalma* from the Greek verb *psallein,* "to play the harp." ATHENAEUS has two pertinent references to this interpretation. He quotes ARISTOXENOS,the reputed musicologist of Antiquity: "the *magadis* and *pēktis* may be played without a plectrum, by simply plucking with the fingers (*dia psalmou parechestai tēn cheiran*)."[158] In another passage, he quotes the actor Eupolis who states that *diapsellein trigōnois* "signifies a strong play on the triangular harp."[159]

Judging from these statements, *diapsalma* is either an interlude of stringed instruments (like *diaulion* is an interlude of pipes [*auloi*] between two choral stanzas), or it signifies a ritornello of stringed instruments played forcefully, while formerly they accompanied softly the voices. Accordingly, DELITZSCH maintains that *selah* indicates "a transition from *piano* to *forte*."[160]

The talmudic sages declare that *selah* is synonymous with *neẓaḥ* and *vaʿed;* all three words would mean continuation in eternity.[161]

More numerous are the nuances in the interpretations of modern commentators. JAHN and others attach to the term the meaning of our *da capo.* DELITZSCH thinks that it represents a marginal note, but of another kind, namely a *nota bene* for the singers or of the choir leader to remind them of a certain manner of interpretation (whichever this may have been). [162]

PFEIFFER, ROSENMÜLLER and other commentators explain the word as a pause for the singers, during which the instrumentalists would perform alone. GESENIUS, HENGSTENBERG, THOLUCK and others derive the word from the verb *shala,* "to be still," and render it as "pause in singing." DELITZSCH, on the contrary, says that

> "there is but one verbal stem with which *selah* can be combined, *viz. salal* or *salah.* The primary notion of this verbal stem is that of lifting up [your voice], from which . . . comes the general meaning for *selah,* of a musical rise."[163]

EWALD and DE WETTE also derive *selah* from these two verbs and, accordingly, interpret it as a *crescendo* for the instrumentalists, or as a signal for the musicians to give a strong attack.

> "*Selah* means 'rise! up!', implying for the performers to play 'loud! accentuated!' If therefore the phrase signifies 'play loud!', its correlated implication would be that the singing should stop during this interlude."[164]

HERDER believes that *selah* means neither a *da capo,* nor an instrumental interlude, but a different mood achieved by increased dynamics, by changing the tempo, and by the transition into another melody.[165]

RIEHM maintains that *selah* is found almost exclusively at places where the preceding passage needs a strong emphasis, or shows a deeper emotional stress, or arrives at a strong change of mood, or when a sharply contrasting idea is introduced. In RIEHM's belief, this would support the assumption that such places gain momentum by loud music. The idea seems to be corroborated by Ps. 9:17, where *selah* is preceded by the term *higgayon,* "Interlude."

Other expounders opine that *selah* is the abbreviated Hebrew version or the transliteration (with the letter *p* omitted) of the Greek *psallē,* "play!", this being an instruction given by Greek music masters to their performers when an instrumental interlude was required.

BUDDE asserts that *selah* indicated the place in the psalmodic text where actions of benediction or prostration, stressed by music, interrupted or closed the singing.

All these interpretations have one thing in common, namely that *selah* stands for a break in the singing and indicates, at the same time, some kind of intermezzo. The implication of an interlude is all the more obvious as *selah* never appears at the beginning of a psalm, but mostly within the text, and only four times at the end (Pss. 3, 9, 24, 26). The exegetic explanation of the last-named exceptions is that these four psalms are probably incomplete in the canonical text; either some verses which originally followed *selah* have been deleted, or, in an earlier order of the Psalter, some psalms, now separated, belonged together. There is a conclusive proof to this effect in the SEPTUAGINT. There, Pss. 9 and 10 constitute a single psalm, and so *selah* does not stand at the end of Ps. 9, but appears within the text of a large psalm.

The possibility should not be excluded that the ritual act which must have always been connected with *selah,* has occasionally taken place at the end of certain psalms. In these instances, the indication would have the significance of an instrumental postlude. Its locative counter-part, however, the instrumental prelude, seems to have been unknown in Ancient Israel, for neither the Scriptures, nor the post-biblical literature contain the slightest reference to it.

It should also be mentioned that some scholars of note consider *selah* as an indication of a strophic structure of the respective psalms.[166] Although many psalms, as well as other parts of the Scriptures, show definite strophic organization,[167] it is highly improbable that such a structural division of the text would be indicated exclusively in the Psalter (and once in Hab. 3), and that the term *selah* would refer to such a poetic treatment. The fact that *selah* does not appear in all the psalms showing a definite strophic structure, especially at places where a strophic division is manifest, excludes its interpretation in this sense.

The division of the psalm-text by the *selah* interludes (or whatever these may have been) is quite irregular and does not allow any conjecture as to the rules of their application. There are only a few instances where the psalms are broken up by such interludes into more or less equal sections. Seldom do the psalmodic contents themselves justify any preceding or following instrumental intermezzi. Sometimes *selah* enhances markedly the impact of a dramatic phrase, by which the psalmist brings his idea to an end; sometimes it is difficult, or even impossible, to discover why the term stands at a place where there does not seem to be the slightest inducement for an interlude. Therefore, unless we assume that *selah* has been distributed indiscriminately or erroneously between the psalmodic verses, we must admit that the reason for its insertion into the Masoretic text represents an insoluble riddle.

It is possible, and even probable, that the word does not stand in every place where an interlude of some kind would actually be called for. The preserved old manuscripts are quite inconsistent with regard to *selah*. The chances are that this word which originally did not belong to the text and had no bearing on the contents of the psalm, was not handled by the *soferim* with the same care as the text itself, at least prior to the fixed Hebrew canon. Too, there are, in this respect, some obvious errors of the copyists, for in the various Bible versions the word has changed places. For instance, in the Masoretic text *selah* stands after Ps. 57:4; in the SEPTUAGINT after 57:3;—the Hebrew text has *selah* after Ps. 61:5; the SEPTUAGINT after 61:4. Sometimes the word appears manifestly at a wrong place, like in Ps. 68:8;

according to the logic of the text, 68:9 would be more appropriate; also *selah* would stand better after Ps. 88:11 than after 88:10. In Ps. 55:20, *selah* stands even in the middle of a phrase, disrupting the whole sentence. Almost contrary to the sense of the phrase is the location of *selah* in Ps. 57:4.[168]

In various codices and manuscripts a number of *Selah* have been found which apparently are correct, but which are missing in the Masoretic text. The canonical arrangement, therefore, does not furnish a definite clue as to where and how often a break in psalmodic singing might actually have occurred at the Temple service.

The simplest explanation of *selah,* generally considered authentic, is hinted by the Talmudic tradition:

> "Ben Arza clashed the cymbal and the Levites broke forth into singing. When they reached a break in the singing they blew upon the trumpets and the people prostrated themselves; at every break there was a blowing of the trumpet and at every blowing of the trumpet a prostration. This was the rite of the daily Whole-offering in the service of the House of our God."[169]

KIMḤI's interpretation, which derives *selah* from the verb *salal,* "to lift up," "to start anew," comes practically to the same conclusion. Accordingly, *selah* would be an instruction for the musicians, who until then accompanied the singing softly, to start forcefully, using trumpets and percussion instruments (*viz.* cymbals). During this loud music the singing was supposed to stop.

This interpretation seems to be quite logical if we take into account a simple practical necessity that arises from the physical limitation of the average human voice. The main burden of music in the Temple ritual, rather extensive as a rule, rested upon the shoulders of the levitical singers (*cf.* 1 Chron. 16:37,40). Even with the greatest devotion of the singers to their service, there would be a natural limit to the endurance of their vocal cords. In lengthy performances—and psalm-singing was precisely of this kind—solo as well as choir singers needed a short repose for recuperation. These breaks in singing might have caused the resorting to instrumental interludes indicated by *selah.*

However logical some of the above explanations may appear, they have never been considered as conclusive.

One of such sophisticated theories was the interpretation of *selah* in the special sense of the verb *salal,* "start anew the praises." According to this hypothesis, at the place indicated by *selah,* a musical doxology has been inserted, a sort of variation on the previously sung melody, during which—contrary to the above interpretations—the ensemble music would stop altogether and the gap thus created would be bridged by the melismatic song of a freely improvising soloist.

The talent for improvisation of the Jewish singer is repeatedly attested in the Old Testament. The "prophesying of the prophets with a psaltery and a harp" (1 Sam. 10:5; 19:20; 2 Kings 3:15, etc.) probably was such an improvisation.

Yet, the idea of free improvisation in Temple music in the sense of doxology as used in the later Christian liturgy, is groundless.

The music of the Temple developed on a rigorously traditional basis. The external as well as the internal order of the liturgical music was regulated by strict rules. Just as the sacred ceremonies were minutely fixed in all details, so nothing was left to chance in their musical counterparts. The musical liturgy was prepared as conscientiously as the rest of the sacred service.

It may safely be assumed that responsible leaders watched sternly lest any fortuitous or arbitrary changes, additions or omissions, should infiltrate into the performances. The strict orthodoxy of the liturgy, the fanatic clinging to the ancient musical heritage, the rigorous professional pride of a well-organized guild of singers, all this is in direct opposition to the very idea that improvisation in the sacred music was permitted or even tolerated. Just the contrary is true. As soon as a song and its accompaniment had been "composed," *i.e.* agreed upon in all details, the music was virtually just as sacrosanct as the divine rites themselves. All this disqualifies the conjecture of an interpolated doxology in the sense of a musical improvisation.

Another theory tries to derive *selah* from the Assyrian word *ẓalla,* "invocation," "prayer." That Jewish liturgy should have tolerated the insertion of prayers into psalm-singing is highly doubtful, to say the least.

Some commentators think that the three consonants forming the word in Hebrew represent an acrostic. Accordingly, *S-L-H* would be taken as the initial letters for *sob le-ma'alah ha-shar,* "singer, go back to the beginning," *i.e.* it would be an instruction for a *da capo* in to-day's sense.

Another interpretation is based upon the assonance of the root of *selah* with the noun *sal,* "basket." From this it is concluded that *selah* may have been a musical instrument, possibly a drum, in the shape of a basket.[170] According to this hypothesis, such drum was used for signal purposes, perhaps as an indication to the priests to continue with the sacrifical ceremonies. The choir leader would give the instruction to one of the musicians placed close to this drum: go "to the *sal,*" in Hebrew *la-sal.* In Hebrew grammar the inversion of consonants is a frequent occurrence; *h* at the end of a word is sometimes exchanged with *l* at the beginning. Following this rule, *la-sal* would be transformed into *selah,* resulting in the meaning exposed above.

One commentator tries to justify this strange hypothesis by referring to the fact that drums in the shape of pots have been used in India, in the shape of barrels in China, and that our modern orchestra has drums in the shape of kettles. From this analogy, this commentator infers the possible existence in the sanctuary in Jerusalem of a drum in the shape of a basket.[171] Yet, neither the Bible, nor JOSEPHUS, nor any other contemporary writer have ever referred to such a signal instrument in Ancient Israel, and especially in the Temple. Such theories, therefore, have no foundation.

Sometimes *selah* is placed after a mere part of the sentence, or in the midst of a parable or allegory as in Ps. 55:8 and 55:20. Thus, biblical criticism is fully justified in maintaining that an instrumental interlude at such spots would completely disrupt the meaning of the phrase. There was much speculation whether the insertion of *selah* in these and similar places has been done haphazardly, or whether it had some definite purpose. Some commentators assume that such a purpose might have been to illustrate, as it were, with musical means the psalmodic text which had just been sung.

This assumption brought forth some strange hypotheses. One of them is propounded by STAINER:

> "*Selah* is always a musical interlude, but not always what is known to modern critic as 'pure music.' Where it separates stanzas it may be mere sound appealing by the beauty of its melody or by combination of instruments; more often it represents what we should call 'programme music,' and is consciously and deliberately descriptive of the text which it accompanies."[172]

To be sure, program-music is by no means a modern or Occidental achievement. Its beginnings may be traced as far back as the 6th century B.C.E. At the artistic festivals of Delphi, the auletes used to illustrate musically Apollo's fight with the dragon. SAKADAS, a famous aulos virtuoso, has obtained the prize with such a composition, the *nomos pythikos,* at the first pythic competition (586 B.C.E.). Centuries later, this melody still was highly praised. TIMOSTHENES, admiral of Ptolemy II (283-246 B.C.E.), gave a detailed description of it, which is preserved by STRABO. Two other writers of Antiquity, PAUSANIAS and JULIUS POLLUX, also mention this famous melody. Other historical records, originating in the 4th century B.C.E., furnish additional evidence about the accomplishments of Greek virtuoso performers of dithyrambs, who were expected to depict with instrumental or vocal means storm, gale, the singing of birds, etc., of which the rendering of a sea storm by the instrumental virtuoso TIMOTHEUS is a prominent example.

Attempts of the same kind have been attested throughout the Middle Ages, continuing uninterruptedly until modern times. Composers of all epochs tried to stimulate the imagination of their audiences by using associative means, such as titles, descriptions, and sometimes by underscoring their lyrics with characteristic rhythms.

Between such tonal pictures and a hypothetical program-music at the Jewish Temple there is an impassable abyss. The Greek, and most of the medieval attempts at depicting events and actions with musical means, have been performed at secular occasions and aimed to amuse the audiences at festivals and, in the Middle Ages, at popular feasts and fairs. They served to demonstrate the virtuosity of the auletes, or the skill of the juggler-musicians of later times. Moreover, such musical displays have always been caused by or associated with material motives. The Greek dithyramb-virtuosi did not play out of enthusiasm for art, but for awards offered, the amount of which sometimes has been quite considerable. The medieval jugglers played to earn their living. The musical images produced by these jugglers have been, as to their aim, mere musical tricks designed to stimulate the generosity of their audiences. It is obvious, therefore, that the nature of such Greek and medieval productions of program-music has been entirely different from that of Jewish sacred music.

The hypothesis that program-music has been performed in the Temple would presuppose a tonal art aiming at the presentation of picturesque musical effects, that is, something wholly extraneous to the cult. As a matter of fact, however, the principal, if not exclusive, goal of Hebrew sacred music consisted in praising the Lord with singing and playing. Program-music in the sanctuary would represent a procedure entirely opposite to the religious conception of the Jews, to their ritual, and also to the character of Temple music itself. Therefore, the assumption of program-music within the service, and as a part of the ritual, cannot be justified either historically, or religiously, and least of all ethically.

The confusion of ideas which prevailed in assuming that program-music in Jewish cult was possible, or even probable, created some further eccentric off-spring. E. CAPEL CURE,[173] and after him W. W. LONGFORD,[174] are not satisfied with merely postulating that *selah* is program-music. They go as far as to describe exactly its specific characteristics. They maintain, in fact, that the contents of the psalms, indeed the thoughts expressed in the verse preceding the *selah,* determined the nature and quality of the latter. CAPEL CURE supports his hypothesis with notions taken over directly from RICHARD WAGNER's technique of applying leading motives in his music dramas. CAPEL CURE's *selahs* have even names borrowed literally from WAGNER's phraseology:

> "Besides the Flight and Storm motive, which we ascribe to the harps and clapping hands and feet . . . , and besides the Death motive (probably given out on reed pipes) which illustrate so many psalms with its cruel suggestiveness, . . . there are two other *selahs* in constant use—the Sacrifice and War *selahs*—both with trumpets, though probably with different sorts of trumpets."[175]

In reading this description, one gets the impression of perusing one of those numerous 19th century booklets of music appreciation analyzing WAGNER's "Ring," whose authors toiled to popularize the "leitmotiv"-principle of WAGNER's "art work of the future," and in which musical hermeneutics brought forth the most whimsical conclusions.

The identification of Temple music of Ancient Israel with modern music drama is quite conspicuous in CAPEL CURE's following arguments:

> "With what eloquent effect the *selah* could be used by one who was both artist and prophet may be seen in Habakkuk's hymn (Hab. 3). Nowhere else in the Old Testament is anything like our modern libretto to be found, where obviously the words are written with conscious regard to the effect and colour of the accompanying music."[176]

Here, CAPEL CURE intimates that prophet Habakkuk composed his poem with the preconceived idea of applying specific musical effects, like WAGNER used to do when he wrote his libretti.

In order to lend force to his program-music hypothesis, CAPEL CURE appends a musical description of a *selah,* which reads as an analytical review of a symphonic poem by RICHARD STRAUSS:

> "It is a most vivid picture of a tropical storm which, however, depends on the orchestra for its fullest effect." Thereafter comes a lengthy characterization of the "devastating storm, the wild melody, being sustained and reinforced, . . . receives a thrilling intensification from the Death *selah,* which immediately follows."[177]

In conclusion, CAPEL CURE summarizes this theory in the following statement:

"In this interpretation of the word *selah,* it will be seen that no excessive demand is made on the technique or resources of primitive performers: but—while every effect was produced by the simplest means —the instrumentalists of the Temple did for the singers what the artist does when he adds colour to the outlines: in fact, so much do some psalms depend upon their instrumental performance, that many of the phrases are only intelligible with the due understanding of their *selahs;* while in all cases where the *selah* is not a mere symphony between stanzas, the interludes deepen the glowing intensity of the words as much as Wagner's music glorifies his libretti."[178]

The comparison between the biblical *selah* and WAGNER's music dramas shows the twisted ways followed by some modern expounders in order to make plausible their peculiar ideology.

ILLUSTRATION No. 37
Levitical singing groups in the First Temple, as depicted in the Codex of Kosmas Indikopleustes, Cod. Vat. Graec. 699. (After K. J. Zenner, *Die Chorgesänge im Buche der Psalmen,* Freiburg i.B., 1896).

° ° °

Not all modern interpretations of *selah* go such befuddled ways as those mentioned above. Some of them are guided by the spirit of music, therefore they cannot fail to arrive at more logical conclusions. Among them a new theory, based upon well-established musical principles, deserves a closer scrutiny.

In a remarkable essay, K. J. ZENNER[179] refers to a pertinent graphic illustration in the CODEX of KOSMAS INDIKOPLEUSTES, (first half of the 6th century C.E.) which is preserved in the Vatican. In this illustration various groups of singers are portrayed who perform songs antiphonally.[180] (Illustr. 37).

Antiphonal singing, as we know, is frequently attested in the Old Testament and represents one of the Jewish forms of vocal art.

From this ancient Jewish usage, ZENNER derives his interesting theory as a possible explanation of *selah.*

As mentioned earlier, the SEPTUAGINT translates *selah* as *diapsalma.* The usual and somewhat free explanation of *diapsalma* is *dia* in *psallein,* that is a "break in singing," while the modern expounders are rather bent upon the conception of *psallein dia, i.e.* "to play between (singing)" hence the idea of an "interlude."

Following ZENNER's theory, the logical interpretation is contained in CHRYSOSTOM's phrase: *autē hē diadochē tou psalmou ekaleito diapsalma,* "such a division of the psalm was called *diapsalma.*" ZENNER refers to etymology and grammar. Just as *dialogos* is the kind of *legein,* "to speak," which is done between two persons (*dia* derived from *dyo,* "two"), so is *diapsalma* the kind of *psallein,* "to play (with singing)," which takes place alternately between two: "singing in a duet" ("Zwiegesang").

> "Thus, we have in *selah,* resp. in *diapsalma,* an evidence repeated more than seventy times that psalms have been performed by several choral groups, with precise indication of the places where the groups were supposed to alternate. The wonderful musical interludes, sweet and soft, or passionate and stormy, created by the imagination of expounders, are gone; in their place, a prosaic and sober explanation remains which, in its simplicity and veracity, represents a deeper insight."

According to KOSMAS, *selah,* resp. *diapsalma,* stands always *kata ton meson tou psalmou,* "within the psalm." But we have already pointed out that in the canonical text as well as in the various translations several *selahs* stand at the end, so in Pss. 3, 9, 24, 46. This would suggest that prior to the canon the psalms have been assembled in different groups. Even the SEPTUAGINT shows, in many instances, divergences from the Masoretic text. Should we consider KOSMAS' indications authentic, we would be bound to assume that in the original setup *selah* stood always within the psalmodic text.

KOSMAS avers that there were six groups of singers to alternate. In the Holy Writ, as we know, there is not the slightest indication to that effect. ZENNER claims, however, that the very construction of Ps. 1 yields certain internal evidences supporting the assumption that it was performed by six choral groups.[181]

Wherever *selah* makes its appearance, the alternation of the choral groups would be logical; but *selah* is not applied to all the places where the text seems to be appropriate for changing the groups. Relatively, numerous choral psalms do not contain *selah* at all. Following ZENNER's idea *selah* should have been used much more frequently, and he himself admits that the lacking of *selah* in so many places endangers his reasoning.

However, he invalidates these objections by referring to the following arguments in support of his theory:

(1) He starts with the question whether the various Bible versions contain all the *selahs* which were primarily indicated. He refers to the fact that sometimes important words are missing in old manuscripts, words which indeed would be essential to the correct meaning of a sentence. Human errors are unavoidable even in a holy book. Such enigmatic words like *selah,* irrelevant to the sense of a phrase, and probably not considered "inspired" like the text itself, have met the same destiny, and in fact even to a higher degree. In the Codex Vaticanus there are several *selahs* (*e.g.* Pss. 34:11, 80:8), which seem to stand in conformity with the principle under consideration, but are missing in the Hebrew text. In Greek minuscule manuscripts JAKOB discovered twelve additional *selahs,* which have not been preserved in other manuscripts.[182] Furthermore, the *Psalterium vetus,* the first, Old Latin, translation of the Psalter, preserved in the Codex St. Germani, contains some additional *selahs.*[183]

Once in a while, a correct *selah* may be hidden in a wrong spelling (for instance, *kaleh* in Ps. 74:11). The difference between the number of *selahs* as they might have originally been applied and as theoretical considerations would require, is—as ZENNER thinks—less than it may appear at first sight.

(2) Since *selah* has been a *nota bene* for the singers, it might have primitively been inscribed into copies alone, which were used for rehearsals and in actual service.

(3) Why was not *selah* indicated in all the places? Why was it sometimes left out altogether? Because this was an instruction intended for professional singers who, under normal circumstances, would know what to do even without it. At all times, professional musicians knew quite a number of *termini technici* which were self-explanatory to them; thus, the leaders of music could easily refrain from writing them down without endangering the desired artistic results.

With these arguments, ZENNER thinks to have proven that *selah* indicated the change of the performing groups in antiphonal singing. KOSMAS' illustration, CHRYSOSTOM's allusion to a similar procedure, as well as philological and exegetical reasons offer strong support for his assumption.

MOWINCKEL also deals extensively with *selah.*[184] His findings do not reveal anything new, therefore a short reference to them will suffice.

MOWINCKEL establishes a parallelism between *s-l-l-* and *shir* by pointing to Ps. 68, verse 5. To sing and to extol—which, in this connotation, mean exclamations of adoration—are the most appropriate media to praise the Lord and pay Him homage (*cp.* also Pss. 147:7; 81:2 ff, and similar passages). MOWINCKEL derives his interpretation of *selah* from this parallelism, and suggests as equivalent the paraphrase: "to render homage to Yahveh with ritual exclamations." He considers as self-evident that music belonged to this ceremony, as indicated by the synonymous words *s-l-l* and *shir*.

Selah is the only term which the English versions, old and recent, did not even attempt to translate. Those which do not take over the term phonetically, like *Wycliffe, Douay, Moulton* and *Moffat,* leave it out altogether in the psalms as well as in Habakkuk.

6. HIGGAYON

The examination of the term *higgayon* (Ps. 9:17) has been assigned to this place, since its meaning is closely connected with that of *selah*.

When appearing in immediate succession, the two terms are translated by the SEPTUAGINT as *ōdē diapsalmatos,* by SYMMACHOS as *melos diapsalmatos,* both in the literal meaning of "song of the (or: as) interlude." AQUILA's rendering is *ōdē aei,* that of THEODOTION *phthongē aei,* both "song for eternity." The VULGATE does not give any translation and even omits the original words. JEROME uses the paraphrase (*corruit impius*) *sonitu sempiterno,* "(the wicked is snared by) the eternal sound." The Targum applies the circumlocution "the righteous men exult in eternity." Thus, even in olden times there was no unanimous interpretation of this dual term.

The various metamorphoses of the word *higgayon* appear in some other places of the Old Testament, but only once again in a musical sense, in Ps. 92:4. There, it characterizes etymologically the rustling sound of the harp: *ʿale higgayon bekinnor,* "(sing praises unto the Lord) with a solemn sound upon the harp." In Isa. 31:4, a noun derived from the same root signifies "the growling of the lion," in Isa. 38:11 "the moaning of a dove," in Isa. 16:7 "the wailing of the sorely stricken," and in Jer. 48:31 "the howling and moaning of the damned."

The root of the word is *hagah,* meaning "to murmur," "to growl," in general "to produce a low sound." Applied to music, the verb is believed to be an instruction for the musicians to keep the accompaniment in subdued and solemn tone colors.

Besides this basic meaning, the verb has another implication, "to meditate," "to muse." According to ancient philosophical conceptions, thought mutters in the heart and talks in undertones. Thus, the affinity of both meanings becomes obvious. In Ps. 15:19, the differently punctuated word is translated as "meditation."

The interpretations of the term by biblical exegetes oscillate between these two imports. GESENIUS defines *higgayon* as the low, rustling sound of the harp, which conforms to the sense of Ps. 92:4. Other commentators, however, attach to it the meaning of pause, silence, meditation.

The fact that *higgayon* appears in the Psalter conjointly with *selah* led to the almost unanimous belief that both represent certain musical instructions, which either belong together or complement each other.[185] Should this be correct, the question arises why they are used only once in this dual form. There are three possible explanations:

(1) *Higgayon selah* is the term in its complete form, and *selah* would merely be an abbreviation of it;

(2) *Higgayon* is a gloss to, or synonym of, *selah,* and both terms are basically identical, so that the shortened form does not alter their meaning;

(3) Perhaps an earlier order of the Psalter had Ps. 9 put in a place where the complete expression *higgayon selah* appeared for the first time. Since its correct meaning was thus established, the psalm editors used only the abbreviated form in subsequent passages,—and so *selah* remained alone. In the final order of the Psalter, Ps. 9 has been put to its present place, so that other psalms in which *selah* stood alone preceded it. But the necessity of inserting the dual term at the place where it appeared for the first time in the final order of the Psalter may have been overlooked.

Psalm commentators attach various implications to the dual terms. THOLUCK, HENGSTENBERG,[186] and others interpret the words as an instruction for the singers to immerse in a meditation, during which the music would be silent. THOLUCK translates "meditate!" and adds the following comment:

> "This again is a place where the singing left off to allow the music to play loud, and where an opportunity was given for a meditation, as the term expressly required."[187]

GLASER holds an opposite view.[188] He thinks that *selah* signifies the entrance of percussion or shaking instruments at the end of a section of the psalms, and that *ʿale higgayon bekinnor* (Ps. 92:4) calls for a solemn, gentle rustle of the harp, consequently a subdued instrumental accompaniment. As to the *higgayon selah,* it represents for him a somewhat contrary combination of all instruments producing a resounding intermezzo. He alludes to 1 Chron. 15:16 as a descriptive illustration of such a practice.

It has been mentioned repeatedly that MOWINCKEL tends to interpret the terms in the headings mainly as ritual acts or as instructions to such acts. He has a similar explanation for the *higgayon.*[189] It signifies for him a reminder to interrupt the singing, insert exclamations of the chorus or of the congregation, and emphasize these exclamations with loud music. This break would serve as a support, or a stress for certain highlights of the psalm, which appear at the end of the preceding verses. Such ritual exclamations are: *ʾamen, hallelujah, laneẓaḥ, ḳadosh hu,* and they constituted, after MOWINCKEL, the participation of the congregation in the performance of psalms.

He interprets SEPTUAGINT's translation *diapsalma* in the same sense as "exclamations with an interlude." A variant of the Greek word, *hypopsalma* (quoted by BAETHGEN),[190] comes even closer to the notion: "an exclamation of the congregation as an assent," in the sense of the worshippers' response.

From all this MOWINCKEL concludes that *higgayon* is an instruction for exclamations such as "for ever," or "in all eternity," which, with the rustling of harps, and together with the "interlude" (*selah*), represented a single and unified ritual action.

Just as the early translators of the Old Testament failed to disclose the exact meaning of the word, the English versions, too, refrained from using an equivalent and, like for *selah* have taken over the expression phonetically from the original. *Wycliffe, Douay, Moulton* and *Moffat* have left out the term entirely. LUTHER alone tried to reproduce in German the hypothetic meaning of the term by translating it as "Zwischenspiel," "interlude."

V. SINGING IN ANCIENT ISRAEL

1. SINGING IN THE EARLY HISTORY OF THE JEWISH PEOPLE

Contrary to the "invented" instrumental music (Gen. 4:21), singing is as old as humanity itself. According to post-biblical Jewish legends, singing existed even prior to the creation of man: the song of the angels praising God after the act of creating the world constituted the celestial parallel to the terrestrial song of praise exalting the Lord.[1]

Among primitive peoples joy, grief, love, triumph, and the inexhaustible gamut of human emotions manifest themselves in crooning, shouting, impassioned speech, and somewhat later, in more or less regularly accented declamation which modern scholars consider to be the archetype of artistic singing. With gradually growing civilization, other causes prevailed in releasing song from the human soul: sorcery, exorcism, healing, ritual, every day's work, besides the festival events in the life of the individual and the community. Among these, the most important functions assigned to singing were prompted by religious rites.

According to the naive belief of primitive man, ordinary speech is not sufficient for the intercourse with supernatural beings, on whom, supposedly, his fate depends. The same belief prevailed largely in later religious usage. Thus, in reciting the ritual formulae, in addressing the deity, in prayers and supplications, the ordinary speech would undergo transformation by overflowing instinctively into accentuated declamation.

This engendered a manifold melodic and rhythmic remodeling of the worshipper's voice, and thus created the first element of singing.[2] Gradually, some specific formulae of speech-melody emerged, primitive melodic patterns crystallized, which may be considered as forerunners of "tunes." Between this stage and the "song," as a form of art, there is still a long but more or less straight development, which can easily be followed up.

In the early life of every people acts of worship and religious ceremonies are the primary sources of organized singing. The musical sentiment of the deeply religious Jewish people likewise manifested itself in songs far back in their history. Side by side, however, the Israelites also developed the faculty of embellishing their secular life with organized singing.

> "This natural tendency of man to singing is conspicuous among the Semitic race and especially among the Hebrews, the more so as their life and actions have their roots in the depths of subjectivity and in their intrinsic feelings. The abundance of a vivid sentiment, coupled with the unconscious urge for an emotional outlet, qualify them particularly for the cultivation of poetry and music, which are precisely the ones among the arts that originate from the depths of emotional life."[3]

o
o o

Since the written records about the primeval existence of the Jewish people are more replete with myth than history, we are informed relatively late about the purely cultural manifestations of the Hebrews, including their singing. As in their poetry, so also in their music the early evolutionary phases are concealed from our observation, and when any tangible products in these domains suddenly emerge they reveal already forms of art which are advanced stages of long and organic development. Especially their music, as it appears for the first time in historical records, reveals already a cultural level that represents a well integrated phenomenon of popular life.

In the earliest history of Israel singing was not restricted to certain classes, social strata or professions; it was the possession of the entire community. When great historical events have taken place and the people's emotions were remorselessly tightened, it sufficed for a leader to start the liberating song in order to release the tension through common singing.

The earliest poems of ancient peoples have all been sung. "Song and tale" ("Singen und Sagen") is the external form of early poetry of all peoples. The folkbards have been the preservers of the art-form of sung poetry. In the primitive stage, singing is normally performed with an instrumental background. As EWALD states,

> "real singing cannot be conceived, from its very inception, without some kind of musical accompaniment; even now, one imagines of hearing in the inanimate parts of some of the ancient Hebrew verses the music inherent to it."[4]

Modern biblical exegesis favors the theory that, although there is no positive evidence sustaining the belief,

> "one must not overlook the possibility that considerable portions of the stories of Genesis were sung in verse by minstrels before they were retold in prose by biblical authors. If such was the case, the extant poetic sections of the stories may be a survival from some preliterary stage."[5]

This would be in conformity with the view of some modern literary historians that "poetry," as an artistic expression of elated human sentiments, constitutes a preliminary stage to "prose," the narrative style of common speech; at best, the two are considered as "sisters of equal rights."[6] For our subject, this implies that "poetry" was sung, "prose" recited. However, there might have been only a slight difference between the singing of poetry and the recitation of a narrative, as carried in the exalted speech of the ancient folkbards.

o
o o

Israel has been a theocratic state *par excellence.* It therefore stands to reason that singing should have been closely interlinked with the evolution of theocracy.

> "Always when the acts of the Lord have resulted in great historical events, singing broke forth as a resonance produced by the divine revelation in the hearts of a people faithful to the covenant."[7]

Since the concept of theocracy goes far back into the primeval history of the Jewish people, the sources of sacred song must also be looked for in times prior to the national existence of the Jews. Owing to the scarcity of historical data, mere conjectures are possible with regard to the pre-Mosaic period. But considering the interrelation of Jewish culture with that of Egypt, it is safe to assume that the sacred song of the Egyptians has left a strong imprint upon that of the Jews.

Ritual prayers offered up with singing, or rather with chanting, have been used in all ancient religions. The Sumerians enunciated longer and shorter formulae of prayers with singing; some of their texts have been preserved. The sacred services of the Babylonians and Assyrians contained numerous hymn-like songs.[8] For the well-being of the king and for temple-dedications, the Babylonians recited litanies, which unmistakably show a responsorial form.[9] This warrants the conclusion that the recitations were processional hymns chanted antiphonally by a priestly chorus and the congregation.

Even assuming that these and similar evidences furnished by the history of religions are to be considered, in some measure, as precursors of the liturgical singing of the Hebrews, the influence of heathen rites upon Jewish musical practice should not be overestimated. The religious institutions of other ancient peoples have been so different from the patriarchal cult of the Israelites that this fact alone must have greatly diminished the penetration of pagan musico-liturgical elements into Jewish worship.

In early times the heads of families have been the qualified stewards of the priestly functions. The rites of this epoch must have been simple, rudimentary, and without elaborate ceremonies. Accordingly, the singing in such patriarchal rites, too, must have been rather primitive. There are allusions to singing liturgical formulae of these rites in the indications *kara shem ʾAdonay*, or *kara b'shem ʾAdonay*, "to call the name of the Lord," or "to call upon the name of the Lord," which might have constituted the essential musical part of the simplest organized worship (Gen. 12:8; 13:4; 26:25; 33:20). As in other ancient Oriental religions, the core of such short prayers and chants might have been the mere calling and joining the various names of God.[10] This was probably performed in an accentuated speech-melody, characteristic of the primitive worship of Orientals.

Science has established rather stable and uniform criteria for the beginnings of sacred singing. However, some new theories cropped up concerning the origin of secular singing.[11] According to one of these, singing has not sprung from the interrelation between speech and music, but from some specific extra-musical rhythmic actions of every day's working procedures.[12] Another theory asserts that

> "the oldest civilized peoples used chanted speech as a means for memorizing in order to transmit to future generations their laws and teachings, and also the glorious deeds of their national heroes."[13]

According to this idea, Jewish secular singing sprang from the two last mentioned sources. And just as in primitive civilizations there was no sharp borderline between poetry and prose, there was not too conspicuous a distinction either between emotional speech and singing.

> "Among the ancients, singing meant infusing into the voice an inflexion proper to the meaning of the words. Any kind of inflexion

of the spoken word was then called singing [*i.e.* chanting]."[14]

As we know, the rhythmic shaping of speech requires a stressed diction, an increased intensity of expression, a richer deployment of the accents inherent to the word and sentence. Eventually, the elongation of the vowels served as the last link toward the establishment of a declamatory artifice, which was already close to real singing, since the vowels of human speech and the musical sounds are of a kindred origin.

This artifice is the norm which we have to take into account when facing the earliest testimony of the Bible concerning secular singing. It goes as far back as the "invention" of music by Jubal. The same biblical passage which informs us about the three primeval professions and crafts, including music, contains the first secular "song" of Jewish history, known as "Lamech's song." (Gen. 4:23,24).[15] Whether the text of this poem, as quoted by the chronicler, is in reality a fragment of a more extensive bardic ballad, as surmised by some historians,[16] is a matter of conjecture. At any rate, it is the oldest Jewish specimen of a secular song, primitive and crude, to be sure, but already presented unmistakably in a poetic form:

> ("And Lamech said unto his wives:)
> Adah and Zillah, hear my voice;
> Ye wives of Lamech, hearken unto my speech;
> For I have slain a man for wounding me,
> And a young man for bruising me;
> If Cain shall be avenged sevenfold,
> Truly Lamech seventy and sevenfold."

If this savage and brutal song still has more or less a legendary tint, historical reality presents itself soon in the biblical text. Laban's reproachful speech when he overtakes Jacob in his flight, contains a reference to a secular song already in its proper sense:

> "Wherefore didst thous flee secretly and outwit me; and didst not tell me, that I might have sent thee away with mirth and with songs, with tabret and with harp?" (Gen. 31:27).

To understand the abyss gaping between Lamech's uncouth song of hatred and Laban's suggested song of mirth, we must compare the mental stage of a primitive man with the markedly higher stage of civilization at the time of the patriarchs Laban and Jacob. There, a crude and barbarous song, which has little to do with "art"; here, singing accompanied by instrumental music, a clearly recognizable artistic manifestation against an ethical background: it testifies to a beautiful custom of patriarchal times,—escorting a friend with music and singing.

From this biblical passage BUDDE draws the conclusion that already in heroic times Israel might have had a guild of singers, by which he evidently means folkbards. These were poets and singer-musicians who, besides possessing a creative gift, have been compilers of many folksongs and ballads, which they performed on suitable occasions. To support his assumption, BUDDE refers to Gen. 4:21 (the Jubal legend) and, as a definite, though later, "referential" proof of it, to Num. 21:27: "Wherefore they that speak in parables [*i.e.* the poets] say . . ." From this, he draws the conclusion that "in ancient times music and poetry have been closely interlinked, one without the other cannot be conceived . . . Such songs and ballads of unknown poets have been sung by itinerant bards all around the country. No doubt, these bards represented a spiritual power and were considered the strongest levers of public opinion, especially in times of great national decisions."[17]

One of the most beautiful, and artistically the most relevant, song of the Old Testament is the one offered as a thanksgiving to the Lord by Moses and the people of Israel after their miraculous escape at the Red Sea (Exod. 15:1-21). Modern biblical criticism is in doubt whether the passage through the Red Sea is truly responsible for the creation of this song. It is surmised that, originally, it must have been shorter and that it has acquired its final form only after the Israelites settled in Cana'an.[18] But whether created earlier or later, whether taken over from a more ancient book, as some exegetes believe, whether its scriptural form is different from the original one, all this in no way belittles its importance. Actually, it is the first religious national song found in the Bible, and born of the stirring emotions on the occasion of an overwhelming event; as such, it is the starting point of a development which culminated in latter days' musical achievements of the people of Israel.

As for its musical rendition, it is safe to assume that the Song at the Red Sea has been sung by Moses and the people responsorially. There is no direct reference to this in the biblical text, to be sure, although later rabbinical sources confirm explicitly this kind of rendition.[19] Yet, the Bible itself contains an indirect proof for the responsorial form of the *Shirah*: the verse following immediately Moses' song states that the women used this manner of singing:

> "And Miriam the prophetess, the sister of Aaron, took a timbrel in her hand; and all the women went out after her with timbrels and with dances. And Miriam sang unto them:[20]
>
> Sing ye to the Lord, for He is highly exalted:
> The horse and his rider hath He thrown into the sea"

(Exod. 15:20-21), which apparently is a repetition of Moses' own lines.

Just as Miriam, Moses' and Aaron's sister, "sang unto the women," so Moses might have led the men in singing. From there on, responsorial and antiphonal singing always occurred whenever large assemblies, choral groups, congregations, or masses of people took part in religious or secular singing; it soon became the most favorite species of choral art. According to the prophetic vision, the seraphim, too, have sung responsorially:

> "And one called unto another, and said: Holy, holy, holy, is the Lord of hosts; the whole earth is full of His glory" (Isa. 6:3).

Responsorial and antiphonal singing reached their highest liturgical significance in psalmody; they were later transplanted from the Temple into the Synagogue and, consequently, were also adopted by the Christian liturgy, where they soon became one of the most important outlets of religious emotions.

The songs of praise and triumph of Moses and Miriam were simply spontaneous religious outbursts, but not yet ritual songs in the proper sense.

Liturgical song, as such, came into being when Israel, through the covenant on the Sinai, became the "chosen" people and, through this, met its ultimate destiny. From there on, Israel, as a theocratic nation, possessed not only its own religion, but also its own form of cult, the dignity of which transfigured all former ritual actions, and its liturgical music as well. From theocracy sprang the higher ethical meaning of Israel's sacred singing, a meaning which is generally lacking in other religions of Antiquity.

2. SINGING IN HEROIC TIMES

The subsequent heroic age of Israel brought forth numerous war-, triumph-, and other bardic songs, in which the happiness about the conquest of a new homeland, the enthusiasm about the deeds of famous national heroes have found their crystallization in poetic form. Ancient songs of minstrels, interspersed with occasional historic reports, used to be compiled in books,[21] most of which, unfortunately, have been lost. But the Scriptures preserved some vestigial fragments from these ancient books in the form of quotations by biblical chroniclers, which proves that they have actually existed.

One of such compilations may have been *Sefer milḥamot Adonay,* "The Book of the Wars of the Lord," from which the biblical scribe quotes two passages (Num. 21:14,15 and 21:27-30). These songs celebrate Israel's victory over the Moabites and the defeat at Heshbon of Sihon, king of the Amorites. Another collection of minstrels' songs has been apparently *Sefer ha-yashar,* "The Book of the Righteous," mentioned in two places of the Old Testament (Josh. 10:13 and 2 Sam. 1:18).[22] To this collection belonged David's lament over Saul and Jonathan, known as the "Song of the Bow," a poem of truly antique grandeur and power.[23] In its partly elegiac, partly dramatic verses, David expresses ungrudgingly his mourning for Saul and his son, and glorifies the never failing bow of Jonathan. This might have been the reason why David ordered "to teach the sons of Judah (the song of) the bow," the poem having been designed to become a popular song that would preserve the glorious memory of the two heroes and, at the same time, serve as a national dirge. According to a recent conjecture,

> "it has been sung as a processional song . . . at the transport of the bones of Saul and Jonathan from Jabesh-gilead to the tomb at Zel(a" (2 Sam. 21:12-14).[24]

Still another vestige pertaining to a lost historical document may be traced in the Lord's commandment to Moses to perpetuate in a book the victory over the Amalekites (Exod. 17:14). It is not evident from the biblical text whether this book has ever been written. Possibly it is identical with the afore-mentioned "Book of the Wars of the Lord."

According to BUDDE, there is a high internal probability that none else than King Solomon ordered, or supervised, the compilation of ancient songs.

> "It would be fitting for the first sovereign, who united the entire people under his peaceful sceptre, to collect and preserve literary testimonies of his glory. There is no need to refer to David's personal gifts in order to prove that at the court of Jerusalem poetry and music have been cultivated and sponsored . . . The particular literary fame

of Solomon, as attested to in 1 Kings 5:12 ff, and which eventually assumed legendary proportions, may have manifested itself in such clear-sighted efforts toward the preservation of the ancient spiritual treasures of his people."[25]

Generally, folkbards would recite at banquets ancient tales and sing heroic ballads. The vivid prosaic descriptions by the biblical chroniclers of the Exodus from Egypt and other outstanding national events seem to reflect the spirit of such ancient bardic songs, dealing with similar subjects.

Primitive marching songs are already mentioned soon after the Exodus from Egypt, during the wanderings in the desert. At breaking up the camp and at putting up a new camp, the people would dash into vigorous songs:

> "And it came to pass, when the ark set forward, that Moses said: 'Rise up, O Lord, and let Thine enemies be scattered; and let them that hate Thee flee before Thee.' And when it rested, he said: 'Return, O Lord, unto the ten thousands of the families of Israel'." (Num. 10:35,36).

The analogy with the general practice of those times warrants the conclusion that Moses did not sing all this by himself. The ark of the covenant was carried like a banner in front of the marching crowds, and at such solemn processions the people would intone the first song. The second song might have been rendered responsorially. Both songs, owing to their popular character, have partially been incorporated into the Psalter (see Ps. 68:2).

Marching songs pertaining to the later epoch of Israel's history are likewise mentioned in the Bible. When King Jehoshaphat has set forth with his army against the Ammonites and Moabites,

> "he appointed them that should sing unto the Lord, and praise in the beauty of holiness, as they went out before the army, and say: 'Give thanks unto the Lord, for His mercy endureth for ever'." (2 Chron. 20:21).

Thus went the army to battle, led by the stimulating song of the Levites, who marched ahead in sumptuous robes. After the victory.

> "they returned, every man of Judah and Jerusalem, and Jehoshaphat in the forefront of them, to go back to Jerusalem with joy . . . And they came to Jerusalem with psalteries and harps and trumpets unto the house of the Lord" (2 Chron. 20:27,28).

Another category of secular songs, mentioned frequently in the Scriptures, is the one connected with work. Such songs can be found among all peoples, in all epochs, and on all levels of civilization.

The Hebrews too, have known the enlivening effect of common worksongs, and the Bible contains numerous examples of their use; in some instances, even their textual fragments are preserved in the Scriptures.[26]

There are numerous references in the Bible to joyous singing at the harvest and vintage; the joys of the harvest festival are alluded to in Exod. 23:16, and in Isa. 9:2.

> "The men of Shechem went out into the field, and gathered their vineyards, and trod the grapes and held festival" (Judg. 9:27). ". . . and in the vineyards there shall be no singing" (Isa. 16:10). "The new

> vine faileth, the vine fadeth, all the merry-hearted do sigh. The mirth of tabrets ceaseth, the noise of them that rejoice endeth, the joy of the harp ceaseth. They drink not wine with a song" (Isa. 24:7-9). "The Lord . . . giveth a shout (*ya'aneh*), as they that thread the grapes" (Jer. 25:30).

Furthermore, traces of a vintage song are preserved in the following passage:

> "As, when wine is found in the cluster, one saith: 'Destroy it not, for a blessing is in it'." (Isa. 65:8).

The Bible mentions, or indirectly alludes to, several other worksongs, one of these being the song of the masons laying the corner-stone (Job 38:7), or the top-stone (Zech. 4:7; *cf.* also Ezra 3:10,11). Some biblical exegetes believe that the prophetic answer of the guard,

> "the morning cometh, and also the night—If ye will inquire, inquire ye; return, come" (Isa. 21:12)

represents a sort of song of the night-watchman.[27]

Another species in the secular repertoire of the Jews was the song of triumph. On the occasion of great national victories, such songs gushed forth spontaneously from the tense emotions of the people and from the urge of manifesting them in an unreserved fashion. These items have been intoned mostly by women, receiving with songs and dances the returning victor and his army. Deborah's paean (Judg. 5) is such a spontaneous manifestation. Even though, as the Bible indicates, the victorious general Barak participated in this song, Deborah was, in reality, the leader of the singing, as evidenced unmistakably by two passages. Deborah was asked by the people: "Awake, awake, Deborah; awake, awake, utter a song" (Verse 12). And as an introduction to her song, Deborah said:

> "I, unto the Lord will I sing (*'azammer*) to the Lord, the God of Israel" (verse 3).

Compared with these powerful songs, particularly their overwhelming expressiveness, Hannah's song of praise (1 Sam. 2) may appear somewhat pale, at least outwardly. It is also outcharmed by the poetic transport of many a psalm. Nevertheless, it is a remarkable example of early hymnic poetry of the Hebrews, which later developed into a luxuriant growth in the Book of Psalms.[28]

3. RESPONSORIAL AND ANTIPHONAL SINGING

In the above mentioned heroic songs, bardic poets glorified outstanding national events. The festivities on such occasions have had a strong religious background, for the songs of victory represented, at the same time, songs of praise in honor of the most High, songs of thanksgiving for His miraculous deeds. Such feasts of victory were eminently suitable to strengthen the religious sentiment of the participants and to foster the feeling of national communion. For this purpose, the crowd, which was practically identical with the people in its entirety, has been granted the privilege of participating in the singing, customarily in antiphonal form.

The simple device of stressing the basic thought of a verse by exchanging exclamations or repetitions existed very early among the Israelites. The same custom can be observed among most of the ancient Oriental peoples. For instance, in the Babylonian-Assyrian liturgy stereotyped formulae of acclamations (probably sung) served to introduce certain ceremonies.[29] The recurrent refrains in Assyrian hymns seem to indicate that these have been sung responsorially by a priest as the precentor, with the answering chorus, or alternating choral groups. In the songs of Rigveda, entire verses have been repeated word for word, or with minor changes only, as a refrain.[30] It is therefore evident that the Israelites have taken over this liturgico-musical practice from other peoples.

On the occasion of a national event, the participation of the individual in the singing gave him a vivid notion and experience of active co-operation and kindled his feeling of belonging to the same ethnic community. Through this, such partly national, partly religious festivals acquired a definite social aspect.

> "This trend, to be sure, is manifest wherever religiously bent people are grouped together in a common social environment. If religion is to be considered one of the strongest cementing powers of collective life and communal consciousness, singing in joint religious manifestations must be adjudged the same binding force."[31]

This social moment is even more conspicuous on occasions when antiphonal singing is artistically synchronized with the dance of women. The "Song at the Red Sea," mentioned before (p. 72), may serve as a case in point.

The "singing and dancing" around the golden calf has also been a manifestation in which the entire people participated. (Exod. 32:18,19). Here, however, the chronicler reports a relapse of the Israelites into the Egyptian pagan practices with worshipping an idol and with ritual customs, which were familiar to the Hebrews from their recent place of slavery. It is obvious that the "Song at the Red Sea" and the subsequent dance by which the women paid homage to the Lord are manifestations of a religion infinitely higher in ethical implications, and its forms are of a much more spiritual and dignified nature than those of the pagan worship around the golden calf. Both ritual manifestations, however, the Jewish as well as the pagan, used identical musical means and forms, namely antiphonal singing, and dancing, a sign that Egyptian ritual customs made an indelible imprint upon Jewish religious folk-ceremonies.[32]

At secular occasions, too, antiphonal singing has been a frequent occurrence, so for instance at the return of King Saul from the victorious battle against the Philistines.

> "The women came out of all the cities of Israel, singing and dancing, to meet king Saul, with timbrels, with joy, and with three-stringed instruments. And the women sang one to another in their play, and said:
>
> Saul hath slain his thousands,
> And David his ten thousands." (1 Sam. 18:6,7).

This solemn reception with antiphonal singing is also reported by the chronicler in two other passages of the same book (1 Sam. 21:12 and 29:5).

With the institution of a regular musical service in the cult by David and Solomon, antiphonal singing—although not mentioned directly—has been introduced into the official liturgy and became, from the outset, an essential feature of sacred musical performances. Quite a number of biblical passages, especially those in the Psalter, allude repeatedly to antiphonal singing, even if in a roundabout way.

The musical service held at the solemn laying of the foundation of the Second Temple has taken place with antiphonal singing. (Ezra 3:10,11).

In the big procession which took place at the dedication of the newly erected walls around Jerusalem, two choral groups sang antiphonally. (Neh. 12:31-42). The singing has been performed

> "according to the commandment of David the man of God, ward against ward," *i.e.* antiphonally (Neh. 12:24).

Antiphonal singing retained its full liturgical significance far into talmudic times, proof of which is the frequent reference to it in the early rabbinic literature.[33]

Apart from celebrations of victory and other joyful national events, antiphonal singing is also referred to at funeral functions. The ceremony of mourning has been minutely regulated in Ancient Israel. At public funerals the people manifested their sympathy by exclamations like those in David's lament over Saul and Jonathan: "How are the mighty fallen!" (2 Sam. 1:19,25,27). King Josiah, who met a hero's death on the battlefield, was lamented by the entire nation,

> "and all the singing men and singing women spoke of Josiah in their lamentations, unto this day; and they made them an ordinance in Israel" (2 Chron. 35:25).

The same biblical passage gives evidence of a "Book of Lamentations," (*ḳinot*), not referred to elsewhere in the Scriptures.[34]

The antiphonal funeral wailing of the Hebrews has analogies among other ancient peoples. Thus, a report about the funeral of an Assyrian king mentions mourning songs performed by a music-master and assisting female singers, in which the mourners participated antiphonally:

> "The wives [of the deceased] wailed, the friends responded."[35]

The wailings at private funerals of the Israelites have likewise been carried out antiphonally. The women of the house were assisted by professional mourning women. These were called "wise women" (*Douay, Jewish Version*), "cunning women" (*Authorized Version, Moulton, Harkavy*), "skillful women" (*American and Revised Standard Versions*), or "well-skilled in dirges" (*Moffat*), and constituted a special profession of female musicians, obvious from a biblical passage, on which BUDDE comments as follows:

> "As a parallel to *mekonenot* ("wailing women") stands the term *hakamot* ("wise women") in Jer. 9:16 [9:17]. This term testifies to the fact that this profession was not restricted to mere routine functions, . . . but that it constituted real art and that the *ḳinah* was an actual song, based upon lyrics with logical contents, written in a poetic form, and performed with a musical setup. A further proof of this fact is

the invitation in verse 19: 'Teach your daughters wailing, and every one her neighbour lamentation'."[36]

The professional mourners cried for men *hoi᾽ahi, hoi᾽adon,* or *hoi hodoh,* "Ah my brother!", "Ah lord!", resp. "Ah his glory!", and for women, *hoi᾽ahot,* "Ah sister!" (1 Kings 13:30; Jer. 22:18; Am. 5:16). Such lamentations belonged to mourning rites of all Semitic peoples of Antiquity; their peculiar penta-accentual verse-form, so different rhythmically from other poetry, can be found already in early Hebrew literature.[37] The lamentations have always been performed responsorially or antiphonally. There is evidence of this in the Scriptures:

> "And the land shall mourn, every family apart; the family of the house of David apart, and their wives apart; the family of the house of Nathan apart, and their wives apart; the family of the house of Levi apart, and their wives apart; the family of the Shimeites apart, and their wives apart; all the families that remain, every family apart, and their wives apart" (Zech. 12:12-14).[38]

The institution of professional wailing women and, with it, the custom of funeral lamentations still existed in Mishnaic times.[39]

4. CREATION OF THE SACRED MUSICAL SERVICE

In the pre-Davidic era, singing originated partly from certain ritual necessities, and partly from the common national consciousness. With the institution of the organized Temple music by David and its further development by Solomon, the ethos of singing changed fundamentally. It ceased to be merely the sounding upshot of the common experience. It was elevated to an *art* and became co-ordinated with poetry, another artistic manifestation permitted and even encouraged among the Jews by their religious laws. In Solomon's Temple, with its sumptous ritual appeal to all the senses of the worshippers, singing became the centre of musical attraction.

The "song of praise" developed into the tone-symbol of faith in God and of the worship of the Eternal. The pent-up creative urge of the Jewish spirit turned to this new art-form. Poets and musicians vied with each other to enrich the sacred service with a splendorous artistic investiture. The endeavor to serve God in word and tone, to praise His glory with singing and playing, led to the creation of immortal art works, the most outstanding of which is the Book of Psalms.

The central feature of Jewish Temple ceremonies was the sacrifice. From the very inception of the organized sacred service, sacrifice was closely connected with music. Singing was considered an integral and indispensable part of the sacrifice; lack of singing even invalidated the sacrificial action.[40]

Owing to the paramount importance of singing in the sacred service it is only natural that the Bible should refer to it quite frequently. The reports of the chroniclers about singing in the ritual and also about the Levites, as the chief representatives of the sacred vocal art, belong to the most momentous informations we possess about the music practice of Ancient Israel.

Besides religious songs of praise and repentance, psalms, hymns, elegies, and educational songs, the Bible mentions practically all the current species of secular songs. Among the secular songs referred to in the Scriptures two species are virtually missing and, curiously enough, just those which have a particular significance in the family life: the cradle song and the children's song. The latter has certain points of contact with levitical singing; therefore it may be appropriate to investigate this apparent biblical omission in connection with singing in the sacred service.

It would be surprising if a people whose entire tradition and education have been based upon a patriarchal form of living and whose social consciousness has been centered in the family, would not have known the species of songs which are most intimately connected with family life. Though the Scriptural text does not mention children's songs specifically, there is ample evidence that such songs have been a current feature in biblical times. Zach. 8:5 says, for instance, that

"boys and girls are playing in the broad places of the city."

The original Hebrew word for "playing" is *m'saḥaḳim, i.e.* precisely as in 1 Chron. 13:8, where it has a definite—vocal and instrumental—connotation (parallel in 2 Sam. 6:5, here, however, without singing). The same word appears again in 1 Sam. 18:7, though in the feminine gender (*ham'saḥaḳot*) and likewise in connection with singing, dancing, and playing musical instruments.

Some commentators refer also to Job 21:11,12 as a proof for children's song in the Bible. The passage reads:

> "They send forth their little ones like a flock, and their children dance (*y'raḳḳedun*); they sing to the timbrel and harp (*yiseu b'tof v'kinnor*), and rejoice at the pipe (*v'yismeḥu l'ḳol ʿugab*)."[41]

The "dancing" of the children has supposedly the meaning of "dancing *and* singing," an assumption based upon the SEPTUAGINT's translation, using for the Hebrew original *propaizousin,* a derivative of *paizō.* This Greek verb has several meanings: "to play (on an instrument)," "to dance," and "to sing."[42] Furthermore, verse 12 of SEPTUAGINT's translation reads: *euphrainontai phōnē psalmou,* which, interpreted literally, would mean "rejoice at the sound of a *song.*" Here, we are confronted with a seemingly incorrect translation of the SEPTAUGINT,[43] since the Hebrew original *ḳol ʿugab* refers to "the sound of the pipe." Thus, despite SEPTUAGINT's *propaizousin,* the passage in Job cannot constitute—even indirectly—a proof of children's singing.

If we may reason from the Old Testament about children's songs only in a roundabout way,[44] the early rabbinic literature contains definite references to them, and thus we may infer retrospectively, and quite legitimately, many permanent family customs in biblical times from their later observance in Jewish life. The rabbinic writers even report that boys participated in the levitical choir. We do not know why the biblical chroniclers passed in silence this important feature of the levitical music organization. The assumption, however, that boys participated in the levitical choir at an early epoch, possibly already in the First Temple, is inevitable if we consider how a levitical singer had to be brought up to achieve professional mastery.

The singers were admitted into the levitical choir when thirty years old

(1 Chron. 23:3).[45] This means that only when they reached this mature age, could they become full fledged members of the levitical guild of singers. The mere fact that the singers were admitted at this relatively late age, and that they were then called "skillful" (Hebr. *meibin*, "experts," LUTHER: "Meister"; 1 Chron. 25:7), proves that their years of schooling must have been long and arduous. Otherwise they could easily start their professional career at the age of twenty-five or even sooner.

Their time to serve was twenty years, until they reached the age of fifty, when the vocal qualities of a singer generally start to decline. Prior to their admittance, they had to pass a five years' apprenticeship.[46] Such a relatively short period of preparation (beginning supposedly at the age of twenty-five) appears inadequate in view of the fact that the Israelites have not known a musical notation (at least in our Occidental and practically efficient sense); for the levitical singers had to memorize the entire voluminous and complex musical ritual in order to master all its details. To achieve this goal, the actual training must have been considerably longer than the prescribed five years, and thus was bound to start at a much earlier age, most probably in childhood. This is proven by the Mishnah:

> "None that was not of age could enter the Temple Court to take part in the [Temple-] service save only when the Levites stood up to sing; and they [the children] did not join the singing with harp and lyre, but with the mouth alone to add spice to the music. R. Eliezer b. Jacob says: They did not help to make up the required number [*i.e.* twelve Levites standing on the Platform], nor did they stand on the Platform; but they used to stand on the ground so that their heads were between the feet of the Levites; and they used to be called the Levites' tormentors (*ẓoʿare*)."[47]

Ẓoʿare is a play upon words, originated by RASHI and BERTINORO. The assonance with *soʿade,* "helper," has given rise to the interpretation that the little singers, owing to their vocal quality ("to add spice to the music"), may have annoyed the adult singers, to wit made them jealous.[48] Thus, the levitical singers might have considered "the little ones" as dangerous competitors.

While the levitical singers accompanied themselves on lyres and harps, the boys sang "with the mouth alone"; by implication, this seems to indicate that they had the lead in singing, or at least that they doubled up the melody in the upper octave. In this tessitura, the pitch level of the boys was identical with that of the female voice; so it came to pass that after women had been eliminated from the levitical choir owing to a growing anti-feminine tendency of the priesthood, boys have taken over their functions. This gives the real significance to the controversial term *ʿal-ʿalamot,* to be found in the Book of Psalms and elsewhere in the Bible; this historical fact supplies evidence for the correct meaning of the term: "in the vocal range of maidens," *i.e.* in the bright treble of women—or boys.

To be sure, the rabbinic references to the use of boy-singers in the levitical choir imply the practice of the Second Temple; it is safe to assume, however, that the usage has already been instituted in the First Temple. Without an appropriately long training, the high artistic level and the famous musical precision of the levitical performances, repeatedly attested in the Scriptures, could not have been achieved.

The singing of the choir-boys in artistic ensembles warrants the assumption, if only by implication, that children in general might have had their own songs. This is corroborated by two parallel allusions to children's songs in the New Testament (Matth. 11:17 and Luke 7:32), from which we may infer, retrospectively, the existence of similar customs among Jews during the Old Testament era. For cradle songs, on the other hand, we have a direct, even if non-Jewish evidence: the "work-song" for nurses, mentioned by JOHN CHRYSOSTOM.[42] Although this item, too, refers to post-biblical times, we may assume *per analogiam* that cradle songs had been used in Ancient Israel, this being, in fact, a universal practice the world over, and at all times.

With male, female, and boys' voices, the Levites possessed all the elements essential for the tonal differentiation and coloring of choral singing on a high artistic level.

5. PSALM-SINGING

The most momentous feature of sacred singing in Israel, the summit of Jewish musical culture, was psalm-singing. The inward poetic and musical inspiration of the Jewish people centered wholly in the creation of psalms. The fact that other ancient Oriental peoples had also written and sung psalms does not alter the truth that the Israelites were the first to impart to this vocal form the artistic and ethical loftiness which even now, after millennia, exercises an irresistible sway upon the human mind.

> "Psalm-singing was the starting point for the higher development of Jewish music. Like poetry, tonal art, too, was governed by the supreme influence of religion; therefore, singing and playing have had primarily a serene, solemn, but by no means dull or gloomy character."[50]

We have to take this character into consideration if we are going to examine psalm-singing studiously.

As exposed in an earlier chapter, the Psalter was a collection of lyrico-religious poems, which were gradually adapted to ritual purposes. With the institution of an elaborate ceremonial of the sacred service and with the establishment of Temple music as an integral part of the ritual, the Psalter—even in its primitive and simple form—became the liturgical hymnal of Israel. This might have well been a powerful incentive for the creative urge of psalm-writers. It is significant that the early rabbinic literature mentions singing and playing as one of the sources of psalm-writing.[51]

In the early period of Temple music, psalm-singing had been the exclusive prerogative of professional levitical singers, both in the capacity of soloists and choristers. The Psalter has been originally designed for their use. Yet, as time went by, the mere passive participation of the worshippers in the divine service might not have satisfied the inner craving for a more rapturous communion with the ritual. This brought forth their desire to join the Levites in the songs of praise, which became reality when the worshippers began first to interject single words (acclamations), and then to repeat entire verses (refrains). This is the origin of the active participation of the congregation in liturgical singing, and from this primitive popular usage responsorial and antiphonal singing gradually developed in the sacred service.

The Babylonian exile was a period of suffering for the people, but this tribulation prepared them effectually for a deeper understanding of the religious and ethical values contained in the Psalter. In the ordeal of collective fate, the individual was bound to realize the import of the liberating and comforting song; only then could the psalms become real folksongs. After the return from the exile the Psalter ceased to be used exclusively by the sanctuary; it served the entire community for devotion and consolation.

> "Sprang from revelations of the sacred history of Israel, reflecting the religious background of the people, and speaking a language which emanated from the disclosure of intrinsic emotions, the psalms have been the best and most beautiful prayers and songs of the community,"[52] as well as of the individual.

Thus, the psalms have gradually become the common property of all Jews wherever they lived. In the period of the Second Temple, music and singing belonged undoubtedly to the subjects of general instruction in the schools.[53] It is obvious, therefore, that the psalms, or popular songs imbued with religious spirit, as they may be called, were best suited to foster music instruction on a large scale.

Some commentators maintain that the Psalter did not represent for the Jews a hymnal in the modern sense, but was merely a collection of poetry serving as prayers.[54] It is reasoned that the common people could hardly have been able to sing and perform such songs properly, since the psalms have had an irregular metrical setup and were not partitioned into easily grasped symmetrical strophes like, for instance, the hymns of later Christian congregations; therefore, as the reasoning goes, they had to be performed more or less in a recitative-like manner. This amounts to cantillation, a style and technique which conflicts allegedly with the principle of popular singing.

This, however, is but partly correct. For there are good reasons to believe that the people could actually participate in the levitical singing routine even beyond simple acclamations and refrainlike responses. One must recall that the basis of Oriental music is the *maḳamat,* ("tunes" or "melodicles"), which constituted the melodic skeleton of psalm-singing. The principal tunes have been known practically to everybody; this is a foregone conclusion in view of the high standard of music culture in Ancient Israel. It is therefore not too far-fetched to suppose that the people, or at least large sections of it, were able to follow the conventional melodic patterns.[55] This assumption is supported by an unmistakable evidence in the Book of Psalms. Its *shire ha-maʿalot,* "songs of the ascent," (Pss. 120-134) have been expressly designed to be sung by people marching in processions or pilgrimages. It is immediately evident that the melodic pattern of these psalms must have been based upon relatively simple and well-known tunes. Furthermore, the musical rendition of certain psalms actually requires an appropriate, and even substantial, participation of the congregation, as one may well judge from the poetic setup of some psalm-texts. Thus, Pss. 44, 47, 80, 99, 144 (verses 1-11) contain responses after each verse. Refrains for the congregation are frequently indicated at the beginning (Pss. 106, 107); sometimes both at the beginning and the end (Pss. 103, 104, 118). Ps. 136 is a perfect specimen of responsorial singing between the precentor (soloist) and the congregation (chorus) after each verse. Apart from responses specifically indicated by the text itself, refrain-like acclamations and similar psalmodic formulae have been spontaneously and rather frequently used by the congregants in other psalms as well. Such places have been designated mainly by the tradition of the Temple. To ensure a uniform response, the congregation received—at least in the Second Temple— a signal by winking with a piece of cloth.[56]

More substantial than such short acclamations were the responses of the congregation with the jubilant *Hallelujah,* applied sometimes at the beginning of a psalm, sometimes at the end, sometimes in both places. The opening lines of Ps. 113 show even three such acclamations:

> "Praise ye the Lord (*Hallelujah!*). Praise, (*Hallelu*) O ye servants of the Lord, praise (*Hallelu*) the name of the Lord!"

The most significant responses, however, were the doxologies of the worshippers, the lengthy glorifications attached at the end of each book of the Psalter (Pss. 41, 72, 89, 106). Considering its meaning and purpose, the last verse of Ps. 150 may likewise be taken as belonging to this category (and perhaps even the entire psalm as an elaborate and worthy conclusion of all five books). In these doxologies, the active participation of the congregation is at the same time a musical and a ritual necessity. This becomes evident from an example, which may be considered typical. 1 Chron. 16:23-36 is a song of praise, which in its contents, sometimes even in its wording, is quite similar to Ps. 96. It may even be assumed that the chronicler had the intention to present a slightly expanded version of this psalm. Above all, the psalm ends without a doxology, whereas the chronicler has appended one to his altered version. We may well assume that the psalm, too, has been sung in this way, and this, if warranted, would lead us to the conclusion that doxologies have been sometimes added to psalms which carry no indications to this effect.

o
o o

Religious singing has not been restricted to ritual occasions or to official public festivities. The intrinsic urge of the Jewish people to express its religious sentiment with singing, soon created the custom of embellishing private feasts with songs. According to ancient beliefs, people eating and drinking together in company were united spiritually in close friendship, and this feeling of solidarity was bound to manifest itself in singing jointly. The song was supposed to enhance the pleasures of a meal, and the Orientals enjoyed singing at banquets just as much as they were fond of perfumes, wreaths and other stimulants for increasing the joys of life. Especially the common sacrificial meals, connected with religious festivals, in which rich and poor participated with their families and friends, have taken place in high spirits and always with singing.

Among the festive celebrations, the historically and nationally significant Passover meal was outstanding in its embellishment with singing. The Pesaḥ-Haggadah, though fully developed only in the Midrashic era, might still contain remnants of certain songs which had been sung at the Passover meal in ancient times.[57]

At this meal, besides other songs, portions of the *Hallel* have been sung. All the participants joined in singing the first portion of the so-called "Egyptian *Hallel*" (Pss. 113, 114).[58] In pouring the fourth cup of wine, the second portion of this *Hallel,* Pss. 115-118, was intoned. This was followed by the so-called "Great *Hallel*" (Pss. 120-136). A passage of the Palestinian Gemarah, in which the contents of this song of praise are discussed, contains a reference to the effect that the precentor always sang the first half of a verse, the participants responding with the second half.[59] Perhaps the prophet Jeremiah has already alluded to these responses (Jer. 33:11).

The strongly developed consciousness of Israel as the people and community of God has found in singing the adequate expression for its spiritual yearnings. This is the reason why popular singing in small and large groups gained such a universal significance at religious feasts as well as in devotional pastime in the home.

o
o o

As mentioned earlier, the culminating point of the sacred ceremony at the Temple was the sacrifice. Each sacrificial action has had its own musical setting and specifically selected psalms. Gradually, a tradition has developd for the performance of particular psalms for the various sacrifices. Thus, the daily burnt, expiatory, laudatory offerings and libations had all a different musical layout, which was strictly regulated like any other part of the ritual.

The detailed descriptions of the Temple's musical liturgy, as furnished by the Bible, the Apocrypha, and the rabbinic literature, enable us to gain a clear insight into the sacrificial musical customs.[60]

The daily burnt-offering was performed with a rich musical display. It seems, however, that a specific psalm was not designed for this sacrificial act, whereas all other parts of the ritual had their own psalms. We find in the Mishnah a late description of this most important daily ritual.[61]

There was a different psalm assigned for each day. The Mishnah contains detailed indications as to the psalms designed for the week days, as well as for the Sabbath and the high holidays.[62]

On the first day of the week, Ps. 24 was sung in remembrance of the first day of the creation. On the second day the Levites sang Ps. 48, on the third Ps. 82, on the fourth Ps. 94, on the fifth Ps. 81, on the sixth Ps. 93, and on the Sabbath Ps. 92.[63] With the exception of the first day of the week, no reason is given for the choice of the daily psalms.

Specific psalms were also assigned for the festivals. One of the psalms (30) contains in its heading an indication with regard to its use at a particular (dedicational) liturgical ceremony.

The psalm of the day was intoned as soon as the high priest started to pour out the drink-offering.[64] It was sung traditionally in three sections; between these the singers and instrumentalists made a break, two priests sounded the sacred trumpets, and on this signal the people prostrated themselves for adoration.

In the morning and evening services of the Sabbath the sacrificial offerings were more numerous than on weekdays; they amounted for each of these services to as much as for the daily morning and evening services together.[65] Consequently, the musical setting of the Sabbath service, too, was much more elaborate and colorful. At the pouring out of the libation the Levites sang Ps. 92 which—like the psalm for the drink-offering on week days—was rendered in three sections, with blasts of trumpets and prostration after each section. At the additional drink-offering on the Sabbath the Levites intoned the "Song of Moses" (Deuter. 32). This was divided into six portions, verses 1-6, 7-13, 13-18, 19-28, 29-39, and 40-52, each one of these being still further broken up into three parts. After each of these subdivisions the priests gave three blasts of trumpets, and the people prostrated themselves. The psalm provided for the New Moon was sung only on weekdays; if a Sabbath fell on the New Moon, they sang the Sabbath-psalm. In the Sabbath-eve service they sang, in addition, the "Song at the Red Sea" (Exod. 15).

After the offerings have been finished, the Levites sang Ps. 105:1-5 in the morning service, and Ps. 96 in the evening service.

Calling the Name of God was always performed by the high priest to the accompaniment of levitical singing.[66]

All these were public offerings and their volume alone was considerable. Yet, it was dwarfed by the abundance of private offerings. Sacrificial gifts by individuals were offered all year round in such quantities that it was necessary to establish for them special offering ceremonies in addition to the regular services. These private offerings constituted a special feature of the Temple rites at Jerusalem. And with the approach of the high holidays the volume of private offerings became so huge that even the increased number of the officiating priests could hardly attend to the sacrifices with all the required ritualistic formalities.[67] The minute observation of the sacrificial rites was, according to the conception of Israel, the principal means of securing God's favor, and therefore the Levites, even levitical singers, were frequently obliged to assist the overburdened priests in the preparation of the sacrificial victims (*cp.* 2 Chr. 29:34). Since the offerings have always been accompanied by the singing of the Levites, the normal daily task of the levitical choir alone must have been considerable. On high holidays, the Levites must have had an uninterrupted musical service altogether.

As time passed, the functions of the levitical choir would be identified, as it were, with the sacrificial rite itself. Thus, the thank-offering was called *todah* ("praise"), and, eventually, the choir which regularly furnished the musical background for these daily offerings was itself called *todah* (Neh. 12:31-40).

o o o

Among the psalms sung at the high holidays, the group of the *Hallel*-psalms occupied the most prominent place. To this group belonged the "Egyptian *Hallel*," as Pss. 113-118 are called in the rabbinic literature, the "Great *Hallel*," Pss. 120-136, and Pss. 146-148, specifically called the *Hallel*-psalms."

At the Passover feast, during the offering of the paschal lamb, the "Great *Hallel*," or parts thereof, were sung. Ps. 135 has been considered particularly appropriate for this occasion because of the mentioning of Israel's liberation from the Egyptian yoke (verses 8 and 9).

At the Feast of Tabernacles Ps. 118:25 ff was sung at every morning-service. While the levitical choir was singing, the worshippers encompassed the altar and swayed the *lulab* carried in their hands. Subsequently the priests sounded the trumpets and on this signal the congregation retreated from the altar with the repeated exclamation "Homage [lit. 'Beauty'] to thee, O Altar!".[68]

At this festival three symbolic ceremonies, richly adorned with music, gained a paramount importance, although they were not connected directly with the Temple worship. To these belonged the ceremony of carrying wood for the burnt-offerings, the rite of water libation, and, finally, the popular festivity of *Bet ha-She'uba* (or *Sho'eba*), which took place at night in the Court of Women, with an abundant display of singing, playing instruments, and dance.

At the ceremony of carrying wood, which was held in the vineyards around Jerusalem, maidens in white garments and young men performed songs antiphonally and indulged in round-dances.[69]

The rite of the water libation is described minutely in the rabbinic literature.[70] We are told that a priest would go with a golden pitcher to the Siloam-pond, and after filling it would return to the Water-Gate. In entering the gate, the people would sing:

> "Therefore with joy shall we draw water out of the wells of salvation" (Isa. 12:3).

The procured water, together with a libation of wine, was then poured out as a drink-offering on the altar. During this ceremony the priests sounded the trumpets, whereupon the music started and the Levites sang the *Hallel*, as on the Passover festival. On this occasion, however, the *Hallel* was accompanied by pipes (*ḥalilim*), except on the first day of the festival and on the Sabbath day. After the sacrificial offerings, the priests marched around the altar in a solemn procession and sang Ps. 118:25:

> "We beseech Thee, O Lord, save now! We beseech Thee, O Lord, make us now to prosper!"

On the seventh day of the festival, the altar was thus encompassed seven times.[71]

The conclusion of the first day of the Feast of Tabernacles was a popular entertainment, the magnificence of which is intimated in the following Mishnaic comment:

> "He that never has seen the joy of the *Bet ha-She'ubah*, has never in his life seen joy."[72]

In the brilliantly illuminated Court of Women, with a multitude of women in its gallery, the most prominent Israelites, among them learned and famous rabbis, performed—like David did long before them—religious dances with burning torches and sang antiphonally hymns and songs of praise. The Levites were standing on the fifteen steps leading up from the Court of the Women to the Court of the Israelites, and accompanied the singing and dancing with instruments. According to another tradition, the Levites sang on this occasion the fifteen psalms called "Songs of the Degrees" (Pss. 120-134).[73] The rejoicing lasted until the cock-crow, when two priests gave a trumpet signal at the Nicanor-Gate. Then the participants turned toward East and the priests recited:

> "Our fathers turned with their backs toward the Temple of the Lord and their faces toward the east, and they worshipped the sun toward the east; but as for us, our eyes are turned toward the Lord. R. Judah says: They used to repeat the words 'We are the Lord's, and our eyes are turned to the Lord'."[74]

The *Hallel* was likewise sung with the accompaniment of *ḥalilim* at the prescribed sacrificial rites on the Feast of Weeks. During these particular ceremonies the levitical choir boys sang together with their fathers. The people participated in these songs as on Passover.

The New Moon was celebrated in the Temple with special offerings (Num. 28:11-15), at which the priests sounded the trumpets. The celebration of the New Moon in the seventh month, however, was considered a higher holiday, and on this occasion, when the drink-offering was poured out, Ps. 81 was sung. For the sacrificial rites at the evening service of this feast, a special psalm, the 29th, has been provided.

The Book of the Maccabees relates that the re-dedication of the Temple, after its desecration by ANTIOCHUS EPIPHANES, was celebrated "with songs and harps and lutes and with cymbals" (1 Macc. 4:54). In addition, rabbinic sources report that at this event the *Hallel* was sung.[75] Many commentators believe that Ps. 50 containing the sub-title "A song at the Dedication of the House," was sung at this re-dedication, but the claim of some exegetes that this psalm has been specially written for that occasion, cannot be proven. It seems more likely that the psalm had served for similar purposes already in the period of the Judaean kings. The frequent apostasy of the Jewish people and its penitent return to the true faith, together with the repeated re-dedication of the desecrated Temple, lend a strong probability to this supposition. Should the psalm have been written prior to the Babylonian exile, as some expositors maintain, it would probably have also been used at the dedication of the post-exilic Second Temple.

The Israelites have made regular pilgrimages to Jerusalem, at which singing and music was prevailing. Especially after the return from the Babylonian captivity, such journeys were considered essential for maintaining and enhancing the feeling of national and religious unity among the repatriates. PHILO reports that many thousands from numerous cities came yearly to the Temple from all provinces, by land, and by sea.[76] In the non-canonical "Psalterium Salomonis," written allegedly in the 1st century B.C.E., there is a poetical description (Ps. 11), showing how from East and West, from North and from the islands, the scattered worshippers of Israel assembled and took off for Jerusalem.

The pilgrimage three times a year to Jerusalem for the high holidays was a religious ordinance, to which every adult Jew was subjected.[77] The prophet Isaiah refers to the music and singing on such occasions:

> "Ye shall have a song as in the night when a feast is hallowed; and gladness of heart, as when one goeth with the pipe to come into the mountain of the Lord, to the Rock of Israel" (Isa. 30:29).

The psalmist, too, mentions the joys of pilgrimages:

> "These things I remember, and pour out my soul within me, how I passed on with the throng, and led them to the house of God, with the voice of joy and praise (*b'ḳol ꞉innah v'todah*), with a multitude that kept holiday" (Ps. 42:5).

Of this pilgrimage EDERSHEIM gives a detailed description which contains a vivid account about the role of singing during this religious procession,[78] and is, in its essentials, a paraphrase of the Mishnaic report about the semi-annual pilgrimages of the ʾ*Anshe Maʿamad* (see p. 184 ff.)

6. MUSIC IN THE SYNAGOGUE

While the Temple existed, psalm-singing has been the ritual background and, at the same time, the artistic adornment of the principal action of the cult, the sacrifice. To be sure, sacrificial prayers and songs have not been exclusive features of the Jewish religion alone; they are to be found in the rites of all ancient peoples. The difference, however, between these and the Jewish sacrificial ritual was

> "that the levitical singers invested the whole worship at the Temple with a spiritual character unknown before as they accompanied the sacrificial cult with their hymnal song and their elevating music."[79]

Unlike the Temple, the Synagogue had no altar, therefore it could not perform sacrificial rites. This, however, could not possibly prevent the transplantation of psalm-singing from the Temple into the Synagogue.

The origin of the Synagogue is shrouded in obscurity. And even though it must have been an age-old Jewish institution,[80] we possess historical records about the Synagogue only from a relatively late period immediately preceding the Christian era, when it already represented the central form of Jewish worship. According to rabbinic tradition, the origin of the Synagogue was traced back to Moses.[81]

The original aim of Sabbath meetings was not divine service, but rather study of the law. This explains why, even in later times, a mere subordinate role has been assigned to the worship and praise of Yahveh in the Synagogue as compared with religious instruction. The Mishnah contains detailed indications with regard to the reading of the Torah and the Prophets in the Sabbath meetings, whereas psalm-singing is not mentioned at all.

The earliest historical references to the Synagogue worship by a coeval witness are to be found in PHILO's writings.[82] Among these, the following passage strikes immediately one's eye:

> "Moses commanded the people to gather on the seventh day in a meeting place and to listen with awe and reverence to the lecture of the law, so that everybody would understand its meaning. And in fact,

they meet regularly and sit together, the crowd generally being silent, except when it is usual to join in with the reading."[83]

This description contains a distinct allusion ("to join in") to the active participation of the congregation in the lection which, in those days, already proceeded customarily in the form of cantillation; this participation might be taken as the first recognizable element of responsorial chanting in the Synagogue.[84]

A pertinent information concerning the purpose of the Synagogue—and, incidentally, the nature of its musical manifestations—is contained in another statement of PHILO, which testifies to the fact that the Sabbath meetings of his time have not been restricted exclusively to the instruction of the law. In this reference, he characterizes the Synagogue as a place of worship and prayer, adding that the participants perform "hymns, songs and canticles (*hymnoi, paianes, ōdais*)."[85]

No other medium has been more effective in creating the "communion of the soul with God," so characteristic of the Synagogue worship, than music and singing. The religious leaders of the people must have recognized this soon enough once they did not object to the transplantation of the music from the Temple into the Synagogue.

Apart from these psychological motives, there were also artistic considerations in the back of the gradual introduction of music into the Synagogue. With the Sabbath meetings firmly established as regular institutions of learning and worship, the congregations might have increasingly become aware of the fact that the emotional part of common worship has been disdainfully neglected. The contrast between the artistically stimulating service of the Temple and the essentially sober synagogal meetings, might have become too conspicuous. Thus a marked tendency might have fairly soon arisen towards lifting up the artistic standard of the Synagogue service, whenever the limited space and the modest musical means of the houses of worship outside of Jerusalem have made this possible. By no means can it be assumed that the Synagogue

> "completely renounced the aiding hand of religious rites designed to stimulate the senses."[86]

Just the contrary is true.

Psalm-singing, the tonal aspect of religious expression, was always considered an indispensable stimulant for adoration, and therefore it must have been introduced without much delay into Synagogue worship. Although singing of psalms did not constitute here a musical background to sacrificial ceremonies—for these were lacking in the Synagogue—it served an essentially similar purpose: to praise God in a form arising directly from the soul, namely with the aid of songs.[87]

With the destruction of the sanctuary by the Romans, the Jewish religion and all its established customs, including singing, would have been in extreme danger of being dissipated, had not the Synagogue become that institution that succeeded in maintaining the tradition.

> "Unlike the Temple, a synagogue could not be destroyed by an enemy. With the burning of the Temple, its entire sacrificial system

was obliterated. The destruction of any number of synagogue buildings entailed no change in the established liturgy or mode of worship. The Jews assembled anywhere in public or private were the real *synagōgē* which could conduct regular services like that held in the largest and most gorgeous structure."[88]

Centuries later, St. AUGUSTINE had to acknowledge admiringly:

"The Jews, although vanquished by the Romans, have not been destroyed. All the nations subjugated by the Romans adopted the laws of the Romans; this nation has been vanquished and, nevertheless, retained its laws and, inasmuch as it pertains to the worship of God, has preserved the ancestral customs and ritual."[89]

In these customs and ritual the traditional music was certainly included, as evidenced by innumerable references to it in the talmudic and patristic literature.

o
o o

From the time of the Second Temple, there are no direct contemporary records about the sacred service and psalm-singing in the Synagogue. Our knowledge of the early synagogal ritual is based on talmudic sources. These inform us that to lections, benedictions and short prayers, first mere portions of psalms and, eventually, entire psalms have been added.

The rabbinic tractate *Sopherim* contains numerous indications with regard to the use of psalms in the early Synagogue. It informs us about the psalms sung at various functions and about the reasons for their choice. We read there, for instance, that the Hallelujah-response has been ejaculated one hundred and twenty-three times by the congregation.[90] We find the confirmation of this in another place of the Talmud.[91] The verses of the *Hallel,* divided according to their poetical structure, give indeed the figure one hundred and twenty-three.[92]

Except for the fact that it was not accompanied by musical instruments, the singing in the early Synagogue was not essentially different from that of the Temple. The tonal system of the songs and the manner of their rendition were certainly identical; this is a foregone conclusion in view of the fact that at the inception of the Synagogue the levitical singers provided also for the musical part of the Synagogue service, which was held in the Temple court itself.

The Talmud gives a substantial description about the daily schedule of the levitical singers on a festival day. The report is based upon the authority of a prominent teacher, R. JOSHUA ben ḤANANIAH, and states:

"On the Feast of Water-Drawing . . . the first hour [was occupied] with the daily morning sacrifice; from there [we proceeded] to prayers; from there [we proceeded] to the additional sacrifice, then to the "House of Study,"[93] then the eating and drinking, then the afternoon prayer, then the daily evening sacrifice, and after that the Rejoicing at the place of the Water-Drawing."[94]

This report proves conclusively that, at least in the Synagogue which was established within the Sanctuary, the musical part of the service has been virtually identical with that of the Temple, if we discount, of course, the musical settings for sacrifices, which simply had no place in the Synagogue. This service was held in the court of squared stones, *lishkat ha-gasit,* where worshippers played and received daily instruction. Its head was called *Rosh ha-k'neset* and its chief functionary *ḥazzan ha-k'neset.*[95]

The instrumental part of the Temple music consisted mainly in accompanying the vocal numbers; therefore, the lack or reduction of instrumental music in the Synagogue after the destruction of the Temple would have had no influence upon the fundamental character of the sacred songs.[96] The talmudic statement that "the song may be sung even without the [attending] sacrifice,"[97] applies, no doubt, to the extensive practice of the Synagogue. While the Temple flourished, and adequately trained instrumentalists for the Jerusalem Synagogue, or Synagogues, were at hand, it is safe to assume that there has been no marked difference between their musical service and that of the Temple possibly with the sole exception of an increased number of musicians for the latter.[98] To be sure, psalm-singing in the Synagogue may have been reduced in quantity, but it served the same purpose: to enhance the religious devotion of the congregants. Even when instrumental music was eventually abolished in the Synagogue, singing survived unchanged, at least temporarily.

It is generally assumed that in the early Synagogues outside of Jerusalem singing was unaccompanied from the very outset. This, however, is only partly true. Certainly, in smaller communities, musicians able to accompany the complex Temple songs in a satisfactory fashion must have been lacking. But in the larger cities there might have been musicians sufficient in number and quality to meet the artistic requirements of sacred music. This assumption is corroborated by an unmistakable reference in the Mishnah. Among other instructions pertaining to music, the rabbinic writer indicates how to handle broken strings of the *kinnorot* and *nebalim;* he says that

> "they might tie up a string [of a musical instrument] in the Temple, but not in the province."[99]

This instruction proves that "in the province," *i.e.* in Synagogues outside of Jerusalem, singing was accompanied by the traditional Temple instruments. Moreover, the second part of the instruction,

> "and *in either place* it is forbidden to tie it up for the first time"

[*i.e.* before the playing started][100] confirms the fact that whenever musicians were available, outside of Jerusalem, instrumental music was a regular feature in the Synagogue service.

Continuing the synagogal practice, the Judaeo-Christians probably accompanied their psalm-singing with instruments as well. To be sure, the heathen population might have done this independently just as the Jews did. Nevertheless, it is logical to assume that the practice of the Judaeo-Christians originated largely from the Temple and Synagogue and not from pagan worship. The continuation of the Jewish tradition by the early Christians is proven repeatedly in the writings of the early Church Fathers.

Despite its official banishment after the national catastrophe in 70 C.E., the instrumental music in the Synagogue was indeed never completely abandoned, at least in some larger localities, as some well attested documents stemming from the Middle Ages, and even from much later times, unmistakably prove. Thus, BENJAMIN of TUDELA from Navarra, who in 1160-73 has made extensive travels in the Orient, reports in his diary about the musical practice in the Synagogue of Bagdad.[101] He refers to the learned Rabbi ELEAZAR ben ẒEMACH,

> "the master of one of the ten Hebrew colleges in Bagdad of that time, who was a descendant of the prophet Samuel and a man who knows the melodies that were sung in the Temple of Jerusalem during the time of its existence."[102]

A man with such claims was probably bent on rendering the ancient melodies in the traditional manner of the Temple; that is, with accompaniment. And in fact, there exists historical evidence to the effect that during the intermediate days of the Feast of Tabernacles, singing in the Synagogue of Bagdad was accompanied by instruments.[103]

Rabbi PETAḤYAH of REGENSBURG [Ratisbon] was another traveler, who toured the Orient in the 12th century. He furnishes a valuable description of the customs of the Jews whom he visited in Babylonia, Ashur, Media, and Persia.[104] His observations contain various details concerning synagogal music in the places referred to, among them the statement that psalm-singing was accompanied by instruments.[105]

In the book *Noga Ẓedeḳ,* published in Dessau in 1818, reference is made to medieval historical records, stating that as late as the 15th century, on the island of Corfu, the *Shemā* was accompanied with music (*b'niggun ha-musiḳa*).[106] And in the *Sidur Amsterdam*[107] there is an indication that in the Meisel-Synagogue at Prague

> "they used to play [in the Friday evening service] before *Lekah Dodi* a lovely melody by R. Solomon Singer with organ (*b'ʿugab*) and string instruments (*u-binebalim*)."[108]

All this is conclusive evidence that the playing of instruments in the Synagogue survived in some form, if only in isolated instances. Since the musical practice of the Temple, at least in its larger outlines, was taken over by the Synagogue, and this includes the use of instruments, it is certain that the Judaeo-Christians, too, continued the tradition of the Temple.[109]

The importance of the musical practice in the Synagogue cannot be overestimated if we consider the multitude of such houses of prayer and devotion, called in those times *didaskaleia, proseuchē* or *proseuktēria,* meaning "Houses of Study," or also *sabbateion,* "House of Sabbath." In most cities with a larger Jewish population there were several of these, and in some places even numerous Synagogues. According to the rabbinic tradition, Jerusalem had, at the time of its destruction by the Romans, 394,[110] and following another tradition, 480 Synagogues.[111] Every trade and profession had their own Synagogues in Jerusalem, where the members met for services.[112] The Jews from other cities, especially the Jews whose vernacular was Greek, for instance those from Cyrene, Alexandria, Cilicia, Tarsus, etc., possessed their own houses of prayer in Jerusalem,[113] as well as in other larger cities of Palestine. Tiberias had 13 Synagogues.[114] Alexandria had numerous Synagogues in various districts of the city.[115] At the time of Augustus, there were quite a number of Synagogues in

Rome.[116] The inscriptions of six of these Roman Synagogues are preserved.[117] In his travels through Asia-Minor and Greece, Apostle Paul has found Jewish Synagogues everywhere; in larger cities, like Damascus, Salamis on Cyprus, etc., even several of them.[118]

According to rabbinic tradition, every Synagogue in Jerusalem was provided with a grammar school and also a school for higher learning,[119] in which young people were instructed in the law and the poetical books of the Scriptures. The same may have been true, if to a lesser degree, for the numerous Synagogues in the provinces. The instruction of sacred texts always proceeded with the aid of singing, as stated explicitly by the Talmud:

> "If one reads the Scripture without a melody or repeats the Mishnah without a tune, of him the Scripture says, 'Wherefore I gave them also statutes that were not good.' "[120]

This method was based upon two practical considerations. On the one hand, chanting of the Scriptural text was looked upon as essential for clarity, the syntactical intelligibility and, not in the least, for the solemnity of the lection; on the other, the live experience showed that studying with chanting was infinitely more effective than the spoken word alone, in memorizing the text. Since the tradition was transmitted exclusively by oral means, chanting became an indispensable mnemotechnical aid in learning lengthy passages from the Scriptures.

One can, therefore, readily realize, how much the numerous houses of study, affiliated with the Synagogues, were bound to contribute towards the preservation and dissemination of Jewish singing.

7. THE ʾANSHE MAʿAMAD

From all that has been said above, it is obvious that the tradition of Temple-singing has been largely adhered to in the Synagogues of Jerusalem and its immediate neighborhood. How was this tradition carried, however, to far off communities, and how was it kept alive in such localities? This question is answered by the Mishnah.

It tells us about the institution of the *ʾAnshe Maʿamad,* an organization of laymen, delegates of the people, established mainly for the purpose of transplanting to far off places the routine of Temple liturgy in its authentic form. As Mishnah states, the institution had been created simultaneously with the organized Temple service:

> "The first prophets [David and Solomon] ordained twenty-four Courses, and for every Course there was a *Maʿamad* in Jerusalem, made up of priests, Levites, and Israelites [laymen]. When the time was come for a Course to go up, the priests and the Levites thereof went up to Jerusalem, and the Israelites that were of the selfsame Course came together unto their own cities."[121]

ʾAnshe is derived from the Hebrew noun *ʾish,* "man," *Maʿamad* means literally "place of standing." This was a term to designate a group of representatives from remote districts, corresponding to the twenty-four Courses of priests and Levites (1 Chron. 23:6; 25:7 ff). Matching these Courses, the country was divided into twenty-four sections. Each section had to delegate twice a year, always for a week, a representative to Jerusalem, who had to attend the Temple services and to participate in the sacrificial rites. What was the purpose of this participation? Doubtless, to make the *Ma'amad* thoroughly familiar with the details of liturgic usage. Back in their home towns, they would see to it that in their own place of worship, *i.e.* Synagogue, the rites, customs and songs should be performed according to the tradition of the Temple. The *Ma'amad* participated, so it says, in regular "refreshing courses," and received twice a year practical instruction in the liturgical ceremonial. They brought back with them the knowledge of the sacred routine and so, through their journey to Jerusalem twice a year, they helped to safeguard the tradition.

To disassociate these travels from presentiments of toil and weariness, and also to make the prescribed "courses" attractive to the participants, the courses have been timed so as to coincide with the seasonal events on which the people used to make pilgrimages to the holy city, in order to participate in the joyous festivals held on these occasions. The priests of the Temple knew how to render the journey of the *Ma'amad,* as well as their stay in the city, so attractive that they would regularly and gladly come to the courses. The journey itself had the appearance of a religious pilgrimage with music and singing. In Jerusalem, the *Ma'amad* attended the two most important and joyful annual festivals of the theocratic state: the offering of the first fruits in the spring, and the thanksgiving for the harvest in the fall, which also inaugurated the new year.

It was a particularly adroit psychological approach of the clergy to flatter the *Ma'amad's* personal vanity. These delegates from the provinces have been escorted to Jerusalem with solemn ceremonies and were received there with almost royal honors. They must have surely felt to be persons of standing, who have come to the holy city on an official and important mission. This might have aroused in them, apart from religious duty, a personal incentive. Certainly, no delegate would miss, without a serious reason, the opportunity to be honored and extolled by the priesthood and the people.

The Mishnah contains a detailed delineation of the pilgrimage of the *Ma'amad*:

> "[The men of] all the smaller towns that belonged to the *Ma'amad* gathered together in the town of the *Ma'amad* and spent the night in the open place of the town and came not into the houses; and early in the morning the officer [of the *Ma'amad*] said, 'Arise ye and let us go up to Zion unto [the house of] the Lord our God' [Jer. 31:6]. They that were near [to Jerusalem] brought fresh figs and grapes, and they that were far off brought dried figs and raisins. Before them went the ox [intended as a Peace-offering], having its horns overlaid with gold and a wreath of olive-leaves on its head. The pipe (*ḥalil*) was played before them until they drew nigh to Jerusalem. When they had drawn nigh to Jerusalem they sent messengers before them and bedecked their First-fruits. The rulers and the prefects [*i.e.* the chiefs of the priests and of the Levites] and the treasurers of the Temple went

forth to meet them. According to the honor due to them that came in they used to go forth. And all the craftsmen in Jerusalem used to rise up before them and greet them, saying, 'Brethren, men of such-and-such a place, ye are welcome!' The pipe was played before them until they reached the Temple Mount. When they reached the Temple Mount even Agrippa, the king, would take his basket on his shoulder and enter in as far as the Temple Court. When they reached the Temple Court, the Levites sang the song, 'I will extol Thee, O Lord, for Thou hast raised me up, and hast not suffered mine enemies to rejoice over me.'" (Ps. 30:2.)[122]

The Mishnah also informs us about the manner in which the instruction of the *Ma'amad* has taken place:

"Beforetime all that could recite [the prescribed words] recited them, and all that could not recite them rehearsed (*makrin*) the words [after the priest]; but when these [that could not recite them] refrained [out of shame] from bringing [their First-fruits] it was ordained that both, they that could recite them and they that could not, should rehearse the words [after the priest]."[123]

The term *makrin,* "to rehearse," (lit. "to repeat" after the reader) is an unmistakable sign that the liturgical text with all its particularities, consequently also with its cantillation, would be rehearsed until it was well anchored in the memory of the *Ma'amad.* Even more than for young people, the memorizing of lengthy passages with the aid of cantillation served as an effective mnemonic device for adults. Therefore, the *Ma'amad* must have been the most effective intermediary for the dissemination of liturgical chants all over the places inhabited by Jews.

To be sure, our sources do not reveal anything about the *Ma'amad* having received direct instruction in liturgical singing. It may be reasonably assumed, however, that this important phase of the ritual has not been neglected, especially when even a cursory musical instruction of some individuals, among the *Ma'amad,* with auspicious backgrounds could be expected to yield a modicum of practical results. An indirect evidence of this is the indication in the Mishnah that the *Ma'amad* were bound to assist at the sacrificial ceremonies. The Synagogue, as we know, had no sacrifices. What was then the purpose of this ruling? Evidently, to give those *Ma'amad* who had a certain musical knowledge, some insight into the substance and the technique of levitical singing.

It could be rightly argued that an "instruction" twice a year for only a week each time would hardly be sufficient to obtain even a smattering in the complex art of levitical singing. It must be stressed, however, that the basic melodic style of Jewish sacred singing was in no way different from Oriental singing in general. Anyone familiar to some extent with the rudiments of Oriental song could, without too much difficulty, grasp the most evident characteristics of Temple singing. Furthermore, it may well be surmised that the *Ma'amad* had been selected mostly from among such men who already had some preliminary notions about singing. However short the time allotted to such refreshing courses may have been, the intense and regular coaching might have accomplished its purpose, at least to a certain extent.

The institution of the *ʾAnshe Maʿamad* cannot be overestimated in the matter of dissemination and preservation of the Jewish sacred song. Through it, the knowledge of Temple melodies was carried into the farthest Jewish communities, and even if these melodies might not have been transmitted everywhere in their spotless purity, the *Maʿamad,* while they flourished, stood as the legitimate guardians of the musical tradition of the Temple.

8. SINGING OF JEWISH SECTS

In the concluding centuries of Israel's national existence singing, sacred as well as secular, attained a towering significance among the artistic manifestations of Jewish life. It is not surprising, therefore, that it has penetrated the hard core of the Jewish religious sects which, despite all their forms of living being so different from those of the average population, adhered strictly to the traditional musical practice as handed down by the forefathers.

Among the Jewish sects there were two, the Essenes and the Therapeutae, about which certain coeval historical records are preserved. Of these, the extant reports concerning the singing of the Essenes are rather scanty, but they afford nevertheless some insight into their world of music and the spiritual background connected with it.

The Essenes were a community of men,[124] mostly of mature age, who led a self-denying and godly life, renounced all mundane possessions and sustained a frugal existence based upon the strict observance of the rigid Mosaic laws. Their day started always with prayers and singing hymns.

> "Before sun-rising they speak not a word about profane matters, but offer up certain prayers, which they have received from their forefathers, as if they supplicated it to rise."[125] "After breakfast, when he [the priest] has a second time offered up supplication, as at the beginning, so at the conclusion of their meal they praise God in hymns."[126]

HYPPOLYTUS (2nd half of the 2nd century, d.c. 230 C.E.) gives even some indications about the character of these hymns, quoting the content of one of them:

> "From thee [comes] father, and through thee [comes] mother, two names immortal, progenitors of Aeons, O denizen of heaven thou illustrious man."[127]

PORPHYRY (233-c.304 C.E.) who, in his statements about the Essenes, follows in general JOSEPHUS' indications, adds to this a significant remark, saying that

> "they devote the Sabbath to singing praises to God and to rest."[128]

To this direct information we may add some pertinent details contained in the apocryphal book *"The Testament of Job,"* which KAUFMAN KOHLER calls *"An Essene Midrash on the Book of Job."*[129] It comprises some musical references, which, at first sight, seem to be unconnected with the practice of the Essenes. But, as KOHLER points out,

> "the Testament of Job belongs to a class of writings which are so pronouncedly Essene in character that the late Rabbinical schools felt

more or less forcibly called upon to disown or ignore them, while those sects . . . treasured them as precious depositories of great mysteries."[130]

It is related, for instance, that when Job invited the poor guests of his house to festive meals, he reminded them, under the sound of six harps and a ten-stringed cithara that they should give praise to the Lord. This strongly suggests that this has been exactly the practice of the Essenes.[131] For this purpose Job employed musicians all day, and when they were tired he took himself the cithara and played sacred music for his guests, "to give them respite from their labor."[132]

In a later chapter it is related that "a whole army sang in a chorus a royal song of lamentation," full of Essenic notions of hell, Satan's realm, and of Paradise, the seat of the blsesed.[133] About which KOHLER remarks that

> "it is a psalm such as only these Essene brotherhoods could have composed."[134]

To the sphere of Essenic thought and practice belongs also the aggadic tale that when the daughters of Job became entranced they

> "sang angelic hymns in the voice of angels, chanting forth the angelic praise of God while dancing."

One of the daughters even "sang in the language of the Cherubim," intimating a rapture of a supernatural character, which might very well have been akin to the religious fervour of the Essenes when chanting their hymns.

In these Midrashic tales music also plays an essential part when Job was about to end his earthly life. On his bed of sickness

> "after three days he saw the holy angels come for his soul, and instantly he rose and took the cithara and gave it to his daughter Yemima (Yemima=Day). And to Kassia (Kassia=Perfume) he gave a censer, and to Amalthea's Horn (=Music) he gave a timbrel in order that they might bless the holy angels who came for his soul. And they took these, and sang, and played on the psaltery, and praised and glorified God *in the holy dialect.*"[135]

If we disregard the metaphoric connotations of this passage, it may very well be assumed that the singing, playing of instruments, and praising God in an exalted language might have been similar to the funeral rites of the Essenes.

o o o

A particularly important role has been assigned to singing at the friendship- and love-feast, the *agapē,* of religious companies and sects. PHILO describes vividly such an *agapē* of the Therapeutae, the other Jewish sect which, like that of the Essenes, distinguished itself by a pious and God-fearing life. As PHILO reports,[136] the feast started with prayers, after which one of the participants expounded a passage from the Scriptures or a religious topic that was submitted to him. The didactic exercises were followed by singing, after which a frugal supper was offered. Then the nocturnal celebration started. The participants rised simultaneously, forming two choruses, one of men and one of women, and intoned hymns in honor of God, which were enlivened with round-dances. Finally, seized by the purest love of God, they united into a single chorus. PHILO states furthermore that the Therapeutae did not confine themselves to the performance of ancient synagogal and other Jewish sacred songs, but that—after the model of these songs—

> "they composed hymns and psalms to God, of many measures and set to many melodies, which they of necessity arranged in more dignified rhythms."[137]

Finally, we have scant records about the music practice of another Jewish sect, the Samaritans. In their sacred services psalm-singing alternated with readings from the law.[138]

o
o o

Love of music and the practice of it were similar among the early Christians, who in those days were generally looked upon as mere Jewish sectarians. And since they considered themselves to be full-fledged members of the Jewish faith, it was only natural that the early Christians continued using the songs of the Jewish liturgy.

The first Judaeo-Christians have held their services in the Temple (Acts 2:46,47; 3:1; 5:42; 21:26; 22:17; 24:17,18), or in the Synagogue (Acts 22:19; 26:11).

> "At the conclusion of the Sabbath, the Christians would gather together in their houses for the *agapē*. Throughout the night they would keep watch, reading the Scriptures, praying, singing psalms. In the early hours of dawn the Mass would be celebrated, after which the faithful resort to the Temple in order to assist at the offering of the Jewish sacrifice."[139]

It is a wide-spread belief that the artful singing of the levitical choir with its complex instrumental accompaniment could not have been taken over by the primitive liturgy of the first Christian congregations; whereas the supposedly simpler form of cantillation, as practiced in the Synagogue, could very well be regarded as the prototype of the Christian sacred song. This, however, is only partially true, for—as shown earlier—singing in the Temple and in the Synagogue have been basically similar in their contents, form, and technique, the only difference between them being the richer and more constant instrumental accompaniment of the former. Thus, whether we consider the liturgical song of the Christians as stemming from the Temple or the Synagogue, is a matter of only secondary importance.

In the New Testament psalm-singing is mentioned only in two passages (1 Cor. 14:26; James 5:13). But the reports of the Early Church Fathers about the meetings of the first Christians comprise numerous references to the paramount importance attached by the new religion to psalm-singing, as practiced in the traditional, *i.e.* Jewish, manner.[140]

As at the *agapē* of the Therapeutae, singing among the first Christians represented that element of worship, which was best suited to create and enhance the feeling of close communion between the congregants. The songs have been simple, unaffected, like popular melodies. The simplicity of singing in the Synagogue, in which every one was able to participate, was imitated by the early Christians. Apart from community singing, in which all took part, some of the excessively inspired individuals would give vent to the collective emotions of the worshippers in improvised chants. Such "new songs," kindled by the stirring enthusiasm of the people, passed from mouth to mouth, to become eventually the common property of the congregation. As a matter of fact, the first Christian songs have been either ancient synagogal chants, or were based upon Jewish "tunes," which were familiar to everybody at those times. Owing to the suddenly changed spiritual approach of the worshippers and to the uncommon manner of creating these items, they were considered to be "inspired songs," somewhat different from those of the ancient tradition. Some of their texts have been actually written down by the devout brethren,[141] and served as the basis for the primitive Christian liturgy.

The different categories of the above mentioned songs are the *psalmoi, hymnoi* and *ōdai pneumatikai,* mentioned by Apostle Paul (Eph. 5:19; Col. 3:16). He calls "psalms" the songs, which go under this name in the Old Testament, but also the songs of praise and thanksgiving specially composed by adepts of the new Christian faith, and the character of which resembles, in some way, that of the ancient Jewish psalms. The term "hymns" refers probably to biblical canticles, like Exod. 15, Judges 5, Isaiah 38, and indicates songs in a popular vein. The songs called *ōdai pneumatikai,* "spiritual songs," however, were the free effusions of religious ecstasy, songs which were either wordless or else drew their subjects from the Scriptures and leaned heavier on the liturgy than the more popular *psalmoi* and *hymnoi.*

9. THE SCROLLS DISCOVERED AT THE DEAD SEA

This chapter would be incomplete without mentioning another Jewish sect which came into light and fame through the discoveries of ancient Hebrew scrolls found since 1947 in a number of caves on the shores of the Dead Sea, seven and a half miles south of Jericho, in a place called *Khirbet Qumrān.*

At this place a monastic Jewish community might have flourished from about 100 B.C.E. to 68 C.E., according to some authorities. Extensive excavations have unearthed a city of ruins and the remnants of a large cemetery testifying to a highly developed communal organization. The community in question is generally called the "Qumrān Sect" after the name of the site of these ruins.

The discovered scrolls raised a considerable stir among biblical scholars, both Jewish and non-Jewish, mainly because of the still unsettled question about their origin and the time their authors are supposed to have lived. One group of scholars places them into the pre-Christian era,[142] by which the musical references contained in them would rightfully belong to the scope of our investigations. Another group, however, maintains that the scrolls could not have been composed at that time as, judging from a number of evidences, they represent typical karaitic literature.[143] The Karaites were a Jewish sect which seems to have arisen around the 7th century of our era and, according to ZEITLIN, who is the chief advocate of their authorship, the scrolls were composed sometime between the 7th and 12th century. This, naturally, would place the musical references in the scrolls outside of our investigation, unless we project them back, historically, that is, try to tie them up with the musical usage of the ancient Hebrews and consider them, possibly, as late remnants of similar practices of the Jewry of the Second Commonwealth.

In the present stage of the clashing opinions it is difficult to take sides. Inasmuch, however, as the musical references in the scrolls are contained in genuinely Jewish writings and, furthermore, as they might reflect, even if retrospectively, the Jewish musical culture of the era presented in our study, we feel justified to incorporate them into our investigations.

o
o o

Among the discovered scrolls there is an elaborate treatise in which the rules and laws of the Qumrān brotherhood are laid down in all their minutest details and which, therefore, is called by modern scholars the *Manual of Discipline.* Its eleven columns regulate every phase of the communal life of the members of this pious group, who lived strictly according to what they believed to be the divine ordinances. It was a priestly community inasmuch as it was directed by priest-like superiors, who called themselves "the Sons of Ẓadok", the descendants of David's high priest. Hence, the Qumrān Sect is also called "the Ẓadokites".

This sect shows distinct affinities with that of the Essenes;[144] so much so, in fact, that some modern scholars consider the Ẓadokites and the Essenes to be one and the same Jewish sect.

The assumption of the latter opinion would force us to conclude that the musical practice of the Ẓadokites was identical with that of the Essenes. The question arises, however, whether the discovered documents justify such an assumption from the musical point of view. This would be tantamount to asking whether there are any references in the Dead Sea Scrolls affording us some insight into the musical practice of the Qumrān Sect, and thus enabling us to make comparisons with that of the Essenes. Unfortunately, the Scrolls contain but scattered references to music, which do not vastly enrich our knowledge of the musical practice of this Jewish sect.

On the other hand, there are indications which are apt to minimize considerably the value even of the few musical references found in the Dead Sea Scrolls. SOLOMON ZEITLIN expressed serious doubts as to the authenticity of the discovered documents. In a number of essays, scrutinizing the subject historically and linguistically, he endeavored to show that the Dead Sea Scrolls are erroneously placed into the pre-Christian era. Taking into account their ideas, language, grammar, orthography, paleography and other characteristics, ZEITLIN concluded that these scrolls are typical karaite literature.[145] He supposes that they were placed much later into the caves, where they have been found recently.[146]

Regardless of the outcome of this controversy between the two opposite factions of biblical scholarship, we cannot shun the necessity of discussing the musical references found in the scrolls, be it only for the sake of completeness. We have to leave it to further investigations whether these references are likely to shed any new light upon the musical practice of the pre-Christian Jewish sects or have merely an historical value in fortifying the widely accepted opinion that the ancient musical culture of the Jews lived forth in the medieval period.

o
o o

Among the musical references of the scrolls the most numerous and the most significant are those to be found in two treatises, the *Psalms* (or *Hymns*) *of Thanksgiving* and *The War Between the Sons of Light and the Sons of Darkness.*

Like many poems of the Psalter, several of these later hymns open with the formula "I give thanks unto the Lord". Some other poems begin with the phrase "Blessed are Thou". "Blessing", in Hebrew Antiquity, has denoted not only a formula of benediction, but also a specific type of religious poetry. Accordingly, GASTER suggests as an adequate title of this collection of hymns *Blessings and Thanksgivings* (*Berakot v'Hodayot*), a title which corresponds to the form as well as to the contents of these post-biblical psalms.[147]

We may safely assume that these newly composed religious poems were performed more or less similarly to those of the canonical Psalter, that is in an appropriate musical setting, and either accompanied or unaccompanied by instruments.

Let us now look into the role that music plays in these new psalms.[148]

Psalm II (column II:11 of the scroll) contains the expression

"A song (*neginah*) was I unto transgressors".[149]

This is evidently an allusion to Job 30:9 and Lam. 3:14, where the same word, but in the form *neginatam,* is used in the meaning of a "song of derision".

Psalm IX (V:13) mentions another kind of "song":

"Thou hast heard my cry,
and in my sighing discerned
the song (*rinnat*) of my pain".

It is doubtful, however, whether "song" in this context has any musical connotation.

A genuine musical reference is contained in Psalm X (V:30):

"They thundered abuse of me
to the tune of the harp (*b'kinnor*),
and in jingles (*neginot*) chorused (*yaḥad*) their jeers".

This might refer to some mocking or satirical song destined to make the complaining author (or psalmist) the laughing-stock of a company of drunken revelers.

Psalm XVII (XI:5) uses some musical metaphors in a highly descriptive way:

"For Thou hast made me to know Thy deep, deep truth,
and to divine Thy wondrous works,
and hast put in my mouth the power to praise,

and psalmody (*hodot*)[150] on my tongue,
and hast given me lips unmarred
and readiness of song (*rinnah*),
that I may sing (*va'azammrah*) of Thy lovingkindness
and rehearse (*esoḥaḥah*)[151] Thy might all the day
and continually bless Thy name".

Psalm XVII (XI:14) applies still another musical metaphor:

"Thou hast granted it unto man . . .
to stand in one company before Thee
with the host everlasting and the spirits of knowledge
and the choir indivisible (*b'yaḥad rinnah*)" [literally:
those versed in "concerted song"].

The psalmist obviously refers here to the Jewish Morning service on Weekdays which alludes to the angelic choir as "all of them opening their mouth in holiness and purity, in song and chant . . ."

The author of Psalm XVIII (XI:22-27) makes use of the "moaning sound of the harp" (similarly to Isa. 16:11), thus characterizing musically the affliction of his soul:

"These things went to my heart
and touched me to the bone,
that I raised a bitter lament
and made doleful moan and groan
and plied my harp (*kinnor*) in mournful dirge . . .[152]
But suddenly I perceived
that there was no more affliction
to rack me with pain.
Then did I ply (*ʾazammerah*) my harp (*kinnor*)
with music of salvation,
and my lyre (*nebel*) to the tune of joy;
yea, I plied the pipe (*ḥalil*) and the flute[153]
in praise without cease.
Albeit none among all Thy works
can rehearse (*y'hulal*) the full tale of Thy mercies (or "wonders"),
yet, in the mouths of them all
may Thy name be praised;
to the meed of their understanding
they yet may bless Thee for ever
and chorus (*yaḥad*) their songs (*rinnah*) of triumph
all the day long".

Here, the psalmist uses the well-known biblical pattern of associating the transition from sadness to joy with the sound qualities of various musical instruments (cf. Ps. 30:11, a.o.).

To the main body of poems of this collection of *Psalms of Thanksgiving*, GASTER prefixes another one, which in the *Manual of Discipline* stands at the end. It is evidently a recapitulation, sometimes verbatim, of the rules of the Brotherhood, and it is assumed that it was a hymn chanted by the initiants when they were formally admitted to the community. Therefore, GASTER thinks its proper place to be at the head of the hymn book and, accordingly, he calls it *The Hymn of the Initiants.*[154]

Its Stanza 10 (according to GASTER's arrangement) reads:

"I shall hold it as one of the laws
 engraven of old on the tablets
to offer to God as my fruits—
 the praises of my tongue,
and to cull for Him as my tithe
 —the skilled music of my lips" (*ʾazammerah bedat*).[155]

GASTER's translation is quite arbitrary. It gives, in a rather free interpretation, only a vague idea of the Hebrew original. Furthermore, it leaves out entirely the reference to three musical instruments mentioned in the Hebrew text: *kinnor, nebel* and *ḥalil.*

DUPONT-SOMMER, in his rendering of this passage, approaches more closely the meaning of the original:[156]

"For as long as I exist
 the engraved Ordinance shall be upon my tongue
As a fruit of praise,
 and the offering of my lips.
I will sing (*ʾazammerah*) with knowledge,[157]
 and my lyre[158] will vibrate the Glory of God
And my lute (*kinnor*) and my harp (*nibli*)
 for the holy Order of which He is the author.
And I will raise the flute (*ḥalil*) of my lips
 on account of his righteous cord".

Still, even this translation does not follow exactly the original text. We add, therefore, a literal rendering of the Hebrew passages, without venturing to express ourselves in a poetic form:

"I will sing (*ʾazammerah*) with knowledge
 and all my singing (*neginati*) [will be] to the Glory of God.
And the lyre (*kinnor*) [and] my harp (*nibli*)
 for the perfection (*tikun*) of His Holiness.
And I will raise the flute (*ḥalil*) of my lips
 in the cord of His judgment."

The idea of praising God in singing is expressed in several other verses of this same hymn, so for instance in Stanza 16:

"When first I go or come,
when I sit and when I rise,
when I lie down on my couch
I will sing (*ʾarannenah*) unto Him."

Also in Stanza 18:

"Whenever distress breaks out,
 I still will praise Him;
and when His salvation comes,
 join the chorus of praise (*ʾarannenah yaḥad*)."

In Psalm VI (III:19-22) GASTER translates two different Hebrew phrases in the same way: "to praise Thy name in their chorus," which reads in the original *v'labo b'yaḥad,* and shortly after *l'halel shimḥah b'yaḥad.*

It should be mentioned, furthermore, that GASTER uses frequently the expression "to rehearse" in his translations. This seems to imply some sort of musical connotation which, however, is completely lacking in the original. GASTER applies this translation, among others, for the Hebrew words *ʾesoḥaḥa* (Psalm XVII, col. X, line 5), *y'hulah* (Psalm XVIII, XI:26), *dab'ru* (The Oration of Moses), *m'bor'kim* and *m'sap'rim* (Manual of Discipline, I:16 ff), as well as in other places.

The *Manual* refers to the morning and evening prayers of the Zadokites. The pious member of the Covenant exercises his fundamental obligation unswervingly:

"With the coming of day and night
    I shall come ever anew
    into God's Covenant;
and when evening and morning depart,
    I will recite (*ʾemor*) His Ordinance" (col.X.).[159]
[or, in Gaster's translation:
    "shall observe how He sets their bounds."][160]

What the author of this hymn wants to express by "recite," is clearly shown by an indication in another treatise which describes the manner of performing the daily prayers. *The Book of Jubilees* (or *Seasons*) deals with the division of the year into four seasons of three months each, establishing a chronological system for a specific calendar for the Sect of the Covenant. This book starts with:

"During the periods, I shall chant the Ordinance" (after
    Dupont-Sommer).

Thus, it is clearly established that the daily prayers were rendered in a chanting fashion.

In the *War Between the Sons of Light and the Sons of Darkness* it is stated that before the battle the priest intones a warlike song, the text of which consists mostly of biblical quotations (X:1 ff).[161] After the battle the entire army shall intone "the hymn of return . . . and they shall extol His Name in joyful unison" (or, after GASTER, "together with joy," *y'rannenu kulam,* XIV:2). (About further musical references in the *War* see p. 338, 499 ff).

o
o o

All in all, neither the *Psalms of Thanksgiving* nor the *Manual of Discipline* or the other tractates reveal anything that cannot be found either in the Scriptures or in the early rabbinic writings. Thus, except the rather hypothetic use of trumpet signals as reflected in an imaginary battle (see pp. 500 ff), the musical implications of this newly discovered literature have largely a mere corroborative value in the description of the ancient musical culture of biblical and post-biblical Jewry.

10. CHRISTIAN PSALM-SINGING IN TALMUDIC TIMES

We have followed the development of Jewish singing unto the cross-road where it merges with the liturgy of the new Christian community and becomes the assistant of the new religion. From here to the later historical stage where the original Jewish song has been conspicuously transformed and became the tonal symbol of the new Church, there was still a long way. At first, its ethos remained unchanged, its substance and its form having not been subject to any essential modification. The development of music was slow and hesitant in those days. Even the different languages (Greek, Latin, Syriac, etc.) could not alter substantially the character of the Jewish song. Inasmuch as psalms did not have a quantitative metric structure (see later), the melodic pattern of Jewish singing could adapt itself easily to the rhythm of other languages.

Only in the course of several centuries has Jewish singing been gradually transformed. It has lost more and more its Oriental-Jewish characteristics and, through a slow metamorphosis, became assimilated to the new liturgic use, eventually merging completely with the alien Christian liturgical singing. At this stage of evolution it remained temporarily hidden to historical observation and emerged only in recent times in its original state, when the affinity of the Temple song of Ancient Israel with the liturgical song of the early Christian Church has been rediscovered by musicologists.

However, prior to its complete transformation, the Temple song of Ancient Israel exercised for a long period a beneficial influence upon the liturgical music of the new Church. The reliable patristic chroniclers of the new faith have properly appreciated the religious, moral and ethical qualities of Jewish Temple singing. Their writings are full of praise for psalm-singing in the ancient Davidic style, that is in the tradition of the Temple.

> "Patristic utterances on liturgical music give an important insight into the character of its predecessor, the Temple music of the Hebrews. The early Church Fathers lived in a period following relatively closely on the heels of the times during which Hebrew Temple music still flourished. The continuation of tradition and the clinging to old customs and practices were axioms of the early Christian church. Jesus himself said of the new religion: 'I am not come to destroy, but to fulfill' (Matthew 5:17). Consequently, everything the early Church Fathers say about the liturgical music of the first centuries sheds light on Jewish music, and especially on Jewish song itself, which lived on practically unchanged in early Christian liturgy."[162]

Numerous passages in the patristic literature refer to the ancient Jewish tradition of psalm-singing. AUGUSTINE (354-430 C.E.) speaks of the "old [Jewish] usage of singing in the church,"[163] and states explicitly that the "Alleluja was chanted according to the old [Jewish] tradition."[164] EUSEBIUS PAMPHILIUS of CAESAREA (ca. 260-ca. 340 C.E.), in his "History of the Church," describes "the divine mission of the apostolic men of his [Philo's] day, who were, it appears, of Hebrew origin, and thus still preserved most of the ancient customs [musical ones as well] in a strictly Jewish manner."[165] HERMIAS SOZOMENES SALAMENES (fl. 443) reports that JOHN CHRYSOSTOM "introduced antiphonal chanting [according to the Hebrew tradition] in Constantinople."[166]

He also relates that

"BARDESANES [d.233] and his son HARMONIOS composed a complete gnostic Psalter of 150 psalms to be sung to the lyre (*ad lyrae cantum*) [*i.e.* in the ancient Jewish fashion]."[167]

As AUGUSTINE says,

"hymns and psalms should be sung according to the Oriental [Jewish] custom,"[168]

and CASSIODORUS (ca. 480-ca. 575 C.E.) gives us a description of psalmody "as sung in the traditional manner."[169] ISIDORE of SEVILLE (ca. 560-636 C.E.), too, describes in detail the responsorial psalmody in its original form and confirms the antiquity of this special usage.[170]

No wonder that singing of psalms in the traditional Jewish style spread quickly in the new religion. AUGUSTINE states that

"though verily they be already sung all over the world (the psalms of David, these faithful songs, these sounds of devotion)."[171]

ANASTASIUS (9th century), in his

"History of the Roman popes," tells that ST. DAMASUS "ordered psalms to be sung by day and by night in all the churches."[172]

According to EUSEBIUS PAMPHILIUS of CAESAREA,

"the command to sing psalms applies to all Churches among the various nations,"[173]

and another assertion of EUSEBIUS testifies to the pleasure shown by the people for this new experience:

"Throughout the whole world, in towns and villages and in the fields also, in short, in the whole Church, the people . . . sing to the one God . . . hymns and psalms with a loud voice, so that the psalm-singers are heard by those standing outside [the place of worship]."[174]

That these have been the ancient Jewish traditional psalms is attested by Pope LEO I (LEO the GREAT, d. 461):

"Davidic psalms are sung everywhere in the Church with all the piety."[175]

Both sexes, of all ages, participated in psalm-singing. AMBROSE (4th century) refers to responsorial singing of psalms by men, women, maidens, and children,[176] and observes in particular:

"But they [the women] also do well to sing their psalms: it is sweet for every age and suitable for either sex . . . and it is a great bond of unity when all the people rise their voices in one chorus."[177]

THEODORET (ca. 393-ca. 457 C.E.) ordered men and women of all ages to sing psalms and hymns.[178] VENANTIUS FORTUNATUS (d.ca. 600) reports that

"clergy, laymen, and even children, join together in the singing of psalms."[179]

At the time of BASIL the GREAT (ca. 330-379 C.E.) certain transformations must have already taken place in the original psalm melodies because of their reworking for the usage of his contemporaries.

"Therefore, the melodies of the psalms were adapted for us [Christians] by the use of Modes, so that young boys as well as mature men enjoy them, so to say, as if they were singing the psalms to their [familiar] tunes."[180]

Needless to say, the sheer fact of "adaptation" mentioned in this passage betrays most unmistakably the purely Jewish rendition of psalms by Christian congregations prior to this initial and probably cautious change.

JEROME (ca. 340-420 C.E.) says that

"even little girls were obliged to sing psalms."[181]

The average psalms must have been known so well that anyone was able to sing them without difficulty and with all the desired perfection. This is confirmed by JOHN CHRYSOSTOM (347?-407 C.E.):

"though men and women, young and old, are different, when they sing hymns, their voices are influenced by the Spirit in such a way that the melody sounds as if sung by one voice."[182]

Singing psalms by laymen has been a matter of the heart and sentiment; with the clergy and other servants of the new religion, on the other hand, it soon became a religious duty. JEROME, in a letter to the monk RUSTICUS, gives him the advice, which sounds almost like a command:

"Thou must learn the psalms word for word by heart."[183]

And in another letter to the virgin EUSTOCHIUS, he commends the nuns of the convent of St. Paula, but says that

"no sister may remain, if she does not know the psalms."[184]

How extensive psalm-singing has become among the servants of the Church at those times, is evident from the report of JOHN CASSIAN (360-435 C.E.), in which he states that

"many Eastern monks used to sing 20 or 30 psalms and more each night."[185]

Comments on responsorial and antiphonal singing interlace the writings of the early Fathers of the Church like red yarns. Numerous statements attest to the continuity of this ancient Jewish style of singing. AMBROSE describes the responsorial singing of psalms, as practiced by men, women, maidens and children.[186] AUGUSTINE states that the psalms have been intoned by the precentor, while the congregation answered responsorially.[187] EUSEBIUS quotes from PHILO's *Peri biou theorētikou* ("On the contemplative life") and praises the antiphonal singing of the Therapeutae.[188] BASIL the GREAT makes a precise distinction between the two forms of singing alternately:

"Divided into two groups . . . people sing [the psalms] antiphonally . . . Then again after entrusting to one person to lead the chant, the rest sing the response; and so having passed the night in a variety of psalm-singing . . . as the day begins to dawn all in common, as of one voice and one heart, intone the psalm of confession to the Lord."[189]

CHRYSOSTOM[190] and CASSIODORUS[191] likewise report about responsorial singing, and ISIDORE of SEVILLE confirms

"the great antiquity of this particular usage,"[192]

as well as the fact that

"the singing of the Alleluia descends from the liturgy of the Hebrews."[193]

TERTULLIAN (ca. 150-ca. 230 C.E.), too, makes reference to the singing of the *Alleluia* and of the psalms in responsorial form.[194]

CASSIODORUS describes the lengthy Alleluia-jubili:

"The tongue of the singers rejoices in it; joyfully the community repeats it; and . . . it is renewed in ever varying melismata (*tropis*)."[195]

And JOHN CASSIAN states that

"certain psalms were lengthened by antiphones and the addition of special 'modulations.' "[196]

According to SOCRATES of CONSTANTINOPLE (fl. 5. century), it was St. IGNATIUS of ANTIOCH who introduced into the Church the ancient usage of singing hymns and psalms antiphonally.[197] In his *"History of the Church,"* THEODORET names two men, FLAVIANUS and DIODOROS,

"who were the first to teach the antiphonal singing of Davidic hymns, the choir of the singers being divided into parts."[198]

As mentioned earlier, apart from Davidic psalms, soon new hymns and psalms have been created, born out of the inspiration of individual poets; PHILO reports already about the Therapeutae that

"they do not confine themselves to contemplation but also compose hymns and psalms of God in all sorts of metres and melodies which they write down in solemn rhythms as best they can."[199]

EUSEBIUS states that Psalms used to be adapted to new melodies:

"When some one had started to sing a psalm to a soft melody, the congregation, at first, would listen in silence, and only sing in chorus the last verses of the hymn."[200]

TERTULLIAN mentions also that the devout brethren used to sing hymns and psalms of their own creation:

"After . . . bringing of lights, each is asked to stand forth and sing, as he can, a hymn to God, either one of the holy Scriptures or one of his own composing."[201]

From the very beginning, such new songs have been zealously collected by those among the brethren who were able to write down their texts, as stated by EUSEBIUS:

"The psalms and songs of the brethren were compiled by the faithful from the earliest days."[202]

These have been

"the new songs, the songs of the Levites, with their eternal strain that bears the name of God and which gave order and harmony to the universe,"

as CLEMENT of ALEXANDRIA (d.ca. 215) says.[203] In another passage he calls them

"at the same time psalmodic and prophetic,"[204]

an interpretation shared by JOHN CHRYSOSTOM, who likewise characterizes them as

"prophetic songs."[205]

In accordance with early Christian propensities, EUSEBIUS attributes mystical significance to psalm-singing.[206]

Not all "new songs" had been considered worthy to become the common property of the new Church, but only those which were in conformity with the ancient Jewish spirit. St. PAUL and STEPHEN (1st century) have already set up certain rules for the monks of their times, which contain precise instructions concerning these new songs:

> "Nobody may either meditate upon or recite responses and antiphones in the congregation, which are sung by some of their own musical setting and which are not taken from canonical Scripture."[207]

The Church Fathers branded all "new songs" contrary to the essence of Jewish tradition as heretical. So ATHANASIUS (ca. 298-373 C.E.)

> "disapproves of ARIUS' exquisite heretical songs [so different from the Jewish chant],"[208]
>
> and EPIPHANIUS (ca. 315-403 C.E.)
>
> "condemns the heretic psalms composed by HIERAKAS, which do not conform to the ancient [Jewish] tradition."[209]

TERTULLIAN tells us that

> "the apostates MARCION and VALENTINUS spread heretical psalms [different from those composed by David],"[210]

whereas PAULUS SAMOSATENUS

> "abolished [in his congregation] the singing of hymns . . . which had been written recently by composers of the day,"[211]

and reinstituted the ancient Hebrew tradition.

Singing of psalms has been for the new Christians one of the strongest stimulants for religious exaltation and furnished all the participants with an emotional experience which is reflected again and again in the writings of the Church Fathers. AUGUSTINE speaks of

> "the great delight of the brethren, singing together [sacred songs] both with voice and hearts."[212]

LEO the GREAT, too, describes minutely

> "the emotional effect of congregational singing,"[213]

likewise EUSEBIUS, who gives a vivid delineation of the

> "variety of psalmodic melodies and the delight of the brethren in them."[214]

All these utterances provide only some general notions about the character of psalm-singing of that epoch. The Church Fathers afford, however, many a valuable hint about the melodies of these songs, which must have been apparently quite attractive. GREGORY NAZIANZEN (ca. 330-ca. 390 C.E.) characterizes the psalms as "angelic,"[215] this certainly being related to the melodies, as evidenced by another coeval report. PAMBO, abbot of the Egyptian monastery of Nitria, a contemporary of GREGORY,

> "reproached one of his monks for listening to the magnificent chants at the monastery of St. Mark in Alexandria with the purpose of introducing these chants into his own monastery."[216]

According to the instructions of St. PAUL and STEPHEN,

> "the manner of singing psalms . . . always be . . . with a sweet

melody."[217]

AUGUSTINE describes the emotional power of these melodies in the famous passage of his "Confessions," in which he says:

> "How abundantly did I weep to hear those hymns and canticles of thine, being touched to the very quick by the voice of the sweet church song."[218]

To be sure, this conflicts somewhat with ISIDORE's characterization of psalm-singing in the early Church:

> "In the primitive church psalms were sung in such a way that the singer made his voice resound by only a slight inflection, so that it was rather solemn declamation than singing."[219]

But it is obvious that ISIDORE's statement refers to the earliest times of the new religion, and probably in one particular locality, whereas the other reports quoted above represent the later, a more developed stage of psalm-singing. This assumption is corroborated by a statement of AUGUSTINE, who says that

> "ATHANASIUS, Bishop of Alexandria, caused the reader of the psalm to sound it forth with so little warbling (*modico flexu*) of the voice, as that it was nearer to speaking, than to singing,"[220]

and at the very same time praises

> "the old [Jewish] usage of singing in the Church, when they [the psalms] are set off [*i.e.* sung] with a clear voice and a suitable modulation."[221]

"Suitable modulation" indicates unmistakably the melodic character of singing, as contrasting to the speech-melody, or cantillation of earlier times.

The emotional power of psalm-singing has been carried at times so far that words to the melody were considered superfluous. Solo-singers, in a sort of religious ecstasy, dropped the consonants, so that their singing acquired a mystic implication which suited very well the intentions of the early Church. These are the songs of which AUGUSTINE says:

> "He who rejoices needs no words; for the song of delight is without words."[222]

In two places of his writings, JOHN CHRYSOSTOM expresses the same idea in a somewhat altered form:

> "It is allowed to sing psalms without words, as long as the mind resounds within. For, we do not sing for men, but for God who can hear even our hearts and penetrate into the secrets of our soul."[223]

The most customary of these wordless hymns has been the singing of the *"Alleluiah."* It consisted in leaving out the consonants and pronouncing only the vowels A E U I A; later, these vowels have been replaced by those of the doxology, *Seculorum amen,* E U O U A E.[224] Such wordless ecstatic songs were called *jubilus,* songs of praise to exalt the Eternal, gushing forth from the most elevated religious emotions, as characterized so pertinently by JEROME:

> "*jubilus* is [the song] which cannot be expressed or understood either in words, or in syllables, or in letters, or in [any] other [speech] utterance."[225]

We do not know whether the ancient Israelites availed themselves of such wordless singing, although its occasional interjection during frenzied prophetic ecstasies would be quite in keeping with the customary Oriental practices. (*Cf.* 1 Corinth. 14:7,8,9,15). A faint allusion to this may be found in AUGUSTINE's report that the "'*Alleluia*' was chanted according to the ancient [Jewish] tradition."[226] It is, however, more likely that this statement implied the structure of the melody rather than wordless singing, which—in all probability—was born with the new religion.

In general, the highest significance has been attributed to the words, *i.e.* to the psalmodic text. The Hebrew tongue, the language of David, was venerated and cherished in early Christian times, and we know examples that people learned Hebrew with the specific purpose of singing the psalms in the original tongue and thus enjoy them the more. JEROME, for instance, reports about the virgin BLAESILLA, who died at an early age:

> "She overcame the difficulties of the Hebrew language in order to teach and sing psalmody together with her mother [PAULA]."[227]

And when PAULA died, JEROME also bestowed high praise upon her, saying:

> "She wanted to teach Hebrew and succeeded in it so notably that she could sing the psalms in Hebrew."[228]

That the melodic rendition of original psalm texts, in these two instances, was bound to be Hebrew as well, may of course be taken for granted.

Relatively soon psalms have been sung not only for religious purposes, but also in all kinds of secular occasions. Among these, psalm-singing in daily life may be mentioned specifically, because it constituted a wide-spread usage among working people. Its aim was mainly to alleviate manual work, or render more pleasant the working procedure of certain professions.

JOHN CHRYSOSTOM tells about this usage[229] in mentioning some of the professions in which singing was customary. The professions referred to by him are without exception of the kind in which singing would facilitate the work by its rhythmic regularity: nurses rocking babies, wagoners driving animals, vintagers treading grapes, sailors pulling the oars, weavers tossing the shuttle. Psalm-singing in all these cases has only a slight religious motivation; in reality, it represents largely a species of secular work song. CHRYSOSTOM's statement proves how closely religious and secular singing have been interwoven in those times.[230]

The early rabbinic literature, too, mentions work songs, without specifying them, however, as "psalms." As a talmudic report states:

> "The singing of sailors and ploughmen is permitted, but that of weavers is prohibited."[231]

To this passage RASHI adds the following comment: "Sailors and ploughmen sing to facilitate their work, whereas weavers sing out of frivolity."[232]

In order to draw a line between psalm-singing for religious use and for secular purposes, the Fathers of the Church have been compelled to make a sharp distinction between these two usages. Already AUGUSTINE stresses the difference between the ordinary "singing" and "psalmody."[233] ATHANASIUS distinguishes exactly "hymns" and "psalms" in the following words:

> "Since the Lord wished the spiritual harmony in the soul to be ex-

pressed symbolically by adding melody to the words, He decreed that hymns be sung with melody and psalms be chanted."[234]

According to this definition, hymns seem to have been the more popular tunes, sung also in secular life, whereas psalms represented the strictly religious type. Even more minutely are these two kinds of songs described by DIDYMUS of ALEXANDRIA (309?-394 C.E.):

> "Psalm is a hymn which is sung to the [accompaniment of the] instrument called psaltery or else cithara."[235]

This seems to indicate that the religious psalms have been accompanied, according to the ancient tradition of the Temple, by the *kithara* or *lyra*. Yet, there also must have been unaccompanied religious psalms, since DIDYMUS says in the same passage that

> "he who [follows] the practical way of life, sings psalmody; he who [follows] the spiritual way of life sings [without accompaniment]."[236]

We see from all this ambiguity that the terms "hymns" and "psalms" have not been too clearly distinguished, and the Church Fathers used them rather indiscriminately. One species, however, the "spiritual songs," *ōdai pneumatikai*, has been used exclusively on religious occasions; they are already mentioned in the New Testament (Ephes. 5:19; Col. 3:16) and constitute in the writings of the Church Fathers the third category of songs, in addition to the hymns and psalms.

This distinction corresponds to the definition made as far back as in ARISTOTLE's times:

> "We accept the classification of melodies made by some philosophers, as ethical melodies, melodies of action, and passionate melodies (*ta men ēthika ta de praktika ta d'enthousiastika*)."[237]

The "ethical melodies" could be likened to the "psalms," the "melodies of action" to the secular "hymns," and the "passionate melodies" to the "spiritual songs."

Psalm-singing in the daily life is frequently attested in the patristic literature. CLEMENT of ALEXANDRIA says:

> "At a banquet we [the Christians] drink to each other's health singing psalms responsively."[238]

JOHN CHRYSOSTOM, too, tells of

> "singing sacred hymns and spiritual songs at banquets."[239]

In a moralizing tendency, CLEMENT of ALEXANDRIA shows the deep cleavage between the music of the heathen revelers at their wild feasts, and the ardent, dignified singing of the Christians at their banquets. He scoffs at

> "the burlesque singing, the instrumental music, choirs, and dances at banquets,"

and puts as a worthy contrast to it the sedate manner of Christian singing:

> "The Christians, however, teach and admonish one another in all wisdom, in psalms, and hymns, and spiritual songs, singing with grace in your heart to God. And even if you wish to sing and play to the harp or the lyre, there is no blame. Thou shalt imitate the righteous Hebrew king in his thanksgiving to God."[240]

Like DIDYMUS after him, CLEMENT testifies that there existed accompanied and unaccompanied hymns and psalms, which proves that Christian singing partly followed the usage of the Temple (accompanied psalms), and partly that of many Synagogues (unaccompanied psalms). In the opinion of the Church Fathers, the accompaniment by instruments does not seem to have affected the ethical value of psalm-singing; singing was the essential part, accompaniment merely a subordinate factor. And this was true for the sacred as well as for the secular psalm-singing.

In early Christian times, the secular psalm-singing has had, besides its function as a bond between the individual and the religious community, the same significance as the popular song in the life of the peoples in later centuries. Accordingly, the melodies of the psalms may have been simple, so that anybody could sing them without difficulty. This explains why the psalms could be sung "in the morning and evening,"[241] and that certain psalms were so popular that they

> "were known to nearly everyone by heart, and were sung daily in the evening assembly by old and young."[242]

TERTULLIAN

> "admonishes Christian married people to emulate one another in singing psalms and hymns, not only in the congregation but also in the family and home,"[243]

which indicates on the one hand that they have been extensively used, and, on the other hand, that they could be sung easily, both these facts pointing quite explicitly to their popular character. In the family, such psalms or psalm-like songs would even be sung "before retiring."[244]

Finally, the Church Fathers report that psalms have been sung at funeral ceremonies, which is another indication of the simplicity and popular melodic character of such songs. JOHN CHRYSOSTOM states that

> "psalms were sung at their [the Christians] funerals."[245]

GREGORY the GREAT (509-604) confirms this usage.[246] JEROME, referring to the death of FABIOLA, mentions that "they sang psalms" at her funeral.[247] About the form of such funeral songs AUGUSTINE reports that "EUODIUS took up the psalter [at funeral rites] and began to sing, the whole house [*i.e.* congregation] answering him,"[248] which points to a responsorial style.

o
o o

All this is merely a selection from the multitude of references in the patristic literature about early Christian psalm-singing, as well as about its immediate predecessor, the psalm-singing of the ancient Hebrews. In view of this abundance of historical records, it is surprising that it took nearly two millennia to discover the true sources of Christian singing. Not till our time, and through the assiduous work of a few scholars, have the affinities between Jewish and Christian psalmody been firmly established. Fortunate musical discoveries in recent decades brought forth the factual proof as to how closely both were interrelated.

Moreover, a diligent comparison between the preserved biblical chants of the Jews and the earliest Christian melodies handed down to us in the

Ambrosian and Gregorian collections, throws a bright light into one of the darkest historical domains of ancient music. Through this research, the musical world of Ancient Israel, long considered extinct, has experienced a resurgence, a veritable rebirth, such as we would not have dared to imagine a few decades ago.

11. ATTEMPTS AT RECONSTRUCTING THE ANCIENT JEWISH SONGS

Attempts have not been lacking to revive by speculation, or by artificial devices, this allegedly engulfed world of music. For the mystery which enshrouded it always was—and still remains—too intriguing to be left unsolved for ever. One refused to believe that with the destruction of the Temple of Jerusalem Jewish song has been irretrievably lost. It seemed improbable that such an extensive musical practice as that of the Hebrews, could do without any musical notation. As a result, scholars have searched eagerly to discover some indications for a system of notation which—if deciphered—might bring ancient Jewish music back to life. Some of the attempts in this respect deserve a brief mention, at least for the sake of curiosity, if for no other reason.

In this enumeration, we can easily dispense with discussing the first known such attempt made in the 18th century by JOHANN CHRISTOPH SPEIDEL,[249] who tried to prove, merely theoretically, that the Hebrews were acquainted with part-singing and that they called the notes by the names of their vowels.

Toward the end of the same century, CONRAD GOTTLOB ANTON has endeavored to bring about the resurgence, in modern notation, of ancient Jewish melodies.[250] ANTON discusses ancient Jewish music mainly in terms of harmonic structures, in accordance with the views of his own time. The musical examples of his pamphlet, that is the Jewish melodies "reconstructed" by him, appear exactly like Protestant chorales in a four part setting, without possessing, of course, either the genuine spirit or the religious power of such Church hymns.

About half a century later, LEOPOLD HAUPT tried to reconstruct melodies of six Old Testament psalms by availing himself of the Hebraic accentual signs (*ta'amim*).[251] He, too, invested his reconstructed melodies with a stiffly conventional harmonic setup in four parts, typical for his period. The resulting musical product turned out to be a weak imitation of the style of Mendelssohn or of his followers, which is all that can be said of his plainly abortive attempt at reconstructing the "ancient Oriental" songs.

A short time later, LEOPOLD ARENDS sought to prove the possibility of reviving the vocal music of Ancient Israel.[252] He approached the problem from another angle, first by interpreting the Hebrew letters, consonants and vowels, as music notes. Thereupon, he committed a basic error in assuming the Oriental music to have been using our Western keys, major and minor, which obviously constitutes not only an anachronism, but also a glaring misunderstanding of the intrinsic character of Oriental music. One single sentence of ARENDS should be quoted to demonstrate his attitude to this problem:

"The melodic pattern in the minor key has not been used in the Babylonian exile alone; we find it already in David's elegy on Saul's and Jonathan's death (2 Sam. 1:19-27)."[253]

Moreover, ARENDS' musical examples show a flagrant misconception of the Jewish-Oriental melos. The melodic curve of his reconstructed Hebrew melodies is full of wide intervallic skips, such as octaves, sevenths, sixths, which is contrary to the character of Oriental music. His musical example No. 1 (p. 115) contain almost no stepwise diatonic progressions, only wide intervals; the same is true of example No. 5 (p. 122), and of others. The average range of ARENDS' reconstructed melodies is one octave and a fourth, which is difficult for singers having no professional voice training. And lastly, the "accompaniments" supplied by ARENDS for his melodies,— patterns of broken chords in the style of piano exercises for beginners—are curious examples of how the basic characteristics of Oriental music, in general, and Jewish music, in particular, can be so grossly misunderstood.

In more recent times, HEINRICH BERL scrutinized the problem of reviving vocal music of the biblical past.[254] His argument is that such attempts have to start with linguistic considerations. As a principle, he believes in the possibility of reconstruction. Vocal music, to which he attaches in this connection the term "consonal music," is—as he thinks—mainly speech-song ("Sprechgesang"). He maintains that alphabetical letters as well as grammatical signs and accents have equivalent and naturally inherent tonal values which can be disclosed. According to BERL, attempts at reconstruction are basically feasible if they originate from the innate rhythmic laws of human speech. In his opinion, to language must be granted the same musical elements as to the music itself, when the latter is detached from the spoken or chanted word.

"Here, in ancient Hebrew vocal music, this is especially true since, as already established, it has originally been pure speech-melody. [*i.e.* chanting]; therefore, it was based not so much upon the melos in the proper sense, as upon rhythm."[255]

As we see, BERL's definitions deal mainly with theoretical premises. However, the crucial practical question as to *how* such a reconstruction could be effectuated, is not answered by theorizings of this kind.

Lately, OTTO GLASER tried to clarify somewhat the situation and to answer the question whether or not ancient Jewish song can be revived.[256] Similar to other "reconstructers," he failed to suggest anything practical toward the solution of the problem under consideration.

This problem is aptly defined by JOSEPH YASSER.[257] As he points out, it is centered not so much in an outright discovery of some supposedly preserved melodies than in becoming aware of

"the changes perpetrated—consciously or not—by individual performers at different historical stages." . . . "To ensure greater accuracy in the matter of weeding out the many extraneous melodic accretions from any traditional chant selected for reconstruction, one must be guided especially by the following threefold observation concerning the structure and the relative age of the Hebrew liturgical melody. As one moves back into the historical past, one finds, *first,* that the number of notes used in any given type of this melody grows smaller; *second,* that its range becomes narrower; and, *third,* that semitones are encountered in it less frequently. This, naturally, is but a very broad observation, . . . but it may be safely applied, as a working rule, to all average cases."

YASSER considers this merely as a general norm. He thinks, however, that it is a practical way of procedure, and he supports his theory with some pertinent musical examples.

12. THE NATURE OF ORIENTAL SONG–MAḲAMAT

Nearly all the scholars who have ever indulged in attempts at reconstruction, or who plumbed theoretically its possibilities, proceeded in their reasonings from our Western musical notions and availed themselves of the musical notation as used in Occidental music. However, the aesthetic standards of Oriental music—and the ancient Jewish song belongs to this category—differ quite appreciably from those of Occidental music, so that none can be interpreted technically to the full extent in the terms of the other. This being so, the true approach to Oriental music, in general, has to be established before the innate characteristics of Jewish music, in particular, can be investigated.

As the first step along this path, one would be expected, of course, to determine the basic nature of Oriental music. But in so far as ancient Jewish singing is concerned, the Bible itself furnishes the most important data in this respect.

The headings of the psalms contain a number of specific terms which apparently have no bearing whatever on the text of the psalm. The majority of the psalm-commentators consider these terms to be the names, or the initial words, of certain popular songs, and the preposition *le* or *ʾal* before them would represent, according to this accepted interpretation, the instruction to sing the psalms in question after the melody of these songs.

From the musical standpoint. this would be a highly satisfactory solution of what has long been considered as the psalm-headings enigma. It has been frequently argued, however, that many difficulties lie on the path of this explanation. How did our forefathers manage, for instance, to adapt a specific melody to the text of a psalm, considering that certain psalms are very extensive; that most of the psalms have no strophic structure; and that the verses of the psalms, moreover, display immense differences as to the number of their syllables and their meter? But all these objections are easily surmounted, if one begins the investigation of Oriental music on proper grounds.

Thus, such terms as "song" or "melody" in the accepted Occidental sense cannot be applied to the musical rendition of the psalms. Oriental music does not know the regularly articulated melodic structure characterized in Western music by motives, phrases. sentences, groups of measures, half-periods, periods, sequences, etc.

Ancient Oriental music is determined by the principle of standard motifs, or thematic kernels, within some basic scale-forms. These are stereotyped musical patterns, melodic formulae ("melodicles"), comprising sometimes only a few notes. Owing to a specific musical ear of the Orientals, so different from ours, these "tunes" are considered as independent melodic units, easily recognizable by anybody.

This principle of "tunes" is the foundation of the entire musical conception of the Orient, and it has been preserved to these days in the *maḳam,* a song-type of the Arabic-Persian cultural sphere.

Maḳam signifies, strictly, a "tone," and in a wider sense a "musical tune." *Maḳamat* is an organized melodic system showing how the single *maḳams* are put together, and it constitutes the basis of Oriental music theory.[258] Each *maḳam* is an independent melodic unit, composed of some specifically built motivic elements, the basic form of which is invariable. The artistry of the Oriental musician consists in his ability to embellish a *maḳam* with constantly changing variations and to create by this device a new artful musical product.

With all his inspiration and imagination, the performer is never allowed to deviate from the original *maḳam,* and especially to blunder into another *maḳam.* The indivisible union of the specific scale-form and the tune represent an entity which the trained ear recognizes infallibly as this or that *maḳam.* The Oriental ear considers any musical piece as strange and unartistic if it does not display the characteristic motives and phrases of some pre-selected *maḳam.*

Ancient Jewish music is a product of the general Oriental musical culture, and therefore subject to the same laws. Thus, the principle of the *maḳamat* must also be applied to Jewish music, and, in this case, should perhaps be given the name of *nussḥaot,* a derivative of *nussaḥ,* which is the late Hebrew equivalent of *maḳam.*

The Book of Psalms furnishes us a rather tangible evidence to the actual use of the principle in question. The above mentioned terms in their headings must have been largely the names of certain *maḳams-nussḥaot* to be applied for the musical elaboration of those psalms. In the light of this interpretation, there remains nothing enigmatic or inexplainable about these terms. It is quite obvious that the levitical singers used specific *maḳams* for different psalms, and through their skill of variation, familiar to any trained singer of those days, they were able to adapt without difficulty these "melodic kernels" to verses, whether short or long.

The main prerequisite for this procedure would be the people's perfect familiarity with such *maḳams,* so that they could be used as musical patterns for the psalms not merely by the actual performers, but also by future generations. The tunes mentioned in the Psalter seem to have been such generally known *maḳam*-types, which were popular during a relatively long period, and which fell into oblivion only after several centuries, owing to external circumstances, like wars, political unrest, apostasy from Yahveh's religion, perhaps also the Bablyonian exile, etc.

Biblical commentators agree that the latter portion of the Psalter originated, or has been compiled, several centuries after the initial portion. It is indeed striking that all the specific names for the melody-types referred to above appear in the first three books of the Psalter. In fact, after Ps. 88 no such names are found in the headings. This, of course, is a clear indication that the *makams* which had primitively been used for the psalms, have fallen into oblivion in the lapse of centuries, so that the later writers and singers of psalms could no longer use them.

Another reason might have been that, as time passed, other *makam*-types cropped up and became popular. The fact, however, that the older *makams* had been forgotten, would reasonably deter the writers and singers of psalms from prescribing for the later books any specific *makams.* It might rather have been left to the judgment of the performers to select the appropriate *makam* for a psalm. This seems to have been the musical practice of the Second Temple, especially so in the concluding centuries of its existence, when the last two books of the Psalter have been given their final order.

Despite the fact that these last books contain no indications of *makams,* we have positive knowledge that quite a number of psalms based on them had been sung in the Temple as well as in religious feasts outside the Temple. Consequently, there must have actually existed appropriate "tunes" for their musical rendition, and these were the "oral" *makams,* so to say, widely known at that time.

It would not even be too far-fetched to assume that most of the vocal music which has been preserved after the destruction of the Jewish national existence and subsequently taken over by the new Christian congregation, represented such *makam*-types.

Makam is by no means identical with the tropal motif (*ta'am*) of the cantillation. The latter of the two, generally permanent in its appearance, is strictly connected with the syntactical order of the biblical sentence; whereas the former, even though always retaining a distinctly recognizable melodic pattern, is more or less freely varied and freely applied to a given text by the performer.[259]

The technique used in a *"makamic"* type of song is likened by ERIC WERNER to the somewhat modern device of "leading motifs," which, as he thinks, can easily be discovered in the Synagogue chant as well as in the Gregorian plain-song in the form of "migrating melisms."[260] *Makam* and *"leitmotif,"* however, are notions which are worlds away from each other. And, in attributing to the *makams* certain "hermeneutical purposes," WERNER adopts the very idea of the hypothetic program-music in Jewish liturgy, which has been refuted earlier (see p. 152 ff). WERNER goes also too far in designating the melismatic style of the variation principle as the oldest form of "absolute" music, "entirely emancipated from meter, syllable, word or sentence." "Absolute music" is a contemporary notion, which cannot be applied either for the music of the biblical, or the post-biblical period.

13. THE CHARACTER OF ANCIENT JEWISH SONG

The variation principle of Oriental music, and especially of Oriental singing, affords a disclosure of many features that concern the character of ancient Jewish singing.

For the Orientals the interpretation of their music is of paramount importance.[261] According to our Western conception of music, the main thing is the art product, that is the musical texture worked out in the most minute details and put down in written form, which is considered as final and immutable. Consequently, any unmotivated infringement upon the finished product, that is any arbitrary alteration of the musical substance, is considered an unlawful trespassing of the creator's rights.[262] The interpretation of the art product assumes, in the Western world, only a secondary importance, however indispensable it may be in actual practice.

In Oriental music, however, its interpretation is the primary factor, the principal thing, almost more important than the original musical idea. The latter constitutes no more than a kernel, out of which the skilled performer creates the art work by his inspired rendition.

> "The manner in which the performer interprets it, tells the Oriental listener that a musical idea has been awakened to a real, flourishing life; the interpretation infuses his idea with flesh and blood; without it, it is merely an empty, barren skeleton, a rigid dead structure of bones."[263]

This "flourishing life," this "flesh and blood" is identical, for the Oriental feeling, with the artistry of the performer who adorns a melodic kernel with all kinds of embellishments: coloraturas, melisms, gruppetti, runs, trills, repetitions of tones, portamenti, glissandi, etc. Particularly the portamento and glissando are, as with all primitive peoples, the paramount feature of artistic Oriental performance, which is loaded, especially at the beginning and the end, with all kinds of ornaments, so that the melodic kernel is sometimes overgrown beyond immediate recognition.

The Oriental listener is capable of separating entirely the rendition of the song from the melody itself. About this RABINDRANATH TAGORE makes some pertinent remarks:

> "In our country the understanding portion of the audience think no harm in keeping the performance up to standard by dint of their own imagination. For the same reason they do not mind any harshness of voice or uncouthness of gesture in the exponent of a perfectly formed melody; on the contrary, they seem sometimes to be of opinion that such minor external defects serve better to set off the internal perfection of the composition."[264]

This approach of the Oriental man to his own music is stressed and complemented by the following observations of HERMANN KEYSERLING after listening to the Hindu *ragas*:

> "Nothing intentional, no definite shape, no beginning, no end; a surge and undulation of the eternally flowing stream of life. Therefore, always the same effect upon the listener: it is not wearisome, could last forever, since nobody ever gets tired of life."[265]

And yet, a *raga*—the Hindu parallel of a *maḳam*—consists only of a few tones, compared with an Occidental piece of music.

Both descriptions throw light upon the essence of Hindu music. The same principle, however, may be applied to the entire Mid-Eastern music and it is also basically true for the character of the music in Ancient Irsael.

o
o o

In talmudic times, there was a clearcut differentiation between the various types of psalmody. In a lengthy discussion about the singing of the "Hallel," learned rabbis distinguished between three different forms of psalmody: the responsorial singing (*roshe peraḳim*), the antiphonal alternation (*bahade hadade*=reading "with each other"), and the chanting speech-melody (*haḳri*ʿ*ya* or *hiḳra*).[266] An even more minute definition of antiphonal singing, *zamre bahade,* can be found in the much later book of IBN BALʿAM (11th century), in which he discusses the accents (*ta*ʿ*amim*) of the three poetical books of the Bible, Psalms, Proverbs and Job.[267]

A certain type of speech-melody, coming rather close to cantillation, was evidently known in Ezra's times (5th century B.C.E.). A solemn public reading of the Torah was undertaken by Ezra and by numerous Levites whose names are mentioned by the biblical chronicler. The report about this event—the earliest of its kind— states that

> "they read in the book, in the Law of God, distinctly, and they gave the sense, and caused them to understand the reading" (Neh. 8:8).

"Reading distinctly" is a clear indication of a rhythmic articulation and melodic inflexion of the spoken words, which—according to the Oriental conception—are indispensable for an expressive declamation. Only a reading that makes use of these elements of cantillation could have possibly exerted such an effect that "all the people wept." (Neh. 8:9).

Furthermore, as mentioned earlier, cantillation was a superior mnemonic device for memorizing lengthy passages. In talmudic times, the study of the Bible and Mishnah was done with chanting. R. PETAḤYAH of REGENSBURG, who, in the 12th century, made extensive voyages in the Orient, observed that in the places visited by him the entire Talmud was recited in a singing tone (*v'kol ha-talmud be-niggun*). The chanting practice has been preserved until our days in studying the *Halaka.*

The Talmud does not institute specific rules for cantillation, which seems to indicate that its coeval practice might already have had certain traditional norms. This is evidenced by some allusions of talmudic writers.[268] Thus, there is the well-known maxim of R. JOḤANAʿAN:

> "If one reads the Scripture without a melody (*ne*ʿ*ima*) or repeats the Mishnah without a tune (*zimrah*), of him the Scripture says: 'Wherefore I gave them also statutes that were not good' (Ezek. 20:25)."[269]

R. AKIBA, too, recommends to study the law with chanting and advises the student:

> "Chant it every day! Chant it every day!"[270]

This has been interpreted in the sense that the student ought to repeat incessantly his subject like a song in order to make it stick to the memory.

According to the talmudic conception, the elements of song have been *ne'ima,* the melody proper, *ta'am,* the prosody, and *hagbeah ḳol,* the pitch level without which a precise intonation was not possible. In order to ensure the correct pitch, the levitical musicians have used an instrument which gave the required tone for the singers at the beginning of every music piece.[271]

Latter-day theories deprived the talmudic *ne'ima* of its original meaning as the melody proper; they understood it to be cantillation in general,[272] and "sweetness" of the singing voice in particular.[273] The character of the Pentateuch cantillation as performed in those days is clearly indicated by the Midrash when it qualifies the reading of the Torah as "shouting with joy (*i.e.* singing)," *rinnah shel torah.*[274]

The Masoretic accentual signs (*ta'amim*), introduced primarily as graphic symbols of the syntax, in the sense of our signs of interpunction, became gradually associated with the concurrently used tropal motifs. Though the signs originated in the post-talmudic centuries, it is possible that their underlying motifs stem from the musical tradition of the early Synagogue.[275] For the three great poetical books (Psalms, Proverbs, Job) the accentual signs have been fixed by a statute. For the Psalms and Proverbs a simple manner of rendition has been provided, which was later also applied to the text of Job not designed originally to be interpreted in chanting.[276]

o o o

In examining the tonal elements of the music in Ancient Israel, we have to remember that Oriental music in general does not confine itself to the conventional octave-scale of seven tones with intercalated intervals of whole- and half-steps. The tonal system of the Orientals also includes different steps and intervals; our scales, our limited classification of the keys in two main categories, major and minor, is unknown in the Orient. Oriental music is based on "modes," consisting in part of intervals different from those of Western tempered system. We hear therefore in Oriental music, especially in vocal music, all kinds of intermediate "microtonic" intervals, which sound strange to our ears and are difficult or even impossible to reproduce in our musical notation, but which appear quite normal to the Oriental ear.

Fundamentally, singing in Ancient Israel has been largely pentatonic, not in the sense of Western patterns as governed by our major and minor keys, but based on a succession of intervals forming a perfectly independent and self-sufficient scalar structure.[277] This is especially evident from what may be taken as probably the oldest extant relics of Hebrew music, namely, the so-called "tropal motifs" of Pentateuch cantillation as chanted to this day by the Persian and Yemenite Jews and recorded some 50 years ago by A. Z. IDELSOHN.[278]

The true nature of these motifs may best be grasped from their following modified presentation by JOSEPH YASSER, who has brought them, for elucidation, to a uniform key-signature level and in the order of their gradually increasing complexity. The Persian and Yemenite cantillation motifs are found, in this presentation, on staves I and II respectively. To further facilitate their comprehension, YASSER has appended underneath these two motivic sets their basic scales (staves I[a] and II[b]) and has placed the latter's component tones in the order of their initial appearance in the motifs right above them. The notes of the motifs that fall upon the two ornamental tones (E and B flat) of the pentatonic scale are marked either by asterisks or arrows on their normally unstable or occasionally stable character respectively.[279]

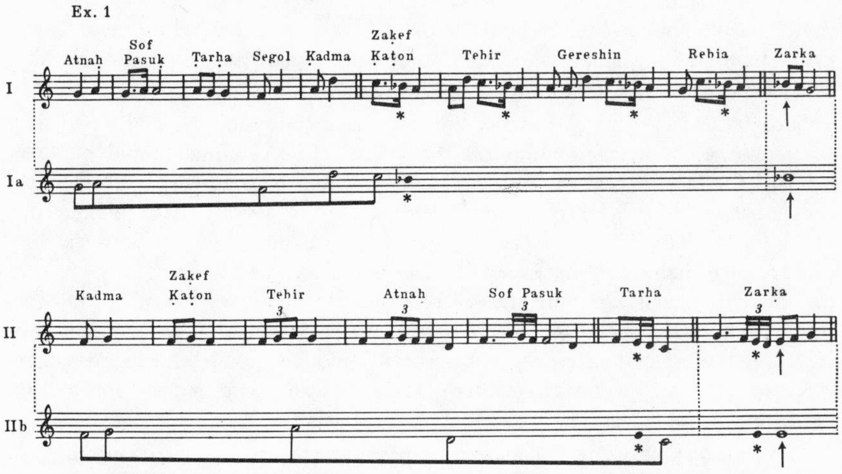

Perhaps a somewhat more advanced Hebrew variant of these two scale species, with conspicuous pentatonic elements still in evidence, but at the same time also manifesting a certain amount of increased diatonic "anticipations," might have been the one referred to by CLEMENT of ALEXANDRIA when he admonishes his fellow religionists to avoid the chromatic and theatrical melodies of the heathens (*i.e.* Greeks) and advised them to return to the "spiritual songs," that is, the traditional psalm-singing of David.[280] He cites as an example worthy of imitation the ancient Greek drinking song:

> "Among the ancient Greeks, in their banquets over brimming cups, a song was called *skolion,* after the manner of the Hebrew psalms, all together raising the paean with the voice, and sometimes taking turns in the song while they drank healths round; while those that were more musical than the rest sang to the lyre."[281]

CLEMENT defines the mode of this song as "Doric" and "Spondaic," in accordance with the rule that songs which accompanied the libation (*spondē*) had to be sung in the *tropos spondeiakos.*

The intervallic structure of this particular mode (E, G, A, B, C, D, E, or E, F, G, A, B, D, E), with one of the two conventional semitones missing either in the lower or the upper tetrachord, clearly shows that the *tropos spondeiakos* belongs to the intermediate evolutionary stage between the pure pentatonic and the ordinary diatonic scale. CURT SACHS, too, seems to cling to this view when he says that

> "the *tropos spondeiakos* was certainly not pentatonic, but hexatonic—either as a direct remnant of older pentatonics, or as an indirect remnant suggested by the pentatonic tuning of the lyre."[282]

However, ERIC WERNER holds an opposite opinion considering the *tropos spondeiakos* to bear merely

> "a certain superficial similarity to pentatonic scales,"

their characteristic elements both in the Gregorian and the European-Jewish chant being, as he believes, of much later origin than the *tropos* itself which represents "actually a modification of the Dorian [diatonic] mode."[283]

Such indeed is often the immediate impression one may get while perusing the writings of ancient authors on this point. However, one should not lose sight of the fact that, at the historical period when these authors were tackling occasionally the subject of *tropos spondeiakos,* it already had become the general—and largely still surviving—custom to expound "retrospectively" in conventional diatonic terms even the older scales that had not yet fully reached the diatonic stage. Judging from its definitely indicated construction, the *tropos spondeiakos* belonged precisely to the last-named category, and for this reason it represented in reality not a coeval "modification" but rather a close precursor of the full-fledged Dorian diatonic scale (the latter forming, in the Greek connotation, a "white-key" E to E series).

This rectified historical perspective provides us, then, with certain important data as to the tonal basis and character of ancient psalm-singing at least during the closing centuries of the Jewish national existence. It goes without saying that inasmuch as the *tropos spondeiakos* has heralded, by way of evolution, the advent of the Dorian diatonic scale (and then, of course, has been used, for a while, side by side with it), it was bound to possess some of the latter's external and internal traits. In their fully developed state, these "Dorian" traits were considered by Greek philosophers and historians, like PLATO, ARISTOTLE, PLUTARCH, ATHENAEUS, and others, particularly appropriate for the education of the youth, in opposition to both "Asiatic" modes, the Phrygian and Lydian,[284] which were classified as "corrupting the morals."

Among the numerous utterances concerning the ethos of the Dorian mode, we quote a typical example from ARISTOTLE,[285] which affords a clear insight regarding the attitude of the Greek philosophers to the educational value of this mode. ARISTOTLE reproaches SOCRATES[286] for repudiating the pipe (*aulos*) as unfit for the education of the youth, while he indulged in the Phrygian mode. And he continues:

> "For the Phrygian mode has the same effect among harmonies as the flute among instruments—both are violently exciting and emotional (*orgiastikai kai pathētikai*). . . . All agree that the Dorian mode is more sedate and of a specially manly character."

The comparison made by CLEMENT between the *skolion* and the ancient Hebrew psalm-singing, both set in the Dorian mode, furnishes us the indirect proof that ancient Jewish music had a sedate, proportioned, dignified character, despite the technique of ornamentation which it must have possessed as a member of the Oriental musical family.

o
o o

As to the nature of choral singing in Ancient Israel, it was obviously monophonic, having had one single melodic line without harmony. This, of course, is true of all the music of Antiquity, and Oriental music in particular rejects even to-day any harmony in the Western sense as being foreign to its inner nature. But within this monophony, the imagination of the Orientals with its characteristic predilection for adornment displays musical patterns of great variety and rich colors. As a result, the monophony of Oriental music can in no way be identified with monotony, if we listen to it under proper conditions and with the right attitude.

According to our Occidental theory, music has three basic elements: melody, harmony and rhythm, to which tone-color is sometimes added as a subordinate factor. It follows from this classification that Oriental music lacks one of the important elements of art-music as we understand it: harmony. One should remember, however, that our "harmonic," or many-voiced music is only a few centuries old, while monophonic music, ordinarily considered as "primitive," is probably as old as human civilization itself. With all its "primitivity"—or what appears as such to Western ears—Oriental music exhibits, among other features, a variety of intervallic divisions which cannot exactly be expressed in our supposedly well developed musical notation. Oriental music has its own artistic and aesthetic norms, and it makes up in other ways for the lack of harmony and polyphony (see below).

The homophony of ancient Jewish music has been repeatedly linked with a misunderstood biblical passage in which the chronicler reports about the musical performance at the dedication of Solomon's Temple, in which

> "it came even to pass, when the trumpeters and singers were as one, to make one sound to be heard in praising and thanking the Lord" . . . (2 Chron. 5:13).[287]

The vocal monophony together with the precision of the instrumental accompaniment gave rise to the idea that this "unity" constituted a specific objective of Jewish sacred music.[288] According to this explanation, the solemn unison conforms with Jewish civilizatory trends and reflects the Jewish monistic conception of the world which in every part aims at unity.

This interpretation is based on a patently erroneous premise. Monophony is neither a product of Jewish cultivation, nor is it rooted in civilisatory trends of the Jewish people. It is simply a common feature of Oriental music. The unity ("one sound") emphasized in the above biblical sentence designates the meticulous precision, the supreme perfection of the performance and constitutes a specific praise of the Levitical singers by the reporting chronicler.

The true unity of Jewish music, and especially of Jewish singing, manifested itself in something entirely different from monophony. This unity is revealed by the fact that at any place where music and songs were performed in honor of Yahveh, the procedure was in complete conformity with the sacred practice of the Temple in Jerusalem. Just as the texts of the lections, prayers, blessings had to be identical everywhere, so it was scrupulously observed that the melodies used for psalms and other songs should always and everywhere be the same. This is the essence of the Midrashic statement that

> "Israel recites the *Shemʿā* with one mouth, one voice, one chant,"

which means in complete uniformity.[289] This principle of absolute homogeneity may justly be extended to all sacred songs of Ancient Israel.

o
o o

As mentioned above, the aesthetic pleasure in listening to music can early be discovered among the Israelites. David was called *naʿayim zimrat*, "the sweet singer" (*Jewish Version*), or "the sweet psalmist" (*Authorized, American* and *Revised Standard Versions* and *Moulton*), whereas *Douay* has "the excellent psalmist," and *Moffat* "whom Israel's lyrics love to sing" (2 Sam. 23:1).[290]

The notion of "beautiful singing," however with its psychological effect upon the human soul, came only later to full bloom. This is the immediate consequence of the Jewish attitude towards music as a source of pleasure. Such attitude is clearly discernible in talmudic writings, despite some scruples of latter-day rabbis raising their voices against the abuses of musical enjoyment which had spread in certain social strata of that period.

Beautiful singing was produced by a fine voice, and according to the rabbinical conception, the possession of a fine voice involved the religious duty to serve God with it. The biblical verse *kabed ʾet ʾAdonay meḥoneḥa,*

> "honour your God with all thy possessions" (Proverbs 3:9)

was interpreted in the sense that whoever possessed a fine voice had the obligation to devote his precious possession to the service of the Lord.[291] The Talmud asks:

> "Who is considered conversant with prayers? . . . Who is skilled in chanting, who has a pleasant voice (*ḳol ʿareb*)"[292]

The rabbinic literature names two of the last teachers of the Mishnah, ḤIYYA BAR ADA and RAB, who had fine voices and, accordingly, served as leaders of prayers, *i.e.* as precentors.[293] HYGROS ben LEVI was said to have had a special *neʿimah* ("sweetness") in his voice.[294] Despite the fact that his vocal qualities have been differently appraised by another talmudic report,[295] he must have been a singer of exceptional rank.

Levitical singers became disqualified with the deterioration of their voice, be it on account of their increasing age, or owing to other reasons which may have affected their vocal production.[296] Someone with an unattractive voice was considered unfit for the function of a precentor:

> "You would not be qualified to chant [lit. "for the platform"], because your voice is thick [hoarse]."[297]

Considering the paramount importance of a fine voice for the sacred service and also its appreciation as a phenomenon of art, it is surprising that the sages seemed to be undecided whether in the Temple service instrumental music or singing should be crowned with pre-eminence. On this subject numerous and lengthy rabbinical discussions have taken place, as reported in the talmudic literature.[298] Some held the opinion that the musical service (*shirah*) subsisted mainly in vocal music (*bepeh*), the instrument (*kle*) serving merely to sweeten the voice (*ḳol*); whereas, in the opinion of others, the character of Temple music was essentially instrumental. There was even a difference of opinion whether singing on the Sabbat was prohibited or not. Since levitical singing was generally accompanied by instruments, some over-zealous rabbis ventured to derive from the prohibition of playing instruments on the Sabbat, the prohibition of singing as well.[299] Finally, a middle-of-the-road decision was adopted, which apparently satisfied everyone:

> "Vocal music is dominant, and the instrument [is used] to sweeten the sound [by accompaniment]."[300]

o
o o

In moral, religious, and philosophical writings of the Jews we find over and over again notions borrowed from singing. In legends, parables, metaphors the sages avail themselves preferentially of figurative idioms with characteristic musical coloration in order to express distinctly their attitude toward singing.

A shrewd understanding for the import of singing as an expression of divine wisdom is contained in the following rabbinical statement:

> "There are three things through which God distinguished men from each other, through the voice (*be-ḳol*), through the melody (*be-ne-ʿimah*), and through the appearance (*be-morah*)."[301]

Under "voice" we have to understand the language, under "melody" the ability to sing.

The rabbis held that the joy of regained liberty manifests itself in spontaneous singing. An Aggadic interpretation of the term *bakosharot* (Ps. 68:7) elaborates:

> "He [God] bringeth out the prisoners into prosperity (*bakosharot*). What does *bakosharot* mean? Weeping (*beki*) and song (*shirot*): he who desires utters song, and he who does not, weeps."[302]

The explanation of this passage is that God, when he frees the captives, bestows upon them anew the faculty of singing.

Deep wisdom is contained in a Aggadic saying which characterizes the ethos of singing in the following manner:

> "Whosoever is singing songs with a troubled heart is like one who is teaching an unworthy pupil."[303]

The Gemarah not only considers singing to be the expression of joy of living, but also attributes to it the power of raising divine enthusiasm. It states:

> "What type of worship is done with joy and good heart? You should say: it is song."[304]

Phenomena of nature are often portrayed by the rabbis in terms of musical metaphors. As in the Bible itself, such portrayals are distinguished by their perspicuity as well as by poetic charm:

> "The valleys also are covered over with corn, they [the ears of corn]

shout for joy, yea, they sing. When do the ears of corn burst into song? In Nisan."[305]

o
o o

The sacred service was permeated with singing, in which the chanting of the precentor alternated with the responses of the congregation. Cantillation was the intermediate form of rendition between a monotonous accentuated speech-melody of the lection and a melodic pattern characteristic of a folk tune. With the aid of cantillation it was possible to convey the scriptural text in all its minute shadings; this manner of singing was equally suitable for recounting, in an enlivened ballad-like manner, the prosaic historical facts, numbers, names, etc., and for reproducing with stirring pathos the emotions of psalms and parts of other poetical books.

We are informed by the rabbinical writers that Ancient Israel has made precise distinctions between the different kinds of sacred singing. In general, the plain, unsophisticated style of chanting was considered appropriate for the musical rendition of prayers.[306] Among the different kinds of singing they distinguished the solemn type (*shirah*), the ecstatic song of praise (*hallel* or *halila*), and the simple manner of chanting which was used for the psalmody and for the study of Mishnah (*zimrah*). Among these types, *shirah* was the simplest and most popular one;—*halila* was more adorned with melisms, corresponding to its hymnic character;—while *zimrah* was the usual term for biblical cantillation, for the "perpetual melody," which survived the ages and still is used for chanting today.[307] *Ne'imah,* moreover, denoted the "sweetness" of singing, the emotion, the rapture of the worshipper which he might have experienced while listening to the music of his people, or which emerged from his overflowing heart when he approached his Creator with songs.

Late until medieval times the notion of supernatural beauty of singing has been preserved unchanged. In the book of the Mystics, *Tikuni Zohar* (XI, p. 45), there is a parallel between singing and celestial life:

"There are in heaven sacred places,
Which open only by song and chant."

o
o o

Both the Bible and the Talmud provide us with ample information concerning the nature of religious singing; about the character of secular singing, howover, we have only a summary knowledge, as transmitted through the somewhat general references found in the biblical and post-biblical sources.

Contrary to sacred music on its higher stage, secular music in Ancient Israel was used simply for "utilitarian purposes" (*Gebrauchsmusik*). Its essence was largely characterized by the co-operation, and even actual participation, of the individual in the collective music making. Despite the pleasure which it dispensed to all concerned, secular music could not be granted the privilege of passive enjoyment which, in its higher developed phase, was the characteristic of sacred music. The highly artistic structure of levitical singing excluded *a priori* the extensive participation of a non-Levite. Therefore, the rôle of the people at large was confined to a passive listening, which they gradually learned to enjoy. As a consequence, religious singing possessed all the criteria of an autonomous art, while secular singing was and remained heteronomous.

All sources testify to the joy and cheerfulness which secular singing dispensed in Israel. Whether people sang alone or in groups, whether with or without instrumental accompaniment, whether singing was done to help the day's work, to invigorate dance, to enliven a family celebration, or a public festival, it always gushed forth from the enthusiasm of a joyful heart.

After a jaunty banquet, the participants would burst into songs. According to rabbinical teachers, the talmudic term *ʾepikomon* signifies merry songs performed after the Passah meal.[308] The word is derived from the Greek *kommoō,* "to beautify," "to embellish," the noun of which is *kommos,* "decoration," and the term *ʾepikomon* was adopted by the Aramaean language and interpreted in post-biblical times as the joy of singing, which "beautifies" the feast after the meal.

At the ordination of rabbis, the participating colleagues performed merry songs:

> "When they ordained him [R. ZIRA], they [the schoolmen] sang before him."[309]

At solemn receptions of high religious dignitaries, singing belonged to the ceremonies honoring the distinguished guest:

> "When R. ABBAHU arrived at the Emperor's Court [in Caesarea] from College, the ladies of the Court went out to receive him and sang to him: 'Great man of thy people, leader of thy nation, lantern of light, thy coming be blessed with peace.' "[310]

The singing of the rabbis as accompaniment to the torch-dance at the feast of water-libation has been one of the highlights of the Festival of Tabernacles.[311]

The rabbis made a clear distinction between legitimate singing and the type of song which bordered upon, or plainly degenerated into, frivolity, as evidenced by the following maxim:

> "Whatever tune the singer may sing, it does not enter the ear of the dancer [the reveller]; whatever tune the singer may sing, the foolish son pays no attention [*i.e.* he ignores advice]."[312]

Singing played an all-important role at the most joyful event in the life of the individual, the wedding. At no other festive occasion was there more abundant singing than at weddings. At all times, there existed wedding songs as may be learnt from all sorts of allusions in the Scriptures, *e.g.* Jer. 7:34, 16:9, 25:10, 33:11, and in Revel. 18:23.

Wise and virtuous rabbis did not consider it below their dignity to adorn the wedding ceremonies with their songs; they sang alone or in groups in honor of the bridal couple and sometimes topped off the songs with dances.

> "At the marriage feast of MAR, the son of RABINA, . . . the Rabbis said to R. HAMNUNA ZUṬI: 'Let the master sing for us.' "[313]

At the same wedding a group of rabbis participated in singing.[314] Occasional fragments of wedding songs are preserved in some of the rabbinical writings as for instance:

"How does one dance [*i.e.* what does one sing] before the bride? . . . Bet Hillel says: 'Beautiful and graceful bride!' "[315]

Or:

"Neither paint nor rouge nor [hair-] dye, yet radiating charm."[316]

Wedding songs seem to have been different in Babylonia and Israel, for R. DIMI, returning to Babylonia from visiting the mother country, reported:

"Thus they sing before the bride in the West [*i.e.* in Israel]: 'No powder and no paint and no waving [of the hair], and still a graceful gazelle.' "[317]

When the political situation deteriorated, joyous singing at weddings had to be curtailed:

"When the Sanhedrin ceased, singing (*shir*) ceased at wedding-feasts."[318]

Despite this restriction, however, the merriment at weddings seems to have continued unabated, for it was necessary to issue a new interdiction:

"During the war of VESPASIAN (67-70 C.E.) they forbade the crowns of the bridegroom and the [wedding] drum."[319]

The Aggadah looked upon the wedding song as an indispensable element of joy:

"The ministering angels assembled and came to listen like people who assemble and come to watch the [musical] entertainment of a bride-groom and bride at a wedding."[320]

Considering the paramount importance of singing at weddings, as expressed in the above statements, it is surprising that the Bible mentions this primeval custom only in passing (Jer. 7:34; 16:9; 25:10; 33:11; also Ps. 45, the superscription of which, "A Song of Loves" really means "A Song for Weddings.").

And yet, the Bible contains a rich assortment of wedding songs, when one grasps the true sense of a document that has been almost generally misunderstood and misinterpreted. We refer to the "Song of Songs," or using the implication of the Hebrew title; *Shir ha-Shirim,* "The most beautiful Song (of Solomon)." A complete re-examination and re-evaluation of its contents leaves no doubt as to the fact that the book has been accepted into the canon merely because of its later allegorical interpretation.

"For it is a collection of wedding and love songs, so roguish, so sensual, so naughty, as used and still in use in civic life by all unspoiled peoples —and not only in the glowing South—at weddings, and only at this occasion."[321]

The book deals from one end to the other with love between the two sexes, and this in an incredibly earthy, even sensuous manner. It certainly must have been a formidably difficult task to attribute an allegorical meaning to erotic folksongs of this kind.

"But the book carries the name of Solomon, which made it a venerable remnant from the times of divine inspiration. These were the times from which no other but sacred writings have been preserved . . . Thus, there was nothing left except resorting to allegorical interpretation, and this naturally construed the whole contents of the book as Yahveh's love for Israel and His matrimony to His people, a favorite idea of the prophets since Hosea's times."[322]

Solomon is only nominally the author of the "Song of Songs." In reality, the author is the people itself. Just as popular poetry generally comes into being, so the "Song of Songs" might have originated and developed gradually from the life and feeling of unsophisticated people. It may have been first crystallized into single little songs, which were subsequently collected by scribes and embodied into a book. It follows the general rule of Antiquity in that the name of a compiler or editor was not preserved.[323] Instead of the real compilers, the name of the patron of arts and sciences,—King Solomon—has been attached to the book. It is also possible that Solomon himself ordered the compilation of these scattered wedding songs, for which reason the book carries his name. It is quite certain that the question of whether or not the "Song of Sons" belongs to the canon would never have arisen if Solomon's name were not in the title.

Solomon's authorship is highly questionable if we examine closely the contents of the songs. His name is mentioned, it is true, in 1:5; 3:7-11; 8:1 ff, but always in the third person. In 1:4,12, and 7:6 a king without a specific name is referred to. In none of these passages does Solomon speak himself, but it is always spoken of him, an indication that he is to be eliminated as the possible author. It is quite obvious that the motive for ascribing the collection to Solomon had been

> "the urge to possess some literary product from the golden epoch of Israel."[324]

Neither Solomon's name, nor the adoption of the book into the canon can alter the fact that we are confronted here with wedding songs, now loaded with facetious, and now with erotic, contents. They are genuine folksongs, composed by unknown, naive popular poets, and as such, they constitute the pure type of "utilitarian music."

In this connection it is revealing to find an indication in the rabbinic literature to the effect that its contemporaries considered the "Song of Songs" as a purely secular book. Young men used even to sing some stanzas of this poem as love ditties in public taverns, which aroused the ire of some zealous rabbis.[325]

In modern times "Song of Songs" has repeatedly been interpreted as a dramatic play with the accompaniment of music, song and dance, and performed with actors, choral and dancing groups.[326] All these ventures fail to understand the real meaning of this biblical book and the intrinsic lyric quality of its poems. Just as the Book of Psalms is the most exquisite collection of religious poetry, so for the unprejudiced reader the "Song of Songs" represents the finest compilation of secular poetry in the Old Testament. This fact is in no way altered either by allegorical interpretations, or by moralizing connotations which were associated surreptitiously with the book in the 18th century in order to justify its ancient admission into the canon, this being also the case with the "Proverbs." Least of all is it possible for the different attempts at the "dramatization" of the *Shir ha-Shirim* to undo the lucky circumstance that, because of canonization, a marvelous example of secular lyric poetry of

Ancient Israel has been preserved, which otherwise would have unfailingly been marked for destruction as it was the case with other secular offshoots of Hebrew poetry.

o
o o

How universal singing must have been in Jewish life, may be judged from the following talmudic passage:

> "The song of thanksgiving was [sung to the accompaniment of] lutes, lyres, and cymbals at every corner and upon every great stone in Jerusalem."[327]

And when the prophets threaten God's punishment for the disobedience and wantonness of the people, they announce, as the severest of all punishments, the changing of merry singing into mourning and lamentation. (Amos 8:10; *cf.* Job 30:31; opposite act Ps. 30:11).

Just as for the ordinary people singing constituted a necessity of every day's life, so its spiritual leaders, the sages and rabbis, fully appreciated the moral values of singing. Later, however, as it was said above, particularly in the Hellenistic period, some rigorously austere rabbis showed a more severe, even hostile attitude toward secular singing. Under Greek influence, the universal joy of singing has been degraded to a level where it has become a servant of sybaritic epicureanism and a constant companion of drinking-bouts. Such corrupt debaucheries are stirringly depicted in Amos 6:4-6 and Isa. 5:11,12. The following rabbinical passage refers to such kind of revelry, though here singing is not expressly mentioned:

> "Whoever drinks [wine] to the accompaniment of four musical instruments, brings five punishments to the world."[328]

It was against singing at occasions of this sort that the rabbis poured out their wrath and admonitions:

> "RABA said: 'When there is a song in a house there is destruction on its threshold.' "[329] "RAB went even further: 'An ear which listens to song should be torn off.' "[330]

The four instruments mentioned in Isa. 5:12, generally used at feasts, are "the harp and the psaltery, the tabret and the pipe." Tabret and pipe have been the instruments for dancing, whereas harp and psaltery were commonly used to accompany singing. Therefore, the above talmudic passage implicitly condemns also singing at such wanton feasts.

The sages have apparently been alarmed by the unseemly attitude displayed, within certain social circles, toward singing which deteriorated to a point where the aesthetic pleasure turned into a mere voluptuous sensation. For moral reasons they felt themselves justified to strive indomitably against this kind of licentious singing. In this desperate battle, the sensuous charm of the female voice was castigated with especial severity:

> "Listening to a woman's voice [song] is a sexual incitement."[331]
> "When men sing and women join in, it is licentiousness; when women sing and men join in, it is like fire in tow."[332]

As might have been expected, a sharp distinction was made by the rabbis between religious and secular singing. The latter was considered to be the root of all evil. This is pointedly expressed by the Talmud:

> "He who recites a verse of the Song of Songs and treats it as a [secular] air (*zemer*), brings evil upon the world."[333]

The true meaning of this saying is elucidated by RASHI's comment: *zemer* is the secular, *i.e.* demoralizing song; it is required, naturally, that the verses of the Song of Songs should be sung "with their traditional cantillation (*neginah aḥeret*)."

The following parable refers also to the destructive effects of debased music: "Thy children have made me as a harp (*kinnor*) upon which they frivolously (*leẓim*) play (*menagnim*)."[334] By *leẓim,* the talmudic writer characterizes the ungodly ones, symbolizing the pernicious influence of secular music.[335]

Yet, when immorality threatens to destroy the world, it can be saved from ruin by sacred singing. This is expressed in the following Midrashic maxim:

> "Profane songs of love and lust are sufficient cause to destroy the world, but Israel's religious song saves it."[336]

o
o o

As long as the Sanhedrin existed, it could check such social abuses as the widely expanding pleasure-hunting of the masses. Later, the restraint was no longer effective, so the Talmud complains:

> "In olden times the fear of the Sanhedrin was over them; so they did not sing [*i.e.* revel]. Now the fear of the Sanhedrin is not over them, so they sing."[337]

It is evident that the warnings of the sages were addressed not against singing as such, but only against the pagan influences, which brought about such revelries. In view of the hostility of the rabbis against the heretic and demoralizing song of the Greeks, it is not surprising to find in the Talmud the statement that "*laẓ* (the Greek language) is good for *zemer.*"[338] As mentioned above, *zemer* meant the frivolous, lascivious singing according to the talmudic conception. Therefore, the belief that the Greek language is particularly suitable for this kind of singing, corroborates the view that the general rabbinical hostility against the abuses of music practice was a consequence of Hellenic penetration into Jewish life.

The semantic change undergone by the word *zemer* since the biblical times is quite conspicuous (*cp.* p. 388). In a later epoch, *zemirot* meant the intimate form of song, the singing at home, in general the music of the Jewish family, while the diminutive word *zemerl* has been introduced eventually in the Yiddish vernacular for a secular tune or—if of devotional character—for a non-liturgical melody.

The rabbinical attitude toward Greek song manifests itself most significantly in the case of the notorious ELISHA ben ABUYA, whose apostasy is attributed to the fact that "Greek song did not cease from his mouth" (according to RASHI, "from his house"). The rabbinical contempt for ELISHA ben ABUYA went so far that subsequently he was referred to only as "AḤER" (the "other one"), like as someone whose very name was sinful to pronounce. The anathema raised against AḤER went so far that another talmudic teacher, R.

MEIR, "who learnt tradition at the mouth of AḤER," was also subjected to the ban. After AḤER's death, even his daughter was deprived of the safeguard of religion.[339]

In general, however, the rabbis have been sensible enough not to hinder too burdensomely the people's pleasure of singing. As a matter of fact, an opposite policy in this respect has even brought forth evil consequences on one occasion, as recounted rather curiously in the rabbinical literature. For some reason, which is not divulged by the Talmud, R. HUNA had forbidden secular singing. As a result, all mundane feasts ceased, for singing was an indispensable part of such festivities. Thereupon a social calamity ensued, and, together with an economic crisis, took such proportions that the prices of the most essential commodities fell to a bottomless low.

> "Hundred geese were priced at a *zuz* and a hundred *se'ahs* of wheat at a *zuz* and there was no demand for them [even at that price]."

R. ḤISDA, successor to R. HUNA, was more understanding and abolished his predecessor's prohibition of singing. Immediately, the prices rose again:

> "A goose was required [even at the high price of] a *zuz* but was not to be found."[340]

This talmudic report, however spurious it may appear, is symptomatic for the cheerful conception of life among the Israelites, with its invariable "leitmotif" of merry singing.

Even long after the destruction of the Temple, the opinions of the sages were divided as to whether all secular singing or merely singing accompanied by instruments has to be expressly prohibited. To settle this question,

> "An inquiry was once addressed to the Exilarch MAR ʿUKBA: (3rd cent. C.E.) 'Where does the Scripture tell us that it is forbidden [in these times] to sing [at carousals]?' He sent back [the following quotation] written on lines: Hosea IX:1.[341] Should he not rather have sent the following: Isaiah 24:9?[342] From this verse I should conclude that only musical instruments are forbidden, but not song."[343]

Evidently enough, rabbinical astuteness and discernment always found ways and means to justify and maintain secular singing. The joy of it could not be extirpated among the Israelites, despite the most severe interdictions.

This joy is beautifully expressed in a poetical sentence of "Ecclesiasticus":

> "A concert of musick in a banquet of wine is as a signet
> of carbuncle set in gold.
> As a signet of an emerald set in work of gold, so is the
> melody of musick with pleasant wine."
> (Ecclus. 32:5,6.).

The pleasure of listening to singing and music is evidenced by two further maxims from the same book·

> "Wine and musick rejoice the heart,"

and

> "The pipe and the psaltery make sweet melody."
> (Ecclus. 40:20,21).[344]

Even if the amount of the mundane pleasures derived from the solemn occasion did not actually measure up to it, it was the joy of singing which compensated the participants for the shortage. The Talmud reports that once in a Passah meal

> "there was [only] as much as an olive of the Passover-offering [to eat], yet the *Hallel* split the roofs! [it was sung with such gusto]."[345]

o
o o

In the religious conception of the Jews singing was not only a mundane, but also a celestial institution. According to a talmudic legend, three groups of angels sang daily songs of praise in honor of the Most High.[346] And the same talmudic passage attributes to the angel who wrestled with Jacob (Gen. 32:26) the following words:

> "I am an angel, and from the day that I was created my time to sing praises [to the Lord] had not come until now."[347]

This passage, incidentally, would point indirectly to the existence of an immense multitude of singing angels, according to Jewish conception. Curiously enough, God prefers the greater amount of mundane singing to that of the angelic, for

> "the ministering angels sing praises but once a day, whereas Israel sings praises to the Lord every hour."[348]

According to the naive conception of the Midrash, God is so pleased with singing as such that

> "every day the Holy One . . . creates a band of new angels who utter a new song before Him and then pass away."[349]

And the singing of His chosen people is so agreeable to the Lord that

> "whenever God hears Israel's song He calls the Heavenly host to listen."[350]

Even if the Lord has a resentment against His people, he is softened when He hears the singing of Israel:

> "When Israel . . . praise and extol God, He listens to their voices and is appeased."[351]

There were some tragic occurrences in the life of Israel on which God prohibited singing to the host of His angels: "On three occasions the Ministering Angels wished to utter song before the Holy One . . . , but He would not let them [*viz.* at the Flood, at the drowning of the Egyptians in the Red Sea, at the destruction of the Temple]."[352]

According to the legend, the Lord Himself indulges in singing:

> "When the Levites started playing and addressed the whole Israel with high voice (*ḳol rom*), you should not read *ḳol rom,* but *keḳolo shel rom,* like the voice of the High One. We learn from this that the Lord himself participates in their music."[353]

This corroborates most strongly the rabbinical contention that singing is of divine origin.

Thus closes the great cycle which, in the conception of Ancient Israel, has been assigned to singing: even before the creation of the world there has been singing in heaven;—in the mundane life, singing is inseparable from man whose joys and sorrows it reflects;—as a symbol of its inherent divine nature, singing returns eventually to the source of everything that is lofty and sublime, into the celestial regions.

o
o o

Celestial singing is connected with the mystic idea of the exultant song of stars and other celestial bodies as may be found in early biblical poetry. Expressions like "when the morning stars sang together" (Job 38:7) and "Sing, O Heavens" (Isa. 49:13) reflect the teaching of the Ancient Orient about the "Harmony of Spheres." According to it, the seven planets in passing the zodiac, produce the seven tones of the basic musical scale as discovered independently and expounded by ancient theorists.

The music theory of Antiquity, even though it is usually associated with the Hellenes, has actually originated in the Orient and thencefrom was brought over to Greece where it has been developed onto a complex system. PYTHAGORAS seems to have been largely instrumental in the introduction of that theory, since it is a well-known fact that he had had strong leanings towards borrowing his ideas from Oriental sources. In medieval mysticism the "Harmony of the Spheres" has subsequently evolved into a rather complicated and widely disseminated doctrine, in which Jewish mystics have had their due share.[354]

The early translators of the Bible assumed the poets of the Old Testament to have been familiar with the ancient Oriental teaching of "Harmony of the Spheres." Thus, the verse in "Song of Songs" 6:10, "clear as the sun," is translated by AQUILA as "sounding as the sun." The VULGATE renders Job 38:37, "who can pour out the bottles of the heaven" with the paraphrase *concentum coeli quis dormire faciet,* "who will reduce to silence the music of the heaven?"

Three further biblical passages explicitly mention the sounding world of the celestial bodies. Ezekiel 1:24 says of the Cherubim:

> "I heard the noise of their wings like the noise of great waters, like the voice of the Almighty."

And the psalmist exults:

> "The heavens declare the glory of God, and the firmament showeth His handiwork; day unto day uttereth speech . . . their line[355] is gone out through all the earth, and their words to the end of the world" (Ps. 19:1-5).

The same idea is expressed in an even more concrete form in Ps. 148:3:

> "Praise ye Him, sun and moon; praise Him, all ye stars of light; praise Him ye heaven of heavens."

Talmudic writers adopted the biblical conception that the movement of celestial bodies produces certain sounds. According to the theory of the Israelites the sound is like a flash of fire which, emanating from the producing body, travels directly to the listener's ear.[356] Vocal music, preferring sustained tones, has the same talmudic name as the echo (*babarah*).[357]

Aside from the stars and planets, the Talmud attributes to the sun the production of its own sounds, which—to be sure—are interpreted less in a musical than in a naturalistic sense. Among the sounds which could allegedly be heard from Jerusalem to Jericho, the Mishnah mentions

> "the sound of the *magrephah;* . . . the voice of Gabini the herald; the sound of the flute; the noise of the cymbal; the sound of the singing; the sound of the *shofar;* and some say, even the voice of the high priest when he pronounced the Name on the day of Atonement."[358]

In a commentary to this passage, a rabbinical writer expresses his astonishment that such phenomena could take place in daytime, since a sound is less audible in the day than in the silence of the night:

> "Why is the voice of a man not heard by day as it is heard by night? Because of the revolution [*lit.* "the wheel"] of the sun which saws in the sky like a carpenter sawing cedars."[359]

14. THE HEBREW MELODY

The destruction of the Jerusalem sanctuary by the Romans and the annihilation of the Jewish national state spelled the greatest disaster in the entire history of the Jews. The people of Israel, defeated, humiliated, driven into slavery, or dispersed beyond hope of recovery, were in danger of being wiped out not only physically, but also culturally and spiritually. The national mourning for the lost sanctuary, decreed by the sages, prohibited music, singing, and all sorts of pleasurable diversion. This prohibition, had it been carried out rigorously, would have amounted to the complete disappearance of Jewish music.

To be sure, the fate of ancient instrumental music was sealed for ever, since no artistic activity which depends entirely on perpetuity of its practice, has a chance to survive after a few decades of forced cessation.

But if the ruined instrumental music of the Jews could never be retrieved, vocal music—fortunately—was spared the same bitter fate. Singing happened to be an inborn urge to the Jews; its roots penetrated so deeply into the soul of the people that the common fate of the nation could not prevent the individual from expressing in singing his natural sentiments, his sorrow, longing, hope, and trust in God.

Besides, religious singing—in contrast to secular singing—has never ceased. To be sure, the rabbinical prohibition of music embraced all kinds of musical manifestations. Singing in the sacred service, however, as a spontaneous expression of Jewish piety, has withstood the most rigorous ban. Furthermore, the rabbinical authorities themselves were at variance as to whether singing was to be radically abolished or not. Some advocated a complete prohibition;[360] others maintained that only instrumental music, but not singing, had to be banned.[361] Curiously enough, the net result of all these controversies turned out to be that singing in the cult and in intimate religious celebrations, never was seriously menaced.[362]

o
o o

Despite this historical evidence, an almost unanimous belief prevailed until the recent decades that the song of the biblical era has been irremediably lost.

Even at a relatively recent time CORNILL says:

> "Both the secular and temple music of Ancient Israel have long since died out in silence. Not one tone has remained alive, not one of her melodies do we hear."[363]

Music scholars were convinced that no attempts at reconstruction would ever succeed in reviving this supposedly vanished world of sounds.

This belief was completely shattered by the tremendous research work done, in the first place, by ABRAHAM ZEVI IDELSOHN (1882-1938). It is his distinctive merit to have proven that remnants of ancient Hebrew music still exist in our days, practically untouched by time and circumstances.

On his extended journeys in the Orient, IDELSOHN has found in Yemen, Babylonia, Persia, Buchara, Daghestan, and in other places, Jewish tribes who seceded from the mother-country mostly during the times of the kings, and established for themselves a new home in these foreign countries. They lived there in a complete religious and cultural isolation and preserved through the millennia their national and religious characteristics, and also their songs.

IDELSOHN has collected these songs and, apart from fixing these in modern musical notation, also recorded them on discs. His publications[364] constituted an unexpected wealth of information about ancient Jewish singing and have created a real sensation in the world of comparative musicology. The results of IDELSOHN's research, despite some debatable points with regard to his methodology, are recognized to-day as the foundation of our knowledge of ancient Jewish song. They have actually opened entirely new vistas for further research in the field of Jewish music.

IDELSOHN was one of the first to prove that there are striking parallels between ancient Hebrew songs and those of the early Christian Church. Some of the melodies of the Yemenite and Babylonian Jews, which he notated for the first time, show for instance the closest conformity with Gregorian chants. As a result, there remains to-day not a shadow of doubt that the early Christian liturgy has taken over a great many of its songs from the melodic repertory of the Temple, or the Synagogue, or both.

In the early medieval period, the chants of the Christian ritual were collected and preserved in crude musical notation, first by AMBROSE, bishop of Milan (333-397), and later by Pope GREGORY I (590-604) or whoever did this in their name. These songs of early Latin Christianity remained virtually unchanged to this day and are still in use in the liturgy of the Church in their original form.

IDELSOHN showed a whole array of similarities between Jewish and Gregorian psalmodies and lamentations, as well as between various intonations of the Christian Church and Jewish Pentateuch cantillation and prayer tunes.[365] PETER WAGNER, one of the most outstanding scholars in the field of Gregorian plain-song, likewise proved the conformity of these Jewish songs with those of the Latin ritual.[366]

> "The Yemenite Pentateuch-tune, for instance, used also for certain psalms, could very well constitute a Gregorian psalm-chant with its *Initium*, its *Tenor* [reciting note], its *Mediante* and *Finalis*." (Mus. ex. 2).

Example 2. After Peter Wagner

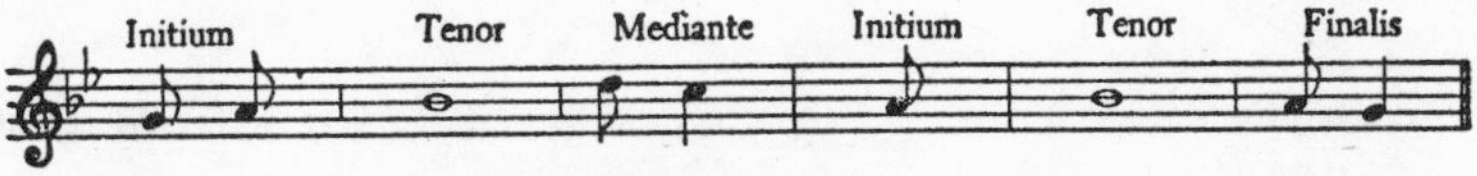

Compare with Idelsohn, *Thesaurus,* Vol. I:

No. 11

No. 202 Exodus 12:21-22

The same holds true for the Sabbath psalmody, which is sung by the entire congregation standing:

Example 3. (After Peter Wagner)

Compare with Idelsohn, Thesaurus, Vol. I:

NO. 16 (PSALM 8:1)

NO. 20 (SABBATH HYMN)

NO. 21 (SABBATH HYMN)

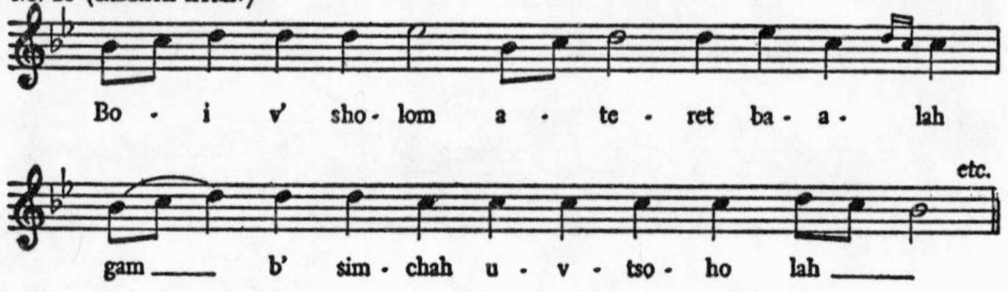

NO. 19 (PSALM 29:1)

No. 23

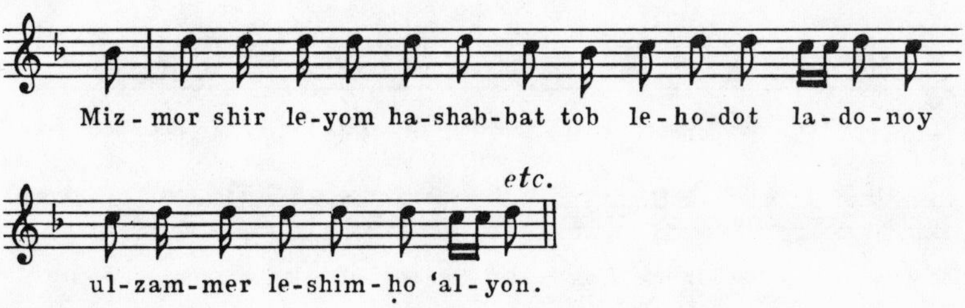
Miz - mor shir le-yom ha-shab-bat tob le-ho-dot la-do-noy
etc.
ul-zam-mer le-shim-ḥo 'al-yon.

Compare the above melodies with the following Gregorian Chant:

PSALM 45:2 GREGORIAN

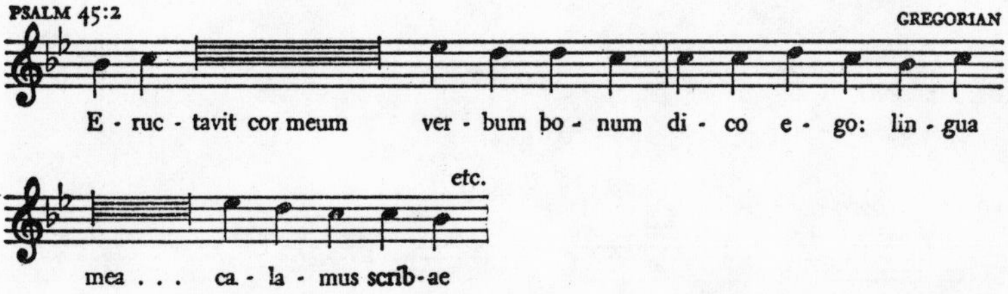
E - ruc - tavit cor meum ver - bum bo - num di - co e - go: lin - gua
etc.
mea . . . ca - la - mus scrib-ae

As PETER WAGNER maintains, such parallelisms in the structure of psalmodic formulae and the similarities with Gregorian chants cannot possibly be considered as coincidental phenomena of two independent lines of evolution. There is only one possibility: the influence of one upon the other. He leaves the question open, however, whether the influence of the synagogal music upon Church music has been a direct or indirect one.

> "It is thinkable, at any rate, that the Jewish community in Rome, for instance, assumed the role of a mediator; it is more appropriate, however, to follow the analogy of the liturgical history and to conclude from it that the Jewish synagogal tradition served as the pattern for psalm-singing in all Christian congregations, the Syrians, the Armenians, the Greeks, consequently also the Latins."[367]

In the above quoted examples, PETER WAGNER has established merely a melodic pattern, by reducing the conformities to the simplest structural formula. These parallels are indeed more striking if we compare more extensive portions of the chants, or even entire melodies. Here are some examples revealing the similarity of Gregorian chants with ancient Jewish songs: (Mus. ex. 5).

Idelsohn, *Thesaurus,* Vol 1. No. 38

Mus. ex. No. 5

Mus. ex. No. 6

Further similar melodies may be found in Idelsohn, *Thesaurus,* Vol I, Nos. 96-108.

Compare all these melodies with the following Gregorian Chant:

Similarities between the following Gregorian chant and the Jewish priestly blessing are self-evident:

Mus. Ex. No. 7

IDELSOHN adduces comparative tables for songs of the Oriental Jews to show that their patterns follow certain ancient Jewish modes. The songs of the Persian, Yemenite, Babylonian-Sephardic and, on the other hand, East-European-Ashkenazic Jews show indeed incontestable resemblances.[368] The mutual conformity of the songs of these widely separated Jewish groups is the irrefutable evidence of their common origin as well as of their old age, which reaches far back into Antiquity.

o o o

CURT SACHS has made pertinent observations with regard to this newly discovered ancient Jewish song.[369] According to him, the conformities as shown above, are the conclusive proof that

> "Gregorian music has been taken over mostly from ancient Jewish music, by which the tonal art of the Jewish people assumes a predominant role in the history of music."

SACHS offers a general analysis of these tunes and concludes that they are tetrachordal, modal, and pentatonic.

> "*Tetrachordal*: the melodies are constructed within the intervallic frame of a fourth, two of which, combined disjunctly, constitute an octave. These tetrachords are basically identical with those called Dorian, Phrygian and Lydian in the music theory of the Hellenes, and the melodies in question are mostly in these modes.—*Pentatonic, with no half steps*: like many other ancient folk melodies the world over, these ritual tunes of the Jews are based on a scale consisting primarily of minor thirds and whole steps; when occasionally half steps occur, they pass by in a quick progression; they never constitute essential steps.—*Modal*: the interval of a minor third appears at different places within the tetrachordal structure, . . . so that in the subsequent diatonic constructions the complementary tone may be put either higher or lower."

SACHS refers to the well-known statement of CLEMENT of ALEXANDRIA (ca. 200 C.E.), according to which the Dorian element prevails in Jewish singing.[370] This is taken by SACHS as a proof of the predominantly dignified and lofty character of ancient Jewish music. He does not doubt, furthermore, that

> "the characteristics attributed to the different modes by the Greeks have been applied in approximately the same manner by the Israelites."

In analyzing the ancient Jewish melodies, SACHS has found that their modes are determined by the character of the songs. Thus, epic melodies (narrations of the Pentateuch) are generally Dorian,—lyric chants (lamentations) are Phrygian,—and jubilant songs of praise are Lydian.[371]

Furthermore, SACHS stresses the point

> "that the mere notation of the melodies does not convey a sufficient idea about the nature of this ancient art. We definitely have to stimulate our imagination by evoking the peculiarly animated, swinging, expressionistic interpretation of this type of music in the Orient."

Finally, SACHS states that

> "one may conclude from a general rule that the liturgical melodies that survived in these far-off countries testify not only to the music of Solomon's Temple, but also to the folk music of Ancient Israel. For both must be branches of the same tree."

SACHS' closing statement is especially important for the following reason. We know that the Yemenite, Babylonian and other displaced Jewish tribes emigrated from the mother-country either long before the Babylonian exile, or just when Jerusalem was conquered by NEBUCHADREZZAR, in order to avoid captivity and slavery. Consequently, the songs they took with them must have been those of the First Temple. Thus, the remaining ancient Hebrew melodies, as found by IDELSOHN, are extant examples of that pre-Babylonian period. The fact is indisputable that certain songs of the Temple survived in the Synagogue. Consequently, it makes no difference whether the first Judaeo-Christians borrowed their songs from the Temple or from the Synagogue.

It is astonishing that, except in musicology, IDELSOHN's life-work has exerted but little influence in other fields of biblical research. Our knowledge of the musical culture of Ancient Israel, especially its sacred music, is based in part on reports and statements of the author (or authors) of the Book of Chronicles I and II, who is generally considered to have been a Levite, or even a levitical singer, in view of his intimate familiarity with the musical practice of the Temple.

Some modern scholars, however, are disinclined to accept these authors as reliable writers of Jewish history. Thus, ROBERT H. PFEIFFER considers all, or most, of the Chronicler's tales about the Temple music of David and Solomon spurious, or grossly exaggerated. Although he admits that

> "it is unfair . . . to dismiss the Chronicler with a shrug of the shoulders as a distorter of facts."[372]

In PFEIFFER's estimation, the chronicler has modelled the institutions of the Temple, and consequently those of the sacred musical service, after the pattern of

> "the small Jewish community of Jerusalem in the middle of the third century B.C.E., (the supposed date of the Books of Chronicles).[373]

However, even PFEIFFER cannot deny the fact that

> "sacred songs were sung by the accompaniment of psalteries in the ancient Israelitic sanctuaries, at least as early as the middle of the eighth century (Am. 5:23), but, if we believe Amos, this music was crude and noisy."[374]

(There is no need to discuss the "crude and noisy" character of these sacred songs. It is obvious that what Amos meant was something quite different).

From all this, PFEIFFER draws the conclusion that

> "since the organization of the musical parts of the service could not be attributed to Moses, the alleged author of the Pentateuch, the chronicler selected David, known to be a poet and musician, as the organizer of the singers' and musicians' guild and composer of hymns."[375]

In trying to disprove the existence of an organized musical service already in David's and Solomon's time, PFEIFFER musters all the evidence *against* it. He overlooks, however, the historical facts and is unaware of their implications, both of which might attest *for* this fact. Among these, Samuel's "schools of prophets" is one of the most important. As will be shown in a subsequent section, these "schools" were the veritable centers of music instruction on a large scale, preparing hundreds of "students" for their future career as singers and musicians. David's musical organization was the logical sequel of such concentrated pedagogical efforts, designed to provide the sacred service with highly qualified professional musicians.

Another historical fact is corroborated by SENNAḤERIB's demand to deliver Hezekiah's famous singers as a ransom for sparing the besieged city of Jerusalem. The artistry of these singers must have been quite different from that of Amos' "crude and noisy" songs, if SENNAḤERIB valued them higher than the pillage and plundering of the enemy's conquered capital city.

Finally, IDELSOHN's recent discoveries may serve as an eloquent, though indirect, proof that the musical culture, and with it the musical organization of Ancient Israel, has been much older than PFEIFFER would have us believe.

o o o

Since the time of IDELSOHN's publications, comparative musicology, biblical accentuology, musico-liturgical research, and other related fields of study are showing an ever-growing interest in ancient Jewish music. Several important works, published in recent decades about the subject, have enlarged considerably our knowledge about the nature of this music, so that we have to-day a rather clear picture concerning the form and character of ancient Jewish song.

Quite apart from the representatives of musicological research, several scholars in other domains of science have been attracted by the subject of Jewish music and have attempted to contribute, from their point of view, to the clarification of certain questions in connection with it. Among their publications, some of which appeared even prior to those of IDELSOHN's, three essays deserve special attention, inasmuch as they try to shed light upon the problem of Jewish music from the angle of neighboring scholarly disciplines.

o o o

EDUARD SIEVERS ventures to determine the character of ancient Jewish song on linguistic and metrical grounds.[376] He starts his deliberations from the accents (*ta'amim*) and thinks that their inventors must have had in mind a manner of speech akin to our oratorical declamation,

> "which, however, shows at the same time certain attempts at marking clearly the melodical aspect. Otherwise it would be difficult to under-

> stand how these accentual signs could have developed in the long run into pure signs for musical notes and series of notes."[377]

SIEVERS does not attribute a definite melodic implication to the accentual syllables alone as indicated by the *ta'amim;* he thinks that the musical contents of the phrases were determined just as much by the unaccented syllables,

> "the melodic line of which was left to the natural feeling of the performer,"

this being indeed a rather vague interpretation. SIEVERS considers this practice as

> "a compromise between the natural and the stylized, or artificial, melody,"

which, basically, corresponds to the Oriental principle of *makamat,* interpreted from the linguistic point of view.

In summarizing his views, SIEVERS states that it is

> "possible, and even probable, that as a principle, the 'singing' of the ancient Hebrews did in no way parallel the modern art-singing; it must be rather relegated to an elementary stage of art, in which the melo-rhythmic pattern was governed by the specific irrational rhythm and the natural speech-melody of the spoken word."

He admits that, with this statement, he does not proclaim anything basically new, for—as he says—

> "the Hebrews practiced more 'a sort of cantillation' than 'singing' in the proper sense."[378]

While making this statement, SIEVERS commits two grave errors; first, in trying to draw a comparison between two radically different musical conceptions, those of the Orient and Occident, and secondly, in assigning to the singing of the Hebrews "an elementary stage." It would indeed be more appropriate to investigate the subject in question not in the light of philological considerations alone but also from the angle of Oriental musical practice, and quite independently from any artistic or aesthetic prejudices of the Occidental world.

According to SIEVERS, the two divergent extremes of speech-rhythm are "the artistic declamation ("der kunstmässige Sprechvortrag") and real singing ("eigentlicher Gesang")." He fails, however, to determine precisely the characteristics of either one, although he admits that there exist some intermediary and transitory stages between these extremes.[379] To be properly understood, the musical terminology used by SIEVERS would need certain clarifications and occasional rectification.

Furthermore, instead of defining cantillation as an art form belonging to the low or early stage of development, SIEVERS should have considered it a specifically Jewish and, more widely, a characteristic Oriental vocal art form. For everything we know about singing in Ancient Israel proves that the tonal art of the Jews has been far above the "low stage of development." He does not seem to be aware of the fact that, according to the conception of the Orientals, the full-bodied *recitativo*-like singing represents a higher category of art as compared to our tonal, square-shaped melody. This is a principle, which retains its unchanging validity on every stage of development of Oriental music.

OSKAR FLEISCHER interprets ancient Jewish singing as a specific art governed by the accentual signs.[380] He considers these signs, however, not as a useful device for linguistic purposes, but as an effective expedient for the musical practice itself. He sees in these signs, just as he does in the early medieval neumes, cheironomic movements reproduced graphically, that is to say, movements of the hand by which the choir leaders of those days used to indicate the rising and falling of the voice and—in general—the fluctuations of the melodic line.

FLEISCHER refers to the fact attested in the rabbinical literature that in Ancient Israel the vocal rendition of the *ta'amim,* presently known as cantillation, was taught by motions of the hand.[381] AARON ben ASHER mentions specifically that these motions were at the origin of the written accents.[382] To quote merely one example, the accent *shalshelet* ("chain"), a zig-zag line ⌇ , representing a tremolating figure, was performed by a quivering motion of the hand. FLEISCHER states that cheironomy has been applied by the Jews for the most part in singing instruction, which prior to the introduction of the written *ta'amim,* had been imparted solely by oral methods. However, since the system of accents has never achieved the status of a completely independent pedagogical discipline, oral teaching has continued to play a highly important part in keeping alive the tradition even in the following centuries and, in the final analysis, it has actually preserved the Hebrew musical heritage.

FLEISCHER alludes to the significant fact that the oldest Latin neumes are to be found in the Lamentations of Jeremiah. He claims that since this can hardly be a mere coincidence, it must be taken as an indication of a definite relationship between ancient Jewish singing and that of the early Christian Church.[383]

> "No other portion of the Hebrew Bible could have been more appropriate than these songs for expressing the feeling of a nation about the destruction of the Jewish state as well as the liberty of the Jewish people. Dispersed and enslaved after the ruin of their state, the Jews were too deeply aware of the prophet's words with which they could bewail their misery day by day. If any poems of the Old Testament could express adequately the sentiments of misfortune, these were the Lamentations of Jeremiah; and if in any such poems the song of the Temple could be preserved, these were the Lamentations. These songs have been the easier learned by the Christians, since they were originally in the same situation as the Jews, and because many other remnants of ancient Jewish customs have also been taken over by the Christian liturgy. For let us remember that it was not a single melody or a melodic formula which has been preserved in the Lamentations, but a musical form, a pattern of recitation, a model for declamation. With

the singing of the Lamentations, the Christian Church has adopted an age old musical principle."

FLEISCHER also points out another proof for the close affinity between the early Christian liturgy and ancient Jewish Temple song: the continuity of using Hebrew letter-names in the Latin text of the Lamentations. These letter names, heading as ordinal numbers the chapters of the Hebrew original, were considered in the Christian liturgy as equal in ritual value to the Latin text and have been sung, like the text itself, as late as the 8th century.[384]

Here are some examples for such Hebrew letter-names, sung in the liturgy of the early Church: Mus. Ex. No. 8

What is the reason that such words, unessential for the contents of the songs and incomprehensible to the singers, should have been preserved in the liturgical text for such a long time? There is no other explanation than that the tradition of ancient Jewish singing was so strong in the first centuries of the common era that the Christians must have shunned the idea of eliminating from their liturgy even such unimportant details as the Hebrew chapter numbers. FLEISCHER refers to the fact that

> "at those times, there seems to have been only a little understanding of the Hebrew language among the dignitaries of the Latin Church,—and even less among the people! What meaning must the Christian congregation have had attributed to these Hebrew words which they sang? While they have had their logical meaning in the original Hebrew, they were meaningless words of stammering for the people speaking Latin . . . Were they and their group-neumes not hallowed, because of their age, around the year 700, no neumator in the world would have ever thought of setting them into music."[385]

The musical setup of the Lamentations is, without doubt, of ancient Jewish origin. Not only has it been adopted in its original form by the Latin Church, but it was kept alive even in the Jewish musical liturgy, though in a restricted way, after the destruction of the Temple.

In tracing back the musical liturgy of the early medieval Church to the music practice of the primitive Judaeo-Christians, and in maintaining the close relationship between the ancient Jewish and early Christian singing, FLEISCHER arrives at the same conclusion, which we have inferred from the facts of an historico-religious nature, namely that the pattern and quality of early Christian and Jewish psalmody must have been identical.

o
o o

ARNO NADEL ventures to apply a philosophical-metaphysical approach to the problem of Jewish singing.[386] He designates as the most outstanding feature of Jewish singing its recitativic character. This he derives ultimately from factors of a supernatural, mystico-religious order. Oriental man

> "does not pour anything into solid forms when he comes into communion with his God, when his soul is boundless and without constraint, when he bows humbly, with no earthly strings attached, before the lofty sphere of the Almighty. He sings loosely, being almost in another region,"

hence the swinging, de-materialized, almost unreal, eternally flowing melodic current of Jewish cantillation.

NADEL attempts to assemble the features of Jewish music into a distinctive pattern, and classifies them as seven "characters," divided into four "principal characters," and three "subordinate characters":

Principal characters:

1. The recitativic,
2. the melodic-diatonic,
3. the anapaestic,
4. the parallelistic.

Subordinate characters:

1. The meditative,
2. the mixed character of the keys (or modes),
3. the changing character of the rhythms.

With these "characters," NADEL intends to establish not anything scholarly or abstract,

> "but the nature of Jewish music and, as a matter of fact, of Jewish soul in general, as it has manifested itself for millennia and will continue to express itself within a reasonable space of time."

In summarizing, NADEL explains the deeper sense of his schematic pattern:

> "The 'recitativic' corresponds to the unbound nature of the Jewish soul, the 'melodic-diatonic' to its perpetual singing and humming, the 'anapaestic' to its seeking, striving and affirming, the 'parallelistic' to its philosophy, to its questioning and answering, the 'meditative' to its mysticism—and the 'changing of keys and rhythms' to its restless roaming in the world."

Obviously, this is a highly subjective and detached approach to Jewish music, which on the whole can hardly claim any significant meaning except for those absorbed in purely cabalistic speculations. According to NADEL's conception, the problem of Jewish music, in the final analysis, is nothing less than the problem of Judaism itself,—a rather debatable statement.

o
o o

Such and similar attempts have a relatively minor value for the investigation of Jewish singing, and have been exposed here merely for the purpose of showing the different approaches to the problem. Since IDELSOHN's publications, Jewish musical research has found its own and generally workable method which makes further groping and seeking unnecessary. We are indeed fortunate nowadays in being able to base our investigations upon living musical material and in possessing a modicum of authentic facts and ideas about the ancient Jewish music.

In general, the melodies collected by IDELSOHN are typical examples of the Oriental variation principle. Inasmuch as we consider PETER WAGNER's structural formulae of Hebrew melodies as representing certain *maḳam*-types, the songs built upon these patterns must be taken as fully crystallized melodies. In them the *maḳam* had already been treated with the variation-technique, as a result of which they constitute perfectly accomplished compositions ("durchkomponierte Singweisen"), at least in the Oriental meaning of the word. They reflect the skill and art of the Oriental for variation, which characterizes ancient Jewish singing to the same extent as it does the singing of the entire Arabian-Persian civilization, and—through adaptation and transplantation—also the entire Christian-Oriental liturgy: the Coptic, Abyssinian, Syriac, Maronite, and Armenian Church song.

o
o o

This chapter would be incomplete without mentioning the latest serious attempt at grasping the concrete essence of the ancient cantillation as it has been put forth by SOLOMON ROSOWSKY in his extensive treatise "The Cantillation of the Bible" (New York, 1957). ROSOWSKY's approach differs radically from that of IDELSOHN and other scholars of the same persuasion. For his fundamental and empirically obtained collection of the Pentateuch chant (in the Lithuanian-Israeli version) has been subjected by him to a critical scrutiny not only *after* its final notation but—quite unprecedentedly—*prior* to it as well.

To accomplish the latter task, ROSOWSKY has availed himself of an objective method of cross-examination directed at the reputedly qualified cantillators of the Bible, with whom he came into close contact in the course of his long research. Through the comparison of the different variants of all the *ta'amim* (as performed repeatedly by these cantillators under specially pre-arranged conditions) and the resulting rigorous elimination of the untrustworthy material, ROSOWSKY claims to have had procured the purest and the most reliable version of the biblical chant, at least within a single Jewish group. With this as a basis, he has worked out subsequently a rationally organized system of cantillation that is supposed to express adequately, and in artistic form, the entire set of syntactical relations with all their minutest details pertaining to the scriptural text.

15. THE HEBREW RHYTHM

Until relatively recent times, most scholars investigating the character of ancient Jewish music, approached the problem mainly from its melodic angle.

Its other essential element—rhythm,—has been subjected but sporadically to a comprehensive inquiry. All the endeavors to determine the Hebrew rhythm have been restricted mostly to the field of Hebrew poetry and, more specifically, to a purely external counting of its syllables, words and stress-accents. It is obvious that the complete disregard for any other approach to metrics impaired the research along these lines from the very outset. Especially the close affinity between the declamatory and musical implications of Hebrew poetry have been either superficially treated or wholly ignored. Language and meter, however, are closely interlinked in the music of Ancient Israel. Biblical poetry, which embraces the lyric episodes of the Old Testament, was principally poetry designed for singing. It is therefore manifest that these songs were strongly, if not decisively, influenced by the intrinsic rhythm of the language. Without deviating too much from our basic subject, it will be necessary to touch as briefly as possible upon some general notions of poetry and metrics, in order to determine the nature and character of Hebrew rhythm, and its application to singing.

It must be stated beforehand that the principle of any investigation pertaining to Hebrew rhythm must be based upon the specific rhythmical predilections of the Orientals, so different from ours. According to Western conception, rhythm is governed by inter-tonal "time-units," the sum total of which constitutes larger metric entities. These time-units consist of longer and shorter rhythmic pulsations (beats), which actually predetermine the pace or *tempo* of music. The larger entities are known in our Western musical terminology as measures, groups of measures, phrases, periods, etc., all these notions being foreign to the Orientals.[387]

Oriental vocal music does not know any conscious beats, or "counts," in the Western sense, consequently it has no metric units bound by bar-lines. Oriental rhythm has a different basis. To gain a clear understanding of it, one must recall that Oriental music does not know harmony in the Occidental sense. This is quite lucidly stated by SACHS:

> "What harmony means to the West, the almost breathlike change from tension to relaxation, is in the East provided by rhythm. In avoiding the deadly inertia of evenness, rhythm helps an otherwise autonomous melody to breathe in and out—just as harmony does in the West."[388]

In other words, in the East the lacking harmonic element in music is compensated by rhythm. We may well understand, therefore, the supreme significance of the rhythmical background in Oriental singing, and also the intrinsic role of percussion instruments in the aesthetics of Oriental music. Most of its tunes, whether sung or played, are accompanied by percussion instruments, and if such are not available, clapping of hands by the participants serves as a sufficient means to enhance the musical feeling of the Orientals. Even such primitive rhythmic devices as clapping of hands, stamping of feet, etc., constitute elements of amplified musical pleasure for the Orientals and afford them aesthetic satisfaction, which the Western audiences derive pre-eminently through the combination of the three main ingredients of Occidental music: melody, harmony, and rhythm.

Surprisingly enough, there is no equivalent in Biblical Hebrew for the term "rhythm," despite the fact that Ancient Israel cultivated intensely all rhythmic arts, such as poetry, music, singing, and dancing. For the various manifestations of dance the Jews used no less than twenty-two different expressions.[389] Nevertheless, one will look in vain for a Hebrew designation of rhythm which is the basic element of dancing. Nor does one find any such term in Hebrew poetry and music. We must therefore turn to the language itself and seek to approach the rhythmical aspect of Jewish music from the linguistic angle.

The preparatory work in this respect was started, though somewhat hesitatingly, by the great biblical scholars of the 19th century, mainly by HEINRICH EWALD, KARL BUDDE, CARL FRIEDRICH KEIL, HERMAN HUPFELD, and others. Only in more recent times do we witness a scientific trend, promoted by outstanding rhythmologists, to investigate the meter and rhythm of Hebrew poetry, and thereby to disclose the intimate interrelation between Hebrew versification and music. The latter objective is, of course, particularly significant for our own subject. Among the modern scholars who paved the way into this rather unexplored field, three should be mentioned as having undertaken the basic pioneering work: EDUARD SIEVERS, ELCANON ISAACS, and WILLIAM R. ARNOLD. Their learned studies contain valuable new material and constitute the basis for further research in this unexploited domain. The importance of their writings is scarcely minimized by the fact that they sometimes arrive at contradictory conclusions. Furthermore, they betray a common weakness of being guided mainly by philological considerations, which frequently impair the musical implications of their research. For, to use SACHS' words,

> "they have analyzed texts and nothing but texts . . . Even the music-minded Eduard Sievers in his monumental work, has clung to the philological aspect."[390]

This is by no means surprising, because at the time these scholars approached the problem,

> "the musical facets of the question were unknown to the rhythmologists."[391]

In the meantime, fortunate discoveries in the field of ancient Jewish music opened up unexpected horizons. Especially IDELSOHN's publications[392] afford to-day a deep insight into the nature of ancient Jewish singing. Availing himself of this invaluable material in conjunction with his own profound knowledge of the music of Antiquity, CURT SACHS, in a scholarly study, has delineated for the first time the musical aspects of Hebrew rhythm.[393]

o o o

It is common knowledge that the canon of the Old Testament comprises prosaic and poetic portions. The decision itself, however, as to what constitutes "poetry," and what is "prose," has been rather uncertain. The reason is that, for the most part, linguistic and stylistic criteria alone were being applied to the two categories which, in this case, can hardly be distinguished more than on the basis of very general principles. The psalms, for instance are unanimously considered as "poetry," whereas the narrative books (with the exception of the occasional song-like episodes) are just as unanimously declared to be "prose." The "poetic" portions of the Bible are supposed to be recognized by their particular idiom, by a richer vocabulary and by a special syntax; accordingly, they are believed to be distinguished by a "poetic" style, while all this, or most of it, is allegedly lacking in the "prosaic" portions. It is obvious, however, that even an "uninspired" text can acquire certain poetic characteristics when clothed in an elated language. For instance, the device of *parallelismus membrorum,* used frequently in the Scriptures and employed repeatedly in antiphonal singing, is very appropriate for enhancing the impressiveness of the style, even in so-called "prosaic" portions.

Any style elevated above the daily language may be considered "poetic," without actually being "poetry." Lofty ideas may lift even pure prose to a level where it becomes almost akin to poetry in the spiritual or aesthetic sense. This comparison alone shows that the notions of poetry and prose are highly flexible when defined according to the stylistic features of the text. The difficulties disappear, however, if the criterion of what constitutes poetry or prose is the accepted notion of the *metric* quality of the text. Meter alone, regular or irregular, should be taken as the real characteristic of the poetic form. Accordingly, all portions of the Old Testament outside of the pure narrations or pronouncements of law, are classified nowadays as poetry, to which belong aside from the psalms, the Proverbs, the Song of Songs, the Lamentations, Ecclesiastes and Job, important sections of the Prophets, and—among the Apocrypha—parts of Ecclesiasticus (Ben Sirach), Judith, Tobit, and a few others.

The metric form of a text is already by itself a bidding for its musical rendition. Among the metrical parts of the Bible there are numerous poems with an unmistakable song-like character. Without any doubt, these poems have been sung in Israel, in conformity with the general practice of ancient peoples, who always performed versified texts with singing. Furthermore, in Jewish usage this is directly attested by the fact that a great part of the Psalter, the Song of Songs, many hymn-like poems, such as Moses' and Miriam's songs at the Red Sea, Deborah's and Judith's triumphant paeans, and many others, have been rendered with singing.

In contrast to these song-like poems, there are the narrative or didactic portions, considered as "poetry for recitation." Between the two, there are the intermediate poetic forms like some writings of the Prophets, which may be taken as belonging to both categories. Also certain parts of Job, Lamentations and Ecclesiastes contain, besides metric texts, intermediate patterns between poetry and prose.

Except for the manifestly song-like portions, it is difficult to discover any regular forms of Hebrew rhythm, inasmuch as the latter lacks any rigorous stability and thus allows all kinds of subjective interpretations. Matters are furthermore aggravated by the fact that there exist no traditional criteria with regard to the difference between "poetic" and "prosaic" texts. True, JOSEPHUS refers a few times to the metrical form of Hebrew poetry,[394] but this has no bearing upon our subject, since it does not reveal anything about the musical rendering of these poems. Furthermore, JOSEPHUS, in characterizing Hebrew poetry, uses terms familiar to his Greek readers, such as trimeters, pentameters, hexameters, all these being metrical forms of quantitative poetry, whereas Hebrew poetry is basically accentual.

PHILO's essays contain a single, and very vague, reference to the meter of ancient Jewish singing. In his description of the rites of the Therapeutae, we find the statement that the members of this Jewish sect

> "do not confine themselves to contemplation but also compose hymns and psalms to God in all sorts of *meters* and melodies which they write down in solemn *rhythms* as best they can."[395]

PHILO's reference is of such a general nature that it does not warrant any conclusion with regard to Hebrew rhythm.

Then, there are a few allusions to Hebrew rhythm in EUSEBIUS' writings. He characterizes the Song of Moses and the 118th (119th) Psalm as verses composed in what the Greeks call the "heroic" meter, *i.e.* hexameters of sixteen syllables. Otherwise he considers the Hebrew poetry to be written in trimeters.[396]

His assertion is contradicted by JULIAN who, in a hypothetic dialogue with CYRIL of ALEXANDRIA, tries to prove that the Hebrews, being devoid of all culture, could not have composed poetry in metrical form.[397]

JOHN CHRYSOSTOM's writings, too, contain some allusions to an allegedly metric structure of Hebrew poetry. Thus, referring to David, CHRYSOSTOM says that

> "the virtuous, just and prophetic king, when moved by the Holy Spirit, composed the Book of 150 psalms in metric form, according to the meter of his own language, and sang them with melody, with rhythm, and with [the accompaniment of] divers instruments, with dancing and singing groups" (*canebat cum modulatione, cumque rhythmo, instrumentisque diversis, choreis et cantionibus*).[398]

This vague reference to Hebrew versification reappears with abbreviations in the following passage from one of CHRYSOSTOM's dubious works:

> "When he was moved by the Spirit, he composed in metric form psalms that corresponded to his topic."[399]

Furthermore, there are some hints concerning Hebrew versification in JEROME's writings. In his "*Prologue to the Book of Job,*" he refers to PHILO, JOSEPHUS, ORIGEN and EUSEBIUS as proving allegedly that the Psalter, the Lamentations of Jeremiah, and almost all the song-like poems of the Scriptures are metrical compositions, similar to the odes of HORACE, PINDAR, ALCAEUS and SAPPHO. He is even more explicit with regard to the Book of Job, in stating that chapter 1 to chapter 3:3, and again chapter 42:7-17 are written in prose (*prosa oratio est*), contrary to the remaining and, consequently, major portion of the book. The latter shows, in his estimation, a verse-form based on hexameters, with dactyls and spondees, interrupted occasionally by characteristically Hebrew interpolations of other verse-feet, containing a dissimilar number of syllables, but the same quantitative value (*non earundem syllabarum, sed eorundem temporum*).[400]

Another allusion to Hebrew meter is to be found in JEROME's *Epistola ad*

Paulam, in which he refers to the four alphabetical psalms (111, 112, 119, and 145). He considers the first two written in trimeter iambics, the other in tetrameter iambics, similar to Moses' Song in Deuter. 32. The four alphabetical acrostics in Lamentations are also written, according to JEROME, in verse form. The first of these shows a kind of Sapphic meter; the second contains periods in the so-called "heroic measure" (*heroici comma*); the third is composed in trimeters, and the fourth is like the first and second.

In the same letter, JEROME alludes to the alphabetical poem in the Book of Proberbs, 31:10-31 (popularly known as King Lemuel's "*Song of the Virtuous Woman*") which, in his estimation, is composed in tetrameter iambics.[401]

Lastly, in the Preface to the second book of his Latin translation of EUSEBIUS' Greek "*Chronica*,"[402] JEROME compares the meters of the Psalter to those of PINDAR'S and HORACE'S poems,

> "now running in iambics, now ringing with Alcaics, now swelling with Sapphics, now beginning with a half foot,"

and ends up his scrutiny with the oratorical question:

> "What is more beautiful than the song of Deuteronomy and Isaiah? What is more sublime than Solomon? What more perfect than Job?"

JEROME's conclusion is that

> "all these, as JOSEPHUS and ORIGEN testify, are written in hexameters and pentameters."

There can be little doubt that JEROME's statements concerning the meter of Hebrew poetry hint merely at its external resemblance to the laws of Greek classical poetry.[403]

Among other references in the early patristic literature concerning the rhythmical organization of Hebrew poetry, that of GREGORY of NYSSA is particularly significant, inasmuch as he denies expressly (and quite correctly) any resemblance of Hebrew poetical verses to classic meters.[404] On the other hand, AUGUSTINE says that those skilled in the Hebrew language believe the Psalter to be written in meter. This statement, however, is invalidated by AUGUSTINE's admission that he was completely ignorant of Hebrew and could not, therefore, verify his own assertion.[405]

Finally, we have a reference concerning this subject by ISIDORE of SEVILLE to the effect that the Song of Moses was composed in the "heroic" meter, and the Book of Job in dactyls and spondees.[406] There is no need for refuting this strange assertion, which follows ostensibly the endeavors of early medieval patristic writers to establish some resemblance between Hebrew and classic versification.[407]

o
o o

Turning now to the opinions of modern scholars concerning the Hebrew rhythm, we come across two main schools of thought diametrically opposed to each other. One is based upon the rigorous *mora* system, the other upon the spontaneous distribution of accented and unaccented syllables. The *morae* (the *chronoi prōtoi*, as ARISTOXENOS calls them) are imaginary "counts" (like the conventional beats in Western musical practice), by which a definite time value is attributed to every vowel: one *mora* to a short vowel (including the *sh'va* and *ḥatef*),[408] two *morae* to a long vowel.[409]

According to the *mora* system, which ISAACS calls the *atnaḥ* meter (using the name of the Hebrew accent *atnaḥ,* ֑ "rester")[410] or pause meter, the Hebrew meter is based on the number of *morae,* and not on the number of syllables. In this system, an accented syllable counts as two *morae,* an unaccented syllable as one.[411] This system follows the theory of the Greek metricists, who applied to their rhythmical units a mathematical arrangement, according to which the syllables were deemed long or short, a long syllable being equal to two short syllables.

The other school of metricists considers Hebrew poetry to be set to a free accentual rhythm, whether the verses (or lines of the text) show a symmetrical arrangement of feet or not. As ARNOLD says,

> "the only time lengths that can contribute to the rhythm of the Hebrew poetry, are the intervals between accents,"[412]

which means that, basically, Hebrew rhythm is not determined by the number of syllables, but by the word-accent. This word-accent, and with it the rhythmic organization of the Hebrew verse,

> "depends not on the relative position of the prominent syllable with respect to the surrounding syllables, but on a certain relative position of the important syllable in the verse."[413]

Comparing the two systems, ISAACS terms classical verse "mechanical," Hebrew verse "dynamic,"[414] which formulation touches the focal point of the whole problem. Because of this dynamism it is the accented syllable that has the paramount importance in Hebrew meter and not the syllable of long duration.

For the rhythmization of poetry pure and simple, the *mora* system might have its advantages. For music, however, and especially for singing, (with the exclusion of dance-songs), it is impractical, since Oriental music does not know beats or counts (*morae*) of uniform length, as these are applied in poetry. A mere glance at any of the Oriental melodies of IDELSOHN's *Thesaurus* will show that the notated eighth notes have no uniformly established time values, some being of a longer, some of a shorter duration. The quarter notes, too, have very rarely the double value of eighth notes, which would be, however, the rule prevailing in the quantitative system. For the purposes of Jewish music, therefore, the only possible basis for rhythmization is that of the free accentual rhythm.

But even for poetry the accentual rhythm becomes of an increased significance, if one wants to establish a close relationship between the rhythmization and the contents of the text. This is clearly expressed by SACHS when he says about the accentual rhythm that

> "it never squeezed emotion or meaning into formal, regular patterns of meter or stress. No frigid, monotonous sequence of uniform iambs or dactyls, no constant number of feet in a verse, no even distribution of accents was allowed to distract attention from the words themselves and to dilute the power of diction. Every word, indeed every sentence,

kept its natural flow without interference of any kind from outside. Biblical poetry was naturalistic and in a way almost an uplifted, poetical prose."[415]

o
o o

The Hebrew verse consists generally of two distinct parts, called half-verses, and divided ordinarily into an equal number of two, three or four feet. Each foot, in turn, contains *one* accented syllable (tonal accent) and a variable number of unaccented syllables.

The following verse is an example of the equal division into two half-verses of four feet each:[416]

ʿadáh v'ẓilláh shemáʿan ḳoli || neshé lémeḥ haʾazennáh ʾimratí

(Adah and Zíllah, heár my voice ||
wíves of Lámech, give eár to my wórd).
(Lamech's song; Gen. 4:23)

Follows an example for the equal division into three feet of each half-verse:

haʿazínu ha-shamáyim v'ʾadabbérah ||
v'tishmá ha-ʾáreẓ ʾimre-fí ||
yaʿaráf kammatár liḳ'ḥí || tizzál kattál ʾimratí

(Give eár, O heávens   And let the eárth hear ||
and I will speák   the wórds of my móuth; ||
Let my teáching come,   let my spéech descénd ||
dówn like the raín,   like the déw).
(Moses' song of praise; Deuter. 32:1,2).

The following example shows a dipodic arrangement of the half-verses:

b'nót yisraél || ʾel-shaúl b'ḳénah ||
hammalbish'kém shani ʿim-ʿadaním ||
hammaʿaléh ʿadi zahháb ||
ʿal l'bush'kén . . . . .

(O daúghters of Israel || Wéep over Sául ||
who clóthed you in púrple || And óther delíghts; ||
Plac'd órnaments of góld || Upón your appárel . . . .
(From David's lament over Saul and Jonathan; 2 Sam. 1:24).

These examples have intentionally been chosen from texts that show strophic, *i.e.* folk-like structure. But among texts which do not show a strophic division, there are also numerous verses divided into equal numbers of feet (see *infra*).

The strophes generally show regular metric pattern, but there are also poems with uneven stanzas, which differ from those with even stanzas only in form, not in principle.

o
o o

There is a widespread dissension, among leading metricists, about the use of strophic structures in the Old Testament. Some consider certain portions as "strophic," while others hold the opposite view.[417]

This controversy would have had only a secondary or no importance at all for our subject, were it not for an essential musical consideration involved in it. The strophic structure of Hebrew poetry has a definite significance for the music (and musical rendition) of these poems. They have a generally well rounded melodic pattern, ending with a distinct concluding formula (something akin to the "full cadence" of Western music), as we find it in most folksongs. Furthermore, the strophic structure certainly facilitated the adaptation of the melody to the text and enabled the singer-composers to shape their melodic lines into square, popular type songs, which were easily retained in the memory of average audiences.

Similar to many elements of their cultural and artistic institutions, the Hebrews probably have also borrowed the strophic technique of their verses from other nations with which they entertained close relations. Until recent times, however, some metricists were inclined to believe that

> "there is nothing in the history of Semitic poetry to lead us, in advance, to expect strophes."[418]

This is the more surprising since already at the end of the last century HEINRICH ZIMMERN published the results of his investigations of Babylonian poetry, in which he submitted sufficient proof for regular metric organization. Especially in the Babylonian creation-story, he demonstrated the almost invariable pattern of two connected verses, each of which was composed of two half-verses.[419]

BREASTED, ERMAN, and ALBRIGHT have found evidences of strophic structure in Egyptian poetry. The meaning of some texts show that now and then three or four lines belong together. This is particularly obvious in the Egyptian poem "*Dispute with his Soul of One who is tired of Life.*"[420]

But the most convincing historical evidence of strophic structure in ancient Oriental versification has recently been disclosed in the "*Ras Shamra*" poems. HARRIS shows that in these poems

> "there is always an intimate connection between the structure of the stanzas and their meaning."[421]

MONTGOMERY went even further along this path in maintaining that he has found a highly developed "choric" art in the poem "*The Conflict of Baal and the Waters*."[422] This leads to the conclusion that such verses must have been sung to the accompaniment of dances, just as described in many biblical passages. Hence, it would not be too far-fetched to assume that it has also been a standing practice among Hebrew poets to give their verses a strophic structure whenever this was deemed suitable.

Hebrew poetry shows indeed a multitude of strophic sections, since any verse of the Bible of at least two full lines expressing a sufficiently homogeneous idea may legitimately be considered a strophe according to modern metricists. The stanza-like structures in the proper sense of the term are the "songs" and folk-like poems which we find sometimes interpolated within the narrative portions. The particular location of these items suggests that they are remnants of ancient bardic songs.

A number of Hebrew poems, or lengthy portions of poetic structure, have, as a rule, a permanent meter throughout their texts (poems of even meters).

Others show, even in short sections, more or less frequently changing verse-forms (poems of changing, or mixed meters). Between the two, there are transitory forms, in which the alternation of meter occurs sporadically.

For a long time, the changing meters have not been recognized by biblical philology as legitimate verse-forms, therefore the term "poetry" was restricted to texts which displayed, at least to some extent, constant meters. Thus, the prophetic texts were considered mostly "prose," as having no "verse-like patterns." Only after modern rhythmologists admitted the use of mixed meters in poetic texts, have the prophetic texts been recognized as "poetry."

The Old Testament contains song-texts with an unbroken regularity of meter, among which those with verses of three feet seem to be particularly typical. On the other hand, there are poems of a less conspicuous song-like character, especially in the Prophets, for which the free alternation of verses of different lengths seems to be just as typical. The verses of regular length are more appropriate for singing, while those of irregular structure suggest a manner of rendition in an exalted, dithyrambic declamation, close to chanting, as they probably have been performed in Israel.

For the evenly shaped verses of the Old Testament, the most appropriate examples are to be found among the poems which were born of the spirit of song, composed for song, and performed in singing: the psalms. We shall now cite at random a few examples of this category.[423]

Psalm 2 has verses of six feet throughout, except the first half of verse 12, which has only four feet.[424] Most of these hexapodic verses have a regular division of 3:3. Verses 5 and 6, though having six feet each, show a different distribution, the former 4:2, the latter 2:2:2.

Psalm 5 is pentapodic, with the exception of the second half of verse 12, which shows a structure of 2:2:2, and of the last verse, having a distribution of 3:3.

Psalm 10 follows the 4:3 meter throughout.

Psalm 18 (identical with 2 Sam. 22) shows in nearly all its fifty-one verses the structure 3:3; the few exceptions are verses 26 and 27, having four feet each, and verse 31, which—owing probably to a later interpolation—is extended to 3:3:3:2.

Psalms 111 and 112 are composed in regular 3:3 meter.

We may also cite a few examples from the Scriptural books outside the Psalter.

Proverbs 2 and 3 have a regular hexapodic arrangement with 3:3 structure as a rule; exceptions are verses 13, 14 and 18 of Prov. 3, (with a 2:2:2 distribution), while verses 2 and 3 of Prov. 3 have irregular meters.

Job 6 and 7 show an almost unchanged structure of 3:3, with slight modifications in 6:4 and 10 (3:3:3), in 7:4 (3:3:3) and 7:5 (4:3).

But even the narrative or "prosaic" portion of the Old Testament contain lengthy passages with a uniformly even meter. A metrical analysis of Num. 23 (*Bala'am's parables*) shows a regular 3:3 structure; exception is the second half of verse 23 (2:2:2).

The forty-three verses of Moses' Song (Deuter. 32) are almost exclusively arranged in 3:3 meter; exceptions are verses 24 and 29 (2:2:2), the second half of verse 30, verse 31, and the first half of verse 32, with a pentapodic setup each.

The prophetic books, too, contain sometimes regular metric constructions, like Nahum 2:1-5 (3:2); merely the second half of verse 4 is shortened to 2:2.

All the above examples warrant two reasonable conclusions:

(1) The portion of the Scriptures which are supposed to be *sung* show a rather regular metric structure, which remains mostly unchanged within a definite section of the poem. This is of paramount importance for the principle of variation as generally applied in the singing of the Orient. The skill of the Oriental singer in using a *maḳam,* that is a small and constantly varied melodic kernel for attractive melodic patterns (attractive at least for the Oriental listener), has certainly been furthered considerably by the regular metric organization of such biblical verses. The musical phase, conditioned by the metrical phase, has thus become, as it were, the reflected image of the contents of the verse. The conformity of both, music and meter, explains why the Jewish singers have so readily understood the technique of a highly artistic melodic elaboration even in lengthy passages of the text (and certain psalms indeed show considerable lengths!). They only had to follow the regular rhythms of the metrical arrangement of the words (and of the meaning of the words) in order to enliven their *maḳams* (the "melodicles") with perpetually new variations. In Oriental music, this parallels the Western concept of a "thoroughly composed" ("durchkomponierte") melody. Thus, the close affinity between the art of poetry and the art of singing in Ancient Israel is again significantly emphasized. This affinity also assures us that the levitical singers must have had the lion's share in the shaping of the poetical portions of the Scriptures, especially of the Psalter.

(2) Even such "non-poetical" portions of the text which are supposed to have been rendered in an exalted speech, show sometimes a fairly regular metric structure. These portions might have been performed in ancient times in the form of chanting, which admits a definite conclusion that meter and cantillation conditioned each other mutually. As SACHS says,

> "Oriental-Jewish cantillation of the Scriptures confirms, but also supplements the results of philology."[425]

Despite such clear evidence, the character and the technique of cantillation have for a long time been misunderstood and misinterpreted by representatives of metrical science. Even such a prominent scholar as SIEVERS commits the basic error in attributing

> "a relatively subordinate role to the specifically musical (or melodic) element of the so-called singing," (*i.e.* cantillation), and in considering this singing merely "as a hybrid kind of rendition," for—as he maintains—"one cannot assume that the songs of that epoch have been "thoroughly composed" ("durchkomponiert") in the modern sense."[426]

Evidently enough, SIEVERS' blunder stems from his constant application of normative Western principles to Hebrew (*i.e.* Oriental) music. In adapting the *maḳam* to the ever-changing necessities of a freely applied metric structure, the Oriental artist achieves in principle the same "final" ("durchkomponiert") shape of *his* musical pattern as the Occidental composer in applying the normative element of "form" according to our Western conception.

Of the numerous portions of the biblical text kept in even meters, or nearly so, the didactic poems (like Job and the Proverbs) were evidently taught to the youth. This pedagogical procedure may have been greatly facilitated by the regular metric structure of the material in question. The texts with changing meters comprise the Prophets and Ecclesiastes; certain of their narrative portions, like Jonah 1, and also some song-like patterns, are broken up into strictly separated single parts which imparts to them a folksong-like character. To this category belongs particularly the "Song of Songs." Here the formula of changing meter appears indeed so consistently applied that one cannot help surmising its intentional application on the part of the author (or authors). Thus Canticles 1:2-4 is an independent little song, which shows clearly a repeated use of the same structure 3:3 || 3:3 || 2;—or Canticles 8:5-6, with the same meter, 5 || 3:3 || 3, appearing twice in succession. Lamentations 1 uses repeatedly the metrical type 5:4:4. Such an "organized" irregularity infuses the text with an almost strophic character. SIEVERS maintains quite correctly that the changing meter suggests a popular device, while the even verses may point to a more developed stage of poetry.

o
o o

ISAACS establishes three periods of Hebrew poetry which, considered merely in their historical perspective,—would bear no significance upon our subject, were it not for some musical implications connected with this particular classification.[427] According to ISAACS' chronology, the first period of Hebrew poetry was that of the "war-song"; the second cultivated mainly its "lyric" quality; while in the third, and last period, which started with the rise of prophetic literature, the "subjective lyric" character of the poems was transmuted into what ISAACS calls an objective "lyric of peoples."

If we apply ISAACS' historical classification to the musical styles of the three periods, we may designate his first period as that of the simple, powerful and stirring bardic songs of the heroic age, like the Song at the Red Sea, Deborah's paean, and the like. The second period would be that of the highly developed variation technique of the Oriental *maḳam*-principle, in which the greatest latitude was given to the subjective lyricism of singers and composers. The artistic products of this period would be best exemplified by the achievements, poetic as well as musical, of the psalmists. The third period, the "lyric of peoples," would be characterized by popular, folksong-type melodies, for which the *Shire ha-ma'alot,* the unsophisticated songs of the pilgrims, but also the songs in popular vein of the Canticles would afford appropriate illustrations.

Although SACHS considers ISAACS' chronological conclusions rather doubtful,[428] he nevertheless admits that the older, epic poetry of the Bible has an unmistakable choral character which, by implication, fits at least ISAACS' first period.

o
o o

In scrutinizing the text of the Old Testament, one discovers fairly soon that the majority of the Hebrew verses start with one or several unstressed syllables and end on a stressed one. The characteristics of the Hebrew verse are determined originally by the Hebrew *word* and thus, in a roundabout way, become normative for the Hebrew verse. In accordance with their beginning and end, therefore, Hebrew versification shows "rising" (or "ascending") rhythms, having a iambic (◡ —, ♪ ♩) or anapaestic (◡◡—, ♪ ♪ ♩) character, without falling, however, into the rigidity of the classical quantitative verse-feet. Musically speaking, this would indicate that the Hebrew song phrase generally starts with an up-beat, that is with one or several unaccented pick-up notes.

Sometimes we find in the Hebrew verse after the last pronounced stress still another unaccented or half-mute syllable; this stands mostly for a *pause* at the end of a metrical unit, as found frequently in Hebrew versification. This is again an original feature of the Hebrew *word,* but the fact that an unaccented syllable stands at the end of a metrical unit is purely coincidental. A relatively long pause is a characteristic of the Hebrew verse-ending or half-verse ending. This has had an increased significance for the singer-performers, since this pause gave them the opportunity to lengthen the last accented syllable by melismatic figures, thus imparting to the end of the verse (or half-verse) a particular grammatical stress and musical embellishment.

o o o

In the rhythmical structure of Hebrew poetry three different subdivisions of the verse can be identified with a certain regularity, namely *stichoi* of four, three and two feet.[429] Some rhythmologists consider the four feet *stichos* as a duplication of a two foot unit, by which the basic forms would be reduced to two types, *stichoi* of three feet and two feet. Frequently the two are combined so that the two units of a verse are of different length, the first having three feet, the second two feet.

When this metrical device is applied consistently for a longer period, as for instance in Lamentations, we are confronted with a specific Hebrew verse form, that of the *ḳinah* (threnody). BUDDE, and with him many metricists, consider this verse form typical for the Hebrew lament, and infer that all lamentations or lament-like songs of the Old Testament are kept in this verse form, called "elegiac pentameter" ("pentameter," to be sure, not in its classical, quantitative meaning). BUDDE avers that

> "wherever a *ḳinah* is applied, we find the same rhythm, which proves that this is the stationary rhythm of the *ḳinah,* based upon a fixed melody, which corresponds exactly to the meter produced by a longer and shorter musical phrase. This is a foregone conclusion, despite the fact that we know nothing about the music itself.[430] The fact that for an artful funeral lament there existed such a fixed melody, and that the latter superimposed these characteristic rhythms upon the text, explains why the prophets used this verse-form whenever they wanted to convey a deep impression with their laments."[431]

Examples of the elegiac pentameter are Lament. 2:1 ff; 3:1 ff; 4:1 ff, and many others. BUDDE is basically right in assuming that the same meter is also applied to the laments, or more precisely, to the lament-like prophecies in the prophetical books. These, indeed, contain numerous lengthy passages in pentameter, like for instance Isa. 1:10 ff; 13:2 ff; 14:4 ff; 37:22 ff; 38:10 ff; 40:9-16; Jer. 2:30 ff; 3:1 ff; Hos. 14:1-8; Amos 3:1 ff; Jonah 2:3 ff Micah 1:13 ff; Nahum 2:1 ff; Zephaniah 1:11 ff, and many others.

Pentametric structure, however, is by no means restricted to the Lamentations and the Prophets. Frequently, this meter appears in other portions of the Scriptures, as for instance in Ps. 5:1 ff, Ps. 42, in Canticles 1:9 ff; 3:6 ff; 4:1 ff; 8:1 ff; etc. If we may attribute a lament-like character to the beginning of Ps. 5, a short glance to the other passages quoted above, especially from the Canticles, suffices to realize that the mood expressed therein is not lament-like at all. As stated above (p. 250), the irregular meter is one of the characteristics of popular poetry. This might explain the fact that the folk-like poems of the Canticles make use of this meter.

ISAACS tries to attribute the mourning effect of Lamentations partly to the *ḳinah* meter, and partly to the frequent use of "rising feet" (see p. 251). "But mostly," as he thinks, "to the predominance of the long *a* sound."[432] As proof, he refers to the fact that in the first verse of Lamentations there are 18 long *a* sounds to the total of 33 vowel sounds. This would be a valuable observation indeed, if it were corroborated by similar occurrences throughout the Lamentations. As he states, however,

> "this ratio in other verses varies; sometimes another vowel sound is more important."[433]

It seems, therefore, that the accumulation of the *a* sound in the first verse of the Lamentations is merely accidental. ISAACS indicates, furthermore, that in other portions of the Scriptures, such as in Isa. 14:4 ff, Isa. 40:9-16, Ps. 42, which show also the *ḳinah* meter, the extensive use of other vowels or vowel combinations is prevalent.[434]

On the other hand, ISAACS makes the interesting observation that

> "where the pain in Lamentations is no longer of mourning, but grows lyric, long *a* decreases and long *i* and *e* are more prominent."[435]

So for instance Lament. 1:15 has 19 long *i* and *e* sounds to a total of 39 vowel sounds. It is not inconceivable that the Hebrew poets might have used this device purposely, in order to reproduce certain moods by way of assonances. This, in turn, gives rise to the possibility that the musicians, composers as well as singers, may have availed themselves of this peculiarity. Whether the accumulation of certain vowel sounds affected in any way the melodic character of the songs used for the texts of the Lamentations, cannot be verified without an extensive comparative study of the texts and their melodies. Such an analysis is beyond the scope of this study.

BUDDE's theoretical considerations have been confirmed a few decades later by IDELSOHN's publications. In his notations of the *ḳinot,* collected among the Babylonian ,Yemenite and Persian Jews, this meter recurs rather often, even if not throughout the entire melodies. It is, of course, well-nigh impossible to reproduce, in our Western musical notation, the exact time values and all the rhythmical subtleties of the songs recorded. Even in this relatively incomplete form, some verses of the melodies show a definite pentametric structure (*e.g. Thesaurus,* vol. III (Persian), No. 98, p. 42; vol. I (Yemenite), No. 58, p. 32; vol. I (Yemenite), No. 60, p. 33 and others).

It should be mentioned at this point that, with all the merits of IDELSOHN's publications, the handling of his material for analytical purposes requires utmost caution.

o o o

In summing up the characteristics of Hebrew meter in its application to vocal music, we may state that

(1) the musical rhythm of ancient Jewish song was governed by the inherent rhythmic laws of the Hebrew language, as expressed particularly in the meter of Hebrew poetry;

(2) unlike ancient Greek or Latin meter, Hebrew meter is not quantitative; it is based on free accentual rhythm, that is, on the relative position of the accented syllable within the verse;

(3) any attempt to reproduce Hebrew rhythmization in terms of ancient quantitative meter is futile and doomed to failure from the very start;

(4) the metrical structure of Hebrew poetry designed to be *sung,* facilitated for the Jewish singers the elaboration of their *maḳams,* regardless of the textual lengths, thus establishing a close interrelation between poetry and singing in Ancient Israel;

(5) the accentual character of Hebrew meter enabled the singers to adapt one and the same melodic kernel to verses of varied length, in simply following the accentual divisions of Hebrew versification;

(6) the narrative portions of the Scriptures, which sometimes show regular metric structures, have been rendered in Israel in a chant-like fashion;

(7) Hebrew verses mostly show a "rising" rhythmical pattern, which suggests that Hebrew melodies generally started with an up-beat, that is, with one or more unaccented pick-up notes;

(8) the frequently applied strophic structure of Hebrew versification furthered the formation of folk-type melodic patterns. It may be assumed that the most ancient folksongs possessed a rather square melodic shape, which differed markedly from the free recitative style of biblical cantillation, and thus greatly eased the rendition of such songs by average and non-professional performers.

16. THE DYNAMICS OF HEBREW SINGING

A somewhat erroneous conception concerning the dynamics of ancient Hebrew singing prevailed for a long time. In analogy to the early Babylonian and Assyrian music, the singing of the Jews is often taken to be loud, noisy, even turbulent. This idea might have originated from the general conception of the ancient Orient that God's attention must be roused by loud praying and singing (*cp.* as a contrast 1 Sam. 1:13). Surely the Israelites did sing at times with a loud voice; in fact, the chroniclers describe more than one solemn occasion in which great masses of singers participated. But the volume of sound of such mammoth choirs was simply proportionate to the number of performers, without necessarily degenerating into crude bawling, as will be presently seen.

One such description of the chroniclers relates that Asa, king of Judah (914-874 B.C.E.), and the people of Israel

> "swore unto the Lord with a loud voice (*b'ḳol gadol*), and with shouting (*ubiteru'ah*), and with trumpets (*ubiḥaẓoẓerot*), and with horns (*ub'shofarot*),"

to renew the covenant with the God of their fathers "with all their heart and with all their soul" (2 Chron. 15:12-14). And the chronicler adds: "And all Judah rejoiced at the oath." (*ibid.* 15:15). It is obvious that the solemn occasion warranted the pouring out the singers' elated feelings with an increased fervor. For this the chronicler probably did not find a more appropriate word than *gadol,* "big," the meaning of which, however, is not necessarily "loud." The sounding of the trumpets and horns, which must have really been loud on this occasion, has no direct bearing upon the levitical *singing.* As at all important state functions or solemn religious festivities, trumpets and horns in this particular passage were the symbols of royal or priestly dignity; their function, if they did not indicate prostrations of the worshippers, was mainly to enhance the solemnity with their powerful blasts.

Another similar description relates that

> "the Levites, of the children of the Korahites, and of the children of the Kohatites, stood up to praise the Lord, the God of Israel, with an exceeding loud voice (*b'ḳol gadol l'ma'alah,*)" (2 Chron. 20:19).

Again, the occasion at which this sacred service took place—God's promise of Jehoshaphat's victory over the Moabites and Ammonites—makes it obvious that the Levites' "exceedingly loud" singing was but the natural and dignified outflow of their gratitude for the reassuring encouragement. By no means do these two biblical passages constitute a "proof" for crude and noisy singing of the Levites.

The prophetical pronouncement of God's words

> "and I cause the noise of thy songs (*hamon shirayiḥ*) to cease" (Ezek. 26:13),

is sometimes also cited as an indication for the loud singing of the Israelites. However, the context clearly shows that this passage applies to the sinful revelers of Tyre, the city upon which the Lord "will bring NEBUCHADREZZAR king of Babylon" (Ezek. 26:7), in order to punish the ungodliness of its inhabitants.

As a further proof of the "loud" singing of the Hebrews, Psalm 22:6 is cited: "Unto Thee they cried, and escaped." To be sure, the Hebrew word *za'ak* signifies "to cry," "to shout," but it is very doubtful whether this psalm-verse may be interpreted in a musical sense, *i.e.* as "singing." It is rather to be assumed that the psalmist means the desperate calls for help of a distressed people and not singing in the proper sense.

Psalm 42:2, too, is unjustly quoted as a proof of the "loud" singing of the Israelites. This was originated by LUTHER's translation. "Meine Seele schreit (cries), Gott zu Dir. "The Hebrew word *ta'arog* means "to yearn," "to languish," "to pant," and, accordingly, the English versions translate correctly:

> "As the hart panteth after the water brooks, so panteth my soul after Thee, O God."

Finally, some passages are cited from the Book of Maccabees which allegedly give evidence to the effect that the singing of the Hebrews has been loud and noisy.

> "Then cried they with a loud voice toward heaven, saying, 'What shall we do with these, and whither shall we carry them away?' " (1 Macc. 3:50).

There is hardly any need in proving that "crying" cannot be understood here in the sense of singing. The following passage, too, has no singing connotation:

> "Then sounded they with trumpets, and cried with a loud voice" (1 Macc. 3:54).

Here, warriors are spoken of, going to battle, their crying, therefore, being perfectly understandable. Shortly thereafter, real singing is described; when they returned victorious after the battle,

> "they sung a song of thanksgiving, and praised the Lord in heaven" (1 Macc. 4:24).

But seeing the desecrated altar,

> "they made great lamentation . . . and cried toward heaven" (1 Macc. 4:39,40).

It is evident that crying, again, has no connection with singing. In the battle

> "thy sounded their trumpets, and cried with prayer" (1 Macc. 5:33).

This passage, too, does not imply singing, and the same is true of the following passage:

> "Wherefore cry ye now unto heaven, that ye may be delivered from the hand of your enemies (1 Macc. 9:46).

Here, doubtless, the chronicler means the desperate invocations for help of the afflicted people and no singing in a musical sense.

Thus, it is obvious that anything cited from the Bible and the Apocrypha as a proof for the noisy, unartistic singing of the Israelites does not actually refer to singing at all. On the contrary, it can be asserted without hesitation that the outstanding feature of art-singing in Ancient Israel has been euphony and refinement. The preponderance of soft instruments, harps and lyres, as accompaniment in the cult, may serve as the most eloquent proof to this effect.

Noisy, dionysiacal singing is not thinkable, as a general rule, without a corresponding instrumentation. Shrill pipes, glaring horns, noisy percussion instruments are connected intrinsically with orgiastic singing. Nowhere are there such reports about Jewish Temple music, about Jewish sacred singing.

In the Second Temple, instrumental music was restricted to the bare minimum required for a large and open-air hall. In every-day's service

> "they blew never less than twenty-one blasts in the Temple and never more than forty-eight [in a day]. They played on never less than two harps or more than six, and on never less than two flutes or more than twelve."[436]

On the Sabbath and on the two days of *Rosh ha-Shanah,* the number of the instrumentalists has been increased.

"There were never less than two trumpets, and their number could be increased without end; there were never less than nine lyres, and their number could be increased without end."[437]

Furthermore,

"on twelve days in the year was the flute (*ḥalil*) played before the Altar: at the slaughtering of the Second Passover-offering, on the first Festival-day of Passover, and on the Festival-day of Pentecost and on the eight days of the Feast [of Tabernacles]."[438]

As for percussion instruments, only a pair of cymbals was admitted.[439] Clearly, the erstwhile showy and grandiose character of Solomon's Temple music has been transformed into the quiet, solemn and dignified quality, as preserved in the memory of Mishnaic tradition.

17. PERFORMER AND AUDIENCE

Considering the comprehensive character and the minute precision which prevail in the early rabbinic literature with regard to reporting and expounding the law and the Jewish customs, it is surprising that this literature does not contain a description of such an important religious institution as sacred music. True enough, musical details, important and not too important, are frequently discussed in Mishnah and Talmud; but the essence of Jewish music, its system, its tonalities, and so forth, are passed in complete silence. Likewise, we have no information whatever about the ethical side of Jewish musical practice, especially the highly important psychological and aesthetic approach of the Jews to tonal art.

Despite all this, we find there a few casual descriptions, sometimes in the form of anecdotes, which afford a certain insight into the cultural relation between music and other aspects of the intellectual life in Ancient Israel.

The musical leaders of the Second Temple, as we know, were bent on keeping the form and expression of singing as plain and dignified as possible. Nevertheless, certain bad habits infiltrated the liturgical singing, which sometimes even endangered its sacred character. Among these, one may mention the nasal tone production and vibrato of the voice which, though generally recognized in the Orient as accepted features of art-singing, got out of hand in the long run. The dignified character of Temple music, however, was mainly imperiled by a gradually evolving predilection for virtuosity of certain singers.

The vibrato, that is the artificial tremolo of the voice, produced by a mechanical trick applied from outside, is to be found already in high Antiquity. Its technique may be grasped from an earlier mentioned Assyrian bas relief which portrays a band of musicians and singers, among them a singing woman who exerts with her fingers a pressure upon her throat and cheeks. We find the same device depicted in Egyptian paintings of singers.[440] This expedient was supposed to produce particularly sharp and shrill sounds and also to increase mechanically the natural vibrato of the voice. This kind of tremolo is still used in our times by Arabian singers and is considered by them as a favorite means of art-singing. Its discriminate employment would not constitute, therefore,—especially in the Orient,—an improper or illicit manner of singing.

The nasal tone-production, too, is a well known mannerism both in the Near- and Far-East. It has always been one of the characteristic features of Oriental singing and this must have prevailed in Ancient Israel as well.

What abuse has sometimes been made in the Temple with these two characteristic manners of singing becomes evident from a report of the Mishnah.[441] There, mention is made of a curious new technique of singing, supposedly having been "invented" by the principal of the levitical singers, HYGROS ben LEVI, apparently a famous singer-virtuoso of his time. He guarded his "invention" so jealously that he refused to teach it to others. The Talmud ventures to characterize this singing technique, but gives only a very superficial and incomplete description of it.[442] According to this report,

> "when he [HYGROS ben LEVI] tuned his voice to a trill, he would put his thumb into his mouth and place his finger [on the division line] between the two parts of the moustache, so that his brethren, the priests, staggered backward with a sudden movement" [enchanted with the beauty of the singing, or startled by the power of his voice].[443]

Maybe this singing-virtuoso used still other tricks, which escaped the rabbis' observation and which the "inventor" has kept secret in order to protect himself from imitation. The fact that he did not want to divulge his secret, enraged the sages, so that "his memory was kept in dishonor."[444]

The Tosefta tries to save the honor of HYGROS ben LEVI. For his refusal to teach his art to others, an apology is offered, which too obviously seeks to find a seemingly religious motivation for HYGROS ben LEVI's unlevitical behavior:

> "HYGROS ben LEVI was an expert in song, but he did not want to teach it to anyone. They asked why? He answered: 'In my father's house they knew that the *Bet ha-Migdash* (the Temple) will be destroyed and they did not want to teach so that they would not give the same songs in honor of idolatry."[445]

In this apology no mention is being made of a special singing manner, but merely of singing in general, just as in the altered version of Tal.Yer. *Shekalim* V:2 (see Note 443). The excuse of HYGROS ben LEVI, however, is not too convincing, for his stubborn refusal is incompatible with the most elementary duty of the levitical singers: to teach their art to the coming generation. Consequently, the Talmud might have been right in assuming that HYGROS' refusal was motivated by selfish reasons.

This is only a single but by no means unique case for the gradual growth of all sorts of personal vanity in the sacred musical service. As a result of the exaggerated importance attributed by the singers to their own accomplishments and of the admiration bestowed upon them by the worshippers, they began to put their own person more and more into the forefront at the expense of the sacred service. Thus it happened that shallow virtuosity with all its pitiful trimmings, its small and big bad habits, has eventually penetrated and gained a firm footing in the sacred music.

This became possible only because the community had manifested at that time an unmistakable aesthetical attitude toward the accomplishments of the levitical singers. For what period can the existence of this particular attitude in Jewish musical practice be definitely proven for the first time?

The earliest forms of communal musical activity were based exclusively on co-operation. In ancient times, musical activity meant performing, assisting, but not passive listening. Only after a long period and after an accumulated experience has the aural faculty obtained the same importance as the activation of the muscular sense in the musical action, and it required again a long development before the aural faculty became the more important and, eventually, the predominant factor in music.[446]

At the primitive stage, any music is "utilitarian music," or "music for practical use," the production of which is necessitated by factors of environment or social conditions.[447] There is a long way of evolution from this "Gebrauchsmusik" stage to that in which music represents for the listener a product of art involving the element of artistic enjoyment. The importance of tonal art in the life of the Jewish people, the impregnation of the individual as well as the community with music in all its aspects, was responsible for the fact that Israel passed relatively soon the phases of development from the heteronomous to the autonomous "music as art phenomenon." We find the proof for this in the Bible itself.

At the time when regular musical practice in Israel had been in its beginnings, even prior to the creation of an organized sacred musical service, we already discover the attitude toward the enjoyment of music in the words of old Barzillai when he speaks of the temporal and spiritual goods of life to be aspired for:

> "Can I discern between good and bad? can thy servant taste what I eat or what I drink? can I hear any more the voice of singing men and singing women?" (2 Sam. 19:36).

Even more emphatically is this attitude exposed in the book of "Ecclesiastes," where music is declared to be indispensable to the enhancement of pleasure of life:

> "I got me men-singers and women-singers, and the delights of the sons of men, as musical instruments, and that of all sorts" (2:8).[448]

And when the prophet speaks of the chosen one of the Lord who should be

> "as a love song of one that hath a pleasant voice, and can play well on an instrument" (Ezek. 33:32),

this metaphor is an unmistakable sign that for the Israelites of those times listening to fine singing and to alluring music definitely included the element of enjoyment.

Ancient Israel knew already a purely aesthetic approach to music as an art product. The sense of appreciation for the absolute beauties of music is attested by a talmudic reference. In the night before the Day of Atonement psalms and proverbs of Solomon have been performed in the Temple for the high-priest, since the beauties (*ta'aman*) of the melodies were considered the most appropriate means for driving away sleep.[449] The fact that beautiful music was considered powerful enough to influence the listener physically, as well as psychically, proves that the notion of enjoyment of music has entered the mind and sentiment of the Israelites.

We read furthermore in the Talmud that "the Exilarch *Mar* *ʿUḳba* in Babylonia would retire and rise with music" [with songs of Israel which they used to play before him].[450] The meaning of this ceremony seems to be first of all an external action: honoring a highly placed person. However, it also shows clearly that the sages considered music to be indispensable for the enjoyment of life. Here, too, the attitude of pleasure toward music is obvious.

These biblical and talmudic passages show that the function of music in Ancient Israel underwent gradually a complete conversion. At first it served religion, helped all day's work, was an indispensable attribute of popular merriment; then, it liberated itself more and more from this servitude and developed into an independent art phenomenon. But even as such, it remained imbedded in the consciousness of the nation and never lost its intimate bond with the life of the people.

The character of Temple music, too, gradually became transformed. In the Second Temple, particularly, it remained no longer "utilitarian music" as it used to be largely in the early times of David and Solomon when they instituted the regular sacred musical service. Music attained more and more the character of an autonomous art and, in this phase of its evolution, it became the most powerful stimulus in the artistic life of the Jewish people. Its external and intrinsic qualities procured for the Jewish musician an enviable and well deserved reputation in the ancient Orient.

18. THE ETHOS OF SINGING IN ANCIENT ISRAEL

The interpretation of songs in Ancient Israel has not been outwardly different from that of the other peoples of Antiquity in the Near-East and—except some unavoidable changes—from that of present day's practice in the same area.

However, with all the similarity between Jewish singing and that of their neighbors, there was a deep-seated difference between them. This difference has been nurtured by the particular ethos of the Jewish song. Music and singing have been considered by certain peoples as useful and practical forms of art, constituting in part an external adornment of life, and in part an essential element for the education of the youth. Their importance with the Jews lies in an entirely different field.

Despite the fact that music among the Hebrews represents essentially "utilitarian music,"—though in a higher sense—it is not wholly covered by the "activity" and the "co-operation." Also, in Jewish music the principles of "enjoyment," or of "aesthetic pleasure," even though explicitly manifest, are not the decisive criteria. The roots of the Jewish musical art go deeper; its ultimate meaning can rather be found in the spiritual, ethical sphere.

In Ancient Israel, music—especially singing—means: to serve God, to exalt God with sounds. Singing, in whatever form, is for the Jew the religious creed expressed in sounds, the palpable affirmation of his close connection with the Eternal, the union in harmonious sounds of the Creator with His creation.

This ethical concept of music and singing has appeared for the first time in Antiquity with the Jewish people and represents one of the great accomplishments of the human spirit. Opinions are sometimes expressed to the effect that Jewish music has not been an original creation, that all its elements have been taken over from other peoples, or at least have been influenced by foreign civilizations. However, it is not so much the vessel, the external form which has to be taken into consideration, as rather what the Jews have been able to achieve by filling this vessel with the fruits of their own spiritual endeavors.

They have attached to their music the imprint of a mysterious, almost supernatural art, that is ultimately rooted in God, that could be explained neither by the intellect nor by the sentiment, but which has its justification in the divine pleasure which human singing offers to the Creator Himself. This pleasure was refracted to mankind through God's grace, giving to human life splendor, bliss, and spiritual rapture.

Thus, through the mutual conjunction of service to God, and God's grace to mankind, music becomes the source of all mundane happiness. This is the supreme significance of Jewish singing, as an unmistakable testimony of its blending with the Universe, of its merging with the notion of God in the ultimate mystery of all existence.

No other people of Antiquity shows in its song more thoroughly than do the Jews the fundamental forces which rise from the depths of the soul. The mysterious emanations of psychic impulsions are exposed in the Jewish song with elementary power.

The theocratic order of Israel has given to Jewish faith and, with it, to Jewish life their extraneous, manifest, and strongly united national aspect. The sacred service has offered to the Jew his spiritual content, his moral foundation, his intellectual stir. Music, however, and especially singing, has bestowed upon him the higher consecration, the halo of transfiguration. Through music, he was elevated to spheres where he could experience the oneness with God, this being an ethical conception exclusive with the Jews, and one that opened up, in the practice of musical art, spiritual domains unknown theretofore.

Through the power of music the Jew merged with his God, became united with the Universe. This constitutes the high ethics of the Jewish conception of art, and because of it Jewish musical genius proved to be worthy of being counted among the greatest spiritual factors of Antiquity.

CLASSIFICATION OF HEBREW INSTRUMENTS

Idiophones and Membranophones	Aerophones			Chordophones			
	Woodwinds	*Horns*	*Trumpets*	*Lyres*	*Harps*	*Lutes*	*Zithers*
tof	ʿugab			kinnor			
meẓiltayim	ḥalil			ʿasor			
ẓelẓelim	maḥol	shofar	ḥaẓoẓerot	shushan	nebel	neginot (?)	pesanterin
shalishim	neḥilot (?)	ḳeren		ḳathros	gittit	sabbeka	
menaʿanʿim	neḳeb (?)	yobel					
paʿamonim	mashroḳita			*pandura*			
meẓillot	ʿalamot (?)			*ḥinga*			
	sumponyah (?)			*baṭon*			
ṭabla				*ʾadrabolin* (?)			
ʿerus	*ʾabub*						
ṭanbura	*magrephah* (?)						
rebiʿit	*barbolin* (*korablin*)						
zog	*ḳalameyles*						
niktimon							
ḳarḳasch							
sharḳuḳita							

The names in italics are mentioned only in the rabbinical literature.

VI. THE MUSICAL INSTRUMENTS

Principles of Classification

Musicology of the 19th century has established a system of classification for musical instruments that was based on their external features. Consequently, the musical instruments have been divided into three main categories:

1) Stringed instruments,

2) Wind instruments, and

3) Percussive, shaking and rattling instruments.

Modern science of instruments follows different principles; to-day's classification is based on the manner of tone production in each category. Accordingly, we distinguish today:

1) *Idiophones,* of which the body itself, if beaten, shaken or scraped produces the sound.

2) *Membranophones,* the tone production of which is caused by beating an animal or artificial skin stretched over a frame. To this category belong all the different kinds of drums; also certain exotic instruments, the membranes of which are activated by vibration of air or blowing on them.

3) *Aerophones,* the tones of which are produced by supplying air (either by blowing or by a mechanical device, such as bellows). This category comprises all woodwinds, brass instruments, the pneumatic organ, the harmonium, the accordion and similar instruments.

4) *Chordophones,* all string instruments, whether played with a bow, plucked with the fingers, or beaten by sticks or a hammer mechanism. To this category belong the families of the harps, lutes, guitars, the piano, as well as its forerunners (virginal, clavichord, cembalo, etc.).

5) *Electrophones,* the latest category of instruments, which came into being in our century, the tone of which is produced by electrical currents· We distinguish two kinds: the electro-mechanical type, whose sound is created in a normal way, but transformed into electrical vibrations,—and the electronic instruments proper, whose sound is the result of oscillating electrical currents. Into the first category belong all the instruments whose normally produced sound is either reinforced or transformed into another tone color,—the last category comprises the electronic instruments which produce the so-called "ether-waves," such as the Theremin, Ondes Martenot, Sphaerophone, Trautonium, Emicon, etc. To this category belong also the electronic organs, which have been widely used in the last decades as substitutes for the pipe organs.

o
o o

Contemporary classification cannot be applied to the instruments of Ancient Israel. First of all, the electronic instruments have to be eliminated altogether. Then, the idiophones and membranophones of the Hebrews can be put into the same category, without jeopardizing their basic characteristics.

Consequently, in our study the instruments of Ancient Israel will be classified according to the older principle and will be distributed into the three former groups, despite the fact that this system is considered obsolete by musicology:

1) Strings,
2) Winds,
3) Instruments of percussion.

According to their actual use in the musical practice of the ancient Hebrews, the string instruments are of paramount importance, therefore they will be discussed first. The wind instruments will follow, and finally, the instruments of percussion will be investigated.

In each category, the instruments mentioned in the Bible will be treated first,—while those of the post-biblical literature will be analyzed after the biblical instruments.

This classification, intentionally differing from that customary to-day, corresponds to the historical implications of Israel's use of its instruments and will afford a better insight into the liturgical and sociological aspects of the music culture of the ancient Hebrews.

General Observations

Despite all the importance of music in the popular life of the ancient Hebrews, the biblical chroniclers, unlike the writers of other nations, have not revealed to us anything about the nature of their coeval musical instruments. Their reports do not contain any indications as to the form and technique of these instruments, and scarcely any allusions to their sound qualities. Here and there an adjective, such as "sweet," "pleasant," "solemn," and the like, is all we learn about their sonorities.

The chroniclers restrict themselves mainly to mentioning the names of the instruments. But with the lapse of time even this primary knowledge was dimmed to such an extent that already the early rabbinic writers were in doubt whether some of the names referred to a stringed or a wind instrument. In some cases the differences of opinion were even more conspicuous, some rabbinic authorities defining, for instance, a given term as the name of a music instrument, while others understood it to be something of an extra-musical nature.

The extant authentic illustrations of instruments of Ancient Israel are few and scarcely appropriate for conveying a clear idea about their shape and musical qualities.[1] Therefore, our sole reliable, though incomplete, source in this respect is the abundant pictorial material preserved in the antiquities of the peoples with whom the Israelites were closely associated and whose musical practice they have in no small measure absorbed.

The pictorial representations in Egyptian, Babylonian, Assyrian, and partly also in Greek and Roman antiquities, furnish us a working basis for drawing reasonable conclusions about the instruments of the ancient Hebrews. The etymology of the Hebrew names of instruments affords valuable information as to their origin, and sometimes also their sound quality.

o
o o

The names of the "first" instruments should not be understood literally. Jubal's two instruments, *kinnor* and *ʿugab,* do not represent single species of instruments, but are general terms for stringed and wind instruments. Percussion instruments, such as drums, hollow tree-trunks, concussion-sticks, as well as horns of animals, hollow reeds and sea-shells producing primitive sounds when blown into, must have already existed when the instruments with distinct pitch had been allegedly invented.

All in all, the Bible mentions sixteen musical instruments as having been used in Ancient Israel. The Book of Daniel refers furthermore to six instruments, which were played at King NEBUCHADREZZAR's court; their names, however, characterize them as non-Jewish instruments. In the Targumim and in the talmudic literature we find sixteen additional names of instruments not mentioned in the Scriptures. It must be assumed that these are instruments of the Gaonic centuries whose use the rabbinic scribes have partly projected back into the biblical period. However, since they were actually used by the Israelites, it is in order to examine them in our study. Finally, it should be mentioned that ABRAHAM DA PORTALEONE, in his treatise *Shilṭe ha-Gibborim* (Mantua, 1612), names thirty-four instruments which were allegedly known and used in Ancient Israel. It is obvious that the majority of these names represent instruments of PORTALEONE's own time, which he arbitrarily places back into the biblical period.

o
o o

As to the material used for the construction of instruments, there are some scanty data in the Scriptures. The *ḥaẓoẓerot* were made of beaten silver (*kesef miḳshah,* Num. 10:2). The shofar was made either from the horn of the ram, or of that of the wild goat, the *ḳeren* from the horn of neat. The *meẓiltayim* (cymbals) were of brass (*neḥoshet*). The stringed instruments were made of wood, but the indication that David's instruments were manufactured of fir wood (*ʿoẓe beroshim,* 2 Sam. 6:5),[2] might be based on an erroneous translation, since the fir wood is not too widespread in the Orient. It is rather to be assumed that under this term the cypress wood is meant, since this tree, like the cedar, is common on the Lebanon.[3] The *Jewish Version* is the only one which renders correctly "all manner of instruments made of cypress wood."[4]

Solomon has ordered instruments made of precious woods, "and there were none such seen before in the land of Judah" (1 Kings 10:11 ff; 2 Chron. 9:10 ff), namely of *ʾalmuggim* (sandal wood),[5] which King Hiram had sent from Ophir (Ethiopia) to Solomon, together with gold and precious stones, for the construction of the Temple. This was the red sandal wood, counted among the precious materials of Antiquity.[6] In two other passages of the Scriptures the word is spelled with inverted consonants as *ʾalgummim* (2 Chron. 2:7 and 9:11). From this ALBRIGHT concludes that *ʾalgum* is the correct name;[7] he derives it from the Arabian *kum* ("gum," *ʾal* is the Arabian article), taken over by the Greeks as *kommi* and by the Romans as *gummi*.[8]

JOSEPHUS reports that the *kinnorot* and *nebalim* have been made of *ēlektron.*[9] The latter name was given by the Greeks to an alloy made of gold and silver. Yellow amber, too, was called *ēlektron.* It is highly improbable that the body of stringed instruments was made of metal or amber. The chances are that *ēlektron* was used for ornaments, as we see on *kitharas* in Greek pictorial representations.

o
o o

Ḳol meant originally the human voice, especially the singing voice. Eventually, this word received an extended meaning, indicating the sound of instruments as well.

Music for the Jews has been "sweet" (in Aram. *ḥali*), the instrument was "well sounding" (*ḳalifonon,* which is manifestly the phonetic transliteration of the Greek *kalliphōnon*).[10]

o
o o

On Sabbath, no playing of instruments was permitted except for the accompaniment of singing at worship.[11] According to a Mishnaic passage dealing with the prohibitions on Sabbath, it was forbidden "to clap the hands (*safaḳ*), or slap the thighs (*tipaḥ*), or stamp the feet (*raḳad*)."[12] Though this passage refers unmistakably to dancing, likewise prohibited on Sabbath, the Gemara furnishes another interpretation: "It is a preventive measure lest one might repair (*tiḳḳen*) a musical instrument."[13]

o
o o

The stringed and wind instruments, when not in use, were wrapped in napkins,[14] or kept in special receptacles, called *teḳ* (from the Greek *thēkē*). There were different kinds of receptacles for *kinnorot* and *nebalim.*[15] Wind instruments were kept either in "cases for pipes," (*teḳ*),[16] or in "bags for pipes" (*ḥemat*).[17] In the regulations for cleanliness, there was even a distinction made as to whether an instrument was laid in its case from above or from the side:

> "The case for the double-flute (*sumponyah*), if this is put from above, is susceptible to uncleanness; if from the side it is not susceptible. The case for pipes (*ḥalilim*) R. Judah declares not susceptible, since they are put in from the side."[18]

To prevent any misinterpretation, the rabbinic scribe sums up the instructions as follows:

> "This is the general rule: What is made as a case is susceptible to uncleanness; what is made only as a covering is not susceptible."[19]

o
o o

Finally, we have to refer to a bewildering error, which is to be found in some English editions of JOSEPHUS' works. In these publications, the chapter in which JOSEPHUS describes the Temple instruments, contains a wrong translation of the Greek word *plēktron;* thus, the English text states erroneously that the *kinnor* has been played with a bow.[20] However, the bow as a tone producing implement has been unknown in Greek and

Hebrew Antiquity.[21] In general it must be stated that JOSEPHUS' reports and descriptions contain some erroneous facts and sometimes gross exaggerations.[22] His indications, therefore—especially those dealing with the music of the Hebrews—must be used with a certain caution.

A. INSTRUMENTS MENTIONED IN THE BIBLE

(a) Stringed Instruments

1. KINNOR

The *kinnor* is one of the two instruments the "invention" of which is ascribed to Jubal. It was "David's harp," the preferred instrument in Israel's music practice. The word has two plural-forms, one masculine, *kinnorim,* and one feminine, *kinnorot,* an unexplainable peculiarity not to be found with any other name of instruments.

The opinions are widely divided with regard to the etymology of the word. SACHS thinks its origin to be unknown.[23] GALPIN, on the contrary, sees a clear assonance between the Egyptian term of the lyre, *kn-an-aul* and the word *kinnor.*[24] He refers furthermore to the fact that in the Arabic version of the Bible *kinnor* is frequently rendered as *kissari,* representing a phonetic transformation of the Greek *kithara. Kissari* is also the name of the Ethiopian lyre.

According to GRESSMANN, *kinnor* is connected etymologically with the Syrian *kenārā* and the Arabic-Persian *kunar,* both terms for "lotus."[25] The wood of the lotus-plant, highly resistant and not subject to rot, was used in the Orient for all kinds of utensils. Thus, it might have been used for making musical instruments as well. GRESSMANN concludes that the name of the instrument (*kinnor*) was derived from the material of which it has been made, a frequent procedure in the Orient. In Greek, too, *lōtos* is at once the name of the plant and the flute made of lotus-wood.[26] SOPATROS confirms that harp-like instruments have been made of lotus-wood.[27]

The instrument of the Phoenicians, played by their legendary hero, KINNYRAS, was called *kinnor.* From Phoenicia the word might have come to the Greeks who used it first in the substantive form *kinnyra,* from which the verb *kinnyrai,* "to lament," has been derived. The Hebrews have taken over the word from the Syrian; thus, the Hebrew *kinnor* and the Greek *kinnyra* are both of Oriental origin.

In Ancient Israel, a town on Lake Genezaret was called *Kinnorot*; the lake's ancient name was *Yam Kinnorot.* The tradition explains that the lake had the shape of a lyre (*kinnor*), which allegedly was the reason for the lake's name. However, the lake has not the slightest resemblance to a lyre, it resembles a harp, though. In later times other explanations cropped up, among them those that the inhabitants of the town excelled in playing the *kinnor*, or else that they have been experts in building such instruments. The latter assumption is not improbable, since Antiquity knew several cities the names of which indicated the principal trade of their inhabitants.[28]

The rabbinical authorities, too, tried to establish some sort of relationship between the word *kinnor* and the town Kinnorot on Lake Genezaret; their interpretations, however, are extremely far-fetched. One of these is:

> "Kinneret is Genesar. Why is its name Kinneret? Because its fruits are sweet as the sound of the *kinnor*."[29]

GRESSMANN'S etymological derivation of the word *kinnor* from the Syrian term of the lotus-plant is corroborated by another talmudic explanation of the name of the town Kinnorot. The Palestinian Talmud states:

> "Kinneret is Genesar. R. Levi objected: It is written (Josh. 12:3) 'And the plane extends to the sea of Kinneret.' Does it follow from this that there were two places called Genesar? Or perhaps there were only two autonomous districts, as Beth-Yerah and Sennabris, which produce lotus plants (*kinnorim*)."[30]

From this, and from the above quoted talmudic allusion to the city's fruits, GRESSMANN concludes that the name of the town might originally have had the meaning of "City of Lotus."[31]

For the origin of the instrument itself SACHS submits his own hypothesis. He first points out a relationship between the ancient Jewish lyres and those of the Cretic-Mycenaean cult; then he refers to the hired soldiers, named *Kreti,* in the body-guard of king David (2 Sam. 15:18; 20:7,23; 1 Kings 1:38; "Cheretites," in the English versions). From this SACHS derives a general historical conclusion attesting to the similarity of form between Cretic and Hebrew instruments.[32]

o
o o

The Bible mentions *kinnor* in forty-two places. In the early translations of the Bible, the word is rendered in most different ways. The SEPTUAGINT translates it twenty times as *kithara,* namely in the Psalms, Job and Isaiah; seventeen times as *kinnyra,* in the Books of Samuel, Kings and Chronicles; in 1 Chron. 15:21, the original *kinnor ʿal ha sheminit* is Grecized with some phonetic likeness as *kinnyra amasenith*; in one instance the translation uses the general term for all musical instruments, *organon* (Ps. 137:2); and in five places *psaltērion* (Gen. 4:21; Pss. 49:5; 81:3; 149:3; Ezech. 26:13), despite the fact that *psaltērion* is the Greek equivalent for the *nebel.*

The VULGATE translates nearly always (thirty-seven times) as *cithara,* 1 Chron. 15:21 as *cithara pro octava,* two places as *lyra* (1 Chron. 15:16; 16:5), two other places *psalterium* (Pss. 49:5; 149:3), and once as *organum* (Ps. 137:2).

AQUILA, SYMMACHOS and THEODOTION use either *kithara,* or *psaltērion,* never *kinnyra.* The Syrian Peshitta has thirty-seven times *kinora,* in five places the word is left out altogether. The Targumim have twenty-seven times *kinora,* (or *kinnora*), once *ḥinga* (Gen. 31:27).[33] The Arabian translation uses mostly *kissari* (*kithara*), or *psantir* (*psalterium*), in a few places also *tanburū.*

o
o o

Since the biblical scribes do not reveal anything about the shape of the *kinnor*, and since no authentic pictures of the instrument are found among

Hebrew antiquities, the opinions about its nature are quite controversial. Whereas some take it for a lute- or guitar-like instrument, others believe it had the form of a harp. FÉTIS, leaning on classical sources, thinks that the *kinnor* was identical with the small, portable, nine stringed *trigōnon*.[34] But ARISTOXENOS (fl. 4th century B.C.E.) clearly distinguishes the *trigōnon* from other harp-like instruments, among them from the *enneachordon*, the "nine-stringed" lyre. ATHENAEUS states:

> "Aristoxenos calls foreign all stringed instruments bearing the names of *phoinix, pēktis, magadis, sambykē, trigōnon, klepsiambos, skindapsos* and the "nine-stringed" (*enneachordon*)."[35]

AMBROS, too, thinks the *kinnor* was identical with the *trigōnon*, which he describes correctly as an instrument with four strings.[36]

In contradistinction, WEISS refers justly to the fact that

> "it would be incomprehensible if the highly talented Semitic people of the Israelites had chosen as its favorite instrument the small trigon-harp, which had only an insignificant sounding body and produced therefore thin and weak sounds, after they had been familiar in Egypt with the much more voluminous sounds of the kitharas and harps, which they certainly have heard on numerous occasions."[37]

According to ATHENAEUS,[38] and JUVENAL,[39] the *trigōnon* has been a Syrian invention. It is known that the Israelites have had an age-long cultural intercourse with the Syrians. Jacob's father-in-law, Laban, was a Syrian, and the *kinnor* was a familiar instrument among them. From this it was concluded that this instrument was introduced into Jewish usage by Jacob or his immediate descendants. In Egypt a triangular harp with nine strings, called *kinnyra* by DIODOR of SICILY, has been used at worship.[40] Against the above opinion of ARISTOXENOS, that of DIODOR, who lived three centuries later, has only a minor value. The Egyptians might have had a nine-stringed harp which, however, was by no means identical with the Syrian *trigōnon*.

PORTALEONE describes the *kinnor* as a large harp with forty-seven strings.[41] This large number of strings would presuppose such a big body that the instrument certainly could not have been carried easily, nor could it have been played in marching, nor even "hanged upon the willows," as it is said —though symbolically— in Ps. 137:2. The small triangular harp would have satisfied more readily all these requirements. Nevertheless, modern research has arrived at the conclusion that the *kinnor* was not a harp-like instrument, not even a type of lute with a long-necked finger-board, as sometimes asserted, but an instrument similar to the Greek *kithara*.[42] This opinion is based mainly upon SEPTUAGINT'S translation, given above. WEISS maintains that if we know the nature of the ancient Greek *kithara*, we have a good idea about the Jewish *kinnor* itself.[43]

To corroborate the point that the writers of the SEPTUAGINT identified the biblical *kinnor* with the Greek *kithara*, WEISS refers to quite a few details from the history of this instrument, as they present themselves in Egyptian and Assyrian antiquities.[44]

Probably the earliest known picture of an Egyptian *kithara* has been found in a sepulchral grotto at Beni-Hassan. (see illus. 33).

Furthermore, WEISS mentions a picture from the time between the 12th and 18th Dynasty found in a tomb in the vicinity of Thebes. It shows a harp-playing precentor, another harp-player, and a *kithara*-player, whose instrument resembles the crude form of the Semitic *kithara*.[45]

In Assyrian antiquities, too, the *kithara* is frequently depicted. Its simplest type appears in a picture which shows three Semitic captives making music, while guarded by an Assyrian warrior. The comparison of these captives with similar figures of the obelisk of SHALMANEZAR II has led to the conclusion that both pictures represent Semites· On other Assyrian monuments the same instrument is reproduced in a slightly modified form.[46]

LAYARD discovered an obelisk of black basalt, on which two *kithara*-players and two cymbal players are portrayed. (see illus. 16).

The monument, according to its inscription, originates from the time of ASHUR-IDANNI-PAL (668-626 B.C.E.) A bas-relief found at Kuyundchik represents four musicians, two of these playing *kitharas* of different shapes; a third musician beats a drum, a fourth the cymbals. (see illus. 18).

From all this historical evidence, WEISS draws the conclusion

> "that the *kithara* originally has been not an Egyptian instrument, but one brought there by Semites. It is also certain that the use of the instrument has been wide-spread among Asiatic peoples, as proven conclusively by Assyriology."[47]

It is generally assumed that the *kithara* originated from Asiatic countries. The instrument was widely known in South-West Asia, as proven by pictorial representations from archaic times, found at Nineveh and elsewhere. (see illus. 28).

In addition, the Asian origin of the *kithara* is hinted by the fact that the Greek writers have frequently substituted the term *asias*, "Asiatic lyre," or "Asiatic harp," for the *kithara*.[48] PLUTARCH says also:

> "It was called the Asian harp (*kithara*), because the Lesbian harpers bordering upon Asia always made use of it."[49]

Finally, Jewish coins of the epoch of the high priest Simeon (132-135 C.E.) show pictures of the *kinnor*, which are quite similar to Greek *kitharas*. (See illus. 30 and 31).

As these coins were made during the second Maccabaean revolt, it might be questionable whether the instruments depicted on them still represent the authentic form of the ancient biblical *kinnor*. However, WEISS points out justly that the Orientals are very conservative in their customs and manners; this is particularly true of the Jewish cult, clinging strictly to traditional forms. The Jewish religious institutions, ceremonies, and also the instruments have scarcely been subjected to any substantial changes during many centuries.

> "The improvements applied gradually to the Greek *kithara* have certainly influenced the Asian prototype of the instrument. The resonant body might have been enlarged, by which the sound became more voluminous; the number of strings might have been increased, the mechanism of tuning perfected, the whole instrument artfully embellished, according to the aesthetic sense of the Greeks: all these non-essential changes did not alter the fundamental structure of the

instrument. We might assume, therefore, with reasonable probability, that the biblical *kinnor* is reproduced on these coins, at least in its basic form."[50] (see illus. 35).

On the other hand, BATHJA BAYER cautions us about adhering too strictly to the concept of the "unchanging East."[51] This might be valid for certain aspects of general life, but not where artifacts and musical instruments are concerned. The basic "types may remain for a long time," but even they may be subject to incisive modifications. As she thinks, "the only lyre-form suitable to King David's time and culture is the one depicted on the Philistine vase from Megiddo (about 1000 B.C.E.)." (*Cp.* the form of this lyre with that on the vase of about 1025, found at Megiddo. Illus. 32).

We have a description of the *kinnor* from a 12th century commentary on the Book of Daniel by ABRAHAM ben MEIR ibn EZRA, who asserts that the instrument had the shape of the Jewish candelabrum, the *menorah.* SACHS considers this indication credible, since the Jewish candelabrum, with its parallel arms disposed in a half-circle, resembles the Asiatic and the early Greek *kithara.*[52] These *kitharas* are, chronologically as well as geographically, rather close to the *kinnor.*

All the pictures on the coins of Bar Kokba reveal a rather bulky resonant body, upon which the strings are stretched. The early Fathers of the Church, in describing the biblical instrument, agree that the sounding-box of the *kinnor* was at its bottom, whereas the psaltery (*nebel*) had it on its top.

Depending on the particular shape of the sounding-box, the Church Fathers called it *testudo* (turtle), *tympanum* (drum), or, in general, *cavamen* (cavity), *lignum cavum, concavitas ligni* (hollow wood), or, figuratively, *sonora concavitas* (resounding cavity), *bucca sonora* (sonorous cheek, or mouth) and *obesus venter* (stout belly).[53]

Their opinions also differ greatly as to the details. Thus, JEROME says that the *kithara* has been played without a plectrum,[54] whereas CHRYSOSTOM[55] and BASIL[56] maintain the opposite view. AUGUSTINE'S remark, however, *utrumque hoc manibus portatur et tangitur* ("both are carried and played by the hands"),[57] seems to corroborate JEROME'S statement. In the spurious letter ascribed to JEROME,[58] it is said that the *kithara* had twenty-four strings. Yet, in his authentic writings, JEROME claims that

> "the *cithara* . . . has six strings . . . several of which have a singing tone, others [produce] a humming [sound]."[59]

The latter indication suggests that the *kithara* has had some thin and some thicker strings.

Furthermore, in the spurious letter to Dardanus it is said that the *kithara* is shaped *in modum Deltae literae,* "in the form of the [Greek] letter Δ," which would allow certain conclusions concerning its relationship to the above mentioned *trigōnon.* ISIDORE, and with him later Church Fathers, accepted the triangular form to be authentic, and so this belief has survived throughout the Middle Ages.[60] ISIDORE adds that this instrument has been the *cithara barbarica,* "the Berber *kithara,*" or, at least, has been similar to it. But ISIDORE lived in a relatively later epoch (c. 560-636 C.E.), and thus had no direct knowledge of the instrument. He also likens the *kithara* to the human chest and says that, in the Dorian language, the chest was called *kithara*.[61]

According to CHRYSOSTOM, the *kithara* was "moved (*kineitai*) from the bottom, the *psaltērion* from above."[62] As some expounders think,

> "whether this refers to the method of carrying the instrument, or to the moving (*i.e.* striking) the strings is not evident."[63]

The chances are, however, that *kineitai* implies the manner of playing, if we consider the indications of the Church Fathers as reliable, according to which the *kithara* had its sounding-box at the bottom and the *psaltērion* on top. The verb *kineitai* ("to move," *i.e.* "to sound") seems to refer to the spot where the strings were plugged, that is at the bottom, close to the sounding-box, where probably the best sonority could be achieved.

Though the descriptions of the Church Fathers indicate the main features of the *kinnor*, the opinions of the biblical scholars are divided even in the fundamental question of the instrumental category to which the *kinnor* may have belonged. Among the older expounders, PFEIFFER thinks that it was a lute or guitar.[64] Quite a number of more modern commentators follow this belief, *e.g.* SAALSCHÜTZ, SCHNEIDER, KEIL, DELITZSCH, STAINER, and others. PORTALEONE, however, and with him AMBROS, HUTCHINSON, HAUPT, and others, claim it to have been a harp. ENGEL, KITTO, WEISS, WELLHAUSEN, BENZINGER, and SACHS, after scrupulous examination of all the involved factors, conclude that the *kinnor* was a *kithara* or *lyra*. As SACHS says, "the last doubt is silenced by the fact that *k·nn·r*[65] designated the same lyre in Egypt."[66] Etymology and history corroborate this opinion.

Kithara and *lyra* represent essentially the same type of instrument; the difference lies mainly in their size. The *kithara* was the larger of the two, thus having also a lower and more voluminous sound; this may be concluded from its larger side-arms, mostly hollow, and therefore producing an increased resonance. The player, when marching, hung the *kithara* with a strap around his shoulders. The *lyra* was the smaller, more delicate type; the side-arms, mostly of one piece, were fixed directly upon the sounding-box. On Bar Kokba's coins both types are reproduced. (See illus. 30 and 31).

The ancient descriptions and also the opinions of virtually all ancient and modern commentators are unanimous in considering the *kinnor* to have been a stringed instrument. The more astonishing therefore is it to find one opinion to the contrary expressed by a reputed scholar. MOVERS refers to the passage in Isaiah, "wherefore my heart moaneth like a harp (*kinnor*) for Moab," (Isa. 16:11), and points out that the same passage is "translated" by Jeremiah as follows: "Therefore my heart moaneth for Moab like pipes (*ḥalilim*)" (Jer. 48:36). From the fact that both passages indicate "music for mourning," MOVERS draws the conclusion that *kinnor* sometimes was the term for a wind instrument, since pipes have always been used at Jewish funerals.[67] In addition, he refers to some Greek writers, who classify the *kinyra* as a mourning instrument.[68] We know that the threnodies (*thrēnoi*) of the Greek dramatic plays, possibly also the lamentations at Greek funerals, were accompanied on the *lyra* or *kithara*; among the Israelites, however, such a use of the *kinnor* is not reported either in biblical or post-biblical sources.

MOVERS' assumption that one biblical passage is the "translation" of another one, has no foundation at all. Both prophets have described their lament for Moab in a different way. Jeremiah has compared the moaning of the heart to the sound of the usual instrument for lamentations, the *ḥalil*, whereas Isaiah applied for his simile the rustling sound of the low strings of the *kinnor*. Both prophets are using here a poetic metaphor; by no means do these prophetical passages warrant a conclusion that the term *kinnor* has ever been used to designate a non-stringed instrument.

o

o o

For the act of playing the *kinnor* the rabbinic writers are using the verb *hiḳḳish*, "to touch," "to strike," the same as for sounding percussion instruments. The Midrash quotes an order of NEBUCHADREZZAR issued to the Jewish captives in Babylonia: "and you shall, in my presence, strike your *kinnorot*."[69] According to KRAUSS, this

> "seems to imply the playing with a plectrum, for which a reference has been lacking so far."[70]

But already JOSEPHUS stated that the *kinnor* was played with the plectrum.[71] "To strike" a stringed instrument is by no means an idiomatic expression found exclusively in the Hebrew language; other languages, too, like the Greek, German, etc., use for playing the harp, the zither, the guitar and mandolin the verb "to strike."

In addition, KRAUSS thinks that ordinary people may have played the *kinnor* with a plectrum, whereas the Levites, in preserving the ancient custom, might have manipulated the instrument with their bare fingers, like an harp. Yet, it is unlikely that the same instrument has been played differently for sacred and secular use.[72]

o

o o

Minnim (sing. *men*) and *yeter*, in post-biblical literature *nimin* (evidently influenced by the Greek *nēma* = string) are terms designating strings, but refer, figuratively, to stringed instruments in general (*cf.* Ps. 150:4). They were made of sheeps' guts, sometimes also of plant-fibers.[73] According to a rabbinic source, the strings of the *nebalim* were made of the "entrails" (*meyav*), and those of the *kinnorot* of the "chitterlings" (*b'ne meyav*, lit. the "sons of sheep gut").[74] By the latter term the tripes are meant, the portions of the entrails lying directly below the stomach of the animals which, in sheep, are particularly thin.

Strings of metal were unknown in Antiquity. There is an indication, however, in the patristic literature, which apparently contradicts this fact. We read in ST. BASIL'S Greek *Homily upon the First Psalm*:

> *tē kithara men gar kai tē lyra kathōten ho chalkos hypēchei pros to plēktron*, etc.

In MIGNE'S Latin *Patrologia* this is translated as

> *nam citharae ac lyrae aes ex inferiori parte sonitum edit ad plectrum; psalterium vero a parte superiori concinnae suae modulationis originem ducit,*[75]

which—Englished literally—would give the sense of

"the brass wires of the cithara and the lyra sound from below with the plectrum, etc."[76]

There exists, however, a modified translation of BASIL'S tractate into Latin by RUFINUS (c. 340-410 C.E.), in which this passage is more explicitly treated:

cithara namque lyra ex inferiori parte aes vel tympanum habens, resonat ac resultat ad plectrum; psalterium vero harmonicas de superioribus habere fertur aptatas, et sonorum causas desuper dare.[77]

Apparently, RUFINUS used for his translation some other Greek text, which explains the addition of the word *tympanum,* missing in the original. Yet, which parts of the instruments BASIL and RUFINUS might have referred to by *aes vel tympanum,* is merely a matter of surmise. One may think of a metal cross-bar or a metal bridge and, accordingly, we suggest the following tentative translations of the two different versions:

MIGNE: The metal bridge of the cithara and lyra emits the sound from the lower part by use of the plectrum; the psaltery, however, has the source of its sound from the upper part.

RUFINUS: The cithara and lyra, having their metal bridge or the skin cover of their sound-chest on the lower part, resound and reverberate by use of the plectrum; the psaltery, however, is said to produce its sounds from the upper parts and originates therefore its tone from above.

Yet, to what part of the instruments the Greek word *chalkos,* "brass," or its Latin equivalent *aes,* refer actually, cannot be established beyond doubt. It is certain, however, that in BASIL's time (c. 330-379 C.E.) there existed no strings of metal.[78]

o
o o

The pins or pegs, on which the strings were fastened, were called *niḳtimon.*[79] The same word was used also to indicate the pegs of drums, which held the skin stretched. The frame or arm of harp-like instruments, on which the pegs were fastened, was called *marḳof.*[80] None of the two words appears in the Old Testament, therefore they must have been introduced initially in the post-biblical era.

Several expounders interpret *marḳof* as a toy, possibly a wooden horse. The Mishnaic text uses the word together with a group of musical instruments,[81] and refers to it as the "singer's *marḳof*."[82] The interpretation as a toy seems, therefore, to be erroneous. Judging from the context, one may assume that it indicates an object connected with a musical instrument, perhaps the frame, or another part, of the lyra.

o
o o

We find in the Mishnah precise instructions when and how a broken string could be tied up:

"They might tie up a string [of a musical instrument] in the Temple, but not in the province [*i.e.* in the sacred service outside of Jerusalem]; and in either place it is forbidden to tie it up for a first time. [*i.e.* at the beginning, before the playing started]."[83]

In commenting on this statement, the Gemara explains:

"A Levite on whose *kinnor* a string is broken may not knot it. R. Simeon says: He should splice it. R Simeon ben Eliezer says: This does not allow the tone to come out clearly [*i.e.* when a string is knotted in the middle]; but one should loosen the string at the bottom and wind it around the top, or loosen it at the top and wind it around the bottom."[84]

The purpose of these discussions was to find the best method in fastening a broken string so that the sounding length of it be free from knots and loops and produce again a good sound. Yet, even these explicit instructions do not explain why the knotting of a broken string was permitted at the services in Jerusalem, but prohibited at those in the province. Perhaps the concession in the latter instance has been due to the fact that, contrary to the huge Jerusalem sanctuary, those in the provinces used a single player for each group of instruments, so that a broken string in any single instance would actually be detrimental to the established procedures of the sacred service.

It was considered important that the instruments accompanying the songs during the sacrifices be in perfect order, because any irregularity—like a broken string, for instance—would invalidate the sacrifice. Therefore the Talmud says:

"If a *nima* (string) broke, they retied it three times on the peg properly."[85]

o
o o

The opinions of the commentators are widely divided also with regard to the number of the strings on the *kinnor.* Between the statement of JEROME (six) and that of PORTALEONE (forty-seven), there seems to be no possible compromise. It is self-evident, however, that owing to the absence of authentic historical data, PORTALEONE describes the harp of his own epoch, which since the Middle Ages was already a markedly developed instrument. This becomes evident from certain details of his lengthy description, as for instance when he mentions "four round windows" (obviously sounding holes) in the resonance body, or the "iron pegs," around which the strings were twisted, etc.

On the Jewish coins mentioned above, mostly three, sometimes five or six strings are sufficiently visible. Since the coins of that epoch have been executed rather crudely, the number of strings depicted on them can hardly be considered conclusive. The same doubt is warranted with regard to the statement in the spurious Dardanus letter, according to which the *kithara* had twenty-four strings.[86] On the other hand, JEROME's assertion that the ordinary *kithara* had six strings might come closer to the truth.[87] JOSEPHUS, however, submits again a different number:

"The *kinyra* is an instrument provided with ten strings (*chordais*),

> struck with the plectrum. The *nabla* has twelve sounds (*phthongous*) and is plucked with the fingers."[88]

The ten-stringed *kinnor* of JOSEPHUS would correspond to the ten-stringea instrument, *ʿasor,* mentioned in the Bible. According to some expositors, the controversial term *sheminit* (1 Chron. 15:21; Pss. 6:1; 12:1) would designate a variety of the *kinnor with eight strings.*[89] It is probable that several types of *kinnorot,* different in size and in the number of strings have been used by the ancient Hebrews. This might explain the divergences in the existing descriptions.

The early rabbinic sages, too, are far from unanimous with regard to the number of strings used for the *kinnor* and *nebel,* the reason being that, similar to the early translators of the Scriptures, they were not sufficiently familiar with the described instruments. They frequently confound the *kinnor* wth the *nebel,* and vice versa, so that it is never too clear which one of the two instruments is referred to in their writings. Sometimes they assert that both instruments are practically identical:

> "*Nebel* and *kinnor* are the same with the only difference of more strings for the former."[90]

According to R. JUDAH, the harp of the Sanctuary has had seven strings. "The harp of the messianic days" will have eight strings, and "the harp of the world to come" ten strings.[91] It is obvious that these indications have but a symbolic meaning. Yet in another passage of the Midrash the number of strings of the "ordinary harp" is given as ten.[92]

o o o

To play stringed instruments was called *naggen* (1 Sam. 16:16 ff; 18:10; Isa. 23:16, etc.), which indicated the plucking of the strings with the fingers, but sometimes also with the plectrum, made of quill, wood, bone, or metal. It was reported about David that he "played with his hand" (*niggen b'yado*) the *kinnor* before the ailing king Saul, and also on other occasions (1 Sam. 16:16; 16:23; 18:10; 19:9). This specifically repeated indication intimates that it might have been something uncommon, at variance with the general usage.[93] Accordingly, this passage is frequently commented as a performance "without a plectrum," which furthermore is corroborated by the fact that, on these occasions, David did not sing but merely played. Such a harp-like manner of playing the lyre is in fact attested by the practice in Egypt and Greece. The Hellenes called the play on the *kithara* with the fingers alone *psilē kitharisis,* whereas the accompaniment to singing with plectrum was called *kitharōdia.* The difference between the two might have been that in the accompaniment (with the plectrum) the player could pluck only one tone, or string at a time; he therefore merely supported, *i.e.* doubled, the melodic line. Whereas in playing a solo (with the fingers), he had the possibility of striking simultaneously several strings. This gave to his playing more volume, and to his interpretation more expression and artistic value. This indeed may explain the salutary effect of *kinnor* music upon the sick king Saul. David's playing "with his hand" might have represented a special skill in those days—a fact that is suggested by the chronicler's stressing it four times.

The Hebrew term designating the playing of a stringed instrument, especially of the *kinnor,* as an accompaniment to singing (the Greek *kitharōdia*) is *zammer* (Pss. 71:22,23; 98:5; 147:7; 149:3).[94] A further expression for playing of stringed instruments is to be found in 1 Chron. 15:28: *mash'miy'im binebalim v'kinnorot.* Translated literally, *hishmiy'a* means "to make a noise," "sounding aloud," and, in a figurative sense, "to strike up a tune," "to make music."

o
o o

In Ancient Israel the *kinnor* was largely the instrument of joy and gaiety (Job. 21:12). It seems to have been more ancient and more generally used than the *nebel.* As early as in the times of the patriarchs it was the customary instrument at family festivities (Gen. 31:27); it was played by shepherds (1 Sam. 16:16) and by women (specifically by "harlots," Isa. 23:16); it was the dispenser of joy at merry banquets, at popular feasts, and at celebrations of victories and coronations.

As mentioned above, there is no reference in the Old Testament that it was ever played at funerals or accompanied lamentation. David's mourning song for Saul and Jonathan (2 Sam. 1:17), his laments for Abner (2 Sam. 3:28), Amnon (2 Sam. 13:31), and Absalom (2 Sam. 19:1) [18:33]) do not contain any indications or even oblique implications of accompanying instruments. A passage in the Book of Job (30:31) is sometimes interpreted in the sense that the *kinnor* supplied the musical background at funerals:

> "Therefore is my harp (*kinnor*) turned to mourning, and my pipe (*'ugab*) into the voice of them that weep."

But it is evident that the two instruments are used here merely as a poetical metaphor, similar to Isa. 16:11 and Jer. 48:36; by no means does this passage imply the participation of *kinnorot* at funeral ceremonies.

The *kinnor* becomes silent when the joy ceases (Ps. 137:2). As punishment for the people's transgressions, the prophets threaten that the sound of the *kinnor* would no longer be heard (Isa. 24:8; Ezek. 26:13).

King David was the most famous *kinnor*-player in Israel's history; only Jeduthun-Ethan came close to him as a virtuoso on the instrument. It is understandable, therefore, that David and his "harp" became the subjects of many legendary tales. As the Midrash and the Talmud relate, a *kinnor* was suspended above his bed; at midnight, the north wind used to sweep over the strings which started to sound by themselves.[95] Or, as another version has it, David would rise at midnight to play his instrument.[96]

o
o o

The sound of the *kinnor* is called in the Bible "pleasant" or "sweet" (*na'ayim,* Ps. 81:3), and "solemn" (*higgayon,* Ps. 92:4), and in the Talmud "sweet" (*ḥali*).[97] The playing of the *kinnor* is termed "joy" (*masos,* Isa.

24:8). In general, the stringed instruments (*minni*) are considered as dispensers of gladness and delight (Ps. 45:9).[98]

o
o o

The *kinnor* was the favorite instrument of the rich and refined people, though not exclusively. It served not only for enhancing the joys at banquets, but playing the instrument belonged to the choicest pleasures of life. There must have existed *kinnor*-teachers who instructed these epicureans of the ancient elite. A passage of Amos (6:5) shows that in the 9th Cent. B.C.E. playing the *kinnor* was considered more or less a novelty, and that there must have been quite a number of clumsy amateurs in the higher strata of society.[99] Its frequent use at the carousals of wealthy revelers was considered by the prophets a defilement of an instrument designed for sacred use. When the prophets raised their voice against the abuses of wealth, against debauchery and sybaritic life, they thundered also against singing and music as mediums for carnal pleasures. As a concomitant phenomenon of the voluptuous revelries, the *kinnor* was also smitten by their anathema. This attitude however, did not impair its significance in the sacred service. As one of the principal instruments of the cult, supplying the accompaniment for levitical singing, the *kinnor* retained an unchallenged esteem throughout the entire existence of the Temple.

The talmudic sages disagreed as to the suitability of instruments in the sacred service. The general prohibition of music after the destruction of the Sanctuary in Jerusalem was handled by the rabbis now rigorously, now leniently, so that by this hesitant interpretation instrumental music was not abruptly eliminated. However, in post-biblical times a gradually increasing hostility of the rabbis against ever growing pagan influences in religion made itself felt quite prominently. These influences were associated with the wide-spread use of certain instruments and contributed substantially to the unyielding rabbinic enmity toward instrumental music. As ERIC WERNER puts it:

> "The post-biblical hostility of rabbinic Judaism toward all instrumental music was not so much an expression of grief over the loss of the Temple and land as a policy of defense for Judaism against pagan cults, especially against the orgiastic mysteries of Asia Minor, wherein certain musical instruments were recognized attributes of the deities."[100]

It is evident, therefore, that the rabbis as well as the prophets demonstrated the same hostile attitude not so much against instrumental music itself, as against its scurrilous and alarming abuses.

o
o o

The rendering of *kinnor* in the English Bibles shows the same variety and vagueness as in the early classical versions. *Wycliffe* translates mostly as "harpe," but in Ps. 49:5 a "sauter" (early), or "sautree" (later), and in Ps. 149:3 as "sautre," all three terms being the Old-English spellings of "psaltery"; then "salm" in 81:2 and "instruments" (early), or "orguns" (later) in Ps. 137:2.

Douay mostly renders *kinnor* as "harp," but in some instances as "psaltery" (Pss. 49:5 [48:5]; 81.2 [80:2]; 149:3) once as "cittern" (1 Kings 10:12), and in one passage *kinnor* is replaced by the generic term "instruments" (Ps. 137:2 [136:2]).

The *Authorized Version* likewise uses "harp," with the sole exception of Ps. 33:2, where the Hebrew term is translated as "psaltery."

We know to-day that the *kinnor* did not belong to the family of harps. And it is quite apparent that the early English translations persisted in this error simply because at that time the distinction between the various categories of stringed instruments was not as clear as it is to-day. It is surprising, therefore, that the modern translations, among them the *Jewish* and *American Versions* and *Moulton* should cling conservatively to the translations as "harp."

Moffat was the first in rendering the *kinnor* correctly as "lyre," but he sometimes also used "harp" 1 Chron. 15:21; Ps. 137:2), or "lute" (2 Sam. 6:5; Isa. 24:8), and in two places he paraphrases an entire verse, without even mentioning *kinnor* (Job 30:31: "my dances turn to dirges, my lyrics to lament," and Isa. 16:11: "I thrill with pity for poor Moab, my heart is stirred for Kir-ḥeres").

The *Revised Standard Version* is the most consistent of all English translations, using correctly "lyres," except in two places (Ps. 150:3 and Isa. 23.16), where for no obvious reasons *kinnor* is rendered as "harp."

2. NEBEL

The other stringed instrument for the accompaniment of singing, mentioned frequently (twenty-seven times) in the Scriptures, is the *nebel* (plur. *nebalim*). In its original meaning, the word signifies "to inflate," "to bulge," therefore in the Hebrew language *nebel* is also the term for the leathern bottle and other bulky vessels holding water, milk, wine, and also pots made of clay.[101] Thus, the SEPTUAGINT translates the word twice as *askos*, "skin bottle" (1 Sam. 10:3; Jer. 13:12). The skin bottle and the jug have similar belly-shaped forms and thus, the term indicating utensils of this shape, might have been applied to the instrument.

The Semitic word *nebel* passed into Greek and Latin as *nabla, nablion* and *nablium* and served, as among the Hebrews, as the term for a stringed instrument of a bulky shape. In the Greek version the *b* has been transformed into a *v,* and so eventually the instrument was called *navla* or *naula*.

The Hellenes attributed the invention of this instrument to the Phoenicians,[102] more precisely to the inhabitants of Sidon, a Phoenician city famous in Antiquity for its music. According to EUSEBIUS, however, the *nabla* or *nablium* was invented by the Cappadocians, who allegedly constructed it after Assyrian models.[103]

Biblical and post-biblical sources leave no doubt that the *nebel* was a stringed instrument. In connection with *nebel* the prophet Amos uses the verg *paraṭ*, literally "to pluck fruits," by which term the manner of playing the instrument, i.e. plucking with the fingers, is clearly expressed.[104] JOSEPHUS states that the *nebel* has twelve strings, which are played with bare fingers.[105] OVID,[106]

POLLUX[107] and other classical writers likewise mention it among the stringed instruments. Nevertheless, some later commentators maintain that it was a wind instrument.[108]

PORTALEONE identifies the *nebel* with the Italian lute of his time. He describes minutely the fingerboard, the sounding box, the arrangement of the strings, and gives in general a portrayal of an instrument which is manifestly an image of the coeval *Chitarrone* or *Liuto chitarronato*. It goes without saying that this description is without any foundation.[109]

The early translations of the Bible contain only very vague indications with regard to the nature of the instrument. The SEPTUATGINT has five different ways of rendering *nebel*: fourteen times as *nabla, nablē,* or *nablion* (in the historical books), eight times as *psaltērion,* once *kithara* (Ps. 81:2), twice *organon* (Am. 5:23; 6:5), and once *kle nebel* with *skeyos psalmou* (Ps. 71:22). The passage in Isa. 14:11, *hemyat nebaleḥo,* "the noise of thy psalteries," is paraphrased as *hē pollē euphrosynē sou,* "thy loud festivity."

The VULGATE has seventeen times *psalterium,* four times *lyra,* three times *nablium,* once *cithara,* and in one passage the word is mistranslated as *cadaver tua* ("thy corpse") (Isa. 14:11).[110] In Ps. 71:22, *kle nebel* is rendered as *vasum psalmi.*

The Peshiṭṭa translates thirteen times, *ḳitara,* four times *kinora,* twice *nabla,* paraphrases twice, and omits the word entirely six times. The Targum has ten times *nibla,* twice *nebel* (2 Sam. 6:5; Isa. 5:12), twice *kinora* (Am. 5:23, Ps. 92:4), and in one place the word is paraphrased (Isa. 14:11).

Later—especially patristic—sources declare that the *psaltērion* and the *nabla* are identical. In the spurious Dardanus letter it is said:

> "*Psalterium quoque Hebraice nablon, Graece autem psalterion, Latine laudatorium dicitur*" ("The psaltery, which is called *nablon* in Hebrew, *psaltērion* in Greek, is considered in Latin [usage] a laudatory [instrument]").[111]

EUSEBIUS is even more explicit in stating that *psalterium citharae species,* "the psaltery is a species of the *kithara.*"[112] HILARIUS, too, declares that both instruments are identical.[113] SUIDAS of Byzantium (10th century C.E.) confirms this explicitly,[114] and SAʿADIA (12th century) maintains that the *pesanterin* mentioned in the Book of Daniel is the same as the *nebel.*[115]

Though the writings of the early Church Fathers mention frequently the *psaltērion,* their descriptions are hardly elucidative with regard to the shape and nature of the instrument. Only in one detail do the Church Fathers agree, namely that the *nebel* had its sounding-box on the upper part, while the *kinnor* had it at the bottom. In Greek music, the word *psaltērion* applied apparently to an entire family of more or less similar instruments and, in a wider sense, to stringed instruments in general. Among the numerous proofs to this effect, those quoted by ATHENAEUS deserve special consideration.

In the chapters dealing with music, ATHENAEUS enumerates a multitude of stringed instruments: *magadis, barbiton, baromos, pandura, trigōnon, sambykē, iambikē, phoinix, klepsiambos, skindapsos,* the "nine-stringed," the "three-stringed," *kithara, lyra,* the "two-stringed *pēktis,*" *lyrophoinikos, epigoneion,* etc. These names would suggest a great number of multifarious stringed instruments. Yet EUPHORION declares that

> "the instruments with many strings varied only in their names."[116]

Other writers confirm that in many cases the same instrument is called differently. APOLLODOROS says, for instance:

> "What we call to-day a *psaltērion* is the *magadis*."[117]

EUPHORION states

> "that the instrument known as the *magadis* is very old, but in more recent times its construction was altered and its name changed to *sambykē*."[118] ALEXANDROS of KYTHERA "perfected the *psaltērion* with a large number of strings."[119] JOUBA "also mentions the *lyrophoinikos*, and the *epigoneion*, which to-day has been re-fashioned into an upright *psaltērion* (*psaltērion orthion*)."[120]

Among the statements of other writers we may quote that of VARRO, who calls the *nebel* an *orthopsallium* (according to another spelling *orthopsaltium*), an "upright psaltery."[121] This would lead one to the conclusion that the psaltery may have been generally played in a horizontal, not in an upright position. However, still another spelling gives the name of the instrument *orthopsalticum*, meaning "high-pitched," which seems to refer to a smaller species of *nebel* with a higher range. Should such a "pygmy harp" have existed in Antiquity—and ATHENAEUS' enumeration seems to point to it—this might greatly contribute to the solution of the *nebalim* *ʿal-ʿalamot* problem. As a matter of fact, such an instrument might disentangle the rather unnatural (and uncustomary) situation in which the tonal range of some harps is apparently higher than that of the lyre.

Even the normal *kinnor* does not seem to have been the soprano-member of the "plucked strings" family. In some instances it was larger, therefore also lower in pitch, than the *nebel* (see p. 283). It appears indeed as if the tonal ranges of the *nebel*, the *kinnor*, and the *orthopsalticum* would have corresponded approximately (and respectively) to those of the violoncello, the viola, and the violin of the "bowed strings" family. There was, however, no parallel in importance of the instruments themselves between these two groups (*cf.* p. 126).

Besides ATHENAEUS, some other ancient writers classify certain string instruments as belonging to the family of psalteries. HESYCHIOS counts the *pandourion* among them,[122] POLLUX also the *pēlēx*.[123] According to OVID, the *nabla* was played with both hands like a harp:

> "Learn also to sweep with both hands the genial Phoenician harp (*nabla*); suitable is it to merry-making."[124]

SUIDAS, too, places the *nabla* among the psalteries and, furthermore, explicitly declares that the *psaltērion* is not a single species of an instrument, but embraces an entire family of stringed instruments.[125]

All these unanimous testimonies prove that the ancient instruments played with both hands without a plectrum were called by the generic name of *psaltērion*, and have been variously shaped harps. They might have shown differences with regard to size, number of strings, volume, sonority, and tuning.

However, their construction and technique of playing must have followed the same pattern.

The similarities and differences of the various species of this family are stressed by several other writers, likewise quoted by ATHENAEUS.

> "The *pēktis* and the *magadis* are the same instrument, as ARISTOXENOS declares."[126] Also "MENAICHMOS, in his work *On Artists,* asserts that *pēktis* is the same as the *magadis.*"[127] But "DIOGENES, the tragic poet thinks that the *pēktis* differed from the *magadis.*"[128] "PHILLIS of DELOS also maintains that the *pēktis* is different from the *magadis.*"[129]

It is generally assumed that the *magadis* had twenty strings. ANAKREON says, for instance:

> "With *magadis* in hand I sing to its twenty strings.[130] But "TELESTES in '*Hymenaios*' indicates that the *magadis* has five strings."[131]

The *pēktis* is supposed to have had two strings only. This small number of strings produced "a barbaric music," as SOPATROS says,[132] which means that playing on two strings sounded so primitive for the refined Hellenic ears that they considered it "barbaric." Therefore, the *pēktis* was soon displaced by instruments with more strings, such as the *nabla* and *sambykē.*

In view of so many testimonies to the contrary, it is peculiar that some ancient writers declared the *magadis* to be a pipe or flute.[133] This obvious error was brought about by the Greek virtuosi of that epoch who discovered a technique how to produce harmonics on the strings of harp-like instruments.[134] This manner of playing was called *syrigmos* or *syrigma;* the derivation of the word from *syrinx,* the Pan's pipe, is obvious, and this might have been the reason that Greek writers, not familiar with the nature of this technique, likened the *magadis* to a pipe or flute.[135] But ATHENAEUS states, without being able to explain the contradiction:

> "The *magadis* is certainly an instrument like the harp as ANAKREON makes clear."[136]

Nevertheless, the error subsisted for a long time, and even in recent times the idea cropped up again that the *nebel* is a wind instrument.[137]

WEISS points out pertinently the double meaning of the word *psalterium* as it appears from ancient sources.

> "In the strict sense, it signifies a particular stringed instrument that was played by the fingers of both hands, therefore it was easily accessible from both sides, had several strings, and a harp-like shape. In a wider sense, instruments were also called psalteries, the strings of which were stretched above a sounding body, and which, therefore, could be played only from one side, and with a plectrum."[138]

WEISS thinks that the Arabian *santir,* a kind of dulcimer, depicted in several Assyrian antiquities, might have been such an instrument in the latter sense. He admits, however, that this could not have been identical with the biblical *nebel,* since all the sources indicate that the *nebel* has been played with the fingers and thus must have belonged to the family of harps.

Nevertheless, the idea has been persistently maintained that the *nebel* has not been a harp, but a dulcimer, an offshoot of which is preserved in the modern cymbal (*cimbalom*) of the Hungarian gypsy-music. This opinion rests upon the assumption that dulcimer-like instruments existed already in Antiquity, as evidenced by numerous pictorial documents. The most revealing of these is the bas-relief found in ASHUR-IDANNI-PAL's palace at Kuyundchik, on which eleven instrumentalists and fifteen singers are portrayed. Among these instruments is one resembling a dulcimer, which some modern scholars consider the biblical *nebel.*[139]

The spurious Dardanus letter mentions the *nebel* as having *forma quadrata.* The dulcimer had indeed a square sounding-box. This gave additional support to the assumption that the *psaltērion,* therefore also the *nebel,* have been identical with the *santir,* a low and lengthy box with flat bottom and slightly convex body, above which the strings were stretched.

This opinion, however, is strictly contradicted by the explicit statement of the Church Fathers, according to which the sounding-box of the psaltery was placed above. This flat shape would also be conflicting with the etymology of the Hebrew word *nebel,* indicating manifestly something bulging, belly-like. SACHS admits the possibility that the resounding arm of the instrument was placed on the upper part of it, so that it might have resembled an Oriental utricle-like vessel.[140] An allusion in Amos 6:5 seems to indicate that the rounded off body of the *nebel* was covered with animal skin.[141] This would have given the instrument even more resemblance with an utricle and would explain the fact that later writers erroneously identified the *nebel* with a bag-pipe.

As the rabbinical writers assert, the *nebel* was larger than the *kinnor;* it must have been, therefore, the lower pitched and stronger type. This is corroborated by the Mishnaic statement that the strings of the *nebel* have been made of the entrails (*meyav*) of sheep, and those of the *kinnor* of the chitterlings (*b'ne meyav*), which produced respectively thicker and thinner strings.[142] The Talmud also says that the sound of the *nebel* has been stronger than that of the *kinnor.*[143]

Assuming these rabbinic statements to be correct, SACHS made the significant observation that the biblical passage 1 Chron. 15:20,21 has been constantly misunderstood, and therefore erroneously translated.[144] In this passage the chronicler reports about two singing groups of the Davidic music organization, one of which performed *binebalim ʿal ʿalamot* "with psalteries set to Alamoth," the other *b'kinnorot ʿal ha-sheminit,* "with harps on (*Revised Version* "set to") the Sheminith." Since the *nebel* is supposed to have been the larger, therefore lower sounding instrument, the *kinnor* generally had the lead, which means that the *kinnor* doubled the melody, while the *nebel* had a more subordinate, accompanying function. Hence SACHS concludes that in this passage *nebel* should be translated as "harp," and *kinnor* as "lyre," or "psaltery," therefore contrary to traditional translations.

This controversy, however, is more apparent than real. As mentioned earlier in our study,[145] the names *kinnor* and *nebel* are mostly used by the chroniclers (and rabbinic writers) without any specifications, referring obviously to the conventional types of these instruments. It is therefore striking to find, in these four places (1 Chron. 15:20,21, and Pss. 6, 12, 46), the names of these instruments coupled with some qualifying term. The chances are that the biblical chronicler, as well as the psalmists, who most probably belonged to the musicians' guild, wanted to indicate some special type of string instruments, in these instances a smaller type of *nebel,* sounding higher (*ʿal ʿalamot* = in the range of maidens' voices), and a larger, therefore lower type of *kinnor* which, rather uncommonly, assumed accompanying functions.[146]

The Hebrew collective term for string instruments, *kle shir,* opens the possibility that, besides the instruments mentioned in the Scriptures, other species of the same family may have existed. Two of these might have been a small *nebel* and a larger *kinnor,* as indicated by the terms under scrutiny.

Though this conclusion is no more than a surmise, it might very well correspond to actual facts and, at the same time, clarify the prevailing confusion with regard to the current translations of this biblical passage, as pointed out by SACHS.

Biblical exegesis and musicology have not found as yet a thoroughly satisfactory explanation of the term *sheminit.* It is commonly known, however, that the Greek music theory has incorporated a scale of eight notes, whatever was its specific application in actual practice. As mentioned earlier, the Greek system was based upon two conjunct tetrachords, the last note of one being the initial note of the other, or else two disjunct tetrachords with no common note. The latter combination produced a scale that included the eighth tone, or the octave, this being essentially the high-pitched duplication of the first. To be sure, "octave" is a later name; the Greeks called it *dia pasōn.* Numerous Greek writers use this term in the sense of the "eighth tone."[147]

But the most conclusive evidence for this is the "invention" reported by ATHENAEUS. This was the special manner of *kithara*-playing, called *syrigma* to which we referred above and which consisted in the device of touching slightly the plucked string exactly in the middle, whereby the second partial, that is the octave, was produced. Such technique of obtaining audible harmonics represents until today one of the artful devices in playing the harp. ATHENAEUS states:

> "PHILLIS of DELOS, in the second book of his work *On Music. . .* says: LYSANDER of SIKYON was the first harp-player to institute the new art of solo-playing, tuning his strings high and making the tone full and rich, in fact giving that flute-like tone (*tēn enaulon kitharisin*) to the string which EPIGONOS and his school were the first to adopt. He abolished the meagre simplicity prevailing among the solo-harpists (*psilois kitharisin*), and introduced in his harp-playing highly-coloured variations, also *iambi,* the *magadis* and the *syrigmos,* as it is called."[148]

We know, furthermore, that the music notation of the Hellenes provided specific signs for high notes, be they sung by maidens and boys, or for the above mentioned *syrigma,* as well as for playing all high species of *auloi.*[149]

The final proof, however, for the theoretical knowledge of the octave and its practical application is furnished by the *magadis.* It had twenty strings,[150] but only ten different tones, the seven basic notes and some chromatic alterations, which were duplicated in the "octave" (*dia pasōn*):

> "PHILLIS of DELOS, in the second book of his work *On Music . . .* says: The *magadides* are those [instruments] with which they sang notes an

octave apart (*dia pasōn*), the parts assigned to the singers being adjusted in equal intervals."[151]

The effect was the doubling in the octave, as boys and men sang together.

ARISTOXENOS declares explicitly:

dia to dyo genōn bama kai bia pasōn echein tēn synōdian andrōn to kai paidōn, "because with the two kinds of instruments [the *magadis* and the *barbitos*] played together and at the interval of an octave there is perfect unison of men's and boys' voices."[152]

This manner of playing or singing together the higher and lower parts, or voices, was called in Greek *magadizein,* a verb, the etymology and function of which is clearly indicated by what was exposed above. ARISTOTLE uses already the term: "They *magadize* in the octave (*dia pasōn*)."[153] ATHENAEUS refers repeatedly to this manner of playing.[154] This doubling of tones in the octave induced TRYPHON to state:

"That named *magadis* can produce at the same moment a high and a low tone (*en tautō oxyn kai baryn phthongon*)."[155]

Not an original Greek instrument, the *magadis* was probably brought from Assyria. The musicologist ARISTOXENOS,[156] and the writer of tragedies DIOGENES[157] mention it among the "foreign" instruments, EUPHORION among the "ancient" ones.[158] In preserved Assyrian pictorial representations there is indeed one of which has the same number of strings (twenty) as the *magadis* played by ANAKREON.[159]

Though we know that the Hellenes have imported and adapted many foreign instruments, their attitude toward them was not always favorable, or even tolerant. The Asiatic *magadis* with its many strings, so different from the traditional domestic instruments, had soon stirred up the displeasure of conservative patriots. ATHENAEUS reports an episode, which is characteristic of this attitude:

"Thimoteos of Miletos is held by most authorities to have adopted an arrangement of strings with too great a number, namely the *magadis;* wherefore he was even about to be disciplined by the Lakedemonians for trying to corrupt their ancient music, and some one was on the point of cutting away his superfluous strings when he pointed to a small image of Apollo among them holding a lyre with the same number of arrangements of strings as his own, and so was acquitted."[160]

Just as the *magadis* has been adopted by the Greeks, the same could have happened with the Hebrews. Though there is no mention of it in our sources, it is by no means inconceivable that the Hebrews, too, knew a harp with many strings. As in the case of the ultra-conservative Lakedemonians, such a "foreign" instrument might have greatly displeased the traditionally inclined guardians of the Jewish religious institutions; but they evidently had more success than the Lakedemonians in removing such an "intruder," since there is no vestige of an instrument with so many strings in the musical practice of Ancient Israel.

Should, however, such an instrument have been known to the Hebrews, be it only for a relatively short period, they could have become familiar with the idea, and also with the technique, of *magadizein.* Then it might be possible that *sheminit* would signify the same thing in the music practice of the Hebrews as *magadizein* did among the Hellenes, namely singing the same melody an octave apart by high and low voices, as well as playing it similarly upon shorter and longer strings, distributed eventually among two separate instruments. The hostility of the Israelites toward the foreign *magadis* has perhaps abolished the use of it; the technique of vocal and instrumental *magadizein,* however, was not done away with, and might have subsisted for a certain time at least.

Lately a new theory about the meaning of the word *sheminit* has developed. It has been brought in relationship with the Byzantine term *octoechos,* the eight Psalm Tones of the Byzantine Church. However, "direct comparison between these with the Psalm Tones of the Synagogue is impossible, since the Synagogue had never fully implemented the theoretical postulate of eight distinct Tones."[161] Nevertheless, it is possible that the Hebrews used eight modes in their liturgy and that some of them were assigned to particular groups of the Levites. *Sheminit,* therefore, might have indicated that a certain Psalm had to be sung in the eighth mode by this group.

Another hypothesis for the explanation of *sheminit* might have been that this term was closely associated with the Jewish calendar and may have referred to one of the eight melodic formulae designed to be sung as part of some seasonal observance.

o
o o

The spurious Dardanus letter states that the psaltery had the form of the Greek letter *Delta.* This statement has been taken over by a number of medieval ecclesiastical writers, who draw on the alleged authority of JEROME.[162] This indication, however, is contrary to the description given by the early Church Fathers, according to which the *psaltērion* had its sounding box above. The Greek letter *Delta,* or a similar geometric figure, excludes a bulky sounding body on the upper part. Should we take the description of the Church Fathers for granted, we would be bound to consider the statement of the unknown author of the Dardanus letter as an error.

Matters are different, however, if we take into account the fact that the initial biblical mention of the *nebel* takes place at a relatively late period (1 Sam. 10:5). This might suggest that the Israelites did not bring along this particular instrument from Egypt, but became acquainted with it through their intercourse with Asiatic peoples. Indeed, some Assyrian angular harps have a form similar to that of a *Delta.* A certain oblique position of this instrument, when played, could in fact intimate as though its sounding-box were placed above.

The diversity of shapes of the stringed instruments in Egyptian and Assyrian-Babylonian pictures testify to the fact that these species must have been also different in size and the number of strings, as well as in tuning. The same situation might have prevailed in Israel's music practice. The headings of Ps. 6 (*bineginot ʿal ha-sheminit*) and Ps. 12 (*ʿal ha-sheminit,* with omission of the name of an instrument), the analogous terms in 1 Chron. 15:21 (*bekinnorot* ʿ*al ha-sheminit*) and 1 Chron. 15:20 (*binebalim* ʿ*al* ʿ*alamot*), as well as 1 Chron. 16:5 (*kle nebalim*), strongly support this assumption.

o
o o

The Bible furnishes three indications as to the number of strings on some of the instruments: in Ps. 92:4, ʿ*ale* ʿ*asor v'* ʿ*ale nebel*, "with an instrument of ten strings, and with the psaltery"; in Pss. 33:2 and 144:9, *nebel* ʿ*asor*, "psaltery of ten strings." The first passage refers to two different instruments, one having ten strings, *and* the *nebel*, whereas the two other passages suggest that there existed also a *nebel* with ten strings. The SEPTUAGINT translates Ps. 92:4 as *en dekachordō psaltēriō*, JEROME, however, as *in decachordo et in psalterio*, a definite and more accurate indication that there are two different instruments involved.

In the rabbinic literature, there are only isolated references to the number of strings of the *nebel*. In general, it is said that

> "the difference between *nebel* and *kinnor* is that one (*nebel*) has more strings than the other."[163]

The same talmudic passage contains further elaboration of the fact that the *nebel* had more strings than the other instruments of the same category:

> "R. Ḥiyya ben Abba said:
> Why was its name called *nebel?* Because it put to shame [excelled] (*ḥilḳin*) many a musical instrument. R. Huna in the name of R. Joseph (said): Because of a skin that is not dressed and because of its many strings it put to shame many a musical instrument."[164]

As we see, the assumption according to which the sounding body of the *nebel* was covered with an animal membrane, was still maintained in the talmudic epoch. This assumption originates from the expression in Amos 6:5, *ha-porṭim* ʿ*al-pi ha-nebel*, "that thrum on the psaltery." It is, however, by no means an established fact that the verb *paraṭ* refers here to a drum-like manner of playing, since its original meaning is "to pluck fruits," which clearly indicates the plucking of strings.[165] Some expositors think, however, that *pi ha-nebel* refers to an opening in the sound-box.[166]

The Bible informs us about the use of the *nebel* in the cult. From the Mishnah we learn that *nebalim* were used for secular purposes as well, and that they were also played by women. A significant statement says:

> "The harps (*nebalim*) of the female singer (*ha-sharah*) [*i.e.* for secular use] are unclean; the harps of the sons of Levi [*i.e.* for liturgical use] are clean."[167]

Among the Greeks, the *nabla* was likewise played by women; such female musicians were called *nablistai*.[168]

o
o o

In view of such numerous descriptions of the *nebel*, and more so of the abundant pictorial material concerning harp-like instruments in Egyptian and

Assyrian archaeological discoveries, it is astonishing that the opinions of biblical scholars with regard to the character of the biblical *nebel* show the greatest divergences. PFEIFFER, FORKEL, JAHN, CORNILL, and others, think it was a lyre; SCHNEIDER, SAALSCHÜTZ, RIEHM, DELITZSCH, and WEISS consider it to have been a harp; PORTALEONE, ENGEL, and others maintain that it was a lute; KITTO holds that it was either a harp or a lyre, whereas BENZINGER believes it was the name of the harp as well as the lute. AMBROS, on the other hand, identifies it with the Assyrian dulcimer (*santir, pesantir*). THEODOR REINACH opines that the *psaltērion* was identical with the small Greek triangular harp, the *trigōnon,*[169] For support, he refers to a passage in ARISTOTLE, "*en trigōnis psaltēriois.*"[170] However, this text ascribed to ARISTOTLE is considered spurious.

All these opinions have at least one thing in common, namely that they understand *nebel* to be a stringed instrument.

Yet, some commentators believe that the *nebel* was a wind instrument. This opinion stems in particular from a misunderstood statement of JOSEPHUS in which the difference between the *kinnor* and *nebel* is reduced to the fact that the former instrument has

> "ten strings" (*chordai*), and the latter "twelve sounds" (*phthongous*).[171]

The latter Greek expression (sing. *phthongos*), generally a sound as distinguished from a "voice" (*phōnē*), seemed to be for some exegetes an indication that it refers to pipes with reeds, similar to those of an organ. But this assumption is invalidated by the simple fact that Antiquity did not know organ pipes with reeds (or vibrating tongues). In describing the water-organ (*hydraulis*) of ARCHIMEDES, TERTULLIAN mentions many of its details, such as

> "limbs, parts, bands, passages for the notes, outlets for their sounds, combinations for their harmony, and the array of its pipes,"

but he does not refer to the reeds (or tongues) of the pipes, which certainly would be quite conspicuous, had they actually existed.[172] The descriptions of the *hydraulis* by other ancient writers[173] are equally devoid of any references to possible reeds of its pipes.

Other commentators, however, believe that the Greek verb *krouein,*[174] used by JOSEPHUS to characterize the manner of playing the *nabla,* may indicate that the fingers of the player "struck" the holes of a wind instrument. This explanation, too, is manifestly erroneous, since it is obvious that the two verbs *typtetai* and *krouetai* served JOSEPHUS for expressing the difference in the manner of sound production: the playing with the plectrum for the *kinnor,* and the striking (plucking) with the bare fingers for the *nebel* respectively.

What could have been the reason for JOSEPHUS' differentiation between *chordai* and *phthongous,* since both terms applied to stringed instruments? It is not improbable that he thereby intended to characterize the difference between their basic sonorities. For the strings plucked with the fingers have had certainly a more muffled sound than the sharp tones of the *kinnor* produced by the plectrum.

Other commentators, of ancient and more recent times, give various reasons for the assumption that the *nebel* was a wind instrument. IBN EZRA opines that the *nebel* has had ten openings, and concludes from this that these were the holes of a wind instrument.[175] The rabbinic descriptions of instruments do not reveal in general an intimate knowledge of their construction. If the *nebel* has had indeed ten openings, these must have been the sound-holes of the resounding box.[176]

In more recent times, MICHAEL PRÄTORIUS has declared that *nebel* was a sort of bagpipe.[177] The same opinion is shared by GUILLAUME A. VILLOTEAU, who identifies the *nebel* with the Arabian *zukkarah,* still existing in Egypt; this is a wind-bag of ram's skin with two inserted pipes, the bells of which are curved at their upper end.[179] The original meaning of the word *nebel,* "skin bottle," which, in this capacity, could well supply the air for the bagpipe, might have been the reason for VILLOTEAU's identifying the biblical *nebel* with the Arabian instrument. For further proof, he refers to an obviously misunderstood passage of ATHENAEUS, who quotes the following verse from SOPATROS' comedy *Pylai* (*The Portal*): *Oute tou Sidoniou nabla laryngophōnos enkechordōtai typos*; translated correctly, it has the following meaning: "Nor has the deep-toned thrum of the Sidonian *nabla* passed from the strings."[179] The word *laryngophōnos* has erroneously created the idea of a flute-like instrument, which was even stressed by another verse of SOPATROS:

> "In the articulation of its lines the *nebla* is not pretty (*eumelēs*);[180] fixed in its ribs is lifeless lotus wood, which gives forth a breathing music (*empnoun aniei mousan*)."[181]

It is obvious, however, that the tube-like lotuswood served merely to enhance the resonance of the instrument, like the hollow side-arms of the *lyra* or *kithara.*[182]

Thus, we see that in ancient as in more modern times there has been a wide divergence of opinion even about the basic question whether the *nebel* was a stringed or a wind instrument.

As late as our time, the *nebel* was considered to be a wind instrument. IDELSOHN thinks that the term used in 1 Chron. 15:20, *nebel ʿal ʿalamot,* refers to a kind of bagpipe. *Nebel* would be the bag on which the pipes were fastened. He considers *ʿalamot* to be a double-flute, and derives it from the Assyrian word *ʿelamu,*

> "usually employed to two bodies close together and yet parted,"

and opines that this "precisely fits the structure of the double-pipe."[183]

Yet, apart from the numerous descriptions of the early Church Fathers, there are two classical testimonies discarding any doubt that the *nebel* was a stringed instrument. OVID says that the player of the *nabla* sweeps with both hands over the strings,[184] and JOSEPHUS states explicitly that the *nabla* was played not with the plectrum, but with the fingers.[185] Some historians argue that JOSEPHUS' statement conflicts with the general evolutionary process, according to which stringed instruments were played originally with the fingers, and only at a later stage with a plectrum. This is incorrect, since playing with a plectrum does not necessarily indicate a later stage of development. Kitharas and lyres have been played from the very outset with the plectrum, while harp-like instruments have been sounded in the earlier as well as in the later age with the fingers. For both manners of playing there are numerous pictorial documents in Egyptian and Assyrian antiquities.

All the factors considered, there can hardly be any doubt that the *nebel* was the upright, portable angular harp. It might have existed in various sizes with tunings involving different intervallic arrangements, but its basic form has been modified only in some minor details throughout the centuries.

o
o o

Nebel is translated in the principal English version in six different ways, as "psaltery" (spelled sawtree, sautre, or sawtrye in the early translations), "psalm," "harp," "lute," "gittern," and "viol." The *Wycliffe Version* has mostly "sawtree," (or "sautre"), in three passages "gittern" (1 Chron. 15:20; 15:28; and Isa. 5:12). In two places this word is used in the Old-English spelling "sitols" (for "citerns"), and "sitols to syngeris" (2 Sam. 6:5; 1 Kings 10:12). The earlier version uses for Isa. 5:12 "syngende instrument," for Amos 5:23 "harpe," and for Amos 6:5 "voice of psautrie" (early), or "vois of sautree" (later). Since *Wycliffe* followed closely the VULGATE, Isa. 14:11 is also mistranslated as "careyn" ("carcass," the Latin "*cadaver*").

The *Douay Version* has mostly "psaltery," once "lute" (2 Sam. 6:5), once "lyre" (Isa. 5:12), twice "harp" (Amos. 5:23, and 6:5), and mistranslates, like the VULGATE, Isa. 14:11 as "carcass."

The *Authorized Version* and *Harkavy* use for the most part "psaltery," in four places "viol" (Isa. 5:12; 14:11; Amos 5:23; 6:5). The *American Version* and *Moulton* also translate mostly as "psaltery," except for Isa. 14:11, Amos 5:23, 6:5 ("viol"), and Isa. 5:12 ("lute").

Most consistent are the *Jewish Version,* using exclusively "psaltery," and the *Moffat Version,* using almost exclusively "lute." Surprisingly, the last-mentioned version paraphrases the passage of Isa. 14:11 as "peals of music."

The *Revised Standard Version* is the only one which classifies the instrument correctly and, with one exception ("lute," in Ps. 150:3), uses throughout the appropriate term, "harp."

Kle nebel is rendered by most versions simply as "psaltery," by the *Douay Version* as "instruments of psaltery." *Wycliffe* has "orgyns of sawtree" (early), and "orguns on the sautrie" (later) for Ps. 33:2, and "vesselis of salm" (early) and "instrumentis of salm" (later) for Ps. 71:22.

The *Revised Standard Version* uses for *kle nebel* the same word ("harp") as for *nebel* alone.

3. ʿASOR

The word *ʿasor* appears only three times in the Old Testament, in Pss. 33:2, 92:4, and 144:9. It is considered generally as a derivative from a root meaning "ten." Since *ʿasor* is always mentioned in connection with some other stringed instrument, the early translators of the Bible have considered the notion of "ten" as referring to the number of strings of this instrument and, consequently, translated the latter as *en dekachordō,* or *psaltērion dekachordōn*

(SEPTUAGINT), and *psalterium decem chordarum,* or *in decachordo psalterio* (VULGATE). The later Latin translations follow the VULGATE; the Chaldaean, Syrian and Arabian versions have also adopted the idea of the earlier translators that *nebel-ʿasor* was an instrument of ten strings.

The correct definition of the instrument is rendered more difficult by the fact that in all three biblical passages *ʿasor* is connected with another instrument. Pss. 33 and 144 have *nebel ʿasor,* with no *maḳef* (the Hebrew hyphen) appearing between the two words. From this, the early translators conclude that *ʿasor* is an adjective to *nebel,* and translated accordingly "*nebel* of ten strings." Ps. 92, on the other hand, has *ʿale-ʿasor vaʿale-nebel.* JEROME was the first to recognize that this might have referred to two different instruments and, thus, he translated this passage *in decachordo et in psalterio.* In his exegetical writings he distinguishes between the *cithara* of six strings and the psaltery of ten strings, and thus again takes the *ʿasor* to be an adjective to *nebel,* as in Psalms 33 and 144.[186] The ancient translators of the Bible follow mostly his rendition.

WEISS thinks that the words *nebel ʿasor* belong together, designating an instrument that was distinguished from the ordinary *nebel* by a different number of strings, or a more voluminous corpus.[187]

SACHS' opinion about the characteristics of the instrument differs considerably from the traditional interpretation. In examining the possibilities as to which category of instruments the *ʿasor* might belong, he arrives at the conclusion that it must have been a sort of zither.

> "Zithers did not exist either in Egypt or in Assyria, the two great monarchies of the Near East. But Israel's most civilized neighbors, the Phoenicians, used a strange type of zither. Two specimens of this instrument are carved on a beautiful ivory pyxis of the 8th century B.C. in the British Museum, No. 118,179, which came from the Southeast Palace at Nimrud in Assyria, and was taken for Assyrian until recently when his Phoenician origin was recognized. On this relief the backs of the two zithers cannot be seen, and it is impossible to determine whether they are flat or bulgy. The front, on the contrary, is distinct; it consists of a small rectangular frame with strings across and running parallel to the smaller sides. The position is upright in the player's hand, and the female musician plays with the bare fingers. The main point is the number of strings: probably ten on one zither, and clearly ten on the other one. The *ʿasor* might have been such a Phoenician zither."[188]

SACHS' opinion contradicts that of GALPIN.[189] The latter examines the word philologically and claims that *ʿasor* is a misspelled, and misunderstood, or else a dialectical form of *ʿashor,* "Assyrian." He refers to the fact that the Hebrew letter *shin* (ש) have been used formerly without much discrimination for both consonants *s* and *sh,* and that the *ʿayyin* (ע) and *ʾaleph* (א), the initial letters of the two words, have also been frequently interchanged in ancient times. From all this he concludes that *ʿashor* was the name of the Assyrian harp, which was taken over by the Hebrews.

Furthermore, GALPIN broaches another possibility in referring to a Sumerian instrument, *eshirtu,* "the 'ten-stringed' (horizontal) angle-harp," which likewise seems to correspond to the biblical *ʿasor.*[190] GALPIN's assumption is supported by an archaeological discovery, which allows an insight into the musical terminology of ancient Oriental peoples.

LANGDON has published a detailed description of a slab found in Assur, containing a long list of Sumerian liturgies.[191] These liturgies were called *tegû,* meaning "flute-songs"; each of these liturgies was a series (*ishkaratu*) of several songs, called *zamaru.* Among these songs there are work-songs, love-songs, songs for shepherds, songs of wisdom, etc. The catalogue contains also precise indications showing that these songs have been performed with instrumental accompaniments. There are in this list *shi-id-ru sha ib-bu-be,* "recitation with pipe," *te-gu-ú* "songs with the reed-pipe," *shir-gid-da-mesh,* "songs with the long flute," and *za-ma-ru a-da-pu,* "songs with the hand-drum."

Number 45 of these inscriptions reads: 23 *iratu sha e-shir-te Akkad-*(*ki*), "23 songs of the breast" (love-songs) "for the instrument of ten" (strings) "in Semitic."[192] As LANGDON states, *e-shir* or *a-shir* is the name of the Assyrian-Babylonian harp of ten strings, taken over by the Hebrews, who called it *ʿasor* or *ʿashor.* This statement would indeed provide the word *ʿasor* with a correct etymological interpretation, compatible at the same time with the number "ten," as well as with the Assyrian origin of the instrument.

Modern commentators never had any doubt that *nebel* and *ʿasor* were actually two different instruments, but no agreement was reached about the exact nature of the latter. To mention only a few examples, FÉTIS identifies the *ʿasor* with the small bow-harp found by WILKINSON in Upper-Egypt,[193] ENGEL with the Syrian trigon-harp,[194] HARENBERG with the *magadis.*[195]

GALPIN's and LANGDON's investigations open the possibility that the *ʿasor* was the ten-stringed harp taken over from the Assyrians. Nevertheless, SACHS' interpretation must be credited with the greater probability, since the biblical text in Ps. 92 indicates clearly that *nebel* and *ʿasor* were two different instruments, which would not apply conclusively to instruments of the same type with the only difference in the number of their strings.

The two trends in interpreting *ʿasor* (1) as the name of an independent instrument, and (2) as a qualification defining a certain variant of *nebel,* prevail in all English translations of the Bible.

Wycliffe uses for Ps. 33:2 "sautrie on ten cordis" (early), and "sautre of ten strengis" (later); for Ps. 92:4 "ten cordid sautre" (early), and "sautrie of ten cordis" (later); for Ps. 144:9 "ten cordid sautre" (early), and "sautrie of ten strings" (later).

Douay has "(sing to him with) the psaltery, the instrument of ten strings" for Ps. 33:2; "upon an instrument of ten strings, upon the psaltery" for Ps. 92:4; "on the psaltery, *and* an instrument of ten strings" (like the VULGATE) for Ps. 144:9.

The *Authorized Version* and *Harkavy* always render *ʿasor* as an "instrument of ten strings." the *Jewish Version* combines *nebel* and *ʿasor* as "psaltery of ten strings" in Pss. 33:2 and 144:9, and sets "instrument of ten strings" for *ʿasor* alone in Ps. 92:4.

The *American Version* likewise telescopes *nebel ʿasor* into "psaltery of ten strings" in two passages, but separates them in Ps. 92:4 as "with an instrument of ten strings, *and* with the psaltery."

Moulton has invariably "psaltery of ten strings," *Moffat* "ten-stringed lute." The *Revised Standard Version* uses "harp of ten strings" (Ps. 33:2), and "ten-stringed harp" (Ps. 144:9) for *nebel ʿasor,* and "lute" for *ʿasor* alone in Ps. 92:4.

4. GITTIT

The term *gittit,* found in the headings of Pss. 8, 81 and 84, has been mostly taken as referring to a musical instrument. The literal meaning of the word is "that from Geth." Thus *ʿal ha-gittit* would represent an instruction for accompanying the psalms in question with an instrument originating from Geth. As we know, David has stayed for some time in the Philistinian city of Geth (or Gath, *cf.* 1 Sam. 27:2; 29:3), and so he might well have brought this indigenous instrument (a sort of lute) to his own country.

This traditional explanation is based principally upon the translation of the Targum: "on the zither, that came from Gath" (to Ps. 8).

Another interpretation uses also the name of that city, but explains *gittit* not as an instrument, but as the name of a song, or a joyous tune, "perhaps a march of the Gittite guard."[196] In this case, *ʿal ha-gittit* would signify that the melody of this song should be used for the three psalms referred to. Such an assumption, however, is fallacious, since it is inconceivable that the priests, bent on preserving the purity of the cult, would ever have openly permitted any psalm—a portion of the sacred ceremony—to be sung to a Philistine, heathen melody.

There exists still another and even more implausible interpretation connected with the city of Geth. It assumes the word *gittit* to imply "a choir of female singers from Geth," which David brought with him on his return from this city. In other words, the three psalms were "given to the class of young women, or songstresses of Geth, to be sung by them."[197] The Bible itself is quoted as furnishing a historical evidence for this assumption. As the chronicler reports, David held in his army six hundred warriors from Geth (2 Sam. 15:18), who had been faithfully devoted to him in luck and adversity (2 Sam. 15:21). There is, however, an abysmal difference between foreign mercenaries in the army and non-Jewish songstresses in the cult. The singing women of the sacred service have been exclusively Jewish; the female members of the Temple choir were the wives and daughters of the levitical singers.[198] The very idea of employing Philistine songstresses in the cult would have certainly been considered by the priests as a sacrilege and would have been opposed violently. This hypothesis must be, therefore, rejected as wholly untenable.

Even though REDSLOB[199] and GESENIUS[200] consider *gittit* to be a musical instrument, they derive its name not from the city of Geth, but from the verb *naggen,* "to touch the strings," the infinitive of which, *genet,* with the affixed syllable, *it,* led allegedly to the creation of the word *gittit.* The feminine ending together with the inversion and assimilation of the consonants, resulted in a meaning which—similar to that of *neginah*—would signify in general the playing of stringed instruments. Thus, the terms *bineginot* and *ʿal ha-gittit* would have an identical meaning, "accompanied by stringed instruments."[201]

The Hebrew word *gat* has still another meaning, "a press," "a vine press," or rather "a trough," "a vat," in which the grapes were trodden with the feet.[202] SEPTUAGINT follows this meaning and translates *ʿal ha-gittit* as *hyper tōn lēnōn,* "upon the wine-pressers" (alluding possibly to a song performed on this occasion). Using another preposition, the VULGATE renders that expression as *pro torcularibus,* "for the wine-treaders." JEROME, AQUILA, and the Midrash have likewise adopted this idea (for Pss. 81 and 84); therefore, many modern commentators are inclined to look upon this version as the most probable one. BAETHGEN advocates a slight change of the vocalization for all three psalm-headings and, consequently, suggests the translation: "with the wine-treaders," which—according to his idea—could be paraphrased as "for the Feast of Tabernacles."[203]

This interpretation would imply that the three psalms under consideration had been sung at Tabernacles during the procedure of treading the new wine, a conception justifiable at most for Ps. 81, if we take into account the contents of the psalm; the texts of the other psalms, however, (8 and 84) do not contain anything suggestive of their possible performance at the harvest thanksgiving festival, or, specifically, while treading the grapes. To be sure, the existence of work songs is frequently attested in Antiquity. The Hebrews, too, had such songs, especially those intended for the vintage season.[204] Yet, it is highly improbable that the melody and rhythm required for a specific bodily function (such as the treading of grapes) and having the purpose of facilitating a strenuous physical work, could have served as a musical pattern for a psalm of the cult.[205]

JAHN is of the opinion that *gittit* was "an instrument played at the treading out of the grapes." He furnishes, however no indication which kind of instrument this might have been.[206]

IBN EZRA interprets *gittit* as a *piyyut* (whatever its contents), the initial word of which was *gittit.*[207] His idea has some probability, since other terms in the headings of the psalms, which have no relationship to the contents of the poems, are likewise explained as the initial words of songs, the tunes of which served as melodic pattern for the psalms.

OESTERLEY thinks that *ha-gittit* might indicate a vintage song. Its melody must have been well-known to everybody, he says, and this might have been the reason why the psalmist wanted it to be used for his poem.

The book of Joel contains a songlike passage:

> "Put ye in the sickle, for the harvest is ripe; come tread ye, for the winepress is full, the vats overflow." (4:13).

In this passage, the Hebrew word for "winepress" is *gat.* From these allusions OESTERLEY concludes that *gittit* meant indeed a vintage song.[208]

For THIRTLE's theory of *gittit* see p. 134.

MOWINCKEL scrutinizes several possibilities with regard to *gittit,* adding some hypotheses of his own. He finally comes to the frank conclusion that none of them represents a usable solution.[209]

LUTHER's translation follows the idea of an accompanying instrument: "on the *gittit,* to lead the song" ("auf der Gittith, vorzusingen"); whereas among the English Bibles the *Jewish Version* alone renders the word unequivocally in the sense of a musical instrument: "upon the Gittith." The *Authorized Version* and *Harkavy* translate "upon Gittith," the *American Version* "set to the Gittith," and the *Revised Standard Version* "according to The Gittith," leaving open the question whether the term refers to an instrument or to the title of a song. *Moffat* interprets the term musically as "set to a vintage melody." Whereas most of the ancient English versions follow the idea of a "winepress"; accordingly, *Wycliffe* translates the term in Ps. 8 "for the pressis" (early), and "for pressours" (later); in Ps. 81 "for the pressis" (early), and "in the pressours" (later); and in Ps. 84 the same for the early version, whereas the later version omits the word altogether. *Douay* has likewise "for the presses" (Ps. 8), and "for the winepresses" (Pss. 81 and 84).

5. SABBEKA

One of the biblical books mentions repeatedly the *sabbeka* as one of the instruments played at King NEBUCHADREZZAR's court (Dan. 3:5,7,10,15).[210] It is generally agreed that this instrument is identical with the Greek *sambykē* (spelled also *zambykē* or *zambikē*) and the Roman *sambuca.* The Hellenes as well as the Romans used the instrument mainly to enhance the exuberance of their banquets.[211] It was also one of the instruments used by girls of questionable repute, who were called by the Greeks *sambykistēs* or *sambykistria,*[212] and by the Romans *sambucisti, sambucistriae,* or *sambucinae.*[213]

The word *sabbeka* is commonly derived from *sambucus,* "elder," the wood of which, when dried, was very strong and durable, hence appropriate for musical instruments. The naming of an instrument after the material which served for its construction has been a frequent practice in Antiquity.

Another etymological explanation brings the word into contact with the Hebrew verb *sabak,* "to interweave," "to interlace," from which the noun *seboko,* "wicker-work," "lattice-work" was built.[214] According to this interpretation, the name of the instrument would refer to its twined strings. Yet, most of the stringed instruments of Antiquity had twined strings; it is therefore difficult to understand why this particular instrument should have been brought in relation with "wicker-work."

ATHENAEUS[215] and, following him, SUIDAS[216] claim that IBYKOS, the Greek poet from Rhegium, has "invented" the *sambykē.* Another statement of ATHENAEUS names a certain SAMBYX, likewise a Greek, as its inventor.[217] Other writers, however, maintain unanimously that the *sambykē* was a "barbaric,"[218] *i.e.,* a "foreign" instrument;[219] it may have, therefore, originated in Asia. A further evidence to this effect is the testimony of EUPHORION, who mentions specifically that the instrument was used by the Parths and Troglodytes.[220]

The very name of the instrument seems to indicate its Asiatic, or better, Semitic origin. The double *b* in the Semitic form has been transformed in Greek and Ltain into the diphthong *mb,* as with the word *ambubajae,* the

Syrian flute-girls, the name of whom is derived from the Semitic term *ʿabub* or *ʿabbub* (pipe).

The ancient sources reveal that the *sabbeka* was of a triangular form,[221] and that it had four strings,[222] its tone having been high and harsh.[223] Yet, PLATO defines the *sambykē* as a *polychordon, i.e.* a "many-stringed" instrument. This would seem to be in agreement with EUPHORION's statement that the *sambykē* was merely a later form of the *magadis*:

> "The instrument known as the *magadis* was very old, but in more recent times its construction was altered and its name changed to *sambykē*."[224]

According to MENAICHMOS and ARISTOXENOS, the *magadis* and *pēktis* were identical instruments.[225] (Thus, we would have here already three different names for the same instrument). This, however, seems very improbable, since the *magadis* had twenty strings, the *pēktis* only two. At most, one would be justified in assuming that the *sambykē* and the *trigōnon* were identical, both having had the same number of strings. This is corroborated by the additional statements of SUIDAS and VITRUVIUS, who declared that the *sambykē* had a triangular form. The high pitch of the *sambykē* may explain the fact that it was the preferred instrument for the accompaniment of female voices.

ATHENAEUS informs us that the word *sambykē* had still another meaning. There existed in Antiquity a siege mechanism, allegedly invented by ARCHIMEDES at the beleaguerment of Syracuse.

> "It was called *sambykē* because, when raised aloft, its appearance as a united whole becomes that of a ship and a ladder, and the appearance of the musical *sambykē* is somewhat similar."[226]

According to this comparison, the musical instrument must have had a bulging sound-box similar to a ship's body, whereas its side arms must have reminded one of the siege machine. Judging from this description, RIEHM thinks that the *sambykē* was akin to a peculiar Egyptian instrument, standing between a harp and a lute, the neck of which was bent,[227] whereas SACHS declares that the only instrument resembling this form was the horizontal angular harp.[228]

Even if we accept a Semitic origin of the word *sabbeka,* it may be assumed with certainty that such an instrument was not used by the ancient Israelites. This is evidenced first by the fact that, except in the Book of Daniel, it is not mentioned elsewhere in the Bible. The Book of Daniel was originally written not entirely in Hebrew, but partly in Aramaic,[229] and it relates events which occurred four centuries earlier. Daniel and the Babylonian King NEBUCHADREZZAR flourished in the first half of the 6th century B.C.E., whereas the Book of Daniel originated in the middle of the 2nd century. Furthermore, Daniel mentions *sabbeka* among foreign instruments of a pagan country and on an occasion which, by its very nature, must have appeared repugnant to the Jews—the erection and worship of an idol set up by NEBUCHADREZZAR. It may be taken for granted, therefore, that the *sabbeka* had no part in Israel's musical practice. Merely the fact that it is mentioned in one of the canonical books is the reason why it has been examined at all by biblical commentators.

Despite the multitude of Greek and Roman descriptions, the expounders are not in agreement as to the real nature of the *sabbeka*. ISIDORE of SEVILLE defines it as a bagpipe:

> "*Sambuca in musicis species est symphoniarum. Est enim genus ligni fragilis, unde et tibiae componuntur,*" "the sambuca is a kind of musical instrument. It is made of brittle wood, of which also its pipes are put together."[230]

IBN EZRA (1088-1180 C.E.) explains it as *maḥol,* an instrument of the family of pipes.[231] SAʿADIA (12th century) declares that the *sabbeka* was the *ʿugab,* a kind of oboe.[232] Among other commentators, GESENIUS claims that the *sabbeka* was similar to the *nebel,* therefore it was a harp-like instrument;[233] ENGEL maintains that it was a kind of guitar,[234] KITTO that it was a harp or lyre,[235] WORMAN thinks that it was a "triangular" instrument, or possibly the Assyrian dulcimer,[236] while GEVAERT identifies it with the *lyrophoininx,* the Phoenician lyre.[237]

Yet, all the classical evidence, which in this case is more abundant and more detailed than for any other instrument, drives one strongly to the conclusion that the *sabbeka,* played at NEBUCHADREZZAR's court, was a horizontal angular harp, similar to the triangular, four-stringed and high-pitched *sambykē* of the Hellenes.

The SEPTUAGINT translates the word by its Greek equivalent *sambykē,* the VULGATE by the Latin form *sambuca;* the later Greek and Latin translators follow their example. Curiously, the Peshiṭṭa omits the word in the enumeration of the instruments as NEBUCHADREZZAR's court.

Among the English Bibles, the *Jewish* and *Revised Standard Versions* render *sabbeka* as "trigon," *Wycliffe* and *Harkavy* as "sambuke," *Moffat* as "harp," the *Authorized Version* and the other principal translations, however, as "sackbut," an instrument which would correspond to today's trombone. It is obvious that the last-mentioned translation was caused solely by the superficial phonetic similarity with the word *sabbeka.* The "sackbut" is a relatively recent instrument, not to be found in England prior to the beginning of the 16th century. In the English medieval literature *sambuca* represents a woodwind instrument with reeds, like the "shawm," hence a species of oboe. In the Psalter of Boulogne (9th century) there is an illustration of the *sambuca,* depicting it correctly as a stringed instrument.

6. PESANTERIN

Another instrument played at the court of NEBUCHADREZZAR, and mentioned in the same verses of the Book of Daniel (3:5,7,10,15), was the *pesanterin.* Owing to the phonetic affinity with the Greek *psaltērion,* it has been widely assumed that both instruments were identical. Since the majority of the biblical expounders define the *psaltērion* as the biblical *nebel,* the belief has been long entertained that the Babylonian *pesanterin* was the same instrument as the Hebrew *nebel.*

In opposition to this belief, it must again be emphasized that the Book of Daniel enumerates foreign, heathen instruments, which were not in use in Israel's music practice. The instruments of the Jews of biblical times had similar names also in the Aramaean language, at least in their basic form;

hence, if both instruments were identical, it would not have been necessary for the chronicler to use the unknown word *pesanterin* for the well-known *nebel.* It is obvious furthermore, that the chronicler has intentionally mentioned here exotic instruments, in order to stress the alien character of the idolatrous ceremony.

To clear up the existing confusion created by the exchange of the names, it is necessary to recall that the Greek word *psaltērion* is derived from the verb *psallein,* "to move by touching," "to pull," "to twitch." Applied to music, *psallein* has the meaning "to play the *nebel*" (with the bare fingers), other terms for which are *plēktein, krēkein,* or *krouein,* in contrast "to play the *kinnor* with the plectrum." All the stringed instruments played with the bare fingers were called in Greek *organa psaltika.* The Romans, too, had different terms for the two manners of playing stringed instruments. They called playing with the plectrum *foris canere,* and with fingers alone, *intus canere.*[238]

ATHENAEUS uses various verbal expressions for playing a harp-like instrument:

> "EPIGONEIOS being very talented, he could play on the harp (*epsallēn*) with the bare hand without a plectrum."[239]

Also:

> "ARISTOXENOS says that the *magadis* and the *pēktis* may be played without the plectrum, by simply plucking (*dia psalmou*) with the fingers."[240]

If Daniel's *pesanterin* were identical with the Greek *psaltērion,* it must have been a harp-like instrument. There are, however, weighty arguments against this assumption. To be sure, *pesanterin* is phonetically affined to *psaltērion,* but its etymology points to a quite different root, namely to the Arabian *santir,* the name of a kind of dulcimer. *Pi-santir* means in Arabian "small *santir,*" and this is the term that has been taken over by the Chaldaean (or Aramaean) language.

A corroborative evidence of it is to be found in the picture of a group of

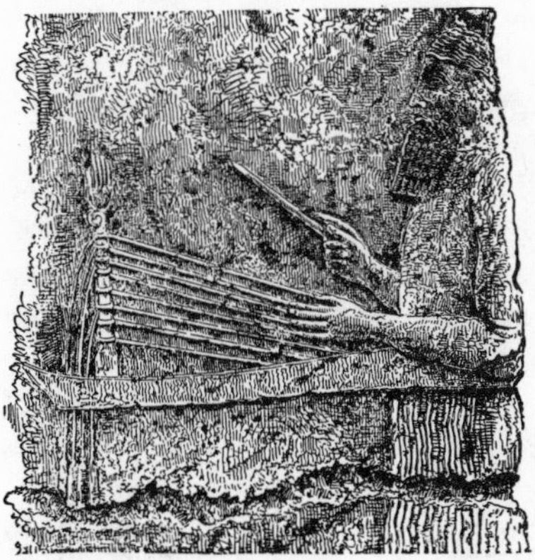

ILLUSTRATION NO. 38
Assyrian dulcimer player. Stone-relief (ca. 7. cent. B.C.E.). British Museum. (After Sir John Stainer, *The Music of the Bible,* London, 1914).

musicians found in the ruins of Nineveh. This picture shows, among other instrumentalists, a musician playing a seemingly square instrument, which he holds horizontally before him; its eight strings are stretched above a slightly arched sound box. This box has ten small round openings, evidently sound-holes. The player strikes the strings with a rather large stick, whereas in Oriental pictures the plectrum has a considerably smaller size. Whether the player plucks with his left hand the strings, or stops them, as is usual with dulcimer-like instruments (f.e. the zither), cannot be fully ascertained. (Illus. 38).

From this picture and from the etymology of the word *pesanterin* it becomes evident that the Semitic peoples of Antiquity have known a dulcimer-like instrument. The doubt is, therefore, amply justified about the assumption of WETZSTEIN, STAINER, AMBROS and some other scholars that Daniel's *pesanterin* and the biblical *nebel* have been identical. Their claim stems, evidently, from SA῾ADIA who identifies *pesanterin* with the *nebel*.[241]

IBN EZRA tries to explain Daniel's foreign terms *ḳathros, sabbeka, pesanterin* and *sumponyah* by identifying them with the biblical instruments *kinnor, maḥol, minnim* and *῾ugab*. By this, he may have somewhat contributed to an easier comprehension of these non-Jewish instruments, but, on the other hand, he certainly destroyed the exotic flavor of Daniel's story. In this connection, it is revealing that unlike other rabbinic writers, IBN EZRA does not identify *pesanterin* with the *nebel*, but uses, for the Aramaic word, the Hebrew generic term for stringed instruments, *minnim*.[242]

In more recent times VILLOTEAU referred specifically to the Arabian root of the word *pesanterin*.[243] His idea was adopted, among others, by FÉTIS, who not only declares that the Assyrian *pesanterin* and the Arabian *santir* have been identical, but extends this also to the biblical *nebel*, which to him was apparently likewise a dulcimer-like instrument.[244] Since numerous coeval descriptions afford a fairly clear idea about the nature of the *nebel*, or psaltery, FÉTIS' opinion merits quotation merely as a matter of curiosity.

Strangely enough, PFEIFFER and WEISS consider Daniel's *pesanterin* to be the *nebel* or *kinnor*, and others interpret it as a harp. GALPIN defines it correctly as a dulcimer-like instrument.[245]

The *santir* must have been known and used by Oriental peoples much earlier than the *psaltērion* by the Greeks. This is corroborated by the picture of the instrument on the archaeological discovery described above. This picture represents an event which took place ca. the 7th century B.C.E. Furthermore, most of the instruments in the Book of Daniel reveal their Asiatic origin, despite their names, akin to Greek terms. It would be far more logical to assume that the Hellenes have taken over these instruments from Asiatic peoples, improving and embellishing them as many other things imported from the Orient. ATHENAEUS states, for instance:

> "ALEXANDROS of KYTHERA [a famous musician living in Ephesus] perfected the *psaltērion* with a larger number of strings."[246]

Also:

> "The *epigoneion* has been re-fashioned into an upright psaltery (*psaltērion orthion*)."[247]

In time, the improved instruments found their way back to their country of origin and were introduced there with their Greek names, at most with some phonetic transformations caused by the different idioms. Such transformations are obvious in the names of *gingra* (*ginera, kinnor*), *aulos* (*ḥalalu, ḥalil*), *ḳeras* (*ḳeren*), *ḳathros* (*kithara*) *ambubaja* (*imbubu, ʾabbub*), etc.

The last doubts about the fact that the biblical *nebel* and Daniel's *pesanterin* were two different instruments must vanish in the light of the unanimous statement of the early Church Fathers that the *nebel* (called by them *psaltērion*) had its sounding body on the upper part, which would not have been possible with the Arabian or Syrian *santir.*

The SEPTUAGINT renders *pesanterin* as *psaltērion,* the VULGATE as *psalterium;* all the early Greek and Latin translations follow them without exception. The Peshiṭṭa translates it as *kinora.* Most of the English Bibles use "psaltery." *Wycliffe* spells the word in its archaic form as "sautrie" or "sawtrie." *Moffat* sets "lute," and the *Revised Standard Version* "harp."

Since the *pesanterin* seems to have been a different instrument from all the above mentioned string species, an English translation as "dulcimer" could very well be conceivable.

7. ḲATHROS

Still another instrument played at NEBUCHADREZZAR's court and mentioned in Daniel (3:5,7,10,15) is the *ḳathros* (or *ḳithros*). It seems easy, at first sight, to explain this term as the Green *kithara.* Consequently biblical exegesis considers unanimously the word as the transformed name of the Greek instrument.

Yet, this assumption, though basically correct, does not provide us with any indication either to the form or the character of the instrument named by Daniel. Almost no other instrument of the ancients has had so many varieties as the *kithara.* Its name was identical, or similar, among the different peoples which warrants a logical conclusion about its common origin in all instances. But already in Antiquity, and more so in subsequent times, the name indicated instruments of the most varied types.

The Arabian *kuitra* was a species of lute; the Persian *kitar* a long-necked guitar; the Nubian *kissar* a lyre and, furthermore, the Egyptians called the *kissar* also *gytarah barbaryeh,* "Berber's guitar." However, the Greek *kithara,* as also the Roman *cithara,* was a lyre.

The origin of the word points to the Far-East. In Sanskrit, *katur* means "four," in Persian *chutara* means "four-stringed," and the Hindus have a popular instrument called *si-tar,* the "three-stringed instrument," a kind of long-necked lute, invented allegedly in the 12th century C.E., but which is manifestly of ancient Asiatic origin.

After the instrument had been taken over by the music-makers of the Occident, its name as well as shape were subjected to the most incisive transformations. *Guitern* (Old-French), *gythorn* (Old-English), *gittern, cithern, cither, ghiterra,* or *chiterra* (Italian), *Zither* (German), are all transformed varieties (in names or substance, or both) of the ancient *kithara.* One has to recall only the Italian *chiterra* or *chitarrone* and the German *Zither,* which, as time passed, developed to entire different types of instruments.

As mentioned earlier, the Hellenes have frequently taken over from the

Orientals many inventions, including musical instruments, improved them by their higher artisanship, and then brought the developed products back to the country of their origin, mostly with their Greek names. After Troy's downfall, many Aeolian and Ionian colonies have settled down in Asia-Minor; this accounts for their acquaintance with Asiatic instruments, resulting in their exchange and transformation.

Things were not different with the Israelites. There is a significant passage in the Old Testament characterizing pertinently the mutual exchange of goods, the intensive trade of the Mediterranean peoples with one another. The various peoples traded or bartered

> "silver, iron, tin, and lead; vessels of brass; horses and mules; ivory and ebony; carbuncles, purple, fine linen, and coral, and rubies; wheat, and balsam, and honey, and oil and balm; wine, and white wool, and yarn; massive iron, cassia, and calmus; precious clothes for riding; lambs, and rams, and goats; spices, and precious stones, and gold; gorgeous fabrics, and richly woven work" (Ezek. 27:12-24).

There can be no doubt that musical instruments of the various trading peoples, representing part and parcel of the luxury of Orientals, likewise belonged to these "riches," "wares," and "merchandize" (Ezek. 27:27).

It would not be too far-fetched to assume that the Assyrian *ḳathros* (or *ḳithros*), named in Daniel, was such an "exchanged" instrument, akin to the Greek *kithara,* but maybe in a more developed form.

Ibn Ezra identifies Daniel's *ḳathros* with the biblical *kinnor.*[248] He is right insofar as it belonged to the lyre-family. However, it is obvious that the two instruments could not have been identical, since—we may repeat again —Daniel's instruments were all of an exotic type, as used at pagan worship and, consequently, they did not belong to Israel's music practice.

The early translators of the Bible follow the assonance with the Greek word and render the *ḳathros* as *kithara* or *cithara* in the Latin versions. The English Bibles, old and new, including the *Jewish Version,* use "harp." Only *Moffat* and the *Revised Standard Version* render it appropriately as "lyre."

8. NEGINOT

The word *neginot* has been subjected to the most contradictory interpretations of ancient and modern biblical expositors. The general meaning of the term (*bineginot* or *ʿal-neginot* = to sing to the accompaniment of stringed instruments, but also simply "song") has been scrutinized in an earlier chapter.[249] However, since *neginot* is frequently interpreted as a music instrument, or a family of such, it is necessary to examine it anew in this light. The word is to be found in the headings of Pss. 4, 6, 54, 55, 61, 67, 76; furthermore in Lament. 3:14; 5:14; Isa. 38.20; Ps. 77.7; Hab. 3:12 and Job 30:9.

The renditions of the early Bible translators already show great discrepancies with regard to the meaning of the word. The Septuagint and Theodotion translate it generally as *en hymnois,* the Vulgate as *in carminibus,* Jerome *in psalmis,* Aquila *en psalmois,* Symmachos *dia psaltērion.* But even the Septuagint does not always follow the same pattern, since it translates Ezek. 33:32 (*naggen*) as *psaltērion,* and Job 30:9 (*neginatam*) as *kithara.*

These various renditions created a confusion which has not been dissipated even in our time. Nevertheless, the root of the word refers unmistakably to its real meaning. Etymologically, *neginot* is derived from the verb *naggen,* "to touch," "to strike," indicating clearly the manner of playing stringed instruments.

In 1 Sam. 16:16; 18:10, but more so in Ps. 68:26, the minstrels (*nogenim*) are distinctly separated from the singers (*sharim*), which should dispel any doubt as to their different functions. The musical juxtaposition is so obvious here that this alone should suffice for a logical explanation of the term.

All the other derivations of the word from the verb *nagan,* "to twist," "to twine together," from *nagah,* "to shine," also that of FÜRST, who identifies the root *gan* with the Latin *can-ere,* "to sing," are arbitrary and downright erroneous.[250]

There is no doubt whatever about the meaning of *neginot* as "stringed instruments," or "music with the accompaniment of strings." This meaning is unmistakably conveyed by the headings of the psalms, as well as by a few other biblical passages, where the harp-player is called *menaggen* (1 Sam. 16:16, 2 Kings 3:15; Ps. 68:26).

Nevertheless, because of various nuances of the word in several biblical contexts, a difference of opinion has arisen concerning its real meaning. In Ps. 69:13, *neginot* is interpreted as "song of the drunkards"; in Job 30:9 and in Lament. 3:14,63, the word is transformed into *manginah* and *manginatam,* and means in these passages "their song" (*i.e.* a "satirical song") in the sense of derision. This secondary meaning, however, appears only in these isolated cases. All the other passages in which the biblical chroniclers use the word, refer unmistakably—at least in the music practice of Ancient Israel—to stringed instruments for the accompaniment of singing.

In post-biblical times *neginot* obtained a different meaning. It was applied to individual biblical accents (grammatical and tropal), whose graphical signs probably developed from cheironomic practice.[251] Subsequently, *neginah* (plur. *neginot*) was adopted for the whole system of biblical cantillation.

For the transformation of the literal meaning of the word SACHS furnishes a pertinent explanation.[252] He compares the Hebrew word in its various mutations with the Greek verb *krouein,* meaning also "to strike," especially "to strike the strings." However, the noun built of this verb, *krouma,* does not signify an instrument, but that what is played on it, hence the melody itself. And this is, as SACHS holds, also the exact meaning of the post-biblical term *neginot.* This word may be considered as the older form of *niggun,* which implies a definite category of Jewish song.

Viewed from this angle, it is strange that PORTALEONE still commits the error of considering the *neginot* to be an ancient Jewish instrument.[253] Particularly so, since in PORTALEONE's time (16th-17th century) the meaning of *neginot* as referring to the system of accents and to their application for biblical cantillation must have already been quite widely known.

For the translations of the term in the English Bibles see pp. 119 ff.

9. SHUSHAN

The headings of Pss. 45, 60, 69 and 80 contain the word *shushan* (or *shoshan*), explained by almost all biblical exegetists as the initial word of a popular song, whose melody has been utilized for these psalms. As DELITZSCH suggests, this popular song has started with the verse "A lily is the testimony," or "Lilies are the testimonies."[254]

Some expounders, however, define *shushan* as an instrument, basing their opinions upon RASHI, who attaches to the word a double meaning: (1) he derives it from *shesh,* "six," which points allegedly to an instrument of six strings, and (2) he considers this instrument to have been in the shape of a lily.

In one respect GESENIUS follows RASHI's interpretation, namely in that he believes *shushan* to have been a musical instrument in the shape of a lily. In support of his view, GESENIUS alludes to the fact that there exists a species of lilies, *Lilium Martagon,* "Turk's cap," or "Turban-shaped lily," which, as he thinks, has the forms of cymbals. He also ventures another hypothesis, namely that the blossom and the stalk of the flower show a certain similarity to a wind instrument, "possibly the trumpet or flute" (he certainly means the oboe).[255] In Pss. 60 and 80 *shushan* is coupled with *ʿedut,* and from this GESENIUS concludes that the twin term signifies "pipe (flute) for the song," or "to accompany the song."[256]

ROMANOFF, too, opines that the instrument might have had a lily-shaped form. He identifies it with the lyre depicted on some coins issued during the second Maccabaean revolt, or on those of JOHN and ALEXANDER JANNAEUS.[257]

Other expositors think *shoshannim* would indicate "lily-shaped bells," or "cymbals in the form of a lily."[258] It is difficult, however, to conceive cymbals in this form, because cymbals, in order to be stricken together, need straight surfaces and flat brims, which cannot be reconciled with the shape of a lily.

LANGDON also considers *shushan* as an instrument, but on an entirely different basis.[259] He first explains a particularity of the Babylonian language, which uses ordinals for naming an instrument according to the number of its strings. Thus, an instrument of six strings, or six tones, would be called the instrument "of the sixths," one with three strings, or three tones, would be called *shushan,* this being the Babylonian word for "one-third." As LANGDON reasons out, the word is derived from the Sumerian *shush,* "one-sixth," which, together with Semitic dual-ending *an,* would constitute the word *shushan,* meaning, two-sixths," that is "one-third."

After this philological excursion, however, LANGDON enters the domain of surmise. He concludes that this instrument with three tones might have been a flute having three holes, and supposes that an instrument in the shape of an ox-head, found in Babylonian excavations, might have been the *shushan.* As a further proof of his hypothesis, he claims that this ancient instrument when blown into, produces the three tones of a C major triad, and concludes from this that it may be called an "instrument of thirds." But intervals named as thirds, and even more so diatonic triads, were unknown notions in Antiquity, which alone invalidates LANGDON's theory. In addition, he main-

ILLUSTRATION NO. 39.
Instrument in the shape of an ox-head. Found at Birs Nimrud, Babylonia (ca. 9. cent. B.C.E.). Royal Asiatic Society, London (After Carl Engel, *The Music of the Most Ancient Nations,* London, 1864).

tains that the Babylonian term *shushan* was taken over by the Hebrews, and so we find it in four psalm-headings as *shushan* or *shoshan.*

The traditional explanation, according to which *shushan,* "lily," is the initial word of a popular song, LANGDON considers to be erroneous; also the interpretation maintaining that *shushan* is an "instrument from Susa."[260] He thinks, however, that he might have found a solution for the controversial term *ʿal ha-sheminit,* in applying to it the analogy of *shushan,* the three-stringed instrument. He holds that the indications in the headings of Pss. 6 and 12 refer to an instrument "with eight tones," or "eight strings," and this, applied to the passage *bekinnorot ʿal ha-sheminit* (1 Chron. 15:21), would justify the translation "with lyres upon the instrument of eight," *i.e.* upon eight-stringed lyres.

Thus, philological considerations sometimes lead to musical conclusions, which are meant to be logical, but actually—as in this instance—create more confusion than contribute to a rational solution.

For THIRTLE's interpretation of *shushan* see p. 134.

By analogy with other psalm-headings containing terms which have no connection with the contents of the psalms, the most simple and musically the most plausible explanation of the term *shushan* is that which interprets it as the title or the initial word of a popular song.

For the translations of the term in the English Bibles see p. 134.

10. KLE SHIR AND COGNATE TERMS

The general term for musical instruments used in the Old Testament is *kle* (lit. "tool"), plur. *kelim. Kle ʿoz* means "loud instrument" (2 Chron. 30:21),[261] *kle David* an "instrument (ordained) by (or for) David." (2 Chron. 29:26). In another biblical passage David is referred as saying "instruments which I made," translated by the SEPTUAGINT as "musical instruments which he [David] had made." (1 Chron. 23:5). Some expounders maintain that these instruments have been "invented" by David, trying to justify this interpretation by the statement of JOSEPHUS: "He [David] also made instruments of music,"[262] and furthermore by the apocryphal Psalm 151, in which the following two verses (2 and 3) are put into the mouth of David:

"My hands made the organ, and my fingers jointed the psaltery."[263] No elaborate proof is needed for the taking that David cannot be considered either as the inventor or builder of these instruments. It is not unlikely, however, that instruments may have been built under David's supervision.[264]

The most important combination of words, in which *kle* is used, is *kle shir,* or *kle ha-shir* (2 Chron. 5:13; 7:6; 23:13), "instruments of (or for) the song," and *kle shir David* (Neh. 12:36). This designates an entire group, or family, of stringed instruments, considered as the most appropriate to accompany singing.

Another combination with *kle,* also applied to stringed instruments, is *kle nebel* (Ps. 71:22), with the variant *kle nebalim* (1 Chron. 16:5). Some commentators consider another variant *kle minnim,* from the extra-canonical book of Ecclesiasticus 39:20, as belonging to this category. This book was originally written partly in Aramaic (verses 2:4 to 7:28) and has been fully preserved in a Greek translation. However, a number of its original Hebrew pages have been discovered by SCHECHTER in the Genizah of a Synagogue at Cairo, which made it possible to reconstruct the original form of the whole book.[265] *Kle minnim* can be considered therefore to be an authentic Hebrew term of biblical times.

Further collective names for instruments accompanying singing were *neginot* (see preceding chapter) and *minnim,* "strings," (Ps. 150:4), the latter being also the meaning of *minni* or *minne* (lit. "my strings") in Ps. 45:9.[266]

Finally, the stringed instruments are also paraphrased as *le-sharim,* "for the singers" (1 Kings 10:12; 2 Chron. 9:11), indicating clearly their accompanying function.

The talmudic literature calls these instruments *kle zemer,*[267] with the variants *minne zemer,*[268] and *minne kle zemer.*[269] The talmudic term *zimra demana,* interpreted by KRAUSS as an "instrumental song," *i.e.* singing with the accompaniment of instruments,[270] does not exactly belong to this category, but since singing was mostly accompanied by stringed instruments, there is at least a connection between it and the other respective terms.

Explaining the meaning of the talmudic *nimin,* RASHI says: *nimin shel kinnor, ḳordes b'laz* ("*nimin* [stands] for *kinnor,* [which means] strings in French").[271] *Cordes,* in medieval as in modern French, is the generic term for stringed instruments. In another commentary, RASHI uses a different collective term for *minne kle zemer* ("stringed instruments"), namely *ḥarpa,* the French *harpe.*[272]

The biblical books, and also the early rabbinical writings, do not leave any doubts that singing in Ancient Israel, particularly the singing of the Levites, has always been accompanied by stringed instruments. In contrast to this, it is difficult to understand how RASHI could assert, while interpreting a talmudic comment, that levitical song has been accompanied by brass instruments. In describing the Last Judgment, the Talmud says:

> "The Holy One . . . spake thus to them: 'Commence [the destruction] from the place where song is uttered before me' ".

Upon which RASHI comments:

"Start with the Levites who utter song to the accompaniment of musical instruments of brass (*bikle neḥoshet*)."[273]

This does not only contradict all known reports, but is virtually impossible for musical reasons. The only brass (or metal) instruments the Hebrews used were the *ḥaẓoẓerot* (trumpets), which could produce merely a limited number of natural harmonics and, consequently, were unable to "accompany" the artful and complex levitical songs.[274] The trumpet blasts in the sacred service had a different significance and were not designed for accompaniment to singing. The cymbals, moreover, indicating the beginning of the singing and, at most, introducing certain ritual ceremonies, were even less appropriate for the accompaniment of singing.[275]

In a few instances the psalm-headings contain indications which imply that sometimes other than stringed instruments were used to accompany signing. Yet, these must have been exceptions. The character of singing, especially that in the sacred service, required soft and smooth instruments for the accompaniment, in contradistinction to other ancient Oriental peoples, whose liturgical singing had an orgiastic character and, therefore, was accompanied preferably by noisy instruments.

From this point of view, the term *kle shir* and other expressions referring to the same category of instruments, have a particular significance in the music practice of Ancient Israel. They serve as unmistakable evidence of the ethos of Jewish singing and particularly of the high esteem the Israelites showed from the very outset for the most beautiful of all music instruments, the human voice.

o o o

Since the meaning of *kle shir* never gave rise to any differences of interpretation, one would expect that the early translators of the Bible had no difficulties at all in finding some uniform terms for it in their respective languages. However, just the contrary is true. For in nearly every case, the expression *kle shir* has been translated with somewhat different nuances. Here is a synopsis of the different renditions of the term in the principal Greek and Latin translations:

	SEPTUAGINT	VULGATE
1 Chr.15:16	*en organois*	*in organis musicorum*
1 Chr.16:5	*en organois nablais*	*super organa psalterii*
2 Chr.5:13	*kai en tō anaphōnein phōnē mia tou exomologeisthai*	*et diversi generis musicorum concinentibus*
2 Chr·7:6	*organois ōdōn Kyriou*	*organis carminum Domini*
2 Chr.23:13	*en tois organois ōdoi*	*diversi generis organis concinentem*
2 Chr.29:26	*organois David*	*organa David*
2 Chr.30:21	*en organois*	*organa*

2 Chr.34:12	*en organois ōdōn*	*Levitae scientes organis canere*
Ps.71:22	*en skeyei psalmou* (for *kle nebel*)	*in vasis psalmi*
Neh.12:36	*en ōdais David*	*in vasis cantici David*
Am.6:5	left out, or—possibly—transferred to the first half of the verse.[276]	*vasa cantici*

o
o o

The English Bibles, though keeping within the concept of "musical instruments," or "instruments of music," apply various nuances for no obvious reasons. Among the oldest English translations, *Wycliffe* has "dyuerse kynde of musikis," "orgyns of dytees of the Lord" (early), "orguns of songs of the Lord" (later), "orgyns of dyuerse maner" (early), "orguns of dyuerse kynde" (later), "vesselis of the song of Dauid" (early), and "instrumentis of song of Dauid" (later). The *Douay Version* renders "musical instruments," "instruments of divers kind," "instruments of David," "instruments of music of the Lord." The *Authorized Version* and most of the modern translations use the same expressions (*Harkavy*: instruments *ordained* by David), with the variant "loud instruments" for 2 Chron. 30:21. *Douay* interprets this verse as "instruments (that agreed to their office)," *Moffat* and the *Revised Standard Version* as "(singing) with all their might." Thus, with the exception of *Wycliffe* (for 2 Chron. 7:6, later version, and Neh. 12:36, both versions), all the English translations miss the idea of "instruments for the song."

The important qualification *kle nebel* is neglected in most of the modern versions, which render the double term by the single word "psalteries," whereas *Moffat* renders "lutes" (1 Chron. 16:5) and "lyre" (Ps. 71:22), and the *Revised Standard Version* "lyre" for both places. *Douay* is more precise in defining *kle nebel* as "instruments of psaltery," following obviously *Wycliffe's* translations "orgyns of sawtree" (early), and "orguns, on the sautrie" (later) for 1 Chron. 16:5, and "vesselis of salm" (early), and "instruments of salm" (later) for Ps. 71:22.

o
o o

In addition to the above generic terms for the different families of stringed instruments, it remains to examine a biblical expression which, from earliest times, has been subjected to the most diversified and contradictory interpretations. This is the obscure Aramaic word *daḥavan* in Daniel 6:19 (18), which in many English versions is translated as "instruments of music."

Etymologically, the word stems from the verb *daḥah,* "to thrust," "to push," "to knock."[277] This meaning is probably responsible for the wholly inadequate interpretation of *daḥavan* as "musical instruments of *percussion,*" which conflicts both with the basic sense of the word itself and of the biblical passage that contains it.

The classical Bible translations render the word in an entirely non-musical sense, the SEPTUAGINT and THEODOTION as *edesma,* "food," the VULGATE and other Latin versions as *cibus,* "meat," "food," the Peshiṭṭa also as "food."

Some modern commentators maintain that "food" in these translations should be understood "in a figurative sense," that is, as a sort of entertainment or amusement which, among other things, includes music and dancing.[278] It is difficult to understand why "food" should not be taken here at its face value, since it harmonizes perfectly with the biblical tale that the king "passed the night fasting," consequently there were no "foods" brought before him.

There is, however, another, and somewhat hidden meaning ingrained in *daḥavan.* The verb *daḥah* means in Arabian *subiecit feminam.*[279] Its Aramaic equivalent seems therefore to refer to the favorite entertainment of Oriental rulers—self amusement with dancing girls, who, apart from their professional functions, served them also as concubines. This idea, which would naturally imply the use of musical instruments in association with dance performances, was first brought up by SA'ADIA (12th century) and, later, taken over, in less candid form, as "diversions," by many modern translators.

A brief listing of some biblical translations of the word *daḥavan* will illustrate the existing controversial opinions:

Wycliffe has "and metis be not brought to byfore hym" (early and later versions); *Douay* sets "and meat was not set before him."

The *Authorized Version, Harkavy* and *Moulton* translate "instruments of music," the *American Version* "instruments of music" in the text, and "dancing girls" in a note, *Moffat* has "dancing girls."

The *Jewish* and the *Revised Standard Versions,* Goodspeed's *The Short Bible* (Chicago, 1933), J. J. Slotki's translation (London, 1951), and others have "diversions."

LUTHER follows the early translators and renders *daḥavan* as "Essen," ("food"), while the French Bibles give the preference to "instruments de musique."

In the light of these translations, the interpretations of the medieval rabbinic authorities have hardly more than a curiosity value. RASHI explains *daḥavan* as "table" (*i.e.* "boards"),[280] IBN EZRA as "instruments of music,"[281] or "stringed instruments,"[282] LEVI ben GERSON as "they drive away sorrows."[283]

Considering these widely divergent interpretations, we can scarcely do better than to accept the non-committal translation of the obscure word in question as "diversions."

(b) Wind Instruments

11. 'UGAB

The *'ugab* is one of the two instruments mentioned in the earliest musical reference of the Bible, their initial use having been attributed to Jubal, (the "father," or patron of the musical profession) (Gen. 4:21). The word is used furthermore in Job 21:12, 30:31, and in Ps. 150:4.

The diversity of rendering the word *'ugab* in the ancient and modern translations brought about glaring discrepancies in interpreting the nature of the instrument. Owing perhaps to the *'ugab*'s sensuous sonority, the etymology of its name might involve the Hebrew verb *ʿagab,* "to have inordinate affection," "to be charming." This etymology seems to indicate a flute-like instrument, since in ancient times as well as in all primitive civilizations the flute is closely connected with love-charm.[284]

The derivation from *ʿagab* brought forth still another interpretation. In contrast to the popular instrument of the Israelites, the *ḥalil,* the meaning "to be charming" seems to indicate a smaller type of pipe, the tone of which was considered more pleasant than that of the shrill *ḥalil.*

Other commentators think that the word is derived from the Arabic *ʿakab* (or *ʿajaba*), "to blow."[285] Some philologists, however, are doubtful whether such an Arabic root exists at all.[286]

R. KIMḤI's blunt statement that *ʿugab* is simply "a musical instrument," is too general for a serviceable definition.[287] GESENIUS defines it as *an instrumentum quod inflatur, fistula eaque fortasse duplex, vel multiplex,* "an instrument, which is played by blowing, probably a double or multiple pipe."[288]

Many expositors, among them PFEIFFER, FORKEL, JAHN, ENGEL, and others, identify the *ʿugab* with the Greek *syrinx,* the Pan's pipe. CALMET furnishes even a detailed and purely imaginary description of the instrument by saying that it was

> "the ancient organ, that is, a kind of flute composed of several pipes of different size, attached to one another, . . . that gave a harmonious sound when blown into, by passing them successively below the lower lip."[289]

STAINER considers the interpretation of *ʿugab* as *syrinx* to be "reasonable," since the wide use of the latter as a shepherd instrument of Antiquity has been attested in many parts of Asia.[290] This statement, however, is invalidated by STAINER himself when he adds that it would be strange if such an instrument were to be used for the sacred service of the Temple. Yet, it is unquestionable that the *ʿugab* was used in Jewish cult, as evidenced by Psalm 150:4, in which *ʿugab* and *minnim* are mentioned as instruments of worship, even if in the generic sense of wind and string species.

SACHS rejects the supposed identity between the *ʿugab* and the *syrinx,* since the initial trace of a Pan's pipe in the Near-East can be found only two millennia after the epoch indicated by the story of Genesis. Judging from the dark tone color of the word *ʿugab,* possibly imitating the *u*-like tone quality of the instrument, SACHS opines that it might have been a lengthy, rather wide, vertical flute.[291] Such an instrument, ordinarily played by shepherds, might have been conceivably known in Canaʿan, since its use is attested in Mesopotamia, Egypt and in ancient Arabian countries.

But SACHS' theory concerning the sonority of the *ʿugab* is contradicted by biblical statements. It appears indeed from the context of the two passages in Job (21:12 and 30:31) that the *ʿugab* must have had a joyous tone character. The faculty of tonal differentiation by the Israelites is repeatedly attested, directly and indirectly, by biblical chroniclers.[292] Hence the *u*-like sound produced by a larger type of flute would have hardly been viewed by them as joyous.

According to Mishnah, *ʿugab* used to be one of the two instruments played in the First Temple. Its alleged disadvantage was that, owing to its delicate construction, it could not be repaired if damaged. Thus, it has been condemned to extinction and was subsequently replaced by the heavier sounding and more solidly built *ʿabub*.[293]

KRAUSS, drawing on PORTALEONE, declares that the *ʿugab* was a bagpipe.[294] Other modern commentators, like WINER[295] and CORNILL[296] are of the same opinion. Yet, no trace of bagpipes can be firmly established at the time when the biblical text was written down.[297] Even with lesser reason can it be assumed that bagpipes were used in the earliest history of Israel, with which the initial mention of the *ʿugab* is associated (Gen. 4:21). For according to available evidences, the bagpipe was definitely unknown in Israel prior to the Greek and Roman epoch.[298]

The SEPTUAGINT translates *ʿugab* in three different ways, as *kithara* (Gen. 4:21), *psalmos* (Job 21:12, 30:31), and *organon* (Ps. 150:4). The VULGATE sets always *organum;* the Peshiṭṭa has also three different translations, *z'mara, mine ḥalyata* (*i.e.* "sweet sounding strings"), and *kinora;* while the Targum renders *ʿugab* as *ʾabbuba.*

The ancient English versions, but also some modern ones, follow the SEPTUAGINT and VULGATE translations, and render the word as "orgon," "orgun," "orgne" (*Wycliffe*), and "organ" (*Douay, Authorized Version* and *Harkavy*). This, of course, is a manifest anachronism. In Greek and Latin, instruments are called generally *organon mousikōn,* resp. *organum musicum,* the term *organon* having been in those days the generic name for all kinds of music instruments. The narrower use of the term "organ" for the instrument with rows of pipes of a different pitch, activated by a specific mechanism, came into being in a later period.[299] Practically all modern versions translate now correctly as "pipe." For no obvious reason, *Moffat* uses "flute" for Ps. 150:4.

The Talmud identifies *ʿugab* with the Greek *hydraulis,* but its identity with the *ʿugab* is unfeasible.

In all probability, the word *ʿugab* did not refer to a specific instrument at all, but to a whole family of some type. This is clearly indicated in Ps. 150:4, which reads:

> "Praise Him with stringed instruments (*minnim*) and the pipe (*ʿugab*)."

"Stringed instrument" is here manifestly a collective term. The parallelistic construction of biblical poetry makes it almost certain that *ʿugab* refers here to the family of wind-instruments. SACHS opines that, although *ʿugab* may have been originally the name of an individual instrument (the vertical flute, as he thinks), the meaning of the word might have later been extended to all types of flutes and pipes, similarly to the Egyptian usage, where *ma·t* first signified the vertical flute, and later all pipes, including oboes and clarinets.[300]

The manner of tone-production on wind instruments was called *ḥikkah* in talmudic times.(See pp. 393, 435).

12. ḤALIL

The word *ḥalil,* plur. *ḥalilim,* generally, but erroneously, translated as "flute," or "flute-like instruments," occurs six times in the Old Testament: in 1 Sam. 10:5; 1 Kings 1:40; Isa. 5:12; 30:29, and Jer. 48:36, twice in the last mentioned passage.

Etymologically it is derived from the verb *ḥalal,* "to pierce," hence the original meaning of the word is "hollow tube." This is a clear indication of the material from which the first flute-like instruments were made: bulrush and other reed-like plants. As indicated earlier, it was a frequent usage in Antiquity to name an instrument after its material. This applies, for instance, to the Greek flute *lōtos,* made of lotus-wood, the Roman pipe *tibia,* made from the shin-bone (Lat. *tibia*), and the shawm *calamus,* made from reed having the same name. There are several examples of this practice in later times as well.

Judging from its described nature and sonority, the *ḥalil* was akin to the full-fledged Greek *aulos;* both had a double-reed mouthpiece, hence they did not belong to the family of flutes, but to that of the shawm, the precursor of later times' oboe.

The *ḥalil,* as well as the *aulos,* are of Asiatic origin. The Babylonians had known it under the name of *malilu,* and used it mainly as an instrument for lamentations.[301] The Assyrian name for it was *ḥalḥalattu* and *ḥalalu,* the player was called *mutta-ḥalalu.* Another term designating the same instrument was *imbubu,* or *ebubu,* found in a text from Assur ca. 800 B.C.E.). This word is likewise Semitic, and corresponds to the later Hebrew and Syrian *ʾabub.*

Auloi without a mouthpiece, that is flutes in the proper sense of the word, seem to have been known by the Hellenes at a very early epoch. According to PLUTARCH, such instruments existed in the mythical age of Orpheus.[302] The *aulos* with a mouthpiece was brought from Phrygia to Greece by OLYMPOS around 800 B.C.E.

Already in Antiquity, the flute has an extended history, having been developed from simple to rather elaborate forms. In Egyptian and Assyrian pictorial representations we see simple longitudinal flutes, of various lengths; also transversal flutes, played like those of to-day; furthermore, nose-flutes, and double-flutes of two types, either with parallel tubes, or with tubes set at an angle, but blown simultaneously. Besides, the Syrians, or more precisely the Phoenicians, have known a small, span long pipe, called *gingras,* the tone of which was shrill and lamenting; it was used mainly in wailings for Adonis, who therefore was also called *Gingras* by the Phoenicians.[303]

Whether one or the other of these instruments corresponded to the primitive *ḥalil,* we do not know exactly. Perhaps *ḥalil* included several of them, or possibly covered an entire family of pipes.

The *ḥalil* is one of the few Jewish instruments of which we possess a coeval pictorial reproduction. A small bronze figure, found at Megiddo, a city of Ancient Israel, represents a flute-girl. (Illus. 36). It is assumed that this figure originates from biblical times and, therefore, depicts a Jewish instrument.[304] This sculpture does not afford a precise idea about the nature of the *ḥalil,* so that we again have to rely upon comparisons and analogies with similar instruments of other peoples.

In Antiquity, flutes and other pipes were made of reed or wood. Sometimes the wood was covered with metal ornaments, preferably of gold or silver. Only occasionally were flutes made entirely of metal. The University Museum in Philadelphia has such a metal made instrument consisting of two slender silver-tubes, each with four finger-holes. Except for the lacking mouthpiece, the instrument is similar to the double-oboes used by the Egyptians, which are seen in numerous sepulchral pictures. It was discovered in the royal tombs of ʾUr, and its time is set around 2800 B.C.E.[305]

The Mishnah mentions *ḥalilim* of solid metal as well as of wood covered with metal:

> "If a spindle, distaff, rod, double-flute (*sumponyah*), or pipe (*ḥalil*) are made of metal, they are susceptible to uncleanness; but if they are only plated they are not susceptible."[306]

In this passage, the instrument called *sumponyah* cannot be identified with certainty; "double-flute" is merely the interpretation of the translator (*Danby*).

Another Mishnaic passage states that flutes made of reed were preferred to metal flutes:

> ". . . on the Feast of Tabernacles they did not play on a flute (or pipe) of bronze (*be-ʾabub shel neḥoshet*), but on a flute (pipe) of reed (*be-ʾabub shel ḳoneh*), because its sound is sweeter (*ʿareb*)."[307]

In this passage, too, it cannot be ascertained whether the English translation renders correctly the meaning of the original text.[308]

Commenting upon this passage, the Gemara quotes the opinion of a rabbinic authority, according to which the *ḥalil* and *ʾabub* are identical instruments:

> "Why does the passage use *ḥalil* in the beginning and *ʾabub* in the end? R. Pappa said: '*Ḥalil* and *ʾabub* are the same.' Why is it called *ḥalil?* Because its sound is sweet (*ḥali*)."[309]

This statement seems to confirm the suggestion offered above that the Hebrew terms for pipes referred to families rather than to individual instruments.

A rabbinic tradition maintains that

> "there was a flute (*ʾabub*) in the sanctuary, which was smooth, made of reed, and dated from the times of Moses. At the king's command it was overlaid with gold, but its sound was no longer sweet. They removed the overlay and its sound became sweet as it was before."[310]

Contrary to this rabbinical statement, many commentators assert that there were no *ḥalilim* used in the First Temple, since in the counting of the Temple instruments, *ḥalil* is not mentioned.[311] This assertion, however, is disproved not only by the rabbinic tradition, but also by some biblical passages, which confirm the use of *ḥalilim* in the early ritual. One of them is 1 Sam. 10:5, in which *ḥalil* is mentioned as one of the instruments played by "a band of prophets." To prophesy with the accompaniment of music was in a way a ritual action, and the "band of prophets" were the pupils in Samuel's schools of prophets.[312] The musical organization of these schools served as prototype for the forthcoming Davidic and Solomonic sacred musical institutions. It is unlikely that an instrument like the *ḥalil* having been used ritually in times of

Samuel and Saul, was to be abandoned in David's sacred music, which was established soon afterwards.

Furthermore, the use of the *ḥalil* in religious ceremonies is directly referred to in Isa. 30:29:

> "Ye shall have a song as in the night when a feast is hallowed; and gladness of heart, as when one goeth with the pipe (*ḥalil*) to come into the mountain of the Lord, to the Rock of Israel."

The talmudic tradition states that "the *ḥalil* was played at the sacrificial altar twelve times during the year."[313]

And the Mishnah contains precise indications as to the ceremonies in which this has taken place.[314]

2 Chron. 7:6 and 29:26,27 mention *kle David,* "the instrument (ordained by, or for) David." This generic term enlarges the terminology for instrumental groups which used to accompany singing, the *kle shir, neginot, minnim,* or *le-sharim.* The assumption crops up automatically that the Israelites may have also had some generic terms for wind instruments. One of them was probably *ʿugab* (Ps. 150:4), *kle David* might possibly be another. A later rabbinical commentary confirms the assumption that the term *ḥalil,* too, has been used in this meaning. In describing the Feast of *Bet ha-Sheʿubah,* the Mishnah refers to

> "the flute-playing, sometimes five and sometimes six days,—this is the flute-playing at the *Bet ha-Sheʿubah,* which overrides neither a Sabbath nor a Festival-day."[315]

In his commentary to this passage, OBADIAH of BERTINORO says:

> "Many kinds of musical instruments (*minne zemer*) were there, but because the sound of the flute (*ḥalil*) was more audible than the rest, all of them are called by its name."[316]

Ḥalil, ʿugab and *ʾabub* are the three words found in Bible and in rabbinical writings which indicate wind instruments, individually as well as collectively. Judging from the fact that the Israelites used to clearly separate sacred and secular objects, we may assume that *ḥalil* and *ʾugab* were the pipes used in the ritual, whereas *ʿabub* was the name of similar instruments in popular usage. The sanctuary was rather conservative with regard to the material of which the instruments were made. As a matter of fact, it preferred pipes made from reed, unlike the secular instruments, which were made from thigh-bones of sheep,[317] or of metal.[318] Pipes of wood and bone were frequently adorned with gold and other ornaments.

The sanctuary used the single pipe of oboe-type. For secular occasions, such as banquets, and especially for popular festivities, the small Syrian, span long pipe was the favorite wind instrument which, in Hebrew usage, seems to have had a joyous sound, contrary to that of the Phoenician lamenting pipe, the *gingras.* The popularity of this species of pipe was certainly enhanced by the fact that its technique must have been simple and easy to master (*Cp.* 1 Kings 1:40).

It cannot be stated unequivocally whether or not the Israelites used double-oboes, despite some vague hints to this effect in the rabbinic literature. We come across, for instance, the Mishnaic term *ḳanafayim,* "wings," which is interpreted by some commentators as pointing to the two pipes of a double-oboe.[319] Accordingly, some modern translators identify the instrument *sumponyah,* having had allegedly such *ḳanafayim,* as "double-flute." It will be shown later that *sumponyah* could not possibly have been such an instrument.[320]

However, the assumption that the Israelites have known the double-oboe is somewhat supported by another controversial Mishnaic passage. In the instructions with regard to playing the pipe at sacred services it is said:

> "They ended [the music] only with a single flute (*beʾabub yeḥidi*), since this made the better close (*maḥaliḳ yafah*),"

or, according to another translation,

> "to make the end agreeable."[321]

Some expounders interpret this passage in the sense that Oriental music considered solo playing as the most beautiful ending of a piece, an idea not corroborated by historical evidences. SACHS gives a more plausible explanation, based upon the nature of the instrument.[322] He considers this Mishnaic text as proving that the instrument was a double-oboe; when playing on one of its pipes, certain tonal interferences, caused by slight differences of pitch, could be avoided, which probably was not the case, as a rule, when both pipes were played simultaneously. Therefore the end sounded "more agreeable."

This interpretation has two weak points: first, one pipe of the double-oboe was a drone-pipe, which could not have created tonal interferences with the pipe playing the melody; then, both pipes of the double-oboe were played simultaneously using the same mouthpiece; thus, the player could not discard one of the pipes.

There is, however, another logical explanation for *ʾabub yeḥidi.* A talmudic passage indicates the allowable number of players for each category of instruments.[323] The respective regulation for *ḥalilim* was: no less than two, and no more than twelve in each service. The reed instruments had evidently some unevenness in their tuning, created either by slight differences of their dimensions, or by minute deviations in the boring of the finger-holes. These differences of pitch were not too disturbing as long as the *ḥalilim* played together with the Levitical singing. However, in solo instrumental endings that must mostly have taken place after the choir finished singing, these differences came clearly to the fore. Therefore, as a remedy, the solo-playing with only one instrument was preferred.

o
o o

Most of the English Bibles use "flute" for *ḥalil,* referring apparently to an instrument with one tube. The *Revised Standard Version* uses "flute" for 1 Sam. 10:5, and Isa. 5:12, and "pipe" for all other passages. Quite astounding is *Moffat's* rendition as "flute" for 1 Sam. 10:5, and Isa. 5:12, "music" for Isa. 30:29, "my heart thrills with pity" (with no instrument named) for Jer. 48:36, and his omission of the word in 1 Kings 1:40.

The early version of *Wycliffe* mistranslates the term as "trompe," "trump or bras," "pipe of bras," and "soun of trumpits," whereas the later version sets correctly "pipe," and "sown of pipis."

LUTHER translates always "Flöten," the French Bibles "flûtes." SACHS points, however, to the historical fact that before 1000 B.C.E. flutes were unknown in the Near East.[324] There are no flutes depicted in any Babylonian, Assyrian, Persian, Phoenician, Hittite, Egyptian, Greek, or Etruscan monuments. Everywhere in Antiquity pipers used the double-oboe. From this SACHS infers that the Jewish pipe has also been such a double-oboe. *Ḥalil* is translated by the SEPTUAGINT mostly as *aulos,* by the VULGATE as *tibia,* both terms referring to an oboe-type instrument, though not necessarily to the double-oboe.

To be sure, PLUTARCH maintains that *auloi* without a mouthpiece, consequently flutes, existed in Greece already in a legendary age.[325] Yet, if this is not pure myth, it may be assumed that he projected back into earlier times the actual situation of his own epoch, as it frequently happens in ancient historiography.

If one still may doubt whether *ḥalilim* were used in Solomon's Temple, this would be wholly unfounded with regard to the post-exilic sanctuary, since we have direct evidence of their use in the Second Temple. Some of these proofs have been cited above (pp. 311 ff).

R. MEIR says about the players of *ḥalilim* that "they were slaves (*nethinim*)[326] of the priests. R. JOSE says:

> "They were from the families of Bet ha-Pegarim and Bet Zipporya and from Emmaus, and they were eligible to give [their daughters] in marriage to the priestly stock. R. Ḥanina b. Antigonous said: They were Levites."[327]

From the fact that the *nethinim* were originally slaves, attending to the menial work connected with the sacrifices, the conclusion was sometimes drawn that the Levites have performed only the vocal part of the sacred service, while the instrumental accompaniment, as a subordinate function, has been entrusted to slaves. But numerous biblical passages attest to the fact that the Levites have been at once singers and instrumentalists. The above rabbinic discussion, moreover, reverses any assumption that the instrumental accompaniment would have had merely an accessory character, and therefore assigned to others than Levites.

As shown above, the talmudic scribes stated that the *ḥalil* was played twelve times on different days in the sanctuary.[328] Another tradition, however, has it that the *ḥalil* was used twice daily in the Temple, namely for the accompaniment of the psalm of the day at the libation in the morning and evening services. One of the Tannaites considers the "flute" even as an integral part of this sacrifice.[329]

On the Sabbath, however, it was prohibited to play the *ḥalil* in the Temple, since it was not considered as belonging to the same category as "sacred" instruments as the *kinnor* and *nebel.*[330]

The sonority or timbre of the *ḥalil* must have been shrill and penetrating similar to all the instruments of the oboe-type blown with a mouthpiece of reed. The Mishnah reports that when *ḥalilim* were played in the sanctuary, their sound was heard in Jericho.[331] This certainly cannot be taken literally. But it may serve as an oblique indication that the piercing sound was heard at a considerable distance, which could certainly not have been the case with the smoother sound of flutes. This explains also the difference between the *ḥalil* and *ʿugab*: the former, belonging to the shawm-family, had a penetrating sound, whereas the "sweeter" *ʿugab* might have been a pipe of the flute-species (see p. 308).

In Ancient Israel the *ḥalil* was pre-eminently the instrument of joy and gaiety; it was played at all merry occasions, such as festivals, banquets, popular entertainments, coronations, etc. The Bible does not refer to it as having been used at weddings, but there is an indication to this effect in the Mishnah:

> "if a man hired . . . pipes for a bride (*ḥalilim l'kallah*)."[332]

Since this usage certainly did not originate in Mishnaic times, we may assume retrospectively to the use of *ḥalilim* at weddings in the biblical period.

At the Feast of Tabernacles wealthy people frequently hired *ḥalil*-players for their domestic entertainment, in order to enhance the splendor of the festival.[333] On other holidays, too, *ḥalil*-players would be used to increase the joy of the feast; such a use of the instrument was even considered sacred.

The use of the *ḥalil* must have been very popular, since it was played not only by professional musicians, but also by the common people:

> "and the people piped with pipes (*m'ḥalilim baḥalilim*), and rejoiced with great joy, so that the earth rent with the sound of them" (1 Kings 1:40).

At the thanksgiving for the harvest as well as at the offering of the first fruits, the playing of *ḥalilim* in the solemn procession of the participants was mandatory:

> "Ye shall have a song as in the night when a feast is hallowed; and gladness of heart, as when one goeth with the pipe (*beḥalil*) to come into the mountain of the Lord, to the Rock of Israel" (Isa. 30:29).

The use of the *ḥalil* in such ceremonies is again attested in Mishnaic times.

Even though the *ḥalil* was mainly the instrument of exuberant joy, we are told that its tone frequently turned over into wailing and assumed by this a mournful character; it was therefore considered also the appropriate instrument for funeral ceremonies. In Egypt and Babylonia, too, it was played on joyful occasions as well as at funerals. In a Sumerian hymn of atonement, the penitent says:

> "Like the reed Nâ, I am in sadness";

and in the lament of Ishtar for Tammuz the goddess moans:

> "A reed of lamentation (*gi-er-ra*) is my heart."[334]

ARISTOTLE expresses the same idea:

> "Why do those who are sad and those who are enjoying themselves both make use of the flute (*aulontai*)?"[335]

In his prophecy, describing figuratively the disconsolation and mourning about the destruction of Moab, Jeremiah avails himself of the wailing sound of the *ḥalil* for enhancing the expressive power of his simile:

> "Therefore my heart moaneth for Moab like pipes (*ḥalilim*), and my heart moaneth like pipes from the men of Kir-heres; . . . On all the house-tops of Moab and in the broad places thereof there is lamentation everywhere." (Jer. 48:36,38).

Even the poorest man in Israel had to hire for the funeral of his wife at least two *ḥalil*-players and a wailing woman.[336] What is more, the Talmud states that if there were no Jewish players available for a funeral, Gentiles would be used for this purpose:

> "If a Gentile brings reed-pipes (*ḥalilim*) on the Sabbath, one must not bewail an Israelite on them, unless they come from a near place."[337]

The shrill and penetrating sound of the *ḥalil* was able to create a state of ecstasy. It is related in the apocryphal Thomas-Acts that a Jewish flute-girl, standing behind the apostle, played the pipe for a long time, until the apostle reached such a state. The words uttered in his rapture were incomprehensible to anyone but the flute-girl.[338]

Despite its sharp sound, Israelites were extremely fond of the instrument. There must have been professionals who mastered it in an artistic way, and these naturally would be much in favor with lovers of music. A talmudic saying expresses clearly the pleasure experienced by true music lovers from listening to an artistic performance of a piper, in contrast to the lack of appreciation on the part of an uneducated listener:

> "A flute (*ʾabub*) is musical to nobles; but give it to weavers, they will not have it."[339]

Originally, the form of the *ḥalil* has been cylindric, like the oboes depicted on Egyptian and Babylonian antiquities. In later times, the *ḥalil* has acquired a conic shape. Jewish coins issued during Bar Kokba's revolt against the emperor Hadrian (132-135 C.E.), show a pair of Jewish wind instruments. The general opinion about them is that they represent trumpets in a somewhat shortened form. According to SACHS, the stout shape, the reed-like mouth-piece, the disk serving to support the lips, the funnel-shaped bell indicate a similar, modern Arabian instrument, the *zamr,* a sort of oboe.[340] He supports this theory by a later Arabian source. The book *Kitab ʾalgani* (7th century C.E.) refers to the *mizmar,* or *zmar,* and the *duff* (*tof*) as the instruments the Jewish tribes of Al-Hijaz would use in their wars.[341]

In later biblical times, the *ḥalil* was considered by the spiritual leaders of the Israelites as an emotionally exciting instrument, just as the Hellenes termed the *aulos* as *orgiastikos* and *pathētikos.* Greek philosophers frowned upon the instrument as pernicious for the manners, especially as destructive for the character of young men. STRABO paraphrases this in the following way:

> "The Korybantes [name of the Phrygian priests of Cybele] in their caverns invented this hide-stretched circlet [*i.e.* the tabret], and blent its Bacchic revelry with the high-pitched, sweet-sounding breath of Phrygian flutes (*auloi*)."[342]

The "Bacchic revelry" was brought about mainly by the exciting sounds of the *auloi,* which explains the aversion of the philosophers against the instrument.

The attitude of the rabbis toward the *ḥalil* might have been similar. The word *zimri,* the correct meaning of which is "flute-player," has a secondary meaning, "lewd person."[343] It is possible, however, that this second meaning of the word is due to the assonance with the name Zimri, a person mentioned in Num. 25:14, who had to pay with his life for his lewdness.

The hostility against the orgiastic *aulos* and against the similarly sounding *ḥalil* is still reflected in the writings of the early Church Fathers. CLEMENT of ALEXANDRIA warns the Christians of the chromatic (*i.e.* orgiastic) and burlesque melodies of the heathens and commands them to return to the traditional, diatonic psalmody of David.[344] Since the singing in such revelries was always accompanied by the *aulos* (or *ḥalil*), CLEMENT turns at the same time also against the instrument.

The SEPTUAGINT translates *ḥalil* five times as *aulos* and once paraphrases it as *en chorois,* "with dances" (1 Kings 1:40); the other Greek versions have mostly *aulos.* The VULGATE and other Latin Bibles render it always as *tibia.* The translations of the Peshiṭṭa and the Targumin are peculiar. The Peshiṭṭa omits the word in one passage (Jer. 48:36), translates five times erroneously, namely twice as *pelaga,* "tambourine," (1 Sam. 10:5; Isa. 5:12), once as *rebiy(a,* "timbrel," (1 Kings 1:40), *haduta,* "dancer, reveller," (Isa. 30:29), and *kinora* (Jer. 48:36). The Targum renders it as *)abuba* in Isa. 5:12; 30:29, as *ẓelẓelin,* "cymbals," in 1 Sam. 10:5, as *ḥinga,* "circle, dancing, chorus," in 1 Kings 1:40, as *kinora* for the first part of Jer. 48:36, and *zimra)abbubin* for the second part of the same verse.[345]

Such frequent irregularities of the translations into Hebrew dialects are puzzling. They reveal the significant fact that in an epoch that was still relatively close to biblical times the knowledge about such a popular instrument as the *ḥalil* must have been completely lost to many translators.

13. NEKEB

Ezekiel 28:13 uses the word *neḳeb,* which is interpreted by many biblical expounders as a "flute" or flute-like instrument.

The earliest translations of the Bible, however, do not attach to the word any musical connotation. The SEPTUAGINT renders the full expression that includes it (*tuppeḥo v'neḳebeḥo*) as *eneplēsas tous thēsaurous,* which would mean "workmanship of thy treasures." The VULGATE translates similarly as *opus decoris tui et foramina tua; foramen,* too, has no musical meaning, it stands for an "opening," or "aperture," produced by boring a hole.

The etymology of *neḳeb* points to a root signifying something "hollow." This could mean a hollow tube (hence the interpretation as "flute") just as well as the hollow cavities in which precious stones are set. Thus, already JEROME translated the word as *pala gemmarum,* "the setting of thy precious stones." Following this interpretation, STAINER has suggested to replace the usual translation of the English Bibles ("of thy tabrets and of thy pipes") by another, corresponding to JEROME's idea,

> "the workmanship of the jewels, and the setting of the stones."[346]

The *Jewish Version,* following closely the Masoretic text, gives a translation akin to that of the SEPTUAGINT: "the workmanship of thy settings and of thy sockets," the *Authorized Version, Moulton* and *Harkavy,* somewhat similarly, "the workmanship of thy tabrets and of thy pipes," whereas *Moffat* has "their setting wrought in gold," leaving out the second half of the sentence and marking it with dots (. . .). The *Revised Standard Version* translates "wrought in gold were your settings and your engravings."

The *Douay Version* paraphrases circumstantially "gold the work of thy beauty: and thy pipes were prepared in the day that thou wast created." *Wycliffe* follows a similar trend by setting "and gold the work of thi fairnes, and thin hollis ben mad redy" (early), and "also gold (was) the werk of thi fairness, and thin hollis wern maad redi" (later).

Most of these translations stem from the doubt as to whether *neḳeb* refers to a musical instrument at all. When the Old Testament mentions the tabret and pipe, this instrumental combination is usually expressed as *tof v'ḥalil* (1 Sam. 10:5; Isa. 5:12). The interpretation of *neḳeb* as "flute" does not fit very well the context in which the word is used by Ezekiel. This biblical passage relates about the abundant wealth of the king of Tyre, his precious stones and splendid jewels. It is true that musical instruments have belonged to Oriental luxury and were counted among the treasures of a princely court; nevertheless, nothing seems to indicate that, in this particular case, *neḳeb* should be interpreted in this sense.

The word *tof,* too, does not refer here to the biblical tabret. In the Latin language, *tympanum* sometimes indicates objects having similarity with the hand-drum.[347] The same holds true for the Hebrew *tof.* The frame into which precious stones were set, could have suggested a similarity with the cavity of a drum. Instead of an animal skin, this cavity was covered with the stone.

The majority of the biblical exegetes, including GESENIUS, agree that *neḳeb* does not refer to music.[348] Nevertheless, the idea of a musical instrument has been persistently maintained by some scholars. The reason for this is LUTHER's translation ("dein Paukenwerk und Pfeifen") as well as that of the *Authorized Version* (see above). FÉTIS, for instance, thinks that *neḳeb* was a double-flute,[349] AMBROS that it was a larger type of flute,[350] and JAHN interprets it as a specific kind of flute, known even in our days by the Turks under the name of *nay.*[351]

All these interpretations, however, are not borne out by historical and linguistic considerations, in the light of which the word *neḳeb* does not seem to carry any musical implication.

14. NEḤILOT

The expression *ʾel ha-neḥilot* is used only once in the Bible, in the heading of Psalm 5. A somewhat related indication, *bineginot,* appearing in the superscription of six psalms, is generally explained as an instruction to accompany the respective psalms with stringed instruments. By analogy, some expounders think that *neḥilot,* referring to flutes or pipes, stands for an instruction to accompany this psalm with such instruments.

This opinion is based upon the etymology of the word; its root, *ḥalal,* "to pierce," is the same from which *ḥalil* is derived. The perforation does not refer to the finger-holes of the instrument, but to its body which is hollow. In the Greek language, too, *aulos* means the instrument as well as a "tube" in general.

The interpretation of the word in the sense of an instruction for the accompaniment of the psalm would therefore be acceptable philologically as well as musically. The more surprising is it that the early translators of the Bible attach to *neḥilot* entirely different meanings. In fact their renditions have no musical connotations altogether. They were quoted on p. 128.

On the other hand, the Targum to the psalms interprets the term in a musical sense, rendering it as ʾ*al ḥingin,* "with flutes."[352] However, in other Targumim this Aramaic word is used for *meḥolot,* "dances" (to Exod. 32:19; Judg. 11:34). Sometimes *meḥolot* is considered to be a corrupt variant of *neḥilot* (*mem* instead of *nun*), produced by an erring scribe. In this case, its meaning would be "with round dances."

Some talmudic expounders give the word another meaning, deriving it from *naḥil,* "beehive." According to R. David KIMḤI, it is the title of a song, the melody of which is similar to the buzzing of bees, and R. HAY asserts that it refers to a musical instrument, the sound of which conjures *leroshiḳat deborim,* "the humming of the bees." R. REGGIO interprets it as a song dealing with bees.

The rabbinic explanations are rather vague, but they still attach to the word a meaning in conformity with the musical character of the psalm, this being in sharp contrast with the extra-musical interpretations of the early translators.

Among modern commentators, JAHN[353] and SAALSCHÜTZ[354] define *neḥilot* as a double-flute (or double-oboe), though not in the sense of two pipes put at an angle, as used by the Egyptians, Assyrians and Hellenes, but implying two parallel tubes of different length.

On the contrary, EWALD thinks that the whole interpretation of *neḥilot* as flutes is untenable, since the latter are "nowhere" mentioned in the sacred music of Ancient Israel. It is unnecessary to disprove this assertion in view of the several direct and indirect biblical references attesting to the use of woodwind instruments in rites, even prior to the First Temple (*e.g.* 1 Sam. 10:5; furthermore Isa. 30:29; Ps. 150:4, etc.). Moreover, the use of *ḥalilim* in the Second Temple is sufficiently evidenced in the rabbinic literature.[355]

KRAUSS, too, maintains that *ḥalilim* have not been used at all in the sacred service, and tries to explain their exclusion by the supposition that the sound of the instrument was susceptible of creating an ecstatic mood.[356] This opinion, however, is likewise repudiated by the numerous references of the rabbinic scribes to the use of *ḥalilim* in ritual ceremonies, within and without the sacred service itself.

THIRTLE, who connects *neḥilot* with Ps. 4, opines that there is nothing to prove that the term *neḥilot* is in any way related to *ḥalil,* or to any other word having the meaning of "flute." He also doubts that it refers to a tune or melody, or to a catchword of some popular song.[357] He invokes linguistic arguments to prove his point. In early times, before the *soferim* and Masoretes added the punctuation marks, the word was composed of four consonants, *nḥlt.* With full points, the word was written as *neḥalot,* meaning "inheritances." Only in succeeding centuries was the idea conceived that a musical instrument could be meant and, accordingly, the later punctuators changed it to *neḥilot.* The translators of the SEPTUAGINT knew only the older version and thus rendered the word with the meaning of "heritage," which was followed by all other early versions. THIRTLE finds a logical explanation for this meaning of the word; "inheritance," in this connection, refers to "the commemoration of the coming into possession of the Land of Promise as the people of God."[358] (*Cp.* Num. 26:53, 56; 33:54; 36:2; Josh. 11:23; 14:1,2).

Even if we assume that *neḥilot* applies to Ps. 4, the contents and the mood of this poem seem to bear out the conception that it might have been accompanied by pipes. It is highly probable that the later punctuators of the Bible knew the tradition of the Temple and changed the vowel points accordingly.

Since the majority of the commentators agree that *neḥilot* represents a collective term for wind instruments, we are justified to assume that the expression *ʾel ha-neḥilot* is an instruction for accompanying Psalm 5 with woodwinds (pipes), in contradistinction to most of the other psalms for which stringed instruments were generally used, or expressly prescribed.

The English translations of the term are given on p. 129.

15. ʿALAMOT

The meaning of this word has already been substantially examined in one of the preceding sections.[359] However, in addition to the opinions of many commentators scrutinized there, one more must be added, namely that which attaches to *ʿalamot* the meaning of a wind instrument, notably a double-oboe. It is therefore mandatory to ponder over the term once again at this place.

There is a striking but apparently fortuitous assonance between *ʿalamot* and the Greek *elymos,* a term used by the Hellenes for a type of double-oboe with pipes of different length, the *aulos elymos.* As PINDAR relates, the *elymos* has been brought from Assyria to Phrygia; from there, the Alexandrians have taken over the instrument,[360] and in this roundabout way it came to be known in Greece.

Thus, the word *elymos* would be of Assyrian origin, derived, as it seems from the verb *elamu,* "to stay opposite." In Assyrian this verb signifies two similar objects, which are close to, and yet separated from one another. This would correspond, for instance, to the form of a double-oboe with a single mouthpiece and two pipes, the latter being connected at an angle. Pictures of such double-pipes are frequently found on ancient Oriental bas-reliefs, carvings and wall paintings, also on Greek amphorae and Etruscan vases. The Assyrian word has an etymological parallel in Arabic, *ʿalama* meaning "open lips" or "separated lips."

While maintaining its Assyrian origin, ERIC WERNER suggests that *ʿalamot* might have been derived from the Assyrian *ḥalimu,* meaning "wooden."[361] At first sight, this even seems to be corroborated by PINDAR's testimony, who states that the *aulos elymos* has been made from a special kind of wood.

The double-oboe has played an important role in the music of the Egyptians, Assyrians and Hellenes; apart from a multitude of pictorial representations, the descriptions of the orchestras and bands of these peoples frequently make mention of it. The Old Testament, however, does not contain any direct reference to such an instrument, though the word *ʿalamot* appears in several biblical passages.

Of the various interpretations of the word, that of GRAETZ too belongs to this chapter. He identifies *ʿalamot* in Ps. 46:1 and 1 Chron. 15:20 as an instrument from Elam.[362] Based upon SEPTUAGINT's translation, *nablai epi alaimōth,* GREATZ thinks that the expression *ʿal-mut labben* in the heading of Psalm 9 would better be "corrected" to *ʿal ʿalamot nebel,* in resemblance to *nebalim ʿal alamot* of 1 Chron. 15:20.[363] However, there does not seem to be reason enough for such a radical emendation of the text, since a conventional interpretation of the heading of Ps. 9 does not involve insurmountable obstacles.

Among the instruments of the Second Temple there is no mention of *ʿalamot.* But the instruments of Solomon's Temple have admittedly been reinstated in the Second Temple. So, had there existed a double-oboe named *ʿalamot* in the First Temple, one would also have been used in the post-exilic sanctuary. Everything depends on whether or not it would be legitimate to attach the meaning of a double-oboe to *ʿalamot.* To be sure, the rabbinic literature confirms the use of the double-oboe in the Second Temple, but it calls this instrument by a different name (*ʾabub*), so that even this confirmation is not a definite proof that *ʿalamot* was in fact the double-oboe.[364]

For a correct interpretation of the word we must rely on the biblical context. And here we find a psalmodic verse, that is quite unambiguous:

> "The singers (*sharim*) go before, the minstrels (*neginim*) follow after, in the midst of damsels playing upon timbrels (*ʿalamot tofefot*)" (Ps. 68:26).

ʿAlamot is the plural of *ʿalmah,* "maiden," "damsel," and *ʿalamot tofefot* are the "dancing girls," accompanying their dance with *tuppim,* the traditional hand-drums of Ancient Israel. We might also recall the parallel in Arabic, where *ʿālmah* has a similar meaning of "an educated singing and playing girl."

Insofar as we attach to *ʿalamot* a musical meaning, connected at the same time with the notion of *ʿalmah,* "maiden," the most natural explanation for *nebalim ʿal ʿalamot* (1 Chron. 15:20) seems to be the one holding that it refers to a string instrument in the range of "maidens' voices," *i.e.* "in the high pitch,"—"high" according to our Occidental concept, of course.

Most of the English Bibles have avoided the pitfalls of a dubious translation of the controversial term and have taken over the word phonetically from the Hebrew. Accordingly, we have in the English versions the variations "set to Alamoth," "upon Alamoth," "on Alamoth," "according to Alamoth," leaving open the interpretation of the term as the name of a musical instrument. *Douay* is more explicit in this regard, setting "mysteries upon psalteries," and defining the other category of instruments (*kinnorot ʿal ha-sheminit*) as "(a song of victory) for the octave upon harps." *Wycliffe,* following closely the VULGATE, translates "for the priue thingis" (early), and "for gongthis" (later) for Ps. 46, "in orgnys sungyn priue thingis" (early), and "sungun pryuetees in giternes" (later) for 1 Chron. 15:20.

The most unequivocal translation for both types of instruments is that of *Moffat,* giving a precise definition of their contrasting nature: "lutes set for soprano voices," and "harps set for bass voices." Ps. 68:26 is rendered in all English Bibles as "damsels," "maidens," and "girls."

16. MAḤOL

The derivation of the word *maḥol* from the verb *ḥul,* "to dance in a circle," "to whirl," seems to be quite obvious.[365] In Arabic, too, *ḥala* means "to whirl." Despite the fact that among the early translators of the Bible, AQUILA, SYMMACHOS, THEODOTION and JEROME have followed this meaning, some ancient and modern biblical expounders explain the word as a musical, especially a woodwind, instrument.

This interpretation of *maḥol* recurs again and again in the commentaries of rabbinic writers. PIRKE d'Rabbi ELIEZER (fl. 2nd century C.E.) comments on Exod. 15:20:

> "And where did they get *tuppim* and *meḥolot* in the desert? . . . At the time of their exodus from Egypt they made *tuppim* and *meḥolot.*"

Consequently, he considers *meḥolot* to be objects, evidently musical instruments, that were made by the Israelites. IBN EZRA (1088-1180 C.E.) opines that *meḥolot* was a popular species of a flute, serving as accompaniment to dancing. RASHI (1040-1105 C.E.) derives the word from *ḥalal,* "to pierce," and maintains that it signifies a "pierced," therefore flute-like instrument.

PFEIFFER, following RASHI, connects *maḥol* also with the *ḥalil* and asserts that both were similar instruments.[366] His main argument is that in all the biblical passages containing this word its translation as "flute" would give a "good sense." Thus, Miriam leading the choir of women, would march "with timbrels and flutes" (Exod. 15:20); Jephtha's daughter would greet her victorious father "with tabrets and flutes" (Judg. 11:34); the daughters of Shiloh would dance "with flutes" (Judg. 21:21); in the same way, the virgins of Israel would rejoice "in piping" (Jer. 31:4,13); moreover, for *b'tof umaḥol* (Ps. 150:4) PFEIFFER sees no other possible interpretation than "with timbrels and flutes," and this despite the fact that he had already explained *ʿugab* of the same verse as a collective term for woodwinds. For all other passages where *maḥol* is used in the biblical text (Exod. 32:19; Pss. 30:12; 149:3; Lam. 5:15; Cant. 7:1), he offers similar interpretations.

Most of these are completely arbitrary. In the Orient, playing the tabret by women was the typical accompaniment for dancing from pristine times on. The joyful excitement of the masses would find its adequate outlet in the women's round dance. This dance, the *maḥol,* cannot be interpreted as a "flute," as PFEIFFER does, without destroying its original significance. HERDER states that

> "music and dancing, animated feelings uttered in words, require gesture to give the expression its highest effect."[367]

He thereby gives a pertinent characterization of the three sisters of art in Ancient Israel: poetry, music and dancing. By eliminating dance from this partnership, PFEIFFER misunderstands completely the basic idea of the threefold artistic manifestations of Jewish music.

HERDER is responsible for SAALSCHÜTZ's opinion, according to which *maḥol* stands not for a single instrument, but for the combination of music, poetry and dance· He takes *maḥalot* and *maḥol* to have the same meaning; both refer to a solemn procession, as intimated by the verb *ḥul,* "to go (or dance) in a circle," and both imply the processional encompassing of the altar, at which ceremony psalms headed by these words were supposedly sung.[368] However, apart from these psalms, none of the biblical passages quoted above can be interpreted in the sense of going around the altar.

Several of these passages do not permit an interpretation in the sense of "flutes," or "pipes." So, for instance, Exod. 32:19, which does not imply an orderly dance accompanied by instruments, but a savage skipping of idolaters around the golden calf. In Ps. 30:12, *maḥol,* "dancing," stands as a symbolic contrast to "mourning," in other words, as the expression of joy, succeeding the affliction. And to set "flute" instead of "the dance of Maḥanaim" (Cant. 7:1), would be completely nonsensical.[369]

In other biblical passages, however, the interpretation of *maḥol* as "flute" would not be conflicting with the meaning of the text. The Syrian version of the Bible translates the word in several places as *repha'ah,* the name of a species of flute which exists even to-day in Syria. The Targumim, too, translate *maḥalat* as *ḥinga,* a term designating a dance, but also a flute-like instrument.[370]

GESENIUS' hypothesis that the word served as a term for some stringed instrument, possibly the "lyre," or "guitar" (as an accompaniment for singing), can be entirely discarded, since there do not exist even the slightest indications to this effect.[371]

For the assumption that *maḥol* might refer to the *ḥalil,* there is some definite probability. The *ḥalil* served in Ancient Israel for two wholly opposite purposes. On the one hand, it was a wide-spread popular instrument, played at all joyous festivities ("and all the people piped with pipes," 1 Kings 1:40); on the other, it was the typical instrument for mourning, never lacking at any funeral. The *ḥalil* as a mourning and lamenting instrument is attested in quite a number of biblical and post-biblical sources.[372] Furthermore, *ḥalil* as an *accompanying* instrument is mentioned in Isa. 30:29:

> "Ye shall have a song as in the night when a feast is hallowed; and gladness of heart, as when one goeth with the pipe (*ḥalil*) to come into the mountain of the Lord, to the Rock of Israel."

In contradistinction to this, the use of the *ḥalil* in the Temple service is not attested directly. Yet, the mention of the *'ugab* among the instruments serving to God's praise (Ps. 150:4) is an indirect proof that woodwinds were used for the accompaniment of sacred singing. The direct confirmation that *ḥalilim* were indeed used in the sacred service is to be found in the early rabbinic literature.[373]

In the light of these arguments, the assumption seems to be justified that the term *'al maḥalot* in the superscriptions of Pss. 53 and 88 refers indeed to the musical rendition of these psalms, indicating the accompaniment with woodwinds. Nothing conflicts with this theory from the musical point of view, since, owing to the mournful character of both psalms, the special use of the *ḥalil* as a lamenting instrument would be appropriate. The prophet Jeremiah, too, expresses the same idea in using the metaphor:

> "Therefore my heart moaneth for Moab like pipes, and my heart moaneth like pipes for the men of Kir-ḥeres" (Jer. 48:36).

The "moaning" of *ḥalilim* might have been just the tone color considered appropriate by the psalmist, or the performers, to enhance the words with the suitable musical background.

The old as well as the more recent translations have taken over the term phonetically from the Hebrew. LUTHER tried to reproduce the meaning of the original, but gave both passages a completely different interpretation. Ps. 53 he rendered as: "im Chor umeinander vorzusingen" ("to sing in choir responsively"), and Ps. 88: "von der Schwachheit des Elenden" ("about the weakness of the miserable one").

LOUIS SEGOND's modern French version of the Scriptures does justice to the musical implication of the term in translating *ʿal maḥalat* in the sense of an instruction for the musical performance and rendering it "avec les flûtes."

The translations of the English Bibles are quoted on p. 128.

17. MASHROḲITA

Among the instruments at NEBUCHADREZZAR's court, the chronicler mentions the *mashroḳita* (Dan. 3:5,7,10,15). The word could be derived from the Hebrew *sharaḳ,* "to hiss," "to whistle." Nevertheless, it is generally assumed that *mashroḳita* refers to a foreign instrument, since it was played at the consecration of a pagan idol, an occasion which, by its very nature, must have appeared abominable to the Israelites. We have already mentioned that, in order to stress the heathen character of this feast, the chronicler has selected intentionally names of instruments that were either not used by the Hebrews, or were generally unknown to them, so that they would be considered "exotic." One of these was the *mashroḳita.*

Translators and expounders were in doubt about the real nature of this instrument. The first Greek translations interpreted the word as *syrinx,* thus identifying the instrument with the Pan's pipe of the Hellenes. (There is even a phonetic affinity between the two words: *syrinx—sharaḳ*). The *syrinx* had a row of pipes of different length, which when played produced a hissing sound. This peculiarity seemed to justify the derivation of the word from the Hebrew *sharaḳ.*

Yet, it is questionable whether the name of an instrument not in use in Ancient Israel could be derived from a Hebrew root. It seems more probable that a similar onomatopoetic verb may have existed also in other Semitic languages, so that *mashroḳita* could have conceivably originated from a non-Hebraic root.[374]

It cannot be said with certainty whether this instrument was in fact identical with the Pan's pipe. PFEIFFER[375] and FORKEL[376] believe it was the *syrinx,* others define it as a flute,[377] AMBROS as a double-flute,[378] while JAHN identifies it with the *ʿugab.*[379]

SACHS supposes the *mashroḳita* to be a woodwind instrument, probably the double-oboe.[380] Should there be any connection between the name of the instrument and the Semitic root *sharaḳ,* it is striking that among all wind instruments the transversal flute and the Pan's pipe are the only ones which produce the sound by "piping," or "whistling," whereas all the others, the mouthpiece of which is held between the lips, are played by "blowing." This difference of tone production is precisely expressed by ATHENAEUS; "to play the flute (*aulos*)," that is, to blow with a mouthpiece, is called by him *aulein;* "to play the Pan's pipe (*syrinx*)," that is "to pipe," is called *syrizein.*[381]

Any attempt to arrive at a working conclusion with regard to the true meaning of *mashroḳita* is beset by well-nigh insurmountable difficulties. For want of a more definite solution, we have practically no other choice than to follow the interpretation of the early translators and identify the *mashroḳita* with the *syrinx*.

The Greek versions of the Scriptures translate without exception as *syrinx,* the VULGATE and most of the early Latin versions as *fistula.* The English translations, including *Wycliffe,* use either "pipe," or "flute," thus missing the significant point of the Book of Daniel, in which the exotic character of the instrument is attached to it by its very name.

It is rather curious that, in later times, the name *mashroḳita* was used by the Jews for the ordinary piano. Using the name of a biblical wind instrument for a modern and completely different type of instrument is, of course, devoid of any logic. But this practice can be frequently observed in the nomenclature of Hebrew instruments, caused by the lack of discrimination in musical matters on the part of the rabbinic writers.

The surprising thing, however, is that some other historians too, show sometimes a regrettable lack of reliability in describing or portraying ancient instruments. This is evidenced by a significant example. In a modern work about the music of biblical times, there is an illustration of the *mashroḳita* taken over from a treatise of the 17th century. In this treatise, however, the illustration is supposed to represent the *magrephah;* (or the *hydraulis*) moreover, the illustration itself is manifestly a result of pure fancy.[382]

18. SUMPONYAH

This instrument is not mentioned in the Hebrew text of the Bible. It appears in the Book of Daniel among those played in NEBUCHADREZZAR's orchestra (3:5,10,15). Whereas all the other instruments are mentioned four times (verses 5,7,10,15), the *sumponyah* is omitted in verse 7, this being generally taken as an error of a scribe subsequently perpetuated in the masoretic text. The early Greek and Latin translators, and also the *Authorized* and *Revised Standard Versions* tried to emendate the text by inserting the missing word. The *Jewish Version* and other modern translations follow closely the masoretic text, leaving out the word in verse 7.[383]

A further evidence for the carelessness of the Aramaic author, or his copyists, is the fact that the word *sumponyah* is spelled differently in all three places. Verse 3 has *sumponyah,* verse 10 *sipunya,* and verse 15 *sumponyah* with *vav* after *pe.*

Until to-day the opinions are divided whether or not *sumponyah* represents a mere transliteration of the Greek word *symphōnia.* The doubt has been occasioned mainly by the fact that the Syrian Greeks knew an instrument which they called *samponia.* This name has been preserved until our time in Italy, where the bagpipe is called *sampugna* or *zampugna.* It is difficult to ascertain whether the Syrian *samponia* and the Chaldaean *sumponyah* had been original terms or phonetic adaptations of the Greek word. The instrument itself might well have been one of those which the Hellenes have taken over from the Orient, improved them technically, and then traded them back, with new Greek names, to the country of their origin.[384]

The original meaning of the Greek word *symphōnia* is "sounding together," specifically the simultaneous playing of instruments, or voices, producing a concord. ARISTOTLE and PLATO use the word in the sense of "simultaneous sound," or "harmony of tones," more precisely as a consonant harmony of two tones forming the intervals of a fourth (*dia tessarōn*), a fifth (*dia pente*), or an octave (*dia pasōn*). POLYBIUS (c. 201-c. 120 B.C.E.) interprets it already, in a wider sense, as a concert (or band) either of vocal or instrumental music, or both.[385]

In the writings of the early Greek philosophers the word does not as yet indicate a musical instrument, especially not the bagpipe. This instrument does not appear before the 4th century B.C.E., and then not under the name of *symphōnia.* ARISTOPHANES (c. 448-385 B.C.E.), in his comedy *"Lysistrata,"* mentions the *physetēria* ("bellow") and the *physallidēs* ("bladder pipes") as the instruments accompanying the dances. The plural form of the last named word seems to indicate that the instrument may have had two, possibly more sounding pipes.

The word *symphōnia* as a term referring to a single musical instrument appears first with ATHENAEUS. He uses the name rather frequently, but the context in which it appears in the different places does not indicate clearly the nature of the instrument. His descriptions do not even give us a clue as to whether he alludes to a stringed, wind, or percussion instrument.

In his description of the nocturne revelries of the eccentric king ANTIOCHUS EPIPHANES (reigned 175-168 B.C.E.), ATHENAEUS quotes POLYBIUS:

> "Whenever he heard that any of the young men were at an entertainment, he would come in quite unceremoniously with a fife (*meta keratiou*) and a procession [or band] of musicians (*symphōnias*)."[386]

Symphōnia in this sentence is interpreted mostly as "bagpipe." This instrument, however, had already at least two sounding pipes; the addition of another wind instrument, the *keration,* to such an ensemble would therefore be highly improbable.[387]

In another passage of ATHENAEUS the licentious behavior of ANTIOCHUS is described somewhat differently:

> "When the symphony gave the signal, he would leap up and dance naked and act with the jesters, so that every one departed in shame."[388]

Here *symphōnia* is used alone, so that its interpretation as bagpipe might not be excluded.

In the following description, however, *symphōnia* is again coupled with other wind instruments, contradicting the idea of the "bagpipe":

> "Two dancers entered the orchestra with castanets (*meta symphōnias*), and four boxers mounted upon the stage accompanied by trumpeters (*salpinktōn*) and horn-players (*bykanistōn*)."[389]

"Castanets" is the interpretation of the modern translator[390] who, to support his rendition, refers to a similar passage, in which POLYBIUS uses the word *symphōnia* evidently in the sense of a percussion instrument, possibly a sistrum.[391]

The explanation of *symphōnia* as a percussive instrument is vitiated, however, by other descriptions of ATHENAEUS, in which these types of instruments are always called by their exact names. So, for instance:

> "PROTAGORIDES of KYZIKOS says: He has laid fingers to every instrument, one after the other—castanets (*krotalōn*), tambourine (*phanon*, corrupt, probably *tympanon*), *pandura*, and on the sweet single-pipe (*monaulos*)."[392]

Also in the following passage:

> "The *magōdos* [the actor who impersonates male and female roles] has tambourines (*tympana*) and cymbals (*kymbala*)."[393]

ATHENAEUS mentions also "bronze-cheeked castanets" (*chalkopara krembala*) —which would be better rendered in English as "rattles"—and for playing these instruments he uses the verb *krembalizein, i.e.,* "to shake the *krembala*."[394] It is therefore quite doubtful whether *symphōnia* in the above passage refers to a percussion instrument.

Moreover, the following passage completely excludes the interpretation of *symphōnia* either as a bagpipe or a percussion instrument:

> "Since the term 'concerted music' (*synaulia*) is unknown to many persons, I must tell its meaning: It was a kind of contest in harmony (*symphōnia*), flute-music (*aulou*) and dance-rhythm (*rhythmou*) exactly corresponding, with no singer adding words to the performance."[395]

From all these descriptions of ATHENAEUS one thing at least emerges unmistakably: at that epoch *symphōnia* was not the bagpipe, nor any percussion instrument, probably not even the name of some individual instrument at all.

Not before the flourishing of Roman writers (1st century B.C.E.) do we have precise information about the bagpipe. In Rome of the emperors (1st century C.E.) this instrument was called *tibia utricularis, utricularium,* or *chorus. Symphonia* meant something entirely different for the Romans. In the writing of HORACE (65-8 B.C.E.), CICERO (106-43 B.C.E.), SENECA (4 B.C.E.-65 C.E.), PLINY (23-79 C.E.), and others, the word is used in the sense of "concord," and also "company of musicians." HORACE says that a *symphonia* (*i.e.* "band") "out-of-tune" spoils the feast. CICERO calls "musical parties" *symphoniae.* In defending Verrem, he quotes in his favor that

> "in their convivials he used to sing with them in concert (or with a band.)"[396]

SENECA relates of singing with the accompaniment of a band (*symphonia*).

During the time of the Caesars the bagpipe was already wide-spread in Rome, but it was held in low esteem on account of its vulgar sonority. VOPISCUS relates in "The Life of Carinus" that at a popular festival a hundred bagpipers took part.[397] With a biting sarcasm SENECA remarked that a *pythaules* (a player of the bagpipe) is valued higher in the theater than the philosophers in the schools.[398] MARTIAL says about the famous flute-player CANUS:

"Do you believe . . . that CANUS longs to be a bagpipe-player (*ascaules*)?"[399]

This ironic question shows that even Romans, trailing in music behind the Hellenes, ascribed to the instrument a lower artistic quality.

NERO (emp. 54-68 C.E.), notorious for having considered himself a great musician, had a predilection for the bagpipe. DIO CHRYSOSTOMOS, a contemporary of SUETONIUS, relates that NERO

"knew how to play the pipe with his mouth and the bag thrust under his arms."

SUETONIUS, in his "Life of the Roman Caesars," reports about NERO that

"towards the end of his life he has publicly vowed that if he retained his power he would at the games in celebration of his victory give a performance on the water-organ (*hydraulis*), the flute (*choraulos*) and the bagpipe (*utricularium*)."[400]

In the Latin parlance of the early Middle Ages *symphonia* meant a music instrument. But about the real nature of it the opinions were at wide variance. According to PRUDENTIUS (c. 400 C.E.), it was a double-oboe, akin to those used by the Egyptians as a signal instrument in battles. VENANTIUS FORTUNATUS (d. c. 600 C.E.) describes it as a pipe "swelled by its own wind" ("*tibia plena suo flatu*"), which would allow the interpretation in the sense of a bagpipe. But according to ISIDORE of SEVILLE (c. 560-636 C.E.), the *symphonia* was a kind of *tympanum,*

"a hollow wood, covered with skin on either end, that the musicians strike with sticks (*virgulis*) from both sides."[401]

As ISIDORE states, one skin was larger than the other, so that *in ea concordia gravis et acuti suavissimus cantus* was produced. However, it is difficult to imagine how it should have been possible to produce "a most pleasing melody" (*suavissimus cantus*) on a drum with two different sized skins, one of them sounding high, the other low.

In French poetry of the Middle Ages we find an instrument, the name of which, *chifonie,* could also be derived from *symphonia* by dropping the *m.* This was the hurdy-gurdy, a wide-spread and popular stringed instrument. In a later epoch, the clavichord was likewise called *symphonia.*

o
o o

On the Jewish side, the Mishnah contains various details concerning Daniel's *sumponyah,* which, however do not afford a clear idea about its nature. Some of these details would permit an inference in favor of a bagpipe, whereas others would exclude it altogether.

In ruling about the precepts for cleanness, the Mishnah states:

"If a spindle, distaff, rod, double-flute (*sumponyah*), or pipe (*ḥalil*) are made of metal, they are susceptible of uncleanness; but if they are only plated they are not susceptible; but in either case if the double-flute has a groove (*bet ḳibul*) for the 'wing' (*ḳanafayim*) it is susceptible."[402]

The rendering of *sumponyah* as "double-flute" is the translator's interpretation

(*Danby*). It was mentioned above that *ḥalil* was sometimes rendered as "double-flute" (see p. 313); an identical translation of *sumponyah* must be considered as arbitrary.

We know from other Mishnaic passages that there existed flute-like instruments (pipes) made of metal.[403] But a metallic bagpipe is a contradiction in terms, unless the qualification refers only to the sounding pipes, which could have well been made of metal.

The rendition of *ḳanafayim* as "wings" is highly doubtful, despite numerous attempts to explain it thusly. *Ḳanaf,* in singular, means a "wing"' or something similar protruding, like the arm or foot of an object. The plural ending . . . *ayim* indicates a duality, but the nature of this duality is difficult to establish, unless we assume that it refers in this case to the two pipes of a bagpipe. Other commentators, however, think that *ḳanafayim* indicates the two pipes, set at an angle, of a double-flute, or double-oboe.[404] Again another interpretation explains it as the two arms of a harp or lyre. This assumption, though not corroborated by any source material, would be a plausible explanation, corresponding to the original meaning of the word as well as to a certain quality of its form. Here, however, the term is applied to a wind instrument, the two arms of which could imply only the two pipes of a double-oboe.[405]

According to rabbinic indications, the *ḳanafayim* were connected (*ḥabar*) with one another at the mouthpiece (*meẓufit* or *meẓubit*) by a cavity (*bet ḳibul*), and yet separated by a stalk (*ḳab*); the *ḳab* seems to have been a single short tube from which the two pipes emerged and into which also the mouthpiece was inserted. The mouthpiece itself was a separate part of the mechanism and was called, according to its shape, "cup" (*ḳos*).[406] Except the *sumponyah* and the *ḥalil, ḳos* is mentioned only in connection with the *shofar,* all the other wind instruments having had mostly mouthpieces of reed, which were called by the generic name of *meẓufit.*

At variance with the above Mishnaic indication, *bet ḳibul* is sometimes explained as the receptacle in which the *sumponyah* was kept when not in use. This, however, is an error, since in another passage of the Mishnah such a receptacle is called *teḳ sumponyah.*[407] *Bet ḳibul* must have had therefore another meaning. DANBY translates: "a groove for the 'wing'," by which he understands "a cavity containing a vibrating tongue," as he explains in a note. (He means probably the vibrating tongues used in metal pipes with a single beating reed striking a frame). DANBY's explanation is manifestly erroneous, since beating tongues of reed or metal are not attested in Antiquity. Thus, with regard to the meaning of *bet ḳibul,* only surmises are possible.

In another passage of the same tractate the bagpipe is mentioned apparently by another name. In discussing the regulations for cleanness, *ḥemat ḥalilim* is mentioned among various other objects.[408] This term is translated by DANBY as "bagpipes." The question arises, however, why the rabbinic writer, if he really meant by this the *sumponyah* (allegedly the bagpipe), used another name for it. As SACHS thinks,

> "it is hard to believe that the author of this tractate, which lists all kinds of objects as being pure or impure, would have listed the bag-

pipe, or, rather, one sort of bagpipe, not with other musical instruments, but with mortars and troughs."[409]

It is true that in the above quoted passage *sumponyah* is also listed together with non-musical objects (spindle, distaff, rod), but SACHS justly refers to the fact that a bagpipe should be called *ḥalil ḥemet* rather than *ḥemat ḥalilim,* the correct meaning of which is "bag for pipes," that is a receptacle in which pipes were kept or carried, as depicted frequently on Greek vases.[410]

Thus, the rabbinic literature, too, does not furnish us with a conclusive solution of the meaning of *sumponyah.*

Among medieval Jewish biblical commentators IBN EZRA identifies *sumponyah* with the biblical *ʿugab.*[411] SAʿADIA, however, defines the *sumponyah* as the instrument of shepherds and adds that it was activated by a bag.[412] He describes this bag somewhat circumstantially as *bet ha-sumponot,* "the house of the pipes," on which the pipes themselves were fastened. SAʿADIA lived in the 12th century, and therefore cannot be considered a dependable describer of an instrument of biblical times. Evidently enough, his views in this respect were influenced by the bagpipe of his own epoch.

The strongest argument against the interpretation of the *sumponyah* as bagpipe is the historical fact that at the epoch of NEBUCHADREZZAR (first half of the 6th century B.C.E.) there existed no such instrument.[413] At first sight, this fact seems to be refuted by a bas-relief found in the excavations of a Hittite palace at Eyuk. In this carving a musician is portrayed, playing to all appearances a bagpipe. At closer scrutiny, however, the picture turns out to be a representation of a court-jester, or a lute player with a monkey.[414] Two pendent objects of the carving could indeed be taken on the surface as the "pipes" of a bagpipe, but they are in reality ribbons of the animal, or of the lute-like instrument.

ILLUSTRATION NO. 40

Hittite lutanist. Stone-relief found at Eyuk (Middle of the 2. millennium B.C.E.). University Museum, Philadelphia (After Sir John Stainer, *The Music of the Bible,* London, 1914).

As SACHS maintains, *sumponyah* was neither a bagpipe, nor a wind instrument at all.[415] He refers to the fact that in the Book of Daniel the instruments are listed four times.[416] First the wind instruments are mentioned (*ḳarna, mashroḳita*), then the string instruments (*ḳathros, sambyḳe, pesanterin*), and then only the *sumponyah* together with "all kinds of music." If we consider the usual order resorted to by biblical chroniclers, we find that music instruments are always mentioned in groups according to their species. In Daniel, *sumponyah* is invariably separated from the wind instruments by the group of string instruments. Therefore, it is questionable whether it is a wind instrument, or even a musical instrument altogether.

o
o o

In the time of the Roman emperors *consonare, consonantia* was the term used to indicate the singing of choral groups, or the playing together of pipes and other instruments, therefore what we call to-day a group of musicians (orchestra, band, ensemble).

This becomes evident from the text of St. Luke's Gospel, in which *symphōnia* is used in the parable of the prodigal son (15:25), having there the meaning of "singing" or "music." The *Authorized Version* translates:

> "Now his elder son was in the field: and as he came and drew nigh to the house, he heard musick and dancing."

JEROME, in commenting on this biblical passage, says:

> "The *symphonia* is not a kind of instrument, as some Latin writers think, but it means concordant harmony. It is expressed in Latin by *consonantia*."

This explanation, written in 407 C.E., has a particular importance, because JEROME, through his long sojourn in the Orient, has known the languages and customs of most of the peoples of the Near-East; therefore, better than anyone else, he was qualified to rectify the erroneous usage of the word.

JEROME's interpretation is corroborated by AMBROSE, who says that "the strings of the *cithara* are of different length, but (they produce) a concordant harmony."[417]

A similar, though figurative, use of the term *consonantia* may be found in TERTULLIAN's writings. He speaks of *consonantia prophetis,* by which he characterizes the spiritual harmony emanating from the teachings of the Jewish prophets.[418]

In the spurious letter to Dardanus, the bagpipe, called there *chorus,* is briefly described.[419] Already the contrast with *symphonia* as explained in the authentic writings of JEROME, should have convinced the commentators that *symphonia* and *chorus* could certainly not be identical. *Consonantia,* in the sense of an orchestral group, is then the most pertinent explanation of *symphonia,* historically as well as linguistically, since neither in Greek nor in Latin is there an equivalent term for our Occidental notion of "orchestra."

A similar interpretation of *sumponyah* in Daniel imposes itself automatically. First, the chronicler enumerates the individual instruments, playing alone. Then, they all play together, a procedure expressed logically by *sumponyah,* in the Greek meaning of the word. Finally, *v'ḳol zenė zimra,* "all kinds of instruments," indicates that to those already mentioned, the percussion instruments were added, drums, cymbals, sistra, etc., which were never lacking on festival celebrations in the Orient.

Following this order of thought, GALPIN suggests an appropriate translation for the passage in Daniel; he renders *sumponyah* as "full consort," a term used in the 16th and 17th centuries for the ensemble playing of instrumentalists. The translation suggested by him would be:

> "at what time ye hear the sound of the trumpet, flute, lyre, rote, psaltery, and the full consort, even of all kind of music."[420]

This is quite a logical explanation and corresponds exactly to the Oriental practice of a musical performance, in which first the solo instruments played alone, joining their forces together at the end of a piece.[421]

The controversy as to whether *symphōnia* was a bagpipe or not survived even until recent times, despite all evidence to the contrary. PHILLIPS BARRY maintains the *symphōnia* was the bagpipe.[422] GEORGE MOORE, answering this article, tries to prove this opinion to be erroneous.[423] This controversy is the more astonishing, as the above quoted passage of St. Luke's Gospel should exclude not only the idea of the bagpipe, but even the identification of the *symphōnia* with any kind of instrument.

Despite all opinions to the contrary, a modern musicological work identifies the *sumponyah* with the bagpipe.[424]

The English Bibles interpret *sumponyah* in the sense of a musical instrument, but with the most diversified meanings. Thus, *Wycliffe* translates "sawtrie" and "sautrie" (early), and "symphonye" (later), *Douay* "symphony," the *Authorized* and *American Versions, Moulton* and *Harkavy* "dulcimer." Despite all the evidence to the contrary, *Moffat,* the *Jewish* and *Revised Standard Versions* use for *sumponyah* "bagpipe," *Moffat* and the *Jewish Version* omitting, the *Revised Standard Version* adding the word in verse 7.

19. ḤAẒOẒERAH

The word *ḥaẓoẓerah* (plur. *ḥaẓoẓerot*) is derived etymologically from the verb *ḥaẓar,* "to be present." In the Pi'el form, *ḥaẓoẓerah* would signify the "convoker." In Arabian, the same root, *ḥeẓār,* has a similar meaning; in the applied form it refers to "calling a meeting," since the sound of the trumpet usually summoned the people. A similar Arabic root signifies "narrow," also "to howl," "to hoot" out of excitement and anxiety, by which the trumpet's shape as well as its sound are well characterized.

GESENIUS considers the word to be an onomatopoeic construction, in which the duplication of certain consonants, especially the sybilants, would imitate some of the characteristic sonority traits of the instrument.[425] One could also cite some other onomatopoeic names of Jewish instruments, especially of the percussion class. They came into being as approximate phonetic imitations of the sound produced by their respective instrument, such as *tof* (timbrel), *ẓilẓal* and *meẓiltayim* (cymbals), *shalishim* (sistrum). Other ancient languages, too, have such sound-imitating words, like *mormorō* (murmuring) in Greek, *tintinnabulum* (little bell) in Latin, and others.

The *ḥaẓoẓerah* was a long straight trumpet, built by the Israelites after Egyptian models. There, it was a familiar instrument long before the biblical Exodus, since we find pictorial reproductions of it in the oldest and well preserved monuments of the New Kingdom, as early as 1414 B.C.E.

In TUT-ANKH-AMEN's tomb two trumpets have been found, one of silver, the other of bronze. The Musée du Louvre in Paris houses another ancient Egyptian trumpet of gilt bronze, which is dated about 1000 years later.[426] The Pharaoh TUT-ANKH-AMEN reigned about the year 1360 B.C.E., a little over a century before the Exodus of the Israelites from Egypt occurred,—c. 1240 B.C.E., according to many present-day authorities.[427] Thus, the Israelites were resident in Egypt before, during, and after the age of TUT-ANKH-AMEN, which makes it logical to assume that they have taken over their trumpets from the Egyptians.

Furthermore, trumpets were used also by the Assyrians, as evidenced by bas-reliefs found in excavated monuments.

JOSEPHUS gives a detailed description of the instrument, which agrees essentially with the pictorial representations on Egyptian antiquities.[428] According to this description, the *ḥaẓoẓerah* was one ell long, its straight tube being somewhat wider than that of the *ḥalil* and still further widened at the lower end into a bell. The mouthpiece was rather broad. Thus, the form of the instrument was identical with to-days' signal-trumpets, which we call "herald's trumpets."

ILLUSTRATION NO. 41.

Trumpets found in Tut-Ankh-Amen's tomb. Left to right: Silver trumpet; its wooden core; bronze trumpet; its wooden core. Museum Cairo (After Hans Hickmann, *Musikgeschichte in Bildern*, Leipzig, 1961).

JEROME's description is more general; but he also states that the instrument was made either of bronze or silver (*de aere vel argento*).[429]

The *ḥaẓoẓerah* is the only Jewish instrument of which we possess at least one contemporary picture and some others not too far removed historically. The Arch of Triumph of the emperor Titus in Rome, erected after the victory over the Jews and the destruction of the sanctuary in Jerusalem, shows the captured implements of the Temple, carried in a triumphal procession. Among them, the two sacred silver trumpets are depicted, which the sculptor must have copied from the originals. Several coins issued during the Maccabaean revolt (132-135 C.E.) show on their face two trumpets, which are designed rather clumsily and are shortened considerably, probably to fit into the face of a small coin. It is characteristic, in this reproduction, that right below the mouthpiece the tube is widened like a bell, serving obviously to reinforce the tone.[430] On the Arch of Triumph of Titus the mouthpieces of the sacred trumpets are hidden, which makes it impossible to ascertain iconographically whether these instruments have had a similar device.

According to Greek and Roman sources the trumpet was invented by the Etruscans, the first bronze-casters of the Mediterranean.[431] The Egyptians must have become familiar with the instrument through their cultural intercourse with the Etruscans. From Egypt, the trumpet was taken over by the Tyrrhennian peoples and thence by the Greeks and Romans.[432]

The Hellenes called the trumpet *salpinx;* it was made of metal, in contrast to the *keratinē* ("horn"), which was made of animal horn.

The Romans had four different types of trumpets: the *tuba,* with a straight tube; the *buccina,* with a curved tube; the *cornu,* in the form of the letter C; and the *lituus,* the military signal instrument, with a straight tube, the bell of which was bent upward. All were made of metal, with the exception of the *cornu,* which—as the name indicates—was made originally of neat's horn, but later also of metal.[433]

Like the Egyptian trumpet, the Jewish *ḥaẓoẓerah* was made of metal, either of bronze or, for the sacred trumpets, of beaten silver (*kesef miḳshah*).[434] The SEPTUAGINT translates this term as *elatas,* "hammered silver," the Syrian version is *nesaḥ,* "cast silver."

As we have seen, the form of the trumpet was known to Moses and the Jewish people from Egypt. Therefore, when—according to the Scriptures—God commanded Moses to make two trumpets (Num. 10:2), only the material was indicated together with instructions how to use the instrument on different occasions, but the shape of it was not mentioned at all. The fact that God commanded two trumpets is the reason that the Bible uses the word, with one exception,[435] in the plural form, as *ḥaẓoẓerot.*

The sounding of the *ḥaẓoẓerot* was the exclusive privilege of Aaron's descendants:

> "And the sons of Aaron, the priests, shall blow the trumpets; and they shall be to you for a statute for ever throughout your generations" (Num. 10:8).

They adhered strictly to this privilege (2 Chron. 5:12 ff; 7:6; 13:12,14; Ezra 3:10; Neh. 12:35,41). The players of trumpets were called *ḥaẓoẓerim* (2 Chron. 5:13; 29:28). The prerogatives of the Aaronites applied only to the sacred trumpets of the ritual, for on secular occasions trumpets were blown also by others than priests; so, for instance, by royal heralds (2 Kings 11:14; 2 Chron. 23:13). The Bible does not reveal as to whether these were the same trumpets of silver or of some other metal. Since the silver trumpets belonged to the *kle ha-ḳodesh*, "the holy vessels," (Num. 31:6; 2 Kings 12:14), it would be logical to assume that the trumpets used on secular occasions were made of bronze, like the Egyptian instruments.

Similar to the loud instruments of other ancient Oriental peoples, the original purpose of the Jewish trumpets may have been to draw the attention of the deity to the ritual action and to the worshippers. Thus, the sound of the *ḥaẓoẓerot* served as means for a persistent invocation of God. A carved picture on an Egyptian coffin from later Roman times shows a trumpet-player,

> "blowing the trumpet before, one rather should say up to, Osiris, and this is done with the same purpose."[436]

Although with the subsequent maturing of Jewish religious concepts the loud invocation of God, (apart from the trumpet calls), was gradually abandoned,[437] we still find the anachronistic custom of the loud call in the relatively late epoch of the Maccabaean revolt (middle of the 2nd century C.E.). On that occasion, the sacred trumpets were blown and the people called, reportedly, with loud voice to implore God's assistance (1 Macc. 4:40; 5:33; 16:8).

A spiritually higher purpose of the trumpets transpires from the command that their blowing should be undertaken *leziḥaron*, "for a memorial before your God" Num. 10:10), that is, as a symbolic reminder of God's presence amidst the people. This would be a reversal of the primitive and originally pagan calculation to arouse the attention of the deity by noise, shouting and loud instruments.

The manner of blowing the trumpets is described in the Bible in all its essentials for various ocacsions (Num. 10:2-10): to gather the congregation to the tent of meeting, to cause the camps to set forward, to invite the princes for a gathering, to sound alarm in danger, to give a signal when going to war. All this refers to the secular use of the instrument.

We know that the Egyptian trumpet was mainly used as a signal instrument in and before the battle. KIRBY suggests, therefore, that the instructions given by the Lord to Moses for the use of the trumpets and which Moses adopted for his own people, represent the code of signals employed by the Egyptian army, or, at least, some modification of it.

> "There is abundant evidence that Moses was thoroughly familiar with everything that appertained to Egyptian life, and it would have been very natural for him to adapt for his own people a system which he knew by experience would work well."

Moreover, KIRBY holds that

> "the fact that there were *two* trumpets found in the tomb of Tut-Ankh-Amen, and that *two* trumpets were made by Moses for the use of his army, would appear to lend additional force" to his suggestion.[438]

As to their sacred functions, the trumpets were blown at all religious feasts, the New Moon, the daily burnt and peace-offerings as well as all important ritual ceremonies. They were used at the transfer of the ark of the covenant to Jerusalem (1 Chr. 15:24; 16:6,42), the dedication of Solomon's Temple (2 Chron. 5:12; 7:6), the laying of the foundation of the Second Temple (Ezra 3:10), the dedication of the newly erected walls around Jerusalem (Neh. 12:35,41), and in general whenever the people were joyous and celebrated feasts (2 Kings 11:14; 2 Chron. 23:13; 1 Chron. 13:8; 15:24,28; 16:42; Ezra 3:10; Ps. 98:6, etc.).

In the daily sacred service the trumpets had the essential function of indicating the prostration of the worshippers. To be sure, references to this effect are lacking in the Scriptures. But the rabbinic scribes mention explicitly that this was a ritual custom in the Second Temple:

> "Ben Arza clashed the cymbal and the Levites broke forth into singing. When they reached a break in the singing they [the priests] blew upon the trumpets and all the people prostrated themselves; at every break there was a blowing of the trumpet and at every blowing of the trumpet a prostration. This was the rite of the Daily Whole-offering in the service to the House of our God."[439]

Since we have a good reason to believe that the routine of the Second Temple's daily services was merely the continuation of that of Solomon's Temple, we may safely assume that the functions of the *ḥaẓoẓerot* were identical in both sanctuaries.

A talmudic passage indicates that the two sacred trumpets used at various rites were exactly of the same dimensions.[440] This was an obvious necessity, since the trumpets were blown mostly in pairs with the intention of producing powerful unisons.

In a contemporary musicological work there is the assertion that in Ancient Israel the trumpets were "perhaps" blown *in two parts.* It is unnecessary to refute this idea. Besides, polyphony in the Western sense was unknown in Antiquity.[441]

At first, the trumpet-players may not have exceeded the three or four easily produceable tones of the natural series, beginning with the second partial, *i.e.* the octave of the fundamental, and the upper fifth, octave and possibly, the tenth (c'-g'-c''-e''). At this primitive stage, the *ḥaẓoẓerot* must have been used primarily for signal purposes, both within and without the sanctuary. Their tone color must have been coarse and uneven, like the primitive trumpets of other ancient peoples. AESCHYLOS (525-456 B.C.E.), in his tragedy "Eumenides," calls the tone of the *salpinx* "yelling" (*diatoros*), and Roman authors characterize the tone of the *tuba* (the straight trumpet, similar to the *ḥaẓoẓerah*) as *horribilis, raucus, rudis,* or *terribilis.*[442] PLUTARCH (c. 46-c. 120 C.E.) compares the tone of the Egyptian trumpet with "an ass' bray."[443]

However, as the priestly Jewish trumpeters have gradually developed their technique and learned particularly how to produce additional partials, the *ḥaẓoẓerah* might have well surmounted its initial stage as a mere signal instrument and risen into the sphere of more artistic playing. That this is not merely a surmise is evidenced by the grandiose musical performance at the dedication of Solomon's Temple, in which, together with more than four hundred singers and musicians, one hundred and twenty priestly trumpeters have participated.

The chronicler reports about this memorable event that the music was performed with such a perfection

> "that trumpeters and singers were as one, to make one sound to be heard in praising and thanking the Lord" (2 Chron. 5:13).

Must it be assumed that the role of the hundred and twenty priestly trumpeters has been confined to the mere production of three or four natural harmonics? If we evaluate correctly the Chronicler's description, it may indeed not be too far-fetched to conclude that at least some of these trumpet-players have been sufficiently skilled for using their instrument in a more elaborate way.

KIRBY reminds us of the well-known fact that

> "short and relatively wide tubes favour the production of the fundamental and the lower partials of the harmonic series; long and relatively narrow tubes favour the production of the higher partials only."[444]

It is not inconceivable that these acoustic phenomena might have been known to the ancient Jewish trumpeters, who made an appropriate use of them.

The construction and probably the sound of the *ḥaẓoẓerah* was basically identical with that of to-day's natural trumpets, the sole difference being that the biblical instrument was not curved. It was put together of several limbs (*praḳim*), which sometimes fell apart (*hitpareḳ*).[445]

o
o o

The number of trumpets in the daily sacred service was at least two, at high holidays and other important religious festivals their number could be increased without restriction. Whether or not one hundred and twenty trumpeters have actually participated at the dedication of Solomon's Temple, cannot be positively ascertained. Still it is quite likely that all the trumpet-playing priests have been summoned for this important event; and their number must have been considerable, even if we make a certain allowance for the well-meant exaggerations of biblical chroniclers.

o
o o

For the trumpet blasts, the biblical text uses mostly two terms, *teḳiʿah* and *teruʿah* (Num. 10:2 ff). The root *ruʿah* has the meaning "to be agitated," "to make noise." Consequently, *teruʿah* would indicate a series of acute, crashing, staccato-like blasts. The opposite, *teḳiʿah,* implies the use of sustained, long drawn tones. With the passing of time, however, the two terms have been interpreted in a different way.[446] According to the purpose of the trumpet blasts, they were drawn by one or both instruments.

The use of the trumpets in the First Temple is attested mainly by 1 Chron. 13:8; 15:24,28; 16:6,42. and 2 Chron. 5:12; 29:26 ff, for the Second Temple by Ezra. 3:10; Neh. 12:35,41, and Psalm 98.6. A number of references in the early rabbinic literature give us a clear picture about the important functions of the instrument in the ritual.

In the Second Temple, the *ḥaẓoẓerot* were sounded three times in immediate succession at the opening of the outer gates, in order to convoke the priests and Levites. At the rite of Tabernacles

> "two priests stood at the Nicanor Gate, leading from the Court of the Israelites to the Court of the Women with two trumpets in their hands; at cock-crow they blew a sustained, a quavering and another sustained blast (*teḳiʿah, teruʿah, teḳiʿah*). When they reached the tenth step they again blew a sustained, a quavering and another sustained blast. When they reached the Court [of the Women] they again blew a sustained, a quavering and another sustained blast."[447]

The Mishnah gives precise indications as to the exact number of blasts which had to be drawn on the various ritual ceremonies:

> "They blew never less than twenty-one blasts in the Temple [in a day] and never more than forty-eight. On all days they blew twenty-one blasts: three at the opening of the gates, nine at the morning Daily Whole-offering, and nine at the evening Daily Whole-offering. At the Additional offerings [on Sabbaths, New Moons, and Festival-days] they blew nine more blasts. On the eve of Sabbath they used to blow six more blasts, three to cause the people to cease from work and three to mark the break between the sacred and the profane. [*i.e.* to mark the entering of the Sabbath]."[448]
>
> "If the eve of Sabbath fell within the [week of the] Feast [of Tabernacles], they blew forty-eight blasts; three at the opening of the gates, three at the upper [Nikanor] gate, three at the lower gate ['that leads to the East'], three at the water-drawing, three at the Altar, nine at the morning Daily Whole-offering, nine at the evening Daily Whole-offering, nine at the Additional-offerings, three to cause the people to cease from work, and three to mark the break between the sacred and the profane."[449]

Further rabbinic regulations concerning the ritual use of the *ḥaẓoẓerot* and to the number of the blasts, which was akin to the use of the *shofarot,* will be found in the following chapter.

As we see from the two last rabbinic quotations, the *ḥaẓoẓerot* (just as the *shofarot,* about which later) were the instruments of announcing the Sabbath. They were sounded by the *ḥazzan ha-kenesset* (the superintendent of the Temple) from a roof at the highest place of the city, so that the people working in the fields could hear the call.[450] Between the start of the Sabbath-call (*naṭal*) and its ending (*gamar*) some time elapsed, in which any work just begun had to be finished. With the end of the trumpet-call the Sabbath started and every activity definitely ceased.

o
o o

Some other calls, too, seem to have existed for various purposes, if the fanciful descriptions of war signals in the recently discovered Dead Sea Scrolls may be taken as reflecting their use in actual life.

One of these scrolls found in a cave at Qumrān contains a detailed strategic plan for an apocalyptic war to be fought between *The Sons of Light and the Sons of Darkness.*[451] Notwithstanding its manifestly imaginary character, this description is considered by some biblical scholars—and even modern military strategists—as "largely conforming to standard Roman patterns of military organizations, procedure and strategy."[452]

It is not impossible that some of these trumpet calls might have been copied from actual Roman military signals, as for instance, the "trumpets of assembly" (see below), which reminds us of the analogous Roman *tuba concionis*. This, however, is merely a surmise.

In order to evaluate correctly the musical references given in this *Rule of Battle*, we have to quote them in full:[453]

VIII:1-14.[454] ". . . The trumpets (*ḥaẓoẓerot*) shall keep sounding for the slingers until they have hurled a full seven times. Then the priests shall blow (*vitekeu*) the [signal of] recall (*ḥaẓoẓerot hamashob*) for them, and they shall return [lit. come] to the first line to take their stand in their assigned position. Thereupon the priests shall sound (*v'takeu*) a blast on the trumpets (*ḥaẓoẓerot*) [on the signal] of assembly, and the squadron of infantry shall go forth from the gaps and take up position between the lines [the Jewish and the enemy lines], and on their flanks shall be horsemen to the right and to the left. The priests shall then sound (*v'takeu*) upon the trumpets (*ḥaẓoẓerot*) a quavering blast (*kol meroded*) the signal for the battle formation . . . And when they have taken up position in three lines, the priests shall sound (*yitekeu*) a second blast—a low, subdued [sustained?] (*kol noaḥ*) signal for the advance to the enemy line. Thereupon they are to grasp their weapons. Then the priests are to sound (*yariu*) six trumpets (*ḥaẓoẓerot*) used for rousing to the slaughter—a sharp insistent [or: agitated] (*kol ḥad tarud*) signal for directing the battle. And the Levites and all the men with rams' horns (*shofarot*) are to sound a single blast [or: sound in unison] (*kol eḥad*)—a great war-blast to strike terror into the heart of the enemy. At the sound of that blast (*kol ha-teru'ah*), the war-darts are to issue to fell the slain. Then they shall accelerate (*yaḥishu*) the sound of the rams' horns (*kol ha-shofarot*), and the priests shall blow upon the trumpets (*ḥaẓoẓerot*) a sharp, insistent [or: agitated] sound (*kol ḥad tarud*) to direct the wings of the battle, until they have hurled their darts into the enemy line seven times. Thereupon the priests shall sound upon the trumpets (*ḥaẓoẓerot*) the signal to recall—a low, quavering, subdued [or: sustained] sound (*kol noaḥ meroded*). In such fashion shall the priests blow (*yitekeu*) the signals for the three squadrons . . ."

This *Rule of Battle* intimates that the priests and Levites have been assigned quite an important role in the battle, namely to direct the operations of the troops in the midst of the combatants. In giving appropriate signals with trumpet and *shofar* blasts, they marked the different phases of the engagement. Priests and Levites as strategists,—a peculiar role, though not entirely novel. It may be considered as a mere elaboration, or even as a more detailed description, of the older practice, as found especially in 2 Chron. 13:12,14, but partly also in Num. 10:1 ff; Josh. 6:3 ff and Judg. 7:8, 16, 18-20, 22.

Looking into the purely musical aspect of this detailed "order of battle," we realize that the priest-strategists had at their disposal seven different kinds of blasts: for the assembly, the advance, the attack, the ambush, the pursuit, the reassembly and the recall. Such blasts must have had some conspicuous rhythmic or other characteristics, without which their specific purpose could not have been recognized by the fighting men.

The imaginary character of this *War* becomes even more manifest by further detailed indications about the inscriptions, evidently symbolic, which were allegedly applied to the trumpets of assembly and war. None of our biblical or post-biblical sources ever mentions inscriptions on musical instruments and such a custom is not known to have existed in the ancient Near-East. The only allusion to an inscription on an object belonging to the family of musical instruments is to be found in Zech. 14:20, where it is said that the *meẓillot,* hung on horses, carried the inscription *ḳodesh le-YHVH,* evidently a superstitious practice for the protection of the useful animals against evil spirits (see p. 386). It would be more difficult to apply inscriptions on trumpets, especially in view of the fact that some of these alleged inscriptions are rather lengthy. Nevertheless, the passage in Zechariah may be considered as an indication that such custom might have existed, even if historically unrecorded.

This is what the scrolls tell about the inscriptions:[455]

> III:1 ff. "On the trumpets (*ḥaẓoẓerot*) of assembly for the entire community, they shall write: *The Enlisted of God.*
>
> "On the trumpets of assembly for commanders they shall write: *The Princes of God.*
>
> "On the trumpets of enrollment they shall write: *The Order of God.*
>
> "On the trumpets of the dignitaries they shall write: *The Heads of the Families of the Community.*
>
> "When they assemble at the house of meeting, they shall write: *The Testimonies of God for the Sacred Council.*
>
> "On the trumpets of the camps they shall write: *The peace of God be in the camp of His Saints.*
>
> "On the trumpets of breaking camp they shall write: *The Power of God is able to scatter the enemy and to put to flight all who hate righteousness. He recompenses loyalty and [requites] them that hate Him.*
>
> "On the trumpets for marshalling the battle they shall write: *The marshalled squadrons of God are able to wreak His angry vengeance upon all the Sons of Darkness.*
>
> "On the trumpets of assembly for the infantry, when the gates of war are opened for them to go out to the enemy line, they shall write: *A Memorial of the vengeance to be exacted in the Era of God* [*cp.* Lev. 23:24; Num. 10:10].
>
> "On the trumpets of the slain they shall write: *The Force of God's Power in Battle is able to fell all the faithless slain.*
>
> "On the trumpets of ambush they shall write: *The Mysteries of God are able to destroy wickedness.*
>
> "On the trumpets of pursuit they shall write: *God has smitten all*

> *the Sons of Darkness. He will not turn back His anger until He has destroyed them.*
>
> "And when they return from the battle to rejoin the ranks they shall write on the trumpets of recall: *God hath gathered them.*
>
> "And on the trumpets which signal the way of return from the war against the enemy and the way back to the community of Jerusalem, they shall write: *The Rejoicing of God at the return of peace* [or: *at a safe return*].

Not only the trumpets but also the standards to be used in the battle are said to have had their appropriate inscriptions. There were such mottos for the entire army, as well as for all categories of combatants, for all sizes of groups,—different inscriptions for the camp commanders, for squadrons of thousand, of hundred, of fifty, and

> "On the standard of [the group of] ten they shall write: *Songs* [or: *hymns*] (*rinnot*) of God on the ten stringed harp (*nebel* ʿ*asor*), together with the names of the commander of the ten, and of the nine men under his command."

Of all the numerous standards, only that of this group has an inscription with a musical implication. It may have had certain numerological reasons, establishing an esoteric relation between the smallest group of combatants and the number of strings on the ʿ*asor,* and thus vesting such a small group with a supernatural power for subduing the enemy.

o
o o

After the collapse of the Jewish national existence and in the subsequent general abashment, some musical notions have disappeared from the people's mind, others became confused owing to the lack of familiarity with them. So we find a talmudic statement reflecting this chaotic state with reference to the nomenclature of certain instruments:

> "The following three groups of words are changed in meaning after the destruction of the Temple: . . . What was formerly called *ḥaẓoẓarta* [*ḥaẓoẓerah* in the Aramaic dialect] was called *shifurta* [*shofar* in Aramaic], and what was formerly called *shifurta* became *ḥaẓoẓarta.*"[456]

Curiously enough, the rabbinic writer himself confounds the two instruments interpreting Num. 10:10 ("ye shall blow with trumpets," *baḥaẓoẓerot*) as the duty of blowing the *shofar.*

The Talmud recounts a peculiar and manifestly fictitious story that, at the time of Ezra, priests with golden trumpets stood on the walls and on the broken ramparts of Jerusalem, fanning the zeal of the people with *teḳiʿah* and *teruʿah* blasts for building the new wall. A priest who had no trumpet in his hand was considered to be no priest at all, and the inhabitants of Jerusalem made a good profit by renting to the priests trumpets for a gold denarius a piece.[457]

A legend of this sort could have originated only in the mind of someone completely unfamiliar with the religious and musical tradition. For trumpets made of noble metal were not judiciously accessible to anyone except the priests, their long and honorable privilege being both to play and to guard the instruments. No ordinary citizens were likely to have trumpets in their possession even by chance, since this has never been a popular instrument, let alone the fact that the expression "golden trumpets" belongs quite obviously to those naive exaggerations found so often in the rabbinic literature.

o
o o

The Old Testament mentions *ḥaẓoẓerot* twenty-nine times. The SEPTUAGINT translates the word twenty-seven times as *salpinx,* never as *keratinē,* since the latter instrument was made of animal horn. The word is left out entirely in 2 Chron. 5:13, whereas in Hos. 5:8 both *shofar* and *ḥaẓoẓerah* are rendered by one single expression: *salpisate salpingi,* "blow with trumpets." In Psalm 98:6, where the Hebrew text mentions both instruments together (*baḥaẓoẓerot v'ḳol shofar*), the SEPTUAGINT clearly distinguishes: *en salpinxin elatais, kai phōnē salpingos keratinēs,* "with silver trumpets, and with the sound of trumpets (made) of horn." The VULGATE puts *tuba* twenty-seven times, 2 Chron. 5:13 is mistranslated, and in Ps. 98:6 it paraphrases: *in tubis ductilibus, et voce tubae corneae.*

The Targumim use the Aramaic form *ḥaẓoẓarta,* the Peshiṭṭa has fifteen times *ḳarna,* "horn," the other places are either mistranslated or paraphrased.

English versions scarcely show any discrimination with regard to the two basically different instruments *ḥaẓoẓerah* and *shofar.* These are translated quite arbitrarily as "trump," "tromp," "trumpet," "bugle," "cornet," or "shawm,"[458] with the variants for 2 Chron. 13:12 of "trumpets of alarm" (*Moulton*), "bugles of alarm" (*Moffat*), and "battle trumpets" (*Revised Standard Version*). The *Jewish* and the *Revised Standard Versions* are the only ones which always render *ḥaẓoẓerah* correctly as "trumpet."

The double term in Ps. 98:6 *baḥaẓoẓerot v'ḳol shofar* is rendered by *Wycliffe* as "in trumpis betun out, and in vois of the hornene trumpe" (*early*), and "in trumpis betun out with hamer, and in vois of a trumpe of horn" (later), thus correctly distinguishing between the *ḥaẓoẓerah* made of metal and the *shofar* made of animal horn.

The *Douay Version* has "with long trumpets, and sound of cornet," *Moffat* "with bugle and with cornet," whereas the *Authorized Version* and *Harkavy* translate "with trumpets and sound of cornet." All these last-mentioned translations do not take into account that the trumpets, bugles and cornets are instruments of the same category, made of brass, their pairing being therefore wholly inappropriate for expressing the basic difference between the *ḥaẓoẓerot* and *shofarot.* Only the *Jewish* and *Revised Standard Versions* give a correct rendering of the dual expression by setting "with trumpets and the sound of horn."

20. SHOFAR

The *shofar* is the only instrument of Ancient Israel that survived the millennia in its original form and which is still used in the Jewish liturgy, although with greatly curtailed functions.

The Hebrews have taken over the *shofar* from the Assyrians. The word itself is derived from the Assyrian *shapparu,* "wild goat" (of the ibex family). More often, however, the Jewish *shofar* (plur. *shofarot*)[459] is made of a ram's horn; as in some other instances, the instrument received its name after the original material from which it was made.[460]

Another etymological interpretation of the word likewise uses the idea of the material: *shu* and *far* would refer respectively to what is "empty" and "hollow" in the neat, namely the horn. However, the ancient Hebrews have not recognized the ritual validity of *shofarot* made of neat's horn,[461] only those made of ram's horn and of the wild goat.

The original form of the *shofar* was a curved one like that of the natural ram's horn. Later, a special mechanic procedure would change the shape of the natural horn, thereby producing straight *shofarot* with a distinct bend only close to the bell. In the Second Temple both species, curved and straight, were used.

> "The *shofar* [blown in the Temple] at New Year [was made from the horn] of the wild goat, straight with its mouthpiece overlaid with gold. And at the sides [of them that blew the *shofar*] were two [that blew upon] *ḥaẓoẓerot*. The *shofar* blew a long note and the *ḥaẓoẓerot* a short note, since the duty of the day fell on the *shofar*.
>
> "[The *shofarot*] of days of fasting were ram's horns, rounded, with their mouthpieces overlaid with silver. And between them were two [that blew upon] *ḥaẓoẓerot.* The *shofar* blew a short note and the *ḥaẓoẓerot* a long note, since the duty of the day fell on the *ḥaẓoẓerot.*
>
> "The Year of the Jubilee is like the New Year in the blowing of the *shofar,* and in the Benedictions. R. Judah says: At the New Year they use ram's horns and at the Year of Jubilee wild goat's horns."[462]

After the destruction of the Temple by the Romans the embellishment of *shofarot* with gold and silver or with other showy ornaments was prohibited, and in its plain form the instrument still exists and functions.

Primitively, the Israelites connected the blowing of the *shofar* with magic and sorcery; similar customs prevail among practically all primitive peoples and at all periods.[463] At a later historical stage the blowing of the *shofar* on New Year's day was supposed to remind God symbolically of his promise given to Abraham, Isaac and Jacob. The blowing on other days was also in the nature of a symbolic action: the faithful should remember the ram sacrificed by Abraham instead of his son (Gen. 22:13).

After the burning of the sanctuary in Jerusalem, all music was prohibited as a sign of mourning. Only the blowing of the *shofar* was permitted, but this practice had now a messianic significance and was connected with the providential hope that at some future time the prophet Elijah will sound the "*shofar* of deliverance," thereby announcing the advent of the Messiah.

Medieval philosophers and mystics have attributed certain moralizing and occult meanings to the custom of blowing the *shofar.* SA'ADIA GAON (892-942 C.E.) invested the sound of the *shofar* with the faculty of raising awe and devotion in the heart and soul of people. Furthermore, the sounding of the *shofar* was supposed to remind man of his duties toward God. MAIMONIDES

(1135-1204) interprets the custom in a similar way.[464] He holds that blowing the *shofar* "has a deep meaning, as if saying:

> "Awake, awake, O sleepers, from your sleep; O slumberers, arouse ye from your slumber; and examine your deeds, return in repentance, and remember your Creator."[465]

The book of the medieval mystics, the Zohar, holds that "the sound of the *shofar* awakens the Higher Mercy."[466]

o
o o

The primitive *shofarot* were made by cutting off the tip of the natural horn, or boring a hole into it. The instrument made in this way had no mouthpiece and could produce only crude sustained tones. The *shofar* with a mouthpiece (*ḳos,* "cup") represents a more developed form of the instrument. But even in this improved form the *shofar* tones were limited usually to two in number (sometimes to three), these being the second, third and fourth partials, *i.e.* the octave, the upper fifth, and the second octave of the fundamental (c'-g'- c", for instance). It goes without saying that the *shofar* could not carry out any musical assignment in the artistic sense, and therefore was restricted to the simple function as a signal instrument.

That the ancient Israelites nevertheless might have attributed some elements of aesthetic pleasure to blowing the *shofar* is intimated by a talmudic passage. One of the eminent rabbis discusses the possibility of someone "playing [the *shofar*] for the sake of a song" (*ha-toke'a loshir*),[467] an indication that has only a slight probability, unless we assume that in the concept of the Jews the religious duty of sounding the instrument was connected at the same time with some artistic gratification.[468] In his commentary to this passage, Rashi mentions that he has heard from one of his teachers, R. Isaac ben Jehudah, another version of it: *ha-toke'a leshed* (with an exchange of the letters ר and ד). This would give the passage an entirely different meaning, *viz.*: "one who blows (or plays) to chase away the evil spirit (*shed*)." Such a magic interpretation of the text would naturally divest the playing of the *shofar* of any aesthetic implication. Rashi himself is inclined to retain the musical meaning and mentions the other version merely because it stems from a highly respected rabbinic authority. Whether *shir* or *shed,* however, it is hardly possible to attribute to the blowing of the *shofar* any higher artistic significance.

o
o o

More than for any other instrument, the rabbinic authorities have given precise instructions as to how to manufacture, repair, and use the *shofarot* and, especially, to establish beyond doubt their ritual validity. The Gemara says:[469]

> "If the horn was too long and it has been shortened, it is valid. If it has been scraped till it becomes thin like a wafer, it is valid. If it is overlaid at the spot where the mouth is applied, it is valid. If it is overlaid with gold on the inside, it is not valid, if on the outside, if the sound is thereby changed from what it was before, it is not

valid, but otherwise it is valid. If it had a hole which has been stopped up, if this interferes with the blast it is not valid, but otherwise it is valid. If one *shofar* is put inside of another *shofar,* if one can hear the sound of the inner one he thereby performs his religious duty, but if he hears the sound of the outer one he does not thereby perform his religious duty."

It is difficult to establish whether putting a *shofar* into another served merely

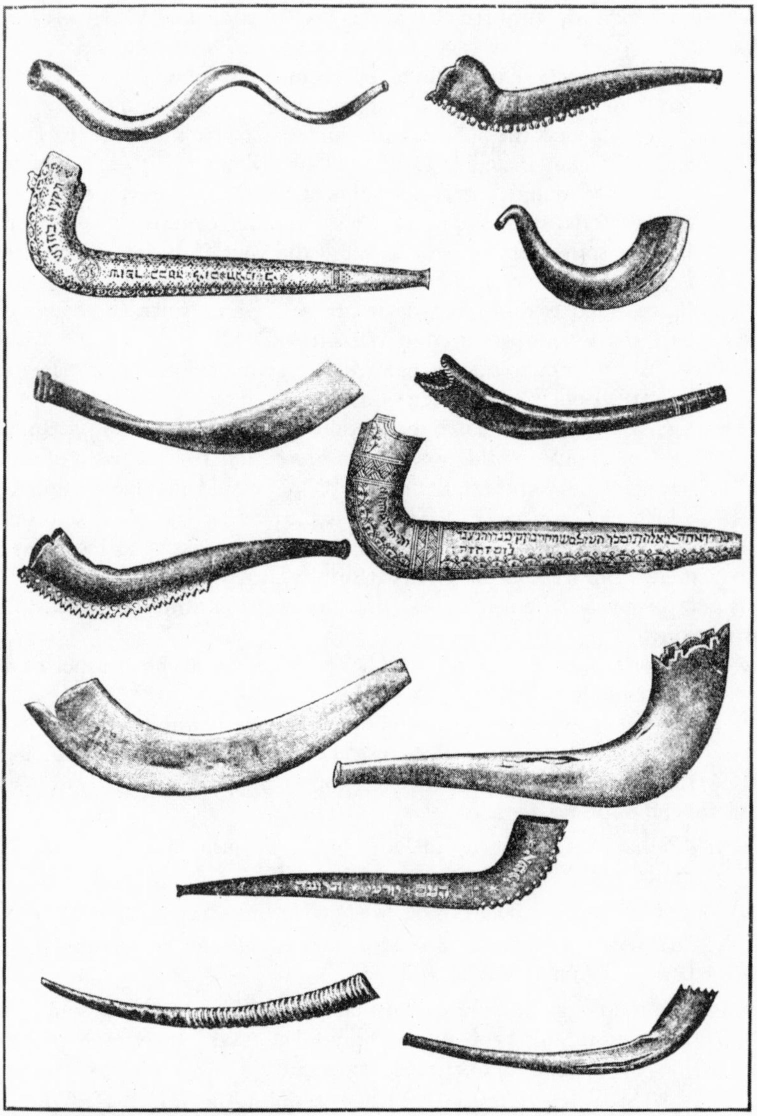

ILLUSTRATION NO. 42
Different shapes of the *shofar* (After Jewish Encyclopedia, vol. XI).

to increase the resonance of the instrument, or whether it had some connection with ancient magic customs.

There must have been all kinds of transformations applied to the natural horn. It could be scraped to make it smooth. Its curved form could be straightened. The bony portion of the skull, in which the horn was imbedded, could be chiseled out and left on the horn itself; by this, obviously, an increased resonance and a greater volume of sound was intended. Even damaged *shofarot,* if expertly repaired, could be used again. The Gemara further advises:[470]

> "If he turns it inside out [by means of softening it with hot water] and blows it, he does not thereby perform his religious duty . . . even if he widened the narrow part and narrowed the wide part. If there was a hole in it and it is stopped up, whether with his own material or another material, it is not valid. R. Nathan, however, says if with its own material it is valid, but if with another material it is not valid . . . If it is split lengthwise it is not valid, but if breadthwise, if enough is left to produce a blast it is valid, but otherwise it is not valid . . . If its sound is thin or thick or dry, it is valid, since all sounds emitted by a *shofar* can pass muster. [*i.e.* are valid]."
>
> "A *shofar* may not be painted over with colors, but ornaments may be carved on it, also inscriptions."[471]

The Gemara mentions some restrictions for sounding the instrument:[472]

> "One should not blow with a *shofar* taken from a burnt-offering . . . neither from a peace-offering . . . One should not blow with a *shofar* which has been used for idolatrous purposes . . . neither with one from a devoted city . . . One who is interdicted by vow to have any enjoyment from a *shofar* may yet perform with it the ritual blowing."

A certain musical element in blowing the *shofar* is implied by the following instruction:

> "If one blew the *shofar* simply to make music, he has performed his religious duty."[473]

The same idea is expressed also in another passage of the Gemara:

> "One who blows to make musical sounds [*i.e.* without religious intention] does hereby fulfill his religious obligation."

And the rabbinic scribe adds:

> "Perhaps our authority includes 'making music' also under the head of 'practising'."[474]

A rather obscure passage of the Mishnah refers to a peculiar ritual custom

> "to blow the *shofar* in a cistern or in a cellar or in a large jar [better: barrel] (Aram. *pithos*)."[475]

Even the chronologically close commentary of the Gemara betrays an ignorance about the true meaning of this custom. The sages therefore narrowed its application by certain sophisticated arguments:

> "This rule applies only to those standing on the edge of the pit, but those standing in the pit perform their religious duty thereby . . . If one blows into a pit or a cistern or a barrel, if he hears the sound of

the *shofar* [pure] he has performed his religious duty, but if he hears the echo he has not performed his religious duty."[476]

To all appearances the custom is a remnant of some primitive Hebrew ritual, connected with magic and sorcery, and will therefore be examined in a subsequent section.[477]

On religious occasions the *shofar* was blown only by priests and Levites, in secular events sometimes also on feast days by laymen, children, and in cases of emergency even by women. The Mishnah says:

> "Children need not be stopped from blowing; on the contrary, they may be helped till they learn how to blow."[478]

To which the Gemara adds:

> "This would imply that women are stopped. But it has been taught: Neither children nor women need to be stopped from blowing the *shofar* on the Festival."[479]

This last indication seems to restrict this rule to the most important religious feast of the year, the Festival of Tabernacles.

Since the *shofar* was frequently blown on other than ritual occasions, it is to be assumed that, contrary to the *shofarot* of the sacred service the mouthpieces of which were overlaid with gold and silver, the instruments used on secular occasions had their mouthpieces overlaid with base metal. Acocrding to Mishnaic views, all the *shofarot* of the sacred service were implicitly "clean," regardless of construction, whereas those in secular use were subjected to the regulations concerning cleanness.[480]

o
o o

Similar to the *ḥaẓoẓerot,* there were precise instructions for blowing the *shofar.* Their correct meaning, however, was not always interpreted in like manner. Originally, the sustained tone was called *mashaḥ* (Exod. 19:13; Josh. 6:5), and, inferentially, the short blast *teki'ah.* But the Mishnah interprets *teki'ah* as the sustained tone, and this meaning remained uncontested after the 3rd century.

About the manner of blowing *teru'ah,* the rabbinic opinions were divided for a long time; some claimed that it implies short (staccato-like) blasts; others maintained that the term refers to a sort of agitato (tremolo, vibrato) on a sustained tone. Finally, R. ABBAHU of CAESAREA in Palestine (4th century) has found a way out: he called the short staccato-blasts with alternating tones *shebarim,* and the tremolo on the same tone *teru'ah.* R. AWIRA and RABINA first dissented, but ABBAHU's regulation was eventually adopted,[481] and this meaning of the two terms prevails to this day.

o
o o

The rabbinic writings contain abundant information with regard to blowing the *shofar* on religious occasions.

The manner of sounding the instrument on various festival days, together with complementary *ḥaẓoẓerot*-blasts, was already mentioned above.

Here follow some other pertinent instructions in the rabbinic literature:

> "The whole day [New Year and Day of Atonement] is valid for

reading the Scroll, and for reciting the *Hallel* [Pss. 113-118], and for blowing the *shofar*."[482]

In order to prevent some infringements of the rabbinic law, it was stated explicitly that

"for the sake of a *shofar* for the New Year none may pass beyond the Sabbath limit [*i.e.* carrying a *shofar*], . . . nor may one cut it [in order to improve it]."[483]

Not quite comprehensible is the following regulation of the rabbinic authorities:

"If a festival day of the New Year fell on a Sabbath they might blow the *shofar* in the Holy City but not in the provinces."

This applied only for the time when the sanctuary in Jerusalem still existed, since the same Mishnaic passage says that

"after the Temple was destroyed Rabban JOḤANAN b. ZAKKAI ordained that they might blow it wheresover there was a court [*i.e.* a congregation]."[484]

The prohibition of blowing the *shofar* outside of Jerusalem was restricted, however, by the following ordinance:

"In this also Jerusalem surpassed Jabneh in that they could blow the *shofar* in any city that could see Jerusalem and they could hear [the *shofar* in Jerusalem] and that was near [within the Sabbath limit], and that was able to come [to Jerusalem]; but at Jabneh they could blow it only in the court."[485]

The ritual of blowing the *shofar* on New Year was strictly regulated in connection with other rites.

"As for the order of the Benedictions a man recites 'the Fathers', 'Power,' and 'the Hallowing of the Name,' and combines them with the Sovereignty verses [the *Malkuyot*]; but he does not then sound the *shofar;* [he then recites] 'the Hallowing of the Day,' and sounds the *shofar;* [he then recites] the Remembrance verses [the *Zikronot*] and sounds the *shofar;* [he then recites] the *Shofar* verses [the two benedictions spoken usually before sounding the *shofar* (Ps. 47)] and sounds the *shofar* . . . So R. Joḥanan b. Nuri."[486]

R. AKIBA's opinion, which is quoted subsequently by the Mishnah, differed in some details from that of R. JOḤANAN, especially after which parts of the ritual the *shofar* should be sounded.

In the order of *shofar*-blasts in the *Rosh ha-Shanah* service there were two different ways of blowing the *teki'ot*-series, one called *teki'ot di-meyushab* (sitting series), the other *teki'ot de-me'ummad* (standing series), the latter being sounded during the *'Amidah* (the standing prayers). With regard to the division of these series and their placing in the *'Amidah,* R. MAR-AMRAM ben SHESHNA, Gaon of Sura (869-881 C.E.), and compiler of the liturgy of the European Jews, instituted the following order: *teki'ah, shebarim, teru'ah* three times for *malkuyot; teki'ah, shebarim, teki'ah* three times for *zikronot;* and *teki'ah, teru'ah, teki'ah* three times for *shofarot.*

However, one of the Tosafists, Rabbenu JACOB TAM, introduced a new custom to the effect that *teki'ah, shebarim, teru'ah, teki'ah* should be sounded three times for either *malkuyot, zikronot* or *shofarot.*[487] The Sephardic and West-German Ashkenazic Jewry adopted the tradition established by R. AMRAM, while in the East-European countries the order of Rabbenu TAM prevailed.

o
o o

There is a significant talmudic discussion about the question why a series of *shofar*-blasts is sounded first sitting and then twice standing. The rabbis say: "It is to confuse the Accuser (in Hebrew 'Satan')."[488] The meaning of this statement is somewhat obscure, despite RASHI's commentary to the passage:

> "The devotion of the Jews to the precepts nullifies Satan's accusations against them."

In the rabbinic thinking the second and third series of *shofar*-blasts were intended to bewilder and stagger Satan who, considering the first series as a mere compliance with the Law, is surprised by the second series, assuming that it announces the advent of the Messiah. Listening to the third series, Satan becomes afraid that the Resurrection is going to take place, with which his power over the Jews will cease. Thus, it is obvious that the repeated series of *shofar*-blasts were caused originally by the superstitious belief that the sound of the *shofar* has the power of bewildering and chasing away evil spirits, in this instance the Accuser.[489]

On *Rosh ha-Shanah* the *shofar* was originally blown in the early part (*Shaḥarit*) of the morning service, but subsequently was transferred to a later hour in the *Musaf* portion.[490] The reason for this was a tragic occurrence, related in the Talmud. It seems that the Jewish *shofar*-blasts resembled the military signals of the Roman army stationed in Palestine. As a result, the Roman authorities once suspected that the Jews were preparing an attack on them and that the *shofar*-blasts served to call the men together. So, in order to prevent an armed revolt, troops were unexpectedly dispatched in the early morning to the synagogues, where a real carnage was committed among the worshipping Jews, before even an explanation could be given. Therefore, in succeeding years the *shofar*-blasts were omitted in the *Shaḥarit* and deferred to the *Musaf* where it was obvious that they served merely for ritual use.[491] In his commentary to this passage RASHI adds:

> "The Romans issued an ordinance that the *shofar* should not be blown at all, and in order to enforce this prohibition, they sent out spies every six hours."

It seems, however, that the Jewish religious leaders gradually succeeded to persuade the occupation authorities that the *shofar*-blasts had merely a ritual significance, because in subsequent years it was again allowed to sound the *shofar* in the *Shaḥarit*. But even after the original order was eventually restored, the sounding of the *shofar* in the *Musaf* was retained as a supplement to the early morning blowing.

The question regarding the rules as applied on days of fasting is answered by the Sages:

"On these days they blow the *shofar* and close the shops."[492]

After involved religious ceremonies and prayers on such days, they recited twenty-four Benedictions, namely the "Eighteen" of daily use, adding to them six more: "the Remembrance and the *Shofar* verses."

On the rite of the Willow-branch, that is in preparing the Feast of Tabernacles, a procession went to the place below Jerusalem called *Moẓa;* there

> "they cut themselves young willow-branches. They came and set these up at the sides of the Altar so that their tops were bent over the Altar. They then blew [on the *shofar*] a sustained, a quavering, and another sustained blast."[493]

At the ceremony of the Water-libation

> "they used to fill a golden jar holding three *logs* with water from Siloam. When they reached the Water Gate they blew [on the *shofar*] a sustained, a quavering and another sustained blast."[499]

For the *Habdalah*-ceremony, marking the end of a Sabbath or Festival day and the entering in of an ordinary day, there were likewise specific regulations with regard to blowing the *shofar*:

> "Whenever the *shofar* is blown no *Habdalah* prayer is recited; and where the *Habdalah* prayer is recited no *shofar* is blown. Thus, if a Festival day falls on a Friday the *shofar* is blown and the *Habdalah* prayer is recited; but if on the day after the Sabbath, the *Habdalah* prayer is recited and no *shofar* is blown."[495]

Like for the *ḥaẓoẓerot,* the daily number of blasts on the *shofarot* was also strictly regulated:

> "Never less than twenty-one, and never more than forty-eight."[496]

This ordinance had its increased importance after the destruction of the Temple by the Romans when the *ḥaẓoẓerot* as sacred instrument ceased to be used in the divine service, and their functions had to be taken over by the *shofar,* the only trumpet-like instrument ever used in the Synagogue.

However, this regulation of the *shofar*-blasts engendered all kinds of interpretations, owing to the fact that some rabbis, poorly versed in musical matters, considered the group of *teki'ah, teru'ah, teki'ah* as *one* sound, others holding that each blast represents a *separate* sound. The Gemara, commenting on Mishnah, *'Arakin* II:3, states, for instance:

> "R. Judah said: One who sounds a smaller number of blasts may not sound less than seven [*i.e.* three times seven], and one who sounds a larger number must not exceed sixteen [*i.e.* three times sixteen]. . . . R. Judah says: *teki'ah, teru'ah, teki'ah* constitutes one sound [and consequently are to be sounded without a break between them], whereas the Sages hold: *teki'ah* is a separate sound, so is *teru'ah,* and so the [second] *teki'ah* [and consequently are to be separated from each other by a small pause]."[497]

The Mishnah contains rather detailed indications as to the relative metric value of these *shofar*-blasts. Commenting upon these indications the Gemara establishes the relationship of the duration of the various *shofar*-calls in the following way:

> "The length of the *teki'ah* is equal to three *teru'ahs* . . . The length

of the *teru'ah* is equal to the length of three *yebabot* . . . But it has been taught, 'The length of the *teru'ah* is equal to three *shebarim* [lit. 'breakings']."[498]

But this regulation, too, was sometimes differently interpreted, as evidenced by the same Mishnaic passage:

"If a man blew the first blast, then prolonged the second blast equal to two, that is reckoned to him only as one blast."[499]

ILLUSTRATION NO. 43
Probably the oldest known *shofar*-calls, in a Hebrew manuscript of the 13. century, the *Codex Adler* (in the Jewish Theological Seminary of America, New York, cat. No. 932).

In this Mishnaic passage the Aramaic word for *teru'ah,* "alarm blast," is *yebabah* (plur. *yebabot*). Targum Onkelos to Lev. 23:24 uses this word as translation for *teru'ah.* The Gemara is uncertain whether this term means an outcry (*yelalah*), or a moaning sound (*genihah*). The former was supposed to be composed of three connected short sounds; the latter, of nine very short notes divided into three disconnected or broken sounds (*shebarim*).[500]

To-day's synagogue service uses four different kinds of sounding the *shofar*:

teki'ah ("blast"), a relatively short pick-up note on the tonic, leading to a sustained note on the fifth and ending, on some *shofarot,* with the higher octave of the tonic;

shebarim ("breaks"), alternating rapidly the tonic and fifth, ending with a sustained note on the fifth;

teru'ah ("din"), a rapid staccato-like repetition of the short notes on the tonic, ending with a long note on the fifth;

teki'ah gedolah ("great blast"), basically identical with the *teki'ah,* but using longer note values, and ending with a long sustained note on the fifth or, on some *shofarot,* on the higher octave.

As in the case of the *ta'amim* (accents) of the Jewish cantillation, the medieval *soferim* established a neume-like notation for the *shofar*-calls. Probably the oldest known signs for *shofar* tones are contained in a Hebrew manuscript of the 13th century, the *Codex Adler,* in the Library of the Jewish Theological Seminary in New York (No. 932, fol. 21 b). Other medieval notations of *shofar* tones may be found in a late 14th century manuscript, the *Codex Shem,* No. 74 (in the Parma Library), and in Juan de Gara's *Mahzor* (publ. in Venice, 1587, p. 190).

The Parma notation, called in the *Codex Shem "Simani Noti,"* is reproduced in Solomon Sulzer, *Shir Zion* (Vienna, 1838, 1865), vol. II, p. 257. It is identical with the notation of the *Codex Adler.*

This is how the three types of *shofar*-calls, to be read from right to left, appear in these manuscripts:

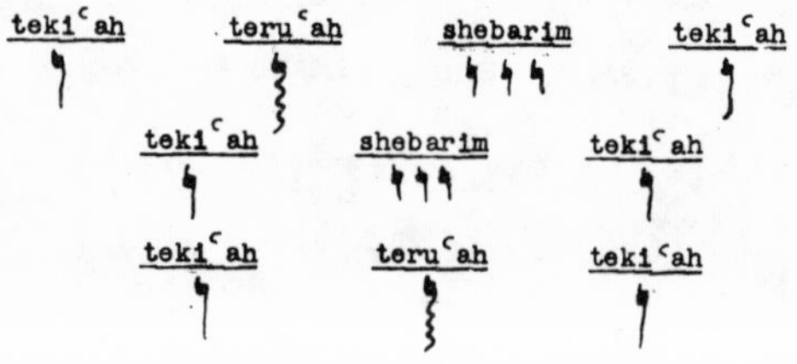

The *shofar* used in to-day's Jewish ritual is normally a straight tube, about fourteen to fifteen inches in length, with the widened bell bent slightly side-wise. Since its interior is rather rough and the instrument is blown mostly through a mouthpiece of irregular shape, its pitch is highly variable and not always distinct. The *shofarot* vary also as to the number of their available harmonics. Some can produce only two, possibly three, and rarely four sounds of their respective natural series.

Here are in musical notations the basic patterns of *shofar*-calls as heard in the modern synagogues which, however, show many variants according to the origin and background of the *baʿale tokeʿah,* as the *shofar*-players are called.

SHOFAR-CALLS

Example 9. *ASHKENAZIM* after Francis Lyon Cohen (in *JE,* XI, p. 306)

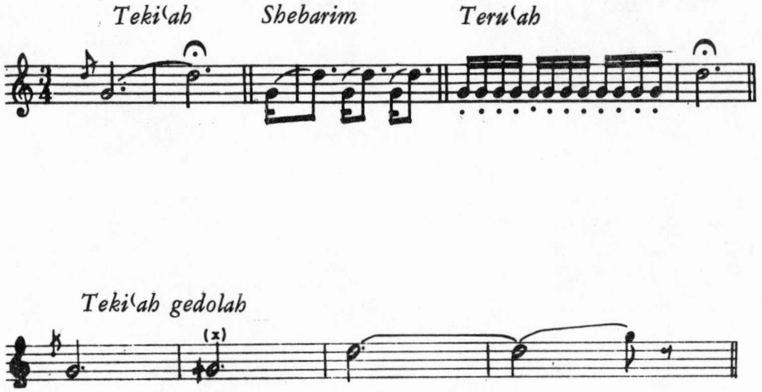

(x) This note is quite irregular and could have been produced only as a distortion of the tonic by means of some extra lip pressure. It is a foreign note in the natural series of harmonics and certainly not typical for *shofar* tones. F. L. Cohen must have heard it played by some local performer on a particular instrument, and should not have quoted it among traditional *shofar*-calls.

Example 10. *SEPHARDIM* after Francis Lyon Cohen (*ibid.*)

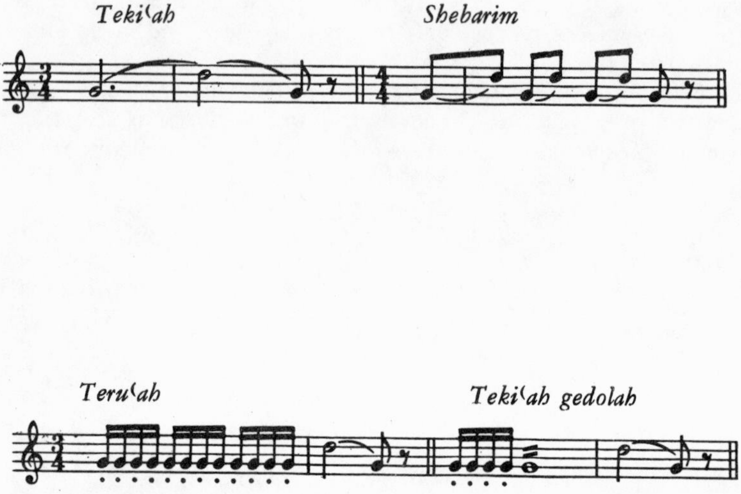

In this example there is no difference between *teruʿah* and *tekiʿah gedolah,* except for more staccato notes on the tonic of the latter. Sephardic *baʿale tokeʿah* doubt the authenticity of this call, since the *tekiʿah gedolah* is supposed to be a prolongated *tekiʿah.*

Example 11.

SEPHARDIM

As heard on an ancient *shofar* without mouthpiece, blown by a *baʿal tokeʿah* from Israel. The fundamental tone of this instrument was

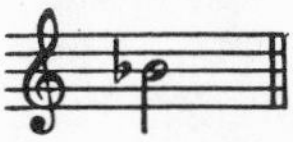

and the following example was transposed a minor third down.

Example 12.

after Solomon Sulzer, *Schir Zion* (Vienna, 1938, 1865), vol. II, p. 257.

The Parma notation of *shofar*-calls is interpreted by Sulzer in the following way:

While explaining this notation, Sulzer says that the ancient *Quilisma*-sign ⦚ represents in reality a *trill,* not a rapid tone-repetition, as used generally. In his compositions for the *shofar* ceremony, Sulzer notates the *shofar*-calls according to this interpretation.

Example 13. after Abraham Beer, *Baal Tefillah* (Gothenburg, 1877), p. 254.

Ex. 13 cont.

Second Version

Example 14. after E. J. Stark, *Shofar*-Service (San Francisco, 1905), pp. 6 ff.

The *shofar*-calls of Stark's Service are written for a *trombone.* In Stark's notation these calls sound an octave lower than quoted above:

Example 15.

LITHUANIAN VERSION

as heard in the Fairfax Synagogue at Los Angeles, on a centuries old *shofar,* blown by a former choir singer and *baʿal tokeʿah* of the Great Synagogue at Vilna. The fundamental tone of this instrument was:

the following example was transposed a minor third up.

This example is acoustically enigmatic. The three initial notes might be explained as harmonics 4-6-9. Or else the uppermost note may be due to an unusual shape of the instrument (see Kirby's statement on p. 337). However, the outward appearance of the instrument did not reveal any particularity accounting for the uppermost note.

Example 16.

In Appendix V. to Stainer's "The Music of the Bible" (London, 1914, p. 225), F. W. Galpin gives the following *shofar*-calls, which he "copied down from those sounded by the *shofar*-player in the London Western Synagogue." The persistent fourth throughout, without any other interval, is certainly unusual.

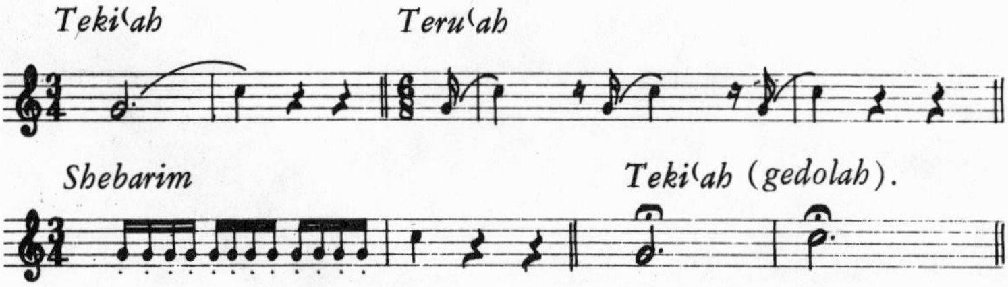

Example 17.

For the sake of curiosity, we add a strange type of *shofar*-calls, as used in Edward Elgar's oratorio "The Apostles" (pp. 19-20). They are rhythmically the same as the ordinary *tekiʿah, shebarim* and *teruʿah* blasts, but the interval is consistently a major sixth, quite unusual on regular *shofarot*. It must be assumed, however, that the composer has heard this *shofar*-call played somewhere.

The Yemenite Jews have huge *shofarot,* sometimes a yard long, straight or twisted. Their calls are basically identical with those of the Ashkenazim.

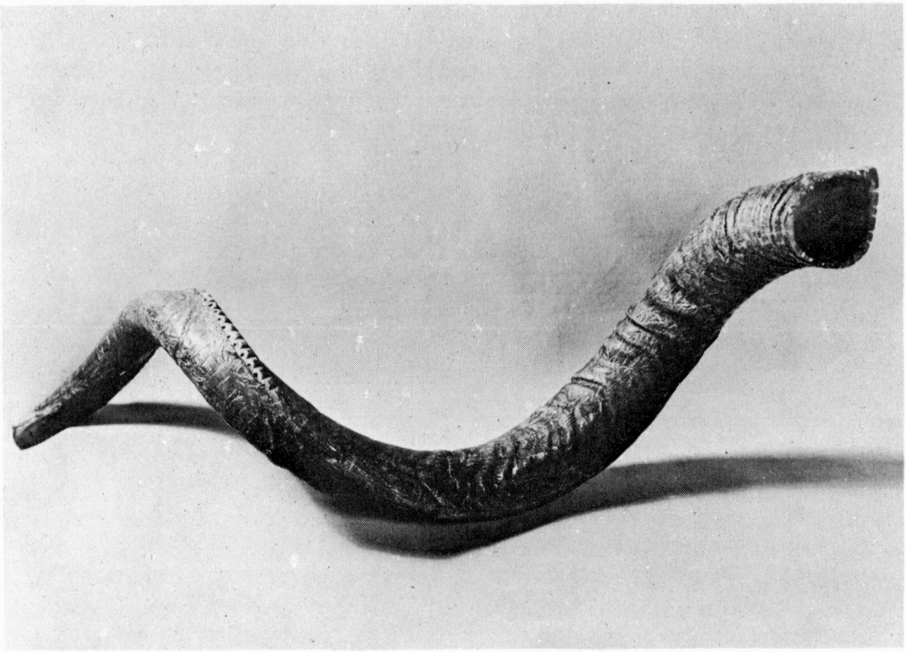

ILLUSTRATION No. 44
Yemenite *shofar,* richly carved with quotations from the Bible, about 54 inches long, 4 inches wide. (Courtesy of the Mount Sinai Memorial Park, Los Angeles, Calif.)

Of all the Israelitic instruments the *shofar* is mentioned most frequently in the Bible (seventy-two times), thus indicating its paramount importance in the religious as well as in the secular life of the Jewish people.[501]

The religious use of the *shofar* is attested by the following biblical occurrences: transfer of the ark of the covenant by David (2 Sam. 6:15; 1 Chron. 15:28); renewal of the covenant by King Asa (2 Chron. 15:14); announcement of the new Moon (Ps. 81:4); thanksgiving to God for His miraculous deeds (Pss. 98:6; 150:3).

Among secular festivities, at which the *shofar* was sounded, the following events may be mentioned: Absalom's accession to the throne (2 Sam. 15:10); Solomon's ointment as king (1 Kings 1:34); Jehu's accession to the crown (2 Kings 9:13)·

In times of war the *shofar* was the regular signal instrument, for assembling the warriors, attacking the enemy, pursuing the vanquished, or announcing the victory. The role played by the *shofar* in wars is evident from the following biblical narrations: Ehud's fight against the Moabites (Judg. 3:27); Gideon's war against the Midianites, on which occasion, as we are told, three hundred warriors have blown the *shofar* (Judg. 6:34; 7:22 ff); Saul's combat against the Philistines (1 Sam. 13:3); Joab's fight against Abner (2 Sam. 2:28); Sheba's revolt (2 Sam. 20:1); warning of impending war (Jer. 4:5; 4:21; 6:1; 6:17; Ezek. 33:3-6); rallying the nation to combat(Jer. 51:27); recounting the terrors of war (Jer. 4:19,21); a horse scenting war at the call of the *shofar* (Job. 39:24,25); announcing the end of combat (2 Sam. 18:16; 20:22); silence of the *shofar* implying peace, not disturbed by any anxiety of war or hunger of bread (Jer. 42:14).

The well-known episode of the siege of Jericho (Josh. 6), in which the *shofarot* played a decisive role, is left out in the present synopsis, since these "trumpets" belonged to a different category of instruments, as will be shown in the following chapter.

Other biblical occurrences that include references to the use of *shofarot* are: the warning sound of the horn upon the return of the Israelites from the Babylonian exile, and their erection of the new Jerusalem walls (Neh. 4:12); the *shofar*-call preparing the people for the coming Day of Judgment (Joel 2:1,15; Ezek. 7:14); the prophets' frequent use of the *shofar*-sound as a musical symbol for the expected horrors on that momentous occasion (Isa. 18:3; 27:13; 58:1; Hos. 5:8; 8:1; Zeph. 1:16); blowing the *shofar* as harbinger of destruction and despair (Am. 2:2); announcing the return of the repentant people by blowing the horn (Jer. 4:5); increasingly loud *shofar*-blasts on the Sinai keeping the people away from the mountain, upon which God communicates with Moses (Exod. 19:16,19; 20:15); description of God as a glorious warrior who, by blowing the *shofar,* will reveal Himself in His whole majesty to the people (Zech. 9:14).

The secular use of the *shofar* demonstrates its two basic groups of practical functions, one of those being connected with ancient magic customs, which have survived incognizantly with the people, and the other symbolizing fateful and heroic events of tragic nature, such as wars, national disasters, but also some important political events.

In post-biblical times the use of the *shofar* has been even more diverse. To begin with, *shofar*-blasts, together with trumpet-blasts, kept on announcing the approach of the Sabbath.[502] Besides the *ḥalil,* the *shofar* was used at funerals. According to ancient Jewish conception,

> "at the death of a person, spirits and demons are supposed to be present. Either they wish to get back into the body, or to take the body with them as a prey."[503]

The sound of the *shofar* was invested with the magic power to frighten off the evil spirits. The Talmud mentions even a specific kind of *shofar,* the *shipura deshikta,* "funerary bugle."[504] However, the Sages do not reveal whether this kind of instrument was a changed form of the biblical *shofar,* and what were its characteristics.

Furthermore, the *shofar* was used at procedures of excommunication. The blowing announced the anathema or its abrogation. A talmudic passage states:

> "A toot [the blowing of the *shofar* at banning] binds and a toot releases."[505]

The faculty of preventing nature catastrophes was also attributed to the *shofar.*[506] This again is connected with the belief in magic and sorcery, but in the long run their original meaning was lost and survived only subconsciously in the minds of the Israelites.

The blowing of the *shofar* at droughts, disasters and natural catastrophes had a partly religious, partly secular significance, besides its original meaning, as stated above. On such occasions the rabbis ordered special fast days; the ordinances issued by them contain detailed instructions as to the use of the *shofar.*[507]

Finally, the Talmud refers to a peculiar custom, also partly religious and partly secular. It was usual to hold public prayers with blowing the *shofar* in times of impending economic calamity, such as the decline in trade or decrease of money's buying power. Thus, we read that

> "linen garments in Babylon and wine and oil in Palestine have become so cheap that ten are sold [at the price of] six."[508]

This amounted to a drop of forty percent of the commercial values which, even in a relatively primitive economy affected both the public affairs and the interests of the individual producers. Public prayers were, therefore, in order, and the part the *shofar* played in these manifestations was akin to that of the magic *shofar*-calls: to draw the attention of the deity to the sacred ceremony, or the worshippers, or both.

Toward the end of Israel's national existence a latent struggle developed between priestly and secular forces with regard to the elimination of the *ḥaẓoẓerot* in the sacred service in favor of the *shofar.*[509] This struggle was automatically decided with the destruction of the Temple by the Romans. Since the *ḥaẓoẓerah* was the instrument associated with the ceremonies of the daily sacrifices, permissible only in the Jerusalem sanctuary, their complete cessation has also terminated the use of the *ḥaẓoẓerot.* The *shofar,* on the other hand, continued to perform its normal functions as heretofore, that is, to announce the New Year, to carry out certain rites on the Day of Atonement, to usher in the New Moon, to introduce the Sabbath. In addition, it took over all the functions fulfilled by the *ḥaẓoẓerot* outside the sanctuary. Thus the *shofar* became, and remained, to this day the only ancient musical instrument in the Jewish sacred ritual.

o
o o

And now one may ask how did it actually come about that of all Jewish instruments used in the sacred service the *shofar* alone has survived. During all the biblical centuries, and often under the most adverse circumstances, the Jews have maintained not only their religious institutions, but also their musical tradition, including the actual music practice. The period of the Babylonian exile may serve as the most striking case in point. Would it then not be rather expectable that after the annihilation of their national existence in the year 70 C.E., the Jews should have also succeeded in preserving their musical culture in the dispersion? Not merely their songs, but also their instrumental music has been an integral part of their religious institutions. If it was possible to keep alive the musical tradition in the Babylonian captivity, why was this not possible in the Diaspora?

First, it must be remembered that, as a sign of mourning for the lost sanctuary, the rabbinic authorities abolished "loud singing," meaning the public practice of music. Despite this prohibition, the private practice of secular music would probably still have been preserved under average conditions, since love of music was too deeply ingrained in the Jewish soul to be easily extinguished. However, a pernicious combination of factors has brought about a situation which not even the strictest rabbinic measures would have achieved.

To understand the intrinsic reasons for this, it suffices to cast a glance at the specific difference between the situation in the Captivity and the Diaspora.

In the Babylonian exile, despite all oppression, the Jews lived as a compact religious and cultural group; they were able, therefore, to preserve at least their spiritual life intact; despite all the hardships of their precarious existence, they were never menaced with the extinction of their religion.

Subsequently, they gained gradually more freedom to pursue their civic activities; their human dignity was restored; their religious institutions (with the exception of the sacrifice) were re-established. Their musical practice, too, did not suffer any radical changes. Thus, their music survived the captivity almost intact.

Following their defeat by the Romans, the Jews were dispersed all over the known part of the globe, mostly in small, incoherent groups, a circumstance that does not usually favor a homogeneous musical culture. Not only were they social outcasts living mostly under economic duress, but their religious institutions were menaced by an unprecedented sectarian factionalism, and mainly by the rising Christianity. To be sure, immediately after the downfall of the Jewish national state, JOḤANAN ben ZAKKAI and his adepts united their efforts to create in Jabneh a central institution for the preservation and continuation of Jewish life under the changed circumstances. Their aim was no less than to supplant for the lost Jewish state a sort of supra-national leadership by creating a supreme authority with the purpose of concentrating all Jewish energies toward one goal: religious and spiritual survival, with the exclusion of all social implications that did not serve directly their higher end. To what extent they succeeded, is evidenced by the subsequent destiny of Jewry, showing to the world the complete religious unity of a people, torn nationally to shreds, but unbroken in spirit.

History shows us also where Jabneh failed: in the preservation of the ancient musical heritage of the Jewish people. We understand, of course, that the solicitude of the new spiritual leaders of Judaism was focussed on a great many and—in their opinion—much more important elements of Jewish life than music, despite all the love the Jews showed for their tonal art during all the centuries of their independent national life.

The odds were simply against those, among the dispersed Jews, who might have succeeded in saving their beloved instruments,—*kinnor, nebel, ḥalil*— and taking these along with them into the exile. Soon, the fragile instruments must have largely deteriorated, the strings broken, and the reed-mouthpieces worn out. Cracks, splits and other damages of the wooden parts could no longer be repaired. Making of instruments, a needless handicraft, has disappeared, for who would indeed have asked for musical instruments in the misery and abasement of the Diaspora.

The same was true of music instruction, both religious and secular, once a flourishing profession in Ancient Israel. When "loud singing" was abolished, the urge for instrumental music making decreased more and more. Even the Jews' normally strong longing for musical activity could not remedy the situation. The *kle shir,* the instruments which accompanied the singing in the Temple and in secular life, could no longer be used, and so the necessity of learning and teaching them became extinct. The knowledge of their technique waned more and more until eventually it fell into complete oblivion. And this, in turn has still further aggravated the decline of the entire culture of practical music.

What has remained was solely a rather primitive instrument of religious import, easy to make from the horn of certain domestic animals, and which could be handled by anybody without much study. Furthermore, there remained in the subconscious of the Jews certain residues of ancient magic and sorcery, long connected with the use of the *shofar,* and which in the national tragedy were felt even more keenly. To this was added the messianic significance attributed in the Diaspora to the *shofar.* Thus it came about that from all the biblical instruments the *shofar* alone has survived.

o
o o

The ancient as well as new translations are just as arbitrary with regard to the rendition of this word as of the *ḥaẓoẓerah.* Thus, the SEPTUAGINT translates *shofar* forty-two times as *salpinx* (the term for the trumpet), once omits the word, and in 1 Chron. 15:28 takes it over phonetically as *sōpher.* In Josh. 6:8 *v'taḳe'u bashofarot* is rendered as *kai sēmainetōsan eutonōs* ("and blow a long blast"); in Josh. 6:9 *taḳe'u ha-shofarot* is omitted; and in Hos.

8:1 the original half-verse, which contains *'al ḥikkaḥo shofar,* is missing altogether in the SEPTUAGINT.

The VULGATE translates thirty-eight times as *buccina,* twenty-nine times as *tuba,* both being terms for the trumpet. In Ps. 98:6, where *ḥaẓoẓerot* and *shofar* are mentioned together, *shofar* is paraphrased as *tuba cornea.* Four times the word is omitted. Most of the other Latin versions follow the VULGATE.

The Targum uses sixty-three times *shofara,* three times *ḳarna,* and once omits the word. The Peshiṭṭa translates now *ḳarna,* and now *shifura* (or *shipura*).

Inasmuch as even the early translators, who were close to biblical times, confound frequently the *shofar* with the *ḥaẓoẓerah,* it is not surprising to find the same inconsistencies in the rabbinic literature. It is said, for instance: "*haẓoẓerot ha-teru'ah* ('alarm trumpets') are *shofarot.*"[510] The complete confusion of the two instruments, so different in many respects, has been mentioned in the preceding chapter (p. 341)

In the English translations, too, the rendition of *shofar* is unreasonably arbitrary. *Wycliffe* uses "trumpe" (early) and "clarioun" (later), *Douay* "trumpet." The *Authorized Version* renders mostly "trumpet," sometimes "trumpet of rams' horn" (in Josh. 6). The *American* and *Revised Standard Versions,* also *Moulton,* use "trumpet," "loud trumpet," and "rams' horn," whereas *Moffat* mingles indiscriminately "rams' horns," "trumpets," "loud trumpet blast," "bugles," "trumpets and rams' horns," "rams' horns as trumpets," "blast," "sound the alarm," etc. *Harkavy's* translation is also quite inconsistent; he uses mostly "trumpet," sometimes "sounding trumpet" (Lev. 25:9), and "trumpets of rams' horns" (Josh. 6). The most logical rendition is that of the *Jewish Version,* which always sets "rams' horn" for *shofar,* and "the voice of the horn" for *ḳol shofar.* But even this version, while following so conscientiously the Masoretic text, misses a correct translation for *ḳeren ha-yobel* and *shofar ha-yobel* (Josh. 6:5,6), for which it uses the same term as for *shofar.* (See subsequent chapters).

Shofar teru'ah is rendered as "trumpet," "loud trumpet," "loud trumpet-blast" (*Moffat*), and "the blast of horns" (*Jewish Version*). *Yom teru'ah* (Lev. 23:24; Num. 29:1) is paraphrased by all English versions (the translations are given above).

After all such discrepancies, it is not surprising to find in the above mentioned musicological work the *shofar* termed "the second species of trumpets."[511]

21. KEREN

The literal meaning of the word *ḳeren* is "firm," "solid," originating from the verb *ḳeren,* "to be firm." It refers to the hard horn of the neat in contrast to the soft flesh of this bovine cattle. Thus, logically the meaning of the word was transferred to the name of the instrument made from neat's horn.

Besides, *ḳeren* is used in the biblical text in more than one extra-musical sense. In Gen. 22:13 the word appears in its original meaning as "horn" of an animal, in this case of a ram:

"Abraham . . . behold behind him a ram caught in the thicket by his horns."

In Lev. 4:7,18,25 *ḳeren* also stands for the "horn" of an animal, this time probably that of a steer, used as an adornment of the four corners of the altar. Apart from aesthetic considerations, the attachment of animal's horns to the altar may have served as a symbol for power, force, and light, as expressed by Jeremiah (48:25), Habakkuk (3:4), and in Ps. 89:18. In 1 Sam. 16:1 and 1 Kings 1:39 *ḳeren* indicates a vessel made from the horn of a steer to hold the oil for the anointment of the king. In Jer. 48:25 and in Ps. 89:18 *ḳeren* stands symbolically for power and dignity,[512] whereas in Ps. 75:5,6 "to lift up the horn" means, figuratively, "to become arrogant and insolent. In the sense of something exalted, *ḳeren* in Isa. 5:1 means the summit of a mountain, and in Hab. 3:4 it symbolizes the majestic rays of the sun and the light. All these meanings are based upon the notion of being "firm," "robust," and "powerful." (Illustr. 45, 46).

The implication of *ḳeren* as an instrument made from animal horn, and one being "powerful," *i.e.* "loud," is thus self-evident. Nevertheless, its translation was handled from the very beginning with little or no care at all. It was mostly considered a synonym of *shofar* despite the obvious etymological difference between the two words and, consequently, the ancient as well as

ILLUSTRATION NO. 45
"Moses." Sculpture by Claus Sluter (d. 1406). Museum, Dijon.

ILLUSTRATION NO. 46
"Moses." Scultpure by Michelangelo (1513-16). the church San Piero di Vincoli, Rome.

the modern translators confound almost constantly both instruments. In the Greek versions *shofar* and *ḳeren* are indiscriminately translated as *keratinē* (from *keras,* "horn") or *salpinx,* in the Latin versions as *tuba* and *buccina,* the same words as used for the *ḥaẓoẓerah.* Many translations do not even make any distinction between the *ḥaẓoẓerah* made of metal, and instruments made from animal horn—*shofar, ḳeren,* and *yobel* (see the following chapter).

JEROME tries to remove the confusion created by the indiscriminate translations of the first Bible versions, by describing the two instruments more precisely:

> "*Buccina pastoralis est, et cornu recurvo efficitur, unde et proprie hebraice* shofar, *graece* keratinē *appellatur. Tuba autem de aere conficitur vel argento, quae in bellis et solemnitatibus concrepabant.*"
>
> ("The *buccina* is the instrument of the shepherds, made from curved horn, therefore it is called in Hebrew *shofar,* in Greek *keratinē.* The *tuba,* however, is made of brass or silver, and its resounding tone is used in wars and festivities.")[513]

Yet, JEROME does not distinguish between the various species of the animal horn, so that he also does not clear up completely the existing doubts.

It is surprising that the differences between the varieties of horns are not sufficiently understood, since the rabbinic literature contains both direct and indirect references to their true nature. The Mishnah states, for instance:

> "All *shofarot* are valid, except neat horns, because they are [properly] called *ḳeren.*"[514]

And the Gemara confirms:

> "All *shofarot* are called both *shofar* and *ḳeren,* whereas neat horns are called *ḳeren* but are not called *shofar.*"[515]

Two further passages of the rabbinic scribes try to determine indirectly the various species of horns. The Mishnah says:

> "The Year of the Jubilee is like the New Year in the blowing of the *shofar* and in the Benedictions. R. Judah says: 'At the New Year they use rams' horns and at the Year of Jubilee wild goats' horns'."[516]

Apart from the differences in material, the differences in form are taken into consideration by the rabbinic prescriptions for cleanness:

> "A curved horn (*ḳeren*) is susceptible to uncleanness whereas a straight one is unsusceptible, but if its mouthpiece is of metal it is susceptible. Its wide [metal] end [bell] R. Tarfon declares susceptible, but the Sages declare it unsusceptible. When they are joined together the whole is susceptible."[517]

It is rather puzzling why the straight horn should be clean and the curved horn unclean. The explanation may be learned from an analogy with other objects, as treated in the Mishnaic tractate *Kelim* ("Vessels"). Objects made of wood and other non-metallic materials (here of animal horn) are considered "clean"; whenever such objects have metal parts or ornaments, they are subject to the stipulations of "uncleanness."[518]

The same passage states furthermore that there existed certain types of horns, put together (*hirḳib*) of several pieces. These pieces could be either of horn or metal, so that the same instrument could have parts of both materials, like for instance mouthpieces and bells of metal on a body of fibrous horn. Moreover, the rabbinic writer says that if the body of the instrument fell apart, it could again be put together (*heḥzir*). The manufacturing of the curved horn (*ḳeren ʿagulah*) required a higher skill of craftsmanship than that of the straight horn (*ḳeren peshuṭah*).[519]

Similar to the *shofar,* the *ḳeren* served as a signal instrument; it was made exclusively of neat horn and apparently had no metal parts whatsoever.[520] Since the biblical text never connects the word *ḳeren* with the sacred service, it may be safely assumed that it was exclusively a secular instrument.

On one occasion the Midrash mentions the *ḳeren* together with the trumpets of the Romans and Greeks.[521] The rabbinic scribes use the names of these trumpets phonetically adapted to the Aramaean language as *buḳinus* and *salpirgasi,*[522] they refer, of course to the *buccina* and *salpinx.*

Since the word *ḳeren* is generally considered to be synonymous with *shofar,* the English versions do not make any distinction between the two and translate indiscriminately "trumpe," "trumpet," "clarioun," "horn," "rams' horn," and "bugle."

The majority of the English translations render the Aramaic *ḳarna* as "horn," *Wycliffe* and *Douay* as "trumpe" and "trumpet," respectively, and the *American Version* as "cornet."

22. YOBEL

The term *yobel,* alone and together with *shanat,* as *Shanat ha-yobel,* appears in Lev. 25:9-54 for the first time in the Bible. There, is signifies the termination of forty-nine years, that is of seven Sabbatical years. The fiftieth year was called *Shanat ha-yobel,* the Year of the Jubilee, the holy year, in which all inhabitants of the country had to be freed and all property restored to the original proprietor.

The Year of the Jubilee was announced with the blowing of the *shofar teruʿah* (Lev. 25:9), translated "the blast of the horn" by the *Jewish Version,* "sounding trumpet" by the *Authorized Version, Douay* and *Harkavy,* "loud trumpet" by the *American* and *Revised Standard Versions* and *Moulton,* "loud trumpet blast" by *Moffat.* On the first day of the seventh month, *i.e.* on the Day of Atonement, the Year of the Jubilee was ushered in with blasts of horns in the whole country. (Num. 29:1).

The Hebrew word *yobel,* which in Lev. 25:12, 13, 28 indicates the Year of the Jubilee, is used elsewhere to designate, jointly with the terms *mashaḥ* and *ḳeren,* a sustained blast of the horn (Josh. 6:5); it is therefore obvious that the year was associated with the specific manner of its announcement. For the same reason, the first day of the seventh month was called *yom teruʿah,* (Num. 29:1) paraphrased by all English versions in a more or less appropriate way. Thus, *Wycliffe* puts "with sownynge trompes" (early) and "sownynge with trumpis" (later), for Leviticus, "the day of noyse it is, and of trompes" (early), and "for it is the day of sownyng, and of trumpis" (later), for Numeri. *Douay* translates "a memorial, with the sound of trumpets" (Lev.), and "the day of the sounding and of the trumpets" (Num.).

The *Authorized Version* and *Harkavy* have "a memorial of blowing of trumpets" (Lev.), and "a day of blowing the trumpets" (Num.). The *American Version* and *Moulton* use "a memorial of blowing of trumpets" (Lev.), and "a day of blowing of trumpets" (Num.). *Moffat* has "a day of remembrance accompanied by a trumpet blast" (Lev.), and "a day for the blowing of the bugles" (Num.). The most logical translation is that of the *Jewish Version,* "a memorial proclaimed with the blast of horns" (Lev.), and "a day of blowing the horn" (Num.). Whereas the *Revised Standard Version* once more uses an erroneous translation for *shofar,* in setting "a memorial proclaimed with blast of trumpets" (Lev.), and "a day for you to blow the trumpets" (Num.).

LUTHER calls *Shanat ha-yobel* appropriately "Halljahr," the "Year of Sounding." However, the translation of the VULGATE, *annus jubilei,* or *jubilus* (hence the generally accepted term of Jubilee) is merely phonetically associated with the Hebrew *yobel,* but implies the meaning of "Jubilee," as a festive occasion, which originally was lacking in the Hebrew term.[523]

It was generally assumed that the *shofar* which would announce the Year of Jubilee was the ordinary instrument used for other solemn occasions. This belief, however, is erroneous, as is obvious from the specific name of the instrument, *shofar teru'ah,* a word-combination not found elsewhere in the biblical text. In all the other passages *shofar* is used either together with the verb *taḳe'o* ("to blow"), or with the noun *ḳol* ("voice"). The coupling of *shofar* with *teru'ah* must therefore have had a particular reason.

The word *teru'ah* in itself means "alarm"; it is used in this sense in Jer. 4:19, *teru'at milḥamot,* "alarm of war," and in Zeph. 1:16, *yom shofar v'teru'ah,* "a day of the horn and alarm." Therefore, it would be quite appropriate to render *shofar teru'ah* in Lev. 25:9 as "horn of alarm." This instrument has been correctly considered by some commentators to be a "horn with the big blast," that is an instrument with a far greater sound volume than produced by ordinary *shofarot.* The same significance may be attributed to Lev. 23:24, in which the term *zikaron teru'ah,* "a memorial proclaimed with the blast of the horn" (*Jewish Translation*) seems to refer to an exceptionally powerful instrument; also to Josh. 6:4,5, about which RIEHM says, for instance:

> "For announcing the Year of the Jubilee, there existed apparently quite a number of a specific type of horn."[524]

And indeed, the siege of Jericho and the magic action used at this occurrence, testify to the fact that the horns used there belonged to a specific type. To prove our point, we may quote verses 4-6, 8-9, 13, 16 and 20 of Chapter 6 of Joshua, with the original Hebrew terms used there:

> "Seven priests shall bear seven rams' horns (*shofarot ha-yobelim*) before the ark; and the seventh day ye shall compass the city seven times, and the priests shall blow with the horns (*yiteḳe'u bashofarot*). And it shall be that when they make a long blast with the rams' horns (*bimashaḥ beḳeren ha-yobel*), and when ye hear the sound of the horn (*et-ḳol ha-shofar*), all the people shall shout with a great shout (*teru'ah gedolah*) . . . Let seven priests bear seven rams' horns (*shofarot yobelim*) . . .

"The seven priests bearing the seven rams' horns (*shofarot ha-yobelim*) before the [ark of the] Lord passed on, and blew with the horns (*v'take'u bashofarot*) . . . And the armed men went before the priests that blew the horns (*tiḳe'u ha-shofarot*), and the rearward went after the ark, [the priests] blowing with the horns (*v'taḳo'a bashofarot*) continually . . .

"And the seven priests bearing the seven rams' horns (*shofarot ha-yobelim*) before the ark of the Lord went on continually, and blew with the horns (*v'taḳe'u bashofarot*); and the armed men went before them; and the rearward came after the ark of the Lord, [the priests] blowing with the horns (*v'taḳo'a bashofarot*) continually . . .

"And it came to pass at the seventh time, when the priests blew with the horns (*taḳe'u bashofarot*), that Joshua said unto the people . . .

"So the people shouted, and [the priests] blew with the horns (*vayitiḳe'u bashofarot*). And it came to pass, when the people heard the sound of the horn (*ḳol ha-shofar*), that the people shouted with a great shout (*teru'ah gedolah*), and the wall fell down flat."

It is striking that in verses 4,5,6,8, and 13, in which the horn is mentioned repeatedly, the name of the instrument, be it *shofar* or *ḳeren,* always appears first together with *yobel,* and later alone. This is by no means fortuitous, but rather a clear indication that the biblical chronicler, using five times the epithet *yobel,* wanted to stress again and again the fact that a specific type of horn, supposedly much louder than the ordinarily used *shofar* or *ḳeren* was meant. Such an intensely powerful instrument, however, was bound to have a larger shape. And this seems to be the explanation for the epithet *ha-yobel,* which refers to a species of horn distinguished by its large dimensions.

That this is not a mere surmise, becomes evident from a Mishnaic statement, in which such a larger horn type is explicitly mentioned.[525]

Evidently enough, the solution of the whole enigma resides in the wide resounding bell of metal, referred to in this Mishnaic passage. For this part of the horn could be put on and taken off and, functioning like a megaphone, not only increased considerably the sound of the instrument, but imparted to it the hollow, gruesome tone quality, thus investing the magic occurrence at Jericho with its specific flavor.

The dramatic description of Moses' ascension of the Mount Sinai (Exod. 19:13,16,19) contains a further indication that such a larger horn type with a resounding bell might have been meant which, together with lightning and thunder, would create the mystic tonal background for God's revelation. It is significant how the biblical chronicler intimates the gradually increasing sound of such a big horn. Verse 13 says: *bim'shoḥ ha-yobel hemmah,* "when the horn soundeth long,"—verse 16: *v'ḳol shofar ḥazaḳ m''od,* "and the voice of the horn exceedingly loud,"—verse 19: *vay'hi ḳol ha-shofar holeḥ v'ḥazaḳ m''od,* "and when the voice of the horn waxed louder and louder." By these three differently graded indications the chronicler seems to convey the idea of a continuous *crescendo* of the horn sound, matching the uproar of the elements.

R. JUDAH's statement that

"at the New Year they use rams' horns and at the Year of Jubilee wild goats' horns,"[526]

might be correct in itself, without refuting our hypothesis. The characteristic feature of the *yobel* was in any case the metal sound bell, which could be applied to the *shofar* as well as to the *ḳeren.* It may, therefore, be assumed with reasonable certainty that the term *yobel* implied an instrument put together of several parts,[527] the most important of which was apparently the sound bell.[528]

o
o o

Both the earlier and later translations of the Scriptures do even less justice to the meaning of *yobel* than to the other species of the *shofar.* The more astounding is the interpretation of the SEPTUAGINT, which stems from the idea that in the Year of the Jubilee the slaves were set free and that the liberation was symbolized by blowing the horn. Accordingly, *yobel* is translated as *aphaseōs sēmasia,* literally "signal for liberation" (Lev. 25:11-13).

It is worthy of note that, whereas the modern English Bibles, and even the otherwise meticulous *Jewish Version,* do not make any distinction between *shofar, ḳeren* and *yobel,* the ancient English versions clearly distinguished at least *yobel* as a different instrument. *Wycliffe* has even two parallel terms for it in the early as well as in the later versions; it is surprising, therefore, that all the modern translations simply ignored this important distinction. For Joshua 6:5 *Wycliffe* has "the voyce of the trompe lenger and thicker ful sowneth" (early), and "the vois of the trumpe schal sowne lengere, and more be whiles" later); for verse 6, "trompes of the iubilees" early), and "clariouns of iubilee" (later). *Ha-yobelim* in verse 4 is rendered simply as "trompes" in the early version, but as "trumpe with clariouns" in the later one.

Douay has "trumpets, which are used in the jubilee," and "trumpets of the jubilee" for verses 4, 6 and 13.

o
o o

It is vitally important to clarify the obvious difference between the meaning of the three varieties of horns mentioned in the Scriptures. Inasmuch as the word *shofar* has been widely adopted in the English language, it would be most practical to use it phonetically in all the passages where it stands in the Hebrew text, or to render it uniformly as "rams' horn." The equivalent for *ḳeren* ought to be "horn," or more precisely, "neat's horn." The adequate translation of *yobel* would be "horn of the Jubilee," or "high-sounding horn." This rendition would refer to the special occasion on which the instrument was blown and also indicate unequivocally its difference from the two other species of horns.

(c) Percussion, shaking and rattling instruments

The linguistic form for the names of these instruments is predominantly onomatopoeic, not merely in Ancient Israel, but practically in the entire

Oriental Antiquity and, in part, among the Greeks and Romans. Quite a number of words already formed in Antiquity has been adopted by the Western world and can be traced even to-day in almost all European languages.

23. TOF

Tof, plur. *tuppim,* is a collective term for all kinds of hand-drums of the ancient Hebrews. The word is of Assyrian origin (*tuppu*); the precursors of the Assyrians, the Sumerians, also called the handdrum *dup* or *tup,* and one species of it *adapa.*[529] In the Arabian, too, the handdrum is called *duff.*

Since the Scriptures do not contain any indications as to the form of the instrument, we have to rely on analogies with similar instruments of other ancient Oriental peoples and on the pictorial reproductions provided by Egyptian and Assyrian antiquities.[530]

Percussion instruments constitute one of the most characteristic features of the ancient Oriental music, both sacred and secular.

> "Some tablets of clay engraved with cuneiform writing . . . give information of drums, on their outstanding role and importance—indeed, on the ritual veneration that they were granted."[531]

The Egyptians and Assyrians had many varieties of drums, such as the small circular hand-drum, the square-shaped species with lightly arched bays on the four sides, furthermore the long cylindric form, hanging on ribbons from the necks of the performers, and played either with both palms or with two slightly curbed sticks. (Illustr. 47, 48)

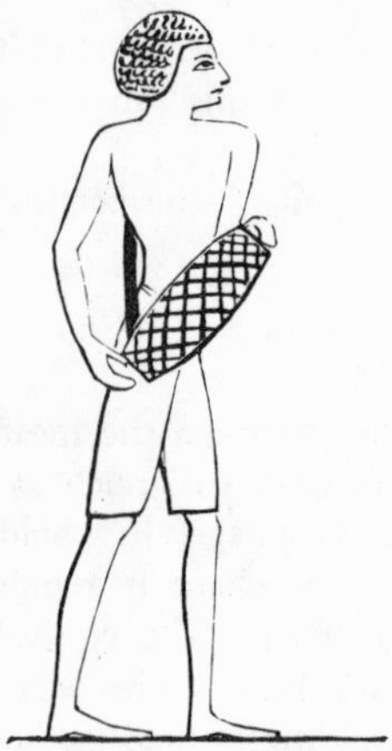

ILLUSTRATION NO. 47.

Egyptian hand-drum (After Carl Engel, *The Music of the Most Ancient Nations,* London, 1864).

ILLUSTRATION NO. 48.

Assyrian hand-drum (After Carl Engel, *The Music of the Most Ancient Nations,* London, 1864).

If we apply the forms reproduced in Oriental antiquities to the Jewish usage, we may assume that the *tof* consisted of a wooden or metal hoop, covered with an animal skin (ordinarily of a ram or wild goat), and that it was played either with the fingers or with the clenched fist. The Bible and the rabbinical literature give no hints as to the playing of *tuppim* with sticks. Nor do we know whether there were metal rings or small metal plates fastened to the hoop in order to produce a tingling sound, as on the later tambourine. Also there is no evidence whatever whether the *tof* had a skin only on one side or on both.

The *tof* was the most primitive, consequently the most common instrument of Ancient Israel, that could easily be played by anybody. In Egyptian monuments the hand-drum is played mostly by women, in Assyrian pictures also by men. In Israel it was played by girls and women, though there are some biblical indications that men, too, might have played the instrument occasionally (1 Sam. 10:5; 2 Sam. 6:5; 1 Chron. 13:8).

Dancing was an important element at many performances of Jewish music.[532] Joy and merriment of the individual and of the community were usually released in rhythmical motions of the participants, and the leadership in the orderly dancing routine was entrusted to girls and women as a rule. The rhythmical background to dances was furnished by hand-drums, and this explains why the instrument was played in Ancient Israel mostly by girls and women. Already in pristine times the *tof* was the symbol of joy. When Laban censures Jacob for his stealthy flight with his daughters Rachel and Leah, he says to him reproachfully:

> "Wherefore didst thou flee secretly, and outwit me; and didst not tell me, that I might have sent thee away with mirth and with songs, with tabrets (*tuppim*) and with harps (*kinnorot*)?" (Gen. 31:27).

Already in the early history of the Jews the *tof* was used in religious ceremonies. At the primitive stage of the Jewish religion we witness dance as one of the three elements (along with singing and playing) that served to glorify God. As in Egypt, the ritual dance was performed exclusively by women who, of course, accompanied themselves with *tuppim*. Later, priestly redactors have tried to eliminate from the biblical text anything that could remind one of this primitive ritual. This zealous expurgation went hand-in-hand with the elimination of women dancers from ritual ceremonies.

The role of the *tuppim* in the dancing customs of Ancient Israel will be examined in a subsequent section. Here it will suffice to state in a general way that at religious, semi-religious, and secular festivities, dancing, and with it the use of *tuppim,* are repeatedly attested in the Scriptures (Exod. 15; Judg. 11:34; 1 Sam. 18:6; 2 Sam. 6:5; 1 Chron. 13:8; Jer. 31:4; Isa. 5:12; 24:8; 30:32; Pss. 68:26; 81:3; 149:2,3; 150:3,4; 1 Macc. 9:39).

Frequently, modern commentators identify the *tof* with the tambourine of our days.[533] However, the hand-drum with small metal plates on a wooden frame is not authenticated prior to the beginning of the 13th century. Moreover, the correct name of this instrument is "tambour de basque," whereas "tambourine" signifies the oblong, cylindric drum of the Provence, which has no jingling metal discs.[534]

The Greek word for the hand-drum was *typanon,* transformed in later times into *tympanon.* The original form *typanon* shows clearly the connection of the word with the Semitic *tof* and the Arabian *duff.* The Romans have adopted the Greek word as *tympanum.*

The word *tof* in the meaning of the hand-drum appears fifteen times in the Bible. In another place where the word is used, it has no musical connotation (Ezek. 28:13). (See also p. 318.)

Among the patristic writers ISIDORE of SEVILLE furnishes a description of the hand-drum,[535] which, however, does not reveal anything that is not evident from ancient sources and pictorial representations.

In his treatise *Shilṭe ha-Gibborim,* PORTALEONE gives shorter and longer descriptions of the Jewish instruments mentioned in the Bible and in rabbinic writings.[536] But these descriptions, apart from being manifestly influenced by the music practice of his own time, are full of glaring mistakes, as for instance when he calls the *shofar* "a kind of flute," the *magrepha* a "clapper," or when he identifies the *mashrikuta* (*sic!*) with a "reed flute."

Actually startling, however, is his description of the hand-drum:

> "The drum is called in Greek *kymbalon,* in Latin *cymbalum,* in Italian *cymbalo.*"

(Follows a lengthy excursion about the pronounciation of the consonant C by the Greeks, Romans, and Italians). Then he continues:

> "The drum received its name from its shape, since it is built like a small ship, called in Greek *kymba* . . . Thus, the drum is called *kymbalon,* because it is similar to a small ship without a deck; it is made of brass, copper or other metal, is long and narrow, tapering on both ends, its middle part being broader and bulging out. This instrument was used particularly by the Egyptian priests in the temple of the mother goddess, called *dea vesta.* It represented the solid earth, and was considered a deity. Apart from the priests, it was frequently used when humans wanted to express their joy by striking it; this hollow, metallic vessel was played with a stick of iron or copper, alternatively using strong and weak beats, with fast rolls, then again slowly and calmly, so that these different beats produced various sounds. This is the *tof* (drum), according to the opinion of Jewish scholars. Our Rabbis . . . maintain (Mishnah, *Kinnim* III:6) that it was a skin stretched over a wooden or other frame. R. Josua says that there is an adage: 'When it is alive, it has one voice, when it is dead, it has seven.' What are these seven voices? Its two horns become two trumpets, its two thigh-bones two flutes, its skin becomes a drum, its entrails a *nablon* (a combination of harp and bagpipe),[537] its chitterlings harp strings. Consequently, the drum, according to the opinion of our Rabbis and also to that of the sages of other peoples, is without any doubt an instrument of minor value, not suitable in any way for purposes of artistic music."

It is strange that PORTALEONE, who certainly was thoroughly familiar with the Scriptures, completely missed the relationship between the *tof* and the dance in Ancient Israel. At least, his treatise does not contain anything referring to it.

o
o o

The SEPTUAGINT translates *tof* as *tympanon,* with the exception of Job 21:12, where the word is strangely rendered as *psaltērion,* and 1 Kings 1:40, where instead of the name of the instrument the act of dancing (*en chorois*) is used as translation. The VULGATE and other ancient Latin versions have always *tympanum.* The Peshiṭṭa sets three times *rebiy'a* (Isa. 5:12; Ps. 149:3; 1 Chron. 13:8), on other places *pelaga.*[538] The Targum renders it as *tuppa* (in the plural *tuppin* or *tuppaya*), and in Isa. 5:12 it mistranslates as *ḳathros.*

In modern English versions *tof* is translated as "tabret," "timbrel," "drums," and "tambourine" (*Moffat*). *Wycliffe* has "timbre" (early) and "tympan" (later); he translates the end of Ps. 86:26 as "tympanystriss" (early), and "syngynge in tympans" (later).

For the different, non-musical translation of *tuppeḥo v'neḳebeḥo* (Ezek. 28:13) see p. 317 ff.

24. MEẒILTAYIM, ẒELẒELIM

The only percussion instruments admitted unreservedly in the sacred service were the bronze cymbals, which—owing to their duality—were named in the plural form as *meẓiltayim* or *ẓelẓelim.* Both words originate from the verb *ẓalal,* "to resound," "to tingle,"[539] and are manifestly onomatopoeic constructions; the noun derived from it has the meaning of "tingling," "ringing," or "clanging."

The fact that in numerous Assyrian bas-reliefs cymbals are depicted gave rise to the opinion that these instruments originated in Assyria. But practically all peoples of early Antiquity have known cymbals made of metal. The instruments on Assyrian pictures show two different forms: the flat, saucer-like shape, held upright and played in striking them sideways, and the more bulging, bell-like shape with long handles, which were played vertically. The Egyptian cymbals had a broad, flat rim and a large bulge in the center, that helped to enhance the resonance. They were held upright and played sideways. The Jewish *ẓelẓelim* might have been similar; according to JOSEPHUS, they were large bronze plates (*kymbala te ēn platea kai megala chalkea*) played with both hands.[540] This corroborates the biblical statement that the cymbals of the Temple were made of brass (*meẓiltayim neḥoshet*) "to sound aloud" (1 Chron. 15:19). (Illustr. 49, 50)

The Greek cymbals were made of a bronze-alloy. ATHENAEUS mentions them together with other percussion instruments for the dancing of women:

> "I hear the turban-wearing women of Asian Kybēle, the daughters of the rich Phrygians, with drums (*tympanois*), and bull-roarers (*rhomboisi*) and booming of bronze cymbals (*chalkotypōn kymbalōn*) in their two hands make loud din."[541]

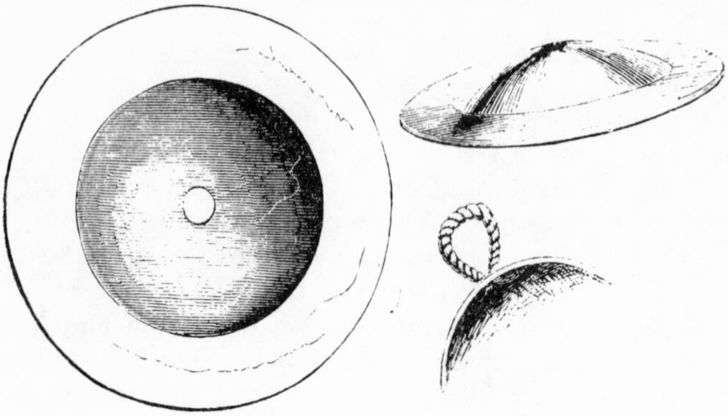

ILLUSTRATION NO. 49
Egyptian bronze cymbals, five inches and a half in diameter (After Carl Engel, *The Music of the Most Ancient Nations,* London, 1864).

ILLUSTRATION NO. 50
Assyrian cymbals (After Carl Engel, *The Music of the Most Ancient Nations,* London, 1864).

In the New Testament the apostle Paul distinguishes between *chalkos ēchōn,* "sounding brass" and *kymbalon alalazon,* "tinkling cymbal" (1 Corinth. 13:1). The first term is usually interpreted as "a brazen instrument, a trumpet," whereas the second seems to imply the Greek cymbals of those days. It is more probable, however, that the apostle's metaphor refers to the Jewish cymbals and that his opposition of the two terms is an intentional parallel, if not a direct quotation, of the two kinds of cymbals, *ẓilẓele shemʿā* and *ẓilẓele teruʿah,* as mentioned in Psalm 150, verse 5. (see p. 379).

Meẓiltayim appears for the first time in the Bible at the transfer of the ark of the covenant to Jerusalem (2 Sam. 6:5, and the corresponding passage in 1 Chron. 13:8). At that time, they were probably no more than noise making instruments, designed to enhance by their bright and metallic sound the general rejoicing. At the institution of the regular sacred music, however, the *meẓiltayim* acquired an important ritual function. They are usually interpreted as having been "played" by the three precentors Heman, Asaph and Jeditun-Ethan, each heading a group of singers, and supposedly "leading," *i.e.* "conducting" their respective groups by beating the cymbal (1 Chron. 15:19).

In other words, according to this interpretation, shared incidentally by many commentators,

"the cymbals apparently served the purpose of a baton in the hand of

> a modern orchestra leader marking the rhythm with their sharp penetrating tone and so holding together the whole."[542]

Moffat goes even so far as to express this idea in his translation of 1 Chron. 15:19,

> "of the singers, Heman, Asaph and Ethan had to beat time with bronze cymbals,"

and 16:6: "Asaph always beating time with cymbals." All this, however, represents a complete misunderstanding of the nature of Oriental music.

To be sure, the music practice of the Occident furnishes many examples for the loud marking of the musical beats, such as hitting the floor with a thick staff, beating the measure on the stand with a music scroll or with the violin bow, stamping the feet, etc. Nevertheless, it is wrong to assume that beating the cymbals might have served the same purpose. Jewish, and in general Oriental, song was not strictly metrical like our Western music, but represented an accentual cantillation with many intentional and unintentional irregularities. The musical phrase, the melodic structure, were not governed by ironclad measures or groups of measures (a system unknown to Orientals), therefore marking of the "beats," as we understand it, could not be applied in the music of the Temple.[543]

SAALSCHÜTZ opines that the choir leaders of the Israelites might have used small metal castanets for their "beats."[544] Even if we were to admit that choir singing of the Levites was led by audible means, the delicate sound of small cymbals must certainly have been much too soft for keeping together choral groups, especially when a greater number of singers have participated in the service. As accompaniment to dancing, such small cymbals might have given a sufficient rhythmical support and in fact were used in Antiquity frequently by female dancers. As an audible help in leading choral singing they were even less appropriate than the large and loud sounding cymbals.

In Jewish rites, as in those of the ancient Orient in general, the clashing of cymbals aimed originally to draw the attention of the deity to the worshippers. In later Jewish ceremonies, the sounding of cymbals was the signal for starting the choir-singing, as attested repeatedly in the rabbinic literature.

In the Davidic music service Asaph was the *primus inter pares* of the three precentors and choral leaders. He alone had the distinction of indicating the start of the singing with sounding the cymbal (1 Chron. 16:5). Both other leaders came to the fore only in the course of later ritual actions (1 Chron. 16:42). In the final organization of the Temple music by David, the privilege of clashing the cymbals was extended to all three precentors (1 Chron. 25:1,6). At the dedication of Solomon's Temple, the chronicler mentions once more their names, together with their functions (2 Chron. 5:12,13). Cymbal-playing Levites are mentioned again at the re-dedication of the Temple by Hezekiah, without, however, citing any names this time (2 Chron. 29:25).

In 2 Chron. 30:21 cymbals are not mentioned together with the other instruments. Since, however, this passage refers to a Passah feast, just as 2 Chron. 29:25, it may be assumed with certainty that the term *bikle ʿoz*, "[singing] with loud instruments," includes the ritual use of cymbals too.

"Levites the sons [*i.e.* descendants] of Asaph with cymbals" are alluded to once more at the laying of the foundation-stone for the Second Temple (Ezra 3:10). Also at the dedication of the newly erected walls of Jerusalem (Neh. 12:27).

Psalm 150, itemizing all the instruments used in the sacred service, mentions two different kinds of cymbals, the *ẓilẓele shem'ā* and the *ẓilẓele teru'ah.* Their difference might have been in their size, perhaps also in their material. The *ẓilẓele shem'ā* were perhaps the smaller brass instruments, having a brighter sound, and played by vertical motion. The *ẓilẓele teru'ah* may have been larger instruments, made of bronze (a heavier metal), held in an upright position when played, their sound being harsh and penetrating.[545]

The rabbinic literature uses both names of the instrument, *meẓiltayim* as well as *ẓilẓal,* the latter one in singular. This is explained in the Talmud in the sense that

> "there were two cymbals, but since only one action was necessary, and one man could do it, the singular is used."[546]

In another passage, the Mishnah states explicitly that one pair of cymbals was used in the Second Temple:

> "There were never less than two trumpets, and their number could be increased without end; there were never less than nine lyres, and their number could be increased without end; but of cymbals there was but one."[547]

The Israelites did not seem to know how to prepare the proper alloy for cymbals (and also for some other metal objects). When once the cymbals of the Temple were damaged, foreign artisans had to be called for repairing them. The Talmud reports about this:

> "There was a cymbal (*ẓilẓal*) in the Sanctuary from the days of Moses, made of bronze, and its sound was pleasant; then it became damaged. The Sages sent for craftsmen from Alexandria in Egypt, and they mended it, but its sound was not pleasant any more. Thereupon they removed the improvement and its sound became as pleasant as it was before."[548]

Other instruments, too, after they were repaired, had to be brought back to their original state, since their sound qualities have been impaired (see p. 311).

In the chapter "Temple Music on New Moon" of his *Shilṭe ha-Gibborim,* PORTALEONE ventures to reconstruct minutely the musical procedure at the ancient sacred service the way he imagined it to have taken place on that occasion. Cymbals play an essential role in this description; it may therefore be in order to quote it here in full:

> "Since on the day of the New Moon more trumpets, musicians and singers were employed, I want to submit to you a delineation of their rightful functions. Eighteen Levites are standing in a straight line on the steps. The first sings in *unisono,* the second in *ditono* or *semiditono,* the third sings the part called *diafente perfeto,* the fourth *diapason,* the fifth *doppioditono* or *semiditono,* the sixth *doppiodiafente,* that is *diapason* combined with *diafente perfeto.* These perform the first part of the singing.
>
> The seventh to twelfth [of the Levites], corresponding to the first to

sixth, join in the second part, the thirteenth to eighteenth in the third part.

In front of the singers there are, also in a straight line, eighteen musicians; one with a ten-stringed *nablon,* two to five with harps, and the sixth again with a ten-stringed *nablon.* These play during the first part, the seventh to twelfth [musician] and the thirteenth to eighteenth, with the same distribution of instruments, during the second and third part, respectively.

In the center before the musicians stands the player of castanets [Portaleone means the cymbal-player]. Right and left of him, in a straight line, there are nine trumpeters on each side. You should know, however, that every trumpeter endeavors to play the same tones as sung by the singers; thus, three trumpets blow *unisono,* three *ditono* or *semiditono,* three *diafente perfeto,* and three *doppiodiafente,* in order to achieve harmony and avoid a confused chaos of tones.

Then the castanet-player emits a sound, thereby introducing the singing. This starts with six voices, accompanied by two *nablon* and four harps. After they have finished a section, the blowing of all eighteen trumpets takes place together with the sounding of the castanets, which are played three times alone in a simple *diapason.* Thereupon the people prostrate themselves.

After this, the castanet-player again performs alone, in order to carry over the tone of the first six singers to that of the second group of six, likewise accompanied by two *nablon* and four harps.

The same occurs after the next section, whereupon the remaining six singers perform to the accompaniment of the third group of instruments.

When this section approaches the end, all eighteen singers and musicians sing and play together; at the closing, all eighteen trumpets blow, together with the sounding of the castanets, in a simple *diapason* three times—as mentioned before—and the people prostrate themselves."

In this description PORTALEONE mingles indiscriminately fancy and reality, absurdity and truth. The application of his Italian musical terms is just as abstruse as the manner of explaining the blowing of ancient Jewish trumpets, or attributing to castanets (*i.e.* cymbals) the faculty of "carrying over the tone" to singers from one section to the other.

In view of the incongruity of his opinions, it is incomprehensible that PORTALEONE's essay could, in all seriousness, be considered the result of a "fine and comprehensive erudition."[549]

Yet, even without a close examination it is easy to figure out that the *meẓiltayim* used by the Levites could not possibly be castanet-like instruments. The main purpose of playing the cymbals was originally to draw the attention of the deity upon the worshippers and, eventually, to announce the beginning of the levitical singing. For either purpose, the delicate sound of a wooden or metal clapper was scarcely sufficient. Besides, the terminology, Hebrew as well as Greek and Latin, definitely repudiates the idea of small castanets. *Ẓilẓele shemʿā* and *teruʿah, kymbala euēcha, cymbala jubilationis,* etc., all presuppose large and powerfully sounding instruments. Moreover, JOSEPHUS' description leaves no doubt whatever that it was a large (*megala*) instrument. Similarly, the scattered references to *ẓilẓal* in the rabbinical literature take large cymbals for granted. For instance, the *meẓiltayim* are mentioned among those instruments, which contributed essentially to the general rejoicing at the Feast of *Bet ha-She'uba*.[550] Furthermore, the *ẓilẓal* was one of the Temple instruments the sound of which—according to rabbinical statements—could be heard as far as Jericho,[551] which would have been quite impossible with a small rattling instrument.

In the enumeration of the various functionaries of the Second Temple, Ben Arza's name is specifically mentioned, indicating that "he was over the cymbal."[552] This is repeated in another Mishnaic passage,[553] a sign that in the Second Temple, too, striking the cymbals was considered such an important ritual function that the rabbinic scribes even perpetuated the name of the player.

Although the cymbals were mainly ritual instruments, their use outside the Temple on semi-religious, or secular, occasions is attested twice in the Bible and once in the Talmud. At the transfer of the ark of the covenant to Jerusalem

> "all the house of Israel played before the Lord with all manners of instruments made of cypress-wood, and with harps, and with psalteries, and with timbrels, and with sistra, and with cymbals" (2 Sam. 6:5).

And in the corresponding report by the later chronicler:

> "And David and all Israel played before God with all their might; even with songs, and with harps, and with psalteries, and with timbrels, and with cymbals, and with trumpets" (1 Chron. 13:8).

The Talmud describes a popular feats, in which

> "the song of thanksgiving was [accompanied] by lutes, lyres, and cymbals (*ẓelẓelim*) at every corner and upon every great stone in Jerusalem."[554]

RASHI, in his commentary to Tal. Bab., *'Arakin* 10 b, calls the *ẓilẓal* by the term of his own time—*ẓinbes*.[555] The same is true of OBADIAH of BERTINORO who, in commenting on Mishnah, *Tamid* III:8 and VII:3, identifies *ẓilẓal* with the 15th century *ẓimbali*.

Ẓelẓelim are mentioned three times in the Old Testament (2 Sam. 6:5, and twice in Ps. 150:5). The other term, *meẓiltayim*, occurs thirteen times in the Bible. The SEPTUAGINT translates both terms as *kymbala*, in Neh. 12:27 in the participle as *kymbalizontes*. In 2 Sam. 6:5, the SEPTUAGINT mistranslates as *auloi*. *Ẓilẓele shem'ā* is rendered as *kymbala euēcha*, *ẓilẓele teru'ah* as *kymbala alalagmou*. The VULGATE sets always *cymbala*, in Ps. 150:5 *cymbala bene sonante* for *ẓilẓele shem'ā*, and *cymbala jubilationis* for *ẓilẓele teru'ah*. *Meẓiltayim neḥoshet*, "cymbals of brass," mentioned in 1 Chron. 15:19, are rendered by the SEPTUAGINT as *kymbala chalka*, by the VULGATE as *cymbala aenei*. The Targum uses generally *ẓilẓalon*, the Peshiṭṭa *ẓiẓela*, but sometimes omits the word or mistranslates it, as for instance *shifura* in Ezra 3:10.

Since the nature of the instrument has never aroused any doubt, the English versions always translate its name as "cymbals." *Ẓilẓele shem'ā* is rendered by

Wycliffe as "in cymbalis wel sounende" (early), and "in cymbalis sownynge wel" (later); *Douay* has "high sounding cymbals"; the *Authorized* and *American Versions, Harkavy* and *Moulton* "loud cymbals"; the *Jewish Version* "loud-sounding cymbals," the *Revised Standard Version* "sounding cymbals," and *Moffat* "resounding cymbals." *Ẓilẓele teruʿah* is interpreted by *Wycliffe* as "in cymbalis of huge ioging" (early), and "in cymbalis of iubilacioun" (later); by *Douay* as "in cymbals of joy"; by the *Authorized* and *American Versions* as well as by *Harkavy* as "high sounding cymbals"; by *Moulton* as "sounding cymbals"; by *Moffat* as "clash of cymbals"; by the *Jewish Version* as "clanging cymbals," and by the *Revised Standard Version* as "loud clashing cymbals."

25. SHALISHIM

This word appears only once in the Bible, in 1 Sam. 18:6. At the reception of King Saul and David, after the victorious campaign against the Philistines,

> "the women came out of all the cities of Israel, singing and dancing, to meet king Saul, with timbrels (*betuppim*), with joy and with three-stringed instruments" (*bashalishim*).

It has long been accepted that the word is somehow connected with the Hebrew *shalosh,* "three," or *shlosha,* "three times." Yet, how should this concept be associated with a musical instrument is still a matter of vague speculation. In fact, this very vagueness challenges in no small measure the validity of the concept itself.

A faint historical support for the latter may be found in a description of the Egyptian sistrum by APULEIUS:

> "[The goddess Isis] had in her right hand a timbrel of brass, a flat piece of metal curved in a manner of a girdle, wherein passed many rods through the periphery of it; and when with her arm she moved these triple chords [better: rods], they gave forth a shrill and clear sound."[556]

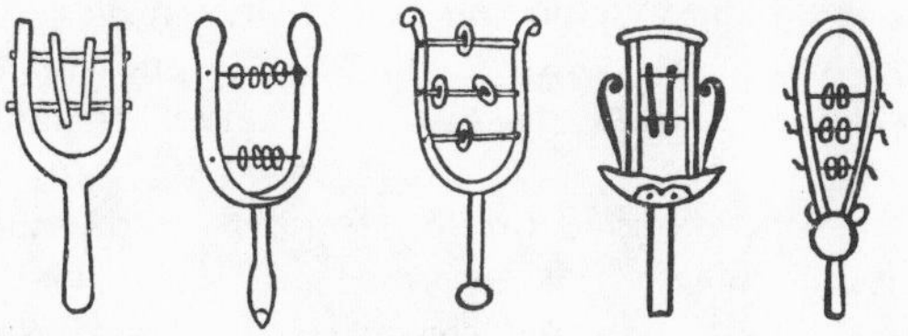

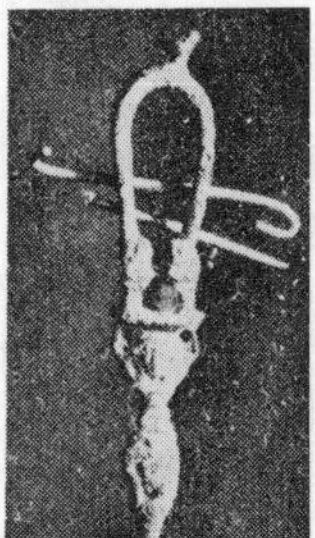

ILLUSTRATION NO. 51

Different kinds of sistra. Berlin Museum (After Francis W. Galpin, *The Music of the Sumerians . . .* , Cambridge, 1937).

The three movable rods mentioned in this description would seem to open the possibility of a parallel musical relation between the Hebrew term *shalishim* and the number "three."

Biblical commentators base their interpretation on the number "three," but otherwise their opinions are widely divided. PORTALEONE defines *shalishim* as a wooden, oblong, round and hollow stringed instrument with three strings.[557] PFEIFFER thinks they were castanets.[558] FORKEL interprets the word as a three-stringed instrument,[559] referring to GIULIO BARTOLOCCI who, in his *Bibliotheca magna Rabbinica* (Rome, 1675-1693) asserts

> "*hoc nomen shalishim esse nomen commune instrumentis trichordis diversorum generum*" ("the name *shalishim* is the generic term for three-stringed instruments of different types").[560]

GESENIUS and JAHN view it as a triangle,[561] NOWACK as cymbals.[562] HAUPT maintains that the word designates a small triangular harp like the Greek *trigōnon.*[563] GRESSMANN sees a connection between *shalishim* and the Arabian *taslis,* meaning "adorned with rings," and hence concludes that the Hebrew instrument is identical with or similar to our modern tambourine.[564] It was explained, however, that the existence of the tambourine is not attested prior to the beginning of the 13th century (see p. 373).

Shalish in Isa. 40:12 indicates a small measure for grain, one third of the *ephah.*[565] From this, GLASER concludes that *shalishim* may also stand for a fractional number and, consequently, refers to an instrument with three strings.[566] GALPIN even states that this instrument is the three-stringed guitar.[567] His arguments, however, are not too convincing:

> "The long-necked lute or guitar appears in the carvings of Assyria as early as 2500 B.C. . . . and in Hittite sculpture before 1000 B.C. . . . That the Hebrews should have remained unacquainted with this Oriental lute or guitar, appears most improbable, and there can be little doubt that the word *shalishim* meaning '*three*'*;* and translated in the margin of the Authorized Version 'three-stringed instruments,' denotes this guitar."

GALPIN's reasons have two weak points. First, not the *shalishim,* but the root *shalosh* from which the word is derived means "three." Then, GALPIN refers to a marginal note in the *Authorized Version* as a proof. One can agree with him that the Hebrews possibly knew the long-necked guitar, since it was used by the Egyptians.[568] There is, however, no positive evidence that such an instrument was familiar to the Hebrews. GALPIN's theory, therefore, is hardly tenable.

SACHS has his own hypothesis concerning *shalishim.* He refers to the noteworthy fact that in this biblical passage *tof* is separated from *shalishim,* a procedure never applied by the biblical poets and chroniclers in enumerating similar objects or notions. He thinks, therefore, that the word cannot refer to a musical instrument at all.

> "Possibly the word indicates some form of a dance, as dance names composed with 'three' are not unusual, such as the Roman *tripudium* of the priests of Mars, the old German *Treialtrei* and the Austrian *Dreysteyrer,*"[569]

The Talmud does not contain any reference to or explanation of the word;

the Targum translates it as *zelzelin,* and therefore interprets it as cymbals.

The Greek translations render it as *kymbala,* likewise "cymbals," while the Latin versions use *sistrum.* Since the Sumerians and their successors the Assyrians, as well as the Egyptians all had instruments of the *sistrum*-type, it would be conceivable that the Hebrews have taken over such an instrument from one of the two last named peoples. Quite unwittingly, SACHS furnishes a substantial support for this assumption in his mention of the *sistrata turba* of the Egyptians, " 'the sistrum-shaking crowd' of women, who shook it when they worshipped the bovine goddess Ḥatḥor."[570] For this could apparently serve as an analogy to the biblical description of women and girls receiving Saul and David dancing, with *tuppim* and shaking *shalishim.* Yet, among the Jewish instruments there is another one, the *mena'an'im,* which is generally identified with the sistrum. It is not likely that the Hebrews should have had two entirely different names for the same instrument.

WEISS, however, offers a solution that does justice to the etymology of the word (*shalosh=three*), and at the same time sustains the idea of the *sistrum.*[571] He interprets *shalishim* as a *sistrum* with three rods, or a rod with three rings. Since SACHS likewise points out several kinds of *sistra,*[572] among them one with three rods, WEISS' assumption seems to be plausible.

OESTERLEY, on the contrary, doubts that the instrument was a *sistrum.*[573] He also argues against the assumption of a "three-stringed instrument," as some modern English versions translate the *shalishim.* To his mind,

> "the suggestion may be hazarded that it was a form of drum, differing from this in having the skin drawn over three pieces of stick fixed together in triangular shape. This would be easier to construct than the circular-shaped *tof.*"

This opinion is not corroborated by any pictorial representation of Antiquity, and is quoted here merely for the sake of completeness.

It is rather doubtful whether the word *shalishim* has been really derived from *shalosh.*[574] The chances are, in fact, that the assonance between the two words is of a purely fortuitous nature, though instruments with names of double derivation are not uncommon in the Hebrew language.[575] A vital bit of evidence in the matter of defining the instrument in question is furnished by its very name, strongly imitative of its sound. This being so, it would seem to be more reasonable to assume that, owing to its onomatopoeic characteristics, the word *shalishim* refers to a shaking or rattling instrument. Such point of view would naturally give a definite credence to the interpretation of WEISS, in preference to all others.

It is worth mentioning that the Talmud identifies *shalishim* with the little bells adorning the garment of the high priests, which are called in the Bible *pa'amonim.*[576] This seems to be one of those terminological confusions so frequently observed in the rabbinic literature.

The uncertainty of opinions of biblical exegesis manifests itself also in the translations of the English versions. *Wycliffe* sets "(tymbers of gladness) and in trumpis" (early), and "(tympans of gladnesse) and in trumpis" (later); thus, he interprets the term as a wind instrument. *Douay* also mistranslates "(timbrels of joy), and cornets." Most of the modern versions have "instruments of music," the *American* and *Revised Standard Versions* adding, in a marginal note, "triangles, or three-stringed instruments." The *Jewish Version* has "three-stringed instruments," whereas *Moffat* interprets the word erroneously as "cymbals."

26. MENA'AN'IM

This word appears in the biblical text only in 2 Sam. 6:5. It originates from the verb *nu'a,* "to shake," "to move about," similarly to its Greek equivalent *seistron,* which derives from the verb *seiō.*[577]

Despite this unequivocal etymology, PFEIFFER thinks that the word indicates a wind instrument.[578] He supports his theory by two parallel passages, in which the transfer of the ark of the covenant is reported (2 Sam. 6:5 and 1 Chron. 13:8). In the first of these, *mena'an'im* but no *ḥaẓoẓerot* are mentioned among the instruments of the festive procession; in the second, it is the reverse. Since both reports describe the same event, the same instruments should logically be mentioned, according to PFEIFFER. This assumption, however, is by no means justified. Even if we would disregard the difference between the chronological appearance of the two biblical books, there is no compelling reason why two chroniclers should relate the same occurrence in identical words. It is rather to be assumed that in the first report, perhaps out of negligence of a scribe, *ḥaẓoẓerot* were omitted, while in the second, the *sistrum* was not mentioned specifically.[579]

Mena'an'im signify a shaking instrument, like the Egyptian *sistrum,* though maybe not so richly adorned. It consisted of a metal frame, in which rods were inserted, carrying loose rings. The frame had a handle, which was held while shaking the instrument, and thereby creating a tinkling sound. (Illustr. 51, 52).

ILLUSTRATION NO. 52

The Egyptian goddess Bastet (or Bubastis) holding a sistrum (After Adolf Erman, *Die ägyptische Religion,* Berlin, 1905).

Some years ago *sistra* were excavated from Sumerian tombs. Consequently it must have been known to the Babylonians and Assyrians as well. The Israelites might have taken them over either from Egypt or Babylonia.

The SEPTUAGINT mistranslates *mena'an'im* as *kymbala* (cymbals). In fact, not merely this term, but the whole passage in 2 Sam. 6:5, referring to music, is differently worded by the Greeks. The Hebrew original says:

> . . . *b'kol ʿoẓe beroshim ubekinnorot ubinebalim ubetuppim ubimenaʿanʿim ubeẓelẓelim* (". . . with all manner of instruments made of cypress-wood, and with harps, and with psalteries, and with timbrels, and with sistra, and with cymbals"). The SEPTUGINT has: . . . *en organois hērmosmenois en ischyi, kai en ōdais* [not in the Hebrew text], *kai en kinyrais, kai en nablais, kai en tympanois, kai en kymbalois* [wrong translation], *kai en aulois* [not in the Hebrew text].

It seems that the translators of the SEPTUAGINT used an earlier Bible version, which was later discarded. It is also possible that they omitted *menaʿanʿim,* by which *kymbala* would stand at least at its correct place; in order to make up the number of instruments, *aulos* was added arbitrarily at the end, not figuring in the Hebrew original.

The VULGATE and the other Latin versions always translate *menaʿanʿim* as *sistra.* Peculiar are the translations of the Peshiṭṭa as *rebiyʿa,* and of the Targum as *rebiʿin,* owing to the striking assonance with the instrument *rebiʿit,* mentioned only in the Mishnah, which seems to refer to a large type of drums (see chapter 41).

Among the English renditions, *Wycliffe* has "trumpis" (both versions), *Douay,* "cornets," both being patent mistranslations. The *Authorized Version* follows *Douay* in this error. The *Jewish Version* and *Harkavy* set "sistrum," *Moulton,* the *American* and *Revised Standard Versions* "castanet" with a footnote addition, or "*sistra,*" in the latter instance. *Moffat* interprets the word as "rattles."

27. PAʿAMONIM

The word *paʿamonim* is derived from the verb *paʿam,* "to strike." In Exod. 28:33,34 and 39:25,26, it signifies the little bells attached to the lower seam of the high priest's purple garment, in order that

> "the sound thereof shall be heard when he goeth in unto the holy place before the Lord, and when he cometh out, that he die not" (Exod. 28:35).

These bells were made of gold and they had a bright, yet unobtrusive sound, just loud enough to indicate the whereabouts of the high priest, but not to interfere with the sacred ceremony itself.

The biblical indication "that he die not" is, like some other elements of the Jewish ritual, a remnant from pristine times, when superstition and magic were closely linked with the crude religion of the Hebrews. Similar indications can be found in the customs of other peoples of Antiquity and of primitive peoples in general.

SACHS interprets it as a remnant of primitive magic:

> "Here, as everywhere, the bell is used as a defense against evil spirits. The demons like to frequent sanctuaries and thresholds. Therefore, the high priest does not have to be protected when he is in the holy place, but when he *goeth in* and *cometh out.*"[580]

Another interpretation of the indication will be given in the section "Music and Superstition," p. 502.

The Hellenistic age, with its philosophy so different from that of the Bible, attributed a transcendental meaning to the function of the *pa'amonim,* as well as to other liturgical customs. PHILO says:

> "The bells represent the harmonious alliance of these two [earth and water], since life cannot be produced by earth without water or by water without the substance of earth, but only by the union and combination of both."[581]

Yet, PHILO does not reveal how both elements of the Greek conception of nature, earth and water, are causally connected with the *pa'amonim.*

English Bibles translate *pa'amonim* more or less uniformly as "bells of gold," "golden bells," "little bells" (*Douay*), and "bells of pure gold" for Exod. 39:25. *Wycliffe* has the word in the Old-English spelling as "litel belles," (early), "smale bellis" (later), and for Exod. 39:25 "litil bellis of moost puyr gold" (early), and "litle bellis of purest gold" (later).

28. MEẒILLOT

This word is mentioned in Zech. 14:20 and is rendered generally as "bells," which were hung upon horses. It is derived from the same root as *meẓiltayim* and *ẓelẓelim* and, like these two names, is of an onomatopoetic nature. Similar to all noise making instruments of pristine ages, these bells had the purpose of keeping away evil spirits and demons from their bearers, in this case from useful domestic animals.

A pictorial analogy to this effect is found in an Assyrian bas-relief. There we see horses, carrying little bells with clappers around their necks. This seems to have been a common usage in Assyria. An Assyrian carving in the British Museum shows two horses hauling a carriage, each having six bells in various sizes around its neck.[582]

Contrary to the dainty *pa'amonim* on the high priest's garment, the Jewish *meẓillot* must have been larger and more compact, since they were supposed to carry an inscription according to the biblical text: "In that day shall there be upon the bells of the horses: HOLY UNTO THE LORD." It is indeed difficult to imagine how an inscription could have been put upon little round bells. Judging from the entire chapter 14 of Zechariah, the allusion of the prophet must have had only a symbolical meaning.

However, according to WEISS, the inscription upon the *meẓillot* should be interpreted literally. In fact, he even reasons out the possibility of placing such an inscription. As he thinks, *meẓillot* refers not to bells but to small plates, akin the one on the high priest's tiara, which might have carried an inscription *ḳodesh le*-YHVH.[583] We possess ancient pictorial reproductions showing harnesses of horses adorned not only with bells, but also with buckles, which look like small cymbals.[584] It was surely much easier to place inscriptions of a certain length on such plates, or buckles, than on bells.

The SEPTUAGINT as well as the VULGATE fail to do justice to the musical meaning of the word; they translate as *chalinos,* resp. *frenum,* meaning "bridle" or "rein." All English Bibles, however, use "bells," with the exception of *Wycliffe* and *Douay,* which—following the VULGATE—render the word as "bridil," resp. "bridle."

o
o o

The *pa'amonim* and *meẓillot* were no musical instruments in the proper sense of the word. They did not serve musical or artistic aims; their purpose has been to exert by their sound an extra-musical, in this instance, magic effect. In the primitive stages of music, the borderline between noise and music is often hazy. Especially when musical elements are introduced into the cult, it is sometimes difficult to establish where noise ends and music commences.

Originally, *pa'amonim* as well as *meẓillot* have had some music-like functions in the service of magic, therefore in this primitive stage they represent to a certain extent musical instruments. Consequently, they are generally considered as belonging to the instruments of the ancient Israelites.

B. INSTRUMENTS MENTIONED IN POST-BIBLICAL LITERATURE

In addition to the instruments mentioned in the biblical books, quite a number of instruments appear in the rabbinic writings. But only in isolated instances are the Sages giving information about the nature of these instruments. Sometimes they are being identified with biblical instruments. In other instances it is possible to grasp their character by comparing them with ancient Jewish instruments of the same, or similar categories. For the most part, however, the descriptions of the rabbis are not factual and frequently misleading, so that it is rarely possible to draw any conclusions as to their real nature.

To be sure, the rabbinic scribes were not supposed to possess a thorough knowledge of music in general, and of instruments in particular. Yet, in view of the carefulness and precision, even pedantry, applied by them frequently in describing the minutest items of the daily life, this sheer ignorance in musical matters, and especially with regard to musical instruments, is simply astounding.

This being so, the rabbinic indications about music and musical instruments can be used only with extreme caution. A highly critical approach to them will therefore be our guiding principle in the following scrutiny. Even so, it will be sometimes difficult, if not impossible, to define with a reasonable probability the nature of instruments mentioned in the Mishnah and the Talmud.

o
o o

(a) Stringed Instruments

29. PANDURA

According to talmudic statements, music in the life of shepherds had a double function: *first,* to alleviate the monotony of the profession and to embellish the daily life of its members, and *second,* to rally the flocks by musical sounds. All this was attained by singing (*zemer*) and by playing instruments, especially the *ʾabub roʿeh,* "shepherd's pipe." As the Talmud states, the shepherds used still another instrument, the *pandura.*[585]

This word originates from the Sumerian *pan-tur,* meaning "bow-small," or "small bow."[586] The Sumerian term in itself indicates a small stringed instrument.

The ancient peoples of the Near-East knew a species of three-stringed lute with a small corpus and long neck. The *pandura* might well have been such an instrument. Coeval writers[587] call the instrument either an Assyrian, or a Cappadocian, or even an Egyptian lute. VARRO derives the *pandura* erroneously from Pan and calls it "Pan's strings."[588] Obviously he confounds it with the Pan's pipe, the Greek name of which was *syrinx.* PYTHAGORAS says "that the Troglodytes[589] make the *pandura* out of the mangrove which grows in the sea."[590] The wood of the mangrove-plant was hard and resistant, hence well suited for the making of music instruments. The plant had aerial roots in arched fashion; the pictures of it and the preserved instruments made of this wood show the arched form of the *pandura;* we understand, therefore, why the Troglodytes used this wood for making the instruments.[591]

ISIDORE of SEVILLE voices an entirely different opinion. He says that the *pandura* was named after its inventor (*pandura ab inventore vocata*), and supports his assertion by a manifestly misunderstood verse of VIRGIL, which apparently suggested to him the idea that Pan has been the "inventor" of the instrument.[592] It is evident, at any rate, that in this verse of VIRGIL, the "Pan's pipe" (*calamos plures*), and certainly not a stringed instrument is meant.

According to SACHS, the *pandura* might have been introduced from Cappadocia to Greece. The Hellenes called it *trichordon,* "three-stringed"; besides, they also used for it the foreign name *pandura.*[593]

WEISS thinks that the *pandura* is identical with the Arabian *ṭanbūr* and that the name *pan-tur* originated merely by a transposition of the letters of the word *ṭanbūr.*[594] The Persians, too, knew a species of lute called *ṭanbūr*; this was, however, different from the Arabian instrument. The Persian lute had a broad neck and a relatively large body, while the Arabian *ṭanbūr,* and also the *pandura,* had a long slender neck and a small corpus.[595]

The Talmud does not furnish any explanation why Jewish shepherds did not use for their pastime one of the ancient Hebrew stringed instruments (*kinnor, nebel, ʿasor*), but rather preferred a foreign instrument. Among all the stringed instruments of the Egyptians, Assyrians, Babylonians, Hellenes, and also the Hebrews, the *pandura,* with its very small resounding body and, consequently, weak tone, might have been the least suitable instrument for shepherds. They lived mostly in the open air; the delicate sound of such an instrument was bound to be rather lost in the wide pastures.

Yet, there must have been some practical reasons for the choice of just such an instrument. It was small, convenient to carry and relatively easy to learn, since it had only three strings. The *kinnor* and *nebel,* having had more strings, required a higher skill in playing, probably exceeding the capacities of simple shepherds.[596] Moreover, the construction of the *kinnor* and *nebel* was much more involved, and thus may have presented difficulties in maintaining the usability of these instruments in the primitive life of shepherds.

Therefore, despite the *pandura's* lack of sonority in the open air, the Talmudic report about it as the favorite instrument of shepherds, has a certain credibility.

30. ḤINGA

A fantastic talmudic tale that relates a fight between mortals and demons contains the word *ḥinga* which, in this connection, seems to indicate some kind of a music instrument. The tale reads:

> "A certain town-official went and stood by a sorb-bush near a town, whereupon he was set upon by sixty demons and his life was in danger. He then went to a scholar who did not know that it was a sorb-bush haunted by sixty demons, and so he wrote a one-demon amulet for it. Then he heard how they [the demons] suspended a *ḥinga* on it [the tree] and sing thus: 'The man's turban is like a scholar's [yet] we have examined the man [and find] that he does not know which benediction to recite.' "[597]

According to JASTROW, *ḥinga* has three different meanings: (1) a circle, dancing, chorus, feast; (2) the dancing place in the vineyards; (3) a musical instrument.[598] He thinks that

> "perhaps they [the demons] danced in chorus around the tree."[599]

This, however, does not tally with the talmudic indication that "they suspended it on the tree." It seems rather that an object is meant, possibly an instrument, which was hung on the tree. But what kind of instrument this might have been can only be surmised.

By a remote analogy one could think of a harp-like instrument. As the psalmist says, the Israelites in the Babylonian exile "hanged up their harps upon the willows" (Ps. 137:2). To be sure, this is not to be understood literally; the psalmist uses this metaphor merely to indicate that in the captivity the Hebrews abandoned their music, especially the singing in public of the "songs of Zion." But an indirect evidence that *ḥinga* was perhaps a stringed instrument may be deduced from the statement that the demons intoned a song to it. As we know, singing in Ancient Israel was accompanied mainly by stringed instruments (*kle shir*). It would be conceivable, therefore, that *ḥinga* was a later variety of the *kinnor* or *nebel.* This conjecture is somewhat corroborated by the fact that Targum Onkelos to Gen. 31:27 renders *kinnor* as *ḥinga,* although in the case of Gen. 4:21 the same word *kinnor* is translated as *kinnora.* At any rate, this would lead to the assumption that the Aramaic *ḥinga* may have been another name for the *kinnor.* However, one of the Targumim to 1 Kings 1:40 uses *ḥinga* as a translation for the *ḥalil.* Furthermore, the Targum to the psalms translates the heading of Ps. 5, *ʾel ha-neḥilo,* as *ʿal ḥingin,* "with flutes." And in other Targumim (*e.g.* to Exod. 32:19, Judg. 11:34), *ḥinga* is used for *meḥolot,* "dances."

It has been repeatedly mentioned how arbitrarily the translators of the Targumim and of the Peshiṭṭa handled the rendering of the names of music instruments.[600] Nevertheless, it is surprising to find that *ḥinga* is used now as the term for a stringed instrument, now for a wind instrument, while its original meaning seems to refer rather to some action of dancing. This is one of the contradictions which occur so frequently in the rabbinic literature.

31. BAṬON (BAṬNON)

About the instrument *baṭon* (or *baṭnon*), mentioned in the Mishnah,[601] we know only as much as a later commentator, OBADIAH of BERTINORO, imparts to us. According to him, it was a large guitar (*ẓithra*) hung over the performer's body or carried in front of it.

Etymologically, the word may be derived from the Hebrew noun *beṭen*, meaning "belly," an "empty" or "hollow" object, also the "belly of a column," or a "protuberance."[602] It is probable, therefore, that *baṭon* refers either to the bulging form of the instrument, or to the circumstance that it was played at the height of the waist, in contrast to other instruments of a similar category, like the *pandura*, which were held before the breast. KRAUSS thinks that the *baṭon* was a large type of harp, held before the body, but admits that the name might as well refer to the belly-like shape of an instrument.[603]

Another species of ancient Oriental instruments, likewise held before the body at the height of the waist, was the zither. According to SACHS, the Egyptians did not have zither-like instruments.[604] But Israel's neighbors, the Phoenicians, knew a kind of zither. It would be possible, therefore, that such an instrument has found its way to Israel as well. There are no means, however, of finding out whether the *baṭon* was such a zither-like instrument, or belonged rather to a type of guitars.

It may be surmised that there was some connection between BERTINORO's *ẓithra* and the Phoenician zither, but conjectures in this regard would be merely theoretical.

In modern Hebrew *baṭnon* signifies a "very large *kinnor* [a stringed instrument] with a heavy voice," that is the bass-viol.[605]

32. ʾADRABOLIN (ʾARDABALIS or ʾADRABLIS)

As a commentary to Gen. 4:21, the Midrash uses two Aramaic names of instruments. The biblical passage reads:

> "And his brother's name was Jubal, he was the father of all such as handle the harp (*kinnor*) and the pipe (*ʿugab*)," and the Midrash comments: "that is organplayers (*ʾadrabolin*) and flutists (*barbolin,* also spelled *korablin* and *karkalin*)."[606]

This interpretation of the two instruments mentioned initially in the Bible would indicate that the Aramaic term for the biblical *kinnor* was supposedly *ʾadrabolin,* and for the *ʿugab-ḥalil* the word *barbolin* (or its variants).[607]

In another passage of the Midrash, too, *ʾadrabolin* and *barbolin* (*korablin*) are mentioned together, but here with a completely different meaning.[608] This passage refers to the biblical tale of the destruction of Sodom. As the Scriptures say, God sent two of his angels to Lot summoning him and his family to flee the city, doomed by the Lord for the immorality of its inhabitants.

"And Lot went out, and spoke to his sons-in-law, who were to marry his daughters, 'Up, get you out of this place; for the Lord will destroy the city.' But he seemed unto his sons-in-law to be jesting." (Gen. 19:14).

In the Midrashic comment to this biblical passage, the sons-in law, astonished by Lot's urgent behest, ask him:

"How, there are organs and cymbals (*ʾadrabolin u-korablin*) in the land, and such land should be destroyed?"[609]

Both English renditions (to Gen. 4:21 and 19:14) are erroneous. In the latter one, *ʾadrabolin* is again translated as "organs," but *korablin* as "cymbals." While in the former quotation the Aramaic *ʾadrabolin* was used as an equivalent for the Hebrew *kinnor,* a stringed instrument, here it is used for the *hydraulis,* that is, the water-organ of the ancients with pipes, and therefore a wind instrument.

It is generally assumed by commentators of the Talmud that *ʾadrabolin* (and its numerous other spellings *ʾardabalis, hardulis, ʾadrikolin,* etc.) are the corruptedly transliterated Greek word *hydraulis.* The similarity of sound, together with the frequent inversion of the letters *u* (*v*) and *b* in the Greek language, lend a positive probability to this assumption. Judging from the reports of some talmudic writers, the *hydraulis* was known to the Hebrews, and it is even maintained that, under the name of *magrephah,* it was used in Herod's Temple. This, however, is denied by other Sages, and moreover there are weighty arguments against this assumption.[610]

RASHI's commentary to Midrash, *Genesis* L:9 is apt to increase the prevailing differences of opinion. In this comment he defines both instruments, *ʾadrabolin* and *korablin* as *mine zemer,* "instruments for the song." An identical idea is expressed in a commentary of the *Matenoth Kehunah* to the same passage. This explanation, too, states that both names refer to *mine kle zemer,* "instruments to [accompany] the song." The English renditions in the Midrash of *korablin* as "cymbals" cannot be harmonized with either RASHI or the *Matenoth Kehunah.*

It is difficult to find one's way out from this maze of contradictory opinions. First of all, there seems to be no doubt that the Aramaic *ʾadrabolin* (and its various spellings) are in fact corrupted transliterations of the Greek word *hydraulis.* Yet, the assumption that the Aramaic *ʾadrabolin* is the equivalent for the Hebrew *kinnor* cannot be maintained. It is not to be supposed that the Midrashic scribes were so ignorant of musical instruments as to confound the *kinnor* with the water-organ of their time. (We leave here out of consideration the *poetica licentia* of legendary tales, which indulge in transferring a rather developed and complicated instrument of the talmudic epoch, such as the *hydraulis,* back into the primitive situation of the earliest biblical times).

Nevertheless, the Midrashic juxtaposition of the two names (*ʾabrabolin u-korablin*), in characterizing two different categories of biblical instruments, cannot be simply dismissed. Generally speaking, both categories (strings and winds) are standing always as contrasting groups in the biblical text.[611] It should be assumed that this is also the true meaning and purpose of the Midrashic comment to Gen. 4:21.

As will be seen subsequently, *korablin* (or *barbolin*) seems definitely to refer to a flute-like instrument, or to a player of such, or else to be a collective term for woodwinds. In this case, *ʾadrabolin* must have signified the other category of instruments, the strings. How the Midrashic scribe managed to confound the water-organ with stringed instruments, in this instance with the *kinnor,* is a mystery which defies a logical explanation.

As for the Midrashic comment to the other biblical passage (Gen. 19:14), it reveals the rabbinic attitude toward the revelries of certain strata of society, in which organ-players and flutists were a common feature. The rabbinic anathema, therefore, was hurled not merely against the feasts as such, but also against the instruments used on such occasions. This is the real meaning of the Midrashic concept that Sodom had to be destroyed because "there were *ʾadrabolin* and *korablin* in the land."

The confusion with regard to the interpretation of both names of instruments was even increased by the statement of one of the early Amoraim, R. SIMEON ben LAḲISH (d. 275 C.E.), who declared that "the *ʿugab* was the *ʾirdablis* (or *ʾidrablis*)," meaning, of course, the *hydraulis.*[612] It was repeatedly pointed out that the statements of the rabbinic writers about instruments have to be taken with utmost caution. Yet SIMEON ben LAḲISH was certainly qualified to know the *hydraulis* better. For in his youth he used to be a gladiator in the Roman circus, where he must have had the opportunity of seeing and hearing the *hydraulis,* a characteristic musical instrument at such popular shows of those days.[613] The fact that he confounds the *ʿugab,* a small and delicate instrument, with the voluminous and noisy *hydraulis,* is not only an obvious error, but a further proof that relatively soon after the destruction of the sanctuary the knowledge of biblical instruments had been lost or was completely eclipsed by the different musical practice of the talmudic age.

In contradistinction to the erroneous interpretation of R. SIMEON ben LAḲISH, the logical meaning of the names of both instruments, *ʾadrabolin* and *korablin,* corresponding to the biblical text of Gen. 4:21, comes clearly to the fore. In the Midrashic concept, *ʾadrabolin* referred to some stringed instrument, or to a generic term for such, while *korablin* signified the pipe, or a pipe-player, or was also a collective name for woodwinds, as will be shown later.

As for the other Midrashic passage where the two names appear together, the only explanation that presents itself is that this comment had been written by a different scribe who seems to have been ignorant of how his predecessor interpreted in Aramaic the two instruments in Gen. 4:21. For the latter passage (to Gen. 19:14) we must therefore accept *ʾadrabolin* at its face value as referring to the *hydraulis* of the talmudic age.

(b) Wind Instruments

33. ʾABUB

The term *ʾabub* (pl. *ʾabubim*) is used by rabbinical writers as a synonym of *ḥalil* and *ʿugab.* According to R. PAPPA, all these words designate the same instrument, the pipe (or oboe).[614] As the Talmud says, *ʾabub roʿeh,* "shepherd's pipe," was one of the three implements in use with shepherds.[615]

Etymologically, ʾ*abub* is derived from a verb which means "to bore," "to hollow out." The word is related to the name of the Akkadian (Semitic) *imbubu,* a pipe-like instrument, brought to Syria, where eventually it became one of the domestic instruments. From there, the Israelites might have taken it over.

According to the rabbinic tradition, "there was a flute (ʾ*abub*) in the sanctuary."[616] If there really were among the instruments of the cult one dating back to Moses' times, the biblical chroniclers would have hardly failed to mention this venerable item. It is clearly one of those legendary tales so frequently encountered in the talmudic literature.

According to a Mishnaic description there were ʾ*abubim* entirely of metal, being different from those of reed by their stronger sound:

> "And they did not play on a pipe of bronze (ʾ*abub shel neḥoshet*), but on a reed-pipe (ʾ*abub shel ḳoneh*), since its sound was sweeter (ʾ*areb.*")[617]

In his commentary to this passage MAIMONIDES says that the ʾ*abub* was a pipe of reed with a mouthpiece of metal or reed. Considering the conventional technique of building musical instruments, it is not quite easy to figure out how a woodwind instrument could have had a mouthpiece of metal.

As to the widely commented rabbinic statement that a solo instrumental passage at the end of a musical piece, played ordinarily by the ʾ*abub,* has been performed only with a single instrument, see pp. 313 ff

In the later period of the Second Temple the soft ʿ*ugab* might have been permanently supplanted by the more vigorous sound of the Syrian ʾ*abub.*

The intoning of wind instruments was called *hiḳḳah,* "to strike." According to KRAUSS, however, this word signified the beginning of a musical piece by percussion instruments.[618] This is only partly correct. True, cymbals were mostly used to indicate the start of a musical piece, and especially of singing; this, however, has nothing to do with the intonation itself. It is rather to be assumed that *hiḳḳah* refers to the manner of tone-production on wind instruments which, as commonly known, is achieved by some sort of striking of the tongue. In the Mishnah, the word *hiḳḳah* is used in connection with the ʾ*abub,* supposedly "struck" by the Nethinim to give the signal (evidently an initial tone) for the start of choral singing.[619] A similar usage was well known among the Greeks and Romans, who indicated with a pitch-pipe (*tonorion*), or with an ivory flageolet (*eburneole fistula*) the initial tone for singers, and even the general pitch-level for orators.[620]

A wide-spread renown, or rather notoriety, had been gained in Antiquity by the Syrian ʾ*abub*-playing girls, not so much owing to their artistry than because of their immoral life. As HORACE and SUETONIUS report, the *ambubajae,* the flute-girls, lived in the basement of the Roman circus which, for this reason, was surnamed *ambubajarum collegia;* their musical activity (playing the pipe) was merely a pretence for their ignoble trade. Probably such Syrian flute-girls have found their way also to Israel. It is understandable, therefore, that the anathema of the rabbinic Sages against immoral life in general, applied also against the musical instruments themselves, implements of this kind of life.

This gives a particular significance to the surprised question of Lot's sons-in-law:

> "There are organ-players and flute-players in the land and such land ought to be destroyed?"[621]

which, indicating the impending destruction of Sodom, is in reality a rabbinic ban in disguised form.

34. MAGREPHAH

No instrument supposedly known to the Israelites has to its credit so many contradictory reports as the *magrephah.* It is considered largely, though not unanimously, to have been identical with, or at least substantially close to, the Greek *hydraulis,* the water-organ. However, while the basic construction of the last-named instrument may fairly well be deduced from the ancient Greek and Latin sources, the various descriptions of the *magrephah* in the rabbinic literature are so fragmentary and confusing that it is impossible to gain from them a clear idea about the instrument itself as a whole.

It is worth while noting that, in their direct references to the Greek *hydraulis,* the rabbinic writers avail themselves persistently of its variously spelt, or misspelt, Semitic transliterations, such as *ʾardablis, ʾardabalis,*[622] *hardulis* and *hirdolim.*[623] (The two last names came into being through the exchange of the guttural vowels א and ה, and of the labial letters ב and ו).[624] On the other hand, the term *magrephah,* whether or not we take it as implying a Hebrew-Aramaic synonym of *hydraulis,* has no variants in the rabbinic literature.

The ancient existence, in the Mediterranean area, of the pneumatic organ, an enlarged species of the Pan's pipe, activated by bellows, is attested by some excavated objects dating, in some instances, before the 4th century B.C.E.[625] In the 3rd century B.C.E. emerges a technical improvement of it, the *hydraulis,* its air flow having been regulated by a water-pressure mechanism. ATHENAEUS quotes ARISTOTLE:

> "The *hydraulis* may be described as a wind instrument, since wind is forced into it by water. For the pipes are set low in water, and as the water is briskly agitated by a boy, air is released in the pipes through certain valves which fit into the pipes from one side of the organ to the other, and a pleasant sound is produced."[626]

It is difficult to establish beyond doubt whether anyone of the two organs just referred to is of Egyptian or Babylonian-Assyrian origin. It is assumed, however, that a primitive form of the pneumatic pipe-organ was known in Mesopotamia and has been taken over eventually by the Hellenes. In Greek and later Latin writings the instrument is frequently mentioned under various names. Several historians, like PHILON (fl. 150 B.C.E.), VITRUVIUS (fl. 70 B.C.E.), and others, furnish rather profuse and essentially accordant descriptions of it.[627] (Illustr. 53, 54).

Among musicologists and modern talmudic scholars there are two schools of thought with regard to the problem of *magrephah-hydraulis.* Some hold that the two names refer to the same instrument, *i.e.* that *magrephah* was the

ILLUSTRATION NO. 53.
A terra-cotta figurine, showing a Syrian piper singing and playing. Another musician, seemingly a dwarf (or a child) plays the cymbals (last century B.C.E.) After Hans Hickman, *Musicologie Pharaonique,* Kehl a.Rh., 1956).

ILLUSTRATION NO. 54
Primtiive organ (probably 1. cent. C.E.) Museum, Arles (After William G. Gratton Flood, *The Story of the Bagpipe,* New York, 1911).

Hebrew-Aramaic term for the Greek water-organ;[628] others think that they indicated two different instruments. This latter opinion is based mainly on a talmudic passage, which quotes the statements of two rabbinic authorities about the basic question whether or not some instrument of the pipe-work category has been used in the Temple.[629] This passage reads:

> "R. SIMEON b. GAMALIEL said: There was no *hirdolim* in the Sanctuary. (What is *hirdolim*?) ABAYE said: A musical instrument (*ṭabla gurgana*) worked by pressure [of water] because its sound was heavy (*ʾab*) and disturbed the music.[630] RABBAH b. SHILAH, in the name of MATTENAH, on the authority of SAMUEL, said: There was a *magrephah* in the Sanctuary; it had ten holes, each of which produced ten different kinds of sounds, with the result that the whole amounted to one hundred kinds of sounds. A Tanna taught: It was one cubit (*ʾammah*) long, one cubit high, from it projected a handle (*ḳuta*), which had ten holes. Each of them produced one hundred kinds of sounds. Said R. NAḤMAN bar ISAAC: To remember whose teaching it is: 'The *baraitha* exaggerates.' "[631]

As we see, R. SIMEON answers the question in the negative, whereas R. RABBAH b. SHILAH, drawing upon the authority of two famous rabbis, maintains that there was indeed a pipe-work in the Temple. R. SIMEON lived around 135 C.E., R. RABBAH two centuries later; his two witnesses, R. MATTENAH and R.

SAMUEL around the year 200 C.E. Consequently, none of them could attest from their own observation the existence or non-existence either of the *hydraulis* or the *magrephah* in the Sanctuary.

It is argued that in the above cited talmudic passage R. SIMEON spoke of the *hydraulis,* whereas R. RABBAH b. SHILAH, whose opinion in the talmudic text is separated from that of R. SIMEON by the remark of ABAYE NAHMANI, spoke of the *magrephah.* From this the conclusion was drawn that the two rabbis spoke of two *different* instruments and that by collating their opinions in one paragraph, the talmudic scribe allegedly was trying to clarify specifically for his readers which one of these two instruments was used in the Temple, and not whether some sort of untraditional instrument was played in the Sanctuary at all.

Let us now scrutinize the question whether the two names refer to the same instrument or not.

Favoring the assumption that R. SIMEON and RABBAH b. SHILAH spoke of different instruments is the complete lack of any historical evidence, either in rabbinic or other coeval sources, that the Greek *hydraulis* was ever called *magrephah* in Aramaean. Just the contrary seems to be true; the Greek word was manifestly transplanted phonetically into the Aramaean, with some mutations in spelling, conditioned by the changed idiom. Furthermore, it is argued that ABAYE NAḤMANI's epithet *ṭabla gurgana,* meaning literally an "organ-instrument," applied merely to the *hydraulis,* not to the *magrephah* of the immediately following sentence in the same rabbinic passage.

Against the assumption that the two first-named rabbis spoke of different instruments it may be pointed out that the description of the *magrephah* as given by RABBAH b. SHILAH unquestionably refers to a pipe-work instrument. The *hydraulis* having been a wind instrument fed by water-pressure, it is conceivable that the term *magrephah* might be the name of the other species of ancient pipe-works, the pneumatic organ.[632] And just as there is no historic evidence that the rabbis called the Greek *hydraulis* by the name of *magrephah,* nothing alludes in the talmudic text either that R. SIMEON and RABBAH b. SHILAH spoke of different instruments; they may have merely applied to them different names, as in the statement of ABAYE, which stands between those of the aforementioned Sages.

Concerning the character and purpose of the *magrephah* there are several contradictory hypotheses, which will be discussed presently.

As for the actual existence, or non-existence, of either the *magrephah* or *hydraulis* in the Sanctuary, it is striking that neither the Apocrypha, nor the writings of PHILO and JOSEPHUS and their contemporaries contain the slightest allusion to such an instrument. It would seem that the musical and other implements of the sacred service must have been well known at least to the two Jewish writers, who both lived during the last decades of the Third Temple. Their complete silence on this score is the more significant since the rabbinic writers concur in their descriptions that the sound of the instrument in question was extremely loud, and this could have hardly remained unnoticed.

A detailed, though manifestly spurious, description of the *magrephah* can be found in PORTALEONE's *Shilṭe ha-Gibborim.*[633] PORTALEONE has obviously striven to avail himself largely of the talmudic indications. Nevertheless, his account contains quite a number of relatively modern traits. As a result, he succeeded in depicting more faithfully the organ of his epoch than that of the talmudic age.

The term *magrephah,* mentioned in various chapters of the rabbinic literature, is considered by many talmudic scholars as referring to altogether different objects. This opinion might have originated by RASHI, who was the first to liken the *magrephah* to a shovel made of brass, which was used for removing the ashes and cinders from the altar.[634] To clean it from the slags, the attendants would cast or throw it (to the floor?), thereby producing a sound, which—increased perhaps by the resonance of the vault or the walls of the court—was so loud that, according to one rabbinic statement,[635]

> "no one could hear the voice of his neighbor in Jerusalem because of the sound of the *magrephah,*" and it was added elsewhere that[636] "from Jericho they could hear the sound of the *magrephah.*"

RASHI does not limit himself to the extra-musical interpretation of this word, for he also adds that

> "there are possibly two sorts of *magrephot,* one for the ashes [the shovel] and one for music."[637]

Furthermore, he has a third explanation of the term, identifying the *magrephah* (or the *hydraulis*) with "a set of bells."[638] This certainly contributes to the existing confusion about the real nature of the instrument.

It was probably RASHI's opinion that induced PORTALEONE to speak of two species of *magrephot,* namely the *magrephah of 'Arakin,* and the *magrephah of Tamid,* respectively.[639] The former of the two was likened to some pipe-work instrument, having had

> "ten holes and every hole emitted ten different sounds."[640]

The latter was considered to be an altar-cleaning implement[641] or as a modern commentator thinks,

> "a utensil shaped like a shovel serving the purpose of a signal-gong."[642]

All the non-Jewish authors of later times, ATHANASIUS KIRCHER,[643] CASPAR PRINTZ,[644] and others, follow more or less PORTALEONE's description of the *magrephah,* but are still more influenced in this respect by the technically developed organ of their times. KIRCHER, for instance, does not hesitate to assert that the *magrephah* was "similar to our church organ," a statement which needless to say, lacks any historical perspective.

Some more recent commentators are inclined to interpret the *magrephah* as a sort of signal instrument. So PFEIFFER, who says that the instrument was a hand-drum or a kettle-drum.[645] JASTROW, too, thinks that it was "a sort of *tympanum.*"[646] As mentioned above, DANBY identifies it with a signal-gong. JOSEPH YASSER holds that the *magrephah* was a pipe-work, but not an organ of any kind serving musical purposes. In a private letter to the author, he describes it as a noise-making signal instrument, consisting of a great number of small and shrill pipes, activated pneumatically, and pitched rather indiscriminately to fractional intervals within a high and narrow range (probably less than an octave). All the pipes were sounding *simultaneously,* according to this view which, among other considerations (see *infra* p. 403), explains allegedly the interference of the instrument with the audibility of the human speech (referred to in rabbinic writings), such phenomenon being eminently characteristic of high-pitched instrumental tones.[647]

FARMER alludes to the alternate use of the Latin word *projicio* (akin to the Mishnaic *zaraḳ; cf.* note 635) which, besides its regular meaning ("to throw," "to project"), has a metaphoric sense, "to expel, drive out, obtrude, utter."[648] This seems to support YASSER's hypothesis. Yet FARMER does not exclude the possibility either that the *magrephah of Tamid* might have been the same instrument as the *magrephah of ʿArakin* (see p. 403). He thinks as more probable, however, that the *magrephah of ʿArakin* was a pneumatic organ.[649] Yet, even if we may interpret the talmudic statement as referring to a pneumatic organ (or pipe-work), there remains still a serious doubt about the admissibility of such an interpretation, since it is rather improbable that such an instrument (even in its crude form for signal purposes) could have been used in the Temple.

As the Mishnah states, the *magrephah* was cast or thrown (*zaraḳ*) between the vestibule (or porch) and the Temple itself, and

> "it was used for three things: when a priest heard the noise of it he knew that his brethren the priests had entered in to prostrate themselves, and he ran and came also; and when a Levite heard the noise of it he knew that his brethren the Levites were gone to sing, and he ran and came also; and [when he heard the noise of it] the chief of the *maʿamad* made the unclean to stand at the Eastern Gate."[650]

Therefore, whatever the *magrephah* might have been, a drum, a gong, or a pipe-work, its purpose, according to the Mishnah, was to give a loud signal. We have to ask again, however, how such a powerful signal summoning to important ritual functions in the daily service could have remained unnoticed by coeval historians such as PHILO and JOSEPHUS, so as to pass them in complete silence.

The rabbinic commentaries, at least those which assert that there *was* a *magrephah* in the Sanctuary, concur in declaring that its sound was very powerful, from which it has been frequently concluded that it must have been a rather voluminous instrument. Yet, according to rabbinic descriptions (divulging only its *two* dimensions), it was one ʾ*ammah* (an ell of 21 inches) wide and had the same height.[651] This description would seem to point to a relatively small, though not necessarily a weak sounding, instrument, if we take the measurements for those of the wind-box. PORTALEONE completes these measurements in saying that the length of the box was 2½ ʾ*ammah* (ca. 53 inches),[652] for which statement there is no evidence in the rabbinic literature.

The indication about the immense tone-volume of the *magrephah* seems to be greatly exaggerated. Theoretically, it might not have been impossible to hear in Jericho a very loud instrument played in Jerusalem, especially at night time and under favorable atmospheric conditions. Jericho was only three *parasangs* (nine or ten miles) from Jerusalem,[653] but according to the Mishnah eight *parasangs* (about twenty-five miles).[654] The plausibility of the statement, however, is considerably minced by the Mishnaic text itself. For if it might have been possible to hear a very loud instrument from a distance of three *parasangs,* then it is impossible, as the Mishnah asserts, that

> "from Jericho they could hear the noise of the opening of the great gate; from Jericho they could hear the noise of the wooden device which Ben Katin made for the laver; from Jericho they could hear the sound of the flute (*ḥalil*); from Jericho they could hear the noise of the cymbal (*ẓilẓal*); from Jericho they could hear the sound of the singing (*shir*) [of the Levites]; from Jericho they could hear the sound of the *shofar;* and some say, even the voice of the High Priest when he pronounced the Name on the Day of Atonement; from Jericho they could smell the smell at the compounding of the incense."[655]

This last statement in particular is liable to destroy completely the credibility of the above recounting, proving that the whole passage had merely a figurative meaning.

The spurious letter to Dardanus relates, among others, that the Jewish "organ" could be heard

> *ab Jerusalem usque ad montem oliveti et amplius,* "from Jerusalem to the Mount of Olives and farther."[656]

This statement would be more likely, since Jerusalem is separated from the Mount of Olives only by the Valley of Kidron. It is unnecessary, however, to point out that the unknown author of this spurious letter could not have based his statement upon a personal observation, since he lived either in JEROME's time (340-420 C.E.), or somewhat later.

As the Palestinian Talmud states, the reason why the *hydraulis* (spelled in this place *ʾardabalim*) was not used in the Sanctuary was that its heavy sound "spoils the sweetness of the singing" (*mipne shehayʾa soreaḥ ha-neʿimah*).[657] Yet, ATHENAEUS (fl. end of 2nd and beginning of 3rd centuries C.E.) gives quite a different description of the sound quality of the instrument:

> "There was heard from a neighboring house the sound of a water-organ (*hydraulis*); it was very sweet and joyous (*hēdys kai terpnos*), so that we all turned our attention to it, charmed by its tunefulness (*emmelais*)."[658]

ATHENAEUS describes the sound of an instrument which he heard himself; it must have been small of size, suited for domestic use, therefore its sound might have been indeed soft and pleasant. Contrary to ATHENAEUS, the rabbinic writers follow the oral "tradition," that is they report from hearsay.

From all that we know about the early organs of Antiquity, it may be inferred that the tone quality of the *hydraulis,* and also that of the pneumatic organ, must have been rough and shrill.[659] And this would certainly warrant their exclusion from the solemn and sedate music of the Jewish sacred service. In the era of the Roman emperors the water-organ was the favorite instrument at spectacular circus shows. Perhaps the recollection of it evoked the idea among the later rabbinic writers that the *magrephah,* too, was a noisy instrument, capable of destroying the "sweetness" of the melody.[660]

Had the *magrephah* been a shovel, or an instrument used only for signal purposes, there could not have been any connection between it and levitical singing, consequently it could not have spoiled the "sweetness" of the song. This exposes another incoherence in the rabbinic reporting. The sacred service used mainly the *kle shir*, "instruments for the song" (strings, sometimes woodwinds) as accompaniment for levitical singing. It is rather improbable that the musical practice of the Second or even the Third Temple would have abandoned this usage of many centuries hallowed by tradition and entrust the accompaniment of the sacred songs to a rather clumsy pipe-work instrument.

According to rabbinic descriptions, the *magrephah* had ten holes (*neḳeb*), each of these holes emitting ten different tones, so that the instrument could produce the total of one hundred different tones. In order to understand the inadequate account of writers evidently unfamiliar with the construction of musical instruments, we have to substitute for "holes" the word "grooves," and will then realize that these may have been the air-supplying cavities in which the pipes (*koneh*) were set horizontally or vertically, ten pipes for each groove, so that the instrument could indeed (theoretically at least) produce one hundred tones.[661]

The Palestinian Talmud contains a verbatim discussion about the *magrephah* of two learned rabbis, RAB and SAMUEL, one of whom said that the instrument had ten holes each producing one hundred different sounds, the other that it had one hundred holes, each emitting ten sounds, amounting in both cases to one thousand different tones.[662] The Babylonian Talmud quotes a similar statement by an anonymous rabbinic authority who, however, amplifies it with such an unconventional detail by placing the alluded ten holes in the instrument's "handle" that it creates still another and grave difficulty for the satisfactory solution of our problem. R. NAḤMAN bar ISAAC felt even induced to utter his characteristic warning that "the *baraitha* exaggerates" (see p. 395). Exaggerations of this kind are due to the commonly known inclination of the rabbinic writers to attribute retrospectively grandiose and exalted qualities to the institutions of the Temple.

On the other hand, the origin of the above talmudic statement has been hypothetically explained by the following historical reference that stems from a non-Jewish source:

> "The Byzantines nicknamed the organ 'the instrument of a thousand voices,' a phrase which has been borrowed by the Jews, as it was by the Arabs and Persians."[663]

The famous Arabic writer on music, ʾAL MASʿUDI (d. ca. 957) mentions this term in his work *"The Book of the Golden Prairies and the Mines of Precious Stones"*:

> "Among the instruments of the Byzantines are mentioned: the organ having sixteen strings [evidently: pipes], which has a big range of sound; it comes from Greece; furthermore, the *kiliophon* with twenty-four strings [pipes]; this word denotes 'thousand tones.' "[664]

This, however, is rather implausible as far as the time element is taken into consideration. For the Byzantine empire was consolidated after the completion of the Talmud (499 C.E.). Things are different, however, if we assume that this nickname existed already earlier in the Orient and was taken over by the Israelites as well as by other peoples, including the Byzantines.

Another erroneous belief should be mentioned here, because it was long held to have reasonable grounds. Some commentators considered Daniel's *mashroḳita* (Dan. 3:5,7,10,15) as being identical with the *magrephah.* This error was initiated by ATHANASIUS KIRCHER, who furnishes a detailed description and an "illustration" of the *mashroḳita,* giving the impression of an organ-like instrument.[665] KIRCHER's delineation, made two thousand years after the event related by Daniel and not supported by any historical evidence, must be considered by any critical observer as an obvious product of pure imagination. Nevertheless, quite a number of later authors had accepted KIRCHER's theory as authentic and taken it over as an historical fact.[666]

There is one point in which the rabbinical descriptions concur, namely that the instrument (or whatever it might have been) had a handle (*ḳuta*). This was probably the main reason why at least the *magrephah of Tamid* has been identified with a shovel. The idea has even a sort of etymological justification. For the root of *magrephah* is *garaph,* a verb with a double meaning, "to carry, to sweep away," and "to grasp."[667] From this verb a substantive was formed and, according to this etymology, the *magrephah* became identified with a shovel.

The indications of the rabbis about this handle are extremely vague. In fact, the compiler of the Mishnah offers no other explanation except that it was the stick of a shovel, and a later talmudic personage, as we already know, made a further "elucidating" remark that the handle of the *magrephah* harboured the sound-producing part of the entire mechanism. Anyone even superficially familiar with the construction of a pipe-work instrument could easily realize that regardless of any other possible functions, the handle might have been the necessary device for pumping the air.

This obvious, though largely overlooked consideration is indeed one of the essential mainstays of a theory of JOSEPH YASSER, according to which the act of "throwing" (or "flinging," or "casting," in other translations) the *magrephah* between two spots might well have involved the back-and-forth *swinging* of the handle which pumped the air for the instrument and which, incidentally, may conceivably have been shaped like a shovel. By mentioning the porch and the altar, the Mishnaic scribe might have simply indicated the *direction* in which the swinging has taken place.

It would be quite possible, in YASSER's opinion, for such a shovel-shaped and presumably hollowed handle to serve as an air canal connected with bellows and, at its fanned-out end, as a small wind-chest holding on one of its sides 100 tiny and horizontally fastened pipes. These might have been economically distributed among the separate and circularly arranged ranks, each such "bunch" of ten pipes being inserted into a single collective groove. The round form of these grooves, inevitable under the described conditions, would naturally impress any layman as a hole-like cavity,—hence the redundant rabbinic references to the entire set as "ten holes." (Illustr. 55).

It goes without saying that YASSER's theory, if accepted, would obviate the frequently recurrent speculation as to how the *magrephah* with its rather complex mechanism, involving many pipes and other delicate parts, could have been thrown to the ground or elsewhere (the Mishnaic word *zaraḳ* pointing

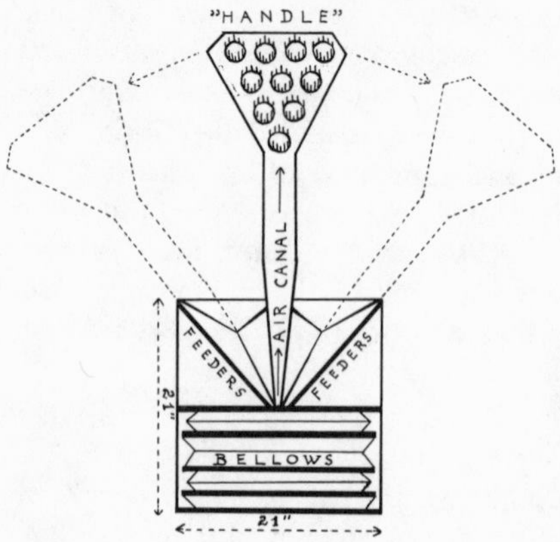

ILLUSTRATION NO. 55.

The Magrephah (After Joseph Yasser, *The Magrephah of the Herodian Temple,* in *Journal of the American Musicological Society,* Richmond, Va. 1960).

to such an act, according to some Western interpreters)[668] without suffering serious damage. True enough, the text of the Mishnah does not contain anything intimating "floor" or "ground."[669] But it is difficult to imagine how an object cast or thrown in the air could have landed elsewhere than on the ground, unless it was connected loosely with another and stable object which prevented such "landing" and, at the same time, did not interfere with its movement. It would likewise become unnecessary to figure out how the throwing of the *magrephah,* if it indicated a plain shovel, could have produced such a loud sound as to be heard in Jericho, or drown out the conversation of neighbors in Jerusalem.

A peculiar opinion is expressed in a modern work, conjecturing that the verb *zaraḳ,* "to throw," should possibly be read, with a minor change, as *sharaḳ,* "to pipe." This, applied to the sounding of the *hydraulis,* might have had a grain of logic.[670] However, *sharaḳ* in talmudic Hebrew signifies "to hiss," "to whistle," "to quack," and is applied in rabbinic writings mostly to sounds produced by animals, so for frogs,[671] for birds,[672] etc. Furthermore, there are serious linguistic arguments against transforming *vezorḳah* into a similar construction using the verb *sharaḳ;* the parallel grammatical form would be *veshorak,* which could hardly be harmonized with the spelling of the word in the original Mishnaic text.

There is still another reason against the hypothetic use of the verb *sharaḳ* in this place. As the Mishnah states, it was the *priest* who would start the operation of the *magrephah.*[673] Should we assume that the instrument was not "cast" but "piped" (*i.e.* played), it would amount to transforming the priest into a musician—an obvious, and unthinkable, deviation of the strict priestly tradition.

A Medieval source gives a different explanation of the meaning of *zaraḳ* in the Mishnah:

> "ABRAHAM ben DAVID [of Posquières, France, 12th century] declares . . . that . . . *zaraḳ* here does not mean 'to throw,' but—figuratively—'to eject suddenly and simultaneously its sounds,' similar to [the meaning of the verb in another talmudic passage] *nizreḳah mipi ha-ḥaborah* (Tal.Bab., *Pesaḥim* 64 a)."[674]

The translation of this latter passage is:

> "It was thrown out from the mouth of the company," interpreted by the modern English translator as "all the scholars unanimously declared."[675]

A similar idea concerning the meaning of *zaraḳ* is expressed by FARMER, who ventures the hypothesis that the *magrephah of Tamid* was possibly the same instrument as the *magrephah of ʿArakin.* He seems to have found a connection between the two in the verb *zaraḳ* and puts the question:

> "Why should *zaraḳ* not be used in a figurative sense in the same way as we speak of 'throwing the voice'?"[676]

As an oblique illustration, he refers to Hos. 7:9 where, as he asserts, *zaraḳ* likewise has a figurative sense, although—as he adds—not in the latter meaning. In reality, however, there is no obvious parallel between the use of *Tamid's zaraḳ* ("to cast, to throw") and that of the same verb in Hosea, where it refers to hairs "sprinkled" with gray.[677]

YASSER bolsters his theory with the above mentioned two passages, maintaining that *Tamid's zaraḳ* implied a highly conspicuous (to the worshippers at least) pendulum-like movement of the handle of the *magrephah* between the Porch and the Altar, that 'threw out' (or 'sprinkled'; cf. note 635) all the tones of this instrument simultaneously.[678]

Among talmudic scholars, KRAUSS tries to clarify the various notions about the talmudic *hydraulis,* without finding, however, a useful solution[679] As a matter of fact, his statements are rather apt to increase the existing confusion in this respect. He refers to R. ABAYE NAḤMANI (d. 338 C.E.), who declared that the *hydraulis* was identical with the *ṭabla.* In KRAUSS' opinion this rabbi must have committed an "error," since *ṭabla* was the name of a percussion instrument, and KRAUSS considers it strange that the *hydraulis* should have been so completely misinterpreted. He overlooks, however, the fact that the word *ṭabla* had rather frequently the meaning of "musical instrument" in general (see p. 409), and that the dual term *ṭabla gurgana,* as shown above (p. 395), signified an "organ-instrument." Yet, KRAUSS opines that the complementary term *gurgana* meant simply "the receptacle or the sound-box of the mechanism."

It is difficult indeed to pick out from such a mass of contradictory statements a kernel of historical truth or even a remote probability. But manifestly enough, Hellenistic Jewry must have known the Greek water-organ. Its invention is ordinarily ascribed to the engineer KTESIBIOS of Alexandria (2nd half of the 3rd century B.C.E.).[680] According to other sources, however, it was invented by PLATO (338-348 B.C.E.), ARISTOTLE (384-322 B.C.E.), or ARCHIMEDES (287-212 B.C.E.).[681] One certain thing emerges from these historical references, namely that the *hydraulis* was either a Greek invention, or that it was mechanically improved by the Hellenes.

It is certain that the Israelites considered the *hydraulis* to be a pagan instrument. An historical and repeatedly mentioned fact is that Hellenism has made great strides in the concluding centuries of Jewish national existence, particularly among the inhabitants of the big cities, who entertained daily contact with the Greeks. The inroads of Hellenism into the ancient Jewish mores and manners were frowned upon by the priests, the guardians of the sacred tradition. The Sanctuary was strictly opposed to the introduction into the rites of any Hellenistic ideas or customs. The attitude of the servants of the true faith against Hellenism is aptly characterized by the contempt shown by the Sages against Greek song. The Talmud says about the apostate ELISHA ben ABUYA:

> "Greek song did not cease from his mouth."[682]

The moral turpitude of this renegade is ascribed to his predilection for Greek, that is, heathen song.

In the long run, this hostility went so far that even the instruments already used in the First Temple aroused the enmity of some priestly zealots. In a document from the Hellenistic period of Israel it is said:

> "They [the faithful] do not pour blood of sacrifices upon the altar; no tympanon is sounded, nor cymbals, nor the aulos with its many holes, instruments full of frenzied tones, nor the whistling of a pan's pipe is heard, imitating the serpent, nor the trumpet calling to war in wild tones."[683]

Nevertheless, in a modern essay about Jewish music we find this positive statement:

> "The organ was used regularly in the Second Temple and is called *Magrephah.* The tractate *ʿArakin* gives us a fairly good description of the *Magrephah.*"[684]

Is it then conceivable that the priests, faithful to the tradition, would have tolerated the introduction into the Sanctuary of a Hellenistic musical instrument, regardless of its practical purpose? There are, on the contrary, good reasons to believe that the *hydraulis* was opposed by the religious purists of that epoch just as mercilessly as the "Christian" organ of later times, and even to-day, by the orthodox Jews. The *magrephah,* on the other hand, might have been more acceptable to the Temple authorities, if we believe it to have represented a sheer noise-making contrivance bereft of any musical implication.

Be it as it may, one is not surprised to find the opinions of the rabbis so radically divided about the basic question whether or not there was a *hydraulis* or *magrephah* in the Temple.

On the other hand, nothing opposes the assumption that the *magrephah,* in the meaning of a shovel, was one of the implements used in the Temple service. The daily cleaning of the altar from ashes, slags and other remnants of the sacrifices was an obvious necessity, for which the shovel or jagging iron could very well have been a utensil called *magrephah.*

It can easily be reconciled with the rabbinic statement that there was no *magrephah* in the Temple, if we apply this term either to the pneumatic organ, or as a synonym to the Greek *hydraulis.* And as for its powerful sound, this may be considered as one of the frequent exaggerations of rabbinical scribes which, as shown above, is even shattered by the Mishnaic text itself.

As for the use of the *hydraulis* by the Jews outside the Sanctuary, there are reasons to believe that this may have happened at some secular occasions. The Israelites in big cities were more inclined to adopt certain Greek customs than the inhabitants of the countryside. Thus, there are a few references in the Midrashim to the effect that players of water-organs (*ʾadrablin-hydraulai*) and pipers (*korablin-choraulai*) have been employed at festivities.[685] From this, KRAUSS concludes that the saying "there are organ-players and flute-players in the land" is a mere figure of speech, which means in fact that the inhabitants of the place in question live riotously.[686] To be sure, the Midrash does not clarify whether such itinerant organ-players and pipers were Jewish or non-Jewish. But probably the latter was the case, since we know that gentile musicians were frequently employed at Jewish weddings especially on the Sabbath when playing of instruments was forbidden to the Jews.

o
o o

All the above presented evidence warrants the assumption that there was no *magrephah* in the Temple, at least not in the sense of an organ-like instrument. True, SACHS opines that a vague possibility remains that such an instrument was used in the last period of the Third Temple, without having found any evidence for it.[687] The introduction of such an instrument just before the last tragic fight of Israel for her national survival would certainly not have remained unnoticed by the contemporary historians like JOSEPHUS and PHILO. The fact that they pass over this in complete silence may serve as the proof that the Tannaim and Amoraim, and after them the medieval writers, projected back into biblical times the organ-like instruments of their own times.

35. BARBOLIN (KORBALIN, KORABLIN, or KARKALIN)

As shown above (chapter 32), two Midrashic passages mention *barbolin* (or its numerous variants) together with *ʾadrabolin*.[688] Their juxtaposition suggests that these two terms imply two different types of instruments.

The etymology of the word is obvious. In one of these passages (Gen. L:9), *barbolin* appears merely as a corruption of the word *korablin*, which can easily be identified with the Greek *choraulēs* (*chorablēs*), the term for "flute-player."[689] In a further metamorphosis, *korablin* might have changed to *sorbalin*, *borbalin*, and was eventually incorporated as *barbolin* into the Aramaean language.[690]

Another, and even simpler explanation as to how *korablin* might have mutated into *barbolin* is that by an understandable inaccuracy of a rabbinic scribe the initial letter כ may have been taken for a ב, so that the word כרבלין could easily be read as ברבלין.

For the Midrashic passage: "There are organs and cymbals (*ʾadrabolin u-barbolin*) in the land . . ."[691] JASTROW suggests the following translation:

> "There are *hydraules*-players and flute-players in the land, and such land should be destroyed."

This explanation of *barbolin* is logical; it is obvious that it refers to pipe-players, or that it may be a collective term for woodwind instruments.

JASTROW's translation may be correct for L:9, but does not take into consideration the meaning of the other passage (XXIII:3), referring to Gen. 4:21, in which the juxtaposition of the two categories of biblical instrument, *kinnor* and *ʿugab*, should be expressed also in Aramaic. If *barbolin* refers to the pipe or pipe-players (as it unmistakably does), *ʾadrabolin* should necessarily be the term for a stringed instrument, or a family of these. It should also be recalled that in his commentary to this passage, RASHI characterized *ʾadrabolin* as well as *barbolin* (this latter word in a different spelling) as *mine zemer*, "instruments for the song,"[692] one of them referring, by inference, to stringed instruments. Thus, neither the extant translations of the Midrashim, nor JASTROW's suggestion do justice to the unmistakable and radical difference in the meaning of the two terms.

Though this has no bearing on the real or alleged meaning of the term, it is worth while to mention that RASHI, in his commentary to L:9, spells the word as *karkalin*, defining it as *mine zemer*, but with an entirely different meaning. He brings it in connection with David's dance on the occasion of transferring the ark of covenant to Jerusalem (2 Sam. 6:14) and says that *karkalin* refers to David's dancing, the Hebrew verb for which is *karker*. If this meaning still seems to have some justification, RASHI's other interpretation of the word, in the same sentence, attributes to it the sense of "singing," which tallies neither with the idea of *mine zemer*, nor with that of dancing.

For the rest, we refer to our exposition in chapter 32 of this section, in which we have advanced the opinion that in both Midrashic passages *barbolin* signifies the pipe, pipe-like instruments, or pipe-players.

36. ḲALAMEYLES

The word *ḳalameyls* (or *ḳalameyles*) serves RASHI as an explanation of the biblical *ḥalil*.[693] He maintains that this instrument, supposedly well known in his own time, was identical with the *ḥalil*.

The medieval French word is obviously derived from the Greek *kalamos*, or from its Latin equivalent *calamus* ("reed"). Both denote in Antiquity, besides the plant itself, an oboe-like instrument made of reed. ATHENAEUS mentions some instrument of this kind, the name of which is rather similar to that of RASHI's *ḳalameyls*:

> "Precisely, then, as they call persons who play on a reed-pipe (*kalamos*) *kalamaulae*, so do they call those who play the *rhappa*, which is also a reed, *rhappaulae*, as Amerias of Makedōn tells us in his *Glōssais*."[694]

In the French literature of the 12th century the instruments made of reed are called *chalamele* (the *chalumeau* of a later epoch), which included, to be sure, flutes, oboes, and especially Pan's pipes. Several medieval French poets mention an instrument *chalameles* with seven pipes.[695] This would obviously refer to the Pan's pipe, so different from the *ḥalil*. Yet, RASHI says that *ḳalameyls* was the name of a pipe-like instrument in *laz*, the spoken language of his time.

However, the biblical *ḥalil* and the *chalumeau* of RASHI's time (1040-1105) must have differed so markedly in form and sound that RASHI's assertion, actually identifying the two instruments, cannot be accepted at its face value. Perhaps RASHI intended merely to convey to his contemporaries the sound character of the *ḥalil* by comparing it with a more familiar instrument of his own epoch.

The only conclusion we may draw from RASHI's statement is that the Gaonim frequently substituted the nomenclature of their coeval instruments for those of the Bible, thereby creating a certain confusion among later commentators, not well versed in musical matters and especially in details concerning the nature of the various musical instruments.

(c) Percussion, Shaking and Rattling Instruments

37. NIḲTIMON (NIḲATMON)

In several Mishnaic passages we come across the word *niḳtimon* which—judging from the context—seems to indicate the pegs on which the strings were fastened. Yet, the true meaning of the word is not established beyond doubt. Some commentators interpret it as a music instrument, and thus warrant its close examination at this point.

The etymology of the word refers to *ʾanḳitmin,* meaning in general the protruding arm of an object, or something in the form of a human foot or leg. JASTROW interprets *ʾanḳitmin*[696] as well as *niḳatmon*[697] as a "musical instrument resembling a wooden leg." However, the rabbinic literature furnishes many other explanations of the term.

In discussing the prescriptions for cleanness, the Mishnah says that

> "the lute (*baṭnon*), the *niḳtimon* and the drum (*ʾerus*) are susceptible to uncleanness."[698]

Assuming that *niḳtimon* were the pegs for the strings, it is difficult to understand why this particular part of the instrument should have been subject to a special regulation. If the instrument itself was unclean, its parts were likewise unclean without referring to them specifically. The association of *niḳtimon* with two instruments (lute and drum) in this passage, seems to indicate that it may have rather been the name of an instrument different from the two others.

This becomes even more obvious from another passage of the Mishnah:

> "Clogs (*ʾanḳatmin*) are susceptible to uncleanness; and none may go out with them [on the Sabbath]."[699]

It would be oddly irrelevant to infer from this context that clogs or pegs of a stringed instrument are implied here. What reason could prevail upon anyone to go out on the Sabbath with only a single part of an instrument, and a small one at that? However, if the entire instrument is subject to uncleanness, there would be no sense in mentioning specifically one of its parts. We are thus driven to the conclusion that the word signifies something entirely different from the pegs for the strings. As in some other instances, the comparative method of the history of musical instruments, as applied in this particular case by SACHS, offers here a logical solution of the problem. His interpretation comes close to a satisfactory explanation of the seemingly enigmatic word:

> "If this term does mean an instrument, it might refer to those typical Egyptian clappers of wood or ivory which were carved to form a human arm with the hand and which were exclusively played by women; or to the boot-shaped clappers of the Greek."[700]

Cautiously SACHS adds: "But this is nothing more than a suggestion." It is probable, however, that the word refers indeed to a kind of clapper, since such instrument is mentioned also in another passage of the early rabbinic literature:

> "One may not ring a bell (*zog*) or a clapper (*ḳarḳash*) for a child on the Sabbath."[701]

PORTALEONE's interpretation of the term *ʿoẓe beroshim* as "sticks of fir-wood," in the sense of a clapper instrument,[702] although offered long after the talmudic age, seems to confirm the assumption that the Israelites, like other peoples of Antiquity, have known clapper instruments.[703] On the other hand, PORTALEONE's assertion that the *magrephah* was also a "clapper," is manifestly untenable.

If we assume with SACHS, and other commentators, that *niḳtimon* indicates a sort of a clapper, then RASHI's commentary may be mentioned here merely for the sake of curiosity, since it has no historical foundation and is obviously influenced by his own time. He defines *niḳatmon* as

> "a sort of instrument for the song (*niggun*), made in the form of a wooden foot (or an artificial leg)."[704]

As mentioned above, clappers in this shape have existed in Egypt. The clapper, however, cannot be considered "a sort of instrument for the song." A string or wind instrument in the shape of a human arm or foot was not known in Antiquity.

In so far as the word *niḳatmon* is concerned, RASHI still takes into consideration its original meaning which implies a musical instrument or a part of it. However, his interpretation of the other terminological variants, *ʾanḳatmin* (*ʾanḳitmin,* also *luḳitmin*) is entirely extra-musical.[705] He defines *ʾanḳatmin* as an object

> "like a funny mask which they put on the face of people in order to frighten the children."[706]

And he gives still another explanation: an imitation of a donkey's head that the merrymakers carried on their shoulders.[707] This furnishes indeed an insight into the origin of the term. *ʾAnḳitmin* is the corrupted Greek expression *onos kat' ōmon,* literally "donkey on the shoulder." These three Greek words were contracted in Aramaic into two, resulting in *onos ḳatmon,*[708] and, subsequently, in *ʾanḳatmon* or *ʾanḳatmin.* Evidently, in talmudic times merrymakers carried such contraptions on their shoulders at fancy masquerades. In the life of the ancient Israelites nothing of the like is attested. Especially images of animals, reminding too much of ancient idols and, in general, of heathen practices, were abhorred by Jews faithful to their religion. It seems, however, that in talmudic times the old religious prohibitions were somewhat eased, and evidently such customs have wormed themselves gradually into Jewish life. The Palestinian Talmud explains the term as *ḥamra deyoda,* "donkey carried in the hand,"[709] whereas the Babylonian Talmud follows more precisely the Greek original by defining the term as *ḥamra dakofa,* "donkey on the shoulder."[710]

Thus, RASHI's commentaries give us a satisfactory explanation at least of the origin and the true meaning of the word, but fail to provide an unequivocal answer to the question which instrument, if any, may be hidden under the term *niḳtimon or ʾanḳatmin.*

SACHS' interpretation comes closest to a satisfactory solution, and therefore it may be assumed with a certain probability that, if a musical instrument is meant by it, the term indicates clappers made of wood or bone.

38. ṬABLA

An instrument named *ṭabla* is mentioned in several rabbinic writings. About its nature and character, however, there are only vague and largely incompatible opinions.

In India, the word *ṭabla* has been signifying anciently a drum-like instrument, known in various shapes. In Arabia and in other Islamic countries, kettledrums are called generally *ṭabl* to this day.[711]

In the Assyrian language there is a similar word, *tabalu,* implying a drum. It is taken by some to be the equivalent of the Arabian *duff* and the Aramaic *ṭuppa,* both being names of the timbrel. The Assyrian word has supposedly been taken over as *tabala* (or *tabla*) by the Greek language.[712]

It seems likely that *ṭabla* is somehow connected with the Greek *tabla,* which generally means "something square."

More light on the word is shed by AUGUSTINE (354-430 C.E.).[713] He first states that

> " 'organ' is a general name for all instruments of music, although usage has now obtained that those are specially called 'organ' which are inflated with bellows."

And then, with regard to Psalm 150, he adds: "But I do not think that this kind is meant here." After examining and explaining the various organ-like instruments of his time, he says:

> "Those which are called 'organs,' especially with us at present, the ancients called the *plinthion achordon* (stringless *plinthion*), and the *plinthion aulētichon* (flute-like *plinthion*)."

The *plinthos* was the square wind-chest of the early organs and, in a figurative sense, *plinthos* was used as a generic term for music instruments, like *organon* in Greek, *organum* in Latin, *kle* and *minnim* in Hebrew. FARMER opines that the Greek *tabla* is a synonym for *plinthos,* consequently *ṭabla* is also a collective term for music instruments.[714]

This is confirmed by a talmudic passage stating that

> "the *hydraulis* was a musical instrument (*ṭabla*) worked by pressure [of water]."[715]

In another passage, too, *ṭabla* is used as a generic term for music instruments:

> "And Rabbi Simeon ben Gamaliel says that there was no *hydraulis* (other spellings: *hirdolim, hirdablis, hirdaulis*) in the Temple. What is *hirdolim?* Abaye says it is a musical instrument (*ṭabla*) like the organ (*gurgrana*)."[716]

THEODORET's interpretation of the word is quite different from that of AUGUSTINE.[717] According to him, *tabla* were *tintinnabula multa ligno appensa agitare,*

> "many bells hung from a wooden frame to be shaken."

A similar explanation can also be found in the Talmud:

> "When Rab died, R. Isaac ben Bisna decreed that none should bring

myrtles and palm-branches to a wedding feast to the sound of the *ṭabla*."[718]

A note of the English translator to this passage, obviously influenced by RASHI's commentary, indicates that the *ṭabla* is

"a bell or a collection of bells forming an instrument specially used at public processions, weddings, etc."

The Talmud contains numerous references to dances at weddings. Dances were always accompanied with tabrets and other percussion instruments.[719]

The same meaning is expressed by the following saying:

"At sixty as at six, the sound of a timbrel (*ṭabla*) makes her nimble [lit. 'run']."[720]

"Nimble" signifies here the eagerness to participate at a wedding ceremony, which included dances accompanied by timbrels. RASHI, commenting on this passage, tries to give a precise definition of the instrument. He says the *ṭabla* was *ḳishḳush ha-zog* (in another spelling *ḳashḳash* or *ḳarḳash*), that is "wedding bells," which would be shaken.[721] In the belief of Orientals

"the tinkling of its jingles could chase away evil spirits."[722]

It is very probable that in pristine times the use of such an instrument at weddings was based upon this superstition.

At numerous other places RASHI gives explanations about the meaning of *ṭabla*. In his commentary on the word *ʾerus,* he says it is a *ṭabla deḥad puma,* ("a bell with one clapper"), which means *zog ha-meḳashḳesh.*[723] In another passage he identifies *ṭabla* with the medieval French word *ʾasḳilṭa* ("bells"), a term by which, however, he defines (in different spellings as *ʾesḳeleṭ* and *ʾesḳaliṭa*) another instrument, the *zog.*[724] And still in another place he obviously uses ABAYE's definition (see above) in calling it *ṭabla gurgrana,* which is, as he says, *ʾaisḳliṭa.*

Interpreting *ṭabla deḥad puma,* RASHI gives a further explanation: "it is *ḳishḳush lo bezog,*" and adds:

"in French (*belaz*) we call that *ʾesḳada* (or *ʾasḳada*)."[725]

Thus, despite numerous attempts at explaining the word *ṭabla,* RASHI too does not provide us with an unequivocal meaning of it.

Finally, there is a definition of *ṭabla* in another talmudic passage:

"*Ḳol ṭabla* is *ʾesḳalina.* What is *ʾesḳalina?* In another tongue (*belaz*) it means that they used to sound a voice (*ḳol*) calling the people to come and celebrate with the groom."[726]

This comment is by RASHI's grandson, RASHBAM (R. SAMUEL ben MEIR, c. 1085-1174) who, after his grandfather's death, finished his commentaries on this tractate of the Talmud.

More obvious is the meaning of the word as an instrument used at weddings in the following passage:

"[If] he [could] hear the sound of the bells (*ṭabla*), he should have come [with a gift]."[727]

A late medieval comment to *ḳol ṭabla* in this passage by BACH (R. YOEL SIRKES, 1561-1640) says:

"They used to hang from the top of the roof a pair of bells to invite the people [to the wedding]."

And the modern translator adds in a note that this was an instrument

> "from which bells were suspended, used at bridal and other processions."

Another talmudic passage gives for *ṭabla* an entirely different explanation. A rabbinic writer uses the word *ʾerus* as a synonym for *tof* and asks:

> "What means *ʾerus?* R. Eleazar says: 'A drum (*ṭabla*) with a *single* bell' [lit. 'mouth']. Rabbah ben Huna made a drum (*ṭanbura*) for his son; his father came and broke it, saying to him, 'It might be substituted for a drum (*ṭabla*) with a single bell.' "[728]

This indication might rather suggest a flat handdrum having a skin only on one side which, therefore, in its construction and sound is substantially different from a shaking instrument.

All the contradictions disappear, however, if we interpret *ṭabla,* according to the Greek analogy, as the generic term for a certain category of instruments, in this instance for percussion instruments. In Assyrian, too, the word *tabalu* was not only the name of the hand-drum, but of the cymbals as well.[729] The same Assyrian term seems to have been used in the sense of a collective name for all percussion instruments. A hypothetical extension of this interpretation to the talmudic *ṭabla* would make it possible to apply this word to the ancient *tof,* the sistrum-like *menaʿanʿim,* and also to the later type of shaking instruments, such as the bells hung on a wooden frame.

A very curious interpretation of the *ṭabla* is given by KRAUSS. Because of the often-repeated reference in the Talmud that at wedding celebrations *ḥalilim* were played,[730] he feels himself

> "justified to assume that, contrary to the general opinion, the *ṭabla* played at weddings was not the timbrel, but some kind of a flute."[731]

Shortly afterwards, however, he contradicts his own statement by saying that

> "according to all evidence, the Syrian *ṭabla* was a hand-drum or timbrel, consequently a percussion instrument,"

and even supports this assertion with a series of quotations from the Targumim.[732]

In a fantastic tale of the Talmud, the *ṭabla* was invested with the magic power of bringing the dead back to life. To confirm the authenticity of such occurrence even a rabbinic authority such as RAB is quoted as an eye-witness. The statement reads:

> "Rab said to R. Ḥiyya: 'I myself saw an Arabian traveller take a sword and cut up a camel; then he rang (*ṭaraf*) a bell (*ṭabla*), at which the camel arose.' "[733]

It is obvious that RAB was taken into some trick hatched by an Oriental magician. Here, we are mainly interested in the fact that the sounding of the *ṭabla* was brought about by an action characterized by the word *ṭaraf, i.e.* "to hit," which evidently refers to a percussion instrument.

After having invested the *ṭabla* with the double meaning of *ḥalil* and timbrel, KRAUSS has found for it a third interpretation. As he says,

> "an authoritative explanation maintains that *ṭabla,* at least in some passages, refers to a bell, like a school-bell, used to assemble the pupils in the house of study."[734]

The sound of this kind of bells seems to have been ideologically connected with some scholarly distinction, as shown by the example of two outstanding rabbis, who both had at the same time curious dreams, which are related *in extenso* in the Talmud:

> "R. Pappa and R. Huna the son of R. Joshua both had dreams. R. Pappa dreamt that he went into a marsh and he became head of an academy. R. Huna, the son of R. Joshua dreamt that he went into a forest and he became head of the collegiates. Some say that both dreamt they went into a marsh, but R. Pappa who was carrying a *ṭabla* became the head of the academy, while R. Huna ben R. Joshua who did not carry a *ṭabla* became only the head of the collegiates."[735]

It is difficult to understand, how the carrying of a *ṭabla* could cause, even in a dream, one scholar to receive a high distinction, while another who had no *ṭabla* was selected for a lower rank. The translator, in a note, suggests that in this case the *ṭabla* might have been a kind of bell such as was used for announcing the approach of a man of distinction.

The real form of the *ṭabla* is easily disclosed once we realize the purpose of the instrument. It was doubtless played at weddings to enhance the general rejoicing. This manifested itself mainly in dances,

> "performed in a multitude of forms, and by both sexes."[736]

We are safe in following here the majority of the commentators who take the *ṭabla* to be a hand-drum with the same functions as those of the biblical *tof*. The instrument was probably bedecked in later times with all sorts of ornaments, maybe also with little bells hung upon it. This might have been responsible for the opinion that the *ṭabla* was a bell or a bell-like instrument.

39. ʾERUS (ʾIRUS)

The word *ʾerus* is mentioned in two Mishnaic passages and indicates in both places a drum-like instrument:

> "During the war of Vespasian they forbade the crowns of the bridegroom and the [wedding] drum (*ʾerus*);"[737]—and: "The lute (*baṭnon*), the *nikṭimon* and the drum (*ʾerus*) are susceptible to uncleanness."[738]

The derivation of the word from the Hebrew *ʾaras* (in Aramaic *ʾarus*), "to betroth," would correspond to the meaning of an instrument used generally at weddings.

Nevertheless, KRAUSS offers here an entirely different explanation.[739] He derives it from the Latin *aes-ris,* or from an imaginary Greek word *airos*. In Latin, *aes,* "brass," signifies also the metal bells and from this KRAUSS concludes that *ʾerus* was such a bell. For a support of his opinion he refers to Rabbi ELEAZAR's interpretation of this term as *ṭabla deḥad puma,* "bell with one clapper [or tongue]."[740] RASHI gives a similar explanation of *ʾerus*:

> "Bell with one clapper, used at wedding ceremonies."[741]

In another commentary to *ʾerus,* RASHI examines R. ELEAZAR's expression *ṭabla deḥad puma,* and interprets it as *zog ha-meḳashḳesh,* "a knocking clapper."[742] KRAUSS maintains that "*aes-ris* is thereby unequivocally explained."[743] This assertion, however, contradicts the meaning of *ʾerus* as "drum," given by the rabbinic writers.

MAIMONIDES interprets the *ʾerus* as a round tambourine (*ṭanburi*), with small metal plates fastened to the wooden frame, which produce a joyous tinkling when shaken. KRAUSS' explanation conflicts with that of MAIMONIDES inasmuch as a drum with a wooden frame could not have been made of brass, and a "single clapper" producing the sound is not characteristic of the tambourine. We may recall, however, that the tambourine was a relatively late instrument that might have existed in MAIMONIDES' time (1153-1204), but cannot be attested in talmudic ages.[744]

RASHI's explanation as "bell with one clapper" may be just as erroneous as MAIMONIDES' interpretation of *ʾerus*. Since KRAUSS' opinion is based mainly on that of RASHI, his hypothesis is likewise untenable.

Several commentators hazarded a supposition that the *ʾerus* must have been a rather voluminous drum, since—according to a rabbinic source—the wailing women would sit upon it at funerals:

> "The drum is susceptible to uncleanness as being something that is sat upon, since the wailing woman sits thereon."[745]

However, the drum referred to in this quotation was not the *ʾerus*, but the *rebiʿit* (see *infra*). This invalidates the reason for considering the *ʾerus* as a large drum.

We probably will come closest to the truth by assuming that the *ʾerus* was a small, brightly adorned hand-drum, used at weddings for the accompaniment of the dancing and for enhancing the general rejoicing. It may have been a more developed and showy type of the biblical *tof*.

A curious parallel should be mentioned at this point. The word *shushan*, "lily" in Hebrew, which is used in the headings of Pss. 45, 60, 69, and 80, has been explained by several commentators as an instrument having had the form of a lily.[746] *ʾErus* is an Aramaean word, but the Hebrew also knows a word *ʾirus* (or *ʾeirus*), designating the plant "Iris."[747] It would be unwarranted, of course, to draw from this fortuitous assonance any conclusions of a musical kind. The Hebrew *ʾeirus* might have been taken over from the Greek-Latin vocabulary of botanics, and has no connection whatever with the Aramaic *ʾerus*. Moreover, an instrument in the form of, or similar to that of the plant Iris is unknown.

40. ṬANBURA (ṬANBURI)

The instrument *ṭanbura* is used in the Talmud in a connection which among rabbinic and later commentators gave rise to all kinds of misinterpretations.

As an indirect illustration of the various types of drums, we may extend a bit the earlier quoted talmudic passage in which a rabbinic scribe relates a supposedly authentic occurrence:

> "RABBAH ben R. HUNA made a drum (*ṭanbura*) for [the wedding of] his son; his father [*i.e.* the bridegroom's grandfather] came and broke it, saying to him, 'It might be substituted for a drum (*ṭabla*) with a single bell. Go, make for him [an instrument by stretching the skin] over the mouth of a pitcher or over the mouth of a *kefiz* [a vessel of the capacity of three *log*]'."[748]

The meaning of this tale is somewhat difficult to unravel. It may have meant to show that the head of the family (the grandfather) observed faithfully the prohibition, according to which

> "during the war of Vespasian they forbade the crowns of the bridegroom and the [wedding] drum (*ʾerus*)."[749]

But, on the other hand, the rejoicing at the wedding should not be curtailed by eliminating the dancing. Thus, R. HUNA's father (R. JOSHUA) applied a sort of talmudic casuistry by stretching the skin of a drum over the mouth of a pitcher of clay or a large measuring vessel. By this, the "instrument" could not be considered a drum in the proper sense, so that the prohibition was not violated and, at the same time, an instrument for the accompaniment of the dances was not lacking either.

In the above rabbinic passage three different names are used for a specific category of drums, *ʾerus, ṭabla,* and *ṭanbura.* The last-named instrument which was broken by R. HUNA's father, was apparently the *ʾerus,* even though it is called here *ṭanbura.* This opinion is held by RASHI, calling the instrument *ṭanburah,*[750] and also by OBADIAH of BERTINORO who, in his commentary, says that

> "in the spoken language' *ʾerus* is called *ṭanburi.*"[751]

Yet, in the talmudic epoch the term *ṭanbur* (or *ṭambur*) did not refer to a percussion instrument but to a long-necked lute.[752] OBADIAH lived long after the talmudic age (second half of the 15th century), and his commentaries and similes were intended to give to his own contemporaries some idea about the ancient Jewish instruments. His comments, however, have the erratic tendency to identify the much more developed instruments with those of talmudic—sometimes also of biblical—times, and thus are apt to create confusion and misunderstanding.

Even KRAUSS looks with suspicion upon the word *ṭanbura* (or *ṭanburi*), because of its similarity to the French *tambour* or *tambourine.* He claims that, according to some ancient commentators, the repeatedly occurring talmudic word *ṭanbura* may have been used erroneously for *rebubah* which means something "hollow, and in this specific case a bell."[753] This claim of KRAUSS, however, is not supported by any linguistic evidence.

As to the word *rebubah* itself, JASTROW considers it to be

> "the name of a musical instrument, a sort of tambourine."[754]

Another spelling of the word is *rekubah,* and HAI GAON cites two further variants, *dekoba* and *dekuba.*[755] Still another spelling, or rather corruption, seems to be the variant *babuyʾa,* to be found in the Talmud[756] which, according to JASTROW, means a

> "mirror, hence (from its shape) a musical instrument, a little drum, tympanum."[757]

All these variants seem to refer to a small handdrum, such as the *ʾerus.*

Another rabbinic source, the *ʾAruk,*[758] commenting upon *ʾerus,*[759] interprets it as the word *koba,* the shortened form of *dekoba.* The *ʾAruk* furnishes a detailed explanation of *koba*:

> "One makes a round, hollow vessel of clay, one ell long, upon the mouth

of which guts of animals are stretched, and which is covered with an animal skin; when stricken, which occurs at weddings and funerals, it produces a pleasant sound."

From this description, which impresses one as an instruction for making the instrument, two things become evident: (1) the instrument named *koba* was quite large and therefore it could not have been identical with the *ʾerus,* the small handdrum used at weddings; it is more probable that the *koba* was the large drum-type, identified by us with the *rebiʿit,* apparently used at funerals;[760] (2) the *koba* had a device like our modern snaredrums; the snare-effect has been produced by the combined vibrations of the animal skin and the tightly stretched strings, which touched lightly the skin itself. This might have been the "pleasant sound," referred to by the *ʾAruk.*[761]

This, however, conflicts with the meaning and purpose of the drum at funerals, namely to enhance the gloomy mood of the mourning ceremony by the muffled and hollow sound of a large-sized drum. One may perhaps overcome this inconsistency by assuming that the snaring device could be turned on and off according to the needs, just as on our modern snaredrums.

41. REBIʿIT

We find this term in one of the Mishnaic discussions dealing with prescriptions for cleanness, which reads as follows:

> "The viol-case (*teḳ nebalim*) and the lyre-case (*teḳ kinnorot*), . . . the singer's *marḳof* (*marḳof shel zemer*), the clappers of the wailing women (*rebiʿit shel ʾalit*) . . . are not susceptible to uncleanness."[762]

Unlike this prescription, another passage of the same tractate stipulates:

> "The drum (*ʾerus*) is susceptible to uncleanness as being something that is sat upon, since the wailing woman (*ʾalit*) sits thereon."[763]

Thus, we have two different instruments, allegedly used by the wailing women in their profession, one of which was considered clean and the other unclean. On the other hand, there are no other indications whatever in our sources that wailing women would use clappers at funerals. The English translation is inaccurate, just as is the translation of *nebalim* as "viols." Yet, the rabbinic statements about the wailing women sitting on their instrument while resting occasionally from their duties, are probably authentic. What kind of instrument might it have been on which an adult person could sit?

The earlier examination of the term *ʾerus* has led us to the conclusion that it referred to a small adorned hand-drum, played at weddings, perhaps a slightly developed descendant of the biblical *tof.* It would be, of course, impossible to sit on such a small and frail instrument. Therefore, it was figured, the drum of the wailing women must have been the larger and more robust *rebiʿit.* The rabbinic writers have apparently confounded the nomenclature of the two instruments, which is not at all surprising in view of their many other musical inconsistencies.

Consequently, it would be in order to replace, in the above quoted Mishnaic passage, the word *ʾerus* by the more correct *rebitʿit,* an instrument on which it was possible to sit; and this substitution would also explain why such an instrument was considered "unclean." However, the reason would still be obscure why the "*rebiʿit* of the wailing women" (wrongly translated as "clappers") were considered to be "clean," unless we assume that *rebiʿit* actually referred to another type of instrument,—a hypothesis that has no foundation.

There is a striking assonance between *rebiʿit* and two other expressions of the Targumim and the Peshiṭṭa. They are the *rebiʿin* of the former, and the *rebiyʿa* of the latter, both being rendition (in Aramaic and Syrian) of the biblical *menaʿanʿim* (2 Sam. 6:5), which is interpreted unanimously as sistra.[764]

According to MAIMONIDES, the *rebiʿin* were two wooden sticks, struck together rhythmically, and thus representing a clapper instrument. For such sticks there is an analogy in Egypt; in a mural painting harvesters are portrayed using "concussion sticks."[765] The striking of such sticks had the purpose to expedite the work of the reapers by uniform rhythmical sounds. It is probable that, owing to their long stay in Egypt, the Israelites, too, were familiar with this device. (Illustr. 59)

The passages of the Mishnah, however, in which *rebiʿit* is mentioned, do not harmonize with the idea of "concussion sticks." Sistrum would be a better interpretation; but for the use of sistra in Jewish funerals there is no reference at all in the rabbinic literature. MAIMONIDES' interpretation, too, does not fit the idea of *menaʿanʿim,* that is of a sistrum-like instrument.

Nevertheless, KRAUSS identifies the *rebiʿin* with the *rebiʿit,* and holding the Targum's translation to be correct, concludes therefrom that a *menaʿanʿim*-like instrument has been used at Jewish funerals.[766] He endeavors to support his assertion with a parallel use of the sistra in the service of the Egyptian Isis, in which the clattering sound of the instrument was supposed to chase away the death-inducing Typhon.

"If, according to the Mishnah, wailing women have played the *rebiʿit,*" KRAUSS argues, then

"the purpose of it might have originally been the same as in Egypt."

He gives, however, no explanation how it should have been possible to "sit" on a sistrum-like instrument.

Yet, apart from this interpretation, KRAUSS tries to explain the word still in another fashion.[767] In Hebrew, *rebiʿit* means "a quart [of a measure]." From this, KRAUSS infers that the word implies a "bell-like instrument," having either the form of this measure, consequently being hollow and bell-shaped, or else that it referred directly to a customary measure of the Babylonians, called *ḳapiẓa,* the Persian *ḳawiẓ* (in Greek *kapithē*).[768] Such an interpretation might be acceptable insofar as musical instruments frequently owed their names either to their shapes similar to those of other objects (like *nebel, baṭon*), or to the material used for their making (*ḳeren*), consequently to extra-musical reasons.

Whether KRAUSS is right with his explanation or not, nothing opposes the assumption that the term *rebiʿit* referred to a drum-like instrument. It may have had an oblong, or bell-like shape, and was certainly of a rather large size and a deep tone. The hollow sound quality of such an instrument might have blended better with the gloomy mood of the mourning ceremony than the lively tone of the *ʾerus,* or the shrill rattling of the sistrum. In assuming that the *rebiʿit* was such an instrument, the rabbinical statement, according to which the wailing women sat upon it during the funerals, becomes quite credible.

In a contemporary Yiddish translation of the Mishnah there is a peculiar interpretation of *rebiʿit.* It is said:

> "*Rebiʿit shel ʾalit*: di tatsenheltser fun de klog-frau (klogerin); dos zenen tsve heltser, vi tatsen, mit velkher di klog-frau paukt tsu ven zi beklogt a met." ("The wooden cymbals of the wailing woman; those are two pieces of wood, like saucers, beaten by the wailing woman when she laments on a funeral").[769]

It is obvious that this interpretation is without any foundation. It is quoted merely for the sake of curiosity.

As we see, the rabbinic literature uses rather indiscriminately the terms *ʾerus ṭabla, ṭanbura, rebubah, dekoba, koba,* and *rebiʿit,* to which the Aramaic and Syriac Bible translations *rebiyʿa* (*rebiʿin*), *pelaga,* and *tuppa* could be added. All these terms designate hand-drums which, in all probability, could be distinguished merely by some differences in their shape, size, and construction.

42. ZOG

Zog is an instrument frequently mentioned in the rabbinic literature. The Hebrew word signifies "shell" in general, also the transparent "skin" of the grape, and refers in this particular case to the form of the instrument. The skin of the grape has a spheric form, and this must have been the shape of little bells, called *zogin* (or *zogim*). In the inside, these bells had either loose, movable pebbles, or fastened clappers called *ʾambol, ʾanbol, ʾenbol,* also *ʾinbol.*[770] The assonance with the similar Greek term *embolon* is unmistakable.

The talmudic *zog* is essentially the same implement as the biblical *paʿamonim,* the little bells on the high priest's garment, as evident from a rabbinic description:

> "Seventy-two bells (*zogin*) containing seventy-two clappers (*ʾenbolin*) were brought and hung thereon, thirty-six on each side. R. Dosa said on the authority of R. Judah: 'There were thirty-six, eighteen on each side'."[771]

In his commentary to this passage, RASHI says that the talmudic *zogin* were called *ʾesḳaliṭa* in his epoch.[772] It is evident that RASHI—like other later rabbinic commentators—refers to some coeval instrument in order to facilitate, by way of comparison, the understanding of a biblical or talmudic instrument.

Manifestly, the *zog* of talmudic times was a metal sphere of various sizes with several holes or slits, like our sleigh-bells. For wealthy or distinguished people *zogin* were sometimes made of gold, as also were their clappers, or these were at least gold plated.[773]

Zogin were used in Jewish life for manifold purposes. Fastened on house doors, they signalled the entrance of people; hung on the neck or on the garment of slaves, also on the neck or on the harness of domestic animals, they indicated their whereabouts; fixed on a mortar and on a wagon pulled by animals, they were supposed to facilitate the working procedure by their rhythmic tinkling. The garments of the rich were adorned with bells and they were even hung on locks of distinguished persons.[774]

A rabbinic scribe uses the word *zog* for a child's clapper:

> "The clappers (*zogin*) from the ʿ*arisah* (cradle) can be taken out [on Sabbath] if it does not produce a sound; if it does produce a sound it is prohibited."[775]

Yet, it is more probable that *zogin* means here "bells," not "clapper." But it will be shown in the next chapter that children's clappers did exist in Ancient Israel.

Apart from *paʾamonim,* the talmudic term *zogin* was applied also to the biblical *meẓillot* (Zech. 14:20), which indicated the bells hung upon horses and other domestic animals. Other rabbinic writings likewise refer to this custom. Among the prohibitions to be observed on Sabbath the following are pertinent to *zogin*:

> "An animal may not go out . . . with a bell (*zog*) around its neck nor with a bell (*zog*) on its coat . . . An animal's bell is unclean."[776]—"The ass may not go out . . . with a bell (*zog*) even though it is plugged (*paḳuk*)."[777]—"A door [bell] (*zog*) appointed for an animal ['s use] is unclean."[778]

And the Midrash says:

> "When the heathen saw the wonders and mighty deeds that God wrought with Hananiah and his companions, they took their idols and broke them, and made them into bells (*zogin paʿamonim*) which they hung on their dogs and their asses, and when they tinkled (*meḳarḳashin*) they said: . . ."[779]

Among the prescriptions for cleanness, the Mishnah contains an instruction which is rather obscure:

> "These parts in a wagon are susceptible to uncleanness: . . . the clapper (ʾ*anbol*)."[780]

As mentioned above, ʾ*anbol* was the clapper, or tongue, of the *zog;* consequently, if one part of an object is unclean, the whole should be unclean, or vice versa. It seems, however, that in this passage ʾ*anbol* does not refer to *zog,* but indicates some part of the wagon, perhaps its pole.

A talmudic passage contains the peculiar opinion that a bell (*zog*) with a clapper (ʾ*inbol*) is unclean, without a clapper, however, it is clean, and this despite the explicit statement that both parts belong together.[781]

It is difficult to find a reason for such a strange regulation.

The manner of sound production of the *zog* is expressed by the verb *hiḳḳish,* "to ring," or "to strike" [the bell].[782] KRAUSS concludes from this that the instrument, besides its function of producing certain noises, was sometimes used for musical purposes as well,[783] an opinion which is quite debatable.

The widespread use of bells on doors, garments and domestic animals had, apart from its evidently practical reason, another, more veiled significance. It should be remembered that the *paʿamonim* on the high priest's garment had originally the magic purpose of protecting the sacred person from the harmful influence of evil demons.[784] Likewise the *meẓillot* hung on domestic animals, were magic means for their protection. It is obvious that the use of the post-biblical *zogin* had the same purpose. Even if the rabbinic literature does not refer to this openly, the magic power of the tinkling bells is implicit in all these statements. There is even an indirect proof of this:

> "[On the Sabbath] sons may go out with bindings and the sons of kings [may go out] with little bells (*zogin*); and so may any one, but the Sages spoke only of the actual custom."[785] And also: "The Master said: '[He may] not [go out] with a bell (*zog*) around his neck, but he may go out with the bell (*zog*) on his garment.' "[786]

At first sight, the meaning of these indications is rather obscure. It becomes, however, unmistakably clear from the context of this Mishnaic chapter which deals with preventive means of sympathetic magic against disaster, sickness and, in general, against evil influences. The Gemara discusses extensively the prescriptions compulsory for men, women and children for their protection when leaving the house on Sabbath. Since all active anti-demoniac precautions exercised on weekdays were forbidden on Sabbath, the hanging of bells upon oneself remained the only measure that safeguarded the individual automatically against the evil spirits.[787] The same belief was underlying the use of bells on doors, since it was easy for a malevolent demon to sneak into the house together with an entering person. The bells were designed to prevent this.

Thus, we see how ancient heathen superstition survived in a veiled form, both in religious and in secular customs, even far into post-biblical times.

43. ḲARḲASH (ḲASHḲASH)

The Aramaic verb *ḳarḳash* means "to strike," "to knock"; the substantive built from this verb should, therefore, indicate an instrument the sound of which is produced by striking it. Despite this clear etymology, the only—if late—rabbinic commentator, RASHI, gives quite a different interpretation of it.

In commenting on the talmudic saying:

> "At sixty as at six, the sound of a timbrel (*ṭabla*) makes her nimble,"[788]

he maintains that the *ṭabla* was a *ḳishḳush ha-zog* (in other spellings *ḳashḳash* or *ḳarḳash*), *i.e.* "wedding bells," that were shaken like the tambourine.

This explanation is obviously erroneous for historical as well as for reasons inherent in the nature of the instrument itself. Historically, it constitutes an anachronism, since insturments of the tambourine-type (hand-drums with small metal plates fastened on their frame) are not attested prior to the 13th century, as mentioned repeatedly. As to the tone production of the instrument, it is quite a difference whether it is achieved by striking or shaking it. Among biblical instruments, the *tof*, *meẓiltayim* and *ẓelẓelim* were percussion instruments, the *shalishim*, *mena'an'im*, *pa'amonim* and *meẓillot* shaking or rattling instruments. The meaning of the word *ḳarḳash* conflicts therefore with RASHI's interpretation.

It is not impossible that RASHI actually had in mind a shaking or rattling instrument, like, for instance, the "crescent" of Janizary bands of his time. This instrument originated in Central Asia and "traveled both east to China and west to Turkey."[789]

A more meaningful interpretation of the instrument is given by KRAUSS, who explains *ḳarḳash* as a special sort of clapper.[790] He does not think that *ḳarḳash* is a bell, since it has no tongue and its form is reminiscent of a saucer. It is common knowledge that little bells are generally spherical. On the other hand, there might have been in ancient times an instrument, consisting of two or more round, saucer-shaped wood or metal plates which, when struck together, produced a clappering sound. Such a procedure is quite fittingly expressed by the Aramaic verb *meḳarḳashin.*[791] Thus, the functional meaning of the word corroborates somewhat the nature of the instrument. The word *ḳarḳash* as well as its variants in spelling, *ḳashḳash* and *ḳishḳush,* are onomatopoeic constructions; the letter *ḳ* used twice in each one of them is clearly imitative of clappers, whereas the names of shaking instruments usually contain sybilants, like the Greek *seistron,* the Latin *sistrum,* the Hebrew *shalishim, meẓillot,* etc.

Such clappers (*ḳarḳash*) were given to children, or sounded before them, in order to calm them down. This was probably the reason why it was allowed to carry them on Sabbath.[792] Little bells were also hung on cradles, having had the same purpose as bells on doors or garments.[793]

It may be assumed with certainty that *ḳarḳash* and *zog* referred to two different types of clappers. The latter represents the bell type, sounding by itself, that is by the movements of those who carried it, whereas the *ḳarḳash* must have been the clapper which had to be activated, *i.e.* stricken, always anew. The strongly sound-imitating word *ḳarḳash* may serve as an indirect proof that, similar to other ancient Oriental peoples, the Israelites knew clappers and that one species of them might have been the *ḳarḳash.*

44. SHARḲUḲITA

According to a talmudic indication, the leading goat had around its neck a bell, called in Aramaic *sharḳuḳita.*[794] With the Hebrew *meẓillot* and *pa‘amonim,* and with the Aramaic *zog,* we have altogether four terms referring apparently to the same kind of objects, namely to bells which used to be hung on the neck of domestic animals.

The word *sharḳuḳita* is derived from the Hebrew verb *sharaḳ,* "to hiss," "to pipe," "to whistle," which is also the original word for the instrument *mashroḳita,* named four times in the Book of Daniel. The peculiar thing about these two Aramaic words, however, is that *mashroḳita* indicates a wind instrument, whereas *sharḳuḳita,* if the Talmud is correct, seems to refer to a shaking instrument. Both words are onomatopoeic constructions, although it is difficult to understand how both actions, the whistling of a pipe and the tinkling of a bell, should have been expressed imitatively with the same sybilant sounds.

The Talmud declares that *mashḳoḳit* (evidently a corrupted spelling of *mashroḳit*) is the same as *sharḳuḳita,* and gives in the first place a rather vague explanation of the instrument by stating that

> "you hang a *zog* around the neck of a big sheep."[795]

However, another interpretation in the same paragraph says explicitly that it was a wind instrument:

> "[it is] a hollow instrument like the horn of a steer which the shepherds use to call together the animals."[796]

These contradictory statements, made almost in the same breath, render it difficult to determine which definition might be the correct one.

JASTROW's explanation is also rather vague, leaving open the possibility for both talmudic versions. Disregarding the above misspelling, he says that the *mashkokita* were

> "the shepherd's principal implements, such as the staff, the bell, the pipe, etc."[797]

Whereas KRAUSS is more inclined to the belief that the *sharkukita* was a flute, "or something alike,"[798] or else, more precisely, "the Pan's pipe."[799] For this assumption there is even a vague corroboration in the Bible. Judg. 5:16 contains the expression *sherikot 'adarim,* "the pipings for the flock;"—*sherikot* has the same root as the Aramaic *sharkukita.*

From all this only one thing emerges as certain, namely that *sharkukita* implies an instrument having had some function in the life of shepherds. But whether this was the pipe, the Pan's pipe, the horn, or bells, cannot be positively determined from the rabbinic indications. We must always be aware that the rabbinic scribes have had little familiarity, if any, with musical matters, so that their reports abound in inaccuracies and contradictions.

VII. THE ORCHESTRA

For a long time, biblical exegesis and musicology concentrated a good deal of attention upon the individual musical instruments of Ancient Israel. Countless attempts have been made to explain their precise nomenclature, to discover their shape, and to resuscitate their respective timbres; on the other hand, their manifold *ensemble* characteristics have been commented upon only in a cursory fashion.[1] However, the whole picture pertaining to our general subject would remain incomplete without shedding some light upon the nature and sheer sounding effect of the ancient Jewish orchestra groups as compared to those of our modern instrumental ensembles, large and small.

Good orchestral sound has its own intrinsic laws, its own technique. To make an orchestra "sound," some other factors are needed besides assembling a sufficient number of instrumentalists and having an adequate number of rehearsals. It is a matter of common knowledge that the good sound effect depends mainly on the appropriate choice of instruments and an expert blending of the various tone colors. Now, what can one say in this respect with regard to the possible taste and actual practice of the ancient Israelites?

One of the earliest references in the Old Testament already points distinctly to music making in an ensemble fashion. Laban's reproachful speech when he overtakes Jacob on his flight, implies, apparently, a band of musicians, designed to accompany singing at the joyous escort of a friend (Gen. 31:27). Thus, small instrumental ensembles might have already existed in patriarchal times.

All the other descriptions in the early history of the Jews at which we could conceivably surmise the use of such ensembles,[2] are too vague for drawing any definite conclusions on that score. We may only conjecture that at triumphant festivities, in which huge choral masses took part, an adequate orchestral body might have participated. There are, however, no direct evidences to that effect in the Bible.

Singing in Israel was generally accompanied by stringed instruments (*kle shir*), occasionally in combination with woodwinds, like the pipes (*ḥalilim*). As mentioned repeatedly, the lack of early biblical references to groups of musicians might well represent intentional omissions of the chroniclers, who did not deem it necessary to report self-evident things.

The initial biblical mention of a real orchestral group is to be found in the announcement of Samuel to Saul (1 Sam. 10:5). A procession of prophets,[3] coming from the sanctuary, a procedure which took place each day at the same hour, "prophesied," *i.e.* "sang" sacred songs with the accompaniment of instruments. The combination of instruments used in these processions, *nebel, tof, ḥalil* and *kinnor,* as well as their number, which must have been quite substantial in view of the expression "band of prophets," warrants the assumption that for the first time in the Old Testament we are confronted with something approaching a real orchestra.

In this connection, one recalls the ancient stone-carved picture of an Elamite court orchestra welcoming in 650 B.C.E. the Assyrian conqueror. It represents indeed an instrumental ensemble rather similar to that of the band of Hebrew prophets, and includes seven harps, one psaltery, two double-oboes and a hand-drum. (Illust. 27)

Considering the many points of contact between the various civilizations of the Near-East, this analogy in the formation of orchestra groups is scarcely incidental. Especially so, since we know that the Israelite musicians have willingly taken over from their neighbors everything that squared with their own ideas of good sound effect. In the long run, they would adapt, of course, the borrowed elements to their own needs. Whatever did not meet with their artistic approval, they either repudiated,—as for instance the noisy and orgiastic music of the Ishtar cult,—or transformed to a greater or lesser degree, like a goodly number of Canaʿanite customs found in their new abode.

The above report about an orchestra of the pre-Davidic times is rather general in its presentation. But soon thereafter the chronicler furnishes us with greater details pertaining to king David's orchestra. At the solemn procession on the occasion of bringing in the ark of the covenant to Jerusalem

> "David and all the house of Israel played before the Lord with all manner of instruments made of cypress-wood, and with harps, and with psalteries, and with timbrels, and with sistra, and with cymbals" (2 Sam. 6:5).

Only a few verses away, the chronicler adds: "with the sound of the horn (*ubeḳol shofar*)" (2 Sam. 6:15). A report in a later book, again describing the same solemnity, enlarges the instrumentation:

> "And David and all Israel played before God with all their might; even with songs and with harps, and with psalteries, and with timbrels, and with cymbals, and with trumpets (*b'ḥaẓoẓerot*)" (1 Chron. 13:8).

It might appear odd at first that in both reports the most popular instrument, the pipe (*ḥalil*), is passed in silence. But then one comes across the reassuring expression "all manner of instruments" which refers, of course, to all those instruments in popular usage, not mentioned specifically in the biblical text.

If we consider the fact that practically "all the house of Israel" took part in this procession and that anyone familiar with music served the sacred cause either with singing, or playing an instrument, or both, it is safe to assume that on this occasion a huge group of musicians provided also the orchestral part.

The next important step in the development of orchestral practice in Ancient Israel has taken place when the regular sacred musical service was inaugurated by David. The orchestra supplying the musical accompaniment at this early stage of the sacred service is not only minutely described with the number of the participants, but the names of the musicians, as well as the singers, are cited by the chronicler together with the instruments they played (1 Chron. 15:16ff).

This orchestra comprised three cymbal-players (*meẓiltayim neḥoshet*=cymbals of brass), this function being entrusted to the three vocal leaders, Heman, Asaph and Ethan, eight harp-players (*nebalim ʿal-ʿalamot*), and six lyre-players (*kinnorot ʿal ha-sheminit*), quite apart from the seven priests who sounded the sacred silver-trumpets (*ḥaẓoẓerot*) when the orchestra was silent. This was an ensemble of seventeen musicians, "all that were skillful" on their instruments

(1 Chron. 25:7), consequently a perfectly adequate group for the relatively restricted space of David's sanctuary.

This orchestra, similar to the group of singers, represented merely a small section of the huge number of skilled singers and musicians, about which the Bible informs us. King David ordained a census of the Levites from the age of thirty and more, this age having been fixed by the law for the entry to the levitical choir. Of these, no less than four thousand Levites from the total number of thirty eight thousand were selected. (1 Chron. 23:5). All these musicians might have previously participated at the transfer of the Ark of the Covenant to Jerusalem. Here we have indeed an indirect evidence of huge choir masses and a mammoth orchestra taking part in a solemn procession.

From this multitude of skilled musicians David and the "captains of the host" made a select choice.

> "They separated for the service certain of the sons of Asaph, and of Heman, and of Jeduthun,[4] who should prophesy with harps, with psalteries, and with cymbals . . . And the number of them, with their brethren that were instructed in singing unto the Lord, even all that were skillful,[5] was two hundred fourscore and eight" (1 Chron. 25:1,7).

These singer-musicians were divided into twenty-four "wards," (*i.e.* groups) of twelve singers each, under the leadership of a precentor for each group, whose names are cited by the chronicler (1 Chron. 25:9-31). In order to avoid jealousy and disputes as to precedence, they used to cast the lot

> "ward against ward, as well the small as the great, the teacher as the scholar" (1 Chron. 25:8),

and by this democratic procedure a just order of precedence was established.

These twenty-four groups have participated, by turns, in the musical service of the cult, one group for each service on weekdays, several groups on Sabbath and high holidays, their actual number depending upon the solemnity of the occasion. According to a later source, the minimum number of the singers was twelve; the maximum was not limited.[6] This, however, applied only to singers, for the number of instrumentalists was regulated differently:

> "They played on never less than two harps (*nebalim*) or more than six, and on never less than two flutes (*ḥalilim*) or more than twelve.[7]"

And also:

> "There were never less than two trumpets, and their number could be increased without end; there were never less than nine lyres (*kinnorot*), and their number could be increased without end; but of cymbals there was but one [*i.e.* one pair]."[8]

Each singer who also played a stringed instrument (and most of them were certainly able to do so) was supposed to accompany his own singing. This ruling would guarantee a balanced proportion between singing and its orchestral background, meticulously observed by the ancient Israelites in their sacred services.

Ḥalilim would be played on twelve days of the year.[9] The artistic implication of this regulation is obvious: the music of the regular services was solemn with largely subdued orchestral colors, as evidenced by the predominance of stringed instruments. But at the great joyful festivals the general character of the accompanying orchestra has been enlivened by the added bright colors of pipes. The joyful mood created thereby among the masses of worshippers is attested in a rabbinical commentary:

> "'The flute-playing, sometimes five and sometimes six days'—this is the flute-playing at the *Bet ha-She'ubah* . . . He that never has seen the joy of the *Bet ha-She'ubah* has never in his life seen joy."[10]

Blowing the priestly trumpets together with the orchestral music seems to have occurred only at some particularly solemn occasions (2 Chron. 5:12 ff; 29:26 ff). Otherwise, the priests sounded the trumpets merely in the breaks between singing; in most cases the blowing of trumpets had a ritual rather than a musical purpose, inasmuch as it indicated the places during the ceremonial when the worshippers had to prostrate themselves.

As mentioned above, the singers and musicians selected by king David were "all that were skillful," "altogether masters." This mastery was maintained invariably on a high level by the strict discipline of the guild of musicians and by constant music rehearsals. For these the Levites were provided with special rooms, as stated in the Bible (Ezek. 40:44) and in the rabbinic literature.[11]

o
o o

Levitical musicians had to be supplied for musical services three times daily,[12] at the morning- and evening-sacrifices, and at the additional sacrifices which took place during the day. This continuous practice kept all the groups occupied at regular intervals and was one of the reasons for the unswerving high standard of the musical performances. Another reason was the methodical and never relinquishing work which the Levites surely carried on at their rehearsals, thereby insuring the artistic quality of their accomplishments.

The Israelites must have taken for granted the constant high quality of the Temple music, since generally there is no reference to this feature in the Old Testament. The single exception to the rule is afforded by the chronicler's report about the uncommon perfection of the musical performance at the dedication of Solomon's newly erected Temple. First, the biblical scribe relates that

> "the Levites who were singers, all of them, even Asaph, Heman, Jeduthun, and their sons and their brethren, arrayed in fine linen, with cymbals and psalteries and harps, stood at the east end of the altar, and with them a hundred and twenty priests sounding with trumpets" (2 Chron. 5:12).

This indicates that a large choir and a similarly large orchestra must have been used at the dedication; "all of them" means evidently that all the twenty-four groups have taken part on this solemn occasion.

The available space in Solomon's Temple was scarcely sufficient for 288 singer-musicians and 120 trumpet-sounding priests, together with the other numerous ministers and their assistants at the sacrificial rites. We know, however, that outside of the Temple proper, there was a second platform in the Court of the Israelites,[13] which could hold larger masses of performers, as generally used at Sabbath and high holiday services. It is safe to assume, therefore, that at the dedication of the Temple singers and musicians have been placed there, so that the huge congregation of worshippers have had their full share in the musical performance.

o
o o

From there on, levitical singing was accompanied on all solemn occasions by an adequate orchestra. Orchestral performance, like singing, was an indispensable element of every festivity.

After his victory against the Ammonites and Moabites, king Jehoshaphat entered Jerusalem

> "with psalteries and harps and trumpets" (2 Chron. 20:28).

There can hardly be any doubt that on this occasion, as at other similar events, a large body of performers had been used, even if the chronicler does not refer to it in so many words.

Prior to this solemn procession to David's city, Jehoshaphat assembled his army and the people in a valley where they rested to give thanks to the Almighty for His mercy and assistance:

> "And on the fourth day they assembled themselves in the valley of Berakah; for they blessed the Lord; therefore the name of that place was called the Valley of Berakah [Blessing], unto this day" (2 Chron. 20:26).[14]

The fact that the chronicler mentions specifically this "camp service" leads to the assumption that it might have been one of those occasions on which a large choir and a similarly large orchestra have been featured. An average kind of celebration of triumph, taking place in the open air with singing and music, would scarcely have induced the king to call the place, in eternal memory, *ʿEmeḳ Berakah,* "The Valley of Blessing." Thus we see how extra-musical indications may sometimes throw significant light upon the character and importance of musical events.

At the coronation of the young king Joash

> "all the people of the land rejoiced, and blew with trumpets; the singers also [played] on instruments of music, and led the singing of praise" (2 Chron. 23:13).

The employment of a large body of musicians in this instance is particularly emphasized by VULGATE's translation of the passage:

> *clangentem tubis, et diversi generis organis concinentem,* "with trumpets blowing, and all kinds of instruments playing together."

Influenced by the energetic and resolute high priest Jehoiada, king Joash reinstituted the true faith of Yahveh. The high priest immediately called forth

> "to appoint the offices of the house of the Lord under the hand of the priests and the Levites, whom David had distributed in the house of the Lord" (2 Chron. 23:18).

The music of the sanctuary, singing as well as orchestral playing, was re-established as of yore "according to the direction of David" (*ibid.*)

After Jehoiada's death, however, the weak king Joash abandoned the true faith. His successors, too, were addicted—with some interruptions—to ungodliness and idolatry. One hundred and thirty years passed before Yahveh's religion was restored again, together with the ancient sacred service and its traditional music. This happened under king Hezekiah (2 Chron. 29:3,4). The King addressed the singers in a solemn speech, ordering that the ancient service be resumed. And once more, this time after an interruption of more than a century, the complex musical apparatus of the Temple functioned in complete perfection. (2 Chron. 29:25-30).

This narration reveals several facts significant for the appreciation of the levitical musical practice. First of all, it is obvious that "the instruments of David" (more correctly "the instruments ordained by David"), consequently the original instruments of Solomon's Temple, have been carefully preserved by the Levites, so that they could be used even after this long period and in spite of all the vicissitudes of the extraneous circumstances. Secondly, the singing as well as the orchestral practice of the Levites was kept alive during all this time, a minor miracle in itself. Finally, the ancient traditional songs were kept in their pristine purity, waiting only for the appropriate moment to resound again to the praise of the Lord.

The music of the Temple was restored by Hezekiah just as it had been in Solomon's Temple. It may be assumed, therefore, that the composition of the orchestra was similar to that of the ancient times. At the re-dedication of the Temple the number of the musicians of the orchestra must have been quite considerable, as evidenced by an indication of the chronicler. At the Passover-Feast, celebrated by Hezekiah and all Israel for the first time after the restoration of Yahveh's service, a large choir and a similarly large orchestra have been used:

> "and the Levites and the priests praised the Lord day by day, singing with loud instruments (*bikle ʿoz*) unto the Lord" (2 Chron. 30:21).

"Loud instruments" seems to indicate not merely the addition of wind instruments, but also that string instruments have been used in a larger number than usual.

Evidently, the king was greatly impressed by these splendid musical performances, since he did not spare his praises. The chronicler paraphrases this with the circumlocution,

> "he spoke encouragingly[15] unto all the Levites that were skillful in the service of the Lord" (2 Chron. 30:22).

The Passover celebration, with its brilliant musical concomitance, has made such a deep impression upon all the worshippers that the congregation took the quite unusual decision "to keep other seven days" (2 Chron. 30:23). This caused

> "great joy in Jerusalem; for since the time of Solomon the son of David king of Israel there was not like in Jerusalem" (2 Chron. 30:26).

The event referred to by the chronicler was the celebration at the dedication of Solomon's Temple, which also lasted two weeks.

The word concerning such artistic accomplishments must soon have been spread around, carrying the fame of Jewish music and Jewish musicians far beyond the frontiers of Israel. In a tragic hour of Israel's history a fateful role was assigned to Hezekiah's musicians. When SENNAḤERIB besieged Jerusalem in 701 B.C.C.,[16] Hezekiah could avert the destruction of the holy city by surrendering—apart from a large contribution of 30 talents of gold and 300 talents of silver and of other treasures—his famous male and female singers, and with them probably his court orchestra as well, since most of these vocal artists were also instrumentalists, this having been a common practice in Oriental royal courts.[17] How great must have been the value of these musicians if an Oriental ruler, in exchange for them, and other treasures, was ready to refrain from the rudimentary impulsion of a conqueror to capturing and pillaging the enemy's capital!

Under the reign of Manasseh and Amon (Hezekiah's son and grandson) Israel again turned to idolatry. After fifty-seven years of paganism, it was king Josiah who restored the true faith. He ordered the repair of the Temple, dilapidated under his predecessors, and reinstituted the sacred service. The vessels of the ritual, too, especially the musical instruments, must have been damaged to a point where they were no more in a usable condition. The instruments, however, have eventually been repaired and, significantly enough, under the supervision of Levites "that had skill with instruments of music," as the biblical text says. (2 Chron. 34:12). This indeed is a highly important statement, since it suddenly divulges a bit of valuable information about a profession in Ancient Israel not mentioned elsewhere, namely the making and repairing of musical instruments. It proves that none else but the levitical musicians themselves were able to take care of their own instruments, and that they kept alive this proficiency through all the centuries, in auspicious as well as in perilous times.

The solicitude of king Josiah in restoring the Temple, its institutions, and also the implements of the sacred service, resulted in the resumption of the orchestral performances in their former glory. Music regained its traditional importance in the service, (2 Chron. 35:15). The celebration of Passover, following the repair work, was so overwhelming that it eclipsed all former feasts. (2 Chron. 35:18). Such splendor would have been unattainable without the greatly stimulating instrumental accompaniment to levitical singing; the praise bestowed by the chronicler upon the whole festival may therefore be extended in a large measure to the Temple orchestra.

During his entire reign Josiah had been a solicitous patron of music and musicians. When only thirty-nine years old, he met a hero's death on the battlefield against the Pharaoh Neko and was lamented by all his musicians:

> "And all the singing men and singing women spoke of Josiah in their lamentations, unto this day; and they made them an ordinance in Israel" (2 Chron. 35:25).

Funeral lamentations have been, as we know, accompanied by playing the *ḥalilim;* we may assume, therefore, that in honoring Josiah's memory orchestral music, too, has had its share. Through these yearly lamenting exercises, the memory of Josiah, the promoter of music, was kept alive. Even centuries later this art loving monarch was not forgotten, as it may be learned from the book of Jesus Sirach:

"The memorial of Josiah is like the incense prepared by the work of the apothecary; it shall be sweet as honey in every mouth, and as music in a banquet of wine" (Ecclus. 49:1,2).

During the Babylonian captivity collective music making (*i.e.* ensemble playing, in to-day's term) was evidently restrained. "Upon the willows . . . we hanged our harps," as the psalmist says significantly (Ps. 137:2). Nevertheless, "the harps" (meaning musical instruments in general) were hanged upon the willows only metaphoricallv. For, at the return of the Jews to their homeland, there were among the repatriates one hundred and twenty-eight levitical singer-musicians, and two hundred additional male and female secular singers (Ezra 2:65). Inasmuch as the singers in Israel were at the same time instrumentalists, we may conclude that during the forty-eight years of captivity instrumental playing, individual and in groups, has zealously continued in secret. This may not have been pursued to the same extent as in the native country, where the demand for liturgical and secular musicians has always been considerable,—but in a sufficient manner to keep the tradition alive.

It would not be too far-fetched to assume that not only among the Levites, but also among the two hundred secular male and female singers referred to above, there were quite a few who mastered various instruments. It is not surprising, therefore, that in the fertile soil of the re-established musical practice, especially after the completion of the new Temple, the musical culture of Ancient Israel, both vocal and instrumental, soon flourished again.

o
o o

It is rather strange that, contrary to sacred musical performances, one comes but sporadically across any direct references to secular music making in the Old Testament. It almost appears as if any substantial report in this respect, because of its common familiarity, would be considered superfluous by the chroniclers. In point of fact, we find only indirect references to that effect, but they enable us to draw some general conclusions regarding the activity of secular musicians.

The feasts of the revelers have always been accompanied with music:

"they sing to the timbrel and harp, and rejoice at the sound of the pipe" (Job 21:12);—"and the harp and the psaltery, the tabret and the pipe, and wine, are in their feasts" (Isa. 5:12).

When joy is transformed into mourning, music, too, ceases:

"The mirth of tabrets ceaseth, the noise of them that rejoice endeth, the joy of the harp ceaseth, they drink not wine with a song" (Isa. 24:8).

To be sure, the groups of musicians playing on such occasions did not form an "orchestra" in the proper sense, particularly if we compare them with the substantial musical forces of the Temple, or with the huge instrumental groups during the outstanding religious and national festivities. But as small "bands," where personnel might have changed depending on the circumstances, they represent the typical "ensemble music" of Ancient Israel. As such, they were largely responsible for the dissemination of secular musical culture in biblical times.

Through the widespread music-making within various groups, private music instruction must have benefited in no small measure. Young people were likely to be attracted by the possibility of devoting their instrumental skill to the service of general rejoicing. Furthermore, there have obviously been some material advantages connected with playing in small bands, since secular musicians used to be somehow remunerated for their services. The young men playing music (Lament. 5:14) might have been mainly amateurs. They represented, however, the basic stock from which groups of musicians were recruited, and it stands to reason that at great popular festivals they have been the leaders of the playing and singing crowds. Such a popular feast is characterized by the chronicler when he reports that at the coronation of king Solomon

> "the people piped with pipes, and rejoiced with great joy, so that the earth rent with the sound of them" (1 Kings 1:40).

o
o o

The already familiar indications in the Book of Daniel concerning King NEBUCHADREZZAR's court orchestra (Dan. 3:5,7,10,15), however interesting in themselves, are hardly of any value for assessing the orchestral practice in Ancient Israel. To be sure, they show the instrumentation of an Oriental court orchestra. And considering the close cultural relationship between Babylonia and Israel, one might be tempted to assume at first sight that the orchestral practice of the mighty neighbor have had exerted a powerful influence upon the analogue institutions of the small country. However, just the contrary is true in this particular case. For the orchestral practice of Israel has developed according to quite different principles. As if intending to stress the "exotic" character of the depicted milieu, the author of the Book of Daniel uses the names of pagan instruments known in the land of Israel perhaps by hearsay, but which were certainly not familiar among its average inhabitants. The names of Greek and Asiatic instruments, transformed into the Aramaean dialect, *ḳarna, mashroḳita, ḳathros, sabbeka, pesanterin,* and *sumponyah*[18] have been completely foreign to the Jewish people.

Apart from the Book of Daniel, NEBUCHADREZZAR's orchestra is referred to also in the Midrash, though with less details:

> "Nebuchadrezzar tried to entice Daniel, saying to him, 'Will you not bow down to the image, for it is strong and real? Come and see what it can do.' He said to him, 'and you will bow down to it yourself.' What did the wicked king do? He took the plate of the high priest [which he wore on his forehead] and put it in the mouth of the image, and then brought together all manner of musicians (*ḳol mine zimra*) who played hymns (*meḳalsin*) to it."[19]

Ḳol mine zimra is a collective term in the talmudic literature, referring to orchestral performances, in which the various instruments are not named individually.

o
o o

With regard to orchestral playing of the ancient Hebrews, the Book of Psalms affords important disclosures. To be sure, it does not furnish detailed descriptions pertaining to the composition of orchestra groups and the number of musicians, such as we find in the Books of the Kings and the Chronicles. The indications of the Psalter, however, carry weight for other reasons. Just as they help us in getting a valuable insight into certain *termini technici* of the musical practice in Ancient Israel, so they contain significant allusions to the diversity of Jewish ensemble music and especially to the differentiation of its orchestral colors.

We have already referred to the fact that the music of biblical Jewry was not uniform in its tone color, *i.e.* was not performed with some invariable combination of instruments. Quite on the contrary, this combination was selected according to the mood of the text underlying the melody.

This is precisely the sense in which the headings of the psalms must be understood, when, in some instances, they indicate "with string music" in general (Pss. 4, 6, 55, 61, 67), and in others merely a certain category of strings, like the lyre (*kinnor*) for Pss. 43:4; 71:22; 98:5; 147:7; 149:3,—the harp (or psaltery) (*nebel*) for Ps. 71:22,—*sheminit* (Ps. 12),—*ʿalamot* (Ps. 46), —*gittit* (Pss. 8, 81, 84),—or the eight-stringed lyre, the ten-stringed lyre and the harp (*kinnor, ʿasor, nebel*) for Pss. 33:2 and 92:4. The indication *ʾel ha-neḥilot* (Ps. 5) seems to imply the accompaniment of singing with one or several kinds of woodwind instruments, whereas Ps. 150, this apotheosis of Israel's religious devotion, requires the use of the full orchestra, with all the instruments named individually, or their families collectively.

It is unlikely that the instructions given in these headings imply each time the accompaniment with only one of the quoted instruments. A single string instrument, for instance, in the relatively vast and roofless Temple hall would have been almost inaudible. The chances are therefore that the indications in question refer to the use of strings in groups, which is tantamount to saying that sacred songs must have been accompanied by a string orchestra in various combinations. Thus we are driven to the conclusion that the levitical orchestra in general had at its disposal tonal effects of differentiated colors. Should we ever be able to discover the true meaning of some hitherto unexplainable terms in the headings of the psalms, we would probably get a further insight into the acute faculty of the Israelites for tonal discrimination.

These instructions for various instrumental combinations are in no way to be taken as fortuitous or arbitrary. Originally, they might have been motivated in part by some intimate interrelation of the psalmodic texts and their musical settings. But having, unfortunately, no precise idea about the actual sounding of the ancient Jewish instruments, we lack the aesthetic gauge for discovering the specific choice of instruments for any given psalm. We may assume, nevertheless, that this choice has been made in each case after careful artistic considerations.

> "The decisions concerning the number of instruments to be used have always been made with the view of ensuring the ensemble effect of the orchestra," says KRAUSS.[20]

This bears out the correct meaning of the talmudic saying that "the instruments were but to sweeten the voice," by which the acoustic relationship between singing and accompaniment is pertinently characterized.[21]

The *ḥalilim,* combined with stringed instruments, have been played in the Temple on twelve different days during the entire year.[22] In the musical performance of the prophetic students (1 Sam. 10:5) and at the banquets of the revelers (Isa. 5:12) pipes and drums are mentioned together with string music. Only in the Books of the Chronicles do we find combinations of horns, trumpets and percussive instruments together with strings (1 Chron. 15:28, 2 Chron. 5:12 ff; 20:28; 29: 26 ff). The soaring music of great religious and national events shows an even richer combination of all kinds of instruments.

Whatever else is found in the Psalter in connection with the orchestral playing of Ancient Israel is practically a reiteration of what has been exposed above. One passage, however, deserves a special consideration, because it reveals some pertinent facts concerning the actual arrangement of various musical groups in mammoth performances.

In describing a solemn procession with singing, playing and dancing, the psalmist states:

> "The singers go before, the minstrels follow after, in the midst of damsels playing upon timbrels" (Ps. 68:26).

This passage should be interpreted as follows:

> "The singers go before; the minstrels are at the rear; they are separated by a group of damsels playing upon timbrels (*i.e. dancing*)."

This appears to be a sensible and practical way of distributing the three groups, each playing a different piece of music, and not one and the same composition as might seem at first sight. The orchestra, having been obviously assigned an independent task in this instance, was segregated from the marching singers at the head of the procession by the intermediate group of the dancing girls. Thus, the ensembles of singers and minstrels did not disturb one another. Since the procession took place in the open, the sounds of the two groups did not mix and each could be listened to separately without any mutual interferences. Evidently enough, the groups of performers were distributed, on this occasion, acocrding to a carefully pre-arranged plan. We may conclude therefore that in other instances, too, the placement of musicians—an important item in artistic performances—was handled with logic and discernment.

The Book of Psalms is concluded with the enumeration of the sacred instruments used in the Temple orchestra (Ps. 150:3-5). In contradistinction to the foreign, pagan instruments mentioned in the Book of Daniel, the list of Ps. 150 contains only Jewish instruments: the *shofar;* the *nebel,* the *kinnor,* as single stringed instruments, and *minnim* as a collective term for all kinds of string instruments. The family of wood-winds is indicated by the generic name of *ʿugab.* Among percussive instruments the *tof* and two kinds of cymbals (*ẓilẓele shemʿā* and *ẓilẓele teruah*) are mentioned. The priestly silver trumpets (*ḥaẓoẓerot*) are not included in this enumeration, since they did not belong to the levitical orchestra proper. However, even though the *ḥaẓoẓerot* are not mentioned here specifically, it is certain that at a feast in which all the musical forces participated, the trumpets have had their proper share in announcing the sacrificial rites and the prostrations of the worshippers.

o
o o

The scrutiny of the orchestral practice in Ancient Israel would be incomplete without considering the factor that was mainly responsible for the outstanding efficiency of the entire musical apparatus, namely the leader of the music, the conductor.

We do not know exactly whether the "composition" of music, the rehearsals and the leading in actual performance have been carried out by the same individual, or were assigned to different persons. It would be logical, however, to assume that those among the levitical musicians who were particularly gifted, received a special education that would help them to distinguish themselves in all three capacities, as composers, rehearsers, and conductors.

Leaders of the music (*menaẓẓeaḥ*) are frequently mentioned in the biblical text; some of them are quoted even by their names. The singing coryphees of the Davidic musical service, Asaph, Heman and Jeduthun-Ethan, have been at the same time the "leading conductors" of the sacred singing. This is evidenced by their earned distinction of striking the cymbals (1 Chron. 15:19), the details of which have already been discussed.

Over these three "conductors," a "general music director" was installed:

> "Chenaniah, Chief of the Levites was over the song; he was master in the song, because he was skillful" (1 Chron. 15:22).[23]

This seems to indicate that he was the actual leader of the performances, whereas the preparatory work in the rehearsals has been the duty of the three precentors, just alluded to.

For the seventeen singer-musicians of the Davidic music ensemble one conductor with three assistants for the rehearsals, might have been adequate. For the two hundred and eighty-eight singer-musicians of Solomon's Temple, four conductors would have been appallingly insufficient, not only as leaders for the multitude of musical performances, but even more so for the greatly increased number of rehearsals, essential for maintaining the artistic quality of the rendition.

All this explains why in the ultimate organization of Solomon's music service each of the newly established twenty-four groups of performers, consisting of twelve singers each, have had their own leader (their names are quoted in 1 Chron. 25:9-31). Thus, Solomon's Temple had twenty-four conductors, who were subordinated to the three chief conductors Asaph, Heman and Jeduthun-Ethan as unmistakably and repeatedly stated by the choniclers (1 Chron. 25:2,3,6).

"General music director" Chenaniah, "master of the singers in the song" of the Davidic music (1 Chron. 15:22,27) seems not to have been alive at the final organization of the musical service, since his name no longer appears at this stage. True enough, there is among the twenty-four group leaders one Ḥananiah, the principal of the eighteenth ward. But apart from the different spelling of his name (ח instead of כ), it is quite improbable that the former supreme leader of the music had been assigned, in the new order, the role of a mere group prefect; particularly so, since his former assistants, Asaph, Heman and Jeduthun-Ethan, have become the leading masters of the entire musical service in Solomon's Temple.

o
o o

That a larger group of singers or musicians has to be conducted by a leader in order to perform with the required rhythmic precision is an axiom valid in ancient times just as it is to-day. But how was music actually "conducted" in Ancient Israel? To answer this question, we have to resort again to analogies found in the musical practice of other peoples of Antiquity. Particularly significant, in this respect, are the institutions of the Egyptians which have mostly influenced the musical practice of the Hebrews.

In excavated Egyptian bas-reliefs and paintings, dancers, processions and festivals are reproduced, in which all kinds of noise making instruments, clappers, cymbals, sistra, handdrums, and also time-beaters are depicted.[24] This has led many to the conclusion that, in ancient times, music was led by precentors with the aid of loud rhythmical instruments, consequently by way of beating the measure. But all these illustrations refer to secular music, which was always joyous, therefore noisy. The sacred music of the Egyptians, on the other hand, was solemn, sedate, and certainly could not have been "conducted" by noise-making instruments. Since the character of Jewish Temple music was somewhat similar to that of the Egyptians, obviously the same technique of leading must have been applied by both, a technique witnessed in the music practice of Antiquity and of early Christian times, far into the Middle Ages: the cheironomy.

This was a manner of leading the singing, that consisted pre-eminently in the manual indication of the fall and rise of the melody; also some of the dynamic degrees have been conveyed by various positions of the fingers.[25] Even occasional movements of the head would indicate certain details of the rendition.[26] All these motions of the arms, the fingers and the head represented mainly mnemotechnical means for the visual delineation of the familiar melodic line and of its interpretation, in the absence of any precise musical notation. Eventually, these cheironomic motions were reproduced in graphic signs, from which the medieval neumes, the precursors of the later musical notation, have originated.[27]

The analogy with the musical practice of ancient Oriental peoples strongly suggests that the art music of the Israelites has been led in a similar fashion. The rabbinical literature even contains some positive evidence to the effect that the Hebrews availed themselves of cheironomy. Thus, it is stated directly that in the cantillation of the Torah, the high and the low pitch as well as the connecting links of the melodic line were expressed by motions of the hand (*hir'eh*). R. NAḤMAN bar ISAAC mentions that the right hand used to indicate cheironomically the *ta'amim* of the Torah.[28] In his commentary to this passage, RASHI confirms that he himself saw Torah-readers from Ereẓ Israel who would use cheironomic signs. As he states, these readers would reproduce the *neginot* of the Torah, the Prophets and the Hagiographa, and the motions they would use were imitations of the written forms of the *ta'amim,* such as the *pashta, dargah, shofar, mapeḥ* etc. Thus, they indicated the melodic fluctuations of the voice, thereby conveying not only the correct meaning of the words, but also the "sweetness" of the *ta'amim.*

o
o o

Before the leader actually started the music, the correct pitch for the voice had to be given. The instrument used for this purpose was the *'abub;* "striking" the note was called *hikkah.* Since the pitch-note did not belong to the musical piece itself, it was not considered, naturally, as a part of the sacred service. This being so, its emission was entrusted to the *nethinim* (or *nethunim*), who are sometimes considered as having belonged to the class of slaves. However, they were no slaves in the direct sense, though they had to take care of certain functions of an inferior category.[29] A rabbinical discussion about them states that they were Levites.[30] Functionaries of the Temple who were allowed to give their daughters in marriage to the priests, the highest dignitaries of the Temple hierarchy, could not possibly be slaves, even if originally they were admitted in this capacity into the service of the sanctuary. If nothing else, the Mosaic law would have freed them anyhow after six years (Exod. 21:2; Deuter. 15:12).

The above rabbinic discussion is responsible for the belief that besides the levitical musicians, others, not belonging to the musicians' guild, would participate in the sacred music. Even KRAUSS supports this idea.[31] This, however, is altogether erroneous, since the strong spirit of caste among the levitical musicians and the strict rules of their guild precluded the participation of any outsider who did not belong to their organization. "The players of instruments of music," mentioned in this discussion, were indeed the *nethinim,* who were, however, in charge of the subordinate task referred to above.[32] Singing and playing instruments, on the other hand, was the exclusive privilege of the levitical musicians.

The Hebrew term *haḥalik,* "to glide off," was used in the rabbinical literature for the act of ending a musical piece.[33] KRAUSS gives this term an entirely misconceived explanation. He thinks that the hand of the player slowly glides off from the instrument, *i.e.* from the holes of the pipe.[34] The playing of a wind instrument, however, is stopped simply by the discontinuation of the air supply. Besides, the meaning of this passage refers to something entirely different:

> "and they closed the playing with one pipe only, since this made the better close."[35]

o
o o

As mentioned repeatedly, the artistic standard of the levitical performances was maintained by permanent and meticulous rehearsals. Where and how did these rehearsals take place? Rehearsal rooms are mentioned in the Bible as well as in the rabbinic literature.

> "And within the inner gate were the chambers of the singers (*sharim*)[36]

in the inner court, which was at the side of the north gate" (Ezek. 40:44).

The Mishnah is even more explicit:

"And there were chambers beneath the Court of the Israelites which opened into the Court of the Women, and there the Levites played upon harps and lyres and the cymbals and all instruments of music."[37]

"Played" implies here the act of rehearsing, which evidently was so assiduous that even one of the Temple gates was named after the music resounding there all the time whenever the sacred service was not in progress:

"And opposite them on the north, counting from the west [were]: the Gate of Jeconiah, the Gate of the Offering, the Gate of the Women, and the Gate of Singing."[38]

This precise indication corroborates the above biblical passage; it is certain therefore that Ezekiel also refers to the rehearsal chambers of the musicians.[39]

The Mishnaic "Gate Tadi" (sometimes spelt "Gate Tari") has been called "The Gate of the Poets," because the authors of the psalms, who were composers at the same time, used to teach their newly created melodies to the singers in a separate chamber.[40]

The musical performances of the Temple took place on a raised platform (*dukan*). There is no mention of it in the Bible, but the rabbinic writings repeatedly refer to it:

"There were never less than twelve Levites standing on the Platform."[41] "Levites only were allowed to ascend the Platform."[42] "[The children] did not stay on the Platform but they used to stand on the ground so that their heads were between the feet of the Levites."[43]

In the long run, the Platform became synonymous with levitical singing itself, as we read in the Talmud:

"If you were a Levite, you would not be qualified for the Platform [*i.e.* to chant], because your voice is thick [hoarse]."[44]

The platform was divided into gradually heightened levels, so that all the singers could see the leader, and furthermore, were themselves visible to the congregation.

For musical performances on a large scale, a second platform would be erected in the Court of the Israelites:

"There was a step one cubit high, and the Platform was set thereon, and on it were three [other] steps each half a cubit high; thus the Court of the Priests was two cubits and a hand higher than the Court of the Israelites."[45]

This platform was used for special performances in the open air at which a multitude of artists, as well as great masses of worshippers have taken part.

This platform was not identical with another location for the great musical performances of the Levites, namely the fifteen steps leading from the Court of the Women up to the Court of the Israelites. About this, the Mishnah states:

"Beforetime [the Court of the Women] was free of buildings, and [afterward] they surrounded it with a gallery, so that the women should behold from above and the men from below and that they should not mingle together. Fifteen steps led up from within into the Court of the

Israelites, corresponding to the fifteen Songs of Ascent in the psalms, and upon them the Levites used to sing."[46]

This is the place where the famous nocturnal festivity of *Bet ha-She'ubah* used to take place, with torch dances, singing and playing.

Referring to the rehearsal work of the Levites, PORTALEONE ventures the belief that they were taught music theoretically and practically from books.[47] There is not the slightest ground for such an assumption. Biblical as well as post-biblical sources reveal nothing about the existence of Jewish music theory, and less so about books pertaining to it. JOSEPHUS, the conscientious chronicler of the Jewish customs, would certainly not have passed over in silence the existence of such an important book. And PHILO, who shows in his numerous treatises a good knowledge of the Greek music theory of his time, would also have alluded without doubt to such a book of the Jews.

o
o o

The rehearsals of the levitical musicians might have proceeded in much the same manner as they do in our times with groups of singers or musicians who cannot read music; by a way of a lengthy and laborious drill.[48] Taking into consideration the great freedom and flexibility of Oriental tunes, we may infer that the results of the rehearsals must have depended mainly upon the skill and efficiency of the leaders.

The work of the music master was not restricted to rehearsing the chants and their instrumental accompaniment. His was yet another important task: to compose the music numbers. However, one should not conceive this "composition" in the sense of to-day's practice, *i.e.* as some precise fixation of music in writing. Yet, the lack of such precise fixation at that historical period does not exclude the possibility that the levitical music masters might have developed some primitive means to retain in writing their musical ideas, at least in general outlines. The simplest of such means might have been the reproduction of the cheironomic motions in graphic form, to which we referred above.

A number of hitherto unexplained marginal signs in the "*Book of Isaiah*" of the so-called St. Marks' Scroll, found at the Dead Sea, have caused ERIC WERNER to ponder upon them as possible historic forerunners of the later Masoretic accentuation, the ekphonetic notation of the Hebrew Scriptures. In his deliberations, based on Mme R. PARALIKOVA VERDEIL's study, *La musique Byzantine che les Bulgares et les Russes*,[49] WERNER points out certain paleographic similarities between the signs of the St. Marks' Scroll and the Byzantine neumes as applied to the *Kontakia*, a hymn type of the 5th-7th centuries, and to some Slavonic chants.[50] However, the question is still not cleared beyond doubt whether the Dead Sea Scrolls originated in pre-Christian times, or—as a number of biblical scholars maintain—are the product of Karaitic writers who flourished in the 7th-10th centuries.[51] Therefore, it would be too early to decide authoritatively whether these signs are merely forerunners of both the Byzantine and the medieval Hebrew notation or whether they have been taken over from the fully developed Byzantine ekphonetic signs. At any rate,

WERNER's investigation is a noteworthy attempt at finding some preliminary historical interpretation for the enigmatic scroll-signs.

o
o o

Whatever the method of "composing" the music of the sacred songs might have been, it is certain that the arrangement of the musical material was not the accomplishment of an individual, but represented the net result of team-work. This is a logical conclusion if we consider the fact that all levitical musicians, or at least most of them, were "skillful" ("all of them masters"), that all received the same thorough musical education, and that the leader of a group was merely the *primus inter pares*. Thus, the levitical "composition" might have gradually crystallized during the rehearsals by a procedure of co-operation, by mutual suggesting, trying out, accepting, rejecting, improving, on musical ideas, until a result satisfactory for all concerned was achieved.

o
o o

The character and the form of levitical singing has been examined in a previous section. But what can be said about the instrumental accompaniment to singing? We can only assume that for the most part the melodic line of the songs was duplicated by instruments, wherever this was practically feasible. Inasmuch as woodwind instruments of those days may have not been sufficiently developed in the technical sense, it would have been difficult for them to follow the melismatic subtleties of the Oriental songs. Stringed instruments were more in a position to do so. By occasional stopping the strings it would be quite possible to fill in the intervallic gaps and thereby to support the melodic line at least in its general contours.

Yet, this method of doubling the melody in unison might not have exhausted the possibilities of levitical orchestral accompaniment. It may well be surmised that another and more involved system of accompaniment also existed, for which there are no indications in our sources, to be sure, but which has manifestly come to the fore in the latest musicological research.

CURT SACHS was struck by the observation that in the picture of the Elamite court orchestra[52] the fingers of harp players seem to touch simultaneously different strings. Stimulated by this discovery, he extended his investigations to other pictorial representations of Egyptian and Assyrian harp-players, in which the position of the fingers is clearly discernible. After a thorough examination, he arrived at the conclusion that in Assyria, in the 7th century B.C.E., the simultaneous production of two tones a fifth apart can be identified on these harps. In Egyptian pictures from about 1000 B.C.E., SACHS believes to have discovered not only the intervals of fifths, but also fourths, octaves and unisons.[53] To quote SACHS' own words,

> "it is probable that this means an incidental stress of essential notes rather than a continuous accompaniment in parallels."[54]

If SACHS' theory is plausible—and there are good reasons to believe that it is—then the assumption might not be far-fetched that the Israelites, too, knew simultaneous combinations of two different sounds and that these were used in their art music, *i.e.* for the most part in the Temple music, especially in its orchestral part.

This opens up new vistas in the interpretation of the two controversial biblical terms *nebalim ʿal-ʿalamot* and *kinnorot ʿal-ha-sheminit.* We have tried to explain the first term as "harps carrying the top-voice melody," the second as "accompanying lyres."[55] SACHS' conclusions may serve as corroborative evidence for our assumption. His theory of two-tone combinations used in Antiquity does not invalidate the fact that Oriental music—ancient as well as modern—is basically monophonic, unharmonized. Occasionally sounded intervals amidst continuous unisons do not constitute a definite harmony; and even should we assume that certain vocal phases of the melodic line have been reinforced instrumentally by parallel motions in fifths, fourths or octaves, this would not constitute an essential deviation from the principle of monody as practiced in Antiquity.[56] There exists an analogy of this practice in the early medieval *organum,* which was based upon singing in parallel fifths, fourths and octaves.[57] This manner of singing was even known in ancient Rome and was called *paraphonia.*[58]

Two classical references testify to the existence in Antiquity of performing music in two different parts. Both are to be found in VARRO's works. In his treatise about the Latin language, he explains the different forms of *canere,* "to sing," defining *accanit* as "he sings to (something)," and *succanit* (the grammatical contraction of *sub-canit*) as "he sings a second part" (different from the first).[59] In another passage, he refers to the two pipes of the *tibia* (double-oboe), stating that the melody was played on the right pipe, called *incentiva,* and the accompaniment on the left, or *succentiva.*[60] In the same chapter he says metaphorically that

> "the shepherd's life is the treble (*incentiva*) to which the farmer's life plays the accompaniment (*succentiva*)."[61]

HICKMANN goes even further back in history. From Egyptian pictorial representations he sets out to prove that the Egyptians knew about polyphony.[62] In the first place, he assumes that Egyptian musicians were familiar with the principle of the "*basso ostinato.*" According to HICKMANN, the technique of the ensemble playing of the Egyptians was heterophonic. This supposedly consisted of the participants performing a theme with variations all in all *simultaneously,* not one variation after the other,—a questionable assertion. Another rudimentary polyphony might have been created, still according to HICKMANN, that the choir singers did not wait for the end of a solo-passage, but came in over it too soon.[63] HICKMANN calls this "involuntary polyphony," a highly debatable theory. Even if such occurrences might have happened (for which there is no historical evidence), they must have been accidental. The principle of polyphony cannot be based on this.

For the "*ostinato*" technique HICKMANN refers to pictures found in tombs. The double-oboe indicates clearly that the player used one pipe for the melody, while the other one served as an accompanying drone. HICKMANN calls this "real polyphony," which, however, constitutes polyphony merely to a limited degree. More convincing, in this regard, are pictures showing several musicians; the positions of the harpists' fingers seem to indicate that they play different melodic lines. The same picture also shows several "conductors," leading the vocalists and instrumentalists with cheironomic movements; the different positions of the hands and fingers intimate indeed the idea of two-part singing. In a relief from a tomb at Sukkârah, HICKMANN even draws the conclusion of three-part singing.[64]

Furthermore, he refers to a terra-cotta figurine from the 1st cent. C.E. (see illustr. 53.) This statuette represents two musicians,—one of them, evidently a midget or a child, plays cymbals, the other, sitting, holds a pan's pipe to his lips. This instrument is connected by a flexible pipe to a pedal-mechanism, activated by the player's right foot. According to SACHS, this figurine represents a primitive pneumatic organ, indicated by the number of pipes (10). Blowing of the pan's pipe by the player seems to have been unnecessary, and his open mouth indicates that the player may have sang simultaneously. From this, HICKMANN draws the conclusion that there is the evidence of an early vocal and instrumental polyphony, primitive to be sure, but unmistakable.[65]

After having established, as he thinks, the principle of polyphony, he uses this as a stepping stone to prove from numerous pictorial representations that there existed in Egypt a polyphony at least of string instruments. In a picture of several harp players, the different positions of hands and fingers clearly show that possibly several simultaneous melodic lines were being performed, or else an instrumental accompaniment was being played to a song, or instrumental melody.

Should we accept the theory that in the music practice of Ancient Israel some of the instruments merely duplicated the vocal melody, while other supplied a rudimentary but not a unisonal accompaniment, it would also be reasonable to conclude that one of the tasks of the levitical music masters during the rehearsals—and by no means the least important one—must have been the determination of tones and intervals, which had to be produced by the accompanying instruments.

From all this we may now gain a rather clear idea as to how the rehearsals of the Levites might have proceeded. In the first phase, the music was "composed," which means that the most important part of it, the vocal melody-line, was established in co-operation with all concerned. Then, the instruments duplicating the vocal melody in unison were coached. Subsequently, the functions of the accompanying instruments were fixed note for note. All this was practiced and repeated until everybody mastered all details assigned to him. Finally, everything was rehearsed together, over and over again, until the desired perfection was achieved. This methodical and conscientious, never relenting technique is the secret of the high artistic standard of the levitical performances, unparalleled in Antiquity.

VIII. THE DANCE

The triplicity of music as manifested in singing, playing and dancing, represents the basic principle of the ancient Jewish conception of the tonal art. These three musical streams spring from the same original source and tend toward the same common aim: the glorification of God.

Dance is as old as music itself. Dance originated from the perpetual need of man to express his emotions in the form of bodily movements. If these emotions accumulate and reach a high degree of intensity, the body starts moving involuntarily, as it were.

Among primitive peoples dance is generally induced by acoustic means. Clapping of hands, stamping of feet, the rhythmic beat of noise-making instruments evoke almost unfailingly some sort of bodily movements which may be considered as the archaic type of dancing. From this initial stage to dancing as a true and civilized art form in its various manifestations there is still a long way. In principle, however, there is no radical difference between primitive dancing, on the one hand, and the dance of a higher artistic order, on the other.

Like all religious, cultural and social institutions of the Hebrews, their dance, too, reveals certain features which had their origin in similar customs of neighboring nations. Therefore, in order to assess adequately the dance of the ancient Israelites, we have to cast a glance upon the analogous artistic occupation of other peoples who have had close cultural interrelations with Israel.

Religious dancing must have been most spectacularly developed among the Phoenicians, since they have had a special deity for the dance, *Ba'al Markod,* "Ba'al (or Lord) of Dancing."[1] He was called so either because the Phoenicians believed that he was the creator of the dance, or because—contrary to other deities—he was mostly hallowed by dancing,[2] particularly in bacchantic dances that were performed in his honor.[3]

The Babylonian New Year's festivities used to be celebrated with processions, dramatic plays, mimic presentations by choral groups, and recitations performed by priests, as well as by laymen.[4] In the extant written monuments of the Babylonians dance is not specially mentioned, to be sure; but the history of ancient Oriental religions as well as the conventional analogy with the customs of other Semitic peoples point strongly to the probability of dance performances at Babylonian joyous festivals.

As for Assyria, we have positive historical evidence about the role of dancing in the life of its people. In Assyrian excavations, numerous pictorial representations of dancing men and women have been found. In the palace of ASHUR-IDANNI-PAL a procession is depicted, which is led by men playing harps; some of them have their feet raised, executing manifestly dancing steps. They are followed by a group of women, whose raised arms seem to take part in dancing and mimic evolutions. The subsequent group of children are clapping their hands, a customary means in the Orient for the rhythmical accompaniment of dancing. The entire group represents a band of musicians, singers and

ILLUSTRATION NO. 56
Ritual dance-procession of the Hittites in a single file. Rock-relief at Boghazkoei. (After Fritz Hommel, *Geschichte Babyloniens und Assyriens,* Berlin, 1885-88).

dancers, in their characteristic "triple" manifestation at an ancient Oriental court. (Illustr. 27).

An inscription on a rock from about 2000 B.C.E., discovered at Boghazkoei in Cappadocia, helps us to obtain a valid insight into the ritual dance of the Hittites. (Illustr. 56). In the middle portion of the carving, gods and goddesses are graphically depicted; processions of men and women, from the left and the right side respectively, are advancing towards them. The men, with partly raised feet, perform dance steps. The presence of gods, whose names are given in hieroglyphic signs, makes it certain that the picture represents a ritual dance. Other Hittite discoveries show similar groups, honoring the deities with dances.

Similar to the Assyrians, the Egyptians alloted quite an essential role to the dance in their religious rites. The large temples maintained a special class of male and female dancers. Numerous Egyptian pictures show ritual dancers performing their parts either in a solemn manner, with rolling steps and raised arms, or in wild ecstasy, with their sinisterly contorted bodies making almost the impression of acrobatic displays. (Illustrations 57, 58).

The dance in Egypt, as in Phoenicia, was considered of divine origin. ḤATḤOR, the mother of HORUS, was the goddess of heavens, of trees, and of love.[5] She was also the goddess of music and of dancing and is frequently depicted with a small boy, shaking a sistrum in front of her. The priests of ḤATḤOR are represented "dancing and clattering castanets."[6] Dance and music constituted the joy of the goddess BASTET (or BUBASTIS, as the Hellenes called her). She is generally depicted holding a sistrum, the attribute of dancing girls in Egypt.[7] (Illustr. 52).

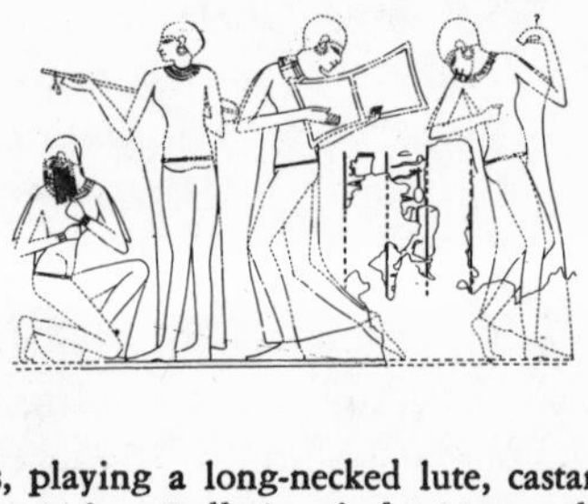

ILLUSTRATION NO. 57
Egyptian dancers and musicians, playing a long-necked lute, castanets and a square-shaped hand-drum (After *Bulletin of the Metropolitan Museum,* New York, 1928).

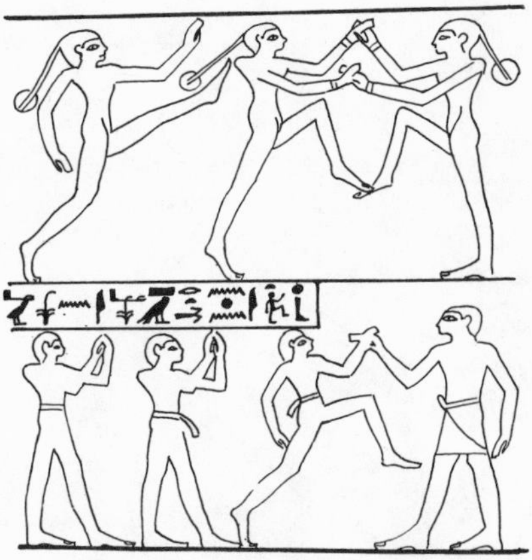

ILLUSTRATION NO. 58

Ritual dances in Egypt (After *Bulletin of the Metropolitan Museum,* New York, 1928).

A custom frequently reproduced on the doors of Egyptian temples is the ritual dance performed by the king while offering sacrificial gifts in honor of the deity.[8] (Illustr. 60).

Apart from religious festivals celebrated in the temples, there were in Egypt abundant secular feasts at which dance was never lacking. After the ingathering of the harvest, the husbandmen, marching in a solemn procession, would offer to the deity the first fruits of the land and perform dances of fertility in honor of the gods.[9] In gratitude for the yearly overflowing of the Nile, the Egyptians offered their thanks to god Ptah with dance ceremonies. During these evolutions, the dancers held small sticks in their hands, which they struck together, thus providing their performances with rhythmic support.[10] (Illustr. 59)

ILLUSTRATION NO. 59

Dancing Egyptian harvesters, using concussion sticks. (V. Dynasty, 2563-2423 B.C.E.) (After Curt Sachs, *The History of Musical Instruments,* New York, 1940).

Many of these dance performances, needless to say, must have been witnessed repeatedly by the Jewish people, who lived for more than four centuries under the Egyptian rule.

No wonder therefore that the Egyptian dance has left its strong imprint on that of the Israelites, except that the frankly technical abuses of the former never have been imitated by the latter. All the other characteristics of the sacred as well as the secular dance of the Egyptians can be found almost without changes in Jewish customs. Like their close neighbors, the Israelites honored their God with dances as well. David's ecstatic dance before the ark of the covenant is akin to that of the sacrificial dance of the Egyptian kings. The ritual dance of the Hebrews was similar to that of the classical period of the Egyptian religion, sedate and dignified. In both religions, processional forms

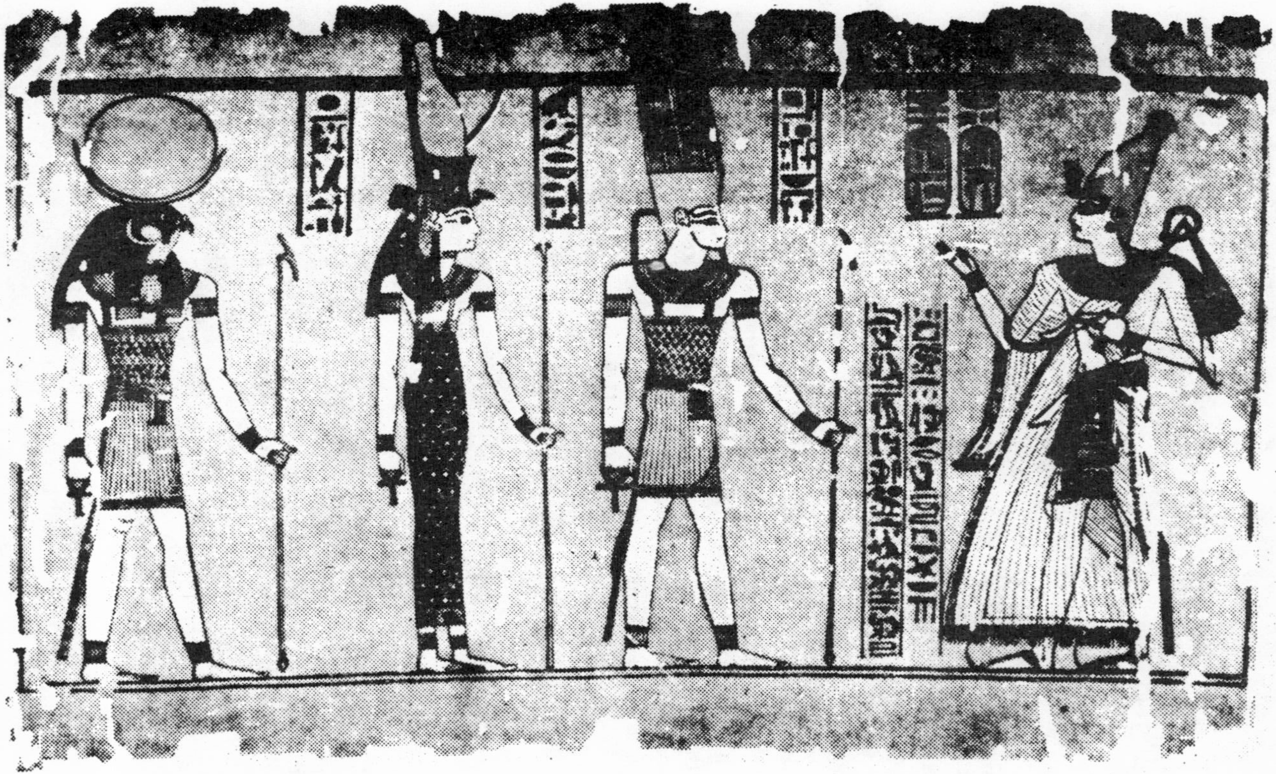

ILLUSTRATION NO. 60

Sacrificial dance of the Egyptian Pharaoh, offering to the gods Amon, Mut and Khonsu. Inscription in hieroglyphics: "He offers incense before the statue of the god, while the priest recites from the mysterious book of the 'Dances of Min.'" (After Adolf Erman, *La Réligion des Egyptiens,* Paris, 1952).

of dance have been used in ritual ceremonies. Joyous national festivals were always adorned with popular dancing. The thanksgiving festival at the ingathering of the harvest was celebrated by both peoples with rites aimed at fertility, the main feature of which consisted in dancing evolutions. When the harvest was brought in, the husbandmen in Israel celebrated the Feast of the Lord, as the Egyptians did, with dances, using

> "branches of palmtrees, and boughs of thick trees, and willows of the brooks" (Lev. 23:40).

As in Egypt, dance was never lacking at any festivity of the nobles and rich. Even the belief of the Egyptians that their gods themselves indulged in dancing, has its parallel in the conception of the Jews. All these common traits inspire the belief that the dance of the Israelites has not only been decisively influenced by that of the Egyptians, but was perhaps taken over entirely from them.

The dance of the Hellenes, however, might have exerted but little influence, if any, upon that of the Israelites. True, the Greeks, like the Egyptians, have already established in the primeval times a relation between the dance and their deities. APOLLO, ARES, DIONYSOS, PAN, ARTEMIS, have all been known as dancers; even ZEUS and HERA have occasionally indulged in dances. Countless historical records, literary as well as pictorial, inform us about the dance of the Hellenes and attest to the importance they attributed to it in their religious and secular life.

The Hebrews of the biblical times have never lived in close communion with the Greeks, except in some large cities. At any rate, cultural relations between the two have not been so intimately interlinked as in the case of the Hebrews and their immediate neighbors, the Phoenicians, Syrians, Babylonians, etc. The hellenistic period of the history of Israel took place at a time when the religious and national characteristics of Judaism have already been most strongly consolidated—in fact, almost to the point of inflexible rigidity. As a result, the people, or at least the broadest strata of it, were no longer susceptible to foreign influences. The Jewish nation, subject to stringent religious laws and led by a fanatic priesthood, kept aloof from the pagan hellenistic notions in religious as well as in secular matters. That is why any inroads of Greek dance customs into Jewish life can scarcely be detected. Anything reported in this respect in later sources (*e.g.* in the New Testament) points not to a Jewish but to a heathen usage, and as such it has no value for the appraisal of the Jewish dance.

1. The Terminology of Dance.

Dance is mentioned in countless passages of biblical and post-biblical literature. This alone would prove its outstanding importance in Jewish religious and secular life. Even more light is thrown upon the significance of dance in Ancient Israel by the fact that biblical Hebrew has no less than twelve verbs to express the act of dancing. Should we add to this the numerous terms found in the rabbinic literature pertaining to this occupation, it could be properly stated that no other ancient language possesses this wealth of expressions describing the various aspects of dancing.

(1) The most frequently used word is *ḥul* or *ḥil,* "to whirl"; from this root the noun *maḥol,* "dance," is derived.—"If the daughters of Shiloh come out to dance in the dances" (Judg. 21:21,23).—"And whether they sing or dance" (Ps. 87:7).—The word signifies also the "writhing" or "twisting" of a woman at childbirth, (Isa. 26:17) or the "writhing" of a person in great pain (Isa. 13:8; 23:5; Jer. 51:29). When the word is used in the sense of dancing, it refers to the turning and twisting of the body, in a sort of brisk dancing motion.

(2) *Saḥaḳ* (in the intensive form *siḥeḳ*) and *ẓaḥaḳ* (*ẓiḥeḳ*) means literally "to laugh," "to play," "to make merry," "to make sport" (in Greek *paixein,* in Latin *ludere*); in a figurative sense it means, however, "to dance."—"And Samson made sport [danced] before them" (Judg. 16:25).—"And Sarah saw the son of Hagar . . . making sport [dancing]" (Gen. 21:9).—"And David and all the house of Israel played [danced] before God with all their might" (2 Sam. 6:5).—"Before the Lord I will make merry [dance]" (2 Sam. 6:21).—"And David and all Israel played [danced] before God with all their might" (1 Chron. 13:8).—". . . king David dancing and playing" (1 Chron. 15:29).—In the meaning "to play": "Wilt thou play with him as with a bird?" (Job. 40:29).—In the meaning "to make merry" : "I sat not in the assembly of them that make merry" (Jer. 15:17).—"The voice of them that make merry" (Jer. 30:19).—"Thou shalt again be adorned with thy tabrets, and shalt go forth in the dances of them that make merry" (Jer. 31:4).—"And the broad places of the city shall be full of boys and girls playing [making merry] in the broad places thereof" (Zech. 8:5).—In the proper meaning of dancing: "And the women sang one to another in their play [*i.e.* dance]" (1 Sam. 18:7).—In the intensive form *ẓiḥeḳ*: "And the people sat down to eat and to drink, and rose up to make merry" (Exod. 32:6). As we see, dance has been an ever present entertainment at any joyous occasion; therefore "to make merry" and "to dance" are synonymous terms in Hebrew.

(3) *Ḥagag,* in the strict sense, means "to celebrate a *ḥag,* a festival." Primitively, *ḥag* was the term for a feast combined with a solemn procession, or with a devout dance in the sanctuary. Therefore, the expression in Ps. 42:5 "to keep a holiday," (*i.e.* "to observe a *ḥag*") means the same as "to visit the sanctuary" (Exod. 23: 14-17). Ancient Jewish colloquial usage considered the words festival and dance as belonging together, and thus *ḥagag* obtained automatically the meaning of dance:

> "They were spread abroad, over all the ground, eating, drinking, and feasting [dancing]" (1 Sam. 30:16).

In Job 26:10 and Isa. 19:17, the word is used metaphorically.

(4) *Karar* (in the intensive form *kirker*), "to whirl about," "to rotate," occurs in the Bible only once in the sense of dancing: "And David danced before the Lord with all his might" (2 Sam. 6:14). The Targum to Isa. 64:20 uses a noun derived from this verb, *kirkeran* (fem. plur.), "dances."

(5) As a synonym of *karar,* the same biblical passage uses the verb *pazaz* (also in the intensive form *pizzez*), in its strict sense "leaping," and applied to dance, "to dance hopping" :

> ". . . Michal the daughter of Saul looked out at the window, and saw

king David leaping and dancing before the Lord" (2 Sam. 6:16).

(6) Another verb, *raḳad* (in the intensive form *riḳḳed*) means "to skip about"; applied to dancing, it is to be found in the following biblical passages: "Michal . . . saw king David dancing and making merry" (1 Chron. 15:29). —"And their children dance" (Job 21:11).—"A time to mourn, and a time to dance" (Eccles. 3:4).—"And satyrs shall dance there" (Isa. 13:21).—"On the tops of the mountains do they leap" (Joel 2:5).—In Ps. 29:6 the word indicates "the skipping of a calf."—In the Midrash it is said that "when a man plans a sin, Satan dances encouragingly before him."[11] The Aramaic word for dancing is here *riḳḳudin,* derived from *raḳad.*[12]

(7) *Dalag* has the same meaning as *raḳad,* "to leap," "to skip about": "Then shall the lame man leap as a hart" (Isa. 35:6).—"Leaping upon the mountains" (Cant. 2:8).—In another passage, the word signifies a sort of skipping step of a pagan ritualistic character: "In the same day also will I punish all those that leap over the treshold" (Zeph. 1:9). This step must have been connected with some heathen superstition, as one may infer from 1 Sam. 5:5, where a similar custom is mentioned at the entering of Dagon's temple in Ashdod. The custom was evidently a remnant from the ancient pagan religion of the Hebrews and therefore prohibited, even subjected to punishment.

(8) *Ḳafaẓ* is synonymous to *dalag* and is used as its parallel expression: "Leaping upon the mountains (*dalag*), skipping upon the hills (*ḳafaẓ*)" (Cant. 2:8). The word, in the sense of dancing, is used in this passage only.

(9) The word *ẓalʿa* is likewise used but once in the Bible "And the sun rose upon him as he [Jacob] passed over Peniel, and he limped upon his thigh" (Gen. 32:32). It indicates some sort of limping ritual dance; as the burial location of Kish, Saul and Jonathan, *Ẓelʿa* may have been an ancient sanctuary, where this peculiar limping dance was performed. The latter used to take place at the rise of the sun (*cp.* verse 31), which suggests that in primeval times it might have been some kind of ritual action in the religion of sun worshippers.

(10) *Duẓ* is used once in the biblical text in the sense of "to leap":
"And dismay danceth before him" (Job. 41:14).

(11) *Pasaḥ* (in the intensive form *pisseaḥ*) is derived from a root, the proper meaning of which is "to pass over," "to spare," "to save"; in this sense it is used in Exod. 12:11,23,27, and in Isa. 31:5. In connection with the Passover-Festival, the word is mentioned in many other passages of the Bible (Lev. 23:5; Num. 28:16; 33:3; Deuter. 16:2,6; Josh. 5:10,11, etc.). A second meaning of the word *pasaḥ* is "to limp," consequently also "to dance in a limping fashion," which suggests a religious ceremony, possibly a limping ritual dance from the early stage of the Jewish religion. (*Cp.* the limping dance of the priests of Baʿal at the Mount Carmel, 1 Kings 18:26). Some biblical commentators, therefore, maintain that *Pesaḥ,* the Passover-Feast, owes its name to the peculiar limping dance usually performed on this festival.[13]

(12) *Sabab* means "to move round" (a sacred object), "to encircle" (the altar), and it is a solemn procession, or a pantomimic evolution, rather than a dance in the strict sense:

"So will I compass Thine altar, O Lord" (Ps. 26:6).

Encircling the sacred places, like the altar, sacred trees, also cities, seems to have been an ancient ritual custom, based upon the idea of the "magic circle." The psalmodic verse

"Walk about Zion, and go around about her" (Ps. 48:13)

intimates the consecration of the city by way of ritual encircling. Whereas the repeated encircling of Jericho (Josh. 6) seems to indicate the belief in the power of an ancient magic custom, as is immediately evident from verse 17:

"And the city shall be devoted [*Harkavy*: 'accursed'], even it and all that is therein, to the Lord."

The custom of ritual processions around a holy place or a sacred object has survived the biblical times. This is manifest from a talmudic statement that on the Feast of Tabernacles, following the sacrifices, the priests walked in a procession around the altar, while Levites sang Ps. 118:25. The first six days of the feast they encompassed the altar once daily, on the seventh day seven times.[14] This must surely have been a primeval ritual institution, like all the other similar customs mentioned in the Old Testament. Their origin goes back to magic and sorcery.

(13) In the Midrash we come across a non-biblical word *ḥolah*:

"R. Berekiah and R. Helbo . . . said in the name of R. Ḥanina: In the Time to Come, the Holy One, blessed be He, will lead (*ḥolah*) the chorus of the righteous . . . It is written *ḥolah* [*i.e.* 'round dance'] —and they will dance around Him like young maidens."[15]

The word might be a transmuted form of *maḥol* or *maḥolah,* a linguistic procedure for which there are many analogous instances in the Hebrew. All these variants are derived from the same root, *ḥul.*

(14) We find in the Targumim an additional term for dance, *ṭafaẓ* or *ṭafas.*[16] Its meaning is "to leap," and it corresponds to the biblical *ḳafaẓ.* As Krauss thinks, this was the most primitive way of dancing, a simple skipping or jumping, without a specific rhythm, and was used in the ritual as well as at joyous wedding celebrations.[17]

(15) The word *raḳʿa* seems to allude to an ancient ritual at funerals. It is used in 2 Sam. 22:43 and Ezek. 6:11 in the sense of "stamping with the feet," but has, in these biblical passages, no connotation of dancing. In the talmudic literature, however, this particular connotation emerges unmistakably. In post-biblical times it was an exequial custom on the part of the mourners to accompany the funeral oration with rhythmic stamping the ground. There are certain indications that, at primeval burials, it was customary for the survivors, men as well as women, to honor the deceased with dances.[18] This ancient custom was eventually confined to merely stamping the floor. The word *raḳʿa* is derived from the verb *raḳad* (see No. 6).

Further terms in the talmudic literature, having a more or less obvious connection with the dance, are:

(16) *Ḳarʿṭa,* meaning the boundless skipping and hopping, as Satan would do in dancing, according to the imagination of the Hebrews.[19] Originated from the Greek verb *skirtaō*="to spring, leap, bound," the word was transplanted in a phonetically modified form into the Aramaic.

(17) *Ḥaddes*, or *haddes*, means "to dance on tiptoe," as used for dancing before the bridal couple.[20]

(18) *Shavar* signifies "to leap"; it is an additional synonym for the numerous other expressions indicating a similar action.[21] In a broader stnse, the word is interpreted as "leaper on [or with] a rope."[22]

(19) *Ḥanag* is a kind of a round dance and is used as a synonym *of ḥolah*. *Ḥanag* has always been accompanied by instrumental music; its musical background was called *ḥanagnay*ʾ*a*, or *ḥanagt*ʾ*a* in Aramaean.[23] From this word the Aramaic term *ḥinga* might have derived, its different meanings being "a circle, dancing, chorus, feast."[24]

(20) *Sanaṭ* means literally "to tease," but it is closely associated with the idea of dancing, signifying a kind of saltatorial entertainment in which all the participants would engage in mutual teasing.[25]

(21) ʾ*Afaẓ* might be a variant of *ṭafaẓ;* there seems to be no indication for any other derivation, and it is used in the same sense.[26]

(22) For the sake of completeness it should be mentioned that the part of the Jewish population influenced by hellenistic culture, *i.e.* mainly the inhabitants of the great cities, called the refined dancer, especially among the professionals, by the term ʾ*arkestes*.[27] This is merely the transliteration into Aramaic of the Greek word for dancer *orchēstēs*.

The Talmud contains no minute description of the various species of dance, with the only exception of the word *riḳḳud,* probably because it is most frequently mentioned in rabbinical texts. The rabbinic writer explains the difference between *ḳipuẓ* (from *ḳafaẓ*), "to leap," and *raḳad,* "to dance."[28] At the first, both feet are lifted, or pulled, simultaneously from the ground (*ʿaḳar*), at the second, the feet are placed alternately one before the other (*heniaḥ*).

Nothing testifies more emphatically to the paramount importance of dance in the life and mind of the Jewish people than this overabundance of terms designating the various forms and phases of dancing.

2. The Forms of the Sacred Dance.

The somewhat sparse mention of the religious dance in the Old Testament might suggest at first sight that this procedure has been assigned only a minor role in the ritual. This, however, is by no means the case. The fact alone that of the twelve terms in biblical Hebrew, enumerated above, eleven refer to sacred dance and merely one to secular dance, proves quite eloquently that the former of the two categories must have played an essential part in the cult.

Religious dance can be found very early in biblical tales. After the miraculous passage of the Red Sea, and immediately following Moses' song of praise,

> "Miriam, the prophetess, the sister of Aaron, took a timbrel in her hand; and all the women went out after her with timbrels and with dances." (Exod. 15:20).

Here, dance is the solemn conclusion of thanksgiving to God and represents undoubtedly a ritual action, although not in the strict sense of a sacred ceremony, since in those heroic times a thoroughly organized sacred service did not exist as yet. But the dance in honor of God has had already at the early stage of Jewish religion a definite ritual connotation; it has certainly originated in the similar sacred ceremonies of the Egyptian religion. In the eventual elaborate development of the Jewish sacred service, other ritual actions (sacrifices, benedictions, songs of praise, etc.) took precedence, without, however, completely obscuring dancing.

The dance at the Red Sea has been combined with singing:

> "And Miriam sang unto them" (Exod. 15:21).

The union of both arts, singing and dancing, is here by no means a fortuitous occurrence; both gushed forth from the same psychic impulse. It is a typical example of a ritual "song for dancing," or, to put it in another way, an example of a religious hymn presented with dancing evolutions.

There can be no doubt that this sacred dance has taken place in a solemn and dignified manner, especially when compared with an event reported shortly afterwards in the Bible, *viz.,*

> "the notorious pagan dance performed around the golden calf" (Exod. 32:6) .

When Moses heard

> "the noise of them that sing," and saw "the calf and the dancing,"

he became so enraged

> ("his anger waxed hot") that he broke the tables of the law which he brought from Sinai (Exod. 32:19).

The biblical narrator dilates intentionally upon the unrestrained character of this "dance around the calf," in order to emphasize the sacrilege of idolatry. A later description of a heathen dance by the priests of Baʿal who "limped about the altar," on the Mount Carmel (1 Kings 18:26), likewise characterizes an un-Jewish, barbarous custom.

On the Feast of the Lord, the daughters of Shiloh used "to come out to dance in the dances" (Judg. 21:21). Though the Bible does not qualify these dances expressly as belonging to the ritual, there can hardly be any doubt that they were sacred dances, since the occasion, the annual Feast of the Lord, has been one of the most important religious festivals.

The best known example of sacred dance in Jewish history is that of David on the occasion of bringing in the ark of the covenant to Jerusalem. Representing one of the most outstanding events in Israel's religious and national existence, it is mentioned no less than three times in the Bible.

> "And David danced before the Lord with all his might" (2 Sam. 6:14);

also:

> "And David and all Israel played [*i.e.* danced] before God with all their might; even with songs, and with harps, and with psalteries, and with timbrels, and with cymbals, and with trumpets" (1 Chron. 13:8, and 15:28).

The first two of these descriptions contain the expression "with all his (or their) might," pointing to a degree of rapture which probably reaches a religious ecstasy. David's dance is a ritual action *kat' exochen,* that manifests his sublime adoration of God. What no music, not even singing is able to express, becomes reality through the elemental power in David's exalted dance. At this moment, rising above anything mundane, David the king represents the concentrated religious feeling of the entire Jewish people. (Cp. the sacrificial dance of the Egyptian Pharaoh) (Illustr. 60).

The deeper meaning of this ritual dance is a sort of corporeal merging with the infinite God, which becomes manifest in David's answer to his wife Michal who

> "despised him in her heart" as she "looked out at the window, and saw king David leaping and dancing before the Lord" (2 Sam. 6:16).

To her mockery David replied:

> "Before the Lord will I make merry; and I will be yet more vile than thus, and will be base in mine own sight" (2 Sam. 6:21,22).

Apart from this answer, the self-abasement of the anointed king before God manifests itself also externally by David's laying off his royal ornaments, and presenting himself only "girded with a linen ephod," the garment of the priests, to the Lord. At this moment, David is not the chosen leader and crowned king of the nation, but the humble servant of his God, standing unadorned, bare of his regalia, absorbed completely in adoration.

In other passages of the Old Testament, dance as an element of the sacred ceremonial is mentioned but cursorily and in a rather veiled fashion. It seems almost as though the overzealous purifiers of the Bible have considered dance to be incompatible with the sacred character of the text, or looked upon dance pre-eminently as a secular occupation. No wonder that they sought to eliminate anything that would have referred directly to it. Nevertheless, a few allusions remained, proving unequivocally the survival of dancing in the sacred service. Especially the Psalter, which underwent only minor changes by purgers, contains repeated references to sacred dance.

The dance of worshippers around the altar is mentioned in the following psalmodic verse:

> "I will wash my hands in innocence; so will I compass Thine altar, O Lord" (Ps. 26:6).

A counterpart to it is the solemn procession to the altar:

> "Order the festival procession with boughs, even to the horns of the altar" (Ps. 118:27).[29]

Other psalmodic verses refer directly to the sacred dance:

> "Sing aloud unto God our strength; shout unto the God of Jacob. Take up the melody, and sound the timbrel, the sweet harp with the psaltery" (Ps. 81:2,3).

"Sound the timbrel" points unmistakably to the ritual dance as a complement to singing praises.—Furthermore:

> "The singers go before, the minstrels follow after, in the midst of damsels playing upon timbrels" (Ps. 68:26).[30]—"And whether they sing or dance, all my thoughts are in Thee [my Lord]" (Ps. 87:7).

—The two concluding psalms contain direct proofs of the recourse to dancing in sacred ceremonies:

> "Let them praise His name in the dance, let them sing praises unto Him with the timbrel and harp" (Ps. 149:3);—and "Praise Him with the timbrel and dance" (Ps. 150:4).

The dance in the ritual ceremony might have been confined only to some symbolically suggestive dancing evolutions. One has to imagine it more in the manner of a solemn display, using rhythmical gestures and pantomimic motions of the arms and the body, as reproduced on numerous Egyptian pictures. The Jewish sacred dance, as an element of the ritual, must have been radically different from David's ecstatic dance before the ark. Here, the rapture was justified by the extraordinary event; in the regular service the sacred dance might have well taken place in a quiet, sedate way, adapting itself to the solemn character of the Temple ritual.

Not only in Egypt, but already in earlier times, sacred dance represented a prominent feature among religious ceremonies. In Sumeria religious dances were performed in various ways, having been accompanied either by flutes or lyres, depending on circumstances. As LANGDON conjectures,

> "in the early period [of Sumer] the flute songs were attended by processional movements on the part of the singers and flute players; on the other hand the songs to the lyre were attended by bowings, prostrations and swaying. Some such distinction must have existed in these liturgies for we find flute-hymns called *kidudu,* that is 'walking, or procession,' and lyre hymns called *ki-shub,* that is 'bowing, falling.' . . . We may, perhaps, conclude that the Sumerian choirs moved in procession while the flute liturgies were being performed."[31]

We may observe something similar in the sacred dance of the Hebrews. In Israel, too, dancing was incorporated into the musical manifestations of the sacred service; therefore, there must have been a close interrelation between sacred music and sacred dance. K. J. ZENNER investigated this relationship and published his findings in a remarkable study.[32]

According to his belief, dance played in the sacred ritual a much more significant role than the few allusions in the Psalter suggest. As a support for his assertion, ZENNER refers to the Christian *Codex Kosmas* (1st half of 6th century), preserved in the Vatican, where it is stated that the psalms have been "sung, played and danced" (*adontes kai psallontes kai orchoumenoi*). ZENNER sees a positive proof for this in the psalm-heading *ʾal maḥalot* (Pss. 53:1; 88:1), rendered by the SEPTUAGINT phonetically as *hyper Maeleth,* that is without an exact translation. But AQUILA actually translates it as *epi choreia,* SYMMACHOS as *dia chorou,* THEODOTION and QUINTILIANUS as *hyper choreias,* JEROME as *pro choro* (53:1) and *per chorum* (88:1). In all these translations dancing is unmistakably expressed.

Furthermore, as mentioned earlier, there is a conclusive evidence for performing psalms with accompanying dances in JOHN CHRYSOSTOM's writings (see p. 155 and Illustr. 37).

According to ZENNER, Pss. 26:6, 118:27, and also 43:4 are unmistakable indications for sacred dance. Moreover, the verse in Ps. 68:26, "The singers go before, the minstrels follows after, in the midst of damsels playing upon timbrels" is, in ZENNER's opinion, the conclusive proof that the psalms have been not merely sung, but also danced, *ēdon meta orchēseōs,* as the *Codex Kosmas* states.

Then, ZENNER advances his hypothesis, according to which the psalms are qualified as "lyric dances" ("Reigenlyrik") in the Old Testament. He shows that there have been, in classical Antiquity, lyric dances, representing

> "the result of the co-operation of three arts, poetry, music, and mimic."

These items have been performed by choirs, accompanied by instruments, and enlivened pantomimically by dancing evolutions and appropriate motions of the arms:

> "Religion was the factor that created these single arts and succeeded to unite them in this beautiful alliance."

ZENNER points out the parallel phenomenon of the Greek orchestics (our modern "choreography") stemming from the same source as did the Jewish lyric dances. WESTPHAL offers a pertinent reasoning with regard to the interrelation between these three arts in Antiquity, which corroborates ZENNER's theory:

> "The source of poetry in the pristine life of ancient peoples is religion. In the religious intercourse with the deity, the speech was elevated to more animated forms, which—in contrast to the regular usage of the language—developed a poetic manner of expression: the prayer, the praise of the deity created *poetry;* the speech addressed to the gods was invested with multifarious accents, the increased intensity of the declamation led to singing, to the *melody;* ultimately, the place where man addressed the deity was the altar, on which the sacrifices were burned and which was encompassed by the singers in a solemn procession; this movement around the altar constitutes the beginnings of the *orchestics*; the religious dance of the ancients, considering its causes, is nothing but a sacred procession to the sacrifices and a sacrificial dance (*cf.* Ps. 118:27). This explains how the three Music sisters of art, poetry, music, and orchestics came into being."[33]

Also SACHS stresses the numerous facets of the Greek complex art of orchestics,

> "in which words, music, dancing, marching, and gestures combined the expressions of the mind and the body."[34]

According to the conception of classical Antiquity, orchestics were considered an indivisible unity of all these different artistic manifestations.

All of which would seem to support strongly ZENNER's theory. Yet, conservative biblical exegetes look upon the mutual influence of the three arts merely as an occasional, fortuitous phenomenon. In their opinion, nothing proves that the lyric dance brought forth a specific art form, which would owe its existence exclusively to the combination of the three arts in question.

Nevertheless, ZENNER maintains vigorously that the Hebrews, specially gifted by nature for lyric arts, have known and practiced lyric dances. He offers the following proofs *per analogiam,* which in their rigorous logic constitute a strong support for his theory.

To begin with, he refers to the frontispiece of the *Codex Kosmas* which shows a pictorial reproduction of the *orchēsis,* the performance of choral songs with pantomimic evolutions. (Illustr. 37). Thus, lyric dances of Antiquity in general are preserved even in a pictorial form.

ZENNER sees a further actual proof for his assumption in the term *leshabbeḥa,* by which the Targumim translate the superscription *lamenaẓẓeaḥ* ("for the leader") in the psalms. LAGARDE has already alluded to the fact that the Arabian verbal form *shebaḥ,* "he praised God," is phonetically similar to *sabaḥa,* which means "he swam."[35] In this connection one comes across the revealing fact that the Arabian word *tasbiḥ,* the noun of the verb *shebaḥ* indicating the praise of God, prescribes motions of the hands and arms which markedly resemble those of a swimming person. ZENNER alludes to a similar custom in Catholic rites; for the orations, the gloria and the prefatio of the Holy Mass, the early Roman Church has prescribed certain motions of the hands which, even to-day, manifestly show similarity with those of a swimmer. The Church might have taken over this custom from the Synagogue. ZENNER surmises, therefore, that the expression *leshabbeḥa* of the Targumim may well indicate the pantomimic manner of performing certain psalms.

One finds analogies to this effect also in Egypt. ERMAN refers to the Egyptian use of certain "dance tours," that is, various positions and evolutions, which were ordinarily applied when two or more people danced together.[36] These motions would express a specific idea, therefore they had particular names. Among others, ERMAN mentions one "tour" which was called "column." Other "tours" represented the wind, swinging over the trees and bending down the reeds,—or the abduction of a belle,—or the mystery of the birth, as expressed by hieroglyphic inscriptions.

ZENNER asks the question (without answering it, however) whether certain expressions in the headings of the psalms, such as *ʿal ʾayyelet ha-shaḥar* (Ps. 22), or *ʿal shoshannim* (Pss. 45,69,80) do not actually represent instructions for using a specific "dance tour" in the performance of these psalms. He refers to the analogy that the Hellenes knew a special kind of dance which they called *krinon* ("lily"). Would it not be possible that the psalm-heading *ʿal shoshannim* meant a similar instruction?

The time when lyric dances allegedly flourished in Ancient Israel is placed by ZENNER into the pre-exilic period of Jewish history. Among other proofs to this effect, he cites the magnificent religious festivities of David and Solomon. The Babylonian exile caused, according to ZENNER, the discontinuation of the lyric dance together with other institutions not directly connected with the ritual of the service. The sacred dance itself, however, was not touched by this decline and survived for a while—perhaps in a changed form—as proven by post-biblical sources.

It may safely be assumed that at least some of the psalms have been sung *and* danced. For this the evidence furnished by KOSMAS INDIKOPLEUSTES constitutes the strongest support. Another reasoning for this assumption may be based upon the possibility that certain psalms have been used for the purposes of expiation, purification and healing. MOWINCKEL, especially, believes in the ancient attribution of this power to a number of psalms and avers that they have been sung with the purpose of healing sickness and alleviating sufferings.[37] It might well be that dancing evolutions of the participants coupled with corresponding pantomimic gestures, were considered appropriate for enhancing the effectiveness of such supplications.[38] OESTERLEY points out the commonly known fact that, in primitive religions, the sacred dance

> "is an appeal to the pity of the god. Not very far removed from this is the idea of compulsion upon the god; . . . and it is quite possible that in some cases the sacred dance was believed to have the effect of coercing the god to do what was required of him."[39]

Among the ancient sacred dances that used to be performed around some devoted objects, the one connected with well-springs is occasionally implied in the Old Testament, without however being directly described or even specifically mentioned. The reason for this peculiar situation is that

> "the priestly historians and legislators resolutely excluded, as far as possible, everything that could infer any similarity between the worship of Yahveh and that of heathen deities."[40]

Nevertheless, the custom in question must have been so deeply rooted in the religious consciousness of the Israelites that dancing around particularly venerated objects has been cultivated as much after this "editorial exclusion" as before it. Analogies with similar customs of other Semitic peoples support this assumption.[41]

Thus, the Greek writer NILUS (or NEILOS, fl. ca. C.E.) reports that when nomadic Arabs have found a well, this important event was celebrated with songs and dances.[42] A similar celebration must have taken place when Moses, at God's command, led the people to a well in the desert (Num. 21:16-18). As a proof of the importance of the occasion, the biblical chonicler quoted the "Song of the Well" textually; however, the sacred dance appertaining to it, as self-evident, was not mentioned specifically, as it occurs so often in the biblical text.

Another form of sacred dance of the Israelites is revealed in 1 Sam. 10:5 :

> "Thou shalt meet a band (*ḥebel*) of prophets[43] coming down from the high place (*bamah*) with a psaltery, and a timbrel, and a pipe, and a harp, before them; and they will be prophesying."

The translation of *ḥebel* as "band" or "company" is not accurate, since the proper meaning of the word is "rope," "cord," or "string." The same word used in Josh. 2:15 gives the correct meaning:

> "Then she let them down by a cord (*ḥebel*) through the window."

If we apply this meaning to the prophets coming down from the sanctuary, it would indicate that they marched in a single file. Such a procession in a single row, accompanied by singing and playing, especially of the *tof* (hand-drum), suggests unmistakably that this evolution must have taken place in some form of dancing.[44]

The dancing of the early Israelite prophets assumed the form of ecstatic bodily movements. They whirled themselves into a state of frenzy; in this mood they pronounced their prophecies, and even infested the onlookers with their rapturous dancing (1 Sam. 19:20-24). When Saul danced wildly, the people asked:

> "Is Saul also among the prophets? And the Spirit of the Lord came upon him, and turned him into another man" (1 Sam. 10:5,7,11).

Singing as accompaniment to dancing has been self-evident in Ancient Israel, so that biblical chroniclers mention but cursorily the combination of both. Examples for this are Miriam's dance with the women of Israel after the passage of the Red Sea (Exod. 15:20,21), the dancing and singing of the women welcoming Saul and David after their victory against the Philistines (1 Sam. 18:6,7; 21:12; 29:5), and others. On all these occasions the people danced in groups, just as the singing was performed by choirs. However, there were sometimes solo singers accompanying the dancing, which may well be termed as "songs for the dance" in the proper sense of the word (*cf.* Ps. 26:7). A typical example for this category can be found in the Midrash:

> "Na'amah was a woman of different stamp, for her name denotes that she sang (*man'amet*) to the timbrel (*tof*) in honor of idolatry."[45]

To be sure, singing and dancing are here performed in the service of a pagan worship. There have been, however, many heathen elements in the Jewish religion, which were eventually adapted to its higher ethical aims, so that the solo-song for the dance may well be taken as having had a perfectly legitimate place in the sacred as well as in the secular customs of the Israelites.

Similar to other ritualistic acts, men and women were generally separated at religious dances. One single biblical report seems to indicate the joint dance of both sexes, this being the dance around the golden calf (Exod. 32:6,19). This, however, is not an Israelitic dance in the strict sense, since it occurs at an idolatrous feast; hence the exception to the rule.

After the destruction of the Jerusalem sanctuary, music, and apparently also dancing, have ceased to exist as parts of the religious rites, and even in secular life. But a custom such as the dance, which was deeply rooted in the popular consciousness of the Jews, could not be completely eradicated from the ritual, and even less so from secular usage. The early rabbinic literature furnishes the proof that after the religious and national catastrophe which befell Judaism with its crushing defeat by the Romans, dance still survived in the religion as well as in secular life. This will be demonstrated in a subsequent chapter.

3. The Dance at Religious Festivals.

As long as the Israelites were nomadic shepherds and were not compelled to rely on agriculture for their principal means of existence, they did not have any festivals that are connected with harvest. It is supposed that they took over such festivals from the residents of Cana'an after the conquest of the new homeland; subsequently, they celebrated these festivals in honor of their own God.

The Jewish festival cycle was governed by the seasonal changes of the soil's production, and aimed at their religious consecration. Thus, the three great events in the life of the husbandmen, all celebrated with profuse festivities, were the offering of the first fruits, the end of the harvesting, and the ingathering of the entire harvest. Each of these feasts was called *ḥag,* a term indicating that the essential feature of these festivals was the religious dance around the sanctuary.

The names of the three principal agricultural festivals just referred to were:

(1) *Ḥag ha-mazzot,* the feast of the unleavened bread, the spring festival, the feast of the newly awakened nature, "when the sickle was first put to the standing corn," and when the first fruits were offered to God (Deuter. 16:9). The *ḥag ha-pasaḥ,* "the Feast of Passover," was originally the spring festival of nomadic Jews, at which the first-born animals of the flocks were sacrificed (Exod. 34:19). In latter days' agricultural existence of Israel both festivals were combined, in which merely the exodus from Egypt was celebrated (*cp.* Ezek. 45:21).

(2) *Ḥag shabuot,* "the Feast of Weeks" (Exod. 34:22; Deuter. 16:10), or *ḥag ha-ḳazir,* "the Feast of Harvest" (Exod. 23:16), which took place seven weeks after the *ḥag ha-pasaḥ,* as the harvest was completed.

(3) *Sukkot,* "the Feast of Tabernacles," called also *ḥag ha-ʾasif,* "the Feast of Ingathering," the festival of thanksgiving,

> "at the end of the year, when thou gatherest in thy labours out of the field" (Exod. 23:16).

Prior to the centralization of the national-religious cult at Jerusalem (620 B.C.E.) the festivals of the nomadic Jews were not held on specific days of the year. After they settled in Canaʿan, however, they adopted the dates of the agricultural festivals of the residents of the land.

Originally, the three festivals had the same religious importance. The Mosaic law prescribed that all men visit the sanctuary on each one of them (Exod. 23:17; 34:23). As time passed, the Feast of Tabernacles gained precedence, becoming the outstanding festival in Israel, called "the Feast of the Lord," or simply "the Feast" (Lev. 23:39,41; Judg. 21:19; 1 Kings 8:2; 12:32, etc.).

As already mentioned, in all these *ḥagim* dance was an essential element of the religious celebration. When the daughters of Shiloh "came out into the vineyards to dance in the dances," this event took place "on the feast of the Lord," which was held "from year to year in Shiloh" (Judg. 21:19)[46]

The biblical scribe reports in a cursory way about this custom, but the rabbinic literature describes it more extensively. According to RABBAN SIMEON ben GAMALIEL

> "there were no happier days for Israel than the 15th of Ab and the Day of Atonement, for on them the daughters of Jerusalem used to go forth in white raiments; and these were borrowed, that none should be abashed which had them not; [hence] all the raiments required immersion [*i.e.* they were newly washed]. And the daughters of Jerusalem went forth to dance in the vineyards. And what did they say? 'Young man, lift up thine eyes and see what thou wouldest choose for thyself: set not thine eyes on beauty, but set thine eyes on family.' "[47]

The ditty sung on this occasion has been paraphrased and versified by EDERSHEIM.[48]

Dancing at the vintage was instituted in early times and, judging from biblical accounts, must have been a wide-spread practice. The birth place of the prophet Elisha, *ʾAbel Meḥolah* ("the field of dancing") (1 Kings 19:16) may have been a locality where such feasts with sacred dances took place regularly. When the Day of Atonement had been transformed into mourning for the destroyed sanctuary, the dancing, connected with the former, was abolished altogether.

Rabbi ELIEZER ben HYRCANUS (1st century C.E.) dilates upon the feast on the 15th of Ab;[49] according to his testimony, the worshippers brought wood for the altar in quantity that was sufficient for the burnt-offerings through the whole coming year. JOSEPHUS, too, mentions this feast, which he calls in Greek *xylophoria,* "the Feast of carrying wood."[50] Apart from its practical purpose, this was a ritualistic practice, which has been performed in a solemn procession, possibly with some pantomimic evolutions. It may be counted, therefore, among the religious ceremonies interspersed with dance elements.

Among the other festivals in which dance had an essential part, the Sukkot-Feast deserves particular mention. On this day, immediately following the sacrifices, the altar was encompassed in a solemn dancing evolution,[51] during which the Levites sang Ps. 118:25.[52] On the seventh day, called *Hoshʿana Rabbah,* the altar was encompassed seven times.[53] The procession was concluded in addressing directly the altar:

> "Homage [lit. 'Beauty'] to thee, O Altar!", or "To Thee O Lord and to thee, O Altar!"[54]

At the most outstanding religious-national festival of the Maccabaean period, the re-dedication of the Temple, a dance-like procession, was a part of the sacred ritual. (2 Macc. 10:7).[55]

Curiously enough, the Bible does not mention a religious ceremony which—judging from rabbinic tales—must have been the crowning event at the Feast of Tabernacles. This was the rite of *Bet ha-Sheʾubah,* observed in the night between the first and second day of the festival, at which a torch-dance was performed in the Court of the Women. The court was then illuminated by chandeliers of four arms, and

> "countless Levites [played] on harps, lyres, cymbals and trumpets and instruments of music."

Before a large audience

> "men of piety and good works[56] [*i.e.* rabbis and distinguished laymen] used to dance with burning torches in their hands, singing songs and praises."[57]

Dancing and singing at the Feast of Tabernacles seem to have served the sole purpose of celebrating joyfully the ingathering of the harvest and to thank God with music. It may be surmised, however, that this festival, or at least some of its ritual actions, had their origin in earlier magic customs. This is corroborated by the rabbinical description of the water libation, which represented an important ceremony of the *Bet ha-Sheʾubah.*[58]

On this occasion water was drawn from the pond Shiloam (or Shiloah) and carried in a solemn procession to the Temple. When the cortège arrived at one of the Temple gates (called "Water Gate"), several priests blew a unisonous trumpet blast. In the Temple, the water was poured out on the altar, with the priests again sounding the trumpets. This ceremony was performed similarly on all seven days of the festival. The analogy with the technique of imitative magic is unmistakable in the procedure of water libation. The purpose of any magical act is to achieve the desired effect by reproducing it on a smaller scale. The rabbinical writers themselves admit that the aim of the ceremony has been to secure rain for the coming year:

> "The Holy One, blessed be He! said: 'Pour out water before Me at the Feast, in order that the rains of the year may be blessed to you."[59]

Judging from this rabbinic statement, the custom of water libation was established in obedience to God's own commandment. It is, however, easy to discover that this is giving merely a modified interpretation to the ancient rain magic incorporated into the ritual custom of the Jewish religion on its more developed stage.

The belief in the magic effect of the ceremony is evidenced by the fact that the talmudic writers indicate the occasions and even the specific prayers which were supposedly most efficacious in exercising "the Power of Rain." As the Mishnah says:

> "We make mention of 'The Power of Rain' in the [benediction] 'the Resurrection of the Dead'."[60]

The best time to utter prayers asking for rain was the Festival of Tabernacles, when the first autumnal rains were expected anyhow. The rabbis were divided only on the point as to which day might be the most favorable for such prayers:

> "From what time do they make mention of 'the Power of Rain'? R. Eliezer says: From the First Festival-day of the Feast [of Tabernacles]. R. Joshua says: From the last Festival-day of the Feast."[61]

The "men of good works"[62] who performed the torch-dance at the *Bet ha-She'ubab* were apparently considered capable of exercising, through their prayers, songs and dances, the "Power of Rain" and thus putting into effect the sympathetic rain magic. The term "men of good works" is also interpreted as "men of might," or "workers of miracles."[63] R. ḤANINA ben DOSA was supposed to be such a man. When called to sick persons, he was able, reputedly, to foretell who should live and who should die.[64] Whoever could perform such miracles, was credited with the faculty of obtaining the most auspicious results from the rain magic through the religious power inherent to his dance.

Singing, instrumental music and dancing, combined with the specific spell of the nocturnal scenery, must have created such a rapturous state of mind upon all participants, performers as well as onlookers, that one may well understand why one of the rabbinical writers was induced to exclaim:

> "He that has never seen the joy of *Bet ha-She'ubab* has never in his life seen joy."[65]

The general sentiment at this feast must have been a sort of religious ecstasy, a familiar phenomenon at nocturnal ritualistic feasts in the ancient and in present-day Orient, as well as in primitive religions in general.

At the Festival of Purim dancing again was an outstanding feature. Originally, Purim was the perpetuation of the ancient Persian *Farvardigān* festival in which dance played an essential part, and which was transmitted to the Jews by the Babylonians. The Hebrew name of the festival was explained by two different folk-etymologies, one deriving from the Akkadian *purruru,* "to destroy," and the other from the Babylonian *pūru,* "lot."[66] The word Purim is the Hebrew plural of the Babylonian *pūru,* as LEWY proved beyond doubt.[67]

The generally accepted justification for the incorporation of this feast into the calendar of Jewish festivals was the Purim tale which, despite its foreign origin and its thoroughly legendary character, has been earnestly taken by the Jews for an historical narrative.

The sources of the Esther story may be found in the Babylonian mythology, as the names of the principal characters indubitably prove. Mordechai is *Marduk,* Esther is *Ishtar,* both being the names of the supreme god and goddess in the Babylonian pantheon. Haman is identical with *Hamman* (or *Humman*), the supreme god of the Elamites, whose capital city Susa (or Shushan) is the scene of the Esther story. Even Vashti is supposed to be the name of an Elamite deity, slightly misspelled as *Mashti.*[68]

The Purim festival was probably brought back to the homeland by the repatriates from the Babylonian exile and continued to be celebrated by the Jews after the return. It was likely to exercise an irresistible influence upon the minds of a people, living under conditions of austerity and in dire need of psychological stimulants such as were able to kindle the imagination and the patriotic sentiments of the nation. The story has certainly circulated among the Israelites long before the book was written and, together with the celebration of the feast in Israel, it became deeply rooted in the national consciousness of the Jews. The written form probably constituted but the last step toward the general acceptance by the Jews of the Esther legend as an historical fact. The story of the canonization of this wholly secular book corroborates our assumption.

The outstanding feature of the Purim festival was frolicking, even boisterousness, with jokers in all kinds of disguise, human as well as animal, with masquerades, joyous cortèges and, of course, with a good deal of dancing. On these days everybody danced, rich and poor, men and women, young and old. The casual saying "On Purim everything is allowed" became in the long run a general rule in Jewish customs, even to a point of transgressing the Mosaic laws. Thus, at the popular Purim masquerading, men would disguise as women and *vice versa,* which is strictly prohibited by religious laws (Deuter. 22:5).[69]

Judging from a talmudic report, a pagan custom, common to many primitive religions, survived in one of the ceremonies of Purim. This was the "leaping through fire."[70] In Babylonian countries there existed a custom, called in Aramaean *meshavarta depuriy)a,* the "jumping place of Purim." According to a Gaonic explanation this involved the following procedure: Four or five days before Purim young men would make an effigy of Haman and hang it on the roof. On Purim itself they would set on a bonfire and cast the effigy into it, while standing around, joking and singing. Thereafter, they would jump over the fire above a hoop placed upon the burning stake.[71] This hoop was called the "place of jumping," *dereḥ ha-ʿabarah.* The custom itself was a remnant of an ancient fire-dance, practiced in many primitive religions.[72] Its magic meaning was the destruction of the demon by fire. The existence of this custom may have been widespread, because in 408 C.E. the Emperor THEODOSIUS II issued a decree forbidding the Jews of the Byzantine Empire to practice it. Despite this prohibition, the fire-dance survived in many countries. It might have been so strongly rooted among the superstitious practices of medieval Jewry that it could not be extirpated. R. NATHAN ben JEḤIEL of Rome (1035-1106) mentioned that the custom continued among the Italian Jews in the same manner as among the Byzantine Jews.[73]

4. Dance in Popular Usage.

In primitive religions the deity was not only the originator of human existence, but the sole being who determined and guided the fate of the people as well as that of the individual. Joyous and sorrowful events of life were caused by the deity, and therefore blessings as well as supplications for absolution had to be offered to him in strictly prescribed ritual ceremonies, which included dance as one of their major elements.[74]

Originally, the sacrificial dance, the expiatory dance, the dance at celebrations of victory, at weddings, at funerals, at the harvest festival, all were of sacred character. However, with the gradual development of religion, merely those dances preserved this character which were incorporated directly or indirectly in ritual ceremonies. The others gradually lost their liturgical implications and became part and parcel of popular customs. At this stage, they were but loosely connected with religion, and may therefore be classified as secular dances, constituting the essential element of all popular festivities. On these occasions, joy and gladness, sometimes also the sorrow of the individual and of the masses, manifest themselves most conspicuously in dancing.

The frequent derivation of biblical female names from the dance constitutes a parallel to the numerous Hebrew terms expressing the dancing action itself. We find, for instance, repeatedly the names *Maḥelah* and *Maḥalat* in the biblical text. *Maḥelah* was the daughter of Zelophehad (Num. 26:33), *Maḥalat* Esau's wife, the grand-daughter of Abraham (Gen. 28:9), and also Rehoboam's wife, David's grand-daughter, had the same name (2 Chron. 11:18). A similar name for males, *Maḥelon,* appears in Ruth 1:2. Whether the levitical family of the *Maḥelites* (Num. 26:58) likewise derived their name from dance, cannot be said with certainty. Yet, it is not impossible that in the early history of Israel this family distinguished itself particularly in dancing, hence this name was given to the clan.

Among all the secular festivities, it was the wedding at which, because of its joyful character, dance fulfilled the most prominent function. Rabbinic writers state repeatedly that "they dance before her [*i.e.* the bride], they play before her,"[75] and the scribes furnish all kinds of information as to how the dances and the appropriate songs and recitations have been performed on such occasions.

The participants of the bridal street-procession danced all along the way until they arrived at the house of the wedding. Only in times of a national catastrophe, as during the war of Vespasian (69 C.E.), could it happen that "the crown of the bridegroom and the [wedding] drum (ʾ*erus*)," that means dancing at weddings, were prohibited.[76] Respected rabbis did not consider it below their dignity to dance before the bridal couple, and several of them were so famous for their artful dancing that the rabbinic writers gave them special praise. One of them was

> "R. JEREMIAH of the branch," so called because he used to dance on weddings with a crown on his head, braided of branches of olive-trees.[77]

Another was

> "R. SAMUEL ben R. ISAAC, the man who used to dance on [or 'with'] three branches [before bridal couples]."[78]

Again another was

> R. JUDAH ben ILAʿI who "used to take a myrtle twig and dance before the bride and say [*i.e. sing*]: 'Beautiful and graceful bride.' "[79]

The most distinguished rabbi of his time, RABBAN SIMEON ben GAMALIEL, must have been a virtuoso in dancing and, at the same time, an expert juggler. At the Feast of *Bet ha-Sheʾubah* he performed a torch dance with eight burning torches, throwing them alternately in the air, catching them, and none of them touched the ground when he prostrated himself, touched the floor with his fingertips, kissed the ground and leaped up again.[80]

The Talmud reports about other sages who displayed their skill in juggling on this feast, as well as on other joyous occasions.

> "R. LEVI [on the rejoicing on Water Drawing] used to juggle in the presence of Rabbi JUDAH I. with eight knives, R. SAMUEL before King SHAPUR with eight glasses of wine [without spilling any of their contents], and ABAYE before RABBAH with eight eggs or, as some say with four eggs."[81]

All these jugglings have nothing in common with the dance, but they show that respected scholars did not hesitate to put themselves into the service of general rejoicing, be it only with their special skill as jugglers.

The wedding customs among Babylonian Jews differed from those living in Israel, since the Talmud discusses the question "how does one dance before the bride?" A distinguished visitor,

> "R. DIMI came [to Babylonia] and said: Thus they sing before the bride in the West [*i.e.* in Israel]: 'No powder and no paint, and no waving [of the hair], and still a graceful gazelle.' "[82]

Famous rabbis used to dance before the bridal couples not merely for the sake of rejoicing, but in order to honor the bride. The dance before a person or an object had the ancient ritual meaning of honoring this person or object. One danced in honor of God, or the people, or the bride, or also of the deceased (see below). One danced before people of standing, just as one sang or played for them.

Sometimes the rabbinical wedding dancers received a reward, as we see in the Midrash:

> "R. SIMEON ben LAḲISH received an invitation from a neighbour, [and going to him] saw men stand up and dance and clap their hands,

and receive food and drink. He exclaimed, 'This is good; I too will stand up and dance and sing.' He stood up, danced and sang, and they gave him a cask of wine."[83]

There is not the slightest allusion either in biblical or in post-biblical sources that Ancient Israel cultivated dramatic plays with singing and dancing. Nevertheless, numerous attempts have been made to interpret in this sense one of the biblical books, the "Song of Songs." According to this concept, the Canticles represent a dramatic play, with acting persons, groups of singers and dancers, which—as it was asserted in all seriousness—has been actually performed on the stage in Ancient Israel. Since in this alleged play the dance was supposed to have had a leading role, it may not be improper to deal here with these attempts.

We know that in the ancient Near-East it was a religious custom to usher in the New Year with a sort of dramatic play representing the combat of the New against the Old.

In Egypt, such "mystery plays" were based upon the Osiris myth, but these were expanded liturgical ceremonies rather than dramatic representations in the strict sense.[84] In ancient Babylon, the New Year festival comprised the recital, possibly also some kind of staging, of the primordial myth relating how MARDUK, the supreme deity and patron of the city, defeated TIAMAT, who challenged the authority of the gods. A similar myth existed in Cana'an, as recorded in the *Ras Shamra* clay tablets, originating from the 14th century B.C.E. and discovered 1929 in Syria. They preserve a tale in which the Cana'anite supreme god, BA'AL, lord of fertility, defeats YAM, the god of water, and MOT, the god of death. The tablets do not reveal, however, whether this rite was only recited or also enacted at the New Year celebration in Cana'an. In Assyria one may find historical records of pantomimic representations with choirs and acting persons, played by priests and laymen.[85]

All these plays, however, have been not so much *theatrical* dramas, as personified representations taken from the mythology of these peoples, rites in histrionic disguise, somewhat akin to the medieval Easter plays of the Christian Church. Not before Hellenic times did the dramatic idea develop to its full bloom.

By analogy, one would be inclined to assume that the ancient Israelites, too, have had dramatic plays, at least in some primitive form.[86] There are, however, momentous arguments against such assumption.

The literary achievements of the Israelites have manifested themselves mainly in the domain of lyricism. Dramatic art was not in the least appropriate to their innate nature. Even apart from this psychological factor, one has to consider the all-round lack of historical evidence with regard to the existence of dramatic plays in Ancient Israel. As in the life of other ancient peoples, plays of this order would have constituted such important events in Israel's existence that they could not possibly have been passed in silence by biblical and post-biblical chroniclers. JOSEPHUS and PHILO, too, make no mention whatever of Jewish theatrical performances.

The initial trace of a theater in Jerusalem dates from the times of HEROD, but this, of course, was one established after Greek models. The furious indignation which the high priest JASON incurred because of his attempt at introducing Greek gymnastic games is a significant symptom for the hostility and even repugnance which the traditionally raised Jewry felt for such spectacles.

The most weighty argument against dramatic plays, however, may be found in Israel's religious laws. For the Mosaic law expressly prohibits the imitation (pictorial as well as corporeal) of persons and objects, which is the very essence of any scenic representation. To be sure, the letter of the law says only

> "thou shalt not *make* unto thee a graven image, nor any manner of likeness, of any thing that is in heaven above, or that is in the earth beneath" (Exod. 20:4; *cp.* Lev. 26:1).

But in the strictly religious sense the *making* of an image was extended to all kinds of reproduction or imitation of persons and objects. The priesthood, as the traditional authority for the enforcement of the law, would certainly have opposed with all its might any such activities in which the personification, *i.e.* imitation of other individuals cannot possibly be avoided.

The idea of the dramatic character of the Canticles goes back to ORIGEN (c.185-c.254 C.E.), whose followers gave the book an intermediate position between the dramatic and lyric creations. They called it "a nuptial poem composed in dramatic form" and "regarded it as a dramatic epithalamium celebrating Solomon's marriage with Pharaoh's daughter."[87] However, the most obvious historical considerations invalidate this assumption. According to modern biblical expositors, the time of origin of the Canticles is about 250 B.C.E., which in itself disproves Solomon's authorship as well as the use of the poem at Solomon's wedding.

Nevertheless, the idea was kept alive for centuries. The first attempt in modern times at the dramatization of the "Song of Songs" was that of an Englishman, JOHN BLAND (d. 1788), a teacher of Hebrew, as he called himself. He wrote a play in seven scenes, which was printed in 1750.

Since then, there is an uninterrupted string of dramatizations, even up to our days. After this initial attempt, there were in the late 18th and early 19th centuries three ventures to dramatize the "Canticles" : by K. F. STÄUDLIN (1792), AMMON (1795), and F. W. C. UMBREIT (1820). Among these, STÄUDLIN's attempt deserves attention for his "arrangement" of the 'Canticles' in thirteen "scenes," though not strictly in the sense of a theatrical play.[88] His outlay was followed closely by HEINRICH AUGUST EWALD. He has been among the first who not only perpetrated the idea that the "Canticles" represent a dramatic play, but also developed an elaborate theatrical plot to make his theory plausible.[89]

EWALD's interpretation brought forth immediately a number of similar attempts.[90] Among these ERNEST RENAN's dramatization attracted the greatest attention because of the author's worldwide fame as a scholar and historian.[91] RENAN supplied the text with a multitude of scenic instructions, and also appended a thoroughly elaborated scenario which reads like the script book of a theatrical producer.

Even in our days the fancy of dramatizing the Canticles did not slacken, despite all the previous attempts which mostly had an ephemeral life. The latest one of the series is LEROY WATERMAN's arrangement as a real play for the theatre, which actually has been performed on the American stage.[92]

An intermediate approach to the Canticles has been attempted by MOULTON.[93] He characterizes the "Song of Songs" as "a suite of seven idyls," a literary form, which he places between a drama and lyric poetry. This definition seems to re-echo, at least in part, a hypothesis advanced by LESSING (1777) and later elaborated by H. GRAETZ (1871) to the effect that the "Song of Songs" has been written under the direct influence of THEOCRITUS, a Greek pastoral poet of the 3rd century B.C.E., famous for his "Idyls."[94]

Summarizing his evaluation of the poem's characteristics, MOULTON maintains that

> "the whole is not part of a dramatic scene occurring at the moment, but a reminiscence. The effect may be styled a dramatic reminiscence,"

and according to this, he interprets the Canticles as a "spiritual drama."[95]

In contradistinction to these attempts at dramatization, the fundamental fact cannot be overlooked that the "Song of Songs" is actually an anthology of lyric poems, of humoristic, roguish, even erotic wedding songs, depicting

> "with brilliant imagination and consummate art the thrills, delights, torments, and dreams of love between man and woman—love in bud and full bloom—against the background of the charming Palestinian countryside in the springtime."[96]

The contemporaries of those who compiled the Canticles certainly understood better the basic character of the poems than did the later generations, whose minds were biased by its manifold allegorical and moralizing interpretations. The early readers of the "Song of Songs" have indeed taken the love poems in their literal meaning, and young men used to sing them as erotic ditties in wine houses. This attitude, naturally, constituted a "sacrilege" in view of the canonicity of the book,—a fact that aroused the raging ire of Rabbi AKIBA (d. 132 C.E.), as we learn from the rabbinical literature.[97]

The conclusive refutation of the claim that the Canticles represented a dramatic play is furnished by the findings of J. G. WETZSTEIN, who, as a long time resident of Damascus and its vicinities, has studied the customs and manners of the population and has been considered as one of the authorities in the domain of Oriental ethnology.[98] The analogies between the wedding customs of the Syrians, as observed by him, and the allusion to wedding entertainments contained in the "Song of Songs," are so striking that they merit a brief discussion at this point.

The bridegroom and the bride are called king and queen during the seven days of the wedding festivities, beginning with the morning on which they rise as a young couple. They take their seat on the only available large sized wooden implement, the thrashing-floor, which serves the royal couple as a throne. During the entire seven day period carrying the name of "royal week," dances, jokes and plays are performed before this throne. In this entertainment, the major role is assigned to the songs describing the young marital bliss of the newlyweds. These songs dealing mostly with the beauty of the young couple and their wedding ornaments, refer to the bride as "the most beautiful of the women." In addition, dances are performed in her honor.

In the "Song of Songs," too, the newlyweds are referred to as the "young royal couple," and the allusions to erotic matters in the Canticles (for instance to "the dance of Maḥanaim") represent nothing else but more or less rude jokes that are customary, as a rule, at all the rustic wedding feasts. The expression "daughters of Jerusalem" in the Canticles indicates companions of the bride, with whom she might have performed a group dance, which is quite usual at weddings in general, and those in the countryside in particular.[99] Finally, the "Shulammite" stands for none else than "Abishag the Shunammite," the virgin from Shunem, who—according to 1 Kings 1:3—was considered the most beautiful of the daughters of Israel and was chosen to become king David's last wife. She was proverbial in Israel for her perfect female beauty, and this is the reason why the poet (or poets) of the Canticles have given this name to the heroine, that is to the bride.[100]

With this, the whole castle in the air of a "dramatic play" falls to pieces. From king and queen, from Solomon and his bride the Shunammite, nothing remains but jesting wedding songs and a dancing entertainment, in which the bride was possibly engaged in a dance, similar to that performed on Arabian wedding nights, when the bride, in all her finery, used to burst forth in a sword dance and, later on, in a torch dance.

o
o o

Regardless of its musical background, the secular dance in Ancient Israel was often accompanied by clapping of hands (*safaḳ*), by striking the thighs (*ṭipaḥ*), or by stamping the feet (*raḳʿa*). If no musicians were available for wedding dances, the rhythmical support could always be supplied by a vigorous clapping of hands (*mesapḳin,* or *ẓilẓal bekaf*), or by snapping the thumb and the middle finger (*ʾeẓbʿa ẓeredah*).[101] These terms, incidentally, are in great part Aramaic, and thus refer essentially to their usage in talmudic times. It would not be too bold to assume, however, that the customs in question were adhered to in biblical times and constituted the authentic dance practice of Ancient Israel.

On Sabbath, secular music and dancing were prohibited and with them such rhythmic impulsions.[102]

According to Aggadic ideas, even the angels danced in heaven. Hosts of angels performed a round-dance (*ḥul*) for Jacob on his journey home, and danced (*raḳad*) before him.[103] In Jacob's vision of the celestial ladder

> "the angels of God (Hananiah, Michael, and Azariah) [danced] ascending on it [the ladder], exalting him and debasing him, dancing (*ʾafaz*), leaping (*ḳafaẓ*) and teasing him (*sanaṭ*)."[104]

Dancing has also been indulged in by Satan, whom the rabbis call the "arch-robber" (*ʾarkilistes,* the Greek word *archilēstēs* taken over phonetically). In exuberant revelries the main entertainment, aside from eating and drinking, has been dancing; the diabolic, demoralizing effect of such carousals is expressed in the following rabbinic maxim:

> "Wherever you find eating and drinking, the arch-robber [Satan] cuts his capers [is dancing]."[105]

The word used here for dancing, *kart'a* (obviously derived from the Greek *skirtaō*) indicates the unbridled leaping and skipping, as by one who is intoxicated. At the dance around the golden calf, Satan mingles with the circling (*ḥigeg*) and swaying (*gaḥan*) masses, he leaps (*ṭafaz*) and jumps (*shavar*).

Jewish Aggadic fancy goes even so far as to state that sometimes God Himself dances.[106] The same idea is set forth by other rabbinic authorities, in a more or less embellished form. According to these descriptions, in the Time to Come, the heavenly hosts will be the dancers, and the people of the righteous the onlookers. The righteous follow rapturously the motions of the divine leader of the dance, point to Him with their fingers and compare it with the dance of young maidens. In the general rejoicing, they surround the leader of the dance and perform around Him a round-dance.[107]

o
o o

The attitude of the rabbis toward the dance has not always been so favorable as we might assume from the above quotations. Especially after the eventual intrusion of Greek dance customs into certain strata of the Jewish population, some rabbis have changed thoroughly their opinion about dancing. The professional dancer, in particular, aroused the ire of the sages, as may be seen from the following contemptuous remark:

> "The ʾ*arkestes* is the emptiest of the empty."[108]

Other talmudic passages express this hostility even more indignantly:

> "Every scholar who feasts much in every place, eventually destroys his home, widows his wife, orphans his young, forgets his learning . . . Said Abaye: He is called a heater of ovens. Rabba said: A tavern dancer! R. Pappa said: A plate licker."[109]

R. Naḥman's servant, Daru, is characterized in terms of contempt, as "a notorious dancer in the wine houses."[110] Scorn and disdain are contained in the following talmudic saying:

> "Thereupon a voice cried out: 'Thou leaper, son of a leaper, leap.' "[111]

The word used here, *shavar,* means literally "to leap," but in a figurative sense it is interpreted as a "leaper on [or with] a rope,"[112] It refers therefore to the lowest class of dancers and jokers, akin to medieval itinerant musicians and jugglers. Such entertainers roved around in taverns and public places of Babylonia and, while performing their grotesque dances, they indulged in certain "manners" (*gavne* in Aramaic). These are interpreted as some sort of gestures or motions with the head,[113] but actually they might have been certain "dance tours," similar to those mentioned above.[114] The Talmud even hints at such "tours" as it characterizes the performances of such jokers in the following terms:

> "Loss of time would be where he was a dancer in wine houses and has to make gestures by moving his head."[115]

In his commentary to this passage, RASHI says

> "that these gestures were of a comic sort in order to make people laugh,"

and calls such dancers *ha-leẓonim,* "merry-makers."

The Talmud states furthermore that dances have been sometimes performed at night, as, for instance, the torch dance at the Feast of *Bet ha-She'ubah.* Pharaoh's daughters performed eighty dances (*rikkudin*) at her wedding night with king Solomon.[116] Robbers breaking into Laban's house, danced (*ḳarṭ'a*) the whole night.[117] From these isolated occurrences KRAUSS concludes that dancing has been mainly a nocturnal entertainment.[118]

In contradistinction to these nocturnal entertainments, the vast majority of dances reported in the Bible and in the talmudic literature took place in daytime. Such was, for instance, the dance celebrated every year in the vineyards by the maidens of Jerusalem and Shiloh on the 15th of Ab.[119] All the popular festivities and celebrations of victory were held in daytime. The victory against the Egyptians after the crossing of the Red Sea was celebrated in daytime with singing and dancing (Exod. 15:20). Jephtha's daughter received her victorious father with her playmates in daylight "with timbrels and with dances" (Judg. 11:34). When Saul and David returned victorious from their war against the Philistines,

> "the women came out of all the cities of Israel, singing and dancing, to meet king Saul, with timbrels, with joy, and with three-stringed instruments. And the women sang one to another in their play [*i.e.* dance]." (1 Sam. 18:6,7).

This victory dance with antiphonal singing, performed in daytime, is also mentioned in two other passages of the same book (21:12 and 29:5).

The welcome of the returning victor by dancing and singing women is an ancient custom; with these performances they not only celebrate the victor, but also offer thanksgiving to the deity, to whom the victory is solely ascribed.

Even victorious enemies have been welcomed by the citizens of conquered cities with singing and dancing,—manifestly under coercion. Thus, the victorious Holofernes was received by the subjugated population "with garlands and dances and timbrels (Judith 3:10)."[120]

The round-dance was the most typical and popular one in Israel. It was performed mainly by young maidens, either alone (Exod. 15:20; Judg. 11:34; *cp.* Matth. 14:6), or in groups (Judg. 21:12; Jer. 31:4,13). Older women, too, participated occasionally in the dances (1 Sam. 18:6,7), and sometimes the round-dance was performed by the entire people (Exod. 32:6,19; Jud. 3:10, etc.). Dancing children are mentioned only once or twice in the Old Testament (Job 21:11; Zech. 8:5; *cp.* Matth. 11:7; Luke 7:32). Young men would form their own group in dancing, and so would also the elderly men (Jer. 31:13).

Toward the end of the Second Temple, however,—evidently under Roman influence,—dancing of men alone was considered indecent. CICERO says that

> "no man ever dances when sober, unless perhaps he be a madman."[121]

As CORNELIUS NEPOS reports, the leading statesmen never indulge in music and would consider the dancing of men a depravity.[122] SUETONIUS related the story about a quaestor of the senate who,

> "because he took pleasure in puppet-like gesturing and dancing, was removed by Domitian out of the senate."[123]

ANTIPATER, SALOME's son, accused ARCHELAUS that he is getting drunk at night and, in this state, performs bacchantic dances.[124]

The orgiastic as well as the grotesque dance was not appropriate to Jewish customs. Already in their early history, the Israelites refused to take over such dances from the Assyrians and Babylonians, and so they also succeeded in later times to keep their dances dignified and well mannered, even on the most joyous occasions.

o
o o

In the life of husbandmen, dance played an important role. At the harvest festival, at the vintage and other happy events in the yearly cycle of fertility, dancing was always crowning the celebration (Judg. 9:27; Isa. 16:10; Jer. 25:30). The dance of the maidens of Shiloh in the vineyards on the Feast of the Lord [*i.e.* on the harvest festival] belonged to these annual celebrations (Judg. 21:21).

Apart from its direct purpose of offering thanksgiving to the Lord for His bounty, dancing at these agricultural festivals has had a veiled magic significance. Dances at such feasts have been mostly performed with green branches, by which—according to the concepts of the ancients—the carrier of live vegetation became the symbol of fertility. To be sure, the Jewish religion has interpreted this custom as a commandment of God:

> "And ye shall take you on the first day [of the Feast of Tabernacles] the fruit of goodly trees, branches of palm-trees, and boughs of thick trees, and willows of the brooks, and ye shall rejoice before the Lord your God seven days" (Lev. 23:40).

Nevertheless, this custom was actually a remnant of the ancient superstitious belief in sympathetic magic. The fact that the magical practice aimed at fertility, though in an altered form, has been admitted into the Jewish religion, shows how deeply the belief in the power of fertility dances has been rooted among the Israelites. A similar act of sympathetic magic in the rite of the Water Libation (*Bet ha-She'ubab*) has already been described above.

The war dance, or the dance preceding the battle, frequently resorted to by Oriental peoples, had a double aim: first, to create physical excitement and thereby to stir up the courage of the warriors; secondly, it was a demonstration of power and ferocity, in order to impress the enemy troops and to strike terror among them.[125] But originally, the war dance was motivated by magic considerations, namely to appease the souls of the killed enemies, or ward off the spirits who protected them.

The Old Testament does not mention war dances. But among all the Semitic peoples the very idea of war usually had some sort of religious connotation, and so we read also in the annals of Israel that the warriors "consecrate themselves" before joining the battle (Isa. 13:3). "To prepare" oneself for the battle (Jer. 6:4) has the same significance as "to sanctify, or consecrate" the war. A veiled mention of a war dance might be contained in Ezek. 6:11: "Smite with thy hand, and stamp with thy foot" (*u-raḳ'a b'ragleḥo*), which alludes to a dancing ceremony in preparation of the battle. Before the battle "burnt-offerings" and "peace-offerings" have been presented (1 Sam. 13:9,10), and after the battle the booty, or a portion of it, was "consecrated," or "dedicated" to the Lord (1 Sam. 15:21; 2 Sam. 8:11; 1 Chron. 18:11).

In which particular form this "consecration" of the warriors before the battle took place is not related by the biblical chroniclers, except that the soldiers participated in a sacrificial ceremony, through which God was to be induced to support them in the battle and to secure victory for them. One can hardly doubt that, similar to other Semitic peoples, the ancient Israelites, too, resorted to dancing during such sacrificial rites.

5. Dance at Funerals.

As in the case of war dances, there is no mention, in the Old Testament, of dances at funerals. Indirectly, however, by analogy and by certain allusions in post-biblical writings, it may be assumed that the Israelites honored not only the living, but also the dead with dances.

In Egypt, dances in honor of the deceased constituted a well-known ancient custom.[126] We have abundant written documents concerning Egyptian funeral dances, which are also reproduced in many paintings and reliefs, especially those of the 18th to the 20th dynasty.[127] In general, dancing and singing girls as well as wailing women were never lacking at Egyptian funerals.[128] (Illustr. 61).

ILLUSTRATION NO. 61

Egyptian funeral dance. Relief from a tomb in the Necropolis of Sukkarah (XIX. Dynasty, 1320-1200 B.C.E.) (After Hans Hickman, *Musikgeschichte in Bildern*, Leipzig, 1961).

Originally, dancing at funerals had a magic motivation. In primitive cultures the spirit of the deceased was supposed to have a hostile attitude toward the survivors. The funeral ceremony, including the dance, was intended to appease this hostility and, if possible, transform it into benevolence. The dance was also believed to be an effective means of restraining the spirit of the deceased from going astray. Above all, some peoples believed that the deceased was surrounded by all sorts of evil demons who sought to get hold of him or of his spirit. The dance was supposed to possess the power of keeping away the evil demons from the departed one. Significantly, such dances have been performed in the form of a circle; the "magic circle" was meant to protect not only the deceased, but also the participants of the funeral from the influence of evil demons.[129]

What might have been the reason for the complete silence of the biblical chroniclers about this ancient custom? The simplest explanation is that dances at funerals, like many other practices, were self-evident in Ancient Israel, so that the scribes considered their specific mention superfluous. Another reason might have been that such ritual dances evoked the memory of the ancient pagan religion of the Jews, so that the biblical authors, and later the editors, tried to eliminate any allusion to it from the sacred text. It is a well established fact that this text has been repeatedly, and sometimes even radically, purified from the remnants of ancient pagan and magic customs.

The fact that dances at funerals existed in Ancient Israel for many centuries is substantiated by more than a single evidence. Thus, the Bible also passes over in silence other customs at funerals, like piping the *ḥalilim,* lacerating of one's body as a sign of mourning, (later replaced by the tearing of garments), cutting of the hairs, taking off the footwear, etc. Here, too, silence does not indicate that these customs have been unknown.

Rabbinical writers relate that, at funeral ceremonies, the mourners clapped their hands (*safaḳ*), and beat rhythmically their thighs and other limbs (*ṭipaḥ*).[130] All these, as we already know, were habitual practices during secular dances, and they have also been used in dances honoring the dead. Even when funeral dances have been abolished, these former attributes of the dance survived.

Another proof of dances at Jewish funerals is the fact that at mourning ceremonies the same instruments were played which, in Ancient Israel, were used regularly for the accompaniment to dances, namely the *ḥalilim* and the hand-drum. The use at funerals of at least two *ḥalilim* was in the rabbinical law a ritual ordinance for rich and poor.[131] The other instrument generally used at mourning ceremonies was the *rebi'it*. The dull sound of this rather large drum must have blended appropriately with the gloomy mood of those ceremonies.

Professional wailing women were already known in Egypt.[132] The implements destined for the tombs were carried in a solemn procession, followed by priests and wailing women.[133] The Israelites must have taken over the custom of wailing women from the Egyptians, although it was also adhered to by ancient peoples in the neighboring countries. In Babylonia, for instance, the sacrifices in memory of the deceased always took place with funeral music and mourning ceremonies performed by professional lamenters.[134] Wailing men and women intoned the funeral songs, the mourners expressed their grief by loud moans, tore their garments, pulled their beards, clipped their hair, and cut themselves with knives. As early as in the Gudea-inscriptions (ca. 2350 B.C.E.), found at Lagash, psalms of lamentation and wailing women are mentioned.[135] The Greeks, too, had wailing women at funerals.[136]

The Bible and the rabbinic literature frequently mention wailing women. The musical side of their profession will be investigated in another chapter of this study.[137] Apart from their musical functions, however, wailing women must have adhered to certain dance customs, as intimated by Mishnaic instructions which also contain a circumstantial evidence for dancing at funerals: During festival days

> "the women may sing dirges but they may not clap their hands. R. Ishmael says: 'They that are near to the bier may clap their hands'."[138]

In the following passage the festival days are minutely indicated:

> "On the first days of the months and at [the Feast of] Dedication [*i.e.* *Ḥanukkah*] and at *Purim* they may sing lamentations [*i.e.* sing in choir] and clap their hands [for the dance]; but during none of them may they wail [*i.e.* sing responsively]. After the corpse has been buried they may not sing lamentations or clap their hands."[139]

This last instruction shows that lamenting songs and dances were allowed only during the funeral procession and the mourning ceremony itself, but had to end as soon as the deceased was buried.

As already mentioned, another custom at Jewish funerals, which certainly sprang from dancing, flourished in talmudic and post-tadmudic times. It consisted in the mourners' monotonous rhythmic stamping the ground during the entire funeral oration. Originally, this might have been a religious dance in honor of the dead, reduced, as time passed, to this simplified mechanical form, in which the idea of honoring the deceased was retained merely in the subconscious mind of the mourners. This peculiar hangover of a dance act is expressed by the rabbinical scribes with the word *raḳ'a,* the same which is used in the Bible for stamping the feet (2 Sam. 22:43; Ezek. 6:11). The Talmud has still another expression for stamping with the feet:

> "*Tipah* is clapping one's hand [to indicate a dance rhythm], and that of *ḳillus* is [tapping] with the foot [in mourning]."[140]

In the biblical text the word *raḳ'a* has no dancing connotation. Possibly the same was also true of the rabbinic writings, since the stamping with the feet has not been dancing in the proper sense, but at most a vague remembrance of an ancient funeral rite. Its implication as a dancing ceremony, however, is betrayed by the fact that it was performed by the entire funeral gathering, as it was customary among other peoples who honored their deceased ones with dancing.

Whereas in dances among the Jews both sexes were commonly separated, at funeral ceremonies men and women performed these veiled dancing steps together, in addition to certain pantomimic gestures with the hands and fingers.[141] Apart from this collective honoring the dead with dancing, there must have existed individual mourning dances in honor of the deceased. We find, for instance, a rabbinic reference to a woman who performed a dance before the picture of her dead son. The Talmud uses here the word *raḳad,* the same as for stamping with the feet at funerals.[142]

It is worthy of note that the modern Sephardim (the Spanish and Portuguese Jews), still cling to a peculiar custom at their funeral rites, that strongly reminds one of a processional dance. This is the act of walking seven times around the bier, during which seven short prayers are recited or chanted, each one ending with the words:

> "And continually may he walk in the land of life, and may his soul rest in the bond of life."[143]

The procession around the bier is apparently a remnant of an ancient dance act. Its direct purpose of keeping away evil demons from the dead and the mourners through the power of the magic circle fell into oblivion as time passed, so that merely the external form of it survived. There might be also a bit of imitative magic in *walking* around the bier and in the prayers' wish that the deceased may *walk* in the land of life. Curiously enough, this custom has entirely disappeared among the Ashkenazim (the German, Polish, Russian, Hungarian, and Rumanian Jews), and can be traced only among the Eastern Ḥasidim. But this Sephardic custom is an unmistakable sign that dancing at funerals represents a primeval custom which, in a transmuted form, survived to our own days.

6. The Metaphoric Use of Dance Terms.

Apart from the rich vocabulary, there is still another indication of the paramount importance of the dance in the feeling and thinking of the Jewish people. We refer to their frequent use of dance terms and expressions in similes, parables, metaphors, both in the poetical and in the daily language. With all these resourceful figures of speech, the biblical scribes attain sometimes an extraordinary descriptive power, which is especially noticeable in the prophetic books.

When joy of life disappears,

> "The joy of our heart is ceased; our dance is turned into mourning" (Lament. 5:15).

When God punishes His people,

> "The mirth of tabrets [*i.e.* dancing] ceaseth, the noise of them that rejoice endeth, the joy of the harp ceaseth, they drink not wine with song" (Isa. 24:8,9).

After the tribulations of the people are over,

> "the voice of mirth and the voice of gladness, the voice of the bridegroom and the voice of the bride" will be heard again (Jer. 25:10),

and the "virgin Israel" will hear God's pronouncement:

> "Again shalt thou be adorned with thy tabrets, and shalt go forth in the dances of them that make merry" (Jer. 31:4). "Then shall the virgin rejoice in the dance, and the young men and the old together, for I will turn their mourning into joy, and will comfort them, and make them rejoice from their sorrow" (Jer. 31:13).

The dance used in biblical metaphors is often imbued with an even more descriptive force. The tale about the Leviathan, for instance, contains this highly impressive simile: "In his neck abideth strength, and dismay ('terror,' *Revised Version*) danceth before him" (Job 41:13).

Deep wisdom is manifest in the proverb:

> "To everything there is a season, and a time for every purpose under the heaven: . . . A time to weep, and a time to laugh; a time to mourn, and a time to dance" (Eccl. 3:4).

One of the "Proverbs" (26:7) contains a simile, which is best expressed in LUTHER's translation:

> "Wie einem Krüppel das Tanzen, also stehet dem Narren an, von Weisheit reden" ("Like the dancing of a lame; so is a parable in the mouth of fools").

There is an allusion to the questionable morals of dancing girls:

> "Use not much the company of a woman that is a singer, lest thou be taken with her attempts" (Ecclus. 9:4).

The numerous similes in talmudic writings, in which the idea of dancing is used for censuring an impious or immoral conduct of life, have been quoted above.[144]

The "Song of Songs" contains a reference to a seemingly peculiar kind of Jewish dance (7:1), [6:13], the "dance of Maḥanaim," which has been interpreted erroneously by all biblical expositors. Even the generally reliable *Jewish Translation* is not doing justice to the passage, rendering it as

> "What will you see in the Shulammite? As it were a dance of two companies."

The *Authorized Version* misses even more the original idea:

> "What will ye see in the Shulamite? As it were the company of two armies."

Douay translates "companies of camps," and *Moffat*—following apparently the idea of the customary Arabian wedding dance—sets "sword-dance." Erroneous is also the rendition of the *Revised Standard Version* as "a dance before two armies." The *American Version, Moulton* and *Harkavy* give at least a correct rendering, in adopting phonetically the Hebrew original:

> "Why will ye look upon the Shulammite, as upon the dance of Mahanaim?" (*meḥolot ha-maḥanayim*).

For the sake of completeness we add *Wycliffe's* translations:

> "What shalt thou seen in Sunamyte, but queres of tentes?" (early), and "What schalt thou se in the Sunamyte, no but cumpeneyes of oostis?" (later).

Without reference to an earlier biblical passage, in which the word *maḥanayim* is used for the first time, the simile in the "Song of Songs" is bound to remain incomprehensible. In the story of Jacob's flight from Laban, the chronicler relates the eventual reconciliation of the two patriarchs. After which

> "early in the morning Laban rose up, and kissed his sons and his daughters, and blessed them. And Laban departed, and returned unto his place. And Jacob went on his way, and the angels of God met him. And Jacob said when he saw them: 'This is God's camp' (*maḥaneh*).

And he called the name of that place *Maḥanaim* (literally 'two camps')." (Gen. 32:1-3).

What Jacob saw in his vision were two groups of angels who—similar to antiphonal singing—performed a sort of "antichoreic" dance ("one to another"), *i.e.* in two groups which alternately led the dancing. Therefore Jacob called the place *Maḥanaim*, "Two Camps."

Modern biblical exegises misses completely the meaning of the term and its application in the Canticles. Thus, RENAN explains *Maḥanaim* as

> "an ancient city celebrated for its bayaderes and for the orgiastic cults which were practiced there."[145]

MORRIS JASTROW Jr. interprets it as

> "the dance in the camp," "a dance or a 'round' in the camp, which may have been the technical name for the sword dance of the bride, which would be danced by the bride in the presence of those who form the camp."[146]

Even more fallacious is LEROY WATERMAN's explanation:

> "This may refer to a traditional war dance between two armies before they joined battle."[147]

However, the true interpretation of the "dance of Maḥanaim" in the Canticles becomes simple and natural, if this expression is read in close connection with its related context as presented in the Hebrew numeration of verses:[148]

7:1b "Why will ye look upon the Shulammite,
As upon the *dance of Maḥanaim?*"

7:2 "How beautiful are thy feet in sandals,
O prince's daughter!
The joints of thy thighs are like jewels,
The work of the hands of a cunning workman."

7:3 "Thy navel is like a round goblet,
Wherein no mingled wine is wanting:
Thy belly is like an heap of wheat
Set about with lilies."

7:4 "Thy *two breasts* are like *two fawns*
That are *twins* of a roe," etc.

Verse 2, immediately following the "dance of Maḥanaim," deals with the dancing Shulammite, and the subsequent verses form a single dithyramb to the beauty and charm of the dancing maiden. Among these, the pertinent simile of verse 4 to the two dancing groups of angels in Genesis 32:1-3 lends itself most logically and irresistibly. The "dance of Maḥanaim" is nothing else but a reference to the breasts of the Shulammite, which are swaying rhythmically in her dance, like the two groups of angels in Jacob's vision.

This explanation fully conforms with the roguishly erotic character of the wedding songs, compiled in the Canticles, and at the same time unriddles the hitherto misconstrued expression in the biblical text.

Should one put together these multifarious details into a composite picture, one would surely admit that dance played the same significant part in the life of Ancient Israel as music and singing. As a concurrent expression of any popular celebration, dance was always the most effective physical release of the psychic tension, especially when a common feeling of happiness pervaded the masses. Voice, instrument, and body, the natural media for singing, playing, and dancing, have been united in the music of Ancient Israel into an indivisible entity. In them, collectively, music in the broader sense became a reality.

IX. MUSIC INSTRUCTION

1. The Roots of Jewish Music Culture.

In pristine times, the music of the Hebrews was not likely to differ much from that of other nomadic peoples of the Near East. Israel being a people of herdsmen, its music was restricted mainly to the singing and playing of shepherds, who would use some simple instruments, appropriate to the primitive forms of life. At this stage, Israel's music, like that of any nomadic people, was not so much a phenomenon of "art," as a practical tool. Thus, the shepherds of patriarchal times have used the *ʿugab* and *kinnor* for mere pastime, and the horn for rallying the flock.

The familiarity with this primitive music and the skill of performing it could be obtained practically by anyone without too much difficulty. A casual succession of tones (it was scarcely a melody as yet in the proper sense) on a reed-instrument, the few sustained or resounding blasts on an instrument made from the horn of sheep or neat, a rudimentary "support" of the faltering vocal pitch on some crude stringed instrument,—this was basically all that was required from a "musician" of those times.

As in the case of all nomadic peoples, the primitive Hebrews not excluded, no specific aptitude for music can be taken for granted. Nor does the music of patriarchal times show any conspicuous features. It can be assumed that it was utilitarian music pure and simple.

It is a fateful trait in the history of the Jewish people that every national disaster has always released its hitherto unsuspected energies and capacities. Their life during the four centuries of Egyptian slavery may be taken as a case in point. It is common knowledge that from Egyptian civilization the Jews have adopted everything in conformity with their own individuality. The chapters of the book of Exodus, recounting the life of the Israelites in the desert, testify to the far-reaching Egyptian influence upon them long after their departure from Egypt.

This must have been particularly true with regard to the art of music, in which, the Egyptians were the leaders of that epoch. The pictures and bas-reliefs in the tombs of kings, priests and court-dignitaries point to a highly developed musical culture. The instruments depicted on the walls and those actually found in the tombs show beautiful forms, are well constructed in the technical sense and must have produced good sound qualities.

Such pictorial representations are preserved from all periods of Egyptian history. They portray singers, dancers, flutists, harp- and lute-players, single and in groups, in scenes of public and private life. We see among them pictures of singing groups led by precentors or conductors, who apparently delineate the melodic line with motions of their hands. All this seems to be the precursor of the eventual musical practice of the Israelites, both sacred and secular.

From the Egyptians, the Jews must have learned the importance of music in popular life; they became familiar with the highly developed musical instruments; there, the inborn musical sense of the Jews must have received its initial and most decisive incentive. The Hebrews may well have had a natural aptitude for music. But the approach to it as an *art* first dawned upon them in Egypt.

After the Jews settled in Cana'an, their musical development progressed with extraordinary rapidity. This certainly would be unthinkable without their previous acquisition, in Egypt, of an efficient method of teaching music.

We are informed by STRABO about the compulsory instruction of the Egyptians, who, among other subjects, were taught stories, songs, and a specific kind of music right from their childhood. He also relates that the poets and musicians in Egypt considered themselves to be improvers of manners.

> "Even the musicians, when they give instruction in singing, in lyre-playing, or in flute-playing, lay claim to this virtue, for they maintain that these studies tend to discipline and correct the character."[1]

All this indicates a well planned and developed system of music instruction in Egypt.

At the time of the biblical Exodus, the development of Egyptian music had not yet reached its zenith. However, the Israelites had already gathered enough experience to build and form their own tonal art.

Although the ethos of Jewish music, at least in its later stage, is quite different from that of Egypt, the external features of the music of both are almost identical. The Jewish instruments are constructed after Egyptian patterns, even though they were later subjected to still other influences, particularly Babylonian and Assyrian. The harps and lyres of the Hebrews were similar to those reproduced in Egyptian tombs. The wind instruments of the Israelites, flutes, oboes, trumpets, also their percussive instruments, seem to have been the same as the ones painted or sculptured by the Egyptians long before biblical chroniclers have mentioned them. Solely the *shofar* is of purely Semitic origin.

Not only the musical instruments of the Hebrews were taken over from Egypt; their whole musical setup followed more or less the Egyptian pattern. Musical performances at court and in the homes of the nobles are a common trait of both peoples. Like the Egyptians, the Hebrews embellished their banquets with singing and playing of instruments. Wandering minstrels, performing songs with instrumental accompaniment, are reported in Egypt. The Hebrews, too, had such folk-bards, who enjoyed great popularity among the masses. Occasional disparaging remarks about them in the early rabbinic literature lead to the conclusion that the popularity of such minstrels has aroused the ire of the puritanically minded religious leaders of the nation. Female dancers, whose performances were accompanied by singing, as well as by cymbals, hand-drums and other shaking and rattling instruments, are a common feature in the popular customs of both nations.

The part music played in the Egyptian religion has been even more important. The musical service in the temples was provided by large choral groups; these comprised sometimes entire families. Solo vocalists sang the hymns, the chorus answered responsively. A special characteristic of the Egyptian ritual was the sacred temple-dance, accompanied by instrumental music. Religious processions around the altar with singing and pantomimic evolutions, were among musically colored ritual ceremonies.

Many characteristics of the Egyptian ritual music were transplanted into the Jewish Temple music, even if with a greater spiritualized significance, according to the philosophical and ethical nature of the Hebrew sacred acts. The focal point of Jewish sacred ceremonies was the sacrifice, and this was understood not only in the material sense, as a way of offering all sorts of gifts,—but also as a spiritual sacrifice through the fervent devotedness of man to his Creator. Something quite novel in the latter setting was music as a sounding sacrifice which involved the exaltation of the Most High with singing, playing, and dancing.

The external features of the music practice of both nations are known from coeval sources; about the intrinsic nature of their music, however, we possess only indirect and incomplete information. The outward appearance of the Egyptian instruments, for instance, and—by analogy—those of Israel, may be learned from the numerous pictorial reproductions. But our sources do not reveal anything pertaining to the existence or non-existence of any musical notation among the Egyptians or the Hebrews.[2] Also there is not the slightest indication whether they have had a system of keys or modes.[3] Had the Egyptians possessed any elaborate musical system, we would certainly know about it through written records. About all the sciences of the Egyptians, mathematics, geometry, astronomy, natural history, etc. written documents are preserved, in which priestly scribes stored the knowledge of those times for their own use and for future generations. Although music has been a part of those sciences, there is nothing in these records concerning any musical system.

Written documents are also lacking about the nature and organized system of ancient Jewish music. Whatever is found in the Bible, as well as in the early rabbinic literature and the writings of the early Church Fathers concerning the music of the Israelites, deals mostly with its external features, but does not divulge any information about its intrinsic characteristics and its possible tonal system.

2. The Beginning of Music Instruction.

At the exodus of the Israelites from Egypt, the foundation of their later musical culture must already have existed in its rough outlines. Following their liberation from bondage, the Jewish people wandered for forty years in the desert, living under the most depraved conditions, suffering hardships and privations, and fighting off enemies. In this austere existence, the spiritual life of the Israelites seems to have been rudely interrupted, if not wholly extinct.

And yet, after having found a permanent home in Cana'an, the Jewish people relatively soon developed a substantial musical culture, which would be inconceivable without assuming that, during all the time spent in the desert, they did not forget what they had learned in Egypt.

How was it possible indeed that these four momentous decades did not extinguish the love and practice of music, or even cause any conspicuous harm? How did the Hebrews succeed in keeping alive their musical knowledge and skill under all these hardships? Their innate love for music is one, but by no means a sufficient explanation of this fact. There must have been a strong will, a driving force in the back of it, a vigilant eye which watched to see that the people's familiarity with matters musical be preserved undiminished. This will, this force emanated from the greatest hero of Jewish history—Moses.

According to tradition, Moses was educated by the Egyptian priestly caste and, as MANETHO reports, for some time he has discharged priestly functions in the temple of Heliopolis. His name, originally, was said to have been OSARSIPH, after the god OSIRIS, the patron of Heliopolis. Since Moses was educated by the priests, he was bound to be thoroughly conversant with the musical art of the Egyptians.[4] PHILO puts particular stress upon Moses' knowledge of theoretical and practical music:

> "Arithmetic, geometry, the lore of metre, rhythm and harmony [*i.e.* poetry], and the whole subject of music as shown by the use of instruments or in textbooks and treatises of a more special character, were imparted to him by learned Egyptians."[5]

It is obvious that PHILO relies merely on the tradition, for he could not have had any direct information about Moses' education. In all probability his judgment is based upon the instruction of young men of his own time. It is possible that, at least in part, PHILO leans on PLATO, who quotes mathematics, music, and dance as subjects belonging to general education in Egypt.[6]

Among the Fathers of the Church, JUSTIN MARTYR refers particularly to MOSES' education in Egypt:

> "Moses also is depicted as a very ancient and venerable leader of the Jews by such writers of Athenian history as Hellanicus, Philochoros, Castor, Thallus and Alexander Polyhistor, as well as by the learned Jewish historians Philo and Josephus . . ."
>
> "These writers, who do not belong to our religion [*i.e.* Christianity], affirmed that their information was gathered from Egyptian priests, among whom Moses was born and educated; in fact, he was given a very thorough Egyptian education, since he was the adopted son of a king's daughter."[7]

We know that the Egyptians established special schools for liturgical music; one of such "Academies for Sacred Music" was maintained in ancient Memphis.[8] If Moses was actually educated for priestly functions, he must have had a thorough knowledge of the musical art of his time.

According to ancient belief, only the most expert musicians were able to perceive the harmony of the spheres. The Hellenes attributed this faculty to PYTHAGORAS. Ancient Arabic tradition conferred this honor also upon Moses. Such a faculty has, of course, no bearing upon Moses' musicianship, since it adds nothing either to his creative talent or to his practical knowledge. It testifies, however, to the fact that, as a musician, Moses was revered not only in the Jewish but also in the Arabic world. In the Islamic Orient he was even considered the patron of pipers.

Apart from his general musical knowledge, Moses must have surely had impressive creative gifts. Only an inspired artist could write and sing a piece of poetry such as the exulting "Song at the Red Sea" (Exod. 15), which even to-day, after several millennia, is overwhelming in its grandeur. Let us recall that, in those heroic times, the folk-bards were at once poets, composers and performers; therefore, the first artistic achievement of Moses, as related by the biblical chronicler, tallies perfectly with the general conception of the "artist-musician" of that epoch. The song of praise (Deuter. 32), composed and "sung" by Moses shortly before his death, is just as sublime as the song born forty years earlier from the experience of a divine miracle after passing the Red Sea.

Moses' sister Miriam, too, must have been well versed in musical art, as intimated by the term "prophetess."[9] After Moses had finished his song of thanksgiving, she followed it up by her own song and dance (Exod. 15:20,21).

We know that in Egypt the sacred temple dances as well as the secular dances, were entrusted mainly to females. Pictures in tombs furnish ample documentary evidence to that effect. The dancing Israelite women, led by Miriam, did not represent, therefore, anything unusual in this respect. They simply continued the custom acquired originally in Egypt.

Things stand differently, however, with the "singing" of Miriam. In Antiquity, Orientals of distinction, be they Egyptians, Arabs, or Syrians, did not indulge in musical activity except on sporadic occasions, and then only for sacred purposes. To satisfy their need for music, they employed professional musicians, belonging mostly to the caste of slaves. Temple musicians, being a privileged class because of their ritual functions, formed an exception to this rule.

Moses, his brother Aaron and his sister Miriam, were of levitical ancestry (Exod. 2:1). Yet, Moses could not have acquired the music tradition of the Levites in his paternal home, even if such a tradition existed already at that time, since he was a Jewish foundling brought up as the son of Pharaoh's daughter. The Bible does not relate anything concerning Aaron's musical background.

But how about Miriam's musical education? That she must have been familiar with matters musical becomes evident from the biblical phrase, "and Miriam sang unto them," that is, she was the leader of song.

As already mentioned, Miriam is termed by the biblical chronicler as "prophetess." What did "prophet" (or "prophetess") mean in the early history of the Jewish people? A man (or woman) who feels, suffers, speaks for the masses, an eloquent interpreter of the beliefs and sentiments of the people and who, in addition, possesses all the qualities of a national leader. These qualities embrace a specific oratorical talent as well as mastery in music, or at least in singing. In biblical parlance, "prophet" or "seer" has often the same meaning as "musician" or "singer."[10] The early history of Israel knows chosen men, who were masters in musical art. They are nearly always called "prophets" by the chroniclers. No wonder, therefore, that the same epithet is applied to Miriam as well. It indicates her mastery in music and singing. And there is a great probability that she owes this mastery to none else than her brother Moses.

As a matter of fact, Moses might have imparted musical instruction and inspiration not only to his sister but also to other individuals among his compatriots. The evidence is contained in the biblical report:

"So Moses wrote this song the same day, and taught it the children of Israel" (Deuter. 31:22).[11]

Another biblical passage furnishes a tangible proof that during the wandering in the desert a sort of musical instruction must have taken place:

"Write this for a memorial in the book and rehearse (*v'sim*) it in the ears of Joshua" (Exod. 17:14).[12]

These words are particularly significant since they are ascribed to God Himself. The instruction "to rehearse," therefore, stems directly from God's commandment. It is easy to discover in this primitive precept a distinct method of oral tradition[13] which is even more explicit in Deuter. 31:19,22. In fact, not only in heroic times, but during all the existence of music culture in Ancient Israel, oral tradition was the exclusive method of instruction. It consisted in constant repetition ("rehearsing") of text and music, until both were rooted indelibly in the memory.

One may safely assume that even in the desert the Israelites continued to practice music, and this despite all their incredible hardships. This means that they kept alive all the musical knowledge acquired in Egypt; and also that they knew how to keep in good condition the musical instruments brought by them from Egypt. This explains why their musical culture in the new homeland came to a vivid bloom in such a relatively short time.

It may further be taken for granted that the man who gave to his people the law, has also seen to it that this people should not give up, or neglect, their intellectual possessions. This man, past master in the musical art of those times, was qualified as none else to become the music instructor of his people. Moses, the liberator of his people, the first law-giver of Israel, must therefore be considered as the first music educator of the Hebrews and, apart from that, as the originator of Jewish music culture in general.

3. The Schools of Prophets.

After the immediate necessities of economic life had been taken care of in the new homeland, the musical development of Israel took a rapid and thriving turn. Soon, music ceased to be the concern of a few. It became the possession of everybody: the people wanted to enjoy music and, at any rate, to be active in music one way or another. This created the first big problem in Israel's musical life: that of music instruction.

That there must have existed during the entire national life of Israel a widespread and systematic music instruction, becomes obvious from the ultimate results: a musical culture, justly famous in Antiquity. There are only scanty reports as to how this instruction has taken place, who the teachers were, and what were the social implications of Jewish musical education. However, in scrutinizing closely even these few data, we may infer quite a number of pertinent facts.

There are no indications in the Pentateuch (except the two passages in Exod. 17:14 and Deuter. 31:19,22), in the books of Joshua, the Judges, and Ruth, how music was taught in Ancient Israel. The initial reference to it, still rather veiled, may be found in the first book of Samuel. There we learn about

"a band of prophets coming down from the high place with a psaltery,

> and a timbrel, and a pipe, and a harp, before them; and they will be prophesying" (1 Sam. 10:5).

But what does this procession of prophets, "prophesying" with musical accompaniment actually imply? Israel's history gives the answer to this question.

After Samuel's political goal was fulfilled with the victory over his enemies, the return of the ark of the covenant, and the appointment of a king over Israel, he solemnly laid down his office as the judge of the nation. His work as a statesman was finished, as far as his own time was concerned. A man like Samuel, however, fired with a glowing love for his people, animated by his high mission for which he considered himself chosen by providence, could not be satisfied with the role of an inactive observer. Politically, nothing was to be accomplished by him any more; as a chosen prophet and a towering spirit of his epoch, he henceforth devoted himself to the intellectual education of the nation. In his solemn appeal addressed to the entire people on the occasion of his retirement, he stated: "I will instruct you in the good and the right way" (1 Sam. 12:23).

The idea is not new. It is quite similarly expressed in the Pentateuch (Deut. 6:18; 12:28), and also has its place in the poem composed and "sung" by Moses shortly before his death (Deut. 32:4). Thus, Samuel merely continued the tradition, established by Moses, that the leaders of the people, the prophets, those privileged by the Lord, had to serve as intellectual educators of the nation. Yet, the manner Samuel carried out this duty is as new as it is unique in the cultural history of Israel.

Samuel realized that the education of the people could only be safeguarded if a staff of enthusiastic and capable disciples were to be brought up for the continuation of the work begun by him. In order to create this staff, Samuel had founded a special school, or college, with the aim of preparing men not belonging to the priestly class for the sheer educational task. Samuel alone possessed the necessary popularity and authority, and also the required knowledge, to embark on such a venture. With this, Samuel, even after he retired from public affairs, remained the spiritual leader of his nation. Around him assembled a group of enthusiastic men of various ages who understood him and were prepared to place themselves unreservedly into the service of the great idea.

HERDER was the first who plainly recognized and appreciated the great design of the schools of prophets. In pertinent observations he describes Samuel's educational goals as follows:

> "It is undeniable that Samuel employed the first tranquil period in the organization of the state, as far as he was able, for commencing also the intellectual cultivation of his people. He established the schools for the Prophets; and though we need not adopt the extravagant conceptions sometimes formed on them, yet their organization by Samuel was marked with wisdom. He sought to bring the arts of cultivation, which then consisted of music and poetry, from the exclusive possession of a single tribe into general use. 'The hill of God' resounded with the songs of the Prophets, *i.e.* the pupils of a free system of rational instruction and wisdom. They dwelt in simple cottages (*nayot*), which have been very

incorrectly translated schools, and conveyed the notion of something corresponding to our own schools of learning. They were simply assemblages of young men, or those of maturer age, practising themselves under the direction of Samuel, who was the judge and father of the state, in what then pertained to national cultivation, not therefore, in ravings concerning the future, nor in barren litanies connected with the service of the temple."[14]

One cannot help assuming the existence of one or several such "schools," when one finds, in the biblical text, a sudden and unexplained upsurge of large choirs and orchestras, that is of thoroughly organized and trained musical groups, which would be virtually inconceivable without a preliminary and long methodical preparation. Therefore, there was bound to be an institution devoted to musical instruction, possibly even prior to Samuel's times, although one comes across its earliest mention only in the Book of Samuel.

Similar schools of music are known to have existed among other nations of Antiquity, far back in times of Sumeria.[15] It may well be possible, therefore, that the Israelites were aware of the usefulness of such institutions already in their primitive history.

In the light of such ample historical evidence, it is somewhat strange to find, among certain biblical exegetes, a tendency to deny flatly the existence of schools of prophets. For instance, the eminent biblical scholar, RIEHM, says:

"Whatever is asserted in this respect about those societies of prophets existing at several places in the times of Samuel, Elijah and Elisha, is mostly based upon fantasy, resulting from the mistaken name of *schools of prophets,* by which in our school-conscious time we termed those institutions, and for which any evidence based upon a source is lacking. Those societies served for sustaining the great prophets in times when the prophetic activity was centered mainly in creating the external structure of the sacred service. When, however, around the year 800 this external practice was replaced by the inspired word as the main agent of prophetic activity, there is no mention of them any more, although, if they were really schools, there would have been just then abundant opportunity for their work."[16]

Here, a historic fact is manifestly misunderstood. With the creation of the regular Temple music by David and Solomon, the levitical guild of musicians (about which more presently) took over those educational functions in music and singing, formerly entrusted to the schools of prophets. Consequently, these have simply lost their necessity and significance as institutions of musical education. This is the reason that they are no longer mentioned in the biblical books.

On the other hand, RIEHM concedes that

"the societies of prophets, even if not being schools, were nevertheless the central points from which, apart from a stimulus for religious life, also religious instruction among the people was disseminated."[17]

And finally, in another place, RIEHM admits unreservedly not only the existence, but also the eminent practical aim of the schools of prophets.[18]

Whether we call these institutions "societies," or "guilds," or "schools," whether we use for them the later term "sons of prophets" (2 Kings 2:3,5; 4:1; 6:1), is irrelevant. RIEHM calls

> "the relationship between these mature, in part married, companions and the prophets [namely their 'teachers'] themselves as a relation of a spiritual communion based upon piety,"

by which the correct approach to the understanding of the whole institution is established.[19] At any rate, it is a stark fact that in these societies *instruction* was given, that men were prepared for specific religious functions, to which principally music belonged. Therefore, their character as schools is undeniably proven.

Following the model of Samuel's school, institutions of the same order were soon organized in other places. The principals of these schools were "holy men," that is men inspired by the spirit of God, who were called "fathers." The first of these was Samuel himself (1 Sam. 19:20); later, one finds among them such great prophets as Elijah (2 Kings 2:12) and Elisha (2 Kings 6:1).[20] The pupils were called "sons of prophets" (2 Kings 6:1).[21] They lived together with their teachers (2 Kings 4:38) and led a frugal life. They built themselves primitive wooden huts (2 Kings 6:1,2), which in time grew into small villages. There were among these pupils more mature men, sometimes married and with children, others were young and unmarried. They came from all strata of the people, from every tribe of Israel. The sole prerequisite for admission was the wish and the aptitude for learning, the voluntary submission to the common discipline, and devotion to the religious and national ideals of Israel.

The participants of these institutions of learning sometimes were entrusted with the task of carrying prophetic messages to the people (2 Kings 9:1). Yet, they were called prophets only in a wider sense. They were not expected to possess real prophetic gifts.

The pupils of the schools were instructed in the Law, in the Scriptures, and in psalm-singing. At the same time, stress was laid upon learning to play an instrument for the accompaniment of singing (*kle shir*) (1 Chron. 25:1,7). As we gather from a later source, the instruction in the schools of prophets was done by proverbs, riddles, parables, rhythmic recitations, by chanting sacred and secular poems, and by singing songs.[22]

A specific care was devoted to instruction in music. Not all the pupils learned to play an instrument, only those who showed some aptitude for it. Singing, however, seems to have been taught to all of them, since common participation in vocal ensembles was a regular feature in the gatherings and processions of the prophet-pupils. Such choral singing with instrumental accompaniment, called "prophesying" in the Bible, must have exercised a fascinating, even suggestive effect upon the people of those times, as evidenced by the experiences of Saul and his messengers (1 Sam. 19:20-24).

Samuel's association of prophets represents doubtless the first *public music school* in human history. Music education in the liturgical schools of Sumeria and Egypt cannot be considered as public instruction, since it was restricted to the members of the priestly class, whereas in Israel anyone who so desired was accepted in these associations, or schools. The fact that other subjects besides music used to be taught there did not alter their basic status as regular music schools. It is undeniable that the "sons of prophets" received systematic and thorough music education, as one may well judge from the outcome of their studies.

The locality where the first school of this order was established carried the name of Nayoth in Ramah. *Nayoth* means "huts," "dwellings"; it was the name of a settlement in the neighborhood of Ramah, which, in the course of time, increased considerably. From *Nayoth, i.e.* from their dwellings, the "sons of prophets" would march every morning and evening in a solemn procession to a high place (*bamah*), where an altar was erected and sacred ceremonies were performed. This "hill of God" (1 Sam. 10:5) was a ritual institution created by Samuel, a place of devotion and prayer, maintained by the "sons of prophets," but it was also used by the people as a place of pilgrimage (1 Sam. 10:3).

> "On a high place one is nearest to the deity, there one likes to worship, there one builds temples and altars to it. Rituals on high places have been preserved until late in Antiquity, especially in Syria . . . The Old Testament refers frequently to Jewish rites on high places, only the tradition of Jerusalem, as codified in Deuteronomy, considers any ritual on the high places as heathen service. But even the sanctuary of Jerusalem was originally such an high place."[23]

From the high place at Ramah came the solemn procession described by Samuel in his "prophecy" on the occasion of the anointment of Saul as king of Israel (1 Sam. 10:5). This portion of Samuel's prophecy is not a prediction in the proper sense. For Samuel knew the daily "routine" of his disciples, so that whatever he foretold Saul was nothing else but the events taking place daily at the same hour.[24]

But Samuel's prophecy is important for us for another reason. It shows which instruments have been taught in this "Conservatory of music": the *nebel* (harp), the *kinnor* (lyre), the *ḥalil* (oboe or pipe), and the *tof* (timbrel). All these are instruments known to the Hebrews from Egypt; the long life in the desert has not impaired their skill in handling them, as evidenced by the historical facts.

We do not know who were the teachers in Samuel's schools of prophets. Contrary to the masters and precentors in the subsequent Davidic and Solomonic music organizations, whose names are actually given by biblical chroniclers, the Books of Samuel do not reveal anything about such teachers. It is quite probable, however, that some of the advanced pupils were teachers at the same time. They might have organized regular courses for instruction, probably under the supervision of Samuel himself.

In these courses the main subjects were poetry and music. For this purpose, the various collections of poems, bardic songs, popular lore, fairy tales and legends may have been used, as they still existed in heroic times. Unfortunately, these collections, probably assembled in book form in those days, have been lost; we know of them merely from a few incidental remarks in biblical texts.[25] It appears almost as if these old folk-books have been destroyed purposely, in order to be replaced by a single, authoritative book, written by priestly functionaries. Yet, the fact remains that in these schools not merely poetry preserved from olden times had been taught, but also the art of writing such poetry with special emphasis on its rhythmic construction, perhaps also the art of setting this poetry to music. Thus, the way was paved for the future national poets of hymns, the psalmists. It is certain that "the sons of prophets" were in a way the pioneers of Hebrew liturgical and secular poetry as a thoroughly organized art, which was destined to rise ultimately to the universal significance in world's literature.

o
o o

With his school, Samuel set new spiritual goals to Jewish life. The repercussions of his educational and cultural endeavours were manifold and far-reaching. Without any doubt, Samuel's national institution exerted a prevailing influence upon the religious and moral development of the Jewish people. This influence makes itself felt centuries later in the teachings of Israel's great literary prophets, Isaiah, Jeremiah, Zechariah, and others. Their active work is the proof that Samuel's idea remained alive even centuries after his schools of prophets ceased to exist.

While Samuel was alive, the fame of his school must have surely served as a powerful attraction for the entire nation within and without its geographical boundaries. From far and wide the disciples came in great numbers, so that in due course the colony at Ramah could not possibly admit all the neophytes. As a result, similar schools sprung up in Gibeah, Beth-el, Gilgal, Mizpah, Jericho, perhaps also in Carmel and probably in many other places. Samuel's maxim

"I will instruct you in the good and the right way"

was the guiding principle for all those educated in these schools. Like their master, they all were, in major as in minor things, unselfish servants of their people, and they tilled the ground from which thereafter a rich crop was bound to rise.

Whereas the intellectual repercussions of Samuel's educational activity in general made themselves felt to the full extent only after a certain lapse of time, his influence in the field of music brought forth immediate and important consequences.

As we know from biblical history, David escaped from Saul's persecutions by taking refuge in Nayoth at Ramah, where he was in hiding for a certain time (1 Sam. 19:18). When he came to that place, he had already established for himself a fame as a *kinnor*-player, and his creative gifts as a poet and musician were certainly rather developed at that time. Consequently, his artistry might not have been enriched directly by his staying at Ramah. His enforced sojourn in Nayoth, however, had another fateful significance for Jewish music. There the plans seem to have originated and matured which eventually led to the creation of the Temple music as a permanent ritual institution.

It does not require much effort to imagine how both men, the older one, wise with knowledge, and the younger one, full of ardent initiative, held long discussions about bringing to life a new important element of the ritual action,—organized sacred music. Prior to this, music in the rites was already a well-established factor of worship. However, the institution to be created henceforth was something higher, loftier: music was planned to be not merely a subordinate element in the ritual, not merely the stereotyped tonal background for sacred ceremonies. It was to be elevated to an integral part of the divine cult and co-ordinated with the other sacred actions. Music was planned to be associated inseparably with the sacrifice; it was, in a way, to become itself a sort of tonal sacrifice.

Even RIEHM, who—as we have seen—expressed doubts as to the very existence of schools of prophets, was compelled to recognize that

> "music seems to have been admitted on a large scale into the sacred service only in the so-called schools of prophets. In their common habitation (1 Sam. 19:20) and on their ritual pilgrimages (1 Sam. 10:5), the practice of the sacred tonal art, singing as well as playing of all kinds of instruments, was one of the principal occupations of these religious fraternities. And it was David, past master in the *kinnor* and in psalm-singing, who has introduced art singing accompanied with instruments into the divine service of the nation's sanctuary."[26]

Singers and instrumentalists were available in great numbers in Ramah and in the other schools, so that, once the plans were drawn up, their realization was assured. The institution of *organized* sacred music represents a revolutionary innovation. The creation of liturgical music as an equal partner with all other ritual ceremonies is the most important turning point in the history of Jewish music. We do not know whether the plan for this decisive reform originated with Samuel. But it is not unlikely that this promoter, full of ideas, cherished for a long time such plans and that these came to full bloom only when David sojourned at Ramah. At any rate, David with the energy peculiar to him, was the right man to put such ideas into action.

The pattern for the future organization of the Temple music was already extant in its bud. The school of prophets at Ramah was its actual prototype. There, musical art must have reached a high level for those times, owing to an orderly and thoughtful instruction developed in this institution. David could do nothing better than to avail himself of a system that had its crucial test at Ramah, and to apply it, on a larger scale, to the future sacred musical organization.

And so we soon witness the flourishing ritual music of the sanctury, an innovation which artistically, ethically, and from the angle of internal and external organization was exemplary.

David's new musical setup gained its intrinsic power not merely from the schools of prophets. Apart from these professional or semi-professional places of musical culture, there existed already at those times a wide-spread and independent secular music practice, deeply rooted in popular life. We don't know whether Ramah has influenced, or stimulated, this popular musical art to any extent. There are indications, however, that this may well have been the case, if we evaluate correctly certain biblical passages.

The first historical account about such a wide-spread popular musical practice is contained in the sumptuous description of David's bringing of the ark of the covenant to Jerusalem, (historians put this event into the year 1002 B.C.E.) An interesting point concerning this solemn cortège is that the people marched in it "even with songs." This whole description promptly suggests a broad musical culture, which would scarcely be conceivable without an adequate preparatory work of musical educators. And who would have been more qualified for such a task than the "sons of prophets"? Thus, it stands to reason that the prophet-students, apart from the instruction of professional musicians (all the "students" of these schools must be in fact considered as such), also took zealous care of the musical education of the people itself. About the success of their endeavors the above two biblical passages offer a substantial evidence.

These passages cite most of the instruments which used to be played by the "sons of prophets" in their daily processions and which, consequently, were taught in the schools. The *ḥaẓoẓerot,* referred to in the Chronicles, were the sacred silver trumpets, played in the ritual by the Aaronites as their exclusive privilege.

The omission of the *ḥalilim* ("pipes") on this occasion might be explained by a somewhat summary reporting, since another biblical passage points to this instrument as being widely used in those days (*cp.* p. 423, 1 Sam. 10:5, and 1 Kings 1:40).

4. Levitical Music Instruction.

The schools of prophets may have flourished for some time after Samuel's death, although one no longer comes across any direct biblical references either to their existence or permanent disbanding. But judging from certain timid allusions, their activity may well have continued for a while. However, for the musical practice, and especially for professional music instruction, their significance gradually decreased.

The attraction emanating from the royal residence, the atmosphere of courtly life, the splendor of the newly created sacred musical service drew the choice musicians to Jerusalem. The schools of prophets ceased to be regarded as the privileged institutions for musical education. They were replaced—to use a modern term—by the "Academy of Music," a regular school for liturgical education with religious music as the main subject of its curriculum, in which hundreds of students were continuously trained for a professional career.

Contrary to the all-embracing musical instruction in the school of prophets, the levitical music instruction was one-sided throughout. It was restricted, in fact, to liturgical music alone, excluding anything of a secular nature. It produced excellent singers and musicians, to be sure, but neglected the art of poetry. Those among the Levites who happened to possess a poetical gift, created out of their own inspirations; the general course of instruction seems to have excluded poetry as a subject.

Thus, the beautiful ancient bardic songs, cultivated with so much zeal by the "sons of prophets," fell gradually into oblivion. Soon, there remained only a faint memory of the erstwhile treasures of heroic poetry, and had not the biblical text mentioned occasionally the title of one of the old books, we would have no knowledge whatever that such collections had existed at all in Israel's heroic times.

Levitical music instruction aimed at practical performing; in this field, the teachers were thoroughly successful. By this method, the art and skill of the Levites were preserved on a high level from generation to generation. Men, women, and boys were prepared meticulously for sacred music.

As mentioned earlier, the levitical singers were admitted to the Temple service having reached their thirtieth year and after an apprenticeship of five years.[27] Such a preparatory period, rather extensive for those times, shows unequivocally how seriously the levitical music masters regarded their profession. In reality, the period of preparation must have been even a longer one, since most of the levitical singers already started their activity as choir-boys (see further below).

There is no doubt that women, too, participated in levitical music, at least in its early period. Later editors of the biblical books, manifestly biased by anti-feminine tendencies, have suppressed most of the data pertaining to this point. Nevertheless, certain clues allowing definite conclusions on the part women played in Temple music, remained unaffected.

A peculiar opinion has been advanced to the effect that a special music school for women existed in Ancient Israel. GALPIN claims to have found certain indications for this assumption in biblical passages and especially in some headings of the psalms.[28] To be sure, women and girls must have received instruction in musical art as long as they took part in levitical singing. However, the existence of a special school for them is not supported by historical evidence. It is logical to assume, therefore, that the musical education of both sexes proceeded jointly, even though there might have been once in a while separate rehearsals for the women's voices, as it is sometimes considered practical even to-day.

The participation of boy-singers in the Temple choir is not attested in the Bible itself. Mishnah, however, furnishes the information (fully discussed on pp. 171 ff) that boys of the Levites were admitted into the choir.

The method of teaching applied by the levitical music masters must have been thorough and adequate, as we may conclude from the quality of the Temple music, which has remained unchanged for centuries.

The educational activity of the Levites did not always proceed under favorable external circumstances. We already know of the frequent apostasy of Jewish kings, worshipping pagan deities, which caused spasmodic interruptions of the sacred service, and which sometimes lasted several decades, in one case even more than a century. The history of the Jewish people after Solomon's death is full of such vicissitudes. Yet, when following such interruptions the levitical singer-musicians were re-established in their functions, their mastery shone as bright as before. This indeed may serve as the best proof that music instruction continued in secret, and with undiminished zeal, frequently endangering even the very lives of its adepts.

Then a national disaster struck the Jewish people. NEBUCHADREZZAR conquered Jerusalem, destroyed the sanctuary, and carried off the flower of the nation into captivity. On the surface, this constituted the extinction of Jewish music, the sacred as well as the secular. Musical education, instruction in music, seemingly lost their aim and purpose. In Babylonia

> "we hanged upon the willows our harps, for . . . how shall we sing the Lord's song in a foreign land?" (Ps. 137:4).

In reality, however, practice of music, and with it instruction in music, continued unabatedly, despite—and perhaps even because—of all the tragic circumstances.

The Levites were not the only ones who kept alive the musical art during the Babylonian captivity. The secular musicians vied with the Levites in the preservation of the popular musical practice, which must have had a sufficient number of teachers and pupils for several generations. For, when after forty-eight years of captivity the first repatriates marched back to their old homestead, there were among them one hundred and twenty-eight levitical singers, the descendants of the ancient musical dynasties, and in addition two hundred male and female secular singers and musicians (Ezra 2:41,65).

A substantial part of the Israelites remained voluntarily in Babylonia. Freed from fetters of slavery, living under favorable economic conditions, they were able to maintain unrestrictedly their cherished musical activity. Thus, we may take it for granted that musical instruction, liturgical and secular, was greatly stimulated among Babylonian Jews, both during and after the period of captivity.

About eighty years after the first stream of repatriates, a second group of Israelites returned to Zion. Among the immigrants there was again a number of levitical singers (Ezra 7:7), but also of secular musicians, even though the latter are not mentioned specifically this time. Their presence, however, may be inferred indirectly from Neh. 7:73, where the enumeration of the Temple dignitaries (priests, Levites, porters, singers, Nethinim) is followed after "singers" by the somewhat puzzling interpolation "and some of the people." This would be manifestly superfluous in view of the comprehensive definition "and all Israel" that terminates the entire phrase. However, the correct meaning of the interpolation referred to presents itself logically if it is completed by the qualification "some *singers* of the people," *i.e.* non-levitical singers.

Even after this second repatriation quite many Israelites still remained in Babylonia. And all extant evidences seem to indicate that a substantial number of musicians also stayed behind to take care of the musical needs of the remaining Jews. Thus, besides the newly awakened musical culture in the Jewish homeland, there was a parallel phenomenon flourishing among the Israelites who had chosen Babylonia as their permanent domicile. The music of the homeland has been irretrievably lost after the destruction of the Jewish national state; that of the Babylonian splinter group has been preserved until our own days, as proven by fortunate discoveries of recent times.[29]

Until the Roman conquest which brought about the annihilation of Israel's independent existence, qualified music instruction with what may be defined as a "high average of output" has been the solid foundation of Jewish musical culture. As a result, we find such supreme exponents of vocal art as Asaph,

Heman and Jeduthun-Ethan in the early history of Temple music. Thereafter outstanding soloists are no longer mentioned. It seems that the educators of Jewish music held it more important to keep up a uniformly high average of knowledge among their students, than to breed virtuosi. It is due to this principle that Jewish music enjoyed an enviable reputation in Antiquity, which was denied to far more powerful nations. In the last analysis, the honor for it belongs to the highly effective music education of Ancient Israel. The method of it was developed by the Jewish music masters, whose achievements may indeed be counted among the most outstanding in the domain of Hebrew art.

5. Sociology of Music Instruction.

In addition to artistic considerations, the sociological aspect of musical education in Ancient Israel, dealing primarily with the economic situation in this particular field, calls for a brief examination.

Similar to what takes place in any other profession, the economic factor in music instruction is regulated by the natural interplay between demand and supply. An intensive cultivation of music opens automatically a large field for music teachers as well. And their dependence on earnings from their professional practice is operative, naturally, to the full extent even in such a relatively uncomplicated economic system as that of Ancient Israel.

How did the music teacher make a living in Israel? What sources of income has he had? With regard to levitical musicians, the answer is self-evident. For from the very beginning they have been taken care of by the population itself. The singers received their "portion" out of the duty designed for the priests and Levites (2 Chron. 31:4). As an essential part of their revenues, they received farming land, by which the sustaining basis of their economic existence was assured. After the return from the Babylonian exile, the provision of foreign kings procured them additional income and other economic advantages. Among these, most important was the edict, issued by CYRUS and confirmed by DARIUS, stipulating that

> "let it be given them day by day without fail . . . that which they have need of" (Ezra 6:8,9).

This represents practically a regular "salary." Thus, throughout the entire existence of the state of Israel, the levitical musicians were free from any concern regarding their economic necessities; they could, therefore, pursue their teaching activity without any remuneration. The education of the young generation was considered an integral part of their public service.

Things were different with secular musicians. In general, they were dependent on the income earned through their professional work. But very few might have lived merely by their activity as teachers. They were mainly performing musicians, playing at popular or private festivities, at weddings, banquets, funerals, etc. Another source of their income might have been the manufacturing and repairing of musical instruments. Among the multiple trades and professions mentioned in the Bible and in the rabbinic literature, that of builders of instruments is lacking. Nevertheless, this profession must have existed; for with a few possible exceptions the multitude of instruments of all kinds used in the ritual service as well as in secular life could have hardly been imported from foreign lands.

The assumption is not far-fetched that the biblical chroniclers considered it to be self-evident for a musician to build and to repair his own instrument. This idea is referred to in several biblical passages:

> "And the Levites stood also with instruments of music of the Lord, which David the king has made [*i.e.* ordered]" (2 Chron. 7:6);—
> "Solomon made [ordered] of the sandal-wood . . . harps and psalteries for the singers" (1 Kings 10:12; 2 Chron. 9:11);—

and when the Temple was repaired under king Josiah, the instruments of music, too, were restored by the Levites "that had skill with instruments of music" (2 Chron. 34:12). Only in one recorded instance (described on p. 378) was a repair of the Temple instruments entrusted to foreign craftsmen.

The early rabbinic literature refers repeatedly to repairing of instruments,[30] without mentioning, however, the profession of builders of instruments. Thus, we are driven to the only possible conclusion that many secular musicians have also manufactured instruments for their own and for public use. This in fact, might have well served them as an additional and perhaps even substantial source of income. The levitical musicians, on the other hand, had to build and maintain in good shape their instruments as part of their service, and without an additional remuneration, of course.

It is largely a matter of conjecture whether the "wages" which the secular musician received for playing at public or private festivities, as well as the "fee" for lessons, were paid to him in money or natural products. There are good reasons to believe, however, that the last-mentioned form was prevalent in Ancient Israel, which is the customary practice in all human societies based on primitive economies.

The Bible does not contain any data pertaining to payment for music instruction. But the early rabbinic literature refers to it several times. We are informed, for instance, that the office of the schoolmaster (who was also the music teacher) has been a full time job, keeping him busy on week days as well as on the Sabbath:

> "A schoolmaster (*ḥazzan*) may look where the children are reading but he himself may not read [on the Sabbath]."[31]

It is certain, therefore, that he received payment for his services.

"Practicing" an instrument is clearly distinguished in the Talmud from "playing" it. Thus, anyone blowing the *shofar* merely for the sake of practice (probably as a hobby) does not fulfill his religious duties.[32]

Among the subjects taught to children was cantillation of the Scriptures. The opinions of the rabbis were divided whether the teacher was allowed to accept payment for this particular task. Some rabbis opined that the teacher was prohibited to accept payment for teaching to read the Torah, but could receive payment for teaching the rules of punctuation and phrase structure of the biblical text, both of which also included automatically their perennial musical companion—the Scriptural cantillation. Others insisted that the fee for teaching the punctuation of the Torah, though not of other portions of the Scriptures, be excluded. Still others maintained that the fee is justified in any case, since it does not constitute a payment for the teaching itself, but merely for supervising the children in the school. From this discussion, carried on rather extensively in the Talmud,[33] we may gather that there existed even a regular weekly or monthly payment for teaching the punctuation, which included also cantillation.

The following talmudic passage, too, refers to teaching cantillation (or maybe some kind of regulated psalmody):

> "[They sing the Hallel] like a school-teacher [whose class was usually in the Synagogue and so he acted as a precentor] who recites the *Shem'ā* in the Synagogue, *viz.*, he begins and they respond after him."[34]

Apart from cantillation, the Talmud repeatedly refers indirectly to teaching the blowing of the *shofar*.[35]

A special subject of music instruction might have been the art of mournful wailing performed exclusively by women. That they were actually taught in it is evident from the biblical passage:

> "Teach your daughter wailing, and every one her neighbour lamentation" (Jer. 9:19).

It is obvious that in this case the teachers were the wailing women themselves, having acquired already the necessary experience.[36]

The Levites were bound by duty to teach their art to others. A refusal to fulfill this obligation was considered a flagrant breach of professional ethics. In the long recorded history of Temple music it happened only once that a singer refused to teach his art to anybody. This was the case of the singer-virtuoso HYGROS ben LEVI, already discussed on an earlier occasion.[37]

o o o

By way of summary, it may be said that musical instruction has been a regular institution and a decisive factor in both the liturgical and secular musical culture of Ancient Israel. The invariably high artistic quality of musical performances presupposes an excellent method in back of this instruction which, in turn, points to the specific pedagogical talent of the Jewish music masters. If Israel was able to preserve its music despite all the vicissitudes of fate, it owes this in no less degree to its innate aptitude for musical education, which remained vigorous and efficient during all the centuries of national life, as well as the entire period of Dispersion.

X. THE SUPERNATURAL POWER OF MUSIC

1. Music and Superstition.

Every primitive religion, based either on worship of natural phenomena, or on idolatry, is invariably tinged with superstition and adheres to all sorts of magic rites as a safeguard against evil spirits and demons. Even the ancient Jewish religion, with its conception of God entirely different from that of all other Oriental religions, had to struggle with a goodly amount of superstitious beliefs before—and in no small measure after—attaining its mature spiritual sublimity. In many instances, these beliefs were tacitly tolerated by priests and prophets who remained powerless in their effort to expel magic radically from the people's consciousness. At the time when Jewish religion seemingly achieved the final victory in its struggle for supremacy, the belief in magic still was strongly rooted in Jewish minds. As late as in talmudic times the religion still was tinted with ancient magical beliefs, as evidenced by numerous references in rabbinical writings.

While representing an advanced stage of their religion, the sacrificial ceremonies of the Israelites were obviously under the spell of analogous rites of neighboring cults. To be sure, the prayers used in these sacrifices were addressed to the invisible Yahveh, but most of the ceremonies accompanying them were unquestionably of pagan, magical origin. And once the magical elements had been incorporated—however disguisedly—into the official Jewish religion, it was virtually impossible to abolish them, even at a later time.

The evidence of this is furnished by the Bible itself. One would think that the faith in an almighty God should have sufficed to abrogate magic as a superfluous and useless practice. Just the contrary, however, is proved by the biblical text. The early draft of the Bible might have contained quite a number of references to magic and acts of sorcery. But countless editors, whose hands can be traced in almost all the parts of the Old Testament, seeked to eliminate anything that might have alluded to ancient pagan rites. The priestly purifiers took great pains either in suppressing references to magic practices or, if this was unfeasible, in beclouding them to a point when they became well-nigh unrecognizable.

There is still another reason why some of the ancient beliefs and customs have remained untouched in the Bible. Similar to what has invariably taken place in other religions, the Jewish priests considered it sometimes advantageous to retain certain popular superstitions, interpreting them, however, in accordance with the new religious laws, so that the originally pagan custom continued to serve exactly its primitive purpose. Thus, we find in the Jewish religion several heathen practices in an altered form, with an added moralizing tendency. The identity with the primitive forms of these customs is easy to discover in most cases. For instance, in the early phase of the Jewish religion we find holy cities, sacred trees and stones, "high-places" (former pagan places of worship), *teraphim* (idols) and *ephod* (amulets and other objects as protection against evil influences).

With all that, however, one must not lose sight of the essential difference between religion and magic which is most obvious in sacrificial rites. We know the high ethical meaning bestowed upon sacrifices at the developed stage of the Jewish religion. Yet, what was the original aim of the sacrifice?

> "The purpose of sacrifice at the lowest was to placate or appease the wrath of the gods. It was most frequently a sacrificial feast in which gods and men met on terms of friendship. It had an ethical element; it was capable of considerable [spiritual] significance. Sacrifice was a religious act; magic was not. Magic sought to coerce, not persuade the gods. It was without an ethical motive and not infrequently accompanied by subterfuge and trickery. It assumed that the gods were weaker or less subtle than men."[1]

In primitive religion, music was still subservient to superstition and constituted an important aid to magic practices. In fact, music was inseparable from magic, serving as one of the most potent agents in creating the appropriate tonal background for occult ceremonies. Magic was the first step of bringing mankind closer to the invisible world, which it did not understand and which instilled it with fear. Man sought to overcome this fear by magical practices, and in these practices music—whatever its nature in those ceremonies—played an essential part. It is evident, therefore, that music is much older in the service of magic and sorcery than in religion. Which indeed is quite natural if we consider the fact that magic, owing to its universal practice and its identical forms everywhere, is one of the most ancient phases of human civilization.

The history of religions explains the evolution of the Jewish religion from its primitive stage, at which it still worshipped spirits and demons, until it reached the ethical heights of the belief in a single and eternal God. The role of music at the primitive stage of Jewish religion deserves a closer scrutiny, inasmuch as the remnants of the magical effects of music were preserved in the later, more enlightened periods of Jewish life. The examination of such remains, necessary for the full understanding of Jewish musical culture, will help us, at the same time, to unravel some seemingly obscure passages of the biblical text.

o
o o

The invocation of the deity with a loud voice or with noisy instruments was a primeval custom in all primitive religions. There are countless examples of it in history and anthropology. The same custom prevailed also in the early Jewish religion; it was the original aim of the prayer. One does not talk to God, but "invokes" Him (*ḳarʾa*), "shouts to Him" (*ẓaʿak*), or "exults" Him (*teruʿah*).[2] When Hannah, mother of prophet Samuel, says a silent prayer in the sanctuary, this appears to the high priest as something extraordinary:

> "As she prayed long before the Lord, Eli watched her mouth. Now Hannah, she spoke in her heart; only her lips moved, but her voice could not be heard; therefore Eli thought she had been drunken" (1 Sam. 1:12,13).

The silent prayer, the invocation of God in the heart and soul ("I poured out my soul before the Lord," in Hannah's words), was a later custom, that presupposed a higher, loftier conception of God. In primitive religions the rule of invoking the deity was: the louder, the better! When the human voice was not powerful enough, one resorted to the use of musical instruments.[3] Most of the Oriental peoples availed themselves of percussion instruments for this purpose,—the Jews used an instrument the sound of which was closest to the human shrieking voice, the *shofar*.

In secular use, the call of the *shofar* had a thoroughly practical purpose. Whether it called the warriors to assemble, or was encouraging them for the battle, whether it sounded at solemn state affairs, or enhanced the joy of popular festivals, or else announced to the people an impending disaster, it was always used with a definite utilitarian aim; it was the universal signal instrument. There was nothing mysterious, nothing magical in its use, nothing that did not conform to its general character as a musical instrument. Things were different, however, as soon as the *shofar* was used in the rites, or when its sound was the accompaniment or symbol of supernatural occurrences.

The aim of blowing the horn in the cult was primarily the same as of the invocation with a loud voice: to attract the attention of the deity and to invite its presence. This is powerfully expressed in the description of the idolatrous ceremonies at Mount Carmel, in which the chronicler jeered at the pagan rites of Ba⁽al:

> "And it came to pass at noon that Elijah mocked them, and said: 'Cry aloud; for he is god; either he is musing, or he is gone aside, or he is in a journey, or peradventure he sleepeth, and must be awaken.' " (1 Kings 18:27).

Another function of the instrument was to imitate the sound of natural phenomena, or to be used at rites which were conceived for such purposes. At the festival of *Bet ha-she⁾ubah,* water was drawn from the pond of Shiloah (or Shiloam); it was brought, under *shofar*-blasts, into the Temple and poured solemnly into the spouts of the altar.[4] According to rabbinical tradition, the aim of this "water libation" has been to secure fertilizing rain for the coming year. The meaning of the rite was sympathetic rain magic, as used frequently by primitive peoples. The natural phenomenon was supposed to be brought about by imitating it on a smaller scale. At this ceremony, the task of the *shofar* was to reproduce the sounds of nature, such as the howling of wind, the rumbling of thunder, and thus produce the desired effect.[5]

At the same festival, the playing of pipes (*ḥalilim*) was an important feature, referred to specifically in rabbinic writings.[6] On the surface, piping had merely the function of an accompaniment for the dancers, whose performances were a usual sight at this festival. Apart from that, however, playing the pipes had a hidden, magic meaning. The sharp, exciting sound of the *ḥalilim* was intended to put the participating "men of might"[7] into such a state of frenzy that they would, in their delirium, perform "miracles," in this case, secure rain. Thus, the desired rain was to be obtained on the one hand, through the sympathetic magical act, and on the other hand, through the religious ecstasy of the dancing men. This example shows how religion and magic sometimes supplement each other.

At this festival, distinguished rabbis performed a dance with burning torches.

According to superstitious belief, burning lights were suitable to chase away demons; they were favorite means against hostile influences of evil spirits.[8] Similar customs have been preserved among the Jews until the late medieval era. In nuptial ceremonies, for instance, which took place during daytime, young men would precede the bridal procession with lighted torches or candles, throwing them into the air. Noisy and often cacophonous music gave to the custom its real significance: chasing away the evil demons.[9]

Ancient Israel celebrated the New Moon with loud blasts of horn:

> ". . . in your new moons, ye shall blow with trumpets over your burnt-offerings, and over the sacrifices of your peace-offerings" (Num. 10:10).

The real meaning of blowing the horn at the new moon was to chase away the darkness by the magic power of sound, a belief for which many analogies among primitive peoples can be found.

According to tradition, the *shofar* had to be blown on the Eve of New Year. This had to be done at night time so as to be effective against evil powers capable to prevent the rise of the sun in the New Year.[10] Mishnah has preserved certain allusions to the effect that the blowing of the *shofar* on New Year's Eve had some relation to the ancient worship of the sun.[11]

An important role has been attributed to the *shofar* in the fight against enemies of Israel and of the true religion. According to the views of the Orientals, the enemies were assisted in the battle by spirits and demons. What could be easier, therefore, than to vanquish the enemy by chasing away the spirits with the aid of loud horn-blasts. This was the magic meaning of blowing the *shofar* before and during the battle, quite apart from its importance as a signal instrument.

In the vivid imagination of the prophets, the *shofar* is sometimes blown by the Lord Himself, in order to frighten His enemies, or to lead the scattered hosts of the faithful ones back to His sanctuary:

> "And the Lord God will blow the horn, and will go with whirlwinds of the south. The Lord of hosts will defend them" (Zech, 9:14,15).

God blowing the *shofar,*—quite a thrilling picture of the divine grandeur!

o
o o

In the magic customs of all peoples, numbers play an important part. In the ancient Orient, especially, the magic of numbers was widespread. Mystic qualities were attributed to certain numbers, that were capable, allegedly, to destroy men or bring them supernatural aid. An incantation had to be repeated exactly according to the magic number to be effective against evil spirits.

The mystic number *three* is present in all religions and is used in all magic practices. It manifests itself, for instance, in the trinity of God or of the gods, common to many religions; in the Jewish conception of three archangels, three holy cities, three biblical festivals.

> "The number three occurs more often in magical texts than any other. Actions and incantations were to be performed three hours before

sunrise, or three days before the new moon, or three days in succession; preparatory rites were to last three days; the magical act comprised three stages, or required three objects; diviners could obtain answers to only three questions at any time; the great Ineffable Name consists of 72 triads of letters; any experience that was repeated thrice was regarded as portent; incantations were most often to be recited three times. The number three came to be recognized as a mark of magic, so that 'anything that is repeated three times is magical' was a frequently quoted rule."[12]

Many other magic "triplicities" could be easily cited.

Besides the preferred number three, *seven* was the favorite mystic figure in the conception of the ancient Orient. The figure had an esoteric relationship with the music of Antiquity,—the seven notes of the diatonic scale were identified with the seven tones of the planets, the differences of pitch being produced by the different periods and speeds of revolution of the planets. This is the "Harmony of the Spheres," a notion which can be found often in the literature of Antiquity and of the Middle Ages.[13]

In Jewish thinking the number seven had a predominant role.[14] According to the Bible, the Universe was created in seven days (six days work, one day rest). After seven times seven years, on the tenth day of the seventh month of the 49th year (in the old calendar on New Year's day of the 50th year), the Year of Jubilee had to be announced with the blowing of the "great horn," the *Shofar ha-yobel* (or *ḳeren ha-yobel*). In his dream, Pharaoh saw seven fat cows, which were devoured by seven lean cows (Gen. 41). In his vision, Ezekiel saw seven men (Ezek. 9:2); he stayed seven days with the prisoners at the river Chebar (Ezek. 3:15). When Elijah went up to Mount Carmel to provide for rain, he had to send his servant seven times to the summit, before he saw the rain-bringing cloud on the horizon (1 Kings 18:44).

On the seventh day of the Feast of Tabernacles, the altar had to be encircled seven times by the priests,[15] which, naturally, was also bound to be reflected in some seven-fold musical form accompanying this ritual act. "The Book of the Secrets of Enoch" mentions the ancient Jewish legend of the seven heavens.[16] The Jewish Gnostics conceived the heavens through which the mystic passes before reaching the Throne World (the center of mystic knowledge) as divided in seven palaces, with attendants and gate-keepers in each. Magical seals and formulas are to be used to enter each palace.

Even to-day, at Jewish weddings, the *Ḥazzan* chants seven blessings.

The significance of the number seven becomes particularly obvious at the conquest of Jericho. As the chronicler reports, the Lord said to Joshua:

> "Ye shall compass the city, all the men of war, going about the city once. Thus shalt thou do six days. And seven priests shall bear seven rams' horns (*shofarot ha-yobelim*)[17] before the ark; and the seventh day ye shall compass the city seven times, and the priests shall blow with the horns. And it shall be, that when they make a long blast with the rams' horn, and when ye hear the sound of the horn, all the people shall shout with a great shout; and the wall of the city shall fall down

flat, and the people shall go up every man straight before him" (Josh. 6:4,5).

Here, the magic of numbers is unmistakable. The assumption that seven *shofarot* (or *yobel*-horns), together wtih the great shout of the people, would cause the crumbling of the walls of the city, is a phenomenon that cannot be explained without the people's belief in magic. The essence of magic is to substitute a wishful action for an objective fact and to assume that a real connection exists between the two. The description of the chronicler, however, seeks to obscure somewhat the magic effect of blowing the *shofar,* by crediting the crumbling of the walls to the almightiness of God. Since nothing is impossible to Him, such a "miracle," as announced by the Lord Himself, could easily be explained. Then, why the magic number seven, mentioned four times? Why the blowing of the *shofar* at all? These are obviously the vestigial remains of the ancient belief in magic and sorcery, suppressed as far as possible in the Jewish religion at its relatively developed stage.

We disregard the reason why the story of Jericho had been retained in this form by the chronicler. As it stands, it is a significant example of ancient magical practices in the Jewish religion.

A similar application of the magic power of the number seven is to be found in the recently discovered Dead Sea Scrolls. *The War Between the Sons of Light and the Sons of Darkness,* one of the tractates of these Scrolls, describes an imaginary battle, already referred to in another connection, in which this number, applied to the most different objects and actions, constitutes a decisive factor for subduing the evil forces. The "strategy" of this battle is governed almost exclusively by the number seven.[18] Each front line has to be seven deep; the length of the spears has to be seven cubits; after having attacked seven times, the combatants return to their positions; the first squadron shall fling seven war-darts into the enemy line; they shall hurl such darts seven times in all (IV:3-VI:6). The seven battle lines shall be flanked, in turn, . . . by cavalry; there will be seven hundred [of them] on the one side and seven hundred on the other (VI:7). When the lines of the battle are drawn up . . . there shall come into the lines seven priests of the descendants of Aaron . . . One priest shall go before all troops of the line to encourage them in the battle, while in the hands of the other six shall be the trumpets for calling to arms (*ḥaẓoẓerot ha-mikra*), the memorial trumpets (*ḥaẓoẓerot ha-zikaron*), and the trumpets for sounding the charge (*ḥaẓoẓerot ha-mirdaf*), and the trumpets for recall (*ḥaẓoẓerot ha-measef*). And when the priests go out between the lines, seven Levites shall go out with them, and in their hands shall be seven rams' horns of jubilee (*shofarot ha-yobel*) (VII:8). The trumpets shall keep sounding (*tiḳeʿu*) for the slingers until they have hurled a full seven times (VIII:1).

It is obvious that this *Rule of Battle* is based almost exclusively upon mystico-magical conceptions. All these actions, carried out seven times, are supposed to have a supernatural efficacy, the same as in the biblical tale of the conquest of Jericho. But whereas the battle of Jericho still had some semblance of an historical occurrence, here the "liturgy of war" has an entirely fictional appearance, which would make its application in a real battle utterly impossible.

It is an ideal set of rules, made by some "arm-chair-strategist," which are reflecting the entire conception of this *War* as a sort of wishful thinking on his part.

o
o o

In the late talmudic and gaonic times the number seven still retained its magic connotation. Thus, it was customary at the return from funerals that the mourners stopped and sat down seven times.[19] In later times, Psalm 91, verse 11 was recited during these holds; this verse has seven words, and at every hold one word was added. It was openly admitted that the reason for this custom was to confuse and shake off the evil spirits that followed the mourners on their way home.[20]

Even in our time, the magic figure seven can be discovered in Jewish customs. At the funeral rites of Sephardic Jews, the bier is encircled seven times, while the mourners recite or chant seven supplications.[21]

o
o o

The translocating power of music is also recounted in the mythology of other ancient peoples. A Greek legend contains an analogy to the destruction of Jericho, though in reverse. In an epigram of MARTIAL a legend is related according to which Apollo has built the walls of Troy by playing the harp.[22] CLEMENT of ALEXANDRIA preserved the myth about Amphion of Thebes, whose playing on the lyre has built the walls of Thebes. The sound of the lyre caused the stones of the wall to move by themselves to their right place.[23] Whether for destruction, or for construction, in each case it was the magic effect of music that performed such miracles.

The talmudic literature, too, contains several references to the belief in the magic power of music. The miracle of Jericho is reported to have been repeated on another occasion:

> "R. Ammi said, that the noise of the harp strings (played by the Jews rebelling against the Persians [Rashi's commentary]) about Caesarea-Mazaca burst the walls of Laodicea."[24]

Magic and sorcery is apparently connected with a custom mentioned by the Talmud:

> "When a man goes on a trip he . . . takes the *shofar* and blows it."[25]

A note of the translator of the Mishnah (*Danby*) explains that the purpose of this procedure was

> "to satisfy his [the traveler's] religious obligation."

It is obvious, however, that here the blowing of the *shofar* had a magic purpose, namely to chase away hostile demons who would otherwise accompany and harm the defenseless traveler.

The following tale, in which music has a decisive role, reads like black magic of the Middle Ages:

> "Said R. Joseph to him: 'Take that Writ, put it into a jar, take it to a graveyard and hoot into it a thousand *shippur* [hornblasts] on forty days.' He went and did so. The jar burst and the domineering bull died."[26]

A somewhat similar purpose might be underlying to the ritual custom, quoted above (see p. 346), to blow a *shofar* in a cistern, a cellar, or in a large barrel. The superstitious belief populated such dark places with all kinds of malevolent sprites, who were to be frightened and chased away by sounding the horn, or even killed by the magic power of the *shofar*-blasts.

There is even an example in the Talmud for the belief in the resurrecting power of music; what is more, this tale is corroborated by a distinguished "eye-witness":

> "Rab said to R. Ḥiyya: 'I myself saw an Arabian traveller take a sword and cut up a camel; then he rang a bell (*ṭabla*), at which the camel arose."[27]

In this case, "music" consisted merely in the ringing of a bell. In principle, however, there is no difference between this primitive "music" and ORPHEUS' harp-playing, both producing the same result, the resurrection of the dead.

o
o o

Among primitive peoples sound and music are not merely means to arouse the attention of the deity or to invoke the gods, they also serve as effective protection against the wrath of gods and against acts of revenge by offended demons. The latter cannot endure some specific noises and loud music, therefore these are considered the best safeguard against their pernicious influence. One of such "protective" noises is that of the little bells on the garment of the Hebrew high priest described in an earlier chapter (p. 386).

To this we may now add that the Jewish religious law emphatically debars any human attempts of seeing God. Whoever ventures to do so must die (Exod. 19:21). Even direct listening to God's voice brings immediate death to a common mortal (Deuter. 18:16). Only someone exceptional, like Moses, was privileged to communicate eye to eye with the Creator. Any other human being, even one in such a sacred function as that of the high priest, was strictly subject to this law. However, during his ministration, the high priest had once a year to enter the holy of the holies, God's own dwelling. Thus, he might have chanced inadvertently upon the sight of God, on these occasions; but this would have instantaneously caused his death,[28] as it actually happened to the men of Beth-shemesh who were smitten by God "because they had gazed upon the ark of the Lord," *i.e.* they had made an attempt of looking inside the ark (1 Sam. 6:19). The bells on the high priest's garment have had primitively the purpose of forewarning the deity, supposed to be present in some form in its earthly dwelling, so that no entering human being could see it.[29]

A similar custom is reported in the Greek religion. Those who wanted to consult the oracle in Delphi were allowed to enter Apollo's sanctuary only with their heads covered and with the accompaniment of loud music, in order not to see and hear things not destined for mortals. Here, the pristine interrelation between music and magic is even more obvious than in the tinkling sound of small bells on the high priest's garment: it stemmed from the awe of the deity, fear of the danger to see god or listen to his voice unexpectedly. In the later development of Jewish rites the primitive aim of the bells had evidently disappeared, and they were merely regarded as ornaments on the high priest's attire. It is manifest, however, that they did not originate from an aesthetic need, but from a superstitious belief.

For the use of noise making instruments as means to chase away evil spirits and demons there are numerous examples in ancient and modern times, in the Orient as well as in other parts of the globe. The Egyptian sistrum has had, according to PLUTARCH, a double aim: to draw the attention of the worshippers to the sacred acts, and to chase away the hostile spirits. LUCIAN mentions a similar custom:

> to frighten evil demons, the worshippers shook "a thing of brass [a bronze sistrum] that sounds great and shrill when it is stirred."[30]

At the festivals of Bacchus and at the feast of the Saturnalia and Lupercalia of the Romans, the processions always took place with abundant use of cymbals, bells, sistra and other noise producing instruments, in order to chase away harmful demons who could have rendered ineffective the ceremonies aimed at fertility.

The original purpose of children's clappers might also have been to protect the youngster from the evil influence of envious demons.

The Talmud recounts an occurrence, in which an evil spirit was driven away by sounding the *shofar*:

> "The reason why one does not sit under a drain pipe was that there was waste water there, but my Master has told me, it is because demons are to be found there. Certain carriers were once carrying a barrel of wine. Wishing to take a rest they put it down under a drain pipe, whereupon the barrel burst, so they came to Mar, son of R. Ashi. He brought forth trumpets (*shipure*) and exorcised the demon."[31]

The Chinese used to beat the tamtam, to clank chains, to let off fire-works in daytime in order to chase away demons. At eclipses of the sun and of the moon, they augment considerably the noise to drive away the dragon that menaces to devour the brightness of celestial bodies. Among the Abyssinian Christians, the sistrum was used as a clapper against demons, and even in the Catholic church there are vestiges of the ancient superstitious fear of demons. A liturgical formula used at the consecration of church-bells has its origin in this fear.[32] In the Catholic services of Maundy Thursday and Good Friday, the bells, normally used in the ritual, are substituted by wooden clappers.[33] The meaning of all these customs was to ward off the harmful influence of malevolent demons who, according to primitive superstition, were believed to be present at all times and in all places.

o
o o

Nowhere in the Bible is the power of music to drive away evil spirits exposed more explicitly than in the reports about David's playing the *kinnor* to cure the sick king Saul. At the period when the biblical text has been put down in writing, music has already lost its primitive function as an element of magic. Yet, the memory of it was still strong enough for attributing Saul's healing to the effect of music. In other words, music did not cease to be considered a potent magic procedure in subduing evil spirits and forcing them to leave their human victims.

As one may infer from the biblical reports, Saul was first possessed by Yahveh's spirit, a state of mind called by Greek philosophers "enthusiastic." Later, however, he was plagued by onsets of melancholia and was afflicted by frequent fits of madness:

> "Now the spirit of the Lord had departed from Saul, and an evil spirit from the Lord terrified him"[34] (1 Sam. 16:14).

The tradition interprets Saul's ailment as God's punishment for committed wrongs. Speaking in psychiatric terms, however, the causal connection between the two conditions of Saul, the enthusiastic and the melancholic, is easily recognizable. Frequent enthusiastic excitement of high-strung individuals often leads to madness. Persons disposed to ecstasy, sometimes display a morbid sentiment, oscillating between violent outbursts of excitement and gloomy, completely passive melancholy. The one so afflicted has "visions," is plagued by delusions, becomes a "prophet" in his ecstatic state, and just as at this stage of his malady he is looked upon as blessed by God, so in the opposite state he is regarded as tormented by evil demons.

During one of such depressive spells, Saul's confidants advised the king to give orders

> "to seek out a man who is a skillful player on the harp; and it shall be, when the evil spirit from God cometh upon thee, that he shall play with his hand, and thou shalt be well" (1 Sam. 16:16).

According to ancient belief, music has not only a sedative, but also a stimulating effect, able to increase the morbid impulse and to bring it to a climax. The mechanism of it is that through a violent discharge, music brings about the intended relief. In this particular function, music is not merely a magic practice tending to drive off demons, but an implement of healing, capable of producing a physical relaxation in cases of an overstrained psychic condition. Thus, music may be said to represent a transitory form from magic to medicine, as we observe even today among primitive peoples, where the priest is at the same time magician and medicine man.

In an attack of madness, and under the exciting effect of music, Saul committed an attempt at David's life:

> "And it came to pass on the morrow, that an evil spirit from God came mightily upon Saul, and he raved in the midst of the house; and David played with his hand, as he did day by day; and Saul had his spear in his hand. And Saul cast the spear; for he said: 'I will smite David even to the wall.' And David stepped aside out of his presence twice." (1 Sam. 18:10,11).

After the attempt failed, the desired relaxation in Saul's state of mind must have been accomplished, for shortly afterwards

> "he made him his captain over a thousand,"

an act caused not only by his fear of David (1 Sam. 18:12), but probably also by the remorse highly characteristic of over-excited persons, desirous to make up with increased zeal the wrong committed in a state of frenzy.

In connection with the capacity of music to heal certain diseases, the Talmud tells of an appliance, which caused drops of water to drip continually on a vessel of metal and thereby to produce a monotonous buzzing sound, by which the sick person was put to sleep and, eventually, led to recovery.[35] Although this cannot be considered "music" in the proper sense of the word, the rhythmical monotony produced by this gadget might have had, nevertheless, a certain music-like effect upon the sick body or the sick soul. At any rate, it shows that primitive superstition, in magic as well as in medicine, used semi-musical procedures for its aims.

SACHS makes pertinent observations concerning the relationship of primitive medicine and music:

> "Where the medicine man (*shaman*) performs religious ceremonies, the music approaches the liturgical intonation. And from the chants of the witch doctor it has descended by a long chain of heredity to the liturgy of the higher religion: it lives on in the *Saman* of the Hindu as in the *Leinen* of the Jews and the *Lectio* of the Christian churches."[36]

ATHENAEUS states that music, and particularly certain modes (*modoi*), serve as remedy against specific physical diseases:

> "That music can also heal diseases, Theophrastus has recorded in his work 'On Inspiration' (*Peri Enthousiasmou*): he says that persons subject of sciatica (*ischiakous*) would always be free from its attacks if one played the flute in the Phrygian mode over the part affected."[37]

The idea of the healing power of music was wide-spread among the Jews until the late talmudic times. We find even in the Talmud the mention of a song (*shir peg'ayim*), which was allegedly capable to serve as protection in times of epidemics.[38]

o
o o

When the Hebrews took possession of the promised land, they have found among the resident tribes all sorts of magic and pagan customs, which were irreconcilable with Jewish religious laws. This is clearly implied by the biblical law-giver, admonishing them retrospectively against idolatry, sorcery and divination:

> "When thou art come into the land which the Lord the God giveth thee, thou shalt not learn to do after the abomination of those nations. There shall not be found among you anyone that maketh his son or his daughter to pass through the fire, one that useth divination, a soothsayer, or an enchanter, or a sorcerer, or a charmer, or one that consulteth a ghost or a familiar spirit, or a necromancer. For whosoever doeth these things is an abomination unto the Lord; and because of these abominations the Lord thy God is driving them out from before thee" (Deuter. 18:9-12).

Despite all religious prohibitions, however, idolatry, superstition and magic must have been flourishing among the Hebrews not only before but also long after the conquest of their new homeland. During Saul's reign, magic and divination have reached such proportions that the king was compelled to expulse from the country all the diviners and soothsayers (1 Sam. 28:3). This, however, did not prevent Saul himself to consult a soothsayer, the woman of

En-dor, when he was hard pressed by the Philistines (1 Sam. 28:7 ff). In this nocturnal episode, the biblical narration does not refer to any musical element, to be sure. But in ceremonies aimed at creating the needed mystical mood, music was the most potent agent of the magician, sorcerer, or priest. It served as a sort of psychological opiate for inducing the participants to believe in the *reality* of the magic act. It is therefore probable that the woman of En-dor has infused her conjuration at least with chanting.

Another heathen and superstitious custom was the use of the *teraphim*—small or large portable idols, the *lares* (Roman house gods) of the ancient Hebrews (*cp.* Gen. 31:34). They could be found practically in every family, and were still worshipped—probably with some musical accessories—during the period of the early kings, when the religion of Yahveh was at its peak, and the theocratic state regulated with iron hand the entire spiritual and intellectual life of the nation. Their use in David's household, for instance, is evidenced by the well-known episode at which his wife Michal, in order to mislead Saul's messengers,

> "took the *teraphim,* and laid it in the bed, and put a quilt of goats' hair at the head thereof, and covered it with a cloth" (1 Sam. 19:11 ff).

Of course, the idol served here a good purpose in saving David's life. Nevertheless, it is significant that at the time when the true faith seemed to be firmly established, there have been idols in the house of David, the standard-bearer of Jewish religion, and that the biblical chronicler does not refrain from reporting this fact.

The cult of the *teraphim* must have been alarmingly wide-spread in the 8th century B.C.E., as we may learn from Hosea 3:4, and some two hundred years later another prophet puts contemptuously their veneration into a line with the superstitious practices of soothsayers and diviners (Zech. 10:2).

Even the wisest of all rulers, the God-fearing Solomon, was not exempt from superstition and idolatry. As he

> "went after Ashtoreth the goddess of the Zidonians, and after Milkom the detestation of the Ammonites,"

as he

> "did build a high place for Chemosh the detestation of Moab, in the mount that is before Jerusalem, and for Molech the detestation of the children of Ammon, so did he for all his foreign wives, who offered and sacrificed unto their gods." (1 Kings 11:5 ff).

The biblical chronicler tries to efface the strange aberrations of this wise ruler and merely states that the aging Solomon, besides his own God, tolerated foreign deities. Yet, where idolatry reigns, there is also superstition; and like the king, the people must have been strongly influenced by it, despite all the severe proscriptions of the Mosaic law. Little wonder, then, that other cults, especially the one of the "Queen of the Heaven," *i.e.* of the Babylonian Ishtar, wide-spread in Canaʿan, was once adopted and perpetuated by the Hebrews, regardless of the fiery condemnations lashed against them by the prophet Jeremiah (7:17-18; 44:17-19).

With the worship of foreign deities, the music of these various pagan services was bound to be introduced anew into Jewish life, even if sporadically.

And it must have surely constituted a strange contrast to the dignified Temple music which, in its final form, was one of the great and enduring achievements of king Solomon.

o
o o

Religious laws have prohibited magic and sorcery, but they were not strong enough to prevent their practice. Thus, proof for their use can be found throughout the entire history of Ancient Israel. The older law (Exod. 22:17) has decreed that sorceresses (*mekassefah*) were not allowed to remain alive. Nevertheless, they must have existed all the time, as the prophets testify. Jeremiah considers them enemies of the true faith (Jer. 27:9). Ezekiel describes the evil influence exercised upon credulous people by deceitful sorceresses (Ezek. 13:17-23), and scorns their cheap practices. Nahum ranks them among the social evils of his time (Nah. 3:4), and, in post-exilic times, Malachi mentions them together with adulterers, perjurers, and inhuman employers (Mal. 3:5). Since music, in some form, has been an essential element in all such superstitious practices, the prophets, implicitly, condemn all the musical trickery employed in such pagan ceremonies.

Thus, it is manifest that magic and sorcery were not only religious, but also social problems in Ancient Israel, which the leaders of the nation and of the religion had to take into account. At the summit of religious development, God's protection was considered the best remedy against evils perpetrated by demons and spirits; nevertheless, the traditional magic customs were never entirely abolished. In danger and distress, the Jews tried to obtain God's assistance by prayers; besides, however, the people believed as before in the effectiveness of magic incantations, especially if the musical background applied to them was impressive enough. Even the ritual itself was permeated with magic, since certain psalms, sung in the rites, were supposed to possess anti-magical or preventive power.

In the post-biblical literature, the evidence for fear of demons and for magical actions against evil influences is even more pronounced than in the Bible. The talmudic superstition was indeed so strong and sincere that even pious teachers could not extricate themselves from the idea that the air was full of evil spirits hostile to man, which were lying in wait for him and trying to destroy him. As an immediate result, all sorts of anti-demoniac practices, including their musical counterparts, have flourished at this period as never before.

The decisive fight of the Jewish religion against magic and sorcery was led by the great prophets of Israel. They carried on a relentless battle against superstition.

2. Prophecy and Music

Among all the peoples of Antiquity music was generally considered a divine gift. This explains its constant association with prophecy which, in many instances, was looked upon as something profoundly akin to music in spiritual substance. The classical example of the close relationship between the two is furnished by the Greek mythology.

DIONYSOS, the god of enthusiasm, and the Muses have many common features. The Muses knew not only the past, but also the future ORPHEUS, the famous singer, was the son of the Muses and at the same time the first priest of DIONYSOS. In the mixed Phoenician-Greek religion, as practiced in Cyprus, there is a similar example, KINNYRAS was the earliest musician and singer and at the same time the first priest of APHRODITE; he was also able to foretell the future, just as his daughters, the KINNYRADES.[39] Besides Cyprus, KINNYRAS was worshipped in Byblos and its environs, and particularly in Aphaca, at Lebanon.[40] Through the intercourse of the Phoenicians with the neighbouring peoples, his name came to both the Greeks and the Hebrews. The term for the instrument played by this mythological musician can be easily recognized in the Greek *kinnyra* and the Hebrew *kinnor.*[41]

The affinity between prophecy and music is particularly conspicuous among the Hebrews. It can even be said that Jewish prophecy was born out of the spirit of music. The musician belonging to the levitical fraternity was called a "prophet," a "seer." As a designation for levitical singing, the chroniclers employ the term *nibba,* the same as used to characterize the enthusiastic attitude of the prophets (1 Chron. 25: 1 ff).[42]

The singer-prophet is driven by the spirit of Yahveh (2 Chron. 20:14), therefore he is at the same time *ro'eh,* "seer," or "diviner" [of the future]. Not only the three precentors of David—Asaph, Heman and Jeduthun-Ethan—were such prophets or seers; the chroniclers also mention Gad and Nathan (2 Chron. 29:25).

There is no radical difference between the great national prophets like Isaiah and Amos, and the singer-prophets. The latter pour out their enthusiasm in harmonious sounds; the former clothe their visions into a spoken form, a language which is elated by ecstasy, having a specific melodious undercurrent. In this extraordinary state of mind, the raptured "seer" does not use every day's language, but employs a form of "poetry," or "song." His utterance is called *masa,* a Hebrew word, which appears in 1 Chron. 15:22, 2 Chron. 24:27, Isa. 13:1. Prov. 31:1, and Lam. 2:14, and which was given in our English translations most diversified and seemingly contradictory meanings: song (of the Levites), oracle, prophecy, visions, dreams, revelations, warnings, sayings, but mostly "burden."

These different translations however, are not so incompatible as it may appear on first sight. They all refer to the various forms of a prophetic message (or pronouncement), which weighs like a burden upon the prophet's soul, a burden imposed upon him by the Lord's commandment, and which he transmits to the people in a tangible form, akin to a solemn song of the levitical singers.

o
o o

In the primitive meaning of the word, the prophet, *nabi* (plur. *nebi'im*), had no relationship to music. It implied "speaker," *i.e.* a person who could render eloquently the exalted sentiments of the people. This is what the term signifies when it is used for the first time in the Bible. When Moses entrusted by the Lord with the formidable task of liberating his people intimates his inaptitude for speech, God Himself gives him the advice:

> "Aaron thy brother shall be thy prophet (*nabi*), . . . and Aaron thy brother shall speak unto Pharaoh" (Exod. 7:1,2).

In a former passage, the LORD says about Aaron:

> "And he shall be thy spokesman (*dibber*) unto the people; and it shall come to pass, that he shall be to thee a mouth (*lepeh*)" (Exod. 4:16).

In particular, *nabi* is the man who speaks in the name of God, whom the Lord has chosen as His spokesman in order to proclaim His will to the people. The root *naba,* "to announce," is identical with the verb *naba,* "to gush" (like a well) and, in a figurative sense, "to speak easily, with enthusiasm," as it was generally bestowed upon men enlightened by God.

The SEPTUAGINT always translates *nabi* as *prophētēs.* This word is derived from *prophanai,* "to speak in the name of someone" and, in a wider sense, it originally had the meaning of a "spokesman," and "interpreter." PLATO called the poets the "prophets of the Muses," that is their interpreters.[43] The interpreter and expounder of ARISTOTLE's works was called his "prophet." APOLLO was said to be JUPITER's "prophet," since he was able to render most precisely the thoughts of the supreme god. Following this idea, PHILO says about Moses:

> "Of the divine utterances, some are spoken by God in His own Person with His prophet for interpreter."[44]

The Church Fathers also used the word in this sense. JOHN CHRYSOSTOM stated repeatedly that the prophets were spokesmen of God.

Thus, according to its etymology as well as its general use, the word *nabi* stands for a man enlightened by God and serving as His mediator. He is not necessarily a foreteller of things to come; but it is essential that his word be imbued with divine revelation. As a rule, however, all the Jewish prophets have predicted the future, or at least warned about future consequences, since God infused their speeches with terrifying or hopeful prophecies, depending on whether He wanted to punish or to console His people. Thus, the prophets were called by all sorts of significant terms, such as *ro*ʾ*eh,* "seer," *ḥozeh,* "diviner" [of the future], ʾ*ish ha-ruaḥ,* "man of the (divine) spirit," and ʾ*ish* ʾ*elohim,* "man of God."

The difference between "prophet" and "seer" is clearly defined by the biblical chroniclers:

> "Beforetime in Israel, when a man went to inquire of God, thus he said: 'Come and let us go to the seer'; for he that is now called a prophet (*nabi*) was beforetime called a seer (*ro*ʾ*eh*)" (1 Sam. 9:9).

Consequently, the function of the *ro*ʾ*eh* was mainly that of predicting the future, while the later *nabi* was rather the "spokesman of God." At the time of Amos the stress was again laid more upon the visionary qualities of the prophet, who was supposed to possess the gift of the "second sight"; he then was called *ḥozeh.* Soon, however, the term was tainted with a bad flavor; *ḥozim* were the false prophets who fraudulously attributed themselves certain qualities in order to satisfy their greed (Micah 3:7,11).

The different meanings of the term *nabi,* as exposed in the biblical text, can be then summarized as follows:

(1) The confidant of God (Gen. 20:7; *cp.* Isa. 41:8 ff; Ps. 105:15).

(2) The interpreter of God's thoughts, a spokesman of God (Exod. 7:1; Deut. 18:18; Jer. 15:19).

(3) A singer, musician, poet (Exod. 15:1-20; Judg. 4:4; 5:2 ff; 1 Sam. 10:5 ff; 1 Chron. 25:1 ff; etc.).

(4) A seer who predicts and reveals the hidden events of the future and who has visions of God (Deut. 13:2; 1 Sam. 9:9; 1 Kings 22:7,8; 2 Kings 3:11; etc.).

(5) A madman, possessed by the evil spirit, or pseudo-prophet in a state of frenzy (1 Sam. 18:10; 1 Kings 18:29).

(6) A worker of miracles (Deut. 13:1 ff; Ecclus. 48:14,15; *cp.* 2 Kings 13:21).

According to the fundamental interpretation, however, the prophet was God's spokesman, a mediator between the Lord and His people. This is beautifully expressed by PHILO in a musical metaphor:

> "Under the prophet's words I recognized the voice of the invisible Master whose invisible hand plays on the instrument of human speech."[45]

At another place he says also:

> "For prophets are the interpreters of God, who make full use of their organs of speech to set forth what He wills."[46]

o
o o

Moses was the first of the great prophets (Deut. 18:18). God revealed Himself to Samuel (1 Sam. 3:20). David has had at his court the "seer" (*ḥozeh*) Gad and the "prophet" (*nabi*) Nathan, who told him the past and the future (2 Sam. 7:2; 7:17; 12:1; 12:25; 24:18,19; 1 Kings 1:10; 1:22; 1:32 ff; 2 Chron. 29:25). David himself used to prophesy; in the song of praise, called by the chronicler "the last words of David," he said himself:

> "The spirit of the Lord spoke by me, and His word was upon my tongue" (2 Sam. 23:2).

Besides prophets, there were prophetesses in Israel. The first of them mentioned in the Bible was Moses' sister Miriam (Exod. 15:20). The meaning of "prophecy" here is still that of the heroic age, when the prophet was identical with the singer-musician, that is the folk-bard, not the divinely inspired intermediary of God, as outlined above.

Deborah was a judge in Israel,[47] but was also called by the chronicler a "prophetess" (Judg. 4:4). Similar to Miriam, she owed this distinction to her attributes as a minstrel. Again, there are no indications of Deborah's ability to foretell the future, which goes to show that the term "prophetess" as applied to her was due to her gift as a singer.

After Deborah, there was a centuries-long lack of information about prophetesses. This certainly was due not to their actual absence, but probably to the fact that in the opinion of the chroniclers their importance was eclipsed by that of Miriam and Deborah.

The next woman mentioned as *nebiy'ah* was Isaiah's wife (Isa. 8:3). Many exegetes, both Jewish and non-Jewish, consider her to have been a real prophetess, "even if we know nothing of the prophecies pronounced by her."[48] There are good reasons to assume, however, that Isaiah's wife belonged to the category of folk-bards, just as Miriam and Deborah.

A real prophetess, Huldah, is mentioned in the days of king Josiah (2 Kings 22:14). The king sent messengers to her to ask for an oracle; she proclaimed the Lord's forgiveness to the king because of his remorse and repentance (2 Kings 22:19,20).

After this, prophetesses are mentioned by Ezekiel (Ezek. 13:17-23). But they have apparently belonged to the class of unethical sorceresses and diviners against whom, besides Ezekiel, other prophets poured out their wrath (see above, p. 507).

Finally, we come across the prophetess Noadiah of the post-Babylonian period (Neh. 6:14). We know nothing about her except her name, and there are no indications whether she belonged to the category of minstrels, or else possessed—like Huldah—a gift for true prophecy.

The announcement of the prophet Joel that "your sons and your daughters shall prophesy" (Joel 3:1) has only a symbolical meaning; it is unlikely that prophetesses who could foretell the future things were meant here.

The Old Testament even mentions a prophet who did not belong to the Jewish faith—Bala'am, the author of several exquisite poetic parables.[49] To be sure, the biblical text does not apply to him directly the term of prophet. But the Lord revealed Himself to him, he spoke in the name of God, and his language is very similar to that of the great Jewish prophets (Num. 22 ff). No wonder that early rabbinical writers attributed to him a rank akin to that of Moses.[50]

o
o o

During the early history of Israel, wandering prophets roamed about in groups and excited themselves mutually by music and dance until they arrived at a state of ecstasy. Their fanatic songs, their violent gestures combined with bewitching and probably wordless incantations, the rhythmic beating of drums, the continuous invocations of the deity, all this produced such a fascinating effect upon the onlookers that, by way of mass-suggestion, the state of rapture was eventually transferred to them as well. At times, this has actually reached enormous proportions, so that the persons struck lost all awareness for their surroundings. (1 Sam. 19:20-24; Num. 11:25; 11:26-29).

A most conspicuous collective prophecy directly associated with music is related in the speech of Samuel held at the anointment of Saul as king of Israel (1 Sam. 10:5,6).

o
o o

The Fathers of the Church compared the prophets either to instruments of music which, in the hands of the Holy Spirit, produce harmonious sounds, or to brilliant mirrors of crystal which reflect faithfully the divine thought.

God's communications to His prophets were brought about by three different ways: through the word, through visions, and through dreams. In general, the divine verbal utterance was not given in an articulate language, heard by mortal ears; it was perceived only by the "inner hearing" of the chosen ones. Only on very rare occasions God revealed Himself in a manner that could be heard by outsiders, as at the invocation of Moses from the bush (Exod. 3:4), at addressing Samuel in the Temple (1 Sam. 3:4 ff), and other instances. God's messages received by the prophets in this dual fashion were transmitted to the people either in the form of exalted oracles,[51] or else they were put into writing in the prophetic books and thus preserved for posterity.

o
o o

The ostensible criterion for distinguishing the true and false prophet was that the former's inspiration rose naturally, without a recognizable external cause; whereas the latter needed artificial means to bring about the state of enrapture. This being so, one would expect the activity of the true prophet to depend upon a supernatural ecstasy, upon an irresistible inner compulsion, which only the divine revelation could bestow upon him.

Such conclusions, however, would be by no means correct. For, according to the testimony of the Bible, the inspiration of both, the true and the false prophets, took place spontaneously as well as unconsciously, and sometimes by means of artificial stimulation. The biblical report in 1 Sam. 10:5 alludes certainly to true prophets, in spite of the fact that they prophesied with music, *i.e.* that they created the necessary ecstatic mood with the aid of instruments and dancing. Elisha certainly was a true prophet; nevertheless, he needed music when he was going to give to king Jehoshaphat a prophetic oracle (2 Kings 3:15). We see, on the other hand, that among false prophets the state of ecstasy often came spontaneously and apparently without external means (1 Kings 18:26 ff).

Generally speaking, unless the inspiration of the prophets would take place spontaneously, they had to avail themselves of artificial means for inducing it. The means used by the prophets for a specific purpose of receiving God's answer to a supplication were of two kinds: ritually inspired, and artificial. The former were the oracles by *Urim* and *Thummim* (Excd. 28:30; Lev. 8:8), by holy divination (Num. 23:23; Ezek. 13:23), and by the *Ephod* (Exod. 28:6; 39:2; Judg. 8:27; 2 Sam. 6:14).

There were probably other elements in sacred worship by which oracles could be invoked. MOWINCKEL alludes to a few headings of the psalms, like *ʿal shoshannim* and *ʿal shushan ʿedut* (Pss. 45:1; 60:1; 69:1) as perhaps signifying certain ways to bring about sacred oracles by the use of flowers.[52]

The artificial means of creating ecstasy were fasting, dancing, honey and intoxicating drinks, but primarily music, ensuing from enthusiasm, as ARISTOTLE intimates.[53] Prophecy and music were closely related according to the ideas of Antiquity, not only among the Hellenes and the Hebrews, but also among other peoples. In the cult of Dionysos, music was used to arouse a bacchic frenzy, and the *thyoskooi mainades,* the "raving Maenades," swooned into ecstasy through divine inspiration. They predicted the future "in a prophetic enrapture," as shown by the example of CASSANDRA and PYTHIA.[54]

The main instruments helping to bring about these ecstatic prophecies were the Phrygian *auloi* (oboes). The sharp, penetrating sound of these instruments, together with melismatic melodic formulae characteristic of Oriental music, applying the variation technique to a small thematic kernel (called *maḳam* by the Arabs, *raga* by the Hindus, *neginot* by the Hebrews), were the musical stimuli that created the state of ecstasy. In Ancient Israel, the *ḥalil* was used for the same purpose (1 Sam. 10:5).

Numerous biblical and post-biblical passages testify to the religious ecstasy induced by music. David's enraptured dance on the occasion of bringing home the ark of the covenant belongs to this category (1 Chron. 13:8). Elisha needed music for his prophecy (2 Kings 3:15). The chroniclers firmly believed that religious ecstasy would exert an influence upon the events themselves which otherwise would not occur. Once, when the Levites had put themselves into a state of prophetic rapture by singing hymns, a surprising miracle happened: Israel's enemies, the Moabites, Ammonites and Edomites mutually annihilated themselves (2 Chron. 20:21 ff).

In a later source, the gnostic acts of St. Thomas, there is a passage giving an eloquent description of the ecstatic rapture created by music:

> ". . . The flute girl, holding the flute in her hand, went round them all; and when she came to the place where the apostle was, she stood over him, playing the flute over his head a long time . . . And the apostle began to sing and to repeat this song . . . and what had been said by him they did not understand . . . But the flute-girl alone heard all, for she was Hebrew by race."[55]

Besides the *ḥalilim,* the prophets also used other instruments for evoking ecstasy, such as the psaltery (*nebel*), the lyre (*kinnor*), and the timbrel (*tof*), the last one as rhythmical support for dancing. For music was always serving as the strongest stimulus to men endowed with ecstatic disposition. This is especially true of Orientals who, far more than Western people, are subject to violent changes of mood and, under the impact of music, are even able to commit actions beyond reason. The frantic dance of Mohammedan dervishes, as well as similar acts of worship among Negro tribes of Africa and some other primitive peoples show the exciting effect of music on human behavior. The most striking example of this phenomenon is the enraptured King Saul. His prophetic outpourings reached such a degree of ecstasy that he stripped his clothes and stayed naked for a whole day and a whole night (1 Sam. 19:24).[56] To be sure, the excitement of Saul may be explained to a certain extent by his abnormal psychic disposition which manifested itself in recurrent fits of melancholy and raving madness (1 Sam. 16:14 ff; 18:10). Nevertheless, he undoubtedly belonged to the category of ecstatic *nebi'im.*

o
o o

The state of unconscious and musically stimulated ecstasy, primitively the concomitant phenomenon of prophecy, receded more and more into the background among the later great prophets. There remained merely the innermost and rather unobtrusive possession by the spirit of God, in which state the prophet announced the Lord's message orally.

As a general rule, the authors of the biblical books were not intent on preserving their names for posterity. Anonymity was a common characteristic of literature and poetry in Ancient Orient. As for the prophetic books, in particular, these were in reality not so much the products of the prophets themselves as of their disciples, who were anxious to preserve in writing, for future generations, the teachings of the former—the true heralds of national consciousness. It will probably never be possible to find out how many of the prophetic books were written by the prophets themselves whose name they bear. This circumstance, however, does not belittle their poetic beauty or their intrinsic message, both of which represent eternal and priceless spiritual treasures.

In addition to the prophetic books, the utterances of the prophets are best preserved in the liturgical poems incorporated in the Psalter. Many biblical expositors tried to establish the authorship of certain psalms by way of the most scrupulous stylistic analyses. But this riddle will probably forever be shrouded in mystery. It is possible, however, to identify at least the probable milieu to which the poets of the psalms belonged (see p. 144 ff).

The Oriental poet has always been considered to possess a supernatural gift. Ancient Israel, too, shared this belief and thus, in the imagination of the people, the poet and the prophet were blended into a single notion. The Jewish *nebi'im* were at the same time poets, even though not all of their utterances have been presented in the form of a regular poetry. At any rate, the oracles of the prophets distinguished themselves by a literary language palpably different from ordinary prose. Furthermore, it may safely be assumed that these oracles were musically intoned and presented in a chanting manner, the necessary prerequisite for exerting a stirring effect upon the masses listening to them. All this contributed to the belief, widely shared in the ancient Semitic world, that both prophecy and poetry originate from a supernatural inspiration and must be cast, therefore, into a poetic form.

Just as the prophet was inspired by music, so was the poet. He conveyed his secret message to the sounds of the harp:

> "Hear this, all ye peoples; give ear, all ye inhabitants of the world, both low and high, rich and poor together. My mouth shall speak wisdom, and the meditation of my heart shall be understanding. I will incline my ear to a parable; I will open my dark saying upon the harp" (Ps. 49:2-5).

As may be learned from this and numerous other biblical passages, the poet-prophets proclaimed their messages in the form of a rhythmic-metrical prose, different from the style of ordinary recitation as employed by the biblical scribes, different inasmuch as it had an enhanced ardour and a specific speech-melody. This may be the reason why the liturgical functions of the levitical singers were associated with the verb *nibba,* "to prophesy." (1 Chron. 25:2,3). This is a further indication to the effect that, according to the belief of Ancient Israel, the singers had to be seized with prophetic inspiration and that, consequently, they possessed all the qualities necessary for writing liturgical psalms.

This is why one may assume that the levitical singers were the authors at least of a great portion, if not all the poems of the Psalter. The gift of singing and of writing poetry was summed up under the general term "prophecy" by the Israelites. Therefore, the prophets and seers among the levitical singers mentioned in the Old Testament by their names, such as Asaph, Heman and Jeduthun-Ethan (1 Chron. 25:1-5), Gad and Nathan (2 Sam. 7:2; 7:17; 12:1; 12:25; 24:18,19; 1 Kings 1:10; 1:22; 1:32 ff; 2 Chron. 29:25), Jahaziel (2 Chron. 20:14), and others, must have not only been excellent singer-musicians, but also distinguished poets. Their accomplishments were, in fact, so outstanding even among the generally prominent levitical singers that the chroniclers were induced to preserve their individual names for posterity.

o
o o

The divine power of poetic inspiration applies to all art forms created by the agitation of the soul, and it also constitutes the psychological background for prophecy. Thus, the innermost association between music, poetry, and prophecy becomes manifest. By virtue of its inherent mysterious force, music has the capacity of stirring the human soul to such an extent that those who are susceptible to it "speak with tongues," meaning that they enter a state of rapture displaying the presence of divine revelation. The Arabs believe that the inspiration of the poet and musician derives from a specific demon of poetry and music.[57] In Ancient Israel it was not a demon who brought about the prophetic ecstasy, but the hand of God reposing on the prophet. God's breath permeated the prophet's whole being, His commandment served as an inducement to perform the holy ministry.

Thus, prophecy in Israel, especially in its higher stages, was the manifestation of the religious power ingrained in the human soul; it was a valve through which the religious feeling of the people, often reaching its highest level, strove to escape; it was the visible embodiment of the word, the will, and the omnipotence of God, revealing themselves through His chosen spokesmen.

In all this, music played an essential aiding role. Primitively a subordinate element in magic, and later in healing ceremonies, music, at the higher stage of Jewish religion had the amazing capacity to stir the innermost sentiments of the soul, to awake the supernatural powers of God's chosen men. Thus, music was considered one of the most important factors that enabled humans to participate in the divine revelation.

XI. WOMEN IN THE MUSIC OF ANCIENT ISRAEL

The history of civilization of ancient Orient contains ample documentation about the role women played in the sacred and secular music of the time. Written records as well as pictorial displays testify to the various activities of women as dancers, singers and instrumentalists.

In Egypt, for instance, music in worship was mostly relegated to priestesses.[1] In the New Empire, almost every lady of distinction participated as a singer in one of the temples, performing songs "before the beautiful face of god" to the accompaniment of the sistrum. Every temple had such singers; the most frequently mentioned are those of the god Amon.[2]

Music was assigned a specific importance in worship as well as in social life of the Assyrians and Babylonians; and women took an active part in it. Female singers and musicians are portrayed in many extant pictorial records, the most beautiful of which is perhaps the bas-relief showing the triumphal reception of the victorious Assyrian king ASHUR-IDANNI-PAL entering Susiana. We see there a group of musicians, consisting of five men, six women, and nine singing boys with harps, double-oboes, psaltery (a kind of zither) and a hand-drum.[3]

Judging from biblical sources, the role of women in the musical practice of the Jews was uncontested only in the dance. As singers, they impress one as having been of subordinate importance. And as instrumentalists, their activity is so veiled, even blurred by biblical scribes, that at a superficial glance women seem to have been kept aloof artificially from instrumental music or, worse, to have not shown any aptitude for it.

As mentioned before, the reasons why the role of women in the musical practice of Ancient Israel is rather clouded in our original sources may be discovered only in roundabout ways. One of these is that, as time passed, the biblical text underwent repeated and rather incisive editorial changes. In their purificatory zeal, the priestly chroniclers tried particularly to eliminate anything that might have alluded to or recalled the primitive pagan, pre-Yahvistic rites of the Hebrews. In pristine times women participated frequently in them. With the suppression of the biblical allusions to such practices the references to women as ritual singers and instrumentalists had also to be deleted. Merely faint vestiges of them remained here and there in the Scriptures.

The other reason might have been a gradually developing anti-feminine tendency of the priestly caste, to an extent that women were displaced step by step from any ritual functions. Consequently, the indications in the biblical text that they ever have had a share in the sacred service had also to be effaced or so transformed as to become almost irrecognizable.

The priestly scribes have taken no offense at the role of women in secular music, therefore most of it remained unchanged in the Bible. To this category belonged primarily the part women played as dancers and singers outside the sanctuary.

A reason for the under-estimation of women's ability as instrumentalists might have been the self-conceit and narrow party-spirit of the levitical music guild.[4] Also the elementary instinct of self-preservation might have induced the Levites to eliminate women-musicians, as dangerous competitors, from the Temple ritual. There is no doubt, however, that in olden times, prior to the establishment of the organized Temple service, and even in the First Temple, women regularly participated in the ritual as singers and instrumentalists.

The activity of women as dancers has been examined in an earlier section of this study. Also their role as singers has been discussed previously in a general way. It will be necessary, however, to elucidate the activity of women as singers from a more specific angle.

The Bible does not contain direct indications as to the participation of female singers in the Temple choir. Nevertheless, there are indirect allusions to singing women in the sacred service, among these the statement that in the pre-Davidic sanctuary the women, like the Levites, had to make their appearance at the east-side of the tent and perform certain ritual functions (Exod. 38:8). Is it to be supposed that these were merely subordinate functions, consisting of some menial work? This is rather improbable, since such menial services were assigned to a special class, the *Nethinim,* who originally had been slaves of the Levites.

The "Court of Women"[5] with its metal mirrors and probably other implements testify expressly to the role of women as performers of dances in religious ceremonies. This must have surely been the place in the sanctuary where the dancers for the divine service could lay on a special attire, adorn themselves with a specific head-dress, apply the makeup customary in the Orient, and so forth.

Apart from dancing, the women's part in the cult might have been identical with those of the levitical musicians. Up to the time of David, women were the predominant performers of the reproductive arts.[6] Miriam is the prototype of these women in early Jewish rites (Exod. 15:20). Clues for participation of female singers in worship are found even in the earliest period of Jewish history. It is said of Noah's wife:

> "Naʿamah was a woman of a different stamp, for the name denotes that she sang (*manʿemet*) to the timbrel (*tof*) in honor of idolatry."[7]

Naʿamah's songs (in this case roundelays), still served pagan rites. However, there is no basic difference between these songs and those performed later in honor of Yahveh.

In olden times women seem to have served merely a part time in the sanctuary. Subsequently, the custom developed that young maidens, but mostly widows, devoted themselves permanently to the sacred service.[8] These women were recruited generally from among the wives and daughters of the levitical singers.[9] However, there were some of the priestly families among them as well.

Not before the 18th century has biblical exegesis conceded that, besides serving as dancers, women had been admitted into the Temple service as singers and instrumentalists. One of the first was AUGUSTIN CALMET (1672-1757), describing the role of women in sacred music as follows:

> "In the Temple and in religious ceremonies female musicians have participated together with male musicians. Generally, they were the Levites' daughters. Heman had twelve sons and three daughters, all well versed in music (1 Chron. 25:5). Psalm IX is addressed to Ben or Banaïas, leader of the group of young girls who sang in the Temple . . . The Chaldaean version of Ecclesiastes 2:8, in which Solomon says that "I got me men-singers and women-singers," means Temple singers."

CALMET considers therefore the seventh group of the Davidic music organization as that of the choir of maidens and women.[10]

As mentioned in an earlier chapter, (pp. 490 ff), GALPIN interprets the term *'alamot,* occurring in several passages of the biblical text and in one heading of the Psalter, as an indication that there might have been in Ancient Israel even separate music schools for women.[11] He opines—erroneously, as we already know—that the word *'alamot,* meaning "young maidens" or "separated ones," was the term for a school or a society in which female singers and dancers were educated for sacred service, and in which they led a communal life. In the heroic period women received their music instruction from male and female folk-bards, who were then the legitimate carriers of musical art. In subsequent times, women, just as men, were educated musically in the levitical school. As members of the levitical music guild, women had the same claim to music instruction as men.

In scrutinizing the role of women in the Temple and the Synagogue, SCHECHTER refers to an ancient rabbinic book, in which he had professedly discovered some indications for the participation of women in the levitical choir. He says, that

> "if we were to trust a certain passage in the 'Chapters of R. Eliezer,' we might perhaps conclude that during the First Temple the wives of the Levites formed a part of the choir."[12]

He restricts, however, his statement to saying that

> "the meaning of the passage is too obscure and doubtful for us to be justified in basing on it so important a reference."[13]

It is indeed surprising to find such an extremely cautious statement with regard to the participation of women in the sacred service after the Bible itself, and also PHILO'S writings have furnished quite indubitable evidence to this effect.

The biblical story of the Jews returning from Babylonian captivity contains definite proof that the levitical choir used female singers already in the First Temple. This story has been treated previously in our study; nevertheless, we have to come back to it once more, in order to fully elucidate the subject.

When the Israelites were carried into the Babylonian captivity in 586 B.C.E., following the destruction of Solomon's Temple, the sacred service, the sacrifices, the entire ritual ceremonial, and also its musical background ceased to exist. Temple music became devoid of any purpose; but also popular music, the joyful expression of the people's soul, was condemned to silence in oppression and sorrow.

Yet, when in 538 B.C.E., after an exile of forty-eight years, the first group of repatriates started their march home, there were among them

> "a hundred twenty and eight singers: the children of Asaph,"

that is the descendants of Asaph, and also of the other levitical singers, for which the chronicler uses the name of the most famous precentor of Solomon's Temple (Ezra 2:41). Furthermore, there were in the procession of the repatriates "two hundred singing men and singing women" (Ezra 2:65). The figures in the book of Nehemiah are slightly different; here, the number of the levitical singers, "the children of Asaph," is one hundred forty-eight (Neh. 7:44), and that of the "singing men and singing women" two hundred and forty-five" (Neh. 7:67). For the total number of the repatriates (42,360 and 7337 servants), the number of the returning male and female singers is proportionately considerable. Moreover, we have to bear in mind that not all the Jews living in Babylonia returned to Zion with the first group. A relatively large part remained voluntarily in exile, among them male and female singers as well.

A second group returned to Israel in 458 B.C.E. And still there must have remained, with other parts of the Jewish population, male and female musicians in Babylonia. For we possess documentary evidence that the Jews who settled permanently in Babylon have continued to cultivate the ancient musical tradition. The fortunate musical discoveries made in Babylonia in our own time would not have been possible without the Jewish splinter group's clinging to the ancient musical heritage.

The relatively important number of singers returning with the first repatriates constitutes definite proof that the cultivation of music was continued in the exile, regardless of all hardships. Despite the fact that Jewish liturgical music was for half a century without its ceremonial meaning and purpose, the Levites managed somehow to preserve the ancient tradition, this having been nursed merely by a faint hope of an eventual return to the homeland.

But how about the "singing men and singing women" mentioned specifically by Ezra and Nehemiah? Following RASHI's interpretation, many biblical expositors consider them to have been secular singers who merely accompanied those returning home and, through the medium of their art, alleviated the hardships of the wandering. No doubt, joyous singing had the power to lift the spirit and kindle anew the courage of the repatriates. This, however, would hardly explain the disproportionately large number of "secular" male and female singers in Babylonia.

> "It is not a happy suggestion that the function of these singers was secular. Is it likely that this company of religious enthusiasts, returning to a desolate home, had carried with them this number of singers for secular amusement?"[14]

This objection of PERITZ, however correct in itself, is only partially justified. To understand and appreciate fully the relatively large number of the returning secular singers, we have to realize the aim and purpose of musical culture during the exile. The intense cultivation of liturgical music among the Babylonian captives did not stem exclusively from the urge of preserving the levitical tradition, however desirable this goal might have been. It had still another, deeper meaning: music in the exile represented, as it were, a substitute for the lacking divine service of the Temple. In keeping alive liturgical music, the levitical singers became the legitimate guardians of the religious tradition. Music became the spiritual substitute for the animal sacrifice, to which formerly it furnished the tonal background in the sanctuary. In the exile, the sacrifice was offered symbolically, by way of music, and no longer physically.

Would it not then be logical to suppose that the returning "secular" male and female singers had also been prepared in the exile, at least partially, for the future sacred service? The number of the levitical progeny must have undergone in Babylonia certain fluctuations. The levitical tradition, however, had to be preserved under all circumstances. With this in view, is it too far-fetched to assume that many non-levitical singers have been trained ahead of time as prospective substitutes for the Levites in case the latter would not survive the exile in sufficient number? It is indeed highly probable that the "male singers and female singers" mentioned by Ezra and Nehemiah must have been in part non-levitical *Temple singers,* whose functions have not terminated with the repatriation, but were supposed to start just after the return of Jerusalem.

PERITZ is right in so far as he assumes that the returning non-levitical singers did not accompany the repatriates "for secular amusement" alone. In reality, they represent extra-levitical reserves for the sacred service, the restitution of which was planned for as soon as possible after the return, and for which "women singers" were just as necessary as "men singers."

This is the main significance of Ezra's and Nehemiah's statements which, besides their authenticity as historical records, furnish the irrefutable proof that women participated in the levitical choir from the very beginning, and even after the Babylonian exile, at least for a certain time, in the Second Temple.

A somewhat obscure passage in Amos, too, seems to allude to female singers of the Temple (Am. 8:3). The *Authorized Version, Moulton* and *Harkavy* translate:

> "And the songs of the Temple shall be howlings in that day."

The *Jewish Translation,* on the other hand, renders the passage:

> "And the songs of the palace shall be wailings in that day."[15]

CORNILL maintains that

> "this doubtful passage should according to all probability be translated: 'Then will the women singers in the Temple howl.' "

He reads *sharot,* "female singers," instead of *shirot,* "songs," and concludes from the context that it was the howling of the women in the Temple

> "that may have especially aroused the anger of the puritanical and untaught herdsman of Tekoa [*i.e.* Amos]."[16]

Whether CORNILL's version is right or wrong cannot be decided with certainty. However, this seems to be one of those passages in which the priestly zealots tried to obscure intentionally the participation of women in the cult.

Apart from the above quoted biblical references, PHILO's writings contain further indications pertaining to the role of women in sacred singing. This Judaeo-Hellenistic writer and philosopher lived during the last decades of the Herodian Temple (born ca. 20 B.C.E.)—in a period when the ancient Jewish tradition was still alive. His historical statements have, therefore, a high credibility. His enlightened education protected him from orthodox literal belief in the biblical text as well as from bias with regard to the priestly tradition, in so far as these contradicted the philosophy and the advanced knowledge of natural phenomena accepted by the coeval hellenistic civilization.

The participation of women in the cult as dancers and also, possibly, as singers, is mentioned in several places in his writings.[17]

PHILO's writings do not contain any hint whether in his days women were still employed in the sanctuary. Probably this was no longer the case, as indicated by his remark that the women were

> "resolved to win the prize of high excellence" and "not to be outstripped by the men in holiness."

This might have constituted for the levitical musicians too dangerous a competition, so that women were eliminated gradually from ritual ceremonies.

It is beyond doubt, however, that women and maidens participated as singers in the Davidic and Solomonic music organizations. Even after the return from the Babylonic exile, at least in the first period of the Second Temple, they might have held the same functions, until they were removed and replaced by singing boys.[18]

o
o o

Besides their participation in the Temple choir, women have had in the sanctuary another important function, which is not mentioned in the Bible, to be sure, but which constitutes an indispensable requirement for certain ritual ceremonies.

On the great religious festivities, like the spring festival, the Weeks, the Tabernacles, and even on minor festive occasions, regular pilgrimages to Jerusalem were a standing institution, in which men and women participated in large numbers. After the daytime's religious devotions in the Temple, the festivity was brought to a climax by a popular entertainment, in which dances were the main feature. These dances were performed, according to the ancient custom, by the sexes separately, or by women alone.

> "If numerous women from each of the tribes always took part in these dances on festivals, there must still have been some constantly at the Sanctuary who should know how to lead the dances, and they may have been the same as those who daily performed the sacred music there."[19]

In other words, the female singers belonging to the regular staff of the Temple, took over in the evening gatherings of the religious festivals the function of dance leaders, a role assigned in Ancient Israel from primeval times to women, as we know from the Bible (Exod. 15:20; Judith 3:10, etc.). In addition, EWALD finds it possible to assume with certainty

"that women who sang and played lived there [*i.e.* in the temple]."[20]

This, however, is very doubtful, since the Temple did not contain any living quarters whatsoever. Even the guardians of the gates had to pass the night in the Sanctuary in the most primitive way, sleeping on mats spread out on the floor, as we learn from rabbinic statements. Such primitive accommodations would certainly not have been adequate for the female members of the Temple personnel.

o
o o

The role of women as "prophetesses," *i.e.* as folk-bards has been examined earlier. We refer to our scrutiny in a previous section (see pp. 510 ff).

o
o o

Whereas the part women played in sacred singing can be established from the Scriptures but indirectly, their place in secular music is handled by the biblical chroniclers with much less restraint. Secular female singers (*sharot*) are mentioned in several places of the Bible, *e.g.* 2 Sam. 19:36; Isa. 23:16; Eccl. 2:8, etc. They participated in social entertainments, weddings, banquets, popular festivals, and thus enhanced the joy of living and the pleasure of festivities.

At all times, male and female singers belonged to the attributes of an Oriental royal court. Already in David's entourage there were "singing men and singing women," as evidenced by Barzillai's appeal to the king (2 Sam. 19:36). "Singing men and singing women" are mentioned also in Solomon's (Eccl. 2:8), and in king Josiah's court (2 Chron. 35:25).

The role of the royal singers of both sexes was providential at the siege of Jerusalem by SENNAḤERIB in 701 B.C.E. In Assyrian cuneiform inscriptions the stipulations are preserved, which the victorious SENNAḤERIB imposed upon king Hezekiah in exchange for sparing Jerusalem from being destroyed and pillaged:

> "Together with thirty talents of gold (and) eight-hundred talents of silver, he sent to me to Nineveh, my chief city, precious stones, cosmetics, . . . pure Uknû stones, couches of ivory, thrones of ivory, elephant skins, ivory, Ushû and Urkarinu wood, all kinds of treasures in quantity, and his daughters and women of the palace, and male and female musicians. He sent his messengers to deliver his tribute and to declare his subjection."[21]

As mentioned earlier, it is not obvious from this text whether the singers mentioned among the other "treasures" of the tribute were Hezekiah's court singers or those of the sacred service. It is rather to be assumed, however, that the latter was the case, since the Jewish Temple singers acquired great fame in the ancient Orient. It seems that SENNAḤERIB took advantage of the opportunity to enhance the lustre of his own court by demanding the deliverance of the renowned Israelitic singers. At any rate, this is one of the rare cases in which an Oriental monarch renounced the capture and pillage of the capital of a conquered enemy in bartering it for intangible artistic possessions.

As the reverse side of secular singing of women the fact may be mentioned that singing and playing of certain instruments belonged to the profession of women leading an immoral life (*cp.* Isa. 23:16; Ecclus. 9:4), since this was the general custom with courtesans of ancient Orient.[22]

o
o o

There was in Ancient Israel a musical profession reserved exclusively to the distaff side, that of the wailing women at funerals (*mekonenot* or *ʾalit*). We have already examined this activity of women in connection with the dance. Here we have to elucidate it from the musical point of view.

The wailing women were not just any females participating at funerals, but only those who possessed certain prescribed skills for which they have been specially trained, as it is stated explicitly in the Bible:

> "Teach your daughters wailing (*nehi*), and every one her neighbour lamentation (*ḳinah*)" (Jer. 9:19).

Some of them must have been particularly efficient in this profession, and thus were able to impart a highly emotional character to funeral ceremonies. Such women are alluded to in the biblical passage:

> "Consider ye, and call for the mourning women, that they may come; and send for the wise women[23] that they may come; and let them make haste, and take up a wailing for us" (Jer. 9:16,17).

Amos' remark "proclaim lamentation to such as are skillful of wailing" (Am. 5:16) likewise refers to such specially trained women.

To strike up wailing or lament was called *ʿanah,* "to sing," or "to intone." The procedure was either responsorial, when one began and the others responded, or antiphonal, when two groups alternated. The Mishnah gives a precise definition of both species:

> "What is lamentation (*ʿinnuy*)? When all sing together. And a wailing (*ḳinah*)? When one begins by herself and all respond after her."[24]

For wailing in antiphonal form there is a clear reference in the Bible; according to the prophet Zechariah, at the great lamentation in Jerusalem the house of David, Nathan, Levi, and of the Shimeites will wail apart, "every family apart, and their wives apart" (Zech. 12:12-14).

That wailing has been a distinct profession, is confirmed by the Talmud:

> "In Palestine [it is customary that] whenever a professional lamenter comes round people say: 'Let those who are sore at heart weep with him.'"[25]

Also in another tractate:

> "When R. Ishmael died, a professional mourner commenced thus: 'Ye daughters of Israel, weep over R. Ishmael.'"[26]

The Bible expresses the same idea in a somewhat generalized form:

"Because man goeth to his long home, and the mourners go about the streets" (Eccl. 12:5).

Wailing women accompanied the whole funeral procession and used various songs for different ceremonies in the course of it; every ceremony had its specifically prescribed song. The Talmud quotes the texts of eight such songs.[27] Once the corps was buried the wailing would stop.[28] On certain days of the month and on other special days of the Jewish calendar, the functions of the wailing women were somewhat modified or limited.[29]

It was shown earlier that the activity of the wailing women was qualified not only as a profession, but also as an "art."[30] Some biblical expositors consider them even as "poetesses,"[31] and try to justify this by Jer. 9:16-18. They allude also to the characteristic metrical pattern of the *ḳinot,* common to most of the wailing songs, which warrants their classification as "poetry."[32] Undoubtedly, the profession of the wailing women required a certain training. To consider them as "poetesses," however, is scarcely justified. Generally, they used traditional threnodies, which any woman could learn easily. We cannot endow them with poetical talents since these were not required at all for this profession.

Apart from singing, the wailing women had to perform some additional functions connected with music, which may be reconstructed only in a roundabout way, by some allusions in the rabbinic literature. We learn, for instance, that at funerals they used to clap their hands rhythmically (*safaḳ*).[33] This indicates unmistakably that the wailing women, or at least some of them, performed a sort of a dance, since dancing in Ancient Israel has always been accompanied by clapping of hands. That wailing women have actually danced at funerals is evident from certain rabbinic indications, as demonstrated in the section "The Dance." These indications are accompanied with references to the use of certain percussive instruments (*ʾerus,* and *rebiʿit*), akin to hand-drums, which served as rhythmical support for dancing.

Besides the wailing songs, the musical background of the funeral ceremony contained also the playing of *ḥalilim,* though the latter not necessarily by women. According to a rabbinic advice,

> "even the poorest in Israel should hire [for his wife's funeral] not less than two flutes (*ḥalilim*) and one wailing woman (*meḳonenet*)."[34]

It may be inferred from this that whoever had the means could hire more than two instrumentalists and any number of wailing women. This shows that the volume of music at funerals was determined by the wealth and the social standing of the deceased. Sometimes, when no sufficient number of *ḥalil*-players or skilled wailing women were available in a place, they were fetched from other towns.[35] There is an analogy to this in Greece. There, the Karian wailing women were so much in favor that they were frequently brought from far off places for aristocratic funerals.[36]

Another musical function assigned mainly to women is indicated by the psalmist:

> "The Lord giveth the word; the women that proclaim the tidings are a great host" (Ps. 68:12).[37]

The biblical word used here is *mebasserot* (SEPTUAGINT: *euangelizomenois;* VULGATE: *evangelizantibus*). It alludes to women who used to announce victories and celebrate them with songs, musical instruments and dances.

Such women extolling victories are frequently mentioned in the Old Testament,[38] even though not always with the specific term of *mebasserot.* These victory celebrations of individuals and groups have one thing in common: they have an unmistakable religious background, a further indication of the participation of women in early religious ceremonies and ritual actions. Several of these biblical references preserve fragments of songs performed on such occasions, so in Exod. 15:20 (Miriam's song after the passage of the Red Sea), Judg. 5:4 (Deborah's and Barak's triumphant paean), Judith 15:12 ff, 16:1 ff. The term *mebasserot* apparently indicates a semi-religious function, assigned to women outside the ritual ceremony, since they were the ones who used to welcome the returning warriors and celebrate victory.

o o o

The anti-feminine tendency of the later priestly scribes has manifestly influenced some of the rabbinic sages. In general, the singing of women is appreciated by the talmudic literature as one of the most beautiful divine gifts. Yet, the laxity of morals and customs under Hellenistic-Roman influence, and especially the practices of the courtesans, for whose trade music and singing were widely used requisites, gradually changed the aesthetic and moral attitude of the sages toward that erstwhile appreciation. The rabbis say, for instance, that the voice of a woman has a sensual charm, and is considered dangerous for men:

> "Listening to a woman's voice stirs his passions."[39]

The same idea is expressed even more emphatically by another teacher:

> "R. Joseph said: 'When men sing and women join in, it is licentiousness; when women sing and men join in, it is like fire in tow.' "[40]

Still more intolerant are the following rabbinic statements:

> "Rab said: 'The ear which listens to song should be torn off.' Raba said: 'When there is song in a house there is destruction on its threshold.' "[41]
>
> "The harps where to they [the women] sing (*nible ha-sharah*) are susceptible to uncleanness; but the harps of the sons of Levi (*nible bene Levi*) are not susceptible."[42]

A similar hostility toward singing of women can even be found with MAIMONIDES (1135-1204), who declares that secular music is prohibited, especially if it is performed by singing women.

o o o

The rise of Jewish sects restituted to the singing of women its original significance in the religious usage of Jewry. Generally speaking, these sects followed in their religious customs the tradition of the Temple and Synagogue. The religious song of the sacred service, too, has been taken over by the sectarians.

As we already know from an earlier description (pp. 187 ff), the two best known Jewish sects were the Essenes and the Therapeutae, of which the latter—we may now recall specifically—accepted women in their ranks. It only remains to emphasize at this point that whatever formal position women may have occupied within the ranks of the Therapeutae, their musical participation in the common convocations of this sect seems to have been equal to that of men. A couple of verbatim quotations from PHILO's works, outlined but in a general way on the earlier occasions, will help the reader to form his own conclusions to that effect.

While describing a large community of Therapeutae in the neighborhood of Alexandria (PHILO's home-town) which he must have visited frequently,[43] PHILO informs us among other things, that the members of this sect spend six days of the week in isolation in their locked houses, and on the seventh day they assemble in the common praying hall in which, following the custom of the early Synagogue, *men and women* occupy separate places.[44] The oldest of them reads the Scriptures and gives explanations in a simple, unaffected manner. All listen to his talk in silence and with absorption.

> "When the Speaker thinks he has discoursed enough and both sides feel sure that they have attained their object, . . . universal applause showing a general pleasure in the prospect of what is still to follow. Then the Speaker rises and sings a hymn composed as an address to God, either a new one of his own composition or an old one by poets of an earlier day who have left behind them hymns in many measures and melodies, hexameters and iambics, lyrics suitable for processions or in libations and at the altars, or for the chorus[45] whilst standing or dancing, with careful metrical arrangements to fit the various evolutions. After him all the others take their turn as they are arranged and in the proper order while all the rest listen in complete silence except when they have to chant the closing lines or refrains, for then they all lift up their voices, *men and women alike.*"[46]

After this hour of edification follows a common frugal meal.

> "After the supper they hold the sacred vigil which is conducted in the following way. They rise up all together and standing in the middle of the refectory form themselves first into two choirs, *one of men and one of women,* the leader and precentor chosen from each being the most honoured amongst them and also the most musical. Then they sing hymns to God composed of many measures and set to many melodies, sometimes *chanting together,* sometimes taking up the harmony *antiphonally,* hands and feet keeping time in accompaniment, and rapt with enthusiasm reproduce sometimes the lyrics of the procession, sometimes of the halt and of the wheeling and

counter-wheeling of a choice dance. Then when each choir has separately done its own part in the feast, having drunk as in the Bacchic rites of the strong wine of God's love, they mix and *both together become a single choir,* a copy of the choir set up of old besides the Red Sea in honour of the wonders there wrought . . .

It is on this model above all that the choir of the Therapeutae of *either sex,* note in response to note and voice to voice, *the bass of the men blending with the treble of the women, create a harmonious concent* (*symphonia*), *music in the truest sense.* Lovely are the thoughts, lovely the words and worthy of reverence the choristers, and the end and aim of thoughts, words and choristers alike is piety. Thus they continue till dawn, drunk with this drunkenness in which there is no shame, then not with heavy heads or drowsy eyes but more alert and wakeful than when they came to the banquet, they stand with their faces and whole body turned to the east and when they see the sun rising they stretch their hands up to heaven and pray for bright days and knowledge of the truth and the power of keen sighted thinking. And after the prayers they depart each to his private sanctuary once more to ply the trade and till the field of their wonted philosophy."[47] [*Italics ours everywhere*].

PHILO compares the choric singing and dancing of the Therapeutae with the "Song at the Red Sea," the religious manifestation of thanksgiving, offered to the Almighty by Moses, Miriam, and all the children of Israel after their miraculous escape from the pursuing Egyptian legions. As a matter of fact, the singing and dancing of the Therapeutae has not been merely the imitation of the singing at the Red Sea, but the conscious return to the ancient tradition of the Temple, namely to the epoch when in the musical portion of the divine service men and women had their equal share.

Anti-feminine priestly scribes might have obscured this fact in the biblical books. PHILO's report, interpreted correctly, brings again the participation of women in the Jewish cult to the fore.

XII. MUSIC ORGANIZATION

Similar to the rigorous order permeating the religious, political and social institutions in Ancient Israel, her arts and sciences, too, were subjected to strict regulations. As servants of the supposedly omnipotent religion, they both were strongly influenced by their relationship to the cult. Nevertheless, they also were able to develop some independent traits even in this subordinate position; in fact, they soon increased in scope and importance, and their well-planned intrinsic order invested them with the power of giving Jewish intellectual life new stimuli and impulsions.

Literature and poetry were cultivated systematically by specially trained priestly and levitical families. Architectural activity and that of the formative arts, were furthered, as far as the religious laws permitted, by appreciative rulers. Even the sciences, originally in the fetters of dogmatic narrowness, emancipated themselves gradually to their own productivity.

In Cana^can, the Israelites have found foreign peoples with their indigenous manners, customs, and forms of living. The Bible itself states:

> "The Lord thy God shall bring thee into the land . . . with great and goodly cities, which thou didst not build, and houses full of all good things, which thou didst not fill, and cisterns hewn out, which thou didst not hew, vineyards and olive-trees, which thou didst not plant" (Deuter. 6:10,11).

The fact that the Israelites were able to adjust the foreign civilizations of Cana'an to their own conception of culture and morale, and to amalgamate the divergent forms of life into a homogenous national idea, betrays a skill for organization which, to this extent, was lacking even with greater and more powerful nations of Antiquity.

Among all the domains of cultural life, music was perhaps most efficiently organized, and this by no means as a matter of sheer accident. Considering the importance of music in the cult, in public and private life, it was but natural that both as an art and profession, music should have obtained a practical setup, which secured its permanent stability.

In so far as the organization itself is concerned, it is immaterial that the Israelites owe the basic features of their music—like so many other elements of their civilization—to foreign peoples, particularly the Egyptians and Babylonians. The essential thing is that while adjusting the borrowed elements to their own individuality, they were able to create something entirely new. The sense of order, as such, is the main distinguishing characteristic of Jewish life in Antiquity, and the native aptitude for it was the factor that brought about the rapid bloom of the Jewish state with all its cultural institutions.

This will become evident as we shall now examine the music organization of the Israelites in its historical evolution and will generally establish the correlation between Jewish life and Jewish art.

o
o o

Only the relatively late period of Jewish history furnishes certain data from which we may reasonably infer the existence of a distinct musical organization. To be sure, even the musical situation in remote Antiquity already displays a certain intrinsic order; it also yields some early vestiges of a musical profession. But a few isolated and scanty indications are not sufficient, of course, for ascertaining the nature of the initial music organization in Ancient Israel.

Whether or not we may consider the initial musical reference in the Bible (Gen. 4:21) as implying some sort of organized musical activity at the earliest period of Jewish history, cannot be determined conclusively; and yet the patronymic unification of *all* instrumentalists in this passage would seem to point broadly to such possibility. Furthermore, the mention of two rather developed types of instruments—strings (*kinnor*) and woodwinds (*ʿugab*)—especially in conjunction with their players in an exhaustive plural form, might well allude to a distinct stage of tonal evolution which usually does lead to a proper professional differentiation, and eventually a formal musical organization, within any human society.

More light is shed in this respect by the second musical reference in the Scriptures. Laban's promise of an elaborate send-off

> "with mirth and with songs, with tabret and with harp" (Gen. 31: 27)

warrants certain conjectures pertaining to professional or semi-professional musicians in patriarchal times. To be sure, this indication refers rather to Syrian than to Jewish mores of the period; but the musical customs of the ancient peoples in the Near-East did not show essential differences, especially between close neighbors.

The company of prophets,

> "coming down from the high place with a psaltery, and a timbrel, and a pipe, and a harp, before them" (1 Sam. 10:5)

furnishes already a more substantial insight into the existing musical organization, especially because it already takes place in tangible historic times, close to Saul's enthronement.

The music organization of the brotherhoods of prophets represents a turning point in the history of Jewish music. It was not only the germ, but also the model of the forthcoming and flourishing Temple music of the Davidic and Solomonic eras. The sacred musical service initiated and perpetrated by the two monarchs reveals from its very outset a strong intrinsic order so that the conclusion about a long previous development is well warranted. This development took place during the time of the Judges, when the national and political structure of Israel had acquired decisive forms in all its ramifications. At this period, also the gradually unfolding artistic disposition of the Israelites came distinctly to the fore. This created a demand for art, which, in turn, led to the establishment of educational institutions to that effect. All historical evidence seems to converge into the conclusion that an organized profession of musicians, music instruction, and skilled craftsmen for building instruments, existed already in Samuel's and Saul's times.

Saul, for instance, gives orders to

> "seek out a man who is a skillful player on the harp. . . . Then answered one of the young men and said: 'Behold, I have seen a son of Jesse the Beth-lehemite, that is skillful in playing.' . . . Wherefore Saul sent messengers unto Jesse, and said: 'Send me David thy son, who is with the sheep.' " (1 Sam. 16:16 ff).

A simple shepherd body so extraordinarily well versed in playing the *kinnor* that even the functionaries of the royal court took cognizance of it, should certainly appear as something quite incredible for those times. Things become different, however, when we consider that *kinnor*-playing shepherd boy as no more than a cross-section of the music culture of that epoch. One may well surmise the existence of numerous other players of the *kinnor,* among whom David stood out as being uncommonly talented. But a greater number of minstrels presupposes in turn, a certain order and stability of musical practice and its inevitable corollaries: building of instruments and music instruction.

Apart from its artistic significance, David's musicianship has also a deep sociological meaning. His ability of playing the *kinnor* has been the immediate cause for his invitation to the court, and consequently it was the starting point of his future ascendance. It is questionable whether David would ever have become king of his people and fulfilled his historical role, if his artistry had not opened him the way to the suffering king Saul. The meteor-like rise of David from the simplest life to highest honors would have probably never materialized without his musicianship. The erstwhile shepherd boy as future extolled hero and ruler of his nation,—the leading spirit, whose activity was to become decisive for the religious and intellectual history of Israel,—all this turned out to be the immediate consequence of his artistry.

An indirect allusion to an existing music organization is contained in the answer of old Barzillai to David, when the king has invited him to go with him to Jerusalem:

> "I am this day four-score years old; can I discern between good and bad? can thy servant taste what I eat or what I drink? can I hear any more the voice of singing men and singing women? wherefore then should thy servant be yet a burden unto my lord the king?" (2 Sam. 19:36).

The male and female singers alluded to by Barzillai presuppose logically the existence of some kind of organization that was likely to control the supply of qualified performers for royal courts and aristocratic homes.

The first distinct forms of a regular music organization become apparent within the frame of Samuel's brotherhoods of prophets. The religious, moral and educational aspects of these brotherhoods have been treated earlier in detail. But their sociological implications were no less significant. For their assiduous preparatory work led to the rise of the first *professional* musicians. The associations of prophets served as the bridge, so to say, between the earlier class of unorganized musicians and that of later organized professional artists. They were the preparatory stage to the future guild of musicians, soon to become one of the outstanding features of the cultural life in Ancient Israel. Finally, the systematic educational work of the brotherhoods of prophets paved the way for the institution of the organized Temple music.

There existed, however, a basic difference between the musical setup of the association of prophets and that of the future guild of the levitical singers. The musical practice of the "sons of prophets" was not an end in itself, did not represent a profession in the proper sense; it was a part of a curriculum, which aimed at the well-rounded education of religious leaders of the nation. To be sure, music played an important part in this curriculum. It was supposed to embellish the daily religious processions to the "Hill of God," to glamorize the singing of hymns and psalms of the neophyte prophets, and also to stir up the mood of the performer in the course of "prophesying," which ordinarily took place to the accompaniment of instruments.

The musician's work at the Temple, on the other hand, was already a clear-cut *profession.* It afforded the members of this group their subsistence, gave them economic security; it was, therefore, an entirely different sociological phenomenon. With the creation of organized Temple music, two new highly important factors were added to the ritual and artistic aspects: the economic and the social. Both will be examined later in this study.

As a matter of fact, there must have been groups of more or less substantially trained and organized musicians even before music was established in the Temple as a profession. When the ark of the covenant was transferred to Jerusalem, this solemn procession has been accompanied by numerous and apparently well trained singers in addition to a large, capable orchestra. The pioneering work of the schools of prophets is here unmistakable; evidently, the seed sown by the "sons of prophets" came up in a short time.

In evaluating the accomplishments of this huge group of musicians, it must be taken into consideration that most of them, with the possible exception of the "sons of prophets," were amateurs. Professional musicians, *i.e.* those making a living exclusively or mainly by music, might have existed in those days only in restricted numbers. The numerous singers and instrumentalists in David's solemn procession were dilettanti, lovers of music, from all strata of the people, practicing music for the sheer delight of it. These also included the greater part of the prophet-pupils, who had a musical education but did not enter music as a profession.

Music organization in the proper sense became evident when David established music as an integral part of the sacred service. This organization already displays such a clearly developed setup that we cannot help assuming a rather lengthy evolution which led to it. The assumption that levitical music must have existed in some form before David incorporated it into the ritual, becomes a certainty if we examine the report about the second phase of transferring the ark of the covenant to Jerusalem.

Scared by the mysterious death of ʿUzza, David did not proceed with bringing the ark to Jerusalem, but only to the house of Obed-Edom, where it remained for three months. There might have been still another reason for this delay. As we know,

> "Hiram king of Tyre sent messengers to David, and cedar-trees, and masons, and carpenters, to build him a house" (1 Chron. 14:1).

It is quite conceivable that David used these artisans to prepare a dignified place for the ark (1 Chron. 15:1), and he might have welcomed this interruption in order to complete the building. When this was finally erected,

> "David assembled all Israel at Jerusalem, to bring up the ark of the Lord unto its place, which he prepared for it" (1 Chron. 15:3). "And David spoke to the chief of the Levites to appoint their brethren the singers, with instruments of music, psalteries and harps and cymbals, sounding aloud and lifting up the voice with joy" (1 Chron. 15:16).

According to the commandment of David, the Levites appointed the leaders of the song and the other singer-musicians, all quoted with their names in the biblical text. (1 Chron. 15:17-22).

This detailed account proves abundantly that the levitical organization must have passed a previous extended stage of development, enabling David to select the most qualified men out of the multitude of trained singers. Judging from the precise musical indications of his report, the chronicler himself belonged evidently to the levitical guild, and his substantial details give us a clear idea of the Davidic music organization.

First he mentions the three soloists: Heman, Asaph and Jeduthun-Ethan. These were the three outstanding singer-virtuosi of those days, who were appointed as precentors and, furthermore, were vested with the privilege of striking the brass cymbals, a function which constituted a high distinction.

Then, the chronicler quotes a group "of the second degree," in which a certain number of musicians played *nebalim ʿal-ʿalamot,* an instrument designed to double, and thereby to lead the melody in the upper register. The Levites playing it had the function of group leaders; they were particularly qualified musicians, who had to take care of the correct intonation and precise cues.

Another group of singers played *kinnorot ʿal ha-sheminit,* evidently a larger, and probably lower sounding instrument, having had certain accompanying functions. Whether these functions consisted in simply sustaining the melody in another range, or whether the *kinnorot* stressed the melody by a certain rhythmic support, cannot be established conclusively.

This ensemble of singers and instrumentalists had been trained and rehearsed by the chief of the levitical musicians, Chenaniah, "the master of the singers in the song" (1 Chron. 15:27), who also acted as conductor of the performance.

The formation of the Davidic Temple music,—conductor, solo-singers, group leaders of the choir, several choral groups, and, as an instrumental background, instruments carrying the melody, instruments for the accompaniment,—has an almost modern appearance. It contains germinally all the elements necessary nowadays for a choral performance with orchestral accompaniment,—a proof that the Levites knew the secret of employing their artistic and technical means in a competent way.

In this account, the members of the various choral groups are called "brethren.". This does not refer to any family relationship, in general; "brethren" has here merely the meaning of "comrades" or "colleagues," a term the real significance of which will be manifest in the later, final organization of the Temple musicians.

Besides these levitical singers and musicians quoted by their names, a number of priests also were assigned who sounded the sacred silver trumpets (*ḥaẓoẓerot*) (1 Chron. 15:24).

Thus, the external structure of the musical functions at the Davidic Temple music presents itself as follows:

Conductor and choir-master: Chenaniah;

Solo singers and cymbal players: Heman, Asaph and Ethan;

Eight group leaders with instruments carrying the melodic line;

Six other leaders with accompanying instruments;

Seven priests blowing trumpets.

There was, in addition, the main body of choir singers, which must have been quite large, since David, when making his final choice, selected from them the most competent ones, numbering two hundred eighty-eight (1 Chron. 25:7).

At a superficial glance, the biblical report may leave the impression that the accompaniment of the huge choir masses in the above outdoor procession was entrusted merely to fourteen weakly sounding string instruments. But taken at its face-value, such impression would grossly underestimate the practical musical sense of the Levites. For, after all, it is a matter of the most elementary knowledge that choral masses of immense proportions referred to above have to be accompanied by an adequate number of instrumentalists, in order to intone correctly, and also to stay together melodically and rhythmically. We know that singing instruction in Ancient Israel was mostly coupled with parallel teaching of some accompanying instruments (singing and playing were merely the different phases of expression of the same artistic activity). It is therefore safe to assume that the eight *nebel*-players and the six *kinnor*-players, quoted by their names, were merely respective leaders of similar instrumental groups, just as they were the precentors of a choral group.

In the light of this reasoning, one may well realize that the biblical report does not deal here with a modest instrumental body of fourteen musicians, a number entirely disproportionate not only to the great number of participants but to the importance of the event itself. On the contrary, we have to assume a large orchestra, perhaps several of them, distributed along the procession; and a huge choir of singers, led by the levitical musicians specifically named in the chronicles.

The assumption of a large choral body on this solemn occasion is, in fact, confirmed by the chronicler himself. When David has made his final preparations to select the most qualified singers for his music organization, the number of all the levitical singers is given as four-thousand (1 Chron. 23:5); all these, with some exceptions, might have participated on this memorable occasion.

From the above mentioned seventeen singer-musicians and seven priests David made a scrupulous choice and put the very best of them before the ark when it was finally brought to Jerusalem (1 Chron. 16:5,6). Then follows the most important indication of the chronicler, the announcement of the starting point of the organized musical service:

"Then on that day did David first ordain to give thanks unto the Lord, by the hand of Asaph and his brethren" (1 Chron. 16:7).

Thus, the transfer of the ark of covenant to Jerusalem was at the same time the birth-hour of the organized and permanent Temple music.

From the very beginning, the service of the levitical musicians was strictly regulated (1 Chron. 16:37,42).

By this, the principle of daily musical performances in the sacred service was firmly established and the functions of the temporary office-holders assigned. Now king David could turn to the final organization of the Temple music, according to a carefully prepared plan. Until then, he "appointed" the singers and musicians; from now on, they were "elected" for the permanent service by means of a procedure that was carried out by the representatives of the musicians themselves. With this, the corporate spirit of the musicians is revealed for the first time, the whole significance of which will be manifest in the later development of the music organization.

The chronicler describes the election itself in all its details:

"And David gathered together all the princes of Israel, with the priests and the Levites. And the Levites were numbered, from thirty years old and upward; and their number by their polls, man by man, was thirty and eight thousand" (1 Chron. 23:2,3).

From this number were selected those

"to oversee the work of the house of the Lord," as well as "the officers, judges and doorkeepers," and, finally, the Levites trained in music, "four thousand to praise the Lord 'with instruments which I made to praise therewith' " (1 Chron. 23:5).

If there were four thousand singers and musicians among the Levites, that is in a single tribe of Israel, it is logical to assume that in the entire nation the number of those well-versed in musical matters must have been proportionately higher. This is not at all surprising if we consider that after the gradual decline of the schools of prophets, the musical education was taken over by the levitical music school. Even prior to the creation of the Davidic Temple music, the Levites constituted a special class which assumed the cultivation of musical art to be a kind of privilege. Long before David's time, still during Saul's reign, the Levites seem to have been joined together in a sort of corporation, as evident from the chronicler's report:

"And these are the singers, heads of the fathers' houses of the Levites, who dwelt in the chambers and were free from other service; for they were employed in their work day and night." (1 Chron. 9:33,34).

After David had selected the best qualified singers from the multitude of Levitical musicians, his problem was to build a practical and permanent organism from this mass. For a big and solmen occasion in the open air, like the transfer of the ark of the covenant, a mammoth choir and a large orchestra have been appropriate. For the relatively small "tabernacle," which David erected as a sanctuary, a music service had to be established, adequate to the available space, but ensuring at the same time a well functioning permanent daily routine. The way David solved this problem was exemplary from the artistic point of view as well as from that of practical organization.

From four thousand levitical singers and musicians David selected, after careful scrutiny, and obviously in agreement with the musicians themselves, those

> "that were instructed in singing unto the Lord, even all that were skillful;and the number of them was two hundred fourscore and eight" (1 Chron. 25:7).

This still large choir was divided into twenty-four "wards," or groups of twelve singers each, under the leadership of a precentor for each one. All these twenty-four group leaders are mentioned by their names in the chronicles, a sign of the importance of their office.

Following this arrangement, all those concerned

> "cast lots ward against ward, as well the small as the great, the teacher as the scholar" (1 Chron. 25:8).

Thus, the order of sequence of the groups was determined by lot, by which procedure all disputes for precedence and all personal or professional sensibilities have been eliminated from the very outset.

From now on, the two hundred eighty-eight singers referred to constituted a closed corporation or guild, which had its own rules, its own precepts and the members of which, united by a pronounced class-consciousness, guarded jealously their special privileges. The Temple musicians had their own dwellings and lived in settlements in and around Jerusalem (Eza 2:70; Neh. 7:73; 13:10). As it fitted their sacred office, they represented a prominent and privileged class.

This first election shows, furthermore, that the guild of singers was organized akin to a trade-union. By casting the lot, the young as the old, the teachers as the pupils enjoyed equal rights. Within the corporation, or guild, there were no preferences, no priorities of the older and more experienced ones. The singers admitted to the guild were "all masters"; all had the same privileges and the same duties. Jealousies or disputes of precedence had been eliminated by the voluntary submission of all members to the decision drawn by the lot. Thus, the Temple musicians were, from the very start, a secluded professional group, guarding strictly their prerogatives, enjoying great esteem and gradually acquiring considerable power.

At the first election, the group leaders were chosen exclusively from among the sons of Asaph, Heman and Jedithun (Ethan), not merely because they evidently were best qualified for the sacred service, but probably also to honor through their sons the fathers, who had earned great merits in the shaping of the Temple music.

According to the chronicler, the number of the sons of the three famous singers has been twenty-four (1 Chron. 25:2-5). It would appear, therefore, as if the twenty-four "wards" owed their existence exclusively to the fortuitous circumstance that Aseph, Heman and Jedithun just happened to have twenty-four sons.[1] However, the number of the groups also seems to have coincided with some practical necessities of the sacred service.

The central point of the divine service was the sacrifice; the sacrifice has always been accompanied with singing of the Levites.[2] There were three daily regular services, at morning, *shaḥarit,* at noon, *minḥa,* and in the evening, *ma'arib.* The daily regular sacrifices were offered in the morning and evening services. Besides, there were numerous additional sacrifices, voluntary or expiatory offerings, the volume and nature of which was most diversified. These were offered in the noon service, requiring priestly as well as levitical assistance. Thus, the levitical singers had three regular services a day.

Each "ward" consisted of twelve singer-musicians, a number adequate for the limited capacity of David's sanctuary. In the three daily sacrificial rites one of these groups always provided the musical background. On the Sabbat, according to the increased solemnity of the day, two groups may have participated in each service. The three daily services of one group on weekdays, and the three services of two groups each on the Sabbat give as a result twenty-four services a week, just as many as there were "wards." On the three great yearly festivals, Passover, Weeks, and Tabernacles the number of the groups must have been increased considerably,—probably eight for every service,—so that at these festivals all the twenty-four groups performed on the same day.[3]

The coincidence of the number of groups and of the normal weekly services would lead to the assumption that the groups alternated for each service, so that every group had to provide music for one service a week. This alone would have been a rather comfortable duty for the singers. In reality, the working conditions of the singers have been even more convenient.

According to some vague indications of the chronicler (1 Chron. 9:25), the groups of singers, like those of the priests and porters, alternated weekly. The weekly alternation is confirmed by JOSEPHUS,[4] and reported also by the Mishnah.[5] This would have amounted to a strange situation, namely that each group, after one week's continuous service, would have been unoccupied for twenty-three consecutive weeks, almost half a year, except when they were needed for the high holidays. However, there are weighty artistic and technical reasons against this assumption.

The performances of the Temple singers were justly famous in Antiquity for their artistic perfection. It would have been scarcely possible to attain and maintain this perfection if the singers had had so rare an opportunity to participate in the sacred service. A more frequent schedule was an indispensable necessity for them to become familiarized not only with the complicated ritual, but also with performing *in public.* To be sure, they could be taught during the rehearsals how to master their singing and playing; but it is common knowledge that the criterion of an artistic accomplishment cannot be reached in rehearsals alone, however assiduous they might be, but in the performance itself. For artistic reasons, therefore, the assumption that each group had one continuous service a week, followed by such a long interruption, is highly improbable.

On the other hand, the alternation of the groups after each service would have had other disadvantages. Each of the three daily services was different, not only in the prayers and lections but also with regard to the other ceremonies requiring music. Furthermore, on the different days of the week, the Levites sang different psalms.[6] In the additional sacrifices of the noon-service the accompanying music had to be adapted to the number and nature of the multitude of offerings. All these differences were of such kind that alternating groups would have had difficulties to accommodate themselves to the ever changing necessities. This would certainly have influenced unfavorably the musical rendition. But the perfection of this rendition was precisely the strong point of the levitical singers and the justification of their fame. Therefore, for practical reasons, the idea of the groups alternating after each service must likewise be discarded.

The truth might be found in the middle. A simple solution, satisfying at once the principles of artistry and organization could be reached by assuming that the groups changed every day, in other words, that the three daily services were provided by the same group. For weekdays one, and for Sabbat two groups, would have amounted to a three weeks' turn for each group. After three weeks, the turn would have started with a different group, so that every group would gradually participate in all the week-day services, thus becoming thoroughly familiar with all their particularities. The increased number of services on the high holidays would have shortened somewhat the turn of three weeks, but this would not affect the principle itself.

The advantages of this schedule are obvious. The singers would have had ample opportunity to prepare themselves for the services, *i.e.* to attend the necessary rehearsals, to learn new psalms and also to teach the young generation liturgical singing. Furthermore, they would have had the possibility to till their fields and gardens, a prime economic necessity for the levitical singers for their subsistence.

Though the assumption of the daily alternating groups is not corroborated by any coeval sources, it has a high degree of probability for artistic and organizational as well as for economic reasons.

o
o o

After the solid foundation of Temple music had been laid by David, music as an independent art took an unsuspected rise. Through assiduous, never relenting rehearsals, and through the fanatic zeal of the music leaders, an artistic perfection, unmatched until then in Antiquity, was achieved in a relatively short time.

This perfection must have manifested itself most conspicuously at the consecration of Solomon's newly built Temple, on which occasion apparently all the two hundred and eighty-eight musicians have taken part. The musical coordination of this huge vocal and instrumental ensemble reached such a degree of precision that the generally dispassionate chronicler could not resist to dispense a particular praise:

> "Also the Levites who were the singers, all of them, even Asaph, Heman, Jedithun, and their sons and their brethren, arrayed in fine linen, with cymbals and psalteries and harps, stood at the east end of the altar, and with them hundred and twenty priests sounding with trumpets—it came even to pass, when the trumpeters and singers were as one, to make one sound to be heard in praising and thanking the Lord" (2 Chron. 5:12,13).

"As one" and "one sound" signify here a precision of the performance, which may have appeared extraordinary in view of the multitude of the performers.

This impressive account represents what may perhaps be termed as the first *musical criticism* in the history of human civilization. The "critic," however, does not confine himself to a mere lavishing his praise upon the well-disciplined performers. He also describes the reaction of the "audience," that is of the worshippers, and this, indeed, gives us even a more penetrating, though indirect, insight into the artistic quality of the performance.

As a matter of fact, the uncommon achievement of the musicians created such a lofty transport, almost a mystic ecstasy, among the listeners that they imagined to have seen a cloud filling the house, which was identified with God's presence and believed to represent His actual approbation of the event:

> "And when they lifted up their voice with the trumpets and cymbals and instruments of music, and praised the Lord: 'for He is good, for His mercy endureth for ever'; that then the house was filled with a cloud, even the house of the Lord, so that the priests could not stand to minister by reason of the cloud; for the glory of the Lord filled the house of God" (2 Chron. 5:13,14).

This cloud certainly could not have been the smoke created ordinarily by the burning incense, since this was a regular occurrence in every sacred service. The chronicler's statement, therefore, intimates something quite extraordinary and miraculous. Even if we disregard the miraculous connotation of this report, still the fact of an extraordinary musical event remains, the perfection of which induced the chronicler to express his admiration by way of a metaphoric paraphrase.

This is the only scriptural report according to which God manifested Himself in a symbolically perceptible form to the entire people, and not merely to some chosen mortals. And it is quite significant that this transcendental occurrence was apparently meant by the chronicler to represent a heavenly "reward" for an outstanding musical performance.

Similar to David, Solomon furthered music with fervor and understanding. He kept up the Temple music as a perpetual institution (2 Chron. 8:14). He ordered showy instruments of precious wood for his musicians (1 Kings 10:12; 2 Chron. 9:11).

It may well be surmised that the settlements of the Temple singers in their own villages and colonies are also due to Solomon's initiative, though there are no direct indications thereto in the biblical text. We know, however, that Solomon pursued the founding of cities on a large scale (*cp.* 2 Chron. 8:4 ff). A later source informs us that the Levitical singers returning from Babylonian captivity settled again in the places where they, or their ancestors, dwelt prior to the exile (Ezra 2:70; Neh. 7:73). Thus, it does actually appear that these settlements represented a privilege accorded by the art-loving king Solomon to his singers.

o
o o

It is understandable that the paramount importance of Temple music in Israel's life eclipsed somewhat the secular music and secular musicians. Nevertheless, besides the levitical music organization, a similar institution of the secular musicians has soon evolved. The nature of the latter may be ascertained but indirectly. However, biblical exegesis is almost unanimous in assuming its existence. BUDDE says, for instance:

> "We possess more than one evidence that already in primeval times Israel had a guild of singers, that is people well versed in musical art, who amassed a treasure of songs, of which they availed themselves at will, just as did the singers of Homer, or the medieval wandering minstrels . . . In the introduction of a fragment of a war song it is said: 'Wherefor they that speak in parables say' . . ." (Num. 21:27).[7] "They that speak in parables" (or "in proverbs") have been the poet-singer-musicians, the folkbards, the wandering minstrels of heroic times, who were "the strongest levers of the public opinion, especially in times of national decisions. They were considered as having the insight, just as the *shâir* of the ancient Arabs, who was requested by the tribe to give an efficient oracle when it was going to start a feud."[8]

This ancient institution survived in Israel's subsequent national existence, though in a changed form. In the theocratic state the secular poet-musicians have lost their political significance, but gained all the more in popularity. They became a national institution, without which public and private festivities would have been inconceivable. This procured them the basis for their eventual union into a professional group.

The guild of secular musicians was far from being as coherent and potent as that of the Temple singers; if for no other reason, because the former did not enjoy the same privileges and were not furthered by the kings as were the latter. For the broader dissemination of music among the masses, however, the secular musicians have accomplished infinitely more than the Levites. These have considered themselves a sort of professional elite, admitting only their closest relatives into their caste and keeping out any non-Levite. The secular musicians showed a much more liberal attitude. Their art had its roots in the people and served the people. Anybody having the desire and the aptitude, could partake in their instruction. How widely spread popular music, including the playing of instruments, was in Israel becomes evident from the description of the festivities on the occasion of Solomon's anointment as king, during which "all the people piped with pipes" (1 Kings 1:40).

Through the professional organization of secular musicians a breach was produced in the idea of a single musical caste and in the sole qualification of musicians as members of a family or tribe. From now on, the musical profession was no longer the privilege of a tribe, a class, a guild. Not the birth, nor the fact of belonging to the tribe of Levi were decisive for becoming a musician, but the *aptitude,* the *talent.* Music became a *free lancing profession,* untrammelled by ritual or religious fetters. This was indeed an important metamorphosis historically, artistically, and sociologically.

The repercussions of this change are manifestly evident in a specific case concerning the young David. His spectacular career was largely due to the fact that he was "a skillful player on the harp," and because Saul happened to need such a man to dissipate his melancholia (1 Sam. 16:17 ff).

> "By music, with which was then combined not only poetry, but whatever of cultivation belonged to the age, he had first found access to the person of the king,"

says HERDER.[9] The qualifications of the artist had opened to him the road from the lowest social stratum to honor and fame. The free lance profession and the free competition became from then on the main criteria of the musical artist's career.

o
o o

After Solomon's death the Jewish state has been passing through the heaviest political and religious convulsions. The state was broken up into two kingdoms—of Israel and Judah; in both, good and bad kings succeeded one another, warring between themselves and against foreign enemies, thereby incurring the gravest danger to the existence of the Jewish nation. The religion itself was constantly menaced; fickle kings abandoned the true faith and served foreign deities; again others, moved by pious zeal, tried to bring back the misled people to the right path.

These political vicissitudes, the recurring apostasy and repentant return of the people to Yahveh's cult, had an immediate repercussive effect upon the Temple music. Each time an idolatrous king abandoned the religion of the fathers, the Temple music was condemned to silence and threatened with extinction. Ordinarily, a few years, even a few months of inactivity suffice to jeopardize the stability of a musical tradition. And from this state until complete destruction is only a relatively short way. It must be remembered that the ancient Jewish musical art was based exclusively on oral tradition, which could be preserved only if maintained without interruption.

It is the merit of the professional organization, and at the same time a proof of the artistic consciousness of the Jewish musicians, that they understood how to preserve the traditional musical heritage despite all the adversities of fortune. As has been shown on a previous occasion (pp. 427 ff), after each period of idolatry the music continued to function as though there had been no interruption at all.

In addition to these artistic standards and, in fact, *because* of maintaining them unremittingly on a high level, the musicians' organization was able to keep up, during the many troublesome periods, the material welfare of its members. Thus, they succeeded in impressing king Hezekiah with their inordinate professional skill to such an extent that this newly enthroned ruler himself took measures to secure a reputable livelihood for the singers. As the chronicler reports:

> "He [Hezekiah] commanded the people that dwelt in Jerusalem to give the portion of the priests and the Levites,that they might give themselves to the law of the Lord" (2 Chron. 31:4).

And the people, in grateful acknowledgment of the singers' achievements, brought gifts in such volume that the king had to build new chambers for their storage and appoint for their administration quite a number of new officers, all of whom are mentioned by their names in the chronicles (2 Chron. 31:11-15). These measures did not apply only to the Levites dwelling in Jerusalem; the king's solicitude was extended to the priests and Levites

> "that were in the fields of the open land about their cities, in every city."

These, too, received their share from the people's contributions (2 Chron. 31:19).

This measure provided to support the musicians by an "assessment," that ostensibly was "voluntary," but actually represented a special tax imposed upon the population. The return of this tax was reserved exclusively to the functionaries of the Temple. This assessment corresponds therefore to a kind of "church-tax" in today's sense. From here to the next stage of development, in which the Temple singers were supported by fiscal means, there was merely a short step. It could not last long before the musicians were elevated into the privileged class of state functionaries.

o
o o

It also must have been largely due to the well-calculated efforts of the selfsame musicians' organization that its members were appointed as indispensable experts for the restitution of the ancient sacred instruments of music at the renewal of Yahveh's faith by king Josiah (630-609 B.C.E.). Moreover, in the course of his reign, and probably again under the suggestive influence of this organization, Josiah actually became an ardent patron of musical art. When he died young on the battle field, his loss was deeply mourned by the musicians:

> "And all the singing men and singing women spoke of Josiah in their lamentations, unto this day; and they made them an ordinance in Israel" (2 Chron. 35:25).

This signifies that for this art loving monarch a permanent national day of mourning was established. Only a strong organized professional group could actually introduce this sort of commemoration as an official "ordinance" for the whole people. No other king has ever been honored in this way.

The report shows also that women belonged to the professional corporation of the musicians. Here it is openly admitted that women were fully authorized members of the guild of musicians, having the same privileges and the same duties as men.

o
o o

What the musical organization of the singers accomplished in the Babylonian exile represents the most outstanding page of its history. In a foreign country, in suppression, in working secretly, it succeeded not only to keep up the musical practice, but to preserve intact the ancient tradition, in short, to save Jewish music, sacred as well as secular, from total perdition. During the forty-eight years of captivity the new generations had to be instructed each time anew, the traditional music had to be transmitted from mouth to mouth, from ear to ear. Without foreseeable hope for return into the old homeland, a complex art discipline was kept alive, for which there was apparently no immediate use in the exile, and which was virtually meaningless for Jews deprived of their sanctuary. Without the methodic work of the musicians and the efficiency of their organization Jewish music would have perished irretrievably.

o
o o

The prominent position of the musicians has been evident already in the First Temple; after the return from the exile it has risen even to a higher level.

The first step of the repatriates was to settle again in their ancient domiciles (Ezra 2:70; Neh. 7:73). Significantly enough, in enumerating the various categories of Temple functionaries, the singers are quoted always separately—a proof of their special status. As was mentioned earlier, the priests and Levites have dwelt

> "in the fields of the open land about their cities, in every city" (2 Chron. 31:19),

which points to the existence, before and after the Babylonian exile, of specific settlements for musicians.

After the return, the Temple musicians took again possession of their erstwhile functions. The exercises in singing and playing, never neglected in the exile, were resumed with increased zeal. And so we see that at the laying of the foundation of the new Temple, shortly after the return, the levitical singers provided as before the music to the ceremony (Ezra 3:10,11).

The artistic importance of the levitical singers has not been affected by the Babylonian exile. Socially and economically, their situation has even improved compared with their ancient status. DARIUS and ARTAXERXES have submitted the position of the Temple musicians to a thorough reform, thereby creating an entirely new basis for their existence. In a generous way, they ordered that the Temple singers, supported until then by voluntary contributions of the people, should be elevated to the status of employed functionaries and their subsistence henceforth provided by the royal treasury.

Already king CYRUS, after approving the construction of the new sanctuary with the restitution of the ancient divine service, has decreed that the ministers of the cult, including the singers, should receive regular dues, that is a kind of "salary." These dues were mainly natural products, and have been taken from the king's estates:

> "That of the king's goods, even of the tribute beyond the River, expenses be given with all diligence unto these men, that they not be hindered."

CYRUS ordered that such dues "let be given them day by day without fail" (Ezra 6:8,9), and Darius confirmed explicitly his predecessor's edict.

Soon, the Temple singers became beneficiaries of even richer privileges. About eighty years after the first colony of captives had returned under Zerubbabel, a second followed in 458 B.C.E. under Ezra's leadership (Ezra 7:7). Ezra, the scribe, must have enjoyed specific favors with king ARTAXERXES, because the monarch gave him not only the permission for the second group to return, but

> "the king granted him all his requests,"

and they were by no means small (Ezra. 7:6). The king's edict, which Ezra carried with him in a copy, enumerates all the things the repatriates were allowed to carry along, practically everything they possessed in Babylon, and also what they needed after the return for the perpetuation of their cult,

> "the vessels that are given thee for the service of the house of thy God, . . . and whatsoever more shall be needful for the house of thy God, which thou shalt have occasion to bestow, bestow it out of the king's treasure house" (Ezra 7:19,20).

For the Temple musicians Ezra demonstrated particular solicitude. He received from ARTAXERXES the repeated confirmation of the daily salary for the singers, as guaranteed by his predecessor:

> "For there was a commandment from the king concerning them, and a sure ordinance concerning the singers, as every day required" (Neh. 11:23).

Besides this salary, furnished by the king's treasury, the Temple singers had still another income. Out of gratitude,

> "all Israel in the days of Zerubbabel, and in the days of Nehemiah, gave the portions of the singers and the porters, as every day required" (Neh. 12:47).

The economic welfare of the singers was thus secured from two sides. Their wealth, and with it their influence and social standing, increased accordingly.

Apart from economic advantages, Ezra received from his royal benefactor further rights and privileges. The above quoted edict of ARTAXERXES stipulates:

> "Also we announce to you, that touching any of the priests, and Levites, the singers, porters, Nethinim, or servants of this house of God, it shall not be lawful to impose tribute, impost, or toll, upon them" (Ezra 7:24).

This constituted the exemption of the musicians from all taxes, a privilege surpassing even that which king CYRUS granted to the corporation of the Temple singers. From now on, they were not only state functionaries, but moreover were elevated to the rank of tax-exempt ministers of the sanctuary.

o o o

After the repatriates have settled in their ancient dwellings, they started to rebuild what was destroyed and, having secured their material existence, proceeded to re-establish their religious and national institutions. Surmounting many obstacles, and despite all sorts of intrigues, they have built strong walls around Jerusalem, thus insuring the new sanctuary with an efficient protection. Again,

> "they appointed the porters and the singers and the Levites" (Neh. 7:1).

After having protected Jerusalem with the new walls against hostile attacks, Nehemiah ordered a census of the people, based upon the book of genealogy of the repatriates. The number of Temple singers, "the children of Asaph," which has been hundred and twenty-eight at the first return (Ezra 2:41), has risen to hundred and forty-eight (Neh. 7:44), while the number of secular male and female singers increased from two hundred (Ezra 2:65) to two hundred and forty-five (Neh. 7:67). This increase, considered numerically, is not very substantial for a lapse of more than half a century. The picture changes, however, if we take into account the economic situation prevailing at that period.

The first decades after the return were filled with securing the bare existence and attending to the reconstruction. Rebuilding the national institutions demanded undivided energies of the repatriates. We should not lose sight of the fact, furthermore, that about fifty thousand persons returned to the old home with Zerubbabel, and not more than two thousand with Ezra. For this relatively small population hundred and forty-eight liturgical, and two hundred and forty-five secular musicians represent a high proportional number. It is due merely to the pressing need for musical activity of the Jewish people that all the musicians referred to could make a living. As a proof of the artistic disposition of the Israelites the fact is significant that in these difficult times of national reconstruction, and despite the natural reduction by death, there was even an increase in both categories of musicians—liturgical and secular. This increase clearly shows that the musical culture never was abandoned by the Jews, not even during the most difficult period of struggle for their survival. At the same time, this also explains why, after the return, such a relatively large number of musicians has found means for their livelihood and that their number was increasing at all.

o
o o

Up to this point, we have examined mostly the economic and social situation concerning the liturgical musicians. Let us now scrutinize briefly the very same subject with regard to the secular musicians in Ancient Israel.

Members of this category have been free lance artists, working for remuneration. Their number certainly would not have been too large without the constant presence of a sufficient and remunerative work for them. But even under the most oppressive circumstances, such as was experienced by the Jews in the Babylonian captivity, the latter would never renounce the joys of music. As a result, there was bound to exist, in their midst, a ceaseless demand for the creators and performers of secular music.

The wages paid to the secular musicians, whether in money or in natural products, were the basis of his existence. These wages are determinative of the free lance artistic profession and represent, even in a somewhat rudimentary form, the "honorarium" of the artist. In the history of civilization, this notion received its full impact at a much later epoch, namely, with the beginning of modern concert institutions (middle of the 18th century).[10] But its artistic and social implications already prevail unmistakably in Ancient Israel. In addition to wages, the secular musician of those days might have had some income from making and repairing musical instruments.

All indications favor the assumption that, similar to the musicians of the Temple, secular musicians have likewise been organized in a guild. Its purpose, naturally, would virtually be the same, namely to safeguard the professional interests of its members. As compared with the Levites, the secular musician was, of course, in a less favorable economical position. He was, however, by no means handicapped by this. The secular musician in Israel was not the type of a poor and despised wandering minstrel; he never represented the itinerant miserable profession which in the medieval times brought into discredit popular music.

The secular musician in Israel was a free man; he belonged to a respected and well liked class; he had a remunerative profession; his livelihood was secured by the insatiable craving for music of the Jewish people; he was the recognized representative of popular art, conscious of his mission, and sure of his influence upon his audience. There existed no musical "proletariat," the musician was no "pariah" in Israel. There he was a giver, like the folkbards of heroic times, and on the other side of the "footlights," there was a crowd of enthusiastic and grateful receivers.

Thus, the sociological features of the Jewish secular musician transpire in a form which was far ahead of his time. They show a stage of development for which there is a parallel only in our own epoch. Perhaps more than by the institutions of Temple musicians, the artistic sense of the Jewish people is evidenced by the sociological aspect of the secular musical profession.

o
o o

As employees of the state, exempt from all concern for their livelihood, the post-Babylonian Temple musicians gained not only prosperity, but high authority and increased influence. After Nehemiah's census, long derelict lands seem to have been apportioned anew, giving the officers of the sacred service a considerable share of it. This at least may be concluded from certain indications of the chroniclers. We learn, for instance, that

> "the singers had builded them villages round about Jerusalem" (Neh. 12:29),

where they tilled their fields and gardens. There were such settlements not only around Jerusalem, but also in farther situated places. For the solemn dedication of the new walls of Jerusalem

> "they sought the Levites out of all their places, to bring them to Jerusalem, to keep the dedication with gladness, both with thanksgivings, and with singing, with cymbals, psalteries, and with harps" (Neh. 12:27).

It is evident also from the chronicler's report that the land was settled according to a consistent plan and that the office holders of the Temple received their due share:

> "In the cities of Judah dwelt every one in his possession in their cities, to wit, Israelites, the priests and the Levites, and the Nethinim, and the children of Solomon's servants" (Neh. 11:3).

Even if the apportioning of the ample land in the abandoned regions did not constitute any particular favor towards the functionaries of the Temple, this might have contributed considerably to the welfare and, by implication, to the social rise of the musicians.

The outstanding position of the Temple musicians in Jewish life has led gradually to a rivalry between the priests and singers. And on one recorded occasion of an economic conflict this rivalry brought forth a trial of strength in which the singers obtained full victory. This was a "strike" of the musicians, a stoppage of work due to "non-payment" of their salaries. The chronicler reports about it in detail; his description is so vivid, and he deals so clearly with the motives and consequences of this economic struggle, that it would be almost superfluous to add anything to his account.

It was mentioned above that the Temple musicians received from the royal treasury a regular salary; also that

> "all Israel in the days of Zerubbabel, and in the days of Nehemiah, gave the portions of the singers and the porters, as every day required" (Neh. 12:47).

As time passed these voluntary contributions, together with the regular emoluments, have become so voluminous that the storage rooms for all sorts of products became insufficient and new chambers had to be built for them. The administration of these chambers has been assigned to the priest Eliashib, who had a relative named Tobiah. The latter was

> "the servant, the Ammonite," who was "grieved exceedingly for that there was come a man to seek the welfare of the children of Israel" (Neh. 2:10).

Through intrigues and subterfuges he tried to thwart the construction of the new city walls (Neh. 3:35; 4:2), and even was after Nehemiah's life, by luring him into a pitfall (Neh. 6:10).

This priest Eliashib turned out to be an unfaithful steward of his office. As the chronicler reports,

> "Eliashib the priest, who was appointed over the chambers of the house of God, being allied unto Tobiah, had prepared for him a great chamber, where aforetime they laid the meal-offerings, the frankincense, and the vessels, and the tithes of the corn, the wine, and the oil, which were given by commandment to the Levites, and the singers, and the porters" (Neh. 13:4,5).

Eliashib not only granted to his relative illegal advantages, but, in addition, has withheld the salary due to the Levites and singers.

The complaints against these abuses apparently remained unanswered and so, as a last resort, the musicians proceeded to a stoppage of work "for non-payment of their salary," to use today's legal expression.

At that time Nehemiah happened to be in Babylonia. After his return, he saw

> "the evil that Eliashib had done for Tobiah, in preparing him a chamber in the courts of the house of God" (Neh. 13:7). He learned "that the portions of the Levites had not been given them; so that the Levites and the singers, that did the work, were fled every one to his field" (Neh. 13:10).

In the modern exegesis, this resolute "flight" has been repeatedly explained by the assumption that, deprived of their "portions," the singers could not support themselves in Jerusalem and that the bare necessities of life forced them to withdraw to their dwellings outside the city. At a superficial glance, this might have constituted an excusable reason to abandon the sacred service. A closer scrutiny, however, does not bear out this argument.

The entire situation seems to indicate that the excuse of the singers—the lacking subsistence in Jerusalem—was but a pretext for striking. It is highly unlikely that the Levites and singers could not have been regularly supplied with provisions from their possessions so close to the city. Even those settled farther off could always find ways and means to receive their supply from their own provisions. Furthermore, there might have been a sufficient number of wealthy citizens in Jerusalem who would have been glad to extend hospitality to one or several Levites or singers. The musicians could never have used successfully the pretext of subsistency for any actions that would jeopardize the sacred service.

It is far more logical to assume that this strike represented a pure and simple contest of power between the priests and singers. The obvious abuse carried on by Eliashib—apparently in connivance with his priestly colleagues—induced the musicians to take the law into their own hands. What no other class could afford to venture, the musicians dared to do, relying upon the power of their organization. The guild protected its members from the consequences of the risky step; and their stable "solidarity" eliminated the danger of any "strike-breaking." All these notions of our modern trade unions are clearly manifest in the biblical conflict about wages under consideration.

And so the strike could not end but with the victory of the musicians. When Nehemiah returned from Babylon and saw the abuses, he took measures not against the striking singers, but against the priests who tolerated such abuses:

> "Then contended I with the rulers, and said: 'Why is the house of God forsaken?'" (Neh. 13:11).

Nehemiah's first concern was to reinstitute the interrupted service:

> "And I gathered them together, and set them [*i.e.* the Levites and singers] in their places" (Neh. 13:11).

Through the abusive appropriation, the provisions designed for the Levites and singers must have shrunk badly, so that an appeal was addressed to the people for renewed voluntary contributions:

> "Then brought all Judah the tithe of the corn and the wine and the oil unto the treasuries" (Neh. 13:12).

With the divine service restored, and the livelihood of the singers assured, Nehemiah turned to deserved castigations. The unfaithful Eliashib, and probably also his accomplices, have been deposed,

> "and I made treasurers over the treasuries, Shelemiah the priest, and Zadok the scribe, and of the Levites, Pedaiah, and next to them was Hanan the son of Zaccur, the son of Mattaniah; for they were counted faithful, and their office was to distribute unto their brethren" (Neh. 13:13).

These Levites and singers were actual trustees, elected or appointed for a proper distribution of the provisions and prevention of any misuses in the future.

The quoted analogies with the contemporary struggle of the working classes are by no means fortuitous; nor do they represent an artificial interpretation of the biblical text. Their existence is as real as it could be. All the conventional scrambles between employers and employees are unmistakably present in the chronicler's report: strike for non-payment of wages; solidarity of the strikers; avoidance of penalization of the strikers; and, finally, appointment of trustees in order to prevent further abuses. The incident, described so vividly by the chronicler, represents the very first recorded struggle of workmen in the history of mankind. The fact that the musicians of Israel succeeded to fight it out victoriously is the proof of the external and internal strength of their professional organization.

Toward the end of the sanctuary's existence the levitical singers once again have run the risk of a trial of power with the priestly class. Temporarily, they again obtained complete victory. Eventually, however, this success turned against the victors themselves and became instrumental in the total crumbling of the musicians' organization.

The ever increasing esteem their congregation bestowed upon them, and an overemphasized class-consciousness gradually caused the Temple musicians to consider themselves a sort of professional aristocracy. The inner satisfaction afforded them by their artistry and by being officers of the divine service, as well as their economic independence, did not suffice them any longer. They aspired to more external honors. Conscious of their own influence, and filled with an exorbitant self-reliance, they wanted to be equal in attire and in rank with the immediate ministers of God, the priests. So they demanded of king AGRIPPA II (reigned 53-100 C.E.) the privilege to wear, while in function, the white linen garments of the priests.

This request must at first have encountered considerable resistance. For JOSEPHUS reports about this presumptuous demand with a deep moral indignation.[11] This is understandable, since JOSEPHUS was himself the offspring of a priestly family, and the Aaronites represented the highest class in Israel, the nobility of the nation, as it were. He considered it, therefore, an insolence that the singers should have tried to become the equals of the nobles.

The priests, too, must have been quite indignant about such arrogance. From the priestly point of view, the request of the levitical singers was nothing less than an infringement of the existing divine order. The class differences between the priests and Levites, and even between the various categories of Levites, must have been very prominent in those times. According to a talmudic account, the still young R. JOSHUA, at that time a levitical singer, wanted to help with closing the Temple gates. An older Levite, belonging to the class of the porters (*i.e.* of the guardians of the gates), debarred him from helping, in saying:

> "Turn back, my son; for thou belongst to the class of singers."[12]

The understandable resistance which the unusual request of the levitical musicians encountered among the priests, induced the former to proceed more cautiously this time than in the earlier case of the strike. They knew how to flatter the king's vanity, in persuading him

> "that this would be a work worthy the times of his government, that he might have a memorial of such novelty, as being his doing."[13]

To be sure, the demand of the Levites had to be submitted to a vote of the Sanhedrin. But the authority of this law-giving assembly was already considerably reduced at that time. Furthermore, the king might have exercised the necessary pressure upon the members of this assembly, so that the demand of the Levites has eventually been granted.

Encouraged by the success of the singers, some other functionaries of the Temple have likewise ventured an attack against the traditional order with regard to rank. The levitical helpers in the sacrifices, the liturgs (*leitourgountos*), belonging to the lowest class of the Levites, asked permission to learn psalm-singing at the Temple service. This meant in actual practice that they asked to be instructed in the art of singing by the Levites so as to be accepted eventually into the ranks of the Temple singers. This request, too, has been granted by the king, with the result that these lower Levites not only could ascend into the higher class, but were also privileged to wear the white garment on a par with the priests.[14]

Now the Temple musicians reached the peak of their social position, equal to that of the highest representatives of the Temple hierarchy; they were secured economically, and—as artist—admired, esteemed and loved by high and low.

The class immediately affected by this change, the Aaronites, deeply hurt in their pride, were helpless for the moment against the royal decree, which has been legally approved by the Sanhedrin. JOSEPHUS, however, foresaw and announced almost prophetically, that

> "all this was contrary to the law of our country, which, whenever they have been transgressed, we have never been able to avoid the punishment of such transgression."[15]

The retaliation did not fail to come soon. Since the royal decree could not be made void, the priests tried to hit the singers where they were solely vulnerable, at their livelihood. The priests have always been the stewards of the tithes offered by the people, serving as subsistence for all the officers of the divine service, and which were evenly distributed among all the Temple functionaries. As a retaliatory measure against the Levites, the Aaronites have simply withheld from the singers the portion of the tithes due to them.[16] The singers filed a complaint with the Sanhedrin, but apparently the law-assembly has not done—or perhaps could not do—anything about it.

With the soon befalling national catastrophe, the destruction of the sanctuary by the Romans (70 C.E.), the significance of the levitical singers has considerably decreased, whereas the priests have retained their authority even after the downfall of the Temple service. The Levites have made strenuous efforts to get back their ancient privilege of the tithes. However, despite the fact that their claim has been sustained by distinguished rabbinic authorities, such as R. JOSHUA and R. AKIBA, they could not obtain any concession from the stubborn priests. Thus, they have been left until the 3rd century without their share of the people's contributions.

o
o o

With the annihilation of the Jewish national state the musical organization of Ancient Israel has externally disappeared. Yet, the *talent for organization* of the Jewish musician, its spirit, its enduring power, remained intact in a latent form, and during all the coming centuries has never failed to infuse new breath into Jewish music. It stood the test in peaceful as in stormy periods, always awaking new energies, kindling new flames. This is the historical significance, the last providential message of the music organization of Ancient Israel.

EPILOGUE

The above investigations represent the resumé of our present knowledge of the music culture of Ancient Israel, as it has crystallized during many centuries through the research of innumerable scholars. The object of our scrutiny was to elucidate and expound this accumulated wealth of information from the angle of modern musicology and to-day's music practice. For this purpose, it was necessary to analyze critically the prevailing divergences of opinion and thereby to find a clear path in the labyrinth of plausible doctrines and empty delusions. For some of the problems it will probably never be possible to obtain the ultimate clarity, unless unexpected new discoveries would afford a deeper insight into the life and music of Ancient Israel.

Fortunately, the facts that are acknowledged in today's findings are abundant enough for a formation of usable conclusions at least with regard to the principal questions, and this despite the prevalent opinion that the historic material furnished by our main source of music about Ancient Israel, the Bible, is rather scanty. True, as compared with our knowledge of the ancient Greek music, the biblical information about the music practice of the ancient Hebrews is quite limited in many respects. Yet, if we consider the fact that, with the exception of pictorial documents, only vague written records remained about the music of once great and powerful peoples of Antiquity, like the Egyptians, Assyrians, Babylonians, we have good reason to be grateful for what the biblical chroniclers have bequeathed us about the music of their nation.

The presentation and treatment of our subject was not determined as much by the volume of the preserved material as rather by its intrinsic value. An appreciation of the biblical indications about music with this view in mind, is bound to expose sufficiently their utmost importance. With all the sparsity of reporting, they contain such a wealth of valuable and revealing details that one needs but to interpret them correctly, that is, to detect their historic, psychological and artistic implications in order to obtain a vivid picture of Ancient Israel's music culture.

By a closer examination of the biblical material we arrive frequently to unexpected and surprising vistas. A world unfolds before our eyes that one would not suspect at a superficial glance. We fathom the depths of Israel's musical soul; we see the organizational skill of this people, witness its individuality and resourcefulness in matters musical. With a sympathetic appreciation of the seemingly scarce material, we discover it to be rich and significant, indeed a precious legacy that has been benevolently left to posterity.

The preponderantly philosophical disposition of the Greeks brought forth an important musical system, showing, however, unmistakable signs of purely intellectual construction. Not nature, but logical consideration is at the origin of Greek music. With all its loftiness, it is a scheme without blooming life. It stems from reflection, and not from emotion. It is irrelevant that the great philosophers of the Hellenes ascribed to music high educational value and considered it particularly appropriate to shape the character of young men. It is, and remains, applied philosophy, the last motivation of which is the intellect and not the soul.

By their inner nature, the Israelites have not been philosophically bent. Their creative talents manifested themselves in other domains: in those of the soul and emotions. The characteristic Jewish spirit is responsible for having created a new world outlook (Weltanschauung), a new moral philosophy, which has inaugurated a spiritual revolution and eventually became the rock foundation of the entire Occidental civilization. With the Jewish notion of God as the unique and supreme creative power, with the moral approach of the Jews to all phenomena of life, the thinking, feeling, and the forms of living of the entire civilized world underwent eventually a profound transformation. In contrast to all other ancient peoples, the Israelites became creative not so much through their intellectual capacities, as through the emotional power of their soul. Their music, too, was not the product of reflection, but of intuition, of inspiration.

The music of the Occident is primarily the incarnation of the form-principle. The specific stylistic feature of Oriental music is emotion. Form alone is a notion without life, but it can be spiritualized by the emanations of the soul. Only the subjective capacity of psychic experience bestows upon form its intrinsic substance, its *raison d'être.*

> "This subjective capacity of psychic experience is not the *logos,* but the *ethos;* it is not the *ratio* but the *religio*; is not the *form,* but the *soul.*"[17]

History shows that the Hebrews have not been overly productive in purely intellectual endeavors; their culture was not centered in philosophy, in formal beaux-arts. Their main achievements were in the domain of emotions which brought them to the fore in poetico-musical, prophetic, and religious arts. This is not due, as frequently asserted, to the incapacity of the Jew for formative art products, but to the religious prohibition of making images. The *forte* of Jewish creative spirit lies therefore not in the plastic, but in the emotional arts, such as poetry and music. If this was a handicap in one respect, it represented a definite advantage for the inborn musical genius of the Jews. Philosophically considered, this determines the relationship of the Jews to music.

Yet, still another factor became determinative for this relationship: the correlation between man and his environment. In no other art is the influence of the environment, of the surrounding nature so important as in music.

> "The soul of a landscape is determinative for a people, it decides its entelechy."[18]

To put it in another way, this means that the condition of a people's individuality is largely influenced by the surrounding landscape, which, in turn, brings forth this people's innate potentialities. This becomes evident in the music of the Israelites. As long as they were a people of the desert, leading a nomadic existence, they could not develop a musical art of their own. But once settled in the fertile valleys of Cana'an, and as soon as they assimilated the music of the surrounding indigenous peoples, their own musical art developed rapidly. The entire fervor, the passion of their soul, repressed for a long time, revealed themselves in this new art. From then on, the colorful and luxuriant countryside of their new homestead reflects itself in their music, imparts to it a richness of fantasy, an iridescent variety, which we are seeking in vain in

Greek music, and which resounds even today in the synagogal song, the distant offshoot of ancient Jewish music.

Since the country of origin of the Jewish people is unknown, we have to accept as determinative for the character and ethos of Jewish music, as for Jewish civilization in general, the environment of their adoptive homeland. This country, in which dry deserts alternate with lush valleys, broad plains with rugged mountains, desolate lands with pleasant pastures, is reflected in the Jew's intellectual and artistic productivity. This environment was his greatest incentive,—it became also his destiny.

We witness how Jewish religion, oscillating between extreme severity and utmost kindness, adapts itself to the surrounding world. The most outstanding literary product of the Jews, the Bible, with all its characteristic grandeur, shows a pronounced lyric character. Their arts, austere and mild like the environment, reveal monumental proportions on the one side, losing themselves, on the other, in minute details; it suffices to recall the biblical description of Solomon's Temple, as an example for this particularity.

Music too, though we possess only an indirect insight into its nature, is the true image of Cana'an's variegated scenery. Soaring hymns alternate with intimate songs; the solemn and sedate Temple music is strongly contrasted with the noisy sounds of luxurious feasts; lustre and shade are bordering each other, joy and sorrow follow in close succession in Israel's music.

Jewish music is highly emotional, and in this respect quite contrary to Greek music, the basic principle of which is intellectuality. The motivation of Greek music is speculation rather than intuition, just the opposite of the Jewish approach to musical art. This explains why the Israelites could not invent a music system of their own, could not develop a specific music theory. Music expressed in terms of an exact science was inconceivable to the ancient Hebrews. For the Hellenes, music was a rigid theoretic discipline, while the Hebrews have discovered a new and purely spiritual approach to tonal art: they experienced it as a cosmic phenomenon, as a transcendental gift. Therefore, music never could become a science for them; it was art in its fundamental manifestation and, beyond that, heavenly grace, divine revelation.

The entire future history of Jewish music, in the Dispersion as well as after the Emancipation, is determined by this approach. Occidental music has gradually evolved into an intellectual formalism, whereas Jewish music, having its roots in the human soul, remained emotional until today. This is its weakness perhaps, but this is, at the same time, its greatest force. Both manifest themselves equally in the destiny of Jewry, which, passing through endless tribulations and spiritual growth, has lead to the rebirth of the Jewish nation.

The way pursued by the Jewish people and by Jewish music for nearly two millennia has been thorny, full of seemingly insurmountable obstacles. It is by no means a hazard of circumstances that, just like the Jewish people themselves, so also their music survived all the catastrophes, and that today both, the nation as well as its music, enjoy their revitalization.

NOTES

NOTES TO PROLOGUE AND SECTION I

1. Friedrich Muckle, *Der Geist der jüdischen Kultur und das Abendland* (Vienna, 1923), p. 638.
2. *ibid.*, p. 639.
3. We owe the most complete and up to date description of the music of Sumeria to F. W. Galpin (*See GalpSum*). In the main, our presentation follows Galpin's results.
4. Illustration in *GalpSum*, Frontispiece.
5. Erich Ebeling, *Ein Hymnenkataog aus Assur*, in *JRAS*, (1923). See also *GalpSum*, p. 61.
6. *LangdLit*, pp. XII, XIX.
7. *ibid.*
8. *ibid.*
9. *ibid.*, p. VIII.
10. Langdon mentions 13 instruments, the names of which appear in cuneiform texts. *See LangdLit*, pp. XXXII- XXXIII. Cp. "all manner of instruments" in 2 Sam. 6:5, "all kinds of music" in Dan. 3:5, 7, 10, 15, and similar indications in the Old Testament.
11. *GalpSum*, p. 53.
12. *ibid.*, p. 73.
13. Published in *GalpSum*, Appendix.
14. *GalpSum*, p. 62.
15. Curt Sachs, *The Mystery of the Babylonian Notation*, in *MusQuart* XXVII (Jan. 1941, No. 1), p. 68. See also Note 28 on p. 46, in which reference is made to Sachs' own successful attempt at deciphering Babylonian musical notation.
16. C. W. Harris, *The Hebrew Heritage* (New York, 1935), p. 66.
17. *SachsHist*, p. 94.
18. *ibid.*, p. 90.
19. *ibid.*, p. 141.
20. A. Wiedemann, *Die Religion der alten Aegypter* (Münster i.W., 1890), p. 100.
21. *ChantRelig*, I, p. 487.
22. J. G. Wilkinson, *The Manners and Customs of the Ancient Egyptians* (London, 1878), I, p. 444.
23. The music of the ancient Egyptians, surveyed here in a summary way, was discussed in order to expose some analogies with the music of the Israelites. Detailed information about this subject can be obtained in the special works of Curt Sachs and in some recently published essays of Hans Hickmann.
24. C. Bezold, *Ninive und Babylon* (Bielefeld and Leipzig, 1926), p. 148.
25. A. Jeremias, *Handbuch der altorientalischen Geisteskultur* (Leipzig, 1913), p. 285.
26. *ibid.*
27. *ibid.*
28. Curt Sachs has made a remarkable attempt at deciphering, and reproducing in modern notation, an ancient Babylonian hymn. A clay slab from Assur on the middle Tigris, from the beginning of the 1st millennium B.C.E., contains a poem in Sumerian with certain symbols at the margin which were supposed to be musical signs. (They seem to indicate the accompaniment of the hymn by a harp of 22 strings). Sachs believed he had found the exact meaning of these symbols, and gave the results of his investigations together with a paraphrase, in modern notation, of the melody and accompaniment (*Die Entzifferung einer babylonischen Notenschrift*, in *Sitzungsberichte der Preussichen Akademie der Wissenschaften*, XVIII [1924]; see also Curt Sachs, *Ein babylonischer Hymnus*, in *Archiv für Musikwissenschaft* (1925, Heft 1). Later, he modified and corrected his findings (in *Papers read at the Intern. Congress of Musicology*, New York, 1939, publ. 1944, pp. 161-167). See also *GalpSum*, p. 43.
29. *RiehmHandw*, I, p. 223.

30. J. Hastings, *A Dictionary of the Bible* (New York, 1898-1904), I, p. 368.
31. *ibid.*
32. Preserved in *JosApio,* I, 17, 18, "*ton te tyrannounta Hierosolymōn Salomōna*"
33. Herodotus, *Historia,* II, 44.
34. *Athen,* IV, 175 c.
35. *ibid.,* IV, 183 d, e.
36. Pollux, *Onomasticon,* IV, 59, 76. See also *Athen,* IV, 182 f.
37. Plutarch, *De superstitione,* chap. 12, 171 d. See also J. Quasten, *Musik und Gesang in den Kulten der heidnischen Antike und der christlichen Frühzeit* (Münster i.W., 1930), pp. 36 ff.
38. Lucian, *De Syria Dea,* 43.
39. For the *ambudaiae* of the Roman circus see p. 394.
40. Aristides, *De Musica,* lib. II, chap. 7 (ed. Marcus Meibohm, Amsterdam, 1652), p. 72. See also Rudolf Schäfke, *Aristeides Quintilianus* (Berlin, 1937), pp. 262-263.
41. Lucian, *De Syria Dea,* 27, 50.
42. *SachsDance,* p. 98.
43. Rudolph Westphal, *Geschichte der alten und mittelalterlichen Musik* (Breslau, 1865), p. 3.
44. Pollux, *Onomasticon,* IV, 75.
45. In many translations of the Bible, ancient and recent, as well as in other literary works about the music of Antiquity, the ancient pipes are incorrectly called "flutes." In their construction and sound, they were in fact oboes. The peoples of Antiquity possessed numerous, often dozens of kinds of, oboes, having different tone production, different sonority, and various applications.
46. Tal. Bab., *Ḥagigah* 15 b.
47. *ChantRelig,* I, p. 609.
48. P. Scholz, *Götzendienst und Zauberwesen bei den alten Hebräern* (Regensburg, 1877), pp. 54 ff.
49. Friedrich Baethgen, *Beiträge zur semitischen Religionsgeschichte* (Berlin, 1888), pp. 20 ff. See also P. Scholz, *op. cit.,* p. 162.
50. *BuddeGesch,* p. 23.

NOTES TO SECTION II

1. Stephen Herbert Langdon, *Semitic Mythology (The Mythology of all Races,* vol. V., Boston, 1931), pp. 105, 202.
2. *GressMus,* pp. 3 ff.
3. *SachsHist,* p. 120.
4. According to Sachs, this was possible on lyres (*SachsHist.,* p. 132).

NOTES TO SECTION III

1. This is the interpretation of all works dealing with the literature of the ancient Hebrews. (*HarrisHer,* p. 59). See also the section "Singing."
2. All the quotations of the Old Testament after the *Jewish Translation,* unless indicated otherwise.
3. See p. 500.
4. Among other lost books of the Hebrews we may mention: the Book of Nathan, the Book of Gad, the Book of Yehu, the Book of Shemiah, the Book of Iddo the Seer, etc. See also p. 164.
5. In post-biblical writings there are further examples of work-songs. The Talmud

mentions songs of sailors, ploughmen and weavers (Tal. Bab., *Soṭah* 48 a). In general, any profession based upon an activity having a regular rhythm, possessed its specific work-songs. See also John Chrysostom, *Eis ton Psalmon XLI,* in *PGL,* (LV, col. 156).

6. A "festival" was always accompanied by dances. Luther translates the passage "they made a dance" ("und machten einen Tanz").
7. See the section "Music and Prophecy."
8. For the participation of women in Jewish musical performances, sacred as well as secular, see a subsequent section.
9. Identical with the above mentioned Ethan. See p. 144.
10. Tal. Bab., *Ḥullin* 24 a. The age of 20 years mentioned in 1 Chron. 23:24,27 did not apply to the levitical singers but to the other office-holders among the Levites who did not undergo such a long period of preparation as the singers.
11. The "18 Psalms of Solomon," discovered in the Codex Alexandrinus, have originated much later (probably in the 1st century B.C.E.), and have nothing to do with Solomon except the name.
12. See pp. 546 ff.
13. About these occurrences we are informed by JOSEPHUS *(JosAnt* XX, 9:6). At this time the biblical canon was already firmly established.
14. See also *PhiloLaws,* XII:69.
15. *Cp.* in the post-biblical literature Mishnah, *Sukkah* IV:1-6; Midrash, *Leviticus* XXX:5; Tal. Bab., *Sukkah* 45 a.
16. Heinrich Ewald, Ernest Renan and others consider the "Song of Songs" a dramatic play, that is supposed to have been staged as a kind of festival performance, with the participation of singers, choral groups and dancers, and with instrumental accompaniment. See the section "The Dance," p. 464.
17. See pp. 475.
18. Translation of the *Authorized Version.* However, the musical meaning of the word *shiddah* is doubtful (see pp. 306 ff.) Even more questionable is the musical meaning of the obscure term *dahavan* (Dan. 6:19), which is translated in quite a number of English versions as "instruments of music." See p. 306.
19. E. W. Rice, *Orientalisms in Bible Land* (Philadelphia, 1910), p. 173.
20. See also Tal.Bab., *Mo'ed Kaṭan* 8a; 28 b.
21. Mishnah, *Ketubot* IV:4; Tal.Bab., *Ketubot* 48 a.
22. So the *Authorized Version* and *Harkavy.* The *Jewish Translation* gives to the word *neḳeb* a non-musical meaning: "thy settings and thy sockets." See also p. 317.
23. The bells on the garment of the high priest *(pa'amonim,* Exod. 28:33,34; 39:25,26) had a somewhat different meaning. Their purpose, however, was the same: to protect the bearer.
24. For Nebuchadrezzar's orchestra see in detail the section "The Orchestra" also *SachsHist,* pp. 84 ff.

NOTES TO SECTION IV

1. The Greek version of the Bible contains an additional, non-canonical psalm, which has the number 151 (see p. 145).
2. *SchneidKult,* I, p. 114.
3. Text in N. de G. Davies, *The Rock Tombs of El Amarna* (London, 1908), vol. VI, pp. 29 ff. Translation with the most noticeable parallel passages side by side in James Henry Breasted, *A History of Egypt* (New York, 1905), pp. 371-376. See also A. Erman, *The Literature of the Ancient Egyptians* (London, 1927), pp. 288 ff.
4. *Cf.* T. H. Gaster, *Psalm 29,* in *JQR* (1946-47), vol. 37, pp. 55 ff.

5. According to Josephus *(JosAnt* VII, 12:3), David has not written his psalms separately and for special occasions as their headings would suggest, but all of them toward the end of his life, after he concluded his wars.
6. Tal.Bab., *ʿAbodah Zarah* 24 b.
7. *ThirTitles,* p. 143.
8. SEPTUAGINT is the term of the first Greek translation of the Old Testament. It is mentioned in a letter written in 200 B.C.E., quoted textually by Josephus *(JosAnt* XII, 2:4), therefore it must have been completed at this time. The first Latin translation, called the OLD LATIN version, made by numerous unknown translators, existed prior to the great revision made by St. JEROME (340-420 C.E.) at the close of the 4th century C.E., which, subsequently, was called the VULGATE and which the Latin Church recognized as its Authorized Version of the Bible. The PSALTERIUM VETUS, the old Latin Psalter, was the first book revised by St. JEROME. In the course of his life, St. JEROME published three versions of it. The first, or Roman Psalter, was published at Rome in 383, the second, the so-called Gallic Psalter, at Bethlehem about 387. His best translation is the third, called the Hebrew Psalter (published about 392), which he made directly from the Hebrew original. A post-Septuagint Greek translator of the Old Testament, AQUILA, lived in the 2nd Century C.E. According to talmudic tradition, he was a Greek convert to the Jewish faith, who made his translation under the supervision of R. Akiba or, according to another tradition, under R. Eliezer and R. Joshua. AQUILA's translation, parts of which are only preserved, follows closely the Hebrew original, whereas the SEPTUAGINT sometimes deviates from the Masoretic text and renders many passages in an easier, more poetic form. Among other classical translators of the Old Testament SYMMACHOS, another Greek convert to Judaism, should be mentioned. He lived at the time of the emperor Severus (193-211 C.E.); his translation, preserved only in fragments, is distinguished by utmost clarity. Another early translator, THEODOTION, also a Greek convert, lived in the 2nd century C.E.; his translation originated later than that of AQUILA.

   English translations of Hebrew musical terms are taken in our study from the principal English versions, Protestant, Catholic, and Jewish, both old and new. Such survey affords a good cross-section of terminological renditions found in the English Bibles. The versions used are the following, in a chronological order:

   (1) The Holy Bible . . . in the earliest English Versions Made from the Latin Vulgate by John Wycliffe and his Followers [one of the earliest in the English language, about 1380]. New edition by J. Forshall and F. Madden (Oxford, 1850). It is printed in two parallel columns with two juxtaposed versions, containing the earlier text and its later revision by John Purvey and Nicholas Hereford.

   (2) The Douay Version, translated from the Latin Vulgate (1582), and compared with the Hebrew, Greek and other editions. It was revised by Bishop Challoner (1750), and is now the Authorized Catholic Bible.

   (3) The Authorized King James Version (1611).

   (4) The American Revised Version (first edition 1885, further revised 1901).

   (5) Richard G. Moulton, The Modern Reader's Bible (first edition 1895).

   (6) Alexander Harkavy's translation from the original Hebrew (first edition 1915).

   (7) The Holy Scriptures according to the Masoretic Text, the Jewish translation (first edition 1917).

   (8) James Moffat, A New Translation of the Bible (first edition 1922).

   (9) The Holy Bible. Revised Standard Version (1952).
9. C. A. Briggs, *A Critical and Exegetical Commentary on the Book of Psalms* (New York, 1908-09), p. LIX. The root and its derivatives seem to be found in the other Semitic languages only when derived from the Hebrew. (See R. D. Wilson,

The Headings of the Psalms, in *Princeton Theological Review,* vol. XXIV (1926), p. 361).

10. Ps. 48 ; 66 ; 83 ; 88 ; 108.
11. Ps. 30 ; 65 ; 67 ; 68 ; 75 ; 76 ; 87 : 92.
12. Midrash, *Tehillim* (ed. Buber, 1891), XXIV:7, p. 204.
13. *LangdTerms,* p. 174.
14. *JosWar,* V, 5:3.
15. Mishnah, *Sukkah* V:4 Mishnah, *Middot* II:5; TalBab., *Sukkah* 51a,b.
16. According to Delitzsch, this explanation lacks historical basis and has been built on nothing more substantial than a Talmudic statement, in which a parallel is established between the fifteen steps and the fifteen psalms *(DelPsalms,* III, pp. 257-58).
17. Jerome, *Commentarium in Epistolam ad Galatas,* I, cap. 1, in *PL,* XXVI, col. 354.
18. Wilson, R. D., *The Headings of the Psalms,* in *Princeton Theological Review,* (vol. XXIV 1926), p. 367.
19. *PhiloLaws,* Book I, XIV:76-78.
20. Mishnah, *Sukkah* V:4; Mishnah, *Middot* II:5; Tal.Bab., *Sukkah* 51 a,b.
21. For *maʿamad* see the section "Singing," pp. 184 ff.
22. Mishnah, *Taʿanit* IV:2.
23. *ThirProblems* p, 69.
24. *ibid.,* p. 32.
25. *ibid.,* p. 67.
26. *ibid.,* p. 31.
27. *HerdSpirit,* II, p. 261; *EwDicht,* I, p. 251.
28. *BuddeGesch,* p. 253.
29. *GesHandw,* p. 446. - Fr. Delitzsch, *Biblical Commentary on the Psalms* (Edinburgh, 1892), II, p. 267. - W.M.L. De Wette, *Commentar über die Psalmen* (Heidelberg, 1811), pp. 31, 55 ff. - G. B. Winer, *Biblisches Realwörterbuch* (Leipzig, 1833-38), II, p. 317.
30. Sigmund Mowinckel, *Psalmenstudien* (Kristiania, 1923-26), 6 vols.
31. *MowPsalm,* IV, p. 3-4.
32. *CalmetDict.*
33. W. Hengstenberg, *Commentary on the Psalms* (Edinburgh, 1840-1843), F.A. Tholuck, *Übersetzung und Auslegung der Psalmen* (Halle a.S., 1843).
34. E. F. K. Rosenmüller, *Vocabularium Veteris Testamenti Hebraico-Chaldaicum* (Halle and Magdeburg, 1822).
35. *MowPsalm,* IV, pp. 5-7.
36. *ibid.*
37. *GesLex,* p. 508.
38. R. A. Nicholson, *Literary History of the Arabs* (London, 1914), pp. 101 ff.
39. S. T. Horne, *An Introduction to the Critical Study and Knowledge of the Holy Scriptures* (New York, 1856), II, p. 242. D. d'Herbelot de Molainville, *Bibliothèque orientale; ou, Dictionaire universal . . .* (Paris, 1697), I, pp. 383, 415.
40. Jastrow, however, translated *gelipa teriẓa* as "a well arranged poetry." *JastDict,* p. 249.
41. *ChantRelig,* I, p. 646.
42. Ferdinand Hitzig, *Die Psalmen übersetzt and ausgelegt* (Leipzig and Heidelberg, 1863), I, p. 80.
43. *GesHandw,* p. 423.
44. J. A. Alexander, *The Psalms translated and explained* (New York, 1855), I, p. 111.
45. O. E. W. Oesterley, *A Fresh Approach to the Psalms* (New York, 1937), p. 88, note.
46. C. A. Briggs, *The Book of Psalms* (Edinburgh, 1906), p. LX. *Cf. DelPsalm,* p. 218.

47. *LangdTerms,* p. 184.
48. *ibid.*
49. *MowPsalm,* IV, pp. 4-5.
50. W. Robertson Smith, *The Old Testament in the Jewish Church* (London, 1926), p. 209. The same usage can be found in the Palestinian Hymnology. See S.I.N.P. Land, *Anecdota Syriaca* (Leiden, 1870), IV, pp. 111 ff.
51. Erich Ebeling, *Religiöse Keilinschifttexte aus Assur* (Leipzig, 1918), No. 158. See also *GalpSum,* p. 61.
52. Published in *LangdTerms,* pp. 170 ff.
53. *PfeifferIntro,* p. 644.
54. "Song of the bow" ("Bogenlied") is Luther's translation, adhered to also by the *American Version* and *Moulton.* The *Jewish* and the other principal English versions have: "To teach the sons of Judah the bow."
55. Fr. Baethgen, *Die Psalmen übersetzt und erklärt* (Göttingen, 1897), p. X
56. *ibid.*
57. The verb in Hebrew means "to err"; but in Babylonian and Arabic "to lament." Babylonian has also *shigū,* "lamentation."
58. C. F. Houbigant, *Racines Hébraiques sans points-voyelles; ou Dictionaire Hébraique* . . . (Paris, 1733), p. 165.
59. J. Parkhurst, *An Hebrew and English Lexicon, without Points* . . . (London, 1813), p. 718.
60. This is somewhat similar to the medieval *tonus peregrinus* which implied a "wandering (irregular) mode" because of the *two* (instead of the normal *one)* reciting notes for its first and second half.
61. *DelPsalms,* I, p. 139.
62. *ibid.*
63. *LangdTerms,* p. 175.
64. *GesLex,* p. 993. Another possible derivation would be through association with a root presumably akin to *sha'ag,* "to call out, cry out, sing aloud."
65. *MowPsalms,* IV, p. 7.
66. Ugolino's *Thesaurus antiquitatum sacrarum* (Venice, 1744-67) contains a Latin translation of Portaleone's description of the Temple (vol. IX, cols. 1-564). In this translation, Ugolino committed the error of rendering *kle ha-niggun* as *instrumentis pulsatilibus,* "percussion instruments." An abridged version of *Shilṭe ha-Gibborim* (in Latin) is to be found in vol. XXXII of the *Thesaurus.*
67. *ThirTitles,* pp. 13 ff.
68. "Skillful" is not the exact translation of the Hebrew *meibin.* The correct meaning of the word, in this context, is rather "expert," "well versed."
69. C. G. Cumming, *The Assyrian and Hebrew Hymns of Praise* (New York, 1934), pp. 72-82, 99.
70. G. Beer, *Individual-und Gemeindepsalmen* (Marburg, 1894), pp. XII ff.
71. *ThirProblems,* pp. 295-96.
72. *MowPsalm,* IV, pp. 17-22.
73. *Cp.* also 1 Sam. 16:16 ff; 16:23; 18:10; 2 Kings 3:15, Ps. 33:3; Isa. 23:16; Ezek. 33:32.
74. According to another theory, the root has the meaning "to inflict suffering," therefore *neginah* in the headings would mean "affliction." A. Cowley, *Aramaic Papyri of the Fifth Century B.C.* (Oxford, 1923).
75. *MowPsalm,* IV, 17-22.
76. H. Winckler, *Keilinschriftliches Textbuch zum A.T.* (Leipzig, 1909), 11, p. 45.—E. Schrader, *Die Keilinschriften und das Alte* Testament (Giessen, 1882), pp. 45 ff.—Alfred Jeremias, *The Old Testament in the Light of the Ancient East* (Engl. ed. London, 1911), II, p. 224. For full quotation see p. 522.
77. *ThirTitles,* p. 240.
78. W. O. E. Oesterley, *The Psalms in the Jewish Church* (London, 1910), p. 116.

79. Mishnah, ʿ*Arakin* II:6.
80. *SachsRise,* pp. 69-70.
81. *CornCult,* p. 128.
82. *MowPsalm,* V, pp. 35 ff.
83. *JosAnt,* VII, 12:3.
84. *LangdTerms,* p. 181.
85. Justus Olshausen, *Die Psalmen erklärt* (Leipzig, 1853), p. 27.
86. *GesLex*: *octava* in re musica vocem gravissimam notat, a viris cantatam (nostr. *basso).*
87. In India, musicians had "discovered" the second partial, that is, the harmonic octave, as early as the 2nd millennium B.C.E. The Greek music theory also knew the octave (*dia pasōn*), created by the equal division of a string. Among others, Aristotle confirms this repeatedly: "The string when struck at half its length gives an octave (*dia pasōn*) with the string struck at full length. Just the same thing is true of pipes (*syringos*) the sound produced through the hole in the middle of the pipe makes an octave with the sound obtained over the whole pipe" (*Problēmata,* XIX:23, 919 b).—"In triangular harps (*trigōnois psaltēriois*) with strings of equal tension an octave (*dia pasōn*) is produced when one string is double the other in length" (*ibid.*).—"By dividing the string in half it is found that two *nētēs* are contained in the *hypatē* (*Problēmata* XIX:12, 918 b).
88. For example, Philo shows a good knowledge of Greek music of his time. Theory of music was one of the subjects to be taught any well-educated young man. Philo's writings contain frequent references to the theory and philosophy of Greek music. It seems, on the other hand, that he himself has not been active in music, for any mention of the practical side of the tonal art of his days is lacking in his works. Moreover, the music of his own people is passed over in complete silence in his essays. Yet, it must be assumed that he was conscious of the fact that the Jewish people possessed a music of their own.
89. *ThirTitles,* p. 111.
90. *ibid.,* p. 112.
91. *ibid.*
92. *Encyclopaedia Britannica,* s.v. "Psalms," p. 26.
93. *MowPsalm,* IV, pp. 42 ff.
94. *ThirTitles,* p. 78.
95. *ibid.,* p. 302.
96. For the various interpretations of *maḥalat* as a musical instrument see p. 322.
97. *MowPsalm,* IV, p. 34.
98. ʾ*El is probably* an erroneous spelling for ʿ*al,* as conjectured by the Septuagint's translation, *hyper.*
99. J. A. Alexander, *The Psalms translated and explained* (New York, 1855), I. p. 36.—*BaethPsalm,* p. IX.
100. *MowPsalms,* IV, p. 34.
101. W. O. E. Oesterley, *The Psalms in the Jewish Church* (London, 1910), p. 125.
102. Tal.Bab., *Shabbat* 21 b.
103. *LangdTerms,* pp. 169-191. Also *GalpSum,* p. 61.
104. *GesHandw,* p. 594.
105. J. A. Alexander, *The Psalms translated and explained* (New York, 1855), I, p. 64.
106. H. Graetz, *Kritischer Commentar zu den Psalmen* (Breslau, 1882-83), pp. 71, 85.
107. *MowPsalm,* IV, p. 31.
108. *ThirTitles,* p. 71.
109. *ibid.,* p. 78.
110. Midrash, *Tehillim* (ed. Buber. 1891), p. 182.
111. *MowPsalm,* IV, p. 28.
112. *ThirTitles,* p. 86.
113. Jacob Levy, *Chaldäisches Wörterbuch über die Targumim* (Leipzig, 1867) II, pp. 175, 499.

114. *MowPsalm,* IV, pp. 31 ff.
115. *ibid.,* p. 30.
116. *MowPsalm,* IV, pp. 22 ff.
117. *ʾaven* means "falsehood," "evil," "calamity" (see *GesLex).* The *Authorized, American* and *Jewish Versions, Moulton* and *Harkavy* translate "iniquity," *Moffat* "malice," the *Revised Standard Version* "crime." Mowinckel's translation is arbitrary, to say the least.
118. *ThirTitles,* pp. 90 ff.
119. *ibid.,* p. 171.
120. *EwDicht,* I, part 1, p. 225.
121. It was shown earlier that, in fact, such analogies exist. See pp. 106 ff.
122. *ThirTitles,* p. 103.
123. Two notable exceptions are Wilson and Thirtle. The former uses the "argument from silence," trying to prove that "the omission of the name of David from the heading of a particular psalm does not mean that they thought that David did not write it." *(op. cit.,* p. 393.). "Who other than David may have been their author? No one whom we know." (*ibid.*) Thirtle, on the other hand, attributes most of the psalms to David and Hezekiah, or to the men who wrote for them *(ThirProblems,* p. 106).
124. Hermann Gunkel, *Einleitung in die Psalmen,* (Göttingen, 1928, 1933), pp. 431 ff.
125. *op. cit.,* p. 353.
126. T. . Cheyne, *The Origins and Religious Contents of the Psalter* (London, 1891), pp. 205 ff.
127. B. Duhm, *Die Psalmen* (Tübingen, 1922), pp. XVIII ff.
128. C. A. Briggs, *A Critical and Exegetical Commentary on the Book of Psalms* (New York, 1908-09), p. LXI.
129. *ibid.*
130. W. O. E. Oesterley, *The Psalms in the Jewish Church* (London, 1910), p. 86.
131. *LangdTerms,* p. 169.
132. *BaethPsalms.*
133. *ibid.*
134. *ThirProblems,* p. 146.
135. O. Braun, *Ein Brief des Katholikos Timotheus I über biblische Studien des 9. Jahrhunderts,* in *Oriens Christianus,* I (1901), p. 304.
136. See pp. 190 ff.
137. Carl Ehrt, *Abfassungszeit und Abschluss des Psalters* (Leipzig, 1869), pp. 126 ff.
138. *BuddeGesch,* p. 43.
139. The scholars of the Oriental Churches, especially those of the School of Antioch, believed that David wrote all the psalms. See Theodore of Mopsuestia, in *PG* LXVI, cols. 647-696, and Theodoret, in *PG* LXXXIV, cols. 562, 571.
140. Pss. 3, 4, 7, 8, 11, 18, 19, 24:1-6; 24:7-10, 29, 32, 101. Ps. 18 being identical with 2 Sam. 22. See *EwDicht,* I, part 2, p. 4.
141. *ThirProblems,* p. 311.
142. *PfeifferIntro,* p. 627.
143. *RiehmHandw,* p. 849.
144. *BuddeGesch,* p. 256.
145. *EwDicht,* I, part 1, p. 225. For Jeduthun interpreted as a musical instrument see p. 293, note 206.
146. Paul Anton Lagarde, *Übersicht über die im Aramäischen, Arabischen und Hebräischen übliche Bildung der Nomina* (Göttingen, 1889), p. 121.
147. *MowPsalm,* IV, pp. 8-17.
148. There is a significant analogy to this in 1 Chron. 25:4. The nine names in this verse, Hananiah, Hanani, Eliatath, Giddalti, Romamti-Ezer, Joshbekashah, Mallothi, Hothir, and Mahazioth are considered "clearly artificial," a view derived from a

discovery, namely that these nine names "are arranged so that the consonantal text reads as a doxology" (*PfeifferIntro*, p. 623, note). See p. 534, note (1).

149. *MowPsalms*, V, pp. 39 ff.
150. Syriac sources reveal four other apocryphal psalms, two of them ascribed to David, and one to Hezekiah. (W. Wright, in *Proceedings of the Society of Biblical Archaeology*, June 1887).
151. The Septuagint also associates Ps. 144 with Goliath.
152. The Septuagint contains some additional *selahs* in other passages.
153. *BuddeGesch*, p. 91.
154. Published by P. A. Lagarde, *Novae Psalterii Graeci Editionis Specimen*, in *Abhandlungen der historisch-philologischen Classe der königl. Gesellschaft der Wissenschaften*, (Göttingen, XXXIII, Band, No. 6, 1886), Specimen 10.
155. Augustine, *Enarratio in Psalmum IV*:4, in *PL*, XXXVI, col. 80.
156. John Chrysostom, *Prooimia tōn Psalmon*, in *PGL, LV*, col. 533.
157. Mishnah, *Tamid*, VII:3.
158. *Athen*, XIV, 635 b.
159. *Athen*, IV, 183 e.
160. *DelPsalms*, I, p. 103.
161. Tal.Bab., (*Erubin* 54 a.
162. *DelPsalms*, I, p. 102.
163. *ibid.*
164. *EwDicht*, I, part 1, p. 232.
165. *HerdSpirit*, II, p. 267.
166. *E.g.* J. L. Saalschütz, *Von der Form der hebräischen Poesie* (Königsberg, 1825), 116.—*EwaldDicht*, I, part 1, pp. 138-139.—Julius Ley, *Leitfaden der Metrik der hebräischen Poesie* (Halle a.S., 1887), p. 17—Hubert Grimme, *Psalmenprobleme* (Freiburg, 1902), p. 150.—E. Kautzsch, *Die Poesie und die poetischen Bücher des A.T.* (Tübingen and Leipzig, 1902), pp. 9-10.—M. Berkowitz, *Strophenbau und Responsion in den Psalmen*, in *Wiener Zeitschrift für die Kunde des Morgenlandes*, XVII (1903), p. 232.
167. For this subject see pp. 450 ff.
168. See also p. 151.
169. Mishnah, *Tamid*, VII:3; Tal.Bab., (*Erubin* 54 a.
170. J. Steinberg, *Mishpat ha-*)*Urim* (Vilna, 1896), p. 581.
171. Jacob Beimel, *Some interpretation of the meaning of SELAH*, in *Jewish Music Forum, Bulletin* (1943), p. 7.
172. *StainMus*, p. 92.
173. Quoted in *StainMus*, pp. 90 ff.
174. W. W. Longford, *Music and Religion* (London, 1916), p. 42.
175. *StainMus*, p. 92.
176. *ibid.*, p. 93.
177. *ibid.*
178. *ibid.*, p. 94.
179. K. J. Zenner, *Die Chorgesänge im Buche der Psalmen* (Freiburg i.B., 1896).
180. The picture is reproduced as the Frontispiece of Zenner's book. John Chrysostom alludes to such antiphonal alternation of choral groups in *Prooimia tōn Psalmon*, in *PGL*, LV, col. 531-533. See p. 147.
181. See his notes to the translation of Ps. 1.
182. B. Jakob, *Beiträge zu einer Einleitung in die Psalmen, in Zeitschrift für alttestamentliche Wissenschaft*, XVI, (1896), p. 134.
183. Published by Sabatier. See Jakob, *op. cit.*, pp. 134-35.
184. *MowPsalm*, IV, pp. 10 ff.
185. Thirtle categorically denies any musical implication of the word. As he maintains, "only through an antecedent assumption in favour of a musical instrument has

the word come to be regarded as meaning 'resounding music,' or 'a deep toned instrument'." (*ThirTitles,* p. 148).

186. E. W. Hengstenberg, *Commentary on the Psalms* (Edinburgh, 1851), I, p. 151.
187. F. A. Tholuck, *Übersetzung und Auslegung der Psalmen* (Halle a.d. S., 1843), p. 45.
188. Otto Glaser, *Die ältesten Psalmenmelodien,* in *Zeitschrift für Semistik* (1932-35), VIII-X, pp. 324-25.
189. *MowPsalm,* IV, pp. 9 ff.
190. *BaethPsalms,* p. XXXIX.

O
O O

NOTES TO SECTION V

[1] Tal.Bab., *Ḥullin,* 91 b. *Cp.* Isa 6:3.

[2] *LeitGes,* pp. 1 ff.

[3] *ibid.,* p. 27.

[4] *EwDicht,* I, Part 1, pp. 209-210.

[5] Robert H. Pfeiffer, *Introduction to the Old Testament* (New York, 1941), p. 272.

[6] *SieversMetr,* p. 376.

[7] *LeitGes,* p. 29.

[8] C. Bezold, *Ninive und Babylon* (Bielefeld and Leipzig, 1926), pp. 147 ff.

[9] G. A. Reisner, *Sumerisch-babylonische Hymnen nach Tontafeln aus griechischer Zeit* (Berlin, 1896), p. XV.

[10] K. C. Bähr, *Symbolik des mosaischen Kultes* (Heidelberg, 1837), I, pp. 147 ff.

[11] *Cp.* the works of K. Bücher, *Arbeit und Rhythmus* (Leipzig, 1909), R. Wallaschek, *Anfänge der Tonkunst* (Leipzig, 1903) Stumpf, Carl, *Die Anfänge der Musik* (Leipzig, 1911), etc.

[12] In Sachs' opinion, however, "the all-dominating influence that Bücher assignates to manual work in shaping music and rhythmic organization seems to be greatly exaggerated" (*SachsRhythm,* p. 39).

[13] *LeitGes,* p. 12.

[14] Oskar Fleischer, *Neumenstudien* (Leipzig, 1895), I, p. 43.

[15] *RiehmHandw,* I, p. 805.—*BuddeGesch,* p. 14, etc.

[16] *LeitGes,* p. 26.

[17] *BuddeGesch,* p. 9. Some English Bibles are even more explicit in characterizing those "that speak in parables" or "in proverbs" as folk-bards. Thus, *Moffat* puts "Hence the song and satire of the bards," and the *Revised Standard Version* "Therefore the ballad singers say."

[18] *EwDicht,* I, Part 1, p. 175.

[19] Mishnah, *Soṭah* V:4; Mishnah, *Sukkah* III:10; Tosefta *Soṭah* VI:2; Midrash, *Exodus* XXII:3, XXIII:2-12; Tal. Bab., *Soṭah* 30b; Tal.Yer., *Soṭah* V:4 (24b), etc.

[20] Thus the *Jewish* and *Revised Standard Versions.* The *Authorized* and *American Versions, Moulton* and *Harkavy* have "answered them," *Douay* "she began the song to them," and *Moffat* "Miriam led them in the song."

[21] In their external appearance, these ancient "books" were scrolls, since books, as we know them today, did not exist in Antiquity.

[22] Modern exegesis surmises that the word *y-sh-r* (without vowels), meaning "upright," "righteous," is misspelled and should rather be read *sh-y-r,* "song." This is based upon an interpolation in the Septuagint, after 1 Kings 8:53, lacking in the Hebrew original and also in other translations, which reads: *ouk idou autē gegraptai en bibliō tēs ōdēs,* "as it is written in the Book of Songs." Thus, *sefer ha-yashar* would be in reality *sefer ha-shir,* "The Book of Songs." (Robert H. Pfeiffer, *op. cit.,* p. 272).

[23] "Song of the Bow" only in Luther's translation and in the English *Revised Version.* The *Jewish Translation* has "to teach the sons of Judah the bow." The Septuagint calls it a "funeral ode" to be taught to the children of Judah.

[24] *LeitGes*, p. 35.
[25] *BuddeGesch*, p. 19.
[26] See p. 74.
[27] A. Bertholet, *A History of Hebrew Civilization* (London, 1926), pp. 324-325.
[28] The famous Christian canticle "Magnificat" is closely modelled after the song of Hannah, a fact generally accepted by Christian writers.
[29] C. Bezold, *Ninive und Bablyon* (Bielefeld and Leipzig, 1926), p. 150.
[30] H. Oldenburg, *Rigveda. Textkritische und exegetische Noten, in Abhandlungen der königl. Gesellschaft der Wissenschaften zu Göttingen. Philologisch-Historische Klasse.* N.F. Band XIII, No. 3. (Berlin, 1909-1912), I, pp. 32, 138.
[31] *LeitGes*, p. 38.
[32] Philo gives a pertinent description of the responsorial singing at the Red Sea. See *PhiloMos*, II, 46.
[33] Mishnah, *Soṭah* V:4; *Sukkah* III:10; Tosefta, *Soṭah* VI:2 (ed. Zuckermandel, 1937, p. 303); Midrash, *Exodus* XXIII: XXIII: 2-12; Tal.Bab., *Sukkah* 38 a,b; *Soṭah* 30 b; Tal.Yer., *Soṭah* V:4 (24b), etc.
[34] Lamentations are also mentioned in the extra-canonical 3 Macc. 6:32.
[35] *JerATAO*, p. 361.
[36] K. Budde, *Das hebräische Klagelied, in Zeitschrift für alttestamentliche Wissenschaft* (1882), pp. 24 ff.
[37] On the rhythm of the *ḳinah* see in detail p. 251.
[38] Cp. Matth. 11:17.
[39] Mishnah, *Ketubot* IV:4.
[40] Tal.Bab., *ʿArakin* 11a.
[41] The rendering of the *Jewish Version* of *Yiseu* as "they sing" is inaccurate, since this verb has no musical connotation. Nevertheless, a number of English versions follow the same idea, so the *American* and *Revised Standard Versions, Moulton* and *Moffat*. The last mentioned version reads: "their children flock out to the fields, boys and girls dancing merrily; they sing to the lyre and tambourine, make merry to the music of the pipe." Whereas the *Authorized Version, Douay* and *Harkavy* have "dance and play" instead of "dance and sing." The passage is also rendered as "singing and rejoicing" in the Septuagint for the Hebrew *m'saḥakim* in all the passages referred to above.
[42] Liddel and Scott, *Greek Lexicon*, p. 1288. Derivatives of the same verb are used in the Septuagint for the Hebrew *m'saḥakim* in all the passages referred to above.
[43] It is possible, however, that the original might have been a Hebrew version slightly different from the one we possess to-day.
[44] In the New Testament there are two references to children's dancing: Matt. 11:17; Luc. 7:32.
[45] Tal.Bab., *Ḥullin* 24 a.
[46] *ibid.*
[47] Mishnah, *ʿArakin* II:6; Tal.Bab., *ʿArakin* 13 b.
[48] A variant reads *zeʿirim*, "the little ones" (of the Levites), instead of *zoʿare*, "tormentors."
[49] See Note (229) on p. 202.
[50] *RiehmHandw*, p. 1029.
[51] Tal.Bab., *Pesaḥim* 117 a; Tal.Yer., *Sukkah* III:12 (54 a); Tal.Yer., *Megillah* 1:9 (72 d).
[52] *LeitGes*, p. 55.
[53] Jacob Hamburger, *Real-Enzyklopedie für Bibel und Talmud* (Strelitz, 1883) II, p. 1245.
[54] Hubert Grimme, *Psalmenprobleme* (Freiburg, Schweiz, 1902), p. 146.
[55] The strophic structure of many a psalm certainly facilitated also the common singing. See in detail p. 241.
[56] Mishnah, *Tamid* VII:3.
[57] David Cassel, *Die Pesachhaggada* (Berlin, 1895), pp. I,II.—Leopold Zunz, *Die gottesdienstlichen Vorträge der Juden* (Berlin, 1832), p. 126.
[58] Exod. 6:6-7 mentions four times God's promise to liberate the Jews from the

Egyptian bondage. In reading these verses during the Passah meal, after each allusion to freedom a cup of wine was drunk (*cf.* Tal.Yer. *Pesaḥim* X:1, p. 68 b). A fifth cup, not to be drunk, was placed at the table for the prophet Elijah, harbinger of the Messiah, supposed to be a guest at every Passah meal.

59 Tal.Yer., *Pesaḥim* V:7 (32 c).

60 2 Chron. 29:26-30; Ecclus. 50:15-21; Mishnah, *Tamid* VII, etc.

61 Mishnah, *Tamid* VII:3.

62 Mishnah, *Tamid* VII:4.

63 The Septuagint contains the same indications.

64 Mishnah, *Tamid* VII:3.

65 *Cp.* Num. 29:9,10; *JosAnt* III, 10:1.

66 Tal.Bab., *Ḳiddushin* 71 a.

67 *PhiloMos* II, 41.

68 Mishnah, *Sukkah* IV:5.

69 F. Delitzsch, *Zur Geschichte der jüdischen Poesie* (Leipzig, 1836), pp. 195-196 publishes one of the songs performed on this occasion, according to Mishnaic sources.

70 Mishnah, *Sukkah* IV; Tosefta, *Sukkah* IV (ed. Zuckermandel, 1937, p. 198);Tal. Bab., *Sukkah* 50 b.

71 Mishnah, *Sukkah* IV:5.

72 Mishnah, *Sukkah* V:1.

73 Mishnah, *Middot* II:5.

74 Mishnah, *Sukkah* V:4. *Cp.* Ezek. 8:15,16.

75 Tal.Bab., *Shabbat* 21 b.

76 *PhiloLaws,* I, XIV:76-78.

77 Exod. 23:17; 34:23,24; Lev. 23:35,36; Num. 29:1,7,12; Deuter. 16:16; 31:12.

78 A. Edersheim, *Sketches of Jewish Life in the Days of Christ* (London, 1910), pp. 337 ff.

79 Kaufmann Kohler, *The Origins of the Synagogue and the Church* (New York, 1929), p. 5.

80 This is indicated by a biblical passage and its translation in the Targumim. The Pentateuch reads: "The tent of the meeting afar off the camp" (Exod. 33:7). Targum Onkelos renders the term as "House of Instruction," the Palestinian Talmud "Place of the House of Instruction." In general, the institution is called by the Targumim "The Place of Meeting."

81 Yer. Targum to Exod. 18:20; also to 1 Chron. 16:39. *Cp. JosApio* II:18; *PhiloMos* II: 214-216; Acts 15:21.—About the rabbinic tradition of Sabbath meetings in the pre-Mosaic times of the patriarchs see *KraussSynAlt,* p. 32. The various theories concerning the origin of the Synagogue are discussed in *KraussSynAlt,* chap. 10, pp. 52 ff.

82 *PhiloMos,* II: 214-16.

83 Preserved in Eusebius, *Praeparatio evangelica,* VIII:7, in *PG,* XIII, Col. 951.

84 For further references in Philo's writings concerning the early Sabbath meetings see *PhiloMos,* II:214-216 and *PhiloLaws,* II:62-64.

85 Philo, *In Flaccum.* XIV.

86 Moritz Friedländer, *Synagoge und Kirche in ihren Anfängen* (Berlin, 1908), p. 39.

87 *Jew. Encycl.,* XI, p. 620. Krauss is of the opinion that the Synagogue served as a substitute for the Temple (*KraussSynAlt,* p. 93). This may hold good for periods during which the Temple service was interrupted or completely abandoned, but not for times in which the Temple itself still existed, together with a multitude of Synagogues in Jerusalem and elsewhere.

88 Salo W. Baron, *A Social and Religious History of the Jews* (New York, 1937), I, p. 290.

89 Augustine, *Sermo* 374, 2, in *PL* XXXIX, col. 1667.

90 *Sopherim* (ed. Joel Müller, 1878), XVI: 11,12.

91 Tal.Bab., *Sukkah* 38 b.

92 *Sopherim, ibid.,* note to the passage.

93 As the Synagogue held in the Temple court was called.

94 Tal.Bab., *Sukkah* 53 a.

[95] Tosefta, *Sukkah* IV:22 (ed. Zuckermandel, 1937, p. 199). The Talmud uses the term "the little sanctuary of God" (T. B., *Megillah* 29a), which is frequently identified with the Synagogue in the Temple. Upon this Baron comments: "Although the general talmudic view that the Synagogue dates back to Moses, the patriarchs, or to an even earlier period, is evidently unhistorical, this particular tradition seems to embody a kernel of truth" (Salo W. Baron, *The Jewish Community,* Philadelphia, 1942, III. p. 10).

[96] *KraussTA,* III, p. 76. See also Midrash, *Canticles* VIII:12.

[97] *Tal.Bab., ʿArakin* 11 b.

[98] W.O.E. Oesterley, *The Psalms in the Jewish Church* (London, 1910), pp. 136 ff.

[99] Mishnah, *ʿErubin* X:13; Tosefta to *ʿErubin* XI:19 (p. 154).

[100] *ibid.*

[101] First published 1543 in Constantinople.

[102] For a modern publication of his writings see Manuel Komroff, *The Contemporaries of Marco Polo* . . . (New York, 1928), pp. 252-322.

[103] Leopold Zunz, *Die Ritus des synagogalen Gottesdienstes geschichtlich entwickelt* (Berlin, 1859), p. 57.

[104] Petaḥyah's diary has first been published 1595 at Prague.

[105] For a modern publication of his travel notes see Lazar Grünhut, *Die Rundreise des R. Petachjah aus Regensburg* (Frankfurt a.M., 1904), sect. 18.

[106] *KraussTA,* III, p. 86.

[107] Published by Shabbethai Bass together with *Sifṭe Yeshenim* (Amsterdam, 1680).

[108] *ibid.,* p. 21 b. 196.

[109] See also pp. 196 ff. *Cp.* W.O.E. Oesterley, *The Jews and Judaism during the Greek period* (London, 1941), p. 215.

[110] Tal.Bab., *Ketubot* 105 a.

[111] Tal.Yer., *Megillah* III:1 (73 d). These figures, of course, are greatly exaggerated. It is certain, however, that Jerusalem must have had a considerable number of Synagogues for, in view of the ever increasing population of the city and its suburbs, the capacity of the Temple must have become completely insufficient for the multitude of worshippers. Moreover, when the pilgrimages for the annual festivals took place, the Temple had to be reserved mainly for the pilgrims, so that the native population had to worship in their local Synagogues.

[112] Tal.Yer., *Megillah* III:1 (83 d).

[113] Acts 6:9; *cp.* Tal.Bab., *Megillah* 26 a; Tosefta, *Megillah,* ch. II.

[114] Tal.Bab., *Berakot* 8 a.

[115] Philo, *De Legatione ad Caium,* chap. 20.

[116] *ibid.,* chap. 23.

[117] About the Synagogues in Rome at the time of the emperors see E. Schürer, *Gemeindeverfassung der Juden in Rom* (Leipzig, 1879), pp. 15 ff.

[118] Acts 13:14; 14:1; 17:2,3; 18:19, etc. About Synagogues authenticated in Palestine, Babylonia, Asia-Minor, Egypt, Greece, Italy, North-Africa, etc. (all in all 138), see *KraussSynAlt,* chap. 21-28, pp. 200-207.

[119] Tal.Bab., *Ketubot* 105 a; Tal.Yer., *Megillah* III:1 (73 d).

[120] Tal.Bab., *Megillah* 32 a; see also *Sopherim* (ed. Higger, 1937), III:13, p. 129; *cp.* Tal.Bab., *Shabbat* 106 b. See Rashi's commentary to the passage.

[121] Mishnah, *Taʿanit* IV:2.

[122] Mishnah, *Bikkurim* III:2-5.

[123] *ibid.,* III:7.

[124] "There is also another order of Essenes who, in their way of living, customs, and laws exactly agree with the others, excepting only that they differ from them about marriage." (*JosWars,* II, VIII:13).

[125] *JosWars,* II, VIII:5. A similar statement in Hippolytus, *Tractatus contra omnes haereses,* IX, 16. *Cp.* Christian D. Ginsburg, *The Essenes* (London, 1864), p. 9. Hippolytus' tractate is lost; only two fragments of the original are extant (see *PGL,* X, col. 331). The tractate is referred to by Eusebius, *Historia ecclesiae,* lib. VI, cap. 22 (in *PGL,* XX, col. 575), and Jerome, *Epistola* LXXI, *Ad Lucinium* (in *PL,*

XXII (col. 672). The Editors of Migne's *Patrologia* think, however, that Hippolytus' preserved work *Contra haeresin Noeti* (in *PGL,* X, cols. 803 ff) contains some substantial portions of the lost tractate.

[126] Hippolytus, *ibid.*

[127] This invocation refers to Adam, whom the Essenes venerated particularly. (Hippolytus, *op. cit.,* V, chap. 1.) Some of the preserved ancient prayers of the Essenes are quoted by Chr. D. Ginsburg, *op. cit.,* pp. 69-70.

[128] Porphyry, *Peri apochēs empsychōn* (*On the Abstinence from Animal Food*), IV, 13.

[129] Kaufmann, Kohler, *The Testament of Job,* in *Semitic Studies in Memory of Alexander Kohut* (Berlin, 1897), pp. 264-338.

[130] K. Kohler, *op. cit.,* p. 265.

[131] *ibid.,* p. 319.

[132] *ibid.,* p. 320.

[133] *ibid.,* p. 327.

[134] *ibid.,* p. 285.

[135] *Epsallon kai eulogēsan kai edoxologēsan ton theon en tē exairetō dialektō; ibid.,* p. 337.

[136] *PhiloTher,* III. For a detailed quotation of this report see "Women in the Music of Ancient Israel," pp. 989 ff.

[137] *ibid.*

[138] J. M. Joost, *Geschichte des Judentums und seiner Sekten* (Leipzig, 1857), p. 58.

[139] Richard B. Rackham, *The Acts of the Apostles* (London, 1912), p. 378.

[140] *Cp.* the *"Halleluyah,"* mentioned three times in Rev. 19:1,3,6.

[141] Eusebius, *Historia Ecclesiastica,* V, 28:5, in *PGL,* XX, 514.

[142] A. Dupont-Sommer, Millar Burrows, Theodor H. Gaster, John A. Allegro, a.o.

[143] Solomon Zeitlin, A. Büchler, A. Marmorstein, G. R. Driver, P. R. Weiss, *et alia.*

[144] *Cf. JosWar,* II, 8:2 ff (II, 119 ff); *Jos Ant,* XVIII, 1:5 (XVIII, 18 ff); Philo, *Quod Omnis Probus Liber* (*Every Good Man is Free*), 75 ff.

[145] Solomon Zeitlin, *The Dead Sea Scrolls and Modern Scholarship,* in *JQR,* Monograph Series No. 3 (Philadelphia, 1956), p. XXIII ff.

[145a] Solomon Zeitlin, *op. cit.,* pp. XIII ff.

[146] Before Zeitlin, A. Büchler has already shown that the *Zadokite Fragments,* discovered 1900 by Solomon Schechter in a Genizah at Cairo, and which are very similar in the contents to the recently found *Manual of Discipline,* were a karaitic work, and hence were composed in the Middle Ages (*JQR,* 1913, pp. 429-485). Furthermore, as was mentioned earlier (see p. 141), a Syriac letter from Timotheus I (726-819 C. E.) relates that around 800 C. E. some Hebrew manuscripts were discovered in a cave near the Dead Sea. Also, Jacob al-Kirkisani, a karaitic writer who lived in the 10th century C. E. mentions a sect, which he calls *al-Maghariya,* meaning "Cave-Sect," because their books were discovered in a cave (Leon Nemoy, *Karaite Anthology,* New Haven, 1952, p. 50).

[147] Th. H. Gaster, *The Dead Sea Scriptures in English Translation* (Garden City, N.Y., 1956), pp. 111-112.

[148] The following translations are mainly those found in the English and French publications about the scrolls. They do not follow always the original Hebrew text. The differences are indicated by us in any particular instance.

[149] Translations of Gaster, unless otherwise indicated.

[150] Millar Burrows: "rejoicing."

[151] Millar Burrows: "meditate."

[152] *v'anahah b'kinnor ḳinah* is a superlinear addition by a second scribe, therefore, strictly speaking, it does not belong to the original text.

[153] The Hebrew word for "flute" is lacking in the original.

[154] Th. Gaster, *op. cit.,* p. 113.

[155] To this, Gaster adds the note: "The expression occurs also in the Psalms of Solomon, 15:3. 'The fruit of the lips with the well-tuned instrument of the tongue . . .' There is a subtle play of words in the original, for the Hebrew word)*azammerah* means

at once "cull" (strictly "trim vines"; cf. Lev. 25:3) and "sing" (Gaster, *op. cit.*, p. 204).

156 A. Dupont-Sommer, *The Jewish Sect of Qumran and the Essenes*, transl. from the French by R. D. Barnett (New York, 1955), p. 139.

157 Cp. 1 Cor. 14:15.

158 At this place, there is no instrument mentioned in the original. Dupont-Sommer's translation is a free interpretation of the Hebrew *neginati.*

159 After Dupont-Sommer.

160 The Hebrew world *ḥok* also means "statute," "ordinance."

161 Cp. with 2 Macc. 12:36-37; Judas "sung psalms in his own [Hebrew] language before beating Gorgias' men."

162 See this author's *Bibliography of Jewish Music* (New York, 1951), Introduction p. XXIV.

163 Augustine, *Confessiones*, X:33, in *PL*, XXXII, 800 ff.

164 Augustine, *Enarratio in Psalmum* CVI, 1, in *PL*, XXXVII, 1419.

165 Eusebius, *Ekklēsiastikēs historias*, II:17, in *PGL*, XX, 179.

166 Hermias Sozomenes, *Ekklēsiastikē historia, lib.* VIII, cap. 8., in *PGL*, LXVII, 1535.

167 Sozomenes, *Ekklēsiastikē historia, lib.* III, cap. 16, in *PGL*, LXVII, 1090.

168 Augustine, *Confessiones*, IX:7, in *PL*, XXXII, 770.

169 Cassiodorus, *In Psalterium praefatio*, in *PL*, LXX, 10.

170 Isidore of Seville, *De ecclesiasticis officiis, lib. I, cap.* 5, in *PL*, LXXXIII, 742 ff.

171 Augustine, *Confessiones*, IX:4, in *PL*, XXXII, 766.

172 Anastasius, *Historia de vitis Romanorum Pontificorum*, XXXIX, in *PL*, CXXVIII, 73-74.

173 Eusebius, *Hypomnēmata eis tous Psalmous*, Psalm LXV, verse 2, in *PGL*, XXIII, 647.

174 *ibid.*, verses 7-9, in *PGL*, XXIII, 658.

175 Leo I, *Sermo* IX:4, in *PL*, LIV, 163.

176 Ambrose, *Hexaemeron*, lib. III, chap 5, in *PL*, XIV, 178.

177 Ambrose, *Enarratio* in *Psalmum* I, sec. 9, in *PL*, XIV, 968-69.

178 Theodoret, *Hermēneia eis tous Psalmous, Ps. CXLVIII, verse* 11, in LXXX, 1991.

179 Venantius Fortunatus, *Poema ad clerum Parisiacum*, in *PL*, LXXXVIII, col. 104.

180 Basil the Great, *Homilia in Psalmum primum*, in *PGL*, XXXI, 1724.

181 Jerome, *Epistola CVII, Ad Laetam*, in *PL*, XXII, 871.

182 John Chrysostom, *Homilia eis ton Psalmon CXLV*, in *PGL*, LV, col. 521.

183 Jerome, *Epistola CXXV*, 11, *Ad Rusticum monachum*, in *PL*, XXII, 896.

184 Jerome, *Epistola CVIII, Ad Eustochium virginem*, in *PL*, XXII, 896.

185 John Cassian, *De Coenobiorum institutis*, II:2, in *PL*, XLIX, 78,

186 See note 176.

187 Augustine, *Enarratio in Psalmum XXVI*, 2, *Sermo ad plebem*, in *PL*, XXXVI, 199.

188 Eusebius, *Ekklēsiastikēs historias*, II:17, in *PGL*, XX, 175.

189 Basil the Great, *Epistolē* CCVII, *Tois kata Neokaisareian klērikois* (written 375), in *PGL*, XXXII, 763.

190 John Chrysostom, *Eis ton Psalmon XLI*, in *PGL*, LV, 159.

191 Cassiodorus, *Expositio in Psalterium, Ps. CIV*, in *PL*, *LXX*, 742.

192 Isidore of Seville, *De ecclesiasticis officiis, lib. I, cap.* 10, in *PL*, LXXXIII, 744.

193 *ibid., lib. I, cap.* 13, in *PL*, LXXXIII, 750.

194 Tertullian, *Liber de oratione*, 27, in *PL*, I, 1301.

195 Cassiodorus, *Expositio in Psalterium, Ps. CIX*, in *PL*, LXX, 742.

196 John Cassian, *De Coenobiorum institutis*, II:2, in *PL*, XLIX, 78.

197 Socrates of Constantinople, *Ekklesiastikē historia*, VI:8, in *PGL*, LXVII, 692.

198 Theodoret, *Ekklēsiastikē historia*, II:19, in *PGL*, LXXXII, 1060.

199 *PhiloTher*, III:29.

200 Eusebius, *Ekklēsiatikēs historias*, II:17, in *PGL*, XX, 183.

201 Tertullian, *Apologeticus adversus Gentes pro Christianis, XXXIX*, in *PL*, I, 540. See also note 94, *ibid.*

202 Eusebius, *Ekklēsiastikēs historias*, V:28, in *PGL*, XX, 513.

[203] Clement of Alexandria, *Logos protreptikos pros Hellēnas, I,* in *PGL,* VIII, 55, 58-60.
[204] Clement of Alexandria, *Strōmata,* VI:11, in *PGL,* IX, 310.
[205] John Chrysostom, *Homilias en Antiocheia lechteisai,* in *PG,* XLIX.
[206] Eusebius, *Ekklēsiastikēs historias,* X:3, in *PGL,* XX, 847.
[207] St. Paul and Stephen, *Regula ad Monachos, XIV,* in *PL,* LXVI, 953.
[208] Athanasius, *Epistola de decretis Nicaenae Synodi,* 16, in *PGL,* XXV, 451.
[209] Epiphanius, *Kata haireseōn,* in *PGL,* XLII, 176-177.
[210] Tertullian, *De Carne Christi, XVII* and *XX,* in *PL,* II, 826, 831.
[211] Eusebius, *Ekklēsiastikēs historias,* VII: 30, *Peri tēs kata Paulou espistolēs tōn episkopōn,* in *PGL,* XX, 714.
[212] Augustine, *Confessions,* IX:7, in *PL,* XXXII, 770.
[213] Leo I, *Sermo* XIV:2, in *LIV,* 505.
[214] Eusebius, *Ekklēsiastikēs historias,* VII:24 in *PGL,* XX, 694.
[215] Gregory Nazianzen, *Logoi,* IV:71, in *PGL,* XXXV, 594.
[216] Gerbert, Martin, *Scriptores ecclesiastici,* No. 1206,I,2.
[217] St. Paul and Stephen, *Regula ad Monachos, VII,* in *PL,* LXVI, 954.
[218] Augustine, *Confessiones,* X:33, in *PL,* XXXII, 800.
[219] Isidore of Seville, *De ecclesiasticis officiis, lib I, cap.* 5, *De psalmis,* in *PL,* LXXXIII, 742.
[220] Augustine, *Confessiones,* X:33. *Ut se gerit ad voluptates aurium,* in *PL,* XXXII, 800 ff.
[221] *ibid.*
[222] Augustine, *Enarratio in Psalmum XCIX,* 4, in *PL,* XXXVII, 1272.
[223] John Chrysostom, *Eis tōn Psalmōn XLI,* in *PGL,* LV, 159; and *Protheoria eis tous Psalmous,* in *PGL,* LV, 538.
[224] E. Werner, *The Doxology in Synagogue and Church,* in *HUCA* XIX, (1945-1946), pp. 275-351.
[225] Jerome, *Breviarium in Psalmos, XXXII,* in *PL,* XXVI, col. 970.
[226] Augustine, *Enarratio in Psalmum CVI,* in *PL,* XXXVII, col. 1419.
[227] Jerome, *Epistola XXXIX, Ad Paulam super obitu Blaesillae filiae,* in *PL,* XXII, col. 466.
[228] Jerome, *Epistola CVIII, Ad Eustochium virginem; Epitaphium Paulae matris,* in *PL,* XXII, col. 902.
[229] Chrysostom, *Eis tōn Psalmōn XLI,* in *PGL,* LV, col. 156.
[230] Anton Naegele, *Über Arbeitslieder bei Johannes Chrysostomos,* in *Sächsische Gesellschaft der Wissenschaften zu Leipzig, Philologisch-Historische Klasse, Berichte,* (1905), vol. 57. p. 101-142.
[231] Tal.Bab., *Soṭah* 48 a.
[232] *ibid.*
[233] Augustine, *Enarratio in Psalmum* XCI:3,5, in *PL,* XXXVII, 1173-74.
[234] Athanasius, *Epos Markellinon eis tōn hermēneian tōn Psalmōn,* in *PGL,* XXVII, 39.
[235] Didymos of Alexandria, *Eis Psalmous,* IV:1, in *PGL,* XXXIX, 1166.
[236] *ibid.*
[237] Aristotle, *Politikē,* VIII, 1341 b, 7.
[238] Clement of Alexandria, *Strōmata, VI,* 11, in *PGL,* IX, 311.
[239] John Chrysostom, *Eis ton Psalmon XLI,* 2, in *PGL,* LV, 157.
[240] Clement of Alexandria, *Paidagōgos,* II:4, in *PGL,* VIII, 443.
[241] John Chrysostom, *Eis tōn Psalmōn CXL,* in *PGL,* LV, 427.
[242] *ibid.,* in *PGL,* LV, 426.
[243] Tertullian, *Ad uxorem,* II:9, in *PL,* I, 1417.
[244] Clement of Alexandria, *Strōmata,* VII, 7, in *PGL,* IX, 470.
[245] John Chrysostom, *Eis tas Hagias Martyras;* in *PGL,* L, 634.
[246] Gregory the Great, *Liber Sacramentorum, Notae,* in *PL,* LXXVIII, 468.
[247] Jerome, *Epistola LXXVII, De morte Fabiolae,* in *PL,* XXII, 697.
[248] Augustine, *Confessiones, IX,* 12, in *PL, XXXII,* 776.

[249] Johann Christoph Speidel, *Unverwerfliche Spuren der alten Davidischen Singkunst* (Waiblingen, Stuttgart, 1740).

[250] Conrad Gottlob Anton, *Versuch, die Melodie und Harmonie der alten hebräischen Gesänge zu entziffern,* in Paulus, *Repertorium für Biblische und Morgenländische Litteratur* (Jena, 1790), I,II,III.

[251] Leopold Haupt, *Sechs alttestamantliche Psalmen; mit ihren aus den Accenten entzifferten Singweisen* (Görlitz, Leipzig, 1854).

[252] Leopold Arends, *Über den Sprachgesang der Vorzeit und Herstellbarkeit der althebräischen Vokalmusik* (Berlin, 1867).

[253] *ibid.*, p. 114, note.

[254] Heinrich Berl, *Die Wiederherstellbarkeit der althebräischen Vokalmusik,* in *Der Jude* (Berlin, 1923), VII, 528-544.

[255] *op. cit.*, p. 544.

[256] Otto Glaser, *Die ältesten Psalmmelodien,* in *Zeitschrift für Semistik* (Leipzig, 1932), VIII and X.

[257] Joseph Yasser, *Restoration of Ancient Hebrew Music.* Paper delivered at Temple Emanuel, New York, March 1946; abstract published in *First Ten Years of the Annual Three Choir Festival* (New York, 1946), p. 47.

[258] The following mainly after Guido Adler's *Handbuch der Musikgeschichte* (Frankfurt a.M., 1924), p. 18 ff.

[259] About *maḳam* and *maḳamat* and its signifiicance for the folk and art music of Oriental and Occidental, ancient and modern, peoples, see in detail Bence Szabolcsi, *Bausteine zur Geschichte der Melodie* (Budapest, 1959), pp. 223-235.

[260] Eric Werner, *The Conflict between Hellenism and Judaism in the Music of the Early Christian Church,* in *HUCA* XX (1947), p. 469.

[261] Robert Lach, *Die Musik der Natur- und der orientalischen Kulturvölker,* in Adler's *Handbuch der Musikgeschichte* (Berlin, 1929), I, pp. 28 ff.

[262] An exception from this rule was the practice of the Italian opera buffa of the 17th and 18th centuries, with the ornamental elaboration of its singing parts being left mainly to the performers, which, of course, led to all kinds of abuses.

[263] Robert Lach, *op. cit.*, p. 29.

[264] Rabindranath Tagore, *My reminiscences* (New York, 1917), p. 189.

[265] Hermann Keyserling, *Das Reisetagebuch eines Philosophen* (Darmstadt, 1921), I, p. 399.

[266] Tal.Bab., *Soṭah* 30 b. The responsive practice is described in *Soferim* XIV, 9-10.

[267] Ibn Bal(am, Abu Zakarya Yaḥya, *Sha(ar ta(ame* 3 *Sifre "EMeT,"* new. ed. Amsterdam, 1858.

[268] Tal.Bab., *Shabbat* 106 b, 113 a; Tal.Bab., *(Erubin* 60 a.

[269] Tal.Bab., *Megillah* 32 a.

[270] Tal.Bab., *Sanhedrin* 99 b; Tosefta, *)Ahilot* XVI:8; Tosefta, *Parah* IV:7 (ed. Zuckermandel, 1937, pp. 614, 633).

[271] See p. 435.

[272] *KraussTA,* III, p. 78.

[273] Tal.Yer., *Shekalim* V:2 (48 d).

[274] Midrash, *Exodus* XLVII:5.

[275] According to our present knowledge, the *ta(amim* cannot be traced earlier than the 7th century, therefore they do not belong to the topics of this study. In their earliest form they might have been the graphic reproduction of the choir-leaders' cheironomic movements. (See pp. 423 ff.). For the literature on the subject see the author's *Bibliography of Jewish Music* (New York, 1951).

[276] Fr. Delitzsch, *Biblical Commentary on the Psalms* (Edinburgh, 1892), I, pp. 35-36. A. Ackermann, *Das hermeneutische Element der biblischen Accentuation* (Berlin, 1893), p. 3.

[277] For musical examples of such ancient pentatonic melodies see Bence Szabolcsi, *About Five-Tone-Scales in the Early Hebrew Melodies,* in *Ignace Goldziher Memorial Volume* (Budapest, 1948), part I, pp. 310-12.

278 A. Z. Idelsohn, *Thesaurus,* II, pp. 44, 52.

279 Joseph Yasser, *The Traditional Roots of Jewish Harmony,* in *Proceedings . . . of the Cantors Assembly and the Department of Music of the United Synagogue of America* (New York, 1951), vol. IV, pp. 16-17.

280 Clement of Alexandria, *Paidagōgos,* II:4, in *PG,* VI, col. 245.

281 *ibid.*

282 *SachsRise,* p. 219.

283 Eric Werner, *Notes on the Attitude of the Early Church Fathers toward Hebrew Psalmody,* in *Review of Religion* (May, 1943), pp. 350-351.

284 Hugo Riemann, *Handbuch der Musikgeschichte* (Leipzig, 1923), I, p. 168.

285 Aristotle, *Politikē,* VIII:7, 1342 a, b.

286 Plato, *Politeia,* III, 399 a.

287 Translation of the *Authorized, Jewish,* and *American Versions, Moulton* and *Harkavy. Douay* has "So when they all sounded together, both with trumpets, and voice, and cymbals, and organs, and with divers kind of musical instruments, and lifted up their voice on high the sound was heard afar off." *Moffat* translates "the trumpeters and singers joined in one loud song of praise and thanksgiving to the Eternal," whereas the *Revised Standard Version* stresses "the one sound" even more emphatically in interpreting the Oriental principle of vocal monophony as a "duty of the trumpeters and singers to make themselves heard in unison in praise and thanksgiving to the Lord."

288 *SchneidKult,* I, p. 226.

289 Midrash, *Song of Song* VIII:12.

290 In Ps. 81:3, the sound of the *kinnor* is also described as *na'ayim,* "sweet" (*Moffat, Jewish* and *Revised Standard Versions*), and "pleasant" (*Authorized* and *American Versions, Douay* and *Moulton*). See also p. 405.

291 *Pesiḳta Rabbati,* chap. XXV, p. 127 a. "Honor the Lord with all thy substance" (*JewTransl, AuthVers, Hark*).

292 Tal.Bab., *Ta'anit* 16 a.

293 *Sha'are teshubah.* No. 178. *Pesiḳta* (ed. Solomon Bober, Lyck, 1868), p. 97 a.

294 Tal.Yer., *Shekalim* V:2 (48 d).

295 See p. 257.

296 Midrash, *Numeri* VI:8.

297 Tal.Bab., *Megillah* 24 b.

298 Tal.Bab., *Sukkah* 50 b; 51 a; *Ta'anit* 27 a; *'Arakin* 11 a.

299 Tal.Bab., *'Erubin* 104 a,

300 Tal.Bab., *Sukkah* 51 a.

301 Abott of R. Nathan, chap. IV, end (ed. Schechter, 1945, p. 17).

302 Midrash, *Genesis* LXVIII:4; Tal.Bab., *Sanhedrin* 21 b.

303 Tal.Bab., *Ḥullin* 133 a; *Mishle* 25:20.

304 Tal.Bab., *'Arakin* 11 b.

305 Tal.Bab., *Rosh ha-Shanah* 8 a. In this passage, the Talmud quotes a verse of Ps. 65:14.

306 Tal.Bab., *Giṭṭin* 7 a.

307 For the classification of post-biblical psalmody see p. 211.

308 *KraussTA,* III, p. 78.

309 Tal.Bab., *Sanhedrin* 14 a.

310 *ibid.*

311 Mishnah, *Sukkah* V:4; Mishnah, *Middot* II:5; Tal.Bab., *Sukkah* 51 a,b.

312 Midrash, *Lamentations* XII, p. 17.

313 Tal.Bab., *Berakot* 30 b, 31 a.

314 *ibid.*

315 Tal.Bab., *Ketubot* 16 b.

316 Tal.Bab., *Sanhedrin* 14 a. See Rashi's commentary.

317 Tal.Bab., *Ketubot* 17 a.

318 Mishnah, *Soṭah* IX:11.

319 Mishnah, *Soṭah* IX:14; see also Tal. Bab., *Giṭṭin* 7 a.

320 Tal.Bab., *Ḥagigah* 14 b.

[321] *Budde Gesch*, p. 286.
[322] *ibid.*, p. 188.
[323] See p. 464.
[324] *BuddeGesch*, p. 278.
[325] Tosefta, *Sanhedrin* 12. See p. 142.
[326] See the section "The Dance," pp. 463 ff.
[327] Tal.Bab., *Shebu'ot* 15 b.
[328] Tal.Bab., *Soṭah*, 48 a.
[329] *ibid.*
[330] *ibid.*
[331] Tal.Bab., *Berakot* 24 a.
[332] Tal,Bab., *Soṭah* 48 a.
[333] Tal.Bab., *Sanhedrin* 101 a.
[334] *ibid.*
[335] In the Middle Ages and subsequent centuries the name *leẓim* was applied to the most impudent buffoons and jokers who participated at fairs and other popular merriments.
[336] Midrash, *Song of Songs* VIII:13.
[337] Tal. Yet., *Soṭah* IX:12 (24 b).
[338] Tal. Yer., *Soṭah* VII:2; Tal. Yer., *Megillah* I:11 (71 b).
[339] Tal.Bab., *Ḥagigah* 15 b.
[340] Tal.Bab., *Soṭah* 48 a.
[341] "Rejoice not, O Israel, unto exultation, like the peoples, for thou hast gone astray from thy god."
[342] "The mirth of tabrets ceaseth, the noise of them that rejoice endeth, the joy of the harp ceaseth, they drink not wine with a song."
[343] Tal.Bab., *Giṭṭin* 7 a. See also p. 277.
[344] See also p. 389.
[345] Tal Bab., *Pesaḥim* 85 b; Tal.Yer., *Pesaḥim* VII:11 (35 b).
[346] Tal.Bab., *Ḥullin* 91 b.
[347] *ibid.*
[348] *ibid.*
[349] Midrash, *Lamentations* III:23.
[350] Midrash, *Song of Songs* VIII:13.
[351] Midrash, *Song of Songs*, VIII:14, par. 1.
[352] Midrash, Lamentations (The Proems of the Sages), XXIV.
[353] Tal.Yer., *Soṭah* VII:2 (21 c). *Cf.* Job 35:10, where God is referred to as a "song-giver."
[354] For the Harmony of the Spheres see Albert von Thimus, *Die harmonikale Symbolik des Alterthums* (Cologne, 1868-76).
[355] Septuagint: "their sound" (*phthongos*).
[356] Midrash, *Numeri* XIV:21.
[357] Tal.Yer., *Yoma* I:6 (39 b).
[358] Mishnah, *Tamid* III:8.
[359] Tal.Bab., *Yoma* 20 b.
[360] Tal.Bab., *Soṭah* 48 a.
[361] TalBab., *Giṭṭin* 7 a; *cp* *'Arakin* 11 a; *Sukkah* 51 b; *Ta'anit* 27 a.
[362] *Jew.Encycl.*, IX, p. 120.
[363] C. H. Cornill, *Music in the Old Testament* (Chicago, 1909), p. 25.
[364] Abraham Zevi Idelsohn, *Hebräisch-Orientalischer Melodienschatz* (Jerusalem, Berlin, Vienna, 1914-1932), 10 volumes. The same in an English and in a Hebrew edition.
[365] A. Z. Idelsohn, *Parallelen zwischen gregorianischen und hebräisch-orientalischen Gesangsweisen*, in *Zeitschrift für Musikwissenschaft* (1921-22), pp. 515 ff.
[366] Peter Wagner, *Der gregorianische Gesang*, in Adler's *Handbuch der Musikgeschichte* (Frankfurt a.M., 1930), I, p. 77.
[367] *ibid.*, p. 78.
[368] *IdelJewMus*, Tables XIII and XIII[a] pp. 79-83.

[369] Curt Sachs, *Musik des Altertums* (Breslau, 1924), pp. 31-32. Also his *Musik der Antike,* in *Handbuch der Musikwissenschaft* (Potsdam, 1928), pp. 8-9.

[370] See also p. 213.

[371] A detailed treatment of ancient Jewish song from the view-point of comparative musicology is contained in *SachsRise,* pp. 81-95.

[372] *PfeifferIntro,* p. 806.

[373] *ibid.*

[374] *PfeifferIntro,* p. 789.

[375] *ibid.*

[376] *SieversMetr.*

[377] *ibid.,* p. 96.

[378] *ibid.,* p. 96.

[379] *ibid.,* p. 48.

[380] Oskar Fleischer, *Neumen-Studien* (Leipzig, 1895), I, p. 31.

[381] Tal.Bab., *Berakot* 62 a.—Aaron ben Moses ben Asher, *Diḳduḳe ha-ta'amim* (new ed. Leipzig, 1879), p. 18—Seligman Baer, *Thorath Emeth* (Rödelheim, 1852), p. 4, note.—*Reise des Petaḥja* (ed. Fürth, 1844), p. 47.

[382] *Diḳduḳe,* p. 17.

[383] Fleischer, *op. cit.,* II, pp. 18-19.

[384] *ibid.,* p. 18.

[385] The earliest known neumes are those of the *Biblia Amiantina,* the oldest extant manuscript of the Vulgate, which originated *ca.* 700 C.E. This Bible is preserved in the Biblioteca Mediceo-Laurenziana in Florence.

[386] Arno Nadel, *Jüdische Musik,* in *Der Jude* (Berlin, 1923), VII, pp. 229 ff.

[387] In occidental music, the "measure," representing a metric unit between two bar-lines, is a relatively recent device. As late as in the 16th and partly in the 17th centuries, a "measure" meant something entirely different from our present term; it was not the higher entity of several time-units as pre-determined by the bar-line, but a single unit of this order, in accordance with the original sense of the Latin word *tactus,* meaning "touch" or "beat."

[388] *SachsRhythm,* p. 92.

[389] See the section "The Dance," pp. 445 ff.

[390] *SachsRhythm,* p. 74.

[391] *ibid.*

[392] Abraham Zevi Idelsohn, *Hebräisch-Orientalischer Melodienschatz* (Jerusalem, Berlin, Vienna, 1914-1932), 10 volumes.

[393] Curt Sachs, *Rhythm and Tempo* (New York, 1953), Chapter "Ancient Israel and the Beginnings of the Eastern Church," pp. 68-82.

[394] He says, f.i.: "[After crossing the Red Sea] they passed that whole night in melody (*en hymnois*) and mirth, Moses himself composing in hexameter verse a song to God (*en hexametrō tonō*)" (*JosAnt,* II, 16:4).—"Then he [Moses] recited to them a poem in hexameter verse, which he has moreover bequeathed in a book preserved in the Temple" (*JosAnt,* IV, 8:44).—"David composed songs and hymns to God in varied meters—some he made in trimeters, and others in pentameters" (*JosAnt* VII, 12:3).—It is obvious that Josephus projects back to Moses' and David's times the versification of Greek poetry of his own epoch. It is hardly conceivable that Moses or David would have written poems in Greek meters.

[395] *PhiloTher,* III, 29.

[396] Eusebius, *Praeparatio evangelica,* XI,3, in *PG,* XIII, 1067.

[397] Cyril of Alexandria, *Pro Sancta Christianorum Religione adversus libros athei Juliani liber* VII, 2, in *PGL,* LXXVI, col. 838.

[398] John Chrysostom, *Prooimia tōn Psalmōn,* in *PGL,* LV, 531 ff.

[399] John Chrysostom, *Proemia in Psalmos,* in *PGL,* LV, 533.

[400] Jerome, *Praefatio in librum Job,* in *PL,* XXVII, col. 1141. Another, shorter, Prologue to the same book (in *PL,* XXIX, 63-66), as well as the introduction of his "Commentaries to the Book of Job" (in *PL,* XXVI, col. 656 ff) do not contain any reference to Hebrew poetry.

[401] Jerome, *Epistola XXX. Ad Paulam,* in *PL,* XXII, col. 441 ff.

[402] Jerome, *Praefatio in Librum II Chronicorum Eusebii Pamphilii,* in *PL,* XXVII, col. 223. This "Preface" is written in the form of a letter to Vincentius and Galienus.

[403] The Benedictine Fathers, editors of Jerome's writings in Migne's *Patrologia Latina,* express themselves some doubts about the alleged metrical form of Hebrew poetry as intimated by Jerome. See *Prolegomena in Divinam S. Hieronymi Bibliothecam. Prolegomenon IV. De titulis et capitulis, versibus et metris sacrorum bibliorum,* in *PL,* XXXVIII, col. 1140, note 9, also *ibid.,* col. 154 ff.

[404] Gregory of Nyssa, *Tractatus prior in Psalmorum inscriptiones, IV,* in *PGL,* XLIV, 446.

[405] Augustine, *Epistola VI, ad Memorio,* in *PL* XXXIII, 369.

[406] Isidore of Seville, *Etymologiae, I,* 39, in *PL,* LXXXII, 119.

[407] For further medieval opinions on the alleged Hebrew metrical versification see McClintock and Strong, *Cyclopaedia of Biblical, Theological and Ecclesiastical Literature* (New York, 1883-86), VIII, pp. 321 b ff.

[408] *Sh'va,* the two vertical dots (:) below a vowelless letter, indicates a silent (*i.e.* half-mute) syllable. This is the simple *sh'va. Ḥatef* (lit. "hurried") is a composite *sh'va,* shortening the pronunciation of a vowel by the *sh'va-sign* together with the particular vowel-sign (-:, :.:, or T:). For metrical purposes both fulfill identical functions: they indicate a silent, or a shortened pronunciation of a half-vowel.

[409] The *mora* basis is accepted by a number of metricists, *e.g.* Johann Joachim Bellerman, Levin Saalschütz, Julius Ley, Hubert Grimme, Nivard Schlögl, Elcanon Isaacs,—and rejected by others, *e.g.* Eduard Sievers, Eduard König, Karl Budde, William R. Arnold.

[410] Called by Gesenius *respiratio.*

[411] Elcanon Isaacs, *The Metrical Basis of Hebrew Poetry,* in *American Journ. of Sem. Languages and Liter.* (1918), vol. 35, No. 1, p. 26.

[412] *ArnoldRhythms,* p. 194.

[413] Isaacs, *op. cit.,* p. 29.

[414] *ibid.*

[415] *SachsRhythm,* p. 70.

[416] For the sake of increased clearness, we use here Oesterley's *equirhythmic* translations with marked accents. See O. W. E. Oesterley, *Ancient Hebrew Poems Metrically Translated* (London, 1938). Similar accents are applied to the Hebrew text.

[417] The thoroughly documented dissertation of Charles Franklin Kraft, *The Strophic Structure of Hebrew Poetry* (Chicago, 1938) contains pertinent information on this subject.

[418] Ch. C. Torrey, *The Second Isaiah* (New York, 1928), p. 175.

[419] Heinrich Zimmern, *Ein vorläufiges Wort über babylonische Metrik,* in *Zeitschrift für alttestamentliche Wissenschaft,* VIII (1893), pp. 121-124.

[420] James Henry Breasted, *The Dawn of Conscience* (New York, 1935), pp. 169-177. Adolf Erman, *Die Literatur der Ägypter* (Leipzig, 1923), pp. 9-11.—W. F. Albright, *The Earliest Forms of Hebrew Verse,* in *Journal of the Palestine Oriental Society,* II (1922), pp. 71-72.

[421] Zellig S. Harris, *The Structure of Ras Shamra C,* in *JAOS,* LIV (1934), pp. 80-81.

[422] James A. Montgomery, *Ras Shamra Notes IV,* in *JAOS,* LV (1935), pp. 268, 269.

[423] In these examples we follow, as a rule, Sievers' metrical analyses, even though these have been severely, and not always fairly, criticized by Arnold.

[424] Sievers explains this metric irregularity by a possible textual corruption of verse 12. (*SieversMetr,* p. 502, note 10).

[425] *SachsRhythm,* p. 74.

[426] *SieversMetr,* p. 93.

[427] Isaacs, *op. cit.,* pp. 47 ff.

[428] *SachsRhythm,* p. 77.

429 *Stichos* is the term for any subdivision of a verse. The combination of two or more *stichoi* constitutes the period of the verse, called distich, tristich, etc.

430 This was true for the time when Budde wrote his essay (1882). Idelsohn's *Thesaurus* contains numerous *ḳinot* of Oriental Jews transcribed in modern musical notation. Therefore, we are to-day in a position to lean on authentic musical material, which enables us to determine the melodic and rhythmic characteristics of the biblical *ḳinah*.

431 Karl Budde, *Das hebräische Klagelied,* in *Zeitschrift für alttestamentliche Wissenschaft* (1882), pp. 24 ff.

432 E. Isaacs, *op. cit.,* p. 41.

433 *ibid.*

434 *ibid.*

435 *ibid.*

436 Mishnah, ʿ*Arakin* II:3.

437 *ibid.,* II:5.

438 *ibid.,* II:3.

439 *ibid.,* II:5.

440 *SachsRise,* p. 78.

441 Mishnah, *Yoma* III:11, *cp.* Tal.Yer., *Yoma* III:7 (40 d).

442 Tal. Bab., *Yoma* 38 b.

443 Tal. Yer., *Shekalim* V:2 (48 d) gives a somewhat different description: "Hygros ben Levi was famous for the beauty of his voice. He would put his thumb in his mouth and would produce varied tunes, to the extent that the priests reeled with joy."—Another translation, that of the Soncino Press, attributes to the passage a different meaning: "Hygros ben Levi knew a cadence in song but would not teach it." The translator (Rabbi J. Epstein) gives the following comment in a note: "A somewhat difficult phrase. Evidently in connection with the Temple songs. It may have been a specially composed finale, allowing for individual margins of musical ingenuity." This is a highly subjective interpretation of the translator, for which there is not the slightest indication in the text.

444 Mishnah, *Yoma* III:11.

445 Tosefta, *Yoma* II:2 (ed. Zuckermandel, 1937, p. 185).

446 Richard Wallaschek, *Anfänge der Tonkunst* (Leipzig, 1903), p. 269.

447 See in detail this author's study *Rundfunk und Musikpflege* (Leipzig, 1931), pp. 10 ff.

448 This is the translation of the *Authorized* and *American Versions.* Luther has also attached a musical meaning to the passage: ("die Wonnen des Menschen, allerlei Saitenspiel" ("all kinds of instruments"). Nevertheless, the musical implication of *shiddah v'shiddot,* is doubtful. Accordingly, most of the principal English Bibles translate the term in a non-musical sense. *Douay* has: ("I made me singing men and singing women, and the delights of the sons of men,) cups and vessels (to serve to pour out wine)" The *Jewish Version* translates: ("I got me men-singers and women-singers, and the delights of the sons of men,) women very many," *Moulton* ("I gat me men singers and women singers, and the delights of the sons of men,) concubines very many," *Harkavy* ("I gat me men singers and women singers, and the delights of the sons of men,) mistresses very many," *Moffat* ("I secured singers, both men and women,) and many a mistress (man's delight,)" and the *Revised Standard Version* ("I got singers, both men and women,) and many concubines, (man's delight.)"

449 Tal. Yer., *Yoma* I:6 (39 b).

450 Tal.Yer., *Megillah* III:2 (74 a).

NOTES TO SECTION VI

[1] The preserved pictorial documents are enumerated on pp. 64 ff.

[2] Thus the *Authorized* and *American Versions, Moulton* and *Harkavy. Douay* has simply "made of wood." *Moffat* and the *Revised Standard Version* mistranslate the term as "singing," resp. "with songs." The latter version adds, however, in a marginal note "fir trees."

[3] *RiehmHandw,* I, p. 204. A marginal note of the *American Version* to the passage adds "cypress wood".

[4] Though *beḳol ʿoẓe beroshim* refers unmistabably to instruments of music, some commentators think that the Masoretic text is corrupt and that the passage should better read as *beḳol ʿoz u-beshirim,* "with all their might, and with songs," like the similar passage in 1 Chron. 13:8. This assumption has but little probability; it is even contradicted by the arbitrary substitution of the two consonants *zayyin* ז and *ẓaddi* צ (Wilhelm Nowack, *Lehrbuch der Archäologie* (Freiburg i.B. 1894) I, p. 273, note. See also *FineInstr.* p. 22 and note (2) *supra.*

[5] Translated by the Septuagint as *xyla peykina* (fir wood). The Vulgate, however, renders it as *ligna thyina,* a precious wood of Antiquity.

[6] See also R. Kimḥi, *Commentary on 2 Chron.* 2:7 In Revel. 18:12 *xylon thyion* is mentioned together with other precious objects.

[7] W. F. Albright, *Magan, Meluḥa, Menes and Naram-Sin,* in *Journal of Egyptian Archaeology* (London, 1921), VII, p. 83.

[8] The English Bibles render the word as "almug trees" for 1 Kings 10:11, and "algum trees" for 2 Chron. 9:10 (*American Version, Moulton* and *Harkavy*), or "almug wood," resp. "algum wood" in the *Revised Standard Version.* For both places *Douay* has "thyine trees," the *Jewish Version* "sandal wood."

[9] *JosAnt,* VIII, 3:8.

[10] Targum to 1 Chron. 15:20.

[11] Tal.Bab., *Shabbat* 58 b; Tal.Yer., *Shabbat* VI:I (7 d); Tal. Yer., *Beẓah* V:2 (63 a).

[12] Mishnah, *Beẓah* V:2.

[13] Tal.Bab., *Beẓah* 36 a,b.

[14] Mishnah, *Kelim* XXIV:14.

[15] *ibid.,* XVI:7.

[16] *ibid.,* XVI:8.

[17] *ibid.,* XX:2.

[18] *ibid.,* XVI:8.

[19] *ibid.,* XVI:8.

[20] The first of these translations is that of William Whiston (publ. by A. L. Burt, New York, no date). The same error has been taken over by other editions (*e.g.* publ. by Bigelow, Brown, and Co., New York, no date). The original text reads: *hē men kinyra deka chordais exēmenē typtetai plēktrō* (*JosAnt,* VII, 12:3). The edition of Josephus' works in Loeb's Classical Library (1934) translates the word correctly as "plectrum."

[21] For the earliest use of the bow with stringed instruments see *SachsHist,* pp. 216, 275.

[22] He pretends, for instance, that there have been in the Temple orchestra 200,000 silver trumpets and 40,000 harps and psalteries made of *ēlektron* (*JosAnt,* VIII:3:8).

[23] *SachsHist,* p. 106. But he also points out its connection with the Egyptian lyre *k•nn•r* (*ibid.*) (p. 107).

[24] *StainMus,* p. 25.

[25] *GressMus,* p. 24.

[26] Among the materials used for making *auloi, Pollux* also mentions lotus-wood (IV: 71).

[27] *Athen* IV, 175 c. See also p. 288.

[28] *GressMus,* p. 25.

[29] Tal.Bab., *Megillah* 6 a.

[30] Tal.Yer., *Megillah* I:1 (70 a).

[31] *GressMus,* p. 26.

[32] *SachsGeist,* pp. 162 ff.

[33] For *ḥinga* see chapter 30 of this section.
[34] F. J. Fétis, *Histoire générale de la Musique* (Paris, 1869-1876), I. p. 384.
[35] Athen, IV, 182 f.
[36] A. W. Ambros, *Musikgeschichte* (Breslau, 1862-1882), I, p. 205.
[37] *WeissInstr,* p. 32.
[38] *Athen,* IV, 175 e.
[39] Juvenal, *Satirae,* III.
[40] Diodorus Siculus, *Historica Bibliotheca* (new ed. London, 1933).
[41] *PortShilṭe,* chap. VI.
[42] *WeissInstr,* pp. 31 ff; *SachsHist,* p. 107.
[43] *WeissInstr, ibid.*
[44] *WeissInstr,* pp. 36 ff.
[45] *WeissInstr,* p. 37.
[46] Illustration in Wellhausen, *op. cit.,* p. 227.
[47] *WeissInstr,* p. 39.
[48] Euripides, *Cyclops,* V, 442 (in *The Complete Greek Drama,* New York, 1938, II, p. 408); Aristophanes, *Thesmophoriazusae* (in *Eleven Comedies,* New York, 1943, II, p. 285).
[49] Plutarch, *De Musica,* VI.
[50] *WeissInstr,* p. 41.
[51] *op. cit.,* p. 40.
[52] *SachsHist,* p. 107.
[53] *Augustine, Enarratio* in *Psalmum XLII,* 5, in *PL XXXVI,* col. 479; Jerome, *Breviarium in Ps. XXXII,* in *PL* XXVI, col. 969; Isidore of Seville, *Etymologiae, III,* 22:10,14, in *PL LXXXII,* col. 168-169.
[54] Jerome, *Breviarium in Ps. CXLIX, in PL* XXVI, col. 1342.
[55] Chrysostom, *Eis ton Psalmon XLI,* in *PGL,* LV, col. 155.
[56] Basil, *Homilia eis ton Psalmon* 1, in *PGL,* XXIX, col. 214. The same, in Rufinus' translation, in *PGL,* XXXI, col. 1725-26.
[57] Augustine, *Enarratio in Ps. XLII,* in *PL,* XXXVI, col. 479.
[58] Jerome, *Ad Dardanum de diversis generibus musicorum instrumentis Epistola XXVIII,* in *PL* XXX, col. 215.
[59] Jerome, *Breviarium in Psalmum XXXII,* in *PL* XXVI, col. 969.
[60] See note 162 on p. 286.
[61] Isidore, *Etymologiae,* III, 22:2, in *PL, LXXXII,* col. 167.
[62] Chrysostom *Eis ton Psalmon CXLIX, in PGL,* LV col. 494.
[63] *FineInstr,* p. 32.
[64] A.F. Pfeiffer, *Über die Musik der alten Hebräer* (Erlangen, 1779).
[65] The *kn-an-aul* of Galpin, in *StainMus* p. 373.
[66] *SachsHist,* p. 107.
[67] Franz Karl Movers, *Die Phönizier* (Bonn, 1841-1856), I, p. 243.
[68] *kinyrē, thrēnētikē* (Suidas), *kinyrometha, thrēnoumen* (Suidas), *kinyresthai,* (Hesychios), and others.
[69] Midrash, *Tehillim,* Ps. 137:4.
[70] *KraussTA,* III, p. 86.
[71] *JosAnt,* VII, 12:3.
[72] *KraussTA,* ibid. Here we have to point out an error committed by Finesinger (*Fine Instr,* p. 28). He translates Tal. Bab., *Yoma* 38 b : *umaniah, ʾeẓbaʿo ben hanimin* as "and he places his fingers between the strings," convinced that this refers to the manner of playing the *kinnor.* However, the phrase is here taken out of context. The corresponding places in Mishnah, *Yoma* III:11, Tal.Yer., *Yoma* III:7, and Tal. Yes., *Shekalim* V:2 prove beyond doubt that this description does not refer to a manner of playing the *kinnor,* but to a physiological trick applied by Hygros ben Levi to produce a specific singing tone. The correct translation of the passage should be: "and he places his fingers [on the division line] between the two parts of the moustache." (See the translation of this passage in the Soncino-edition of the Talmud).
[73] *SachsHist,* p. 131.

[74] Tal.Bab., *Kinnim* 25 a. The Mishnah says about Abraham's sacrificial animal: "When it is alive, it has one sound; but when it is dead, it has seven. R. Joshua says: How is its voice multiplies sevenfold? Its two horns become two trumpets (*ḥaẓoẓerot*) [better: *shofarot*]; its two legbones become two flutes (*ḥalilim*); its hide becomes a drum (*tof*); its entrails (*meyav*) are used for harps (*nebalim*); and its chitterlings (*b'ne meyav*) for lyres (*kinnorot*)." (*Kinnim* III:6).

[75] Basil, *Homilia in Psalmum primum,* in *PGL,* XXIX, cols. 213-14.

[76] Oliver Strunk, *Source Reading in Music History* (New York, 1950), p. 66.

[77] Rufinus, *Homilia in Psalmum primum* (Latin translation of a tractate of Basil), in *PGL,* XXXI, cols. 1725-26.

[78] The author is indebted to Prof. Curt Sachs for a letter with some pertinent observations on this subject:

"It is obvious that strings of metal are out of the question. Parallels do intimate, however some other possibilities:

(1) The Chinese *yüe ch'in,* called in popular parlance 'moon-guitar,' has inside a metal spring fastened only on one end, which would correspond indeed to a plectrum from below.

(2) The lute *rabâb* of North-West Africa, related to the medieval *rebec,* has a divided front, on the upper part of brass, on the lower of skin (*aes vel tympanum*). In a similar way, the Egyptian zither *ḳanun* is covered partly with wood, partly with skin.

It is not impossible that BASIL meant a kind of spring similar to that of the Chinese guitar; the literal meaning would fit exactly, and there is no reason for assuming that such a metal reverberating spring should have been restricted to China.

The later author might have thought of one of the Muhammedan partitions of the front part. I cannot conceive a different reason for the incongruent addition of the *tympanum.*"

[79] Mishnah, *Shabbat* VI:8; Mishnah, *Kelim* XV:6.—For another interpretation of this word see chapter 37 of this section.

[80] Mishnah, *Kelim,* XV:6; XVI:7.

[81] Mishnah, *Kelim,* XV:6.

[82] Mishnah, *Kelim,* XVI:7.

[83] Mishnah, ʿ*Erubin* XI:13 (ed. Zuckermandel, 1937, p. 154).

[84] Tal.Yer., ʿ*Erubin* 103a.

[85] Tal.Yer., ʿ*Erubin* X:I (26c).

[86] See note 58 on p. 270.

[87] See note 59 on p. 270.

[88] *JosAnt,* VII, 12:3. For the difference between *chordos* and *phthongos* see the chapter *nebel.*

[89] H. Graetz, *Kritischer Kommentar zu den Psalmen* (Breslau, 1882-1883), p. 85.

[90] Tal.Yer., *Sukkah* V:6 (55 c).

[91] Midrash, *Numeri* XV:11, Tal.Bab., ʿ*Arakin* 13 b.

[92] Midrash, *Tehillim* XCII:7 (ed. Buber, p. 406).

[93] *SachsHist,* p. 108.

[94] *Zamar,* "to touch" or "to strike" the chords of an instrument, hence "to provide accompaniment for singing," (which results, reversely, in singing or chanting with instrumental accompaniment). (*GesLex,* 9th ed., p. 282).

[95] Leopold Löw, in his *Beiträge zur jüdischen Alterthumskunde* (Szegedin, 1875) fully discusses this legend and its relation to the Aeol's harp of the Greeks.

[96] Midrash, *Numeri* XV:16; Midrash, *Lamentations* II:19; Midrash. *Ruth* VI:1; Tal. Bab., *Berakot* 3 b; *Sanhedrin* 16 a; Tal. Yer., *Berakot* I:1 (2 b). *Cf.* also Ps. 119:62.

[97] Tal.Bab., *Megillah* 6 a.

[98] *Minni* is rendered as "stringed instruments" by the *Jewish, American, Revised Standard Versions,* and *Moulton; Moffat* interprets the term as "music of ivory harps." The other principal versions divest the word of any musical meaning, translating "whereby they have made thee glad" (*Authorized Version* and *Harkavy*), and "the daughters of kings [have delighted thee in thy glory]" (*Douay*). Also *Wycliffe*: "fro the

yuer [ivory] housis, of the whiche deliteden thee the doytris of kingus" (early), and ". . . of whiche the douytris of kyngis delitiden thee" (later).

99 *EwDicht*, I, part 1, p. 211.

100 Eric Werner, *The Conflict between Hellenism and Judaism in the Music of the Early Christian Church*, in *HUCA* XX (1947), p. 468.

101 *GesHandw*, p. 481.

102 *Athen*, IV, 175 b.

103 Eusebius, *Praeparatio evangelica*, X:6, in *PGL*, XXI, col. 791.

104 *ha-porṭim*, *ʿal-pi ha-nebel* (Am. 6:5).

105 2*JosAnt*, VII, 12:3.

106 Ovid, *Ars amandi*, III:325.

107 Julius Pollux of Naucratis, *Onomasticon*, IV.

108 See p. 287.

109 *PortShilṭe*, chap. V.

110 Like the Septuagint and the Vulgate, the Targum also paraphrases this passage.

111 Jerome, *Ad Dardanum . . . Epistola XXIII*, see note 58.

112 Eusebius, *Commentarium in Ps. LXXX*, 2, in *PG* XXIII, col. 971.

113 Hilarius, *Tractatus super Psalmos*, *Prolog. in Ps.* 1, in *PL* IX, col. 237.

114 Suidas, *Lexicon* (new ed. by Ada Adler, Leipzig, 1928), s.v. *mousourgoi*, III, p. 45.

115 Saʿadia, *Commentary on Daniel* 3:7. This Saʿadia should not be confused with Saʿadia Gaon (892-942). For *pesanterin* see chapter 6 of this section.

116 *Athen*, XIV, 335 f.

117 *ibid.*, XIV, 636 f.

118 *ibid.*, XIV, 635 a.

119 *ibid.*, IV, 183 c.

120 *ibid.*, IV, 183 d.

121 Varro, *De lingua Latina.*

122 Hesychios of Alexandria, *Lexicon* (new ed. Jena, 1858-1864), III, p. 265, IV, part 1, p. 174.

123 Julius Pollux of Naucratis, *Onomasticon*, IV, 61.

124 Ovid, *Ars amandi*, III, 325.

125 Suidas, *op. cit.*, *ibid.*

126 *Athen*, XIV, 635 e.

127 *ibid.*, XIV, 635 b, d.

128 *ibid.*, XIV, 636 a.

129 *ibid.*, XIV, 636 b.

130 *ibid.*, XIV, 635 c.

131 *ibid.*, XIV, 637 a.

132 *ibid.*, IV, 183 b.

133 Artemidōros (the disciple of Aristophanes) in the second book of his *Doric Dialect* (*Athen*, IV, 182 d); also Didymos in his book on *Flute-Boring* (*Athen*, XIV, 634 e); Tryphōn, who says: "The flute called *magadis*" (*Athen*, XIV, 634 e), and others.

134 This technique is basically the same as used by harp-players in our own time.

135 For *syrigma* see p. 283. *Syrigma* is an exact parallel to harmonics on modern string instruments which are called flageolet-tones, or simply *flageolets*, this being literally the French name for *whistle-flutes.*

136 *hē gar magadis organon esti psaltikon*, *Athen*, XIV, 634 f.

137 See p. 287.

138 *WeissInstr*, p. 54.

139 *AmbrosMus*, I, pp. 206-207, and others.

140 *SachsHist*, p. 116.

141 See p. 286.

142 Mishnah, *Kinnim* III:6.

143 Tal.Bab., *ʿArakin* 13 b.

144 *SachsHist*, p. 116.

145 See pp. 125 and 275.

146 *Cp. Moffat's* translation of 1 Chron. 15:20,21: "lutes set for soprano voices," and

"harps set for bass voices."

147 See note 87 on p. 124.

148 *Athen,* XIV, 638-639.

149 Hugo Riemann, *Handbuch der Musikgeschichte* (Leipzig, 1923), I, p. 244.

150 *Athen,* XIV, 634 c.

151 *ibid.,* XIV, 636 c.

152 *ibid.,* XIV, 635 b.

153 Aristotle, *Problēmata,* XIX:18, 919 a; XIX: 39, 921 a.

154 *Athen,* XIV, 635 a.

155 *ibid.,* XIV, 634 e.

156 *ibid.,* IV, 182 f.

157 *ibid.,* XIV, 636 b.

158 *ibid.,* XIV, 635 a.

159 In the bas-reliefs found at Kuyundchik. Illus. 23.

160 *Athen,* XIV, 636 e,f.

161 Eric Werner, *The Sacred Bridge* (London and New York, 1959), p. 460.

162 Cassiodorus, *Praefatio in Psalterium, IV,* in *PL,* LXX, col. 15; Isidore of Seville, *Etymologiae,* III, 22, in LXXXII, col. 168; Beda, *Interpretatio Psalterii artis cantilenae in PL* XCIII, col. 1099, and others.

163 Tal.Yer., *Sukkah* V:6 (55 c).

164 *ibid.*

165 However, C. F. Keil (*Twelve Minor Prophets,* Edinburgh, 1889, p. 299) translates *paraṭ* as "to strew around,"—an exact opposite of "plucking."

166 *FineInstr,* p. 37.

167 Mishnah, *Kelim* XV:6.

168 *Athen,* IV, 182 c.

169 In Daremberg and Saglio, *Dictionnaire des Antiquités Grecques et Romaines* (Paris, 1875-1919), III, part 2, p. 1448.

170 Aristotle, *Problēmata,* XIX, 23.

171 *JosAnt,* VII, 12:3.

172 Tertullian, *De anima,. XIV,.* in *PL,* II, col. 710 (trans. of the *Ante-Nicene Christian Library,* XV. p. 439).

173 Vitruvius, Herōn, Athenaeus, Julius Pollux, Augustine St., etc.

174 "to strike," "to smite" (also with the fingers), "to strike a stringed instrument," generally "to play an instrument."

175 Ibn Ezra, *Commentary to Isaiah,* V:12.

176 *Cp.* Julius Wellhausen, *The Book of Psalms* (New York 1898), p. 225, fig *v.* The instrument shown there has several openings in the upper part of the resounding box, and these, according to Wellhausen, are supposed to increase the tone volume.

177 Michael Prätorius, *Syntagma musicum* (Wolfenbüttel, 1614-1619), p. 110. *"Nebel =uter, qui compressus collabitur."*

178 Guillaume A. Villoteau, *Description de l'Égypte* (Paris, 1809), XIII, p. 477.

179 *Athen,* IV, 175 c.

180 *eumelēs* has a double meaning: "pretty," and "melodious."

181 *Athen,* IV, 175 c,d.

182 Euripides (*Elektra,* 716) also uses the expression *lōtos de phthongon keladei,* "the din of the lōtos' (flute) sound." This is interpreted as "a pipe inserted in the *nabla*" (See Liddell and Scott, *Greek Lexicon,* I, p. 1070). It is evident, however, that a stringed instrument could not have had a pipe as one of its sounding parts. *Lōtos* refers here manifestly to the hollow side-arms serving to increase the resonance.

183 *IdelJewMus,* pp. 13-14.

184 Ovid, *Ars amandi,* III:325.

185 *JosAnt,* VII, 12:3.

186 Jerome, *Breviarium in Psalmum XXXV,* in *PL,* XXVI, cols. 969-970, and 1318.

187 *WeissInstr.* p. 62.

188 *SachsHist,* p. 118.

189 *StainMus,* p. 42.

[190] *GalpSum,* p. 83, illustr. p. 85, plate XII, fig. 9.
[191] *LangdTerms,* part II, p. 169 ff.
[192] *ibid.,* p. 183.
[193] *FétisHist,* I, p. 388.
[194] *EngMus,* chap. II, pp. 47-51.
[195] In *Miscellanea Lips. nova,* IX, part II.
[196] *Del Psalms,* I, p. 149.
[197] Augustin Calmet, *A Dictionary of the Holy Bible* (Engl. ed. London, 1732), I, p. 619.
[198] See the section "Women in the Music of Ancient Israel."
[199] Gustav Moritz Redslob, *De praecepto musico* (Leipzig, 1831), p. 24.
[200] *GesLex,* p. 386.
[201] The full consecutive chain of supposed verbal transformations would then be: *neginah—naggan—naggen—negenet—genet—genetit—gittit.*
[202] *GesLex,* p. 387.
[203] *BaethPsalm,* p. XVI.
[204] *Cp.* Isa. 16:10; Jer. 25:30; Judg. 9.27.
[205] Apart from the Bible, the patristic and talmudic literature mentions repeatedly psalm-singing in daily life, and especially its wide-spread use among the working people. These items, however, are but in their name religious "psalms." In reality, they were a species of secular, even if "inspired," work-songs (see section "Singing," pp. 202 ff).
[206] Johann Jahn, *Biblical Archaeology* (New York, 1853), p. 103. A few other terms among those found pre-eminently in the headings of the psalms, have been ill-judgedly taken by Jahn as referring to musical instruments, namely: *almuth labben* (Ps. 9:1), *Jeduthun* (Pss. 39:1; 62:1), *mahalath* (Pss. 88:1; 53:1), and *higgayon* (Pss. 9:17; 92:4).
[207] Ibn Ezra, *Commentary to Ps.* 8.
[208] E.O.W. Oesterley, *The Psalms in the Jewish Church* (London, 1910), p. 55.
[209] *MowPsalms,* IV, p. 46.
[210] About Nebuchadrezzar's Orchestra see in detail *GalpSum,* pp. 66-69, and *Sachs-Hist,* pp. 83-85.
[211] *Athen* IV, 129 a; XIV, 634 b.
[212] *ibid., IV,* 175 d.
[213] Livius, XXXIX:6.
[214] *GesLex,* p. 959.
[215] *Athen,* IV, 175 e.
[216] Suidas, *Anthologia,* s.v. *sambykai.*
[217] *Athen,* XIV, 637 b.
[218] Strabo, *Geōgraphikōn,* X, 3:17.
[219] Aristoxenos, in *Athen,* IV, 182 f.
[220] *Athen,* XIV, 634 a.
[221] Vitruvius, *De Architectura,* VI:5; Suidas, *Lexicon* (new ed. Ada Adler, Leipzig, 1928), IV, p. 317; *sambykai:organa mousika trigōna.*
[222] *Athen,* XIV, 634 a.
[223] *ibid.,* 633 f; Aristides Quintilianus, *De Musica.* II, 101.
[224] *Athen,* XIV, 635 a.
[225] *ibid.,* 635 e.
[226] *ibid.,* 634 b.
[227] *RiehmHandw,* II, p. 1036.
[228] *SachsHist,* p. 84.
[229] See note 383, p. 325.
[230] Isidore of Seville, *Etymologiae,* III, 21:7, lu *PL* LXXXII, col. 167.
[231] A. F. Gallé, *Daniel avec Commentaires . . .* (Paris, 1900), p. 32.
[232] Sa(adia, *Commentary on Daniel* 3:5.
[233] *GesHandw,* p. 925.
[234] *EngMus,* p. 286.

235 In *Cyclopedia of Biblical Literature* (Philadelphia, 1861), see art. Music, musical instruments, II, p. 373.

236 In McClintock and Strong, *Cyclopedia of Biblical . . . Literature* (New York, 1883), art. "Musical instruments," VI, p. 767.

237 A. Gevaert, *Histoire et théorie de la musique dans l'Antiquité* (Gand, 1881), II, p. 245.

238 *Aspendius citharista quem omnia intus canere dicebant* (Asconius in Cicero, *In Verrem,* II, 1:20). The player held the instrument in the left arm close to his body and played it with the bare fingers; hence *intus,* "inside." Whereas the right hand, with the plectrum, played farther off from his body; hence, *foris,* "outside."

239 *Athen,* IV, 183 d.

240 *ibid.,* XIV, 635 b.

241 Sa'adia, *Commentary on Daniel* 3:5.

242 A. F. Gallé, *op. cit.,* p. 32.

243 A. Villoteau, *Dissertation sur les diverses espèces d'instruments de musique qu'on remarque parmi les sculptures qui décorent les antiques monuments de l'Egypte,* in *Description de l'Egypte, Antiquités* (Paris, 1809), VI, p. 425.

244 *FétisHist,* II, p. 273.

245 *GalpSum,* p. 67.

246 *Athen,* IV, 183 c.

247 *ibid.,* 183 d.

248 A. F. Gallé. *op. cit.,* p. 32.

249 See p. 119.

250 *Julius Fürst, Librorum Sacrorum Veteris Testamenti concordantiae Hebraicae atque Chaldaicae* (Leipzig, 1840), p. 677.

251 See pp. 236 ff.

252 *SachsHist,* p. 126.

253 *PortShilṭe,* chap. II.

254 *DelPsalm,* II, p. 77.

255 *GesLex,* p. 1004.—Two other species of lilies, the *Lilium Eulinon* and *Isolirion,* have indeed trumpet- or funnel-shaped flowers.

256 For further interpretations of the three terms see pp. 133 ff.

257 Paul Romanoff, *Jewish Symbols on Ancient Jewish Coins,* in *JQR,* XXXIV, p. 306.

258 *DelPsalm,* II, p. 77.

259 *LangdTerms,* pp. 180 ff.

260 *LangdTerms,* p. 181.

261 "Loud instruments" have not been used, in general, to accompany singing in Ancient Israel. Kautzsch suggests, therefore, (*Das Alte Testament,* Tübingen, 1921, IV) the same reading for this passage as for 1 Chron, 13:8: "with a loud voice (*beḳol* 'oz)." Some of the English Bibles follow this reasoning, *e.g. Moffat* and the *Revised Standard Version*: "(singing) with all their might," the latter adding in a marginal note: "with instruments of might." *Douay* has "with instruments that agreed to their office."

262 *JosAnt,* VII, 12:3.

263 "Organ" is here the phonetic transliteration of the Greek word *organon,* the generic term for all instruments of music.

264 Enoch Hutchinson, *Music in the Bible* (Boston, 1864), p. 204.

265 Solomon Schechter, *The Wisdom of Ben Sira. Portions of the Book Ecclesiasticus from Hebrew Manuscripts in the Cairo Genizah Collection* . . . (Cambridge, 1899).

266 The *Jewish, American, Revised Standard Versions* and *Moulton* have "stringed instruments," *Moffat* "music of ivory harps." The other principal English Bibles attribute to *minni* a non-musical sense; "whereby they have made thee glad."

267 Midrash, *Genesis* XXIII:3.

268 *ibid.,* L:9.

269 *ibid.*

270 *KraussTA,* III, p. 81.

271 Tal.Bab., '*Abodah Zarah* 47 a.

272 Tal.Bab., '*Erubin* 103 a.

[273] Tal.Bab., *Shabbot* 55 a.

[274] See p. 336.

[275] Perhaps Rashi meant "with the *assistance* of musical instruments of brass" (*i.e.* upon the signal of cymbals), which would be quite true to facts. The expression "utter song" (not to "sing") hints at the beginning of singing. This, however, is merely a surmise.

[276] The SEPTUAGINT's translation of this verse differs markedly from the Masoretic text. The Hebrew original reads: *ha-porṭim ʿal-pi ha-nebel k'David ḥosh'bu lohem kle-shir* ("that chant to the sound of the viol, *and* invent to themselves instruments of music, like David" [*Moffat* translates: "composing airs like David himself"]), whereas the SEPTUAGINT renders it *hoi epikratountes pros tēn phōnēn tōn organōn hōs estēkota elogisanto kai ouch hōs pheugonta* ("who excel in the sound of musical instruments; they have regarded them as abiding, not as fleeting pleasures",—translation of an anonymous work entitled "*The Septuagint Version of the Old Testament with an English Translation,*" London, 1879, p. 1089).

It is striking that whereas the Hebrew text has two musical references (one in each half-verse), the SEPTUAGINT has only one (in the first half). The Greek equivalent for *kle shir* (*tōn organōn*) seems to be transferred to the first half of the verse and, furthermore, David's name is left out from the SEPTUAGINT version. For all these perceptible differences there is no positive explanation. One may only surmise that the SEPTUAGINT translation was made from an earlier variant of the Hebrew text, which was later discarded and replaced by the extant version.

[277] *GesLex* (1858), p. 220.

[278] Ferdinand Hitzig, *Daniel* (Leipzig, 1850), p. 96.

[279] James A. Montgomery, *A Critical and Exegetical Commentary on the Book of Daniel* (New York, 1927), p. 279, Note. See also *GesLex* (1858), p. 220.

[280] See *Talmudic Lexicon.*

[281] Ibn Ezra, *Commentary on Daniel* 3:5.

[282] S. D. Driver, *The Book of Daniel* (Cambridge, 1905), p. 77.

[283] R. H. Charles, *A Critical and Exegetical Commentary on the Book of Daniel* (Oxford, 1929), p. 160.

[284] *SachsHist,* p. 106.

[285] *WeissIstr,* p. 87.

[286] Cheyne and Black, *Encyclopedia Biblica* (New York, 1899), col. 3229.—J. Hastings, *A Dictionary of the Bible* (Edinburgh, 1896), col. 461 b.

[287] R. Kimḥi, (ed. Biesenthal-Lebrecht), p. 250 b.

[288] *GesThes,* 988 b.

[289] Augustin Calmet, *Dictionnaire historique, critique, chronologique, géographique et litteral de la Bible* (Geneva, 1780), III, pp. 334, 336.

[290] *StainMus,* p. 118. The *Mashroḳita,* too, has been sometimes interpreted as *syrinx.* See p. 324.

[291] *SachsHist,* p. 106.

[292] See pp. 413, 420 ff.

[293] Mishnah, *ʿArakin* II:3.

[294] *KraussTA,* p. 88.

[295] G. B. Winer, *Biblisches Realwörterbuch* (Leipzig, 1833-38), II, p. 146,

[296] K. H. Cornill, *Music in the Old Testament* (Chicago, 1909), p. 12.

[297] *SachsHist,* p. 84.

[298] *ibid.,* p. 121. See also p. 327.

[299] Willi Apel, *Early History of the Organ,* in *Speculum* (1948), vol. 23, No. 2 (April), pp. 191 ff. Also *FarOrg,* pp. 9 ff.

[300] *SachsHist,* p. 106.

[301] Morris Jastrow Jr., *Die Religion Babyloniens und Assyriens* (Giessen, 1905-1912), II, p. 4.

[302] Plutarch, *De Musica,* V.

[303] *Athen,* IV, 174 f, 175 a.

[304] See p. 70. According to Bathyah Bayer, it originates from 900 B.C.E.

305 *SachsHist,* pp. 72 ff.
306 Mishnah, *Kelim* XI:6.
307 Mishnah, *ʿArakin* II:3.
308 See p. 328.
309 Tal.Bab., *ʿArakin* 11 b.
310 . . Tal.Bab., *ʿArakin* 10 b. An analogous statement, in a shorter form, is to be found in Tal.Yer., *Sukkah* V:6 (55 c).
311 The instruments of the First Temple are enumerated in 1 Chron. 15:16,28; 2 Chron. 5:12; 29:25 ff.
312 See the section "Music Instruction."
313 Tal.Yer., *Sukkah* V:1 (55 a).
314 Mishnah, *ʿArakin* II:3.
315 Mishnah, *Sukkah* V:1.
316 Cp. T.B., *Sukkah* 50 b.
317 Mishnah, *Kinnim* III:6.
318 Mishnah, *Kelim* XI:6.
319 *ibid.*
320 See chapter 18 of this section.
321 Mishnah, *ʿArakin* II:3.
322 *SachsHist,* p .120.
323 Tal.Bab., *ʿArakin* 10 b ff.
324 *Sachs Hist,* p. 119.
325 Plutarch, *De Musica* V.
326 *Nathin,* plur. *nethinim,* lit. "given." See 1 Chron. 9:2; Ezra 2:43; 8:20; Neh. 3:26; 10:29. They were descendants of the Gibeonites, whom Joshua made into Temple slaves. *Cp.* Josh. 9:27.
327 Mishnah, *ʿArakin* II:4.
328 Tal.Bab., *ʿArakin* 10 a.
329 Tal.Bab., *Sukkah* 50 b; Tal. Yer., *Sukkah* V:1 (55 a); *cp.* Mishnah, *Sukkah* V:1.
330 Tal. Bab., *Sukkah* 50 b.
331 Mishnah, *Tamid* III:8.
332 Mishnah, *Baba Meẓiʿah* VI:1.
333 Mishnah, *Sukkah* V:1.
334 *GalpSum,* p. 16.
335 Aristotle, *Problēmata,* XIX:1, 917 b.
336 Mishnah, *Ketubot* IV:4; *cp.* Matth. 9:23. Pollux reports about a similar custom among the Karians and Phoenicians (IV, 76); Apuleius (*Metamorphoses* III), Ovid (*Fasti* IV), Sedulius (III), and others, among the Romans and Greeks.
337 Tal.Bab., *Shabbat* 151 a.
338 M. R. James, *The Apocryphal New Testament* (Oxford, 1924), pp. 367-368. See p. 513.
339 Tal.Bab., *Yoma* 20 b.
340 *SachsHist,* p. 120.
341 For a different interpretation of the wind instruments on these coins see pp. 64 ff.
342 Strabo, *Geōgraphikōn,* X, 3:13.
343 *Cp.* the analogy with the *ambubajae* of ancient Rome, p. 394.
344 Clement of Alexandria, *Paidagōgos,* II, 4, in *PGL* VIII, col. 443-446.
345 All these Aramaic names of instruments are examined in subsequent chapters.
346 *StainMus,* p. 101.
347 Plinius, *Historia naturalis,* XXXIII, 52, 146.
348 *GesThes, s.v. neḳeb.*
349 *FétisHist,* I, p. 396.
350 *AmbrosMus,* I, p. 209.
351 J. Jahn, *Biblical Archaeology* (New York, 1853), p. 101.
352 *ḥinga,* "a musical instrument," Hebr. *maḥol,* Aram. *ḥalil* (see *JastDict,* I, p. 458). For *ḥinga* see chap. 30 of this section.
353 J. Jahn, *Biblical Archaeology* (New York, 1853), p. 101.

[354] *SaalForm,* p. 342.
[355] Tal.Bab., (*Arakin* 10 a.
[356] *KraussTA,* III, p. 88.
[357] *ThirTitles,* p. 123.
[358] *ibid.,* p. 172.
[359] See "The Book of Psalms," pp. 120 ff.
[360] *Athen,* IV, 176 f.
[361] *SachsHist,* p. 117.
[362] Elam was the country located on the great plain north of the Persian Gulf and east of the lower Tigris. It is the "Elamtu" of the Babylonians and Assyrians and the "Elymais" of the Hellenes, who also called it "Susiana" from the capital city of Susa (or Shushan).
[363] H. Graetz, *Kritischer Commentar zu den Psalmen* (Breslau, 1882-83), pp. 71, 85.
[364] Tal. Bab., (*Arakin* 10 a.
[365] *GesThes,* s.v. *ḥul.* For *maḥol* see the section "The Dance."
[366] *PfeifferMus.*
[367] *HerdSpirit,* II, p. 193.
[368] *SaalForm,* pp. 361 ff.
[369] For the dance of Maḥanaim see pp. 474 ff.
[370] See note 352.
[371] *GesThes,* p. 476.
[372] Ecclus. 22:6; Matth. 9:23; *JosWar,* III, 9:5; Mishnah, *Ketubot* IV:4; Mishnah, *Baba Meẓi(ah* VI:1; Tal. Bab., *Ketubot* 48 a; Tal. Yer., *Berakot* III:1 (5 d).
[373] Mishnah, *Sukkah* IV:1; V:1; Tal.Bab., *Sukkah* 50 b; (*Arakin* 10 b; Tos. *Sukkah* IV (p. 198); Tal.Yer., *Sukkah* V:1 (55 a).
[374] Another instrument, the *sharḳuḳita,* may be derived from the same root. See chapter 44 of this section.
[375] A. F. Pfeiffer, *Über die Music der alten Hebräer* (Erlangen, 1779).
[376] J. N. Forkel, *Allgemeine Geschichte der Musik* (Leipzig, 1788-1801), I. p. 136.
[377] J. H. Worman, in McClintock and Strong, *Cyclopaedia of Biblical Literature* (New York, 1871-81), VI, p. 770.
[378] *AmbrosMus,* I, p. 209.
[379] J.Jahn, *Biblical Archaeology* (New York, 1853), p. 101.
[380] *SachsHist,* p. 83.
[381] *Athen,* IV, 174 f.
[382] *FarOrg,* pp. 22 ff. See also p. 394.
[383] Portions of the Book of Daniel have been written in Aramaic (verses 2:4 to 7:28). These have been later translated into biblical Hebrew. The events related to in this book have taken place four centuries prior to their appearance in writing (ca. 165 B.C.E.). This was the Hellenistic period in Jewish history; some names of instruments in Daniel are therefore visibly influenced by Greek terms.
[384] See also pp. 298 and 300.
[385] Polybius, *Historiai,* XXVI, 1:4.
[386] *Athen,* V, 139 c.
[387] Another version spells the word *keration* as *kerameion,* or *keramion,* meaning "wine-jar." This would naturally invalidate our argument.
[388] *Athen,* V, 195 f.
[389] *ibid.,* XIV, 615 d.
[390] In Loeb's Classical Library (London).
[391] *Athen,* X, 439 a-d.
[392] *ibid.,* IV, 176 b.
[393] *ibid.,* XIV, 621 c.
[394] *ibid.,* XIV, 636 d.
[395] *ibid.,* XIV, 618 a.
[396] Cicero, *In Verrem,* II, 3:44, chap. 105. *"Cum eius conviviis symphonia caneret."*
[397] Flavius Vopiscus, *The Life of Carus, Carinus and Numerian,* XIX, 2.
[398] Seneca, *Epistola* 76, 4.

[399] Martial, *Epigram* 10, 3:8.
[400] Suetonius, *Nero,* 54.
[401] Isidore, *Etymologiae,* 3:15, in *PL,* LXXXII, col. 169.
[402] Mishnah, *Kelim* XI:6.
[403] Mishnah, *ʿArakin* II:3.
[404] *FineInstr,* p. 55.
[405] In Isa. 18:1 the word *ḳanafayim* is coupled with another word, having originally also a sort of musical connotation, which appears but indirectly in this passage. It is the widely commented expression *ʾereẓ ẓilẓal ḳanafayim.* By this, the prophet alludes to Ethiopia, the country situated beyond the river Kush. The meaning of *ẓilẓal ḳanafayim* is rather obscure, just as is Isaiah's prophecy. Some translations render it as "the country dotted with army wings (*i.e.* divisions) in clashing armour," others as "the land of uproaring waves," again others as "the country of double-shadow." All these are strained translations, which miss the concrete meaning of the term. The ancient biblical translations are not any better. The *Septuagint* and *Vulgate* render it as "land of winged ships," *Luther* as "land moving with sails in the shadow" ("Land das unter Segeln im Schatten fähret"). *Wycliffe* has "Wo to the lond, cymbal of weengus, that is beyunde the flood of Etheope" (early), and "Wo to the lond, the cymbal of wyngis, which is biyende the flood of Ethiopie" (later). The *Authorized Version* and *Harkavy* translate as "land shadowing with wings," the *Jewish Version* "buzzing with wings," *Moffat* as "land of winged fleets." The most probable meaning is that which takes into consideration the swarms of insects, populating the Nile valley, producing in the flight a buzzing sound (*ẓilẓal*=rustling). The most appropriate translations, therefore, are those of *Moulton,* "land of the rustling of wings," and of the *Revised Standard Version,* "the land of rustling wings."
[406] Mishnah, *Kelim* XI:7.
[407] *ibid.,* XVI:8.
[408] *ibid.* XX:2.
[409] *SachsHist,* p. 121.
[410] *ibid.*
[411] A.F. Gallé, *op. cit.,* p. 32.
[412] Saʿadia, *Commentary on Daniel* 3. (About this Saʿadia see Note 115 on p. 279).
[413] *SachsHist,* pp. 84, 141. Among the Sumerian-Babylonian names of instruments Langdon quotes two, *gi-di-takaltu* and *sa-li-ne-lu pagû,* which are supposedly identical with the bagpipe (*LangdLit,* pp. XXXII, XXXIII). This is, however, no more than a surmise, as admitted by Langdon himself, when he attaches a question-mark to his translation.
[414] *SachsHist,* p. 141.
[415] *SachsGeist,* p. 196.
[416] *For sumponyah* omitted in verse 7 see p. 325.
[417] *"Dispares citharae nervi sunt, sed una symphonia."—Ambrose, Enarratio in Psalmum primum,* 9, in *PL,* XIV, col. 969.
[418] Tertullian, *De anima, II,* in *PL,* II, col. 690.
[419] *"Synagogae antiquis temporibus fuit chorus quoque simplex pellis cum duabus cicutis aereis: et per primam inspiratur, per secundam vocem emittit."* Jerome, *op. cit.,* in *PL,* XXX, col. 215.
[420] *GalpSum,* p. 69.
[421] *SachsHist,* p. 85.
[422] Phillips Barry, *On Luke* 15:25, *Symphōnia, Bagpipe,* in *JBL,* XXIII, (1904), pp. 180-210.
[423] George Moore, *Symphōnia Not a Bagpipe,* in *JBL* XXIV (1905), pp. 166-175.
[424] Friedrich Behn, *Musikleben im Altertum . . .* (Stuttgart, 1954), p. 60.
[425] *GesHandw,* p. 253.
[426] All three are described and illustrated in Percival R. Kirby, *The Trumpets of Tut-Ankh-Amen and their Successors,* in *Journal of the Royal Anthropological Institute* (London, 1947), LXXVII, pp. 33 ff.
[427] *ibid.,* p. 43.

[428] "Moses further invented a kind of clarion (*bykanēs*), which he had made for him in silver, on this wise. In length a little short of a cubit, it is a narrow tube, slightly thicker than a flute (*aulos*), with a mouthpiece wide enough to admit the breath and a bell-shaped extremity such as trumpets (*salpinxi*) have. It is called *ḥaẓoẓerah* in the Hebrew tongue." *JosAnt,* III, 12:6.

[429] Jerome, *Commentarium in Hosean,* II:8,9, in *PL* XXV, col. 861.

[430] Sachs claims that this picture represents an oboe-like instrument (*SachsHist,* p. 120). See also p. 316. For a different interpretation see p. 64.

[431] *SachsHist,* p. 145.

[432] Clement of Alexandria, *Paidagōgos,* II, 4, in *PG,* VI, col. 244.

[433] Varro, *De lingua latina,* V, 117. *"Cornua, quod ea, quae nunc sunt ex aere, tunc fiebant bubulo ex cornu."*

[434] The word *miḳshah* in connection with *ḥaẓoẓerah* signifies "beaten" or "hammered." Nevertheless, Stainer suggests (*StainMus,* p. 154) that the word might indicate a curved or round form of the Jewish trumpet, similar to the Roman *buccina.* All descriptions, however, as well as the pictures of the *ḥaẓoẓerah* show the straight form which, therefore, invalidates Stainer's hypothesis. The word *miḳshah* is used in the Bible to designate objects of precious metal, mostly of gold, in the following passages: Exod. 25:31,36; Exod. 37:7,17,22; Num. 8:4; 10:2.

[435] Hosea 5:8. Here, however, the gemination is expressed by the juxtaposition of *shofar and ḥaẓoẓerah.*

[436] *SachsHist,* p. 113.

[437] *Cp.* the derision of the prophet Elijah of the pagan ceremony at the Mount Carmel (1 Kings 18:27); also Hannah's silent prayer (1 Sam. 1:13).

[438] Kirby, *op. cit.,* p. 43.

[439] Mishnah, *Tamid* VII:3, Tal.Bab., (*Erubin* 54 a.

[440] Tal.Yer., *Yoma* VI:1 (43 b).

[441] Friedrich Behn, *op. cit.,* p. 60.

[442] *SachsHist,* p. 146.

[443] *ibid.,* p. 100. As for the "small" trumpets, mentioned by Plutarch, and allegedly blown by the Israelites at their "Bacchus-Festivals," that is at Tabernacles, he was either misinformed, or he has taken the *ḥaẓoẓerot* for the smaller, namely, shorter *shofar.* (*Questiones convivii,* IV, 6).

[444] Kirby, *op. cit.,* p. 44.

[445] Tosefta, *Kelim* (*Baba Meẓi*(*ah*), I:8 (p. 579).

[446] See the next chapter, p. 347.

[447] Mishnah, *Sukkah* V:4.

[448] *ibid.,* V:5.

[449] *ibid.,* V:5; Mishnah, (*Arakin* II:3; Tal. Bab., *Sukkah* 53 a.

[450] Tosefta, *Sukkah* IV:22 (p. 199).

[451] This title is inscribed on one of the scrolls found in 1947.

[452] Th. Gaster, *op. cit.,* p. 277.

[453] Translations mainly after Gaster.

[454] The Roman numerals designate the column of the original Hebrew scrolls which contain this tractate. The interpolations in brackets are my own explanatory remarks.

[455] Translations mainly after Gaster, *op. cit.,* pp. 284-285.

[456] Tal.Bab., *Shabbat* 36 a. Similar indications in Tal.Bab., *Rosh ha-Shanah* 36 a, and Tal. Bab., *Sukkah* 34 a.

[457] *Tosefta, Soṭah* VII:15 (p. 308).

[458] The "shawm" was not a trumpet, but an oboe-like instrument of various sizes. Furthermore, the existence of the "shawm" cannot be attested prior to the 14th century. The affinity of the word with the French "chalumeau" and the German "Schalmei" is unmistakable. All these names are derived from the Latin *calamus,* "reed."

[459] Some modern musicological works use wrongly *shofarim* as plural of *shofar, e.g. Sacht Hist,* pp. 111, 112, and Peter Gradenwitz, *The Music of Israel* (New York, 1949), p. 30.

[460] For different etymological derivations see *GesThes* 1469 b.

[461] Mishnah, *Rosh ha-Shanah* III:2.
[462] *ibid.* III:3-5.
[463] See the chapter "Music and Superstition."
[464] Maimonides, *Hilkot Teshubah* III:4.
[465] Translation by Moses Hyamson.
[466] Zohar, *Emor*, p. 99 b.
[467] Tal.Bab., *Rosh ha-Shanah* 28 a.
[468] *Cf.* the expression "enjoyment" in the same passage (see p. 346).
[469] Tal.Bab., *Rosh ha-Shanah* 27 b, to Mishnah, *Rosh ha-Shanah* III:6.
[470] *ibid.*
[471] Joseph Caro, *Shulḥan ʿAruk, Oraḥ Ḥayyim* 587, 17, note.
[472] Tal.Bab., *Rosh ha-Shanah* 28 a.
[473] *ibid.*
[474] Tal.Bab., *Rosh ha-Shanah* 33 a.
[475] Mishnah, *Rosh ha-Shanah* III:7.
[476] Tal. Bab., *Rosh ha-Shanah* 28 a.
[477] "Superstition and Music." See also *FineShof* and Theodor Reik, *Probleme der Religionspsychologie* (Vienna and Leipzig, 1919), art. "Der Schofar," pp. 178-311.
[478] Mishnah, *Rosh ha-Shanah* IV:8.
[479] Tal.Bab., *Rosh ha-Shanah* 33 a.
[480] "The harps whereto they sing [*i.e.* the harps for secular use] are susceptible to uncleanness; but the harps of the sons of Levi are not susceptible . . . The *markof* [the wooden arm of a harp around which the strings were bound] is not susceptible to uncleanness. The lute, the *niktimon* [clogs for the strings], and the drum are susceptible to uncleanness" (Mishnah, *Kelim* XV:6). Even secular objects, considered "unclean," become "clean" if used for the sacred service, so for instance "the case for pipes" (*Kelim* XVI:8), "a napkin that is used for the harps of the sons of Levi" (*Kelim,* XXIV:14), "bagpipes" [Better bags for pipes,"] (*Kelim,* XX:2). see p. 329.
[481] Tal.Bab., *Rosh ha-Shanah* 34 a.
[482] Mishnah, *Megillah* II:5.
[483] Mishnah, *Rosh ha-Shanah* IV:8.
[484] *ibid.* IV:1. For the meaning here of a "court" *cf.* Mishnah, *Sanhedrin* I:6.
[485] Mishnah, *Rosh ha-Shanah* IV:2.
[486] *ibid.*, IV:5.
[487] Tosefta to *Rosh ha-Shanah* 33 b.
[488] Tal.Bab., *Rosh ha-Shanah* 16 b.
[489] For a parallel to outwitting the evil spirits by musical means among the Chinese see Joseph Yasser, *Rhythmical Structure of Chinese Tunes,* in *Musical Courier* (New York, April 3, 1924).
[490] Tal.Yer., *Rosh ha-Shanah* IV:8 (p. 40).
[491] Tal.Bab., *Rosh ha-Shanah* 32 b.
[492] Mishnah, *Taʿanit* I:6.
[493] Mishnah, *Sukkah* IV:5.
[494] *ibid.* IV:9.
[495] Mishnah, *Ḥullin* I:7.
[496] Mishnah, *Sukkah* V:4. The occasions when these blasts had to be performed are enumerated on p. 338.
[497] Tal.Bab., *ʿArakin* 10 a. A similar statement in Tal.Bab., *Sukkah* 53 b.
[498] Mishnah, *Rosh ha-Shanah* IV:9.—Sachs calls our attention to the revealing fact that "this rule for the relative length of the blasts, formulated at the latest in the Talmudian epoch—that is, the first or second century B.C.E., but probably much earlier—has a striking resemblance to the so-called *modus perfectus* of medieval musical theory, which arranged metric values in threes: *1 (nota) maxima=3 longae=9 breves.* In consequence, the scholastic theory interpreting this trisection as a Christian symbol of Trinity is incorrect." (*SachsHist,* p. 110).
[499] Mishnah, *Rosh ha-Shanah* IV:9.
[500] Tal.Bab., *Rosh ha-Shanah* 33 b.

[501] The Mishnah uses the word *shofar* also to designate the chests (probably indicating their tapering shape) into which were cast money contributions toward the upkeep of the Temple service (*Shekalim* VI:1,5). There were thirteen *shofar*-chests in the Temple, and they had also such chests in the province, *i.e.*, in synagogues outside of Jerusalem (*ibid.* II:1).

[502] Mishnah, *Sukkah* V:5; *ʿArakin* II:3; Tal.Bab., *Sukkah* 53 a; *ʿAbodah Zarah* 70 a; Tosefta, *Sukkah* IV:22 (p. 199). See also p. 338.

[503] *FineShof*, p. 224.

[504] Tal.Bab., *Moʿed Katan* 27 b; *cf.* Tal.Bab., *Megillah* 29 a.

[505] Tal.Bab., *Moʿed Katan* 16 a.

[506] *Fine Shof*, pp. 210 ff.

[507] Mishnah, *Taʿanit* III:1.

[508] Tal.Bab., *Baba Batra* 91 a.

[509] *FineShof*, p. 228.

[510] Tal.Bab., *Soṭah* 43 a.

[511] F. Behn, *op. cit.*, p. 61.

[512] *Cp.* Michelangelo's famous statue of Moses with two horns on his forehead. More than a century prior to Michelangelo, the Dutch sculptor Clause Sluter (d. 1406) represented Moses with horns on his forehead (in the Museum of Dijon).

[513] Jerome, *Commentarium in Hosean, II, 8,9,* in *PL* XXV, col. 861.

[514] Tal.Bab., *Rosh ha-Shanah* 26 a. Deuter. 23:17 also calls the horn of a bullock *ḳeren.*

[515] Mishnah, *Rosh ha-Shanah* III:2.

[516] Mishnah, *Rosh ha-Shanah* III:5.

[517] Mishnah, *Kelim* XI:7.

[518] *Cp.* the following instructions of the Mishnah: "Utensils of metal are susceptible to uncleanness whether they are flat or whether they form a receptacle" (*Kelim* XI:1). "An oven of stone or of metal is not susceptible to uncleanness; yet this last is susceptible by virtue of being a vessel of metal" (*Kelim* V:11). "If a needle or a ring were found embedded in the bottom of an oven, and they were visible but did not project, . . . the oven is unclean" (*Kelim* IX:1). "If a spindle, distaff, rod, double flute, or pipe are made of metal they are susceptible to uncleanness; but if they are only plated they are not susceptible; but in either case if the double flute has a groove for the 'wing' [perhaps a cavity containing a vibrating tongue] it is susceptible" (*Kelim* XI:6). *Cf. Kelim* XII:8, XIII:1, XIV:4, and XVI:17, where other utensils of metal are listed.

[519] Mishnah, *Kelim* XI:7; Tal.Bab., *Shabbat* 47 a.

[520] Jahn maintains that *ḳeren* is one of the oldest instruments, which was originally no more than a neat horn with an opening on its tip. (*JahnArch*, p. 102). See also Varro, *De lingua latina,* V, 117.

[521] Midrash, *Leviticus* XXIX:3,6,10.

[522] The Pesiḳta (ed. Buber, p. 162a) has a different spelling as *salpidim.*

[523] *RiehmHandw*, I, p. 733.

[524] *ibid.*

[525] Mishnah, *Kelim* XI:7.

[526] Mishnah, *Rosh ha-Shanah* III:5.

[527] Mishnah, *Kelim* XI:7; Tal.Bab., *Shabbat* 47 a.

[528] For the conception that *yobel* is connected hypostatically with the name of Jubal see p. 61.

[529] *LangdTerms*, p. 171. "Literary sources give at least twelve Sumerian words with their Akkadian (Semitic) equivalents which must be supposed to designate drums" (*SachsHist*, p. 73).

[530] An exhaustive compilation of ancient sources about percussion instruments is F. A. Lampe's treatise in *UgThes*, XXXII, col. 867-1092, where hundreds of quotations are given.

[531] *SachsHist*, pp. 73-78.

[532] See the section "The Dance."

[533] *CornMus*, p. 6; *SaalArch*, I, p. 276; *WeissInstr*, p. 99, and others.

[534] *SachsHist,* p. 289.

[535] Isidore of Seville, *Etymologiae,* . . . III, 21:10. "*Tympanum est pellis vel corium ligno ex una parte extentum. Est enim pars media symphoniae in similitudine cribri. Tympanum artem quod medium est.*" In *PL,* LXXXII, col. 168.

[536] Chapter V. Reprinted in Winter and Wünsche, *Die jüdische Literatur seit Abschluss des Kanons* (Berlin, 1897), III, pp. 337 ff.

[537] This is Portaleone's commentary to the term *nablon,* messing up the characteristics of two entirely different instruments. It is quite obvious that he translated erroneously the Mishnaic text. The correct translation of the passage is given on p. 272, note 74.

[538] Derived from the Babylonian *balag,* "hand-drum." (*LangdTerms,* p. 169).

[539] *GesLex,* p. 595.

[540] *JosAnt,* VII, 12:3.

[541] *Athen* XIV, 636 a.

[542] *CornCult,* p. 127; *RiehmHandw,* p. 1043, and others.

[543] For the technique of conducting levitical singing see pp. 434 ff.

[544] *SaalArch,* I, pp. 273 ff.

[545] H. Graetz, *Kritischer Kommentar zu den Psalmen,* (Breslau, 1882-83) suggests that *ẓilẓele teru'ah* should better be read as *ḥaẓoẓerot teru'ah,* since, as he says, *teru'ah* is applied only to wind instruments. There is no valid reason, however, why *teru'ah* could not also signify a loud din of a percussion instrument.

[546] Tal.Bab., *'Arakin* 17 b.

[547] Mishnah, *'Arakin* II:5.

[548] Tal.Bab., *'Arakin* 10 b; Tal.Yer., *Sukkah* V:6 (55 c).

[549] Eric Werner, *The Oldest Sources of Synagogal Chant,* in *Proceedings of the American Academy for Jewish Research* (1947), vol. XVI, p. 228 ff.

[550] Mishnah, *Sukkah* V:1,4; Tal.Bab., *Sukkah* 51 a,b.

[551] Mishnah, *Tamid* III:8 and VII:3; Tal.Yer., *Sukkah* V:3 (55 c).

[552] Mishnah, *Shekalim* V:1. Cf. p. 336.

[553] Mishnah, *Tamid* VII:3.

[554] Tal.Bab., *Shebu'ot* 15 b.

[555] Spelled also *ẓinpes* (Tal.Bab., *'Arakin* 13 b) and *ẓenbes* (Tal.Bab., *'Erubin* 104 a). For Tal.Bab., *'Arakin* 10 b Rashi uses also the variant *ẓimbanu* (the Italian *cinbano*).

[556] Apuleius, *Metamorphoses* (*The Golden Ass*), XI:5 (New York, 1927), p. 250.

[557] *PortShilṭe,* chap. II.

[558] *PfeifferMus.*

[559] *ForkelGesch.*

[560] See also *UgThes,* XXXII, p. 470.

[561] *JahnArch.*

[562] *NowackArch.*

[563] In *WellPsalms,* p. 223.

[564] *GressMus,* p. 32.

[565] *GesLex* (1858), p. 1073.

[566] O. Glaser, *Die ältesten Psalmmelodien,* in *Zeitschrift für Semistik* (Leipzig, VIII, 1932), p. 194.

[567] In *StainMus,,* p. 46.

[568] See illustration 9.

[569] *SachsHist,* p. 123.

[570] *ibid.,* p. 89.

[571] *WeissInstr,* p. 104.

[572] *SachsHist,* Sumerian, p. 69, Egyptian, p. 89.

[573] W. O. E. Oesterley, *The Psalms in the Jewish Church* (London, 1910), p. 50.

[574] Gressmann, too, doubts the derivation of *shalishim* from the number "three," (*GressMus,* p. 32).

[575] *E.g. kinnor, from* the Egyptian *k-nn-r,* "lyre," or the Arabic-Persian *kunar,* "lotos," —*'asor,* from the Hebrew term for "ten," or from *'ashor,* meaning "Assyrian,"—*gittit,* (an instrument) from Gath, or from *gat,* a "winepress,"—*sabbeka,* from *sambucus* "elder," or from the verb *sabak,* "to interweave,"—*shushan,* "lily," or (an instrument) from Susa, etc.

[576] Tal.Bab., *Zebaḥim* 88 b.
[577] *GesHandw,* p. 438.
[578] *PfeifferMus.*
[579] A similar seeming discrepancy in reporting the same event by two different biblical authors can be found in the description of the dedication of Solomon's Temple. In 1 Kings 7:51 to 8:65 music instruments are not mentioned; in 2 Chron. 7:6, music instruments and *ḥaẓoẓerot* are specifically named.
[580] *SachsHist,* p. 109.
[581] *PhiloMos,* II, 24:119.
[582] *EngMus,* p. 66.
[583] *WeissInstr,* p. 101.
[584] C. Niebuhr, *Reisebeschreibung nach Arabien* . . . (Copenhague, 1774), II, p. 154, Plate 32.
[585] Tal.Bab., *Soṭah* 48 a.
[586] *SachsHist,* pp. 82, 137.
[587] Pollux IV, Varro VII.
[588] Varro, *De lingua latina,* VIII:33 b.
[589] The Troglodytes were cave dwellers, living from Lydia southward (Strabo XVI:828), especially on the Coast of the Red Sea (Diodorus III:32-33).
[590] *Athen,* IV, 183 f.
[591] Illustration in *SachsHist,* Plate IV, fig. *f, g.*
[592] Isidore of Seville, *Etymologiae XXI:8,* in *PL* LXXXII, col. 167. This verse of Virgil reads: *Pan primus calamos cera conjugere plures instituit, Pan curat oves, oviumque magistros.*
[593] Wilhelm Pape, *Handwörterbuch der griechischen Sprache* (Braunschweig, 1905-1914). The Italian *pandora* and the later French *mandore* (*mandole*) are instruments of a different category and of a later epoch. On the other hand, the *panduri* (or *fandur*) existing even to-day in Georgia (Caucasus), seems to be a direct offspring of the *pandura* of Antiquity. (*SachsHist,* p. 275).
[594] *WeissInstr,* p. 28.
[595] *SachsHist,* pp. 232, 255 ff.
[596] The famous exception was the shepherd-boy David, whose later rise to the king of his people had its starting point in his virtuosity on the *kinnor.*
[597] Tal.Bab., *Pesaḥim* III b.
[598] *JastDict,* I, p. 458.
[599] *ibid.*
[600] See pp. 317.
[601] Mishnah, *Kelim* XV:6.
[602] *GesLex,* p. 124.
[603] *KraussTA,* III, p. 87.
[604] *SachsHist,* pp. 117-118.
[605] Jehudah Gur, *Hebrew Lexicon* (Tel-Aviv, 1947), p. 86.
[606] Midrash, *Genesis* XXIII:3.
[607] The English version of the Midrashim (Soncino Press) renders *'adrabolin* as "organ-players," which in itself is etymologically correct, but as a translation for Gen. 4:21 is erroneous, since it deviates radically from the generally accepted meaning of *kinnor* in the biblical text.
[608] Midrash, *Genesis* L:9.
[609] Translation of the Soncino Press.
[610] See chapter 34 of this section.
[611] 1 Sam. 10:5; 2 Sam. 6:5; 1 Chron. 13:8; 15:24; 15:28; 16:5,6; 25:1,3,5,6; 2 Chron. 5:12,13; 7:6; 20:28; 23:13; 29:25-28; Job 21:12; 30:31; Pss. 81:1-3; 98:5,6; 150:3-5; Isa. 5:12; 30.29,32; Dan. 3:5,7,10,15.
[612] Tal.Yer., *Sukkah* V:6. (55 c).
[613] C. Daremberg and E. Saglio, *Dictionnaire des antiquités grecques et romaines* (Paris, 1877 et seq.), II, p. 1594. Mielziner, M., *Introduction to the Talmud* (New York, 1925), p. 42.

[614] Tal.Bab., ʿ*Arakin* 10 b.
[615] Tal.Bab., *Soṭah* 48 a.
[616] Tal. Bab., ʿ*Arakin* 10 b; an analogous statement, in a shorter form, in Tal.Yer., *Sukkah* V:6 (55 c). See also p. 311.
[617] Mishnah, ʿ*Arakin* II:3.
[618] *KraussTA,* III, p. 81.
[619] Mishnah, ʿ*Arakin,* II:4.
[620] Cicero, *De oratore,* III, 60:225,227.
[621] Midrash, *Genesis* L:9. *Cp.* Isa. 23:15,16.
[622] Tal.Yer., *Sukkah* V:6 (55 c,d).
[623] Tal.Bab., ʿ*Arakin* 10 b.
[624] For another interpretation of the two terms see chapters 32 and 35 of this section.
[625] *FarOrg,* pp. 23-24.
[626] *Athen,* IV, 174 d.
[627] A list of these writers is quoted in *FarOrg* pp. 38 ff.
[628] *e.g. SachsHist,* p. 124.
[629] Tal.Bab., ʿ*Arakin* 10 b, 11 a.
[630] Jastrow renders: "There was no organ used in the Sanctuary because it would interfere with the sweetness of the song."
[631] *Baraitha* is the term for an extraneous or supplementary tradition, belonging, however, to the same period.
[632] Kathleen Schlesinger intimates that the *magrephah* was a pneumatic organ in the second stage of development, but there is no documentary evidence for this hypothesis. Moreover, she holds that "the hydraulic and pneumatic organs of the ancients were practically the same instrument, differing only in the method adopted for the compression of the wind supply" (*Encyclopaedia Britannica,* article *Organ* vol. XVI [1953], p. 891. See also *JewEncycl,* vol. IX, p. 432).
[633] The Hebrew text together with a Latin translation is reprinted in *UgThes,* vol. XXXII. An English version can be found in *FarOrg,* pp. 31 ff.
[634] Rashi uses as explanation for *magrephah* the medieval French word *vadil* (also spelled *vadal*), in the meaning of "shovel" (Tal.Bab., *Shabbat* 20a; 122 b; *Ḥagigah* 20a; *Baba Meẓiʿah* 30 a; ʿ*Arakin* 10 b). In modern French its equivalent would be *videlle,* "jagging iron."
[635] Mishnah, *Tamid* V:6. The original word for "casting" in this passage is *zaraḳ*. Another meaning of the same word is "to sprinkle," (see *JastDict,* p. 415).
[636] Mishnah, *Tamid* V:6.
[637] Tal.Bab., ʿ*Arakin* 10 b, 11 a.
[638] *ibid.* See also p. 410. Rashi says that *hirdolis* should be spelled with a *samek* at the end, whereas the Tosafists hold that the last letter should be a *mem.* This is also the spelling of the Palestinian Talmud. The Midrash Rabba has it with a *nun* at the end and an ʿ*ayyin* at the beginning.
[639] *PortShilṭe,* XXXVI, XLI.
[640] Tal.Bab., ʿ*Arakin* 11 a.
[641] Mishnah, *Tamid* V:6.
[642] Danby in his translation of the Mishnah, p. 587, note. 10.
[643] Athanasius Kircher, *Musurgia Universalis* (Rome, 1650).
[644] Caspar Printz, *Historische Beschreibung der edelen Sing- und Klingkunst* (Dresden, 1690).
[645] *PfeifferMus,* p. 52.
[646] *JastDict,* s.v.
[647] See also: Joseph Yasser, *The Magrepha of the Herodian Temple: a Five-Fold Hypothesis.* In: *Journal of the American Musicological Society,* Vol. 13 (1960), pp. 24-42.
[648] *FarOrg,* p. 36.
[649] *ibid.,* p. 37.
[650] Mishnah, *Tamid* V:6. According to Maimonides, these were the lepers who had been pronounced clean and who were set in readiness at the Eastern Gate to bring their

offerings and to be sprinkled. *Cf.* Mishnah, *Neg'aim* XIV: 8 (See Danby, p. 587, note 12).

651 Tal.Bab., *'Arakin* 11 a.

652 *PortShilṭe, loc. cit.*

653 Tal.Bab., *Yoma* 20 b.

654 Both statements cannot be taken at their face value and are uttered more by way of hyperbole. It is more probable that there might have existed a common saying "from Jerusalem to Jericho" (used also in Luke 10:30), indicating a certain distance, possibly a one day's travel. See John Lightfoot, *Descriptio Templi Hierosolymitani,* in *UgThes,* IX. cols. 750-751.

655 Mishnah, *Tamid* III:8.

656 See note 58 on p. 270.

657 Tal. Yer., *Sukkah* V:6 (55 c,d); Tosefta, *'Arakin* I:13.

658 *Athen,* IV, 174 a.

659 Athenaeus' description seems to refer to an already more developed stage of the instrument.

660 However, Kathleen Schlesinger intimates that the pneumatic organ "was probably not so imperfect at the beginning of our era as has been thought, and which was destined to establish its supremacy in the end" (*Encyclopedia Britannica* [1953], vol. XVI, p. 892).

661 Tal.Bab., *'Arakin* 11 a.

662 Tal.Yer., *Sukkah* V:6 (55 c,d.).

663 Henry George Farmer, *Byzantine Musical Instruments in the Ninth Century* (London, 1925), pp. 5-6.

664 Paris, 1874, vol. VIII, p. 91.

665 Athanasius Kircher, *op. cit.,* I, p. 53. Kathleen Schlesinger calls the instrument *magraḳetha,* erroneously ascribed this expression to Kircher, which he never used. (See *Researches into the Origin of the Organs of the Ancients,* in *Sammelbände der Int. Mus.Ges.,* II [1901], p. 201).

666 *FarOrg,* p. 23. Kircher's illustration of the *magrephah* has been taken over by Caspar Printz, *op. cit., ForkelGesch,* table IV, fig. 42, *SaalForm,* table I, fig. 9, and others.

667 Idelsohn thinks that *magrephah* is derived from the Hebrew word *grophit,* "reed of bulrush." (*IdelJewMus,* p. 496, note 32). And according to J.D. Prince (*Encycl.Bibl.,* III, pp. 3229-30), *magrephah* means a "fork" or "tined shovel," this name having been apparently given to the instrument because of its form, "the pipes of which were thought to resemble tines."

668 John Lightfoot, *Temple Service* (Rotterdam, 1686), VII:3, IX:5. See also *FarOrg,* p. 35.

669 *Natal 'eḥad 'et-ha-magrephah vezorḳah bein ha-ulam velamizbeaḥ.*

670 Peter Gradenwitz, *The Music of Israel* (New York, 1949), p. 56.

671 Tal.Bab., *Sandhedrin* 67 b.

672 Tal.Bab., *Ḥullin* 63 b.

673 "When they [the *priests*] reached the space between the Porch and the Altar, one of them took the 'shovel' and cast it between the Porch and the Altar." (*Tamid* V:6).

674 J. Cohn, MISCHNAJOT, *Die Sechs Ordnungen der Mischna, Teil V* (Berlin, 1925), p. 469, note 42.

675 Soncino Press, *Pesaḥim* 64 a, p. 323 note 3.

676 *FarOrg,* p. 36.

677 See *Harkavy's* translation, and *cf.* note 635 above.

678 According to Grove's Dictionary (1928), vol. III, pp. 736, 739, "the pipes of the early organs are said to have sounded *all together,*" and that even in the eleventh-century organs there were two or perhaps more pipes to each slide controlling the production of a single "note" at a time.

679 *KraussTA,* III, p. 92.

680 *Athen,* IV, 174 d.

681 Coeval descriptions of the ancient organ can be found in Hero, *Pneumatica,* I, 42;

Tertullian, *De anima,* chap. XIV; and Vitruvius, *De architectura,* X, 8.

682 Tal.Bab., *Ḥagigah* 15 b.

683 *Oracula Sibyllina,* VIII, 113. *Cp.* Eric Werner, *The Conflict between Hellenism and Judaism in the Music of the Early Christian Church,* in *HUCA* XX (1947), pp. 416 ff.

684 Eric Werner, *The Jewish Contribution to Music,* in *The Jews, their History, Culture and Religion* (Philadelphia, 1949), vol. III, p. 952.

685 Midrash, *Genesis* L:9.

686 *KraussTA,* III, p. 91.

687 *SachsHist,* p. 124.

688 Midrash, *Genesis* XXIII:3; L:9.

689 *JastDict,* I, p. 625.

690 Other variants of the word are *bidbalin* (XXIII:3, in the Ḥoreb edition), *korbalin* (XXIII:3) and *karkalin* (L:9).

691 "Cymbals" is an erroneous translation of the Soncino Press.

692 See p. 391.

693 Tal.Bab., ʿ*Arakin* 10 b, to Mishnah, ʿ*Arakin* II:3; Tal. Bab., *Ketubot* 64 b; spelled also *yalamels* in Tal.Bab., ʿ*Abodah Zarah* 47 a, and *klimils* in Tal.Bab., ʿ*Arakin* 10 a.

694 *Athen,* IV, 176 d,e.

695 *SachsHist,* p. 288

696 *JastDict,* I, p. 78.

697 *ibid.,* II, p. 908.

698 Mishnah, *Kelim* XV:6.

699 Mishnah, *Shabbat* VI:8.

700 *SachsHist,* p. 109.

701 Tosefta, *Shabbat* XIII (ed. Zuckermandel, 1937, p. 130).

702 *PortShilṭe,* chap. V.

703 About clappers of the Sumerians and Egyptians see *SachsHist,* pp. 69, 88-89, 103. See also chap. 43 of this section.

704 To Mishnah, *Kelim* XV:6.

705 *Luḳitmin* has several other non-musical explanations in rabbinic writings: "An artificial arm (*luḳitmin*) is clean. What is *luḳitmin?* Said R. Abbahu: 'A pulley for loads.' Raba b. Papa said. 'Stilts.' Raba b. R. Huna said: 'A mask.'" (Tal.Bab., *Shabbat* 66 b).

706 Tal.Bab., *Shabbat* 66 b.

707 Mishnah, *Shabbat* VI:8.

708 Tal.Bab., *Shabbat* 66 b.

709 Tal.Yer., *Shabbat* VI:8 (p. 76, Vilna ed.)

710 Tal.Bab., *Shabbat* 66 b.

711 *SachsHist,* pp. 223, 230, 251.

712 *LangdLit,* p. LII.

713 Augustine, *Enarratio in Psalmum CL*:7, in *PL,* XXXVII, col. 1964.

714 *FarOrg.* p. 41.

715 Tal.Bab., ʿ*Arakin* 10 b.

716 *ibid.* 11 a; Tosefta to Tal. Bab., ʿ*Arakin* 11 a.

717 Theodoret, *Hairetikēs kakomythias, IV*:7, in *PG* LXXXIII, col. 426.

718 Tal.Bab., *Shabbat* 110 a.

719 Tal.Bab., *ID*ʿ*ed Katan* 9 b; Tal.Bab., *Baba Batra* 145 b.

720 Tal.Bab., *Mo*ʿ*ed Katan* 9 b.

721 Tal.Bab., *Giṭṭin* 7 a. For *ḳarḳash* see chap. 43.

722 *SachsHist,* p. 437.

723 Tal.Bab., *Giṭṭin* 7 a; *Soṭah* 49 b.

724 Tal.Bab., *Sanhedrin* 67 b. (Vilna ed.)

725 *ibid.*

726 Tal.Bab., *Baba Batra* 145 b. In modern French, the meaning of the medieval ʾ*esḳaliṭa* (and its various spellings) is *clochette,* "bells."

727 *ibid.*
728 Tal.Bab., *Soṭah* 49 a,b.
729 *LangdLit,* p. LII.
730 Tal.Bab., *Shabbat* 110 a; *Mo'ed Katan* 9 b; etc.
731 *KraussTA,* III, p. 92.
732 *ibid.*
733 Tal.Bab., *Sanhedrin* 67 b.
734 *KraussTA,* III, p. 92.
735 Tal.Bab., *Berakot* 57 a.
736 *KraussTA,* II, p. 40.
737 Mishnah, *Soṭah* IX:14.
738 Mishnah, *Kelim* XV:6.
739 *KraussTA,* III, p. 93; II, p. 40.
740 Tal.Bab., *Soṭah* 49 b.
741 *ibid.*
742 Tal.Bab., *Giṭṭin* 7 a. For *zog* see chap. 42.
743 *KraussTA,* III, p. 281, note 112.
744 *SachsHist,* p. 289. See also p. 374.
745 Mishnah, *Kelim* XV:6.
746 See chapter 9.

747 Judah Ibn-Shmuel Kaufman, *English-Hebrew Dictionary* (Tel-Aviv, 1947), p. 365. See also *JastDict,* p. 60, where *)erus* is given the meaning of a "lily with an aromatic root."

748 Tal.Bab., *Soṭah* 49 b.
749 Mishnah, *Soṭah* IX:14; Tal.Bab., *Giṭṭin* 7 a.
750 Tal.Bab., *Soṭah* 49 b.
751 To Mishnah, *Soṭah* IX:14.
752 *SachsHist,* pp. 232, 255 ff. See also p. 388.
753 *KraussTA,* III, p. 93.
754 *JastDict,* II, p. 1440.
755 To Mishnah, *Kelim* XV:6.
756 Tal.Yer., *Ta'anit* I:4 (64 b).
757 *JastDict,* I, p. 136.

758 R. Nathan ben Jeḥiel of Rome, *)Aruk* (publ. 1101). New ed. by Alexander Kohut, *)Aruk ha-Shalem* (Vienna 1878-92), I, p. 94.

759 To Tal.Bab., *Soṭah* 49 b.
760 See the following chapter.

761 A parallel to this can be found in Isidore of Seville's description of the *symphonia* in his *Etymologiae* in *PL,* LXXXII, Col. 169. (For full quotation see note 535). *Symphonia* was the medieval Latin name of the drum, which, according to Isidore's description, also produced a *suavissimus cantus* by the *concordia gravis et acuti* of its membranes, applied on both ends of the drum (See *SachsHist,* p. 289).

762 Mishnah, *Kelim* XVI:7. For *markof* see p. 273.
763 *ibid.* XV:6.
764 *JastDict,* II, p. 1443.
765 Illustration 60.
766 *KraussTA,* III, pp. 93-94.
767 *ibid.*
768 *ibid.* II, p. 394.
769 The Mishnah. Yiddish Translation by Simḥa Petrushka (Montreal, 1949), VI, p. 97.
770 Sifre, *Numeri* 24 (p. 8 a).
771 Tal.Bab., *Zebaḥim* 88 b.

772 Also Tal.Bab., *Baba Kamma* 17 b. For a modern French equivalent of *)eskaliṭa* see note 726 on p. 410.

773 Midrash, *Song of Songs* VII:9.
774 *KraussTA,* III, p. 95.

[775] Tal. Yer., *Shabbat* VI:1 (7 d).
[776] Tal.Bab., *Shabbat* 58 a.
[777] Mishnah, *Shabbat* V:4.
[778] Tal.Bab., *Shabbat* 58 a.
[779] Midrash, *Song of Songs* VII:9.
[780] Mishnah, *Kelim* XIV:4.
[781] Tal.Bab., *Shabbat* 58 b.
[782] Tal.Yer., *Soṭah* I:8 (17 b).
[783] *KraussTA,* III, p. 95.
[784] This, at least is Sachs' interpretation. See chapters 27 and 28 of this section.
[785] Mishnah, *Shabbat* VI:9.
[786] Tal.Bab., *Shabbat* 58 a.
[787] This applied only to humans; for animals there were stricter regulations (Mishnah, *Shabbat* V:4; Tal.Bab., *Shabbat* 58 a). See also p. 408.
[788] Tal.Bab., *Mo'ed Katan* 9 b. In a note to his translation of this passage, Danby gives the following comment: "lit. 'run' to see a wedding ceremony with dances accompanied by instrumental music including hand-drums."
[789] *SachsHist,* p. 437. Illustration on p. 438.
[790] *KraussTA,* III, p. 95.
[791] Midrash, *Song of Songs* VII:9.
[792] Tosefta, *Shabbat* XIII (XIV):16 (ed. Zuckermandel, p. 130).
[793] *KraussTA,* I, p. 65; III, p. 95.
[794] Tal. Yer., *Ḳiddushin* I:4 (65 b).
[795] *ibid.*
[796] *ibid.*
[797] *JastDict,* II, p. 854.
[798] *KraussTA,* II, p. 527, note 984.
[799] *ibid.* III, p. 88.

NOTES TO SECTION VII.

[1] The only exception is "Nebuchadrezzar's Orchestra," mentioned in the Book of Daniel, which has been treated extensively by musicologists. But this group of musicians constituted a pagan, not a Jewish orchestra. See *GalpSum,* pp. 14, 16-17, 40, 55, 66; *SachsHist,* p. 83, and many others.
[2] Exod. 15:20; Judg. 5; 11:34; 21:21; 1 Sam. 18:6,7; 29.5.
[3] Better "pupils of prophets." See the section "Music Instruction."
[4] Identical with the above named Ethan. See pp. 144 ff.
[5] "Altogether masters," in Luther's translation.
[6] Mishnah, *'Arakin* II:6.
[7] *ibid.,* II:3.
[8] *ibid.,* II:5. To be sure, these rabbinic indications refer to the usage of the Second Temple. But they represent conceivably a mere continuation of the practice of the First Temple.
[9] Mishnah, *'Arakin* II:3.
[10] Mishnah, *Sukkah* V:1.
[11] Mishnah, *Middot* II:6.
[12] *Cp.* Daniel 6:11. After the destruction of the Temple, the "Eighteen Benedictions" had to be recited in the Synagogue three times a day, at the very same hours when formerly the three services of the Temple have taken place: in the morning (*shaḥarit*), at noon (*minḥa*), and in the evening (*ma'arib*).
[13] Mishnah, *Middot* II:6. See also p. 436.
[14] Probably today's Wadi Bereikhut.
[15] Luther's translation is: "And Hiskia spoke cordially to all the Levites."
[16] According to Grätz, the year was 711 B.C.E.
[17] For the full quotation of Sennaḥerib's report about Hezekiah's surrender see p. 522.

[18] For all these names see the section "Musical Instruments."
[19] Midrash, *Song of Songs* VII:9.
[20] *KraussTA,* III, p. 84.
[21] Tal.Bab., *Sukkah* 51 a.
[22] Mishnah, *ʿArakin* II:3.
[23] See note 68 on p. 115.
[24] *WilkEgypt,* I, pp. 452, 497-500.
[25] Oskar Fleischer, *Neumenstudien* (Leipzig, 1895), I, p. 35.
[26] *FétisHist,* IV, p. 43.
[27] Fleischer, *op. cit., ibid.* The *taʿamim,* the accents of Jewsih cantillation, are also supposed to have been graphic reproductions of cheironomic signs. However, Eric Werner narrows this supposition in believing "that the earliest Masoretic accents were a combination of signs borrowed from the contemporaneous Syriac system and the older Hebrew cheironomic tradition" (*The Conflict between Hellenism and Judaism in the Music of the Early Christian Church,* XX [1947], p. 453.) See also *IdelJewMus,* p. 67.
[28] Tal.Bab., *Berakot* 62 a.
[29] To *nethinim* see pp. 82 ff.
[30] Mishnah, *ʿArakin* II:4.
[31] *KraussTA,* III, p. 81.
[32] The Greeks and Romans, too, availed themselves of pitch-pipes, called *tonorion,* and these used to indicate the pitch even for orators. See note 620 on p. 394.
[33] Mishnah, *ʿArakin* II:3; Tal.Bab., *ʿArakin* 10 a.
[34] *KraussTA,* III, p. 81.
[35] See p. 313.
[36] So the *Authorized Version, Moulton* and *Harkavy. Douay* has "singing men." The *Jewish Version,* however, interprets the word in a non-musical sense as "for the guard." Yet, the word *sharim* hardly allows any other interpretation but "singers." *Moffat* and the *Revised Standard Version,* following obviously the Septuagint, leave out *sharim* altogether, translating "two chambers in the inner court."
[37] Mishnah, *Middot* II:6.
[38] *ibid.,* and Mishnah, *Shekalim* VI:3.
[39] Such chambers serving as rehearsal rooms and storage places for musical instruments have also existed in Egyptian temples. (*ErmanRel,* p. 213).
[40] Mishnah, *Middot* I:3.
[41] Mishnah, *ʿArakin* II:6.
[42] Tal.Bab., *Sukkah* 51 a.
[43] Mishnah, *ʿArakin* II:6.
[44] Tal.Bab., *Megillah* 24 b.
[45] Mishnah, *Middot* II:6.
[46] *ibid.,* II:5.
[47] *PortShilṭe,* chap. IV.
[48] Workmen's choirs are trained to-day mostly in this fashion; also gipsy bands, the members of which could not read music until recently. Nevertheless, such choral groups and bands sometimes render performances of a high artistic quality.
[49] Published as *Monumenta Musicae Byzantinae Subsidia,* vol. III, (Copenhagen and Boston, 1953).
[50] Eric Werner, *Musical Aspects of the Dead Sea Scrolls,* in *MQ* XLIII, (Jan. 1957), p. 23.
[51] Solomon Zeitlin, *The Dead Sea Scrolls and Modern Scholarship,* in *JQR, Monograph Series No. 3* (Philadelphia, 1956).
[52] Illus. 27.
[53] Curt Sachs, *Zweiklänge im Altertum,* in *Zeitschrift für Johannes Wolf* (Berlin, 1929), pp. 168-170.
[54] *SachsRise,* pp. 99-100.
[55] See pp. 123 ff.
[56] In the Middle Ages monody had a different implication; it was the term for a solo voice accompanied by instruments.

[57] Even to-day, the folksongs of Iceland are sung by the native population in parallel fifths and fourths. This is a remnant of the medieval style of singing, which was introduced into the island by Christian missionaries and which, owing to the geographic isolation of the country, remained unchanged through the centuries. However, the medieval *organum* is essentially a harmonic, not monophonic, phenomenon. Parallel fourths and fifths play in it the same role as parallel thirds and sixths in tertian harmony. See Joseph Yasser, *Medieval Quartal Harmony* (New York, 1938), pp. 70,84,91.

[58] Peter Wagner, *Über die Anfänge des mehrstimmigen Gesanges,* in *ZMW,* IX (1926), pp. 3 ff.

[59] Varro, *De lingua latina,* VI, 75.

[60] Varro, *De agricultura,* I, 2:14-16.

[61] *ibid.*

[62] Hans Hickmann, *Musicologie Pharaonique. Études sur l'évolution de l'art musical dans l'Égypte ancienne* (Kehl am Rhein, 1956), pp. 97 ff.

[63] *op. cit.,* p. 101.

[64] Hans Hickmann, *Ägypten,* in *Musikgeschichte in Bildern,* vol. II, *Musik des Altertums,* Lieferung 1 (Leipzig, 1961) pp. 86, 88, 90.

[65] However, Hickmann indicates that the theory according to which the statuette represents a precursor of the pneumatic organ, has met with serious doubts by Egyptian scholars.

O

O O

NOTES TO SECTION VIII.

[1] Ernest Renan, *Mission de Phénice* (Paris, 1864), pp. 355 ff.

[2] W. Robertson Smith, *Religion of the Semites* (New York, 1894), p. 93.

[3] *ChantRelig,* I, pp. 637, 645.

[4] *SchneidKult,* p. 125.

[5] Kurt Heinrich Sethe, *Urgeschichte und älteste Religionen der Ägypter* (Leipzig, 1930), in *Abhandlungen für die Kunde des Morgenlandes,* XVIII, No. 4.

[6] Hastings, *ERE,* vol. X, p. 294 b.

[7] *ErmanRel,* p. 14. Illustration *ibid.,* p. 15.

[8] H. Kees, *Der Opfertanz des ägyptischen Königs* (Leipzig, 1912), pp. 105 ff. For Egyptian dance rites combined with musical performances see in particular Lucius Apuleius, *Metamorphoses* (*The Golden Ass*), XI:8-17 (Engl. ed. New York, 1927, pp. 253 ff), and Herodotus, *History,* II, 58-60 (transl. by G. Rawlinson, New York, 1939, pp. 101-102).

[9] *ErmanRel,* p. 280.

[10] *ibid.*

[11] Midrash, *Numeri* XX:11.

[12] Midrash, *Leviticus* XII:5.

[13] *SachsDance,* p. 130.

[14] Mishnah, *Sukkah* IV:2.

[15] Midrash, *Leviticus* XI:9; Midrash, *Song of Songs* II:8; Targum to *Ḳohelet* 3:4.

[16] Targum to *Num.* 21:35; Targum to *Cant.* 2:8; Targum to *Ḳohelet* 3:4.

[17] *KraussTA,* III, pp. 101, 285. *Jast Dict,* p. 545 b.

[18] *KraussTA,* III, pp. 67 ff, 483. See also pp. 471 ff.

[19] Midrash, *Genesis* XXXVIII:7.

[20] Tal.Yer., *Pe'ah* I (15 d). The word occurs only in the Vilna edition (1922, p. 4); the Krotoschin edition has for it *meḳales;* the verb *ḳalas* means "to be done honor by a song" (*JastDict,* II, p. 1379).

[21] Targum Jonathan to *Exodus* 32:19.

[22] J. Gur (Grasowsky), *Milon 'Ibri,* 2nd ed. (*Tel-Aviv,* 1947), p. 1007.

[23] Tal.Bab., *Pesaḥim* III b; Targum Yerush. to *Exodus* 15:20; 32:18. (*JastDict,* I, p. 481).

[24] *JastDict,* I, p. 458.

[25] Midrash, *Genesis* LXVIII:13.

[26] *ibid.*

[27] Tal.Yer. *Sukkah* V:4 (55 c); Tal.Yer., *Sanhedrin* II:4 (20 b).

[28] Tal. Yer., *Bezah* V:2 (63 a).

[29] *Moffat's* translation: "Round and round the altar dance, waving your boughs, linked together."

[30] *Douay* translates: "Princes went before joined with singers, in the midst of young damsels playing on timbrels," and *Moffat*: "Singers in front, musicians behind, between them girls with tambourines."

[31] *LangdLit,* pp. XLI, XLII.

[32] K. J. Zenner, *Die Chorgesänge im Buche der Psalmen* (Freiburg i.B., 1896). See also the section "The Book of Psalms," pp. 154 ff.

[33] Rudolph Westphal, *Griechische Harmonik und Melopoeik* (Leipzig, 1886), p. 17.

[34] *SachsRhythm,* p. 29.

[35] Paul von Lagarde, *Orientalia,* in *Abhandlungen der königl. Gesellschaft der Wissenschaften zu Göttingen,* XXIV, (1879), p. 22.

[36] Adolf Erman, *Aegypten und Aegyptisches Leben im Altertum.* Neu bearbeitet von Hermann Ranke (Tübingen, 1923), pp. 281 ff.

[37] *MowPsalm,* IV, pp. 22 ff.

[38] This would be quite similar to what takes place even to-day in shamanistic performances among many primitive peoples the world over.

[39] W.O.E. Oesterley, *The Sacred Dance* (New York, 1923), p. 87.

[40] *HastDict,* I, p. 550 b.

[41] Wilhelm Baudissin, *Studien zur Semitischen Religionsgeschichte* (Leipzig, 1876), II, pp. 154 ff.—W. Robertson Smith, *The Religion of the Semites* (New York, 1894), Lecture V, pp. 150-195.

[42] Neilos, *Narratio V,* in *PG,* LXXIX, col. 650.

[43] Curiously, *Moffat* translates "band of dervishes."

[44] A similar procession in a single file is depicted in the rock-inscription of Boghazkoei (see p. 441), and Illustr. 56.

[45] Midrash, *Genesis* XIII:3. See also p. 518.

[46] Not only Shiloh, but practically every vineyard in Ancient Israel had a "dancing place," used exclusively by women.

[47] Mishnah, *Ta'anit* IV:8, Tal.Bab., *Ta'anit* 31 a.

[48] Published in *HastDict,* I, p. 550 b.

[49] *Megillat Ta'anit* V.

[50] *JosWar,* II, 17:6.

[51] For the ceremony of encompassing the altar see Pss. 26:6; 32:7; 68:26; 81:3; 118:27; also Mishnah, *Sukkah* IV:5.

[52] Mishnah, *Sukkah* IV:1.

[53] *ibid.,* also Midrash, *Leviticus* XXX:5; *cp.* Ps. 119:164.

[54] Mishnah, *Sukkah* IV:5.

[55] Also *JosAnt,* XII, 7:7; XIII, 13:5.

[56] Interpreted as "men of might" or "workers of miracle." See pp. 459, 496.

[57] Mishnah, *Sukkah* V:4.

[58] Mishnah, *Sukkah* IV:9; *Berakot* V:2; Tal.Bab., *Rosh ha-Shanah* 16 a.

[59] Tal.Bab., *Rosh ha-Shanah* 16 a. Examples for rain magic can be found in G. Frazer, *The Golden Bough* (London, 1911-27), I, pp. 247-329.

[60] Mishnah, *Berakot* V:2.

[61] Mishnah, *Ta'anit* I:1.

[62] Mishnah, *Sukkah* V:4.

[63] See Danby's translation of the Mishnah, p. 180, note 2.

[64] Mishnah, *Berakot* V:5.

[65] Mishnah, *Sukkah* V:1.

[66] Julius Levy, *The Feast of the 14th Day of Adar,* in *HUCA,* XIV (1939), pp. 127 ff.

[67] *ibid.,* p. 144. According to Lewy, Mordechai is not even a proper name, but a term denoting worshippers of Marduk as evidenced by the Greek term in 2 Macc. 15:36: *hē Mardochaikē hēmera,* "the day of the worshippers of Marduk." (Lewy, *op. cit.,* p. 131).

[68] *ibid.*, p. 146.
[69] This laxity in observing the law at Purim was partly responsible for the origin of latter days' Purim plays, the only kind of dramatic productions tolerated by the religious leaders of the Jews. See pp. 463 ff.
[70] Tal.Bab., *Sanhedrin* 64 b. See also *KraussTA*, III, p. 102.
[71] Louis Ginzberg, *Genizah-Studies*, in *JQR*, XVI (1903-04), p. 650.
[72] About this custom among the Hebrews and other peoples see *SachsDance*, pp. 71 ff.
[73] *U.J.E.*, III, 458.
[74] For other motivations pertaining to ritual dances see Oesterley, *op. cit.*, pp. 22 ff.
[75] Tal.Bab., *Ketubot* 16 a.
[76] Midrash, *Soṭah* IX:14.
[77] Midrash, *Lamentations* V:16; Midrash, *Ecclesiastes* X:5.
[78] Midrash, *Genesis* LIX:4; Tal.Bab., *Ketubot* 17 a.
[79] Tal.Bab., *Ketubot* 17 a.
[80] Mishnah, *Sukkah* V:4; Tosefta, *Sukkah* IV:4; a somewhat different description of this dance is given in Tal.Bab., *Sukkah* 53 a.
[81] Tal.Bab., *Sukkah* 53 a.
[82] Tal.Bab., *Ketubot* 17 a.
[83] Midrash, *Ecclesiastes* X:19.
[84] *SchneidKult*, p. 58.
[85] *ibid.*, p. 125.
[86] Latter days' Purim plays would seem to lend a certain justification for this hypothesis. "In Geonic times the dramatization of the story of Esther was a well-established custom among the Jews of the Orient" (*Jewish Encyclopedia*, X, p. 279). Similar plays are reported to have been performed by Jews of other countries in the Middle Ages.
[87] *PfeifferIntro*, p. 715.
[88] In Paulus' *Memorabilien* (1792), II.
[89] In the first edition of his *Dichter des Alten Bundes* (Göttingen, 1839), enlarged in the second edition, 1866.
[90] Other dramatizers of the *Canticles* were: F. Böttcher (1850); F. Hitzig (1855); C. D. Ginsburg (1857); Ernest Renan (1860); W. Robertson Smith (1876); J. G. Stickel (1888); S. Oettli (1889); Ch. Bruston (1891); S. R. Driver (1891); E. König (1893); W. F. Adeney (1895); A. Harper (1902); J. W. Rothstein (1911); L. Cicognani (*Il Cantico dei Cantici, Turin,* 1911); S. Minocchi (1924); G. Pouget and J. Guitton (*Le Cantique des Cantiques*, Paris, 1934); A. Hazan (*Le Cantique des Cantiques enfin expliqué*, Paris, 1936); Leroy Waterman (*The Song of Songs, translated and interpreted as a dramatic poem*, Ann Arbor, Mich., 1948).
[91] Ernest Renan, *The Song of Songs* (Engl. transl. by William M. Thomson, London, 1860).
[92] See note 90.
[93] Richard G. Moulton, *The Modern Reader's Bible* (New York, 1924).
[94] Heinrich Graetz, *Shir ha-shirim oder das Salomonische Hohelied* (Wien, 1871), pp. 68 ff.
[95] *Moulton, op. cit.*, pp. 1444 ff. He uses similar terms for the Book of Job (p. 1037), which he calls "a dramatic poem formed in an epic story," and also for the prophecies of Second Isaiah (Isa. 40-66), called by him "a rhapsody or spiritual drama" (p. 513).
[96] *PfeifferIntro*, p. 713.
[97] Tosefta, *Sanhedrin* XII.
[98] J. G. Wetzstein, *Die syrische Dreschtafel*, in Bastian's *Zeitschrift für Ethnologie* (1873), V, pp. 270-302.
[99] G. H. Dalman, *Palästinischer Diwan* (Leipzig, 1901), p. XII.
[100] Another interpretation explains "Schulammite" as the feminine of Solomon, namely "Shelomith," *i.e.* "Solomoness." See Edgar J. Goodspeed, *The Shulammite*, in *American Journal of Semitic Languages and Literature*, vol. 50 (1933-34), pp. 102-104.
[101] *KraussTA*, III, p. 81.
[102] Mishnah, *Beẓah* V:2; Tal.Bab., *Beẓah* 36 b.

[103] Midrash, *Genesis* LXXIV:17; *Song of Songs* VII:2.
[104] Midrash, *Genesis* LXVIII:13.
[105] *ibid.*, XXXVIII:7.
[106] Midrash, *Leviticus* XI:9. For the same dance, the Talmud uses the word *maḥol;* see Tal.Bab., *Taʿanit* 31 a.
[107] Tal.Yer., *Megillah* II:3 (73 b); Tal.Yer., *Moʿed Katan* III:7 (83 b); Midrash, *Song of Songs* I:3, par. 2.
[108] Tal.Yer., *Sanhedrin* II:4 (20 b).
[109] Tal.Bab., *Pesaḥim* 49 a.
[110] Tal.Bab., *Baba Kamma* 97 a.
[111] Tal.Bab., *Sanhedrin* 96 a.
[112] See p. 449.
[113] *KraussTA,* III, p. 100.
[114] See p. 454 ff.
[115] Tal.Bab., *Baba Kamma* 86 a.
[116] Midrash, *Leviticus* XII:5; Tal.Bab., *Shabbat* 56 b.
[117] Midrash, *Genesis* LXXIV:16.
[118] *KraussTA,* III, p. 100.
[119] Mishnah, *Taʿanit* IV:8; Tal.Bab., *Taʿanit* 31 a.
[120] The *Douay Version,* following closely the Vulgate, has: "with garlands and lights, and dances, and timbrels and flutes."
[121] Cicero, *Pro Muren* VI.
[122] Cornelius Nepos, *Vitae*: *Epaminondas,* 15:1.
[123] Suetonius, *Domitian* 8.
[124] *JosWar,* II, 2:5.
[125] Hastings, *ERE,* X, p. 359 b.
[126] *ErmanRel,* p. 121.
[127] Hastings, *ERE,* V, p. 238 a.
[128] *ErmanRel,* p. 131.
[129] *SachsDance,* p. 74.
[130] Mishnah, *Moʿed Katan* III:9.
[131] Mishnah, *Ketubot* IV:4; Tal.Bab., *Ketubot* 48 a.
[132] *ErmanRel,* p. 131.
[133] *ChantRelig,* I, p. 466.
[134] *ibid.,* I, p. 579.
[135] *ibid.,* I, p. 587.
[136] *ibid.,* II, p. 388.
[137] See p. 523.
[138] Mishnah, *Moʿed Katan* III:8; Tal.Bab., *Moʿed Katan* 28 b.
[139] Mishnah, *Moʿed Katan* III:9.
[140] Tal.Bab., *Moʿed Katan* 27 b.
[141] *KraussTA,* II, pp. 67 ff.
[142] *ibid.*
[143] For the description of this ceremony see Moses Gaster, *Daily and Occasional Prayers* (London, 1901), I, p. 197.
[144] See pp. 467 ff.
[145] Ernest Renan, *op. cit.,* p. 119.
[146] Morris Jastrow Jr., *The Song of Songs* (Philadelphia, 1921), p. 218.
[147] Leroy Waterman, *op. cit.,* p. 84.
[148] We use here *Moulton's* translation.

o

o o

NOTES TO SECTION IX.

[1] Strabo, *Geōgraphikōn,* I, 2:3.
[2] The Jewish accents, *taʿamim,* as used for the cantillation of biblical texts, originated in a much later period.

[3] "Key" or "mode" are used here in the broadest sense. In ancient Oriental music "tonality," at least in our Western conception, was unknown. Yet in Occidental music, too, "tonality" is a relatively late development.

[4] *JosApio,* I, 26:9; 28:12; 31:1. A summary of Moses' education is given in the New Testament: "He was instructed in all the wisdom of the Egyptians" (Acts 7:22).

[5] *PhiloMos,* I, 5:23.

[6] Plato, *Nomoi* (*Laws*), 656 d; 799 a; 819 a.

[7] Justin Martyr, *Cohortatio ad Graecos,* IX,X, in *PGL,* VI, cols. 261-62.

[8] Hans Hickmann, *Die ältesten Musikernamen,* in *Musica* (March 1951), V, 3, p. 90.

[9] See pp. 481, 510.

[10] A. A. Wolff, *Der Prophet Habakkuk* (Darmstadt, 1822), p. 41. See also pp. 485, 510, 514.

[11] It is worthy of note that, according to the early Christian tradition, even a number of strangers who excelled in music and poetry—among them Orpheus, Pythagoras and Homer—"had taken advantage of the history of Moses, when they had been in Egypt, and profited by his godliness and his ancestry" (Justin Martyr, *Apologia Prima pro Christianis, 44,* in *PGL,* VI, col. 395).

[12] Translation of the *Jewish, Authorized* and *American Versions,* and *Moulton. Douay* has: "and deliver it to the ears of Josue," *Moffat*: "and read it aloud to Joshua," and the *Revised Standard Version*: "and recite it in the ears of Joshua."

[13] *Cp.* Josephus' statement: "The report goes that even he [Homer] did not leave the poems in writing, but that their memory was preserved in songs, and they were put together afterward" (*JosApio,* I, 1:2).

[14] *HerdSpirit,* II, pp. 217 ff.

[15] See p. 12. *Cp. SachsRise,* pp. 58-59, and *LangdLit,* pp. XII, XIX.

[16] *RiehmHandw,* p. 826. *Cp.* W. Robertson Smith, *The Prophets in Israel . . .* (New York, 1882), p. 85.

[17] *RiehmHandw,* p. 1698.

[18] *ibid.,* p. 1041.

[19] *ibid.,* p. 1233. *Cp.* 2 Kings 2:3,5; 4:1 ff; 4:38; 5.22; 6:1.

[20] Subsequently, the leaders of the levitical singers were likewise called "fathers," and their school termed as "Fathers' houses of the Levites" (1 Chron. 9:33,34). In Sumeria, the headmaster of the school was called "school father," while the pupil was called "school son" (Samuel Noah Kramer, *From the Tablets of Sumer,* Indian Hills, Colo., 1956, p. 5).

[21] It must be well borne in mind that, in the ancient Hebrew parlance, the word "son" (*ben*) did not necessarily imply an offspring in the biological sense. Quite often it had a figurative meaning that was applied to men in general as well as to animals and even to lifeless objects. Such expressions as "sons of God," "son of herd," "son of flame," etc. belong to this category. In the light of this usage, the title "sons of prophets" signified simply a membership in a prophetic order. *Cf. GesLex,* p. 121. In a similar figurative sense, musical tones are called "daughters of music" (Eccl. 12:4).

[22] Eusebius, *Praeparatio evangelica XI:5,* in *PGL,* XXI, col. 854.

[23] *ChantRelig,* I, p. 617.

[24] Still in recent times the character of these fraternities of prophets has been grossly misinterpreted. See Solomon Reinach's misstatement about the "sons of the prophets" in his *Orpheus* (New York, 1941), p. 205. *Moffat* also completely misunderstood the character of this educational institution in calling, in his Bible translation, the "sons of prophets" a "band of dervishes."

[25] See p. 74, note 4.

[26] *RiehmHandw,* p. 1041.

[27] Tal.Bab., *Ḥullin* 24 a. See also pp. 305 ff.

[28] *StainMus,* p. 90. See also p. 518.

[29] See Idelsohn's publications (pp. 228 ff).

[30] Tal.Bab., *Beẓah* 36 b; *ʿArakin* 10 b; Tal.Yer., *Sukkah* V:6 (55 c).

[31] Mishnah, *Shabbat* I:3.

[32] Tal.Bab., *Rosh ha-Shanah* 33 b.

[33] Tal.Bab., *Nedarim* 37 a.
[34] Tal.Bab., *Soṭah* 30 b.
[35] Tal.Bab., *Rosh ha-Shanah* 29 b; *Sukkah* 42 b; *Megillah* 4 b.
[36] See also p. 169.
[37] See pp. 476 ff.

o
o o

NOTES TO SECTION X.

[1] *HarrisHer,* p. 56.
[2] The meaning of *teruʿah* is "noise," and, applied to wind-instruments, the "resounding" blast.
[3] *GressMus,* p. 9.
[4] Mishnah, *Sukkah* IV:9; *Taʿanit* III:1-3; 7-8.
[5] W. Robertson Smith, *Religion of the Semites* (New York, 1894), pp. 147 ff.—Salomon Reinach, *Cultes, Myths et Religion* (Paris, 1904-1923), p. 129.
[6] Mishnah, *Sukkah* IV:1; V:1,4; Tal.Bab., *Sukkah* 50 b; Tal.Yer., *Sukkah* V:1 (55 a).
[7] See p. 459.
[8] *FineShof,* p. 203, note.
[9] Joshua Trachtenberg, *Jewish Magic and Superstition* (New York, 1939), p. 172.
[10] *FineShof,* p. 203.
[11] *ibid.,* p. 204.
[12] J. Trachtenberg, *op. cit.,* p. 119.
[13] H. Winckler, *Arabisch-Semitisch-Orientalisch,* in *MVAG* (1901), pp. 4,5,180.
[14] Other times and other countries had other mystic figures. The magic number of the Cabalists in the Middle Ages was ten. The famous Cabalist Pico della Mirandola established even a relationship between this figure and the music of Ancient Israel: the psaltery had ten strings, there were ten famous psalm-singers (or psalm-authors), the Hebrews possessed ten musical instruments, they knew ten modes which served as melodies to the psalms, etc. (Pico della Mirandola, *"De Magia,"* in *Opera Omnia,* Basel, 1572, p. 174).
[15] Tal.Bab., *Sukkah* 45 a. Philo quotes numerous examples for the significance of the number seven in nature, human life, grammar, philosophy and mythology. See *Nomōn hierōn allēgorias tōn meta tēn hexaēmeron to prōton* (*Allegorical interpretation of Genesis*), II, III, Book I, chap. II, 8 ff.
[16] R. H. Charles, *The Apocrypha and Pseudepigraphia of the Old Testament in English* (Oxford, 1913), II, pp. 342 ff.
[17] *Shofarot* with a particularly powerful sound. See pp. 368 ff.
[18] We use Gaster's translations, *op. cit.* pp. 288 ff.
[19] "No less than seven halts are made for the dead," in Maimonides, *Mishneh Torah* (*The Book of the Judges*), XII:4.
[20] J. Trachtenberg, *op. cit.,* p. 179.
[21] See p. 473.
[22] "These are the cups that once belonged to Laomedon's table: to win these Apollo by his harp playing built the walls of Troy." Martial, *Epigrams,* VIII, 6:5,6.
[23] Clement of Alexandria, *Protreptikos pros Hellēnas, chap. 1,* in *PGL,* VIII, cols. 50-51.
[24] Tal.Bab., *Moʿed Katan* 26 a.
[25] Tal.Yer., *Sukkah* III:10 (53 d). The same with a somewhat different wording in Tal.Bab., *Berakot* 30 a.
[26] Tal.Bab., *Moʿed Katan* 17 a,b.
[27] Tal.Bab., *Sanhedrin* 67 b.
[28] Philo refers to another device designed to avoid the unexpected possibility of seeing God in the sanctuary: "All inside is unseen except by the high priest alone, and indeed he, though charged with the duty of entering once a year, gets no view of anything. For he takes with him a brazier full of lighted coals and incense, and the great quantity of vapour which this naturally gives forth covers everything around it, beclouds

the eyesight and prevents it from being able to penetrate to any distance" (*PhiloLaws*, XIII: 72). See also Philo, *Peri methēs* (*On drunkenness*), XXXIV:136, and *De Gigantibus*, 52.

[29] Sachs gives for the use of *pa'amonim* a different explanation. See p. 384.

[30] Lucian, *De Syria Dea*, 29. For other noise-making protective devices see the chapters on *meẓillot, zog, ḳarḳash* and *sharḳuḳita.*

[31] Tal.Bab., *Ḥullin* 105 b.

[32] *Rituale Romanum*, pp. 107 ff.

[33] *GressMus*, p. 6, note.

[34] "Tormented"' in the *Revised Standard Version.*

[35] Tal.Bab., *'Erubin* 104 a. See also Leopold Löw, *Beiträge zur jüdischen Altertumskunde* (Szeged, 1875), II, p. 304.

[36] *SachsDance*, pp. 201-202.

[37] *Athen*, XIV, 624 a,b.

[38] Tal.Yer., *'Erubin* X:1 (26 c).

[39] W. H. Roscher, *Ausführliches Lexikon der griechischen und römischen Mythologie* (Leipzig, 1884-1919), art. "Kinnyras."

[40] Pindar, *Pythia*, 2:15.—Strabo, *Geōgraphikēn*, XVI:755, 18.—Lucian, *De Syria Dea*, 9.

[41] *SachsHist*, p. 107. Another explanation gives the etymology of both terms of the instrument from the Egyptian root *k·nn·r.*

[42] Unlike other translations, that of *Harkavy* always renders *nibba* as "played," instead of "prophesied."

[43] Plato, *Phaedrus* 262.

[44] *PhiloMos*, II, 35:188.

[45] Philo, *Peri tōn metonomazomenōn* (*On the Change of Names*), XXIV:139.

[46] *PhiloLaws*, Book I, XI:65.

[47] The translation of the Hebrew *shofetim* as "judges" does not represent its conventional meaning. The *shofetim* of Israel have not been officers of a court of justice, but the elected leaders and chief magistrates of the nation. Their functions corresponded to those of the *shupetim*, the regents, of Phoenicia, and to the *sufetès* of Carthage, whose office was similar to that of the Roman consuls.

[48] K.W.E. Nägelsbach, *The Prophet Isaiah* (New York, 1906), see commentary on 8:3.

[49] The four hundred and fifty priests of Ba'al on the Mount Carmel are considered by the chronicler as heathen, *i.e.* false prophets (1 Kings 18:22 ff).

[50] Midrash, *Siphre*, Commentary to Num. 24:10.

[51] Isa. 7:3 ff; 36:21; Jer. 21:1 ff; 28:5; Ezek. 16:1; Amos 7:10, etc.

[52] *MowPsalm*, III, p. 23.

[53] *Poiei tas psychas enthousiastikas*, "makes our souls enthusiastic." Aristotle, *Politics*, 1340 a, 10.

[54] *GressMus*, p. 16.

[55] M. R. James, *The Apocryphal New Testament* (Oxford, 1924), pp. 367-68. *Cp. ZNTW*, III, pp. 287 ff. (Translation of the *Ante-Nicene Library*, XVI, pp. 390 ff).

[56] A parallel to this is the story of the Arabic prince *Abu Said Kukuburi*, lord of Arbella . . . , who "would pass nights in hearing religious music to which he was so sensible that, when excited by its influence, he used to pull off part of his clothes." (See the *Biographical Dictionary* of Ibn Khallikan [13th century], vol. II, p. 538 in the English edition).

[57] J. Goldziher, *Abhandlungen zur arabischen Philologie* (Leiden, 1896-99), I, pp. 3 ff, 15 ff.

o

o o

NOTES TO SECTION XI.

[1] *ErmanRel*, p. 51.

[2] *ibid.*, p. 74.

[3] See Illustr. 27.

[4] Originally, women also belonged to this guild, as is apparent from 2 Chron. 35:25.
[5] Mishnah, *Middot* II:6.
[6] *EwaldAnt,* pp. 285 ff.
[7] Midrash, *Genesis* XXIII:3.
[8] P. Scholz, *Die heiligen Altertümer des Volkes Israel* (Regensburg, 1868), I, p. 36.
[9] *RiehmHandw,* I, p. 447.
[10] *CalmetDict* (French ed., Geneva, 1780), III, p. 335.
[11] In *StainMus,* p. 90.
[12] Solomon Schechter, *Studies in Judaism, 1st series* (Philadelphia, 1896), p. 316.
[13] *ibid.,* p. 317.
[14] Ismar Peritz, *Women in the Ancient Hebrew Cult,* in *JBL* (Syracuse, 1898), p. 148.
[15] *Moffat,* changing the order of the verses, renders the passage as: "(turn your festivals into mourning and your ditties into dirges); the temple hymns shall change to howls." The *American* and *Revised Standard Versions* translate: "The songs of the Temple [note: or palace] shall become wailings in that day." While *Douay* divests the passage of any musical meaning: "and the hinges of the Temple shall screak in that day."
[16] *CornCult,* p. 119.
[17] Philo, *Peri Apoikias* (*On the Migration of Abraham*), XVII, 97. *PhiloMos,* Book II, XXVII, 136.
[18] Mishnah, *ʿArakin* II:6.
[19] *EwaldAnt,* pp. 285-86.
[20] *ibid.,* p. 286.
[21] *WincklerKeil,* II, p. 45.—E. Schrader, *Die Keilinschriften und das Alte Testament* (Giessen, 1882), pp. 45 ff.—*JerATAO* (Engl. ed., London, 1911), II, p. 224.
[22] *Cp.* the *ambubaiae* of ancient Rome and the *aulētridēs* of the Hellenes. See also *PhiloTher,* VII, 58.
[23] The *Authorized Version, Moulton* and *Harkavy* translate "cunning women," the *American* and *Revised Standard Versions* "skillful women," and *Moffat* "Those well-skilled in dirges."
[24] Mishnah, *Moʿed Katan* III:9; Tal.Bab., *Moʿed Katan* 28 b.
[25] Tal.Bab., *Moʿed Katan* 8 a.
[26] Tal.Bab., *Nedarim* 66 b.
[27] Tal.Bab., *Moʿed Katan* 28 b, to Mishnah, *Moʿed Katan* III:9.
[28] Mishnah, *Moʿed Katan* III:9.
[29] *ibid.* See also pp. 472 ff.
[30] See p. 169.
[31] *BuddeGesch,* p. 21.
[32] K. Budde, *Das hebräische Klagelied,* in *Zeitschrift für alttestamentliche Wissenschaft* (1882), pp. 24 ff. For full quotation see pp. 251 ff.
[33] Mishnah, *Moʿed Katan* III:9.
[34] Mishnah, *Ketubot* IV:4; Tal.Bab., *Ketubot* 48 a.
[35] Tal.Yer., *Berakot* III:1, (5 b).
[36] *Athen,* IV, 175 a.
[37] *Douay* translates: "The Lord shall give the word to them that preach good tidings with great power"; the *Authorized Version* and *Harkavy*: "The Lord gave the word: great was the company of those that published it"; the *American Version* and *Moulton*: "The Lord giveth the word; the women that publish the tidings are a great host"; *Moffat*: "When the Lord sent news of victory, the women who told it were a mighty host"; and the *Revised Standard Version*: "The Lord gives the command; great is the host of those who bore the tidings."
[38] Exod. 15:20; Judg. 5:1; 11:34; 1 Sam. 18:6; 21:12; Ps. 68:26; applied to non-Jewish women 2 Sam. 1:20.
[39] Tal.Bab., *Berakot* 24 a.
[40] Tal.Bab., *Soṭah* 48 a.
[41] *ibid.*
[42] Mishnah, *Kelim* XV:6. This might have already been the later usage when women were eliminated from the Temple choir.

[43] For a certain time some scholars considered Philo's essay a forgery of an unknown Christian writer at the end of the 3rd century C.E., who allegedly used Philo's name to project back into the early Christian epoch an imaginary account of a monastic life. However, this theory has been conclusively refuted by modern research.

[44] *PhiloTher*, X, 79-80.

[45] The Greek word used here is *chorikōn,* meaning a "danced hymn," in general "dance song."

[46] *PhiloTher*, X, 79-80.

[47] *ibid.*, XI, 83-89.

o

o o

NOTES TO SECTION XII and EPILOGUE

[1] Whether Heman had fourteen sons, as stated in Verse 4, is rather doubtful..It seems that the chronicler, in order to arrive at the given number of group leaders (24), had invented a few of the names. It is evident that he arbitrarily used some liturgical text (possibly a fragment of a discarded psalm) to construct from it the required number of names. Indeed, if we read consecutively the last nine names of Verse 4, starting with Ḥananiah, and interpret the inherent meaning of the words, we find that the text thus obtained represents a little poem:

"Be gracious unto me, O God,
be gracious unto me.
Thou art my God.
Thou hast increased
and raised up help for him that
sat in distress.
Do thou make the [prophetic]
visions abundant."

According to Ewald (in Keil, *Kommentar zur Chronik,* 1870, p. 200), this was part of an ancient famous oracle, while Haupt (*ZAW,* 1914, vol. 34, pp. 142 ff) opines that it was a fragment of a post-exilic psalm. It is therefore evident that the names of some of the twenty-four group leaders have been artificially created (see also p. 145, note 148).

[2] Tal.Bab., *ʿArakin* 11 a.

[3] Mishnah, *Sukkah* V:6-8, and Obadiah of Bertinoro to *Sukkah* V:5.

[4] *JosAnt,* VII, 14, 7

[5] Mishnah, *Sukkah* V:6; *Taʿanit* IV:2.

[6] Mishnah, *Tamid* VII:4.

[7] *BuddeGesch,* p. 9. Luther translates the passage as "therefore they say in songs," paraphrased by Budde as "therefore the poets sing." In the English Bibles, the *Authorized* and *American Versions, Moulton* and *Harkavy* have "in proverbs," *Douay* omits the reference to minstrels: "therefore it is said in the proverb," whereas *Moffat* sets: "hence the song and satire of the bards," and the *Revised Standard Version*: "therefore the ballad singers say."

[8] *ibid.*

[9] *HerdSpirit,* II, p. 222.

[10] See the author's *Rundfunk und Musikpflege* (Leipzig, 1931), p. 54.

[11] *JosAnt,* XX, 9, 6.

[12] Tal.Bab., *ʿArakin* 11 b.

[13] *JosAnt, ibid.*

[14] *ibid.*

[15] *ibid.*

[16] Heinrich Graetz, *Eine Strafmassnahme gegen die Leviten,* in *MGWJ* XXXV (1886), pp. 97-108.

[17] Heinrich Berl, *Das Judentum in der Musik* (Stuttgart, 1926), p. 85.

[18] *ibid.*, p. 18.

BIBLIOGRAPHY

Aaron ben Moses ben Asher, *Dikduke ha-ta'amim* (new ed. Leipzig, 1879).
Abbot of R. Nathan (ed. S. Schechter, 1945)
Ackermann, Aron, *Das hermeneutische Element der biblischen Accentuation* (Berlin, 1893).
Adler, Guido, *Handbuch der Musikgeschichte* (Berlin, 1929), 2 vols.
Albright, W. A., *The earliest Forms of Hebrew Verse*, in *Journal of the Palestine Oriental Society* (1922), II.
Albright, W. F., *Magan, Meluḫa, Menes and Narâm-Shin*, in *Journal of Egyptian Archaeology* (London, 1921), VII.
Alexander, J. A. *The Psalms translated and explained* (New York, 1855), 2 vols.
Allegro, John Marco, *The Dead Sea Scrolls* (Baltimore, 1956).
)Al-Mas'udi, *Livre des Prairies d'Or et des mines de Pierres Précieuses.* Texte et tranduction par C. Barbier de Maynard (Paris: L'Imprimerie Nationale, 1874), VII.
Ambros, August Wilhelm, *Musikgeschichte* (Breslau, 1862-82), 2 vols.
Ambrose, St., *Enarratio in Ps. I,* in *PL,* XIV.
———— *Hexaemeron,* in *PL,* XIV.
American (Revised) Version of the Bible (The) (New York, 1885, 1901).
Anastasius, *Historia de vitis Romanorum Pontificorum,* XXXIX, in *PL,* CXXVIII.
Anton, Conrad Gottlob, *Versuch, die Melodie und Harmonie der alten hebräischen Gesänge zu entziffern,* in Paulus, *Neues Repertorium für Biblische und Morgenländische Litteratur* (Jena, 1790).
Apel, Willi, *Early History of the Organ,* in *Speculum* (1948), vol. 23, No. 2.
Apuleius, Lucius, *Metamorphoses (The Golden Ass)* (Engl. ed. New York, 1927)).
Arends, Leopold, *Über den Sprachgesang der Vorzeit und Herstellbarkeit der althebräischen Vokalmusik* (Berlin, 1867).
Aristides Quintilianus, *De Musica* (Amsterdam, 1652).
Aristophanes, *Thesmophoriazusae,* in *Eleven Comedies* (New York, 1943), 2 vols.
Aristotle, *Politikē,* VIII.
Aristotle, *Problēmata.*
Arnold, William R., *The Rhythms of the Ancient Hebrews,* in *Old Testament and Semitic Studies in Memory of William Rainey Harper* (Chicago, 1908).
Athanasius, *Epistola de decretis Nicaenae Synodi,* in *PGL* XXV.
———— *Epos Merkellinon eis tōn hermēneian tōn Psalmōn,* in *PGL,* XXVII.
Athenaeus, *Deipnosophistēs (The Sophists at Dinner).*
Augustine, St., *Confessiones,* in *PL,* XXXII.
———— *Enarratio in Ps. IV:4,* in *PL,* XXXVI.
———— *Enarratio in Ps. XXVI, Sermo ad plebem,* in *PL,* XXXVI.
———— *Enarratio in Ps. XLII,* in *PL,* XXXVI.
———— *Enarratio in Ps. XCI,* in *PL,* XXXVII.
———— *Enarratio in Ps. XCIX,* in *PL,* XXXVII.
———— *Enarratio in Ps. CVI,* in *PL,* XXXVII.
———— *Enarratio in Ps. CL,* in *PL,* XXXI.
———— *Epistola CI ad Memorio,* in *PL,* XXXIII.
———— *Sermo 374, 2,* in *PL,* XXXIX.
Baer, Seligman, *Thorath Emeth* (Rödelsheim, 1852).
Baethgen, Friedrich, *Beiträge zur semitischen Religionsgeschichte* (Berlin, 1888).
———— *Die Psalmen übersetzt und erklärt* (Göttingen, 1897).
Bähr, Karl Christian, *Symbolik des mosaischen Kultes* (Heidelberg, 1837).
Baron, Salo Wittmayer, *The Jewish Community* (Philadelphia, 1942), 3 vols.
———— *A Social and Religious History of the Jews* (New York, 1937), 3 vols.
———— *same* (Enlarged edition, Philadelphia, 1957), 8 vols.
Barry, Phillips, *On Luke 15:25. Symphōnia, Bagpipe,* in *JBL* (1904), vol. 23.
Barthélemy, D. and Milik J. T., *Discoveries in the Judaean Desert I, Qumran Cave I* (Oxford, 1955).
Bartolocci, Giulio, *Bibliotheca magna Rabbinica* (Rome, 1675-93), 5 vols.

Basil the Great, *Epistolē CCVII. Tois Kata Neokaisareian klērikois* (written 375), in *PG,* XXXII.
——— *Homilia eis tōn prōton Psalmon,* in *PGL,* XXIX.
——— *same: Homilia in Psalmum primum* (translated into Latin by Rufinus), in *PGL,* XXXI.
Baudissin, Wilhelm von, *Studien zur semitischen Religionsgeschichte* (Leipzig, 1876), 2 vols.
Beda Venerabilis, *Interpretatio Psalterii artis cantilenae,* in *PL,* XCIII.
Beer, G. *Individual-und Gemeindepsalmen* (Marburg, 1894).
Behn, Friedrich, *Musikleben im Altertum und frühen Mittelalter* (Stuttgart, 1954).
Beimel, Jakob, *Some interpretation of the meaning of SELAH,* in *Jewish Music Forum, Bulletin* (1943).
Benzinger, Immanuel, *Hebräische Archaeologie* (Leipzig, 1927).
Benzinger, K., *Musik bei den Hebräern,* in *Realencyclopedie für protestantische Theologie und Kirche,* XIII (Leipzig, 1897-1913).
Berkowitz, M., *Strophenbau und Responsion in den Psalmen,* in *Wiener Zeitschrift für die Kunde des Morgenlandes* (1903), XVII.
Berl, Heinrich, *Das Judentum in der Musik* (Stuttgart, 1926).
——— *Die Wiederherstellbarkeit der althebräischen Vokalmusik,* in *Der Jude* (Berlin, 1923), VII.
Bertholet, Alfred, *A History of Hebrew Civilization* (London, 1926).
Bezold, Carl, *Ninive und Babylon* (Bielefeld and Leipzig, 1926).
Braun, O., *Ein Brief des Katholikos Timotheos I über biblische Studien des 9. Jahrhunderts,* in *Oriens Christianus,* I (1901).
Breasted, James Henry, *Ancient Records of Egypt: The Historical Documents* (Chicago, 1905), 5 vols.
——— *The Dawn of Conscience* (New York, 1935).
——— *A History of Egypt* (New York, 1905).
Briggs, Charles Augustus, *A Critical and Exegetical Commentary on the Book of Psalms* (New York, 1908-09), 2 vols.
Bücher, Karl, *Arbeit und Rhythmus* (Leipzig, 1909).
Budde, Karl, *Geschichte der althebräischen Literatur* (Leipzig, 1906).
——— *Das Hebräische Klagelied,* in *Zeitschrift für alttestamentliche Wissenschaft* (1882).
Budge, Wallis, *From Fetish to God in Ancient Egypt* (Oxford, 1934).
Bulletin of the Metropolitan Museum of Art (New York, 1928).
Burrows, Millar, *The Dead Sea Scrolls* (New York, 1955).
Buttenwieser, Moses, *The Psalms Chronologically Treated with a New Translation* (Chicago, 1938).
Calmet, Augustin, *Dictionnaire historique, critique, chronologique, géographique et litteral de la Bible* (Geneva, 1780). (Engl. ed. Boston, 1832).
——— *Dissertatio in musica instrumenta Hebraeorum,* in *UgThes,* XXXII.
——— *Les Pseaumes* (Paris, 1724).
Caro, Joseph, *Shulḥan ʿAruk. Oraḥ Ḥayyim.*
Cassel, David, *Die Pesachhaggada* (Berlin, 1895).
Cassiodorus, *Expositio in Psalterium, Ps. CIX,* in *PL,* LXX.
——— *In Psalterium praefatio,* in *PL,* LXX.
Chantepie de la Saussaye, Pierre Daniel, *Lehrbuch der Religionsgeschichte* (Tübingen, 1925), 2 vols.
Charles, R. H., *The Apocrypha and Pseudepigraphia of the Old Testament in English* (Oxford, 1913), 2 vols.
Cheyne, Thomas Kelly, *The Origins and Religious Contents of the Psalter* (London, 1891).
Cheyne, Th. K. and J. S. Black, *Encyclopedia Biblica* (New York, 1899), 4 vols.
Cicero, *De oratore.*
——— *In Verrem.*
——— *Pro Muren.*

Cicognani, L., *Il Cantico dei Cantici* (Turin, 1911).
Clement of Alexandria, *Logos protreptikos pros Hellēnas, I,* in *PGL,* VIII.
——— *Paidagōgos, II, 4. Quomodo in conviviis se recreare oportet,* in *PGL,* VIII. Also in *PG,* VI.
——— *Strōmata, VI, 7, 11, VII, 7,* in *PGL,* IX.
Clitarchos, *Scholia in Platonis Minoem,* in Siebenkees, J. Ph., *Anecdota graeca e prestantissimis italicarum bibliothecarum codicibus descriptis* (1798).
Codex Kosmas (in the Vatican Library, Graec. 699).
Cohen, Francis Lyon, *Ancient Musical Tradition of the Synagogue,* in *Musical Association London, Proceedings,* Session 19, (1892-93).
(*The*) *Companion Bible* (London, n.d.).
Cornelius Nepos, *Vitae. Epaminondas.*
Cornill, Karl Heinrich, *The Culture of Ancient Israel* (Chicago, 1914).
——— *Music in the Old Testament* (Chicago, 1909).
Cowley, Sir Arthur Ernest, *Aramaic Papyri of the Fifth Century B.C.* (Oxford, 1923).
Cumming, C. G., *The Assyrian and Hebrew Hymns of Praise* (New York, 1934).
Cyril of Alexandria, *Pro Sancta Christianorum Religione adversus libros athei Juliani liber VII,* in *PGL,* LXXVI.
Daremberg, C. and E. Saglio, *Dictionnaire des Antiquités Grecques et Romaines* (Paris, 1875-1919), 3 vols.
Darmsteter, Arsène and D. S. Blondheim, *Les Gloses françaises dans les Commentaires talmudiques de Raschi* (Paris, 1929).
Davies, N. G. de, *The Rock Tombs of El Amarna* (London, 1908).
Delitzsch, Franz Julius, *Biblical Commentary on the Psalms* (Edinburgh, 1892), 2 vols.
——— *Zur Geschichte der jüdischen Poesie* (Leipzig, 1836).
De Wette, Wilhelm Martin Leberecht, *Commentar über die Psalmen* (Heidelberg, 1811).
Didymus of Alexandria, *Eis Psalmous, IV,* in *PGL,* XXXIX.
Dio Chrysostomos, *Opera omnia.*
Diodorus Siculus, *Historia Bibliotheca.*
Driver, C. G., *The Hebrew Scrolls* (London, 1951).
Driver, S. D., *The Book of Daniel* (Cambridge, 1905).
Duhm, Bernhard, *Die Psalmen* (Tübingen, 1922).
Dupont-Sommer, A., *The Dead Sea Scrolls.* Translated by Margaret Rowley (Oxford, 1950).
——— *The Jewish Sect of Qumran and the Essenes.* Translated from the French by R. D. Barnett (New York, 1955).
Durant, Will, *Our Oriental Heritage* (New York, 1954).
Ebeling, Erich, *Ein Hymnenkatalog aus Assur,* in *JRAS* (1923).
——— *Religiöse Keilinschrifttexte aus Assur* (Leipzig, 1918).
Edersheim, Alfred, *Sketches of Jewish Life in the Days of Christ* (London, 1910).
Ehrt, Carl, *Abfassungszeit und Abschluss des Psalters* (Leipzig, 1869).
Encyclopaedia Britannica.
Engel, Carl, *The Music of the Most Ancient Nations* (London, 1864).
Epiphanius, *Kata haireseōn,* in *PGL,* XLII.
Erman, Adolf, *Aegypten und aegyptisches Leben im Altertum.* Neu bearb. von Hermann Ranke (Tübingen, 1923).
——— *Die Ägyptische Religion* (Berlin, 1905).
——— *Die Literatur der Ägypter* (Leipzig, 1923).
——— *same, Engl. ed. The Literature of the Ancient Egyptians* (London, 1927).
Euripides, *Cyclops,* in *The Complete Greek Drama* (New York, 1938), 2 vols.
——— *Elektra, ibid.*
Eusebius Pamphilius of Caesarea, *Commentarium in Psalmum LXXX,* in *PG,* XXIII.
——— *Ekklesiastikēs historias,* in *PGL,* XX.
——— *Hypomnēmata eis tous Psalmous, Ps. LXV,* in *PGL,* XXIII.
——— *Praeparatio evangelica,* in *PG,* XIII, also in *PGL,* XXI.
Ewald, Heinrich August, *The Antiquities of Israel* (Boston, 1876).

———— *Die Dichter des Alten Bundes* (Göttingen, 1866).
Farmer, Henry George, *Byzantine Musical Instruments in the Ninth Century* (London, 1925).
——— *The Organ of the Ancients. From Eastern Sources (Hebrew, Syriac and Arabic).* (London, 1931).
Fétis, François Joseph, *Histoire générale de la Musique* (Paris, 1867-76), 5 vols.
Finesinger, Sol Baruch, *Musical Instruments in OT,* in *HUCA* (1926), III.
———— *The Shofar,* in *HUCA* (1931-32), VIII-IX.
Finkelstein, Louis, *The Origin of the Synagogue,* in *Proceedings of the American Academy for Jewish Research,* I, (1928-30).
———— *Pharisees* (Philadelphia, 1938), 2 vols.
Fleischer, Oskar, *Neumenstudien* (Leipzig, 1895), 2 vols.
Forkel, Johann Nicholaus, *Allgemeine Geschichte der Musik* (Leipzig, 1788-1801), 2 vols.
Frazer, Sir George, *The Golden Bough* (London, 1911-1927), 13 vols.
Friedländer, Moritz, *Synagoge und Kirche in ihren Anfängen* (Berlin, 1908).
Fritsch, Charles T., *The Qumrān Community. Its History and Scrolls* (New York, 1956).
Fürst, Julius, *Librorum Sacrorum Veteris Testamenti concordantiae Hebraicae atque Chaldaicae* (Leipzig, 1840).
Gallé, A. F., *Daniel avec Commentaires de R. Saadia, Aben-Ezra, Rashi, etc.* (Paris, 1900).
Galpin, Francis William, *The Music of the Sumerians and Their Immediate Successors the Babylonians and Assyrians* (Cambridge, 1937).
Gaster, Moses, *Daily and Occasional Prayers* (London, 1901).
Gaster, Theodor H., *The Dead Sea Scriptures in English Translation* (Garden City, New York, 1956).
———— *Psalm 29* in *JQR* (1946-47), vol. 37.
Gerbert, Martin, *Scriptores ecclesiastici de musica sacra potissimum* (San Blasien, 1784).
Gesenius, Wilhelm, *A Hebrew and English Lexicon of the Old Testament, including the Biblical Chaldee* (Boston, 1906).
———— *Hebräisches und chaldäisches Handwörterbuch über das A.T.* (Leipzig, 1915).
———— *Thesaurus philologicus criticus linguae Hebraeae et Chaldaeae Veteris Testamenti* (vol. II ed. by Aemilius Roediger). (Leipzig, 1829-58), 3 vols.
Gevaert, François Auguste, *Histoire et théorie de la musique dans l'Antiquité* (Gand, 1881).
Ginsburg, Christian David, *The Essenes* (London, 1864).
Ginzberg, Louis, *Genizah-Studies,* in *JQR* (1903-04), XVI.
Glaser, Otto, *Die ältesten Psalmenmelodien,* in *Zeitschrift für Semistik* (Leipzig, 1935), vol. VIII and X.
Goldziher, Ignaz, *Abhandlungen zur arabischen Philologie* (Leyden, 1896-99).
Goodspeed, Edgar J., *The Short Bible* (Chicago, 1933).
———— *The Shulammite,* in *American Journal of Semitic Languages and Literature* (1933-34), vol. 50.
Gradenwitz, Peter, *The Music of Israel* (New York, 1949).
Graetz, Heinrich Hirsch, *Eine Strafmassnahme gegen die Leviten,* in *MGWJ* (1886), XXXV.
———— *History of the Jews* (Engl. ed.) (Philadelphia, 1898), 6 vols.
———— *Kritischer Kommentar zu den Psalmen* (Breslau, 1882-83).
Gregory the Great, *Liber Sacramentorum, Notae,* in *PL,* LXXVIII.
Gregory Nazianzen, *Logoi, IV:71,* in *PGL,* XXXV.
Gregory of Nyssa, *Tractatus prior in Psalmorum inscriptiones, IV,* in *PGL,* XLIV.
Gressmann, Hugo, *Musik und Musikinstrumente im Alten Testament* (Giessen, 1903).
Grimme, Hubert, *Psalmenprobleme* (Freiburg, Schweiz, 1902).
Grünhut, Lazar, *Die Rundreise des R. Petachjah aus Regensburg* (Frankfurt a.M., 1904).
Guillaume, A., *Prophecy and Divination among the Hebrews and other Semites* (New York, 1938).
Gunkel, Hermann, *Einleitung in die Psalmen* (Göttingen, 1928, 1933), 2 vols.

Gur (Grasowsky), Jehudah, *Milon ʾIbri (Hebrew Lexicon)*, 2nd ed. (Tel-Aviv, 1947).
Halliday, W. R., *Greek Divination* (London, 1913).
Hamburger, Jacob, *Real-Enzyklopedie für Bibel und Talmud* (Strelitz, 1883), 2 vols.
Harenberg, Joannes Christoph, *Commentatio de re musica vetutissima, ad illustrandum Scriptores Sacros et exteros accomodata* in *Miscellanea Lipsiensis Nova* (Leipzig, 1753), IX.
Harris, C. W., *The Hebrew Heritage* (New York, 1935).
Harris, Zelig S., *The Structure of Ras Shamra C,* in *JAOS* (1934), LIV.
Hartmann, Henrike, *Die Musik der sumerischen Kultur* (Frankfurt a.M., 1950).
Hastings, James, *A Dictionary of the Bible* (New York, 1898-1904), 4 vols.
——— *Encyclopedia of Religion and Ethics* (New York, 1908-1921), 12 vols.
Haupt, Leopold, *Sechs alttestamentliche Psalmen; mit ihren aus den Accenten entzifferten Singweisen* (Görlitz, Leipzig, 1854).
Hazan, A., *Le Cantique des Cantiques enfin expliqué* (Paris, 1936).
Heaton, E. W., *Everyday Life in Old Testament Times* (New York, 1956).
Hengstenberg, E. W., *Commentary on the Psalms* (Edinburgh, 1851).
Herbelot de Molainville, d'D., *Bibliothèque orientale; ou, Dictionnaire universel . . .* (Paris, 1697), 2 vols.
Herder, Johann Goffried, *The Spirit of Hebrew Poetry.* Transl. by James Marsh (Burlington, 1833), 2 vols.
Hermias Sozomenes, *Ekklēsiastikē historia,* in *PGL,* LXVII.
Hero, *Pneumatica.*
Herodotus, *Historia* (transl. by G. Rawlinson).
Hesychios of Alexandria, *Lexicon* (new ed. Jena, 1858-64), 4 vols.
Hickmann, Hans, *Ägypten,* in *Musikgeschichte in Bildern,* hrsg. von Heinrich Besseler und Max Schneider, Band II, Lieferung 1 (Leipzig, 1961).
——— *Die ältesten Musikernamen,* in *Musica* (March, 1951), V.
——— *Musicologie Pharaonique. Études sur l'évolution de l'art dans l'Egypte ancienne* (Kehl am Rhein, 1956).
Hilarius, *Tractatus super Psalmos. Prolog. in Ps. 1,* in *PL,* IX.
Hippolytus, *Contra haeresin Noeti,* in *PGL,* X.
——— *Tractatus contra omnes haereses* (two fragments only are preserved).
Hitzig, Ferdinand, *Daniel* (Leipzig, 1850).
——— *Die Psalmen übersetzt und ausgelegt* (Leipzig and Heidelberg, 1863).
The Holy Scriptures According to the Masoretic Text. A New Translation (Philadelphia, 1917).
Hommel, Fritz, *Geschichte Babyloniens und Assyriens* (Berlin, 1885-88).
Horace, *Odes.*
Horne, S. T., *An Introduction to the Critical Study and Knowledge of the Holy Scriptures* (New York, 1856), 2 vols.
Houbigant, C. F., *Racines Hébraiques sans points-voyelles; ou, Dictionnaire Hébraique . . .* (Paris, 1733).
Hupfeld, Hermann, *Die Psalmen* (Gotha, 1868).
Ibn Balaʿam, Abu Zakarya Yaḥya, *Shaʿar taʿame 3 Sifre EMeT* (new ed. Amsterdam, 1858).
Ibn Ezra, Abraham ben Meïr, *Commentary on the Book of Daniel.*
——— *Commentary on the Book of Psalms.*
——— *Commentary to Isaiah.*
Idelsohn, Abraham Zevi, *Hebräisch-Orientalischer Melodienschatz* (Jerusalem, Berlin, Vienna, 1914-32), 10 vols.
——— same in English and Hebrew editions.
——— *Jewish Music in its Historical Development* (New York, 1929).
——— *Parallelen zwischen gregorianischen und hebräisch-orientalischen Gesangsweisen,* in *ZMW* (1921-22).
Isaacs, Elcanon, *The Metrical Basis of Hebrew Poetry,* in *American Journal of Semitic Languages and Literature* (1918), XXXV.
Isidore of Seville, *De ecclesiasticis officiis,* in *PL,* LXXXIII.

——— *Etymologiae*, in *PL, LXXXII*.
Jahn, Johann, *Biblical Archaeology* (New York, 1853).
Jakob, B., *Beiträge zu einer Einleitung in die Psalmen*, in *Zeitschrift für alttestamentliche Wissenschaft* (1896), XVI.
James, M. R., *The Apocryphal New Testament* (Oxford, 1924).
Jastrow, Marcus, *A Dictionary of the Targumin, the Talmud Babli and Yerushalmi and the Midrashic Literature* (New York, 1943).
Jastrow, Morris Jr., *Die Religion Babyloniens und Assyriens* (Giessen, 105-12), 2 vols.
——— *The Song of Songs* (Philadelphia, 1921).
Jeremias, Alfred, *Das Alte Testament im Lichte des Alten Orients* (Leipzig, 1903).
——— *Handbuch der altorientalischen Geisteskultur* (Leipzig, 1913).
——— *The Old Testament in the Light of the Ancient East* (Engl. ed. London, 1911).
Jerome, St., *Ad Dardanum de diversis generibus musicorum instrumentis Epistola*, in *PL*, XXX.
——— *Breviarium in Psalmos. Ps. XXXII*, in *PL*, XXVI.
——— *Breviarium in Psalmos. Ps. XXXV*, in *PL*, XXVI.
——— *Breviarium in Psalmos. Ps. CXLIX*, in *PL*, XXVI.
——— *Commentarii in librum Job*, in *PL*, XXVI.
——— *Commentarium in Epistolam ad Galatos, I, cap. 1*, in *PL*, XXVI.
——— *Commentarium in Hosean*, in *PL*, XXV.
——— *Epistola XXXIX. Ad Paulam super obitu Blaesillae filiae*, in *PL*, XXII.
——— *Epistola LXXL. Ad Lucinium*, in *PL*, XXII.
——— *Epistola LXXVII. De morte Fabiolae*, in *PL*, XXII.
——— *Epistola CVII. Ad Laetam*, in *PL*, XXII.
——— *Epistola CVIII. Ad Eustochium Virginem; Epitaphium Paulae matris*, in *PL*, XXII.
——— *Praefatio in Eusebii Pamphilii Chronica*, in *PL*, XXXVII.
——— *Praefatio in librum Job*, in *PL*, XIX.
Jewish Encyclopedia (New York, 1901-06), 12 vols.
John Cassian, *De Coenobiorum institutis*, in *PL*, XLIX.
——— *Expositio in Psalterium. Ps. CIV*, in *PL*, LXX.
John Chrysostom, *Eis tas Hagias Martyras*, in *PGL*, L.
——— *Eis tōn Psalmōn XLI*, in *PGL*, LV.
——— *Eis tōn Psalmōn CXL*, in *PGL*, LV.
——— *Eis tōn Psalmōn CXLIX*, in *PGL*, LV.
——— *Homilia eis tōn Psalmōn CXLV*, in *PGL*, LV.
——— *Homilias en Antoicheia lechtesai*, in *PGL*, XLIX
——— *Prooimia tōn Psalmōn*, in *PGL*, LV.
——— *Protheoria eis tous Psalmous*, in *PGL*, LV.
Josephus Flavius, *Antiquities of the Jews*.
——— *Contra Apionem*.
——— *Wars of the Jews*.
Justin Martyr, *Apologia prima pro Christianis*, in *PGL*, VI.
——— *Cohortatio ad Graecos*, in *PGL*, VI.
Juvenal, *Satirae*.
Karo, Joseph, See Caro, Joseph.
Kaufman, Judah Ibn-Shmuel, *English-Hebrew Dictionary* (Tel-Aviv, 1947).
Kautzsch, E., *Das Alte Testament* (Tübingen, 1921).
——— *Die Poesie und die poetischen Bücher des A.T.*, (Tübingen und Leipzig, 1902).
Kees, Hermann, *Der Opfertanz des ägyptischen Königs* (Leipzig, 1912).
Keil, Karl Friedrich, *Twelve Minor Prophets* (Edinburgh, 1889).
Keyserling, Hermann, *Das Reisetagebuch eines Philosophen* (Darmstadt, 1921).
Kimḥi, David R., (ReDaK), *Commentary on the Book of Chronicles*.
——— *Commentary on the Psalms*.

Kirby, Percival R., *The Trumpets of Tut-Ankh-Amen and their Successors,* in *Journal of the Royal Anthropological Institute* (London), LXXVII.
Kircher, Athanasius, *Musurgia Universalis* (Rome, 1650).
Kirkpatrick, A. F., *The Book of Psalms* (Cambridge, 1927).
Kitto, John, *A Cyclopedia of Biblical Literature* (Philadelphia, 1866), 3 vols.
Knudtzon, J. A., *Die El-Amarna Tafeln* (Leipzig, 1915).
Kohler, Kaufmann, *The Origins of the Synagogue and the Church* (New York, 1929).
——— *The Testament of Job,* in *Semitic Studies in Memory of Alexander Kohut* (Berlin, 1897).
Komroff, Manuel, *The Contemporaries of Marco Polo . . .* (New York, 1928).
Kraft, Charles Franklin, *The Strophic Structure of Hebrew Poetry* (Chicago, 1938).
Kramer, Samuel Noah, *From the Tablets of Sumer* (Indian Hills, Colorado, 1956).
Krauss, Samuel, *Synagogale Altertümer* (Berlin, Vienna, 1922).
——— *Talmudische Archäologie* (Leipzig, 1910-12), 3 vols.
Laborde, Jean Benjamin and P. J. Roussier, *Essai sur la musique ancienne et moderne* (Paris, 1780).
Lach, Robert, *Die Musik der Natur- und der orientalischen Kulturvölker,* in Adler's *Handbuch der Musikgeschichte* (Berlin, 1929), 2 vols.
Lagarde, Paul Anton, *Novae Psalterii Graeci Editionis Specimen,* in *Abhandlungen der historisch-philologischen Classe der königl. Gesellschaft der Wissenschaften* (Göttingen, 1886), vol. XXXIII.
——— *Orientalia,* in *Abhandlungen der königl. Gesellschaft der Wissenschaften zu Göttingen* (1879), vol. XXIV.
——— *Übersicht über die im Aramäischen, Arabischen und Hebräischen übliche Bildung der Nomina* (Göttingen, 1889).
Lampe, Friedrich Adolf, *De cymbalis veterum libri tres . . .* in *UgThes,* XXXII.
Land, S.I.N.P., *Anecdota Syriaca* (Leiden, 1870), 4 vols.
Langdon, Stephen Herbert, *Babylonian and Hebrew Musical Terms,* in *JRAS* (1921), part 2.
——— *Babylonian Liturgies* (Paris, 1913).
——— *Semitic Mythology* (*The Mythology of All Races,* vol. V.). (Boston, 1931).
Layard, Sir Austen Henry, *Discoveries among the ruins of Nineveh and Babylon . . .* (New York, 1853).
Leitner, Franz, *Der gottesdienstliche Volksgesang im jüdischen und christlichen Altertum* (Freiburg i.B., 1906).
Leo I (Leo the Great), *Sermo IX,* in *PL.* LIV.
——— *Sermo XIV,* in *PL,* LIV.
Lepsius, Richard, *Denkmäler aus Ägypten und Äthiopien* (Leipzig, 1897-1913), 2 vols.
Levy, Jacob, *Chaldäisches Wörterbuch über die Targumim* (Leipzig, 1867).
——— *Wörterbuch über die Talmudim und Midraschim* (Berlin and Vienna, 1924), 4 vols.
Lewy, Julius, *The Feast of the 14th Day of Adar,* in *HUCA* (1939), XIV.
Ley, Julius, *Leitfaden der Metrik in der hebräischen Poesie* (Halle a.S., 1887).
Liddell, Henry George and Robert Scott, *Greek Lexicon* (Oxford, 1940).
Lightfoot, John, *Descriptio Templi Hierosolymitani,* in *UgThes,* IX.
Livius, *Ab urbe condita.*
Löhr, Max, *Die Stellung des Weibes zu Jahwe-Religion und -Kult* (Leipzig, 1908).
Longford, W. W., *Music and Religion* (London, 1916).
Löw, Leopold, *Beiträge zur jüdischen Altertumskunde* (Szegedin, 1875).
Lucian of Samosata, *De Syria Dea.*
McClintock, John and James Strong, *Cyclopedia of Biblical . . . Literature* (New York, 1883), 10 vols.
Maimonides, *Hilkot Teshubah.*
——— *Mishneh Torah.*
Martial, *Epigrams.*
Mielziner, M., *Introduction to the Talmud* (New York, 1925).
Migne, Paul, Editor of the writings of the Church Fathers.

Moffat, James, *A New Translation of the Bible* (New York and London), 1922.
Montgomery, James A., *A Critical and Exegetical Commentary on the Book of Daniel* (New York, 1927).
——— *Rās Shamra Notes IV*, in *JAOS* (1935), LV.
Monumenta Musicae Byzantinae Subsidia (Copenhagen and Boston, 1953, see Verdeil R. Paralikova.
Moore, George, *Symphōnia Not a Bagpipe*, in *JBL*, (1905), vol. 24.
Moulton, Richard G., *The Modern Reader's Bible* (New York, 1895).
Movers, Franz Karl, *Die Phönizier* (Bonn, 1841-56), 2 vols.
Mowinckel, Sigmund, *Psalmenstudien* (Kristiania, 1923-26), 6 vols.
Muckle, Friedrich, *Der Geist der jüdischen Kultur und das Abendland* (Vienna, 1923).
Nadel, Arno, *Jüdische Musik*, in *Der Jude* (Berlin, 1923), VII.
Naegele, Anton, *Über Arbeitslieder bei Johannes Chrysostomos*, in *Sächsische Gesellschaft der Wissenschaften zu Leipzig, Philologisch-Historische Klasse, Berichte*, Band 57 (1905).
Nägelsbach, K. W. E., *The Prophet Isaiah* (New York, 1906).
Nathan ben Jeḥiel of Rome, *ʾAruk* (publ. 1101). New ed. by Alexander Kohut, *ʾAruk ha-Shalem* (Vienna, 1878-92).
Naumann, Emil, *The History of Music* (London, n.d.), 2 vols.
Neilos, *Narratio V*, in *PGL*, LXXIX.
Nemoy, Leon, *Karaite Anthology* (New Haven, 1952).
Nicholson, R. A., *Literary History of the Arabs* (London, 1914).
Niebuhr, Carsten, *Reisebeschreibung nach Arabien* . . . (Copenhagen, 1774), 2 vols.
Nowack, Wilhelm, *Lehrbuch der Archäologie* (Freiburg i.B., 1894), 2 vols.
Oesterley, William Oscar Emil, *Ancient Hebrew Poems Metrically translated* (London, 1938).
——— *A Fresh Approach to the Psalms* (New York, 1937).
——— *The Jews and Judaism during the Greek Period* (London, 1941).
——— *The Psalms.* Translated with Text-critical and Exegetical Notes (London, 1955).
——— *The Psalms in the Jewish Church* (London, 1910).
——— *The Sacred Dance* (New York, 1923).
Oesterley, W. O. E. and Th. H. Robinson, *Hebrew Religion* (London, 1930).
Oldenburg, Hermann, *Rigveda. Textkritische und exegetische Noten*, in *Abhandlungen der königl. Gesellschaft der Wissenschaften zu Göttingen, Philologisch-Historische Klasse*, N.F. Band XIII, No. 3 (Berlin, 1909-12).
Olshausen, Justus, *Die Psalmen erklärt* (Leipzig, 1853).
Oracula Sybillina.
Ovid, *Ars amandi.*
——— *Fasti.*
Pape, Wilhelm, *Handwörterbuch der griechischen Sprache* (Braunschweig, 1905-14).
Parkhurst, J., *An Hebrew and English Lexicon, without Points* . . . (London, 1813).
Paul, St. and Stephen, St., *Regula ad Monachos*, XIV, in *PL*, LXVI.
Paulus, . . . , *Memorabilien* (Leipzig, 1792).
Peritz, Ismar, *Women in the Ancient Hebrew Cult*, in *JBL* (1898).
Petrushka, Simḥa, *The Mishnah. Yiddish Translation* (Montreal, 1949).
Pfeiffer, Augustus Friedrich, *Über die Musik der alten Hebräer* (Erlangen, 1779).
Pfeiffer, Robert H., *Introduction to the Old Testament* (New York, 1941).
Philo Judaeus, *De Gigantibus.*
——— *De legatione ad Caium.*
——— *In Flaccum.*
——— *Nomōn hierōn allēgoria tōn meta tēn hexaēmeron to prōton* (*Allegorical interpretation of Genesis*).
——— *Peri apoikias* (*On the Migration of Abraham*).
——— *Peri biou Mouseōs* (*About the Life of Moses*).
——— *Peri biou theorētikou hē iketōn* (*About the Contemplative Life*).
——— *Peri methēs* (*On Drunkenness*).

——— *Peri tōn en merei diatagmatōn* (*On the Special Laws*).
——— *Peri tōn metenozomenōn* (*On the Changes of Names*).
——— *Peri tou panta spudaion eleutheron* (*Every Good Man is Free*).
Pico della Mirandola, Giovanni, *De Magia,* in *Opera Omnia* (Basel, 1572).
Pindar, *Pythia.*
Plato, *Nomoi* (*Laws*).
——— *Phaedrus.*
——— *Politeia.*
Plinius, *Historia naturalis.*
Plutarch, *De Musica.*
——— *De superstitione.*
Pollux, Julius of Naucratis, *Onomasticon.*
Polybius, *Historiai.*
Porphyry, *Peri apochēs empsychōn* (*On the Abstinence from Animal Food*).
Portaleone, Abraham, da, *Shilṭe ha-Gibborim* (Mantua, 1612).
Prätorius, Michael, *Syntagma musicum* (Wolfenbüttel, 1914-18).
Printz, Caspar, *Historische Beschreibung der edelen Sing- und Klingkunst* (Dresden, 1690).
Quasten, J., *Musik und Gesang in den Kulten der heidnischen Antike und der christlichen Frühzeit* (Münster i.W., 1930).
Rabindranath Tagore, see Tagore.
Rackham, Richard B., *The Acts of the Apostles* (London, 1912).
Rawlinson, G., *The Five Great Monarchies of the Ancient World* (New York, 1873), 2 vols.
Redslob, Gustav Moritz, *De praecepto musico* (Leipzig, 1831).
Reik, Theodor, *Probleme der Religionspsychologie* (art. *"Der Schofar"*) (Vienna and Leipzig, 1919).
Reinach, Salomon, *Cultes, Myths et Religion* (Paris, 1904-23).
——— *Orpheus* (New York, 1941).
Reinach, Theodor, in Daremberg and Saglio, *Dictionnaire des Antiquités Grecques et Romaines* (Paris, 1875-1919).
Reisner, Georg Andrew, *Sumerisch-bablyonische Hymnen nach Tontafeln aus griechischer Zeit* (Berlin, 1896).
Renan, Ernest, *History of the People of Israel* (Engl. ed., Boston, 1896), 5 vols.
——— *Mission de Phénice* (Paris, 1864).
——— *The Song of Songs* (Engl. transl. by William M. Thomson). (London, 1860).
Rice, E. W., *Orientalisms in Bible Land* (Philadelphia, 1910).
Riehm, Eduard Carl August, *Handwörterbuch des biblischen Altertums* (Bielefeld and Leipzig, 1893-94).
Riemann, Hugo, *Handbuch der Musikgeschichte* (Leipzig, 1923), 3 vols.
Rituale Romanum.
Robertson Smith, W., *The Old Testament in the Jewish Church* (London, 1926).
——— *The Prophets in Israel* . . . (New York, 1882).
——— *The Religion of the Semites* (New York, 1894).
Robinson, Theodore H., *Prophecy and the Prophets* (London, 1941).
Rödiger, Emil, Ed. of *Gesenius' Hebrew Grammar* (New ed. transl. by T. J. Conant). (New York, 1855).
Romanoff, Paul, *Jewish Symbols on Ancient Jewish Coins,* in *JQR,* XXXIV.
Roscher, Wilhelm Heinrich, *Ausführliches Lexicon der griechischen und römischen Mythologie* (Leipzig, 1884-1919).
Rosenmüller, E. F. K., *Vocabularium Veteris Testamenti Hebraico-Chaldaicum* (Halle and Magdeburg, 1822).
Rosowsky, Solomon, *The Cantillation of the Bible. The Five Books of Moses* (New York, 1957).
Rowley, H. H., *The Zadokite Fragments and the Dead Sea Scrolls* (Oxford, 1955).
Rufinus, *Homilia in Psalmum primum.* Translation into Latin of a tractate by Basil St. in *PGL,* XXXI.

Sa'adia Ben Joseph (Gaon), *Sefer ha-Emunot veha-Deot.*
Sa'adia ben Naḥmani, *Commentary on Daniel.*
Saalschütz, Joseph Levin, *Archäologie der Hebräer,* (Königsberg, 1855).
——— *Von der Form der hebräischen Poesie* (Königsberg, 1925).
——— *Geschichte und Würdigung der Musik bei den Hebräern* (Berlin, 1829).
Sachs, Curt, *Die Entzifferung einer babylonischen Notenschrift,* in *Sitzungsberichte der Preussischen Akademie der Wissenschaften* (Berlin, 1924), XVIII.
——— *Ein babylonischer Hymnus,* in *Archiv für Musikwissenschaft* (1925).
——— *Geist und Werden der Musikinstrumente* (Berlin, 1929).
——— *(The) History of Musical Instruments* (New York, 1940).
——— *Musik der Antike,* in *Handbuch der Musikwissenschaft* (Potsdam, 1928).
——— *Die Musik des Altertums* (Breslau, 1924).
——— *Musikinstrumente des alten Ägypten,* in *Der Alte Orient* (Leipzig, 1920), XXI.
——— *Die Musikinstrumente des Alten Ägypten* (Berlin, 1921).
——— *The Mystery of the Babylonian Notation,* in *MusQuart* (1941), XXVII.
——— *Rhythm and Tempo* (New York, 1953).
——— *The Rise of Music in the Ancient World East and West* (New York, 1943).
——— *The Wellsprings of Music,* ed. by Jaap Kunst (den Haag, 1962).
——— *World History of the Dance* (New York, 1937).
——— *Zweiklänge im Altertum,* in *Zeitschrift für Johannes Wolf* (Berlin, 1929).
Saran, Fr., *Beiträge zur Geschichte der deutschen Sprache und Literatur* (Halle a.S., 1898).
Schäfke, Rudolf, *Aristeides Quintilianus* (Berlin, 1937).
Schechter, Solomon, *Studies in Judaism, 1st Series* (Philadelphia, 1896).
——— *The Wisdom of Ben Sira. Portions of the Book of Ecclesiasticus from Hebrew Manuscripts in the Cairo Genizah Collection . . .* (Cambridge, 1899).
Schletterer, Hans Michel, *Geschichte der geistlichen Dichtung und kirchlichen Tonkunst* (Hannover, 1869).
Schneider, Hermann, *Die Kulturleistungen der Menschheit* (Leipzig, 1931-33), 3 vols.
Schneider, Peter Joseph, *Biblisch-geschichtliche Darstellung der hebräischen Musik, deren Ursprung, Zunahme . . .* (Bonn, 1837).
Scholz, P., *Götzendienst und Zauberwesen bei den alten Hebräern* (Regensburg, 1877)
——— *Die heiligen Altertümer des Volkes Israel* (Regensburg, 1868), 2 vols.
Schrader, Eberhard, *Die Keilinschriften und das Alte Testament* (Giessen, 1882).
Schulz, Alfons, *Kritisches zum Psalter,* in *Alttestamentliche Abhandlungen XII,* 1. (Breslau, 1932).
Schumacher, Gottlieb, *Tell el-Muteselim* (Leipzig, 1908), 2 vols.
Schürer, Emil, *Gemeindeverfassung der Juden in Rom* (Leipzig, 1879).
Sedulius, *Opera omnia.* Ed. by Joh. Huemer (Vienna, 1885).
Segond, Louis, *La Sainte Bible . . . l'Ancien et le Nouveau Testament* (Oxford, 1887).
Sendrey, Alfred, *Bibliography of Jewish Music* (New York, 1951).
——— *Rundfunk und Musikpflege* (Leipzig, 1931).
Seneca, *Epistolae.*
Sethe, Kurt Heinrich, *Urgeschichte und älteste Religionen der Ägypter,* in *Abhandlungen für die Kunde des Morgenlandes* (Leipzig, 1930), XVIII, No. 4.
Sidur Amsterdam, publ. by Shabbetai Bass (Amsterdam, 1680).
Sievers, Eduard, *Metrische Studien. Part I. Studien zur hebräischen Metrik,* in *Abhandlungen der philologisch-historischen Klasse der Königlich Sächsichen Gesellschaft der Wissenschaften* (Leipzig, 1901), XXI, No. 1.
Slotki, J. J., *The Holy Scriptures* (London, 1951).
Socrates of Constantinople, *Ekklēsiastikē historia, VI, 8,* in *PGL,* LXVII.
Sohar
Sopherim, ed. Joel Müller (1878).
Sopherim, ed. Michael Higger (1937).
Sozomenes, *Ekklēsiastikē historia,* in *PGL,* LXVII.

Speidel, Johann Christoph, *Unverwerfliche Spuren der alten davidischen Singkunst* (Waiblingen, Stuttgart, 1740).
Stainer, Sir John, *The Music of the Bible.* New ed. by F. W. Galpin (London, 1914).
Stauder, Wilhelm, *Die Harfen und Leiern der Sumerer* (Frankfurt a.M., 1957).
Steinberg, J., *Mishpat ha-ʾUrim* (Vilna, 1896).
Strabo, *Geōgraphikōn.*
Straham, James, *The Book of Job Interpreted* (Edinburgh, 1913).
Strunk, Oliver, *Source Reading in Music History* (New York, 1950).
Stumpf, Carl, *Die Anfänge der Musik* (Leipzig, 1911).
Suetonius, *Domitian,* in *Vitae Imperatorum Romanorum.*
——— *Nero,* in *Vitae Imperatorum Romanorum.*
Suidas, *Lexicon.* New ed. Ada Adler (Leipzig, 1928).
Sukenik, Eleazar Lipa, *The Dead Sea Scrolls of the Hebrew University* (Jerusalem, 1955).
——— *Megillat Genezot* (Jerusalem, 1950).
Swete, Henry Barclay, *An Introduction to the Old Testament in Greek* (Cambridge, 1914).
Szabolcsi, Bence, *About Five-Tone-Scales in the Early Hebrew Melodies,* in *Ignace Goldziher Memorial Volume* (Budapest, 1948), part I.
Tagore, Rabindranath, *My Reminiscences* (New York, 1917).
Talmudic Lexicon.
Tertullian, *Ad uxorem, II,* in *PL,* I.
——— *Apologeticus adversus Gentes pro Christianis, XXXIX,* in *PL,* I.
——— *De Anima, XIV,* in *PL,* II.
——— *De Carne Christi, XVII, XX,* in *PL* II.
——— *Liber de oratione, 27,* in *PL,* I.
Theodoret, *Ekklēsiastikē historia, II, 19,* in *PGL,* LXXXII.
——— *Hairetikēs kakomythias,* in *PGL,* LXXXIII.
——— *Hermēneia eis tous Psalmous, Ps. CXLVIII,* in *PGL,* LXXX.
Thimus, Albert von, *Die harmonikale Symbolik des Alterthums* (Cologne, 1868-76).
Thirtle, James William, *Old Testament Problems* (London, 1916).
——— *The Titles of the Psalms,* (London, 1904).
Tholuck, F. A., *Übersetzung und Auslegung der Psalmen* (Halle a.S., 1843).
Torrey, Ch. C., *The Second Isaiah* (New York, 1928).
Tosefta. Ed. Zuckermandel (Pasewalk and Treves, 1937).
Trachtenberg, Joshua, *Jewish Magic and Superstition* (New York, 1939).
Ugolino, Biagio (Blasius), *Thesaurus antiquitatum Sacrarum* (Venice, 1744-67), 34 vols.
Varro, *De agricultura.*
——— *De lingua latina.*
Venantius Fortunatus, *Poema ad clerum Parisiacum,* in *PL,* LXXXVIII.
Verdeil, R. Paralikova, *La Musique Byzantine ches les Bulgares et les Russes,* in *Momumenta Musicae Byzantinae Subsidia* (Copenhagen and Boston, 1953), vol. III.
Villoteau, Guillaume André, *Description de l'Égypte* (Paris, 1809), 13 vols.
——— *Dissertation sur les diverses espèces d'instruments de musique qu'on remarque parmi les sculptures qui décorent les antiques monuments de l'Égypte,* in *Description de l'Égypte, Antiquités* (Paris, 1809), vol. VI.
Virgil, *Epigrams.*
Vitruvius, *De Architectura.*
Vopiscus Flavius, *The Life of Carus, Carinus and Numerian,* in *Scriptores Historiae Augustae,* vol. 3.
Wagner, Peter, *Der gregorianische Gesang,* in Adler's *Handbuch der Musikgeschichte* (Frankfurt a.M., 1930).
——— *Über die Anfänge des mehrstimmigen Gesanges,* in *ZMW* (1926), IX.
Wallaschek, Richard, *Anfänge der Tonkunst* (Leipzig, 1903).
——— *Primitive Music* (London, 1893).
Ward, Jules, *Les Origines de la musique* (Lyons, 1865).
Waterman, Leroy, *The Song of Songs, translated and interpreted as a dramatic poem*

(Ann Arbor, Mich., 1948).
Weiser, Artur, *Einleitung in das Alte Testament* (Göttingen, 1949).
——— *The Psalms.* Transl. by Herbert Hartwell (Philadelphia, 1962).
Weiss, Johann, *Die musikalischen Instrumente in den heiligen Schriften des Alten Testaments* (Graz, 1895).
Wellhausen, Julius, *The Book of the Psalms* (New York, 1898).
Werner, Eric, *The Conflict between Hellenism and Judaism in the Early Christian Church,* in *HUCA* (1947), XX.
——— *The Doxology in Synagogue and Church,* in *HUCA* (1945-46), XIX.
——— *The Jewish Contribution to Music,* in *The Jews, their History, Culture and Religion* (Philadelphia, 1949), vol. III.
——— *Musical Aspects of the Dead Sea Scrolls,* in *MQ* (Jan. 1957), vol. XLIII, No. 1.
——— *Notes on the Attitude of the Early Church Fathers toward Hebrew Psalmody,* in *The Review of Religion* (May, 1943).
——— *The Sacred Bridge* (London and New York, 1959).
Westphal, Rudolph, *Geschichte der alten und mittelalterlichen Musik* (Breslau, 1865).
——— *Griechische Harmonik und Melopoeik* (Leipzig, 1886).
Wetzstein, Johann Gottfried, *Die syrische Dreschtafel,* in Bastian's *Zeitschrift für Ethnologie* (1873), V.
Whibley, Charles, *An Essay on Apuleius,* in *Studies in Frankness* (London, 1898).
Wiedemann, A., *Die Religion der alten Ägypter* (Münster i.W., 1890).
Wilkinson, Sir Gardner, *The Manners and Customs of the Ancient Egyptians* (London, 1878), 2 vols.
Wilson, Edmund, *The Scrolls from the Dead Sea* (New York, 1955).
Wilson, Robert Dick, *The Headings of the Psalms,* in *The Princeton Theological Review* (1926), vol. XXIV.
Winckler, Hugo, *Arabisch-Semitisch-Orientalisch,* in *MVAG* (1901).
——— *Keilinschriftliches Textbuch zum A.T.* (Leipzig, 1909), 2 vols.
Winer, G. B., *Biblisches Realwörterbuch* (Leipzig, 1833-38), 2 vols.
Winter, Jakob and August Wünsche, *Die jüdische Literatur seit Abschluss des Kanons* (Berlin, 1897), 3 vols.
Wolff, A. A., *Der Prophet Habakkuk* (Darmstadt, 1822).
Woolley, Sir Leonard, *Excavations at Ur* (New York, 1954).
Worman, J. H., *Music, musical instruments,* in McClintock and Strong, *Cyclopedia of Biblical . . . Literature* (New York, 1883), 10 vols.
Yadin, Yigael, *Megillat Milḥemet B'nei* ʾ*Or bi-B'nei Ḥosheh* (Jerusalem, 1955).
Yasser, Joseph, *Restoration of Ancient Hebrew Music.* Abstract in *First Ten Years of the Annual Three Choir Festival* (New York, 1946).
——— *The Magrepha of the Herodian Temple: A Five-Fold Hypothesis,* in *JAMS* (1960), vol. 13.
——— *Medieval Quartal Harmony* (New York, 1938).
——— *Rhythmical Structure of Chinese Tunes,* in *Musical Courier* (New York, April 3, 1924).
Zeitlin, Solomon, *The Zadokite Fragments,* in *The Jewish Quarterly Review, Monograph Series, No. 1.* (Philadelphia, 1952).
——— *The Dead Sea Scrolls and Modern Scholarship,* in *The Jewish Quarterly Review, Monograph Series, No. 3* (Philadelphia, 1956).
——— *The Idolatry of the Dead Sea Scrolls,* in *The Jewish Quarterly Review, New Series, vol. XLVIII, No. 3* (Philadelphia, 1958).
Zenner, K. J., *Die Chorgesänge im Buche der Psalmen* (Freiburg i.B. 1896).
Zimmern, Heinrich, *Ein vorläufiges Wort über babylonische Metrik,* in *Zeitschrift für alttestamentliche Wissenschaft* (1893), VIII.
——— *Palästina um das Jahr 1400 vor Chr., nach neuen Quellen,* in *Zeitschrift des deutschen Palästina Vereins* (1890), XII.
Zunz, Leopold, *Die gottesdienstlichen Vorträge der Juden* (Berlin, 1832).
——— *Die Ritus des synagogalen Gottesdienstes geschichtlich entwickelt* (Berlin, 1859).

List of Scriptural References

A. From the Bible

1. OLD TESTAMENT

5:1 116, 128, 252, 318, 431
5:2-4 116
5:4 200a
5:5-7 116
5:8-9 116
5:10-11 116
5:12 248
5:12, 13 116
6 118, 126
6:1 118, 124, 274, 282, 285, 300
7 111, 143 (note) 146
7:1 110
8 129, 131, 143 (note) 148, 293
8:1 431
9 116, 130, 131, 146, 148, 149, 155, 157, 517
9:1 107, 130, 293, 321
9:17 157, 293 (note)
10 148, 248
11 143 (note)
12 117, 124, 126
12:1 274, 282, 285, 303, 431
13:6 86
15:19 157
16 64, 109
16:1 105, 107
17:1 96
18 76, 94, 117, 143 (note) 248
18:1 98
18:26, 27 248
18:31 248
19 143 (note)
19:1-5 226
19:13 110
20 146
21 133, 146
22:1 107, 130, 132, 454
22:6 254
24 146, 148, 155, 175
24:1-6 143 (note)
24:3 100
24:7, 10 143 (note)
26 148
26:6 85, 86, 127, 448, 451, 452, 458
26:7 456
27:6 86
28:1 129
28:7 86
29 95, 102, 143, (note) 176
29:6 447
30 93, 100, 175, 176
30:1 98, 99, 129
30:2 124, 186
30:5 86
30:11 193, 222
30:12 91, 322, 323
30:13 85
32 103, 143, (note) 146
32:1 103
32:7 458
32:8 103
33:2 86, 278, 286, 289, 290, 291, 292, 431
33:3 86, 118 (note)
34:11 155
38:1 109,110
39 117, 146
39:1 140, 144, 293
40:4 86
41 117, 173
42 144, 252
42:1 103, 144
42:2 254
42:5 179, 446
43 144
43:4 431, 452
44 144, 146, 173
44:1 103
45 85, 96, 104, 121, 134, 144
45:1 99, 103, 107, 130, 133, 135, 220, 302, 454, 512
45:2 230 (mus. ex.)
45:9 276, 304
45:10-18 122
46 96, 117, 123, 144, 146, 155
46:1 98, 99, 121, 282, 320, 321, 431
47 117, 144, 146, 173, 347
47:6 86
47:7 85
47:8 103, 104
48 131, 144, 146, 175
48:1 98, 99
48:13 448
48:15 131
49 114, 144, 146
49:2-5 140, 514
49:5 86, 267, 277, 578
50 146
51 107
52 107, 126
52:1 103
53 127, 128
53:1 105, 107, 126, 293, 324
54 107, 146
54:1 113, 118, 119, 300
55 135
55:1 103, 118, 119, 300, 431
55:6, 7 107
55:6-8 135
55:8 151
55:20 151
56 136
56:1 104, 105, 106, 107, 130
56:8 135
57 107, 136, 146
57:1 104, 105, 106, 107, 130
57:3 149
57:4 149, 150
57:9 86
57:10 86
58 136
58:1 104, 105, 106, 107, 130

2. NEW TESTAMENT

3. APOCRYPHA

4. TARGUMIM

B. List of References from the Early Rabbinical Literature

(The numbers at the right indicate the pages within the text.)

1. MIDRASH

Genesis
IV:21 390, 391, 392
XIX:14 392
XXIII:3 304, 391, 405, 406, 517
XXXVIII:7 448, 467
L:9 304, 391, 394, 405
LIX:4 462
LXVIII:4 217
LXVIII:13 449, 465
LXXIV:16 468
LXXIV:17 465

Exodus
XXII:3 163, 168
XXIII:2-12 168
XLVII:5 212

Leviticus
XI:9 448, 467
XII:5 447, 467
XXIX:3,6,10 367
XXX:5 87, 458

Numeri
VI:8 216
XIV:21 226
XV:11 275
XV:16 277
XX:11 447

Ruth
VI:1 277

Ecclesiastes
X:5 462
X:19 463

Tehillim p. 182 132
XXIV:7
p. 204 98
p. 407 98
XCII:7 275
Ps. 137:4 271

Canticum
I:3 467
II:8 448
VII:2 465
VII:9 418, 420, 430
VIII:12 181, 216
VIII:13 223, 235
VIII:14 235

Lamentations
II:19 277
III:23 225
V:16 462
XII p. 17 220
The Proems of the Sages,
XXIV 225

2. MISHNAH

(in alphabetical order)

ʿArakin
II:3 256, 309, 311, 312, 313, 329, 338, 363, 393, 406, 424, 425, 432, 435
II:4 314, 394, 435
II:5 256, 378, 424
II:6 122, 424, 436, 521

Baba Meẓiʿah
VI:1 315, 321

Berakot
V:2 458, 459
V:5 459

Beẓah
V:2 265, 465

Bikkurim
III:2-5 186
III:7 186

ʿErubin
X:13 182, 274

Ḥullin
I:7 350

Kelim
V:11 367
XI:1 367
XI:6 311, 312, 313, 328, 367
XI:7 329, 367, 371
XII:8 367
XIII:1 367
XIV:4 367, 419
XV:6 273, 286, 347, 390, 407, 408, 412, 413, 415, 525
XVI:7 265, 273, 415
XVI:8 264, 329, 347
XVI:17 367
XX:2 265, 329, 347
XXIV:14 268, 347

Ketubot
IV:4 92, 169, 316, 323, 471, 524

3. TALMUD BABLI

in alphabetical order)

4. TALMUD YERUSHALMI

(in alphabetical order)
(The page numbers refer to the Krotoschin edition, unless indicated otherwise)

5. TOSEFTA

(Ed. Zuckermandel, 1937)
(in alphabetical order)

6. SMALL TREATISES

(in alphabetical order)

ABBREVIATIONS USED IN THE INDEX

Arab	=	Arabic
Aram.	=	Aramaic
Assyr.	=	Assyrian
Babyl.	=	Babylonian
Byzant.	=	Byzantine
Chin.	=	Chinese
Egypt.	=	Egyptian
Fr.	=	French
Germ.	=	German
Gr.	=	Greek
Hebr.	=	Hebrew
Hung.	=	Hungarian
Ital.	=	Italian
Lat.	=	Latin
Med.	=	Medieval
Pers.	=	Persian
Phoenic.	=	Phoenician
Sanscr.	=	Sanscrit
Sumer.	=	Sumerian
Syr.	=	Syriac
Yidd.	=	Yiddish

Index of Names and Subjects

131ff, 132, 138, 171, 280, 282, 285, 320ff, 423, 431, 439, 518, 532
ʿ*Alamot tofefot* (Hebr.), 321
ʿ*Alamut* (Hebr.), see ʿ*Alamot*
Alarm trumpets, 365
Albright, W. F., 247, 264
Alcaeus, 243
Alexander, J. A., 105, 131, 135, 136
Alexander Jannaeus (100-76 B.C.E.), 302
Alexander Polyhistor, 480
Alexandria, Alexandrian, 183, 200, 201, 320, 378, 526
Alexandros of Kythēra, 280, 298
Al-gar (Sumer.), 37
ʾ*Algum* (Hebr.), 264
ʾ*Al-Hijaz* (Arab.), 316
ʾ*Al ḥingin* (Aram.), 319
ʾ*Alit* (Hebr.), 415, 417, 523ff
ʿ*Al Kālā dh'* . . . (Syr.), 106
ʿAl-Kirkisani, Jacob (10th cent.), 191 (note)
Allegorical interpretations, 220, 221
Allegro, John A., 190 (note)
ʿ*Al-Maghariya* (Syr.), 191 (note)
ʿ*Almah,* ʿ*Alma,* ʿ*Al'meh* (Hebr.)., (Arab.), 121, 321
ʾAl Mas'udi (d.c. 957 C.E.), 401
ʾ*Almuggim* (Hebr.), 264
Almug trees, 264 (note)
ʿ*Almut,* ʿ*al-mut* (Hebr.), see ʿ*Alamot,* also *Mut Labben*
ʿ*Al neginot* (Hebr.), 119, 138
ʿ*Al shiggionot* (Hebr.), see *Shiggayon*
ʿ*Al tashḥet* (Hebr.), 107, 136ff, 139
(ʿ*Al*) *yede*ʿ*ethan* (Hebr.), 144
Amalekites, 164
Amalthea's Horn, 188
ʾ*Ambol,* ʾ*anbol,* ʾ*enbol,* ʾ*inbol* (Aram.), 417, 418
Ambros, August Wilhelm (1816-1876), 271, 287, 298, 318, 324
Ambrose, St. (333-397 C.E.), 197, 198, 228
Ambrosian Chants, 144, 205, 228
Ambubajae (Lat.), 55, 294, 299, 394
Ambubajarum collegia (Lat.), 394
ʾ*Amen* (Hebr.), 158
Amenemhet I (c. 2000-c. 1970 B.C.E.), 95
Amenophis IV (Amenhotep IV) (1375-1358 B.C.E.) see also Ikhnaton, 95
Amerias of Makedōn, 406
American (Revised) Version, 97 (note), 101, 109 (note), 110, 118, 129, 131, 135, 163 (note), 164, 168, 170 (note), 215 (note), 216, 258 (note), 264 (note), 265 (note), 278 (note), 289, 291, 294, 304 (note), 307, 332, 365, 368, 380, 384, 385, 474, 482 (note), 520 (note), 523 (note), 525 (note), 539 (note)
ʿ*Amidah* (Hebr.), 348
ʾ*Ammah* (Hebr.), 395, 399
Ammi, Rabbi (3rd cent. C.E.), 501
Ammon, . . . (18th cent.), 464 (note)
Ammonites, 59, 80, 165, 254, 426, 506, 513, 546
Amnon, 276
Amon (Egyptian god), 444, 516
Amon, King of Judah (640-638 B.C.E.), 427
Amorites, 164
Amos, Prophet (8th cent. B.C.E.), 233, 278, 508, 520, 523
Amousia (Gr.), 55
Amphion of Thebes, 501
Amram ben Sheshna, see Mar Amram ben Sheshna
Anachronism, 133
Anadiplosis (Gr.), 102
ʿ*Anah* (Hebr.), 127, 523
Anakreōn (b.c. 560 B.C.E.), 281, 284
Analysis of ancient Jewish melodies, 212ff
Anastasius (9th cent. C.E.), 197
Anathema, 362
ʾ*Anbol* (Aram.), see ʾ*Ambol*
Anekdoton (Gr.), 105
Angels, 188, 220, 225
Animals, 85
ʾ*Ankitmin,* ʾ*ankatmin, lukitmin* (Aram.), 407, 408
Annus jubilei (Lat.), 363
Anonymity of Authors in Antiquity, 142, 221, 514
ʾ*Anshe Ma*ʿ*amad,* see *Ma*ʿ*amad* (Hebr.)
Anti-feminine tendency of the priesthood, 171, 490, 516, 525, 527
Antilēpsis heōthinē (Gr.), 132
Antioch, City of, 107, 144 (note)
Antiochus Epiphanes (reign. 175-168 B.C.E.), 129, 178, 326
Antipater (d. 40 B.C.E.), 469
Antiphonal Singing, 40, 46, 75, 82, 83, 88, 103, 116, 128, 154, 156, 161, 163, 166ff, 169, 173, 177, 197, 198, 199, 200, 211ff, 468, 475, 478, 523, 526
Anton, Conrad Gottlob (1745-1814), 205
Apel, Willi (1893-   ), 309 (note)
Aphaca, 508
Aphaseōs sēmasia (Gr.), 371
Aphrodite, 508
Apis (Egyptian god), 40
Apollo, 152, 284, 445, 501, 502, 509
Apollodōros (c. 300-c. 260 B.C.E.), 280
Apuleius (Lucius Apuleius) (b. c. 125 C.E.), 315 (note), 381, 444 (note)
Aquila (2nd cent. C.E.), 97, 98, 99, 103, 105, 109, 110, 115, 119, 121, 124, 127, 128, 130, 131, 132, 133, 135, 136, 147, 157, 226, 267, 293, 300, 322, 452
Arabia, 53, 104, 110 (note), 144, 208, 239, 256, 266, 267, 288, 289, 298, 299, 307, 308, 316, 320, 321, 322, 332, 372, 382, 388, 409, 411, 453, 455, 466, 474, 480, 481, 502, 513 (note), 515, 539

B

Benaiah (Ben), Singer, 125, 518
Ben Arza, Singer, 150, 336, 380
Benē Babel (Hebr.), 53
Beni-Hassan, 69, 268
Benjamin of Tudela (12th cent.), 183
Ben Katin, 399
Ben Sira, see Ecclesiasticus, Book of
Benzinger, K. (1865-), 271, 287
Bepeh (Hebr.) 217
Berakot v'hodayot (Hebr.), 192
Berekiah, Rabbi, 448
Berkowitz, M., 149 (note)
Berl, Heinrich, 206, 551 (note)
Bertholet, Alfred (1868-1951), 166 (note)
Bertinoro, see Obadiah of Bertinoro
Beṭen (Hebr.), 390
Bet ha-Pegarim (Hebr.), 314
Bet ha-She'ubah, (Hebr.), 177, 180, 219, 312, 380, 425, 437, 458, 459, 462, 468, 497
Bet ha-Sumponot (Hebr.), 330
Beth-El, 487
Bet Hillel, Rabbi (1st cent. C.E.), 220
Beth-shemesh, 502
Beth-Yeraḥ, 267
Bet ḳibul (Aram.), 328
Betlehem, 96 (note)
Bet Zipporya, 314
Beyn (Aram.), 131
Bezold, Carl (1859-1922), 41 (note), 161 (note), 167 note)
Bible as source for Jewish music, 60ff, 66ff
Biblia Amiantina, 237 (note)
Biblioteca Mediceo-Laurenziana (Florence), 237 (note)
Bidbalin (Aram.), see *Korablin*
Biesenthal-Lebrecht, . . . 307 (note)
Bikle neḥoshet (Hebr.), 305
Bikle 'oz (Hebr.), 303, 376, 427
Bīn (Egypt.), see *Ben*
Bineginot (Hebr.), 119, 138, 293, 318
Bismaya, 44
Bit Yakin, 47
Black, J. Sutherland, 308 (note)
Blaesilla, 202
Bland, John (d. 1788), 464
B'ne meyav (Hebr.), 272, 282
Boghazkeui, 442, 456 (note)
Book of Gad, 74 (note)
Book of Iddo the Seer, 74 (note)
Book of Isaiah (from the Dead Sea Scrolls), 417
Book of Job, 465 (note)
Book of Jubilees (or Seasons), 195
Book of Lamentations, 74, 168
Book of Nathan, 74 (note)
Book of the Righteous, 74, 164
Book of the Secrets of Enoch, 499
Book of Shemiah, 74 (note)
Book of Songs, 164 (note)
Book of the Wars of the Lord, 74, 164
Book of Yehu, 74 (note)
Borbalin (Aram.), see *Korablin*
Borrowed melodies for psalms, 105
Borrowing from other civilizations, 36, 260, 441, 445, 477, 478, 528
Böttcher, F., 464 (note)
Bow, playing stringed instruments with a, 265
Boys' choir, 171, 227
Boy singers in the Levitical choir, 171ff, 490
Braun, O., 141 (note)
Break between the sacred and the profane, 338
Breasted, James Henry (1865-1935), 95 (note), 247 (note)
Briggs, Charles Augustus (1841-1913), 97 (note), 106 (note), 140
British Museum, 290, 386
Broken strings, 182, 274
Brotherhood of prophets, see Schools of prophets
Bruston, Ch., 464 (note)
Bubastis, 443
Bucca sonora (Lat.), 270
Buccina (Lat.), 334, 365, 367, 368
Buchara, 228
Bücher, Karl (1847-1930), 161 (note)
Büchler, A., 190 (note), 191 (note)
Budde, Karl, (1850-1935), 59 (note), 102 (note), 143 (note), 144 (note), 146 (note), 148, 162, 163 (note), 165 (note), 168 (note), 219 (note), 221 (note), 241, 244 (note), 251, 252, 524 (note), 538 (note)
Bugle, 342, 366, 368, 369
Bugles of alarum, 342
Buḳinus (Aram.), 368
Burnt offering, 175, 177, 334, 346, 458, 470, 498
Burrows, Millar, 190 (note), 192 (note)
Byblos (Gebal), 58, 508
Bykanēs (Gr.), 333 (note)
Bykanistos (Gr.), 326
Byzantine, 401, 437, 461
Byzantine music, 285, 437

C

Cabala, 499 (note)
Cadaver tua (Lat.), 279, 289
Caesarea-Mazaca, 219, 501
Cain, 162
Cairo, 304
Calamus (Lat.), 310, 342 (note), 388, 406
Calling the Name of God, 176
Calmet, Augustin (1672-1757), 103, 110, 292 (note), 308, 518
Cana'an, 33, 36, 53, 58, 59, 82, 95, 102, 111, 163, 308, 456, 463, 478, 506, 528, 551, 552
Candelabrum, 270
Canere (Lat.), 301, 439
Canon of the Bible, 108, 142
Cantata, 116

England, 296
En hymnois (Gr.), 119, 120, 300
Enki, 60
Enneachordon (Gr.), 268
En psalmois (Gr.), 119, 120, 300
Ensemble music (Bands), 429, 431
Enthusiastic state of mind, 504, 508, 512
Environment and music, 551
ʿ*Ephah* (measure, Hebr.), 382
Ephesus, 298
ʾ*Ephod* (Hebr.), 495, 512 (note)
Epi agnoēmatōn (Gr.), 110
Epi alaimōth (Gr.), 320
Epi choreia (Gr.), 127, 452
Epigoneion (Gr.), 39, 279, 298
Epigonos, Epigoneios (proper name), 283, 297
Epigram, 105
ʾ*Epikomon* (Aram.), 219
Epi neaniotētōn (Gr.), 121
Epinikios (Gr.), 115
Epiphanius (c. 315-403 C.E.), 200
Epistimōn (Gr.), 103
Epi tēs ogdoēs (Gr.), 124
Epsallēn (Gr.), 297
Epstein, Joseph Lazar, Rabbi (1821-1885), 257 (note)
Equirhythmic translations, 246
Erection of a wall around Jerusalem, 543
ʾ*Erez Kasdim* (Hebr.), see also Chaldaea, 30
ʾ*Erez ẓilẓal kanafayim* (Hebr.), 329 (note)
Erman, Adolf (1854-1937), 95 (note), 247, 436 (note), 443 (note), 454, 470 (note), 471 (note), 516 (note)
Eruditio (Lat.), 103
ʾ*Erus,* ʾ*irus* (Aram.), 407, 410, 411, 412ff, 414, 415, 416, 417, 462, 524
Esau, 481
Escort with musical accompaniment, 72, 162, 422, 529
Eshir, ashir (Babyl., Assyr.), 291
Eshirtu (Sumer.), 290
ʾ*Eskada,* ʾ*askada* (med. Fr.), 410
ʾ*Eskalina* (med. Fr.), 410
ʾ*Eskalita,* ʾ*eskelet* (med. Fr.), see ʾ*Askilta*
ʾ*Esoḥaḥah* (Hebr.), 193, 195
Essenes, 187ff, 191, 526ff
Esther, 460, 463 (note)
Ethan (Jeduthun), Singer, 77, 95, 125, 139, 140, 144, 276, 292 (note), 376, 424, 425, 433, 434, 492, 508, 515, 532, 533, 535, 537
Ethanim (*Nethinim*) (Hebr.), 126
Ethical melodies, 202
Ethiopia, Ethiopian, 264, 266, 329 (note)
Ethos (Gr.), 550, 552
—— of the dance, 476
—— of Jewish music, 258, 259ff, 305, 478, 551
—— of singing, 169, 217, 259ff, 305
Etruscan, 314, 334
Euangelizomenois, (Gr.), 525
Euergetes, King of Egypt (2nd cent. B.C.E.), 142
Eumelēs (Gr.), 288
Euodius, 204
EUOUAE, 201
Euphoriōn, 280, 284, 294
Eupolis, 147
Euripides, (c. 484-407 B.C.E.), 269 (note), 288 (note)
Eusebius Pamphilius of Caesarea (c. 260-c. 340 C.E.), 180 (note), 187 (note), 190 (note), 196, 197, 198, 199, 200, 243, 244, 278, 279, 485 (note)
Eustochius, 198, 202 (note)
Evangelizantibus (Lat.), 525
Ewald, Georg Heinrich August (1803-1875), 87 (note), 101, 111, 124, 136, 142, 143, 144, 148, 149 (note), 160, 163 (note), 241, 277 (note), 319, 464, 517 (note), 521 (note), 535 (note)
Exchange of instruments in Antiquity, 57, 298, 300, 326
Excommunication, 362
Exemption from taxes for the Levitical singers, 543
Exodus from Egypt, 72, 165, 333, 456, 477, 478, 479
Eyuk, 330
ʾ*Ezbʿa ẓeredah* (Aram.), 466
Ezekiel, Prophet (592-570 B.C.E.), 318, 499, 507, 511
Ezra, Scribe (5th cent. B.C.E.), 82, 83, 100, 142, 143, 211, 341, 519, 520, 542, 543, 544
Ezrahite, 140, 144

F

Fabiola, 204
Fairfax Synagogue (Los Angeles), 358 (mus. ex.)
Falsetto-singing, 123
Fame of Jewish singing in Antiquity, 81, 234, 428, 522
Far (Hebr.), 342
Farmer, Henry George (1882-   ), 309 (note), 325 (note), 394 (note), 397 (note), 398, 401 (note), 402, (note), 403, 409
Farwardīgān, Festival of, 459
Fasting, Day of, 350, 363
Fathers' houses, 485 (note), 534
Feast of the Harvest, 457
—— of the Lord, see Tabernacles, Feast of
—— of Weeks, 178, 456
Female singers and musicians, 75, 121, 131, 516, 518, 525
Fertility dances, see Dance of fertility
Festival, see *Ḥag* (Hebr.)
Fétis, François Joseph (1784-1871), 268, 291, 298, 318, 434 (note)
Fifteen steps, 99, 178, 437
Finalis (Lat.), 229

H

d'Herbelot de Molainville, Barthelemy (1625-1695), 105
Herder, Johann Gottfried (1744-1803), 101, 148, 322, 483, 539
Hereditary office of singers, 40, 46
Hereford, Nicholas, 96 (note)
Hermeneutics, musical, 153, 209
Hermias Sozomenes Salamenes (fl. c. 400-443 C.E.), 196
Hero, 404 (note)
Herod (37 B.C.E.-4.C.E.), 391, 464
Herodotus (c. 484-425 B.C.E.), 54 (note), 57, 444 (note)
Herod's Temple, see Third Temple
Heroic meter, 243, 244
Herōn, 287 (note)
Heshbon, 164
Hesychios of Alexandria (5th cent. C.E.), 271 (note), 280
Hexameter, 243, 244
Hexatonic scale, 214
Ḥezār (Arab.), 332
Hezekiah, King of Judah (719-691 B.C.E.), 80, 91, 94, 95, 101, 104, 105, 114, 129, 140 (note), 145 (note), 234, 377, 427, 522, 540
Hickmann, Hans, 41 (note), 439, 440, 480 (note)
Ḥidot (Hebr.), 87
Hierakas, 200
Hierodules, 55
Hieronymus St. (340-420 C.E.), see Jerome St.
Hieropolis, 55
Ḥigeg (Aram.), 467
Higgayon (Hebr.), 116, 148, 156ff, 276, 293 (note)
Higgayon selah (Hebr.), 116, 156
"High" and "low" in Oriental music, 123
High places, 59, 75, 455, 482, 486, 495, 506, 529
High standard of Levitical performances, 78, 427, 435, 440, 490, 526, 537, 538
Hikkah (Aram.), 309, 393, 435
Hikkish (Aram.), 272, 419
Ḥil (Hebr.), see *ḥul*
Hilarius St., Bishop of Poitiers (c. 300-367 C.E.), 279
Ḥilkin (Aram.), 286
Hill of God, 483, 486, 531
Hindu, 210, 299, 505
Ḥinga (Aram.), 269, 317, 319, 323, 389ff, 449
Hippolytus (d.c. 230 C.E.), 147, 187
Hiram King of Tyre (980-947 B.C.E.), 54, 264, 532
Hirdolim (Aram.), see also *hardulis* and *hydraulis*, 394, 395, 397 (note), 409
Hirʾeh (Hebr.), 434
Hirkib (Aram.), 367
Ḥisda, Rabbi (216-308 C.E.), 224
Hishmiyʿa (Hebr.), 276
Historic odes, 93
Hitparek (Hebr.), 338
Hittite, 44, 314, 330, 382, 442
Hitzig, Ferdinand (1807-1875), 105, 307 (note), 464 (note)
Ḥiyya bar Ada (Abba) (3rd cent. C.E.), 217, 286, 411, 502
Hodot (Hebr.), 193
Ḥok (Hebr.), 195 (note)
Ḥolah (Aram.), 448, 449
Holofernes, 468
Holy cities, 495
Homer (12th cent. B.C.E.), 482 (note)
Homophony of Jewish music, 215
Horace (65-8 B.C.E.), 243, 244, 327, 394
Horizontal angular harp, 39, 45
Horn, 53, 61, 72, 80, 82, 85, 87, 89, 91, 92, 254, 255, 264, 334, 342ff, 366, 368, 369, 370, 371, 375, 421, 423, 432, 477, 497, 498, 499, 500
Horne, S. T., 105
Horribilis (Lat.), 336
Horus, 443
Hoshʿana Rabbah (Hebr.), 458
Hoshea, Prophet (733-725 B.C.E.), 221
Hostility toward the dance, 467
—— toward instrumental music, 277
—— toward secular singing, 222, 223
Hothir, Singer, 145 (note)
Houbigant, Charles François (1686-1783), 110
House of Study, 181, 183, 184
Ḥozeh (Hebr.), 509, 510
Ḥul (Sumer.), 38
Ḥul, ḥil (Hebr.), 38, 322, 446, 448, 466
Huldah, Prophetess, 511
Human sacrifices, 54
Humilis et perfectus (Lat.), 105
Humilis et simplex (Lat.), 105
Huna ben Joshua, Rabbi (d.c. 410 C.E.), 224, 286, 412, 414
Hupfeld, Hermann (1796-1866), 142, 241
Hurdy-gurdy, 328
Hutchinson, Enoch, 271, 303 (note)
Hyamson, Moses (1862-), 344 (note)
Hydraulis (Gr.), 287, 309, 328, 391, 392, 394, 403, 404, 406, 409
Hygros ben Levi, Singer, 216, 257, 272 (note), 498
Hymnēsis (Gr.), 97
Hymn of the Initiants, 194
—— to the Sun, 95
Hymnos (Gr.), 180, 190
Hymnus (Lat.), 97, 98, 203
Hypatē (Gr.), 123, 124 (note)
Hyper agnoias (Gr.), 110
—— *akmēs tou hyiou*, 131
—— *choreias* (Gr.), 452
—— *klērodosiōn* (Gr.), 128
—— *klērouchōn* (Gr.), 128
—— *maeleth* (Gr.), 127, 452
—— *peristeras alalou makrysmōn* (Gr.), 135

466, 474, 475
Jacob al-Kirḳisānī, 191 (note)
Jacob ben Meïr Tam, Rabbenu (1100-1171), 348
Jahaziel, Singer, 515
Jahn, Johann (1750-1816), 148, 287, 293, 308, 318, 319, 324, 368 (note), 382
Jakob, B., 156
James, M. R., 316 (note), 513 (note)
Janitzary-bands, 420
Jannaeus, Alexander, 302
Jannaeus, John, 302
Jason, High Priest (2nd cent. C.E.), 464
Jastrow, Marcus (1829-1903), 105 (note), 318 (note), 389, 395 (note), 397 (note), 398, 405, 406, 407, 413 (note), 415, 416 (note), 421 (note), 448 (note), 449 (note)
Jastrow, Morris Jr. (1861-1921), 310 (note), 475
Jeduthun (Jedithun), see Ethan
Jehiel, Singer, 124
Jehoiada, High Priest, 80, 426
Jehoshaphat, King of Judah (874-850 B.C.E.), 80, 165, 254, 425, 512
Jehu, King of Israel (842-815 B.C.E.), 73, 361
Jeiel, Singer, 125
Jephthah's daughter, 75, 322, 468
Jeremiah, Prophet (626-580 B.C.E.), 175, 236, 271, 315, 323, 486, 506, 507
Jeremiah of the Branch, Rabbi, 462
Jeremias, Alfred (1864-1935), 44 (note), 168 (note), 522 (note)
Jericho, 73, 190, 227, 314, 369ff, 380, 397, 399, 402, 448, 487, 499ff, 500, 501
Jeroboam, King of Israel (932-911 B.C.E.), 79
Jerome, St. (340-420 C.E.), 96 (note), 98, 99 (note), 103, 105, 108, 109, 110, 115, 119, 121, 127, 128, 131, 132, 133, 135, 136, 137, 147, 157, 198, 201, 204, 243, 244, 270, 274, 279, 285, 290, 293, 300, 317, 322, 331, 333, 367, 399, 452
Jerusalem, 96 (note), 98, 99, 103, 105, 108, 109, 110, 115, 119, 121, 124, 127, 128, 131, 132, 133, 135, 136, 137, 147, 157, 187 (note), 198, 202, 204, 243, 244, 270, 274, 279, 285, 290, 293, 300, 317, 322, 331, 333, 367, 399, 452
Jesse, the Beth-lehemite, 530
Jesus, 64, 196
Jesus ben Sirah (2nd cent. B.C.E.), 142, 427
Jewish Encyclopedia, 227 (note), 354 (mus. ex.), 396 (note), 463 (note)
Jewish Sects, 186ff, 525
Jewish Theological Seminary (New York), 352
Jewish Translation, 63, 64, 70, 73, 75, 76, 80, 81, 82, 83, 91, 99, 100, 101, 102, 105, 122, 138, 157, 164, 165, 168, 176, 177, 178, 179, 180, 182, 183, 185, 205, 216, 222, 227, 233, 234, 274, 277, 334, 335, 340, 343, 348, 350, 361 (note), 362, 376, 378, 380, 397, 399, 402, 406, 423, 424, 426, 427, 450, 456, 457, 464, 486, 489, 491, 506, 520, 521, 522, 523, 530, 531, 533, 535, 540, 543, 545, 546
Jezrahiah, Chief of the Levitical singers, 115
Joab, 361
Joash, King of Judah (836-797 B.C.E.), 76, 80, 426
Job, Book of, 85, 187, 188, 242, 243, 244, 250, 267, 465 (note)
Joel, Prophet (8th-7th cent. B.C.E.), 293, 511
Joel Sirkes (BACH), Rabbi (1561-1640), 411
Joḥanan, Rabbi (2nd cent. C.E.), 211
Joḥanan ben Nuri, Rabbi (1st-2nd cent. C.E.), 348
Joḥanan ben Zakkai, Rabbi (1st cent. C.E.), 348, 364
John Cassian (360-435), 198, 199
John Chrysostom (347?-407), 74 (note), 147, 154 (note), 155, 172, 196, 198, 199, 201, 202, 203, 204, 243, 270, 271, 452, 509
Jonathan, 164, 168, 206, 245, 276, 447
Jongleur-musicians, 152
Joost, J. M., 189 (note)
Jose, Rabbi (2nd cent. C.E.), 314
Joseph, Rabbi (3rd cent. C.E.), 286, 501, 525
Josephus Flavius (37-c-100 C.E.), 54 (note), 62, 83 (note), 95 (note), 96 (note), 99, 124 (note), 151, 176 (note), 179 (note), 187, 191 (note), 242, 243, 244, 264, 265, 272, 274, 278, 287, 288, 303, 323 note), 333, 376, 380, 397, 399, 405, 437, 458, 464, 469 (note), 479 (note), 482 (note), 536, 548, 549
Joshebekashah, Singer, 145 (note)
Joshua, 314 (note), 369, 482, 499
Joshua ben Ḥananiah, Rabbi (1st-2nd cent.), 96 (note), 181, 548, 549
Joshua, ben Levi, Rabbi (3rd cent. C.E.), 272 (note), 375, 414, 459
Josiah, King of Judah (639-609 B.C.E.), 81, 168, 428, 429, 493, 511, 522, 541
Jouba, 54, 280
Juan de Gara (16th cent.), 352
Jubal, 60, 61, 72, 162, 263, 266, 307, 370 (note), 391
Jubilee, Year of the, 72, 348, 367, 368, 369, 371, 499
Jubilus (Lat.), 201, 367
Judah I, Rabbi (c.135-c-220 C.E.), 178,

Matenoth Kehunah (Hebr.), 391
Mat kaldu (Hebr.), 52
Mattaniah, Singer, 115, 547
Mattenah, Rabbi (fl. c. 200 C.E.), 395
Mattithiah, Singer, 125
Mazaca, 501
Mazzot (Hebr.), 457
M'bor'kim (Hebr.), 195
McClintock, John (1814-1870), 244 (note), 296 (note), 324 (note)
Measure, 240, 377
Mebasserot (Hebr.), 525
Mechanical verse, 245
Media, 183
Mediant (Lat.), 229
Mē diaphteirēs (Gr.), 136
Meditation, 94, 103
Mediterranean, 300, 334, 394
Megiddo, 69, 70, 270, 310
Meholah (Hebr.), 448
Meholot (Hebr.), 138, 319, 390
Meibin (Hebr.), 115 (note), 171
Meibohm, Marcus (1626-1711), 56 (note)
Meïr, Rabbi (c. 100 C.E.), 314
Meisel-Synagogue in Prague, 183
Mekales (Aram.), 449 (note)
Mekalsin (Aram.), 430
Mekarkashin (Aram.), 418, 420
Mekassefah (Hebr.), 507
Mekonenot (Hebr.), 168, 523, 524
Melancholia, 504
Melismatic figures, 150, 218, 251
Melkart, 54
Melōdēma (Gr.), 98, 249
Melodicles, 207
Melodies of action, 203
Melody, 267ff, 453
Melos diapsalmatos (Gr.), 157
Memorizing texts and melodies, 161
Memphis, 480
Men (Hebr.), see *Minnim*
Mena'an'im (Hebr.), 383, 384ff, 411, 416, 420
Menaggen (Hebr.), 120, 223, 301
Menaichmos, 281, 295
Menazzeah (Hebr.), 114ff, 138, 144, 146, 433, 454
Mendelssohn-Bartholdy, Felix (1809-1847), 205
Men of might (workers of miracles), 459, 497
Menorah (Hebr.), 270
Mesapkin (Aram.), 466
Meshavarta depuriy'a (Aram.), 460
Mesopotamia, 47, 308, 395
Messiah, 175 (note), 343, 349
Messianic significance of blowing the *shofar,* 344, 365
Metal strings, 272
Meta ōdēs (Gr.), 110, 111
Metaphors, musical, 90, 91, 92, 217, 272, 276
Meter, metric structure, 173, 196, 242, 250, 377
Meter and music, 250, 377
Metric values of *shofar*-calls, 351 (note)
Meyav (Hebr.), 282, 372
Me-ze (Sumer), 37
Mezillot (Hebr.), 114, 340, 386ff, 387, 418, 419, 420
Meziltayim, zelzelim (Hebr.), 264, 332, 376ff, 378, 386, 420, 423
—— *nehoshet,* 376
Mezufit, mezubit (Aram.), 329
Michael, Angel, 466
Michal, 446, 451, 506
Michelangelo (1475-1564), 366 (note)
Microtonic intervals, 212
Middle Ages, 152
Midian, Midianites, 361
Midrash, 62, 98, 110, 121, 212, 216, 223, 225, 272, 275, 276, 293, 368, 390, 391, 392, 397 (note), 405, 406, 430, 447, 448, 456, 462
Mielziner, M., 392 (note)
Migne, Jacques Paul (1800-1875), 187 (note), 244, 272
Migrating melisms, 209
—— songs, 209
Mikneiah, Singer, 125
Mikshah (Hebr.), 334
Miktab (Hebr.), 106
Miktam (Hebr.), 104ff, 108, 109, 138, 139
Milkom, 506
Mimic presentations, 441
Mine halyata (Syr.), 309
—— *kle zemer* (Aram.), 304, 391
—— *zemer* (Aram.), 304, 312, 391, 406
Minha (Hebr.), 425 (note), 535
Minnim, sing. *men* (Hebr.), 272, 276, 297, 304, 308, 309, 312, 409, 432
Minocchi, S., 463 (note)
Minstrel, 160, 164, 301, 432, 451, 478, 510, 511, 530, 539, 545
Miracle, 538
Miriam the Prophetess, 72, 74, 163, 242, 322, 449, 450, 456, 481, 510, 517, 525, 527
Mirrors for women at the Tabernacle, 517
Mishnah, (Hebr.), 62, 71, 147, 179, 182, 184, 185, 186, 211, 216, 218, 227, 256, 272 (note), 273, 282, 286, 308, 311, 312, 313, 315, 328, 329, 338, 347, 348, 350, 352, 367, (note), 370, 378, 380, 390, 393, 398, 399, 401, 402, 403, 405, 407, 412, 415, 416, 417, 418, 419, 490, 498, 501, 523, 536
Mixed meters, 248
Mizmar (Arab.), 316
Mizmor (Hebr.), 96, 98, 99, 138
Mnemotechnique, mnemonic device, 161, 181, 184, 186, 211, 434
Moab, Moabites, 59, 80, 90, 91, 92, 164,

Singing, 159ff, 227ff, 249, 254
—— angels, 159, 225
—— as a celestial institution, 159, 225, 226
—— as an art, 159, 169, 235, 488
—— as the possession of the entire nation, 160, 222, 482
—— at private festivities, 174
——, bad habits in, 256, 257
——, beauty of, 216, 218
—— boys, 45
—— of divine origin, 225
—— of Jewish Sects, 187ff
—— on the Sabbath, 217
——, primitive sources of, 159, 162
Sipunya (Aram.), see *Sumponyah*
Sistrata turba (Lat.), 383
Sistrum (Lat.), *seistron* (Gr.), 40, 327, 331, 332, 380, 381, 383, 384, 385, 416, 417, 420, 423, 434, 443, 503, 516
Si-tar (Hindu), 299
Sitols (Old Engl.), 289
Skeyos psalmou (Gr.), 279
Skindapsos (Gr.), 268, 269
Skirtaō (Gr.), 448, 467
Skolion (Gr.), 213, 214
SLH (Hebr. root), 151
SLL (Hebr. root), 156
Slotki, J. J., 307
Sluter, Claus (d. 1406), 366 (note)
Snaredrum, 415
So'ade (Hebr.), 171
Sociology of music instruction, 491ff
Sociological aspect of music organization, 530
Socrates (c. 470-c. 399 B.C.E.), 214
—— of Constantinople (fl. 5th cent.), 199
Sodom, 391, 392, 394
Soferim (Hebr.), 145, 149, 319, 352
Solomon, King (reign. 972-932 B.C.E.), 54, 59, 73, 76, 78, 79, 80, 81, 83, 87, 95, 129, 140, 141, 143 144, 165, 168, 169, 184, 215, 220, 221, 232, 233, 244, 256, 259, 264, 321, 336, 337, 361, 377, 384 (note), 425, 427, 430, 433, 454, 464, 466, 468, 484, 486, 490, 493, 506, 507, 518, 519, 521, 522, 529, 537, 538, 539, 540, 545, 552
—— as author, 79, 87, 95, 143, 144, 165, 221, 464
Soncino Press, 257 (note), 272 (note), 391 (note), 403 (note), 405 (note)
Song and tale (*"Singen und Sagen,"* Germ.), 160
—— at the Red Sea, 72, 157, 163, 167, 176, 242, 250, 480, 527
—— of celestial bodies, 226
—— of loves, 103
—— of Moses, 175, 240 (note), 244, 248
—— of praise, 169, 172, 173, 175, 178, 190, 202
—— of Songs as a dramatic play, 221, 462ff
—— see *Shir ha-Shirim*
—— of the Bow, 74, 108, 164
—— of the Virtuous Woman, 244
—— of triumph and victory, 166
—— of the Well, 74, 455
Songs of Ascent, see Degrees, Songs of the
—— in the Bible, different kinds, 84, 85
Sonitu sempiterno (Lat.), 157
Sonora concavitas (Lat.), 270
(The) Sons of Light and the Sons of Darkness, 338ff, 500
Sons of Prophets, 484, 485, 486, 487, 488, 489, 531
—— of Zadok, 191
Sōpatros, 54, 266, 281, 288
Sōpher (Gr.), 365
Sorbalin (Aram.), see *Korablin*
Sorceress, 507, 511
Sorcery, 61, 343, 347, 362, 365, 448, 495, 500, 501, 505, 507
Sound effects of the orchestra, 431
Sounding holes, 274
Sources of income for musicians, 492
—— of singing, 159
Sozomenes, see Hermias Sozomenes
Speaking with tongues, 515
Speech-melody, 72, 75, 159, 161, 206, 211, 218, 235, 514
Speidel, Johann Christoph (18th cent.), 205
Spiritual approach to tonal art, 552
—— songs, see *Odai pneumatikai* (Gr.)
Spondē (Gr.), 213
"Sprechgesang" (Germ.), 206
Staccato blasts (on the *shofar*), 337, 352
Stainer, Sir John (1840-1901), 152, 153 (note), 266 (note), 271, 290 (note), 298, 308, 317, 334 (note), 359 (mus. ex.), 382 (note), 490 (note), 518 (note)
Stamping with the feet, 441, 448, 466, 472, 473
Stanza, see Strophic structure
Stark, Edward J. (1863-1918), 357 (mus. ex.)
Stäudlin, K. F. (18th cent.), 463 (note)
"Steiger," see *Modoi*
Steinberg, J., 151 (note)
Steles erected before the gods, 105
Stēlographia (Gr.), 105
Stephen, St. (1st cent.), 200
Stichos, pl. *stichoi* (Gr.), 251
Stickel, J. G., 463 (note)
Stimulating influence of music, 504
Storm motive, 153
St. Mark's Scroll, 437
Stopping the strings, 45, 438
Strabo (b.c. 63 B.C.E.), 158, 294 (note), 316, 478

Strahan, James, 170 (note)
Strauss, Richard (1864-1949), 153
Strike of the Levitical singers, 84, 545ff
Striking the harp, 271, 272
—— the thighs, 466, 471
Stringed instruments, 266ff, 387ff
Strings, 272, 273
—— of metal, 272, 273
Strong, James (1822-1894), 244 (note), 296 (note), 324 (note)
Strophic structure of the psalms, 110, 149, 173, 207, 246, 253
Strunk, Oliver, 273 (note)
Studying with chanting, 183
Stumpf, Carl (1848-1936), 161 (note)
Subjective lyric poems, 250
Succanere (Lat.), 439
Succentiva (Lat.), 439
Suetonius (1st-2nd cent. C.E.), 328, 394, 469
Sufetes (Lat.), 510 (note)
Suidas (10th cent.), 271 (note), 279, 280, 294, 295
Sukkârah (Arab.), 440
Sukkot, Feast of (Hebr.), see also Tabernacles, 457, 458
Sulamith, see Shulammite
Sulzer, Solomon (1804-1890), 351, 355 (mus. ex.)
Sumeria, Sumerian, 35, 44, 46, 47, 53, 107, 114, 130, 140, 161, 290, 302, 315, 330 (note), 372 (note), 383, 384, 388, 408 (note), 452, 484, 485
Sumerian catalogue of liturgies, 36, 107, 130, 291
—— language considered sacred by the Babylonians, 42
Sumponyah (Aram.), 92, 265, 298, 311, 313, 325, 430
Sun worship, 447, 498
Super octava (Lat.), 124
—— *puellarum* (*modulum*) (Lat.), 121
Superstition, 349, 385, 410, 419, 447, 495ff, 496, 502, 503, 505, 506, 507
Sura, 348
Susa, Shushan, 302, 303, 320 (note), 382 (note), 460
Susiana, capital city of Elam, 320 (note)
Swimming motions of the arms, 454
Sword dance, 466, 474, 475
Symmachos (fl. 193-211 C.E.), 96 (note), 98, 99, 103, 105, 108, 110, 115, 119, 121, 124, 127, 128, 132, 133, 136, 147, 157, 267, 300, 322, 452
Sympathetic magic, 73, 419, 459, 469, 497, 498
Symphōnia (Gr., Lat.), 326, 327, 328, 331, 332, 374 (note), 415 (note), 527
Symphony, 332
Synagogue, 63, 64, 100, 163, 179ff, 185, 186, 189, 209, 212, 228, 232, 285, 349, 350, 361 (note), 454, 494, 526
—— in the Jerusalem Sanctuary, 181
——, Songs of the, 130, 179ff
Synaulia (Gr.), 327
Syneseōs (Gr.), 103
Synēsis (Gr.), 103
Synhedrion (Gr.), see Sanhedrin
Synpsalma (Gr.), 147
Syracuse, 295
Syria, Syrian, 55, 57, 59, 72, 106, 107, 143, 146, 196, 231, 266, 267, 268, 290, 291, 294, 299, 310, 312, 323, 325, 334, 393, 394, 411, 416, 417, 445, 463, 465, 481, 486, 529
Syrian Bible and liturgy, 143, 145, 148, 239, 417
Syrigma, syrigmos (Gr.), 281, 283
Syrinx (Gr.), 125 (note), 281, 308, 324, 325, 388
Syrizein (Gr.), 325
Szabolcsi, Bence, 209 (note), 212 (note)

T

Taʿam (Hebr.), 209, 212, 258
Taʿame ha-neginah (Hebr.), 120
Taʿamim (Hebr.), 120, 205, 211, 212 (note), 235, 236, 239, 352, 434 (note), 479 (note)
Taʿarog (Hebr.), 254
Tabala, tabla (Gr.), 409, 410
Tabalu (Assyr.), 409, 411
Tabernacles, Feast of, 85, 89, 99, 102, 126, 134, 138, 177, 183, 185, 219, 256, 293, 311, 315, 336 (note), 337, 347, 350, 444, 448, 450, 457, 458, 459, 469, 499, 521, 536
Ṭabl (Arab.), 409
Ṭabla (Aram.), 403, 409, 414, 417, 419, 502
Ṭabla deḥad puma (Aram.), 410, 413
Ṭabla gurgana, gurgrana (Aram.), 395, 396, 403, 410
Tabret, 72, 89, 92, 162, 166, 222, 224 (note), 316, 317, 322, 374, 375, 410, 429, 446, 473, 529
Tacitus (c. 55-c. 117 C.E.), 62
Tactus (Lat.), 240 (note)
Ṭafaẓ, ṭafas (Aram.), 448, 449, 467
Tagore, Rabindranath (1861-1941), 210
Tagtug and Dilmun 1 60
Taḳeʿo (Hebr.), 367, 368
Talmud, 62, 130, 211, 212, 218, 223, 225, 226, 256, 272 (note), 276, 282, 304, 309, 316, 336, 341, 344, 349, 362, 363, 378, 380, 382, 383, 388, 389, 391, 393, 400, 401, 404, 409, 410, 411, 414, 418, 421, 449, 462, 468, 472, 473, 494, 501, 502, 503, 504, 523
Tam, Jacob ben Meïr, Rabbenu (1100-1171), 348, 349
Tambour de basque (Fr.), 374
Tambourine (Fr.), 106, 170 (note), 316, 327, 373, 374, 375, 382, 413, 415, 419, 451 (note)
Tamid-Sacrifice, 132

(note), 316, 317, 318, 321, 322, 332, 371ff, 381, 382, 383, 411, 412, 413, 416, 420, 422, 432, 456, 486, 513, 517
Tois alliōthēsomenois eti (Gr.), 133
Toke'a leshed (Hebr.), 344
Toke'a loshir (Hebr.), 344
Tonal elements of the music of Ancient Israel, 213
Tonal sacrifice, 488
Tone colors of the orchestra, 431
Tō nikopoiō (Gr.), 115
Tonorion (Gr.), 394, 435 (note)
Tonus peregrinus (Lat.), 111
Torah (Hebr.), 493
Torah-motifs, 213 (mus. ex.)
Torch dance, 219, 437, 458, 459, 462, 466, 468, 497
Torrey, Charles Cutler (1863-), 247 (note)
Tosefta (Hebr.), 62
Tou anamimnēskein (Gr.), 109
Tou apokrithēnai (Gr.), 127
"Tours" (dances), 454
Towel, waving the, 174
Trachtenberg, Joshua (1904-), 498 (note), 499 (note), 501 (note)
Tradition, musical, 108, 112, 125, 145, 151, 187, 363, 404, 427, 429, 519, 520, 540
Transition from *piano* to *forte,* 148, 150
Translocating power of music, 501
Treialtrei (Germ.), 382
Tremolo on the *shofar,* 347, 352
Triad, Instrument of the, 302
Triangle (Instrument), 382, 384
Trichordon (Gr.), 388
Trigon-harp, 92, 125 (note), 147, 267, 268, 287, 291, 296, 382
Trigōnon (Gr.), 54, 55, 125 (note), 147, 268, 270, 279, 287, 295, 382
Trimeter, 244
Trinity, Symbol of, 350 (note), 498
Triplicity of music in Ancient Israel, 75, 87, 322, 441, 476, 479
Tripudium (Lat.), 382
Triumph, Songs of, 84, 163, 166
Troglodytes, 388
Trombone, 296, 357 (mus. ex.)
Tromp, trump, 313, 342, 365, 368, 371, 383, 385
Tropal motifs, 212, 213 (mus. ex.)
Tropes, see *ta'amim*
Tropos (Gr.), 199
—— *spondeiakos* (Gr.), 213, 214
Troy, 300, 501
Trumpet, 40, 64, 73, 76, 77, 78, 80, 91, 150, 165, 176, 177, 178, 195, 254, 255, 266 (note), 272 (note), 302, 305, 316, 332, 333, 340, 342, 351, 362, 365, 366, 368, 369, 370, 371, 376, 378, 379, 380, 404, 423, 424, 425, 426, 432, 450, 458, 478, 489, 498, 533, 537
Trumpeters, 73, 74, 77, 215, 326, 335, 379, 537
Trumpet signals in the Dead Sea Scrolls, 339
Trumpets, Inscriptions on, 340, 341
—— of alarm, 73, 86, 342, 365
Tryphōn, 281 (note), 284
Tuba (Lat.), 334, 336, 342, 365, 367
—— *concionis* (Lat.), 339
—— *cornea* (Lat.), 342, 365
—— *ductilis* (Lat.), 342
Tup (Sumer.), see *dup*
Tuppa, pl. *tuppin,* or *tuppaya* (Aram.), 375, 409, 417
Tuppu (Assyr.), 372
Turban-shaped lily, 302
Turkey, Turks, 318, 420
Turk's cap, 302
Tut-Ankh-Amen, Pharaoh (reign. c. 1360 B.C.E.), 332, 333
Tympanistriss (Old Engl.), 375
Tympanum (Lat.), 270, 273, 318, 328, 374, 375, 398
Typanon, tympanon (Gr.), 327, 374, 376, 404
Typhon, 416
Typtō (Gr.), 287, 365 (note)
Tyre, City of, 54, 58, 90, 92, 254, 318
Tyrrhenes, 334

U

'*Ugab* (Hebr.), 146, 170, 183, 263, 276, 296, 298, 307ff, 312, 315, 322, 323, 324, 330, 391, 392, 393, 406, 432, 477, 528
Ugolino, Biagio (Blasius, b.c. 1700), 113 (note), 372 (note), 397 (note), 399 (note)
Umbreit, F.W.C. (19th cent.), 463
Uniformity of tone color, 431
Unison, singing in, 123, 124, 126
Unisono (Ital.), 378, 379
Unity of Jewish music, 215
Unni, Singer, 125
"*Unterweisung*" (Germ.), 103
Up-beat, 250, 253
'Ur of Chaldaea ('*ur kasdim*), 36, 53, 311
Urim and *Thummim* (Hebr.), 512
'Usu (City), 58
Usurtesen II, see Sesurtesen II
Utilitarian music, 32, 61, 221, 258, 259, 477, 497
Ut non disperdas (Lat.), 136
Utricularium (Lat.), 327, 328
'Uzza, Singer, 531
'Uzzi, Singer, 83

V

Vadil. vadal (med. Fr.), 397 (note)
Va'ed (Hebr.), 148
Valentinus, Apostate (2nd cent. C.E.), 200
Valley of Berakah, 80, 426

—— of Kidron, 399
Vanity of artists, 117, 257
Variation, Principle of, 208, 209, 210, 239, 249, 250
Varro (116-27 B.C.E.), 280, 334 (note), 368 (note), 388, 439
Vashti, 460
Vasum psalmi (Lat.), 279
Vatican, 154, 452
Venantius Fortunatus (530-c. 609), 197, 328
Venice, 352
Verdeil, R. Paralikova, 437
Vertical angular harp, 39, 45
Vesorkah (Aram.), 402
Vespasian, Emp. (9-79 C.E.), 220, 412, 461
Vesselis of salm (Old. Engl.), 289
Vibrating tongues of pipes, 287, 329, 368 (note)
Vibrato of the singing voice, 45, 256
Victori (Lat.), 115
Videlle (Fr.), 397 (note)
Villoteau, Guillaume André (1759-1839), 288, 298
Vilna, 358 (mus. ex.)
Vincentius, St. (3rd cent. C.E.), 244 (note)
Vintage, Songs of the, 107, 165, 202, 293
Viol, 289, 305 (note), 415
Virgil (70-19 B.C.E.), 388
Virtuosity of the singers, 117, 118, 256
Vitruvius Pollio (fl. 70 B.C.E.), 287 (note), 295, 395, 404 (note)
V'labo b'yaḥad (Hebr.), 195
"*Von den Rosen*" (Germ.), 133
"*Von der Hindin*" (Germ.), 132
"*Von der Jugend*" (Germ.), 121
"*Von der schönen Jugend*" (Germ.), 131
"*Von der stummen Taube*" (Germ.), 135
Vopiscus Flavius (4th cent. C.E.), 327
V'sim (Hebr.), 482
Vulgate, 96, 98, 99, 103, 105, 106, 108, 109, 110, 115, 118, 119, 121, 124, 127, 128, 130, 131, 132, 133, 135, 136, 147, 157, 226, 237 (note), 264 (note), 267, 279, 289, 290, 291, 293, 296, 299, 300, 305ff, 307, 309, 314, 317, 321, 325, 329 (note), 342, 365, 369, 375, 380, 385, 387, 426, 468 (note), 525

W

Wadi Bereikhut (Arab.), 426
Wages of the musicians, 493, 544
Wagner, Peter (1865-1931), 228
Wagner, Richard (1813-1883), 153, 154
Wagoners, Songs of the, 202
Wailing as an "art", 494, 524
—— women, 92, 168, 316, 413, 415, 416, 417, 470, 472, 494, 523
Walking around the bier, 473
Wallaschek, Richard (1860-1917), 161 (note), 258 (note)
Wandering minstrels, 478, 539, 544, 545
—— songs, 110
(The) War between the Sons of Light and the Sons of Darkness, 192, 195, 338ff, 500
War dance, 470, 471, 475
War-*selah*, 153
—— song, 250
Wards of singers, 77, 78, 424, 433, 535, 536, 537
Water drawing, Ceremony of, 181, 338, 350, 461
—— Gate, 177, 350, 458
—— libation, Ceremony of, 99, 177, 219, 338, 350, 458, 459, 462, 469, 497
Waterman, Leroy, 463 (note), 465, 475
Water-organ, 287, 328, 391, 392, 394, 395, 400, 403, 405, see also *hydraulis*
Weavers, Songs of the, 202
Wedding bells, 410, 411, 412, 413, 419 (note)
—— customs, 405, 462, 497
—— dances, 410, 412, 413, 414, 419 (note), 461, 462, 474
—— drum, see *'erus*
—— processions, 410
—— songs, 465, 466, 475
Weeks, Festival of the, 457, 521, 536
Weiss, Johann (1850-1919), 268, 269, 270 (note), 271, 281, 287, 290, 293, 307 (note), 374 (note), 383, 387, 388
—— P.R., 190 (note)
Wellhausen, Julius (1844-1918), 269 (note), 271, 288 (note), 382 (note)
Wells, sacred, 455
Weltanschauung (Germ.), 551
Werner, Eric, 201 (note), 209 (note), 214, 277, 285 (note), 320, 379 (note), 404 (note), 434 (note), 437
Western Synagogue (London), 359 (mus. ex.)
Westphal, Rudolph (1826-1892), 57 (note), 453
Wetzstein, Johann Gottfried (1815-1905), 298, 465
Whiston, William (1667-1752), 265 (note)
Whole-offering, 150, 336, 338
Wiedemann, Alfred (1856-), 40 (note)
"*Wie die Jugend*" (Germ.), 131
Wilkinson, Sir Gardner (1797-1875), 40 (note), 291, 434 (note)
Willow-branch, Rite of the, 350
Wilson, Robert Dick, 98 (note), 100, 140, 142
Winckler, Hugo (1863-1913), 121 (note), 497 (note), 522 (note)
Wind instruments, 307ff, 392ff
Winer, Johan Georg Benedikt (1789-1858), 102, 309
Winter, Jakob (1857-1941), 374 (note)